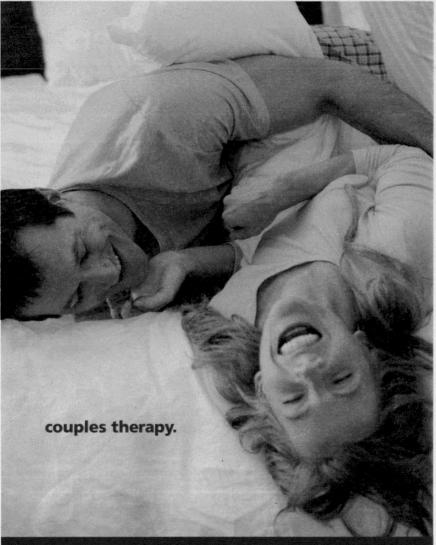

couples therapy.

Remember when you first fell in love? Yeah, it's kind of like that. So jump into Cloud Nine. The Hampton bed experience. A plush, down-like comforter. Crisp white duvet. Soft sheets. And your choice of pillows. **Plus, we offer AAA/CAA rates. For reservations, visit hampton.com or call 1-800-HAMPTON.**

Cozy
Hampton Bed

Complimentary
Hot Breakfast

100% Satisfaction
Guarantee

we love having you here.®

Western Canada & Alaska

Are we meeting your travel needs?
Send written comments to:

AAA Member Comments
1000 AAA Drive, Box 61
Heathrow, FL 32746-5063

Published by AAA Publishing
1000 AAA Drive
Heathrow, FL 32746-5063
Copyright AAA 2008

The publisher is not responsible for changes that occur after publication. TourBook® guides are published for the exclusive use of AAA members. Not for sale.

Advertising Rate and Circulation Information: (407) 444-8280

Printed in the USA by Quebecor World, Buffalo, NY

Photo Credit: (Cover & Title Page) Mount Revelstoke National Park of Canada, BC / © Eero Sorila

Printed on recyclable paper. Please recycle whenever possible.

Mixed Sources
Product group from well-managed forests and other controlled sources
www.fsc.org Cert no. SW-COC-1610
© 1996 Forest Stewardship Council

FSC

Stock #4601

Western Canada & Alaska

4

Leaves You Hanging

Your Travel Authority
Online, On the Road and Every Day

DISCOVER THE KEY TO EASY HOTEL AND RESTAURANT SELECTION

Use the trusted AAA/CAA Diamonds to choose the right hotel or restaurant for your needs, every time.

Quality Assurance
Every AAA/CAA Diamond rated hotel and restaurant has been AAA/CAA Approved by a professional inspector to ensure it offers the cleanliness and comfort members expect.

Easy Selection
AAA/CAA Approved hotels and restaurants receive a rating of One Diamond to Five Diamonds to indicate the level of hospitality — from no-frills hotels and restaurants to full-service resorts and world-class dining.

For more details, go to pages 20-21 or AAA.com/Diamonds

Attractions, lodgings and restaurants are listed on the basis of merit alone after careful evaluation and approval by one of AAA/CAA's full-time, professionally trained Inspectors. Evaluations are unannounced to ensure that we see an establishment just as you would see it.

An establishment's decision to advertise in the TourBook guide has no bearing on its evaluation or rating. Advertising for services or products does not imply AAA endorsement.

All information in this guide was reviewed for accuracy before publication. However, since changes inevitably occur between annual editions, we suggest you work with your AAA travel professional or check on AAA.com to confirm prices and schedules.

How the TourBook Guide is Organized

The TourBook guide is organized into three distinct sections.

The **Points of Interest** section helps you plan daily activities and sightseeing excursions and provides details about the city or attraction you are visiting.

The **Lodgings and Restaurants** section helps you select AAA Approved accommodations and dining facilities meeting your specific needs and expectations.

The **Reference** section provides indexes for locating information within this guide and items to aid the trip planning process.

Locating the Attractions, Lodgings and Restaurants

Attractions, lodgings and restaurants are listed under the city in which they physically are located - or in some cases under the nearest recognized city. Most listings are alphabetically organized by state, province, region or island, then by city and establishment name.

A color is assigned to each state or province so that you can match the color bars at the top of the page to switch from the **Points of Interest** section to the **Lodgings and Restaurants** section.

Spotting maps help you physically locate points of interest, lodgings and restaurants in the major destinations.

The Comprehensive City Index located in the **Reference** section contains an A-to-Z list of cities.

Destination Cities and Destination Areas

Destination cities, established based on government models and local expertise, include metropolitan areas plus nearby vicinity cities. **Destination areas** are regions with broad tourist appeal; several cities will comprise the area.

If a city falls within a destination's vicinity, the city name will appear at its alphabetical location in the book, and a cross reference will give you the exact page on which listings for that city begin.

An orientation map appears at the beginning of each destination section to orient you to that destination.

Understanding the Points of Interest Listing

GEM Designation

A ⬩ indicates the attraction has been rated a AAA GEM, a "must see" point of interest that offers a *Great Experience for Members®*. These attractions have been judged to be of exceptional interest and quality by AAA Inspectors.

A GEM listing page with a brief description of individual GEM attractions follows the Orientation map near the beginning of each state or province Points of Interest section. Cross-references guide the reader to the attraction's listing page.

Discount Savings

The 〔SAVE〕 icon denotes those attractions offering AAA/CAA, AAA MasterCard, AAA VISA or international Show Your Card & Save discount cardholders a discount off the attraction's standard admission. Present your card at the attraction's admission desk.

A list of participating points of interest appears in the Reference section of this guide.

Shopping establishments preceded by a 〔SAVE〕 icon also provide to AAA/CAA members a discount and/or gift with purchase; present your card at the mall's customer service center to receive your benefit.

Exceptions

- Members should inquire in advance concerning the validity of the discount for special rates.
- The 〔SAVE〕 discount may not be used in conjunction with other discounts.
- Attractions that already provide a reduced senior or child rate may not honor the 〔SAVE〕 discount for those age groups.
- All offers are subject to change and may not apply during special events, particular days or seasons or for the entire validity period of the TourBook guide.

Adventure Travel

There are inherent risks with adventure travel activities like air tours, hiking, skiing and white-water rafting. For your own safety, please read and adhere to all safety instructions. Mentions of these activities are for information only and do **not** imply endorsement by AAA.

Shopping areas: Mast General Store, 630 W. King St., operates out of a 1913 building, stocked with a variety of goods including Amish

⬩ **RED OAK** is off I-95 exit 4A, just n. to Dogwood 1812 house has eight 60-foot columns and is furnish 9-7, May 15-Labor Day; 9-5, Apr. 1-May 14 and d of year. Hours may vary; phone ahead. Closed Jan admission 45 minutes before closing. Admission $8; $5 (a MC, VI. Phone (555) 555-5555 or (800) 555-5555.

holiday
10-18); free (on Tues.).

BOONVILLE (B-4) pop. 1,138, elev. 1,066'

⬩ **RED OAK** is off I-95 exit 4A, just n. to Dogwood Dr., then 2 mi. e. to 610 Magnolia St. The 1812 house has eight 60-foot columns and is furnished in period. Allow 1 hour minimum. Daily 9-7, May 15-Labor Day; 9-5, Apr. 1-May 14 and day after Labor Day-Thanksgiving; 10-4, rest of year. Hours may vary; phone ahead. Closed Jan. 1, Easter, Thanksgiving and Dec. 25. Last admission 45 minutes before closing. Admission $8; $5 (ages 6-12 and 66+); $3 (ages 0-5). AX, DS, MC, VI. Phone (555) 555-5555 or (800) 555-5555.

RECREATIONAL ACTIVITIES

White-water Rafting

- **River Adventures**, 1 mi. s. on SR 50. Write P.O. Box 1012, Gale, NC 35244. Trips daily May-Oct. Phone (828) 555-5555.

BREVARD (F-3) pop. 6,789, elev. 2,229'

The town is a popular summer resort at the entrance to Pisgah National Forest (*see place listing p. 166*). Brevard is in an area known as the "Land of Waterfalls," sporting more than 250 named waterfalls such as Laughing Falls and Courthouse Falls. Brevard Music Center offers concerts nightly, last weekend in June to mid

Brevard

RECREATIONAL ACTIVITI

White-water Rafting

- **River Adventures**, 1 mi. s. or Box 1012, Gale, NC 35244. T Phone (828) 555-5555.

Swain Co
Box 509,

white-
begin
Lake
board
tahal
Cl
low
Oct.
VI.

RE
Wh

Directions

Unless otherwise specified, directions are given from the center of town, using the following highway designations:

I=interstate highway   **US**=federal highway
SR=state route   **CR**=county road
FM=farm to market   **FR**=forest road
Mex.=Mexican highway   **Hwy.**=Canadian or
                                 Caribbean highway

Prices and Dates of Operations

Admission prices are quoted without sales tax. Children under the lowest age specified are admitted free when accompanied by an adult. Days, months and age groups written with a hyphen are inclusive.

Prices pertaining to points of interest in the United States are quoted in U.S. dollars; points of interest in Canada are quoted in Canadian dollars; prices for points of interest in Mexico and the Caribbean are quoted as an approximate U.S. dollar equivalent.

Schedules and admission rates may change throughout the validity period of this guide. Check AAA.com for the most current information.

Credit Cards Accepted

AX=American Express   **JC**=Japan Credit Bureau
CB=Carte Blanche   **MC**=MasterCard
DC=Diners Club   **VI**=VISA
DS=Discover

Bulleted Listings

Gambling establishments are evaluated by AAA personnel; casinos within hotels are presented for member information regardless of whether the lodging is AAA Approved.

Recreational activities of a participatory nature (requiring physical exertion or special skills) are not inspected.

Wineries are inspected by AAA Tourism Editors to ensure they meet listing requirements and offer tours.

All are presented in an abbreviated bulleted format for informational purposes.

BOONE — BURLINGTON, NC   125

nty Chamber of Commerce: P.O.
Bryson City, NC 28713; phone (828)

Dr., then 2 mi. e. to 610 Magnolia St. The
ed in period. Allow 1 hour minimum. Daily
y after Labor Day-Thanksgiving; 10-4, rest
1, Easter, Thanksgiving and Dec. 25. Last
es 6-12 and 66+); $3 (ages 0-5). AX, DS,

departing
Bryson City, combines rail and
ater excursions in one outing. The adventure
with a scenic 2-hour train trip across Fontana
the top of Nantahala Gorge. Rafts are then
d for a guided 3-hour trip down the Nan-
River. Lunch is included.
dren under 60 pounds are not permitted. Al-
hours minimum. Trips daily mid-Apr. to late
ares begin at $66; $51 (ages 3-12). DS, MC,
hone (828) 488-2384 or (800) 451-9972.

REATIONAL ACTIVITIES
e-water Rafting

antahala Outdoor Center, 26 mi. s.w. on US
5N. Write 13077 Hwy. 19W, Bryson City, NC
8713. Trips daily Mar.-Oct. Phone (828)
88-2175 or (800) 232-7238.

USA Raft, 12 mi. s. on US 19W. Write 11044 US
19W, Bryson City, NC 28713. Trips daily Mar.-
Sept. Phone (828) 488-3316 or (800) 872-7238.

Wildwater Ltd., 12 mi. s.w. on US 19/74W.
Write P.O. Box 309, Long Creek, SC 29658. Trips
daily Apr.-Oct. Phone (828) 488-2384 or (800)
451-9972.

BURLINGTON (A-5) pop. 44,917, elev. 656'
Burlington is a textile industry center with numer-
outlet shops that attract bargain hunters
es. Clothing, leather goods, towels,
ets and furniture are popular
as a maintenance and re-
Carolina Railroad; the
as a train station and

ES

ty Park, at South
is a 1910 Dentzel
ir detail and intri-
ls still exist world-
SR 50. Write P.O.   s, the hand-carved
ips daily May-Oct.   ffe and reindeer, four
                         . The carousel operates
                         ; phone (336) 222-5030.

Understanding the Lodging Listing

Local Member Value

AAA or SAVE identify hotels that offer members a rate guarantee and up to two free special amenities as part of their Official Appointment partnership with AAA. Rate guarantee: Discounted standard room rate (usually based on last standard room availability) or the lowest public rate available at time of booking for dates of stay. Free special amenity options are included in the listing and could be either: Breakfast, local telephone calls, newspaper, room upgrade, preferred room, high-speed Internet.

Diamond Rating

The number of diamonds informs you of the overall complexity of a lodging's amenities and service. Red indicates an Official Appointment lodging. An [fyi] in place of diamonds indicates the property has not been rated but is included as an "information only" service. A detailed description of each rating level appears on page 20.

Classification

All diamond rated lodgings are classified using three key elements: style of operation, overall concept and service level. See pages 22-23 for details on our classifications.

Rates

The property's standard 2-person rates and effective dates are shown.

Rates are provided to AAA by each lodging and represent the regular (rack) rate or ranges for a standard room. Rates are rounded to the nearest dollar and do not include taxes. U.S., Mexican and Caribbean rates are in U.S. dollars; rates for Canadian lodgings are in Canadian dollars.

Information about cancellation and minimum stay policies is provided in the Terms section of the property's listing.

Online Reservations

This notation indicates AAA/CAA members can conveniently check room availability, validate room rates and make reservations for this property in a secure online environment at AAA.com.

Service Availability

Unit types, amenities and room features preceded by the word "Some" indicate the item is available on a limited basis, potentially within only one unit.

Nationwide Member Value

The blue box in the listing identifies hotel brands that offer an everyday member benefit at all AAA Approved locations. (See page 19 for additional program benefits.)

Spotting Symbol

Black ovals with white numbers are used to locate, or "spot," lodgings on maps we provide for larger cities.

Credit Cards Accepted

AX=American Express   **JC**=Japan Credit Bureau
CB=Carte Blanche   **MC**=MasterCard
DC=Diners Club   **VI**=VISA
DS=Discover

Icons

Lodging icons represent some of the member values, services and facilities offered.

Discounts

- **ASK** May offer discount
- **S$_D$** Offers minimum 10% senior discount to members over 59

Member Services

- Airport transportation
- Pets allowed (call property for restrictions and fees)
- Restaurant on premises
- Restaurant off premises (walking distance)
- 24-hour room service
- Full bar
- Child care
- Accessible features (call property for available services and amenities)

Leisure Activities

- Full-service casino
- Pool
- Health club on premises
- Health club off premises
- Recreational activities

In-Room Amenities

- Designated non-smoking rooms
- VCR
- Movies
- Refrigerator
- Microwave
- Coffee maker
- No air conditioning
- No TV
- No cable TV
- No telephones

Safety Features

(see page 24)
(Mexico and Caribbean only)

- **S** Sprinklers
- **D** Smoke detectors

The presence of the term **SOME UNITS** indicates that any amenity icon in that section is available on a limited basis, potentially in only one unit. The term **FEE** appearing to the left of an amenity icon indicates an extra charge applies.

14

Understanding the Restaurant Listing

Official Appointment

  or indicates our Official Appointment (OA) restaurants. The OA program permits properties to display and advertise the AAA or CAA emblem. We highlight these properties in red to help you quickly identify them. The AAA or CAA Approved sign helps traveling members find restaurants that want member business.

Diamond Rating

The number of diamonds informs you of the overall complexity of food, presentation, service and ambience. Red indicates an Official Appointment restaurant. A detailed description of each diamond level appears on page 21.

Cuisine Type

The cuisine type helps you select a dining facility that caters to your individual taste. AAA currently recognizes more than 90 different cuisine types.

Prices

Rates shown represent the minimum and maximum entree cost per person. Exceptions may include one-of-a-kind or special market priced items. Rates are rounded to the nearest dollar and do not include taxes. U.S., Mexican and Caribbean rates are in U.S. dollars; rates for Canadian restaurants are in Canadian dollars.

Icons

Icons provide additional information about services and facilities.

 No air-conditioning

 Accessible features offered
 (call property for available services and amenities)

 Designated smoking section available

Menus

This notation indicates AAA/CAA members can conveniently view the restaurant's menu in a secure online environment at AAA.com.

Spotting Symbol

White ovals with black numbers serve as restaurant locators and are used to locate, or "spot," restaurants on maps we provide for larger cities.

Classifications

If applicable, a restaurant may be defined as:

Classic - renowned and/or landmark restaurant in business longer than 25 years, known for unique style and ambience.

Historic - properties must meet one of the following criteria:

- Listed on the U.S. National Register of Historic Places
- Designated a U.S. National Historic Landmark
- Located in a U.S. National Register Historic District

Separate criteria designate historic properties in Canada, Mexico and the Caribbean.

Credit Cards Accepted

AX = American Express
CB = Carte Blanche
DC = Diners Club
DS = Discover
JC = Japan Credit Bureau
MC = MasterCard
VI = VISA

ighway, the casual eatery prepares tasty steak, seafood, chicken and **Phone:** 336/299-8850 **Reservations:** accepted. **Hours:** 11:15 am-10 pm, Fri & Sat-11 pm, Sun ress: 601 Friendly Center Rd 27408 **Location:** Jct Wendover Ave, just ar. **Parking:** on-site. **Cards:** AX, DC, DS, MC, VI.

336/547-8868

y expanded to this newly constructed building, located behind a **Phone:** 555/555-5555 ㊸ The atmosphere is informal, yet the menu offerings are cutting ssional. Dressy casual. **Bar:** full bar. **Reservations:** accepted. Sat 5 pm-9 pm. Closed: 12/25; also Sun, Mon & for dinner Super **Location:** I-40, exit 213, 2 mi n, then just e on Hunt Club Rd; **Parking:** on-site. **Cards:** AX, DC, DS, MC, VI. **Classic**

ections include leg of lamb, flank steak, bacon-wrapped filet and many more. Dressy casual. **Bar:** full bar. 30 pm. Closed: 12/25; also Sun. **Address:** 4512 W Market St e mi e on Wendover Ave, exit Holden Rd, just n, then 0.8 mi w.

asually upscale dining atmosphere. The menu features dishes **Phone:** 336/273-7057 ays, such as in stuffed rainbow trout and lamb with honey-mint prepared with flair, including roasted pulled pork, fried chicken bar. **Reservations:** accepted. **Hours:** 11:30 am-9:30 pm, Fri-idays; also Sun. **Address:** 100-D W Washington St 27401 arking: street. **Cards:** AX, DS, MC, VI.

upscale eatery, with the focus of the cuisine on incorporating **Phone:** 336/370-0707 gional American fare. Casual dress. **Bar:** full bar. 30, Fri & Sat-11 pm, Sun 10 am-10 pm. Closed: 11/27, 408 **Location:** Wendover Ave, exit US 220 N/Westover a. **Cards:** AX, DS, MC, VI.

gthy menu of burgers, wraps, sandwiches and hearty pub **Phone:** 336/274-1373 Outdoor seating is offered during warm weather. Casual dnight. Closed: 1/1, 11/27, 12/24, 12/25. **Address:** 345 S a. **Parking:** street. **Cards:** AX, DS, MC, VI.

tastiest and is served with a smile in the comfortable, **Phone:** 336/294-5551 e wine. **Hours:** 11 am-3:30 & 5-9:30 pm. **Address:** 4B eastbound; exit 214 westbound, 1 mi ne, exit Spring X, DS, MC, VI.

s as fish and chips, gourmet sandwiches, the signature **Phone:** 336/299-3649 ck Angus beef. Sauces, dressings and soups are -site brewery. Casual dress. **Bar:** full bar. **Hours:** 11 d: 11/27, 12/25. **Address:** 714 Francis King St 27410 d, just w on Hunt Club Rd, then just n. **Parking:** on-

o this newly constructed building, located behind a **Phone:** 336/297-0950 ere is informal, yet the menu offerings are cutting sy casual. **Bar:** full bar. **Reservations:** accepted n. Closed: 12/25; also Sun, Mon & for dinner Super 40, exit 213, 2 mi n, then just e on Hunt Club Rd; e. **Cards:** AX, DC, DS, MC, VI.

16

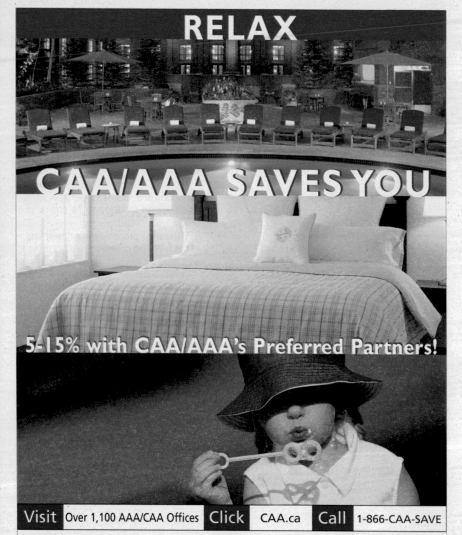

RELAX

CAA/AAA SAVES YOU

5-15% with CAA/AAA's Preferred Partners!

| Visit | Over 1,100 AAA/CAA Offices | Click | CAA.ca | Call | 1-866-CAA-SAVE |

CAA/AAA Preferred Lodging Partners

Aloft
Best Western
Courtyard by Marriott
Element
Fairfield Inn
Four Points by Sheraton
Hyatt Hotels & Resorts
Hyatt Place
Hyatt Summerfield Suites

La Quinta Inn & Suites
Le Meridien
Marriott
Renaissance Hotels & Resorts
Residence Inn
Sheraton Hotels & Resorts
Springhill Suites

St. Regis Hotels & Resorts
The Luxury Collection
TownePlace Suites
W Hotels Worldwide
Westin Hotels & Resorts

– see page 19 for full details.
Visit, Click, Call for member savings.

Lodging Rates Guaranteed

AAA/CAA members are guaranteed they will not be charged more than the maximum regular rate printed in the TourBook guide in each rate range for a standard room. Rates may vary within the range, depending on season and room type. Listed rates are usually based on last standard room availability. Obtain current AAA/CAA member rates and make reservations at AAA.com.

Discounts

Member discounts, when offered, will apply to rates quoted within the rate range and are applicable at the time of booking. Special rates used in advertising, as well as special short-term promotional rates lower than the lowest listed rate in the range, are not subject to additional member discounts.

Exceptions

Rates for properties operating as concessionaires for the U.S. National Park Service are not guaranteed due to governing regulations. Rates in the Mexico TourBook are not guaranteed and may fluctuate based on the exchange rate of the peso.

Lodgings may temporarily increase room rates, not recognize discounts or modify pricing policies during special events. Examples of special events range from Mardi Gras and the Kentucky Derby (including pre-Derby events) to college football games, holidays, holiday periods and state fairs. Although some special events are listed in AAA/CAA TourBook guides and on AAA.com, it is always wise to check in advance with AAA travel professionals for specific dates.

Get the Room You Reserved

When making your reservation, identify yourself as a AAA or CAA member and request written confirmation to guarantee: type of room, rate, dates of stay, and cancellation and refund policies. At registration, show your membership card.

When you find your room is not as specified, and you have written confirmation of reservations for a certain type of accommodation, you should be given the option of choosing a different room or finding one elsewhere. Should you choose to go elsewhere and a refund is refused or resisted, submit the matter to AAA/CAA within 30 days, along with complete documentation, including your reasons for refusing the room and copies of your written confirmation and any receipts or canceled checks associated with this problem.

If you are charged more than the maximum rate listed in the TourBook guide for a standard

room, question the additional charge. If management refuses to adhere to the published rate, pay for the room and submit your receipt and membership number to AAA/CAA within 30 days. Include all pertinent information: dates of stay, rate paid, itemized paid receipts, number of persons in your party and the room number you occupied, and list any extra room equipment used. A refund of the amount paid in excess of the stated maximum will be made if our investigation indicates that unjustified charging occurred.

Deposit, Refund and Cancellation Policies

Most establishments give full deposit refunds if they have been notified at least 48 hours before the normal check-in time. Listing prose will note if more than 48 hours' notice is required for cancellation. Some properties may charge a cancellation or handling fee. When this applies, "cancellation fee imposed" will appear in the listing. If you cancel too late, you have little recourse if a refund is denied.

When an establishment requires full or partial payment in advance and your trip is cut short, a refund may not be given.

When canceling a reservation, phone the lodging immediately. Make a note of the date and time you called, the cancellation number if there is one, and the name of the person who handled the cancellation. If your AAA/CAA club made your reservation, allow them to make the cancellation for you as well, so you will have proof of cancellation.

Check-in and Check-out Times

Check-in and check-out times are shown in the lodging listings, under Terms, only if they are before 10 a.m. or after 3 p.m. respectively.

Members Save With Our Partners

These National Show Your Card & Save® partners provide the listed member benefits. Admission tickets that offer greater discounts may be available for purchase at the local AAA/CAA club. A maximum of six tickets is available at the discount price at the gate. Visit AAA.com/Save to discover all the great Show Your Card & Save® discounts in your area.

SeaWorld, Busch Gardens, Sesame Place
AAA.com/SeaWorld, AAA.com/BuschGardens,
AAA.com/SesamePlace

- Save on admission at the gate, at participating offices, or online
- Save 10% on up-close dining; visit Guest Relations for details

Six Flags
AAA.com/SixFlags

- Save on admission at the gate, at participating offices, or online
- Save 10% on merchandise purchases of $15 or more at in-park stores
- Save 10% on Brunch with Bugs online

Universal Orlando and Universal Studios Hollywood
AAA.com/Universal

- Save on admission at the gate, at participating offices, or online
- Save 10% on select merchandise and dining in-park and at CityWalk Orlando

Gray Line AAA.com/GrayLine

- Save 10% on sightseeing tours of 1 day or less

Restaurant Partner
Savings applies to AAA/CAA members and up to five guests.

Joe's Crab Shack

- Save 10% on food, non-alcoholic beverages and merchandise

Landry's Seafood House, The Crab House, Chart House, Muer Seafood Restaurants, and Aquarium and Downtown Aquarium Restaurants

- Save 10% on food and non-alcoholic beverages at all of the above restaurants
- Save 10% on merchandise at Aquarium and Downtown Aquarium restaurants.

Hard Rock Cafe

- Save 10% on food, non-alcoholic beverages and merchandise at all U.S. and select Canadian and international locations

Tanger Outlet Centers www.tangeroutlet.com

- Save up to 20% on total purchase at select merchants with AAA/CAA coupon booklet
- Member BONUS: FREE $5 gift card for each additional Tanger Outlet Center visited after first within same calendar year
- Show membership card and register at the AAA customer service desk when you visit

Amtrak

- 10% discount on rail fare when booked at least 3 days in advance of travel date

Carey
AAA.com/Carey

- Save 15% on chauffeured ground transportation at over 450 locations worldwide

Grand Canyon Railway

- Save up to 20% on rail fare, hotel accommodations, restaurant and gift shop purchases

AAA Preferred Lodging Partners

EXPECT SAVINGS, SELECTION, AND SATISFACTION

- **Best AAA/CAA member rates for your dates of stay.** Provide valid membership number when placing reservation and show your card at hotel check-in.
- **Satisfaction guarantee.** Notify the property if you are dissatisfied with any part of your stay. If the matter cannot be resolved, you may be entitled to compensation (see page 17).
- **Seasonal promotions and special member offers.** Visit AAA.com to view current offers.
- **Everyday member benefit.*** Look for the blue boxes in the TourBook listings for everyday values offered at all AAA Approved locations.

*Offer good at time of publication: Chains and offers may change without notice. Official Hotel Partner discounts may vary in Mexico and the Caribbean.

| Visit | Over 1,100 AAA Offices | Click | AAA.com | Call | 866-AAA-SAVE |

Understanding the Diamond Ratings

AAA/CAA Inspectors have evaluated and rated each of the 60,000 lodging and restaurant establishments in the TourBook series to ensure quality travel information for our members. All properties must meet AAA's minimum requirements (for lodgings) concerning cleanliness, comfort and security - or - AAA's minimum requirements (for restaurants) pertaining to cleanliness, food preparation and service.

Eligible applicants receive an unannounced evaluation by a AAA/CAA Inspector that includes two distinct components:

- **AAA Approval:** The Inspector first must determine whether the property meets the criteria required to be AAA Approved. Every establishment that meets these strict guidelines offers AAA members the assurance that, regardless of the diamond rating, it provides acceptable quality, cleanliness, service and value.
- **AAA Diamond Rating:** Once an establishment becomes AAA Approved, it is then assigned a rating of one to five diamonds, indicating the extensiveness of its facilities, amenities and services, from basic to moderate to luxury. These diamond ratings guide members in selecting establishments appropriately matched to their needs and expectations.

LODGINGS

1 Diamond

One diamond lodgings typically appeal to the budget-minded traveler. They provide essential, no-frills accommodations and basic comfort and hospitality.

2 Diamond

Two diamond lodgings appeal to family travelers seeking affordable yet more than the basic accommodations. Facilities, decor and amenities are modestly enhanced.

3 Diamond

Three diamond lodgings offer a distinguished style. Properties are multi-faceted, with marked upgrades in physical attributes, amenities and guest comforts.

4 Diamond

Four diamond lodgings are refined and stylish. Physical attributes are upscale. The fundamental hallmarks at this level include an extensive array of amenities combined with a high degree of hospitality, service and attention to detail.

5 Diamond

Five diamond lodgings provide the ultimate in luxury and sophistication. Physical attributes are extraordinary in every manner. Service is meticulous, exceeding guest expectations and maintaining impeccable standards of excellence. Extensive personalized services and amenities provide first-class comfort.

fyi The lodging listings with **fyi** in place of diamonds are included as an *information only* service for members. The icon indicates that a property has not been rated for one or more of the following reasons: too new to rate, under construction, under major renovation, not evaluated, may not meet all AAA requirements.

A property not meeting all AAA requirements is included for either its member value or because it may be the only accommodation available in the area. Listing prose will give insight as to why the **fyi** designation was assigned.

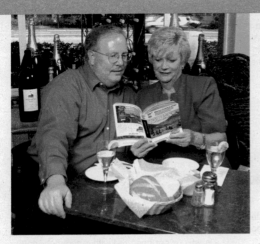

RESTAURANTS

1 Diamond

One diamond restaurants provide simple, familiar specialty food (such as burgers, chicken, pizza or tacos) at an economical price. Often self-service, basic surroundings complement a no-nonsense approach.

2 Diamond

Two diamond restaurants offer a familiar, family-oriented experience. Menu selection includes home-style foods and family favorites, often cooked to order, modestly enhanced and reasonably priced. Service is accommodating yet relaxed, a perfect complement to casual surroundings.

3 Diamond

Three diamond restaurants convey an entry into fine dining and are often positioned as adult-oriented experiences. The atypical menu may feature the latest cooking trends and/or traditional cuisine. Expanded beverage offerings complement the menu. The ambience is well coordinated, comfortable and enhanced by a professional service staff.

4 Diamond

Four diamond restaurants provide a distinctive fine-dining experience that is typically expensive. Surroundings are highly refined with upscale enhancements throughout. Highly creative chefs use imaginative presentations to augment fresh, top-quality ingredients. A proficient service staff meets or exceeds guest expectations. A wine steward may offer menu-specific knowledge to guide selection.

5 Diamond

Five diamond restaurants are luxurious and renowned for consistently providing a world-class experience. Highly acclaimed chefs offer artistic menu selections that are imaginative and unique, using only the finest ingredients available. A maitre d' leads an expert service staff in exceeding guest expectations, attending to every detail in an effortless and unobtrusive manner.

fyi The restaurants with fyi in place of diamonds are included as an *information only* service for members. These listings provide additional dining choices but have not yet been evaluated.

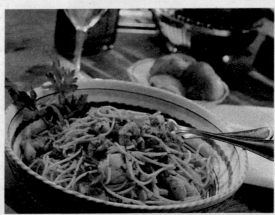

Understanding the Lodging Classifications

To ensure that your lodging needs and preferences are met, we recommend that you consider an establishment's classification when making your travel choices. While the quality and comfort at properties with the same diamond rating should be consistent (regardless of the classification), there are differences in typical decor/theme elements, range of facilities and service levels.

Large-scale Hotel

A multistory establishment with interior room entrances. A variety of guest unit styles is offered. Public areas are spacious and include a variety of facilities such as a restaurant, fitness center, spa, business center, shops or meeting rooms.

Hotel Royal Plaza, Lake Buena Vista, FL

Small-scale Hotel

A multistory establishment typically with interior room entrances. A variety of guest unit styles is offered. Public areas are limited in size and/or the variety of facilities available.

Baymont Inn, Dallas Ft. Worth-Airport N, TX

Motel

A 1- to 3-story establishment typically with exterior room entrances facilitating convenient access to parking. The standard guest units have one bedroom with a bathroom and are typically similar in decor and design throughout. Public areas are limited in size and/or the variety of facilities available.

Best Western Deltona Inn, Deltona, FL

Country Inn

Similar in definition to a bed and breakfast but usually larger in scale, with spacious public areas offering a dining facility that serves at least breakfast and dinner.

Greenville Inn, Greenville, ME

Bed & Breakfast

Small-scale properties emphasizing a high degree of personal touches that provide guests an "at home" feeling. Guest units tend to be individually decorated. Rooms may not include some modern amenities such as televisions and telephones, and may have a shared bathroom. Usually owner-operated with a common room or parlor separate from the innkeeper's living quarters, where guests and operators can interact during evening and breakfast hours. Evening office closures are normal. A Continental or full, hot breakfast is served and is included in the room rate.

1884 Paxton House Inn, Thomasville, GA

Condominium

Vacation-oriented or extended-stay, apartment-style accommodations that are routinely available for rent through a management company. Units vary in design and decor and often contain one or more bedrooms, a living room, full kitchen and an eating area. Studio-type models combine the sleeping and living areas into one room. Typically, basic cleaning supplies, kitchen utensils and complete bed and bath linens are supplied. The guest registration area may be located off-site.

Sands of Kahana, Kahana, Maui, HI

Cabin/Cottage

Vacation-oriented, small-scale, freestanding houses or cabins. Units vary in design and decor and often contain one or more bedrooms, a living room, kitchen, dining area and bathroom. Studio-type models combine the sleeping and living areas into one room. Typically, basic cleaning supplies, kitchen utensils, and complete bed and bath linens are supplied. The guest registration area may be located off-site.

Desert Rose Inn, Bluff, UT

Ranch

Typically a working ranch with an obvious rustic, Western theme. In general, equestrian-related activities are featured, but ranches may

Lost Valley Ranch, Deckers, CO

include other animals and activities as well. A variety of guest unit styles is offered in a family-oriented atmosphere.

Vacation Home

Vacation-oriented or extended-stay, large-scale, freestanding houses that are routinely available for rent through a

ResortQuest, Hilton Head Island, SC

management company. Houses vary in design and decor and often contain two or more bedrooms, a living room, full kitchen, dining room and multiple bathrooms. Typically, basic cleaning supplies, kitchen utensils, and complete bed and bath linens are supplied. The guest registration area may be located off-site.

Lodging Subclassifications

The following are subclassifications that may appear along with the classifications listed previously to provide a more specific description of the lodging.

Casino

Extensive gaming facilities are available such as blackjack, craps, keno and slot machines. Note: This subclassification will not appear beneath its diamond rating in the listing. It will be indicated by a 🎲 icon and will be included in the row of icons immediately below the lodging listing.

Classic

Renowned and landmark properties, older than 50 years, well-known for their unique style and ambience.

Historic

These properties are typically over 75 years of age and exhibit many features of a historic nature with respect to architecture, design, furnishings, public record or acclaim. Properties must meet one of the following criteria:

- Maintained the integrity of the historical aspect
- Listed on the U.S. National Register of Historic Places
- Designated a U.S. National Historic Landmark
- Located in a U.S. National Register Historic District

Separate criteria designate historic properties in Canada, Mexico and the Caribbean.

Vacation Rental

Typically houses, condos, cottages or cabins; these properties are a "home away from home" offering more room and greater value for the money and generally provide the conveniences of home, such as full kitchens and washers/dryers. They are located in resort or popular destination areas within close proximity to major points of interest, attractions, or recreation areas. These properties may require a pre-arranged reservation and check-in at an off-site location. Housekeeping services may be limited or not included.

Resort

Recreation-oriented, geared to vacation travelers seeking a specific destination experience. Travel packages, meal plans, themed entertainment, and social and recreational programs are typically available. Recreational facilities are extensive and may include spa treatments, golf, tennis, skiing, fishing, water sports, etc. Larger resorts may offer a variety of guest accommodations.

Guest Safety

Room Security

In order to be approved for listing in AAA/CAA TourBook guides for the United States and Canada, accommodations must have dead bolt locks on all guest room entry doors and connecting room doors.

If the area outside the guest room door is not visible from inside the room through a window or door panel, viewports must be installed on all guest room entry doors. Bed and breakfast properties and country inns are not required to have viewports. Ground floor and easily accessible sliding doors must be equipped with some type of secondary security locks.

Even with those approval requirements, AAA cannot guarantee guest safety. AAA Inspectors view a percentage of rooms at each property since it is not feasible to evaluate every room in every lodging establishment. Therefore, AAA cannot guarantee that there are working locks on all doors and windows in all guest rooms.

Fire Safety

Because of the highly specialized skills needed to conduct professional fire safety inspections, AAA/CAA Inspectors cannot assess fire safety.

Properties must meet all federal, state/province and local fire codes. Each guest unit in all U.S. and Canadian lodging properties must be equipped with an operational, single-station smoke detector. A AAA/CAA Inspector has evaluated a sampling of the rooms to verify this equipment is in place.

Mexico and the Caribbean

Requirements for some features, such as door locks and smoke detectors/sprinkler systems, differ in Mexico and the Caribbean. If a property met AAA's security requirements at the time of the evaluation, the phrase "Meets AAA guest room security requirements" appears in the listing.

Service Animals

The Americans with Disabilities Act (ADA) prohibits U.S. businesses that serve the public from discriminating against persons with disabilities. Some businesses have mistakenly denied access to persons who use service animals. Businesses must permit entry to guests and their service animals, as well as allow service animals to accompany guests to all public areas of a property.

A property is permitted to ask whether the animal is a service animal or a pet, and whether the guest has a disability. The property may not, however, ask questions about the nature of the disability, the service provided by the animal, or require proof of a disability or certification that the animal is a service animal. These regulations may not apply in Canada, Mexico or the Caribbean.

No fees or deposits, even those normally charged for pets, may be charged for service animals. Service animals fulfill a critical need for their owners—they are not pets.

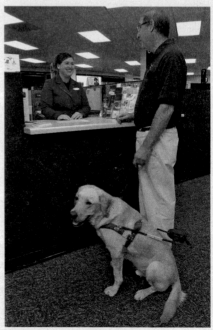

Frank Frand with his seeing eye dog, Cardinal.

Savings for all Seasons

Hertz rents Fords and other fine cars. ® REG. U.S. PAT. OFF. © HERTZ SYSTEM INC. 1999/2006-09.

No matter the season, Hertz offers CAA members exclusive discounts and benefits.

Operating in 150 countries at over 7,600 locations, Hertz makes traveling more convenient and efficient wherever and whenever you go. Hertz offers CAA members discounts up to 20% on car rentals worldwide.

To receive your exclusive CAA member discounts and benefits, mention your CAA membership card at time of reservation and present it at time of rental. **In addition**, to receive a free one car class upgrade on daily, weekly or weekend rental in the United States, Puerto Rico and Canada, mention PC# 969194 at the time of reservation. Offer is valid for vehicle pick-up on or before 12/15/08.

For reservations and program details, call your CAA Travel centre or the Hertz/CAA Desk at **1-800-654-3080.**

With the CAA Visa TravelMoney®
card, worry-free travel is here. Like
travelers cheques, this card has
replacement and refund options,
emergency assistance service, zero
liability, purchase security, and
even luggage protection.

The next time you travel, don't
forget to pack the CAA Visa
TravelMoney® card.

Honey, I lost my wallet.

Without the CAA Visa TravelMoney® card,
their money problems would be monumental.

* Terms and conditions apply, see detailed terms and
conditions provided with your card fulfillment kit.

 Visit your participating CAA office.

Alberta

Camping
Doesn't get better than in Alberta

Shop 'til You Drop
In a mall so large it has a hotel and a water park

The Old West is Alive and Well
For 10 days in the Canadian Rockies during The Calgary Stampede

Variety Unsurpassed
Placid lakes, prairies, red rock canyons, lush forests, and soaring mountains

Lake Louise
Ski it in winter, hike it in summer, admire it all year

Abraham Lake, near Cline River
Travel Alberta

seasons
in the sun

Waterton Lakes National Park
of Canada / © Chuck Haney
Danita Delimont Stock Photography

Alberta is a *happening* place.
In any season you're bound to find
Albertans commemorating some aspect of
their multifaceted province. And with the Canadian
Rockies blocking eastbound Pacific moisture, odds
are great that whatever the event, it will take place
in sunshine.

Winter festivals in Jasper and Banff showcase
snowy weather sports like skiing, sledding and
ice-skating against a backdrop of postcard-beautiful
alpine scenery.

As spring and summer heat things up, Edmonton
earns its reputation as "Canada's Festival City,"
with events celebrating local culture. Laughter and
applause punctuate the Edmonton International
Street Performers Festival, while food lovers can
take a gastronomic trip around the world as they
sample from a spectrum of cuisines during the
Edmonton Heritage Festival.

The bronc-buckin' Calgary Stampede all but
steals the spotlight. Much more than a big-time
rodeo, this Wild West exhibition turns into a huge
outdoor party with parades and a carnival midway.

In autumn Calgary's Spruce Meadows hosts
another exciting equestrian event—the Masters
Tournament, one of the world's most distinguished
show jumping competitions.

Of course, you don't have to trick or treat or
rope a steer if you travel to Alberta. Just visiting
Canada's sunniest province is a special event.

Mirror images of mountain peaks reflected in calm, clear lakes. The twinkling, shimmering dance of lights known as "aurora borealis." Blankets of golden wheat and vivid canola pulled up snugly over the rolling countryside.

Typical visions of the Wild West? Hardly.

But Alberta urges you to stretch the definition of what the Canadian West is all about.

Plenty in the province fits neatly into the Western mold. Take Calgary, for instance. The former cow town's very roots are in ranching and meatpacking. Thousands of folks in denim and 10-gallon hats gather to watch the rough-and-tumble rodeo and chuck wagon races of the 10-day Calgary Stampede. Even the roof of the Saddledome, home of the National Hockey League's Calgary Flames, is in the shape of—you guessed it—a saddle.

But although Calgary is decidedly Western in many ways, it prides itself on having cultivated a personality that's much more well-rounded.

A Multifaceted Identity

In 1988 the world's best athletes united in the city for the Olympic Winter Games. From grizzly bears to wood bison, the renowned Calgary Zoo offers the best chance to see native wildlife. It also is home to more than 4,000 plants and a collection of life-size replicas of dinosaurs in a simulated Mesozoic landscape. Futuristic elevated "pedways" link nearly half of the buildings downtown.

And so it goes with the rest of the province, where such dichotomies are commonplace.

The faintly sweet aroma of 18 varieties of orchids in Cypress Hills Interprovincial Park lends to an air of tranquility and peace. But just a scant hop and skip to the northwest, volatile Medicine Hat harnesses an extensive reserve of natural gas that prompted Rudyard Kipling to describe the city as having "all hell for a basement."

Rafters steel themselves against the raging rapids of the Elbow, Highwood and Kananaskis rivers in Kananaskis Country. Turbulent rushes of water sweeping over rock at Athabasca and Sunwapta falls become imposing towers of irresistible ice to climbers who chink away at them in winter. Amid the chaos, however, canoeists ply the placid, emerald waters of Banff National Park of Canada's

The Hudson's Bay Co. gets fur-trading rights in a portion of what is now Alberta.
1670

Anthony Henday is the first European to visit the area.
1754

Calgary is established as a North West Mounted Police fort.
1875

Library of Congress

1795
Edmonton is founded as a Hudson's Bay trading fort.

Alberta Historical Timeline

Library of Congress

1883
The Canadian Pacific Railway reaches Calgary.

Moraine Lake and gaze upon the 10 glaciated summits that rise around it to provide a serene habitat for elk, deer and bighorn sheep.

The ground in Fort McMurray holds a significant reserve of lucrative oil sands deposits, but most people visit the town for its treasure in the sky: a spectacular view of the northern lights.

A Canadian Melting Pot

Alberta's diversity also stems from the many ethnic currents that run through it.

A strong Ukrainian heritage marks the area east of Edmonton. At the Ukrainian Cultural Heritage Village costumed interpreters demonstrate what life was like for settlers from the 1890s to 1930. The design of Vegreville's famed bronze, gold and silver pysanka, or Ukrainian Easter egg, depicts the people's faith and commemorates the protection provided to them by the Royal Canadian Mounted Police. Museums in Edmonton and Mundare hold collections of cultural items.

West of Edmonton, English-, French- and German-speaking emigrants from central Europe established villages. Murals and a living-history museum in Stony Plain tell their stories.

The history of native cultures is evident at the Head-Smashed-In Buffalo Jump Interpretive Centre near Fort Macleod and in the petroglyphs and pictographs at Writing-on-Stone Provincial Park, near Milk River. Indian Battle Park in Lethbridge details a significant battle between the Cree and Blackfoot Indians.

Traditions of the aboriginal people are remembered in Edmonton's Royal Alberta Museum. The territory around Cypress Hills Interprovincial Park—now home to ruminants, beavers and coyotes—nurtured a community of aborigines more than 7,000 years ago.

Prehistoric denizens of the Red Deer Valley, the dinosaurs, left their mark on the region by way of the fossils left behind in walls of sediment. Drumheller best captures the age along the Dinosaur Trail and through displays in its museums. To the southeast, a fertile fossil bed at Dinosaur Provincial Park contains the remains of 35 species of dinosaurs.

Alberta weaves a rich, vibrant tapestry of cultures, geography and a wealth of experiences. Westward ho.

The province of Alberta is formed.
1905

The first plant to extract synthetic crude oil from oil sands is built in Fort McMurray.
1967

Construction of West Edmonton Mall, one of the world's largest malls, is completed.
1998

Travel Alberta

1988
Calgary hosts the Winter Olympic Games.

2005
Alberta celebrates its 100th year as a Canadian province.

1914
Oil is discovered in the Turner Valley.

Recreation

Alberta is a nature lover's paradise. A place where unspoiled landscapes lend themselves to exploration in any season. A place where midnight summer sunsets in the north cap off long days of rest and relaxation. A place where towering mountains in the west beckon to all who appreciate unrestrained beauty.

Outdoor enthusiasts often look to Alberta's five national parks. Hikers, golfers, boaters, bicyclists, horseback riders, anglers and skiers are among the people who trek to them: Banff, Canada's first national park; Elk Island, an oasis for rare and endangered species; Jasper, a land of glaciers; Waterton Lakes, where the Rockies and prairie meet; and Wood Buffalo, which reaches north into Northwest Territories.

And although the national parks are arguably the most popular spots for recreational escape, sites throughout the grand expanse of untamed Alberta are equally as irresistible.

Experienced guides lead half-day to multiweek **trail riding** expeditions through the Elbow and Sheep valleys in the Kananaskis high country, west of Calgary; Ram Falls, southwest of Rocky Mountain House National Historic Site of Canada; and Cooking Lake-Blackfoot Provincial Recreational Area, east of Edmonton.

Only your imagination limits what you can do in the challenging Rockies. **Hiking, mountain climbing** and **mountain biking** are among the ways to get to know the peaks.

High-Octane Excitement

Pulse-pounding thrills await the adventurous who take on raging rivers for a **whitewater rafting** diversion. Beginners and veterans alike appreciate the draw of the Athabasca, Elbow, Highwood, Kananaskis, Kicking Horse, Red Deer and Sunwapta rivers.

The Blackstone River, a hot spot for **kayaking** in inflatable boats, cuts through the foothills of the Rockies. Slip into the North Saskatchewan River for a memorable **canoeing** experience.

When a blanket of snow covers the majestic Rockies, bundle up and head for the mountains. **Snowshoeing, tobogganing, crosscountry skiing** and **sledding,** which can be done nearly anywhere there's snow, are mainstays of Canadian family fun.

To up the exhilaration factor, take advantage of one of North America's longest ski seasons, which can range from early November to late May in places. Some of the best **downhill skiing** and **snowboarding** the province has to offer is at Marmot Basin, 19 kilometres (12 mi.) south of Jasper; Lake Louise, 57 kilometres (35 mi.) northwest of Banff; Sunshine Village and Banff Mount Norquay, both within 15 minutes of Banff; Fortress Mountain, in Kananaskis Country; and Nakiska, at 90 kilometres (55 mi.) west the closest mountain ski area to Calgary. The boldest of the bold tackle waterfall **ice climbing** or **heliskiing,** in which a helicopter takes skiers to untouched powder.

Leaving a Wake of Powder

Wide, open expanses of windswept grasslands, rolling hills and heavily dusted valleys make for lots of good **snowmobiling,** too. For cheek-reddening mirth, zip through the region around Grande Prairie.

One of Alberta's more popular winter adventures is a trip to Fort McMurray to catch the best view of the awe-inspiring aurora borealis, or "northern lights."

Nearly anywhere you go in the province, you'll find opportunities galore for **fishing.** Alberta's numerous trophy lakes, so designated because of the huge fish that inhabit them, brim with pike, whitefish, perch and walleye. Some notable fly-in trophy lakes are Gardiner and Namur, northwest of Fort McMurray, and Winefred, northeast of Lac La Biche. Head to the Bow River for exceptional trout fly-fishing. Phone (780) 944-0313 for information about regulations and licensing.

For an unforgettable **camping** experience, charter a plane out of Cold Lake, Fort McMurray, Fort Smith, Fort Vermilion, High Level or Lac La Biche and fly to a lodge or camp in the northern lakes.

Recreational Activities

Throughout the TourBook, you may notice a Recreational Activities heading with bulleted listings of recreation-oriented establishments listed underneath. Similar operations also may be mentioned in Destination City recreation sections. Since normal AAA inspection criteria cannot be applied, these establishments are presented only for information. Age, height and weight restrictions may apply. Reservations often are recommended and sometimes are required. Addresses and/or phone numbers are provided so visitors can contact the attraction for additional information.

Fast Facts

POPULATION: 3,290,350.

AREA: 640,045 sq km (247,123 sq mi); ranks 6th.

CAPITAL: Edmonton.

HIGHEST POINT: 3,747 m/12,293 ft., Mount Columbia.

LOWEST POINT: 152 m/499 ft., Salt River at border with the Northwest Territories.

TIME ZONE(S): Mountain. DST.

MINIMUM AGE FOR UNRESTRICTED DRIVER'S LICENSE: 18.

MINIMUM AGE FOR GAMBLING: 18.

SEAT BELT/CHILD RESTRAINT LAWS: Seat belts required for driver and all passengers over age 15. Children ages 6-15 and over 18 kilograms (40 lbs.) required to be in a child restraint or seat belt. Child restraints required for those under age 6 and under 18 kilograms (40 lbs.).

HELMETS FOR MOTORCYCLISTS: Required for all riders.

RADAR DETECTORS: Permitted.

FIREARMS LAWS: By federal law, all nonresidents entering Canada with a firearm must declare their weapon in writing and pay a fee of $25 (Canadian). Contact the Canadian Firearms Centre at (800) 731-4000 to receive a declaration form or for additional information.

HOLIDAYS: Jan. 1; Family Day, Feb. (3rd Mon.); Good Friday; Easter Monday; Victoria Day, May 24 (if a Mon.) or the closest prior Mon.; Canada Day, July 1; Heritage Day, Aug. (1st Mon.); Labour Day, Sept. (1st Mon.); Thanksgiving, Oct. (2nd Mon.); Remembrance Day, Nov. 11; Christmas, Dec. 25; Boxing Day, Dec. 26.

TAXES: Alberta has no provincial sales tax. However, there is a 4 percent tourism levy in addition to the 6 percent national Goods and Services Tax (GST).

INFORMATION CENTERS: Travel Alberta Visitor Centres provide information about accommodations and campgrounds as well as maps. They are located at Canmore on Hwy. 1; Crowsnest Pass on Hwy. 3; Field, British Columbia, on Hwy. 1; Grande Prairie on 106th St.; Hinton on Hwy. 16; Lloydminster on Hwy. 16; Milk River on Hwy. 4; Oyen at the junction of hwys. 9 and 41; Walsh on Hwy. 1; and West Glacier, Mont., at the junction of Hwy. 2 and Going-to-the-Sun Road. Most centers are open daily 9-6, mid-May through Labour Day. A tourism office is open year-round in Canmore.

FURTHER INFORMATION FOR VISITORS:

Travel Alberta
P.O. Box 2500
Edmonton, AB, Canada
T5J 2Z4
(780) 427-4321
(800) 252-3782

RECREATION INFORMATION:

Alberta Tourism, Parks, Recreation and Culture
Parks & Protected Areas
9820 106th St., 2nd Floor
Edmonton, AB, Canada T5K 2J6
(780) 427-3582
(866) 427-3582

FISHING AND HUNTING REGULATIONS:

Sustainable Resource Development Information Centre
9920 108th St., Main Floor
Edmonton, AB, Canada T5K 2M4
(780) 944-0313
(877) 944-0313 (in Alberta)

ALCOHOL CONSUMPTION: Legal age 18.

Alberta
Orientation

N

NOT INTENDED FOR DRIVING.
SEE APPROPRIATE AAA SHEET MAP.

Miles   0   63.2
Kilometers 0   101

Only places listed in the Attractions
section appear on this map.

🚩 See AAA GEM Attractions
🚩 See Chart of Recreation Areas

MEDICINE HAT

CALGARY

Red Deer

Elkwater
16
41
41

Milk River 87
Warner
86

Cardston
Coaldale
Lethbridge 66
5
4

23
46
44
24
60

Clareshom
Nanton 10
2
Fort Macleod 3
6
Pincher Creek 5 2

Waterton Lakes
National Park 11

Municipality of
Crowsnest Pass

Patricia
18
Brooks
42

Hanna
Drumheller
Rosebud
570
36

Stettler
56
Trochu 19 90
21
Irricana
567
9
91

88
High River 23
Okotoks
Longview 7
Bragg Creek 37 35 34 39
40 541
38

Sylvan Lake 76
Markerville 54
Raven
Spruce View 70
Dickson 97

Rocky Mountain House 61
National Historic Site of Canada
14
Banff 32 33 25 40 41
Cochrane
Canmore 36
Kananaskis

Banff National Park
Lake Louise

ICEFIELDS PARKWAY 11

QUEEN
Bow River

CROWSNEST
CANADA
UNITED STATES
MONTANA
ALBERTA
BRITISH COLUMBIA
IDAHO
WASHINGTON

G H I J K L

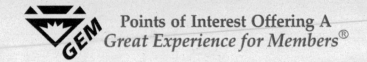

Points of Interest Offering A
Great Experience for Members®

Banff National Park of Canada (G-4)

BANFF NATIONAL PARK OF CANADA—This awe-inspiring wildlife refuge is spectacular in autumn when four-footed residents seem to be reveling in the riotous display of color. See p. 42.

ICEFIELDS PARKWAY (HWY. 93)—This is a really cool scenic drive. See p. 45.

Calgary (H-6)

BUTTERFIELD ACRES CHILDREN'S FARM—Kids, including kids at heart, get to meet and play with newborn animals at this whimsical and educational farm. See p. 52.

CALGARY TOWER—"As far as the eye can see" is all the way to the Rocky Mountains atop this tower. See p. 53.

CALGARY ZOO, BOTANICAL GARDEN & PREHISTORIC PARK—Whoop it up with the cranes and more than 900 animals in this facility partially supported by paintings done by an elephant. See p. 53.

CANADA OLYMPIC PARK—Test your strength, intelligence, accuracy, speed and endurance in simulated athletic competitions in the park's museum. See p. 53.

GLENBOW MUSEUM—You'll find out how cowboys removed their boots when you view early settlement every-day objects. See p. 56.

WHERE THE WORLD MEETS THE WEST

HERITAGE PARK HISTORICAL VILLAGE—Return to the Spartan days of the fur trade, the stark days of settlement and the comforts of the early 20th century at this village. See p. 56.

Cardston (K-6)

REMINGTON CARRIAGE MUSEUM—Experience the transportation of yesterday without being taken for a ride. See p. 62.

Crowsnest Pass (J-5)

FRANK SLIDE INTERPRETIVE CENTRE—Walkways outside the center provide amazing views of the devastation caused by the 1903 rock slide. See p. 62.

Devon (E-6)

CANADIAN PETROLEUM DISCOVERY CENTRE—This attraction is hard to miss; a 53-metre (174-ft.) replica derrick marks the spot of the area's first oil well. See p. 76.

Drumheller (H-7)

ROYAL TYRRELL MUSEUM—Take a high-tech, hands-on journey to the Mesozoic Era and see skeletons of the dinosaurs that lived in the Red Deer River Valley. See p. 64.

Edmonton (E-6)

FORT EDMONTON PARK—This living-history park re-creates periods in Edmonton's history from 1846-1920. See p. 71.

MUTTART CONSERVATORY—The plants in these four pyramids received two green-thumbs-up from our inspector. See p. 72.

ROYAL ALBERTA MUSEUM—Gain insight into the natural and cultural history of Alberta. See p. 72.

TELUS WORLD OF SCIENCE EDMONTON—This ultra-modern building is nearly as thought-provoking as the exhibits it contains. See p. 72.

UKRAINIAN CULTURAL HERITAGE VILLAGE—Restored buildings and living-history demonstrations depict the story of the area's Ukrainian immigrants, who arrived prior to 1930. See p. 72.

WEST EDMONTON MALL—"Shop 'til you drop" takes on a new meaning in this 800-plus store mall that also offers a bungee jump. See p. 73.

Elk Island National Park of Canada (E-7)

ELK ISLAND NATIONAL PARK OF CANADA—Enjoy all sorts of recreational pursuits at the park, which is home to a large herd of plains bison. See p. 78.

Fort Macleod (J-6)

HEAD-SMASHED-IN BUFFALO JUMP INTERPRE-TIVE CENTRE—For at least 6,000 years this site was crucial to the survival of the Plains Indians. See p. 79.

Fort McMurray (A-8)

OIL SANDS DISCOVERY CENTRE—A stop here will tell you everything you always wanted to know about mining oil sands. See p. 79.

Jasper National Park of Canada (E-2, E-3, F-2)

JASPER NATIONAL PARK OF CANADA—Craggy mountain peaks, lush valleys and mirror-smooth lakes make this park a photographer's dream. See p. 81.

JASPER TRAMWAY—Take in spectacular views from atop 2,277-metre (7,470-ft.) Whistlers Mountain. See p. 84.

Lethbridge (J-7)

NIKKA YUKO JAPANESE GARDEN—Discover the beauty and serenity engendered by minimalism in this spot where East meets West. See p. 87.

Longview (I-6)

BAR U RANCH NATIONAL HISTORIC SITE OF CANADA—Formerly one of the country's largest ranching operations, this site commemorates the importance ranching had in the development of Canada. See p. 87.

Medicine Hat (J-8)

MEDICINE HAT CLAY INDUSTRIES NATIONAL HIS-TORIC DISTRICT—Peek inside beehive kilns and learn about the pottery industry that thrived here in the late 19th century. See p. 88.

Patricia (I-8)

DINOSAUR PROVINCIAL PARK—Visit the spectacular grasslands and badlands of this UNESCO World Heritage Site, where dinosaurs played millions of years ago. See p. 89.

Rocky Mountain House National Historic Site of Canada (F-5)

ROCKY MOUNTAIN HOUSE NATIONAL HISTORIC SITE OF CANADA—See the ruins of four failed fur-trading posts at this formerly forested frontier. See p. 91.

Waterton Lakes National Park of Canada (K-5)

WATERTON LAKES NATIONAL PARK OF CANADA—The prairies meet the mountains in this popular summer vacation site. See p. 92.

Wetaskiwin (F-6)

REYNOLDS-ALBERTA MUSEUM—In the summer you can ride in a vintage automobile or airplane at this museum, which presents the history of agriculture, industry and transportation in the province. See p. 94.

Alberta Temperature Averages Maximum/Minimum (Celsius)
From the records of The Weather Channel Interactive, Inc.

	JAN	FEB	MAR	APR	MAY	JUNE	JULY	AUG	SEPT	OCT	NOV	DEC
Banff	-5 / -15	0 / -11	4 / -8	9 / -3	14 / 2	19 / 6	22 / 7	22 / 7	16 / 3	10 / -1	1 / -8	-5 / -14
Calgary	-3 / -16	-1 / -12	3 / -8	11 / -2	17 / 3	21 / 7	23 / 9	23 / 9	17 / 4	13 / -1	3 / -9	-2 / -14
Edmonton	-8 / -17	-4 / -14	1 / -9	10 / -1	17 / 6	21 / 9	23 / 12	22 / 11	16 / 6	11 / 1	-1 / -9	-7 / -15
Jasper	-6 / -16	-1 / -12	4 / -8	10 / -3	15 / 2	19 / 6	22 / 8	22 / 7	16 / 3	10 / -1	0 / -9	-6 / -14

RECREATION AREAS

	MAP LOCATION	CAMPING	PICNICKING	HIKING TRAILS	BOATING	BOAT RAMP	BOAT RENTAL	FISHING	SWIMMING	PETS ON LEASH	BICYCLE TRAILS	WINTER SPORTS	VISITOR CENTER	LODGE/CABINS	FOOD SERVICE
NATIONAL PARKS *(See place listings)*															
Banff (G-4) 6,641 square kilometres. Horse rental.		•	•	•	•	•	•	•	•	•	•	•	•	•	•
Elk Island (E-7) 194 square kilometres.		•	•	•	•	•				•		•	•		•
Jasper (E-2, E-3, F-2) 11,228 square kilometres. Horse rental.		•	•	•	•	•	•	•	•	•	•	•	•	•	•
Waterton Lakes (K-5) 505 square kilometres. Golf; horse rental.		•	•	•	•	•	•	•	•	•	•	•	•	•	•
PROVINCIAL															
Aspen Beach (F-6) 214 hectares on Gull Lake, 17 km w. of Lacombe on Hwy. 12. Golf; outdoor exhibits. *(See Red Deer p. 90)*	**1**	•	•	•	•	•		•	•				•		•
Beauvais Lake (K-6) 1,160 hectares 11 km w. of Pincher Creek on Hwy. 507 and 8 km s. on Hwy. 775. Golf, sailing, windsurfing.	**2**	•	•	•	•	•		•	•	•			•		
Beaverdam (D-9) 88 hectares 5 km e. of Nordegg on Hwy. 11. Canoeing, kayaking.	**3**	•	•	•				•		•			•		
Beaver Lake (C-7) 97 hectares 6 km s.e. of Lac La Biche off Hwy. 36, on the n.e. shore of Beaver Lake.	**4**	•						•	•	•					
Beaver Mines Lake (K-6) 113 hectares 20 km w. of Pincher Creek on Hwy. 507, 10 km s.w. on Hwy. 774, then 5 km s. on access road.	**5**	•	•	•	•			•	•				•		
Big Knife (F-7) 295 hectares 8 km w. and 13 km s. of Forestburg on Hwy. 855. Golf.	**6**	•	•	•				•					•		
Brazeau Reservoir (F-4) 80 hectares 25 km s.w. of Lodgepole along SR 620. Interpretive programs.	**7**	•	•		•	•		•					•		
Calling Lake (C-6) 738 hectares 55 km n. of Athabasca on Hwy. 813. Golf.	**8**	•	•		•	•		•	•				•		
Carson-Pegasus (D-4) 1,209 hectares 6 km w. of Whitecourt on Hwy. 43, 11 km n. on Hwy. 32, then 5 km e. on access road. Golf; amphitheater.	**9**	•	•		•	•	•	•	•				•		•
Chain Lakes (I-6) 409 hectares 38 km s.w. of Nanton on Hwy. 533. Golf.	**10**	•	•		•	•		•		•			•		
Chinook (J-5) 48 hectares 8 km w. of Crowsnest Pass off Hwy. 3. Canoeing, kayaking.	**11**	•	•					•		•					
Cold Lake (C-9) 5,855 hectares 3 km n.e. of Cold Lake off Hwy. 28. Golf; interpretive programs.	**12**	•	•	•	•	•		•	•	•			•		
Cooking Lake-Blackfoot (E-7) 9,700 hectares 24 km e. of Sherwood Park s. of Hwy. 16. Canoeing, golf, kayaking; interpretive programs.	**13**		•	•						•	•	•	•		
Crimson Lake (F-5) 3,209 hectares 14 km w. and 6 km n. of Rocky Mountain House on Hwy. 756. Golf; amphitheater, interpretive programs.	**14**	•	•	•	•	•		•	•	•	•	•	•		•
Cross Lake (D-6) 2,076 hectares 8 km n. and 19 km n.e. of Jarvie off Hwy. 663. Golf; interpretive programs.	**15**	•	•	•	•	•		•	•	•			•		
Cypress Hills (J-9) 20,451 hectares 1.5 km n. of Elkwater on Hwy. 41. Cross-country skiing, golf, tennis; horse rental, interpretive programs, pool. Five horsepower limit for boats. *(See Elkwater p. 78)*	**16**	•	•	•	•	•		•	•	•	•	•	•	•	•
Dillberry Lake (F-9) 1,205 hectares 15 km s. of Chauvin on Hwy. 17 at Alberta/Saskatchewan border. Golf.	**17**	•	•	•	•			•	•	•			•		
Dinosaur (I-8) 8,085 hectares 13 km n.e. of Patricia via Hwy. 210. Historic. Canoeing, kayaking; interpretive programs. *(See Patricia p. 89)*	**18**	•	•	•				•					•		•
Dry Island Buffalo Jump (G-7) 1,598 hectares 15 km e. of Huxley off Hwy. 21 on an access road. Canoeing, golf, kayaking.	**19**	•	•					•	•	•					
Fawcett Lake (West) (C-6) 48 hectares 55 km s.e. of Slave Lake on Hwy. 2, 20 km n. on Hwy. 2A, then 18 km n. on access road. Interpretive programs.	**20**	•	•	•	•	•		•	•	•			•		
Figure Eight Lake (A-3) 90 hectares 25 km w. of Peace River off Hwy. 35.	**21**	•	•					•	•	•			•		
Fish Creek (I-6) 1,189 hectares in Calgary between 37th St. S.W. and the Bow River. Golf; horse rental, interpretive programs.	**22**		•	•				•	•	•	•	•	•		•

RECREATION AREAS

	MAP LOCATION	CAMPING	PICNICKING	HIKING TRAILS	BOATING	BOAT RAMP	BOAT RENTAL	FISHING	SWIMMING	PETS ON LEASH	BICYCLE TRAILS	WINTER SPORTS	VISITOR CENTER	LODGE/CABINS	FOOD SERVICE
French Bay (D-9) 449 hectares 11 km e. and 3 km n. of Cold Lake off Hwy. 55. Golf.	23	•	•		•	•		•	•	•		•			
Garner Lake (D-7) 74 hectares 5 km n. of Spedden off Hwy. 28. Golf; interpretive programs.	24	•	•	•	•	•		•	•	•		•			
Ghost Reservoir (H-5) 24 hectares 18 km w. of Cochrane on Hwy. 1A. Golf, sailing, windsurfing.	25	•	•		•	•	•	•	•	•		•			
Gooseberry Lake (G-8) 52 hectares 12 km n. of Consort on Hwy. 41, then 2 km e. on access road. Golf.	26	•	•					•	•	•					
Gregoire Lake (A-8) 696 hectares 19 km s. of Fort McMurray on Hwy. 63, then 10 km e. on Hwy. 881. Golf.	27	•	•	•	•	•		•	•	•		•			
Hilliard's Bay (B-4) 2,323 hectares 10 km e. of Grouard off Hwy. 750. Golf.	28	•	•	•	•	•		•	•	•		•			
Historic Dunvegan (B-2) 9 hectares off Queen Elizabeth II Hwy. on the n. side of the Peace River beside Dunvegan Suspension Bridge. Golf; interpretive programs. *(See Dunvegan p. 64)*	29	•	•	•	•			•		•		•	•		
Jackfish Lake (F-4) 203 hectares 50 km w. of Rocky Mountain House on Hwy. 11, then 2 km n. on access road. Pier.	30	•	•		•	•		•	•	•		•	•		
Jarvis Bay (G-6) 86 hectares 4 km n. of Sylvan Lake townsite on Hwy. 20. Golf; bicycle rentals.	31	•	•		•			•	•			•		•	•
Kananaskis Country (I-4) *(See place listing p. 85)*															
Bow Valley (H-5) 3,129 hectares 25 km e. of Canmore on Hwy. 1 and .5 km n. on Hwy. 1X. Canoeing, kayaking; bicycle rental, interpretive programs.	32	•	•	•	•	•	•	•		•	•	•	•		•
Canmore Nordic Centre (H-5) 435 hectares 3 km s. of Canmore on Spray Lakes Rd. Interpretive programs.	33		•	•						•	•	•	•		
Elbow Falls (I-5) 96 hectares 30 km w. of Bragg Creek on Hwy. 66. Canoeing, kayaking; interpretive programs.	34	•	•	•				•		•					
Elbow River (I-5) 232 hectares 20 km w. of Bragg Creek on Hwy. 66. Interpretive programs.	35	•	•	•				•		•	•				
Evan-Thomas (H-4) 2,571 hectares 3 km s. of Canmore on Spray Lakes Rd. Interpretive programs.	36		•	•				•		•		•		•	
McLean Creek (H-5) 245 hectares 12 km w. of Bragg Creek on Hwy. 66, then 1.3 km s. on McLean Creek Trail. Interpretive programs.	37	•	•	•				•		•		•			
Peter Lougheed (I-5) 50,142 hectares 43 km s.e. of Canmore on Hwy. 40. Golf; interpretive programs.	38	•	•	•	•	•		•		•	•	•	•	•	•
Sheep River (I-5) 6,191 hectares 25 km w. of Turner Valley on Hwy. 546. Horseback riding; interpretive programs.	39	•	•	•				•		•		•			
Sibbald Lake (H-5) 73 hectares 30 km w. of Canmore on Hwy. 1, 6 km s. on Hwy. 40, then 12 km e. on Hwy. 68. Canoeing, kayaking; amphitheater, interpretive programs.	40	•	•	•	•			•		•		•			
Spray Valley (H-5) 27,452 hectares s.w. of Canmore, surrounding the Spray Lakes Reservoir. Interpretive programs.	41	•	•	•	•			•		•		•			
Kinbrook Island (I-8) 540 hectares 13 km s. of Brooks off Hwy. 873. Golf.	42	•	•		•	•		•	•	•		•			
Lakeland (C-8) 59,030 hectares 13 km e. of Lac La Biche off Hwy. 663. Canoeing, kayaking. *(See Lac La Biche p. 85)*	43	•	•	•	•	•		•	•	•		•			
Lake McGregor (I-7) 140 hectares 20 km n. of Vulcan on Hwy. 23, then 25 km e. on Hwy. 542. Golf, sailing, windsurfing.	44	•	•		•	•		•	•	•					
Lesser Slave Lake (C-5) 7,566 hectares 6 km n. of Slave Lake on Hwy. 88. Golf; interpretive programs. *(See Slave Lake p. 91)*	45	•	•	•	•	•		•	•	•		•			
Little Bow (I-7) 110 hectares 20 km s. of Vulcan on Hwy. 23, 16 km e. on Hwy. 529, then 1 km s. on access road. Golf.	46	•	•		•	•		•	•	•					
Long Lake (D-7) 769 hectares 20 km s. of Boyle on Hwy. 831, then 2 km n.e. on access road. Golf; trail rides.	47	•	•	•	•	•		•	•	•		•	•		•
Maqua Lake (A-8) 135 hectares 27 km s. of Fort McMurray on Hwy. 63, 15 km s. on Hwy. 881, then 10 km s.w. on access road. Canoeing, kayaking.	48		•	•	•			•	•			•			

RECREATION AREAS

	MAP LOCATION	CAMPING	PICNICKING	HIKING TRAILS	BOATING	BOAT RAMP	BOAT RENTAL	FISHING	SWIMMING	PETS ON LEASH	BICYCLE TRAILS	WINTER SPORTS	VISITOR CENTER	LODGE/CABINS	FOOD SERVICE
Medicine Lake (F-5) 24 hectares 47 km n. of Rocky Mountain House on Hwy. 22, then 8 km s.e. on access road.	49	•	•		•	•		•	•	•		•			
Midland (H-7) 599 hectares 6 km w. of Drumheller on Hwy. 838. Canoeing, golf, kayaking; interpretive programs, outdoor exhibits. *(See Drumheller p. 63)*	50		•	•				•		•		•			
Miquelon Lake (E-7) 835 hectares 3 km s. of New Sarepta on Hwy. 21, then 20 km e. on Hwy. 623. Golf; interpretive programs.	51	•	•	•	•				•	•		•	•		
Moonshine Lake (B-2) 1,103 hectares 27 km w. of Spirit River on Hwy. 49, then 7 km n. on Hwy. 725. Golf.	52	•	•	•	•	•		•	•	•		•			
Moose Lake (D-8) 736 hectares 5 km n. of Bonnyville on Hwy. 41, 10 km w. on Hwy. 660, then 2 km s. on access road. Golf.	53	•	•	•	•	•		•	•	•					
Musreau Lake (D-2) 270 hectares 80 km s. of Grande Prairie on Hwy. 40, then 2 km e. on access road.	54	•	•	•	•			•	•	•		•			
North Wabasca (B-6) 77 hectares 38 km n. of Slave Lake on Hwy. 88, 100 km n.e. on Hwy. 754, then 7 km. n. on access road.	55	•	•		•	•		•	•	•		•			
Notikewin (A-3) 9,697 hectares 37 km n. of Manning via Hwy. 35, then 30 km e. on Hwy. 692. Historic. Golf.	56	•	•	•				•		•			•	•	
Obed Lake (E-3) 3,402 hectares 55 km w. of Edson off Hwy. 16.	57	•	•		•	•		•	•						
O'Brien (C-2) 65 hectares 10 km s. of Grande Prairie on Hwy. 40. Golf.	58		•		•			•	•	•					
Paddle River Dam (E-5) 70 hectares 10 km n.w. of Sangudo on Hwy. 43.	59		•		•	•		•	•	•					
Park Lake (J-7) 224 hectares 17 km n.w. of Lethbridge on Hwy. 25, then 5 km n.w. on Hwy. 101. Canoeing, golf, kayaking, sailing.	60	•	•		•	•		•	•	•		•			•
Pembina River (E-5) 167 hectares 2 km n.e. of Entwistle on Hwy. 16A. Canoeing, kayaking; interpretive programs.	61	•	•	•				•	•	•					
Peppers Lake (G-4) 18 hectares 84 km s.e. of Nordegg on Forestry Trunk Rd. (Hwy. 734). Horseback riding.	62	•		•	•			•		•					
Pierre Grey's Lakes (E-2) 633 hectares 37 km s. of Grande Cache off Hwy. 40 on access road. Historic. Scenic.	63	•	•	•	•			•		•			•	•	
Pigeon Lake (F-6) 443 hectares 5 km w. and 10 km n. of Westerose off Hwy. 771. Dogsledding.	64	•	•	•	•	•	•	•	•	•		•			•
Poachers' Landing (C-7) 1,750 hectares 35 km n.e. of Athabasca on Hwy. 55, then 25 km n. on access road. Horseback riding.	65	•	•	•				•		•					
Police Outpost (K-6) 223 hectares 10 km s. and 23 km w. of Cardston on Queen Elizabeth II Hwy.	66	•	•	•				•		•			•	•	
Prairie Creek (G-5) 42 hectares 41 km s.w. of Rocky Mountain House on Hwy. 752. Horseback riding; interpretive programs.	67	•	•	•				•		•					
Queen Elizabeth (A-3) 86 hectares 3 km n. and 5 km w. of Grimshaw off Hwy. 35. Historic. Golf.	68	•	•	•	•				•	•		•			
Ram Falls (G-4) 116 hectares 64 km s. of Nordegg on Forestry Trunk Rd. (Hwy. 734).	69	•	•	•				•		•					•
Red Lodge (G-6) 129 hectares 15 km w. of Bowden on Hwy. 587. Canoeing, kayaking.	70	•	•					•	•	•			•		
Rochon Sands (F-7) 119 hectares 12 km w. of Stettler on Hwy. 12, then 16 km n. on Hwy. 835. Golf.	71	•	•		•	•			•	•					
Saskatoon Island (C-2) 101 hectares 21 km w. of Grande Prairie on Hwy. 43, then 4 km n. on an access road. Golf, water sports.	72	•	•	•		•		•	•	•	•		•		•
Sir Winston Churchill (C-7) 239 hectares 13 km n.e. of Lac La Biche off Hwy. 881. Golf; interpretive programs. *(See Lac La Biche p. 85)*	73	•	•	•	•			•	•	•			•	•	
Smoke Lake (D-3) 53 hectares 9 km s.w. of Fox Creek off Hwy. 43.	74	•	•		•	•		•	•	•			•	•	

RECREATION AREAS

	MAP LOCATION	CAMPING	PICNICKING	HIKING TRAILS	BOATING	BOAT RAMP	BOAT RENTAL	FISHING	SWIMMING	PETS ON LEASH	BICYCLE TRAILS	WINTER SPORTS	VISITOR CENTER	LODGE/CABINS	FOOD SERVICE
Sundance (E-3) 3,712 hectares 56 km n.e. of Hinton on Emerson Creek Rd. Interpretive programs.	75	•	•	•	•			•	•				•		
Sylvan Lake (G-6) 85 hectares 18 km n.w. of Red Deer on Hwy. 11 in town of Sylvan Lake. Golf. *(See Red Deer p. 90)*	76		•	•				•	•	•			•		•
Thunder Lake (D-5) 208 hectares 21 km w. of Barrhead on Hwy. 18. Golf.	77	•	•	•	•	•		•	•	•			•		
Two Lakes (D-1) 1,554 hectares 130 km s.w. of Grande Prairie on Two Lakes Rd.	78	•		•	•	•		•		•			•	•	
Upper Shunda Creek (F-4) 47 hectares 3 km w. of Nordegg off Hwy. 11.	79	•		•				•		•		•	•		
Vermilion (E-8) 759 hectares 1.5 km n. of Vermilion on Hwy. 41 from jct. Hwy. 16, then w. on 50th Ave. following signs. Historic. Canoeing, golf, kayaking.	80	•	•	•	•			•	•	•			•		
Wabamun Lake (E-5) 231 hectares 3 km e. and 1 km s. of Wabamun off Hwy. 16A. Historic. Golf.	81	•	•	•	•	•		•		•	•		•		
Whitney Lakes (D-8) 1,489 hectares 24 km e. of Elk Point off Hwy. 646. Historic. Interpretive programs.	82	•	•	•	•	•		•	•	•	•		•		
William A. Switzer (E-3) 6,268 hectares 3 km w. of Hinton on Hwy. 16, then 19 km n. on Hwy. 40. Historic. Bicycle rentals, interpretive programs.	83	•	•	•	•	•	•	•	•	•	•	•	•	•	•
Williamson (C-3) 17 hectares 17 km w. of Valleyview on Hwy. 43, then 2 km n. on an access road. Golf.	84	•	•	•	•	•		•		•	•		•		
Winagami Lake (B-4) 6,542 hectares 20 km n. of High Prairie on Hwy. 749, 10 km w. on Hwy. 679, then 7 km n. on access road. Golf.	85	•	•	•	•	•		•	•	•		•	•	•	
Woolford (K-7) 35 hectares 50 km s.w. of Lethbridge on Hwy. 5, then 17 km e. on Hwy. 503. Historic. Canoeing, golf, kayaking.	86	•	•	•	•			•		•			•		
Writing-on-Stone (K-8) 1,718 hectares 35 km e. of Milk River off Hwy. 501. Historic. Canoeing, kayaking; interpretive programs. *(See Milk River p. 88)*	87	•	•	•	•			•	•	•			•	•	
Wyndham-Carseland (I-6) 178 hectares 2 km e. and 2 km s. of Carseland on Hwy. 24. Canoeing, golf, kayaking.	88	•	•	•	•	•		•	•	•			•		
Young's Point (C-3) 3,072 hectares 26 km w. of Valleyview on Hwy. 43, then 10 km n.e. on an access road. Golf, water sports; outdoor exhibits.	89	•	•	•	•	•		•	•	•			•		
OTHER															
Content Bridge (G-6) 12 hectares 6 km s. of Nevis on Hwy. 21. Canoeing, kayaking.	90	•	•		•			•		•					•
Eagle Lake Park (H-6) 7 km e. and 6 km s. of Strathmore via Hwy. 1.	91	•	•		•	•		•	•						•
Elks Beach (D-5) 14 km s. of Barrhead on Hwy. 33, then e. on Hwy. 651.	92	•	•		•	•		•							•
Half Moon Lake (E-6) 4 hectares 3 km e. of Sherwood Park on Hwy. 630. Canoeing, kayaking; horse rental.	93	•	•		•	•	•	•	•						•
Hasse Lake (E-6) 81 hectares 5 km w. and 10 km s. of Stony Plain on Hwy. 16.	94		•	•				•	•	•		•			
Pipestone Creek (C-2) 15 km s. of Wembley. Interpretive trails.	95	•	•	•	•			•		•					
Stony Lake (D-8) 158 hectares on Stony Lake, 16 km s.w. of Elk Point off Hwy. 646.	96	•	•		•	•		•	•						
Westward Ho (G-5) 8 km e. of Sundre on Hwy. 27. Canoeing, kayaking.	97	•	•		•			•	•	•					•
Wizard Lake (F-6) 33 hectares 19 km s. of Calmar on Hwy. 795.	98	•	•		•	•		•	•	•					•

Points of Interest

ALDER FLATS (F-5)
pop. 148, elev. 953 m/3,125′

EM-TE TOWN is 3 km (1.9 mi.) s. of jct. hwys. 13 and 22, then 10 km (6.2 mi.) w. on a gravel road following signs. This replica of an 1880s Western ghost town has 27 buildings including a saloon, gazebo, church, blacksmith shop, school, emporium and jail. Trail rides are offered. Food is available. Camping is available. Allow 1 hour minimum. Town open daily 9-6. Admission $7; $5 (ages 12-17 and 65+); $4 (ages 6-11). One-hour trail ride $25. Prices may vary; phone ahead. MC, VI. Phone (780) 388-2166.

BANFF NATIONAL PARK OF CANADA (G-4)

Elevations in the park range from 1,326 metres (4,350 ft.) around the Bow River to 3,612 metres (11,851 ft.) at Mount Forbes. Refer to CAA/AAA maps for additional elevation information.

Banff National Park of Canada is approached from the southeast via the Trans-Canada Hwy. west of Canmore, from the northeast via Hwy. 11 southwest of Abraham Lake, or from the north via Hwy. 93 from Jasper. The park's majestic beauty is inescapable. These routes lead to a region where mountains and the forces of nature inspire awe and command respect.

This is Canada's oldest national park: Evidence suggests that prehistoric habitation dates back 11,000 years. Remnants of the more recent Assiniboine, Blackfoot, Cree, Kootenai and Stoney settlements also have been found in the park. European explorers did not arrive until the early 1800s, and when they did, they argued over the land's resources, prompting the government to establish the park in 1885.

In this 6,641-square-kilometre (2,564-sq.-mi.) section of the Canadian Rockies there are only two main centers of activity: Banff and Lake Louise. The glacial-green Bow River flows through the mountain-ringed valley that is the setting for Banff. The dry, bracing climate, alpine grandeur and mineral hot spring pools enhance Banff's attractiveness.

The town of Banff, granted autonomy from federal jurisdiction Jan. 1, 1990, is within the park. Development within the town is strictly controlled; residents do not own their land but lease it from the park.

Situated 58 kilometres (36 mi.) west of Banff at an elevation of 1,731 metres (5,679 ft.) is icy, blue-green Lake Louise. About 2.4 kilometres (1.5 mi.) long, .6 kilometres (.4 mi.) wide and 90 metres (295 ft.) deep, Lake Louise springs from Victoria Glacier, whose meltwater carries the silt and rock flour that give the lake the opaque turquoise color common to most of the area's waters. The upper portion of the glacier is 60 to 90 metres (197 to 295 ft.) thick; the lower part is 90 metres (295 ft.) at its deepest.

The park's well-known peaks include Rundle, Cascade, Victoria, Lefroy, Temple, Castle, Forbes, Chephren, Hector and the Ten Peaks, all ranging from 2,752 to 3,618 metres (9,030 to 11,870 ft.) above sea level. The upper slopes of the ranges are either bare and rugged or glacier crowned, while the lower slopes are forested. Many mountains are mirrored in Moraine, Peyto and other lakes.

Banff National Park of Canada is a wildlife refuge. Animals are especially visible in the fall; elk, deer and bighorn sheep are most common, while sightings of mountain goats and moose often require binoculars. Bears, wolves, coyotes, lynx and other predators are seen occasionally. Black magpies and other members of the crow family, including the gray jay, Clark's nutcracker and raven, dart through the trees.

Although most of the park's lakes and rivers—particularly the Bow River—sustain healthy fish populations, some lakes cannot due to the "winter kill." This phenomenon occurs when a lake freezes to such a great depth that oxygen is depleted at the bottom of the lake, thereby killing all fish.

Note: Night travelers should be alert for animals on the highways. It is not only dangerous but also against park regulations to feed, molest, touch or tease the animals.

General Information and Activities

The park, which is open all year, has about 354 kilometres (219 mi.) of scenic roads. Hwy. 1 to Vancouver and Hwy. 93S (Banff-Windermere Hwy.) are open year-round, as is the northern end of Hwy. 93N (Icefields Parkway) from Lake Louise to Jasper; check locally for road conditions. One- or multiple-day bus tours of the park's major points of interest also are available.

More than 1,300 kilometres (800 mi.) of trails traverse the park. All activities involving an overnight stay in the back country require a wilderness permit offered at information centers and park warden offices in the Banff and Lake Louise townsites. Public campgrounds in the park are available by reservation, with some sites set aside on a first-come, first-served basis; phone (877) 737-3783, or TTY (866) 787-6221 in Canada.

If such potentially risky activities as mountain climbing or hiking away from designated trails are planned, visitors should register their trips in person at a park warden office or information center. Upon return, notify the warden office or information center in person or by phone. Phone (403) 762-1550 for back-country travel information, including weather and avalanche bulletins.

Lake Louise's waters, about 4 C (39 F), are too cold for swimming but are ideal for boating. Motors are not permitted; motorboats may be used only on Lake Minnewanka. Cruises on Lake Minnewanka are offered during the summer. Skating, skiing, curling and hockey are available in the park in winter.

Park naturalists conduct interpretive programs at major campgrounds most evenings and at key attractions daily throughout the summer. Bankhead, a once-booming mining town 4.8 kilometres (3 mi.) northeast of Banff, has a self-guiding trail with explanatory signs and a mining exhibit. The trail is open daily 24 hours.

Special events include the Banff Mountain Film Festival and the Banff Mountain Book Festival. Both are held late October through early November. The ▽ Banff Summer Arts Festival, held May through August, also provides additional activities for visitors to enjoy.

Throughout the summer guides and outfitters offer fishing, hiking and float trips. Saddle horses are available for trips through the mountains to glacier-fed lakes, and helicopter tours can be arranged outside the park boundaries in Canmore and in Golden, British Columbia.

Information, interpretive program schedules and back-country trail tips are available at Banff Information Centre, (403) 762-1550, 224 Banff Ave., and Lake Louise Information Centre, (403) 522-3833, on Village Road; topographical maps and trail guides are sold at both locations. The Banff center is open daily 8-8, late June to mid-Sept.; hours vary rest of year. The Lake Louise center is open daily 9-7, late June to mid-Sept.; hours vary rest of year. Audio-tape tours by CCInc. Auto Tape Tours are available at the Banff Information Centre at the Friends of Banff outlet; phone (403) 762-8918.

Fishing is permitted; national park fishing permits are sold at park information, administration and warden offices as well as at some boat concessionaires and tackle shops. Check at the information centers in Banff or Lake Louise for a summary of park fishing regulations.

Hunting is strictly prohibited; visitors entering the area must have firearms dismantled. *See Recreation Chart and the AAA/CAA Western Canada & Alaska CampBook.*

ADMISSION to the park for 1 day is $8.90 per person; over 65, $7.65. Admission for two to seven persons in a private vehicle for 1 day is $17.80. An annual pass, valid at all Canadian national parks, is available. AX, MC, VI .

PETS are allowed in the park but must be leashed, crated or physically restrained.

ADDRESS inquiries to the Superintendent, Banff National Park of Canada, P.O. Box 900, Banff, AB, Canada T1L 1K2; phone (403) 762-1550.

Points of Interest

Natural points of interest within the park include hoodoos—mushroom-shaped pillars of glacial silt and clay—east of Banff; Vermilion Lakes and Johnston Canyon to the west; Bow Falls to the south; Mount Norquay, Lake Louise, Moraine Lake and Valley of the Ten Peaks to the northwest via the Trans-Canada Hwy.; and Hector, Bow and Peyto lakes and Bow Summit to the northwest on the Icefields Parkway.

BANFF GONDOLA is 3.2 km (2 mi.) s. of Banff on Mountain Ave. (lower terminal next to the Upper Hot Springs). An enclosed gondola journeys to the top of Sulphur Mountain. The lift rises 701 metres (2,300 ft.) from the 1,585-metre (5,200-ft.) level to the 2,451-metre (8,040-ft.) peak in 8 minutes. An open-air observation deck affords spectacular views of Banff and the surrounding mountains. A self-guiding nature walk leads to other panoramic views.

Food is available. Open daily 7:30 a.m.-9 p.m., early June-day before Labour Day; otherwise varies. Closed 12 days in January for maintenance and Dec. 25. Round-trip fare $26; $13 (ages 6-15). One-way fare (only available June-Sept.) $13; $6.50 (ages 6-15). AX, MC, VI. Phone (403) 762-2523.

BANFF PARK MUSEUM NATIONAL HISTORIC SITE OF CANADA is at 91 Banff Ave. Established in 1895, the collection moved to its present building in 1903. The museum depicts the way natural history exhibits were presented and interpreted at the beginning of the 20th century. Exhibits include mounted animals and mineral specimens.

Allow 30 minutes minimum. Daily 10-6, mid-May to mid-Sept.; 1-5, rest of year. Closed Jan. 1 and Dec. 25-26. Guided tours are given daily at 3, mid-May to mid-Sept. Admission $3.95; $3.45 (ages 65+); $1.95 (ages 6-18); $9.90 (family). Phone (403) 762-1558.

[SAVE] **BANFF UPPER HOT SPRINGS** is 4 km (2.5 mi.) s. of Banff via Mountain Ave. Natural hot springs feed this bathing pool with temperatures ranging between 34 C (93 F) and 42 C (108 F). A day spa is on the premises. Food is available. Swimsuit, towel and locker rentals are available. Allow 1 hour minimum. Daily 9 a.m.-11 p.m., mid-May to early Sept.; 10-10 (also Fri.-Sat. 10-11 p.m.), rest of year. Admission $7.55; $6.60 (ages 3-17 and 65+). Prices may vary; phone ahead. AX, MC, VI. Phone (403) 762-1515 or (800) 767-1611.

BUFFALO NATIONS LUXTON MUSEUM is just w. of Banff Ave. at 1 Birch Ave. This log-fort museum re-creates the era when Europeans first arrived on the Plains to find a culture rich in ceremonies, songs and legends. Arts, crafts, dioramas and displays showcase the historical journey of the Northern Plains people, their culture and the flora and fauna of the surrounding area.

Allow 30 minutes minimum. Daily 11-6, May 1 to mid-Oct.; 1-5, rest of year. Closed Dec. 25. Admission $8; $6 (ages 65+ and students with ID); $2.50 (ages 6-12); $16.50 (family). MC, VI. Phone (403) 762-2388.

THE CASCADE OF TIME GARDENS encircle the Banff National Park of Canada administration building. These gardens are built in a series of rock terraces connected by small cascades that highlight flowers, plants and shrubs, rustic bridges, pavilions and flagged walks. Allow 30 minutes minimum. Free.

CAVE AND BASIN NATIONAL HISTORIC SITE OF CANADA is at 311 Cave Ave. A cave and hot springs were discovered in 1883 by three Canadian Pacific Railway workers. The site consists of naturally occurring warm mineral springs inside the cave and an emerald-colored basin outside. Exhibits, interpretive trails and a 30-minute videotape presentation explain the history of the springs and the development of the national park.

Allow 1 hour minimum. Daily 9-6, mid-May through Sept. 30; Mon.-Fri. 11-4, Sat.-Sun. 9:30-5, rest of year. Closed Jan. 1 and Dec. 25-26. Guided tours are given daily at 3, June-Sept. Admission $3.95; $3.45 (ages 65+); $1.95 (ages 6-18); $9.90 (family). Phone (403) 762-1566.

DISCOVER BANFF TOURS is at 215 Banff Ave. in the Sundance Mall. Passengers also are picked up at area hotels. Various year-round guided tours are offered, including ice walks, snowshoe treks, dogsled trips, sleigh rides, mountain hikes, evening safaris, horseback riding, white-water rafting and nature walks. Some tours include lunch. Canoe rentals and self-guiding tours also are available.

Inquire about cancellation policies. Allow 2-9 hours minimum, depending on tour. Tours depart daily (weather permitting) 7:30 a.m.-10 p.m. Tour times vary; phone ahead. Fee $39-$150. AX, MC, VI. Phone (403) 760-5007 or (877) 565-9372.

ICEFIELDS PARKWAY (HWY. 93) crosses Banff and Jasper national parks. The 230-kilometre (143-mi.) route, which connects the towns of Lake Louise and Jasper, offers spectacular vistas of snowcapped mountains, waterfalls, lakes and rivers

that drain the Columbia Icefields' glacial meltwater to the oceans. While the terrain is rugged, the road is well-engineered to provide a relatively easy drive.

About 76 kilometres (47 mi.) north of Lake Louise at the Saskatchewan River crossing, David Thompson Hwy. (Hwy. 11) meets the Icefields Parkway. Just inside Jasper National Park of Canada is the Athabasca Glacier, a tongue of the Columbia Icefield *(see Jasper National Park of Canada p. 83)*; it comes to within 1.5 kilometres (.9 mi.) of the parkway.

Note: Drivers should be alert for slow or stopped vehicles and animals. Snow tires and/or chains are recommended in winter; check for weather and road conditions. Parkway free; drivers must pay the national park entrance fee regardless of whether they stop inside the park. Phone (403) 762-2088 for weather information or (403) 762-1450 for road condition information.

LAKE LOUISE SIGHTSEEING GONDOLA AND INTERPRETIVE CENTRE is just n. of Hwy. 1 interchange. A lift offers an impressive aerial view of Lake Louise and the mountains of the Continental Divide. At the interpretive center staff members present a brief visitor orientation session; interpretive programs, including guided walks, are offered daily for an additional fee. Ride and dine packages also are offered. Food is available. Open daily 8:30-3:30, May 15-Sept. 30. Gondola $24; $12 (ages 6-15). Interpretive center free. AX, DC, MC, VI. Phone (403) 522-3555.

(SAVE) **LAKE MINNEWANKA BOAT TOURS** is on Lake Minnewanka, 8 km (5 mi.) n.e. of Banff on Hwy. 1, then n. 7 km (4 mi.) from the beginning of Lake Minnewanka Loop. The interpretive sightseeing cruises, in glass-enclosed, heated boats, last 1 hour, 30 minutes. Motorboats can be rented. Charter fishing is available. Cruises depart daily at 10:30, 12:30, 3 and 5, mid-May through first weekend in Oct. (also at 7 p.m., June 23-Labour Day). Fare $40; $20 (ages 5-11). MC, VI. Phone (403) 762-3473.

ROCKY MOUNTAIN RAFT TOURS launch area is reached by buses departing the Banff Park Lodge and the Banff Springs Hotel. Tickets are available at the Banff Springs Hotel concierge desk and at the launch point meeting area below Bow Falls. Scenic 1-hour guided raft tours travel the river in the section of the Bow Valley below Tunnel and Rundle mountains. Raft trips depart daily at 9:20, 11:20,

1:20 and 3:20, mid-May through Labour Day. Fare $38; $15 (ages 0-15). Phone (403) 762-3632.

WALTER PHILLIPS GALLERY is in Glyde Hall at The Banff Centre, 107 Tunnel Mountain Dr. Exhibits contain international and Canadian contemporary art. Media include painting, sculpture, printmaking, textiles, ceramics, photography, video and performance art. Works by established and emerging artists are featured. Open Wed.-Sun. noon-5 (also Thurs. 5-9); closed holidays and between exhibitions. Donations. Phone (403) 762-6281.

SAVE **WHYTE MUSEUM OF THE CANADIAN ROCKIES** is at 111 Bear St. The museum features artwork and cultural and natural history displays detailing the story of the region. On-site are seven historic homes, including the 1931 home of artists and museum founders Peter and Catherine Whyte. Beginnings & Beyond, Heritage Homes, Lives and Legacy, and Luxton Home & Garden guided tours are offered.

Allow 30 minutes minimum. Museum daily 10-5; closed Jan. 1 and Dec. 25. Beginnings & Beyond and Luxton Home & Garden tours are given daily at 1:30, June 1-Labour Day. Lives and Legacy tour is given daily at 11, June 1-Labour Day; Sun. at 1:30, rest of year. Heritage Homes tour is given daily at 11 and 2:30, June 1-Labour Day; Sun. at 2:30, rest of year.

Admission $6; $3.50 (ages 65+ and students with ID); free (ages 0-5); $15 (family, two adults and two children). Heritage Homes or Luxton Home & Garden tour $7. Beginnings & Beyond and Lives and Legacy tours free. Phone (403) 762-2291.

RECREATIONAL ACTIVITIES

Skiing

• **Lake Louise Ski Area** is 60 km (36 mi.) w. of the town of Banff. Write P.O. Box 5, Lake Louise, AB, Canada T1L 1E6. Other activities are offered. Open daily, early Nov.-May 31. Hours vary; phone ahead. Phone (403) 591-7777, (403) 256-8473 or (800) 258-7669.

• **Ski Norquay** is 6 km (4 mi.) n. of the town of Banff on the Mount Norquay access road. Write P.O. Box 1520, Banff, AB, Canada T1L 1B4. Daily 9-4, early Dec. to mid-Apr. (also Fri. 4-9, Jan.-Mar.). Phone (403) 762-4421.

• **Sunshine Village Ski Resort** is 8 km (5 mi.) w. of the town of Banff on Hwy. 1. Write P.O. Box 1510, Banff, AB, Canada T1L 1J5. Daily 9-4, mid-Nov. to late May. Phone (403) 762-6500 or (877) 542-2633.

White-water Rafting

• **Wild Water Adventures** provides pick-up service at Banff and Lake Louise hotels. Write P.O. Box 25, Lake Louise, AB, Canada T0L 1E0. Trips depart twice daily (weather permitting), mid-May to mid-Sept. Phone (403) 522-2211 or (888) 647-6444.

BARRHEAD (D-5)
pop. 4,209, elev. 648 m/2,125'

BARRHEAD CENTENNIAL MUSEUM is at 5629 49th St. Displays depict early area history. Exhibits include farm equipment, pioneer furniture, tools, woodcrafts, a wildlife display, Native artifacts and a collection of African trophies. The museum also serves as a visitor information center. Allow 1 hour minimum. Tues.-Sat. and holidays 10-5; by appointment rest of year. Donations. Phone (780) 674-5203.

BEAVERLODGE (C-1) pop. 2,264

First settled in 1908, Beaverlodge derives its name from the Beaver Indians who made their temporary home, or lodge, in the area. With the arrival of the railway in 1928, a new townsite was created about 1.6 kilometres (1 mi.) northwest of the original hamlet; many original buildings were moved. In the Beaverlodge Valley, the town serves as a gateway to Monkman Pass and is a large agricultural center.

Beaverlodge & District Chamber of Commerce: P.O. Box 303, Beaverlodge, AB, Canada T0H 0C0; phone (780) 354-8785.

SOUTH PEACE CENTENNIAL MUSEUM is 3 km (1.9 mi.) n.w. on Hwy. 43. Pioneer items, equipment and furnishings used in the early 1900s are displayed. A 1928 pioneer house is furnished in period. Other exhibits include a trading post, a general store, a flour mill, a schoolhouse, an Anglican church, a railway caboose, antique steam engines and vintage cars and trucks. Daily 10-6, mid-May to early Sept. Admission $5; free (ages 0-11). Phone (780) 354-8869.

BRAGG CREEK —see Calgary p. 59.

BROOKS (I-8) pop. 12,498

Brooks is surrounded by 105,222 hectares (260,000 acres) of irrigated farmland and more than 404,700 hectares (1 million acres) of rangeland used for cattle grazing. An aqueduct that was operational until 1977 has been preserved as a monument to the engineers and agriculturalists who developed the region. This semiarid shortgrass section of the province is the setting for wildlife and horticultural research centers.

Newell Regional Tourism Association Office and Tourism Information Centre: 208 2nd Ave. W., P.O. Box 1597, Brooks, AB, Canada T1R 1C4; phone (403) 793-8064.

BROOKS AND DISTRICT MUSEUM is .4 km (.2 mi.) w. of Trans-Canada Hwy. Exhibits about early ranchers, homesteaders, the Royal Canadian Mounted Police, railroading and irrigation trace local history from the late 19th and early 20th century. Seventeen buildings, including a log cabin, a schoolhouse and a church, are on the grounds. Allow 1 hour, 30 minutes minimum. Daily 9-5, Victoria Day weekend-Labour Day; by appointment rest of year. Donations. Phone (403) 362-5073.

 DINOSAUR PROVINCIAL PARK— see Patricia p. 89.

Calgary

City Population: 988,193
Elevation: 1,048 m/3,440 ft.

Editor's Picks:

Calgary Tower .... *(see p. 53)*

Calgary Zoo, Botanical Garden &
Prehistoric Park .... *(see p. 53)*

Glenbow Museum .... *(see p. 56)*

Centre Street / © Walter Bibikow / age fotostock

Calgary, once considered a cow town, now is a city of skyscrapers, light-rail transit, shopping complexes and contemporary houses. The city's economy began with—and still includes—ranching and the subsequent meatpacking industry, but the discovery of oil just south of the city in 1914 and just north in 1947 fueled a spurt of growth that turned an agricultural community into a metropolis.

Calgary today boasts a high concentration of head offices, the second largest in Canada. Energy, agriculture, tourism, manufacturing, research and development, and advanced technology comprise Calgary's industrial base.

The region's history of human habitation began almost 10,000 years before the first 19th-century fur and whiskey traders arrived. Indian tribes chose the confluence of the Bow and Elbow rivers as a campsite; emerging as the dominant tribe was the Blackfoot. Their acquisition of horses allowed them to hunt buffalo and fight almost every other prairie tribe with great success. As European settlement increased, so did the friction between the natives and the newcomers.

An 1877 treaty calmed the rough waters, and relative peace among all factions has existed since. Several reservations, including the Tsuu T'ina Reserve south of the city, are near Calgary. Native North Americans have sought to assimilate themselves into Canadian culture while retaining their native heritage.

Chinese were recruited abroad in the early 1900s to build the railroads; once the trains were running, however, Chinese immigration was restricted severely. Oil and money lured many American entrepreneurs who brought the technology and investment funds needed to get Calgary's petroleum industry started. But many of those who came for the money enjoyed the area and stayed, becoming Canadian citizens.

Calgary's modern sophistication is offset by a romantic perception of the past—a past in which the city was established as a North West Mounted Police fort in 1875. The Calgary Stampede, a 10-day Western wingding, is attended by more than a million residents and visitors who relive the days of chuck wagons and lassos. Those days existed more than a century ago, after the North West Mounted Police—the forerunner of today's Royal Canadian Mounted Police—and the railroad brought law, order and homesteaders to a region previously settled by trappers, buffalo hunters and whiskey traders.

Although Calgary's growth has been rapid, it has been practical. The bustling downtown district was designed to accommodate a large amount of activity, even during winter when below-freezing temperatures normally would inhibit commerce. Enclosed walkways called "plus-15s" (they are 15 feet above street level) connect almost half the downtown buildings, making it possible to eat, work, shop or visit neighbors without donning so much as a mitten.

The Stephen Avenue Walk, a pedestrian mall in the city center lined with trees, benches and fountains, is an urban refuge from traffic as well as a

Getting There — *starting on p. 49*

Getting Around — *starting on p. 49*

What To See — *starting on p. 49*

What To Do — *starting on p. 57*

Where To Stay — *starting on p. 393*

Where To Dine — *starting on p. 397*

nice place to enjoy lunch or a stroll in warm weather.

All is not business in Calgary. Music, ballet, theater and plenty of outdoor recreation are readily available. In addition Calgary distinguished itself as host city of the 1988 Winter Olympic Games. Such educational institutions as Mount Royal College, Southern Alberta Institute of Technology and the University of Calgary prepare Canadians for the future. Natural resources and man-made technology continue to drive Calgary in the 21st century.

Getting There

By Car

Two major highways pass through Calgary. Queen Elizabeth II Hwy. runs north and south through the city; Trans-Canada Hwy. provides access from the east and west. Hwy. 1A, which connects Calgary and Cochrane, also serves as an alternate route between Calgary and the towns of Canmore and Banff. Hwy. 8 connects Calgary with Bragg Creek.

Getting Around

Street System

Calgary is divided into quadrants, with Centre Street separating the east and west sectors and the Bow River and Memorial Drive delineating north and south. Streets run north and south, avenues east and west. All are numbered from the intersection of Centre Street and Centre Avenue, just north of downtown. Roads in suburban areas are numbered where they form grids and named where they do not.

The speed limit is 50 kilometres per hour (30 mph) or as posted. A right turn on red after stopping is permitted unless otherwise posted; U-turns are not. Other

The Calgary Stampede
© Hans-Peter Merten / age fotostock

restrictions apply during rush hours in certain areas; be aware of signs, especially in school and playground zones. Pedestrian crosswalks are designated by "X" signs, and motorists must yield to pedestrians.

Parking

Parking is not permitted on major roads in the downtown core during rush hours, between 6:30 and 9 a.m. and 3:30 and 6 p.m. Downtown metered street parking usually is limited to 2 hours at a maximum cost of $3.50 per hour. Pay parking for extended periods is available at numerous locations. Rates for downtown parking lots range from $1.75-$2.50 per half-hour during the day.

What To See

SAVE **AERO SPACE MUSEUM OF CALGARY** is at 4629 McCall Way N.E. In a former Royal Air Force drill hall, the museum contains exhibits about western Canada's aviation history. Aircraft displayed

Destination Calgary

*A*lthough a thriving ranching industry and the discovery of oil helped put Calgary on the map, it was the 1988 Olympic Games that turned all eyes on the former cow town.

*T*oday visitors can travel to an observation terrace in the sky, peruse museums and historic sites and ski in the same park where the games were held.

Travel Alberta

Calgary Zoo, Botanical Garden & Prehistoric Park.
Meet this tiger at Calgary's zoo, which features many rare and endangered species among its 900 residents. (See listing page 53)

The Calgary Stampede.
With such rodeo events as bull riding and steer wrestling, this 10-day celebration revisits the Wild West as both professional riders and cowboys in training enter the corral. (See mention page 59)

Tourism Calgary

Travel Alberta

Aero Space Museum of Calgary.
Get up close and personal with fighter jets and other aircraft at this aerospace museum. (See listing page 49)

See Vicinity map page 53

Cochrane

Calgary

Bragg Creek

Okotoks

Travel Alberta

*P*laces included in this AAA Destination City:

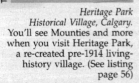

Heritage Park Historical Village, Calgary.
You'll see Mounties and more when you visit Heritage Park, a re-created pre-1914 living-history village. (See listing page 56)

The Informed Traveler

Sales Tax: The federal Goods and Services Tax is 6 percent and applies to most goods, food/beverages and services, including lodgings. Alberta does not have a provincial sales tax but does impose a 4 percent tourism levy.

WHOM TO CALL

Emergency: 911

Police (non-emergency): (403) 266-1234

Fire: (403) 287-4299

Weather: (403) 299-7878

Road Conditions: (403) 246-5853

Hospitals: Foothills Medical Centre, (403) 670-1110, and Rockyview General Hospital, (403) 541-3000.

WHERE TO LOOK

Newspapers

Calgary's daily newspapers are the *Calgary Herald* and the *Calgary Sun,* both morning papers. The national newspapers are *The Globe and Mail* and the *National Post.*

Radio

Calgary radio station CBC (1010 AM) is a member of the Canadian Broadcasting Corp.

Visitor Information

Tourism Calgary: 238 11th Ave. S.E., Room 200, Calgary, AB, Canada T2G 0X8; phone (403) 263-8510 or (800) 661-1678. Visitor information also is available at the Calgary International Airport on the arrivals level; and at the Riley & McCormick Western Store at 220 Stephen Ave. in the Eau Claire Festival Market.

TRANSPORTATION

Air Travel

Calgary International Airport is northeast of downtown. SunDog Tour Co. is one of the companies providing transportation between the airport and downtown. Shuttles between the airport and several major hotels typically operate daily 8:30 a.m.-8:45 p.m.; hours may vary. The one-way fare is $15; under 13, $8. Reservations are required; phone (403) 291-9617. Many hotels also offer free shuttle service for their guests.

Rental Cars

Hertz, downtown or at the airport, offers discounts to CAA and AAA members; phone (403) 233-8366 downtown, (403) 221-1676 at the airport, (800) 263-0600 in Canada or (800) 654-3080 out of Canada.

Rail Service

The nearest VIA Rail stations are in Jasper and Edmonton; phone (506) 857-9830 or (888) 842-7245.

Buses

Greyhound Lines Inc. operates from the depot at 850 16th St. S.W.; phone (800) 661-8747. Red Arrow Express operates luxury motor coaches between Calgary, Red Deer, Edmonton and Fort McMurray; phone (403) 531-0350.

Taxis

Taxi companies include Checker Yellow Cab, (403) 299-9999; Mayfair Taxi, (403) 255-6555; Prestige Limousine, (403) 730-6666; and Yellow Cab, (403) 974-1111. Rates begin at $3 for the first 150 metres (about 1/10 mi.) or portion thereof, plus 20c for each additional 150 metres (about 1/10 mi.) or portion thereof. Cabs can be hailed on the street, but phoning ahead is recommended.

Public Transport

Calgary has both bus and light-rail rapid transit (LRT) service; the latter is free in the downtown core. Calgary Transit's office, 240 7th Ave. S.W., has schedules and maps and sells transit passes. Fares are $2.25 for adults and $1.50 for ages 7-14. Day passes are $6.75; ages 6-14, $4.50. Phone (403) 262-1000.

include an F86 Sabre jet, a Bell 47G helicopter and one of the few remaining World War I Sopwith Triplanes. Also featured are piston and jet aircraft engines, aviation artwork and a Martin Baker ejection seat.

Allow 30 minutes minimum. Daily 10-5; closed Jan. 1 and Dec. 24-26. Admission $7; $4.50 (ages 60+ and students with ID); $3.50 (ages 6-11); $18 (family). AX, MC, VI. Phone (403) 250-3752.

BOW HABITAT STATION is at 1440 17A St. S.E. in Pearce Estate City Park. This eco-park is located along the Bow River and features the Sam Livingston Fish Hatchery, the Pearce Estate Park Interpretive Wetland and a visitor center. The hatchery is one of the largest of its kind, producing 2 to 3 million trout a year, while the wetland showcases Albertan aquatic habitats. In the visitor center interactive exhibits tell about fisheries management and fish culture programs in Alberta.

Note: The site is closed for renovations; reopening is scheduled for early 2009. Allow 30 minutes minimum. Self-guiding tours of the interpretive wetland are available daily 7 a.m.-11 p.m. Donations. Phone (403) 297-6561.

BUTTERFIELD ACRES CHILDREN'S FARM is 3 km (1.9 mi.) n. of Crowchild Tr. at 254077 Rocky Ridge Rd. Visitors can meet and play with animals such as baby goats, rabbits, chicks, calves, sheep, llamas and a 450-pound pig named Scarlet at this whimsical, educational farm. In addition to interactive displays and pony and wagon rides, children also will enjoy trying to milk a goat and playing on a tractor.

Picnicking is permitted. Food is available. Allow 2 hours minimum. Daily 10-4, July-Aug.; Mon.-Fri. 10-2, Sat.-Sun. 10-4, Apr.-June and in Sept. Admission $11.99; $9.99 (ages 65+); $8.99 (ages 1-17). Pony rides $1. MC, VI. Phone (403) 547-3595 or (403) 239-0638.

CALAWAY PARK is 10 km (6 mi.) w. off Trans-Canada Hwy. Springbank Rd. exit. Said to be western Canada's largest outdoor amusement park, it features 32 rides, including a roller coaster, a log ride, bumper boats and skill games. Live stage shows are presented daily. The landscaped grounds include an interactive maze, a miniature golf course, a fishing hole and picnic areas.

Food is available. Kennel, stroller and wheelchair rentals are available. Allow 4 hours minimum. Daily 10-7, July 1-Labour Day weekend; Fri. 5-9, Sat.-Sun. 10-7, Victoria Day weekend-June 30; Mon. and Sat.-Sun. 11-6, day after Labour Day-late Nov. Hours may vary; phone ahead. Admission (includes unlimited rides) $27; $21 (ages 3-6); $19 (ages 50+); $70 (family, four persons). Admission after 2 p.m. $15; free (ages 0-2). Admission after 4 p.m. $12.50; free (ages 0-2). Prices for individual games, the maze, fishing and miniature golf vary. AX, MC, VI. Phone (403) 240-3822.

Calgary Zoo, Botanical Garden & Prehistoric Park / Travel Alberta

To Butterfield Acres Children's Farm · © 2007 NAVTEQ · To Edmonton · University Of Calgary · The Nickle Arts Museum · McMahon Stadium · Confederation Park · Chinese Cultural Centre Museum · Renfrew Athletic Park · Mc Hugh Bluff · Crescent Heights Park · Riley Park · Park Eau Claire Festival Market · Prince's Island Park · Sunnyside · Bank Park · Calgary Zoo, Botanical Garden and Prehistoric Park · Devonian Gardens · Family of Man · TELUS World of Science Calgary · Fort Calgary Historic Park · Glenbow Museum · Grain Academy · Calgary Tower · Central Park · Pengrowth Saddledome · Stampede Casino · Stampede Park · Elbow River Casino · The Military Museum · RAPID TRANSIT STATIONS · To Heritage Park Hist Village & Bar U Nat'l Hist Site · Cash Casino · © AAA · 2129-B

Calgary · Miles 1.2 · Kilometers 1.9

CALGARY TOWER is in Tower Centre at 101 9th Ave. S.W. at Centre St. S. The tower rises 191 metres (626 ft.) above the city. An observation deck and revolving restaurant provide a panorama of the city and the nearby Rocky Mountains. The observation deck features a glass floor and glass walls, which create in visitors the sensation of floating high above the city.

A torch atop the tower burned nonstop during the 1988 Olympic Games; it is illuminated on special occasions. Open daily 7 a.m.-10:30 p.m., June-Sept.; 9-9, rest of year. Hours may vary Oct.-May; phone ahead. Admission $13.50; $11.25 (ages 65+); $10.25 (ages 6-17); $5 (ages 0-5); free (one child age 0-5 with each adult admission). AX, MC, VI. Phone (403) 266-7171.

CALGARY ZOO, BOTANICAL GARDEN & PREHISTORIC PARK is at 1300 Zoo Rd. N.E. at Memorial Dr. and 12th St. E. The zoo is dedicated to conservation, education, recreation and scientific study. Such rare and endangered species as the Siberian tiger and the whooping crane are among more than 900 animals in the zoo. Varied habitats simulate such ecosystems as the boreal forest and an African rainforest and savannah. An Asian elephant is noteworthy for her ability to paint; profits from the sale of her works benefit the environmental enrichment fund.

A tropical aviary and conservatory contains a butterfly garden and more than 4,000 plants. A prehistoric park contains a collection of life-size replicas of dinosaurs in 2.6 hectares (6.5 acres) of re-created Mesozoic landscape. Allow 3 hours minimum. Daily 9-6; closed Dec. 25. Admission $18; $16 (ages 65+); $12 (ages 13-17); $10 (ages 3-12). AX, MC, VI. Phone (403) 232-9300. See color ad p. 55.

CANADA OLYMPIC PARK is off Trans-Canada Hwy. Bowfort Rd. exit. The park, the host area for ski jumping, freestyle skiing, bobsled and luge events at the 1988 Winter Olympic Games, remains a site for year-round sports activities.

In winter visitors can learn to ski and snowboard. During summer guests can try the bobsled/luge track, at speeds up to 95 kilometres per hour (59 mph). Also on the premises is a mountain bike park with more than 25 kilometres (15 mi.) of trails.

A 2-hour self-guiding audio tour is available in several different languages and includes visitor access to the Olympic Hall of Fame and Museum; the Ice House, a training facility where bobsled, skeleton-sled and luge athletes practice; the Olympic

bobsled track; the observation level of the 90-metre (295-ft.) ski-jump tower; and, in summer, a chairlift offering breathtaking scenic views.

Food is available. Allow 2 hours minimum. Self-guiding audio tours are available daily 9-5, July-Aug.; 10-4, rest of year. Self-guiding tour $16; $49 (family). Prices for activities and rides vary. AX, MC, VI. Phone (403) 247-5452.

Olympic Hall of Fame and Museum is at Canada Olympic Park. Exhibits focus on Canada's participation in the Winter Olympic Games from 1924 to the present. A large collection of Olympic torches is on display. The facility also offers such hands-on displays as the Virtual Reality Hockey Shootout, which lets visitors experience firsthand what it's like to be a member of a Canadian Olympic hockey team. Daily 9-5, July-Aug.; 10-4, rest of year. Museum admission included in fee for Canada Olympic Park self-guiding tour. Museum admission only $7. Phone (403) 247-5452.

CHINESE CULTURAL CENTRE MUSEUM is at 197 1st St. S.W. Exhibits represent Chinese culture and history and include sculptures, ceramics and other artifacts dating back thousands of years. Permanently displayed is a replica of the army of terracotta soldiers found during a 1974 excavation at Mount Li in China. The clay archers, bowmen, cavalry, chariots and saddled cavalry horses were found in battle-ready formation guarding the Tomb of Qin Shihuang; each figure is unique. Daily 11-5; closed holidays. Admission $4; $2 (ages 6-12 and 65+). Phone (403) 262-5071.

DEVONIAN GARDENS is on the 4th level of Toronto Dominion Square, 317 7th Ave. S.W. These 1-hectare (2.5-acre) glassed-in, indoor gardens contain 15,700 subtropical trees, plants, fish and turtles as well as waterfalls, fountains and a reflecting pool. Monthly exhibits display works by local artists. A 100-seat amphitheater occasionally hosts shows at noon. Daily 9:30-6 (also Thurs.-Fri. 6-8 p.m.). Free. Phone (403) 221-4681.

FAMILY OF MAN is outside the Calgary Board of Education Building at 515 Macleod Tr. S.E. This grouping of sculpted metal figures stands 6.5 metres (21 ft.) tall. Originally commissioned as part of Great Britain's exhibit for Expo 67, the statues were created by Mario Armengol. Nude and lacking a discernible race, the figures extend their arms and hands in gestures of goodwill and friendship. Daily 24 hours. Free. Phone (403) 268-2489.

FIREFIGHTERS MUSEUM is at 4124 11th St. S.E., n. of 42nd Ave. between Ogden Rd. and Blackfoot Tr. Photographs, artifacts, uniforms and equipment depict the history of the city's firefighters. A collection of 1890-1974 restored fire engines and other equipment also is featured. Allow 1 hour minimum. Thurs.-Mon. 10:30-4, mid-May to mid-Oct. Admission $3; $2 (senior citizens); free (ages 0-11). Phone (403) 246-3322.

SAVE **FORT CALGARY** is at 750 9th Ave. S.E. The 16-hectare (40-acre) riverside park contains a reconstruction of an 1875 North West Mounted Police fort and its 1888 barracks and the Deane House Historic Site, the last remaining building from the site's days as a garrison. Interactive exhibits, costumed interpreters, hands-on activities and audiovisual presentations tell the story of the site, the settlement and the people of Calgary.

Food is available. Daily 9-5; closed Jan. 1, Good Friday and Dec. 24-26. Admission $10.50; $9.50 (ages 65+ and college students with ID); $6.50 (ages 7-17). Prices may vary; phone ahead. AX, MC, VI. Phone (403) 290-1875.

GLENBOW MUSEUM is at 130 9th Ave. S.E., across from the Calgary Tower. The complex includes a museum, an art gallery, a library and archives. Fascinating men and women who contributed to the development of the province are highlighted in Mavericks: An Incorrigible History of Alberta. Niitsitapiisinni: Our Way of Life features artifacts and interactive displays illustrating Blackfoot traditions and values. Other galleries feature exhibits about warriors, gemstones and West Africa; an Asian sculpture gallery and a hands-on art studio also are on-site.

Food is available. Allow 2 hours minimum. Fri.-Wed. 9-5, Thurs. 9-9 (Jan. 1 open noon-5); closed Dec. 25. Admission $14; $12 (college students with ID); $10 (ages 65+); $9 (ages 7-17); $45 (family, two adults and four children). AX, MC, VI. Phone (403) 268-4100.

GRAIN ACADEMY MUSEUM is at Stampede Park off 4th St. S.E. on the second level of Round Up Centre. Visitors can learn about the processes of bringing grain from the field to the table. Highlights include a miniature grain elevator and a working model train that depicts the transportation of grain from the prairie to the Pacific coast. A movie theater and displays describing the history of grain also are featured. Allow 1 hour minimum. Mon.-Fri. 10-4; closed holidays. Free. Parking $10. Phone (403) 263-4594.

HERITAGE PARK HISTORICAL VILLAGE is 2.5 km (1.5 mi.) w. off Queen Elizabeth II Hwy. to 1900 Heritage Dr. S.W. The re-created pre-1914 village is on 27 hectares (66 acres). The village reflects the fur trade of the 1860s, the pre-railway settlements of the 1880s and businesses and residences 1900-14.

Among the park's more than 150 exhibits are a general store, an antique midway, pioneer farm machinery and a Hudson's Bay Co. trading post. Most of the buildings are originals that have been moved to the park. An antique steam train circles the park, and a 200-passenger stern-wheeler cruises Glenmore Reservoir.

Daily 9-5, mid-May through Labour Day; Sat.-Sun. 9-5, day after Labour Day-late Nov. Admission $13.95; $11.95 (senior citizens); $8.95 (ages 3-17); $45.85 (family, two adults and children). Unlimited rides pass $9. Individual ride $3. Prices may vary; phone ahead. AX, MC, VI. Phone (403) 268-8500. *See color ad.*

INGLEWOOD BIRD SANCTUARY is at 2425 9th Ave. S.E. on the Bow River. Self-guiding trails wind throughout the forest, where some 280 species of birds and various mammals have been sighted. Natural history programs and guided nature walks also are offered. Allow 1 hour minimum. Trails daily dawn-dusk. Visitor center daily 10-5, May-Sept.; Tues.-Sun. 10-4, rest of year. Closed Jan. 1, Easter, Nov. 11 and Dec. 24-26. Donations. Phone (403) 268-2489.

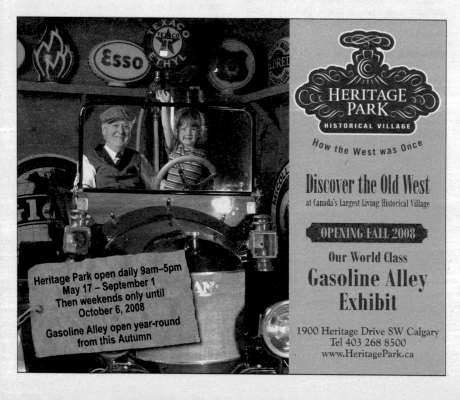

SAVE **THE MILITARY MUSEUMS** is at 4520 Crowchild Tr. S.W., off Flanders Ave. exit. The museum depicts the history of Lord Strathcona's Horse
Regiment—the Royal Canadians; Princess Patricia's
Canadian Light Infantry; The King's Own Calgary
Regiment; and The Calgary Highlanders. Vintage
tanks and carriers are outside. Allow 1 hour minimum. Daily 9:30-4; closed Jan. 1 and Dec. 25. Admission $6; $4 (senior citizens); $3 (ages 7-17); free
(veterans and active military with ID and their families). Phone (403) 974-2850.

THE NICKLE ARTS MUSEUM is on the University
of Calgary campus at 434 Collegiate Blvd. N.W.
Four galleries present changing exhibits of contemporary art textile and numismatic collections. Lectures, gallery talks and other events are offered
throughout the year. Allow 1 hour minimum. Mon.-
Fri. 10-5 (also Thurs. 5-9), Sat. 1-5, Sept.-May;
Mon.-Fri. 10-5, rest of year. Closed holidays. Admission $5; $2 (ages 66+); $1 (ages 7-17); free (stu-
dents with ID and on Tues.). Phone (403) 220-7234.

TELUS WORLD OF SCIENCE CALGARY is at
11th St. and 7th Ave. S.W. Science is at the core of
hands-on exhibits, demonstrations and live theater.
The center presents multimedia productions and
large-format films in the Discovery Dome. The Creative Kids Museum's five exhibit areas focus on the
literary, performing and visual arts.

Daily 9:30-5:30, late June-Aug. 31; Mon.-Thurs.
9:45-4, Fri. 9:45-5; Sat.-Sun. 10-5, rest of year.
Closed Dec. 25. Admission $15; $12 (ages 3-17 and
65+); $49 (family, two adults and four children).
Parking $1.25 per hour, up to $5 for 6 hours. Under
12 must be with an adult. MC, VI. Phone (403)
268-8300.

GAMBLING ESTABLISHMENTS

- **Cash Casino** is at 4040 Blackfoot Tr. S.E. Daily
  10 a.m.-3 a.m.; closed Dec. 25. Phone (403)
  287-1635.
- **Casino Calgary** is at 1420 Meridian Rd. N.E.
  Daily 10 a.m.-3 a.m.; closed Dec. 25. Phone (403)
  248-9467.
- **Elbow River Casino** is at 218 18th Ave. S.E.
  Table games daily noon-3 a.m. Poker daily 24
  hours. Closed Dec. 25. Phone (403) 289-8880.
- **Frank Sisson's Silver Dollar Casino** is at 1010
  42nd Ave. S.E. Daily 10 a.m.-3 a.m.; closed Dec.
  25. Phone (403) 287-1183.
- **Stampede Casino** is at 1801 Big Four Tr. S.E. in
  the Big Four Building in Stampede Park. Daily
  9:30 a.m.-3 a.m.; closed Dec. 25. Phone (403)
  261-0422.

What To Do

Sightseeing

Bus, Train and Van Tours

Brewster Transportation and Tours offers a 4-hour
bus tour of Calgary's attractions as well as trips to
Banff, Lake Louise, Jasper and the Columbia Icefield; phone (403) 221-8242 for schedules and fares.

Rocky Mountaineer Vacations offers scenic vacation packages, including the Rocky Mountaineer, a
2-day, all-daylight, narrated rail tour between Canada's west and the Canadian Rockies. The Rocky
Mountaineer tour departs mid-April to mid-October,
with winter rail trips available in December; phone
(604) 606-7245 or (800) 665-7245.

SAVE Gray Line Calgary provides a variety of excursions featuring the entire area: Banff, Lake Louise, Jasper and the Columbia Icefields; phone (604)
879-3363 or (800) 667-0882.

Walking Tours

Free pamphlets about a self-guiding tour of the
Stephen Avenue Walk are available at the City of
Calgary Municipal Building, 800 Macleod Tr. S.E.,
plaza level, second floor. This pedestrian mall,
which extends from Macleod Trail west along 8th
Avenue to 3rd Street S.W., is a showcase for historic
buildings, many of which are restored. Other pamphlets describing self-guiding walking tours and historic sites also are available.

Sports and Recreation

Calgary was an appropriate choice as host of the
1988 Winter Olympic Games—opportunities for indoor and outdoor recreation abound. For information
about recreational activities, programs and facilities
visitors can phone the city's recreation department
by dialing 311 in Calgary or (403) 268-2489.

In winter public **skiing** facilities at Canada Olympic Park and in numerous areas nearby are available.
Canada Olympic Park *(see attraction listing p. 53)*
also is where to go for other **winter sports,** such as
luge, bobsledding, ski jumping and snowboarding.

At Talisman Centre, 2225 Macleod Tr. S., **swimming, track events** and **weight lifting** are among
the popular activities; phone (403) 233-8393. Similar facilities are offered at the following leisure centers: Eau Claire YMCA, 101 3rd St. S.W.; YWCA,
320 5th Ave. S.E.; Southland Leisure Center, 19th
Street and Southland Drive S.W.; and Village Square
Leisure Center, 2623 56th St. N.E. The latter two
offer wave pools.

Ice-skating is featured during the winter at
Olympic Plaza as well as year-round at more than
two dozen other locations. The Olympic Oval, at
2500 University Dr. N.W., is the site of the 1988
Olympic speed-skating events; skate rentals are
available.

Several parks are in the city, particularly along
the Bow River. Fish Creek Provincial Park *(see Recreation Chart)* has a visitor center and a small lake
providing swimming in summer and ice-skating in
winter. Joggers and bicyclists use the park's extensive trail system. Other recreation sites include
Bowness, Edworthy and Riley parks in northwest
Calgary and Prince's Island Park in the city center.
The 145-hectare (360-acre) Glenmore Reservoir provides ample space for **sailing** and **canoeing;** the
Dragon Boat races are held in late July.

With spectacular natural areas nearby, many visitors to Calgary will be lured to the wilds to enjoy canoeing, **camping, rafting, hiking** and other outdoor pursuits. **Walking** and **bicycling** trails meander through these regions, as do **cross-country skiing** routes. **Tennis** and swimming enthusiasts will find courts and pools throughout Calgary.

Golf lovers can play at more than 40 local courses, including 18 holes at Maple Ridge, 1240 Mapleglade Dr. S.E.; McCall Lake, 1600 32nd Ave. N.E.; McKenzie Meadows, 17215 McKenzie Meadows Dr. S.E.; and Shaganappi Point, 1200 26th St. S.W. Nine-hole courses are at Confederation, 3204 Collingwood Dr. N.W.; Lakeview, 5840 19th St. S.W.; and Richmond Green, 2539 33rd Ave. S.W. Some private courses accept visiting golfers; check locally for greens fees and restrictions.

With names like Flames, Stampeders, Roughnecks and Hitmen, Calgary's major sports teams cannot help but be exciting. The Flames play **ice hockey** at Pengrowth Saddledome in Stampede Park; phone (403) 777-2177.

The local Canadian **Football** League team, the Calgary Stampeders, pounds the turf at McMahon Stadium on Crowchild Trail N.W., off 16th Avenue. Tickets can be obtained by phoning the box office at (403) 289-0258. Ticket prices are $27-$80; over 60 and under 18, $23-$80.

Race City Speedway, 11550 68th St. S.E., features professional and amateur **auto racing** on a dragstrip, a high-banked oval and a 3-kilometre (2-mi.) roadcourse; phone (403) 272-7223. For those wishing to get behind the wheel, Kart World Family Fun Center, 5202 1st St. S.W., offers **go-carts**, which can be rented. Helmets, clothing and instructions are provided. Tamer tracks for children also are available; phone (403) 253-8301.

Spruce Meadows, an outdoor equestrian center and show jumping venue 3 kilometres (2 mi.) west on Hwy. 22X (Spruce Meadows Trail) from Macleod Trail, has world-class programs, including international show jumping events. On days when no shows are scheduled the grounds are open free to the public, daily 9-5. Visitors are invited to wander the grounds, picnic and view horses in the stables; phone (403) 974-4200 for a schedule of Spruce Meadows events.

Shopping

Stephen Avenue Walk, a downtown pedestrian mall, extends from Bankers Hall to the city municipal buildings. This popular spot for people-watching features shops, galleries and restaurants housed within historic buildings. Also downtown, a five-block shopping complex linked by an indoor walkway includes the more than 200 boutiques, department stores and retail chains of Calgary Eaton Centre/TD Square, Bankers Hall, Scotia Centre and Penny Lane Mall.

Unique specialty shops, kiosks and restaurants are the draw at Eau Claire Festival Market, adjacent to the Bow River and Prince's Island Park at 2nd Avenue and 2nd Street S.W.

The trendy Uptown 17th Avenue, a scenic neighborhood and upscale shopping district, features stylish fashion shops, antiques stores and eclectic craft boutiques. The avenue also is home to the exclusive shops at Mount Royal Village. The Kensington district features smaller stores in new and old buildings. Originally Atlantic Avenue, Ninth Avenue S.E. now is lined with antiques and home-furnishings stores, bookstores and cappuccino bars.

Major department stores and a wide variety of chain and specialty stores occupy the city's shopping centers: Chinook Centre at the corner of Macleod Trail and Glenmore Trail S.W., Deerfoot Outlet Mall at 901 64th Ave. N.E., Market Mall at 3625 Shaganappi Tr. N.W., North Hill Mall at 16th Avenue and 14th Street N.W., Northland Village Shoppes at Crowchild Trail N.W. and Shaganappi Trail N.W., Shawnessy Centre at 162nd Avenue and Macleod Trail, Southcentre Mall at Macleod Trail and Anderson Road S.E., Sunridge Mall at 2525 36th St. N.E., Westhills Towne Centre at Stewart Green S.W. off Richmond Road and Sarcee Trail S.W. and Willow Park Village on Macleod Trail S.

Performing Arts

Four of Calgary's most illustrious theater and music companies perform in the Epcor Centre for the Performing Arts at 205 8th Ave. S.E. The center is shared by Alberta Theatre Projects, Theatre Calgary, One Yellow Rabbit Theatre Company and Calgary Philharmonic Orchestra. In addition to four theaters and a concert hall, it contains shops, a restaurant and a coffee bar. For information about performance schedules and ticket sales phone Ticketmaster at (403) 777-0000 or (403) 299-8888.

Southern Alberta Jubilee Auditorium, just south of 14th Avenue and 14th Street N.W., stages a variety of performing arts, including touring companies of Broadway musicals and presentations by Calgary Opera; for details phone the opera company at (403) 262-7286 or the auditorium at (403) 297-8000.

Loose Moose Theatre Company performs adult comedy and drama as well as children's theater; for information phone (403) 265-5682. Pumphouse Theatre, 2140 Pumphouse Ave. S.W., gets its name from the 1913 former pumphouse that the city converted into two theaters; phone (403) 263-0079 for schedule and ticket information. Midday performances take place in the aptly named Lunchbox Theatre on the second level in Bow Valley Square, 205 Fifth Ave. S.W.; phone (403) 265-4292.

A popular dinner theater that often showcases well-known performers in its productions is Stage West, 727 42nd Ave. S.E.; phone (403) 243-6642. Other theater, dance and music companies operate locally; check newspapers for performance schedules.

Special Events

To celebrate the season and showcase local arts, culture and sports, Calgary Winter Festival takes place for 11 days in February. The festival, which takes advantage of the venues from the 1988 Winter

Olympics, features dogsledding, snowboarding and the Winter Village.

Calgary International Children's Festival, which begins the third Wednesday in May and continues for 5 days, draws performers from such locales as Peru, Germany, Russia and Zimbabwe. The festival's many offerings include music, puppetry, dance and storytelling.

Despite a focus on the modern oil and gas industry, Calgary citizens recall their past starting the first Friday after Canada Day (July 1) with ☆ The Calgary Stampede (officially known as The Calgary Exhibition & Stampede). This 10-day Wild West exhibition features a rodeo, chuck wagon races, livestock shows, a re-creation of a Plains Indian village, beach-themed attractions, educational displays, shopping, extreme sports events and a midway. Parades, fireworks, street dancing, pancake breakfasts and other activities create a carnival-like atmosphere.

Families enjoy the cultural and musical events that take place during the ☆ Calgary Folk Music Festival, held for 4 days in late July.

Visitors can sample fine foods and beverages during ☆ Taste of Calgary, which occurs at the Eau Claire Festival Market in August. GlobalFest also takes place in August and features such events as an international fireworks competition and a multicultural celebration. Afrikadey! celebrates African culture through traditional and contemporary music, crafts, food and special scheduled events. Venues for the popular mid-August event are found throughout the area, with festivities concluding at Prince's Island Park.

During Labour Day weekend BBQ on the Bow offers a barbecue competition, live performances by local bands, a children's craft tent, and vendors selling food samples and take-home goods. Jazz musicians and jazz enthusiasts gather in early September at the C-Jazz Festival. Also taking place in early September at the Spruce Meadows outdoor equestrian center, off Hwy. 22X (Spruce Meadows Trail) and Macleod Trail, is the Masters Tournament. Other racing and dressage events are held at the center throughout the year.

The Calgary Vicinity

BRAGG CREEK (I-5) pop. 550

Bragg Creek, 40 kilometres (25 mi.) southwest of Calgary on Hwy. 22, was named after Albert Bragg, a rancher who settled in the area in 1894. Known as the "Gateway to the Kananaskis" for its proximity to the Northern Rockies, the town has been a popular weekend getaway and year-round recreation area since the 1920s. Bragg Creek offers picnic areas, hiking trails, cross-country skiing, campgrounds and scenic Elbow Falls. The area has evolved as an artist's community with sculptors, potters, weavers, painters and other artisans practicing their crafts.

Bragg Creek Chamber of Commerce: P.O. Box 216, Bragg Creek, AB, Canada T0L 0K0; phone (403) 949-0004.

COCHRANE (H-5) pop. 13,760

Cochrane—named for Sen. Matthew Henry Cochrane, who began the first large-scale cattle ranch in the area in the 1880s—is known locally for its homemade ice cream, made by the same family since 1948; hang gliding; horseback riding; and canoe trips down the Bow River. Stoney Indian Reserve, 16 kilometres (10 mi.) west on Hwy. 1A, was the filming site of several movies, including Arthur Penn's "Legends of the Fall" and "Little Big Man," and of the television series "Lonesome Dove."

The downtown's Western-style architecture provides a backdrop for local arts and crafts and specialty shops. Of particular interest is Studio West, a foundry and art gallery where visitors can view the

3,000-year-old sculpting technique known as the "lost wax" process.

Cochrane & District Chamber of Commerce: Unit 6 205 First St. E., Cochrane, AB, Canada T4C 1X6; phone (403) 932-0320.

COCHRANE RANCHE HISTORIC SITE is near jct. hwys. 1A and 22. This 60-hectare (150-acre) site is where Sen. Matthew Cochrane began his large-scale cattle operation in 1881. A visitor center, interpretive programs, walking trails and picnic grounds are available. The "Men of Vision" bronze statue overlooks the grounds. Allow 30 minutes minimum. Daily 9-5, mid-May through Labour Day. Free. Phone (403) 932-4705.

OKOTOKS (I-6)
pop. 17,145, elev. 1,036 m/3,400'

Incorporated in 1904, Okotoks thrived on brick making, lumber and oil distribution in its early days.

Today Okotoks is a commuter community of Calgary. The town gets its name from the Blackfoot name *okatoks,* meaning "rocks." Big Rock, 7 kilometres (4 mi.) west, is the continent's largest known glacial boulder, having been carried here during an ice age.

A popular recreational retreat, Okotoks offers such leisure pursuits as fishing and hiking. Events include a parade and Youth Festival in mid-June and the Coors Pro Rodeo and Western Art Show on Labour Day.

Okotoks & District Chamber of Commerce: 53 N. Railway St., P.O. Box 1053, Okotoks, AB, Canada T1S 1B1; phone (403) 938-2848.

Self-guiding tours: Heritage Walking Tour brochures are available from the information desk at The Station Cultural Centre, 53 N. Railway St.

The Calgary Stampede / © Hans-Peter Merten / age fotostock

This ends listings for the Calgary Vicinity.
The following page resumes the alphabetical listings of cities in Alberta.

CAMROSE (F-7) pop. 15,620

Camrose, first settled around 1900 as a trading post, has a strong sense of its Scandinavian heritage. Known originally as the Hamlet of Sparling, its name was changed to Camrose in 1906. Camrose salutes country music during ⚐ Big Valley Jamboree the first week in August.

Camrose Chamber of Commerce and Tourist Information Centre: 5402 48 Ave., Camrose, AB, Canada T4V 0J7; phone (780) 672-4217.

CAMROSE AND DISTRICT CENTENNIAL MUSEUM is 2 blks. s. of Hwy. 13 at 4522 53 St. at jct. 46th Ave. The museum houses items from Camrose's pioneer days. Buildings include a country school, a fire hall and a restored log pioneer house and church, both furnished in period. A steam engine, a replica of the first newspaper building and a working model of an early threshing machine are displayed.

Tues.-Sun. 9:30-5, Victoria Day-Labour Day; by appointment rest of year. Donations. Phone (780) 672-3298 Victoria Day-Labour Day or (780) 672-5377 for appointments rest of year.

CANMORE (H-4)
pop. 12,039, elev. 1,341 m/4,400′

Established in 1883 as a coal-mining center, Canmore was the first Canadian Pacific Railroad divisional point west of Calgary. The town also was the site of the biathlon and cross-country ski events of the 1988 Winter Olympics. Year-round recreational activities are abundant; fly fishing, rock climbing, snowshoeing and dogsledding are just a few activities visitors can enjoy. Hiking, mountain biking and cross-country skiing are popular along the area's numerous trails.

Tourism Canmore: 907 7th Ave., P.O. Box 8608, Canmore, AB, Canada T1W 3K1; phone (403) 678-1295 or (866) 226-6673.

ALPINE HELICOPTERS LTD. is off Hwy. 1 Canmore exit, following signs to Canmore Municipal Heliport at 91 Bow Valley Tr. Scenic flights over the Canadian Rockies are offered. Passengers can view alpine valleys, glaciers, ice fields, the Continental Divide, Banff National Park of Canada and towering Mount Assiniboine—the "Matterhorn of the Canadian Rockies." Helicopters carry four to six passengers.

Sightseeing flights are offered daily (weather permitting); closed Jan. 1 and Dec. 25-26. Hours vary; phone ahead. Sightseeing flight $219 per passenger (30-minute tour); $189 per passenger (25-minute tour); $95 per passenger (12-minute tour). Reservations are required. Phone (403) 678-4802.

CANMORE MUSEUM AND GEOSCIENCE CENTRE is at 902B 7th Ave. Displays detail Canmore's past through photographs and coal-mining artifacts. The museum also presents a geology exhibit with fossils, rocks, photographs and videos. Historical walking tours are offered.

Allow 30 minutes minimum. Mon.-Tues. noon-5, Wed.-Sun. 10-6, Victoria Day weekend-Labour Day; Mon.-Fri. noon-5, Sat.-Sun. 11-5, rest of year. Closed Jan. 1 and Dec. 25. Admission $3; $2 (ages 65+ and students with ID); free (ages 0-8); $7 (family, two adults and two children). Phone (403) 678-2462.

[SAVE] OH CANADA EH?! DINNER SHOW is at 125 Kananaskis Way. The show provides guests with a humorous take on Canadian culture and tradition. Singing Mounties, lumberjacks, a hockey player as well as other characters serve guests a family-style Canadian meal during the show. Allow 2 hours, 30 minutes minimum. Shows are presented most days at 6:30 p.m., May-Oct.; otherwise varies. Phone ahead to confirm schedule. Admission $66; $33 (ages 6-16). Reservations are required. MC, VI. Phone (403) 609-0004 or (800) 773-0004. *See color ad p. 43.*

RECREATIONAL ACTIVITIES
Dogsledding
- **Snowy Owl Sled Dog Tours** is at 602 Bow Valley Tr. Write P.O. Box 8390, Canmore, AB, Canada T1W 2V2. Trips are offered daily, Nov.-Apr. (weather permitting). Departure times vary; phone ahead. Phone (403) 678-4369 or (888) 311-6874.

Mountain Biking
- **Canadian Rockies Trail Tours** is at 106 Bow Meadows Crescent. Write P.O. Box 8138, Canmore, AB, Canada T1W 2T9. Trips are offered daily, May-Oct. Schedule varies; phone ahead. Phone (403) 760-9521.

White-water Rafting
- **[SAVE] Mirage Adventure Tours Ltd.** departs Canmore Rafting Centre, 20 Lincoln Park. Write P.O. Box 8097, Canmore, AB, Canada T1W 2T8. Other activities are offered. Trips depart daily at 10 and 1:30, May-Sept. Phone (403) 678-4919, or (888) 312-7238 in Alberta, Manitoba and Saskatchewan.

CARDSTON (K-6)
pop. 3,452, elev. 1,185 m/3,888′

A son-in-law of Brigham Young, Charles Ora Card, led 10 Mormon families from Utah into Canada in 1887, hoping to find freedom from American anti-polygamy laws. Settling in Cardston, the immigrants founded the country's first Mormon settlement and named the town after their leader, who became its first mayor.

Cardston Alberta Temple of the Church of Jesus Christ of Latter-day Saints, 348 3rd St. W., was completed and dedicated in 1923. The temple serves a large area of western Canada and Montana; a large percentage of Cardston residents are Mormon. Non-Mormons are not permitted to enter the structure but can tour the grounds, where a visitor center offers information; phone (403) 653-1696.

Cardston & District Chamber of Commerce: P.O. Box 1212, Cardston, AB, Canada T0K 0K0; phone (403) 653-2798.

CHARLES ORA CARD HOME is at 337 Main St. The log cabin of this Mormon leader has been restored and refurnished with hand-carved furniture. Allow 30 minutes minimum. Mon.-Sat. 1:30-5, July-Aug. Donations. Phone (403) 653-3366.

COURTHOUSE MUSEUM is at 89 3rd Ave. W. Displays include local pioneer memorabilia in a stone courthouse dating from 1907. Allow 1 hour minimum. Mon.-Sat. 9-12:30, July-Aug. Donations. Phone (403) 653-3366.

REMINGTON CARRIAGE MUSEUM is at 623 Main St. More than 250 19th- and early 20th-century horse-drawn vehicles are showcased. Interactive displays and exhibit galleries provide the feeling of riding in the horse-drawn transportation of that era, and an introductory multimedia presentation provides an overview of that time.

The exhibit galleries, which include a blacksmith shop and livery stable, carriage factory, carriage dealership, a working restoration shop, frontier settlement and racetrack, depict 19th-century society and its dependence on this mode of transportation. Sound effects, lighting and audiovisual presentations enhance many of the presentations. A working stable shows horses being groomed and harnessed. In summer visitors may schedule 15-minute rides on vintage and reproduction carriages.

Guided tours are available. Picnicking is permitted. Food is available. Allow 1 hour, 30 minutes minimum. Daily 9-6, May 15-Sept. 14; 10-5, rest of year. Closed Jan. 1, Easter and Dec. 24-25. Carriage rides are offered daily 11-noon and 1-5, May 15-Sept. 14. Admission (May 15-Sept. 14) $9; $8 (ages 65+); $5 (ages 7-17); $22 (family, two adults and two children). Admission (rest of year) $8; $7 (ages 65+); $4 (ages 7-17); $22 (family, two adults and two children). Carriage ride $4; $2.50 (ages 4-17); $12 (family, two adults and two children). MC, VI. Phone (403) 653-5139.

CLARESHOLM (J-6) pop. 3,700

CLARESHOLM MUSEUM is on Hwy. 2 at 5126 1st St. W. Displays are housed in a former Canadian Pacific Railway station. The sandstone building features early 20th-century items that represent pioneer life. Town history is highlighted in railway, medical and educational displays. On the grounds are a one-room schoolhouse, a historic log cabin, a caboose, a playground and the Louise McKinney Memorial Gardens. Daily 9:30-5:30, Victoria Day-Aug. 31; 10-5, Sept. 1-second Mon. in Oct.; by appointment rest of year. Donations. Phone (403) 625-3131.

COALDALE (J-7) pop. 6,177

THE ALBERTA BIRDS OF PREY CENTRE is 3 blks. n. of jct. hwys. 3 and 845, then w. on 16th Ave. The center rehabilitates injured and orphaned birds of prey and prepares them for release back into the wild. A captive breeding program returns threatened and endangered species to their native habitats. A self-guiding nature walk provides a close-up view of caged or tethered hawks, falcons, owls, eagles and vultures. Birds fly freely during daily demonstrations.

Guided tours are available. Picnicking is permitted. Allow 1 hour, 30 minutes minimum. Daily 9:30-5, early May-early Sept. Admission $8; $7 (ages 60+); $5 (ages 6-17); $4 (ages 3-5). MC, VI. Phone (403) 345-4262.

COCHRANE—see Calgary p. 59.

COLUMBIA ICEFIELD—
see Jasper National Park of Canada p. 83.

CROWSNEST PASS (J-5) pop. 5,749

An area of wild beauty and haunting legends, the municipality of Crowsnest Pass is an amalgamation of the former coal-mining towns of Bellevue, Blairmore, Coleman, Frank and Hillcrest. Scenic Hwy. 3 through Crowsnest Pass connects Burmis to Fernie, British Columbia, via the Rocky Mountain Range and the Continental Divide.

The area provides visitors with recreational opportunities and stimulates the imagination with such stories as the curse of the Lost Lemon Gold Mine, rum-running and the shoot-out at Bellevue Cafe.

The town of Frank made national headlines April 29, 1903, when close to 70 residents were killed in the dramatic slide of Turtle Mountain on the east side of the pass. Ninety million tons of limestone swept over 1.5 kilometres (.9 mi.) of the valley before dawn, destroying part of the town and burying a mine plant and railway. The old town was at the western edge of the slide; many cellars still are visible.

BELLEVUE UNDERGROUND MINE TOUR is n. off Hwy. 3 Bellevue exit, following signs to the Bellevue Underground Mine access road at 21814 28th Ave. Participants don a miner's helmet and lamp, strap on a battery pack and follow guides along the same path taken by coal miners 1903-61, when this was an active coal mine. The half-hour tour provides insights into the process of coal mining and the events that led to the mine's closing.

Note: The temperature in the mine can reach 7 C (45 F); dress in warm clothing and wear sturdy footwear. Allow 30 minutes minimum. Tours depart daily every 30 minutes 10-5:30, May 15-Labour Day. Fee $6; $5 (ages 6-17 and 65+); $18 (family). MC, VI. Phone (403) 564-4700.

FRANK SLIDE INTERPRETIVE CENTRE is 1.5 km (.9 mi.) n. off Hwy. 3 at w. edge of Frank Slide. The center overlooks the site of the 1903 rockslide. Displays and a 20-minute audiovisual program, "In the Mountain's Shadow," describe area history from early settlement to the decline and fall of the mining industry and the events surrounding the Frank Slide. A 47-minute documentary, "On the Edge of Destruction," also is featured.

Walkways outside the center provide views of the devastation and the surrounding area. A 1.5-kilometre (.9-mi.) self-guiding trail over the slide allows visitors to view the debris. Interpretive programs are offered in summer. Allow 1 hour, 30 minutes minimum. Daily 9-6, May 15-Sept. 14; 10-5, rest of year. Closed Jan. 1, Easter and Dec. 24-25. Admission $9; $8 (ages 65+); $5 (ages 7-17); $22 (family, two adults and children). AX, MC, VI. Phone (403) 562-7388.

LEITCH COLLIERIES PROVINCIAL HISTORIC SITE is 3 km (1.9 mi.) e. of Bellevue on Hwy. 3. Founded in 1907, this was the first wholly Canadian-owned mine. The area was the site of a sophisticated early colliery—a coal mine and the buildings and equipment connected with it. The remains of the power house, washery, mine manager's residence and coke ovens still stand.

Interpretive signs explain the mining and processing methods. Self-guiding tours are available year-round. Interpreters are on-site daily 10-5, mid-May through Labour Day. Donations. Phone (403) 562-7388.

DEVON—*see Edmonton p. 76.*

DICKSON (G-5) pop. 77

DICKSON STORE MUSEUM is at 1928 2nd Ave. Renovated to a style typical of the 1930s, this general store once served as the town post office and a local gathering place. Now operating as a museum, it features exhibits of dry goods, hardware and groceries common to that time. Costumed interpreters also lead visitors through the restored second-floor living quarters.

Allow 30 minutes minimum. Mon.-Sat. 10-5:30, Sun. 12:30-5:30, mid-May through Labour Day; Sat. 10-5:30, Sun. 12:30-5:30, day after Labour Day-last Sun. in Sept. Donations. Phone (403) 728-3355.

DONALDA (F-7) pop. 224

Situated in the heart of Alberta, Donalda was established in 1911 and named after the niece of Donald A. Mann, an official with the Canadian National Railway. It overlooks the scenic Meeting Creek Coulee. The region's unusual Paskapoo sandstone rock formations attract sportsman, hikers, artists and photographers. Donalda also claims an unusual man-made distinction. A 12.8-metre (42-ft.) lamp, said to be the world's largest, was built in the town center by local residents. It glows at the east end of Main Street each evening.

DONALDA & DISTRICT MUSEUM is at Main St. and Railway Ave. More than 900 lamps ranging from the antique bicycle variety to colorful living room types are displayed. Some 40 tiny courting lamps, which hold only an hour's worth of fuel and

were used in the 1800s to signal the end of a suitor's visit, also can be seen. An art gallery, a 1909 railway station and a creamery are included.

Allow 30 minutes minimum. Mon.-Fri. 9-5, Sat.-Sun. 11-5, early May-second Mon. in Oct.; Mon.-Fri. 9-5, rest of year. Admission $3; free (ages 0-14); $5 (family, two adults and children). Phone (403) 883-2100.

DRUMHELLER (H-7) pop. 7,932

About 65 million years before Sam Drumheller began promoting the 1910 townsite later named for him, the surrounding Red Deer Valley was the home of immense dinosaurs. Plant-eating hadrosaurs, flesh-eating tyrannosaurs and their formidable cousins stomped through the swampy lowlands and forests bordering the Mowry Sea, which once covered the North American plains. Fossils of prehistoric creatures often are discovered in the multi-layered sedimentary walls of the valley; several life-size dinosaur replicas can be seen in town.

A larger-than-life version of one of these prehistoric beings, a 25-metre-tall (84-ft.) facsimile of a tyrannosaurus rex, has been built over the top of the Drumheller & District Chamber of Commerce at 60 First Ave. W. Visitors can climb up to a viewing platform in the dinosaur's mouth.

Although the local coal industry founded in 1911 by American Jesse Gouge has declined, remnants of old mines still exist. In Midland Provincial Park *(see Recreation Chart)* off N. Dinosaur Trail (Hwy. 838), a self-guiding walking trail leads to the former site of Midland Mine. Gas and oil wells sporadically dot the nearby rolling prairies, but the shortgrass country is occupied mostly by geese and antelope.

Hoodoos—mushroom-shaped pillars of rock that have been carved into unusual formations by centuries of wind and rain—can be seen 18 km (11 mi.) southeast on Hwy. 10. Because of their fragile nature, climbing these formations is not permitted.

Another nearby remarkable natural site is Horseshoe Canyon, 17 kilometres (11 mi.) southwest on Hwy. 9. Deriving its name from its horseshoe shape, the canyon is in an area of badlands amidst the Alberta prairies. Viewpoints provide opportunities to survey multicolored canyon walls and unusual rock formations.

A natural amphitheater is the site in early July for six performances of The Canadian Badlands Passion Play. In a setting closely resembling the Holy Land, a cast of 150 and a 100-voice choir relate the life of Christ; phone (403) 823-2001 or (888) 823-2001.

Stretching over the Red Deer River, the Rosedale Suspension Bridge on Hwy. 10 originally was used to carry miners across the river to the now-abandoned Star Mine. In 1931 the swinging bridge replaced the original cable car system and was used until the mine closed in 1957. A park with picnic facilities is available.

Drumheller & District Chamber of Commerce: 60 First Ave. W., P.O. Box 999, Drumheller, AB, Canada T0J 0Y0; phone (403) 823-8100 or (866) 823-8100.

ATLAS COAL MINE NATIONAL HISTORIC SITE is 18 km (11 mi.) s.e. on Hwy. 10. This site explores the coal mining history of the Drumheller Valley. Visitors can take a tour of an eight-story wooden tipple (coal screening plant), see restored mine offices, a lamp house and a miner's shack, hike on interpretive trails and climb on antique mining machines. A restored mine locomotive pulling coal cars provides rides through the site.

Allow 1 hour, 30 minutes minimum. Daily 9:30-8:30, July-Aug.; 9:30-5:30, May-June; 10-5, Sept. 1-second Mon. in Oct. (weather permitting). Admission $6; free (ages 0-5); $18 (family, two adults and two children). MC, VI. Phone (403) 822-2220.

DINOSAUR TRAIL (HWY. 838) is a 50-km (30-mi.) circle tour that connects Drumheller and the Red Deer Valley, part of Alberta's Canadian Badlands. The trail is marked. The arid terrain is distinguished by hoodoos—mushroom-shaped rock pillars carved by thousands of years of wind and rain.

A short distance along the north trail is The Little Church, a meditation chapel that holds six visitors. The cable-run Bleriot Ferry crosses the Red Deer River. Highway open daily. The ferry departs on demand, early May through Oct. 31. Highway and ferry free. Phone (866) 823-8100.

Badlands Historical Centre is at 335 1st St. E. Displays focus on pioneer history, the coal-mining boom and the region's ecology. A lapidary collection includes fossils, gems and minerals. Interactive exhibits are available. Daily 9-6, May-Oct. Admission $4; $3 (ages 7-17 and 65+); $12 (family). AX, MC, VI. Phone (403) 823-2593.

HOMESTEAD MUSEUM is .7 km (.5 mi.) n.w. via Hwy. 9 to 901 N. Dinosaur Tr. Pioneer and First Nations items as well as clocks, gramophones, radios, early cars, fine china, jewelry, tractors and farm implements are displayed. There also are collections of military badges, medals and early 20th-century clothing. Allow 1 hour, 30 minutes minimum. Daily 10-5, May 1 to mid.-Oct. (also Fri.-Sun. 5-8, Victoria Day weekend-Labour Day). Admission $5; $3 (ages 6-17 and 65+); $12 (family). Phone (403) 823-2600.

REPTILE WORLD is at 95 3rd Ave. E. Home to more than 150 species of reptiles and amphibians—including snakes, frogs and turtles—the facility features Fred, a 318-kilogram (700-lb.) alligator. Allow 30 minutes minimum. Daily 9 a.m.-10 p.m., July-Aug.; Thurs.-Mon. 10-5, Sun. noon-5, Nov.-Apr.; Thurs.-Mon. 10-6, May-June; Thurs.-Mon. 10-5, rest of year. Closed major holidays. Hours may vary; phone ahead. Admission $6.50; $4.50 (ages 5-17 and 65+); $18 (family, two adults and children). AX, MC, VI. Phone (403) 823-8623.

ROYAL TYRRELL MUSEUM is 6 km (4 mi.) n.w. on N. Dinosaur Tr. (Hwy. 838) in Midland Provincial Park. The museum is in the badlands of the Red Deer River Valley, surrounded by one of the richest fossil deposits in the world. Dinosaurs that once roamed Alberta are now showcased in the museum's Dinosaur Hall, where more than 35 skeletons and lifelike models are displayed.

Fossils, models, computers, DVD centers, a preparation laboratory, hands-on exhibits and an indoor garden illustrate millions of years of geological and biological development. Educational programs are offered Victoria Day weekend through Labour Day. The Cretaceous Garden contains plants that are virtually the same today as they were more than 65 million years ago. The museum also houses a research center and operates a field station near Patricia (see attraction listing p. 89).

Allow 3 hours minimum. Daily 9-9, Victoria Day weekend-Labour Day; daily 10-5, day after Labour Day-second Mon. in Oct.; Tues.-Sun. 10-5, rest of year. Closed Jan. 1 and Dec. 25. Admission $10; $8 (ages 65+); $6 (ages 7-17); $30 (family, two adults and children). MC, VI. Phone (403) 823-7707, or (888) 440-4240 out of Alberta.

DUNVEGAN (B-2)

HISTORIC DUNVEGAN PROVINCIAL PARK is off Queen Elizabeth II Hwy. on the n. side of the Peace River beside Dunvegan Suspension Bridge. The park was a fur-trading post and the site of one of the first Roman Catholic missions in Alberta. Three original buildings remain: the 1877-78 Factor's House, part of the Hudson's Bay Co.'s fort; the 1885 church of St. Charles Mission; and its 1889 rectory.

Guided walks and educational programs explain the site's history. A visitor center offers a video about the history of Dunvegan. Allow 1 hour minimum. Daily 10-6, May 15-Labour Day. Admission $3; $2 (ages 65+); $1.50 (ages 7-17); $8 (family). Phone (780) 835-7150. See Recreation Chart.

Savings for all Seasons

Hertz rents Fords and other fine cars. ® REG. U.S. PAT. OFF. © HERTZ SYSTEM INC. 1999/2008-99.

No matter the season, Hertz offers CAA members exclusive discounts and benefits.

Operating in 150 countries at over 7,600 locations, Hertz makes traveling more convenient and efficient wherever and whenever you go. Hertz offers CAA members discounts up to 20% on car rentals worldwide.

To receive your exclusive CAA member discounts and benefits, mention your CAA membership card at time of reservation and present it at time of rental. **In addition**, to receive a free one car class upgrade on daily, weekly or weekend rental in the United States, Puerto Rico and Canada, mention PC# 969194 at the time of reservation. Offer is valid for vehicle pick-up on or before 12/15/08.

For reservations and program details, call your CAA Travel centre or the Hertz/CAA Desk at **1-800-654-3080.**

Edmonton

City Population: 730,372
Elevation: 670 m/2,198 ft.

Editor's Picks:

Fort Edmonton Park.................(see p. 71)

Royal Alberta Museum ....(see p. 72)

West Edmonton Mall ....(see p. 73)

Alberta Legislature Building / Travel Alberta

Few first-time visitors to Edmonton are prepared for what they discover when they arrive. From trading post to metropolis within some 200 years, this capital city continues to surprise visitors by its size, quality of life, sophistication and its beautiful river valley location.

Edmonton owes its existence to an abundant and varied supply of natural resources, which prompted each of its three major booms. In 1795 the Hudson's Bay Co. founded Fort Edmonton on the banks of the North Saskatchewan River. Traders bartered with Cree and Blackfoot Indians for luxuriant and sought-after pelts of otters, beavers, muskrats, minks and foxes. A trading settlement developed and became the main stopping point on routes to the north and to the Pacific.

This stopping point became a starting point for prospectors rushing to the Klondike for gold; they stocked up on supplies in Edmonton for the harsh trip northward. When gold failed to materialize and many prospectors realized they were not going to get rich, let alone get rich quick, they headed back to Edmonton to settle for a slower but surer way of life.

A bust for prospectors was a boom for Edmonton. The city grew to six times its previous size, making it a prime choice for the provincial capital when Alberta was formed in 1905.

In the years that followed, the capital city earned its nickname, "Gateway to the North," because of its status as a transportation hub and gateway to the regions beyond. In 1915 Edmonton became a major link in the Canadian Pacific Transcontinental Railroad, emerging as an important crossroads stop between east and west as well as north and south.

The city's reputation as a transportation center was reinforced during the 1930s as bush pilots transported vital medical supplies, food and mail to northern communities. And when construction began on the Alaska Hwy. in 1942, Edmonton found itself again in the role of a major distribution and supply center. Edmonton also is an important air travel link.

When the last big boom was fading from memory, the Leduc No. 1 Well gushed forth black crude oil only 40 kilometres (25 mi.) southwest of Edmonton. This discovery in February 1947 was just the beginning. Since then more than 2,250 wells within a 40-kilometre (25-mi.) radius of Edmonton have coaxed the precious natural resource to the surface. Enormous industrial growth resulted; the city's population quadrupled in the 25 years following the Leduc gusher. Today more than 450,000 barrels of crude oil are refined daily in Greater Edmonton.

Edmonton is a city growing in both prosperity and beauty. With about 938,000 residents in the greater metropolitan area, Edmonton has been careful not to sacrifice the natural resource that makes it livable—its green space. Edmonton's river valley parkland is reputed to be the largest stretch of urban parkland in North America, encompassing 7,340 hectares (18,348 acres). The city contains more than 11,000 hectares (27,181 acres) of parkland, playgrounds and open areas.

Getting There — *starting on p. 67*

Getting Around — *starting on p. 67*

What To See — *starting on p. 70*

What To Do — *starting on p. 73*

Where To Stay — *starting on p. 438*

Where To Dine — *starting on p. 439*

Stretches of parks along the North Saskatchewan River Valley let residents spend long summer days enjoying the outdoors. The city park system provides a winter playground for such activities as cross-country skiing, ice-skating, dogsledding and snowshoeing. For visitors who prefer the indoors, an extensive system of underground and overhead "pedways" in the downtown area makes it possible to travel in climate-controlled comfort regardless of the weather; Edmonton Tourism provides pedway maps.

Getting There

By Car

Two major highways run through Edmonton. The Trans-Canada Yellowhead Hwy. (Hwy. 16) provides access from the east and west; Queen Elizabeth II Hwy. runs north and south between Edmonton and Calgary.

Getting Around

Street System

Edmonton's street system is a grid with streets running north and south and avenues running east and west. Most streets and avenues are numbered starting from the southeast corner of the city; a few are named.

Edmonton's street plan includes several traffic circles. When approaching a traffic circle, make sure you are in the correct lane. Use the right lane if you plan to exit, the left lane if you are traveling around the circle. When in the circle, the vehicle on the outside must yield to the vehicle on the inside.

The city speed limit is 50 kilometres per hour (30 mph) or as posted. A right turn on red after stopping

West Edmonton Mall / Travel Alberta

is permitted; U-turns are not. A sign that reads "Bus and Taxi Lane Only" means it is illegal to drive, park or stop any vehicle other than the above in that lane.

Parking

Street parking restrictions vary throughout the city; watch for and heed the signs. Parking is not permitted in the residential areas surrounding Northlands Park, TELUS Field and Commonwealth Stadium during major events; cars parked there will be towed.

Rates for city-operated parking meters are $1-$2 per hour. Most meters are free after 6 p.m. and on Sundays and holidays; however, there are some 24-hour meters.

Rates for downtown parking lots range $1.50-$3 per half-hour during the day. At lots participating in the city's Park in the Heart program, parking costs $2 from 6 p.m. to midnight Monday through Friday and for the first 3 hours on Saturdays and Sundays.

Destination Edmonton

Once a tiny settlement where traders sought to swap for furs with Cree and Blackfoot Indians, today's bustling Edmonton holds its heritage in high regard.

Reminders of the city's past can be found at museums, living-history demonstrations, historic sites and archives. But don't forget to step into the present for a visit to one of the world's largest malls.

Alberta Legislature Building, Edmonton.
The seat of Alberta's provincial government also boasts landscaped grounds—fountains and pools in summer and a skating rink in the winter. (See listing page 70)

Fort Edmonton Park.
Go back in time at this park while you watch costumed interpreters demonstrate crafts and chores of the past. (See listing page 71)

© Richard Cummins
SuperStock

Royal Alberta Museum, Edmonton.
Alberta's natural and human histories are explored in exhibits within the confines of this modern building. (See listing page 72)

Travel Alberta

Edmonton

• Fort Saskatchewan

St. Albert•

Stony Plain

See Vicinity map page 71

•Devon

Muttart Conservatory, Edmonton.
The conservatory's pyramid-shaped greenhouses frame the city's skyline. (See listing page 72)

Places included in this AAA Destination City:

The Informed Traveler

Sales Tax: The federal Goods and Services Tax is 6 percent and applies to most goods, food/beverages and services, including lodgings. Alberta does not have a provincial sales tax but does impose a 4 percent tourism levy.

WHOM TO CALL

Emergency: 911 or (780) 426-3232
Police (non-emergency): (780) 423-4567
Fire: (780) 496-3900
Ambulance: 911 or (780) 426-3232
Distress Line: (780) 482-4357
Weather: (780) 468-4940
Road Reports: (780) 471-6056
Hospitals: Grey Nuns Community Hospital, (780) 450-7000; Misericordia, (780) 930-5611; Royal Alexandra Hospital, (780) 477-4111; University of Alberta Hospital, (780) 407-8822.

WHERE TO LOOK

Newspapers

Edmonton has two daily newspapers, the *Edmonton Journal* and the *Edmonton Sun,* both distributed in the morning. Canada's national newspapers, *The Globe and Mail* and the *National Post,* also are available at newsstands.

Radio

Radio station CBC (740 AM) is a member of Canadian Broadcasting Corp.

Visitor Information

Edmonton Tourism: 9990 Jasper Ave. N.W., Edmonton, AB, Canada T5J 1P7; phone (780) 496-8400 or (800) 463-4667.

Gateway Park Information Center: 2404 Gateway Blvd. S.W./Queen Elizabeth II Hwy., Edmonton, AB, Canada T6W 1A1; phone (780) 496-8400 or (800) 463-4667.

Visitor information also is available at the Edmonton International Airport.

TRANSPORTATION

Air Travel

Edmonton International Airport is 29 kilometres (18 mi.) south of the city center; for information phone (780) 890-8382 or (800) 268-7134. Sky Shuttle service to downtown costs $13 one way and $20 round-trip (phone to confirm fares); phone (780) 465-8515 or (888) 438-2342. Taxi service between the airport and downtown averages $40-$44; a limousine is $48. In addition many hotels offer free shuttle service for their guests.

Rental Cars

Hertz, downtown or at the airport, offers discounts to CAA and AAA members; phone (780) 423-3431 downtown, (780) 890-4435 at the airport, (800) 263-0600 in Canada or (800) 654-3080 out of Canada.

Rail Service

The VIA Rail station is at 12360 121st St.; phone (780) 448-2575 for baggage information, (888) 842-7245 for arrival and departure information.

Buses

The downtown depot for Greyhound Lines Inc. is at 10324 103rd St.; phone (780) 413-8747 or (800) 661-8747. The south side depot is at 5723 104th St. Red Arrow Express offers luxury motor coach service between Edmonton, Calgary, Fort McMurray and Red Deer; phone (780) 424-3339 or (800) 232-1958.

Taxis

Taxi companies include Alberta Co-Op Taxi, (780) 425-2525; Capital Taxi Line Ltd., (780) 423-2425; and Yellow Cab, (780) 462-3456. Taxi rates start at $3.60, plus 20c is charged for each additional 150 metres (about 1/10 mile) or a portion thereof. Taxis can be hailed, but phoning is recommended.

Public Transport

Edmonton Transit System's Churchill Station Information Centre, 99th Street and 102A Avenue, is open Mon.-Fri. 8:30-5:30; phone (780) 496-1611. Buses operate 6 a.m.-1 a.m., Mon.-Sat., 6:30 a.m.-12:30 a.m., Sun. and holidays; hours may be extended for special events. The Light-Rail Transit (LRT) operates 5:30 a.m. to 1 a.m. Fare is $2.50; over 64 and ages 6-17, $2.25. A 1-day pass is $6.75.

Disabled Adult Transit System (DATS) serves those who can't use other transit facilities. Visitors may request a temporary registration number by phoning (780) 496-4570. DATS reservations are accepted up to 3 days in advance.

What To See

ALBERTA AVIATION MUSEUM is at 11410 Kingsway Ave. This hangar was part of a training facility for air crews during World War II. The museum displays 30 historic aircraft including a carefully restored Fairchild 71, a fighter-bomber version of the De Havilland Mosquito, a fully operational Boeing 737 airliner, as well as 1920s biplanes and jet fighters from the Cold War era. Other displays detail the history of aviation in Edmonton and Alberta.

Guided tours are available by appointment. Allow 1 hour minimum. Mon.-Fri. 10-6, Sat.-Sun. and holidays 10-4; closed Jan. 1 and Dec. 25-26 and 31. Admission $9; $7 (ages 60+); $6 (ages 6-17); $24 (family, two adults and four children). AX, MC, VI. Phone (780) 451-1175.

ALBERTA LEGISLATURE BUILDING is at 10800 97th Ave. Public-use parkland, monuments, reflecting pools and fountains surround the building, which was built with sandstone and marble and completed in 1912. Displays outline Alberta's history and parliamentary traditions. Guided 45-minute tours begin in the Legislature Interpretive Centre.

Allow 1 hour minimum. Guided tours are offered daily on the hour 9-noon and every 30 minutes 12:30-4, May 1-Oct. 15; on the hour Mon.-Fri. 9-3, Sat.-Sun. and holidays noon-4, rest of year. Closed Jan. 1, Good Friday and Dec. 25. Free. Phone (780) 427-7362.

ALBERTA RAILWAY MUSEUM is 2 km (1.2 mi.) s. of Hwy. 37 at 24215 34th St. The museum resembles a railway terminal, with a train yard, locomotive and car shops, and a station. More than 60 pieces of rolling stock are displayed. There are many exhibits about railway history, including telegraph systems and railway technology. If volunteer staff is available, some weekends in July and August a 20-minute ride aboard a diesel-powered train is offered (weather permitting).

Guided tours are available. Picnicking is permitted. Allow 1 hour, 30 minutes minimum. Daily 10-5, Victoria Day weekend-Labour Day. Admission $5; $3.50 (students with ID and senior citizens); $2 (ages 3-12). Train ride $4. VI. Phone (780) 472-6229.

[SAVE] **ART GALLERY OF ALBERTA** is at 100-10230 Jasper Ave. at Enterprise Square. The gallery exhibits fine and applied arts, with an emphasis on Canadian historical art and western Canadian contemporary art.

Note: The museum's collections are currently displayed in an interim gallery; a new permanent facility is being constructed on Sir Winston Churchill Square and is set to open in late 2009. Allow 1 hour minimum. Mon.-Fri. 10:30-5 (also Thurs. 5-8), Sat.-Sun. 11-5; closed major holidays. Admission $10; $7 (ages 65+ and students with ID); $5 (ages 6-12); $20 (family, two adults and four children); free (on Thurs. 4-8). MC, VI. Phone (780) 422-6223.

EDMONTON PUBLIC SCHOOLS ARCHIVES AND MUSEUM is at 10425 99th Ave. The archives and museum is in historic 1905 McKay Avenue School, site of the first two sessions of the Alberta Legislature. The building has been carefully restored and

Fort Edmonton Park / Travel Alberta

Edmonton

Miles 0 — 2
Kilometers 0 — 3.2

To Athabasca & St Albert

© 2007 NAVTEQ

features the 1906 legislative chamber, period class-rooms and displays tracing the history of Edmonton public schools.

Also on the grounds is the restored Edmonton 1881 Schoolhouse, the first free public school in Alberta. Allow 1 hour minimum. Tues.-Fri. 12:30-4 (also Wed. 4-9), Sun. 1-4, May-Sept.; Tues.-Fri. 12:30-4, rest of year. Closed holidays. Free. Phone (780) 422-1970.

FORT EDMONTON PARK is at jct. Fox and Whitemud drs. at 7000 143rd. St. Reputed to be Canada's largest living-history park, it depicts Edmonton in four eras: as an 1846 Hudson's Bay Co. fur-trading fort and Cree encampment, as an 1885 settlement, as a developing capital in 1905 and as a 1920 business community.

Costumed interpreters give demonstrations. Visitors may play horseshoes and old-time children's games, ride in antique cars, fire a round in the shooting gallery, learn to bead and sample pioneer foods such as bannock. Steam train and streetcar rides as well as a 1920s-style midway are included.

Food is available. Pets are not permitted. Allow 3 hours minimum. Daily 10-6, late June-Labour Day; Mon.-Fri. 10-4, Sat.-Sun. 10-6, late May-late June; Sun. 10-6, day after Labour Day-Sept. 30. Guided tours are available at 11, noon, 1, 2 and 3. Admission $9.25; $7 (ages 13-17 and 65+); $4.75 (ages 2-12); $29.50 (family, two adults and children). Prices may vary; phone ahead. MC, VI. Phone (780) 496-8787.

JOHN JANZEN NATURE CENTRE is at jct. Fox and Whitemud drs., adjacent to Fort Edmonton Park. The center has exhibits, self-guiding nature trails through the river valley, small animals, hands-on exhibits for children and interpretive programs and events designed to promote awareness and appreciation of wildlife and the environment.

Allow 1 hour minimum. Mon.-Fri. 10-5, Sat.-Sun. and holidays 11-5, late June-Labour Day; Mon.-Fri. 9-4, Sat.-Sun. and holidays 11-5, late May-late June; Mon.-Fri. 9-4, Sat.-Sun. and holidays 1-4, Jan. 1-late May and day after Labour Day-Dec. 23; daily

1-4, rest of year. Closed Jan. 1 and Dec. 25. Admission $1.80; $1.55 (ages 13-17 and 65+); $1.30 (ages 2-12); $4.85 (family). Prices may vary; phone ahead. Phone (780) 496-8787.

MUTTART CONSERVATORY is at 9626 96A St., at the e. end of the James MacDonald Bridge. Four pyramid-shaped glass greenhouses showcase a variety of flora. Palm trees, orchids and hibiscus, typical of warm, moist climates, thrive in the rain forest atmosphere of the Tropical Pyramid, while the Arid Pyramid displays vegetation indigenous to parts of North America and Africa. The Temperate Pyramid shows seasonal changes, and the Show Pyramid features changing floral displays. The conservatory's outdoor grounds can be enjoyed on a stroll.

Food is available. Allow 1 hour minimum. Mon.-Fri. 9-5:30; Sat.-Sun. 11-5:30; closed Dec. 25. Admission $7.75; $6.75 (ages 13-18, ages 65+ and students with ID); $4.25 (ages 2-12); $24.25 (family). Prices may vary; phone ahead. MC, VI. Phone (780) 496-8787.

ROYAL ALBERTA MUSEUM is at 12845 102nd Ave. Alberta's natural and human history museum houses a permanent collection in three main galleries, with changing displays and events scheduled throughout the year.

The Natural History Gallery offers specimens of plants, animals, birds, live insects, fossils and minerals depicting the 1 billion-year odyssey from dinosaurs to rare minerals and gems. A fossil gallery displays extinct beasts from ancient Alberta, while The Bug Room contains live specimens from around the world.

The Syncrude Gallery of Aboriginal Culture tells the story of 11,000 years of aboriginal history. The Wild Alberta gallery encourages visitors to look at Alberta's environment from a different perspective.

Food is available. Allow 2 hours minimum. Daily 9-5; closed Dec. 24-25. Hours may vary during special exhibits. Admission $10; $8 (ages 65+); $7 (students with ID); $5 (ages 7-17); $28 (family, two adults and children); half-price (Sat.-Sun. 9-11). An additional fee may be charged during special exhibits. AX, MC, VI. Phone (780) 453-9100.

RUTHERFORD HOUSE PROVINCIAL HISTORIC SITE is at 11153 Saskatchewan Dr. on the University of Alberta campus. The structure was home to A.C. Rutherford, Alberta's first premier and a founder of the University of Alberta. Completed in 1911, the elegant Jacobethan (a blend of Jacobean and Elizabethan styles) Revival house established a new standard in domestic architecture and marked the end of the pioneer style in Alberta. Historical interpreters in period dress conduct house tours upon request. Events are scheduled throughout the year.

Food is available. Allow 1 hour minimum. Daily 9-5, May 15-Labour Day; Tues.-Sun. noon-5, rest of year. Closed Jan. 1, Good Friday and Dec. 25. Admission $4; $3 (ages 7-17 and 66+); $12 (family). Phone (780) 427-3995.

TELUS WORLD OF SCIENCE EDMONTON is at 142nd St. and 111th Ave. Five galleries house exhibits that explain and explore unusual phenomena: Space Place, which focuses on space exploration; The Body Fantastic, which includes large-scale models of body parts; Mystery Avenue, where visitors must collect and analyze clues to solve a crime; The Greens' House, a living backyard that teaches visitors about nature and conservation; and DiscoveryLand, an interactive area designed for children ages 2 through 8.

In addition visitors enjoy live science demonstrations, an observatory, films offered in an IMAX theater, and planetarium and laser shows presented in the Margaret Zeidler Star Theatre. Weekend visitors can explore the world of computers in the Dow Computer Lab.

Food is available. Center open daily 10-9, July 1-Labour Day; 10-5 (also Fri.-Sat. 5-9), rest of year. Closed Dec. 25. Observatory open daily 1-5 and 6:30-10, July 1-Labour Day; Fri. 7 p.m.-10 p.m., Sat.-Sun. and holidays 1-4 and 7-10, rest of year (weather permitting). Science demonstrations are given daily on the hour noon-4, July 1-Labour Day; Sat.-Sun. and holidays on the hour noon-4, rest of year. IMAX shows are offered daily on the hour beginning at 11.

Admission to exhibit galleries and planetarium or to one IMAX film $12.95; $10.95 (ages 13-17 and 65+); $9.50 (ages 4-12); $47.95 (family, two adults and four children). Combination admission to exhibit galleries, planetarium and one IMAX film $19.50; $16.50 (ages 13-17 and 65+); $14.50 (ages 4-12); $69.95 (family, two adults and four children). MC, VI. Phone (780) 451-3344.

UKRAINIAN CANADIAN ARCHIVES & MUSEUM OF ALBERTA is at 9543 110th Ave. Exhibits trace the history of Alberta's Ukrainian pioneers. Displays include traditional apparel and musical instruments, costumes, Ukrainian currency, photographs, church artifacts and folk art. Allow 1 hour minimum. Tues.-Fri. 10-5, Sat. noon-5; closed national holidays. Hours may vary; phone ahead. Donations. Phone (780) 424-7580.

UKRAINIAN CULTURAL HERITAGE VILLAGE is 50 km (31 mi.) e. on Hwy. 16, 3 km e. of the entrance to Elk Island National Park of Canada. The lifestyle of the region's Ukrainian immigrant population is portrayed in a village re-created to resemble a typical east central Alberta settlement 1892-1930.

Living-history demonstrations center around 34 restored historic buildings, including houses, farm buildings, churches and stores. The site comprises four areas: a town, a farmstead, a rural community and an overview area. Costumed interpreters depicting a wide variety of characters from the turn of the 20th century re-create the lives of those who lived in each of the buildings, demonstrating the settlers' daily routines. Special events are held throughout the summer.

Picnicking is permitted. Allow 2 hours minimum. Daily 10-6, Victoria Day weekend-Labour Day; Sat.-Sun. 10-6, day after Labour Day-second Mon. in Oct. Admission $8; $7 (ages 65+); $4 (ages 7-17); $20 (family, two adults and children). Rates may be increased during special events. MC, VI. Phone (780) 662-3640.

SAVE **UNIVERSITY OF ALBERTA DEVONIAN BO-
TANIC GARDEN** is 14 km (9 mi.) s. on Hwy. 60 from jct. Hwy. 16W and the Devon Hwy. overpass. Comprising 32 hectares (80 acres) of cultivated gardens and 44.5 hectares (110 acres) of natural area, the garden includes a Japanese garden, a butterfly house, ecological reserves and collections of native and alpine plants. Nature trails and guided tram tours also are offered.

Picnicking is permitted. Food is available. Allow 2 hours minimum. Daily 10-9, July-Aug.; 10-6 in June and Sept.; 10-4, in May. Tram tours are given daily on the hour 11-3, July 1-Labour Day (also daily at 4, July-Aug.); Thurs.-Mon. on the hour 11-3, in June; Sat.-Sun. on the hour 11-3, in May. Tram tour schedule may vary; phone ahead. Admission $11; $8 (ages 65+); $6 (ages 13-17); $3 (ages 7-12); half-price (after 6 p.m., July-Aug.). Tram tour $5. Prices may vary. MC, VI. Phone (780) 987-3054 or (780) 987-3055.

VALLEY ZOO is at Buena Vista Rd. (87th Ave.) and 134th St. More than 300 domestic, endangered and exotic animals from around the world call the zoo home. Animal interpretive programs are featured year-round. A merry-go-round, paddle boats, a miniature train and a children's discovery zoo are available in summer.

Food is available. Allow 1 hour, 30 minutes minimum. Daily 9:30-8, late June-Labour Day; daily 9:30-6, early May-late June; Mon.-Fri. 9:30-4, Sat.-Sun. 9:30-6, day after Labour Day-second Mon. in Oct.; daily 9:30-4, rest of year. Closed Dec. 25. Admission $8.50; $6.25 (ages 13-17 and 65+); $4.25 (ages 2-12); $25 (family). Prices may vary; phone ahead. MC, VI. Phone (780) 496-8787.

GEM **WEST EDMONTON MALL** is at jct. 87th Ave. and 170th St. The huge, two-level complex is one of the world's largest shopping centers and contains more than 800 stores and services, 19 movie theaters, more than 100 eateries and nine major theme attractions.

Galaxyland features 25 rides and attractions. Deep Sea Adventure has one of the world's largest indoor lakes and a life-size replica of Christopher Columbus' *Santa Maria*. Sea Life Caverns contains approximately 200 species of marine life. World Waterpark offers more than 2 hectares (5 acres) of indoor fun, including a giant wave pool. The mall also is home to three sea lions; the Ice Palace, an NHL-size ice rink; two miniature golf courses; and a recreation center offering bowling, billiards and arcade games.

Allow a full day. Shops open Mon.-Sat. 10-9, Sun. 11-5, most holidays 10-6. Hours for attractions, theaters and restaurants vary; phone ahead.

Galaxyland unlimited 1-day pass $34.95; $27.95 (ages 55+ and 0-121 centimetres or 0-47 in. tall); $94.95 (family, four persons). Individual ride ticket $1.50. Water park $34.95; $27.95 (ages 3-10 and 55+); $94.95 (family, four persons). Ice Palace $6.95; $4.95 (ages 3-10 and 55+); $16.95 (family, four persons). Miniature golf $10.95; $7.95 (ages 3-10 and 55+). Sea Life Caverns $6.95. AX, MC, VI. Phone (780) 444-5300 or (800) 661-8890 for attractions' hours of operation.

GAMBLING ESTABLISHMENTS

- **Baccarat Casino** is at 10128 104th Ave. N.W. Slots daily 10 a.m.-3 a.m. Table games daily noon-2 a.m. Poker daily 24 hours. Closed Dec. 25. Phone (780) 413-3178 or (877) 616-5695.

- **Casino Edmonton** is at 7055 Argyll Rd. Slot machines daily 10 a.m.-3 a.m. Poker daily 24 hours. Closed Dec. 25. Phone (780) 463-9467.

- **Casino Yellowhead** is at 12464 153rd St. N.W. Slot machines 10 a.m.-3 a.m. Poker daily 24 hours. Closed Dec. 25. Phone (780) 424-9467.

- **Palace Casino** is at 2710 West Edmonton Mall, 8882 170th St. N.W., Upper Level Entrance #9. Table games daily noon-2 a.m. Slots daily 10 a.m.-3 a.m. Poker daily 24 hours. Phone (780) 444-2112.

What To Do

Sightseeing

Bus, Streetcar and Van Tours

Nite Tours offers pub crawls and ghost and graveyard tours; phone (780) 454-0303 or (877) 600-6483.

HIGH LEVEL STREETCAR departs from the Old Strathcona stop at 103rd St. and 84th Ave. and from downtown s. of Jasper Ave. and w. of 109th St. A vintage streetcar takes passengers along the old CPR rail line across the High Level Bridge built 1911-13 to link Old Strathcona and Edmonton. The 3-kilometre (1.9-mi.) trip offers excellent views of the city and the river valley.

Allow 30 minutes minimum. Sun.-Fri. 11-4, Sat. 9-4, late May-Labour Day; Fri.-Sun. 11-4, day after Labour Day-early Oct. Hours extended to 10 p.m. during the Fringe Festival in Aug. Hours may vary; phone ahead. Fare $4; free (ages 0-5); $12 (family, two adults and children). Phone (780) 437-7721.

OUT AN' ABOUT TOURS TRAVEL ADVENTURES excursions depart from local hotels. These 3-hour to 3-day van trips highlight area cultural and historical sites. Downtown Edmonton tour includes the Alberta Legislature Building, Fort Edmonton Park, Muttart Conservatory and the Royal Alberta Museum. Other tours visit such sites as the Ukrainian Cultural Heritage Village, Elk Island National Park

AAA and Motorsports

AAA, a pioneer in the development and growth of auto racing during the first half of the 20th century, has returned to the racetrack. Today the association is the "Official Motor Club" and "Official Roadside Assistance Provider" of 11 tracks owned and operated by the International Speedway Corporation (ISC), which hosts the NASCAR NEXTEL Cup Series and Indy Racing League (IRL) events.

As part of an agreement with ISC, AAA's widely recognized logo appears on track safety and recovery vehicles as well as on track signs, in racing programs and at other promotional venues. ISC, a leading promoter of motorsports activities in the United States, conducts more than 100 events annually. ISC/AAA facilities include California Speedway in Fontana, Calif.; Darlington Raceway in Darlington, S.C.; Daytona International Speedway in Daytona Beach, Fla.; Homestead-Miami Speedway in Homestead, Fla.; Kansas Speedway in Kansas City, Kan.; Martinsville Speedway in Martinsville, Va.; Michigan International Speedway in Cambridge Junction, Mich.; Phoenix International Raceway in Phoenix, Ariz.; Richmond International Raceway in Richmond, Va.; Talladega Superspeedway in Talladega, Ala.; and Watkins Glen International in Watkins Glen, N.Y.

© International Speedway Corporation

of Canada and the North Saskatchewan River Valley, the Royal Tyrrell Museum and the badlands at Drumheller, and the Rocky Mountains.

Some departures require a minimum of two to three persons. Tours depart daily, May 1-second Mon. in Oct.; otherwise varies. Departure times vary; phone ahead. Fare $45-$220; $30-$190 (children). Fares include all applicable admission charges. Reservations are recommended. Phone (780) 909-8687 or (888) 488-8687.

Driving Tours

The most scenic areas in Edmonton are along the North Saskatchewan River Valley. On the south side, the drive north along Saskatchewan Drive from 76th Avenue and 120th Street to 99th Street offers a picturesque trip around the University of Alberta campus. The views from the Royal Alberta Museum, 102nd Avenue and 128th Street, and the residential district of Glenora are impressive.

Walking Tours

Heritage Trail leads from the Shaw Conference Centre to the Alberta Legislature Building, a route that links government and industry by way of Edmonton's past. Old Strathcona, south of the North Saskatchewan River, offers a view of many original buildings and street scenes characteristic of an early 20th-century prairie town. Edmonton Gallery Walk joins nine private art galleries around Jasper Avenue and 124th Street.

Guided walking tours of the 30,000-student University of Alberta are available year-round; phone (780) 492-1648.

Sports and Recreation

Whatever the season, there are opportunities for both indoor and outdoor recreation. The North Saskatchewan River Valley is an oasis of parkland, with 122 kilometres (76 mi.) of trails, four lake systems and 22 parks. Depending on the time of year, you can **golf, hike, jog, cycle, ride horseback, fish, ski (cross-country** and **downhill), skate** or even pan for gold in a park.

The largest park is Capital City Recreation Park, composed of many smaller areas in the center and on the east side of the city. Within the park are 30 kilometres (19 mi.) of paths for **bicycling** and **jogging.** For information about activities and facilities phone Community Services at (780) 496-7275 Monday through Friday.

Playing host to three major sporting events—the Commonwealth Games in 1978, the World University Games in 1983 and the World Championships in Athletics in 2001—has provided Edmonton with a legacy of world-class sporting facilities. Several multiple-purpose centers—including Commonwealth Stadium Sport & Fitness Centre, 11000 Stadium Rd. at 91st Street, (780) 944-7400; Kinsmen Sports Centre, 9100 Walterdale Hill, (780) 944-7400; and Mill Woods Recreation Centre, 7207 28th Ave., (780) 496-2900—offer such activities as **swimming, diving, racquetball, squash** and **track** events.

Bring your set of clubs and try out one of more than 70 **golf** courses scattered about the Edmonton area. Three courses in the city's river valley are Riverside, on Rowland Road (106th Avenue) on the south side of the Dawson Bridge; Rundle Park, in the east end of Edmonton off 118th Avenue and Victoria Trail; and Victoria, said to be the oldest municipal golf course in Canada, on River Valley Road, accessible from Groat Road or from either 109th Street via the Walterdale Bridge from the south, or from 101st Street from the north.

Spectator sports can be enjoyed throughout the year. Castrol Motorsports Park, 2 kilometres (1.2 mi.) west of Queen Elizabeth II Hwy. on Hwy. 19, offers motorsport racing May through September; phone (780) 461-5801 or (780) 955-5540. Northlands Park, 7300 116th Ave., offers a chance to watch **harness racing** from early March to mid-June and from October to mid-December; phone (780) 471-7379 to confirm the dates for the racing schedule. **Thoroughbred racing** takes place from June to October; phone (780) 471-7379.

Note: Policies concerning admittance of children to pari-mutuel betting facilities vary. Phone for information.

Home to four professional sports teams, Edmonton is referred to fondly as the City of Champions. The Edmonton Oilers, several-time Stanley Cup champions of the National **Hockey** League, play from September to April in Rexall Place at 118th Avenue and 74th Street; phone (780) 414-4625. The Edmonton Eskimos **football** team, many times the Grey Cup champions of the Canadian Football League, play at Commonwealth Stadium, 111th Avenue and Stadium Road, from June to November; phone (780) 448-3757.

Northern League **Baseball** is played by the Edmonton Cracker-Cats from April to September at TELUS Field, south of downtown at 96th Avenue and 102nd Street; phone (780) 414-4450. National League **Lacrosse** is played by the Edmonton Rush from January through April in Rexall Place at 118th Avenue and 74th Street; phone (780) 732-7874.

Shopping

For the intrepid shopper, there is nothing like **West Edmonton Mall** (*see attraction listing p. 73*), which occupies a 44-hectare (110-acre) site at 87th Avenue and 170th Street. Inside are more than 800 stores and services.

Once complete, South Edmonton Common will offer about 21 hectares (52 acres) of retail space. Construction of the open-air shopping center at 23rd Avenue and Calgary Trail is ongoing; currently there are more than 100 stores available to shoppers.

For those who want shopping on a less imposing scale, other popular malls include Kingsway Garden Mall, 109th Street and Princess Elizabeth Avenue; Londonderry Mall, 137th Avenue and 66th Street; and Southgate Centre, 111th Street and 51st Avenue.

Downtown offers boutiques and restaurants as well as covered shopping areas joined by enclosed walkways or pedways. The Edmonton City Centre complex between 100th and 103rd streets on 102nd Avenue contains Hudson's Bay Co., 140 other shops and a nine-screen theater among its four glittering floors.

ManuLife Place, 102nd Avenue and 101st Street, contains designer boutiques and Holt Renfrew, an elegant retail store with a quaint in-store cafe. Connected to ManuLife Place is Commerce Place, which features several shops with signature fashions.

Rice Howard Way, an attractive outdoor pedestrian area lined with sidewalk seating and eateries, is downtown at 100th Street and 101A Avenue. It is particularly popular in summer.

At 102nd Avenue and 97th Street, the Chinatown Gate symbolizes friendship and welcomes visitors to Chinatown, which features several ethnic restaurants, shops and outdoor vendors selling fresh produce.

Old Strathcona at Whyte Avenue (82nd Avenue from 99th to 109th streets), the main outdoor shopping street on the south side of the city, has the look of historic Edmonton and offers boutiques, specialty shops, restaurants, bistros and coffee bars.

Don't forget that the major museums have interesting shops with items sometimes impossible to find elsewhere. Of particular interest are the six period shops in Fort Edmonton Park and the shop in the interpretive center at the Alberta Legislature Building.

Performing Arts

Theater season runs from September through May. For live theater visit the Citadel Theatre complex, 99th Street and 101A Avenue, which consists of four theaters, an amphitheater and a beautiful atrium; phone (780) 425-1820. Family-themed theater, produced by Fringe Theatre Adventures, can be enjoyed by all ages in October, December and February at the Arts Barns in Old Strathcona at 103rd Street and 84th Avenue; phone (780) 448-9000.

Prominent Canadian and American performers take to the stage at Mayfield Dinner Theatre at Mayfield Inn & Suites, 166th Street and 109th Avenue; phone (780) 483-4051 or (877) 529-7829. Jubilations Dinner Theatre, in the West Edmonton Mall at the intersection of 87th Avenue and 170th Street, features musical comedy; phone (780) 484-2424.

The Alberta Ballet, (780) 428-6839, and the Edmonton Opera, (780) 429-1000, perform in Northern Alberta Jubilee Auditorium on the University of Alberta campus at 87th Avenue and 114th Street; phone (780) 427-2760 for auditorium information. Phone ahead for updates. The Edmonton Symphony Orchestra, (780) 428-1414, performs at Francis Winspear Centre, 4 Sir Winston Churchill Sq.; phone (780) 428-1414 for concert information. Shaw Conference Centre, Francis Winspear Centre, Northern Alberta Jubilee Auditorium and Rexall Place play host to a variety of concerts ranging from classical music to rock.

The free publications *See Magazine, Vue Magazine* and *Where Edmonton* give detailed, up-to-date information about arts and entertainment in Edmonton, and local newspapers provide current performance information. Ticketmaster outlets handle ticket sales for most sports, recreation, theater and concert events; phone (780) 451-8000.

Special Events

Edmonton offers a smorgasbord of events. Concerts, workshops, club dates and outdoor events characterize the Yardbird Jazz-Festival, held mid- to late June. Also in June The Works Art and Design Festival brings together artists and artisans.

Edmonton Celebrate Canada is a 12-day celebration, beginning late June with National Aboriginal Day. On June 24 are Francophone festivities honoring St. Jean Baptiste. The celebration concludes on Canada Day (July 1), with a full day of events and the Fireworks Finale.

During late June to mid-July the River City Shakespeare Festival presents two shows on alternating nights in William Hawrelak Park. Edmonton International Street Performers Festival in early July offers 10 days of free performances by street acts including magicians, clowns, jugglers, mime artists, musicians and comics.

The city's biggest event is 🐝 Edmonton's Capital EX, a 10-day celebration held in July. Parades, casinos, gold panning, a chuck wagon derby and various other forms of entertainment keep the city alive with activities such as Sunday in the City and A Taste of Edmonton. Another major draw in July is the Rexall Grand Prix of Edmonton, offering racing excitement, concerts, exhibits and live demonstrations.

Colored lights illuminate Great Divide Waterfall on Sunday evenings of summer holiday weekends; the best view is northeast of the High Level Bridge at 109th Street and 97th Avenue.

August brings the world to Canada during the 4-day 🐝 Edmonton Heritage Festival, which offers more than 60 outdoor ethnic pavilions showcasing international music, dance, art and cuisine. Also in August are the 🐝 Edmonton Folk Music Festival; the Cariwest Caribbean Arts Festival; the Labatt Blues Festival; the Dragon Boat Festival; and the 🐝 Edmonton International Fringe Theatre Festival, an 11-day extravaganza of plays, dance, music, mime and street performances.

In September is the Edmonton Symphony Orchestra's 5-day Symphony Under the Sky Festival at Hawrelak Park. Post-summer events include the Edmonton International Film Festival, featuring independent short and feature-length movies in October, the 🐝 Canadian Finals Rodeo in early November, and New Year's Eve special events.

The Edmonton Vicinity

DEVON (E-6) pop. 6,256, elev. 680 m/2,230′

Canada's first planned community, Devon was created by Imperial Oil Resources Ltd. in 1948 to provide accommodations for the workers employed in the company's oilfields. Imperial Leduc No. 1, the area's first well, had just put the town of Devon on the map. The town's name was derived from the Devonian formation, the oil's source, a stratum 1,524 metres (5,000 ft.) underground.

Devon is on the banks of the North Saskatchewan River, where fishing often yields northern pike, walleye and goldeye. Year-round recreational activities include canoeing, cross-country skiing, golf, hiking, ice-skating and swimming.

Town of Devon: 1 Columbia Ave. W., Devon, AB, Canada T9G 1A1; phone (780) 987-8300.

CANADIAN PETROLEUM DISCOVERY CENTRE is 2 km (1.2 mi.) s. on Hwy. 60. The center not only provides insight into the workings of the oil industry but also looks at area history, the story behind Leduc No. 1 and how Canada became self-sufficient in oil production. A 15-minute video presentation, interactive energy displays, geological exhibits, equipment, artifacts, photographs, scale models, murals and an outdoor interpretive trail help explain how oil is produced and refined.

Oilfield veterans are on hand to share their experiences and answer questions. A 53-metre (174-ft.) replica of the original derrick has been erected on the discovery site. Allow 1 hour minimum. Daily 9-5. Admission $8; $7 (ages 65+); $5 (ages 6-18); $20 (family). MC, VI. Phone (780) 987-4323 or (866) 987-4323.

FORT SASKATCHEWAN (E-6) pop. 14,957

FORT SASKATCHEWAN MUSEUM AND HISTORIC SITE is at 10006 100th Ave. A 1909 courthouse contains clothing and documents pertaining to area history, exhibits about the North West Mounted Police and the original courtroom. Also comprising the site are an early 20th-century pioneer house, Dr. T.W.E. Henry's residence built in 1913, a schoolhouse, a church and a blacksmith shop. Displays include a vintage fire truck, antique automobiles, carriages and farm equipment.

Allow 1 hour minimum. Daily 10-4, Victoria Day-Labour Day; Mon.-Fri. 10-4, rest of year. Closed holidays and Dec. 26-31. Admission $4; $3 (ages 61+); free (ages 0-5). Phone (780) 998-1783.

ST. ALBERT (E-6) pop. 57,719

Alberta's oldest non-fortified community, St. Albert was established in 1861. The city is the site of the first cathedral west of Winnipeg. Its founder—Father Albert Lacombe—devoted 62 years to acting as a peacemaker between the Cree and the Blackfoot and as a negotiator between the Blood Indians and the Canadian Pacific Railway.

St. Albert lays claim to western Canada's largest outdoor farmers' market, which operates every Saturday July through September, as well as an interactive water play park and a vibrant arts community.

The Rainmaker Rodeo & Exhibition takes place the fourth weekend in May. The Northern Alberta International Children's Festival—a showcase for performers in theater, music, dance, storytelling and puppetry—is traditionally held the weekend after the rodeo.

St. Albert Business and Tourism Development: 71 St. Albert Rd., St. Albert, AB, Canada T8N 6L5; phone (780) 459-1724.

SAVE **FATHER LACOMBE CHAPEL** is just w. of Queen Elizabeth II Hwy. on St. Vital Ave. The log chapel, built by Father Albert Lacombe and his Métis helpers in 1861, is said to be Alberta's oldest building. Guided tours explain the importance of Lacombe and the St. Albert Roman Catholic Mission to the French/Métis community as well as the priest's role as spiritual leader, peacemaker and negotiator in the 1860s. Tours are conducted in English and French.

Allow 30 minutes minimum. Tours are given daily by request 10-6, May 15-Labour Day. Fee $2; $1.50 (ages 7-17 and senior citizens); $5 (family). Phone (780) 459-7663, or (780) 431-2300 off-season.

MUSÉE HERITAGE MUSEUM is w. of Queen Elizabeth II Hwy. at 5 St. Anne St. in St. Albert Place. Exhibits are dedicated to the heritage of St. Albert. Changing displays are featured. Allow 1 hour minimum. Mon.-Sat. 10-5 (also Sun. 1-5, Sept.-June); closed holidays. Donations. Phone (780) 459-1528.

STONY PLAIN (E-6) pop. 12,363

Plentiful water and abundant fish and game attracted the first settlers to the region in 1881. By 1892 the name of the community itself was changed from Dog Creek to Stony Plain. The Stony Plain of today is an agricultural community.

Murals depicting historical remembrances, events and pioneers prominent in the early settlement of Stony Plain have been painted by local artists on 26 buildings in town. Memories of an early 1900s Christmas from a child's point of view are the basis for one mural, while another shows the multiculturalism of the area's early residents. The Heritage Walk Murals can be seen on a walking tour.

Town of Stony Plain: 4905 51st Ave., Stony Plain, AB, Canada T7Z 1Y1; phone (780) 963-2151.

MULTICULTURAL HERITAGE CENTRE AND OPPERTSHAUSER HOUSE is at 5411 51st St. Restored buildings feature local history and art exhibits, programs and events. The center, built as the area's first high school in 1925, offers regional archives as well as a living-history museum, a demonstration farm, an art gallery and the 1910 Oppertshauser House. Food is available. Allow 30 minutes minimum. Daily 10-4 (also Sun. 4-6); closed Dec. 24-Jan. 2. A country market takes place Sat. 9-1, May-Oct. Donations. Phone (780) 963-2777.

Santa Maria, Deep Sea Adventure, West Edmonton Mall / Travel Alberta

This ends listings for the Edmonton Vicinity.
The following page resumes the alphabetical listings of cities in Alberta.

ELK ISLAND NATIONAL PARK OF CANADA (E-7)

Elevations in the park range from 709 metres (2,326 ft.) at Goose Lake to 754 metres (2,475 ft.) at Tawayik Lake. Refer to CAA/AAA maps for additional elevation information.

About 35 kilometres (22 mi.) east of Edmonton, Elk Island National Park of Canada is reached by Hwy. 15 from the north and Hwy. 16 from the south. The lakes, ponds, forests and meadows of this 194-square-kilometre (75-sq.-mi.) park provide a haven for many species of animals and plants.

The park occupies the Beaver Hills region, which first was settled by Sarcee and Plains Cree Indians. They trapped beavers and hunted bison and elk, as did the European fur traders who arrived between the late 18th and the mid-19th centuries. Soon the animals became nearly extinct, and the natives were forced to seek sustenance elsewhere.

In 1906 five local men asked that the government establish a wildlife refuge to preserve the remaining elk. A year later 400 plains bison were added, while another preserve near Wainwright was being established. Most of these animals later were transferred, but about 50 stayed and produced the plains bison herd of more than 600 that remains today north of Hwy. 16. A herd of several hundred wood bison, a threatened subspecies, is kept separate from this herd south of Hwy. 16.

As the wildlife populations grew, so did the park's area; more land was added to the refuge in 1922, 1947, 1956 and 1978. Many small lakes dot the landscape, but the major bodies are Tawayik and Astotin, the latter being the larger. The lakes and marshes support the more than 250 bird species, including ducks, grebes, gulls, loons, pelicans, swans and terns.

Marsh marigolds and several types of lilies are among several plants rarely seen outside the park. Song birds occupy the many aspen, spruce and birch forests, but few fish inhabit the waters due to low oxygen levels. The herd of elk for which the park was established flourish among the meadows and forests, as do reintroduced colonies of beavers. Deer, moose and coyotes also roam the park.

General Information and Activities

The park is open daily all year. Most recreation facilities center on Astotin Lake, which offers nonmotorized boating, wildlife observations, picnic facilities, a nine-hole golf course, camping, hiking and walking trails. A campground is on the east side of the lake. Interpretive talks, events and displays explain the park's history and features.

A visitor information center is .8 kilometres (.5 mi.) north of Hwy. 16 before the park's south gate entrance. Staff members and displays describe Elk Island and other national parks. The center is open mid-May through Labour Day; phone (780) 922-5790 to confirm schedule.

Camping and picnicking are popular in summer. The park's approximately 100 kilometres (60 mi.) of trails are popular with hikers and cross-country skiers. Hunting and fishing are prohibited. *See Recreation Chart and the AAA/CAA Western Canada & Alaska CampBook.*

ADMISSION to the park is $6.90; over 64, $5.90; ages 6-16, $3.45. Admission for three to seven persons in a private vehicle is $17.30. An annual pass, valid at all Canadian national parks, is available.

PETS must be kept on a leash at all times.

ADDRESS inquiries for additional information to Elk Island National Park of Canada, Site 4, R.R. 1, Fort Saskatchewan, AB, Canada T8L 2N7; phone (780) 992-2950.

UKRAINIAN CULTURAL HERITAGE VILLAGE— *see Edmonton p. 72.*

ELKWATER (J-9) pop. 107

Before Europeans came to the Elkwater region, Assiniboine, Blackfoot, Cree and Sioux shared the land with grizzly bears, wolves, bison and a large number of elk. After settlers and trappers arrived, the wolves and elk were hunted to extinction; the elk population since has been reintroduced. An 1873 massacre of Assiniboine Indians by wolf hunters and whiskey traders prompted the formation of the North West Mounted Police and the establishment of Fort Walsh.

The Cypress Hills area, shared by Alberta and Saskatchewan, is noted for its lodgepole pine forests, water resources and wildlife. The hills, which rise to more than 1,466 metres (4,810 ft.), offer visitors a cool climate, scenic views and diverse flora and fauna. Elkwater serves as the area's hub.

CYPRESS HILLS INTERPROVINCIAL PARK is 1.5 km (.9 mi.) n. on Hwy. 41. Fossils of early mammals dating back 40 million years have been found in the hills. An aboriginal culture flourished in the area for more than 7,000 years. Ruminants, beavers, coyotes and varied birds and plants now live in the park. Park interpreters schedule programs May through September. The visitor center offers information, displays and audiovisual presentations.

Note: The visitor center is under renovation; phone ahead to confirm schedule. Camping is permitted. Grounds daily 24 hours. Visitor center daily 10-5, mid-May through Labour Day. Special events are offered year-round. Free. Phone (403) 893-3833 or (403) 893-3777 for the visitor center, or (403) 893-3782 for camping reservations May-Aug. *See Recreation Chart and Medicine Hat in the AAA/CAA Western Canada & Alaska CampBook.*

FORT MACLEOD (J-6)
pop. 3,072, elev. 955 m/3,133′

In 1874 at the end of their 1,126-kilometre (700-mi.) march through the prairie wilderness to rid western Canada of whiskey traders, the North West

Wherever your travels take you, there's always a Choice hotel nearby. We offer over 4,000 locations across Canada and the United States that suit any travel plan or budget. And as a CAA/AAA member, you'll save when you book ahead. Just contact your local CAA/AAA office, call **800.228.1222** or visit **choicehotels.ca** to book your next stay.

**800.228.1222
choicehotels.ca**

One inch equals a whole lot of Choice hotels.

We'll see you there.
CHOICE HOTELS CANADA™

Mounted Police, now the Royal Canadian Mounted Police, chose the site of what is now Fort Macleod as their first headquarters.

A commanding view of the countryside and the natural protection afforded by the Oldman River made Fort Macleod an important outpost; a cairn at 2nd Avenue and 25th Street commemorates the fort's founding. Guided walking tours of the historic district, ranging from 30 minutes to 1 hour, can be arranged in advance during the summer by contacting the Main Street Office; phone (403) 553-2500, or The Fort Museum of the North West Mounted Police *(see attraction listing)*.

The highland physical geography that made the Fort Macleod outpost successful also helped the Plains Indians survive long before the first traders appeared in the area. In order to kill the buffalo for food, the Plains hunters stampeded them over the high cliffs.

(SAVE) **THE FORT MUSEUM OF THE NORTH WEST MOUNTED POLICE**, 25th St. and 3rd Ave., creates the atmosphere of the original Fort Macleod. Exhibits set among historic structures focus on the history of the North West Mounted Police, southern Alberta natives and pioneer settlers. Of particular interest are the summer Mounted Patrol Musical Rides in which horseback riders in replicas of 1878 RCMP uniforms perform precision movements to music.

Allow 1 hour minimum. Daily 9-6, July 1-Labour Day; daily 9-5, late May-June 30; Wed.-Sun. 10-4, May 1-late May and day after Labour Day-Oct. 31. Musical rides are presented Wed.-Mon. (weather permitting) at 10, 11:30, 2 and 3:30, July 1-Labour Day.

Admission (July 1-Labour Day) $7.50; $7 (ages 65+); $5.50 (ages 12-17); $4.50 (ages 6-11); $22 (family, two adults and four children). Admission (May-June and day after Labour Day-Oct. 31) $6; $5.50 (ages 65+); $4 (ages 12-17); $3 (ages 6-11); $17 (family, two adults and four children). MC, VI. Phone (403) 553-4703 or (866) 273-6841.

HEAD-SMASHED-IN BUFFALO JUMP INTERPRETIVE CENTRE is 3 km (1.9 mi.) n. on Queen Elizabeth II Hwy., then 16 km (SAVE) (10 mi.) w. on Hwy. 785. For at least 6,000 years the Plains Indians stampeded herds of buffalo over sandstone cliffs to their deaths. The hunters then butchered the kill at their campsite below the cliffs. This is one of the oldest, best-preserved buffalo jump sites. A 12-minute film re-creates the hunts.

The site's name is derived from a young brave who stood under a ledge of the cliff to watch the buffalo as they fell past him. As the number of carcasses multiplied, his skull was crushed as he became trapped between the animals and the cliff.

Built into that cliff today is a seven-story interpretive center with displays. Exhibits focus on the geographical and climatic factors affecting these

tribes as well as their lifestyle and history. The hunting site is preserved; short trails lead to the main areas.

Food is available. Allow 2 hours minimum. Daily 9-6, mid-May to mid-Sept.; 10-5, rest of year. Closed Jan. 1, Easter and Dec. 24-25. Admission $9; $8 (ages 66+); $5 (ages 7-17); $22 (family). MC, VI. Phone (403) 553-2731.

FORT McMURRAY (A-8) pop. 47,705

At the confluence of the Clearwater and Athabasca rivers in the fur country of northern Alberta, Fort McMurray began as the home of the Woodland Cree and Chipewyan Indians. In 1778 explorers and fur traders led by Peter Pond opened the vast fur trade region of the Mackenzie River basin. In 1870 Henry John Moberly built a post and named it Fort McMurray after his chief factor, William McMurray of Hudson's Bay Co.

Soon after a steamboat terminus was established near Fort McMurray in 1884, the region's vast resources began to attract attention. Oil sands containing some 1.7 trillion barrels of oil were found around Lake Athabasca. The first commercially successful extractions, however, did not take place until the late 1960s. Since then Fort McMurray has boomed, serving oil recovery plants that now extract from the sands about 600,000 barrels of synthetic crude oil per day.

The city is the southern terminus of the vast water transportation system that navigates Great Slave Lake and the Mackenzie River en route to the Arctic. Logging and tourism further bolster the economy. Fort McMurray is a service center for surrounding areas and the oil sands plants.

Re-creating the city's past is Heritage Park, on the banks of the Hangingstone River just off King Street on Tolen Drive. A museum highlights the history of boat building, aviation, river travel, lumbering, fishing, salt production and fur trading; phone (780) 791-7575.

Fort McMurray Tourism: 400 Sakitawaw Tr., Fort McMurray, AB, Canada T9H 4Z3; phone (780) 791-4336 or (800) 565-3947.

OIL SANDS DISCOVERY CENTRE is at jct. Hwy. 63 and MacKenzie Blvd. Exhibits relate the geology, history and technology (SAVE) of the Athabasca Oil Sands, said to be the world's single largest oil deposit. Oil sands mining, technology and new methods of exploration are explained through interpretive displays, demonstrations and the video presentation "Quest for Energy." Outside in the Industrial Garden are a seven-story bucket-wheel excavator and other pieces of massive mining equipment.

Seasonal bus tours to view the production facilities of Syncrude Canada Ltd. and Suncor Energy depart from the discovery center; reservations for the 3.5-hour tours can be arranged through Fort McMurray Tourism.

Note: Photo ID is required for the bus tour. Allow 1 hour, 30 minutes minimum. Daily 9-5, mid-May to Labour Day; Tues.-Sun. 10-4, rest of year. Closed Jan. 1, Good Friday and Dec. 24-26. Bus tours to Syncrude or Suncor, generally one per day, are given daily, July-Aug.; Thurs.-Mon., in June; Fri.-Sat., in Sept.; Sat., mid-May through May 31.

Discovery center $6; $5 (ages 65+); $4 (ages 7-17); $20 (family, two adults and children). Bus tour (includes admission to Heritage Park and Oil Sands Discovery Centre) $25; $20 (ages 12-17 and 65+). Under 12 are not permitted on the bus tour. Because bus tours are generally given only once a day and are in high demand, make reservations well in advance of your visit. In any event, reservations for the bus tour are required and must be made at least 24 hours in advance. Bus tour prices may vary; phone ahead. MC, VI. Phone (780) 743-7167 for the Oil Sands Discovery Centre, or Fort McMurray Tourism at (780) 791-4336 or (800) 565-3947 for tour reservations.

FORT SASKATCHEWAN—

see Edmonton p. 76.

GIROUXVILLE (B-3) pop. 282

GIROUXVILLE MUSEUM is on Main St. (Hwy. 49). More than 6,000 artifacts tell the story of the indigenous people, devout missionaries and rugged pioneers who lived here. The museum also displays mounted birds and fur-bearing animals and the works of local artists Leon Tremblay and Alfred Gaboury.

Transportation Means of Yesterday includes sleighs, an antique snowmobile, a birch bark canoe and a 1927 Chevrolet truck. Allow 1 hour minimum. Mon.-Fri. 10-5, May-Sept.; by appointment rest of year. Admission $3; $1.50 (ages 6-17). Phone (780) 323-4252.

GRANDE CACHE (D-2) pop. 3,783

Grande Cache was named after a large shipment of furs cached nearby in 1821 by Ignace Giasson, an Iroquois working for Hudson Bay Co. The Grande Cache area historically served as a major trading area for marten, lynx and beaver pelts.

Grande Cache is known for the many recreational activities available nearby. The town is surrounded on three sides by Willmore Wilderness Park, which has the Continental Divide and Jasper National Park of Canada as its western and southern borders, respectively; the park can be accessed only by horseback, mountain bike or by hiking.

Lakes, rivers and mountains are favorites with outdoor enthusiasts, who come for white-water rafting, horseback riding, hiking, kayaking, fishing, canoeing and mountain biking. Pacific Western Helicopter Tours offers various sightseeing trips; phone (780) 827-3911.

Local events accommodate those with an adventurous streak. During the Canadian Death Race, held the first weekend in August, runners must travel 125 kilometres (78 mi.) over rough mountain trails—with part of the race occurring after dusk—and then cross a major river by raft. An accompanying festival offers food, concerts and carnival rides and games.

Interpretive displays in the tourism center, on the south side of Grande Cache, feature dinosaur tracks, artifacts from the ice age and memorabilia from the fur trade era.

Grande Cache Tourism and Interpretive Centre: 9701 100th St., P.O. Box 300, Grande Cache, AB, Canada T0E 0Y0; phone (780) 827-3300 or (888) 827-3790.

RECREATIONAL ACTIVITIES

White-water Rafting

- **Wild Blue Yonder White Water Rafting** is w. off Hwy. 40 in the lobby of the Grand Cache Hotel at 1701 Pine Plaza, following signs. Write P.O. Box 1611, Grande Cache, AB, Canada T0E 0Y0. Trips are available daily, May-Sept. Phone (780) 827-5450 or (877) 945-3786.

GRANDE PRAIRIE (C-2) pop. 47,076

Surrounded by a colorful checkerboard of rich farmland along the gateway to the Alaska Hwy., Grande Prairie serves as the business and transportation center of Alberta's Peace River country.

Glimpses into the Peace River region's past are evident in the Kleskun Hills, just east via Hwy. 43. Erosion of the glacial drift of clay, sand, gravel and boulders has uncovered dinosaur tracks and aquatic fossils embedded in a prehistoric river delta formed more than 70 million years ago.

Local culture and artistry are displayed at The Prairie Art Gallery, 9856 97th Ave., Suite 103; phone (780) 532-8111. Muskoseepi Park has hiking and bicycling trails, picnicking areas and recreation facilities. Other area recreational pursuits include swimming, boating, bird-watching and fishing. A pioneer-oriented event is the Grande Prairie Stompede the first weekend in June. Other festivals celebrated throughout the summer highlight the region's diversity.

Grande Prairie Regional Tourism Association: 11330 106th St. Suite 217, Grande Prairie, AB, Canada T8V 7X9; phone (780) 539-7688 or (866) 202-2202.

Shopping areas: Prairie Mall, 11801 100th St., features Shopper's and Zellers.

GRANDE PRAIRIE MUSEUM is at 102nd St. and 102nd Ave. in Muskoseepi Park. The 10-building village features a one-room schoolhouse, a country store, a church and a log homesteader's cabin. The main exhibit building houses artifacts depicting the life of Peace River area pioneers 1908-16. The gallery also features natural history items and aboriginal artifacts. Open Mon.-Fri. 8:30-4:30, Sat. 10-5, Sun. noon-5. Admission $5; $4 (ages 66+); $3 (ages 6-17); $12 (family, two adults and children); $10 (family, one adult and children). Phone (780) 532-5482.

GAMBLING ESTABLISHMENTS

- **Great Northern Casino** is at 10910-107 A Ave. Mon.-Sat. 10 a.m.-2 a.m., Sun. 10 a.m.-1 a.m. Phone (780) 539-4454.

HANNA (G-7) pop. 2,847

SAVE **HANNA PIONEER VILLAGE & MUSEUM** is at Pioneer Tr. and 4th Ave. E. Restored and partially furnished 19th-century buildings, arranged in a pioneer village setting, include a general store, school, four-room hospital, church, power windmill, Canadian National Railway station, telephone office, ranch house and smithy, and the Hanna archives. Among displays are antique automobiles and farm machinery.

Guided tours are available. Allow 1 hour, 30 minutes minimum. Daily 10-6, June-Aug.; by appointment in May and Sept. Last tour begins 1 hour, 30 minutes before closing. Admission $4; $1 (ages 0-11). Phone (403) 854-4244.

HIGH RIVER (I-6) pop. 10,716

A ranching and farming town, High River counts among its events Little Britches Rodeo and Parade, held Victoria Day weekend in late May, as well as the North American Chuckwagon Championship and the Guy Weadick Memorial Rodeo, both held in June. The winter holiday season is ushered in the first weekend in December with the evening Santa Claus Parade.

High River Tourism and Economic Development: 309B Macleod Tr. S.W., High River, AB, Canada T1V 1Z5; phone (403) 652-2110.

HIGH RIVER HISTORICAL MURALS are at various locations throughout town. Many colorful paintings illustrate area history. The murals present a variety of subjects, ranging from cattle ranching and polo to well-known residents, including W.O. Mitchell and former Prime Minister Joe Clark.

Murals visible daily 24 hours. Brochures are available at the High River Tourism and Economic Development office and from the Museum of the Highwood Mon.-Fri. 10-6, Sat.-Sun. 12:30-5, May-Oct.; otherwise varies. Closed Jan. 1 and Dec. 25. Free. Phone (403) 603-3101.

MUSEUM OF THE HIGHWOOD is at 406 1st St. S.W. The museum takes its name from the nearby Highwood River. Changing exhibits are housed in an 1911 sandstone building once used as a Canadian Pacific Railway station. Displays detail local history, primarily from the mid-19th century to the present. A family discovery room has interactive exhibits.

Allow 30 minutes minimum. Mon.-Sat. 10-5, Sun. 12:30-5, Victoria Day-Labour Day; Wed.-Sat. 11-3, Sun. 12:30-3, rest of year. Closed statutory holidays in the off-season. Admission $3; $2.50 (senior citizens); free (ages 0-15). Phone (403) 652-7156.

IRRICANA (H-6) pop. 1,243

PIONEER ACRES OF ALBERTA MUSEUM is off Hwy. 9, 1 km n., then 1 km w. The museum features one of the largest collections of antique farm equipment in western Canada. It also displays furniture, tools, memorabilia, clothing and vehicles. A collection of early buildings includes a school, a steam-engine shop and a blacksmith shop. Guided tours are available. Allow 1 hour, 30 minutes minimum. Daily 9-5, May 15-Sept. 30. Admission $7; free (ages 0-11). Phone (403) 935-4357.

 JASPER NATIONAL PARK OF CANADA (E-2, E-3, F-2)

See map page 82.

Elevations in the park range from 1,067 metres (3,500 ft.) in the town of Jasper to 3,747 metres (12,293 ft.) at Mount Columbia. Refer to CAA/AAA maps for additional elevation information.

Reached from the east and west via the Yellowhead Hwy. (Hwy. 16) and from the south by the Icefields Parkway (Hwy. 93), Jasper National Park of Canada, Banff National Park of Canada's northern neighbor, was established in 1907. The park was named after Jasper Haws, who was in charge of a Hudson's Bay Co. trading post in 1817.

Less developed and less crowded than Banff National Park of Canada, its 11,228 square kilometres (4,335 sq. mi.) of majestic mountains, valleys and lakes offer equally spectacular views of the Rocky Mountain wilderness. The variety and beauty of its numerous lakes, of which Maligne Lake is the largest, are perhaps the area's chief attractions.

Nature's scenic sculpting process at work can be seen at Athabasca Falls and Sunwapta Falls, both just west of Icefields Parkway south of Jasper. To the east off Hwy. 16 is Miette Hot Springs, where mineral pools are open for bathing Victoria Day weekend through the second Monday in October. Northeast of Jasper 51-metre-deep (170-ft.) Maligne Canyon surrounds the river that carved it over the years.

Park wildlife is as diverse as its peaks and valleys. Mountain goats and bighorn sheep inhabit the crags and highlands, although the sheep frequently wander down within good viewing distance.

The lower slopes and meadows are home to deer, elk, moose and bears, which never should be fed or approached. More elusive are coyotes, wolves, lynx and other predators that usually avoid humans. Lodgepole pines, spruces, poplars and firs forest the area, and eagles, jays, magpies and other birds dot the skies.

Note: Since hunting is illegal, some animals may have lost their fear of human activity; be alert for animals on the highways both day and night, and never feed them.

© AAA
△ RESTHAVEN MTN
2,048 m

© 2007 NAVTEQ

Jasper National Park

Miles
0   23.8
Kilometers
0   38.1

△ CAMPGROUND SITE WITHIN NAT'L. PARK. SEE CAMPBOOK FOR ADDITIONAL LISTINGS IN NEARBY TOWNS.

Willmore

Wilderness

Park

Resthaven Icefield

MT CHOWN 3,331 m

Jasper

To Edmonton

HWY 16

River

To Prince George

MT BESS 3,216 m

Snake River

CONTINENTAL

Snaring

Indian River

National

MT RANEE 2,939 m

MT AEOLUS △ 2,671 m

Entrance

Brulé

Hinton

McLeod River

Holmes River

MT ROBSON 3,954 m
HIGHEST POINT IN THE CANADIAN ROCKIES

Reef Icefield

SALIENT MTN 2,810 m

Brulé Lake

Pocahontas

Jasper Lake

River

Pocahontas

Miette Hot Springs Pool

Jasper-Hinton Airport

47

40   40   40

5

Moose Lake

Valemount

Fraser River

YELLOWHEAD PASS 1,146 m

Yellowhead

Snaring River

16

Miette Hot Springs

SEE INSET MAP FOR DETAIL

LUSCAR MTN 2,601 m

Rocky

To Kamloops

5

PACIFIC MOUNTAIN TIME

TIME

Canoe River

N

BRITISH COLUMBIA   ALBERTA

River

16

Jasper

SIRDAR MTN △ 2,804 m

Medicine Lake

Park

Rocky

River

Wabasso △

MT EDITH CAVELL 3,361 m

MT KERKESUN △ 2,984 m

Maligne

MT BALINHARD 3,130 m

Mountain

SAMSON PK 3,081 m

Honeymoon Lake

Lake

Mt Kerkeslin △

Athabasca River

DIVIDE

ICEFIELDS

MT BRAZEAU 3,470 m

MT DALHOUSIE 2,947 m

River

Forest

Mt Brown Icefield

River

Wood River

Jonas Creek △

SUNWAPTA PK 3,315 m

Brazeau River

PARKWAY

93

Reserve

MT ALBERTA 3,619 m

Chaba Icefield

Athabasca Glacier

Columbia Icefield

Wilcox Creek △

OBSTRUCTION MTN 3,168 m

Pyramid Lake

To Miette Hot Springs Pool

16

Maligne Canyon

To Maligne Lake Boat Tours

TRAMWAY   CNR

River   HWY

YELLOWHEAD

Lake Edith

Lake Annette

MT COLUMBIA 3,747 m
HIGHEST POINT IN ALBERTA

SUNWAPTA PASS 2,055 m

Columbia Icefield

△ MT STEWART 3,313 m

MT CLINE 3,362 m

Patricia Lake

Athabasca River

Lac Beauvert

Ice Explorer on the Athabasca Glacier

MT AMERY 3,329 m

Banff

11

Jasper-Yellowhead Mus & Archives

The Den

Jasper Adventure Centre

CNR   JASPER

ICEFIELDS   River

Maligne Lake Boat Tours

Kinbasket

Bush River

Saskatchewan River Crossing

National

Park

93

To Lake Louise

Lake

RUSTRUM PK 3,283 m

Freshfield Icefield

BOW SUMMIT 2,068 m

Miette River

Wapiti & Wapiti Winter

93

Whistlers △

Jasper

TRAILS

MT FRESHFIELD 3,336 m

SEE BANFF NATIONAL PARK

Wapta Icefield

To Kamloops

1

Blaeberry

To Golden

2012-B

River

Yoho National Park

To Lake Louise

1

General Information and Activities

The park is open all year, though weather conditions in winter make some portions inaccessible except to cross-country skiers and those on snowshoes. Some facilities are open only from May to September or October. A Parks Canada information center is in the townsite of Jasper.

Many hiking trails, including the 11.2-kilometre (7-mi.) trip to Valley of Five Lakes and the loop to Lac Beauvert, depart from Old Fort Point, 1.6 kilometres (1 mi.) east of Jasper on Hwy. 93. The Valley of Five Lakes also can be accessed from the trailhead on the Icefields Parkway, 9 km (6 mi.) south of the townsite.

Hikers and skiers staying overnight in the back country must have a valid back-country use permit. These permits are available at the Parks Canada information center in Jasper and at the Columbia Icefield Centre from early June to mid-October.

Campgrounds are open varying durations: Whistler early May through the second Monday in October; Snaring River mid-May to late September; Wapiti mid-June to mid-September; and Wabasso late June through Labour Day. Limited camping facilities are available in winter at the Wapiti campgrounds. For campground information phone (780) 852-6176.

There are many ways to explore the park's features, either alone or with a guide. One- or multiple-day bus tours to attractions within the park depart from Jasper. Several stables in the Jasper area offer 1-hour and half- and full-day trail rides from mid-May to mid-September and sleigh rides in winter.

Winter sports include curling, skating, tobogganing, ice climbing, snowshoeing and hockey. Cross-country skiing tours operate out of Jasper. Downhill skiing is available at Marmot Basin; cross-country trails also traverse the Maligne and Pyramid lake areas. Interpretive guides share their insights in theatrical productions. Wildlife tours also are available. Audiotape tours by CCInc. Auto Tape Tours are available at the Friends of Jasper store in the Parks Canada information center, 415 Connaught Dr.; phone (780) 852-4767.

Fishing permits can be obtained at information centers, campgrounds and local sport fishing shops. Boats with electric motors are allowed on lakes unless signs indicate otherwise. *See Recreation Chart and the AAA/CAA Western Canada & Alaska Camp-Book.*

ADMISSION to the park for 1 day is $8.90; over 64, $7.65; ages 6-16, $4.45. Admission for two to seven persons in a private vehicle for 1 day is $17.80. An annual pass, valid at Jasper and 10 other western Canada national parks, is available. MC, VI

PETS are allowed in some areas of the park but must be leashed, crated or physically restrained at all times.

ADDRESS inquiries to the Jasper National Park Information Centre, Jasper National Park of Canada, P.O. Box 10, Jasper, AB, Canada T0E 1E0; phone (780) 852-6176. For other area information contact Jasper Park Chamber of Commerce, P.O. Box 98, Jasper, AB, Canada T0E 1E0; phone (780) 852-3858.

Points of Interest

Natural points of interest include Edith and Annette lakes to the east of Jasper; Maligne Canyon, Maligne Lake and Medicine Lake to the northeast; Pyramid and Patricia lakes to the north; and Mount Edith Cavell, with its Angel Glacier, and Athabasca and Sunwapta falls to the south.

COLUMBIA ICEFIELD, just inside the Jasper National Park of Canada boundary next to Banff National Park of Canada, is the largest ice mass in the Rocky Mountains. Its main bulk, about 16 by 24 kilometres (10 by 15 mi.), straddles the Great Divide, part of the British Columbia border and portions of Banff and Jasper national parks. The ice covers about 325 square kilometres (130 sq. mi.) to an estimated depth of 350 metres (1,148 ft.). Three glaciers—Stutfield, Athabasca and Dome—can be seen from Icefields Parkway.

Columbia Icefield Centre is 105 km (64 mi.) s. of Jasper on Hwy. 93. The center overlooks Athabasca and Dome glaciers and offers views of major mountain peaks surrounding the Columbia Icefield. An interpretive center contains models of the ice field and an ice cave. The center offers maps, information and details about interpretive programs. Food is available. Allow 30 minutes minimum. Daily 9-6, May-Sept.; 10-4 in Apr. and Oct. Free. Phone (877) 423-7433.

THE DEN is in the lower level of Whistler's Inn in Jasper. Displayed are more than 150 mounted animals in simulated habitats. All animals shown were native to the area. Allow 30 minutes minimum. Daily 8 a.m.-10 p.m. Admission $3; $2 (ages 6-16 and 61+); $6 (family). Phone (780) 852-3361.

ICE EXPLORER ON THE ATHABASCA GLACIER departs from Columbia Icefield Centre, 105 km (64 mi.) s. of Jasper on Hwy. 93N. Tours provide an opportunity to see and walk on a glaciated ice field formed by snow falling as long ago as 400 years. The bus driver provides anecdotes and information during this 80-minute excursion. Allow 1 hour, 30 minutes minimum. Tours depart daily every 15-30 minutes (weather permitting) 9-5, mid-Apr. to mid-Oct. Fare $38; $19 (ages 6-15); free (ages 0-5 in lap). AX, MC, VI. Phone (877) 423-7433.

 ICEFIELDS PARKWAY— *see Banff National Park of Canada p. 45.*

[SAVE] **JASPER ADVENTURE CENTRE** is on Connaught Dr. in Jasper National Park of Canada. The company offers guided interpretive van tours, wildlife tours and walking tours. Summer adventures include exploration of the Columbia Icefield, Maligne Valley and Morro Peak. Some winter treks encompass such activities as snowshoeing, dogsledding and cross-country skiing. Daily 8-8, May-Sept.; 8-6, rest of year. Closed Dec. 25. Fare $40-$107; half-price (ages 6-14). MC, VI. Phone (780) 852-5595 or (800) 565-7547.

JASPER TRAMWAY is 3 km (1.8 mi.) s. on Hwy. 93, then 4 km (2.5 mi.) w. at Whistlers Mountain Rd. Passengers take a short, narrated tram ride 973 m (3,243 ft.) up into the alpine zone on Whistlers Mountain, where scenic views await. Six surrounding mountain ranges, glacial-fed lakes and the Jasper townsite are visible. Once at the top, visitors may hike to the summit. Interpretive panels describe natural features.

Allow 1 hour minimum. Daily 9-8, late June-late Aug.; 9:30-6:30, late May-late June; 10-5, mid-Apr. to late May and late Aug.-Thanksgiving. Fare $25; $12.50 (ages 5-14); $62.50 (family, two adults and two children). MC, VI. Phone (780) 852-3093. *See color ad.*

JASPER-YELLOWHEAD MUSEUM AND ARCHIVES is at 400 Pyramid Lake Rd. An art gallery features the works of local artists, and exhibits depict Jasper history. Interpretive programs also are included. The archives have photographs, maps and documents. Allow 30 minutes minimum. Daily 10-5, Victoria Day-second Mon. in Oct.; Thurs.-Sun. 10-5, rest of year. Closed Jan. 1 and Dec. 25-26. Admission $4; $3 (ages 65+); free (ages 0-4); $10 (family). Phone (780) 852-3013.

MALIGNE LAKE BOAT TOURS is 48 km (30 mi.) s.e. via Maligne Lake Rd.; tickets can be purchased from the office at 616 Patricia St. in the town of Jasper. The 90-minute tours, which offer a brief stop at Spirit Island, provide exceptional views of Maligne Narrows and insight into area geology and wildlife. Hiking and trout-fishing trips as well as boat, canoe and sea kayak rentals are available June to September. Shuttles are available from the town of Jasper.

Allow 1 hour, 30 minutes minimum. Boat tours depart daily on the hour (weather permitting) 10-5, May-Sept. Boat fare $41; $20 (ages 6-12). Round-trip shuttle fare $32.10; one-way $16.06. AX, MC, VI. Phone (780) 852-3370 for information and shuttle schedule. *See color ad.*

MIETTE HOT SPRINGS POOL is e. on Hwy. 16 from Jasper for 44 km (27.3 mi.) to the Pocahontas Bungalows and jct. Miette Rd., then s. 17 km (11 mi.) on Miette Rd. to its end. Man-made pools are fed by sulfur hot springs, with the water temperature ranging between 38 C (100 F) and 42 C (108 F). One pool is about 1.5 metres (5 ft.) deep; another pool averages one-half metre (18 in.) deep. Visitors also can cool off in two swimming pools.

Wildlife viewing opportunities often are available in the area, and hiking trails are nearby. Picnicking is permitted. Food is available. Changing rooms and bathing suit and towel rentals are available. Allow 30 minutes minimum. Daily 8:30 a.m.-10:30 p.m., mid-June through Labour Day; 10:30-9, early May to mid-June and day after Labour Day to mid-Oct. Admission $7.07; $6.13 (ages 3-17 and 65+). Prices may vary; phone ahead. AX, MC, VI. Phone (780) 866-3939 or (800) 767-1611.

RECREATIONAL ACTIVITIES

Horseback Riding

• **Pyramid Stables** is 4 km (2.5 mi.) n. on Pyramid Lake Rd. Write P.O. Box 1200, Jasper, AB,

Canada T0E 1E0. Daily 8:30-4:30, mid-May to mid-Oct. Phone (780) 852-7433.

- **Skyline Trail Rides Ltd.** departs The Fairmont Jasper Park Lodge on Old Lodge Rd. Write P.O. Box 207, Jasper, AB, Canada T0E 1E0. Daily 9:30-6:30, late Apr.-late Oct. Phone (780) 852-4215 or (888) 852-7787.

White-water Rafting

- SAVE **Jasper Raft Tours** meets at the Chaba Movie Theatre across from the Jasper Train Station at 604 Connaught Dr. Write P.O. Box 398, Jasper, AB, Canada T0E 1E0. Trips depart daily, May 15-Sept. 30. Hours vary; phone ahead. Phone (780) 852-2665 or (888) 553-5628.

- **Rocky Mountain River Guides** is at 626 Connaught Dr. Write P.O. Box 1447, Jasper, AB, Canada T0E 1E0. Trips depart daily, mid-May through Sept. 30. Hours vary; phone ahead. Phone (780) 852-3777 or (866) 952-3777.

KANANASKIS COUNTRY (I-4) pop. 429

Kananaskis Country is a four-season, multiuse recreation area encompassing more than 4,200 square kilometres (1,622 sq. mi.) of mountains and foothills. West of Calgary, the area contains Bow Valley, Bragg Creek, Canmore Nordic Centre, Peter Lougheed, Sheep River and Spray Valley provincial parks. In addition there are Blue Rock, Bow Valley, Don Getty and Elbow-Sheep wildland parks. There are also numerous provincial recreation areas with campgrounds, day use areas and trails *(see Recreation Chart)*.

Year-round recreational activities are offered, including hiking, horseback riding, snowmobiling, kayaking, mountain biking, fishing, snowshoeing and downhill and cross-country skiing. The area begins just south of Hwy. 1 and extends south to the intersection of hwys. 940 and 532. Animals, including elk, deer, bighorn sheep, lynx, moose, mountain goats, bears and porcupines, can be observed in the area.

Three major visitor information centers within Kananaskis Country provide brochures, maps, displays and other travel information. The Barrier Lake Visitor Information Centre is 6.5 kilometres (4 mi.) south of Hwy. 1 on Hwy. 40, and Peter Lougheed Provincial Park Visitor Information Centre is 50 kilometres (31 mi.) south off Hwy. 40 on Kananaskis Lakes Trail. Elbow Valley Visitor Information Centre is 5 kilometres (3 mi.) west of Hwy. 22 on Hwy. 66. Campground amphitheaters offer interpretive programs Wednesday through Sunday evenings in July and August. The area is open daily; however, Hwy. 40 is closed December 1 to June 15 between the Kananaskis Lakes Trail and the junction of hwys. 541 and 940.

Kananaskis Country General Inquiries: Provincial Building, 800 Railway Ave., Suite 201, Canmore, AB, Canada T1W 1P1; phone (403) 678-5508 or (403) 673-3985.

PASSING OF THE LEGENDS MUSEUM is at Rafter 6 Ranch, 2 km (1.2 mi.) s. of Hwy. 1 overpass after the Seebe exit. Exhibits include First Nations, North West Mounted Police and pioneer memorabilia; antique carriages; and artworks. Movies and television commercials have been filmed on the property. Adventure programs, including trail riding, white-water rafting and hiking tours, can be organized at the ranch. Daily 9-5, May-Sept. Admission $5; $3 (ages 5-12 and senior citizens). Phone (403) 673-3622, (403) 264-1251 or (888) 267-2624.

RECREATIONAL ACTIVITIES

Skiing

- **Nakiska Ski Resort** is just n. of Kananaskis Village on Hwy. 40. Write 1505 17th Ave. S.W., Calgary, AB, Canada T2T 0E2. Daily 9-4, early Dec. to mid-Apr. Phone (403) 591-7777, (403) 256-8473 or (800) 258-7669.

LAC LA BICHE (C-7) pop. 2,758

South of town, Portage La Biche was discovered in 1798 by renowned geographer and explorer David Thompson of the North West Co. This area encompasses the land between the Churchill and Athabasca-Mackenzie basins. Soon after its discovery the portage became a key link in Canada's main fur trade routes and a passageway to the Pacific Ocean.

The 1853 founding of Lac La Biche Mission played a vital role in the settlement of the area, which quickly developed into a major transportation center of the north.

Lakeland Provincial Park *(see Recreation Chart)*, 13 kilometres (8 mi.) east off Hwy. 663, provides such recreational opportunities as bicycling, bird-watching, camping, cross-country skiing, fishing, hiking and swimming. The park also offers Alberta's only back-country canoe circuit. Sir Winston Churchill Provincial Park *(see Recreation Chart and the AAA/CAA Western Canada & Alaska Camp-Book)*, 13 km (8 mi.) northeast off Hwy. 881, is the largest of the 12 islands on Lac La Biche and offers opportunities for camping, hiking and bird-watching.

Lac La Biche Regional Community Development Corp.: 10106 102nd Ave., P.O. Box 2188, Lac La Biche, AB, Canada T0A 2C0; phone (780) 623-2662 or (877) 623-9696.

LAKE LOUISE—

see Banff National Park of Canada p. 43.

LEGAL (D-6) pop. 1,192

Best known for its collection of building-sized historical murals, the small town of Legal is 50 kilometres (31 mi.) north of Edmonton. The Francophone community is named after Father Emile Legal, a French bishop, missionary and architect.

The town takes pride in its Francophone pioneer history, as is depicted by its huge outdoor murals. Subject matter ranges from the Grey Nuns—who built the first educational center for rural children—to Alexandre Lavoie, whose court battle helped French-Canadians throughout the country obtain federal services in French.

ACFA and Centralta Community Centre: 5109-46 St., P.O. Box 328, Legal, AB, Canada T0G 1L0; phone (780) 961-3665.

LETHBRIDGE (J-7)
pop. 74,637, elev. 930 m/3,051′

Founded in the 1870s, abundant agricultural resources helped Lethbridge to become one of Alberta's major feedlot and grain distribution centers. The region reportedly receives more hours of sunshine annually than any other spot in Canada and therefore requires irrigation to counterbalance the semiarid climate; more than 400,000 hectares (988,000 acres) produce crops of grain and sugar beets. Livestock, oil and gas also support the economic base.

Numerous parks and green spaces complement the city's commercial enterprises. Two popular areas are Lethbridge Nature Preserve in Indian Battle Park at 3rd Avenue S. and Scenic Drive, and Henderson Park at S. Parkside Drive and Mayor Magrath. The park has a golf course, a 60-acre lake with tennis courts, a picnic area and a campground. Rose and Japanese gardens, a stadium and an ice-skating center are included. Lethbridge holds Whoop-Up Days in summer.

Chinook Country Tourist Association: 2805 Scenic Dr. S., Lethbridge, AB, Canada T1K 5B5; phone (403) 320-1222 or (800) 661-1222.

Shopping areas: Hudson's Bay Co. anchors Lethbridge Centre, off Hwy. 3 at 200 4th Ave. S. Park Place Mall, 1st Avenue S. on Scenic Drive, has more than 100 stores and features Sears.

BREWERY GARDENS is just w. off 1st Ave. S. at Brewery Hill on Scenic Dr. Developed by a former brewery, the gardens present eight floral displays May through the first frost, as well as displays for Easter, Halloween, Remembrance Day and Christmas. The gardens are not walk-through gardens, but are a 1 hectare (2.5 acre) plot on the side of a coulee. Visitors view them across the coulee. Daily dawn-dusk. Free. Phone (403) 320-1223.

GALT MUSEUM & ARCHIVES is at the w. end of 5th Ave. S. Housed in a 1910 building that once served as a hospital, the museum is named for the founder of North Western Coal and Navigation Co. The Discovery Hall exhibit gallery highlights the history of the Kainai people and southern Alberta. The High Level Bridge can be seen from the Viewing Gallery, which overlooks the Oldman River Valley.

Allow 30 minutes minimum. Museum daily 10-6, May 15-Sept. 15; 10-4:30, rest of year. Closed Jan. 1, Easter and Dec. 25. Archives Mon.-Fri. 10-4:30; closed statutory holidays. Admission $5; $4 (students with ID and senior citizens); $3 (ages 7-17); $12 (family, two adults and three children). Phone (403) 320-3898, (403) 320-4258 for recorded information, or (866) 320-3898 in Canada.

INDIAN BATTLE PARK is 1 km (.6 mi.) w. of jct. Scenic Dr. and 3rd Ave. S. under the High Level Bridge. This was the 1870 site of the last intertribal battle in North America, between the Cree and Blackfoot Indians. Within the park are attractions, self-guiding trails and picnic and playground facilities. Daily 7 a.m.-10:30 p.m., May-Sept.; 7 a.m.-8:30 p.m., rest of year. Free.

Coal Banks Interpretive Sites are scattered throughout the city. Five informational signs explain the origin of coal mining in the area. Three of the signs are in or near the park at Helen Schuler Coulee Centre *(see attraction listing)*, by the Elks Recreation Centre, and between the Lodge and the Galt Museum & Archives *(see attraction listing)*. The others are at Brewery Gardens *(see attraction listing)* and on Queen Elizabeth II Hwy. near Kipp. Daily 24 hours. For more information phone Galt Museum & Archives at (403) 320-3898.

Fort Whoop-Up Interpretive Centre is on the river in Indian Battle Park. This is a replica of a fort built in 1869 by American traders in Canadian territory. Trade in guns and illegal alcohol, in addition to reports of an American flag flying in Canada, led to the formation of the North West Mounted Police and to their march west in 1874. Wagon rides through the park are available in summer; they must be booked in advance during winter months.

Allow 30 minutes minimum. Daily 9-5, May 15-Sept. 30; Wed.-Sun. 1-4, Apr. 1-May 14 and in Oct.; Sat.-Sun. 1-4, rest of year. Closed holidays. Guided tours are available Tues.-Sun. at 10:30, 1:30 and 2:30, July-Aug. Admission (June-Sept.) $7; $6 (ages 65+); $5 (ages 13-18); $3 (ages 5-12); $18.69 (family). Admission (rest of year) $5; $4 (ages 65+); $3 (ages 13-18); $2 (ages 5-12); $14 (family). MC, VI. Phone (403) 329-0444.

Helen Schuler Coulee Centre is n. of Indian Battle Park. Desertlike flora and fauna are found on the coulee slopes and in cottonwood forests along the Oldman River. The center is surrounded by the 79-hectare (196-acre) Lethbridge Nature Reserve, home to the great horned owl, porcupines and white-tailed deer. Most of the park is accessible via three self-guiding trails. The center offers seasonal exhibits.

Pets, bicycles, inline skates and skateboards are not permitted. Allow 30 minutes minimum. Daily 10-6, June-Aug.; Tues.-Sun. 1-4 in May and Sept.; Tues.-Sun. 1-4, rest of year. Closed Jan. 1 and Dec. 25. Hours may vary; phone ahead. Free. Phone (403) 320-3064.

The High Level Bridge, in Indian Battle Park, spans the Oldman River. Reputedly this is the longest and highest bridge of its type and construction in North America. The 1909 trestle bridge extends 1.6 kilometres (1 mi.) across the coulees and is 97 metres high (300 ft.). The best place to view the bridge is from the information center/rest area on the west end of 1st Avenue, south of Hwy. 3 on Brewery Hill. Daily 24 hours. Free.

NIKKA YUKO JAPANESE GARDEN is at 9th Ave. and Mayor Magrath Dr. in Henderson Park. Five basic types of traditional Japanese gardens are incorporated into the overall design, which is one of the most authentic of its kind in North America. A pavilion, bridges, a bell tower imported from Japan and cypress wood from Taiwan are featured; paths punctuated by footbridges over ponds and streams weave through the gardens.

Guides in traditional kimonos conduct half-hour tours as needed. Visitors can enjoy ongoing activities such as art exhibits and pruning and gardening techniques. Special events, which take place on select Saturdays at 2, include traditional Japanese art demonstrations of bonsai, flower arranging, origami, sand art and calligraphy. A tea ceremony is offered Sundays at 2.

Allow 1 hour minimum. Daily 9-8, July 1-Labour Day; 9-5, early May-June 30 and day after Labour Day-Sept. 30. Hours may vary; phone ahead. Admission $7; $5 (ages 65+); $4 (ages 6-17). MC, VI. Phone (403) 328-3511.

ST. MARY'S RIVER DAM is 78 km (47 mi.) s. off Hwy. 5. This earth-filled dam is one of the largest in Canada. Water sports and a campground are available. Phone Park Lake Provincial Park at (403) 382-4097 for more information.

SOUTHERN ALBERTA ART GALLERY is at 601 3rd Ave. S. Exhibits showcase works of Canadian and international artists with an emphasis on contemporary art. Allow 30 minutes minimum. Tues.-Sat. 10-5, Sun. 1-5; closed holidays except July 1. Admission $5; $4 (students with ID and senior citizens); free (ages 0-11 and on Sun.). Phone (403) 327-8770.

GAMBLING ESTABLISHMENTS

• **Casino Lethbridge** is at 3756 2nd Ave. S. Daily 9:30 a.m.-3 a.m.; closed Dec. 25. Phone (403) 381-9467.

LLOYDMINSTER—see Saskatchewan p. 266.

LONGVIEW (I-6) pop. 300

BAR U RANCH NATIONAL HISTORIC SITE OF CANADA is 15 km (9 mi.) s. on Hwy. 22. The site focuses on the history of ranching in Canada and the role that occupation played in the country's development. Visitors learn the history of the Bar U Ranch, from the days of open range ranching through its prominence as a breeding center for cattle and Percheron horses to its position as part of a multiple-ranch cattle operation.

The visitor center has exhibits and a presentation about the site, one of Canada's largest ranching operations 1882-1950. Guests can tour the 148-hectare (367-acre) site on foot or via a hay wagon. Historic structures include the 1882-83 saddle horse barn, blacksmith shop, stud horse barn, wintering pens, 1910 cook house, storage sheds and ranch office/post office. Ranch chores are demonstrated.

Food is available. Daily 9-5, Victoria Day-second Mon. in Oct. Admission $7.90; $6.65 (ages 65+); $3.95 (ages 6-16); $19.80 (family). AX, MC, VI. Phone (403) 395-2212, (403) 395-3044, (888) 773-8888, or TTY (866) 787-6221.

MARKERVILLE (G-5) pop. 50

On June 27, 1888, 50 Icelanders from the drought-plagued Dakota Territory crossed the Red Deer River to settle in Markerville, where they hoped to maintain their language and customs. For a time they produced woolen outerwear, pastries, sweets and smoked mutton in the traditional Icelandic manner.

During the 1920s, however, an increase in intermarriage with other ethnic groups and improved transportation diluted their cultural isolation. Less than 10 percent of the population is now of purely Icelandic descent, but many traditional customs are celebrated during heritage days.

HISTORIC MARKERVILLE CREAMERY MUSEUM is off hwys. 781 and 592 on Creamery Way. Begun by 34 Icelandic farmers as a cooperative in 1899 and in operation until 1972, the creamery has been restored to depict the operation as it was in the 1930s. Costumed guides offer tours.

Picnicking is permitted. Food is available. Allow 30 minutes minimum. Mon.-Sat. 10-5:30, Sun. noon-5:30, May 15-Labour Day; by appointment rest of year. Admission $2; $1.50 (ages 7-17 and 65+); $5 (family, two adults and two children). MC, VI. Phone (403) 728-3006.

STEPHANSSON HOUSE PROVINCIAL HISTORIC SITE is 7 km (4 mi.) n., following signs. Historical displays highlight the Icelanders who founded Markerville, including Stephan G. Stephansson, a prominent poet and farmer. His home, restored to its 1927 appearance, contains original furnishings. Costumed guides give 15- to 30-minute tours and demonstrations of 1920s homemaking chores such as spinning.

Self-guiding tours are available. Picnicking is permitted. Allow 30 minutes minimum. Daily 10-6, May 15-Labour Day. Admission $3; $2 (ages 7-17 and 65+); $8 (family, two adults and children). Phone (403) 728-3929 May 15-Labour Day or (780) 427-1787 rest of year.

MEDICINE HAT (J-8)
pop. 56,997, elev. 715 m/2,346'

According to popular legend the name Medicine Hat originated because of a battle between Cree and Blackfoot Indians on the banks of a southern Alberta river. The Cree fought bravely until their medicine man deserted them, losing his headdress in midstream. Believing this to be a bad omen, the Cree put down their weapons and were killed by the Blackfoot. This site became known as "Saamis," which translates as "medicine man's hat."

A buried prehistoric river, or aquifer, serves as a source of unlimited cool water. More than 20 billion cubic metres (26 billion cu. yd.) of natural gas reserves inspired Rudyard Kipling in 1907 to describe Medicine Hat as possessing "all hell for a basement."

Guided tours of Medicine Hat are available through Tourism Medicine Hat. Outdoor opportunities include swimming, boating and fishing at Echo Dale Regional Park. Riverside Waterslides & Amusement Park offers waterslides, miniature golf and go-carts. Circuit cowboys and spectators gather for 4 days in late July for the Medicine Hat Exhibition & Stampede.

Tourism Medicine Hat: 8 Gehring Rd. S.W., Medicine Hat, AB, Canada T1B 4W1; phone (403) 527-6422 or (800) 481-2822.

Self-guiding tours: A map describing a self-guiding tour of downtown Medicine Hat is available from City Hall, 580 1st St. S.E., and Tourism Medicine Hat.

Shopping areas: Medicine Hat Mall, 3292 Dunmore Rd. S.E., features The Bay, Sears and Zellers among its more than 100 stores.

ESPLANADE ARTS & HERITAGE CENTRE, 401 First St. S.E., houses theaters, an art gallery and archives. A museum presents displays that detail the region's cultural heritage; more than 25,000 pieces are exhibited, including Indian artifacts and pioneer items.

Allow 1 hour minimum. Exhibit galleries and box office open Mon.-Fri. 10-5, Sat.-Sun. and holidays noon-5; closed Good Friday and Dec. 25-26. Exhibit galleries $4; $3 (ages 7-17 and students with ID); $12 (family); free (on Thurs.). Prices for shows vary; phone ahead. Phone (403) 502-8580 for the museum or (403) 502-8583 for the art gallery.

MEDICINE HAT CLAY INDUSTRIES NATIONAL HISTORIC DISTRICT is at 713 Medalta Ave. S.E. Brick, tile and pottery manufacturing were prominent industries in Medicine Hat starting in the late 19th century due to a supply of clay deposits, natural gas and the availability of railroad transportation. The city once boasted several potteries, such as Medalta Potteries and Medicine Hat Potteries (later Hycroft China Ltd.). Today only the brick industry remains.

At the Medalta Potteries site, visitors can see beehive kilns constructed in the early 1920s. Artifacts and production machines also are displayed. Allow 2 hours minimum. Daily 9-5, mid-May through Labour Day; Tues.-Sat. 9:30-4:30, rest of year. Guided tours are offered daily on the hour 10-11 and 1-4, mid-May through Labour Day. Self-guiding tours are available Tues.-Sat. 9:30-4:30, rest of year. Admission $8; $6 (ages 7-16, ages 65+ and students with ID); $25 (family). AX, MC, VI. Phone (403) 529-1070.

SAAMIS TEEPEE is at jct. Hwy. 1 and South Ridge Dr. Made of steel, the tepee stands approximately 20 stories high. Storyboards incorporated in the tepee stand 3.6 metres (12 ft.) high and depict Indian history. Used during the 1988 Olympics in Calgary, the tepee was moved to Medicine Hat where it now stands on Saamis Archaeological Site—the location of a 16th-century buffalo camp. Allow 1 hour minimum. Daily 24 hours, Victoria Day weekend-Aug. 31. Donations. Phone (403) 527-6422 or (800) 481-2822.

GAMBLING ESTABLISHMENTS

- **Casino by Van Shaw** is at 1051 Ross Glen Dr. S.E. Daily 10 a.m.-3 a.m.; closed Dec. 25. Phone (403) 504-4584.

MILK RIVER (K-8) pop. 816

Milk River is on the east side of Milk River Ridge, an area more than 1,200 metres (3,900 ft.) high, 39 kilometres (24 mi.) long and 29 kilometres (18 mi.) wide. Quartzite, granite and gneiss rock formations indicate prehistoric glacial action; meltwater carved the Milk River Valley 10,000 years ago. The river, formed from small streams and springs in southwest Alberta and northern Montana, joins the Missouri and Mississippi rivers to flow to the Gulf of Mexico.

Throughout the area and predominantly in Writing-on-Stone Provincial Park *(see attraction listing)* are mushroom-shaped sandstone hoodoos, odd rock formations that once led Indians to believe spirits inhabited the valley.

The Alberta Tourism Information and Interpretive Centre: General Delivery, Milk River, AB, Canada T0K 1M0; phone (800) 252-3782.

WRITING-ON-STONE PROVINCIAL PARK is 35 km (21.9 mi.) e. on Hwy. 501, 7 km (4.5 mi.) s. on Hwy. 130, then 6 km (3.9 mi.) e. on Hwy. 500, following signs. The archeological preserve overlooks the Milk River. Massive sandstone outcrops display pictographs and petroglyphs created by nomadic Shoshone and Blackfoot Indians. Fire-burned stones, broken bones, horn tools and other implements have been found at former campsites. Interpretive programs are presented mid-May to early September.

Note: Temperatures in excess of 40 C (104 F) are often recorded along the trail. Grounds daily 24 hours. Guided 90-minute tours depart daily, mid-May to early Sept. Grounds free. Guided tour $8; $6 (ages 6-17); $25 (family). Phone (403) 647-2364. *See Recreation Chart and the AAA/CAA Western Canada & Alaska CampBook.*

MUNDARE (E-7) pop. 712

BASILIAN FATHERS MUSEUM is 2 km (1.2 mi.) n. of Hwy. 16 on Hwy. 855. Operated by the Basilian Fathers, the museum houses exhibits about Ukrainian immigration and the religious order's work in east central Alberta and throughout Canada.

Guided tours are available. Open Mon.-Fri. 10-4 (also Sat.-Sun. 1-5, July-Aug.); closed holidays Sept.-June. Donations. Phone (780) 764-3887.

NANTON (I-6) pop. 2,055

NANTON LANCASTER SOCIETY AIR MUSEUM is s. on Queen Elizabeth II Hwy. following signs. Exhibits honor Royal Canadian Air Force and Royal Air Force members who waged bombing operations during World War II. Among displays are a Canadian-built Lancaster bomber, other bombers and training planes, simulators, gun turrets and instrumentation and photographs of training aircraft in action. Allow 1 hour minimum. Daily 9-5, May-Oct.; Sat.-Sun. 10-4, Mon.-Fri. by appointment, rest of year. Closed Jan. 1 and Dec. 25-26. Donations. Phone (403) 646-2270.

OKOTOKS—see Calgary p. 60.

PATRICIA (I-8) pop. 114

DINOSAUR PROVINCIAL PARK is 13 km (8 mi.) n.e. via Hwy. 210, following signs.
The park, declared a UNESCO World Heritage Site in 1979, covers 81 square kilometres (31 sq. mi.) of badlands and prairie along the Red Deer River. One of the richest fossil beds in the world, it contains the remains of 39 species of dinosaurs from 75 million years ago as well as crocodile, fish, flying reptile, small mammal and turtle fossils.

Five self-guiding trails explore three habitats: prairie grassland, badlands and riverside. Each offers opportunities for bird-watching. The visitor center contains exhibits, a theater and a preparation lab. Interpretive programs are offered seasonally.

Picnicking is permitted. Camping is permitted. Allow a full day. Grounds daily 24 hours. Visitor center daily 8:30-7, Victoria Day weekend-day before Labour Day; daily 10-5, Labour Day-second Mon. in Oct.; Mon.-Fri. 9-4, rest of year.

Grounds free. Visitor center (includes Royal Tyrrell Museum Field Station) $3; $2.50 (ages 65+); $2 (ages 7-17); $8 (family). Interpretive programs $8; $6 (ages 7-17). Reservations are recommended for interpretive programs. Phone (403) 378-4344, or (403) 378-3700 for camping reservations. *See Recreation Chart and the AAA/CAA Western Canada & Alaska CampBook.*

Royal Tyrrell Museum Field Station is within Dinosaur Provincial Park at the back of the visitor center building. The interpretive center and research facility contains dinosaur skeletons, interpretive displays depicting the park's geological and paleontological resources, a preparation lab and the park administration office. Daily 8:30-7, Victoria Day weekend-day before Labour Day; daily 10-5, Labour Day-second Mon. in Oct.; Mon.-Fri. 9-4, rest of year. Admission included with Dinosaur Provincial Park. Phone (403) 378-4342.

PEACE RIVER (A-3) pop. 6,315

Formed by the confluence of the Smoky and Heart rivers, the Peace River flows north and east of the town of the same name to Lake Athabasca and to the west into British Columbia. The area was known as "The Forks" by trappers and traders in the 1700s and "Sagitawa" (meeting of the waters) by the Cree Indians. On his historic trek across the northern continent, Alexander Mackenzie explored the region and built a fort and wintered here 1792-93.

A wooden statue honors prospector and local legend Henry Fuller "Twelve-Foot" Davis. The Vermont native, known for his generosity and hospitality, achieved great social stature when he mined $15,000 worth of gold from a 3.5-metre (12-ft.) plot between two gold claims. Davis said on his deathbed that he was not afraid to die because "I never kilt nobody, I never stole from nobody and I kept open house for travelers all my life." His grave overlooks the confluence of the Peace, Heart and Smoky rivers.

Nearby forests, rivers and streams make Peace River a popular center for year-round recreation in northern Alberta. Golfing, swimming, canoeing, downhill skiing and dogsledding are all options.

Peace River and District Chamber of Commerce: 9309 100th St., P.O. Box 6599, Peace River, AB, Canada T8S 1S4; phone (780) 624-4166.

PINCHER CREEK (K-6) pop. 3,625

Pincher Creek was established in 1878 by the North West Mounted Police as a horse farm to provide remounts for Fort Macleod *(see place listing p. 78).* The town was named for a pair of pincers that presumably were left behind by prospectors. After hearing that the area had ample grassland, other settlers soon arrived.

Pincher Creek & District Chamber of Economic Development and Information Centre: 1037 Beverly McLachlin Dr., P.O. Box 2287, Pincher Creek, AB, Canada T0K 1W0; phone (403) 627-5855 or (888) 298-5855.

KOOTENAI BROWN PIONEER VILLAGE is at 1037 Bridge Ave. Displays include more than 7,000 local artifacts—including military uniforms, agricultural equipment, jewelry, clothing and books about local history—in 12 historical buildings. On the grounds is the restored log cabin of George "Kootenai" Brown, an Irish adventurer and one of the region's first settlers who helped establish Waterton Lakes National Park of Canada. Other period buildings are on the grounds.

Allow 2 hours minimum. Daily 10-6, Victoria Day weekend-Labour Day; 10-4:30, rest of year. Closed Dec. 24-Jan. 2. Admission $6; $5 (ages 65+); $4 (ages 7-17); free (ages 0-6 with adult); $18 (family). Phone (403) 627-3684.

RECREATIONAL ACTIVITIES
Skiing

• Castle Mountain Resort is off CR 507, just w. on CR 774. Write P.O. Box 610, Pincher Creek,

AB, Canada T0K 1W0. Daily 9-4, mid-Dec. to early Apr. Phone (403) 627-5101.

RAVEN (G-5)

MEDICINE RIVER WILDLIFE CENTRE is 4 km (2.5 mi.) s. of Hwy. 54, then 2 km (1.2 mi.) e. The organization provides rehabilitation for injured and orphaned wildlife. It also serves as an environmental education center, offering a videotape presentation and displays about wildlife. A trail leads to an observation tower that affords excellent bird-watching around a 30-hectare (75-acre) marsh. Allow 1 hour minimum. Daily 10-5, May 1-Labour Day; by appointment rest of year. Donations. Phone (403) 728-3467.

RED DEER (G-6)
pop. 82,772, elev. 905 m/2,969′

Red Deer's name comes from the Cree Indian word *waskasoo*, meaning "elk." Early Scottish settlers mistook the native elk for the red deer of their homeland and the name stuck. A creek and park running through Red Deer still bear the name Waskasoo.

The original settlement was several kilometres upstream on the Red Deer River where the water was shallow and easy to cross. Dr. Leonard Gaetz, a Methodist minister who arrived in 1884, persuaded the Calgary and Edmonton Railway to cross the river on his property by donating half of his land for use as a townsite. The trains came through, and the town took root at its current site. Agriculture and petroleum products are the major local industries.

City Hall Park, 48th Avenue and Ross Street, is a landscaped oasis known for its Christmas light and flower displays. West of town is Sylvan Lake, which accommodates Jarvis Bay and Sylvan Lake parks (*see Recreation Chart*). A noteworthy lake resort north at Gull Lake is Aspen Beach Provincial Park (*see Recreation Chart and Lacombe in the AAA/ CAA Western Canada & Alaska CampBook*).

Lacombe, also north of the city, is the site of the Canadian Agriculture Department's experimental farm; visitors can tour the facility. Red Deer events include the Highland Games in June, International Folk Festival/Canada Day celebrations on July 1 and Westerner Days in mid-July.

Tourism Red Deer: 30A Riverview Park, Red Deer, AB, Canada T4N 1E3; phone (403) 346-0180 or (800) 215-8946.

Self-guiding tours: A brochure outlining a walking tour of historic downtown is available from The Red Deer and District Museum and Archives and from the visitor information center west of Heritage Ranch in Waskasoo Park (*see attraction listings*).

Shopping areas: Bower Place, Gaetz Avenue and 28th Street, is anchored by The Bay and Zellers. Parkland Mall, 67th Street and Gaetz Avenue, has Sears and 120 smaller shops.

ALBERTA SPORTS HALL OF FAME & MUSEUM is on Queen Elizabeth II Hwy., n. of 32nd St. by Heritage Ranch. Alberta's sports history and heroes are celebrated through the display of 7,000 artifacts, archival material and interactive exhibits, including an Alpine ski racer game and a 200-metre (656-ft.) wheelchair race.

Picnicking is permitted. Food is available. Allow 1 hour, 30 minutes minimum. Daily 9-6, Victoria Day weekend-second Mon. in Oct.; 10-5, rest of year. Closed Jan. 1, Good Friday, Easter and Dec. 25-26. Admission $3; $2 (ages 6-17 and 56+); $9 (family, two adults and children). MC, VI. Phone (403) 341-8614.

THE RED DEER AND DISTRICT MUSEUM AND ARCHIVES is at 4525 47A Ave. Galleries tell the story of diverse cultures who lived in the Red Deer River Valley from the days of the First Nations to the start of modern civilization. Changing art exhibits are featured. Daily noon-5; closed holidays. Admission $2; $1 (ages 0-17 and senior citizens); $5 (family). Phone (403) 309-8405.

ST. MARY'S CHURCH is at 6 McMillan Ave. This ultramodern 1968 structure of unusual design is the work of architect Douglas Cardinal. Local architect Graham Leadbeater designed the parish center addition. Alois Peter Marx of Germany created the sculpture displays. Mon.-Fri. 10-4; closed legal holidays. Free. Phone (403) 347-3114.

WASKASOO PARK borders the Red Deer River and runs throughout the city. The park has about 100 kilometres (62 mi.) of both paved and unpaved walking trails. Also within the park are Bower Ponds; the 1911 Victorian Cronquist House Multicultural Centre; Fort Normandeau, with an interpretive center; Heritage Ranch; Kerry Wood Nature Centre, which houses nature displays; and Gaetz Lake Sanctuary, a wildlife preserve. Many recreational pursuits are possible. Picnicking is permitted. Grounds open daily dawn-11 p.m. Grounds free. Phone (403) 342-8159.

GAMBLING ESTABLISHMENTS
- **Cash Casino** is at 6350 67th St. Daily 10 a.m.-2 a.m. (also Fri.-Sat. 2-3 a.m.); closed Dec. 25. Phone (403) 346-3339.
- **Jackpot Casino Ltd.** is at 4950 47th Ave. Daily 10 a.m.-3 a.m. Phone (403) 342-5825.

RECREATIONAL ACTIVITIES
Recreational Complex
- **Collicutt Centre** is at 3031 30th Ave. Write P.O. Box 5008, Red Deer, AB, Canada T4N 3T4. Mon.-Fri. 5:30 a.m.-10:30 p.m., Sat.-Sun. 6:30 a.m.-10:30 p.m., holidays 10-8; closed Dec. 25. Phone (403) 358-7529.

RIMBEY (F-5) pop. 2,252

PAS-KA-POO HISTORICAL PARK is at 5620 51st St. The park's Smithson International Truck Museum features 19 half-ton trucks, a collection of license plates, farm machinery and photographs. A restored village features 10 historic structures and two museums. A 1902 schoolhouse, a 1915 town office, a train station, a replica trapper's cabin, a 1932 homesteader's cottage, a 1908 church, a barbershop and a blacksmith shop are on-site. Each building contains artifacts and memorabilia.

Guided tours are available. Truck museum open daily 10-5; closed Jan. 1 and Dec. 25. Village open daily 10-5, mid-May to early Sept. Admission $5; free (ages 0-11 with adult). Phone (403) 843-2004.

◆ ROCKY MOUNTAIN HOUSE NATIONAL HISTORIC SITE OF CANADA (F-5)

In west central Alberta about 80 kilometres (50 mi.) west of Red Deer on Hwy. 11 and 6 kilometres (4 mi.) west from the town of Rocky Mountain House via Hwy. 11A, following signs, Rocky Mountain House National Historic Site of Canada tells the story of the fur trade era that existed 1799-1875. The site, on the banks of the North Saskatchewan River, protects the remains of four fur-trading posts.

Both the North West Co. and Hudson's Bay Co. were expanding in an attempt to reach the area's native peoples. The two rivals arrived here within a week of each other in 1799, their goal being to stimulate trade with the Kootenai, who were on the western side of the Rocky Mountains. The Blackfoot people blocked the planned trade. Rocky Mountain House traded with eight different aboriginal groups in its 76 years of operation.

Well-known cartographer and fur trader David Thompson used Rocky Mountain House for a time as a base for exploring routes over the mountains. Thompson was the first person of European descent to cross Howse Pass, accomplishing this feat in 1807.

Trade competition remained intense between the two companies until their merger in 1821. The influx of illegal whiskey traders into southern Alberta in 1869 disrupted trade with the aboriginal people, and in 1875 the last of the four posts was abandoned.

Two walking trails along the North Saskatchewan River and through a scenic wooded area connect the remains of the four forts. Eight listening stations and illustrated interpretive panels are spaced along the trail system. A 30-minute walk leads past the two later forts, the reconstructed chimneys at the last fort site, a replica flat-bottom York boat, a Red River cart and a fur press. A longer 90-minute walk travels to the first two forts built at Rocky Mountain House, passing tepees, the 1967 Centennial Canoe Race exhibit and a buffalo viewing area. Visitors often can see deer, coyotes, bluebirds and hawks along the trails.

The visitor center contains exhibits of trade items and aboriginal objects and a theater presenting films. Interpretive programs and special events are offered daily during July and August. Bicycle rentals are available.

The visitor center is open daily 10-5, Victoria Day weekend-Labour Day; hours vary, day after Labour Day-Sept. 30. Admission is $3.95; ages 65+, $3.45; ages 6-16, $1.95. AX, MC, VI. Phone (403) 845-2412.

ROSEBUD (H-7) pop. 109

A pioneer ranching settlement founded in the 1880s, Rosebud has become a thriving cultural center. The community participates in the activities of Rosebud School of the Arts. Rosebud Theatre offers dinner and theater entertainment at matinees and evening performances Wednesday through Saturday from March through December; phone (403) 677-2001 or (800) 267-7553.

Among Rosebud's historic buildings is an early 20th-century Chinese laundry, which now is home to Centennial Museum. The museum displays local memorabilia and an array of western Canadiana. Works by Alberta artists are exhibited in Akokiniskway Art Gallery and other shops along the town's self-guiding historic walking tour.

ST. ALBERT —see Edmonton p. 76.

SLAVE LAKE (C-5) pop. 6,703

Slave Lake is on the southeast shore of Lesser Slave Lake, Alberta's largest auto-accessible lake. Lesser Slave Lake Provincial Park (see Recreation Chart and the AAA/CAA Western Canada & Alaska CampBook), which surrounds a golf course and hugs the lake's east shore, provides snowshoeing and cross-country skiing opportunities in winter and camping, hiking and bird-watching during the summer. Riverboat Daze takes place the second week in July, and the Alberta Open Sand Sculpture Championship is held the third weekend in July.

SMOKY LAKE (D-7) pop. 1,010

[SAVE] VICTORIA SETTLEMENT PROVINCIAL HISTORIC SITE is 10 km (6 mi.) s. on Hwy. 855 and 6 km (3.6 mi.) e. on Victoria Tr. Settlement began in 1862 as a Methodist mission. A Hudson's Bay Co. fur-trading post soon followed, and by the beginning of the 20th century the village was known as Pakan. Guided tours are offered of the 1906 Methodist Church and the 1864 Clerk's Quarters, which is furnished with pioneer articles. A videotape presentation describes local history.

Allow 1 hour minimum. Daily 10-6, May 15-Labour Day. Admission $3; $1.50 (ages 7-16 and 65+); $8 (family, two adults and children). Phone (780) 656-2333.

SPRUCE VIEW (G-5)

Founded at the turn of the 20th century, Spruce View was named for its omnipresent spruce trees. Such recreational opportunities as boating, camping, fishing and picnicking are available at Dickson Dam-North Valley Provincial Recreation Area (see Innisfail in the AAA/CAA Western Canada & Alaska CampBook).

DICKSON DAM VISITOR CENTRE is 6 km (4 mi.) e. on Hwy. 54, following signs. Perched on a hillside, the center offers a bird's-eye view of Dickson Dam. Exhibits and a short video focus on the dam's history and topography. Tues. and Fri. 8-3:30, June-Oct. Free. Phone (403) 227-1106.

STETTLER (G-7) pop. 5,418

Stettler is named after Carl Stettler, a Swiss immigrant who arrived in Alberta in 1903. He helped establish a Swiss community known as Blumenau not far from present-day Stettler. With the arrival of the railroad, the Stettler settlement was established and the residents of Blumenau relocated there.

ALBERTA PRAIRIE RAILWAY EXCURSIONS depart the train station at 47th Ave. and 46th St. Steam- and diesel-powered rail excursions are offered through the Alberta countryside in vintage passenger coaches. Trips last 5 to 6 hours; all include a buffet-style meal at the destination in the summer or on-board dining during the winter. Theme trips also are scheduled.

Trains operate Sat.-Sun. and selected weekdays, May-Oct. Departure times vary. Fare $85-$135; $65-$120 (ages 11-17); $35-$120 (ages 4-10). Reservations are required. AX, MC, VI. Phone (403) 742-2811.

STONY PLAIN—see Edmonton p. 77.

TROCHU (G-6) pop. 1,005

ST. ANN RANCH TRADING CO. PROVINCIAL HISTORIC SITE is .5 km (.3 mi.) s. on King George Ave. This reconstructed 1905 French settlement contains restored historic houses and reproductions of period buildings. The site includes a small school, post office, hospital and chapel. An interpretive center contains displays recounting the history of the settlement, which was founded by aristocratic officers from the French cavalry. Allow 30 minutes minimum. Museum and interpretive center open daily 9-9. Admission $2. Phone (403) 442-3924, or (888) 442-3924 in Canada.

VEGREVILLE (E-7) pop. 5,519

The center of eastern Alberta's Ukrainian culture, Vegreville has the distinction of possessing the largest known *pysanka*, or Easter egg, in the world. The 9.4-metre-high (31-ft.) egg, decorated to reflect Ukrainian folk art, was erected in 1975 for the centennial of the formation of the Royal Canadian Mounted Police in Alberta.

The egg's bronze, gold and silver design, made from more than 3,500 pieces of aluminum, illustrates the local settlers' struggles and the protection the mounted police provided them. Queen Elizabeth and Prince Phillip unveiled the plaque next to the giant egg in Elks/Kinsmen Park during their visit in 1978. The Ukrainian Pysanka Festival is held in early July.

Town of Vegreville Parks, Recreation & Tourism: 4509-48 St., P.O. Box 640, Vegreville, AB, Canada T9C 1K8; phone (780) 632-2606.

WAINWRIGHT (F-8) pop. 5,426

WAINWRIGHT & DISTRICT MUSEUM is at 1001 1st Ave. Displays include items and memorabilia relating to family life in the town since its founding in 1908. The histories of Wood Buffalo National Park of Canada and a local prisoner of war camp also are presented. The museum is housed in an original Canadian National Railway station built in the early 1930s. Allow 30 minutes minimum. Daily 9-5; closed Jan. 1, Good Friday and Dec. 25. Admission $5; $3 (ages 6-17). Phone (780) 842-3115.

WARNER (K-7) pop. 307, elev. 1,017 m/3,336'

DEVIL'S COULEE DINOSAUR HERITAGE MUSEUM is in the County of Warner Administration Building w. off Hwy. 4, following signs. Small fossil fragments found on the Milk River Ridge in 1987 were from a hadrosaur (a duck-billed dinosaur); the location was the first nesting site found in Canada. A 2-hour tour to the dinosaur egg site leaves from the museum. Displays feature a hadrosaur nest, embryo, fossils and models of dinosaurs. Also included is an exhibit about early area settlement.

Note: The nesting site is in a primitive area not suitable for small children or those with mobility or medical problems. Allow 30 minutes minimum for the museum, 3 hours minimum for tour and museum. Museum daily 9-5, Victoria Day weekend-June 30; Wed.-Mon. 9-5, July 1-Labour Day. Tours to the nesting site are given daily at 10 and 1, July 1-Labour Day; Sat.-Sun. at 10 and 1, Victoria Day weekend-June 30 (weather permitting).

Museum admission $3; free (ages 0-5); $10 (family, five persons). Tour to dig site (includes museum admission) $10; $25 (family, five persons). Reservations are recommended for the tour. AX, MC, VI. Phone (403) 642-2118.

⬥ WATERTON LAKES NATIONAL PARK OF CANADA (K-5)

Elevations in the park range from 1,279 metres (4,200 ft.) in the town of Waterton Park to 2,920 metres (9,580 ft.) at Mount Blakiston. Refer to CAA/AAA maps for additional elevation information.

The most direct approach into the national park from the south is over Chief Mountain International Hwy. (SR 17/Hwy. 6) from Glacier National Park in Montana; the park also is accessible via Hwy. 5 from Cardston or Hwy. 6 from Pincher Creek. Covering 505 square kilometres (195 sq. mi.), Waterton Lakes National Park of Canada adjoins Glacier National Park. Together the two parks form Waterton-Glacier International Peace Park. The customs office is open daily 7 a.m.-10 p.m., June 1-Sept. 1; 9-6, Victoria Day weekend-May 31 and Sept. 2-30.

For thousands of years this was aboriginal territory, where the Kootenai and Blackfoot were the primary aboriginal tribes. In 1858 Lt. Thomas Blakiston became the first European on record to explore the area; he named the lakes for Charles Waterton, an 18th-century English naturalist.

Local rancher Fred Godsal, American journalist and naturalist George Bird Grinnell and others lobbied their respective governments in the late 19th century to set aside parts of this wilderness area for future generations. They succeeded, and Waterton Lakes and Glacier national parks were established in 1895 and 1910, respectively.

Waterton Lake is divided into three parts: Upper, Middle and Lower Waterton lakes. The townsite, the location of park headquarters, is on the north shore of Upper Waterton Lake, which juts 4.7 kilometres (3 mi.) into Glacier National Park. The mountains on either side tower 900 to 1,200 metres (3,000 to 4,000 ft.) above the lake. Mount Crandell rises to the north; Sofa Mountain and Vimy Peak are east across the lake.

Wildlife ranging from squirrels and marmots to deer and bears inhabits the park. A small herd of plains bison is in the buffalo paddocks on the northern boundary, 1.6 kilometres (1 mi.) north of the Waterton River Bridge on Hwy. 6. Thousands of waterfowl visit the lakes during spring and fall migrations. Hunting is prohibited.

Among the many rare wildflowers that grace prairie and mountain landscapes are bear grass, pygmy poppy and mountain lady-slipper. Evergreens blanket the slopes and peaks below mountain goat country at an altitude of about 2,286 metres (7,500 ft.).

General Information and Activities

The park is open all year, though most concessions operate only from Victoria Day weekend through the second Monday in October. Red Rock Canyon, 15 kilometres (11 mi.) northwest of Waterton, offers a .7-kilometre (.4-mi.) loop trail along the canyon and a 1-kilometre (.6-mi.) trail to Blakiston Falls. Riding stables are 2.5 kilometres (1.5 mi.) north of town near the main entrance road; horses can be rented.

Just north of the townsite is an 18-hole public golf course that is open daily, Victoria Day weekend through the second Monday in October. A free four-court tennis facility is on Cameron Falls Drive.

The park visitor center, at the junction of the entrance road and Prince of Wales Road, is open daily 8-7, mid-June through Labour Day; 9-5, mid-May to mid-June; 9-4:30, day after Labour Day-second Mon. in Oct. Interpretive display centers at Cameron Lake and the Waterton townsite describe the park's subalpine forest and the history of the International Peace Park. All are open daily 24 hours.

Illustrated talks are given every evening at 8 at the park's indoor theaters. There also are guided walks and other interpretive programs; phone (403) 859-5133.

Those wishing to camp in Waterton's backcountry campsites must obtain a park use permit

($8.90) at the visitor center. You also can register your outing with the Park Warden Service.

Hunting is prohibited. Anglers need a fishing license, which can be obtained along with fishing regulations at the park offices, information center, campgrounds, from park wardens and at service stations in the townsite. Motorboats are permitted on both Upper and Middle Waterton lakes; water skiing, however, is permitted only on Middle Waterton Lake. *See Recreation Chart and the AAA/CAA Western Canada & Alaska CampBook.*

ADMISSION to the park is $6.90; over 64, $5.90; ages 6-16, $3.45. Admission for up to seven persons in a private vehicle is $17.30. An annual pass, valid at all Canadian national parks, is available.

PETS must be leashed at all times while in the park.

ADDRESS inquiries to the Superintendent, Waterton Lakes National Park of Canada, Waterton Park, AB, Canada T0K 2M0; phone (403) 859-2224. *See color ad p. 482.*

WATERTON INTER-NATION SHORELINE CRUISE CO. departs from the Waterton Marina. Narrated sightseeing trips lasting 2.25 hours cross Waterton Lake, which is surrounded by the majestic scenery of the Rocky Mountains. From early June through late September the cruise includes a 30 minute stop at Goat Haunt in Montana; passengers also may stay at Goat Haunt for day-long hiking trips and return on a later boat. A shuttle to Crypt Landing, where hikers are picked up or dropped off, also is available July through August.

Sightseeing trips landing at Goat Haunt depart daily at 10, 1 and 4, early June-late Sept. (also at 7 p.m. July-Aug.). Non-landing sightseeing trips depart daily at 10 and 2:30, early May-early June and late Sept.-second Mon. in Oct. Crypt Landing shuttle trips depart daily at 9 and 10, July-Aug.

DID YOU KNOW

There are more than 400 campgrounds in Alberta.

Sightseeing trip $30; $14 (ages 13-17); $10 (ages 4-12). Crypt Landing shuttle $14; $7 (ages 4-12). Phone (403) 859-2362.

RECREATIONAL ACTIVITIES

Horseback Riding

• **Alpine Stables** is in Waterton Lakes National Park of Canada, following signs. Write P.O. Box 53, Waterton Lakes National Park of Canada, AB, Canada T0K 2M0. Daily 9-5, July-Aug.; 10-5, May-Sept. Hours may vary; phone ahead. Phone (403) 859-2462, or (403) 653-2449 off-season.

WETASKIWIN (F-6) pop. 11,673

Wetaskiwin got its name from a Cree phrase meaning "the hills where peace was made." It is believed that a peace agreement between the warring Cree and Blackfoot tribes was made in the area. A stop between the growing outposts of Calgary and Edmonton, Wetaskiwin flourished due to its proximity to the Canadian Pacific Railway; the city was incorporated in 1906. Today Wetaskiwin boasts progressive commercial, agricultural and industrial ties, while a restored downtown area highlights the community's historic roots.

Wetaskiwin City Hall: 4705 50th Ave., P.O. Box 6210, Wetaskiwin, AB, Canada T9A 2E9; phone (780) 361-4417.

REYNOLDS-ALBERTA MUSEUM is 2 km (1.2 mi.) w. on Hwy. 13. Displays interpret the history of ground and air transportation, agriculture and industry in Alberta. Audiovisual presentations, displays and demonstrations supplement the actual operation of vintage automobiles, bicycles, and farm and industrial machinery. One area features a reproduction of a small drive-in theater, complete with old films, metal speakers and seats shaped like the back end of 1950-era automobiles.

The museum also is home to Canada's Aviation Hall of Fame in a separate exhibit building. Vintage aircraft are displayed. Canadians who have contributed significantly to aviation history are recognized.

Food is available. Allow 2 hours minimum. Daily 10-6, July 1-Labour Day; Tues.-Sun. and Mon. holidays 10-5, rest of year. Closed Jan. 1 and Dec. 24-25. Admission $9; $7 (ages 65+); $5 (ages 7-17); $25 (family, two adults and children). MC, VI. Phone (780) 361-1351 or (800) 661-4726.

WOOD BUFFALO NATIONAL PARK OF CANADA—

see Northwest Territories and Nunavut p. 249.

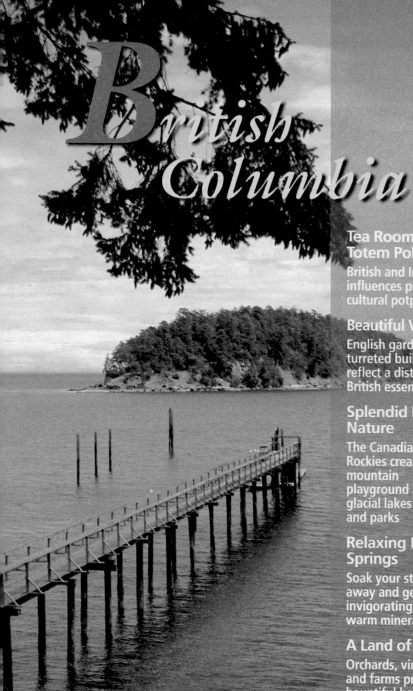

British Columbia

Tea Rooms & Totem Poles

British and Indian influences profile a cultural potpourri

Beautiful Victoria

English gardens and turreted buildings reflect a distinctive British essence

Splendid by Nature

The Canadian Rockies create a mountain playground amid glacial lakes and parks

Relaxing Hot Springs

Soak your stresses away and get an invigorating rush in warm mineral baths

A Land of Plenty

Orchards, vineyards and farms produce bountiful harvests

Mayne Island, Gulf
Islands National Park
Reserve of Canada
© Michael J. Hipple
age fotostock

"a perfect Eden"

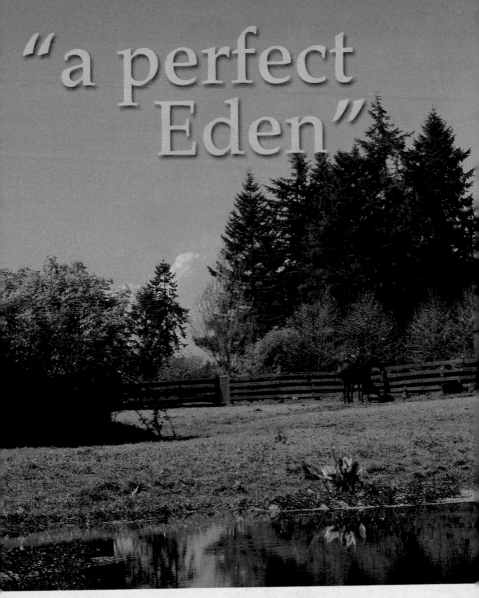

Near Fort Langley / © Eero Sorila

Sailing along Vancouver Island's untamed coast in 1842, James Douglas visited the site of present-day Victoria and reported: "The place itself appears a perfect Eden... one might be pardoned for supposing it had been dropped from the clouds..."

Prophetic words considering that Douglas, who later became colonial governor of British Columbia, was describing the "Garden City" many years before its first flower beds were planted.

Today, Edenic gardens are the province's forte: From Victoria's renowned, blossom-loaded Butchart Gardens to lush Queen Elizabeth Park atop the city of Vancouver's tallest hill, horticultural delights are everywhere.

And if a single apple was enough to tempt Adam and Eve, then they would no doubt have found BC's fertile Okanagan Valley irresistible. Not only do orchards here produce more than a third of Canada's apples, the valley also lures vacationers with sunny weather, sandy lakefront beaches and picturesque rolling hills striped by orderly rows of grapevines.

According to legend, Okanagan Lake even harbors a serpentlike monster called Ogopogo, although unlike the biblical serpent, this elusive beast seems quite shy.

If you were searching for the Garden of Eden on Earth, British Columbia wouldn't be a bad place to start.

"Once upon a time. . ."

For generations, parents have used these four words to introduce children to the fantastic, magic-filled realms of fairy tales. Say them, and a spell is cast, transforming restless young ones into an attentive audience eagerly awaiting a story. Maybe you remember feeling such anticipation yourself.

If not, then a trip to British Columbia might just help recapture that youthful expectation of adventure. Though far removed from the Old World settings popularized in the works of Hans Christian Andersen and the Brothers Grimm, this far western province—with its daunting, snowcapped mountains and mist-filled rain forests—seems to have sprung from the pages of a storybook.

Into the Woods

Walk among centuries-old Douglas firs in MacMillan Provincial Park's Cathedral Grove and it's easy to imagine bumping into Little Red Riding Hood on her way to grandmother's house. Not only will these giants make you feel child-size by comparison; the perpetual twilight created by their lofty, intertwining branches can play tricks on your eyes, too. Look up at the high, dim ceiling of needle-heavy boughs arching overhead, and you'll understand how this grove got its name. Logging may have taken its toll on British Columbia's old-growth forests, but many stands continue to thrive in such havens as Pacific Rim National Park Reserve of Canada and Strathcona Provincial Park, both on Vancouver Island.

Another of these sylvan sanctuaries is in the city of Vancouver's Stanley Park. This urban wilderness embraces an evergreen woodland so extensive that while wandering its paths you might forget you're in the heart of Canada's third largest city. A miniature railway, children's petting zoo and the Vancouver Aquarium make this park a great Sunday getaway for families—and a perfect backdrop for storytelling.

Some of the most interesting tales told in Stanley Park are silently portrayed by stylized figures carved into totem poles. A thicket of these cedar columns loom at the park's eastern edge, and each one communicates its own story, whether it be a family history, a notable event or an age-old myth. Travel along the mainland coast or among British Columbia's offshore islands and you'll find more outstanding examples carved by the Bella Coola,

The Queen Charlotte Islands are occupied by Haida Indians.

© Dewitt Jones/Corbis

1750

George Vancouver, an English explorer, surveys the British Columbian coast.

1792

Spanish explorers first sight the coast of Vancouver Island.

1774

© Bettmann/Corbis

Vancouver Island becomes a crown colony.

1849

1786
The British establish profitable fur trade with local Indians.

British Columbia Historical Timeline

1820
The powerful Hudson's Bay Co. controls fur trading in the Pacific Northwest.

Haida, Kwakwaka'wakw, Nootka, Salish, Tlingit and Tsimshian peoples.

Symbolizing strength and authority, the bears glaring down from totem poles may not be the only ones you see in British Columbia: Grizzlies are common within Mount Revelstoke and Glacier national parks. Part of the Columbia Mountains, the terrain here consists of narrow, steep-walled valleys that fill with snow in winter to create icebound Shangri-Las.

Not far away, in the Canadian Rockies, Kootenay National Park of Canada preserves land that seems equally imbued with magic. At the park's southern end are the Radium Hot Springs, which bubble forth hot, mineral-tinged water no matter what time of year it is.

Enchanted Gardens

On the other hand, changing seasons mean a world of difference at Victoria's flower-crowded Butchart Gardens. As some plants bloom, others fade, producing a dramatic shift in hues seemingly conjured by a wizard's wand. Meandering paths thread among blossoming trees and shrubs, past softly splashing fountains and around countless flower beds in this rainbow-saturated wonderland. Rhododendrons and azaleas enjoy the limelight in spring and early summer; roses steal the show in late June.

Across the Straits of Georgia, Vancouver's VanDusen Botanical Garden is similarly endowed with floral color. Careful tending has transfigured this former golf course into a city showplace of lakes, streams, hedge mazes and whimsical topiary figures.

And what childhood fantasy would be complete without a castle? Victoria boasts two. Turrets, columns and rough sandstone walls lend 19th-century Craigdarroch Castle a medieval air that greatly pleased its builder, Robert Dunsmuir, a wealthy Scottish immigrant and industrialist. Hatley Castle, on the Royal Roads University campus, looks even more like a genuine fortress from the Middle Ages. Topped by battlements, this imposing mansion would be at home in a European fable.

To anyone who has ever been mesmerized by fanciful storybook illustrations, British Columbia should seem delightfully familiar.

Gold is discovered in the Fraser River Valley.
1858
© Gunter Marx/Corbis

The Nisga'a Treaty, British Columbia's first since 1899, ends 20 years of negotiations with the Nisga'a people over land, resources and self-government.
1998

A transcontinental railroad links British Columbia with eastern Canada.
1885

1871
British Columbia becomes the fifth province of the Dominion of Canada.

1986
Vancouver celebrates its centennial with a world's fair, Expo '86.
© Corbis

Recreation

The Rocky Mountain and Cascade ranges, a lush valley, and a system of rivers, lakes and protected ocean waterways are the hallmarks of British Columbia's natural beauty and the sources of unlimited recreational possibilities.

Summer Sojourns

Extended **canoeing** trips await you on the Outside Trail, a chain of lakes in the Kootenay region's Champion Lakes Provincial Park. The coastal area's 57-kilometre (35-mi.) Powell Forest Canoe Route, eight lakes connected by portage routes, begins on Lois Lake and ends at the marina on Powell Lake.

The 116-kilometre (72-mi.) canoeing and **kayaking** circuit (plus portage routes) in Bowron Lake Provincial Park is so popular that reservations are required and daily access is limited to 25 boats. Paddling through this unspoiled wildlife sanctuary could take up to 7 days, depending on the weather or how much time you spend gawking at bears, deer, moose, mountain goats or the beautiful Cariboo Mountains. Approach the park from Wells, which is just north of Barkerville Historic Town. For more information contact BC Parks Cariboo District in Williams Lake; phone (250) 398-4530.

In addition to spectacular mountain scenery, canoeists will find calm, turquoise-colored glacial lakes nestled in the snowcapped Rockies; two of these—O'Hara and the aptly named Emerald—are in Yoho National Park of Canada.

If rushing water is more your speed, try negotiating the Thompson and Fraser rivers. They converge near Lytton, said to be the **white-water rafting** capital of Canada; outfitters and guide services are plentiful. The Chilko and Chilcotin tributaries of the Fraser River, which lie west of Williams Lake, also have a reputation for adventure.

Every region has a network of **hiking** trails that will bring you up close and personal with British Columbia's natural wonders. One of the best coastal hikes is in Pacific Rim National Park Reserve of Canada, on Vancouver Island. The Long Beach Unit, accessed off Hwy. 4 near Ucluelet, offers eight moderately challenging hiking venues ranging from beaches to rain forests. The park's pride and joy—the rugged West Coast Trail—follows the shoreline from Port Renfrew to Bamfield. Only experienced hikers need apply for reservations, which are restricted to 50 per day during the season, May through September.

But that's just the tip of the iceberg when it comes to trekking around the province. Five national and nearly 650 provincial parks and recreation areas are your gateways to discovery.

Take the family **swimming, water skiing** or **windsurfing** inland at one of seven provincial beach parks on Okanagan Lake, or to Osoyoos Lake, the warmest in the province; both are in the desertlike Okanagan Valley.

The valley's climate and terrain invite other types of activities. The Kettle Valley Railway bed, west of Penticton, provides easy **mountain biking**, while tougher trails cross nearby Campbell Mountain and Ellis Ridge.

World-class Wintering

The **skiing** amenities at Whistler and Blackcomb mountains, north of Vancouver, are world renowned. Some 32 high-speed lifts, 200 trails and 12 alpine bowls—all on more than 2,800 hectares (7,000 acres)—make up one of the largest ski resorts in North America. **Snowboarding** and skiing lessons keep the children happy. Off the slopes, adults have unlimited après ski options in Whistler Village's eclectic mix of pubs, dance clubs and culinary nightspots; shops, spas and art galleries also are tucked in the hamlet. Bonus conveniences at the resort include several ski-in/ski-out lodgings.

Gentle slopes and rolling hills in the Okanagan Valley are ideal for snowboarding and **cross-country skiing.** Resorts and community ski areas near the towns of Osoyoos, Oliver, Penticton, Westbank and Kelowna, along the Hwy. 97 corridor, have quite a following; most offer night skiing, too. Some of western Canada's best cross-country skiing is farther north on Hwy. 97, stretching from 100 Mile House to Quesnel and lying west of the Cariboo Mountains. The area is laced with dozens of marked, groomed trails as well as wilderness paths.

Recreational Activities

Throughout the TourBook, you may notice a Recreational Activities heading with bulleted listings of recreation-oriented establishments listed underneath. Similar operations also may be mentioned in Destination City recreation sections. Since normal AAA inspection criteria cannot be applied, these establishments are presented only for information. Age, height and weight restrictions may apply. Reservations often are recommended and sometimes are required. Addresses and/or phone numbers are provided so visitors can contact the attraction for additional information.

Fast Facts

POPULATION: 3,907,738.

AREA: 944,735 sq km (364,762 sq mi); ranks 5th.

CAPITAL: Victoria.

HIGHEST POINT: 4,663 m/15,295 ft., Mount Fairweather.

LOWEST POINT: Sea level, Pacific Ocean.

TIME ZONE(S): Mountain/Pacific. DST in portions of the province.

MINIMUM AGE FOR UNRESTRICTED DRIVER'S LICENSE: 19.

SEAT BELT/CHILD RESTRAINT LAWS: Seat belts required for driver and all passengers ages 15 and older. Children ages 6 through 14, and over 18 kg (40 pounds), are required to be in a child restraint or seat belt; child restraints are required for under 18 kg.

HELMETS FOR MOTORCYCLISTS: Required for all riders.

RADAR DETECTORS: Permitted.

FIREARMS LAWS: By federal law, all nonresidents entering Canada with a firearm must declare their weapon in writing and pay a fee of $25 (Canadian). Contact the Canadian Firearms Centre at (800) 731-4000 to receive a declaration form or for additional information.

HOLIDAYS: Jan. 1; Easter Monday; Victoria Day, May 24 (if a Mon.) or closest prior Mon.; Canada Day, July 1; British Columbia Day, Aug. (1st Mon.); Labour Day, Sept. (1st Mon.); Thanksgiving, Oct. (2nd Mon.); Remembrance Day, Nov. 11; Christmas, Dec. 25; Boxing Day, Dec. 26.

TAXES: British Columbia's provincial sales tax is 7 percent. There also is a provincial room tax of 8 percent to 10 percent on lodgings. A 6 percent Goods and Services Tax (GST) also is levied.

INFORMATION CENTERS: British Columbia has more than 110 visitor information centers throughout the province. Of these more than 80 are open all year and can be found in all major cities including Victoria and Vancouver. The smaller community travel information centers are open June through August. For further information phone Hello BC at (800) 435-5622.

FURTHER INFORMATION FOR VISITORS:

1-800-HELLO BC
200 Burrard St.,
    Plaza Level
Vancouver, BC, Canada
    V6C 3L6
(250) 387-1642
(604) 435-5622 (in
    Greater Vancouver)
(800) 435-5622

RECREATION INFORMATION:

BC Parks
P.O. Box 9398, Stn.
    Prov. Gov't.
Victoria, BC, Canada
    V8W 9M9
(604) 689-9025
(camping reservations in Greater Vancouver) (800) 689-9025 (camping reservations)

FISHING AND HUNTING REGULATIONS:

Ministry of Environment Fish and
    Wildlife Branch
P.O. Box 9391, Stn. Prov. Gov't.
Victoria, BC, Canada V8W 9M8
(250) 387-9771

ALCOHOL CONSUMPTION: Legal age 19.

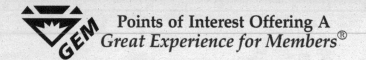

Barkerville Historic Town (F-5)

BARKERVILLE HISTORIC TOWN—The restored 1870s gold rush town features 125 original and reconstructed buildings, such as the Barkerville Hotel and the Wake Up Jake Cafe. See p. 114.

Boston Bar (C-7)

HELL'S GATE AIRTRAM—Descending into the narrowest part of Fraser Canyon, the tram travels a route that lets visitors view fishways, a suspension footbridge and a film about salmon. See p. 114.

Brentwood Bay (H-10)

BUTCHART GARDENS—Among the gardens' most interesting features are the diversity of seasonal flowers, fountains and a sunken garden created on the site of a depleted limestone quarry. See p. 194.

VICTORIA BUTTERFLY GARDENS—Visitors learn about and interact with up to 2,000 exotic free-flying butterflies in this tropical rain forest environment. See p. 194.

Cache Creek (B-7)

HISTORIC HAT CREEK RANCH—Established in 1861, the roadhouse provided food, lodging and supplies to thousands of miners and settlers headed north on the Cariboo Waggon Road. See p. 115.

Chilliwack (H-12)

MINTER GARDENS—At the base of the Coastal Mountain Range, the 11 thematic gardens of the 11-hectare (27-acre) site bloom in bursts of seasonal color. See p. 117.

Fort St. James (E-4)

FORT ST. JAMES NATIONAL HISTORIC SITE OF CANADA—Reconstructed and restored buildings—including the officers' dwelling, fish cache and chicken yard—comprise the former Hudson's Bay Co. trading post. See p. 122.

Fort Steele (C-12)

FORT STEELE HERITAGE TOWN—An operating bakery, restaurant and newspaper office are among the buildings in this representation of a typical 1890-1905 East Kootenay town. See p. 122.

Hudson's Hope (D-4)

PEACE CANYON DAM—At the outlet of Peace River Canyon, the dam uses water that generated electricity at a dam upstream. See p. 128.

W.A.C. BENNETT DAM—Built to produce electrical power for British Columbia, the dam produces a backup that forms the province's largest lake. See p. 128.

Kootenay National Park of Canada (B-12)

KOOTENAY NATIONAL PARK OF CANADA—Extensive faults are responsible for two of the park's significant features: Radium Hot Springs and the Paint Pots. See p. 131.

North Vancouver (G-11)

CAPILANO SUSPENSION BRIDGE—Fear of heights won't keep visitors away from the park's perennial gardens, rain forest, totem park, First Nations carvers and dancers, and the Treetops Adventure. See p. 177.

GROUSE MOUNTAIN—Look down on the town from this recreationally rich gathering spot where activities range from sleigh riding to paragliding. See p. 177.

Pacific Rim National Park Reserve of Canada (I-3)

PACIFIC RIM NATIONAL PARK RESERVE OF CANADA—Sandy beaches, rocky headlands, temperate rain forests and an island archipelago make up this spectacular park on Vancouver's West Coast. See p. 147.

Port Alberni (F-10)

McLEAN MILL NATIONAL HISTORIC SITE—A 1929 steam locomotive transports visitors to this 13-hectare (32-acre) site, which commemorates the early days of British Columbia's logging industry. See p. 148.

Qualicum Beach (F-10)

HORNE LAKE CAVERNS—Guided tours lead visitors underground as they discover the beauty of caves. See p. 151.

Richmond (H-11)

GULF OF GEORGIA CANNERY NATIONAL HISTORIC SITE—Canada's West Coast fishing industry is documented through films, equipment demonstrations and interactive exhibits. See p. 178.

Valemount (F-5)

MOUNT ROBSON PROVINCIAL PARK—Home to the highest peak in the Canadian Rockies, the 224,866-hectare (555,656-acre) park features an abundance of wildlife, scenic views and outdoor activities. See p. 157.

Vancouver (I-4)

H.R. MacMILLAN SPACE CENTRE—Children have fun learning about everything that's space-related. See p. 165

SCIENCE WORLD AT TELUS WORLD OF SCIENCE—Interactive exhibits and demonstrations explain scientific phenomena. See p. 166.

STANLEY PARK—Among the park's highlights are a miniature steam railway, a farmyard for children and totem pole displays. See p. 167.

VANCOUVER AQUARIUM MARINE SCIENCE CENTRE—Aquarium exhibits let visitors learn about endangered species, frogs, beluga whales, sea lions and sea otters. See p. 167.

VANDUSEN BOTANICAL GARDEN—From inside the intricate gardens—set amid lakes, lawns and rock displays—visitors can gaze out upon the mountains and the city. See p. 169.

Victoria (I-4)

CRAIGDARROCH CASTLE—Built 1887-89, this coal baron's 39-room castle contains fine Victorian appointments; a turret leads to a panoramic view of Victoria, the Strait and the Olympic Mountains. See p. 187.

MINIATURE WORLD—Animation, lights and sound bring to life highly detailed miniature scenes that reflect fairy tales, nursery rhymes, historic battles and classic novels. See p. 189.

ROYAL BC MUSEUM—Two floors of displays let visitors explore a frontier town, a coastal rain forest, the First Peoples Gallery and Haida argillite carvings. See p. 189.

ROYAL LONDON WAX MUSEUM—Featured are some 300 wax figures ranging from political and religious leaders to royalty and movie stars. See p. 191.

Yoho National Park of Canada (A-11)

YOHO NATIONAL PARK OF CANADA—Takakkaw Falls, one of the highest falls in Canada, is but one natural wonder that explains how the park got the name *yoho,* an exclamation of astonishment in the Cree Indian language. See p. 198.

RECREATION AREAS

RECREATION AREAS	MAP LOCATION	CAMPING	PICNICKING	HIKING TRAILS	BOATING	BOAT RAMP	BOAT RENTAL	FISHING	SWIMMING	PETS ON LEASH	BICYCLE TRAILS	WINTER SPORTS	VISITOR CENTER	LODGE/CABINS	FOOD SERVICE
NATIONAL PARKS *(See place listings)*															
Glacier (A-10) 1,350 square kilometres.		•	•	•				•		•		•	•	•	•
Gulf Islands (H-10) 33 square kilometres. Golf, kayaking, scuba diving. Recreational activities vary on each island.		•	•	•	•		•	•	•						
Gwaii Haanas (F-1) 1,495 square kilometres. Kayaking.					•								•		
Kootenay (B-12) 1,406 square kilometres.		•	•	•				•	•	•		•	•	•	•
Mount Revelstoke (A-10) 260 square kilometres.		•	•	•				•	•	•		•	•	•	
Pacific Rim (I-3) 510 square kilometres.		•	•	•	•			•	•	•			•		
Yoho (A-11) 1,313 square kilometres. Cross-country skiing; horse rental.		•	•	•	•		•	•	•	•		•	•	•	•
PROVINCIAL															
Adams Lake (B-9) 56 hectares 30 km n. of Chase off Hwy. 1. Archeological sites. Canoeing, scuba diving, water skiing, windsurfing.	**1**	•						•	•	•					
Alice Lake (G-12) 396 hectares 13 km n. of Squamish on Hwy. 99. Canoeing.	**2**	•	•	•				•	•	•	•				
Allison Lake (C-8) 23 hectares 28 km n. of Princeton on Hwy. 5A.	**3**	•						•	•	•					
Arrow Lakes (Shelter Bay) (B-10) 93 hectares on Hwy. 23. *(See Castlegar p. 116)*	**4**	•	•		•			•	•	•					
Babine Lake-Pendleton Bay Marine (E-3) 37 hectares 45 km n. of Burns Lake off Hwy. 16.	**5**	•			•	•		•	•						
Bamberton (H-10) 28 hectares 45 km n. of Victoria off Hwy. 1.	**6**	•	•	•				•	•	•					
Bear Creek (C-9) 178 hectares 9 km n. off Hwy. 97 west of Kelowna.	**7**	•	•	•		•	•	•	•	•					
Beaumont (E-4) 192 hectares, 134 km w. of Prince George.	**8**	•	•	•	•	•		•	•	•					
Big Bar Lake (A-7) 332 hectares 42 km n. of Clinton off Hwy. 97.	**9**	•	•	•	•			•	•	•					
Birkenhead Lake (G-5) 9,755 hectares 56 km n.e. of Pemberton. Cross-country skiing, windsurfing.	**10**	•		•	•			•	•	•		•			
Blanket Creek (B-10) 318 hectares 25 km s. of Revelstoke on Hwy. 23.	**11**	•						•	•	•					
Bowron Lake (F-5) 149,207 hectares 112.5 km e. of Quesnel via a gravel access road off Hwy. 26. Water circuit of connecting lakes.	**12**	•		•	•	•		•	•	•			•	•	
Boya Lake (B-3) 4,597 hectares 50 km n. of Dease Lake. Canoeing, kayaking.	**13**	•		•	•			•	•	•					
Bridge Lake (A-8) 11 hectares 51 km e. of 100 Mile House off Hwy. 24.	**14**	•	•			•		•							
Bromley Rock (C-8) 149 hectares 21 km e. of Princeton off Hwy. 3.	**15**	•	•					•	•						
Bull Canyon (F-4) 369 hectares 6 km w. of Alexis Creek off Hwy. 20.	**16**	•	•	•				•	•						
Canim Beach (A-8) 6 hectares on Canim Lake, 43 km n.e. of 100 Mile House off Hwy. 97. Canoeing, kayaking.	**17**		•	•	•			•	•	•					
Cape Scott (G-2) 22,294 hectares 64 km w. of Port Hardy. Canoeing, hunting, kayaking.	**18**	•		•				•	•	•					
Carp Lake (E-4) 38,149 hectares 32 km s.w. of McLeod Lake off Hwy. 97. Canoeing, hunting, ice fishing, kayaking.	**19**	•		•	•	•		•	•	•			•		
Cathedral (D-8) 33,272 hectares 24 km w. of Keremeos off Hwy. 3. Hunting, mountaineering.	**20**	•	•	•				•	•						
Cedar Point (F-5) 8 hectares 45 km n.e. of Williams Lake off Hwy. 97 on Quesnel Lake. Water skiing; mining displays.	**21**	•	•	•	•	•		•	•	•					•
Champion Lakes (D-10) 1,426 hectares 10 km s. of Castlegar off Hwy. 3B. Cross-country skiing. Power boats prohibited.	**22**	•	•	•	•	•		•	•	•	•	•			

RECREATION AREAS

	MAP LOCATION	CAMPING	PICNICKING	HIKING TRAILS	BOATING	BOAT RAMP	BOAT RENTAL	FISHING	SWIMMING	PETS ON LEASH	BICYCLE TRAILS	WINTER SPORTS	VISITOR CENTER	LODGE/CABINS	FOOD SERVICE
Charlie Lake (D-5) 85 hectares 11 km n. of Fort St. John off Hwy. 97.	23	•	•	•	•	•		•	•	•	•				
Chilliwack Lake (D-7) 9,528 hectares 64 km s.e. of Chilliwack via an access road off Hwy. 1. Hunting, water skiing.	24	•	•	•	•	•		•	•	•					
Cinnemousun Narrows (B-9) 176 hectares 22.5 km n. of Sicamous via boat. Scuba diving, water skiing, windsurfing.	25	•	•	•	•	•		•	•	•				•	
Conkle Lake (D-9) 587 hectares 28 km n.e. of Osoyoos via Hwy. 3, then 26 km to entrance. Windsurfing.	26	•	•	•	•	•		•	•	•			•		
Crooked River (E-5) 970 hectares 70 km n. of Prince George on Hwy. 97. Cross-country skiing, ice fishing, windsurfing. Power boats prohibited.	27	•	•	•	•			•	•	•					
Cultus Lake (I-11) 2,561 hectares 11 km s.w. of Chilliwack off Hwy. 1. Water skiing. *(See Cultus Lake p. 119)*	28	•	•	•	•	•	•	•	•	•					
Cypress (G-11) 3,012 hectares n. of Vancouver off hwys. 1 and 99. Cross-country and downhill skiing, primitive camping. *(See West Vancouver p. 180)*	29	•	•	•						•		•	•		
Dionisio Point (H-10) 142 hectares on Galiano Island via car ferry. Scuba diving. *(See Galiano Island p. 125)*	30	•	•	•	•			•	•	•					
Downing (A-7) 100 hectares 18 km s.w. of Clinton off Hwy. 97.	31	•	•	•	•			•	•						
E.C. Manning (D-8) 70,844 hectares on Hwy. 3 between Hope and Princeton. Scenic. Cross-country and downhill skiing, mountain biking, snowshoeing; canoe, kayak and horse rentals. *(See Hope p. 127)*	32	•	•	•	•	•	•	•	•	•	•	•	•	•	•
Elk Falls (E-10) 1,087 hectares 3 km n.w. of Campbell River off Hwy. 28. *(See Campbell River p. 115)*	33	•	•	•				•	•	•	•	•	•		
Ellison (B-9) 200 hectares on Okanagan Lake, 16 km s.w. of Vernon off Hwy. 97. Rock climbing.	34	•	•	•	•			•	•	•					
Emory Creek (C-7) 15 hectares 18 km n. of Hope on Hwy 1.	35	•						•	•	•					
Englishman River Falls (G-10) 97 hectares 13 km s.w. of Parksville off Hwy. 4.	36	•	•	•				•	•	•					
Fillongley (F-10) 23 hectares on Denman Island via ferry from Buckley Bay. Canoeing, kayaking.	37	•	•	•				•	•	•					
Fintry (C-9) 361 hectares 34 km n. of Kelowna off Hwy. 97. Hunting, scuba diving, water skiing.	38	•	•	•	•			•	•	•				•	
French Beach (H-9) 59 hectares 20 km w. of Sooke off Hwy. 14. Windsurfing.	39	•	•	•				•	•	•					
Garibaldi (G-12) 194,650 hectares accessible by five trails from Hwy. 99. Cross-country skiing. *(See Squamish p. 155)*	40			•				•	•		•	•	•		
Gladstone (D-10) 39,387 hectares 5 km e. of Christina Lake on Hwy. 3. Hunting, scuba diving, water skiing.	41	•	•	•	•			•	•	•					
Golden Ears (H-11) 62,540 hectares 11 km n. of Maple Ridge off Hwy. 7. Water skiing, windsurfing. Horse rental.	42	•	•	•	•			•	•	•	•		•		
Goldpan (B-7) 5 hectares 10 km s. of Spences Bridge adjacent to Hwy. 1 on the east bank of the Thompson River. Canoeing, kayaking.	43	•	•					•		•					
Goldstream (H-10) 477 hectares 16 km n.w. of Victoria via Hwy. 1. Salmon spawning in fall.	44	•	•	•				•	•	•			•	•	
Gordon Bay (G-10) 51 hectares 14 km w. of Lake Cowichan off Hwy. 18. Freshwater diving, water skiing, windsurfing.	45	•	•	•	•			•	•	•					
Green Lake (A-8) 347 hectares 16 km n.e. of Hwy. 97 at 70 Mile House.	46	•	•		•	•		•	•	•					
Gwillim Lake (E-5) 32,458 hectares 56 km. s.e. of Chetwynd on Hwy. 29. Canoeing, kayaking, rock climbing, scuba diving, water skiing, windsurfing.	47	•	•	•	•			•	•	•			•		
Haynes Point (D-9) 38 hectares 2 km s. of Osoyoos on Hwy. 97. Water skiing.	48	•	•	•	•	•	•	•	•	•					
Herald (B-9) 79 hectares 14 km e. of Tappen off Hwy. 1. Scuba diving, water skiing, windsurfing.	49	•	•	•	•	•		•	•	•					

RECREATION AREAS

RECREATION AREAS	MAP LOCATION	CAMPING	PICNICKING	HIKING TRAILS	BOATING	BOAT RAMP	BOAT RENTAL	FISHING	SWIMMING	PETS ON LEASH	BICYCLE TRAILS	WINTER SPORTS	VISITOR CENTER	LODGE/CABINS	FOOD SERVICE
Horsefly Lake (F-5) 148 hectares 65 km e. of 150 Mile House off Hwy. 97. Water skiing.	50	•	•	•	•	•	•	•	•	•					
Inkaneep (D-9) 21 hectares 6 km n. of Oliver on Hwy. 97.	51	•						•		•					
Inland Lake (E-11) 2,763 hectares 12 km n. of Powell River on Inland Lake Rd. Canoeing, kayaking. *(See Powell River p. 149)*	52	•	•	•	•	•		•	•	•			•	•	
Jedediah Island Marine (F-10) 243 hectares between Lasqueti and Texada islands in the Sabine Channel of the Strait of Georgia. Accessible only via boat from Lasqueti Island. Kayaking, primitive camping; sandy bays.	53	•						•	•	•					
Jimsmith Lake (C-11) 14 hectares 5 km w. of Cranbrook off Hwy. 3.	54	•	•	•	•			•	•	•					
Juniper Beach (B-8) 260 hectares 19 km e. of Cache Creek on Hwy. 1.	55	•	•	•				•	•	•					
Kalamalka Lake (C-9) 978 hectares 8 km s. of Vernon off Hwy. 6. Canoeing and kayaking, cross-country skiing, horseback riding, water skiing, wildlife viewing.	56		•	•				•	•	•	•	•			
Kentucky Alleyne (C-8) 144 hectares 38 km s. of Merritt on Hwy. 5A.	57	•			•			•	•	•					
Kettle River (D-9) 179 hectares 5 km n. of Rock Creek on Hwy. 33. Cross-country skiing, snowshoeing.	58	•	•	•				•	•	•		•			
Kikomun Creek (D-12) 682 hectares 64 km s.e. of Cranbrook via Hwy. 3, then 11 km s. to entrance. Canoeing.	59	•	•	•	•	•		•	•	•					
Kilby (C-7) 3 hectares 2 km e. of Harrison Mills on Hwy. 7. Historic. Water skiing.	60	•	•		•	•		•	•	•					
Kinaskan Lake (C-2) 1,800 hectares on Hwy. 37 at Kinaskan Lake.	61	•	•	•	•			•	•	•					
Kleanza Creek (E-3) 269 hectares 15 km e. of Terrace on Hwy. 16. Snowshoeing.	62	•	•	•				•		•			•		
Kokanee Creek (C-11) 260 hectares 19 km e. of Nelson on Hwy. 3A. Cross-country skiing, snowshoeing, water skiing, windsurfing.	63	•	•	•	•			•	•	•			•		
Kokanee Glacier (C-10) 32,035 hectares 19 km n.e. of Nelson on Hwy. 3A. Back- and cross-country skiing, snowshoeing.	64	•	•	•				•					•	•	
Kootenay Lake (Davis Creek/Lost Ledge) (C-11) 343 hectares near Kaslo on Hwy. 31. Water skiing, windsurfing.	65	•	•	•	•	•		•	•	•					
Lac La Hache (G-5) 24 hectares 13 km n. of Lac la Hache on Hwy. 97. Water skiing.	66	•	•	•	•			•	•	•					
Lac Le Jeune (B-8) 213 hectares 37 km s. of Kamloops off Hwy. 5. Nature programs. Cross-country skiing, ice fishing, snowshoeing; canoe rental, playground.	67	•	•	•	•	•	•	•	•	•		•	•	•	•
Lakelse Lake (E-2) 354 hectares 20 km s. of Terrace on Hwy. 37. Canoeing, water skiing, windsurfing.	68	•	•	•	•	•		•	•	•					
Liard River Hot Springs (B-4) 1,082 hectares at Liard River at Km-post 765 on Hwy. 97 (Alaska Hwy.). Playground.	69	•	•	•					•	•					
Little Andrews Bay (E-3) 45 hectares 60 km w. of Hwy. 35, s. of Burns Lake on Oosta Lake.	70	•			•	•		•	•	•					
Little Qualicum Falls (F-10) 440 hectares 19 km w. of Parksville off Hwy. 4. Canoeing, kayaking, scuba diving, water skiing, windsurfing.	71	•	•	•				•	•	•					
Lockhart Beach (C-11) 3 hectares 40 km n. of Creston on Hwy. 3A.	72	•	•	•				•	•	•					
Loveland Bay (E-10) 30 hectares 18 km w. of Campbell River off Hwy. 28.	73	•			•	•		•	•	•					
Mabel Lake (B-9) 187 hectares 60 km n.e. of Vernon via an access road off Hwy. 6.	74	•	•	•	•	•		•	•	•					
Marble Canyon (B-7) 355 hectares 40 km n.w. of Cache Creek off Hwy. 99. Rock climbing.	75	•	•	•				•	•	•					

RECREATION AREAS	MAP LOCATION	CAMPING	PICNICKING	HIKING TRAILS	BOATING	BOAT RAMP	BOAT RENTAL	FISHING	SWIMMING	PETS ON LEASH	BICYCLE TRAILS	WINTER SPORTS	VISITOR CENTER	LODGE/CABINS	FOOD SERVICE
Martha Creek (A-10) 71 hectares 20 km n. of Revelstoke on Hwy. 23. Canoeing, kayaking.	76	•	•	•	•	•		•	•	•					
McConnell Lake (B-8) 102 hectares 35 km s. of Kamloops off Hwy. 5. Canoeing, cross-country skiing, kayaking, ice fishing, snowshoeing.	77		•	•	•	•		•	•	•		•			
Meziadin Lake (D-2) 335 hectares 50 km e. of Stewart off Hwy. 37.	78	•	•		•	•		•	•	•					
Miracle Beach (E-10) 137 hectares 22.5 km n. of Courtenay off Hwy. 19.	79	•	•	•				•	•	•					•
Moberly Lake (D-5) 104 hectares 25 km n.w. of Chetwynd on Hwy. 29.	80	•	•	•	•	•		•	•	•					
Monck (C-8) 92 hectares 22 km n. of Merritt off Hwy. 5A. Water skiing, windsurfing.	81	•	•	•	•	•		•	•	•	•				
Montague Harbour Marine (H-10) 97 hectares 48 km n. of Victoria on Galiano Island via car ferry. (See Galiano Island p. 125)	82	•	•	•	•	•		•	•	•					
Morton Lake (E-10) 74 hectares 27 km n.w. of Campbell River on Hwy. 19.	83	•	•	•	•			•	•	•					
Mount Fernie (C-12) 259 hectares 3 km w. of Fernie on Hwy. 3. (See Fernie p. 120)	84	•	•	•				•		•					
Mount Robson (F-6) 224,866 hectares bordering Jasper National Park of Canada on Hwy. 16. Spelunking; horse rental. (See Valemount p. 157)	85	•	•	•	•	•		•	•	•			•	•	•
Mount Seymour (H-12) 3,508 hectares 15 km n.e. of Vancouver off Hwy. 1. Cross-country skiing. (See Vancouver p. 177)	86	•	•	•				•	•	•	•	•	•		
Moyie Lake (C-11) 91 hectares 20 km s. of Cranbrook on Hwy. 3. Canoeing, kayaking, windsurfing; playground.	87	•	•	•	•	•		•	•	•					
Muncho Lake (B-4) 86,079 hectares on Hwy. 97 at Muncho Lake. Canoeing, kayaking, scuba diving, water skiing.	88	•	•	•	•	•		•	•	•				•	
Naikoon (E-1) 69,166 hectares on n. tip of Graham Island in the Queen Charlotte Islands. (See Queen Charlotte Islands p. 152)	89			•				•	•	•					
Nairn Falls (F-12) 170 hectares 4 km s. of Pemberton on Hwy. 99.	90	•	•	•				•		•					
Nancy Greene (D-10) 203 hectares 29 km n.w. of Rossland via Hwy. 3B. Cross-country skiing, snowshoeing.	91	•	•	•				•	•	•		•			
Newcastle Island Marine (G-10) 336 hectares e. of Nanaimo via passenger ferry. (See Nanaimo p. 134)	92	•	•	•				•	•	•					•
Nicolum River (C-7) 24 hectares 8 km e. of Hope on Hwy. 3.	93	•	•					•		•					
Niskonlith Lake (B-9) 238 hectares 8 km n.w. of Chase off Hwy. 1. Cross-country skiing, ice fishing, scuba diving, snowshoeing, windsurfing.	94	•			•	•		•		•		•			
Norbury Lake (C-12) 97 hectares 16 km s. of jct. hwys. 93 and 95 at Fort Steele.	95	•	•	•				•	•	•					
North Thompson River (A-8) 126 hectares 5 km s. of Clearwater off Hwy. 5.	96	•	•	•				•	•	•					
Okanagan Lake (C-8) 98 hectares 28 km n.w. of Penticton off Hwy. 97. Water skiing, windsurfing.	97	•	•	•				•	•	•				•	•
Okanagan Mountain (C-9) 11,038 hectares 25 km n. of Penticton off Hwy. 97. Canoeing, kayaking, horseback riding, hunting, mountain biking, water skiing.	98	•	•	•				•	•	•		•		•	
One Island Lake (E-6) 59 hectares 30 km s. of Tupper off Hwy. 2. Canoeing, kayaking, scuba diving, water skiing, windsurfing; playground.	99	•	•		•	•		•	•	•					
Otter Lake (C-8) 51 hectares on Otter Lake, 33 km w. of Princeton off Hwy. 5A.	100	•	•	•				•	•	•					
Paarens Beach (E-4) 43 hectares 11 km s.w. of Fort St. James off Hwy. 27. Water skiing, windsurfing.	101	•	•	•	•	•		•	•	•					

RECREATION AREAS

	MAP LOCATION	CAMPING	PICNICKING	HIKING TRAILS	BOATING	BOAT RAMP	BOAT RENTAL	FISHING	SWIMMING	PETS ON LEASH	BICYCLE TRAILS	WINTER SPORTS	VISITOR CENTER	LODGE/CABINS	FOOD SERVICE
Paul Lake (B-8) 670 hectares 5 km n. of Kamloops off Hwy. 5.	102	●	●	●	●	●	●	●	●	●		●			
Pirates Cove Marine (G-10) 31 hectares 16 km s.e. of Nanaimo on DeCourcy Island via boat.	103	●	●	●	●			●	●	●					
Plumper Cove Marine (G-11) 66 hectares on Keats Island. Boat and ferry access only.	104	●	●	●	●			●	●	●	●				
Porpoise Bay (G-11) 61 hectares 4 km n. of Sechelt on East Porpoise Bay Rd.	105	●	●	●				●	●	●					
Porteau Cove (G-11) 50 hectares 38 km n. of Vancouver on Hwy. 99. Scuba diving.	106	●	●	●	●			●	●	●	●				
Premier Lake (C-12) 662 hectares 12 km s. of Skookumchuck via Hwy. 95.	107	●	●	●	●	●		●	●	●					
Prudhomme Lake (E-2) 7 hectares 16 km e. of Prince Rupert on Hwy. 16.	108	●		●				●	●						
Purden Lake (F-5) 2,521 hectares 64 km e. of Prince George off Hwy. 16. Water skiing.	109	●	●	●	●	●		●	●	●					
Rathtrevor Beach (G-10) 347 hectares 3 km s. of Parksville on Hwy. 19. Nature programs. Windsurfing; playground.	110	●	●	●				●	●	●					
Rebecca Spit Marine (E-10) 177 hectares on Quadra Island via ferry from Campbell River, then 5 km e. on Heriot Bay Rd. Scuba diving, windsurfing.	111		●	●	●			●	●	●					
Red Bluff (E-3) 148 hectares 45 km n. of Topley via Hwy. 118.	112	●	●	●	●			●	●	●					
Roberts Creek (G-11) 40 hectares 10 km w. of Gibsons Landing on Hwy. 101.	113	●	●					●	●	●					
Rolley Lake (H-12) 115 hectares 23 km n.w. of Mission off Hwy. 7.	114	●	●	●				●	●	●					
Ruckle (H-10) 486 hectares at Beaver Point on Salt Spring Island via ferry from Swartz Bay. Scuba diving, windsurfing. *(See Salt Spring Island p. 125)*	115	●	●	●				●		●					
Saltery Bay (F-11) 69 hectares 1 km n. of Saltery Bay ferry landing on Hwy. 101. Scuba diving.	116	●	●	●	●	●		●	●	●					
Sasquatch (D-7) 1,217 hectares 6.4 km n. of Harrison Hot Springs via an access road off Hwy. 7. Canoeing, water skiing, windsurfing; playground.	117	●	●	●	●	●	●	●	●	●					
Schoen Lake (H-3) 8,430 hectares 20 km n. of Sayward, 12 km s. of Hwy. 19.	118	●	●	●	●			●	●	●					
Seeley Lake (D-3) 24 hectares 10 km w. of Hazelton on Hwy. 16.	119	●	●	●				●	●	●					
Shuswap Lake (B-9) 149 hectares 19.25 km n. of Squilax. Nature programs. Canoeing, kayaking, snorkeling, water skiing, windsurfing; playground.	120	●	●	●	●	●		●	●	●		●	●		
Silver Beach (A-9) 130 hectares at n. end of Shuswap Lake at Seymour Arm.	121	●		●	●	●		●	●	●					
Skagit Valley (D-7) 27,948 hectares 8 km w. of Hope via Hwy. 1, then 43 km s. on Second Rd. Interpretive programs. Hunting; horse trails, playground.	122	●	●	●		●		●	●	●					
Skihist (B-7) 33 hectares 6 km e. of Lytton on Hwy. 1.	123	●	●	●				●		●	●				
Smelt Bay (E-10) 16 hectares on Cortes Island via ferry from Campbell River. Canoeing, kayaking.	124	●	●		●	●		●		●					
Sowchea Bay (E-4) 13 hectares on Stuart Lake, 20 km w. of Fort St. James off Hwy. 27.	125				●	●		●	●						
Sproat Lake (F-9) 43 hectares 13 km n.w. of Port Alberni on Sproat Lake Rd. Water skiing. *(See Port Alberni p. 148)*	126	●	●		●	●		●	●	●					
Stamp River (F-10) 327 hectares 14 km w. of Port Alberni on Stamp River Rd.	127	●	●	●				●		●					
Stone Mountain (B-4) 25,690 hectares 140 km w. of Fort Nelson on Hwy. 97. Canoeing, kayaking.	128	●	●	●	●	●		●		●		●		●	

RECREATION AREAS

	MAP LOCATION	CAMPING	PICNICKING	HIKING TRAILS	BOATING	BOAT RAMP	BOAT RENTAL	FISHING	SWIMMING	PETS ON LEASH	BICYCLE TRAILS	WINTER SPORTS	VISITOR CENTER	LODGE/CABINS	FOOD SERVICE
Strathcona (E-10) 245,807 hectares 48.25 km w. of Campbell River via Hwy. 28. Cross-country and downhill skiing, mountain biking, rock climbing, snowshoeing, water skiing, windsurfing.	129	•	•	•	•	•		•	•	•	•	•		•	
Swan Lake (D-6) 65 hectares at Tupper, 35 km s.e. of Dawson Creek via Hwy. 2. Canoeing, kayaking, scuba diving, water skiing, windsurfing; playground.	130	•	•	•	•	•		•	•	•					
Syringa (C-10) 4,417 hectares 19 km n.w. of Castlegar off Hwy. 3. Canoeing, kayaking, water skiing, windsurfing; playground. *(See Castlegar p. 116)*	131	•	•	•	•	•		•	•	•					
Taylor Arm (F-10) 71 hectares 23 km n.w. of Port Alberni on Hwy. 4.	132	•	•		•	•		•							
Ten Mile Lake (F-5) 260 hectares 12 km n. of Quesnel on Hwy. 97. Cross-country and water skiing.	133	•	•	•	•	•		•	•	•	•	•			
Top of the World (C-12) 8,790 hectares 48 km n.e. of Kimberley off Hwy. 93. Cross-country skiing, mountain biking, snowshoeing; horse trails.	134	•		•				•		•	•	•		•	
Tudyah Lake (E-4) 56 hectares 9 km n. of McLeod Lake on Hwy. 97.	135	•	•		•	•		•							
Tweedsmuir South (F-3) 506,000 hectares 349 km n.w. of Williams Lake on Hwy. 20. Canoeing circuit, cross-country and downhill skiing.	136	•	•	•	•	•		•	•	•		•		•	
Tyhee Lake (E-3) 33 hectares 10 km e. of Smithers on Hwy. 16. Canoeing, cross-country skiing, kayaking.	137	•	•	•	•	•		•	•	•					
Vaseux Lake (D-9) 12 hectares 25 km s. of Penticton on Hwy. 97. Canoeing, ice fishing, kayaking.	138	•	•	•	•			•	•	•					
Wasa Lake (C-12) 144 hectares 21 km n. of Fort Steele off Hwy. 93/95. Canoeing, water skiing, windsurfing; playground.	139	•	•	•	•	•		•	•	•					
Wells Gray (G-6) 540,000 hectares 30 km n. of Clearwater via an access road off Hwy. 5. Interpretive programs. Canoeing, cross-country skiing, horseback riding, kayaking, snowshoeing; horse rental. *(See Clearwater p. 117)*	140	•	•	•	•			•	•	•	•	•	•		•
West Lake (F-4) 256 hectares 22 km s.w. of Prince George off Hwy. 16.	141		•	•	•	•		•	•	•		•			
Whiskers Point (E-5) 116 hectares 130 km n. of Prince George off Hwy. 97. Canoeing, kayaking, water skiing, windsurfing; nature trail, playground.	142	•	•	•	•	•		•	•	•					
Whiteswan Lake (C-12) 1,994 hectares 25 km s. of Canal Flats off Hwy. 93/95. Canoeing, ice fishing, kayaking.	143	•	•	•	•	•		•	•	•					
Wistaria (E-3) 40 hectares 40 km w. of Hwy. 35, s.w. of Burns Lake on Ootsa Lake.	144	•		•	•			•	•						
Yahk (D-12) 9 hectares on Hwy. 3/93 at Yahk.	145	•	•					•		•					
Yard Creek (B-9) 61 hectares 15 km e. of Sicamous on Hwy. 1.	146	•	•		•										
OTHER															
Berman Lake Park (F-4) 38 hectares 45 km w. of Prince George. Canoeing.	147		•	•				•	•						
Canyon Hot Springs (A-10) Hot mineral springs 35.5 km e. of Revelstoke. *(See Revelstoke p. 152)*	148	•	•	•				•	•	•				•	•
Creston Valley (D-11) 7,000 hectares 9.5 km w. of Creston on Hwy. 3. Bird-watching, canoeing, cross-country skiing, hunting. *(See Creston p. 119)*	149	•	•					•		•	•	•	•		•
Descanso Bay Regional Park (G-10) 16 hectares 1 km e. of Nanaimo on Gabriola Island via ferry. Kayaking.	150	•	•	•				•	•	•					
Fairmont Hot Springs (B-12) Hot mineral springs on Hwy. 95 in Fairmont Hot Springs. Downhill skiing; horse rental. *(See place listing p. 120)*	151	•	•	•	•			•	•		•	•		•	•
Ferry Island (E-2) 61 hectares 1 km e. of Terrace off Hwy. 16. Cross-country skiing.	152	•	•	•	•	•	•	•	•		•		•		

RECREATION AREAS

	MAP LOCATION	CAMPING	PICNICKING	HIKING TRAILS	BOATING	BOAT RAMP	BOAT RENTAL	FISHING	SWIMMING	PETS ON LEASH	BICYCLE TRAILS	WINTER SPORTS	VISITOR CENTER	LODGE/CABINS	FOOD SERVICE
Giscome Portage (E-5) 160 hectares 40 km n. of Prince George. Historic. Cross-country skiing.	153		•					•	•			•			
Green Lake Area (A-8) 347 hectares 16 km n.e. of 70 Mile House on Green Lake Rd. Water skiing; horse rental.	154	•	•	•	•	•		•	•	•					
Harold Mann (E-4) 13 hectares 50 km n.e. of Prince George. Canoeing; nature trail.	155		•												
Harrison Hot Springs (C-7) Hot mineral springs on Harrison Lake, 5 km n. of Hwy. 9. Canoeing, golf, hunting, rock hunting; horse rental. *(See place listing p. 127)*	156	•	•	•	•	•	•	•	•	•	•	•	•	•	•
Kanaka Creek (H-12) 400 hectares 2 km e. of Haney. Canoeing; fish hatchery, horse trails. *(See Maple Ridge p. 175)*	157		•	•				•		•					
Kawkawa Lake (C-7) 7 hectares 5 km e. of Hope off Hwy. 5.	158	•	•		•	•		•	•						
Nakusp Hot Springs (B-10) Hot mineral springs 3 km n. of Nakusp on Hwy. 23, then e. on Hot Springs Rd. Cross-country skiing. *(See Nakusp p. 133)*	159	•	•	•					•	•		•		•	
Ness Lake (E-4) 14 hectares 35 km n.w. of Prince George. Canoeing, cross-country skiing.	160	•	•		•			•				•			
Radium Hot Springs (B-12) Hot mineral springs near the w. entrance of Kootenay National Park of Canada. *(See place listing and Kootenay National Park of Canada p. 131)*	161	•	•	•				•	•	•		•	•	•	•
Whytecliff Park (G-11) 40 acres 22.5 km n.e. of Vancouver on the North Shore. Scuba diving.	162		•	•	•			•	•	•					•
Wilkins Park (F-5) 57 hectares 15 km w. of Prince George. Cross-country skiing; nature trail.	163		•	•	•				•	•		•	•		

British Columbia Temperature Averages
Maximum/Minimum (Celcius)
From the records of The Weather Channel Interactive, Inc.

	JAN	FEB	MAR	APR	MAY	JUNE	JULY	AUG	SEPT	OCT	NOV	DEC
Fort St. John	-11 / -19	-7 / -16	-1 / -11	8 / -2	15 / 3	19 / 8	21 / 10	20 / 9	14 / 4	8 / -1	-3 / -11	-9 / -18
Kamloops	-2 / -9	3 / -5	10 / -2	16 / 2	21 / 7	25 / 11	28 / 13	28 / 13	22 / 8	14 / 3	5 / -2	0 / -7
Prince George	-6 / -14	-1 / -11	4 / -6	11 / -2	16 / 3	19 / 6	22 / 8	21 / 7	16 / 3	9 / -1	1 / -7	-5 / -13
Prince Rupert	4 / -3	6 / -1	7 / 0	9 / 2	12 / 4	14 / 7	16 / 9	16 / 10	15 / 7	11 / 4	7 / 1	4 / -2
Vancouver	6 / 0	8 / 1	9 / 2	12 / 4	16 / 8	19 / 11	22 / 12	22 / 13	18 / 10	13 / 6	9 / 3	6 / 1
Victoria	6 / 0	8 / 1	10 / 2	13 / 3	16 / 6	19 / 9	22 / 11	22 / 11	19 / 8	14 / 5	9 / 2	7 / 1

Points of Interest

108 MILE HOUSE (A-7)

South Cariboo Visitor Info Centre: 422 Hwy. 97, Box 340, 100 Mile House, BC, Canada V0K 2E0; phone (250) 395-5353 or (877) 511-5353.

108 MILE HOUSE HERITAGE SITE is at 4690 Cariboo Tr. The site comprises 8 historical buildings depicting the famous mile houses, which were established as a stopover for weary travelers. With the discovery of gold in 1858 and the influx of miners increasing, the houses served a need by providing meals or a place to sleep. A 1908 log barn and 1890 church also are on-site. Allow 30 minutes minimum. Daily 10-5, Victoria Day through Labor Day weekend. Donations. Phone (250) 791-5288 or (250) 791-1971.

ABBOTSFORD (H-11)
pop. 115,463, elev. 58 m/190′

Abbotsford is the regional shopping center as well as the center of trade and industry for the fruit, livestock, poultry and dairy farms of the surrounding Fraser Valley. Several area industries and farms offer tours, including Clayburn Industries Ltd., at Railway and Pine streets. Castle Park Golf and Games Amusement Park, 36165 N. Parallel Rd., provides a range of family entertainment.

Tourism Abbotsford Visitor Centre: 34561 Delair Rd., Abbotsford, BC, Canada V2S 2E1; phone (604) 859-1721 or (888) 332-2229.

TRETHEWEY HOUSE HERITAGE SITE ON MILL LAKE is at 2313 Ware St., next to John Mahoney Park. Restored and furnished to its 1925 appearance, this Arts and Crafts-style house features reconstructions of a playhouse and a carriage house as well as period gardens.

Guided tours are offered. Allow 30 minutes minimum. House open Mon.-Sat. 1-5, July-Aug.; Mon.-Fri. 1-5, rest of year. Closed statutory holidays. Donations. Phone (604) 853-0313.

AINSWORTH HOT SPRINGS (C-10)
elev. 538 m/1766′

AINSWORTH HOT SPRINGS RESORT is on Hwy. 31. Overlooking Kootenay Lake, the springs feature a natural, odorless mineral cave pool with an average temperature of 40-44 C (104-111 F), and a main pool averaging 35 C (97 F). The cold plunge pool, fed by a natural spring, has an average temperature of 4 C (40 F). Towels can be rented. Food is available. Daily 10-9. Last admission 30 minutes before closing. Admission $8; $7 (ages 13-17 and 65+); $6 (ages 3-12). AX, MC, VI. Phone (250) 229-4212 or (800) 668-1171.

ALDERGROVE—see *Vancouver p. 174.*

ALERT BAY (G-3) pop. 583, elev. 15 m/49′

On crescent-shaped Cormorant Island off Vancouver Island's northeast coast, Alert Bay is a fishing village reached by ferry from Port McNeill *(see place listing p. 148)*. The influence of native cultures is evident in the many totem poles, including a memorial pole for totem carver Chief Mungo Martin.

Christ Church on Front Street is an 1881 cedar church with stained-glass windows that reflect the blending of Indian and European cultures; phone (250) 974-5024 for information from the Travel InfoCentre.

Alert Bay Travel InfoCentre: 116 Fir St., Bag Service 2800, Alert Bay, BC, Canada V0N 1A0; phone (250) 974-5024.

ALERT BAY PUBLIC LIBRARY AND MUSEUM is at 118 Fir St. This small museum houses Kwakwaka'wakw artifacts and items depicting local history. Its archives include Alert Bay newspapers and more than 6,000 photographs. Allow 30 minutes minimum. Mon.-Sat. 1-4, July-Aug.; Mon., Wed. and Fri.-Sat. 1-4, rest of year. Closed holidays. Donations. Phone (250) 974-5721.

TOTEM POLE is near the corner of Park and Wood sts. Erected in 1973, the 53-metre (173-ft.) pole is considered to be the world's tallest. It features 22 figures, including a sun at the top. Binoculars are recommended for viewing. The totem pole stands near the 'Namgis Big House, a Kwakwaka'wakw ceremonial center not open to the public. Allow 30 minutes minimum. Daily dawn-dusk. Free.

U'MISTA CULTURAL CENTRE is 2 km (1.2 mi.) w. of the ferry on Front St. The collection includes elaborately carved masks, traditional and historical carvings, woven cedar pieces, ceremonial regalia, paintings and other artifacts from Indian potlatches—the gift-giving ceremonies that mark such important occasions as birth, marriage and death. There also are films and small galleries with short-term exhibits.

Daily 9-5, Victoria Day-Labour Day; Mon.-Fri. 9-5, rest of year. Admission $5; $4 (ages 66+ and students with ID); $1 (ages 0-11). MC, VI. Phone (250) 974-5403 or (800) 690-8222

ASHCROFT (B-7)
pop. 1,788, elev. 305 m/1,000′

Ashcroft Manor, a roadside house on Cariboo Wagon Road, was named for the English home of its settlers, Clement and Henry Cornwall. The Cornwalls established themselves as cattlemen in 1862 and lived the pioneer life in the style of gentlemen, practicing such rituals as afternoon tea and riding to hounds through sagebrush and scrub in pursuit of coyotes. The manor is south of town on Hwy. 1.

ASHCROFT MUSEUM is at 404 Brink St. Exhibits recount the history of the southern Cariboo, the Indian tribes that first settled Ashcroft. Artifacts and photographs are displayed in the windows of old shops, churches and houses along a board sidewalk, depicting life as it was in Ashcroft's glory days between the first settlement in 1884 and the great fire in 1916. A re-creation of the Hat Creek Mine also is displayed. Daily 9-5, July-Aug.; Thurs.-Mon. 9-5, Apr.-June and Sept.-Oct.; otherwise varies. Closed holidays. Donations. Phone (250) 453-9232.

☜ BARKERVILLE HISTORIC TOWN (F-5)

Barkerville is approximately 80 kilometres (50 mi.) east of Quesnel via Hwy. 26. The restored 1870s gold rush town once had the largest population north of San Francisco and west of Chicago. In those days when more than $50 million of gold—at $16 per ounce—had been mined from the area, soap cost $1 a bar and a dance with a hurdy-gurdy girl cost $1 a whirl.

The town was named for Billy Barker, a Cornish miner who first found gold in large quantities in the early 1860s. Barkerville became a virtual ghost town a few years later when the gold ran out.

The town contains 125 original and reconstructed buildings, including the Barkerville Hotel, St. Saviours Church, the Mason and Daly General Store and the Wake Up Jake Cafe; many are manned by attendants in period dress. Board sidewalks and dirt streets help preserve the essence of the original site.

Theatre Royale presents period melodrama, dance and music Victoria Day-September 30. Treasure seekers can pan for gold at Eldorado Mine. A visitor center presents videos and exhibits about the history of Barkerville. Guided town, Chinatown and cemetery tours as well as living-history programs are offered.

The townsite is open daily 8:30-dusk. Full visitor services operate daily, mid-June through Sept. 30. Pets are not permitted. Admission mid-May through Sept. 30, $13.50; $12.25 (ages 65+); $8 (ages 13-18); $4 (ages 6-12); $28.75 (family). Free rest of year. Phone (250) 994-3332 or (888) 994-3332.

BELLA COOLA (F-2) pop. 788, elev. 590'

BELLA COOLA VALLEY MUSEUM is just e. of jct. MacKenzie Hwy. and Bentinck Ave. at 269 Hwy. 20. The museum, in an 1892 heritage building, contains artifacts and interpretive exhibits about the Bella Coola Valley from the late 18th century, when Europeans first discovered the area's aboriginal people, to the mid-20th century. Guided tours are available. Allow 30 minutes minimum. Daily 9-noon and 1-5, early June-early Sept. Admission $2.50; $2 (students with ID). Phone (250) 799-5767 or (250) 982-2130 in the off-season.

BOSTON BAR (C-7)
pop. 233, elev. 309 m/1,013'

Boston Bar, which began as a gold mining town, was named for a Dutchman who came from Boston to prospect in the 1860s. Because Boston was the home port to many of the ships bringing prospectors, local Indians called the newcomers Boston men. Boston Bar is a logging and trade center, with the Canadian National Railway passing through town. The Canadian Pacific Railway parallels the National on the other side of Fraser River Canyon and passes through the village of North Bend.

Boston Bar is the access point for the Nahatlach Valley, which features the Nahatlach River and a chain of lakes. Recreation includes camping, fishing and white-water rafting.

☜ HELL'S GATE AIRTRAM is 11 km (7 mi.) s. on Hwy. 1 to 43111 Trans-Canada Hwy.

in Fraser River Canyon. The tram descends 153 metres (502 ft.) across the river to the narrowest part of Fraser Canyon and across Hell's Gate Fishways, where millions of salmon annually swim upstream to their spawning grounds. Visitors can see eight fishways from observation decks or a suspension bridge. A film about the life cycle of the salmon is shown at the education center.

Food is available. Allow 1 hour minimum. Daily 10-5, June-Aug., Apr. 11-May 31 and Sept.-Oct. Fare $15.09; $12.26 (ages 65+ and students with ID); $9.43 (ages 6-18). MC, VI. Phone (604) 867-9277.

RECREATIONAL ACTIVITIES
White-water Rafting

• **REO Rafting Adventure Resort** is 18 km (11 mi.) n.w. on Hwy. 1 in Fraser Canyon. Write 845 Spence Way, Anmore, BC, Canada V3H 4Y7. Nahatlach River trips operate May-Sept. Phone (604) 461-7238 or (800) 736-7238.

BOSWELL (C-11) pop. 100, elev. 533 m/1,748'

THE GLASS HOUSE is on Hwy. 3A (Southern Trans-Canada Hwy.). This six-room, castlelike house is made of empty 16-ounce embalming fluid bottles. A funeral director built the house, archway and several terraces on the landscaped lakefront grounds. Allow 30 minutes minimum. Daily 8-8, July-Aug.; 9-5, May-June and Sept. 1 through mid-Oct. Admission $8; $6 (ages 13-19); $5 (ages 6-12). VI. Phone (250) 223-8372.

BRACKENDALE (G-12)
RECREATIONAL ACTIVITIES
White-water Rafting

• **Sunwolf Outdoor Centre—Bald Eagle Rafting** is at 70002 Squamish Valley Rd. Write P.O. Box 244, Brackendale, BC, Canada V0N 1H0. Other activities are available. Daily 8-8, June-Sept.; 9-5, rest of year. Phone (604) 898-1537 or (877) 806-8046.

BRENTWOOD BAY—see Victoria p. 194.

BRIDAL FALLS (I-12) elev. 61 m/200'

DINOTOWN is off Hwy. 1 exit 135 following signs. Geared for ages 2-12, this 5-hectare (12-acre) amusement park features live shows, a train, paddleboats, bumper cars, miniature golf, a parade and a water park. Picnicking is permitted. Food is available. Allow 3 hours minimum. Mon.-Fri. 10-5, Sat.-Sun. 10-7, July-Aug.; Mon.-Fri. 10-5, day after Father's Day-June 30; Sat.-Sun. 10-5, Mother's Day weekend-Father's Day and in Sept. Admission $13; $8.88 (ages 65+); free (ages 0-2). MC, VI. Phone (604) 794-7410 or (604) 794-3733.

TRANS-CANADA WATERSLIDES is at jct. hwys. 1 and 9 on Bridal Falls Rd. The park features 10 waterslides, a giant hot pool, miniature golf course, river ride, and picnic and barbecue facilities. Food is available. Allow 2 hours minimum. Daily 10-7, mid-June through Labour Day; Sat.-Sun. 10-6, late May to mid-June. Hours may vary; phone ahead. Admission $12; free (ages 0-2). Admission after 5 p.m. $7. Admission may vary; phone ahead. MC, VI. Phone (604) 794-7455 or (888) 883-8852 to verify schedule or rates.

BRITANNIA BEACH (G-11)
pop. 300, elev. 6 m/20'

From 1930 to 1935 the Britannia Mine at Britannia Beach was the largest producer of copper in the British Empire. No longer in operation, the mine is now part of the British Columbia Museum of Mining.

BRITISH COLUMBIA MUSEUM OF MINING is on Hwy. 99. An underground mine tunnel ride is a highlight of the museum, which chronicles mining history through hands-on demonstrations and exhibits. On site is a 1921 concentrator mill and a 235-ton super mine truck. Gold panning is included with admission.

The tunnel temperature is a constant 12 C (54 F); warm clothing and comfortable walking shoes are recommended. Hard hats are provided. Allow 1 hour, 30 minutes minimum. Daily 9-4:30, first Sun. in May-second Mon. in Oct.; Mon.-Fri. 9-4:30, rest of year. Admission $14.95; $11.95 (ages 65+ and students with ID); free (ages 0-4). MC, VI. Phone (604) 896-2233 or (800) 896-4044.

BURNABY—see Vancouver p. 174.

CACHE CREEK (B-7)
pop. 1,056, elev. 450 m/1,500'

HISTORIC HAT CREEK RANCH is 11 km (7 mi.) n. on Hwy. 97 at jct. hwys. 97 and 99. The 130-hectare (320-acre) ranch, on one of the few sections of the Cariboo Wagon Road still accessible to the public, consists of more than 20 historic buildings constructed 1863-1915 when the ranch served as a roadhouse for the horse-drawn stagecoaches and freight wagons of the B.C. Express line (known as the B.X.).

Guided tours are offered of the 1860 roadhouse, and visitors can explore a heritage apple orchard, a Shuswap village, a blacksmith shop and a collection of pioneer agricultural machinery. Camping is available. Food is available. Daily 9-6, July-Aug.; 9-5, May-June and in Sept. Admission $9; $8 (ages 55+); $5 (ages 6-12); $20 (family, two adults and three children). Camping $10-$15 per night. MC, VI. Phone (250) 457-9722 or (800) 782-0922.

CAMPBELL RIVER (E-10)
pop. 28,456, elev. 18 m/59'

An important lumber, mining and commercial fishing center, Campbell River is near a noted Vancouver Island timber stand. The Elk Falls Pulp and Paper Mill offers tours in the summer. Campbell River is headquarters of the Tyee Club, whose members must catch a salmon of 30 pounds or more while fishing from a rowboat in the raging waters of Discovery Passage.

Provincial parks preserve the area's natural beauty, typified by waterfalls and mountainous wilderness. At Elk Falls Provincial Park the Campbell River drops 27 metres (90 ft.) into a deep canyon. Strathcona Provincial Park contains Mount Golden Hinde, at 2,200 metres (7,218 ft.) the highest mountain on Vancouver Island, and 440-metre (1,445-ft.) Della Falls, the highest waterfall in Canada. Scuba diving is popular during the winter when the waters are particularly clear. *See Recreation Chart and the AAA/CAA Western Canada & Alaska CampBook.*

The 183-metre-long (600-ft.) Campbell River Fishing Pier, 655 Island Hwy., is available for fishing, strolling or watching the cruise ships pass through the Strait of Georgia.

Campbell River Visitor Centre: 1235 Shoppers Row, P.O. Box 400, Campbell River, BC, Canada V9W 5B6; phone (250) 287-4636 or (877) 286-5705.

[SAVE] **MUSEUM AT CAMPBELL RIVER** is at 470 Island Hwy. with an entrance off 5th Ave. The museum displays artifacts crafted by First Nations peoples of northern Vancouver Island. Exhibits also follow the island's pioneer and industrial history, including vintage logging and fishing equipment and replicas of a pioneer cabin and a float house. The outdoor historical interpretation park includes indigenous plant gardens, a cod fishing boat and a logging steam donkey.

Allow 1 hour minimum. Daily 10-5, mid-May through Sept. 30; Tues.-Sun. noon-5, rest of year. Closed Good Friday, Nov. 11, and Dec. 25 and 31. Admission $6; $4 (students with ID); free (ages 0-5); $15 (family). Phone (250) 287-3103.

QUINSAM RIVER HATCHERY is .5 km (.3 mi.) w. on Hwy. 28, then 2.4 km (1.5 mi.) s. on Quinsam Rd. to 4217 Argonaut Rd. The salmon enhancement project produces pink, coho and chinook salmon and steelhead trout. A display room chronicles the life cycle of a salmon. Facilities include various hatchery sensing containers. Adult salmon viewing is best from mid-September to mid-November. Also available are picnic sites and a network of hiking trails along the river. Daily 8-4. Free. Phone (250) 287-9564.

RECREATIONAL ACTIVITIES

Scuba Diving

- **Abyssal Dive Charters** departs from Quadra Island. Write P.O. Box 747, Quathiaski Cove, BC, Canada V0P 1N0. Other activities are available. Daily 7:30 a.m.-10:30 p.m. Phone (250) 285-2420 or (800) 499-2297.

CASTLEGAR (D-10)
pop. 7,002, elev. 494 m/1,620'

At the junction of hwys. 3 and 3A, Castlegar is considered the crossroads of the Kootenays. Just north is the 51-metre-high (167-ft.) Hugh Keenleyside Dam. The upper and lower Arrow Lakes, created by the dam, offer popular summer recreation areas including Arrow Lakes Provincial Park (Shelter Bay) and Syringa Creek Provincial Park. *See Recreation Chart and the AAA/CAA Western Canada & Alaska CampBook.*

Castlegar Chamber of Commerce: 1995 Sixth Ave., Castlegar, BC, Canada V1N 4B7; phone (250) 365-6313.

[SAVE] **DOUKHOBOR DISCOVERY CENTRE** is opposite the airport just off Hwy. 3A to 112 Heritage Way. The site is a ten-building replica of the communal settlement of the Doukhobors, a pacifist group of Russian immigrants who settled in the area 1908-13. There were about 90 such villages. Highlights include thousands of artifacts reflecting the settlement and an art gallery depicting Doukhobor life. Spinning and weaving demonstrations occur July through September. Allow 30 minutes minimum. Daily 10-5, May-Sept. Admission $8; $5 (students with ID); free (ages 0-5). Phone (250) 365-5327.

KOOTENAY GALLERY OF ART, HISTORY AND SCIENCE is opposite the airport just off Hwy. 3A at 120 Heritage Way, next to Doukhobor Discovery Centre. Two galleries feature rotating historical, scientific and artistic exhibitions of local, national and international origin. Workshops and musical events are held throughout the year. Allow 30 minutes minimum. Daily 10-5, June-Aug.; Wed.-Sat. 10-5, Sun. noon-5, Mar.-May; Wed.-Sat. 10-5, Sun. noon-5, Sept.-Nov.; daily 10-5 in Dec. Closed Easter and Dec. 25. Schedule may change; phone ahead. Admission $2; $1 (students with ID and senior citizens); free (ages 0-11). Phone (250) 365-3337.

ZUCKERBERG ISLAND HERITAGE PARK is at 7th Ave. and 9th St. A suspension bridge leads to the island at the confluence of the Columbia and Kootenay rivers. Walking tours offers such sights as an Indian Kekuli or pit house, a cemetery, a log house, a sculpture of a seated woman carved from a tree stump and the Chapel House with its Russian Orthodox onion dome.

Picnicking is permitted. Allow 30 minutes minimum. Daily 10-5, July-Aug.; Wed-Sun. 10-5, May-June. Island tours are available year-round. Hours may vary; phone ahead to confirm. Admission $2. Phone (250) 365-6440.

CHEMAINUS (G-10) pop. 2,706, elev. 6 m/20'

A lumber and manufacturing town, Chemainus added tourism to its economy with the creation of murals. More than 30 professional paintings on the walls of buildings portray the history of the Chemainus Valley. Subjects range from North American Indians to dramatic depictions of the logging industry.

Begun by local artists, the series of murals has attracted artists from around the world. Walking tour maps can be bought at the kiosk in the central parking area. Prearranged guided tours and horse-drawn carriage tours also are available for a fee; phone (250) 246-5055 or (250) 246-0063.

Chemainus Theatre offers dramas, comedies and musical productions; phone (250) 246-9820 or (800) 565-7738.

Chemainus Chamber of Commerce: 9796 Willow St., P.O. Box 575, Chemainus, BC, Canada V0R 1K0; phone (250) 246-3944.

CHILLIWACK (H-12)
pop. 62,927, elev. 10 m/33'

In the heart of the upper Fraser River Valley, Chilliwack is the center of a prosperous farming and dairy region. The surrounding lakes, rivers, mountains and nearby provincial parks offer such varied recreation as skiing, hiking, fishing, rock hunting and white-water rafting. Scenic views and picnic facilities are available at Chilliwack Lake Provincial Park, 84 kilometres (54 mi.) southeast off Hwy. 1 (see Recreation Chart), and Cultus Lake Provincial Park, 11 kilometres (7 mi.) southwest off Hwy. 1 (see Recreation Chart).

Tourism Chilliwack Visitor Information Centre: 44150 Luckakuck Way, Chilliwack, BC, Canada V2R 4A7; phone (604) 858-8121 or (800) 567-9535.

BRIDAL VEIL FALLS PROVINCIAL PARK is 16 km (10 mi.) e. off Hwy. 1 exit 135, following signs. An easy 15-minute hike leads visitors to a lovely view of the area, characterized by valleys and emerald-colored rounded mountains. The main attraction is the falls, Canada's sixth-highest, which cascade 60 metres (197 ft.) over slick rock and create the appearance of a glassy bridal veil. The park is the former site of Popkum, a 1700s village.

Note: In winter, the falls may freeze and cause the base to be slippery as well as allow rock and ice to fall. Picnicking is permitted. Allow 30 minutes minimum. Daily dawn-dusk. Free.

GREAT BLUE HERON NATURE RESERVE is at 5200 Sumas Prairie Rd. This 130-hectare (321-acre) site includes an interpretive center, an observation tower, fish-spawning channels and a self-guiding interpretive walking trail. More than 90 herons build nests here; painted turtles, tailed frogs, beavers, bald eagles and a variety of other birds also dwell at the reserve. Allow 1 hour minimum. Nature reserve open daily 8-8. Interpretive center open daily 10-4; phone ahead in winter. Donations. Phone (604) 823-6603.

MINTER GARDENS is 19 km (12 mi.) e. on Hwy. 1 to exit 135 (Hwy. 9) at 52892 Bunker Rd. Covering nearly 11 hectares (27 acres), 11 thematic gardens display seasonal colors and plants from around the world. Highlights include an evergreen living maze, topiary sculptures, a Penjing rock collection and two Victorian-style conservatories.

Food is available. Allow 1 hour minimum. Daily 9-7, July-Aug.; 9-6, in June; 9-5:30, May and Sept.; 10-5, Apr. and Oct. Hours are weather permitting; phone to confirm. Admission $14.15; $11.85 (ages 65+); $5.85 (ages 6-12); $8.50 (ages 13-18). AX, MC, VI. Phone (604) 794-7191 or (888) 646-8377.

CLEARWATER (A-8) pop. 3,500

Clearwater gets its name from the clear waters of the nearby Clearwater River. Opportunities for riding, hiking, canoeing, skiing and fishing abound in the surrounding North Thompson Valley.

Wells Gray Provincial Park, north off Hwy. 5, offers a variety of scenery, particularly with regard to water. Scattered throughout its boundaries are five large lakes, two river systems, many streams and waterways and a multitude of waterfalls. Helmcken Falls, which drops 141 metres (465 ft.), is said to be the fourth highest in Canada. At Bailey's Chute Loop in late summer, visitors can view salmon jumping upstream to spawn. Extinct volcanoes and lava beds recall the region's fiery past. *See Recreation Chart and the AAA/CAA Western Canada & Alaska CampBook.*

Clearwater Chamber of Commerce: 425 E. Yellowhead Hwy., P.O. Box 1988, Clearwater, BC, Canada V0E 1N0; phone (250) 674-2646.

RECREATIONAL ACTIVITIES
White-water Rafting

• **Interior Whitewater Expeditions** is w. of Hwy. 5 at Old N. Thompson Hwy. Write P.O. Box 393, Clearwater, BC, Canada V0E 1N0. Daily 8-8, May-Sept. (depending on water level); Mon.-Fri. 9-5, rest of year. Phone (250) 674-3727 or (800) 661-7238.

CLINTON (A-7) pop. 621, elev. 274 m/898′

During the gold rush of the late 1850s and early 1860s Clinton was the junction of several wagon roads leading to northern goldfields. In 1863 Queen Victoria changed the town's name from Junction to Clinton. Retaining much of its frontier look, Clinton is a supply center for surrounding resorts, fishing camps and ranches. Summer activities include boating, fishing and camping at area lakes, which also attract various wildlife.

The Village of Clinton: 1423 Cariboo Hwy., P.O. Box 309, Clinton, BC, Canada V0K 1K0; phone (250) 459-2261.

SOUTH CARIBOO HISTORICAL MUSEUM is at 1419 Cariboo Hwy. Built in 1892, this building has served as the town's schoolhouse and courthouse. Displays include photographs and pioneer artifacts. Allow 30 minutes minimum. Daily 8-8, June-Oct. Schedule may vary; phone ahead. Donations. Phone (250) 459-2442.

COMOX (F-10) pop. 11,172

Comox was founded in the mid-1800s, taking its name from the Salish word *Koumuckthay*, meaning "land of plenty." Once an important port for ships of the Royal Navy, the east coast village became the home of a Royal Air Force base in 1942. CFB Comox maintains search-and-rescue operations, maritime patrols and support of naval and air force defense.

COMOX AIR FORCE MUSEUM is e. on Ryan Rd. following signs to CFB Comox main entrance. Museum displays outline the history of the base and West Coast aviation. Two squadrons continue to fly Cormorant helicopters and Buffalo and Aurora aircraft. Nearby, a heritage aircraft park displays vintage aircraft. Canada's flight pioneers are recognized in a videotape presentation. On weekends visitors may view a Spitfire that is being restored. A comprehensive aviation library also is on site. Allow 30 minutes minimum. Museum daily 10-4. Heritage aircraft park daily 10-4, May-Sept. Closed Jan. 1 and Dec. 25. Museum admission by donations. Heritage aircraft park free. Phone (250) 339-8162.

FILBERG HERITAGE LODGE AND PARK is at 61 Filberg Rd. The 1929 Heritage Lodge and outbuildings stand on 4 hectares (9 acres) of landscaped grounds on Comox Bay. The timber lodge is restored and furnished in period. Rare and exotic trees, rhododendrons and herb gardens adorn the park, which offers 1-hour concerts most Sundays at 2 in July and August. A petting farm is available from mid-June to mid-August.

Food is available. Pets are not permitted. Allow 1 hour minimum. Park open daily 8-dusk. Lodge open daily 10-4, Apr.-Sept.; phone for winter hours. Petting zoo daily 10-4, June 19-Aug. 20. Closed Jan. 1, second Mon. in Oct. and Dec. 25-26. Lodge admission $3; free (ages 0-4). Petting farm $2; free (ages 0-4). Park admission is charged during special events. Phone (250) 339-2715.

COOMBS (F-10) pop. 1,372

Coombs retains the atmosphere of a quaint village settled around 1910. The Coombs General Store, which has operated continuously since the settlement days, and the Old Country Market, which is unusual for the goats that are kept on the roof in summer, are two landmarks.

The town is on Vancouver Island, midway between Little Qualicum River Falls Provincial Park *(see Recreation Chart)* and Englishman River Falls Provincial Park *(see Recreation Chart)*, where there are many recreational opportunities.

BUTTERFLY WORLD & GARDENS is 1 km (.6 mi.) w. on Hwy. 4A at 1080 Winchester Rd. A walk-through tropical garden contains more than 30 species of free-flying butterflies. The insect's life cycle is portrayed through displays. Other exhibits include birds in an outdoor aviary, a Japanese water garden with exotic fish, an orchid garden with some 800 orchids, a petting zoo in the summer and Big Bug Jungle—an insectary housing large live jungle insects.

Allow 30 minutes minimum. Daily 10-5, May-Aug.; 10-4, Mar.-Apr. and Sept.-Oct. Admission $9.75; $8.75 (ages 65+); $5.75 (students with ID); $3.75 (ages 3-12). MC, VI. Phone (250) 248-7026.

COQUITLAM—*see Vancouver p. 174.*

COURTENAY (E-10)
pop. 18,304, elev. 25 m/82′

Courtenay was established in the late 1860s when settlers began a major farming community near the Comox Valley. Known for a garden called the Mile of Flowers, the town is now a year-round recreation area with good skiing and sailing nearby.

The 1989 Puntledge River discovery of the fossilized intact skull of a 14-metre-long (46-ft.) elasmosaur, a long-necked Cretaceous marine reptile 80 million years old, brought Courtenay to the attention of the world of paleontology.

Courtenay is the terminus of the Powell River Ferry, which makes round-trip excursions to the mainland.

Comox Valley Visitor Centre: 2040 Cliffe Ave., Courtenay, BC, Canada V9N 2L3; phone (250) 334-3234 or (888) 357-4471.

COURTENAY AND DISTRICT MUSEUM AND PALAEONTOLOGY CENTRE is at 207 Fourth St., downtown at jct. Fourth St. and Cliffe Ave. Permanent exhibits, enhanced by audiovisuals, focus on native history, exploration, agriculture, logging and pioneer life. A reconstruction of an elasmosaur is displayed along with locally excavated fossil evidence from the age of dinosaurs. The museum has archival material pertaining to the nearby Comox Valley. Guided fossil discovery tours are available.

Allow 1 hour minimum. Mon.-Sat. 10-5, Sun. noon-4, Victoria Day-Labour Day; Tues.-Sat. 10-5, rest of year. Closed Jan. 1, Good Friday and Dec. 25. Donations. Phone (250) 334-0686.

PUNTLEDGE HATCHERY is 3 km (1.9 mi.) w. on Lake Trail Rd., then 2 km (1.2 mi.) n. on Powerhouse Rd. following signs. The hatchery nurtures and releases several varieties of salmon and steelhead trout into the Puntledge River. Photographic displays outline the species' various stages of development. Daily 8-4; closed Jan. 1 and Dec. 25. Free. Phone (250) 703-0907.

RECREATIONAL ACTIVITIES
Skiing

- **Mt. Washington Alpine Resort** is 31 km (19 mi.) n.w. on the Strathcona Pkwy. Write P.O. Box 3069, Courtenay, BC, Canada V9N 5N3. Other activities are available. Daily 9-3:30. Hours may vary; phone ahead to confirm. Phone (250) 338-1386 or (888) 231-1499.

CRANBROOK (C-11)
pop. 18,476, elev. 940 m/3,083′

Cranbrook is the key city of the eastern Kootenays and the center of many circle tours. Nearby lakes, rivers and mountains provide such recreational opportunities as swimming, fishing, hiking, hunting and skiing. A scenic portion of Hwy. 93 runs north from Cranbrook into Alberta to the junction with Hwy. 16 in Jasper.

Cranbrook Chamber of Commerce: 2279 Cranbrook St. (Hwy. 3/95), P.O. Box 84, Cranbrook, BC, Canada V1C 4H6; phone (250) 426-5914 or (800) 222-6174.

Self-guiding tours: Information about driving and walking tours is available from the chamber of commerce.

[SAVE] **CANADIAN MUSEUM OF RAIL TRAVEL** is at 57 Van Horne St. (Hwy. 3/95). The museum restores and preserves vintage Canadian Pacific Railway passenger train sets, including cars from the luxury Trans-Canada Limited. The lifestyle of rail travel is reflected in trains from 1880 to 1955, including cars of state, business and royalty. On the grounds is the original three-story café from the Canadian Pacific Railway's Royal Alexandra Hotel of Winnipeg.

Allow 90 minutes minimum. Museum open daily 9:45-6, early Apr. to mid-Oct.; Tues.-Sat. 10-5, rest of year. Guided tours are given daily every 45 minutes. Last tour begins 45 minutes before closing. Guided tours $14.40; $12.25 (ages 65+); $7.20 (students with ID); $3.40 (children); $36 (family). Phone (250) 489-3918 to verify tour schedule and rates.

GAMBLING ESTABLISHMENTS

- **Casino of the Rockies** is at 7777 Mission Rd. Sun.-Thurs. 10 a.m.-12 a.m., Fri.-Sat. and holidays 10 a.m.-2 a.m.; closed Dec. 25. Phone (250) 417-2772.

CRESTON (D-11)
pop. 4,795, elev. 636 m/2,086′

The unusual Kutenai canoe, which has a bow and stern that both meet the waterline, was used by Indians in the area around Creston in pre-pioneer days. The only other place such a canoe has been found is the Amur River region in southeastern Russia. The canoe's use in this area supports the theory that Asians migrated to North America over a frozen Bering Strait.

In the 1930s about 8,100 hectares (20,000 acres) of land were reclaimed from the Kootenay Delta for agriculture. The Creston Valley floor is now quilted with a variety of seed and root crops, grains and fruit orchards. Other Creston industries include forestry, dairying and brewing.

The Columbia Brewing Co., 6 blocks south on 16th Avenue, offers free narrated tours of its facilities mid-May to mid-October. Complimentary beer is available at the end of the tour. Free guided tours of a candlemaking factory are offered year-round at Kootenay Candles, 1511 Northwest Blvd.

Summit Creek Park, 9 kilometres (6 mi.) west, offers camping, natural history programs and hiking along the old Dewdney Trail, which carried gold seekers from Hope to the Wild Horse goldfields in the 1860s. Mountain Stream Trout Farm and Recreation Area, 7 kilometres (4 mi.) north, features nature trails and ponds stocked with fish for catching and barbecuing on the premises.

Creston Chamber of Commerce: 1607 Canyon St., P.O. Box 268, Creston, BC, Canada V0B 1G0; phone (250) 428-4342 or (866) 528-4342.

[SAVE] **CRESTON AND DISTRICT MUSEUM** is at 219 Devon St. via Hwy. 3A N. The 1957 Stone House, which has four stone fireplaces and walls more than one-third metre (1 ft.) thick, contains more than 10,000 pioneer and Indian artifacts, including a replica of a Kutenai Indian canoe and early agricultural tools. A schoolroom exhibit can be seen in the restored Kingsgate Schoolhouse on the museum grounds. Allow 1 hour minimum. Mon.-Sat. 10-3:30, mid-May to mid-June; daily 10-5, mid-June through Aug. 31; by appointment rest of year. Admission $3; $2 (ages 6-16); $8 (family). Phone (250) 428-9262.

CRESTON VALLEY WILDLIFE MANAGEMENT AREA AND INTERPRETATION CENTRE is 9.5 km (6 mi.) w. on Hwy. 3. The 7,000-hectare (17,297-acre) area permits hiking, seasonal camping, bicycling, hunting, canoeing and picnicking in a managed waterfowl habitat. A variety of programs and canoe trips originate at the Interpretation Centre, which houses natural history displays and a theater.

Center open daily 9-5, May-Oct. The recreation area is open year-round. Donations. Phone (250) 402-6900 or (250) 402-6908. *See Recreation Chart.*

CULTUS LAKE (I-12)
pop. 637, elev. 45 m/150′

Cultus Lake Provincial Park, 11 kilometres (7 miles) southwest of Chilliwack, off Hwy. 1, is a popular recreational area and offers camping, boating, fishing, horseback riding and hiking. *See Recreation Chart.* Cultus Lake Waterpark, Hwy. 1 exit 119A, has giant waterslides, twisting tunnels, pools and inner tube rides; phone (604) 858-7241 for more information.

CUMBERLAND (F-10) pop. 2,618

Cumberland's origins are rooted in the rigors of coal mining. From 1888 until the last of its nine mines closed in 1966, the village produced some 25 million tons of high-grade coal. The lucrative enterprise solidified Cumberland's economy and contributed to its multi-ethnic mix, drawing miners from locations as diverse as England, Scotland, Italy, China and Japan. The village and many of its streets were named for the mining region in England known as Cumbria.

Nestled in the foothills of the Beaufort Mountains and a stone's throw from Comox Lake, Cumberland offers ample snow skiing, hiking, fishing and boating opportunities.

Cumberland Chamber of Commerce and Tourism Information Centre: 2755 Dunsmuir, P.O. Box 250, Cumberland, BC, Canada V0R 1S0; phone (250) 336-8313 or (866) 301-4636.

CUMBERLAND MUSEUM & ARCHIVES is off Hwy. 19 Cumberland exit, 2 km (1.2 mi.) w. on Cumberland Rd./4th St., then just w. to jct. 1st St. and Dunsmuir Ave. Visitors can walk through a replica of a coal mine and view exhibits about Cumberland's mining history. Outdoor heritage tours are offered. Allow 30 minutes minimum. Mon.-Fri. 9-4, Sat.-Sun. 10-4, Jan.-June and Sept.-Dec.; Sun. 10-4, rest of year. Admission $3; $2 (senior citizens); $1 (ages 13-18). Tours $2. Phone (250) 336-2445.

DAWSON CREEK (D-6)
pop. 10,754, elev. 655 m/2,148′

Named for George Mercer Dawson of the Geological Survey of Canada, Dawson Creek was settled in 1912. Growth accelerated during World War II, as this was the southern terminus of the Alaska Hwy. The highway was then called the Alcan Military Hwy., and it served as a supply road to bases in Alaska. The Mile Zero Cairn, which marks the start of the Alaska Hwy., and the Zero Milepost are in the center of town. Alpine skiing, camping, hiking and fishing are popular recreational activities.

Dawson Creek & District Chamber of Commerce: 10201 10th St., Dawson Creek, BC, Canada V1G 3T5; phone (250) 782-4868.

DAWSON CREEK STATION MUSEUM AND VISITORS' INFORMATION CENTRE is at 900 Alaska Ave. Artifacts, fossils and mounted animals and birds from the Peace River region are displayed. Highlights include an early 1900s railway caboose and a 1930s grain elevator as well as an art gallery and a video presentation about construction of the Alaska Highway. Daily 7-6:30, May-Aug.; Mon.-Sat. 9-5 in Sept.; Tues.-Sat. 9-4, rest of year. Closed Jan. 1, Good Friday, Nov. 11 and Dec. 25-26. Admission $2; $5 (family). Phone (250) 782-9595 for the Visitors' Information Centre.

WALTER WRIGHT PIONEER VILLAGE is just w. of jct. Hwy. 97N (Alaska Hwy.) and Hwy. 97S (Hart Hwy.). The complex of pioneer buildings includes a log schoolhouse, log cabin, general store, smithy and two churches. All contain period furnishings. An extensive collection of farm machinery and implements also is featured as well as nine flower gardens, a memorial rose garden and a lake for swimming. Food is available. Allow 1 hour minimum. Daily 9-6, June 1-Sept. 1. Donations. Phone (250) 782-7144.

DELTA—*see Vancouver p. 174.*

DUNCAN (H-10) pop. 4,699, elev. 15 m/49'

Founded in 1887 as Alderlea, Duncan was renamed in 1912 in honor of farmer William Duncan, who gave his land for the original townsite. Settlers were attracted by the promise of copper and coal on nearby Mount Sicker, where abandoned mines and original homesteads still can be seen. The growth of the logging and farming industries brought increasing numbers to Duncan and the Cowichan Valley.

The area around Duncan is known for the handspun woolen sweaters produced by the Cowichan Indians. West on Hwy. 18 is the Cowichan Valley Demonstration Forest with scenic viewpoints and signs describing forest management practices and ecology. More than 80 totem poles dot the town of Duncan.

Duncan-Cowichan Chamber of Commerce: 381 Trans-Canada Hwy., Duncan, BC, Canada V9L 3R5; phone (888) 303-3337.

Shopping areas: Whippletree Junction, a group of shops and boutiques with late 1800s storefronts, is 5 kilometres (3 mi.) south on the Trans-Canada Hwy.

BC FOREST DISCOVERY CENTRE is 1.5 km (1 mi.) n. off Hwy. 1 to 2892 Drinkwater Rd. The site has more than 40 hectares (99 acres) of forest and interactive displays and videotapes depicting British Columbia's forestry heritage, management practices and renewal efforts. In addition to a logging museum there are Douglas fir trees, forestry equipment and an old-time logging camp. A nature trail and a ride on a logging train are available July through August; a Christmas train ride is available in late November and December.

Daily 10-5, July 2-Sept. 1; Thurs.-Mon. 10-4:30, Mar. 21-July 1 and Sept. 2-Oct. 13; Fri.-Sun. 4-9, Nov. 28-Dec. 21. Admission $14; $12 (ages 13-18 and 66+); $9 (ages 5-12). Christmas train $5. MC, VI. Phone (250) 715-1113 or (866) 715-1113.

QUW'UTSUN' CULTURAL AND CONFERENCE CENTRE is 1 blk. w. of Hwy. 1 at 200 Cowichan Way. The 6-acre site consists of a living-history museum and a gallery dedicated to the preservation and dissemination of the culture of the Northwest Coast Indians. Exhibits include numerous totem poles and historical artifacts as well as the Comeakin longhouse and Khenipsen Carving House. Interpretive tours, craft demonstrations and a film presentation also are featured.

Food is available. Allow 1 hour minimum. Daily 10-5, Dec. 1-24; Mon.-Fri. 10-5, Sat.-Sun. 10-4,

holidays 10-3, May-Sept.; Mon.-Fri. 10-4, rest of year. Closed Dec. 25-26. Guided tours are offered on the hour; multimedia presentations begin on the half-hour. Admission $13; $11 (ages 13-18 and 56+); $2 (ages 4-12). Rates may vary; phone ahead. Phone (250) 746-8119 or (877) 746-8119.

ERRINGTON (G-10) pop. 2,122

NORTH ISLAND WILDLIFE RECOVERY ASSOCIATION is .7 km (.4 mi.) e. on Grafton Ave., then .4 km (.25 mi.) n. to 1240 Leffler Rd. Bald eagles, owls, hawks, swans and black bears are among the animals that can be viewed at this 8-acre rehabilitation facility. An eagle flight cage houses eagles waiting to be released into the wild.

A nature museum, wildlife learning center, nature trails and a release pond are on the grounds. Picnicking is permitted. Allow 30 minutes minimum. Daily 9-5, Apr.-Oct. Admission $5; $3 (ages 3-12). MC, VI. Phone (250) 248-8534.

FAIRMONT HOT SPRINGS (B-12) pop. 400, elev. 810 m/2,657'

At the north end of Columbia Lake, Fairmont Hot Springs were discovered about 1840. This popular resort area offers four hot mineral springs with temperatures averaging 35 to 45 C (95 to 113 F). Water sports and alpine and cross-country skiing also are available. *See Recreation Chart and the AAA/CAA Western Canada & Alaska CampBook.*

RECREATIONAL ACTIVITIES
Skiing

- **Fairmont Hot Springs Resort** is on 5225 Fairmont Resort Rd. Write P.O. Box 10, Fairmont Hot Springs, BC, Canada V0B 1L0. Other activities are available. Skiing daily 9:30-4, mid-Dec. to early Apr. Phone (250) 345-6311 or (800) 663-4979.

FERNIE (C-12) pop. 4,611, elev. 1,005 m/3,297'

At the foot of Trinity Mountain in the British Columbia Rockies, Fernie is a year-round recreation center. The many surrounding lakes and mountains provide opportunities for boating, fishing, hiking, camping and skiing. Mount Fernie Provincial Park is 4.8 kilometres (3 mi.) east *(see Recreation Chart and the AAA/CAA Western Canada & Alaska CampBook)*. Prentice and Rotary parks are downtown.

Fernie Chamber of Commerce: 102 Commerce Rd., Fernie, BC, Canada V0B 1M5; phone (250) 423-6868 or (877) 433-7643.

RECREATIONAL ACTIVITIES
Skiing

- **Fernie Alpine Resort** is 5 km (3 mi.) s.w. off Hwy. 3 at 5339 Fernie Ski Hill Rd., Fernie, BC, Canada V0B 1M6. Other activities are offered. Daily 9-4, early Dec. to early Apr. Phone (250) 423-4655 or (800) 258-7669.

White-water rafting

- **Mountain High River Adventures Inc.** collects passengers at Riverside Mountain Lodge at 100 Riverside Way. Write P.O. Box 221, Fernie, BC, Canada V0B 1M0. Other activities are offered. Daily 8-8, May-Sept. Reservations are required. Phone (250) 423-5008 or (877) 423-4555.

FORT LANGLEY (H-12)
pop. 2,641, elev. 12 m/39′

BRITISH COLUMBIA FARM MACHINERY AND AGRICULTURAL MUSEUM is at 9131 King St. This complex of buildings features artifacts and exhibits devoted to the development of farm machinery in British Columbia. Included are a handwrought plow, a threshing machine, carriages and buckboards, and a Tiger-Moth airplane used for crop dusting. A research library also is available. Allow 30 minutes minimum. Daily 10-4, Apr. 1 through mid-Oct. Admission $4; $2 (ages 13-18 and 61+); $2 (ages 6-12). Phone (604) 888-2273.

LANGLEY CENTENNIAL MUSEUM AND NATIONAL EXHIBITION CENTRE is at 9135 King St. Regional artifacts reflect the lifestyle of early explorers, fur traders and First Nations peoples. Re-created period rooms include a parlor, a kitchen and a general store. Displays also feature wood carvings, stone artifacts and baskets from the Coast Salish culture. Changing exhibits focus on art, science and Canadian and world history. Mon.-Sat. 10-4:45, Sun. 1-4:45; closed Good Friday, Easter Monday, Nov. 11 and Dec. 25-Jan. 4. Donations. Phone (604) 888-3922.

FORT LANGLEY NATIONAL HISTORIC SITE OF CANADA (H-11)

Fort Langley National Historic Site of Canada is 6.5 kilometres (4 mi.) north of Langley off Hwy. 1 at 23433 Mavis Ave. The park occupies the Fraser River site of the 19th-century Hudson's Bay Company trading post, an important supply link in the company's network of fur trading forts west of the Rockies. British Columbia was proclaimed a colony from the site in 1858.

The site preserves an original 1840 storehouse and reconstructed Red River-style wooden buildings, including a cooperage and blacksmith's shop and a log palisade. From March to October interpreters in period costumes demonstrate fur-trading activities. A visitor center displays contemporary exhibits and an orientation videotape. Special events are presented throughout the year.

Picnicking is permitted. Allow 1 hour minimum. Daily 9-8, late June-early Sept., daily 10-5, rest of year. Closed Jan. 1 and Dec. 25-26. Admission $7.90; $6.65 (ages 65+); $3.95 (ages 6-16); $19.80 (family). Phone (604) 513-4777.

FORT NELSON (B-5)
pop. 4,188, elev. 405 m/1,350′

Originally a fur-trading post, Fort Nelson thrived with the building of the Alaska Hwy. during World War II. Nearby mountains, lakes, parks, forests and diverse wildlife populations make Fort Nelson a destination for adventurous tourists, anglers and hunters.

Fort Nelson Visitor InfoCentre: 5340 50th Ave. N., Box 196, Fort Nelson, BC, Canada V0C 1R0; phone (250) 774-6400.

FORT NELSON HERITAGE MUSEUM is w. on Hwy. 97. An albino moose is among the stuffed animals displayed at the museum, which chronicles the history of Fort Nelson. Exhibits include vintage cars, photographs of the construction of the Alaska Hwy. and a trapper's log cabin. Allow 30 minutes minimum. Daily 8:30-7:30, mid-May to mid-Sept.; closed July 1 for morning parade. Admission $5; $3 (ages 5-16 and senior citizens); $10 (family). MC, VI. Phone (250) 774-3536.

FORT RODD HILL AND FISGARD LIGHTHOUSE NATIONAL HISTORIC SITES—*see Victoria p. 194.*

FORT ST. JAMES (E-4)
pop. 1,927, elev. 680 m/2,230′

Established in 1806 by Simon Fraser and John Stuart, the fur-trading post of Fort St. James became the capital of New Caledonia in 1821. Furs from outlying New Caledonia posts were brought overland to Fort St. James by dog sled and then shipped south during the spring thaw to the coast by canoe and horse.

During this time George Simpson, governor of the Hudson's Bay Co.'s vast empire, visited the fort. Determined to impress the Carrier Indians, Simpson organized a flamboyant procession complete with flute, bugle and bagpipe players in Highland dress, accompanied by a dog with a music box around its neck. Thereafter, the awe-struck Indians reverently referred to Simpson as the "great chief whose dog sings."

A Roman Catholic mission was founded at the fort in 1843. Services continue to be held in Our Lady of Good Hope Church, which was built in 1873 and is one of the oldest churches in British Columbia.

Mining activity supplemented the capital's trapping enterprises after the discovery of gold in the Omineca region in 1869. Interest in mining rekindled during World War II when the Pinchi Mine a few kilometres north yielded more mercury than any other mine in the British Commonwealth.

A lack of highways and railways prompted Fort St. James to pioneer bush flying as a means of transportation; it has served as an air base since the earliest days of charter flight.

The north shore of Stuart Lake, 16 kilometres (10 mi.) west, features some of the earliest signs of habitation in the form of prehistoric rock paintings just above the high-water mark. Although Fort St. James has emerged from relative wilderness, its surrounding evergreen forests continue to be among the best big-game hunting areas in the province. Alpine skiing is available nearby.

Fort St. James Chamber of Commerce: 115 Douglas Ave., P.O. Box 1164, Fort St. James, BC, Canada V0J 1P0; phone (250) 996-7023.

FORT ST. JAMES NATIONAL HISTORIC SITE OF CANADA is 2 blks. w. of Hwy. 27. Established on the southern shore of Stuart Lake by the North West Co. in 1806, Fort St. James contains one of the largest groups of original wooden buildings from Canada's fur trade. A massive fur warehouse is a noted example of Red River framing. The fully restored Hudson's Bay Co. post on the site served as a hub of commerce between fur traders and the First Nations peoples—and as the capital of New Caledonia, now central British Columbia.

The visitor center provides pictorial displays, artifacts and an audiovisual presentation. Changing exhibits also are offered seasonally. Interpreters in period costume provide living-history demonstrations throughout the day. Food is available. Allow 2 hours minimum. Daily 9-5, mid-May through Sept. 30; by appointment rest of year. Admission $7.90; $6.65 (ages 66+); $3.25 (ages 6-16); $16.25 (family). Prices may vary; phone to confirm. Phone (250) 996-7191.

FORT ST. JOHN (C-6)
pop. 16,034, elev. 695 m/2,280'

One of the oldest European settlements in the province, Fort St. John was established in 1793 as a fur-trading outpost called Rocky Mountain Fort. Residents engage in gas and oil exploration as well as the lumber industry and cattle ranching. There are coalfields to the south and west.

Recreational activities include fishing for Arctic grayling and gray trout in nearby Charlie Lake *(see Recreation Chart and the AAA/CAA Western Canada & Alaska CampBook)*, canoeing the rapids of the Peace River, skiing, and hunting for mountain caribou, mountain goats and black bears in the Rocky Mountain foothills. Floatplanes operating out of Charlie Lake provide access to the wilderness surrounding Fort St. John, and Hwy. 29 provides scenic driving to Chetwynd.

Fort St. John Visitor Centre: 9523-100th St., Fort St. John, BC, Canada V1J 4N4; phone (250) 785-3033 or (877) 785-6037.

FORT STEELE (C-12)
pop. 600, elev. 771 m/2,529'

Founded during the 1864 Kootenay gold rush, Fort Steele, then known as Galbraith's Ferry, became the site of the first North West Mounted Police west of the Rockies. In 1888 the settlement's name was changed to honor police superintendent Samuel Steele, who peacefully settled tensions between European settlers and the Ktunaxa people.

As a result of the mining boom of the 1890s the town became a thriving center of trade, transportation, communication and social activity, with a population of more than 2,000. In 1898 the British Columbia Southern Railroad bypassed Fort Steele in favor of Cranbrook, 16 kilometres (10 mi.) southwest, and the town began its decline. At the end of World War II Fort Steele had fewer than 50 residents.

FORT STEELE HERITAGE TOWN is 3 km (1.9 mi.) s.w. at 9851 Hwy. 93/95. The 11-hectare (27-acre) site preserves an 1890s boomtown. More than 60 restored, reconstructed or original buildings include an operating bakery, restaurant, tinsmith shop, blacksmith shop and newspaper office. Street dramas and demonstrations such as quilting, horse farming and ice cream making help re-create life in the era.

Fort Steele's Clydesdales give wagon rides daily mid-June through Labour Day and perform a six-horse hitch show on July 1. Live entertainment is presented in the Wild Horse Theatre, late June through Labour Day. Steam train rides are available during this time. A visitor reception center contains exhibits about the town's history.

Grounds open daily 9:30-5. Last admission 1 hour before closing. Programs, including street skits depicting daily life of the late 1890s, are presented daily 9:30-5:30, late June-Labour Day. The Wild Horse Theatre show is presented daily at 2, late June-Labour Day.

Admission July-Aug., $14; $13 (ages 65+); $5.50 (ages 13-18); $3.50 (ages 6-12). Admission rest of year $10; $9.50 (ages 65+); $4.50 (ages 13-18); $2.50 (ages 6-12). Phone (250) 417-6000 or (250) 426-7352.

GALIANO ISLAND—
see Gulf Islands National Park Reserve of Canada p. 125.

GIBSONS (G-11) pop. 3,906

SUNSHINE COAST MUSEUM & ARCHIVES is at 716 Winn Rd. Two floors of exhibits explain the history of the Sunshine Coast and its inhabitants. The main floor features displays about the area's maritime past; the upper floor recounts information about the First Nations peoples and pioneers as well as natural history and industries. Allow 1 hour minimum. Tues.-Sat. 10:30-4:30; closed statutory holidays. Donations. Phone (604) 886-8232.

GLACIER NATIONAL PARK OF CANADA (A-10)

Elevations in the park range from 500 metres (1,640 ft.) at Revelstoke to 3,390 metres (11,121 ft.) at Mount Dawson. Refer to CAA/AAA maps for additional elevation information.

West of the Rockies in the southeast, Glacier National Park of Canada and its smaller counterpart

Mount Revelstoke National Park of Canada (see place listing p. 133) encompass portions of the rugged Columbia Mountains. The 1,350 square kilometres (521 sq. mi.) of hard rock terrain present a jagged profile of angular mountains with narrow steep-walled valleys. The steep mountain slopes and enormous snowfall make this region susceptible to avalanches.

Rogers Pass in the heart of the park became the scene of a pitched 19th-century battle between the railroad engineers and these mountains. Sheer walls, numerous slide areas and severe weather proved almost insurmountable obstacles to the completion of Canada's first transcontinental railroad. Some of the largest railroad trestles then known were built to carry the line across raging streams to the summit of this pass across the Selkirks.

From there the tracks crossed to the southern wall of the valley on several loops to avoid the numerous avalanche slopes and the steep downgrade. Despite the ingenuity of its engineers, the new railroad had to be abandoned to the devastating winter forces that closed the pass the first year of construction. Avalanches attaining speeds of up to 325 kilometres (202 mi.) per hour tore up sections of the new track and left other sections buried under tons of snow.

Thirty-one snowsheds were built to shield the track, but even this was not enough. In 1910, 58 men were killed by an avalanche as they were clearing snow from an earlier slide. This incident, mounting costs and the dangerous grades of this section convinced the railroad to tunnel under Mount MacDonald.

The Trans-Canada Hwy. met similar obstacles as it crossed the pass, but the use of mobile howitzers to dislodge potential slides and other methods of controlling avalanches have held the road's position in the pass. Evidence of the struggle to build the railroad is visible from the road and the park's various campgrounds.

Several short trails follow the railroad's progress, winding past the ruins of Glacier House, a 19th-century resort hotel, remains of former snow sheds and the stone pillars that once supported the railroad trestles.

History is only part of the park's attractions. Twelve percent of the park is covered perpetually by snow and ice; more than 400 glaciers are scattered throughout the park. The contrast of the deep green forests and meadows with the glacial whites of these crags makes the park especially scenic.

Towering above the richly wooded valleys, the 3,297-metre (10,817-ft.) Mount Sir Donald rises to the east of the campgrounds, with Eagle and Uto peaks to the north. Day-hiking trails lead toward the Illecillewaet and Asulkan glaciers.

General Information and Activities

The park is open all year, but winter conditions are rigorous. Illecillewaet campground, the center of the park's best ski touring area, and Beaver River picnic area offer limited winter skiing. During the summer some of the popular activities are camping, hiking and mountaineering.

From Illecillewaet campground interpreters lead evening strolls and campfire talks as well as summer hikes that pass through the different life zones of the park's flora and fauna.

In addition, an extensive network of challenging day-hiking trails leads to such attractions as the Illecillewaet and Asulkan glaciers; Mount Abbott, with several fine viewpoints; Mount Tupper; and the Rogers group of peaks.

Grizzly and black bears are common in Glacier National Park of Canada; be cautious and make noise frequently as you hike. Climbers and overnight hikers may register at Rogers Pass Centre before and after every trip. Topographical maps and a hiker's guide also are available. Park use permits can be purchased at the welcome stations and the Rogers Pass Centre. See Recreation Chart and the AAA/CAA Western Canada & Alaska CampBook.

ADMISSION to the park is $6.90; $5.90 (ages 65+); $3.45 (ages 6-16); $17.30 (all occupants of a private vehicle with up to seven people). AX, MC, VI .

PETS are permitted in the park provided they are on a leash at all times.

ADDRESS inquiries to the Superintendent, Glacier and Mount Revelstoke National Parks of Canada, P.O. Box 350, Revelstoke, BC, Canada V0E 2S0; phone (250) 837-7500.

ROGERS PASS CENTRE is 1.3 km (.8 mi.) e. of the Rogers Pass summit. Modeled after the snowsheds that once protected the railroad from avalanches, the visitor center includes a theater, an exhibit hall with railway models and displays about natural history. Allow 30 minutes minimum. Daily 7:30 a.m.-8 p.m., mid-June through Labour Day; daily 8-4, day after Labour Day-Oct. 31 and Dec. 1 through mid-June; Thurs.-Mon. 8-4, in Nov. Schedule may vary; phone ahead. Free. Phone (250) 814-5232.

GOLDEN (A-10) pop. 4,020, elev. 785 m/2,575′

On the Trans-Canada Hwy. at the confluence of the Columbia and Kicking Horse rivers, Golden is near Glacier (see place listing p. 122) and Yoho national parks of Canada (see place listing p. 198) as well as Banff National Park of Canada (see place listing in Alberta p. 42). The community also is an outfitting point for sports enthusiasts.

The Golden and District Museum is at 11th Avenue and 13th Street. The museum is housed in a restored one-room schoolhouse and contains local historical items.

Kicking Horse Country Chamber of Commerce: 500 10th Ave. N., P.O. Box 1320, Golden, BC, Canada V0A 1H0; phone (250) 344-7125 or (800) 622-4653.

RECREATIONAL ACTIVITIES
White-water Rafting

- [SAVE] **Alpine Rafting Co.** is at 1416 Goldenview Rd. Write P.O. Box 1272, Golden, BC, Canada V0A 1H0. Trips depart daily 8 a.m.-9 p.m., mid-May to early Sept. Phone (250) 344-6778 or (888) 599-5299.

- [SAVE] **Glacier Raft Company** is at 612 N. 7th St. Write P.O. Box 428, Golden, BC, Canada V0A 1H0. Trips depart daily at 10 and 1, mid-May to mid-Sept. Phone (250) 344-6521.

GOLD RIVER (H-2)
pop. 1,359, elev. 122 m/400'

At the joining of the Gold and Heber rivers, the town of Gold River was built in 6 months in 1965 for employees of a pulp mill. The town, with its beautiful untamed countryside, has become popular with fishermen, photographers, hikers and campers.

The MV *Uchuck III* departs from the dock on Hwy. 28. The full-day and overnight cruises explore Tahsis, Nootka Sound and Friendly Cove, where Capt. James Cook met Chief Maquinna and the Nootka Indians when he landed on Vancouver Island in 1778; phone (250) 283-2418 for the tourist information center or (250) 283-2207 for the municipal office during off-season.

GRAND FORKS (D-9) pop. 4,054

Settlement at the confluence of the Kettle and Granby rivers began in the late 1800s when copper, gold and silver were discovered in the area. After 20 years of prosperity Grand Forks suffered reverses when the local copper smelter, said to be the largest in the British Empire, closed due to faltering copper prices. The logging industry and seed growing operations later restored stability to the community.

The downtown Boundary District contains preserved historic homes, stores and civic buildings from the settlement period. It is flanked on the south and east by rivers, on the west by 5th Avenue and on the north by 75th Avenue. A walking tour map is available at the Boundary Museum (*see attraction listing*).

Chamber of Commerce of the City of Grand Forks: 7362 Fifth St., P.O. Box 1086, Grand Forks, BC, Canada V0H 1H0; phone (250) 442-2833 or (866) 442-2833.

BOUNDARY MUSEUM is at 7370 Fifth St. The museum depicts the area's history from the late 1800s. Artifacts, maps and photographs show the lifestyles of the Doukhobor and First Nations cultures. Other exhibits include a scale model and display of Grand Forks' Chinatown in the 1900s, a wildlife exhibit and a 1929 fire truck. Note: the museum is closed temporarily; plans are to reopen in 2008 at a new location. Daily 9:30-4:30, June-Aug.; Mon.-Fri. 9:30-4:30, rest of year. Admission $4; $2 (ages 13-17 and 60+); free (ages 0-11 with paying adult); $7 (family). Phone (250) 442-3737.

GULF ISLANDS NATIONAL PARK RESERVE OF CANADA (G-10)

Separated from the San Juan Islands in Washington only by an international boundary, the almost 200 islands of various shapes and sizes that make up the Gulf Islands nestle against the southeast coast of Vancouver Island. Formed by a series of moving land masses beginning about 100 million years ago, today's Gulf Islands are the result of a mass collision of land that produced the long ridges of sandstone, conglomerate and shale that constitute the islands' geology.

The area was discovered by Capt. George Vancouver while on a quest to find a northwest passage to the Orient in 1792. Erroneously named Gulf of Georgia by Vancouver, the water separating Vancouver Island from the southwestern portion of British Columbia was later correctly termed the Strait of Georgia. The islands, however, retained the designation Gulf Islands.

The area features a climate that is sunnier and milder than that found on the nearby mainland. The quiet waters promote a much quieter lifestyle as well, and the islands are a haven from the frantic pace of nearby cities. Each island, though similar in many respects, has its own distinct identity. Easily reached from the mainland, they have become popular weekend retreats offering varying degrees of amenities and activities. Artists and professionals have joined the population of local fishermen who relish the peaceful lifestyle created by the sparkling waters, cliffs, winding roads and parks.

The islands are a haven for various wildlife, including such endangered species as the anatum peregrine falcon, the sharp-tailed snake, Townsend's big-eared bat and the western meadowlark. The southern Gulf Islands are home to the endangered Garry Oak ecosystem. Various shorebirds, waterfowl, great blue herons, seals and sea lions also inhabit the area.

The main components of the southern Gulf Islands are Galiano, Mayne, North and South Pender, Salt Spring and Saturna islands. Although they can be explored by automobile, the best way to experience the islands is by bicycle or foot. The Islands Trust, a governmental agency, is charged with preserving and protecting the islands and waters in the Strait of Georgia.

BC Ferries provides year-round service to the main islands from Tsawwassen, south of Vancouver, and Swartz Bay, near Victoria. Vehicle reservations are recommended for travel between the mainland and the islands, but are not available for travel between Vancouver Island and the Gulf Islands or for inter-island travel. It is advisable to make reservations as far in advance as possible for summer and holiday travel. For schedule information and reservations phone (250) 386-3431 from the Victoria area and outside British Columbia or (888) 223-3779 from elsewhere in the province. Air service also is available.

Established in 2003, Gulf Islands National Park Reserve of Canada protects an island landscape of rocky headlands, forested hills and shorelines studded with colorful tidepools. The park encompasses areas of lands scattered over fifteen larger islands and includes many smaller islets and reefs. Waters adjacent to park lands, extending 200 metres (650 ft.) seaward, also are under Parks Canada management.

The park shares the larger populated islands of Mayne, Saturna and the Penders with communities that offer a range of tourist amenities. Facilities and services inside the national park reserve are currently limited. The populated larger islands are accessible by vehicle, bicycle and BC Ferries from Vancouver and Victoria. The smaller islands are accessible by only boat or kayak. Water taxis also operate in several areas. Many local tour operators offer such recreational opportunities as cycling, kayaking, scuba diving, whale-watching or hiking. Comfortable, sturdy shoes and water are recommended for all hiking excursions.

For more information contact the Gulf Islands National Park Reserve of Canada InfoCentre, 2220 Harbour Rd., Sidney, BC, Canada V8L 2P6; phone (250) 654-4000. *See Recreation Chart.*

Galiano Island (G-10) pop. 1,071

Named after Spanish explorer Dionisio Alcala Galiano, Galiano Island is a long narrow island that is a haven for bird watchers and naturalists. Bicycling, horseback riding, kayaking, fishing, sailing, diving, swimming and hiking are popular recreational activities. The efforts of hikers and cyclists are rewarded with grand vistas and viewpoints. Mount Galiano provides climbers with eye-catching views of the southern Gulf Islands and the Olympic Mountains.

Montague Harbour Marine Provincial Park has 3,000-year-old Indian middens; camping facilities are available at the park as well as at Dionisio Point Provincial Park *(see Recreation Chart and the AAA/ CAA Western Canada & Alaska CampBook).* The Descanso Bay Regional Park offers 30 camping sites *(see Recreation Chart).*

Galiano Island Chamber of Commerce: P.O. Box 73, Galiano Island, BC, Canada V0N 1P0; phone (250) 539-2233.

Mayne Island (H-10) pop. 547

Although visited by the Spanish in the 1790s, it was not until the 1850s that British Capt. George Richards surveyed and mapped the area. Capt. Richards named Mayne Island after his lieutenant, Richard Charles Mayne. During the gold rush of the mid-1800s the island, halfway between Victoria and the mouth of the Fraser River, was a stopping point for miners heading for the riches to be found at the gold fields along the river.

The island is known as a haven for artists and artisans. Small and sparsely settled, Mayne offers quiet beaches and hiking trails; wildflowers; a landscape heavy with trees; seals, sea lions, salmon and sole offshore; and a large variety of birds, from tiny hummingbirds to soaring bald eagles.

Mayne Island Community Chamber of Commerce: P.O. Box 2, Mayne Island, BC, Canada V0N 2J0.

Pender Islands (H-10)

The Penders, consisting of North and South Pender islands, are connected by a one-lane wooden bridge that spans the canal linking Bedwell and Browning harbors. An archeological dig conducted at the time the bridge was built found evidence of island occupation dating back 4,000 years.

The island's 20 public ocean access points and many coves allow ample opportunities for swimming and picnicking. Hiking, boating, fishing, golfing, bicycling, kayaking and scuba diving are other available recreational activities. Roadside stands offer locally grown produce. The view from the summit of Mount Norman is worth the climb.

Tourism Association of Vancouver Island-Pender Islands: 335 Wesley St., Suite 203, Nanaimo, BC, Canada V9R 2T5; phone (250) 754-3500.

Quadra Island (E-10) pop. 2,548

Old totem poles are found within the Indian reservation on Quadra Island, which is reached by a 15-minute ferry ride from Campbell River *(see place listing p. 115).*

Salt Spring Island (H-10) pop. 9,381

Originally called Chuan Island, then Admiral Island, Salt Spring Island is the largest of the Gulf Island group and a popular spot for yachting, cycling, fishing and golfing. Bicycle and kayak rentals are available.

Although it is one of the most developed of the islands, it retains a rural feel. Mount Maxwell Park has a scenic drive leading to 610-metre (2,001-ft.) Baynes Peak. Ruckle Provincial Park *(see Recreation Chart)* offers 7 kilometres (4.3 mi.) of shoreline and has walking trails; bicycling, fishing, kayaking and picnicking are permitted.

The island also features popular Saturday farmers markets and arts and crafts, and is home to many fine artists such as Robert Bateman and Carol Evans. Ganges is the island's commercial hub.

Ferries operate daily from the island's three ferry terminals—between Swartz Bay and Fulford Harbour, between Crofton and Vesuvius Bay and between Long Harbour (the largest of the terminals) and Tsawwassen. For schedules and information phone BC Ferries, (250) 386-3431 from the Victoria area or outside British Columbia or (888) 223-3779 from elsewhere in the province.

Salt Spring Island Travel InfoCentre: 121 Lower Ganges Rd., Salt Spring Island, BC, Canada V8K 2T1; phone (250) 537-5252 or (866) 216-2936.

Saturna Island (H-10) pop. 319

Saturna Island—remote, rugged and sparsely populated—is probably the least visited of the Gulf

Islands. Mountain biking is one of the best ways to see the island. Its bays, beaches and tidal pools offer glimpses of many varieties of marine life. The southernmost of the Gulf Islands, Saturna offers hiking, bicycling and boating opportunities. There is no camping available and lodging is limited.

Tourism Association of Vancouver Island-Saturna Island: 335 Wesley St., Suite 203, Nanaimo, BC, Canada V9R 2T5; phone (250) 754-3500.

GWAII HAANAS NATIONAL PARK RESERVE AND HAIDA HERITAGE SITE (F-1)

Elevations in the park range from sea level along Kunghit and Moresby islands to 1,123 metres (696 ft.) at Mount de la Touche. Refer to CAA/AAA maps for additional elevation information.

Off the British Columbia coast west of Prince Rupert, Gwaii Haanas National Park Reserve and Haida Heritage Site is in the southern part of the Queen Charlotte Islands *(see place listing p. 151)*, a remote island chain. The Queen Charlotte Islands also are known as the Haida Gwaii Islands. This protected area is jointly managed by the Government of Canada and the Council of the Haida Nation.

The 1,470 square kilometres (912 sq. mi.) of Gwaii Haanas National Park Reserve and Haida Heritage Site offer a rich and fascinating diversity of flora, sea creatures and wildlife. Remnants of native village sites on the 138 islands capture the history of the Haida. Haida Gwaii Watchmen basecamps have been established at major sites of cultural significance. Watchmen provide site security and protection of the cultural features.

Access to the park reserve is challenging: The only way to and around Gwaii Haanas is by air or sea. Solo travel is recommended only for the experienced outdoor traveler. Licensed tour operators provide a variety of excursions. Sea kayaking, sailboat and powerboat charters are the most popular ways to tour Gwaii Haanas. There are no maintained trails or designated campsites, and only limited visitor facilities are provided within the park reserve.

The Queen Charlotte Islands can be reached by air from Vancouver and Prince Rupert. BC Ferries also provides year-round service between the islands and Prince Rupert. Arrangements for ferry transportation should be made well in advance and reservations are highly recommended; phone (250) 386-3431 from the Victoria area and outside British Columbia or (888) 223-3779 from elsewhere in the province.

Single-day admission $19.80; $16.80 (senior citizens); $9.90 (children); free (ages 0-16). Reservations are required to visit the reserve May through September. Regulations allow for no more than 12 people on shore in one place at one time.

Note: All visitors must participate in one 60-minute orientation session offered daily at visitor centers in Sandspit and Queen Charlotte; phone (250) 559-8818 to guarantee a place. For more information write to Gwaii Haanas National Park Reserve and Haida Heritage Site, P.O. Box 37, Queen Charlotte, BC, Canada V0T 1S0 or phone (250) 559-8818 or TTY (250) 559-8139.

HAGENSBORG (F-3) elev. 495'

SNOOTLI HATCHERY is 4 km (2.5 mi.) w. on Hwy. 20, following signs. The hatchery raises Chinook, Chum, Coho and Sockeye salmon as well as Steelhead trout for release into local rivers. Allow 30 minutes minimum. Mon.-Fri. 8-4. Guided tours are available 8:30-3:30, June-Sept. Free. Phone (250) 982-2214.

HARRISON HOT SPRINGS (C-7)
pop. 1,343, elev. 11 m/36'

At the foot of Harrison Lake, Harrison Hot Springs *(see Recreation Chart)* is a well-known health and vacation resort with two mineral springs and a sandy beach on the lakeshore. Strong area winds make this a favorite spot for windsurfing. The surrounding mountains are known as Sasquatch country, where sightings of the legendary apelike creature twice the size of a man have been reported dozens of times.

More likely to be found in the mountains are mutton-fat jades, garnets, agates, fossils and gold; the area is renowned among rockhounds.

Harrison Hot Springs Visitor InfoCentre: 499 Hot Springs Rd., P.O. Box 255, Harrison Hot Springs, BC, Canada V0M 1K0; phone (604) 796-5581.

HARRISON MILLS (D-7)
pop. 141, elev. 11 m/36'

KILBY HISTORIC SITE is 1.6 km (.9 mi.) s. of Hwy. 7 at 215 Kilby Rd. Costumed interpreters conduct tours of this 5-acre living-history site, once the heart of a thriving community of lumber mills. The 1906 General Store contains forgotten foodstuffs, a wood stove and the traditional checkerboard. Other highlights include the Heritage Post Office, the Manchester House Hotel and animals of the Waterloo Farm. Food is available. Daily 11-5, May-Sept. Hours vary rest of year; phone ahead. Admission $9; $8 (ages 66+); $7 (ages 6-18). Phone (604) 796-9576.

HAZELTON (D-3) pop. 345, elev. 306 m/1,004'

A showplace of Indian culture, Hazelton originally was called Git-an-maks, meaning "where people fish by torchlight." European settlers arriving in 1872 renamed the area Hazelton, after the profusion of hazelnut trees covering the fertile farmland.

Considered holy by the Gitxsan Indian community, the forest land within a 64.4-kilometre (40-mi.) radius of Hazelton has the province's greatest concentration of standing totem poles, many portrayed in paintings by British Columbia artist Emily Carr.

'KSAN HISTORICAL VILLAGE & MUSEUM is 5 km (3 mi.) s. on Hwy. 62. The Gitxsan Indian village consists of seven tribal houses. The 'Ksan Museum, the Frog House of the Stone Age, the Wolf House or Feast House, the Eagle House, the Fireweed House, the studio, the 'Ksan Shop, and the carving shed and workshop are decorated with paintings, carved interior poles and painted scenes in classic West Coast Indian style.

Guided tours are available. Daily 9-5:30, May 1 to mid-Oct.; Mon.-Fri. 10-4:30, rest of year. Admission $2. Tour $10; $8.50 (ages 66+ and students

with ID). MC, VI. Phone (250) 842-5544 or (877) 842-5518.

HOPE (C-7) pop. 6,184, elev. 39 m/127'

At the entrance to the Fraser River Valley, Hope dates from 1848 when the Hudson's Bay Co. established a fort. The town developed rapidly, especially during the gold rush of 1858. The 1859 Anglican Christ Church is one of the province's oldest churches.

From Hope the Trans-Canada Hwy. leads north to Fraser Canyon *(see Boston Bar p. 114)*. Kawkawa Lake *(see Recreation Chart)*, Lake of the Woods, Mount Hope, Mount Ogilvie and Skagit Valley *(see Recreation Chart)* are just some of the nearby places that offer year-round recreational opportunities.

The result of the 1965 Hope Slide is evident about 16 kilometres (10 mi.) east beside Hwy. 3. A plaque at the edge of the present roadway explains the collapse of the side of Johnson Peak, which buried the highway under 45 metres (148 ft.) of rubble.

The Hope Museum, inside the Hope Visitor Info-Centre, portrays the town's history through native artifacts and historical settings; phone (604) 869-2021. Hope was the location of several films, including "Rambo: First Blood," "Shoot to Kill" with Sidney Poitier, and Disney's "Far From Home: The Adventures of Yellow Dog."

The Hope Arts Gallery, 349 Fort St., features the work of more than 20 artists; phone (604) 869-2408. More art can be found scattered throughout downtown Hope. Wood carvings in such shapes as a gold prospector with his horse to a bald eagle holding a salmon in his talons were created from dying trees with a chainsaw; most are on the grounds of Memorial Park. Brochures about the more than two dozen carvings can be picked up at the Hope Visitor InfoCentre.

Hope Visitor InfoCentre: 919 Water Ave., P.O. Box 370, Hope, BC, Canada V0X 1L0; phone (604) 869-2021.

E.C. MANNING PROVINCIAL PARK is e. on Hwy. 3. The mountain park includes the Hope-Princeton Hwy. (Hwy. 3), a 134-kilometre (83-mi.) ride that climbs from near sea level at Hope to the 1,346-metre (4,416-ft.) summit of Allison Pass. Blackwall Road off Hwy. 3 leads to Cascade Lookout and offers access to a subalpine meadow. Recreational activities include hiking, camping, canoeing, birdwatching, cross-country skiing, mountain biking and horseback riding.

The park is open daily 24 hours. Campgrounds are open May-Oct. Park free. Camping $14-$22 per night. Phone (250) 840-8822 or (800) 330-3321. *See Recreation Chart and the AAA/CAA Western Canada & Alaska CampBook.*

 HELL'S GATE AIRTRAM— *see Boston Bar p. 114.*

OTHELLO-QUINTETTE TUNNELS are off Hwy. 3 exit 170 in Coquihalla Canyon Provincial Park; take

6th St. 1 blk. n. to Kawkawa Lake Rd., then 5 km (3 mi.) e. to Tunnels Rd. Five tunnels were built 1911-16 to complete a railroad through Coquihalla Canyon. The Coquihalla River zigzags through the canyon, presenting a challenge to engineer Andrew McCulloch, who used dynamite to blast through the canyon walls to create the narrow tunnels.

The railway ceased operations in 1959; wooden walkways now bridge the river's serpentine course between the tunnels and allow close-up views of the rushing waters.

Note: Wear shoes with good traction, as the gravel path through the tunnels may be wet and slippery. A flashlight is recommended for visibility. Picnicking is permitted. Allow 1 hour, 30 minutes minimum. Daily dawn-dusk, Apr.-Oct. Free. Parking $1 per hour; $3 per day. Phone (604) 476-9069.

HUDSON'S HOPE (D-4)
pop. 1,039, elev. 520 m/1,706′

Hudson's Hope is one of the oldest settlements in the province: Only two communities on Vancouver Island have been continuously occupied from earlier dates. First discovered in 1793 by Alexander Mackenzie, the area was the site of a small fur-trading post built in 1805. In 1900 the post was moved to the present site of Hudson's Hope on the north side of the Peace River, where it flourished as a center of trade for the Hudson's Bay Co.

Hudson's Hope is an important supplier of hydroelectricity; its two dams generate about 38 percent of the hydropower used in British Columbia. The dams also are major recreation centers for the area.

Hudson's Hope Travel InfoCentre: 9555 Beattie Dr., P.O. Box 330, Hudson's Hope, BC, Canada V0C 1V0; phone (250) 783-9154 mid-May through Aug. 31, or (250) 783-9901 rest of year.

HUDSON'S HOPE MUSEUM is at 9510 Beattie Dr. Housed in a 1942 Hudson's Bay Co. store, the museum contains local artifacts and a collection of prehistoric items including ichthyosaur fossils that were unearthed during construction of the W.A.C. Bennett dam. Outbuildings include an active log church built in 1938, a trapper's cabin, a fur cache and a pioneer house. A steamboiler and other antique machines are displayed on the grounds. Daily 9-5:30, mid-May to early Sept.; Mon.-Fri. 9:30-5, early Apr. to mid-May and early Sept.-early Nov.; by appointment rest of year. Donations. Phone (250) 783-5735.

PEACE CANYON DAM is 4 km (2.5 mi.) s. on Hwy. 29. Completed in 1980, the dam is 50 metres (165 ft.) high and 533 metres (1,750 ft.) long. It reuses water that has generated electricity at the W.A.C. Bennett Dam, 23 kilometres (14 mi.) upstream on the Peace River. Nearby recreational facilities include a campground, picnic facilities and a boat launch to Dinosaur Lake, the dam's reservoir.

Peace Canyon Dam Visitor Centre is next to the powerhouse. Exhibits reflect the area's natural history, its pioneer past and the Peace Canyon Project.

Highlights include a replica of the stern-wheeler SS *Peace River,* a large-scale model of a generating unit, displays about the damming of the Peace River, and mammoth tusks found during excavation. Visitors can view the project's central control system, walk across the dam or visit the observation area on the main floor.

Daily 8-4, Victoria Day-Labour Day; Mon.-Fri. 8-4, rest of year. Closed Jan. 1, Easter, second Mon. in Oct., Nov. 11 and Dec. 25-26. Free. Phone (250) 783-7418.

W.A.C. BENNETT DAM is 21 km (13 mi.) w. on Canyon Dr. following signs. A major hydroelectric project on the Peace River, the dam was completed in 1967 to produce electrical power for British Columbia. It is 183 metres (600 ft.) high, 2 kilometres (1.2 mi.) long and .8 kilometre (.5 mi.) thick at the base. Backup water from the dam forms 164,600-hectare (406,727-acre) Williston Lake, British Columbia's largest lake. Its shoreline stretches for 1,770 kilometres (1,100 mi.).

W.A.C. Bennett Dam Visitor Centre is about 1 km (.6 mi.) s.e. of the dam. Photographs and artifacts chronicle the history and geology of the region and the construction of the dam and powerhouse. A participatory exhibit demonstrates the generation of electricity and magnetism. Underground bus tours into the powerhouse and manifold chambers are available. A 40-minute multimedia presentation also is offered in the theater.

Note: Cameras, purses and bags are not permitted on the tour. Food is available. Center daily 10-6, Victoria Day-Labour Day. Bus tours are available 10:30-4:30. Multimedia presentation offered every hour 10:30-4:30. Last presentation begins at 4:30. Admission $5; $3 (children and senior citizens); $12 (family, two adults and two children); free (ages 0-6). Reservations are required for the tour. Phone (250) 783-5048 or (888) 333-6667.

INVERMERE (B-12) pop. 2,858

In the summer Invermere offers recreational opportunities that include hiking and camping, and fishing, boating and sailboarding on Lake Windermere. Hang gliders often are seen launching off nearby Mount Swansea. Birds can be seen at Wilmer National Wildlife Area, about 5 kilometres (3 mi.) north.

Columbia Valley Chamber of Commerce: 651 Hwy. 93/95, P.O. Box 1019, Invermere, BC, Canada V0A 1K0; phone (250) 342-2844.

WINDERMERE VALLEY MUSEUM is at 622 Third St. Pioneer artifacts and local archives are displayed in a complex in a small park. The six log outbuildings have thematic displays. Allow 1 hour minimum. Tues.-Sat. 10-4, July-Aug.; Mon.-Fri. 1-4, in June and Sept. Donations. Phone (250) 342-9769.

KAMLOOPS (B-8)
pop. 77,281, elev. 345 m/1,131′

Founded in 1812 as a North West Co. depot, Kamloops later was a Hudson's Bay Co. post. Developed where the north and south branches of the Thompson River converge to form Kamloops Lake, Kamloops was named after an Indian word, *cumcloups*, or "the meeting of the waters." During the gold rush of the 1860s the Overlanders reached the city by rafting down the North Thompson.

Since the Cariboo's gold supply disappeared in the 1860s, Kamloops has developed as a center of cattle and sheep ranching.

Lumber is an important natural resource in the area. Weyerhaeuser Canada Ltd., a pulp mill on Mission Flats Road, offers guided tours of its facility in July and August. Ages 0-11 are not permitted; long pants and flat, closed shoes are required. For information or reservations phone (800) 824-4412.

Area lakes offer good fishing; Kamloops trout are known to jump a few feet in the air after being hooked. Outdoor enthusiasts also enjoy golfing, nature trails, boating, kayaking, hiking and mountain biking.

Tourism Kamloops: 1290 W. Trans-Canada Hwy., Kamloops, BC, Canada V2C 6R3; phone (250) 372-8000. *See color ad.*

Self-guiding tours: Kamloops is the site of several historical attractions, including the provincial courthouse and several old houses and churches. Self-guiding tour brochures are available from Kamloops Museum and Archives.

BRITISH COLUMBIA WILDLIFE PARK is 17 km (10 mi.) e. on Hwy. 1 to 9077 Dallas Dr. Sixty-five species of local and endangered wildlife, including grizzly bears, timber wolves, cougars, moose, snakes and birds of prey live in natural habitats at this 50-hectare (120-acre) park. Highlights include interpretive talks, animal encounters, a children's play area and splash park, and seasonal miniature train. Discovery Centre features interactive displays. Wildlights, a holiday light display, is offered in December and January.

Park open daily 8-6, July-Aug.; 8-4:30, rest of year. Train departs daily 9-5, June-Sept.; 9:30-4, Mar. 15-May 31 and in Oct.; 5-9, Dec. 14-Jan. 6. Closed Dec. 25. Admission $12; $11 (ages 13-16 and 66+); $9 (ages 3-12). Train $1. Admission may vary; phone ahead. MC, VI. Phone (250) 573-3242.

SAVE **KAMLOOPS ART GALLERY** is at 465 Victoria St. Works by regional, national and international contemporary and First Nations artists are featured. Exhibits change monthly and include paintings, sculptures, prints, drawings, photographs, video art and First Nations art. Allow 30 minutes minimum. Mon.-Wed. and Fri.-Sat. 10-5, Thurs. 10-9, Sun. noon-4; closed statutory holidays. Admission Oct.-May $3; $3 (couples ages 62+); $2 (ages 62+ and students with ID). Admission rest of year $5; $5 (couples ages 62+); $3 (ages 62+ and students with ID); $8 (family); donations (Thurs. after 5). Admission may vary for certain exhibits; phone ahead. MC, VI. Phone (250) 377-2400.

SAVE **KAMLOOPS HERITAGE RAILWAY** is at #6-510 Lorne St. *The Spirit of Kamloops,* the restored steam locomotive 2141 with its hayrack cars and heritage coach, departs the Canadian National Railway station and carries passengers on a sightseeing tour, passing St. Joseph's Church along the way. Allow 1 hour, 30 minutes minimum. Mon.-Fri. 9-4:30. Hours may vary; phone ahead to confirm.

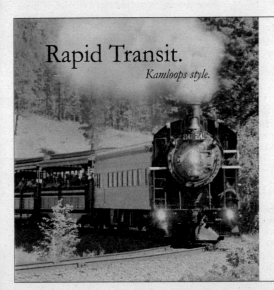

Passengers should arrive 30 minutes prior to departure. Fare $16; $13.50 (ages 61+); $9.50 (ages 5-18). AX, MC, VI. Phone (250) 374-2141.

KAMLOOPS MUSEUM AND ARCHIVES is at 207 Seymour St. The area's history is portrayed in displays of Indian culture, fly-fishing, a reconstructed Hudson's Bay Co. fur-trading cabin, pioneer and Victorian artifacts and tableaux, transportation items and natural history specimens. The archives has collections of photographs and manuscripts.

Guided tours are available. Allow 1 hour minimum. Tues.-Sat. 9:30-4:30; closed holidays. Guided walking tours are available July-Aug. Donations. Phone (250) 828-3576.

ST. JOSEPH'S CHURCH is n. on Mount Paul Way, then w. to end of Chilcotin St. Constructed by Roman Catholic missionaries and the Kamloops Indian Band in the late 19th century, the church has been meticulously renovated. The building's elaborate gilded altar and its many period religious artifacts also have been restored. Allow 30 minutes minimum. Wed.-Sat. 12:30-7:30, July 1-Labour Day. Hours may vary; phone ahead. Donations. Phone (250) 374-7323.

SECWEPEMC MUSEUM AND HERITAGE PARK is at 311-355 Yellowhead Hwy. The 5-hectare (12-acre) park interprets the history and culture of the Secwepemc, or Shuswap, Nation. A walking trail leads through the archeological remains of a 2,000-year-old Shuswap winter village, pit house reconstructions and a summer village. The park also features a museum and ethnobotanical gardens.

Allow 1 hour minimum. Daily 8:30-4:30, June 15-Labour Day; Mon.-Fri. 8:30-4:30, rest of year. Closed Jan. 1 and the last week in Dec. Admission $5; $2 (ages 7-17 and 60+); $12 (family). MC, VI. Phone (250) 828-9801.

GAMBLING ESTABLISHMENTS

- **Lake City Casino** is at 540 Victoria St. Daily 10 a.m.-2 a.m. Phone (250) 372-3336. *See color ad p. 142.*

RECREATIONAL ACTIVITIES

Skiing

- **Sun Peaks Resort** is 54 km (32 mi.) n. on Hwy. 5. Write 3150 Creekside Way, Suite 50, Sun Peaks, BC, Canada V0E 5N0. Other activities are available. Daily 9-5, mid-May to mid-Oct.; 8:30-4:30, mid-Nov. to mid-Apr. Phone (250) 578-7842 or (800) 807-3257.

KASLO (C-11) pop. 1,032, elev. 588 m/1,929'

Kaslo began as a mill site in 1888. Following large silver strikes in 1893 the town quickly expanded to city proportions. A village once again, Kaslo is a distribution center for the Lardeau Valley.

Duncan Dam, 42 kilometres (26 mi.) north, was the first of the three dams constructed by B.C. Hydro in accordance with the Columbia River Treaty,

ratified by British Columbia and the United States in 1964. Southwest of the dam is the Kokanee Spawning Channel, built to compensate for the loss of natural spawning areas resulting from the dam's construction. The 3.2-kilometre (2-mi.) channel, one of the longest in the world, is said to be the first constructed for freshwater fish.

SS *MOYIE* NATIONAL HISTORIC SITE is 1 blk. n. off Hwy. 31 at 324 Front St., following signs. Considered the world's oldest intact passenger sternwheeler, the *Moyie* operated on Kootenay Lake 1898-1957, hauling travelers and freight from Nelson to northern destinations along the shore. It is the last active commercial stern-wheeler in the province and contains artifacts, antiques, a model of Kaslo Harbor, a railway display and a photograph exhibit relating to the history of the vessel and its crew.

Allow 30 minutes minimum. Daily 9-5, mid-May to mid-Oct. Admission $5; $4 (ages 65+ and students with ID); $2 (ages 6-12); $15 (family). MC, VI. Phone (250) 353-2525.

KELOWNA — see Okanagan Valley p. 141

KEREMEOS (D-8) pop. 1,197, elev. 1,356'

The rich soil and desert climate of the Similkameen Valley drew early settlers, who planted the first fruit trees there in 1880. Today Keremeos is considered one of the best fruit-growing regions in British Columbia. Cherries, apples, grapes, peaches and apricots are among the area's bounties.

THE GRIST MILL AT KEREMEOS is 1.5 km (.9 mi.) n.e. on Hwy. 3A, then .8 km (.5 mi.) e. on Upper Bench Rd. Demonstrations of the principles of milling and restoration are offered at this 1877 flour mill, which features a working waterwheel and flume. A visitor center provides a schedule of living-history presentations for the Apple House Theatre and the summer kitchen. On the grounds are Victorian-era gardens, an heirloom apple orchard and heritage wheat fields.

Food is available. Camping is available. Allow 1 hour minimum. Daily 9-5, May-Sept. Admission $7.50; $6.50 (ages 65+); $5.50 (ages 12-18); $4.50 (ages 5-11). Phone (250) 499-2888.

KIMBERLEY (C-11)
pop. 6,484, elev. 1,113 m/3,651'

Kimberley is a winter sports center with a Bavarian theme and a pedestrian mall—the Platzl—complete with wandering minstrels and a huge cuckoo clock. The Kimberley Community Gardens present colorful views June through October.

Built on the slopes of Sullivan and North Star hills, Kimberley is one of Canada's highest cities. It is perhaps best known as the site of the Sullivan Mine, one of the world's largest underground silver, lead and zinc mines. The mine closed in 2001 after 92 years of production, yielding more than $20 billion in ore.

Kimberley Bavarian Society Chamber of Commerce: 270 Kimberley Ave., Kimberley, BC, Canada V1A 3N3; phone (250) 427-3666 or (866) 913-3666.

KIMBERLEY DISTRICT HERITAGE SOCIETY is in the Platzl at 105 Spokane St. Permanent and changing exhibits depict local history and the legacy of mining in the area. Archives are available for research. Tues.-Sat. 9-4:30, July-Aug.; Mon.-Fri. 1-4, rest of year. Closed holidays. Donations. Phone (250) 427-7510.

SULLIVAN MINE & RAILWAY HISTORICAL SOCIETY offers narrated 1-hour train rides departing the lower train station, 2 blks. n.w. of the Platzl. Passengers are transported through the Mark Creek Valley on a narrow-gauge mine track. Interactive mining displays are offered in an underground tunnel. Daily 11-5:30, July-Aug.; 1-4, mid-May through June 30 and in Sept. Hours may vary; phone ahead. Fare $15; $12 (ages 13-18 and 60+); $7 (ages 4-12). MC, VI. Phone (250) 427-0022.

RECREATIONAL ACTIVITIES

Skiing

- **Kimberley Alpine Resort** is above town via Gerry Sorenson Way to 301 North Star Blvd. Write P.O. Box 40, Kimberley, BC, Canada V1A 2Y5. Other activities are offered. Daily 9-4, mid-Dec. to mid-Mar. Phone (250) 427-4881 or (800) 258-7669.

KITIMAT (E-2) pop. 10,285, elev. 130 m/426′

Kitimat is a planned city built in the early 1950s by Alcan Smelters and Chemicals Ltd. The company chose the wilderness site for a new plant because of the area's deepwater harbor, flat land and hydroelectric plant.

Kitimat Chamber of Commerce: 2109 Forest Ave., P.O. Box 214, Kitimat, BC, Canada V8C 2G7; phone (250) 632-6294 or (800) 664-6554.

ALCAN PRIMARY METAL is n. on Hwy. 37. The company offers a videotape presentation and guided 2-hour bus tour of its aluminum smelter, one of the world's largest. Tours depart Mon.-Fri. at 1, June-Aug.; closed holidays. Donations. Reservations are recommended. Phone (250) 639-8259 June-Aug. or (800) 664-6554 rest of year.

KOOTENAY NATIONAL PARK OF CANADA (B-12)

Elevations in the park range from 918 metres (3,011 ft.) at the park entrance to 3,424 metres (11,235 ft.) at Deltaform Mountain. Refer to CAA/AAA maps for additional elevation information.

Straddling the Banff-Windermere Hwy. (Hwy. 93) as it travels down the western slope of the Rocky Mountains, Kootenay National Park of Canada encompasses 1,406 square kilometres (543 sq. mi.).

Following the Vermilion and Kootenay river valleys, this slender 94-kilometre-long (63-mi.) park embraces several significant geologic features; Kootenay National Park of Canada, a World Heritage Site, is representative of the Rocky Mountain landscape.

Extensive faults created two of the park's significant and different features. Radium Hot Springs at the park's southern end resulted from rainwater and runoff being vaporized deep underground. The steam then returned to the surface via the earth's fissures and condensed in these springs, which were popularized by health buffs at the turn of the 20th century.

At the other end of the park are the Paint Pots, cold springs with a spiritual significance rather than physical. The exit holes, formed by the deposits of the iron-laden water, resemble earthen pots; Blackfoot, Stoney and Kootenay Indians once used the bright bronze mud to stain their bodies, decorate their tepees and draw rock paintings once visible near Sinclair Canyon.

Less dramatic are the topographical differences in the park. The Brisco and Stanford ranges intercept much of the coastal moisture bound for the park's southern region, but to the north, beyond Kootenay Crossing, the climate becomes much damper.

The dry southern climate offers winter shelter for animals migrating from the north and provides good grazing conditions for herds of bighorn sheep. Bears, moose, mountain goats and elk are common. Trails ranging from short hikes to overnight treks explore the park's wealth of evergreen forests, alpine meadows, glaciers and lakes.

General Information and Activities

Although the park is open all year, its three main campgrounds are open only from early May to late September. Winter camping is available at Dolly Varden campground. Information about self-guiding walks, trails, features and facilities can be obtained from information centers in the village of Radium Hot Springs and at Vermilion Crossing from Victoria Day weekend through Labour Day and at the gateway or park headquarters during the rest of the year.

Nonmotorized watercraft are permitted on all lakes and rivers in the park. Climbers can register at the information centers, and back-country campers must obtain a wilderness pass. *See Recreation Chart and the AAA/CAA Western Canada & Alaska CampBook.*

ADMISSION to the park is $8.90; $7.65 (ages 65+); $4.45 (ages 6-16); $17.80 (all occupants of a private vehicle with up to seven people). MC, VI .

PETS must be leashed at all times. Pets are permitted in the back-country overnight.

ADDRESS inquiries to the Superintendent, Kootenay National Park of Canada, Box 220, Radium Hot Springs, BC, Canada V0A 1M0; phone (250) 347-9615 or (800) 748-7275.

Points of Interest

MARBLE CANYON is n. of McLeod Meadows along the Vermilion River and 90 m (295 ft.) from the road. The walls of gray limestone and quartzite laced with a stratum of white and gray dolomite make this one of the most beautiful canyons in the park. Tokumm Creek has cut a sheer, narrow cleft to the depth of about 39 metres (128 ft.).

A self-guiding trail follows the top edge of the canyon and leads to a waterfall. Interpretive signs describe the power of water in shaping the canyon's features. Allow 30 minutes minimum.

SAVE **RADIUM HOT SPRINGS** is just n. of the w. entrance to Kootenay National Park of Canada. Water temperatures range from 35 to 47 C (95 to 117 F). There is a hot pool, a cool pool and a 372-square-metre (4,000-sq.-ft.) day spa. Iron oxide also colors the towering sandstone cliffs, giving a perpetual sunset quality.

Pools open daily 9 a.m.-11 p.m., mid-May to mid-Oct.; Sun.-Thurs. noon-9, Fri.-Sat. noon-10, rest of year. Admission $7.50; $6.50 (ages 3-17 and 65+); $20 (family, two adults and two children, each additional child $3.50). MC, VI. Phone (250) 347-9485 or (800) 767-1611. *See place listing p. 152 and Recreation Chart.*

LADYSMITH (G-10)
pop. 6,587, elev. 40 m/131'

On the 49th parallel, Ladysmith is noted for its scenic position between mountain and sea. Founded during the Boer War, Ladysmith was named for a sister city in South Africa. Transfer Beach Park offers a playground, picnic tables and a swimming area watched by lifeguards.

Ladysmith & District Chamber of Commerce: 132C Roberts St., P.O. Box 598, Ladysmith, BC, Canada V9G 1A4; phone (250) 245-2112.

LAKE COWICHAN (G-10) pop. 2,827

KAATZA STATION MUSEUM AND ARCHIVES is at 125 S. Shore Rd. Housed in the renovated Esquimalt and Nanaimo railway station, the museum features murals, exhibits, photographs and archives pertaining to various industries as well as pioneer life in the area. Allow 30 minutes minimum. Daily 10-4, Mother's Day-Labour Day weekend; Mon.-Fri. 9-4, rest of year. Closed Dec. 15-Jan. 15. Schedule may vary; phone ahead. Admission $2; free (ages 0-18). Phone (250) 749-6142.

LANGLEY — *see Vancouver p. 174.*

LILLOOET (B-7) pop. 2,741, elev. 290 m/951'

Lillooet, on the Fraser River, marked the first leg of the Cariboo Wagon Road and was therefore sometimes referred to as "Mile 0." The trail reached north to such destinations as 100 Mile House and 150 Mile House, named for their distances from the start of the trail. In 1859, during the Cariboo Gold Rush, the 15,000 inhabitants of Lillooet made it the most populous city north of San Francisco and west of Chicago. The surrounding area now is of particular interest to rockhounds.

LILLOOET MUSEUM AND VISITOR CENTRE is at 790 Main St. Displays in the former Anglican church include local pioneer relics, farm equipment, Indian artifacts, Chinese utensils and late 19th-century rooms. The museum houses the newspaper equipment collection of Margaret "Ma" Murray, Lillooet's beloved publisher. Daily 9-6, July-Aug.; Tues.-Sat. 10-4, May-June and Sept.-Oct. Donations. Phone (250) 256-4308.

MIYAZAKI HOUSE is at 643 Russell Ln., near jct. Main St. and 6th Ave., following signs. Originally owned by Caspar and Cerise Phair, the late 19th-century house was built in the same architectural style as Mrs. Phair's family home in Ireland. In the 1940s, Dr. Masajiro Miyazaki and his family purchased the house. Visitors will learn about this family's history, including a period when the doctor treated residents of a local Japanese internment camp.

Guided tours are available. Allow 30 minutes minimum. Tues.-Sat. 10-4, June-Aug.; Mon.-Fri. 11-3, rest of year. Donations. Phone (250) 256-6808.

LYTTON (B-7) pop. 319, elev. 199 m/650'

At the junction of the Thompson and Fraser rivers, Lytton derives its livelihood from its location. Indians harvested tons of salmon from this river junction. Their trail along the Fraser became a major route to the gold fields, with Lytton as a base of supplies. This community calls itself the Rafting Capital of Canada and claims some of the warmest weather in the country.

Lytton & District Chamber of Commerce: 400 Fraser St., P.O. Box 460, Lytton, BC, Canada V0K 1Z0; phone (250) 455-2523.

RECREATIONAL ACTIVITIES
White-water Rafting

- **Kumsheen Rafting Resort** is 6 km (4 mi.) n.e. on Trans-Canada Hwy. Write P.O. Box 30, Lytton, BC, Canada V0K 1Z0. Other activities are offered. Trips operate daily 8-8, May-Sept. Phone (250) 455-2296 or (800) 663-6667.

MAPLE RIDGE — *see Vancouver p. 175.*

MAYNE ISLAND —
see Gulf Islands National Park Reserve of Canada p. 125.

MERRITT (C-7) pop. 7,088, elev. 858 m/2,814'

Merritt is known for its many lakes. Of particular interest is Nicola Lake, a large warm-water lake 10 kilometres (6 mi.) north of town. Recreational activities include swimming, fishing, sailing, water skiing and windsurfing. Monck Provincial Park, on the west side of the lake, offers camping and picnic facilities.

Merritt Visitor Centre: 2202 Voght St., P.O. Box 1105, Merritt, BC, Canada V1K 1B8; phone (250) 378-0349.

NICOLA VALLEY MUSEUM ARCHIVES is at 2201 Coldwater Ave. The history of the region is chronicled in exhibits about mining, logging and ranching. Indian and pioneer artifacts are displayed, along with photographs depicting the lives of early settlers. Allow 30 minutes minimum. Mon.-Fri. 9-4:30, July-Aug.; Mon.-Fri. 10-3, rest of year. Closed holidays and Dec. 20-Jan. 3. Hours may vary; phone ahead. Donations. Phone (250) 378-4145.

MISSION—*see Vancouver p. 175.*

MORICETOWN (D-3)
pop. 700, elev. 411 m/1,348′

Moricetown is a Wet'suwet'en community that still practices the traditional hereditary system of governance. Originally known as Kyah Wiget, it was once the largest village of the Bulkley River Carrier tribe, a settlement built some 4,000 years ago. The town later took the name of Father A.G. Morice, a missionary who lived among the Carrier Indians in the late 19th century.

MORICETOWN CANYON is on Hwy. 16. The Bulkley River plunges through this narrow gorge in a series of waterfalls. The canyon was vital to First Nations tribes, whose diet depended on salmon. Visitors can view fish ladders that help five species of salmon reach their annual spawning grounds. During the summer Wet'suwet'en Indians still can be seen gaffing salmon as the fish fight their way upstream. Allow 1 hour minimum.

MOUNT REVELSTOKE NATIONAL PARK OF CANADA (A-10)

Elevations in the park range from 760 metres (2,493 ft.) at the bottom of Mount Revelstoke to 1,920 metres (6,300 ft.) at the Mount Revelstoke summit at Balsam Lake. Refer to CAA/AAA maps for additional elevation information.

On the west edge of the Selkirk Range in southeastern British Columbia, Mount Revelstoke National Park of Canada is 260 square kilometres (100 sq. mi.) of sharp peaks, heavily timbered slopes and flowering meadows. The Selkirk Mountains, flanked on the east by the Purcell Range and on the west by the Monashee Range, are distinguished by their height and geologic complexity.

Erosion by glaciers and the heavy rainfall of the region have carved the rock of the Selkirks into jagged forms. Complementing the park's dense green forests and lush wildflower meadows are glacier-fed streams and lakes as well as the deep snows that blanket the slopes until late June.

Deer inhabit the lower slopes; black and grizzly bears and mountain caribou also may be seen in the park. Most mountain species of birds are represented, including fox sparrows, hermit thrushes and northern hawk owls.

The Trans-Canada Hwy. passes through the southeastern portion of the park for 13 kilometres (8 mi.) and parallels its southern boundary for 18 kilometres (11 mi.).

General Information and Activities

The park is open all year. Visitor facilities and accommodations are available in Revelstoke at the western entrance. A park pass must be purchased at the park kiosk at Rogers Pass Centre.

From Hwy. 1, a 26-kilometre (16-mi.) hard surface road that is open only in summer leads to the summit of Mount Revelstoke, which provides an excellent panoramic view. Along its length are several viewpoints; many wildflowers bloom in August. Picnic areas are available at Monashee, the 8-kilometre (5-mi.) viewpoint on this road, and at Balsam Lake, 1 kilometre (.6 mi.) from the summit. Other picnic areas and nature trails are along the Trans-Canada Hwy.

Recreation includes subalpine hiking, mountain climbing and fishing. More than 44 kilometres (27 mi.) of hiking trails lead to such sites as Miller and Jade lakes. Climbers and hikers traveling off park trails may register with a park warden before and after each trip. Fishing is by permit, available at the park administrative office in Revelstoke. *See Recreation Chart.*

ADMISSION to the park is $6.90; $5.90 (ages 65+); $3.45 (ages 6-16); $17.30 (all occupants of a private vehicle with up to seven people). AX, MC, VI.

PETS are permitted in the park provided they are on leashes at all times.

ADDRESS inquiries to the Superintendent, Mount Revelstoke and Glacier National Parks of Canada, P.O. Box 350, Revelstoke, BC, Canada V0E 2S0; phone (250) 837-7500.

NAKUSP (B-10) pop. 1,698, elev. 914 m/2,998′

Nakusp, on the shore of Upper Arrow Lake between the Selkirk and Monashee mountain ranges, is named for an Indian word meaning "bay of quiet waters." Arrow Lake, part of the Columbia River system, is a popular destination for trout and salmon fishing. Heli-skiing is among the many winter activities offered in the area.

Nakusp Chamber of Commerce: 92 N.W. Sixth Ave., P.O. Box 387, Nakusp, BC, Canada V0G 1R0; phone (250) 265-4234 or (800) 909-8819 within British Columbia.

NAKUSP HOT SPRINGS is 12 km (7 mi.) n. on Nakusp Hot Springs Rd. Several mineral baths are sheltered by an outdoor cedar structure. The temperature of the pools varies from 36 to 41 C (97-107 F). Picnicking is permitted. Food is available. Daily

9:30 a.m.-10 p.m., Friday after Victoria Day-Sept. 30; 10-9:30, rest of year. Admission (one swim) $7.50; $6.50 (ages 6-17 and 61+); $23 (family, two adults and two children, each additional child $4). Day pass $11; $10 (ages 6-17 and 61+); $32 (family, two adults and two children, each additional child $5). MC, VI. Phone (250) 265-4528 or (800) 909-8819. *See Recreation Chart.*

NANAIMO (G-10) pop. 73,000, elev. 30 m/98'

Some 120 kilometres (75 mi.) north of Victoria, Nanaimo began as a Hudson's Bay Co. outpost called Colvilletown, established for miners brought from England and Scotland to mine coal.

A thriving forest products industry and important deep-sea fishing port have replaced coal's economic influence. Nanaimo has made tourism and recreation a part of the economy.

Offshore islands and nearby mountains and lakes provide a variety of recreational opportunities including hiking, swimming, camping and picnicking. During winter and early spring charter companies offer marine wildlife tours to view the bald eagles and sea lions that winter in the area.

Exotic trees provide a setting for picnicking at Harmac Arboretum, 11 kilometres (7 mi.) south at Harmac Pulp Mill and Duke Point roads. Newcastle Island *(see Recreation Chart and the AAA/CAA Western Canada & Alaska CampBook)* is a marine provincial park accessible by a 10-minute ferry ride from Maffeo-Sutton Park, behind the Civic Arena. Automobiles are not permitted; the ferry operates daily on the hour, May 1-second Mon. in Oct.

Salmon sport fishing, scuba diving, windsurfing and sailing are available from Nanaimo's natural harbor, regularly visited by the ferry from Vancouver. An intertidal lagoon park with three lighted water curtains and a 4-kilometre (2.5-mi.) walkway along the seawall graces Nanaimo's waterfront. St. Jean's Custom Cannery is one of three factories where fishing enthusiasts can have their catch canned or smoked.

On a landscaped hillside, Malaspina College offers a view of the city and harbor below and also is the site of Nanaimo Art Gallery. Visitors interested in prehistoric art can see Indian sandstone carvings at Petroglyph Park, 3.25 kilometres (2 mi.) south on scenic Hwy. 1.

Nanaimo is accessible from the mainland by BC Ferries, which sails from Horseshoe Bay to Departure Bay and from Tsawwassen to Duke Point, 8 kilometres (5 mi.) south. For more information phone (888) 223-3779.

Tourism Nanaimo: 2290 Bowen Rd., Nanaimo, BC, Canada V9T 3K7; phone (250) 756-0106 or (800) 663-7337.

NANAIMO ART GALLERY is on the Malaspina University-College campus at 900 Fifth St. Two galleries display local, regional and national exhibits; the second gallery is downtown at 150 Commercial St. New exhibits are installed frequently. Allow 1 hour minimum. Campus gallery Mon.-Fri. 10-5, Sat. noon-4. Downtown gallery Tues.-Sat. 10-5. Closed holidays. Admission $1. Phone (250) 740-6350.

NANAIMO DISTRICT MUSEUM is at 100 Museum Way in the Port of Nanaimo Centre. Exhibits depict local history, including coal mining in Nanaimo, First Nations and the Old Town district. One gallery hosts changing exhibits.

Note: The museum will be closed Jan.-June 2008 and will reopen summer 2008 in its new location at 100 Museum Way. Daily 10-4, Victoria Day weekend-Labour Day; Tues.-Sat. 10-5, rest of year. Closed winter holidays. Hours may vary after reopening; phone ahead. Admission $2; $1.75 (ages 56+ and students with ID); 75c (ages 0-11). Rates may vary after reopening; phone ahead. MC, VI. Phone (250) 753-1821.

The Bastion is on Front St. across from Coast Bastion Hotel. The small fort was built in 1853 to protect early settlers. A display shows how the bastion was used in the 1860s. A noon ceremonial cannon firing is conducted by staff dressed in period costumes. Daily 10-4, Victoria Day weekend-Labour Day weekend; by appointment rest of year. Admission $1. Phone (250) 753-1821.

GAMBLING ESTABLISHMENTS

- **Great Canadian Casinos Nanaimo** is at 620 Terminal Ave. Daily 10 a.m.-2 a.m. Phone (250) 753-3033.

RECREATIONAL ACTIVITIES

Bungee Jumping

- **Wildplay Elements Park** is at 35 Nanaimo River Rd., Nanaimo, BC, Canada V9X 1S5. Other activities are offered. Daily 10-6. Hours may vary; phone ahead. Phone (250) 753-5867 or (888) 668-7874.

Hiking

- **Tracks Outdoor Adventures** is at 2130 Akenhead Rd., Nanaimo, BC, Canada V9X 1T9. Other activities are available. Daily 7:30-7. Tours are given 9-dusk; reservations are required. Phone (250) 754-8732 or (877) 898-8732.

NELSON (C-11) pop. 9,298, elev. 535 m/1,755'

An old iron and silver mining town, Nelson was settled by prospectors in the late 1880s. With the depletion of its mines, the town turned to logging, sawmilling and area trade. However, the legacy of the bonanza days lives on in the more than 350 heritage sites. Most of Nelson's historic commercial buildings are open to the public, but homes are private and closed to visitors.

Nearby parks, lakes, streams and mountains offer all types of summer and winter recreation. Kokanee Creek and Kokanee Glacier provincial parks *(see Recreation Chart and the AAA/CAA Western Canada & Alaska CampBook)* are 19 kilometres (12 mi.) northeast on Hwy. 3A.

Nelson Chamber of Commerce: 225 Hall St., Nelson, BC, Canada V1L 5X4; phone (250) 352-3433 or (877) 663-5706.

Self-guiding tours: Maps detailing walking and driving tours are available from the chamber of commerce.

TOUCHSTONES NELSON MUSEUM OF ART AND HISTORY is at s.e. corner of jct. Vernon and Ward sts. at 502 Vernon St. Formerly The Nelson Museum, this renovated building features permanent visual and interactive exhibitions which examine the area's cultural, developmental and economic history. The Shawn Lamb Archives houses a thorough collection of materials relating to the region's diversified origins. Temporary exhibits and galleries also are available and change monthly.

Mon. and Wed.-Sat. 10-6, Sun. 10-4, Victoria Day weekend-Labour Day weekend; Wed.-Sat. 10-6, Sun. 10-4, rest of year. Closed holidays. Admission $10; $6 (ages 61+ and college students with ID); $4 (ages 7-18); $25 (family). AX, MC, VI. Phone (250) 352-9813.

RECREATIONAL ACTIVITIES

Skiing

• **Whitewater Winter Resort** is 20 km (12 mi.) s. off Hwy. 6. Write P.O. Box 60, Nelson, BC,

Canada V1L 5P7. Daily 9-3:30, early Dec.-early Apr. Phone (250) 354-4944 or (800) 666-9420.

NEW DENVER (C-10)
pop. 538, elev. 555 m/1,850′

NIKKEI INTERNMENT MEMORIAL CENTRE is at 306 Josephine St. Dedicated to remembering the Japanese internment experience during World War II, the center commemorates the 22,000 Nikkei (people of Japanese descent) removed from their British Columbia homes and relocated to camps. Exhibits include a typical two-family shack, an outhouse and a peace garden. Tribute also is paid to the first generation of Japanese who arrived in Canada in 1877.

Allow 30 minutes minimum. Daily 9:30-5, May-Sept. Admission $6; $4 (ages 61+ and students with ID); $12 (family); free (ages 0-5). Phone (250) 358-7288.

NEW WESTMINSTER—*see Vancouver p. 175.*

NORTH VANCOUVER—*see Vancouver p. 176.*

OKANAGAN CENTRE—
see Okanagan Valley p. 142

OKANAGAN FALLS—
see Okanagan Valley p. 142

Okanagan Valley

Kelowna / © Eero Sorila

It's one thing to read about a place; it's quite another to experience it in person. Evocatively written guides and glossy photo books can pique the curiosity and whet the appetite of almost any traveler, but when it comes down to it you really need to get out of the armchair and go. This is certainly true of the Okanagan (oh-ka-NOG-an) Valley; in a province almost embarrassingly gifted with scenic riches, it still manages to stand out.

British Columbia—like much of Canada—is notable for its sheer ruggedness: lofty mountains, expansive forests, rushing rivers. The valley, in contrast, is an anomaly; it could almost be Italy or some other sun-kissed land. The sun does indeed shine warmly, and the azure sky is huge. Tawny bluffs rise from the shores of steel-blue lakes. Scraggly pine trees and compact mounds of silvery gray sagebrush cloak hillsides. Parts of the Okanagan are arid enough to meet the meteorological criteria of a desert, but irrigation has transformed it into one of the most productive fruit- and vegetable-growing regions in North America.

A Land Created by Glaciers

This long, narrow valley was shaped over time by glacial movement. Layers of ice more than a mile thick began retreating some 10,000 years ago, scraping the surface of the land and leaving behind deposits of sediment. Flowing mountain rivers caused innumerable cycles of flooding and erosion. All this water action contributed to a slow but steady accumulation of nutrient-rich soils that over time formed fertile deltas, setting the stage for the valley's eventual blossoming as an agricultural powerhouse.

Impressive mountains, with some peaks topping 3,000 metres (9,800 ft.), flank both sides of the Okanagan Valley—the Monashee range to the east, the Cascades to the west. The mountain systems in this part of North America are oriented in a north-south direction paralleling the Pacific coast, and the intervening valleys follow suit. The entire area is part of the vast Interior Plateau, an uplifted section of the Earth's crust that covers much of British Columbia's southern interior.

One of the Okanagan Valley's many virtues is its topographical variety—everything from desert to grassland to forest. The northern end is wetter and greener, with a panorama of snowcapped mountains rising off in the distance. As you head south into the heart of the valley the trees become more scattered; ponderosa pines speckling the hills are replaced by shrubs like antelope bush and hardy plants like

bunch grass (so named because it grows in individual clumps or tufts rather than forming a uniform carpet), both of which are adapted to a drier climate.

Farther south the Okanagan verges on true desert. In and around Osoyoos the landscape is austere; towering cliffs and bare hillsides flaunt a palette of browns, beiges and grays, and the grasses and other low-growing plants are buffeted by persistent dry winds. The desert plants and animals that inhabit this arid environment are found nowhere else in Canada; the far southern end of the Okanagan Valley lies just above the northernmost reach of the Sonoran Desert, which extends south all the way into Mexico. This also is the country's warmest region, with relatively mild winters, hot summers and abundant sunshine, an ideal combination for irrigation-assisted agriculture.

Between Osoyoos to the east and Princeton to the west is the Similkameen Valley, nestled between steep rocky hills and threaded by the Similkameen River. Although a geographically separate region, it shares the southern Okanagan Valley's dramatic scenery and climatological characteristics. Similkameen country is known for its cattle ranches, horse farms and fruit orchards, and bills itself variously as the "Fruit Stand Capital of Canada" and "BC's Garden of Eden" in an attempt to step out of the better-known Okanagan's shadow.

Hwy. 3, also called the Crowsnest Highway, meanders along the province's southern border from Hope east to the Alberta border. Between Keremos and Osoyoos the highway traverses an area that climatologists classify as a mid-altitude steppe, although it certainly *looks* like a desert. Away from the sweep of the ever-present irrigation sprinklers, this little portion of extreme southern British Columbia—known as Canada's "pocket desert"—is home to sagebrush, prickly pear cactus, Western rattlesnakes and even the odd scorpion, all of which thrive in these desert-like conditions.

The bracing beauty of the Similkameen countryside is particularly evident in the vicinity of Hedley, a small village about 76 kilometres (47 mi.) west of Osoyoos on Hwy. 3. Here the waters of Hedley Creek rush into the Similkameen River. Stemwinder Mountain looms to the west, Nickel Plate Mountain to the east. Marbled cliffs rise up on both sides of the highway (the Similkameen Indians named this area Sna-za-ist, meaning "the striped rock place"). Notes of color are supplied by a bright blue sky, the deep green of flourishing fruit trees and (in season) the gold and purple hues of ripening apricots, peaches, plums and grapes.

About 9 kilometres (5.5 mi.) west of Osoyoos is Spotted Lake, which gets its name from one of the world's highest concentrations of magnesium sulfate, calcium, sodium sulfates and other minerals. In summer much of the lake's water evaporates and the minerals crystallize into circles on the surface that can be white, pale yellow, green or blue, depending on the mineral composition. The lake is on private land, but you can view it from the highway.

The Okanagan Valley's distinguishing feature, in fact, is its chain of long, narrow lakes that stretch from north to south. Created by receding glaciers, they are kept fresh and full by snowmelt and runoff from the mountains that flank both sides of the valley. The largest is Okanagan Lake, which stretches north to south for some 111 kilometres (69 mi.) while averaging just 5 kilometres (3 mi.) wide. Skaha, Vaseux and Osoyoos lakes continue the chain

Tourism Kelowna

to the south. To the east of Okanagan Lake are Kalamalka and Wood lakes; just north is little Swan Lake.

Cattle, Gold, Fruit and Wine

These valleys were first inhabited by the Okanagan Indians, an Interior Salish First Nations tribe. They hunted wild game, fished salmon runs, foraged for roots and berries and traded with other nations. The first European arrivals were fur traders searching for accessible routes to transport their goods to the Pacific. In the early 19th century they ventured north from Fort Okanogan, a Pacific Fur Co. trading post at the confluence of the Okanagan and Columbia rivers in present-day Washington state. Fur caravans were soon heading in and out of the valley region.

When the Oregon Treaty designated the 49th parallel as the border between the United States and the Canadian territory, Osoyoos became a port of entry, and vast herds of cattle were trailed through customs to supply food for miners who panned for

Destination Okanagan Valley

Nature has blessed the Okanagan Valley with fertile soil and sunny weather. Irrigation has transformed this delightfully scenic region into an agricultural wonderland known for its bounteous harvests of apples, apricots, peaches and other fruit.

The Okanagan's picturesque hills also are striped with orderly rows of grapevines; this is British Columbia's premier wine-producing region, and dozens of small wineries are tucked into pastoral rural settings.

© AAA / Ron Willis

Historic O'Keefe Ranch, Vernon.
Owned and operated by the O'Keefe family for 110 years, the mansion at this restored homestead features a priceless collection of silverware and porcelain. (See listing page 146)

© AAA / Ron Willis

Nk'Mip Desert Cultural Centre, Osoyoos.
Built literally into the side of a hill, this state-of-the-art interpretive center has indoor and outdoor exhibits describing Canada's only desert region. (See listing page 143)

Places included in this AAA Destination Area:

placer gold along the Similkameen River. The bunch grass that grew along the river valley provided abundant forage, and ranches began to be established.

Father Charles Pandosy, an Oblate priest, founded a mission in 1859 on the eastern shore of Okanagan Lake. He and his followers endured a harsh first winter—they were forced to shoot their horses for food—but went on to build other missions in the Okanagan Valley, where Father Pandosy instructed the native people in European agricultural techniques in addition to performing baptisms, marriages and funerals.

The discovery of gold on the Fraser River in 1858 resulted in a full-fledged gold rush. British Columbia's southern interior was further opened up with the building of the Caribou Road (now Hwy. 97) and the Dewdney Trail (now Hwy. 3). By the late 19th century the Okanagan and Similkameen valleys were buzzing with gold camps and boom towns that began to spring up along the shores of the region's lakes.

The fruit industry that today is a hallmark of the Okanagan began with difficulty. Apple orchards were planted as early as 1892, but it wasn't until the 1920s that fruit crops proved economically successful. The valley's warm temperatures and long growing season—besides providing Canadians with approximately one-third of their apples—nurtures verdant orchards of apricots, cherries, peaches, pears and plums.

Commercial grape plantings near Kelowna supplied the Okanagan's first wineries. The local wine industry has grown exponentially since the introduction of large-scale irrigation, and almost all of British Columbia's wine comes from the Okanagan region. The diversity of growing conditions—from the hot, sandy desert soils of the south to the deep topsoil and clay of the cooler north, plus distinct microclimates created by the valley's lakes—help ensure a diversity of wines.

Vineyards at the southern end of the valley produce such vintages as Chardonnay, Merlot, Cabernet Sauvignon, Pinot gris and Pinot noir, while vineyards in the central and northern valley specialize in Pinot blanc, Riesling and Gewürztraminer wines. Some grapes are left to freeze on the vine to produce icewine, a rich, sweet dessert wine. One of the Okanagan's most picturesque sights is orderly rows of grapevines, often covering a hillside that overlooks a deep blue lake.

Hwy. 97, which runs the length of British Columbia from the U.S. border just south of Osoyoos north to Watson Lake at the Yukon Territory border, is the principal route through the Okanagan Valley. From Osoyoos it travels north to Penticton, then follows the western shore of Okanagan Lake before crossing the lake on a floating bridge (the largest in the country) that is scheduled to be replaced with an overhead bridge.

Okanagan Lake is said to be the home of Ogopogo, the best known of Canada's unexplained lake

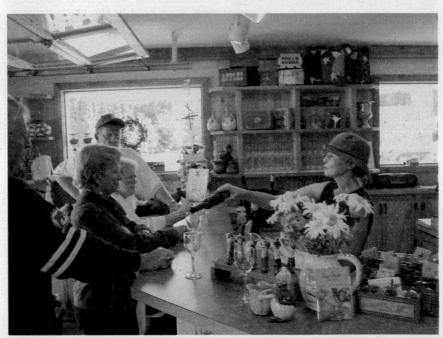

Kelowna Land and Orchard Co., Kelowna / © AAA / Ron Willis

creatures. Sightings of the mythical beast—most often described as 15 to 20 feet long, shaped like a log and with a head resembling that of a horse or goat—date back as far as 1872. Indians believed that Ogopogo's home was small, barren Rattlesnake Island; they claimed that the island's rocky beaches were sometimes strewn with animal parts, presumably dinner remains, and when crossing the lake during bad weather always took along a small animal that would be thrown overboard in order to appease the monster. Interestingly, there are similarities between Okanagan Lake and Scotland's Loch Ness, home of the famed Loch Ness Monster; both bodies of water are long and narrow, and both lie at about the same latitude.

East of the lake Hwy. 97 winds north to Enderby, the unofficial northern end of the valley, before continuing on toward Sicamous. But whether you proceed from south to north or north to south, this 211-kilometre (131 mi.) journey through the heart of the Okanagan is utterly delightful. One minute the highway is running tantalizingly close to a sparkling lakeshore; the next it's in the shadow of a soaring, sagebrush-dotted bluff or looking down on checkerboard farmland. Each bend and turn reveals a new view, and each one is lovely. The scenery alone would be more than enough to recommend this drive, even if you didn't make a single stop.

Year-Round Fun

But of course you *will* want to stop, because this is Canada's No. 1 year-round recreation destination. Dozens of parks ring Okanagan Lake, offering myriad opportunities for hiking, backpacking, mountain biking and camping. Bear Creek Provincial Park *(see Recreation Chart and the AAA/CAA Western Canada & Alaska CampBook)*, about 9 kilometres (6 mi.) west of Kelowna off Hwy. 97, has miles of hiking trails to explore, all beginning from a common trailhead at the park entrance. Bear Creek runs through the bottom of a tree-walled canyon, and the trails above wind past ponderosa pine, Douglas fir, juniper and prickly pear cactus that frame expansive lake views.

The lakes are, of course, ideal for water recreation, whether it's sailing, paddle boating, water skiing, jet skiing, kayaking, canoeing or freshwater fishing. Okanagan Lake is ringed with sandy beaches and sheltered coves, and numerous marina facilities provide equipment rentals.

For a northern Okanagan getaway head out to Kalamalka Lake Provincial Park *(see Recreation Chart)*, about 8 kilometres (5 mi.) southeast of Vernon off Hwy. 6. Kalamalka is known as a "marl lake," a process that begins when the water warms, forming calcium carbonate and limestone crystals that reflect sunlight. The water's distinctive blue-green color is often shot through with ribbons of deep blue, earning it the nickname "lake of a thousand colors." This largely undeveloped park encompasses rolling grasslands and forested ridges where Douglas fir and lodgepole pine grow; a paved trail leads to secluded beaches. Wildlife ranges from mule deer and minks to bobcats and western painted turtles. Bird watching is rewarding, and the spring wildflower display is spectacular.

Nearly 40 golf courses are scattered from Vernon south to Osoyoos, with many of them concentrated around Kelowna. Due to the mild climate most courses open as early as March, and golfers frequently play into November. And this being the Okanagan, it's only natural that water and fruit trees figure into course layouts; the grounds of the Kelowna Springs Golf Club include seven spring-fed lakes, while fairways at the Harvest Golf Club are set in the midst of a huge hillside apple orchard and have prime views of Okanagan Lake.

Kelowna is the Okanagan Valley's largest city and a big summer vacation destination. Water sports—sailing, kayaking, windsurfing, fishing—rule the summer calendar, but downtown Kelowna also offers museums, art galleries, pretty lakeside parks, all kinds of restaurants and a lively nightlife. It makes a convenient base for touring the many small wineries in the vicinity.

Breezy Penticton has the best of both worlds; the north end of town fronts the southern tip of Okanagan Lake, while the south end brushes up against the north shore of Skaha Lake. Lakeside beaches give the city a summery feel, and families flock to Penticton's amusement centers, go-cart tracks, miniature golf course and waterslides. Stroll along Front Street, the original business corridor, which is lined with restaurants and funky little shops.

Situated between Swan, Kalamalka and Okanagan lakes, Vernon started out as a camp on the Okanagan Valley trail during the fur trade years; by the turn of the 20th century it was a bustling ranching center. Downtown Vernon truly earns the description "quaint": The tree-lined, flower-filled streets are packed with historic old buildings and specialty stores selling everything from Victorian crafts to homemade jams. Be sure to search out the 27 outdoor murals—some up to 300 feet long—that depict Okanagan history, folklore and landscapes.

Just a stone's throw from the U.S. border, Osoyoos (oh-SOY-yoos) means, in the local Inkaneep native dialect, "where the water narrows"—a reference to its location spanning a narrow portion of Osoyoos Lake. Vineyards and orchards abound in the surrounding countryside, and the lake is one of Canada's warmest. Stroll along one of the lakeside parks in town while watching windsurfers and parasailing enthusiasts do their thing under sunny summer skies, and it's not that hard to believe you've happened onto some undiscovered Mediterranean resort.

The Okanagan Valley has something to offer regardless of the season. Downhill and cross-country skiers, snowboarders and other winter sports enthusiasts can choose from four ski resorts: Silver Star Mountain Resort, north of Vernon; Big White Ski Resort near Kelowna; Crystal Mountain resort near Westbank; and Apex Mountain Resort, southwest of Penticton.

Spring and summer are seasons to experience the valley's agricultural bounty. In the spring fruit trees are in full glorious bloom. Spring into early summer also is the time when wildflowers make their appearance in the Okanagan's wilderness parks.

Harvest time for the region's famous fruits and vegetables begins in late June and lasts until mid-October. If you're here in the summer or fall stop at one of the ubiquitous roadside fruit stands, which seem almost as plentiful as the trees themselves. Cherries are first in the fruit parade, ripening from late June through mid-July. Peaches appear from mid-July through September; pears in August and September; plums in September; and apples from August through October.

Practically every town in the valley has a farmers market, and you'll want to check out every single one. In addition to all sorts of fruit, the markets offer tomatoes, pumpkins, squash, asparagus, organic preserves, homemade pies, artisanal cheeses, honey, herbs, flowers—just about everything. Most are open April or May through October.

Grapes are harvested September through mid-October, an ideal time to go winery hopping. Most of the Okanagan's roughly 100 wineries can be visited, many have an intriguing history to share, and practically all of them enjoy a picturesque rural setting. Before hitting the tasting bars, pick up information and maps at any local visitor center.

So when should you plan a trip? Come to think of it, just about *any* time is right.

Destinations in this region listed under their own names are Kelowna, Okanagan Centre, Okanagan Falls, Oliver, Osoyoos, Peachland, Penticton, Summerland, Vernon and Westbank.

KELOWNA (C-9)
pop. 96,288, elev. 420 m/1,387'

Kelowna is the center of a fruit and vineyard region around Lake Okanagan, from which one-third of all apples harvested in Canada are shipped. The lake also is known for its legendary monster, the Ogopogo, a Loch Ness type beast reportedly 9 to 21 metres (30-69 ft.) long with a head resembling that of a horse, goat or sheep.

The Kelowna Community Theatre stages productions during fall and winter; phone (250) 763-9018. The Okanagan Symphony Orchestra is another prominent cultural feature; phone (250) 763-7544.

Recreation in the area includes water sports, fishing and golf. City Park on Lake Okanagan is the city's largest park, with a beach, tennis courts and a children's water park.

Tourism Kelowna: 544 Harvey Ave., Kelowna, BC, Canada V1Y 6C9; phone (250) 861-1515 or (800) 663-4345. *See color ad.*

B.C. ORCHARD INDUSTRY MUSEUM is at 1304 Ellis St. The museum traces the development of the orchard industry in the province. A 15-metre (50-ft.) model train layout is displayed. Other displays explain fruit production from planting to processing

and preserving. The Apple Tree Activities Centre is available for children. Allow 30 minutes minimum. Mon.-Fri. 10-5, Sat. 10-4; closed Dec. 25. Donations. Phone (250) 763-0433.

The Wine Museum & VQA Wine Shop is at 1304 Ellis St. Housed in a converted 1917 packing house, the museum displays machines used for pressing and bottling as well as exhibits featuring the history of wine production in the area. Wine tastings are offered. Guided tours are available by appointment. Open Mon.-Fri. 10-6, Sat. 10-5, Sun. and holidays 11-5; closed Jan. 1, Dec. 25-26. Donations. Phone (250) 868-0441.

ELYSIUM GARDENS is at 2834 Belgo Rd. The site covers 3 acres and includes organically grown perennial gardens and a Japanese garden. Featured are herb gardens, cut flower and kitchen gardens, xeriscape gardens, ornamental grasses and rock and scree beds. Dependent on the season, visitors will discover peonies, roses, primroses, tulips, day lilies and hydrangeas in full, fragrant bloom. Mountains and countryside views provide a backdrop for the gardens.

Allow 1 hour minimum. Daily and holidays 9-5, Mar. 31-Sept. 30. Admission $8.50; $4 (students with ID); free (ages 0-11); $18 (family). Phone (250) 491-1368.

GEERT MAAS SCULPTURE GARDENS, GALLERY AND STUDIO is 10 km (6.2 mi.) n. on Hwy. 97N, then 2 km (1.2 mi.) w. on Sexsmith Rd. to 250

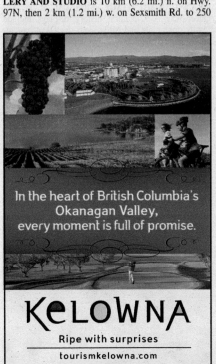

Reynolds Rd. Maas' semi-abstract sculptures of bronze, aluminum, stainless steel, stoneware and mixed media are exhibited in the gallery and in the .4-hectare (1-acre) sculpture garden. The complex contains one of the largest collections of bronze sculptures in Canada.

Medallions, paintings, etchings and reliefs can be seen in the permanent collection; changing exhibits also are offered. Allow 1 hour minimum. Mon.-Sat. 10-5, May 1-Oct. 1; by appointment rest of year. Hours may vary; phone ahead. Donations. Phone (250) 860-7012.

KELOWNA LAND AND ORCHARD CO. is 3 km (1.9 mi.) s. on Gordon Rd., 4 km (2.5 mi.) e. on K.L.O. Rd., then 1 km (.6 mi.) n. on E. Kelowna Rd. to 3002 Dunster Rd. The working orchard offers visitors a chance to see techniques of the past as well as farm animals and current technologies used in growing apples. Self-guiding walking tours and guided covered hay-wagon tours of the orchard are available. Juice samples are included. A cider-making facility also is on site.

Food is available. Allow 30 minutes minimum for the walking tour, 1 hour minimum for the wagon tour. Grounds open daily 8-5, May-Oct. Guided wagon tours depart daily at 11 and 1; at 1, in Oct. Tours $7; $5 (ages 6-16); free (ages 0-5). MC, VI. Phone (250) 763-1091.

OKANAGAN HERITAGE MUSEUM is at 470 Queensway Ave. Natural history displays include fossils, mammals and birds from the Okanagan region. Other permanent exhibits depict human history themes, including First Nations heritage, exploration and settlement, and the cultures of Africa, Asia, the Americas and the Pacific Islands. Mon.-Fri. 10-5; Sat. 10-4. Donations. Phone (250) 763-2417.

GAMBLING ESTABLISHMENTS
- **Lake City Casino** is at 1310 Water St. Daily 10 a.m.-2 a.m. Phone (250) 861-5457. *See color ad.*

RECREATIONAL ACTIVITIES
Skiing
- **Big White Ski Resort** is 54 km (34 mi.) e. on Hwy. 33. Write P.O. Box 2039, Station R, Kelowna, BC, Canada V1X 4K5. Daily 8:45-3:30,

mid-Nov. to mid-Apr. (also Tues.-Sat. 3:30-8, Dec. 17 through mid-Apr.). Phone (250) 765-3101 or (800) 663-2772.

WINERIES
- **CedarCreek Estate Winery** is 12 km (7 mi.) s. at 5445 Lakeshore Rd. following signs. Tastings are available daily 11-5. Tours daily at 11, 2 and 3, May-Oct. Phone (250) 764-8866.
- **Quails' Gate Estate Winery** is at 3303 Boucherie Rd. Daily 10-7, May 1-Oct. 15; 10-5, rest of year. Hours may vary; phone ahead. Closed Jan. 1 and Dec. 25. Tours on the hour daily 11-4, May-Oct. Phone (250) 769-4451 or (800) 420-9463.
- **Summerhill Pyramid Winery** is at 4870 Chute Rd. Daily 9-9. Tours are given on the hour. Phone (250) 764-8000 or (800) 667-3538.

OKANAGAN CENTRE (C-8)
pop. 1,200, elev. 344 m/1,129'

WINERIES
- **Gray Monk Estate Winery** is at 1055 Camp Rd. Tours on the hour daily 11-4, Apr.-Oct.; daily at 2, Nov.-Dec.; Mon.-Sat. at 2 and by appointment, rest of year. Closed Jan. 1 and Dec. 25. Phone (250) 766-3168, or (800) 663-4205 in British Columbia.

OKANAGAN FALLS (C-9)

WINERIES
- **Hawthorne Mountain Vineyards** is 5 km (3 mi.) s.w. on Green Lake Rd. Daily 9-5, May-Oct.; 9-4, rest of year. Closed major holidays. Guided tours are given daily at 11, 1 and 3, May-Oct. Phone (250) 497-8267.

OLIVER (D-9) pop. 4,224, elev. 307 m/1,007'

The northern tip of the American Great Basin Desert, which extends to Mexico, begins at Oliver. Irrigation begun in the 1920s converted the once desertlike valley floor and arid hillsides surrounding the town into productive orchards and vineyards.

Abundant sunshine and little rain provide ideal conditions for growing wine grapes.

The area's climate also promotes numerous recreational activities. An 18-kilometre (11-mi.) paved bicycle trail travels through Oliver's rolling hills and along the Okanagan River. The valley lakes and streams offer boating and fishing. Vaseux Lake and Inkaneep provincial parks *(see Recreation Chart)* are nearby, as are Bear and Madden lakes, known for excellent trout fishing.

The Fairview Townsite, 3 kilometres (1.9 mi.) west on Fairview Road, formerly was the site of an 1880s boomtown. The town disappeared along with the gold in 1906; plaques at the site provide historical information.

Oliver & District Chamber of Commerce: 36205-93 St., P.O. Box 460, Oliver, BC, Canada V0H 1T0; phone (250) 498-6321 or (866) 498-6321.

WINERIES

• **Inniskillin Okanagan Vineyards** is 5 km (3 mi.) s. on Hwy. 97 to Rd. 11 W. Daily 10-5, May-Oct.; 10-4, rest of year. Tours are given daily, Apr.-Oct.; by appointment rest of year. Closed Jan. 1 and Dec. 25-26. Phone (250) 498-6663, or (800) 498-6211.

OSOYOOS (D-9)
pop. 4,295, elev. 335 m/1,099'

From Osoyoos on the east side of Osoyoos Lake, an area of desert sand extends 48 kilometres (30 mi.) north to Skaha Lake and 24 kilometres (15 mi.) west along the Similkameen River. The area's similarity to Spain in climate and terrain inspired the citizens to adopt an Iberian style in their buildings. Despite its arid surroundings, Osoyoos has 19 kilometres (12 mi.) of sandy beach lining one of Canada's warmest freshwater lakes.

Man-made recreational facilities include the Wild Rapids on East Lakeshore Drive, with three large waterslides, five giant hot tubs and two minislides. Skiing is available nearby.

A heavy concentration of minerals, including evaporated copper, silver, gold and sulfate and Epsom salts, can be found at Spotted Lake, west on Crowsnest Hwy. 3, which provides 446 kilometres (277 mi.) of scenic driving all the way to Hope.

Osoyoos & District Chamber of Commerce: 7610 Veterans Way, P.O. Box 227, Osoyoos, BC, Canada V0H 1V0; phone (250) 495-7142.

NK'MIP DESERT CULTURAL CENTRE is at 1000 Rancher Creek Rd. Visitors will experience a desert ecosystem and the traditions of the Okanagan people through interactive exhibits, artifacts, a re-created Okanagan village and self-guiding walking trails. The Village Trail is 1.4 kilometres (.9 mi.) long and has interpretive signs, benches and ramadas; the Loop Trail is 2 kilometres (1.2 mi.) and includes several uphill segments.

Guided tours are available. Allow 1 hour minimum. Daily 9:30-4:30, May-Oct.; Mon.-Sat. 9:30-4:30, rest of year. Admission $12; $8 (ages 6-18); $11 (ages 55+ and students with ID); $36 (family, two adults and two or more children). MC, VI. Phone (250) 495-7901 or (888) 495-8555.

OSOYOOS DESERT CENTRE is 2.9 km (1.9 mi.) n. of jct. hwys. 3 and 97, then 1.2 km (.7 mi.) w. to 14580 146th Ave. The 26.8-hectare (66-acre) ecological, interpretive and education center stands in the Great Basin Desert, which extends from Mexico to Canada. Narrated 60-minute guided tours on the 1.5-kilometre (1-mi.) boardwalk trail allow visitors to learn about rare, threatened and endangered plant and animal species.

Pets are not permitted. Picnic facilities are available. Allow 1 hour, 30 minutes minimum. Open daily 9-5. Guided tours are given Apr.-Oct. Hours may vary; phone ahead to confirm and to inquire about summer evening tours. Admission $7; $6 (ages 65+ and students with ID); $4 (ages 0-12); $15 (family). MC, VI. Phone (250) 495-2470 or (877) 899-0897 within British Columbia.

OSOYOOS MUSEUM is in Gyro Community Park at 19 Park Pl. The museum houses children's art from the Inkameep Day School Art Collection—art and photographs created 1931-43 under the guidance of Anthony Walsh, the teacher and principal who based his teaching on the importance of art in education. Exhibits also include a butterfly collection and an 1892 log building that served as a customs house, jail, school, residence and government office over the years. Allow 1 hour minimum. Daily 10-4, July-Aug. Hours vary rest of year; phone ahead. Last admission 30 minutes before closing. Admission $3; $1 (ages 6-14). Phone (250) 495-2582.

WINERIES

• **Nk'Mip Cellars** is at 1400 Rancher Creek Rd. Daily 9-5, May-Oct.; 10-4, rest of year. Tours daily at 11, 1 and 3. Phone (250) 495-2985.

PEACHLAND (C-8)
pop. 4,654, elev. 366 m/1,200'

Peachland's rolling green countryside is a prosperous fruit growing, farming, lumber producing and mining area. The mining of molybdenum and copper from the Brenda Mines complex in the hills above Hwy. 97 drastically increased Peachland's population during the 1970s.

Nearby mountains, rivers and lakes, including Okanagan Lake *(see Recreation Chart)*, offer abundant opportunities for skiing, hiking, fishing and water sports.

PENTICTON (C-9)
pop. 30,985, elev. 345 m/1,131'

The first orchards in Okanagan Valley were planted by the Oblates at Okanagan Mission 1860-61, and the fruits, especially peaches, became a staple of the area. Tom Ellis established the first cattle ranch in 1865 and it was an empire when he sold it for a hefty sum in 1905; by 1909 orchards had replaced cattle in the agricultural economy. Today Penticton's fruit industry combines with tourism and lumber industries to keep the community strong.

Okanagan and Skaha lakes, at opposite ends of the city, offer ample expanses of shoreline for recreational pursuits. A popular summer activity is floating down the 8-kilometre (5-mi.) river channel from the mouth of Okanagan Lake *(see Recreation Chart and the AAA/ CAA Western Canada & Alaska CampBook)* to Skaha Lake. The channel has rest and picnic areas and is paralleled by a bicycle path and a jogging trail.

Penticton & Wine Country Tourism: 553 Railway St., Penticton, BC, Canada V2A 8S3; phone (250) 493-4055 or (800) 663-5052. *See color ad.*

ART GALLERY OF THE SOUTH OKANAGAN is at 199 Marina Way. Four exhibition halls and an art loft comprise the facility on the shore of Okanagan Lake, where works by professional local, provincial and nationally known artists are displayed. Allow 30 minutes minimum. Tues.-Fri. 10-5, Sat.-Sun. noon-5; closed statutory holidays. Admission $2; free (ages 0-18); free (weekends). MC, VI. Phone (250) 493-2928.

DOMINION RADIO ASTROPHYSICAL OBSERVATORY is 16 km (10 mi.) s.w. on Hwy. 97, then 7 km (4 mi.) s. on White Lake Rd. The site features

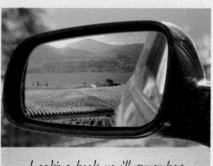

Looking back, you'll remember the pristine beauty. The warmth of our sun. And the people.

If only we could bottle the feeling.

tourismpenticton.com
1-800-663-5052
Okanagan Valley, BC

PENTICTON
& WINE COUNTRY
time to breathe

radio telescopes used to study the universe. A self-guiding tour includes a 26-metre (85-ft.) parabolic antenna and an array of more sophisticated, computer-linked, 9-metre (30-ft.) antennae.

Since automobile ignitions cause radio interference, visitors are asked to leave their vehicles at the road and walk the 600 metres (.4 mi.) to the facility. Allow 30 minutes minimum. Visitor center daily 10-5, Easter weekend-Thanksgiving; Mon.-Fri. 10-5, rest of year. Closed major holidays. Guided tours are given Sun. 2-5, July-Aug. Free. Phone (250) 493-2277.

OKANAGAN INLAND MARINE HERITAGE PARK & SS SICAMOUS RESTORATION SOCIETY is on Okanagan Lake Beach at 1099 Lakeshore Dr. Featured on-site is the *Sicamous*, the last steam-powered sternwheeler to operate on Okanagan Lake. Visitors can experience what once was a major means of transportation in the area. Also on view is the 1914 tugboat SS *Naramata*; it is one of only two tugs from the steam era that has survived in the province.

Allow 30 minutes minimum. Daily 10-9, late June to mid-Sept.; daily 10-4, May 1-late June; Mon.-Fri. 10-4, rest of year. Schedule may vary; phone ahead. Closed mid-Dec. to mid-Jan. Admission $5; $3 (students with ID and senior citizens); $1 (ages 5-12). MC, VI. Phone (250) 492-0403 or (866) 492-0403.

PENTICTON (R.N. ATKINSON) MUSEUM is at 785 Main St. Displays describe the natural and social histories of the southern Okanagan Valley. A historic transportation exhibit about the Kettle Valley Railway is available along with an exhibit about the Canadian military. Summer programs include cemetery walks, heritage tours and children's activities. Allow 1 hour minimum. Tues.-Sat. 10-5; closed holidays. Donations. Phone (250) 490-2451.

GAMBLING ESTABLISHMENTS
- **Lake City Casino** is at 21 Lakeshore Dr. W. Daily 10 a.m.-2 a.m. Phone (250) 487-1280. *See color ad p. 142.*

RECREATIONAL ACTIVITIES
Skiing
- **Apex Mountain Resort** is 32 km (20 mi.) w. on Green Mountain Rd. Write P.O. Box 1060, Penticton, BC, Canada V2A 6J9. Other activities are available. Daily 9-3:30, mid-Nov. through Mar. 30; Sat.-Sun. 11-5, July-Aug. Phone (877) 777-2739.

WINERIES
- **Hillside Estate Winery** is 3 km (2 mi.) n. of jct. McMillan Ave. and Naramata Rd. at 1350 Naramata Rd. Mon.-Wed. 11-4, Thurs.-Sun. 10-5, Apr.-Oct.; Mon.-Sat. 11-4 and Sun. by appointment only, Dec.-Mar. Phone (250) 493-6274 or (888) 923-9463.

SUMMERLAND (C-9)
pop. 10,713, elev. 454 m/1,489′

Surrounded by lush orchards and vineyards, Summerland depends on fruit cultivation as its main industry. Overlooking Okanagan Lake *(see Recreation*

Chart and the AAA/CAA Western Canada & Alaska CampBook), the first commercial orchard in the Okanagan Valley was planted in 1890.

Summerland also was the first town on the lake to employ electricity as an energy source; it was generated by a small hydroelectric plant built on the lakeshore in 1905. These and other historical landmarks are the focus of Summerland Museum on Wharton Street.

Fruit stands are the best way to sample the region's bountiful produce. The public can visit a fruit packing facility at B.C. Fruit Packers Co-op on Jubilee Road, depending on availability of fruit in season (usually June through October).

Giants Head Park on 910-metre (2,986-ft.) Giants Head Mountain offers picnic facilities and views of Summerland, the valley below and Okanagan Lake.

Many beaches, including Sunoka, Peach Orchard *(see the AAA/CAA Western Canada & Alaska Camp-Book)*, Powell and Rotary, line the shores of Okanagan Lake. Also of interest is the Summerland Trout Hatchery, Lakeshore Drive S., where rainbow, brook and Kokanee trout are raised.

Summerland Chamber of Economic Development Tourism: 15600 Hwy. 97, P.O. Box 130, Summerland, BC, Canada V0H 1Z0; phone (250) 494-2686.

SAVE **KETTLE VALLEY STEAM RAILWAY** is 5 km (3 mi.) w. on Prairie Valley Rd. to 18404 Bathville Rd. Passengers take a 1-hour, 45-minute narrated tour on the only preserved portion of the original Kettle Valley Railway Line, which ran from Midway to Hope. The train departs from Prairie Valley Station Thurs.-Mon. at 10:30 and 1:30, June 26-Sept. 1.; Sat.-Mon. at 10:30 and 1:30, mid-May through June 23 and Sept. 6-second Mon. in Oct. Fare $19; $18 (ages 65+); $15 (ages 13-18); $11

(ages 3-12). Fares may vary; phone ahead. MC, VI. Phone (250) 494-8422 or (877) 494-8424.

SUMMERLAND ORNAMENTAL GARDENS is s. on Hwy. 97 to 4200 Hwy. 97 on the grounds of Pacific Agri-Foods Research Centre. Established in 1916, the 300-hectare (741-acre) site specializes in Xeriscape landscaping, the use of drought-tolerant plants. English gardens, roses, meadow plants and wetland plants also are cultivated. A butterfly and hummingbird garden is featured. Picnic facilities are available. Allow 1 hour minimum. Daily 8-8, May-Sept.; 8-dusk, Mar.-Apr. and Oct.-Nov.; otherwise varies. Admission $3. Phone (250) 494-6385.

WINERIES

- **Dirty Laundry Vineyard** is at 7311 Fiske St. Daily 10-5, May-Oct. Hours vary rest of year; phone ahead. Phone (250) 494-8815.

- **Sumac Ridge Estate Winery** is 1 km (.6 mi.) n. at 17403 Hwy. 97. Daily 9-9, Mar.-Dec.; Mon.-Fri. 9-5, Sat.-Sun. 11-5, rest of year. Tours are given daily on the hour 10-noon and 2-4, May-Oct. Phone (250) 494-0451.

VERNON (B-9) pop. 33,494, elev. 383 m/1,256'

At the confluence of five valleys and bounded by three lakes, Vernon is an important shipping and trading center for the Okanagan region. The town's history is portrayed in 26 large murals painted on downtown buildings. On Hwy. 97 at 25th Avenue, Polson Park encompasses a Japanese garden, a Chinese tea house, a floral clock made of 3,500 plants and a children's water park.

Boating, fishing, hiking, mountain biking and golf are popular in summer; winter activities include skiing, dogsledding and snowshoeing. Several recreational opportunities are available at nearby Ellison Provincial

Park *(see Recreation Chart and the AAA/CAA Western Canada & Alaska CampBook)* and Kalamalka Lake Provincial Park *(see Recreation Chart)*.

Silver Star Provincial Park offers mountain biking tours from late June to mid-September. A chairlift to the top of Silver Star Mountain operates daily, July 1 through mid-September.

For relaxation, the Kalamalka Lake viewpoint, 5 kilometres (3 mi.) south of 25th Avenue on Hwy. 97, provides an excellent view of the lake.

Tourism Greater Vernon: 701 Hwy. 97S, Vernon, BC, Canada V1B 3W4; phone (250) 542-1415 or (800) 665-0795. *See color ad p. 145.*

[SAVE] **ATLANTIS WATERSLIDES LTD.** is 8 km (5 mi.) n. on Hwy. 97A at Pleasant Valley Rd. The water park has a slide with 10 flumes of varying lengths and slopes, a giant hot tub, miniature golf and a picnic area. Food is available. Allow 2 hours, 30 minutes minimum. Daily 10-7, early July to mid-Aug.; 10-6, mid-Aug. through early Sept.; 9:30-5, mid-June to early July; 11-5, early June to mid-June. Admission $19; $13 (ages 4-12); $10 (ages 65+); $55 (family, two adults and two children). MC, VI. Phone (250) 549-4121.

GREATER VERNON MUSEUM AND ARCHIVES is at 3009 32nd Ave. Exhibits include local and natural history items, Indian artifacts and period costumes and furniture. The Allan Brooks Gallery features works by the artist and naturalist. Archives and a research facility also are on the premises. Allow 1 hour minimum. Tues.-Sat. 10-5; closed holidays. Donations. Phone (250) 542-3142.

[SAVE] **HISTORIC O'KEEFE RANCH** is at 9380 Hwy 97 N. One of the earliest cattle empires in the Okanagan Valley, the 1867 O'Keefe homestead includes a dozen restored structures. Guided tours are offered of the family's Victorian mansion. Other buildings include a log house, a church, a general store, a blacksmith shop, a cowboy bunk house, barns and tool sheds. A museum depicts the family's history and the ranching way of life.

Picnicking is permitted. Food is available. Allow 1 hour, 30 minutes minimum. Daily 9-6, May 1 through mid-Oct. Admission $12; $11 (ages 65+); $10 (ages 6-18); $30 (family). MC, VI. Phone (250) 542-7868.

OKANAGAN SCIENCE CENTRE is at 2704 Hwy. 6 in Polson Park. Housed in one of the oldest brick schoolhouses in British Columbia, the center features hands-on exhibits focusing on such topics as rocks, fossils, illusions, recycling and the environment. Allow 1 hour minimum. Tues.-Fri. 10-5, Sat. 11-5, Sept.-June; Mon.-Fri. 10-5 (also Thurs. 5-8), rest of year. Admission $7; $4 (ages 6-18 and 66+). Phone (250) 545-3644.

PLANET BEE HONEY FARM, jct. Hwy. 97 and 25th Ave., 1 km (.6 mi.) w. on 25th Ave., just n. on 41st St., then w. to 5011 Bella Vista Rd., provides a variety of tours at several apiaries. Visitors may witness the complex societal structure and diligent work habits of more than 10,000 bees in indoor and outdoor observatories. The Inside the Hive tour allows visitors to don gear and explore a working hive. Free taste samples of honey are available from a selection of global sources.

Picnicking is permitted. Allow 30 minutes minimum. Mon.-Sat. 8-7, Sun. 10-6, July-Aug.; Mon.-Sat. 8:30-5:30, Sun. 10-5:30, rest of year. Closed Dec. 25. Guided tour hours vary; phone ahead. Free. Guided tours $5-$12; $3-$4.50 (ages 4-10); $20 (family). AX, MC, VI. Phone (250) 542-8088 or (877) 233-9675.

VERNON PUBLIC ART GALLERY is at 3228 31st Ave. on the ground level of the Parkade Bldg. Three exhibition rooms feature works of regional and nationally known artists. Free gallery tours are available upon request. Allow 30 minutes minimum. Mon.-Fri. 10-5, Sat. 11-4; closed statutory holidays. Donations. Phone (250) 545-3173.

GAMBLING ESTABLISHMENTS

- **Lake City Casino** is at 4801 27th St. Daily 10 a.m.-2 a.m. Hours vary Dec. 25-26; phone ahead. Phone (250) 545-3505. *See color ad p. 142.*

RECREATIONAL ACTIVITIES

Skiing

- **Silver Star Mountain Resort** is 22 km (15 mi.) n.e. on Silver Star Rd. Write Box 3002, Silver Star Mountain, BC, Canada V1B 3M1. Sun.-Wed. 8:30-3:30, Thurs. and Sat. 8:30-8, Fri. 8:30-9, mid-Nov. through mid-Apr. Other activities are available. Phone (250) 542-0224 for information or (800) 663-4431 for reservations.

WESTBANK (C-9)
pop. 15,700, elev. 411 m/1,348′

Westbank was a link on the fur-trading route from the north-central part of the province, called New Caledonia, to the Columbia River. In the early 1860s fortune seekers en route to the Cariboo gold mines followed the old trail through the Okanagan Valley.

Ideal climatic conditions in the Okanagan Valley nurture Westbank's many orchards and vineyards. Vacationers also are drawn by the favorable weather in the valley. Downhill and cross-country skiing in the surrounding countryside are popular in winter.

Westbank Chamber of Commerce: 2375 Pamela Rd., Unit 4, Westbank, BC, Canada V4T 2H9; phone (250) 768-3378 or (866) 768-3378.

WINERIES

- **Mission Hill Family Estate** is 4.5 km (3 mi.) e. off Hwy. 97 via Boucherie Rd. to 1730 Mission Hill Rd. Daily 9:30-7, June 30-Sept. 2; 10-6, Mar. 31-June 29 and Sept. 4-Oct. 7; 10-5, Oct. 8-Mar. 30. Closed Jan. 1 and Dec. 25-26. Phone (250) 768-6448.

OLIVER—see Okanagan Valley p. 142

OSOYOOS—see Okanagan Valley p. 143

 PACIFIC RIM NATIONAL PARK RESERVE OF CANADA (I-3)

Elevations in the park range from sea level along the Long Beach area to 140 metres (459 ft.) at Radar Hill. Refer to CAA/AAA maps for additional elevation information.

On the west coast of Vancouver Island, Pacific Rim National Park Reserve of Canada consists of three geographically distinct sections with different entry points: the Long Beach unit between Ucluelet and Tofino; the Broken Group Island unit, a cluster of islands in Barkley Sound; and the 75-kilometre-long (47-mi.) West Coast Trail unit between Bamfield and Port Renfrew.

Numerous contrasts exist in the 510-square-kilometre (197-sq.-mi.) reserve, which has sandy beaches, tranquil estuaries and lakes, rugged headlands, dense rain forests and rocky islands. Wildflowers nurtured by the area's moist and temperate climate thrive in an immense old-growth rain forest.

A stopping place for geese and ducks during their yearly migrations, the shoreline zone also accommodates colonies of sea birds and wildlife. Each spring some 20,000 gray whales migrate through the reserve's waters.

General Information and Activities

The reserve is open all year, although many facilities are seasonal. The Long Beach area, about 16 kilometres (10 mi.) west of the junction of Hwy. 4 and the Ucluelet highway, has 19 kilometres (12 mi.) of sandy beach and shoreline which are popular year-round with surfers and beachwalkers; wheelchair-accessible trails are available. Long Beach Information Centre, open mid-March to mid-October, is on Hwy. 4 inside the park boundary. There are self-guiding nature trails in the surrounding rain forest and other interpretive programs. The Wickaninnish Interpretive Centre features displays and films chronicling marine life of the Pacific.

The Broken Group Islands, accessible only by boat, offer pristine wilderness spread over a 100-island cluster in the center of Barkley Sound. Eagles and sea lions are abundant, while varied sea life and sunken ships create a diver's paradise. Camping is available in designated areas on eight islands.

The West Coast Trail, which had its beginnings as an avenue of rescue for shipwrecked sailors, follows the national park's rugged coastline between Port Renfrew and Bamfield. The trail is open to experienced hikers only and offers spectacular coastal scenery along its challenging path. Remnants of former settlements and shipwrecks can be seen along the shoreline.

The West Coast Trail Information and Registration Centres at Pachena Bay near Bamfield and at Port Renfrew are open May through September. Reservations to hike the trail may be made for June 15-Sept. 15; phone (800) 435-5622. *See Recreation Chart and the AAA/CAA Western Canada & Alaska CampBook.*

ADMISSION to the Long Beach area is adults $6.90; senior citizens $5.90; ages 6-16, $3.45; family (up to seven people) $17.30. Camping fee at Long Beach is $16-$25 per person per night. Camping fee at other designated sites is $9 per person per night. West Coast Trail use permit is $110; reservation fee $25 (non-refundable). Ferry fee $15.

ADDRESS inquiries to the Superintendent, Pacific Rim National Park Reserve of Canada, P.O. Box 280, Ucluelet, BC, Canada V0R 3A0; phone (250) 726-7721, or (250) 726-4212 June 1 through mid-Sept.

PARKSVILLE (G-10)
pop. 10,323, elev. 80 m/262'

With its 1.6-kilometre-long (1-mi.) sandy beach on the Strait of Georgia, Parksville is a popular summer resort. Nearby Englishman and Little Qualicum rivers and parks, with scenic waterfalls, provide many opportunities for recreation, as do other area lakes, streams, mountains and parks. Rathtrevor Beach Provincial Park offers a beach, camping and picnicking. *See Recreation Chart and the AAA/CAA Western Canada & Alaska CampBook.*

Parksville & District Chamber of Commerce: 1275 E. Island Hwy., P.O. Box 99, Parksville, BC, Canada V9P 2G3; phone (250) 248-3613.

CRAIG HERITAGE PARK AND MUSEUM is 4 km (2.5 mi.) s. at 1245 E. Island Hwy. The collection of historic buildings includes a church, a log house, a fire station, a turn-of-the-20th-century schoolhouse and two 19th-century post offices. Exhibits inside the buildings depict local history. Allow 30 minutes minimum. Daily 10-4, mid-May through Sept. 30. Admission $4; $3 (ages 13-18 and 65+); $2 (ages 6-12); $6 (family). Phone (250) 248-6966.

PEACHLAND—see Okanagan Valley p. 143

PENDER ISLANDS—
see Gulf Islands National Park Reserve of Canada p. 125.

PENTICTON—see Okanagan Valley p. 143

PORT ALBERNI (F-10)
pop. 17,743, elev. 60 m/197'

A deepwater port and important fishing and lumber shipping center, Port Alberni was discovered in

1791 by Don Pedro Alberni, a Spanish sea captain. Industry began in 1860 when nine workmen arriving on the schooner *Meg Merrilees* built a sawmill on the harbor's edge.

Port Alberni's harbor remains the city's focal point, enhanced by the Alberni Harbour Quay at the foot of Argyle Street. The facility includes shops, an arts and crafts outlet and the MV *Lady Rose* office. From the 1912 CPR Train Station, a logging locomotive takes visitors on a 35-minute journey along the waterfront to McLean Mill National Historic Site *(see attraction listing).*

Surrounded by mountains, lakes and forests, the city is a good base for naturalists and outdoors enthusiasts. Alpine and cross-country skiing are available nearby. Sproat Lake Provincial Park *(see Recreation Chart and the AAA/CAA Western Canada & Alaska CampBook)* features Indian carvings of mythological beasts. There are hundreds of giant Douglas firs, many that date from the late 12th century, at Cathedral Grove in MacMillan Provincial Park, 16 kilometres (10 mi.) east.

The region's natural wonders are protected by the Martin Mars Water Bombers based at Sproat Lake. Designed to combat forest fires, these huge aircraft carry 6,000 imperial gallons (7,206 U.S. gallons) of water.

Alberni Valley Chamber of Commerce: 2533 Port Alberni Hwy., Port Alberni, BC, Canada V9Y 8P2; phone (250) 724-6535.

MARITIME DISCOVERY CENTRE is on the waterfront at 2750 Harbour Rd. Collections relate to First Nations art, culture and community and Vancouver Island's domestic and industrial history. Highlights include an exhibit about the 1964 tidal wave, Nuu Chah Nulth basketry, Alberni Valley folk art, antique photographs and a display chronicling the history of the West Coast Trail. Traveling exhibits also are featured. Daily 10-5, July-Aug.; Mon.-Sat. 10-5 (also Thurs. 5-8), rest of year. Closed statutory holidays. Donations. Phone (250) 723-6164.

SAVE McLEAN MILL NATIONAL HISTORIC SITE is 6 km (10 mi.) w. on Beaver Creek Rd., then 3 km (1.8 mi.) n. to 5633 Smith Rd., following signs. The 13-hectare (32-acre) site preserves a working 1926 steam sawmill that was operated by the R.B. McLean family until 1965. Thirty structures from the early days of British Columbia's forest industry include the camp where loggers and mill employees lived and worked. Interactive guided tours and stage shows and sawmill demonstrations are given Thursday through Monday.

Food is available. Allow 1 hour, 30 minutes minimum. Daily 10-4, mid-June through Labour Day. Hours may vary; phone ahead. Mill and train tours $29; $21.75 (students with ID and senior citizens); $9.75 (ages 5-12). Rates may vary; phone ahead. Reservations are suggested. MC, VI. Phone (250) 723-1376.

SAVE **Alberni Pacific Railway** departs from the CPR Station at Argyle and Kingsway sts. Passengers embark upon a 35-minute train ride to McLean Mill National Historic Site. Trips depart Thurs.-Mon. at 10 and 2, mid-June through Labour Day. Last train leaves the mill at 5. Hours may vary; phone ahead. Round-trip fare (includes mill admission) $29; $21.75 (students with ID and senior citizens); $9.75 (ages 5-12); $75 (family). Rates may vary; phone ahead. MC, VI. Phone (250) 723-1376.

SAVE **MV *LADY ROSE* MARINE SERVICES** docks at the Argyle Pier in the Alberni Harbour Quay at the foot of Argyle St. The packet freighter takes visitors on an all-day cruise. The MV *Lady Rose* and her sister ship, the MV *Frances Barkley,* deliver mail and cargo to isolated villages, fishing resorts and camps. The freighters sail down the Alberni Inlet to Bamfield, Ucluelet and the Broken Group Islands.

Food is available. Sensible shoes and a sweater or light jacket are advisable. Departures to Bamfield Tues. and Thurs.-Sun. at 8 a.m., July-Sept.; Tues., Thurs. and Sat. at 8 a.m., rest of year. Sailings to Ucluelet and Broken Group Islands Mon., Wed. and Fri. at 8 a.m., early June-late Sept. Hours may vary; phone ahead. Ucluelet trip $64; $32 (ages 8-15). Bamfield trip $58; $29 (ages 8-15). All children must be accompanied by an adult. Reservations are recommended in summer. Fares may vary; phone ahead. AX, MC, VI. Phone (250) 723-8313, or (800) 663-7192 Apr.-Sept.

ROBERTSON CREEK FISH HATCHERY is 5 km (3 mi.) w. on Hwy. 4, then 7 km (4 mi.) n.w. on Great Central Lake Rd. The hatchery has an annual output of 8 million chinook and 800,000 coho salmon and 150,000 steelhead trout. Displays explain the fish breeding process from incubation through release. Facilities include outdoor rearing ponds and raceways. Daily 8:30-3:30; closed Dec. 25. Free. Phone (250) 724-6521.

PORT COQUITLAM—*see Vancouver p. 177.*

PORT EDWARD (E-2) pop. 659

The river of mists, as the Indians called the Skeena River, bursts through the Coast Range and empties into the Pacific Ocean near Port Edward. The river provides the community's major commodity, fish, which is processed by local canneries. Salmon and steelhead trout, besides being economic staples, also offer a recreational challenge to anglers.

SAVE **NORTH PACIFIC HISTORIC FISHING VILLAGE** is 10 km (6 mi.) s. of Hwy. 16 at 1889 Skeena Dr. The restored 1889 cannery village includes the main cannery, reduction plant, staff housing and mess house. Artifacts of the fishing industry are displayed throughout the complex. Guided tours and live entertainment also are offered. Food is available. Tues.-Sun. 10-5:30, May-Sept. Hours may vary; phone ahead. Admission $11.95; $9.95 (ages 56+ and students with ID); $7.95 (ages 6-12);

$34.95 (family, two adults and four children). Rates may vary; phone ahead. MC, VI. Phone (250) 628-3538.

PORT McNEILL (H-2)
pop. 2,821, elev. 15 m/49'

In the scenic, untamed wilderness of northern Vancouver Island, Port McNeill occupies a rich lumber and fishing region popular with adventurous hikers, campers, spelunkers, fishermen and other sports enthusiasts.

Of interest to rock collectors and geologists are several nearby natural phenomena, including the Vanishing River, which plunges underground into a maze of caves and tunnels; the Devil's Bath, a huge rock bowl continuously filled by an underground spring; and the Eternal Fountain, which gushes from a rock crevice and then disappears underground again. All are reached by logging roads that are accessible only in summer.

An inter-island ferry operates a shuttle service between Port McNeill, Sointula and Alert Bay *(see place listing p. 113).*

Port McNeill & District Chamber of Commerce: 351 Shelley Crescent, P.O. Box 129, Port McNeill, BC, Canada V0N 2R0; phone (250) 956-3131.

PORT MOODY —*see Vancouver p. 178.*

POUCE COUPE (D-5)
pop. 833, elev. 652 m/2,139'

The village of Pouce Coupe is referred to as the gateway to Peace country because it is one of the first communities travelers will see when entering British Columbia from Alberta.

POUCE COUPE MUSEUM is at 5006 49th Ave. Pioneer artifacts are housed in the former Northern Alberta Railway station. Daily 8-5, May-Aug; by appointment rest of year. Admission $1. Phone (250) 786-5555.

POWELL RIVER (F-11)
pop. 12,983, elev. 55 m/180'

Rich forests and abundant water brought the founders of the Powell River Company to the area in the early 1900s. The townsite is one of the oldest company-built communities in western Canada.

Separated from the mainland by Jervis Inlet, the area offers year-round recreation including freshwater and saltwater fishing, scuba diving, boating, kayaking, hiking and bicycling. The Powell Forest Canoe Route connects eight lakes around the Upper Sunshine Coast region with camping areas along the scenic circuit.

A panorama of the Strait of Malaspina unfolds from the Mount Valentine viewpoint, reached by a rock stairway in the heart of town. Bald eagles can be observed at any time of year, especially in late fall when they are attracted by salmon spawning in

channels and small streams. Also of interest are Sliammon Fish Hatchery and Powell River Salmon Society Spawning Channel.

Guided 2-hour tours of the Catalyst Paper Mill are offered through the Visitor Centre. Part of the tour is outdoors; appropriate dress and low-heeled, closed footwear are advised. Tours depart Mon.-Fri. at 9:30, June-Sept. Children ages 0-9 are not permitted. For information and reservations phone (877) 817-8669.

Powell River Visitor Centre: 4871 Joyce Ave., Unit 111, Powell River, BC, Canada V8A 5P4; phone (604) 485-4701 or (877) 817-8669.

INLAND LAKE PROVINCIAL PARK is 12 km (7 mi.) n. on Inland Lake Rd. In a semi-remote area with abundant and varied wildlife, the park offers wheelchair-accessible facilities for camping, hiking and fishing. A 13-kilometre-long (8-mi.) circuit of crushed limestone with minimal grades has eight picnic and rest areas and six fishing wharves. Amenities include cabins exclusively for use by the physically impaired, and wheelchair-accessible outhouses.

Site open for day use daily 7 a.m.-10 p.m., Apr.-Oct. Hours may vary; phone ahead. Free. Phone (604) 487-4168. *See Recreation Chart.*

POWELL RIVER HISTORICAL MUSEUM AND ARCHIVES is on Marine Ave. across from Willingdon Beach. The museum houses artifacts, archival material and displays about the area's history. A children's treasure hunt is featured. Allow 30 minutes minimum. Daily 9-4:30, June 16-Sept. 1; Mon.-Fri. 9-4:30, rest of year. Closed holidays. Admission $2; $1 (ages 5-12). Phone (604) 485-2222.

PRINCE GEORGE (E-5)
pop. 72,406, elev. 691 m/2,267'

At the confluence of the Nechako and Fraser rivers, the area was visited in 1793 by Alexander Mackenzie in his trek down the Fraser to the Pacific. In 1807 it became the site for Simon Fraser's North West Co. fort. Fraser's canoe brigades soon gave way to paddlewheelers and then railroads, which converged on this important northern crossroads. Prince George remains a major transportation and trade center, a role enhanced by a thriving forest industry.

Despite its urban transformation, the city has retained much of its natural heritage in its 116 parks. Of interest are Fort George Park, which contains a replica of Fraser's trading post; Connaught Park's manicured gardens and scenic views; and Cottonwood Island Park, which includes the Prince George Railway Museum and its collection of railroad artifacts and cars.

Prince George blends its pastoral features with such cultural centers as Studio 2880 and Vanier Hall. Studio 2880, home to six craft guilds, is the site of craft markets and special events throughout the year. Concerts by the Prince George Symphony and by visiting performers are held in Vanier Hall.

These cultural amenities coexist with the more rugged recreational opportunities available in the wilderness that surrounds the city. Nearby lakes, rivers and mountains present an array of activities ranging from rugged back-country hikes and fishing to skiing and ice skating.

Tourism Prince George: 101-1300 First Ave., Prince George, BC, Canada V2L 2Y3; phone (250) 562-3700 or (800) 668-7646.

THE EXPLORATION PLACE AT THE FRASER-FORT GEORGE REGIONAL MUSEUM is at the end of 20th Ave. at 333 Becott Pl. in Fort George Park. Fort George's history and development are explored through such topics as transportation, lumber and the First Nations culture. The Children's Gallery houses life-size dinosaur sculptures, skeletons and a dig pit. The Explorations Gallery features live animals and interactive computers. A SimEx virtual motion theater offers three rides daily. A steam locomotive ride is offered on weekends and holidays.

Allow 1 hour minimum. Daily 10-5, day after Victoria Day-day before second Mon. in Oct.; Wed.-Sun. 10-5, rest of year. Closed Jan. 1 and Dec. 25-26. Museum admission $8.95; $6.95 (ages 60+); $5.95 (ages 3-18); $20.95 (family, two adults and up to four children ages 0-18). Combination ticket with movie ride $10.95; $9.95 (ages 60+ and students with ID); $8.95 (ages 2-12); $29.95 (family, two adults and up to four children ages 0-18). Train rides $1. AX, MC, VI. Phone (250) 562-1612 or (866) 562-1612.

HUBLE HOMESTEAD HISTORIC SITE is 40 km n. of Prince George on Mitchell Rd. The site features several replicas of historic buildings as well as the original homestead of Al and Annie Huble. Along with his business partner Ed Seebach, Huble was instrumental in establishing a community within the Giscome Portage area. Guided tours are available. Allow 1 hour minimum. Daily 10-5, Victoria Day weekend-Labor Day weekend. Donations. Phone (250) 564-7033.

RAILWAY & FORESTRY MUSEUM is at 850 River Rd. The museum houses one of the largest collection of railway-related artifacts in British Columbia. Items, circa 1899-1960s, include a wooden snow plow, locomotives, box cars and cabooses. Picnicking is permitted. Allow 1 hour minimum. Daily 10-5, May-Sept.; Tues.-Sun. 11-4, rest of year. Admission $6; $5 (students and senior citizens); $3 (ages 5-12); $15 (family, two adults and two children). AX, MC, VI. Phone (250) 563-7351.

PRINCE RUPERT (E-2)
pop. 14,643, elev. 50 m/164'

At the turn of the 20th century Prince Rupert existed only in the imagination of Charles Hays, manager of the Grand Trunk Pacific Railway. Hays died with the sinking of the SS *Titanic*, but the Grand Trunk Pacific Railway carried out his intention to build a port to rival Vancouver on this rugged, uninhabited island bordered by a natural harbor. The new site was expected to be successful because it was closer to the Far East than Vancouver and would provide an outlet for the untapped resources of Canada's far north.

Prince Rupert has fulfilled that potential and is now one of Canada's major seaports. It is the southernmost port of the Alaska Ferry System, the northern terminus of the British Columbia Ferry Corp. and the western terminus of the Canadian National Railway. Cruise ships en route to coastal glaciers and fjords also stop at Prince Rupert's harbor, said to be the world's third largest natural ice-free deep-sea harbor.

Before the coming of the railroad the northern coast was home to the Tsimpsean and Haida, cultures whose ancestors inhabited the area for almost 5,000 years. Both are renowned for their stylized artworks, the most familiar of which are totem poles. Many of these graceful monuments are shown in such city parks as Service Park, the colorful terraced Sunken Gardens, and Roosevelt Park with its sweeping views of the Pacific.

On the waterfront, Kwinitsa Railway Stationis a relic of the modern era. Restored and moved from its original location, Kwinitsa is one of the last of the Grand Trunk Pacific Railway stations; inside are exhibits about the railroad's history.

Just beyond the city, climate and soil have stunted and twisted lodgepole pines into a natural bonsai garden at Oliver Lake Provincial Park. Another interesting phenomenon is Butze Rapids, a series of reversing rapids between Wainwright and Morse basins that rival the reversing falls at Saint John, New Brunswick. A dramatic view of the rapids occurs during a falling tide and can be seen from a viewing point on Hwy. 16, which offers scenic driving east to Terrace *(see place listing p. 156)*.

Guided tours are offered during the summer by Farwest Bus Lines Ltd., 225 Second Ave. W. Trans-Provincial Airlines and Northcoast Air Services offer flight tours of the region.

Prince Rupert Visitor Information Centre: 215 Cow Bay Rd., Suite 100, Prince Rupert, BC, Canada V8J 1A2; phone (250) 624-5637 or (800) 667-1994.

Self-guiding tours: A walking tour that includes sunken gardens, the harbor, sections of the downtown area and various attractions is detailed on maps and brochures available from the visitor bureau at the Museum of Northern British Columbia *(see attraction listing)*.

MUSEUM OF NORTHERN BRITISH COLUMBIA is at 100 First Ave. W. and McBride St. Models, maps, graphic displays and an ethnological collection explain pioneer history and the lifestyles of the coastal First Nations groups from prehistoric times through their contacts with Europeans. Changing exhibits are displayed in the art gallery. Of interest are an early 20th-century steamroller and a modern First Nations carving shed with local artists on site.

Daily 9-5, June-Aug.; Tues.-Sat. 9-5, rest of year. Closed Jan. 1 and Dec. 25-26. Admission $5; $2 (students with ID); $1 (ages 6-12); $10 (family). MC, VI. Phone (250) 624-3207, ext. 27.

PRINCETON (C-8) pop. 2,610

Named "Vermilion Forks" by fur traders in the early 1800s, Princeton developed as a ranching and mining outpost in the foothills of the Cascade Mountains. In 1860 the town was renamed to honor a visit by the Prince of Wales. Revitalized downtown storefronts boast murals and facades in keeping with Princeton's Western heritage.

Princeton & District Chamber of Commerce: 105 Hwy. 3, P.O. Box 540, Princeton, BC, Canada V0X 1W0; phone (250) 295-3103.

Self-guiding tours: Maps detailing walking tours are available from the chamber of commerce.

PRINCETON AND DISTRICT MUSEUM AND AR-CHIVES is at 167 Vermilion Ave. The collection includes fossils and minerals, aboriginal baskets, lace and textiles, antique cooking utensils, mining tools and equipment, a large butterfly collection and a stagecoach. Daily 10-7, June-Aug.; 10-5, Apr.-May and Sept.-Oct. Donations. Phone (250) 295-7588.

QUADRA ISLAND—
see Gulf Islands National Park Reserve of Canada p. 125.

QUALICUM BEACH (F-10)
pop. 6,921, elev. 9 m/30'

A popular resort and arts community, Qualicum Beach is known for its white sand beaches. Nearby Little Qualicum Falls, Englishman River Falls *(see Recreation Chart)* and Horne Lake Caves Provincial Park *(see Recreation Chart)* also present abundant recreational opportunities. Salmon and trout are raised at fish hatcheries on the Big and Little Qualicum rivers.

Qualicum Beach Visitor Information Centre: 2711 W. Island Hwy., Qualicum Beach, BC, Canada V9K 2C4; phone (250) 752-9532 or (866) 887-7106.

BIG QUALICUM RIVER HATCHERY is 12 km (7 mi.) n. on Hwy. 19A, then e. on Kenmuir Rd., following signs. Millions of chum, coho and chinook salmon are hatched here each year as part of the country's efforts to restore its salmon population. Steelhead and cutthroat trout also are raised. Visitors can see holding ponds, rearing channels and incubation units. Hiking trails are available. Allow 30 minutes minimum. Daily dawn-dusk. Donations. Phone (250) 757-8412.

HORNE LAKE CAVES is 15 km n. of Qualicum Beach on Hwy. 19 to exit 75 (Horne Lake Rd.), then 14 km w. on a gravel road, following signs to cave parking lot. A part of the Horne Lake Caves Provincial Park, the cave system is considered to be one of the best in Canada. Tours are guided and highlights include crystal formations, ancient fossils and a waterfall.

The 1.5-hour Family Cave Tour teaches about the geology and history of the caves. The interpretive tour starts with a 25-minute walk to the entrance. Once inside the cave, visitors explore the easy passages; no crawling or maneuvering in tight spaces is necessary. Other 3-, 4-, and 5-hour tours also are offered. Self-guiding exploration is available in Horne Lake Main and Lower caves year-round. A helmet and two sources of light are required. Helmets may be rented for $5 each during the summer only.

Note: The caves are mostly undeveloped and do not provide lighting. Floors are rocky and uneven; children ages 0-4 and visitors with mobility issues could encounter difficulty walking. Warm clothing and comfortable boots or shoes are highly recommended, as the caves remain cool even in hot weather. Cameras are permitted. Allow 1 hour, 30 minutes minimum. Tours require a minimum of three people. Family Cave Tour is given on a first-come, first-served basis on the hour 10-5, late June-early Sept.; by appointment rest of year. Closed Jan. 1 and Dec. 25. Last tour leaves at closing. Family Cave Tour admission $17; $15 (ages 0-11). MC, VI. Phone (250) 248-7829 for reservations or (250) 757-8687 for tour information.

MILNER GARDENS AND WOODLANDS, 2179 W. Island Hwy., comprises 24 hectares (60 acres) of Douglas fir woodland and 4 hectares (10 acres) of garden surrounding a gabled heritage house. Visitors may view the dining, sitting and drawing rooms as well as the library. Historical photos, artifacts and keepsakes of visits by members of the Royal family also are displayed.

Allow 1 hour minimum. Daily 10-5, Mother's Day-Labour Day; Thurs.-Sun. and Mon. holidays 10-5, day after Labour Day through mid-Oct. Admission $10; $6 (students with ID); free (ages 0-12 when accompanied by an adult). Phone (250) 752-6153.

QUALICUM BEACH HISTORICAL & MUSEUM SOCIETY is at 587 Beach Rd. Two floors of exhibits highlight the history of Qualicum Beach and Canada. Included in the displays are murals, a diorama of a 1930s kitchen and a paleontology collection. The 1929 Powerhouse building also is on-site and houses a variety of historical items. Allow 30 minutes minimum. Tues.-Sat. 11-4, late May to mid-Sept. Donations. Phone (250) 752-5533.

QUEEN CHARLOTTE ISLANDS (E-1)

The Queen Charlotte Islands were occupied by Haida Indians when Spanish sea captain Juan Pérez sighted the archipelago in 1774. A seafaring and artistic people, the Haida traded sea otter pelts with European traders during the early 1800s. By the late 19th century, however, the Haida had to vacate many of their ancestral villages to escape a devastating smallpox epidemic.

Only a fraction of their original number still inhabit the island—at Haida, near Masset, and Skidegate, near Queen Charlotte City. Continuing their cultural traditions, they carve elaborate works of art from argillite, a black slatelike stone found only in mountain deposits off the coast.

A group of about 150 islands forming an elongated triangle, the Queen Charlotte Islands stretch 250 kilometres (157 mi.) from north to south, 90 kilometres (56 mi.) off the coast of British Columbia. Characterized by fog and low clouds, these islands also are known as the Misty Islands. The towns are small and decidedly rural; the entire population of the Queen Charlotte Islands is about 5,000.

The largest of the islands is Graham. In the north on its broad and flat eastern side are most of the archipelago's communities—Masset, Old Masset, Port Clements, Queen Charlotte City, Skidegate, and Tlell—which are linked by a paved road. An airport is at Masset as well as at Sandspit, on the northeastern tip of Moresby Island.

A temperate marine climate supports dense coniferous forests, which, as the basis of the islands' economy, have been logged extensively. The fish and shellfish in the coastal waters supply the islands' important commercial fishing industry.

Visitors are attracted by the pristine wilderness, the hunting and fishing prospects, kayaking and hiking opportunities, and the handicrafts and art of the Haida. Wildlife is abundant; tiny Sitka deer and bald eagles frequent the shores, and seals, porpoises and whales often appear in the inlets. Bird-watching is a popular activity.

Points of interest include Naikoon Provincial Park (see Recreation Chart) on Graham Island, the remote Haida village sites, the Delkatla Wildlife Sanctuary in Masset, the Haida Heritage Centre at Qay'llnagaay (see attraction listing p. 154) in Skidegate and the various carving sheds in Skidegate and Old Masset.

Permission to visit Haida unoccupied village sites must be obtained from Band Council offices; phone (250) 559-8225.

The Queen Charlotte Islands can be reached by air from Prince Rupert and Vancouver and by ferry from Prince Rupert; phone (250) 386-3431 from the Victoria area and outside British Columbia or (888) 223-3779 from elsewhere in the province. Kayak rentals, fishing charters and various guided boat and land tours are available.

Queen Charlotte Visitor Centre: 3220 Wharf St., P.O. Box 819, Queen Charlotte, BC, Canada V0T 1S0; phone (250) 559-8316.

QUESNEL (F-4)
pop. 10,044, elev. 545 m/1,788'

Discovery of gold in the surrounding area in the 1860s contributed to Quesnel's growth. The city is the center of a popular hunting and fishing region at the junction of the Fraser and Quesnel rivers. Lumber, pulp and plywood manufacturing, tourism, cattle ranching and mining are the city's primary sources of income.

East of the city on Hwy. 26 is a historic remnant of the gold rush days, Barkerville Historic Town (see place listing p. 114), a restored boomtown of that era. Just beyond Barkerville is Bowron Lake

Provincial Park (see Recreation Chart and the AAA/CAA Western Canada & Alaska CampBook), which has a 116-kilometre (72-mi.) canoe circuit of interconnecting lakes. Alpine skiing is available nearby.

Quesnel Visitor Information Centre: 703 Carson Ave., Quesnel, BC, Canada V2J 2B6; phone (250) 992-8716 or (800) 992-4922.

COTTONWOOD HOUSE HISTORIC SITE is 28 km (17 mi.) e. on Hwy. 26. Cottonwood was built 1864-65 as a roadhouse for travelers on the Cariboo Wagon Road en route to the gold fields of Barkerville. The 26-acre site includes a double barn, stable, animals, guesthouse, outbuildings and antique machinery. Costumed interpreters provide tours of cottonwood house and wagon rides. A walking trail winds along the river.

Daily 10-5, May-Aug. Admission (includes wagon ride) $4.50; $3.50 (ages 61+); $2 (ages 13-18). MC, VI. Phone (250) 992-2071.

QUESNEL & DISTRICT MUSEUM AND ARCHIVES is .7 km (.5 mi.) s. on Hwy. 97 at 705 Carson Ave. Marking the area's history from the days of Alexander Mackenzie's explorations and the 1862 gold rush, the museum includes exhibits about pioneer life, a hands-on area for children, artifacts from the Titanic and an archives.

Allow 1 hour minimum. Daily 9-6, May-Aug.; Tues.-Sat. 8:30-4:30, rest of year. Closed statutory holidays. Admission $3; $1.50 (ages 13-17). Phone (250) 992-9580.

RADIUM HOT SPRINGS (B-11)
pop. 583, elev. 805 m/2,641'

Renowned for its mineral hot springs (see Kootenay National Park of Canada p. 131 and Recreation Chart), Radium Hot Springs also is a popular departure point for scenic and white-water river excursions. More than 10 golf courses are in the vicinity.

RECREATIONAL ACTIVITIES
Skiing
- **Panorama Mountain Village** is 12 km (7.5 mi.) w. on Hwy. 95. Write Panorama, BC, Canada V0A 1T0. Other activities are offered. Daily 9-4, Dec.-Apr.; 10-5, June-Labour Day. Phone (800) 663-2929.

White-water Rafting
- **Kootenay River Runners** is at 4987 Hwy. 93. Daily 8 a.m.-10 p.m., early June to mid-Sept. Phone (250) 347-9210 or (800) 599-4399.

REVELSTOKE (B-10)
pop. 7,500, elev. 440 m/1,433'

Revelstoke is at the western end of Rogers Pass, the section of the Trans-Canada Hwy. that traverses Glacier National Park of Canada (see place listing p. 122). Rogers Pass is one of the world's most scenic mountain roads. Downhill skiing is available nearby.

Revelstoke Chamber of Commerce: 204 Campbell Ave., P.O. Box 490, Revelstoke, BC, Canada V0E 2S0; phone (250) 837-5345 or (800) 487-1493.

CANYON HOT SPRINGS is 35.5 km (22 mi.) e. on Hwy. 1. Bathers can dip in a pool of 40 C (104 F) mineral waters or swim in a pool that is 30 C (86 F).

Camping is permitted. Food is available. Daily 9 a.m.-10 p.m., July-Aug.; 9-9, May-June and in Sept. Hours may vary; phone ahead. Day passes $10; $9.50 (ages 5-14 and 60+); $28 (family pass, two adults and two children). Single swim $7.50; $6.50 (ages 5-14 and 60+); $20 (family, two adults and two children). Rates may vary; phone ahead. Phone (250) 837-2420. *See Recreation Chart.*

SAVE **ENCHANTED FOREST** is 32 km (20 mi.) w. on Hwy. 1 to 7060 Trans-Canada Hwy. More than 350 handmade figurines include Old World fairy folk, dragons and dungeons in a natural forest setting with giant cedars, a stump house, a fish pond and a towering tree house that is reputedly one of the province's tallest. Swamp boat rides and a wetland boardwalk including lush vegetation, beaver dams and spawning salmon beds also are offered.

Pets are permitted. Daily 9-8, June 16-Sept. 4; 10-6, late Apr.-June 15 and Sept. 5-Oct. 15 (weather permitting). Admission $7.95; $7.47 (ages 3-15). MC, VI. Phone (250) 837-9477 or (866) 944-9744.

SAVE **REVELSTOKE RAILWAY MUSEUM** is at 719 Track St. W. off Victoria Rd. The building of the Canadian Pacific Railway is traced with artifacts, photographs and original equipment. One of the company's largest steam locomotives is displayed beside a restored 1929 solarium car inside the museum, while the yard features such rolling stock as a caboose, a snow plow and a flange car. A diesel cabin simulator allows visitors to experience the feeling of driving a train.

Allow 30 minutes minimum. Daily 9-8, July-Aug.; Thurs.-Tues. 9-5, Mar.-Apr.; daily 9-5, May-June and Sept.-Oct.; Fri.-Tues. 11-4, rest of year. Closed Jan. 1, Good Friday, Easter, second Mon. in Oct. and Dec. 25-26. Admission $8; $6 (ages 61+); $4 (ages 7-16); $13 (family). MC, VI. Phone (250) 837-6060 or (877) 837-6060.

THREE VALLEY GAP HERITAGE GHOST TOWN is 19 km (12 mi.) w. on Hwy. 1. Near the original site of the 19th-century lumber and mining town of Three Valley are more than 40 relocated buildings including a hotel, a general store, a church, two schoolhouses, a saloon and many examples of hand-crafted log buildings. An exhibit chronicles the history of steam, transportation and communication. Live performances of a musical stage show take place most nights May through September.

Guided 1-hour tours depart daily 9-4, mid-Apr. to mid-Oct. Admission $8.88; $7.01 (ages 65+); $6.54 (ages 12-17); $4.67 (ages 6-11). An additional fee is charged for the stage show; reservations are required. AX, MC, VI. Phone (250) 837-2109 or (888) 667-2109.

RICHMOND—*see Vancouver p. 178.*

ROSSLAND (D-10)
pop. 3,646, elev. 1,039 m/3,408'

The 1890 gold rush on Red Mountain spurred the growth of Rossland from a prospectors' camp to a bustling town with 42 saloons, 17 law firms, four breweries and two distilleries. The area's vast mineral wealth, which supported a booming mining industry for 40 years, produced more than 6 million tons of ore valued at about $125 million.

Camping and picnicking are offered at King George VI Provincial Park, 9.6 kilometres (6 mi.) south near the U.S. border *(see the AAA/CAA Western Canada & Alaska CampBook)*; fishing, swimming and canoeing are available at Nancy Greene Provincial Park, 26 kilometres (16 mi.) northwest at hwys. 3 and 3B *(see Recreation Chart and the AAA/CAA Western Canada & Alaska CampBook)*.

Rossland Chamber of Commerce: 2185 Columbia Ave., P.O. Box 1385, Rossland, BC, Canada V0G 1Y0; phone (250) 362-5666.

ROSSLAND HISTORICAL MUSEUM AND LE ROI MINE is at jct. hwys. 3B and 22. Guided underground mine tours enter a historic Le Roi gold mine. The museum has mining artifacts and rock and mineral samples. There also are outdoor exhibits. Gold panning is offered.

Allow 2 hours minimum. Daily 9-5, mid-May to mid-Sept. Last mine tour departs 90 minutes before closing. Museum $4; $5 (students with ID); $3 (ages 60+); $1.50 (ages 6-13). Mine tours (museum included) $10; $8 (ages 60+ and students with ID); $3 (ages 6-13); $25 (family). AX, MC, VI. Phone (250) 362-7722 or (888) 448-7444.

RECREATIONAL ACTIVITIES
Skiing
- **Red Mountain Ski Area** is 3 km (1.5 mi.) n. on Hwy. 3B. Write P.O. Box 670, Rossland, BC, Canada V0G 1Y0. Daily 8-4:30, Dec. 1-Apr. 6. Phone (250) 362-7384 or (800) 663-0105.

SAANICHTON—*see Victoria p. 194.*

SALT SPRING ISLAND—
see Gulf Islands National Park Reserve of Canada p. 125.

SATURNA ISLAND—
see Gulf Islands National Park Reserve of Canada p. 125.

SECHELT (G-11) pop. 7,775

CHAPMAN CREEK HATCHERY is at 4381 Parkway Dr. Visitors learn about the life-cycle of Pacific salmon. Throughout the facility, interpretive signs communicate the history of the hatchery and its function. Picnicking is permitted. Allow 1 hour minimum. Daily 9-3:30. Donations. Phone (604) 885-4136.

SICAMOUS (B-9)
pop. 2,720, elev. 352 m/1,155'

Flanked by Mara and Shuswap lakes, Sicamous has abundant recreational opportunities, including swimming, fishing, boating and other water sports. Full- and half-day cruises on Shuswap Lake *(see Recreation Chart)* and 2- and 3-hour evening excursions on Mara Lake depart from the public wharf at the foot of Finlayson Street. Houseboats, which can be rented, are a popular way of touring the arms of Shuswap Lake.

At nearby Adams River almost 10 million scarlet sockeye salmon bury their eggs each October; it is one of the largest spawning grounds in the country. Several spawning grounds can be seen at Roderick Haig-Brown Provincial Park.

Sicamous & District Chamber of Commerce: 110 Finlayson St., P.O. Box 346, Sicamous, BC, Canada V0E 2V0; phone (250) 836-3313.

SIDNEY—*see Victoria p. 195.*

SKIDEGATE (E-1) pop. 743

HAIDA HERITAGE CENTRE AT QAY'LLNAGAAY is at Second Beach Rd. Haida art, history and culture are celebrated through audiovisuals and interactive displays. Traditional totem poles representing the 14 clans front the facility; three ancient poles are inside. A canoe house, performing house and carving shed also may be seen. The Haida Gwaii Museum includes exhibits about the Haida's belief in the natural and supernatural as well as plant and wildlife. A collection of argillite carvings and contemporary art is showcased.

Guided tours are available. Food is available. Allow 1 hour minimum. Daily 10-6, June-Aug.; Mon.-Fri. 10-5 in May and Sept.; Tues.-Sat. 10-5, rest of year. Closed Jan. 1, Dec. 25-26 and 31. Admission (includes Haida Gwaii Museum and Haida Heritage Centre) $12; $9 (ages 13-18 and students with ID); $5 (ages 6-12). MC, VI. Phone (250) 559-7885.

SMITHERS (E-3)
pop. 5,414, elev. 520 m/1,706'

Named for A.W. Smithers, one-time chairman of the Grand Trunk Pacific Railway, Smithers owes its location to railway construction crews who in 1913 selected the scenic spot at the base of Hudson Bay Mountain. It became a village in 1921 and officially a town in 1967. Today it is a distribution and supply center for local farms, mills and mines. Murals adorn many buildings within its alpine-style Main Street district.

Smithers is popular as a year-round skiing center thanks to 2,652-metre (8,700-ft.) Hudson Bay Mountain. The town also is a convenient starting point for fossil hunting, fishing, mountain climbing and trail riding.

Smithers District Chamber of Commerce: 1411 Court St., P.O. Box 2379, Smithers, BC, Canada V0J 2N0; phone (250) 847-5072 or (800) 542-6673.

Self-guiding tours: Information about driving and walking tours is available at the chamber of commerce.

ADAMS IGLOO is 10 km (6 mi.) w. on Hwy. 16. Mounted animals and birds native to British Columbia are displayed inside an igloo. Allow 30 minutes minimum. Daily 9-6. Admission $5; $4 (ages 56+); $3 (ages 6-13). MC, VI. Phone (250) 847-3188.

SOOKE—see *Victoria p. 195.*

SPARWOOD (C-12)
pop. 3,812, elev. 1,143 m/3,750′

Once known as a mining town, Sparwood offers guided tours of the Elkview Coal Mine during summer. Popular area recreational activities include fly fishing, white-water rafting, hiking and mountain biking.

Sparwood Chamber of Commerce: 141A Aspen Dr., P.O. Box 1448, Sparwood, BC, Canada V0B 2G0; phone (250) 425-2423 or (877) 485-8185.

SQUAMISH (G-12) pop. 14,247, elev. 5 m/16′

Overshadowed by Stawamus Chief Mountain and other snowcapped peaks, Squamish was named for the Indian word meaning "mother of the wind." It is a popular stopover for tourists and recreation seekers. Rock climbing and windsurfing are popular activities.

Picnic facilities are available 3 kilometres (1.9 mi.) south at Shannon Falls, and camping facilities are available at Alice Lake Park *(see Recreation Chart and the AAA/CAA Western Canada & Alaska CampBook)* 13 kilometres (8 mi.) to the north.

Squamish Chamber of Commerce: 102-38551 Loggers Ln., Squamish, BC, Canada V8B 0H2; phone (604) 815-4994 or (866) 333-2010 within British Columbia.

GARIBALDI PROVINCIAL PARK is accessible by trail from Hwy. 99 or the British Columbia Railway. The 194,650-hectare (480,980-acre) park is a pristine wilderness of peaks, glaciers, meadows, lakes and streams.

Access to the Garibaldi Lake/Black Tusk Area is by a 7.25-kilometre (5-mi.) trail off Hwy. 99, about 37 kilometres (23 mi.) north of Squamish. A gravel road leads 16 kilometres (10 mi.) to the base camp parking lot, where a trail follows Paul Ridge 11.25 kilometres (7 mi.) to the Diamond Head Area. Glacier-fed Cheakamus Lake lies at an elevation of less than 914 metres (2,999 ft.). The park is open all year. Park admission free. Parking $3 per day. Phone (604) 582-5200 for more information. *See Recreation Chart.*

[SAVE] **GLACIER AIR TOURS** is at 46001 Government Rd. at Squamish Municipal Airport. Helicopter and airplane sightseeing flights and glacier-landing flights are offered. The latter may include dining on a glacier. Daily 9-6 (departure times vary), May-Oct.; on demand, rest of year. Fares for sightseeing flights start at $75. Reservations are recommended. MC, VI. Phone (604) 898-9016, or (800) 265-0088 within Canada.

WEST COAST RAILWAY HERITAGE PARK is 1 km (.6 mi.) w. off Hwy. 99 on Industrial Way, n. on Queensway Rd. to 39645 Government Rd. This outdoor museum features more than 60 railway heritage pieces dating to the early 1900s. Displays include steam and diesel locomotives, a sleeping car, caboose, bunk cars and a business car. A restoration exhibit demonstrates the process of restoring old railway cars. Visitors can ride a miniature train on a 7.5-gauge track around the property.

Food is available. Allow 30 minutes minimum. Daily 10-5; closed Jan. 1 and Dec. 25. Miniature train operates daily 11-3. Admission $10; $8.50 (ages 6-18 and 65+); $32 (family, two adults and three children). Miniature railway rides $2. MC, VI. Phone (604) 898-9336.

SUMMERLAND—
see *Okanagan Valley p. 145*

SUNSHINE COAST (H-4)

Lining the western edge of the British Columbia mainland, the Sunshine Coast offers a wide variety of marine and land habitats, from coastal rain forests and rocky beaches to an alpine wilderness with peaks reaching 2,500 metres (8,000 ft.).

Powell River *(see place listing p. 149)*, with more than 100 regional dive sites, exceptionally clear water and deep ocean currents, is called the "Dive Capital of Canada." Desolation Sound's warm, sheltered waters also contribute to the destination's popularity with scuba divers and kayakers. Sechelt *(see place listing p. 154)* is known for its rich artisan community, while Gibsons *(see place listing p. 122)* is home to up to 200 bird species throughout the year.

SURREY—see *Vancouver p. 179.*

TELEGRAPH COVE (H-3) pop. 1,600

The bay community served as the northern terminus of the telegraph line along the coast of Vancouver Island and later became a logging and salmon fishing area. Whale watching, fishing and camping are popular during the summer.

STUBBS ISLAND WHALE WATCHING departs from the end of the boardwalk. For excursions on the Johnstone Strait, vessels are equipped with underwater microphones for listening to whale vocalizations. A Magnificent Seven Marine Mammal tour also is available. Warm clothing is recommended. Allow 4 hours minimum. Daily departures early May to mid-Oct. Hours vary; phone ahead. Mid-day fare $89; $79 (ages 1-12 and 65+). Morning and evening fare $79. Reservations are required. MC, VI. Phone (250) 928-3185 or (800) 665-3066.

WHALE INTERPRETIVE CENTRE is at the end of the boardwalk. Interpreters provide hands-on presentations and share information about and promote awareness of the marine environment. Exhibits include whale skeletons and artifacts. An educational video about marine-life also is featured. Allow 45 minutes minimum. Daily 9-7, May-Sept. Donations. Phone (250) 928-3129.

TERRACE (E-2) pop. 12,109, elev. 215 m/705'

On the banks of the Skeena River, Terrace is a major producer of forest products. The area provides excellent recreational opportunities ranging from hiking on a variety of trails to fishing in nearby rivers and creeks. Among the region's wildlife is a rare species of black bear, the white Kermodei. Native to the area, it is the city's symbol.

Among the most popular recreation areas are Lakelse Lake *(see Recreation Chart and the AAA/ CAA Western Canada & Alaska CampBook)*; Lakelse River, a tributary of the Skeena River that harbors record-size salmon; and Williams Creek, which teems with spawning sockeye each August.

Several places of natural interest are nearby. At the eastern entrance to the city is Ferry Island, a park with hiking trails, swimming and camping *(see Recreation Chart)*. About 20 kilometres (12 mi.) south of Terrace is Mount Layton Hot Springs Resort, which has waterslides and a pool filled with natural hot spring mineral water. Hwy. 16 offers a scenic drive west along the Skeena River to Prince Rupert.

Terrace Visitor InfoCentre: 4511 Keith Ave., Terrace, BC, Canada V8G 1K1; phone (250) 635-2063 or (800) 499-1637.

HERITAGE PARK MUSEUM is at 4702 Kerby Ave. Historic buildings depict the history of pioneers in the region. The structures contain more than 4,000 artifacts pertaining to the life of settlers to the area 1890-1950. Guided tours are available. Allow 1 hour minimum. Daily 10-6, June-Sept.; by appointment rest of year. Tours are given 10:30-4:30. Admission $4; $2 (ages 4-18, ages 61+ and students with ID); $10 (family). Phone (250) 635-4546.

NISGA'A MEMORIAL LAVA BED PROVINCIAL PARK is 4 km (2.5 mi.) w. on Hwy. 16, then 80 km (50 mi.) n. on Kalum Lake Dr. (Nisga'a Hwy.). Drivers should watch for logging trucks.

Miles of lava beds were formed by a volcanic eruption some 250 years ago that destroyed two Nisga'a tribal villages, causing 2,000 deaths. The valley floor resembles the moon's surface. Interpretive trails provide easy access through the park. The New Aiyansh Indian Village, 16 kilometres (10 mi.) north, features totem poles, a tribal council hall and a Nisga'a Lisims government building.

Camping is available. Park daily dawn-dusk, May 1 through mid-Oct. Visitor center daily 10-6, June-early Sept. Guided hiking tours of the volcanic cone are offered on Sat. at 10, mid-June through Aug. 31. Visitor center $2; free (ages 0-12). Park free. Guided hiking tour fee $25; $20 (ages 16-18); $15 (ages 8-15 and 65+); ages 0-7 are not permitted. Phone (250) 798-2277.

TOFINO (I-3) pop. 1,466

A fishing and resort village with sandy beaches, Tofino is on the western side of Vancouver Island at the end of Hwy. 4. The area was the site of Fort Defiance, where Boston fur trader Robert Gray and his men spent the winter of 1791. The fort was stripped and abandoned the next spring, and all that remains are scattered bricks and ruins.

Near Clayoquot Sound and the northern end of Pacific Rim National Park Reserve of Canada, the town's shoreline and waters are popular with scuba divers and beachcombers. In the spring whales often can be seen migrating along the coast. The Whale Centre and Museum at 411 Campbell St. exhibits scientific and artistic displays, photographs and artifacts depicting past and present whale encounters.

Several companies, including Adventures Pacific, (250) 725-2811; Jamie's Whaling Station, (250) 725-3919; [SAVE] Remote Passages, (250) 725-3330; and Sea Trek Tours and Expeditions, (250) 725-4412, offer whale-watching excursions on Clayoquot Sound. Tours lasting up to 2.5 hours may afford sightings of sea lions, porpoises and eagles. Combination whale-watching and hot springs cruises that last approximately 6.5 hours also are available.

Tofino-Long Beach Chamber of Commerce: 1426 Pacific Rim Hwy., P.O. Box 249, Tofino, BC, Canada V0R 2Z0; phone (250) 725-3414.

TOFINO BOTANICAL GARDENS is at 1084 Pacific Rim Hwy. This site consists of 12 acres of gardens that include a children's garden, a medicinal herb garden, 1000-year-old cedar trees, an orchard and a berry patch, and a bird-watching area. An old homestead also is on the grounds. Food is available. Pets and smoking are not permitted. Allow 1 hour minimum. Daily 9-dusk. Admission $10; $6 (students); free (ages 0-12). MC, VI. Phone (250) 725-1220.

TRAIL (D-10) pop. 7,575, elev. 430 m/1,410'

At City Hall a sculptured screen titled "City of Lead and Zinc" illustrates how Trail's mineral and industrial strength steadily developed since the discovery of gold and copper in the area about 1890. Hydroelectric dams along the Kootenay River power extensive mining and smelting operations, dominated by Teck Cominco Ltd.

Trail and District Chamber of Commerce and Visitor Centre: 1199 Bay Ave., Suite 200, Trail, BC, Canada V1R 4A4; phone (250) 368-3144 or (877) 636-9569 within British Columbia.

Self-guiding tours: Brochures for walking tours are available at the chamber of commerce.

TECK COMINCO LTD. tours depart from the Interpretive Centre downtown at 1199 Bay Ave., Suite 200. Guided tours are offered of one of the largest lead-zinc smelters in the world. Long pants, long-sleeved shirts and closed shoes are required; cameras and video equipment are prohibited. Individuals with pacemakers should not attend. Allow 2 hours minimum. Center open daily 9-5, July-Aug.; Mon.-Fri. 9-5, rest of year. Tours depart Mon.-Fri. at 10, July-Aug.; by appointment rest of year. Closed major holidays. Free. Ages 0-11 are not permitted on tours. Phone (250) 368-3144.

UCLUELET (I-3) pop. 1,559

On Barkley Sound, Ucluelet was named for an Indian word meaning "safe harbor." Charter boats for salmon fishing, whale watching, skin diving and nature excursions are available; phone the chamber of commerce. The MV *Lady Rose* makes round trips between Port Alberni and Ucluelet June through September (*see attraction listing in Port Alberni p. 148*). He Tin Kis Park allows visitors to experience a Canadian rain forest and follow a boardwalk trail that leads to the ocean. The 5-kilometre (3-mi.) Wild Pacific Trail passes a lighthouse en route to cliffside ocean views.

Ucluelet Chamber of Commerce: 200 Main St., P.O. Box 428, Ucluelet, BC, Canada V0R 3A0; phone (250) 726-4641.

VALEMOUNT (F-5)
pop. 1,195, elev. 792 m/2,600'

Valemount, the valley in the mountains, offers many activities for outdoor enthusiasts. The village, where the Rocky, Cariboo and Monashee mountain ranges meet, is popular for both summer and winter pursuits, including hiking, rafting, skiing and snowmobiling. The area is rich with birds and other wildlife. Off Hwy. 16 is Mount Terry Fox Provincial Park. A viewing area affords vistas of the peak named for the late athlete.

Village of Valemount Visitor Centre: 735 Cranberry Lake Rd., P.O. Box 168, Valemount, BC, Canada V0E 2Z0; phone (250) 566-4435, or (250) 566-9893 mid-June to mid-Sept.

GEORGE HICKS REGIONAL PARK is off Hwy. 5 at 785 Cranberry Lake Rd. The site offers a bird's-eye view of Chinook salmon as they near the end of a 1,280-kilometre (768-mi.) upstream trip from mid-August to mid-September. Daily mid-May to mid-Sept. Donations. Phone (250) 566-9893.

MOUNT ROBSON PROVINCIAL PARK is on Hwy. 16. Mount Robson, at 3,954 metres (12,972 ft.) is the highest peak in the Canadian Rockies. Other park highlights include glacier-fed lakes, valleys, canyons, waterfalls, rivers and streams. More than 180 species of birds reside here along with deer, moose, bears, elk and caribou. Fishing and hiking are just a few of the outdoor activities to be enjoyed.

Scenic views abound on the many walking and hiking trails. A visitor center is at the Mount Robson viewpoint. Picnicking is permitted. Park open daily 24 hours. Visitor center open May-Sept. Donations. Phone (250) 566-4325. *See Recreation Chart and the AAA/CAA Western Canada & Alaska CampBook.*

ROBSON HELIMAGIC SIGHTSEEING TOURS depart from the Yellowhead Helicopters hangar, 5 km (3 mi.) n. on Hwy. 5 to 3010 Selwyn Rd. Helicopters take passengers on 12-36 minute tours of the Valemount and Mount Robson areas, providing breathtaking views of glaciers, snow-covered mountains, alpine meadows, valleys, waterfalls, lakes and rivers. Heli-skiing, heli-snowshoeing and heli-snowboarding also are offered in winter. Daily 8-dusk. Fare $89-$210. AX, MC, VI. Phone (250) 566-4700 or (877) 454-4700.

R.W. STARRATT WILDLIFE SANCTUARY is 1 km (.6 mi.) s. on Hwy. 5. The refuge is home to a variety of songbirds, waterfowl and other animals. Informational signs line a trail to two viewing platforms. Allow 30 minutes minimum. Daily 9-9, May-Sept. Free. Phone (250) 566-9893.

Vancouver

City Population: 545,671
Elevation: 3 m/10 ft.

Editor's Picks:

Find more AAA top picks at AAA.com

© Eero Sorila

A great port, cultural center and tourist area, Vancouver is the crown jewel of western Canada. The city is dotted lavishly with greenery, posed against the rugged peaks of the perpetually blue Coast Range and ringed with sparkling Pacific waters. Although many think Vancouver occupies Vancouver Island, the city is on the mainland; Vancouver Island lies across the Strait of Georgia and on the island is the provincial capital of Victoria.

The first recorded exploration of the Strait of Georgia and English Bay was made by Don José Narváez in 1791. The second was by Capt. George Vancouver, who sailed into Burrard Inlet in 1792 while searching for the legendary Northwest Passage. At the time of his arrival, the area was a seasonal home for First Nations peoples. Fur traders followed Vancouver; in 1858 came the prospectors in the wake of a gold strike.

A wild community sprang up on the peninsula between the Fraser River and Burrard Inlet. Later that year Royal Engineers sent to keep law and order named the settlement Queensborough. Queensborough became New Westminster, now part of the Vancouver metropolitan area.

Settlers gradually drifted in to populate other parts of the peninsula, and in April 1886, Vancouver, with a population of 2,000, formally became a city. Two months later a fire destroyed the community and caused an estimated $1.3 million in damage. Undaunted by the disaster, residents began rebuilding, and by the year's end the reconstructed community housed approximately 2,500 people.

Two milestones marked Vancouver's rapid progress. On May 23, 1887, the first passenger train to cross the vast Canadian expanses from the East chugged into the city and belched soot and cinders onto an exuberant crowd. In 1891 the great white ships of the Canadian Pacific fleet sailed into Burrard Inlet to inaugurate transpacific shipping and to mark Vancouver as a major world port. The population mushroomed to 100,000 by 1900.

Vancouver has expanded to cover most of the peninsula between Fraser River and Burrard Inlet. Bordered by the Coastal Mountain Range, the downtown area occupies a tiny peninsula jutting into the inlet, with the magnificent harbor to the east and beautiful English Bay to the west. Broad beaches along English Bay enable office workers to join the bathers during lunch hours.

Behind the beaches rise pastel apartment buildings and fine old houses, some with a Tudor influence. Within walking distance is the busy waterfront, where ships of many nations discharge passengers, unload cargo or fill up for the return voyage. Vancouver also is the main terminal for cruise ships traveling to Alaska. Towering bridges link the downtown area with the city and suburbs.

Atop suburban Burnaby Mountain is Simon Fraser University, British Columbia's instant university. Constructed in only 18 months, it is a bold concept of integrated design, with buildings executed in natural materials for a classic effect. One of the most beautifully located universities in North America is the University of British Columbia; from a forested campus its Gothic buildings overlook the Strait of Georgia while the North Shore Mountains form a distant backdrop.

Vancouver's character is West Coast with a liberal Oriental essence. The city's Chinatown is second only to San Francisco's in size in North America. Visitors to Vancouver can watch an engaging cricket match, celebrate Chinese New Year or enjoy a colorful Japanese summer festival—all without leaving town.

Vancouver is a big city—the financial, industrial, shipping and cultural center of Canada's west coast. Rapid growth has been tempered by the gentler influences of the arts and sciences. The city has much that is reminiscent of other parts of Canada and much of Europe as well as the Orient and the United States. The resulting blend is happy, carefree and relaxed.

North Vancouver / © Capilano Suspension Bridge

Getting There

By Car

Hwy. 1 and hwys. 1A and 7 are the major east-west routes to Vancouver. To reach downtown on the Trans-Canada Hwy., use the First Avenue exit or continue to Hastings Street.

Hwy. 99 to S.W. Marine West becomes the major downtown artery, Granville Street. Before becoming a city street, Hwy. 99 begins its journey as I-5 at the Mexican border and crosses through California and the Pacific Northwest.

Aquabus Ltd., (604) 689-5858, provides ferry service between Granville Island, Hornby Street, Yaletown, Stamps Landing and Science World at TELUS World of Science daily 7 a.m.-8 p.m. Times vary according to destination. Fare ranges from $4-$6. The Aquabus from Granville Island to Hornby Street is equipped to carry bicycles for an extra 50c.

Getting Around

Street System

All streets and avenues in downtown Vancouver are named; many are one-way. Outside the business section, east-west avenues are numbered beginning with First Avenue, and north-south streets are named. Addresses begin at Ontario-Carrall streets for all east-west numbering and at Powell-Dundas streets for all north-south numbering.

The downtown peninsula is connected to western Vancouver by the Burrard, Granville and Cambie

Destination Vancouver

The nuances of cosmopolitan Vancouver's multiple cultures are revealed through the arts, in neighborhood preservation and by observing the lifestyle enjoyed by residents.

You'll find ambience in green spaces and historic places; at galleries and gardens; and on beaches, bays and gap-spanning bridges.

© age fotostock / SuperStock

Stanley Park, Vancouver.
A spring flower display delights visitors within this 405-hectare (1,000-acre) natural park. (See listing page 167)

© Barry Winiker / Index Stock

Grouse Mountain, North Vancouver.
An aerial tramway takes visitors to the summit, which offers a panoramic view of the city. (See listing page 177)

© Gibson Stock Photography

Vancouver Aquarium Marine Science Centre.
The aquarium features 60,000 marine animals and is a popular attraction for families. (See listing page 167)

West Vancouver

North Vancouver

See Downtown map page 164

Vancouver

Burnaby

Coquitlam

Port Coquitlam

New Westminster

Maple Ridge

Richmond

Pitt Meadows

Delta

Surrey

Mission

White Rock

Langley

Aldergrove

See Vicinity map page 163

UNITED STATES
CANADA

BRITISH COLUMBIA
WASHINGTON

© Troy & Mary Parlee / Index Stock

Places included in this AAA Destination City:

Science World at Telus World of Science, Vancouver.
Designed for Expo '86, this striking geodesic dome in the forefront houses hands-on exhibits and a movie theater. (See listing page 166)

The Informed Traveler

Sales Tax: British Columbia's provincial sales tax is 7 percent. A room tax of 10 percent on lodgings also is levied in the Vancouver area.

WHOM TO CALL

Emergency: 911

Police (non-emergency): (604) 717-3321

Time and Temperature: (604) 664-9010

Hospitals: British Columbia's Children's Hospital, (604) 875-2345; Mount Saint Joseph Hospital Site, (604) 874-1141; Vancouver Hospital and Health Sciences Centre, (604) 875-4111; Vancouver Hospital and Health Sciences Centre-UBC, (604) 822-7121.

WHERE TO LOOK

Newspapers

The two major daily newspapers, both published in the morning, are the *Province* and the *Vancouver Sun*.

Radio

Vancouver radio stations CBU-AM (690), CBU-FM (105.7), CHQM-FM (103.5), CKCL-FM (104.9), CKLG-FM (96.9) and CKWX-AM (1130) have news and weather reports.

Visitor Information

Vancouver Tourist InfoCentre: 200 Burrard St., Plaza Level, Vancouver, BC, Canada V6C 3L6; phone (604) 683-2000.

Maps, lodging reservations and literature about attractions as well as tickets for tours are available at the Vancouver Tourist InfoCentre which is open daily 8:30-6, Victoria Day weekend through mid-Sept.; Mon.-Sat. 8:30-5, rest of year.

TRANSPORTATION

Air Travel

Vancouver International Airport, in Richmond, is reached via Granville St. and the Arthur Lang Bridge, then Sea Island Way, which leads into Grant McConachie Way. Vancouver Airporter buses run every 20 minutes 8:55 a.m.-9:25 p.m. One-way bus service departs most major downtown hotels every 30 minutes. The fare is $13.50, round trip $21; phone (604) 946-8866 or (800) 668-3141. Taxis average $26 one-way.

Rental Cars

Hertz, at 1128 Seymour St., offers discounts to AAA and CAA members; phone (604) 606-4711, (800) 263-0600 in Canada, or (800) 654-3131 in North America. Additional agencies are listed in the telephone directory.

Rail Service

The Via Rail passenger train terminal is at 1150 Station St.; phone (888) 842-7245 in Canada or in the United States.

Buses

The bus terminal is at 1150 Station St.; phone (604) 482-8747 or (800) 661-8747.

Taxis

Fares start at $2.75, plus $1.50 per kilometre (.6 mi.). Companies include Black Top, (604) 731-1111; MacLure's, (604) 731-9211; Yellow Cab, (604) 681-1111; and Vancouver Taxi, (604) 255-5111.

Public Transport

Translink offers bus service as well as SeaBus and SkyTrain service. *See Public Transportation for details.*

Boats

BC Ferries links Vancouver Island with the rest of the province. Nanaimo and Sunshine Coast ferries leave from Horseshoe Bay, 21 kilometres (13 mi.) west of the city in West Vancouver. From Tsawwassen south of Vancouver automobile/passenger ferries make frequent trips to the southern Gulf Islands, Nanaimo and Swartz Bay, north of Victoria; Vancouver-Victoria bus service is available on most sailings.

For schedules phone the British Columbia Automobile Association, (604) 268-5555, British Columbia Ferries Information Centre, (250) 386-3431 outside British Columbia, (888) 223-3779 in British Columbia, or Tourism Vancouver, (604) 683-2000.

bridges and to North Vancouver and West Vancouver by the Lions Gate and the Iron Workers Memorial (Second Narrows) bridges.

Rush hours are 6-9:30 a.m. and 3-6:30 p.m. Right turns on red are permitted after a stop, unless otherwise posted; drivers must yield to pedestrians and vehicles in the intersection and to city buses pulling into traffic.

Parking

On-street parking, controlled by meter, is restricted on many thoroughfares during rush hours; violators' cars will be towed. Off-street parking is available in lots and garages at rates ranging from $1.25 per half-hour to $11 or more per day. Parking in a school zone between 8 and 5 on any school day is strictly prohibited unless otherwise posted.

Public Transportation

Translink offers bus service to points throughout Vancouver and to all suburban areas; it also offers SeaBus and SkyTrain service as well as the West Coast Express commuter rail.

One-way bus fare within the city ranges from $2.25-$9.25. Exact change is required. Rush hour fares are higher. All-day passes, available from SkyTrain and SeaBus ticket machines, Safeway food stores and 7-11 stores, cost $8, senior citizens $6.

SeaBus service conveys commuters between North Vancouver and the city of Vancouver, connecting with the bus system at the foot of Granville Street; phone (604) 953-3333 Mon.-Sat. 6 a.m.-12:30 a.m., Sun. and holidays 8 a.m.-11 p.m. for more information.

SkyTrain, Vancouver's rapid transit system, runs from Waterfront Station through downtown Vancouver to the suburbs of Burnaby and New Westminster and across the Fraser River to the suburb of Surrey. Trains operate every 5 minutes Mon.-Fri. 5:30 a.m.-midnight, Sat. 6:50 a.m.-12:30 a.m., Sun. 7:50 a.m.-11:30 p.m. A 1-Zone fare (within Vancouver) is $2.25, 2-Zone fare is $3.25 and 3-Zone fare is $4.50. Fares are subject to change. Every SkyTrain station has information panels; phone (604) 953-3333.

What To See

B.C. SPORTS HALL OF FAME AND MUSEUM is at jct. Beatty and Robson sts., Gate A of the B.C. Place Stadium. The history of sports in British Columbia is traced from First Nations traditions to modern Olympic games. Honorees include amateur and professional teams, athletes, journalists and sports pioneers. Interactive galleries provide opportunities for running, climbing, throwing, riding and rowing. Rotating exhibits, a sports library and a stadium tour also are featured.

Daily 10-5. Admission $10; $8 (students and senior citizens); free (ages 0-4); $25 (family). Half-price to B.C. Place Stadium or General Motors Place ticket-holders. Phone (604) 687-5520.

Burnaby / © Eero Sorila

Vancouver & Vicinity

© AAA

Downtown
Vancouver

RAPID TRANSIT
STATIONS

© 2007 NAVTEQ

2221-A

BLOEDEL CONSERVATORY—
see *Queen Elizabeth Park* p. 166.

CHINATOWN—see *Shopping* p. 173.

CHRIST CHURCH CATHEDRAL is at 690 Burrard St. One of Vancouver's oldest stone churches, the cathedral is adorned with English and Canadian stained-glass windows. Mon.-Fri. 10-4. Donations. Phone (604) 682-3848.

CN IMAX THEATRE AT CANADA PLACE is at 201-999 Canada Pl. Various IMAX films are presented on a screen five stories tall. Three-dimensional movies are shown periodically. Food is available. Allow 1 hour minimum. Daily on the hour 11-10. Admission $10.84; $9.90 (ages 66+); $8.96 (ages 3-12). AX, MC, VI. Phone (604) 682-4629 or (800) 582-4629.

DR. SUN YAT-SEN CLASSICAL CHINESE GARDEN is at 578 Carrall St. in the heart of Chinatown. The site is modeled after private classical gardens in the city of Suzhou during the 1368-1644 Ming Dynasty. Most of the garden's elements—from hand-fired roof tiles, carved woodwork and lattice

windows to courtyard pebbles—are from China. Art and horticultural exhibits and demonstrations also are offered. Festivals and concerts are featured throughout the year.

Guided tours are available. Allow 30 minutes minimum. Daily 9:30-7, June 15-Aug. 31; 10-6, May 1-June 14 and in Sept.; 10-4:30, rest of year. Closed Jan.1 and Dec. 25. Admission $9.75; $8 (ages 5-17 and 66+). Admission price includes a tour and tea. Phone (604) 662-3207.

GRANVILLE ISLAND MUSEUMS is at 1502 Duranleau St. Three different museums are located in one building. The Sport Fishing Museum features a large collection of Hardy rods and reels, and historic and contemporary artifacts relating to both fresh and saltwater sport fishing. The Model Ships Museum includes meticulously detailed large-scale model warships, local steamers and tugs. The Model Trains Museum has displays of model and toy trains as well as memorabilia.

Allow 1 hour minimum. Daily 10-5:30, May-Sept.; Tues.-Sun. 10-5:30, rest of year. Admission

$7.50; $6 (ages 66+ and students with ID); $4 (ages 4-11). AX, JC, MC, VI. Phone (604) 683-1939.

HOLY ROSARY CATHEDRAL is at 646 Richards St. between Dunsmuir and W. Georgia sts. The church has stained-glass windows and eight bells hung in the rare English ringing style. Cathedral open Mon.-Sat. 7-6, Sun. 7:30 a.m.-9:30 p.m. Bell ringing Sun. at 10:30, Tues. at 7:30 p.m. Free. Phone (604) 682-6774.

H.R. MacMILLAN SPACE CENTRE is at 1100 Chestnut St. in Vanier Park. The Virtual Voyages motion simulator is among the interactive exhibits and games featured at the center. The Planetarium Star Theatre and Ground-Station Canada present laser light shows and programs dealing with astronomy, solar history and space explorations.

Allow 1 hour, 30 minutes minimum. Daily 10-5, July-Aug.; Tues.-Sun. 10-5, rest of year. Laser shows Thurs.-Sat. at 9:30 p.m. (also Fri.-Sat. at 10:45 p.m.). Closed Dec. 25. Show times may vary; phone for schedule. Admission $15; $10.75 (ages 5-18, ages 65+ and students with ID). Laser light show $9.35. AX, MC, VI. Phone (604) 738-7827.

OLD HASTINGS MILL STORE MUSEUM is at 1575 Alma St. in Hastings Mill Park. The mill was the first industrial facility on the south shore of what is now Vancouver. One of the few buildings to withstand the ravages of the 1886 fire, it contains relics of early Vancouver. Allow 30 minutes minimum. Tues.-Sun. 1-4, mid-Apr. to mid-Sept.; Sat.-Sun. 1-4, rest of year. Guided tours are offered by appointment Mar.-Nov. Donations. Phone (604) 734-1212.

PACIFIC NATIONAL EXHIBITION is on E. Hastings St. between Renfrew and Cassiar sts. The site occupies 58 hectares (144 acres) and is home to Pacific Coliseum, a tradeshow and entertainment complex, and a skateboard park. The Pacific National Exhibition Fair is held in late August. Various trade and hobby shows, rock concerts and sporting events are scheduled throughout the year.

Food is available. Fair daily 11 a.m.-midnight, mid-Aug. through Labour Day. Last admission 1 hour, 30 minutes before closing. Fair admission $15; $5 (ages 65+). Phone (604) 253-2311.

Playland Amusement Park is on E. Hastings St. between Renfrew and Cassiar sts. The 4-hectare (10-acre) park features games, miniature golf and rides, including a large wooden roller coaster and three "extreme rides."

Daily 11 a.m.-midnight, late Aug.-Labour Day; daily 11-9, late June to late Aug.; Sat.-Sun. and holidays 11-7, day after Labour Day-late Sept. (weather permitting). Hours may vary; phone ahead. Park admission $31.75; $15.85 (under 122 centimetres [48 in.] tall); free (ages 0-2 and 61+). $12.67 (parents

when accompanied by a paying child ages 0-12). AX, MC, VI. Phone (604) 253-2311.

QUEEN ELIZABETH PARK is off Cambie St. and W. 33rd Ave. On 167-metre (548-ft.) Little Mountain, the highest point in Vancouver, the park offers magnificent views of the city, harbor and North Shore Mountains. Other highlights include an arboretum; rose, sunken and quarry gardens; tennis courts; and pitch and putt greens. Daily 24 hours. Free.

Bloedel Conservatory is at 33rd Ave. and Cambie St. Climatically varied species of plants grow in a climate-controlled, illuminated triodetic dome 43 metres (141 ft.) in diameter and 21 metres (70 ft.) high. Tropical birds and a fish pond are other highlights. Allow 30 minutes minimum. Mon.-Fri. 9-8, Sat.-Sun. 10-9, Apr.-Sept.; Mon.-Fri. 10-5, rest of year. Closed Dec. 25. Admission $4.50; $3.20 (ages 13-18); $3 (ages 65+); $2.35 (ages 6-12). MC, VI. Phone (604) 257-8570.

ST. ANDREW'S-WESLEY CHURCH is at 1012 Nelson St. The Gothic structure includes many stained-glass windows. Mon.-Fri. 10-4, July-Aug. Donations. Phone (604) 683-4574.

SCIENCE WORLD AT TELUS WORLD OF SCIENCE, 1455 Quebec St., features hands-on exhibits and demonstrations that explain scientific phenomena. The Eureka Gallery explores such subjects as water, air, motion and invention. The Science Theatre features a variety of high-definition video shows throughout the day. The Centre Stage presents science demonstrations daily. Human performance and nature are the subjects of additional galleries. The Kidspace Gallery features activities for children ages 2 through 6. Also of interest is the OMNIMAX Theater that presents nature and science films.

Food is available. Allow 2 hours minimum. Daily 10-6, late June-Labour Day; Mon.-Fri. 10-5, Sat.-Sun. and holidays 10-6, rest of year. Exhibits and Science Theatre $14.50; $10 (ages 4-18, ages 65+ and students with ID). Exhibits, Science Theatre and one OMNIMAX film $19.50; $15 (ages 4-18, ages 65+ and students with ID). OMNIMAX only $11.25; $9 (ages 4-18, ages 65+ and students with ID). Parking $3-$7. Rates may vary; phone ahead. MC, VI. Phone (604) 443-7443.

STANLEY PARK is on the peninsula near the business district. Covering 405 hectares (1,000 acres) in downtown Vancouver, the urban oasis is considered one of the finest natural parks on the continent. Visitors can lawn bowl, watch a cricket match, swim, golf, play tennis or checkers, jog, or go bicycling over some of the 80 kilometres (50 mi.) of roads and trails.

Also featured are a children's farmyard, rose garden, miniature steam railway and totem pole displays. Shows are presented at the open-air theater at Malkin Bowl in July and August. An information booth is in the lower farmyard parking lot on Park Drive just off the Georgia Street entrance. A free shuttle travels between the park's most popular destinations in summer; the shuttles depart from the miniature railway parking lot.

Park open daily 24 hours. Information booth open 10-5, June 15-Sept. 15; 10-4, May 1-June 14 and Sept. 16-second Mon. in Oct. Booth hours may vary; phone ahead. Children's farmyard and railway daily 11-4, June 1-early Sept. and during the holiday season; Sat.-Sun. 11-4, Mar.-May (weather permitting). Shuttle daily 10-6:30, mid-June to mid-Sept. Park admission free. Farmyard and railway each $5; $3.75 (ages 13-18); $3.50 (ages 65+); $2.50 (ages 2-12); family rate is available. Rates may vary; phone ahead. Phone (604) 257-8531 for railway.

Stanley Park Horse-drawn Tours depart from beside the information booth on Park Dr. off the Georgia St. entrance. The narrated, 1-hour tour highlights the park's points of interest. Tours depart daily every 20-30 minutes 9:30-5:30, July 1-Labour Day; 9:40-5, Apr.-June and day after Labour Day-Sept. 30; 9:40-4, Mar. 15-31 and in Oct.; 10:30-3, Mar. 1-14. Fare $24.99; $23.58 (ages 66+ and students with ID); $14.99 (ages 3-12). DC, MC, VI. Phone (604) 681-5115.

Vancouver Aquarium Marine Science Centre is at 845 Avison Way. More than 70,000 marine animals are exhibited, with emphasis on such diverse habitats as the Canadian Arctic, the Amazon Rain Forest and the Pacific Northwest. Sharks, moray eels and colorful fish populate the Tropic Zone, while the Strait of Georgia exhibit features divers interacting with marine life. Programs allowing animal encounters with sea lions, seals, otters and beluga whales are available for an additional fee.

Walk the BC Hydro Salmon Stream in Stanley Park to learn about a salmon's incredible life journey. Other highlights include daily whale and dolphin shows, shark dives and sea otter feedings as well as exhibits that feature sea lions and harbor seals.

Food is available. Allow 2 hours minimum. Daily 9:30-7, late June-Labour Day; 9:30-5, rest of year. Admission $21.95; $16.50 (ages 13-18, ages 65+ and students with ID); $13.50 (ages 4-12). AX, MC, VI. Phone (604) 659-3474. *See color ad.*

UNIVERSITY OF BRITISH COLUMBIA is on Point Grey. Encompassing 2,470 hectares (6,103 acres) overlooking the Strait of Georgia, the university is the largest in the province.

The Pacific Museum of the Earth is just off the West Mall of the university on the main floor of the Earth and Ocean Science Building at 6339 Stores Rd. A highlight of the 30,000-piece mineral and fossil collection is an 80 million-year-old Lambeosaurus dinosaur. Also featured are a 2-metre-long (7-ft.) amethyst tube and a large sedimentary structure. Allow 30 minutes minimum. Mon.-Fri. 9-5; closed statutory holidays. Donations. Phone (604) 822-6992.

UBC Botanical Garden is at 6804 S.W. Marine Dr. More than 10,000 plants from around the world are cultivated on 28 hectares (69 acres). Themed gardens include Asian, alpine, perennial, food, medicinal and native plantings. Nitobe Memorial Garden, one of the most accurately represented Japanese gardens in North America, features a tea garden and stroll garden with seasonal displays of irises, Japanese maples and flowering cherries.

Allow 1 hour minimum. Main garden open daily 10-6. Nitobe Memorial Garden open daily 10-6, mid-Mar. to mid-Oct.; Mon.-Fri. 10-2:30, rest of year. Main garden $7; $5 (senior citizens); $3 (non-UBC students). Nitobe Memorial Garden $5; $4 (senior citizens); $3 (non-UBC students). Phone (604) 822-9666.

UBC Museum of Anthropology is at 6393 N.W. Marine Dr. on the Point Grey Cliffs. Traditional post and beam construction is reflected in this striking concrete and glass building, which houses a major collection of Northwest Coast First Nations artwork. Displays include totem poles, feast dishes and canoes as well as artifacts from around the world. European ceramics also are displayed.

Allow 1 hour minimum. Daily 10-5 (also Tues. 5-9), Victoria Day-Labour Day; Tues.-Sun. 11-5 (also Tues. 5-9), rest of year. Closed Dec. 25-26. Admission $9; $7 (ages 6-18, ages 65+ and students with ID); $5 (ages 0-5). MC, VI. Phone (604) 822-3825.

 VANCOUVER AQUARIUM MARINE SCIENCE CENTRE—see Stanley Park p. 167.

[SAVE] **VANCOUVER ART GALLERY** is at 750 Hornby St. One of the largest art galleries in Western Canada features a full range of national and international art by contemporary artists and major historical figures. Allow 1 hour minimum. Mon., Wed. and Fri.-Sun., 10-5:30 and holidays, Tues. and Thurs. 10-9. Admission $15; $11 (ages 65+); $10 (students with ID); $6 (ages 5-12); free (ages 0-4); $40 (family, two adults and two children); donations (Tues. 5-9). AX, MC, VI. Phone (604) 662-4719. See color ad.

VANCOUVER LOOKOUT AT HARBOUR CENTRE is at 555 W. Hastings St. Two glass elevators ascend the outside of this tower, which is crowned with an observation deck that offers a spectacular panoramic view of the city and outlying districts. Hourly guided tours point out the city's landmarks. The complex includes a revolving restaurant and a shopping mall.

Allow 30 minutes minimum. Skylift elevator runs daily 8:30 a.m.-10:30 p.m., late Apr.-Oct. 31; 9-9, rest of year. Admission $13; $11 (ages 61+); $9 (ages 13-18); $6 (ages 6-12). Rates may vary; phone ahead. Phone (604) 689-0421.

VANCOUVER MARITIME MUSEUM is at 1905 Ogden Ave. at n. foot of Chestnut and Cypress sts. Model ships, naval uniforms and other artifacts relate to man's interaction with the sea. Historic vessels are displayed outside in the harbor. The Alcan

Children's Maritime Discovery Centre features hands-on activities to introduce youngsters to ships and pirates of the sea.

Allow 1 hour minimum. Tues.-Sun. 10-5, Victoria Day-Labour Day; Tues.-Sat. 10-5, Sun. noon-5, rest of year. Museum admission (including the *St. Roch* National Historic Site) $10; $7.50 (ages 6-18 and 65+); $25 (family). MC, VI. Phone (604) 257-8300.

St. Roch National Historic Site is next to the Vancouver Maritime Museum. During World War II the *St. Roch* became the first vessel to travel from the Pacific to the Atlantic via the treacherous Northwest Passage in the Arctic; it completed the round trip in 1944. After the war, the schooner reached its destination via the Panama Canal, becoming the first ship to circumnavigate the North American continent. Preserved in dry dock, the vessel is displayed as it appeared in 1944.

Allow 1 hour minimum. Daily 10-4. Admission is included in the Vancouver Maritime Museum charge. Phone (604) 257-8300.

[SAVE] **VANCOUVER MUSEUM** is at the s.w. end of Burrard St. in Vanier Park at 1100 Chestnut St. Devoted to the art, natural history, anthropology and history of the lower mainland, the museum displays regional artifacts including pieces from First Nations peoples as well as ancient and contemporary objects from around the world. Daily 10-5 (also Thurs. 5-9), July-Aug.; Tues.-Sun. 10-5, (also Thurs. 5-9), rest of year. Closed Dec. 25. Admission $10; $8 (ages 65+ and students with ID); $6.50 (ages 5-17). MC, VI. Phone (604) 736-4431.

[GEM] [SAVE] **VANDUSEN BOTANICAL GARDEN** is at 5251 Oak St. at W. 37th Ave. The 22-hectare (55-acre) area has an outstanding plant collection arranged to show geographical origin and botanical relationships. Gardens are set amid lawns, lakes and rock displays with vistas of the mountains and city. A hedge maze provides entertainment for children.

Food is available. Allow 1 hour minimum. Daily 10-9, June-Aug.; 10-4, Jan.-Feb. and Nov.-Dec.; 10-6, in Apr.; 10-8, in May; 10-5, rest of year.

Closed Dec. 25. Admission Apr.-Sept. $8.25; $8.25 (ages 13-18); $6 (ages 65+); $4.25 (ages 6-12). Admission rest of year $6; $4.50 (ages 13-18 and 65+); $3 (ages 6-12). MC, VI. Phone (604) 878-9274.

What To Do
Sightseeing

Opportunities to watch bustling harbor activities are available at several vantage points in Vancouver. Seaplanes, barges, tugboats, cargo ships, ferries and the SeaBus can be observed from Granville Square at the foot of Granville Street; from Canada Place at the foot of Howe St.; from Lonsdale Quay at the foot of Lonsdale Ave.; and from Stanley Park. Fine views of the city, sea and mountains are available at CypressBowl, Simon Fraser University atop Burnaby Mountain, Grouse Mountain and Queen Elizabeth Park.

Boat Tours

HARBOUR CRUISES departs from the n. foot of Denman St., next to Stanley Park. Scenic 75-minute harbor tours are offered aboard an authentic paddlewheeler. Lunch, dinner and carol ship cruises also are available.

Harbor tours board daily at 11:30, 1 and 2:30, mid-May to mid-Sept.; at 2:30, April 15 through mid-May and mid-Sept. through Oct. 31. Harbor tours $25; $21 (ages 12-17 and 60+); $10 (ages 5-11). Schedule and fares may vary; phone ahead. Phone (604) 688-7246 or (800) 663-1500. *See color ad.*

Bus Tours

SAVE Gray Line West *(see color ad)* offers daily tours of Vancouver, Victoria and Whistler with convenient departures from most major hotels. Its double-decker buses make a continuous loop, stopping at more than 20 attractions and allowing sightseers to reboard. Phone Gray Line West at (604) 879-3363 or (800) 667-0882.

West Coast City and Nature Sightseeing Ltd. features sightseeing trips of the city and its surrounding natural areas in 12- to 30-passenger minibuses. Full-day trips to Victoria and the Whistler resort area also are available; phone (604) 451-1600 or (877) 451-1777.

Industrial Tours

Tours are available of the Vancouver Post Office, (604) 662-5715, 349 W. Georgia St. Reservations are required.

Plane Tours

Another way to see Vancouver and its surroundings is by air. Harbour Air offers flights lasting from 35 minutes to 1.25 hours; departure is from downtown on Coal Harbour Rd., one block west of Canada Place. Fares vary, and reservations are required; phone (604) 274-1277.

Train Tours

Rocky Mountaineer Vacations *(see color ad p. 171)* offers scenic, 2-day, all daylight, narrated rail tours between Vancouver or Whistler, British Columbia, and Banff, Calgary, or Jasper, Alberta.

Westbound or eastbound departures are offered mid-April to mid-October, with winter rail trips available in December. Onboard meals and snacks as well as accommodations in Kamloops or Quesnel are included. A 3-hour trip on the Whistler Mountaineer also is available and runs between Vancouver and Whistler May through October. Phone (604) 606-7245 or (877) 460-3200, or (888) 687-7245 for information about Whistler trips.

Trolley Tours

Trolley tours provide a look at the city at a relaxed pace. The Downtown Historic Railway, comprised of two electric interurban railcars, skirts False Creek between Science World at TELUS World of Science and Granville Island and runs from mid-May to mid-October; phone (604) 665-3903.

THE VANCOUVER TROLLEY CO. departs from many downtown accommodations and attractions. Narrated tours highlight Vancouver's major attractions. Passengers may board, depart or reboard at any stop on the route. Allow 2 hours minimum. Daily 8:40-6, Apr. 1-late Oct.; 9-6, rest of year. A 4-hour sunset tour leaves for Grouse Mountain at 6:15, mid-June to mid-Sept. Day tour pass, valid for one full circuit, $33; $18.50 (ages 4-12). Sunset tour $60; $58 (senior citizens); $47 (ages 13-18); $30 (ages 4-12). A combination ticket is available. Phone (604) 801-5515 or (888) 451-5581. *See color ad.*

Sports and Recreation

Vancouver offers such a diversity of recreational opportunities that anyone with a yen for variety can ski on Grouse Mountain in the morning, golf on the banks of the Fraser River in the afternoon, fish for salmon in Horseshoe Bay at dusk and top off the day with a dip in English Bay.

Vancouver's park system has tennis courts, swimming pools, putting greens, golf courses, lawn bowling greens, hiking paths and a comprehensive bike route. For park information phone the Vancouver Park Board at (604) 257-8400.

Swimming is available along English Bay, which is bordered by beaches from West Point Grey to Stanley Park. Beaches are easily accessible from Northwest Marine Drive in West Point Grey, Point Grey Road in Vancouver West and from Beach Avenue downtown.

White-water rafting is available April through September on the nearby Chilliwack River and a little farther afield on the Lillooet, Fraser and Thompson rivers. Vancouver rafting companies offering day trips as well as multiday trips include REO Rafting Adventure Resort, (604) 461-7238 or (800) 736-7238, and Kumsheen Rafting Resort, (250) 455-2296 or (800) 663-6667. Lotus Land Tours offers **sea kayaking** trips on Indian Arm and **whale-watching** tours from Steveston; phone (604) 684-4922 or (800) 528-3531.

Winter visitors with a penchant for **skiing** can tackle the challenging slopes of Grouse Mountain or Mount Seymour Park in North Vancouver. East of Vancouver are Hemlock Valley and Manning Park ski resorts, offering both downhill and cross-country treks. Cypress Provincial Park in West Vancouver also has cross-country and downhill skiing *(see Recreation Chart)*. Skiers can head north of Vancouver to Whistler and Blackcomb Mountains; site of the 2010 Olympic and Paralympic Winter Games.

When the waters sparkle from the summer sun, Vancouver becomes a **boating** paradise. For visitors without a boat, several companies have craft for hourly or daily rental. For charter yachts phone Harbour Cruises, (604) 688-7246, or Westin Bayshore Yacht Charters, (604) 250-8008. For **fishing** charters and boat rentals phone Sewell's Ltd., (604) 921-3474, at Horseshoe Bay.

Vancouver residents love spectator sports, especially **football, hockey** and **soccer.** The B.C. Lions of the Canadian Football League play before capacity crowds in B.C. Place Stadium. The Canucks of the National Hockey League compete in General Motors Place. For football and hockey ticket information phone TicketMaster, (604) 280-4444. **Baseball** is played by the Vancouver Canadians at Nat Bailey Stadium; phone (604) 872-5232 for schedule and ticket information. Indoor **lacrosse** can be enjoyed at Bill Copeland Sports Centre in Burnaby, (604) 291-1261; and at Queens Park Arena, (604) 777-5111, in New Westminster.

Thoroughbred racing with pari-mutuel betting is held at Hastings Park Race Course on the grounds of the Pacific National Exhibition; phone (604) 254-1631 *(see attraction listing p. 166).*

Note: Policies concerning admittance of children to pari-mutuel betting facilities vary. Phone for information.

Shopping

Befitting an international port, Vancouver has a wealth of marketplaces. These emporiums give definition to a metropolis that can be broken easily into a series of villages. From the cosmopolitan heart of the West End to historic Gastown to exotic Chinatown, Vancouver is a shopper's paradise.

Streets of fashionable boutiques are the signature of the West End. Representative of this area is Robson Street and its high-fashion boutiques. Enhancing the shops are the gardens, pools and waterfalls of Robson Square, a three-block area that stretches from the Vancouver Art Gallery to the glass-tiered pyramid of the Law Courts.

When the pleasure of the outdoors fades with the weather, there are nearby underground malls. The largest of these is Granville Street Mall, which includes Pacific Centre, anchored by the above-ground department stores Holt Renfrew and Sears, and the adjoining Vancouver Centre. Beneath the Hyatt Regency Hotel is Royal Centre with its fashion boutiques.

In Burnaby, MetroTown contains MetroTown Centre, Metropolis and Station Square. The area features more than 550 shops, restaurants and 22 motion-picture theaters. The Crystal Mall, 4500 Kingsway, is a 200-store mall and office complex.

Expo '86 created a world village and left a legacy of buildings and the light rail system known as SkyTrain. SkyTrain and its water counterpart, SeaBus, link two of the city's several marketplaces. Lonsdale Quay and Westminster Quay (in North Vancouver and New Westminster respectively) both offer shops, eateries and promenades along the waterfront.

Near the SeaBus terminal is the former Canadian Pavilion, now Canada Place. The distinctive white sails of this complex embrace the trade and convention center, cruise terminal, a hotel, the Promenade Shops and an IMAX theater.

East of the SeaBus terminal are the restored 19th-century buildings and cobblestone streets of Gastown. Carrall, Powell, Water and Alexander streets meet at Maple Tree Square, defining this historic area and embracing specialty and antique shops, art galleries and restaurants. Most shops are open Sundays. Street vendors add to the area's charm, as does the 1.8-metric-ton (2-ton) Gastown Steam Clock at the corner of Cambie and Water streets.

The warehouses of the reclaimed industrial area of Granville Island have become a refuge for artists and casual shoppers. The centerpiece of this community is Granville Island Market, off W. Fourth Street by False Creek, an open market that offers fresh fruits, vegetables, seafood, meats, gourmet foods, baked goods, many fine restaurants (reservations are recommended), handicrafts and live theater.

Another cluster of abandoned warehouses has been rejuvenated into one of the trendiest areas of Vancouver—Yaletown. Bordered by Nelson and Homer streets and Pacific Boulevard, the community is filled with stores featuring everything from imported designer clothing to home furnishings and giftware by Canadian craftsmen. Old warehouse loading bays have been converted into cafes and restaurants, which use the wide sidewalks for patio dining.

South Vancouver features Oakridge Shopping Centre, 41st and Cambie streets; its vaulted glass ceilings shelter a collection of shops as well as giant fig trees. Across Burrard Inlet in West Vancouver are the twin malls of Park Royal. This complex has more than 190 shops offering everything from furnishings to groceries; the largest store being The Bay.

CHINATOWN centers on E. Pender St. between Carrall and Gore sts. The second largest area of its kind in North America, Chinatown is lined with elaborately carved and gilded shops displaying jade, bamboo, rattan, brassware, silk and brocade. Sidewalk markets feature Oriental produce. Even the phone booths are topped with pagoda roofs. The Chinese Cultural Centre Museum & Archives, 555 Columbia St., has some displays and photographs on its second floor relating to the history of the Chinese in British Columbia; phone (604) 658-8850. During Chinese New Year the streets resound with the din of drums and fireworks.

Performing Arts

The Centre in Vancouver for Performing Arts, 777 Homer St., is a premier facility for theater, dance and music; phone (604) 602-0616 for event information. The Queen Elizabeth Theatre at the intersection of Hamilton and Georgia streets, (604) 665-3050, is home to Ballet British Columbia, (604) 732-5003, and the Vancouver Opera Association, (604) 683-0222. The adjacent Vancouver Playhouse presents professional theater, recitals and chamber music; phone (604) 873-3311. The Vancouver Symphony Orchestra performs at the Orpheum Theatre, Smithe and Granville streets; phone (604) 876-3434 for ticket information.

Other prominent metropolitan theaters presenting dramatic productions include the Arts Club Theatre, on Johnston Street on Granville Island, (604) 687-1644; the Metro Theatre, 1370 S.W. Marine Dr., (604) 266-7191; Studio 58, 100 W. 49th Ave., (604) 323-5227; and the Vancouver East Cultural Centre, 1895 Venables St., (604) 251-1363.

During the summer concerts and musicals are presented in Stanley Park's Malkin Bowl. Kitsilano Showboat at Kitsilano Beach presents an outdoor variety show Monday, Wednesday and Friday at 7:30 p.m. during July and August (weather permitting). For more information phone (604) 734-7332.

Concerts in such genres as classical, country, pop and rock are presented year-round at the Pacific Coliseum, 100 N. Renfrew St., (604) 253-2311, and General Motors Place, 800 Griffiths Way, (604) 899-7444.

The daily papers carry listings of cultural events, as do weekly and monthly magazines. Ticket outlets include Ticketmaster Head Office, 1304 Hornby St.; and Ticketmaster, Pacific Centre Mall, 700 W. Georgia St.

Special Events

Life in a city where your office is only 25 minutes from a ski slope is worth celebrating, and the residents of Vancouver celebrate their setting throughout the year. New Year's Day sees the Polar Bear Swim at English Bay; the event draws many swimmers and hundreds of spectators.

The Vancouver Children's Festival in May ushers in summer, while cultural entertainment sails in with the Canadian International Dragon Boat Festival in mid-June. The Vancouver Folk Music Festival draws fans from as far away as Los Angeles for concerts during mid-July. For 2 weeks in August and staged in seven venues throughout the city, Festival Vancouver runs the gamut in musical offerings including classical, opera, jazz and chamber music. HSBC Celebration of Light features 4 nights of fireworks displays and is held at English Bay the last week of July and the first week in August.

Virtually all facets of life and work in British Columbia are celebrated in the Pacific National Exhibition, held at the Exhibition Grounds from late August through Labour Day. In late September and early October the Oktoberfest is held at the Exhibition Grounds, where the revelry continues into the wee hours.

The Christmas season begins with the Christmas Carol Ships, which lead a flotilla of private watercraft decorated with Christmas lights around the harbor in mid-December. More information about events is available from your CAA or AAA club.

DID YOU KNOW

More than 1.8 million people live in the greater Vancouver area.

The Vancouver Vicinity

ALDERGROVE (H-11)
pop. 11,910, elev. 61 m/200'

A small town on the Lower Fraser Valley's southern side, Aldergrove is near the Fraser River and the Canada-United States border. Dairy, chicken, strawberry and raspberry farms dot the surrounding area. Just northeast of Aldergrove, Bradner grows about 400 varieties of daffodils.

Greater Langley Chamber of Commerce-Aldergrove: 5761 Glover Rd., Suite 1, Langley, BC, Canada V3A 8M8; phone (604) 530-6656.

GREATER VANCOUVER ZOO is at 5048 264th St. The 48-hectare (120-acre) zoo is devoted to the preservation of endangered species. More than 600 animals represent 135 species from around the world, including hippopotami, monkeys, giraffes and tigers. A narrated train ride takes passengers around the zoo's perimeter; a bus tour travels through the North American Wilds exhibit.

Picnicking is permitted. Food is available. Allow 2 hours minimum. Daily 9-7, Apr.-Sept.; 9-4, rest of year. Admission $18; $14 (ages 4-15 and 65+); $60 (family, two adults and two children). Train ride $5. Parking $3. MC, VI. Phone (604) 856-6825.

BURNABY (H-11)
pop. 193,954, elev. 40 m/130'

Burnaby is more than just a suburban, bedroom community of hills, ridges, valleys, plain, and stunning views; it is an urban center which is home to Simon Fraser University and the British Columbia Institute of Technology.

DEER LAKE PARK is 14.5 km (9 mi.) s.e. at 6450 Deer Lake Ave. at Canada Way. The park contains the Century Gardens, with its distinctive rhododendron display and rose gardens. The Shadbolt Centre for the Arts offers community arts programs as well as theater and dance performances in its James Cowan Theatre. Several walking trails provide scenic views throughout the park. Daily 24 hours. Free. Phone (604) 294-7450 or (604) 291-6864.

[SAVE] **Burnaby Village Museum** is off Hwy. 1 Kensington Ave. S. exit to 6501 Deer Lake Ave. The 4-hectare (10-acre) village re-creates the sights and sounds of an 1890-1925 settlement in lower mainland British Columbia. Costumed townspeople welcome visitors to more than 30 shops and homes, including a printshop and schoolhouse. A restored 1912 Parker carousel is on the site.

Food is available. Allow 1 hour minimum. Daily 11-4:30, May 3-Sept. 8; noon-4, Mar. 17-21. Closed Dec. 24-25. Hours vary Nov. 22-Jan. 1; phone ahead. Admission $12; $9 (ages 13-18 and 65+); $6 (ages 6-12). Carousel ride $1.89. Prices and schedule may vary; phone ahead. MC, VI. Phone (604) 293-6500.

COQUITLAM (H-11)
pop. 112,890, elev. 137 m/449'

Named for a type of landlocked salmon, Coquitlam borders Pitt Lake and encompasses Burke Mountain. Recreational opportunities, including swimming, canoeing, hiking and fishing, are available throughout the area.

Nearby parks and lakes include Mundy Park, 4 kilometres (2.5 mi.) south off Mariner Way; Belcarra Park, 15 kilometres (9 mi.) northwest off Ioco and Bedwell Bay roads; Buntzen Lake, 12 kilometres (7 mi.) northwest off East and Sunnyside roads; Minnekhada Regional Park, 13 kilometres (8 mi.) northeast off Victoria Drive and Quarry Road; Town Centre Park and Lafarge Lake, on Pinetree Way just north of Lougheed Hwy.; and Burke Mountain, 11 kilometres (7 mi.) northeast off Coast Meridian and Harper roads.

Visitor InfoCentre/Tri-cities Chamber of Commerce: 1209 Pinetree Way, Coquitlam, BC, Canada V3B 7Y3; phone (604) 464-2716.

DELTA (H-11) pop. 96,950, elev. 10 m/33'

Delta, composed of the three distinct communities of Ladner, Tsawwassen and North Delta, is an amalgam of commerce, fisheries, industry, farmland, beaches and suburban residences. The warm-water beaches on Boundary Bay and Tsawwassen are popular spots for swimming and sunbathing. Other recreational opportunities in the area include fishing for salmon and boating on the Fraser River and the Strait of Georgia.

Delta Chamber of Commerce: 6201 60th Ave., Delta, BC, Canada V4K 4E2; phone (604) 946-4232.

DELTA MUSEUM AND ARCHIVES is at 4858 Delta St. The museum houses marine, fishing and farming exhibits, pioneer and First Nations displays, reconstructed rooms of a late Victorian household and an early 1900s Delta street scene. Allow 1 hour minimum. Museum open Tues.-Sun. 10-4:30. Archives open Tues.-Sat. 10-3; closed Nov. 11 and Dec. 25. Donations. Phone (604) 946-9322.

GEORGE C. REIFEL MIGRATORY BIRD SANCTUARY is at 5191 Robertson Rd. on Westham Island. More than 268 species of birds have been observed at the refuge, which comprises 344 hectares (850 acres) with 4 kilometres (2.5 mi.) of trails. Allow 1 hour minimum. Daily 9-4. Admission $4; $2 (ages 2-14 and 60+). Bird seed 50c per bag. Phone (604) 946-6980.

LANGLEY (H-11) pop. 23,643, elev. 10 m/33'

Langley, the site of a Hudson's Bay Co. fort built in 1840 (see Fort Langley National Historic Site of Canada p. 121), is in an important farming region.

Orchards, strawberry and raspberry farms, horse ranches and dairy, chicken and mink farms make a patchwork of the countryside.

Greater Langley Chamber of Commerce-Langley: Unit One, 5761 Glover Rd., Langley, BC, Canada V3A 8M8; phone (604) 530-6656.

CANADIAN MUSEUM OF FLIGHT is at Hangar 3, 5333 216th St., at the Langley Airport. The museum features a collection of more than 25 aircraft; some restored. Aircraft include a Handley-Page Hampden Bomber, helicopters and jets. The aircraft and artifacts displayed represent Canada's aviation history 1909 to the present day. A collection of other aviation memorabilia as well as a children's activity center is available.

Allow 30 minutes minimum. Daily 10-4; closed Jan. 1 and Dec. 25-26. Admission $5.30; $4.24 (students with ID and ages 60+); free (ages 0-5); $12 (family, two adults and up to five children). MC, VI. Phone (604) 532-0035.

GAMBLING ESTABLISHMENTS

- **Cascades Langley City** is at 20393 Fraser Hwy. Daily 24 hours. Phone (604) 530-2211.

WINERIES

- **Domaine de Chaberton Estate Winery** is at 1064 216th St. Tastings are given daily 10-5:30. Tours are offered at 2 and 4, Feb.-Nov.; at 3, rest of year. (weather permitting). Closed Jan. 1 and Dec. 25-26. Phone (604) 530-1736.

MAPLE RIDGE (H-12)
pop. 63,169, elev. 30 m/98'

Maple Ridge lies on the north shore of the Fraser River, with the Coast Mountains to the north and the Stave and Pitt Rivers forming its east and west boundaries. Snow-capped peaks overlook this Fraser Valley community.

The Fraser River Heritage Walk, which starts at Port Haney Wharf, passes many of the town's notable spots. The Haney House at 11612 224th St. was built in 1876 and contains many furnishings and artifacts owned by three generations of the Haney family. Displays at Maple Ridge Museum, 22520 116th Ave., reflect the history and geography of the area.

Kanaka Creek Regional Park (*see Recreation Chart*) offers hiking and horseback riding trails as well as canoeing, kayaking, fishing and picnic facilities. A fish hatchery is on the grounds. Phone (604) 530-4983. Maple Ridge also has a large per capita horse population and an extensive riding trail system.

Tourism Maple Ridge and Pitt Meadows: 12492 Harris Rd., Pitt Meadows, BC, Canada V3Y 2J4; phone (604) 460-8300 or (877) 465-8300.

UBC MALCOLM KNAPP RESEARCH FOREST is n. at 14500 Silver Valley Rd. Trails of various

lengths lead visitors on tours through the forest, a research facility of the University of British Columbia. Bicycles and pets are not permitted. Daily dawn-dusk. Free. Phone (604) 463-8148.

MISSION (H-12) pop. 31,272, elev. 55 m/180'

Mission developed from a Roman Catholic mission built in 1861 to serve Indian tribes. The site became a popular stopping place for trappers, settlers and other river travelers.

The Fraser River provides opportunities for swimming, fishing, boating and water sports; its sandbars are good for rockhounds in search of agates, jades and garnets. Motocross and boat races are held at Mission Raceway from March through October.

Mission Regional Chamber of Commerce: 34033 Lougheed Hwy., Mission, BC, Canada V2V 5X8; phone (604) 826-6914.

[SAVE] **POWER HOUSE AT STAVE FALLS** is 1.3 km (.8 mi.) w. on Ferndale Ave. from jct. Stave Lake St. and Ferndale Ave., then 12. 9 km (8 mi.) n.w. on Dewdney Trunk Rd. to 31338 Dewdney Trunk Rd. Through interactive science games and historic displays, the facility tells the story of how power helped build British Columbia. Within a 50-seat theater, visitors may start their self-guiding tour with a 9-minute video that introduces life in the early 1900s. On display are generators and turbines within a 1912 generating station.

Allow 1 hour minimum. Daily 10-5, Mar. 15-Oct. 31. Admission $6; $5 (ages 6-8 and ages 55+); $15 (family, two adults and two children). MC, VI. Phone (604) 462-1222.

WESTMINSTER ABBEY is 1.5 km (.9 mi.) e., .7 km (.5 mi.) n. of Hwy. 7 to 34224 Dewdney Trunk Rd. The Seminary of Christ the King is managed by Benedictine monks. Of interest are the view and architecture. Modest dress is required. Allow 30 minutes minimum. Mon.-Sat. 1:30-4:30, Sun. 2-4. Donations. Phone (604) 826-8975.

XÁ:YTEM LONGHOUSE INTERPRETIVE CENTRE is at 35087 Lougheed Hwy. (Hwy. 7). Xá:ytem (pronounced HAY-tum) is said to be British Columbia's oldest known dwelling site. It is evidence of one of many large villages that were once inhabited by the ancestors of today's Stó:lō people. Of note is a replica of a *skumel*, or underground pithouse, and the "Rock"—a physical manifestation of Stó:lō spirituality. Among the items housed at the cedar longhouse are artifacts found at the site.

Guided tours are available. Picnicking is permitted. Allow 1 hour minimum. Mon.-Sun. 9-4:30, July-Aug.; Mon.-Sat. 9-4:30, rest of year. Closed Jan. 1 and Dec. 25-26. Hours may vary, phone ahead. Admission $10; $9 (ages 60+ and students with ID); $7 (ages 0-12). MC, VI. Phone (604) 820-9725.

NEW WESTMINSTER (G-11)
pop. 49,400, elev. 75 m/246'

The oldest incorporated city in Western Canada, New Westminster—also known as the Royal City—

was named by Queen Victoria. Transformed into a boomtown by the lure of gold in 1857, it plunged into a depression when the gold rush subsided in the late 1860s. The city was the provincial capital until 1868.

New Westminster also is known for its architecture. Parts of the city were built by the Royal Engineers, sent in 1855 to keep order in the new crown colony. Former members of this organization later formed the New Westminster Regiment, whose history is recounted in the Museum of the Royal Westminster Regiment at Sixth St. and Queens Ave.; phone (604) 526-5116.

Other places of interest include old houses, many of which survived a devastating fire in 1898. The houses can be toured in May. Tickets must be purchased in advance; for information phone the New Westminster Hyack Festival Association at (604) 522-6894.

Westminster Quay Public Market, on the waterfront, maintains a tradition started in 1892 when farmers, hunters and settlers came to barter for goods. Fresh meat, baked goods, produce and local crafts can be purchased daily.

Antique Alley, on historic Front Street, is known for its heritage buildings housing stores featuring an array of antiques and collectibles.

Also of interest is *Sampson V* Maritime Museum aboard the stern-wheeler berthed on the Fraser River at the foot of Tenth Street. The stern-wheeler, the last steam-powered paddlewheeler to operate on the Fraser, can be toured; phone (604) 522-6894. The Canadian Lacrosse Hall of Fame, which celebrates Canada's national summer sport, is at 65 E. Sixth Ave., junction Sixth Avenue and McBride Boulevard; phone (604) 527-4640.

New Westminster Chamber of Commerce: 601 Queens Ave., New Westminster, BC, Canada V3M 1L1; phone (604) 521-7781 or (604) 526-1905.

JAPANESE FRIENDSHIP GARDEN is next to City Hall at 511 Royal Ave. Waterfalls, pathways and flowering trees and shrubs adorn the garden, which features

DID YOU KNOW

Vancouver's Chinatown is the third largest in North America (after San Francisco and New York).

100 Yoshino cherry trees, a gift from the city of Moriguchi, Japan. Allow 1 hour, 30 minutes minimum. Daily dawn-dusk. Free. Phone (604) 527-4567.

NEW WESTMINSTER MUSEUM AND ARCHIVES is at 302 Royal Ave. This 1864 mansion was built in the San Francisco Gothic Revival style for Capt. William Irving, a pioneer of the riverboat trade on the Fraser River. Furnished in period, the 14-room residence is bedecked in Victorian Christmas decor during December. The adjacent museum features artifacts, local history displays and an 1876 coach built to carry the governor general of Canada to the Cariboo goldfields.

Allow 1 hour minimum. Museum and mansion Wed.-Sun. noon-5, May 1-Labour Day. Archives Wed.-Sun. noon-4:30. Hours may vary; phone ahead. Closed holidays. Donations. Phone (604) 527-4640.

PADDLEWHEELER RIVERBOAT TOURS departs from the boardwalk of the New Westminster Quay Public Market at 139-810 Quayside Dr. Narrated sightseeing tours of various lengths are offered aboard an authentic paddlewheeler. The MV *Native* is a replica of a late 19th-century riverboat that carried passengers on the historic Gold Rush Trail via the Fraser River. Evening entertainment cruises also are available.

Cruises depart daily year-round; phone for schedule. Fare $29.95-$59.95; $26.95-$53.95 (senior citizens); $14.95-$35.95 (ages 6-12); some fares may include meals. Reservations are required. AX, MC, VI. Phone (604) 525-4465 or (877) 825-1302.

QUEENS PARK is at 6th St. and McBride Blvd. in the center of town. The park includes a Salish totem pole, a picnic area, tennis courts, botanical gardens, nature trails, a stadium, an arena and a band shell in which concerts are presented in July and August. Splash pools, playgrounds and a petting zoo are open in summer. In Centennial Lodge, the Art Gallery in the Park features works by emerging and established artists.

Allow 1 hour, 30 minutes minimum. Park open daily dawn-dusk. Art gallery daily 1-5, July-Aug.; Tues.-Sun. 1-5, rest of year. Splash pools daily 10-7, Victoria Day weekend-Labour Day weekend; Sat.-Sun. 10-7, Labour Day-Sept. 30. Petting zoo daily 10-5:30, June-Aug. Donations. Phone (604) 527-4567 for the park or (604) 525-3244 for the gallery.

NORTH VANCOUVER (G-11)
pop. 44,303, elev. 99 m/325'

CAPILANO SALMON HATCHERY is at 4500 Capilano Park Rd. Self-guiding tours allow visitors to view this architecturally acclaimed facility. Displays trace the development of coho, chinook and steelhead salmon. Live adult salmon may be seen in the fish ladder July through November. Scenic picnic areas are available. Allow 30 minutes minimum. Daily 8-8, June-Aug.; 8-7 in May and Sept.; 8-6, in Oct.; 8-4, rest of year. Free. Phone (604) 666-1790.

CAPILANO SUSPENSION BRIDGE is off Hwy. 1 exit 14, then 2 km (1.2 mi.) n. to 3735 Capilano Rd. The swinging 137-metre-long (450-ft.) footbridge spans a 70-metre-deep (230-ft.) densely wooded gorge above the Capilano River. George Grant Mackay, a Scottish civil engineer, built the original bridge in 1889 from hemp rope and cedar planks; the fourth structure on the site is reinforced with steel cables and concrete.

The site features gardens, a totem park, the Treetops Adventure and a story center that displays artifacts of the bridge. The Living Forest includes interactive displays and naturalist exhibits which guide visitors through a West Coast rain forest. Artisans sculpt totem poles and masks in the Big House. First Nations dancers perform and costumed guides offer tours of the park and nature trails daily May through October.

Food is available. Allow 1 hour minimum. Daily 8:30-dusk, May-Oct.; 9-5, rest of year. Closed Dec. 25. Admission $28.95; $26.95 (ages 65+); $22.30 (students with ID); $16.80 (ages 13-16); $8.95 (ages 6-12). AX, MC, VI. Phone (604) 985-7474. *See color ad p. 166.*

GROUSE MOUNTAIN is at 6400 Nancy Greene Way. From a height of 1,100 metres (4,100 ft.), the summit offers a panorama of the city. Skiing, snowshoeing, snowboarding, ice skating and sleigh rides are possible in the winter while helicopter tours are popular in the summer. Sports events and shows take place year-round. An aerial tramway operates all year to the chalet.

Each hour, Theatre in the Sky shows the film "Born to Fly," which provides an eagle's view of southwestern British Columbia. The Grouse Mountain Refuge for Endangered Wildlife is home to two orphaned grizzly bears and a pack of gray wolves. Also offered are a guided Eco Walk, a lumberjack show and a Birds in Motion demonstration.

Picnicking is permitted. Food is available. Allow 1 hour minimum. Grouse Mountain open daily 9 a.m.-10 p.m. Tram $32.95; $30.95 (ages 65+); $18.95 (ages 13-18); $11.95 (ages 5-12). Fares may vary; phone ahead. AX, DC, MC, VI. Phone (604) 984-0661.

LYNN CANYON PARK AND ECOLOGY CENTRE is off Lynn Valley Rd. to the end of Peters Rd., following signs to 3663 Park Rd. The municipal park features paths, natural streams and rivers and a 50-metre-high (166-ft.) suspension bridge spanning a waterfall and the canyon. The ecology center offers films, interactive displays and nature programs. Food is available. Park open daily dawn-dusk; closed Jan. 1 and Dec. 25-26. Ecology center open daily 10-5, June-Sept.; Mon.-Fri. 10-5, Sat.-Sun. and holidays noon-4, rest of year. Donations. Phone (604) 981-3103.

MAPLEWOOD FARM is at 405 Seymour River Pl. This park-farm specializes in the display of domestic farm animals and birds. Visitors may pet the inhabitants of Goathill and Rabbitat and view a cow-milking demonstration. Allow 1 hour minimum.

Daily 10-4, Apr.-Sept.; Tues.-Sun. 10-4, rest of year. Closed Dec. 25. Cow-milking demonstrations daily at 1:15. Admission $4.25; $2.75 (ages 19 months-16 years and 55+). Phone (604) 929-5610.

MOUNT SEYMOUR PROVINCIAL PARK is 24 km (15 mi.) n.e. The scenic area of 3,508 hectares (8,668 acres) is on the slopes of 1,433-metre (4,701-ft.) Mount Seymour. A good highway goes to the 1,006-metre (3,330-ft.) level. Hiking trails and downhill skiing are available in season. Picnicking is permitted. Daily 7 a.m.-11 p.m. Free. Phone (604) 582-5200. *See Recreation Chart.*

NORTH VANCOUVER MUSEUM AND ARCHIVES is in Presentation House at 209 W. Fourth St. The museum's artifacts document the community's growth from pioneer days. Documentary and photographic collections are housed in the archives at 3203 Institute Rd. Allow 1 hour minimum. Museum open Tues.-Sun. noon-5. Archives open Tues.-Sat. noon-5 (closed Sat.-Sun. in Aug.). Complex closed Jan. 1 and Dec. 25. Donations. Phone (604) 990-3700.

PARK & TILFORD GARDENS is at jct. Cotton Rd. and Brooksbank Ave. at 440-333 Brooksbank Ave. Founded in 1969, the three-acre botanical site consists of eight interconnected theme gardens. A variety of both native and exotic floral arrangements leads through arboreal displays and to aviaries, where visitors may see parrots and other tropical birds. An aromatic blend of plant and flower enclosures composes the Rose Garden, home to 24 varieties of plant life and more than 250 rose plants.

Guided tours are available. Allow 1 hour minimum. Daily 9:30-dusk. Free. Phone (604) 984-8200.

ROCKWOOD ADVENTURES RAINFOREST WALKS departs from downtown hotels. Half- and full-day guided nature walks are offered to area ecological destinations including Lynn Canyon, a rain forest in Capilano River Canyon, a coastal forest at Burrard Inlet and Mount Gardner on Bowen Island. All trips include a snack or lunch. Trips daily Apr.-Oct. Fee $75; $66 (senior citizens); $60 (children). Reservations are required. MC, VI. Phone (604) 980-7749 or (888) 236-6606.

RECREATIONAL ACTIVITIES
Kayaking

• **Takaya Tours** depart from off Hwy. 1 exit 23A to Main St. (becomes Dollarton Hwy.), then 3.3 mi. e. to Cates Park docks, following signs. Shuttle transportation is available. Write 4310 Gallant Ave., North Vancouver, BC, Canada V7G 1K8. Daily 9-8, May-Oct. Phone (604) 904-7410 or (604) 936-0236.

PORT COQUITLAM (H-11)
pop. 51,257, elev. 10 m/33′

Port Coquitlam is bordered by the Pitt and Fraser rivers to the east and south and mountains to the north. The rivers were coveted fishing grounds, and in fact, Coquitlam is derived from the Salish word *kwayhquitlum*, which means "red fish in the river," referring to the annual salmon spawning run. Before the 1800s, the area was occupied by the ancestors of the Kwayhquitlum First Nations tribe. With the arrival of the first European settlers, Port Coquitlam began its growth as a farming and logging community.

Opportunities for recreational activities abound. The 29-kilometre (18-mi.) PoCo Trail passes through wooded areas and runs alongside the Pitt River, providing plenty of opportunities to observe waterfowl and other wildlife; the Pitt Dikes can be seen from the trail. Activities such as hiking, jogging, bicycling and horseback riding also can be enjoyed.

PORT MOODY (H-11)
pop. 23,816, elev. 10 m/33′

Port Moody once was the terminus of the Canadian Pacific Railway—the first train from Montréal to the Pacific arrived July 4, 1886. A year later the line was extended 20 kilometres (12 mi.) west to Vancouver. Rocky Point Park on Burrard Inlet offers picnicking, swimming, boating and nature trails.

PORT MOODY STATION MUSEUM is at 2734 Murray St. The museum displays community and railway artifacts and historical information about Port Moody in a former Canadian Pacific Railway depot with working and living areas restored to their early 1900s appearance. A heritage garden, typical of Canadian Pacific Railway stations 1882-1912, is on the grounds. A restored 1921 sleeper car also is on site. Daily 10-5, Victoria Day-Sept. 30; 10-4, rest of year. Closed Jan. 1 and Dec.25-26. Donations. Phone (604) 939-1648.

RICHMOND (H-11) pop. 164,345, elev. 5 m/16′

On an island at the mouth of the Fraser River, Richmond first was settled in 1879. The town grew and prospered with its farming, fishing and waterborne trade industries. Today, Richmond's major industries include aviation, berry farming, high technology and manufacturing.

Golden Village, in central Richmond, affords visitors the opportunity to experience the Asian culture through shopping, dining and festivals.

Steveston, a historic fishing village now part of the southwest corner of Richmond, has been restored and is an area of shops, restaurants and businesses. Hundreds of boats line the docks as fishermen dry their nets and unload their catches for sale. A stroll along the boardwalks and dykes reveals scenic vistas, wildlife, public art and heritage sites.

The Richmond Nature Park, 44 hectares (109 acres) at 11851 Westminster Hwy., has a bird pond, beehive displays, mounted birds, a quaking bog and plants identified by markers. A naturalist conducts hour-long tours of the park on Sunday.

Tourism Richmond: 11980 Deas Thruway, Richmond, BC, Canada V6W 1L1; phone (604) 271-8280 or (877) 247-0777. *See color ad.*

BUDDHIST TEMPLE is at 9160 Steveston Hwy. This working temple offers visitors tranquility through its classical Chinese garden, ponds, small waterfalls and gazebos. A courtyard features bonsai plants and a striking ceramic mural. The temple houses Chinese artifacts that reveal the artisans' skill in sculpture, painting, carpentry and embroidery. Also on site is the Seven Buddha Mural; at 22 metres (73 ft.) long it is said to be the only Buddhist mural of this size in the world. Allow 1 hour minimum. Daily 9:30-5:30. Donations. Phone (604) 274-2822.

GULF OF GEORGIA CANNERY NATIONAL HISTORIC SITE is at 12138 Fourth Ave. in Steveston Village. The 1894 salmon cannery has been restored to serve as an interpretive center for Canada's West Coast fishing industry. Interactive video presentations, guided tours of the plant and replicated 1900-50 canning line, and equipment demonstrations are offered. Every 30 minutes, the Boiler House Theatre presents a film about the West Coast fishing industry.

Mon.-Sat. 10-5, Sun. 11-5, June-Sept.; Thurs.-Sat. 10-5, Sun. 11-5 in May and Sept. 1-Oct. 6. Admission $7.90; $6.65 (ages 65+); $3.95 (ages 6-16). VI. Phone (604) 664-9009.

LONDON HERITAGE FARM is at 6511 Dyke Rd. The restored 1880s house, furnished in period, is the former residence of Charles and Henrietta London. Picnicking is permitted. Allow 1 hour minimum. Mon.-Fri. 10-4, Sat.-Sun. 10-5, July-Aug.; Sat.-Sun. noon-5, Sept.-Dec. and Feb.-June. Donations. Phone (604) 271-5220.

RICHMOND CULTURAL CENTRE is off Granville St. at 7700 Minoru Gate. Home to the Richmond Arts Centre, Archives, Museum and Art Gallery, the center presents programs and events in art, music, drama and dance. The gallery features works from local artists and traveling exhibits. The museum depicts Richmond's history through early household items, personal effects and articles relating to the area's agriculture, dairying, fishing and transportation.

Allow 1 hour minimum. Museum open Mon.-Fri. 9 a.m.-9:30 p.m.; Sat.-Sun. 10-5. Art gallery open Mon.-Fri. 10-6, Sat.-Sun. 10-5. Archives open Mon.-Thurs. 9-4:30. Complex closed holidays. Donations. Phone (604) 231-6457.

STEVESTON SEABREEZE ADVENTURES is at 12551 #1 Rd., bldg. 43. A narrated whale-watching tour departs from historic Steveston village and transits the Fraser River Delta, Strait of Georgia and Gulf Islands. Hydrophones are used to listen to the whales vocalizing. The scenic trip affords passengers an opportunity to view other marine animals and wildlife.

Allow 3 hours minimum. Daily at 9 and 2, mid-June to early Sept.; at 11, early Apr. to mid-June and early Sept.-late Oct. Fare (includes water/coffee and a snack) $105; $95 (students with ID and senior citizens); $69 (ages 4-12). Reservations are suggested. Phone (604) 272-7200.

VANCOUVER WHALE WATCH is at 210-12240 Second Ave. A 40-passenger, semi-covered vessel transports visitors through the Fraser River Delta, Strait of Georgia and Gulf Islands. Led by a naturalist, the narrated tour focuses on killer whales. Hydrophones are used to listen to the whales communicating. Other wildlife such as porpoises, sea lions, seals and eagles also may be seen. Binoculars are provided on loan.

Allow 3 hours minimum. Daily at 9 and 2, mid-June to early Sept.; at 11, early Apr. to mid-June and early Sept.-late Oct. Fare (includes water and a snack) $105; $95 (students with ID and senior citizens); $69 (ages 4-12). Reservations are suggested. Phone (604) 274-9565.

GAMBLING ESTABLISHMENTS

• **River Rock Casino Resort** is at 8811 River Rd. Daily 24 hours. Phone (604) 273-1895 or (877) 473-2818.

SURREY (H-11) pop. 347,825, elev. 80 m/262′

Surrey's sights are popular with nature buffs. Bear Creek Park features a garden area that includes rhododendrons, azaleas, ornamental grasses and bulb displays. A shoreline walk extends from Crescent Beach to Peace Arch Park. Walkers can observe tide pools, dig for clams or watch the myriad native birds.

Surrey Regional Chamber of Commerce: 14439 104th Ave., Suite 101, Surrey, BC, Canada V3R 1M1; phone (604) 581-7130 or (866) 848-7130.

HISTORIC STEWART FARM is at 13723 Crescent Rd. Costumed guides offer tours of an 1890s farmhouse that has been restored to represent Victorian rural life. The site includes a pole barn, heritage gardens and walking trails along the Nicomekl River. Demonstrations, and seasonal special events and programs also are featured. Picnicking is permitted. Allow 30 minutes minimum. Tues.-Fri. 10-4, Sat.-Sun. noon-4, Mar. 1 through mid-Dec.; closed statutory holidays. Donations. Phone (604) 592-6956.

NEWTON WAVE POOL is at 13730 72nd Ave. The indoor aquatic center houses, in addition to the wave pool, two water slides, a wading pool and a lagoon. The complex also includes an exercise, a steam and 465-square-metre (5,000-sq.-ft.) weight room as well as a whirlpool. Tues. and Thurs.-Sat. 12:30-9, Sun. 12:30-8, Mon. and Wed. 1:15-9, early July-early Sept.; Fri.-Sat. 12:30-9, Sun. 12:30-8, Mon. and Wed. 1:15-3:30 and 6-8 p.m., Tues. and Thurs. noon-3:30 and 6-8 p.m., rest of year. Pool admission $5.05; $3.85 (ages 60+ and students ages 19+ with ID); $2.55 (ages 2-18). MC, VI. Phone (604) 501-5540.

REPTILE REFUGE EDUCATION CENTRE is 2 km (1.2 mi.) n. of the Pacific Border Crossing to 1395 176th St. The refuge is a sanctuary for unwanted and abused reptiles and amphibians that once were pets and cannot be returned to their wilderness environments. Visitors can view crocodilians, turtles, lizards and snakes. Cameras are not permitted. Allow 1 hour minimum. Tues.-Sun. 11-5. Admission $8; $7 (students with ID); $6 (ages 0-12 and 56+). Hours and rates may vary; phone ahead. AX, MC, VI. Phone (604) 538-1711.

SURREY MUSEUM is at 17710-56A Ave. Interactive exhibits and a 42-seat theater portray the history of Surrey. A textile library and weaving studio are featured on-site. Changing exhibits are offered. Also on the grounds is the Anderson cabin, the oldest remaining pioneer-era structure in Surrey. The cabin was built in 1872 by Eric Anderson, a Swedish immigrant and one of the first settlers in the area. Allow 1 hour minimum. Tues.-Thurs. 10-6, Fri.-Sat. 10-5; closed statutory holidays and Dec. 24-early Feb. Admission $5; $3.75 (ages 61+ and students with ID); $2.50 (children); free (ages 0-5). Phone (604) 592-6956.

WEST VANCOUVER (G-11) pop. 41,421

CYPRESS PROVINCIAL PARK is off Trans-Canada Hwy. exit 8, then w. following signs. The park encompasses nearly 3,000 hectares (7,403 acres) of mountains, lakes and forests. Winter offers skiing and other snow-related activates, while summer features bird-watching and a wide range of hiking and nature trails. Picnicking is permitted. Daily 24 hours. Free. Phone (604) 924-2200. *See Recreation Chart.*

[SAVE] **SEWELLS SEA SAFARI TOURS** is off Trans-Canada Hwy. at Horseshoe Bay Ferry Terminal, following signs to village. Points of interest on the 2-hour high-speed tour of coastal British Columbia may include Bowyer Island, Pam Rocks—birthing ground to seal pups in July—Ragged Island and The Strait of Georgia. Tours depart daily at 10, 1 and 4, late Apr.-Oct. 31. Fare $67; $59 (ages 65+ and students with ID); $37 (ages 0-11). AX, MC, VI. Phone (604) 921-3474.

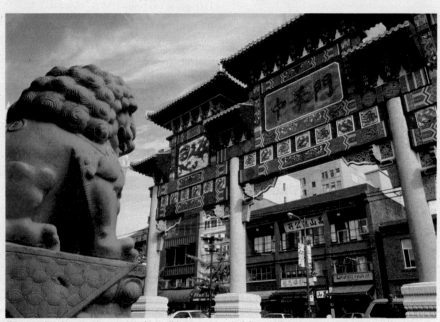

Chinese Cultural Centre Museum & Archives, Chinatown / Connie Coleman / Getty Images

---

This ends listings for the Vancouver Vicinity.
The following resumes the alphabetical listings of cities in British Columbia.

VANDERHOOF (E-4)
pop. 4,390, elev. 915 m/2,050′

When the last spike of the railroad was driven in 1914, the Grand Trunk Pacific Development Company offered land for sale. The decision of where to put the new settlement in the wilderness was decided by Herbert Vanderhoof, a railroad employee, and a town was built in just a few weeks. The site, unfortunately, was a poor choice, as the land flooded every spring. In 1919 the townspeople moved to higher ground on the opposite side of the tracks.

Mr. Vanderhoof's legacy to the town is its name, Dutch for "of the farm." The name is fitting, as farming has always been an economic mainstay in the area.

Vanderhoof District Chamber of Commerce: 2353 Burrard Ave., P.O. Box 126, Vanderhoof, BC, Canada V0J 3A0; phone (250) 567-2124 or (800) 752-4092.

VANDERHOOF HERITAGE MUSEUM is w. on Hwy. 16 to 478 W. First St. The collection of reconstructed buildings depicts rural agriculture in the 1920s. Among the buildings restored and open are the 1914 Board of Trade Building, a café, a police office, a 1914 jail cell and a home typical of those built in the area by early Mennonite settlers. In the town square are examples of farm machines and equipment. Food is available. Allow 30 minutes minimum. Mon.-Sat. 10-5, Victoria Day weekend-Labour Day. Donations. Phone (250) 567-2991.

VERNON—*see Okanagan Valley p. 145*

Victoria

City Population: 74,125
Elevation: 17m/56 ft.

Editor's Picks:

Miniature World . . . . *(see p. 189)*

Royal BC Museum . . . . *(see p. 189)*

Royal London Wax Museum . . . . . *(see p. 191)*

Parliament Buildings
© Mark Gibson / Index Stock / Photolibrary

"To realize Victoria," Rudyard Kipling wrote, "you must take all that the eye admires in Bournemouth, Torquay, the Isle of Wight, the Happy Valley at Hong Kong, the Doon, Sorrento, Camp's Bay, add reminiscences of the Thousand Islands and arrange the whole around the Bay of Naples with some Himalayas for the background."

Yet the capital of British Columbia remains quint-essentially British. Along with its tearooms, double-decker buses, horse-drawn tallyho carriages and shops that sell china and woolens, Victoria proudly claims another, much older culture. Totem poles can be seen throughout local parks, reflecting the city's dual heritage.

Regarded as Canada's gentlest city, Victoria has uncluttered streets, gardens that bloom year-round and hotels that have been serving high tea for decades. Sharing a passion for gardening, Victoria residents tend their prim English gardens. The city's innumerable flower beds and hanging baskets, nurtured by its mild climate, bloom in bright displays while the rest of Canada shivers.

The heart of the city curves around the stone-walled Inner Harbour, alive with bobbing pleasure craft, fishing boats and coastal shipping vessels. Facing the harbor are the Parliament Buildings and the block-long, ivy-covered Empress Hotel.

Emily Carr, a native of Victoria, devoted her artistic career to capturing on canvas the brilliant totem poles carved by the vanishing Indian civilizations of the Pacific coast. Like those she found in deserted Indian villages, the fanciful totems in Thunderbird Park evoke the highly developed ancient culture that dominated the area long before Victoria was settled in the mid-19th century.

Fort Victoria was built by Hudson's Bay Co. in 1843. Six years later Vancouver Island became a crown colony, and as British Columbia's only port, it became a passage to the Cariboo goldfields on the mainland in 1858. Violence around Bastion Square was so commonplace during this rowdy boomtown period that the *Victoria Gazette* reported no deaths "from natural causes in the city during the last 30 days." Local politicians supposedly settled their debates with fist fights on Government Street.

After the gold fever broke, Victoria began to assume its characteristic cool reserve. Lured by modest land prices, English settlers developed their queen's namesake city into a thriving government and commercial center. In 1868 Victoria became the capital of the newly joined crown colonies of Vancouver Island and British Columbia.

Since commercial supremacy passed to Vancouver after the completion of the Canadian Pacific Railway, Victoria has adopted a slower pace with few heavy industries. Victoria's harbor is a center for commercial trade. Lumber and fishing also contribute to the bustle of this port. The dry dock at the Canadian Forces Base-Pacific Command is one of the world's largest.

The city's strong tourism industry is buoyed by the continuous stream of travelers who come by ferry from Washington and throughout British Columbia.

Getting There — starting on p. 183

Getting Around — starting on p. 183

What To See — starting on p. 186

What To Do — starting on p. 192

Where To Stay — starting on p. 639

Where To Dine — starting on p. 660

Whether or not Victoria is more British than Britain remains an ongoing debate among Victoria's residents. Few would contest, however, that nature's blessings have endowed the city with ample charm in its own right. No one understood this better than its native Indians, whose awesome totems continue to speak the land's wonder.

Getting There

By Car

Victoria is the western terminus of the 7,760-kilometre (4,850-mi.) Trans-Canada Hwy. The highway traverses the mainland to Horseshoe Bay in West Vancouver and resumes at the Nanaimo ferry terminal. It then proceeds south along the island's eastern shore to Victoria. Hwy. 17, the other major artery into the city, connects Victoria with the ferry terminals at Swartz Bay and Sidney on the Saanich Peninsula.

By Boat

Several ferry systems connect Vancouver Island and Victoria with mainland Canada and the United States. The most direct route is the Tsawwassen-Swartz Bay automobile/passenger ferry service used by the intercity buses between Vancouver and Victoria. British Columbia Ferries also connects Nanaimo, 111 kilometres (69 mi.) north of Victoria, to Horseshoe Bay in West Vancouver. Phone (250) 386-3431 outside British Columbia or (888) 223-3779 within British Columbia for ferry information or reservations.

Ferries linking the southern end of the island and Victoria with the United States include Black Ball Transport Inc., (250) 386-2202, from Port Angeles,

Tourism Victoria

Wash.; and Washington State Ferries, (206) 464-6400, from Anacortes, Wash., to Sidney. Reservations are available for the Anacortes, Wash., to Sidney route; phone 1 day in advance to determine estimated waiting time.

Connecting Seattle and Victoria is the high-speed passenger ferry, the *Victoria Clipper (see color ad p. 192);* phone (250) 382-8100 or (800) 888-2535.

Departing from the north end of the island at Port Hardy, British Columbia Ferries' vessels voyage through the Inside Passage to Prince Rupert, where they connect with the Alaska State Ferry system. Information can be obtained from British Columbia Ferries, 1112 Fort St., Victoria, BC, Canada V8V 4V2; phone (250) 386-3431 outside British Columbia or (888) 223-3779 within British Columbia.

Getting Around

Street System

Most traffic activity is on Wharf, Government and Belleville streets, which embrace the Inner Harbour. Ferries arrive from Port Angeles, Wash., all

Destination Victoria

*T*he British legacy is indelibly stamped on the city. Here you will find massive stone castles, palatial government buildings, quaint cottages and gardens that bloom almost all year.

*B*ut look closer—another culture has left its mark: Native Indian icons are displayed with equal prominence throughout Victoria.

© CanStock Images / Alamy

Butchart Gardens, Brentwood Bay. One of the Victoria vicinity's "must see" gardens dates to 1904. (See listing page 194)

© Troy & Mary Parlee Index Stock

Craigdarroch Castle, Victoria. The late 19th-century, 39-room castle features stunning views of Victoria, the Strait and the Olympic Mountains. (See listing page 187)

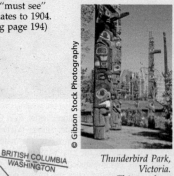

© Gibson Stock Photography

Thunderbird Park, Victoria. This outdoor collection of First Nations totem poles includes many carvings of the mythical thunderbird. (See listing page 191)

See Downtown map page 187

© Buddy Mays Travel Stock Photography

Fisgard Lighthouse, Victoria. The restored 1873 lighthouse is still operational and features historical exhibits. (See mention page 194)

*P*laces included in this AAA Destination City:

The Informed Traveler

Sales Tax: British Columbia's provincial sales tax is 7 percent. A room tax of 10 percent on lodgings also is levied in the Victoria area.

WHOM TO CALL

Emergency: 911
Police (non-emergency): (250) 995-7654
Hospitals: Royal Jubilee Hospital, (250) 370-8000; Victoria General Hospital, (250) 727-4212.

WHERE TO LOOK

Newspapers

Victoria's daily paper is the *Times-Colonist,* which is distributed in the morning.

Radio

Victoria radio stations CBC (90.5 FM), CIOC (98.5 FM), CFUV (102 FM) and C-FAX (1070 AM) have news and weather reports.

Visitor Information

Tourism Victoria Visitor Information Centre: 812 Wharf St., Victoria, BC, Canada V8W 1T3; phone (250) 953-2033 or (800) 663-3883.

The center provides maps and brochures outlining various self-guiding walking and driving tours. The center is open daily 8:30-6:30, mid-May to mid-Sept.; 9-5, rest of year.

TRANSPORTATION

Air Travel

Victoria International Airport is 22 kilometres (12 mi.) north on Hwy. 17 (Patricia Bay Hwy.). Air Canada makes frequent flights to Victoria from Vancouver and Seattle. International air connections are made in Vancouver.

Airport Bus Service runs between the airport and downtown hotels; phone (250) 386-2525. Fare $15; free (ages 0-4).

Rental Cars

Auto rental agencies include Hertz, 1640 Electra Blvd. and 2634 Douglas St., which offers discounts to AAA and CAA members; phone (250) 656-2312 or (250) 360-2822, or (800) 263-0600 in Canada, or (800) 654-3080 out of Canada. Additional agencies are listed in the telephone directory.

Rail Service

From its depot at 450 Pandora Ave., Via Rail has weekday passenger service between Victoria and Courtenay; phone (888) 842-7245 in Canada or in the United States.

Buses

Pacific Coach Lines, 700 Douglas St., provides daily bus service between Vancouver and Victoria via British Columbia Ferry. The vessels transport buses and personal vehicles; phone (604) 662-7575.

Island Coach Lines provides bus transportation between Victoria and Campbell River; Nanaimo; Port Alberni; Port Hardy; and Port McNeill. For information phone (250) 385-4411.

Taxis

Taxis charge $2.85 minimum plus $1.45 per kilometre (.6 mi.). Companies include Blue Bird Cabs, (250) 382-4235; Empress Taxi, (250) 381-2222; and Victoria Taxi, (250) 383-7111.

Public Transport

BC Transit provides bus service for Greater Victoria. Buses serve the downtown area 6:30 a.m.-midnight. Fare $2.25; senior citizens, students and children $1.40. Buses run frequently between downtown and the ferry terminal. For route information phone (250) 382-6161.

Boats

Several ferry systems make connections with mainland Canada and the United States. *See Getting There By Boat for details.*

year and from Seattle in summer. The main east-west streets are Yates, Fort and Johnson. Pandora Avenue, renamed Oak Bay Avenue in midtown, crosses the city from the Inner Harbour to Oak Bay.

Major north-south thoroughfares are Blanshard Street (Hwy. 17) and Douglas Street (Hwy. 1), which begins at Victoria's southern coast along the Juan de Fuca Strait. Dallas Road borders the shore and continues as Beach Drive along Victoria's eastern coast. Many Victoria streets are one-way.

Parking

On-street parking is controlled by meters and posted restrictions Mon.-Sat. 9-6. Vehicles parked on specially posted blocks are subject to towing during rush hours. Downtown off-street parking is available in civic parkades and shopping center lots.

What To See

ART GALLERY OF GREATER VICTORIA is at 1040 Moss St. The gallery presents contemporary, historical and Asian exhibitions, including a permanent Emily Carr exhibition. Daily 10-5 (also Thurs. 5-9); closed Good Friday, Nov. 11 and Dec. 25. Admission $12; $10 (ages 65+ and students with ID); $2 (ages 6-17); donations (first Tues. of each month). Admission may increase for special exhibits. MC, VI. Phone (250) 384-4101.

BASTION SQUARE overlooks the harbor. James Douglas established Fort Victoria on this site in 1843. Restored and preserved buildings from the 19th-century boom days surround a courtyard plaza.

BEACON HILL PARK is at Douglas and Dallas sts. The 74-hectare (183-acre) park features attractive flowerbeds, small lakes, playing fields and lawns that slope to the sea, and a totem pole carved by Chief Mungo Martin. Daily dawn-dusk. Free.

 BUTCHART GARDENS— *see Brentwood Bay p. 194.*

CANADIAN FORCES BASE ESQUIMALT NAVAL & MILITARY MUSEUM is 6 km (4 mi.) w. on Esquimalt Rd., then n. on Admirals Rd. to the main gate of Naden. Historic artifacts, documents and photographs relate to the naval and military heritage of the area. Allow 1 hour minimum. Daily 10-3:30, July-Aug.; Mon.-Fri. 10-3:30, rest of year. Closed statutory holidays and last 2 weeks in Dec. A photo identification card is required. Admission $2; $1 (children, students with ID and senior citizens); $5 (family). Phone (250) 363-4312 or (250) 363-5655.

Esquimalt Navy Base Summer Bus Tour departs from the Canadian Forces Base Esquimalt Naval & Military Museum. A 1-hour tour of the base also passes the harbor, where navy warships can be seen. Mon.-Fri. 8-3, July-Aug. A photo identification card is required. Free. Phone (250) 363-7060.

CENTRE OF THE UNIVERSE is at 5071 W. Saanich Rd. Housed within the Dominion Astrophysical

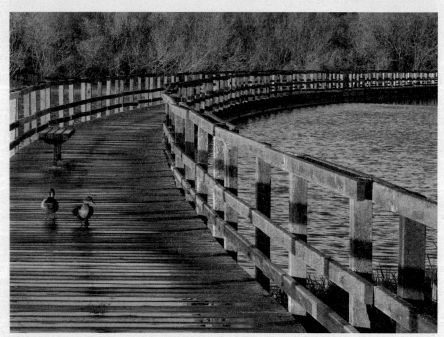

Swan Lake-Christmas Hill Nature Sanctuary / © Don Johnston / age fotostock

Downtown Victoria

Observatory, this interpretive center affords visitors a glimpse into the world of astronomy. The facility offers interactive exhibits, theater presentations and a look at the constellations in the Starlab Planetarium. Visitors may tour the 1.8-metre (5-ft.) Plaskett Telescope.

Guided tours are available. Allow 1 hour, 30 minutes minimum. Tues.-Sat. 3-11, Victoria Day-Labour Day; Tues.-Fri. 1-4:30 and Sat. 3-11, day after Labour Day-Oct. 31; Tues.-Fri. 1-4:30 and Sat. 10-4:30, Mar.-May; Sat. 10-4:30, rest of year. Closed Dec. 24-Jan. 2. Admission $9; $8 (ages 13-18 and 65+); $5 (ages 4-12); free (ages 0-4 when accompanied by a parent); $23 (family, two adults and three children). Admission after 6 p.m. $12; $10 (ages 13-18 and 65+); $7 (ages 4-12); $31 (family, two adults and three children). AX, MC, VI. Phone (250) 363-8262.

CHRIST CHURCH CATHEDRAL is at 911 Quadra St., between Burdett and Rockland sts. The Anglican-Episcopal cathedral is reminiscent of the great Gothic churches of the Middle Ages. Originally founded in 1856, the present cathedral is the third church built on this site. Started in the late 1920s and completed in 1986, it is one of Canada's largest cathedrals. The bells are replicas of those at

Westminster Abbey in London. A labyrinth is on the grounds. Mon.-Sat. 8:30-5:30, Sun. 8-4. Donations. Phone (250) 383-2714.

CRAIGDARROCH CASTLE is at 1050 Joan Crescent St. The sandstone mansion was built in the late 1880s for Robert Dunsmuir, a Scottish immigrant who attained wealth and fame through politics and coal mining. Dunsmuir died before the 39-room castle was completed. The building later served as a military hospital, a college and a music conservatory.

Visitors can appreciate the castle's stained-glass windows, intricate woodwork, ceiling murals and Victorian furnishings. There are numerous staircases, but no elevators. A self-guiding tour includes four floors of the castle and an 87-step climb to the tower, which offers stunning views of Victoria, the Strait and the Olympic Mountains.

Picnicking is permitted. Allow 1 hour minimum. Daily 9-7, June 15-Labour Day; 10-4:30, rest of year. Closed Jan. 1 and Dec. 25-26. Admission $11.50; $10.75 (senior citizens); $7.50 (students with ID); $3.50 (ages 6-18 when accompanied by an adult). MC, VI. Phone (250) 592-5323.

EMILY CARR HOUSE is at 207 Government St. Built in 1864 a few blocks from the harbor, the house was the birthplace of artist and writer Emily Carr. The Victorian residence has been restored to the ambiance the Carr family experienced in the 1870s. Family possessions, including some of Carr's early pottery, are displayed. Daily 11-4, June-Aug.; Tues.-Sat. 11-4, in May and Sept. Last admission is at 4. Admission $5; $3.50 (ages 0-17); $15 (family). Guided tour $10; $5 (ages 0-17); $25 (family). MC, VI. Phone (250) 383-5843.

GLENDALE GARDENS & WOODLAND is off Hwy. 17 West Saanich/Quadra exit, then w. to Beaver Lake Rd., following signs to 505 Quayle Rd. Two hectares (5 acres) of educational gardens feature more than 10,000 plant varieties. Highlights of the developing site include the Winter Garden and the Takata Japanese Garden. The surrounding 36 hectares (90 acres) include forests, wetlands and a haven for migratory birds.

Picnicking is permitted. Allow 1 hour minimum. Daily 8-6, May-Sept.; 8-4, rest of year. Closed Jan. 1 and Dec. 24-26 and 31. Admission $7.50; $5.25 (ages 60+ and students with ID); free (ages 0-15). MC, VI. Phone (250) 479-6162.

GOVERNMENT HOUSE GARDENS is at 1401 Rockland Ave. The grounds in front of the lieutenant governor's residence consist of 5.7 hectares (14 acres) of formal gardens, featuring perennials, herbs, roses, irises, azaleas, rhododendrons and other floral varieties. The property behind the house—which is

closed to the public—covers a 9-hectare (22-acre) rare Garry oak woodland that is native to southeast Vancouver Island.

Picnicking is permitted. Formal gardens daily dawn-dusk. Guided 90-minute tours of the woodland or gardens are available; phone ahead for times. Formal gardens by donations. Guided tours $10. Phone (250) 387-2080.

HATLEY PARK NATIONAL HISTORIC SITE is at 2005 Sooke Rd. The 216.5-hectare (565-acre) Hatley Park estate offers a variety of hands-on, educational visitor experiences. With its preserved old-growth forests, heritage gardens and spectacular vistas that overlook the Esquimalt Lagoon and the Juan de Fuca Strait, the centerpiece of this magnificent site is a 40-room Edwardian home built in 1908. The site also is home to Royal Roads University.

Grounds open daily 10-8, early June-Labour Day; 10-3, rest of year. Museum daily 10-7, early June-Labour Day; 10-4, rest of year. Guided tours of Hatley Castle are available daily 10-3:15, early June-Labour Day; 11-2:30, rest of year. Grounds and museum free. Hatley Castle tours (includes Heritage Gardens) May-Sept. $7-$17. Castle tours rest of year $5-$15. Heritage Gardens admission May-Sept. $6-$9. Gardens rest of year $3-$4.50. Phone (250) 391-2666 or (866) 241-0674.

MARITIME MUSEUM OF BRITISH COLUMBIA is at 28 Bastion Sq. The Pacific Northwest's maritime

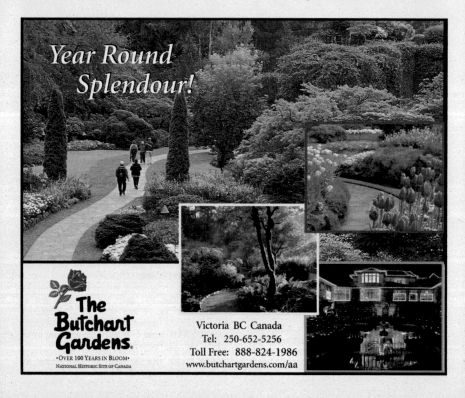

heritage is presented through ship models, figureheads, ships' tools and naval uniforms. Also featured is the 1860 *Tilikum*, an 11-metre (36-ft.) dugout canoe converted to a schooner, which sailed from Victoria to England 1901-04. The museum's 1889 building features one of the oldest operating birdcage elevators in North America.

Allow 1 hour minimum. Daily 9:30-5, mid-June to mid-Sept.; 9:30-4:30, rest of year. Closed Dec. 25. Admission $8; $5 (ages 65+ and students with ID); $3 (ages 6-11). MC, VI. Phone (250) 385-4222.

MINIATURE WORLD is in the Fairmont Empress Hotel at 649 Humboldt St. Animation, lighting and sound effects enhance more than 80 highly detailed miniature scenes. Displays include a circus, two of the world's largest dollhouses, a Swiss Family Robinson tree house and a futuristic space diorama. Scenes illustrate historic battles, fairy tales, nursery rhymes, "Gulliver's Travels" and novels by Charles Dickens. The Great Canadian Railway exhibit re-creates rail transportation in late 19th-century Canada.

Allow 1 hour minimum. Daily 8:30 a.m.-9 p.m., June 30-Labour Day; daily 9-5, day after Labour Day-Apr. 30; Sat.-Sun. 9-7, in May. Closed Dec. 25. Admission $9; $8 (ages 12-18); $7 (ages 5-11). AX, MC, VI. Phone (250) 385-9731.

PACIFIC UNDERSEA GARDENS is at 490 Belleville St. An observation room on the sea bottom allows visitors to view native marine life through large underwater windows. Daily 9-8, mid-June to mid-Sept.; 10-6, mid-Apr. to mid-June; 10-5, rest of year. Admission $9.50; $8.50 (ages 65+); $6.95 (ages 12-17); $5.50 (ages 5-11). MC, VI. Phone (250) 382-5717.

PARLIAMENT BUILDINGS overlook the Inner Harbour and yacht basin. The seat of British Columbia's Legislative Assembly, the buildings have elaborately carved facades and are surrounded by 5 hectares (12 acres) of lawns, gardens, fountains and statues of dignitaries. The rooms have mosaic tile floors, rotundas, stained-glass windows, woodcarvings and murals. Guided tours, conducted in several languages, are given Mon.-Thurs. 9-5, Fri.-Sun. 9-7, Victoria Day-Labour Day; Mon.-Fri. 8:30-5, rest of year. Contact the Tour Coordinator office to confirm times. Closed winter holidays. Free. Phone (250) 387-3046 or (250) 382-1400.

POINT ELLICE HOUSE is at 2616 Pleasant St. Built in 1861, the rambling Italianate residence contains many of its original furnishings. Lawns and a restored 19th-century garden surround the house. Self-guiding audiotapes are available. Food is available. Allow 30 minutes minimum. Daily 11-5, mid-May to mid-Sept.; Thurs. by appointment rest of year. Admission $6.36 (includes tour); $4.24 (ages 12-18); $3.18 (ages 5-11). MC, VI. Phone (250) 380-6506.

PRINCE OF WHALES WHALE WATCHING is at 812 Wharf St. Narrated tours by a marine biologist provides passengers with information about marine life while sitting below cover on-board the 62-foot *Ocean Magic* cruiser. High-speed open-boat tours also are available. Allow 2 hours, 30 minutes minimum. Daily at 8:30, 9:30, 10:30, noon, 1, 2, 3:30, 4:30 and 5:30, May-Oct. Passengers should arrive 30 minutes prior to departure. Fare $74-$89; $69 (ages 0-12). Reservations are required. AX, JC, MC, VI. Phone (250) 383-4882 or (888) 383-4884.

ROYAL BC MUSEUM is next to the parliament buildings at 675 Belleville St. Two floors of displays reflect the human and natural history of British Columbia. An early 1900s frontier town has a theater with silent movies, a saloon, shops and a hotel. The Natural History Gallery showcases the Living Land, Living Sea exhibit with a coastal rain forest display highlighted by live plants and tidal-pool animals as well as a climate change exhibit which explores the province's future climate. The First Peoples Gallery includes an exhibit focusing on the historic Nisga'a agreement and the present-day Nisga'a community, and Haida argillite carvings.

The on-site National Geographic IMAX Theater offers films to complement the natural and human history theme of the museum as well as other exciting IMAX footage. Special exhibits are featured periodically.

Museum open daily 9-5. Theater open daily 10-8. Closed Jan. 1 and Dec. 25. Theater schedule varies;

Some Things Never Change...

...Some Do

Sweethearts - and licensed drivers - since age 16.

For more than 50 years, Peter and Anna have shared a love for the open road. Now, with more time to travel, they're determined to keep tabs on factors that can affect their driving safety.

Using the easy new *AAA Roadwise Review* program on their home computer, the Johnsons are pairing up to check their driving abilities in areas associated with crash risk in older drivers. Repeating the tests periodically will help pinpoint changes in areas such as visual acuity and flexibility. The self-paced program identifies challenges as well as solutions, making driving safer for everyone.

AAA Roadwise Review is available at local AAA/CAA offices. For more information, visit www.AAA.com/publicaffairs.

phone ahead. Museum $14; $9.50 (ages 6-18 and 65+); $37.50 (family, two adults and two children). Combination ticket (Museum and IMAX Theater) $22.50; $17.75 (ages 6-18 and 65+); $5 (ages 0-4); $70 (family, two adults and two children). Admission may increase for special exhibits. AX, MC, VI. Phone (250) 356-7226 or (888) 447-7977. *See color ad p. 189.*

British Columbia Archives is at 655 Belleville St. Extensive public and private records are available to those conducting historical, genealogical or other research. Gardens containing native plants surround the building. The archives are open to the public Mon.-Tues. and Thurs.-Fri. 9:30-4:30; closed 1 week in early May and holidays. Free. Phone (250) 387-5885.

Helmcken House is next to the Royal BC Museum, in Thunderbird Park. One of the oldest houses in British Columbia still on its original site, the 1852 log structure was the home of John Sebastian Helmcken, a surgeon for Hudson's Bay Co. at Fort Victoria and a Father of Confederation. The restored house displays many original furnishings and a fine collection of period medical instruments.

Allow 30 minutes minimum. Daily noon-4, June-Sept.; by appointment rest of year. Hours vary; phone ahead. Free. Phone (250) 356-7226.

The Netherlands Centennial Carillon is at the corner of Government and Belleville sts. The largest carillon in Canada houses 62 bells donated by British Columbians of Dutch origin in celebration of the 1967 Canadian Confederation Centennial and in recognition of Canada's role in the liberation of the Netherlands during World War II. Recitals are held Sun. at 3, Apr.-Dec.; at 7 p.m. July-Aug. Schedule may vary; phone ahead. Free. Phone (250) 356-7226.

Thunderbird Park is at the corner of Douglas and Belleville sts. on the grounds of the Royal BC Museum. The park's collection of Northwest Coast totem poles was established in 1940, and re-carved via the Totem Restoration Program 1950-1990, when the originals began to decay beyond repair. A new Kwakwaka'wakw pole was carved and raised in 2000. Park open daily dawn-dusk. Free. Phone (250) 356-7226 or (888) 447-7977.

ROYAL LONDON WAX MUSEUM is at 470 Belleville in the Inner Harbour opposite the Parliament Buildings. Housed in the former steamship terminal, the museum features some 300 wax figures in more than 50 scenes. Included are Albert Einstein, Mother Teresa, Martin Luther King, Prince William and Princess Diana. Storytelling guides provide historical background about each figure. Themed exhibits include Royalty Row, Storybook Land, Martyrs of Hope, The Galaxy of Stars and The Chamber of Horrors.

A special exhibit with commentary, The Crown Jewels Theatre, displays replicas of the crown jewels of England. Frozen in Time, a multimedia theater presentation, focuses on the search for the Northwest Passage. Allow 1 hour minimum. Daily 9-7:30, May-Aug.; 10-5, rest of year. Closed Dec. 25. Admission $10; $9 (ages 65+); $7 (ages 13-19); $5 (ages 6-12). AX, DC, MC, VI. Phone (250) 388-4461.

SPRINGTIDE WHALE WATCHING is at 1207 Wharf St. Depending on the season and in addition to killer whales, visitors also may encounter sea lions; seals; porpoises; humpback, grey and minke whales as well as a variety of birds. Allow 2 hours minimum. Daily 8:30 a.m.-11 p.m., Apr.-Oct.; 8:30-5, Nov.-Mar. (weather permitting). Tours are offered at 10 and 2. Fare $89; $85 (ages 56+); $59 (ages 3-15). AX, MC, VI. Phone (250) 384-4444 or (800) 470-3474.

UNIVERSITY OF VICTORIA is on McKenzie Ave. at Gordon Head Rd. The 160-hectare (395-acre) campus includes the Mystic Vale Ecological Protection Area, several totems carved by local artists and Finnerty Gardens, known for its collection of more than 200 rhododendron species. A self-guiding walking tour brochure is available from the MacPherson Library loans desk.

Library loans desk Mon.-Thurs. 7:30 a.m.-11 p.m., Fri. 7:30 a.m.-9 p.m., Sat. 10-9, Sun. 10 a.m.-11 p.m., early Sept.-late Apr.; Mon.-Thurs. 8 a.m.-9 p.m., Fri. 8-6, Sat.-Sun. 10-6, rest of year. Guided tours are given Mon.-Sat. at 1, May-Aug.; Mon.-Fri. at 1, rest of year. Free. Parking $1 per hour. Reservations are required for tours. Phone (250) 721-8949.

VICTORIA BUG ZOO is at 631 Courtney St. More than 40 species of insects and spiders from around the world are on display. Highlights include a leafcutter ant farm and the giant African millipede. For the more adventurous, the zoo also provides the opportunity for and an environment conducive to a safe bug-handling experience. Guided tours are available. Allow 30 minutes minimum. Daily 10-6; closed Jan. 1 and Dec. 25. Admission $8; $6 (senior citizens); $7 (students with ID); $5 (ages 3-16). MC, VI. Phone (250) 384-2847.

What To Do

Sightseeing

Boat Tours

Sightseers using Victoria as a base for their travels can explore the Gulf Islands and Vancouver by ferry from Swartz Bay, north of Victoria via Hwy. 17; for schedule and toll phone the British Columbia Ferry Service at (250) 386-3431.

Opportunities for whale watching are offered by several boating companies, the oldest of which is Seacoast Expeditions, 146 Kingston St.; phone (250) 383-2254.

Bus and Carriage Tours

Guided tours of the city in red double-decker buses from London enhance Victoria's British atmosphere. Many of these tour operators are found along Belleville and Menzies streets by the harbor. SAVE Gray Line *(see color ad p. 170)*, 4196 Glanford Ave., (250) 388-6539 or (800) 663-8390, conducts bus tours.

Narrated horse-drawn carriage tours of the city are offered by several companies, including Black Beauty Line Ltd., phone (250) 507-0789; Tallyho, phone (250) 383-5067; and Victoria Carriage Tours, phone (250) 383-2207. All tours leave from the corner of Belleville and Menzies streets.

Driving Tours

The Greater Victoria Visitors Information Centre has information about such scenic drives as Marine Drive along the shoreline, a trip to Sooke Harbour on the west coast and the Malahat Drive, which runs along the east coast and reaches an elevation of 381 metres (1,250 ft.). The trip to Butchart Gardens is one of the most popular drives, following Hwy. 17 and Hwy. 17A through the rural communities and pastoral valleys of the Saanich Peninsula.

Walking Tours

Victoria is the perfect size for visitors keen on walking. A favorite thoroughfare of strollers and shoppers is Government Street, graced by banners and five-globe Victorian lampposts supporting baskets of geraniums and petunias.

Sports and Recreation

The English spirit still is manifest in such games as **lawn bowling** at the corner of Belleville and Douglas streets and **cricket** at Beacon Hill Park. Any notion, however, that Victoria's sports are too staid is dispelled quickly by a **box lacrosse** game. This offspring of the Indian game of *baggataway* is a rough-and-tumble version of field lacrosse confined to a smaller, enclosed area. Canada's Parliament designated boxla, as it also is called, the national sport in 1867. The game is played from April to August at Memorial Arena, 1925 Blanshard.

All-star **wrestling** and **ice hockey,** two other spectator sports that hardly could be considered sedate, also are held at the arena.

Water sports have obvious appeal in this island city. The wide variety of game fish around southern Vancouver Island includes rockfish, lingcod, sole and flounder; fishing licenses are required. Surf **fishing** often yields rewarding catches of salmon and black sea bass. Clamming and oyster harvesting are popular activities on any of the Gulf Islands, which are accessible by ferry from Swartz Bay.

Oak Bay Marina, 1327 Beach Dr., offers fishing charters at an hourly rate. Fishing equipment, a tackle shop and marine store are available; phone (250) 598-3369. Other nearby marinas include Anglers Anchorage Marina, 933 Marchant, Brentwood Bay; North Saanich Marina, 1949 Marina Way, Sidney; and the West Bay Marina, 453 Head St.

Boating is enjoyed in the Strait of Georgia and the Saanich Inlet. Uplands Park on Oak Bay is equipped with boat ramps. Fine beaches border Dallas Road and Beach Drive.

With its scenic coastal location and balmy climate, Victoria offers excellent playing conditions for **golf.** On a peninsula jutting into the Juan de Fuca Strait, Victoria Golf Club is open to members of other clubs.

Other golf clubs include Ardmore (nine holes), 930 Ardmore Dr., North Saanich; Cedar Hill (18 holes), 1400 Derby Rd.; Cordova Bay (18 holes), 5333 Cordova Bay Rd.; Glen Meadows (18 holes), 1050 McTavish Rd.; Green Acres (nine holes), 3970 Metchosin Rd.; Henderson Park (nine holes), 2291 Cedar Hill Crossroad; Mount Douglas (nine holes), 4225 Blenkinsop Rd.; Olympic View Golf Course (18 holes), 643 Latoria Rd.; Prospect Lake (nine holes), 4633 Prospect Lake Rd.; and Royal Oak Golf Club (nine holes), 540 Marsett Pl.

Many parks are scattered throughout Victoria and its surrounding municipalities of Oak Bay, Saanich and Esquimalt. Some offer **swimming,** such as Thetis Lake Park, Mount Work Park, Elk/Beaver Lake Park, Willows Beach Park and Island View Beach Park. Swimmers also might wish to try the Crystal Pool in Central Park.

Hiking, nature and horse trails are found at several parks. For more information contact Victoria Downtown Park; phone (250) 361-0600. Bamberton Provincial Park *(see Recreation Chart and the AAA/ CAA Western Canada & Alaska CampBook)* offers developed recreational facilities, including **camping.**

Swan Lake-Christmas Hill Nature Sanctuary, 6.5 kilometres (4 mi.) north via the Patricia Bay Hwy., can be explored by hiking trails and floating walkways weaving through the area. Excellent views of Victoria and the sea are at Mount Douglas, Mount Tolmie and Beacon Hill Park.

Shopping

Lined with shops carrying English tweeds and fine china, Government Street maintains Victoria's heritage as a trading post of the British Empire. Such shops as E.A. Morris Tobacconist have distinguished Government Street since the 19th century. Established in 1833, Rogers' Chocolate Shop is a Victoria institution that counts British royalty in its clientele. The Rogers' factory, behind the store at 913 Government St., still produces its renowned bittersweet chocolate according to a guarded recipe.

Shoppers determined to bring home something other than a few extra pounds might want to explore the craft and specialty shops in the renovated squares and malls off Government Street. More than 30 quaint stores and restaurants in revitalized old buildings highlight Market Square, bounded by Johnson, Pandora and Store streets.

Trounce Alley, in the downtown core, is a hideaway of eclectic shops. Shops of mid-19th-century architecture display modern items in Bastion Square, once a hangout for prospectors and drifters. An attractive shopping arcade is in Centennial Square off Douglas Street. Nootka Court between Courtney and Humboldt streets contains small arts and crafts shops.

Popular items available in Victoria include handwoven woolens from Ireland and England, hand-knit Cowichan Indian sweaters, Eskimo jade sculpture and Northwest Indian masks and prints. The Bay department stores, 1150 and 3125 Douglas St., sell authentic Cowichan sweaters. Also in Victoria are Hillside Shopping Centre, 1644 Hillside Rd.; Mayfair Shopping Centre, 3147 Douglas St.; and Sears, 3190 Shelbourne St.

In keeping with its Victorian image, Victoria has more than 50 antique shops. Many are found along Government and Fort streets and Oak Bay Avenue.

Performing Arts

McPherson Playhouse in Centennial Square is the center of Vancouver Island's regional and professional theater. The restored old theater regularly presents noontime concerts and musical comedy productions in the evening; phone (250) 386-6121 or (888) 717-6121. The Pacific Opera Victoria, (250) 385-0222, performs at the Royal Theatre.

The Royal Theatre on Broughton Street is the home of the Victoria Symphony Orchestra, (250) 385-6515, which offers a pop and masterworks series September through May. The Victoria Conservatory of Music sometimes offers performances; phone (250) 386-5311.

Comedy revues and music hall shows also are staged frequently at the Belfry, (250) 385-6815, 1291 Gladstone, and the Royal Theatre, (250) 386-6121, 805 Broughton. The University of Victoria Auditorium on Finnerty Road also presents various cultural events; phone (250) 721-8480. Butchart Gardens mounts musical stage shows during the summer. Kaleidoscope Theatre, an open-air theater at the Inner Harbour, also offers summer productions.

Top-name entertainers, rock groups and other performers draw large audiences to Memorial Arena, 1925 Blanshard. A carillon at the Parliament Buildings can be heard daily at 3 during the summer. The

Royal BC Museum's National Geographic IMAX Theater offers big-screen films complementing the museum's natural and human history themes; phone (250) 356-7226.

Special Events

As a city of traditions, Victoria celebrates many events and festivals year after year. Victoria Day, a Canadian national holiday, launches a week of festivities highlighted by a parade. The weekend following Victoria Day features the classic Swiftsure Race, which has drawn an armada of more than 450 sailboats from all over the world since 1930. The

Highlander Games take place in mid-May. The performing arts provide a theme for the Victoria Harbour Festival the last week in May. Boating enthusiasts will enjoy the Classic Boat Festival at Inner Harbour from late August to early September.

Autumn shows off its best colors along the rural Saanich Peninsula, where the Saanich Fair has been held in early September for more than a century. Fall's lower temperatures provide an energy boost for several major sports events, including the Victoria Open PGA Tournament Players Series and the Royal Victoria Marathon.

The Victoria Vicinity

BRENTWOOD BAY (H-10)

BUTCHART GARDENS is 2 km (1.2 mi.) s. on W. Saanich Rd., then w. to 800 Benvenuto Ave. The 22-hectare (55-acre) site contains the Rose Garden, Japanese Garden, Italian Garden, as well as the Star Pond and Ross Fountain. The Sunken Garden was created by the Butcharts on the site of their depleted limestone quarry.

The spring season brings azaleas, tulips, daffodils and other delicate blossoms. Breathtaking roses, annuals and perennials bloom in summer, while bursts of colorful foliage appear in autumn; subtle colored lighting illuminates the gardens June 15 through Sept. 15. July through August, nightly entertainment is offered with fireworks displays Saturday nights. The sparkle of holiday lights and decorations complement the colorful berries on shrubs and trees from Dec. 1 to Jan. 6. An outdoor skating rink, with skate rental, also is available in Waterwheel Square.

Food is available. Allow 2 hours minimum. Gardens open daily at 9; (at 1 on Dec. 25); closing times vary depending on the season. Admission mid-June through Sept. 30, $26.50; $13.25 (ages 13-17); $3 (ages 5-12). Admission varies, rest of year. AX, DC, DS, JC, MC, VI. Phone (250) 652-5256 or (866) 652-4422. *See color ad p. 188.*

VICTORIA BUTTERFLY GARDENS is 2 km (1.2 mi.) s. at jct. Saanich and Keating Cross rds. to 1461 Benvenuto Ave. This 1,110-square-metre (12,000-sq.-ft.) indoor tropical garden was designed specifically for the housing and breeding of more than 35 exotic butterfly and moth species. Guided tours and a videotape explain the transformations the butterflies undergo during their life cycle. More than 300 pupae are imported each week and displayed in the Emerging Room.

Up to 2,000 butterflies—from the 1.3-centimetre-long (.5-in.) Glasswing to the 30.5-centimetre-long (1-ft.) Atlas Moth—fly free among tropical plants and flowers, including an orchid exhibit and a carnivorous bog. Water falls into a stream that is home to fish, tropical ducks and such rare birds as the South African turacos.

Food is available. Allow 1 hour minimum. Daily 9-5:30, May 10-Sept. 1; 9:30-4:30, Mar. 1-May 9 and Sept. 2-Oct. 31. Opening and closing dates may vary; phone ahead. All-day admission $12; $11 (ages 13-18, ages 65+ and students with ID); $6.50 (ages 5-12). MC, VI. Phone (250) 652-3822 or (877) 722-0272.

FORT RODD HILL AND FISGARD LIGHTHOUSE NATIONAL HISTORIC SITES (H-9)

Fourteen kilometres (9 mi.) west of Victoria via Hwy. 1A, Fort Rodd Hill was a coastal artillery fort 1895-1956. Of interest are the loophole walls, underground magazines, artillery stores, command posts, barracks and gun and searchlight emplacements. Audiotape and videotape presentations, along with period rooms, depict life at the fort. The 1860 Fisgard Lighthouse, restored to its 1873 appearance, was the first built on this part of the coast. Still operational, the lighthouse has two floors of historical exhibits. A nature trail follows the paths formerly used by soldiers. Historical exhibits also are featured. Picnic facilities are available.

Allow 1 hour, 30 minutes minimum. Park open daily 10-5:30, Feb.-Oct.; 9-4:30, rest of year. Lighthouse and fort exhibits daily 10-5, Mar.-Oct.; 9-4, rest of year. Closed Jan. 1 and Dec. 25-26. Limited services Nov.-Feb. Admission (includes fort and lighthouse) $3.95; $3.45 (ages 65+); $1.95 (ages 6-16); $10 (family). MC, VI. Phone (250) 478-5849.

SAANICHTON (H-10) elev. 58 m/194′

HERITAGE ACRES (SAANICH HISTORICAL ARTIFACTS SOCIETY) is off Hwy. 17, e. on Island View Dr., then n. to 7321 Lochside Dr. The society is dedicated to maintaining artifacts from the area's rural past on 12 hectares (29 acres) of parkland. A museum exhibits historic household items, furnishings and farm equipment. Also part of the complex are a blacksmith's shop, a sawmill, nature trails and a one-room log cabin. Rides are offered aboard model trains.

Picnicking is permitted. Allow 30 minutes minimum. Daily 10-4, June 1-Labour Day; 9:30-noon, rest of year. Closed Dec. 25. Donations. Admission is charged during events held Father's Day weekend and the third weekend in Sept. Phone (250) 652-5522.

SIDNEY (H-10) pop. 10,929, elev. 9 m/30′

Salish Indians were the earliest known inhabitants of the area now called Sidney. Incorporated into a town in 1967, Sidney is known for its fishing and waterfront activity. Picnicking, beachcombing and camping are popular at Sidney Spit Marine Provincial Park *(see the AAA/CAA Western Canada & Alaska CampBook).*

Saanich Peninsula Chamber of Commerce: 203-2453 Beacon Ave., P.O. Box 2014, Sidney, BC, Canada V8L 1M7; phone (250) 656-3616.

BRITISH COLUMBIA AVIATION MUSEUM is at Victoria Airport at 1910 Norseman Rd. Displays of memorabilia and aircraft include World War II planes and bush planes, a model plane exhibit, photographs and aircraft engines. Guided tours are available. Allow 1 hour minimum. Daily 10-4 May-Sept.; 11-3, rest of year. Closed Jan. 1 and Dec. 25. Admission $7; $5 (ages 6-12 and 66+); $3 (students with ID); free (ages 0-5). VI. Phone (250) 655-3300.

SIDNEY HISTORICAL MUSEUM is at 2423 Beacon Ave. The early lives of Sidney and North Saanich pioneers are portrayed through photographs and artifacts. Allow 1 hour minimum. Daily 10-4. Donations. Phone (250) 655-6355.

SIDNEY MARINE MUSEUM is at 9801 Seaport Pl. The museum traces the story of the biology and evolution of whales and other marine mammals. **Note:** The museum is undergoing renovations and is scheduled to re-open in spring 2009; phone ahead to confirm. Daily 10-4, May-Oct.; Sat.-Sun. 11-3, rest of year. Phone to verify schedule. Donations. Phone (250) 656-1322.

SOOKE (H-10) pop. 8,735, elev. 38 m/125′

A natural harbor off the Juan de Fuca Strait, Sooke was discovered and claimed by the Spanish in 1790. The area, soon traded to the British by treaty, was named after a local Indian tribe, T'Soke. It is a popular fishing site and the center of a large forest industry. A scenic portion of Hwy. 14 runs 43 kilometres (27 mi.) east from Sooke to Victoria.

Sooke Travel InfoCentre: 2070 Phillips Rd., Box 774, Sooke, BC, Canada V0S 1N0; phone (250) 642-6351.

SOOKE REGION MUSEUM is 1 km (.6 mi.) e. on Hwy. 14 at 2070 Phillips Rd. Exhibits about First Nations peoples, early settlers and industrialization illustrate the history and economy of the west coast region. The 1870 Moss Cottage depicts late 19th-century family life. Documentary films are shown. In the summer salmon barbecues are scheduled; reservations are required. Guided tours are available. Allow 30 minutes minimum. Daily 9-5. Museum by donations. Moss Cottage $2; $1 (ages 13+ and students with ID). Lighthouse tours $3; $1.50 (ages 13+ and students with ID). Phone (250) 642-6351.

VIEW ROYAL (H-10)
pop. 7,271, elev. 22 m/72′

CRAIGFLOWER MANOR is at 110 Island Hwy., jct. Admirals Rd. Built in 1856 on an original homestead, the farmhouse is a fine example of early Georgian architecture. The heavy oak door reinforced with iron studs is a reminder of the British class system. Farm animals, on view in the summer, and a kitchen garden complement the atmosphere. The schoolhouse was built by the Craigflower farmhouse workers for their children.

Allow 30 minutes minimum. Daily 11-5, May-Sept. Admission $6; $4 (ages 13-18 and senior citizens). Reservations are required Oct.-Apr. MC. Phone (250) 386-1606.

This ends listings for the Victoria Vicinity.
The following page resumes the alphabetical listings of cities in British Columbia.

VIEW ROYAL—*see Victoria p. 195.*

WARDNER (D-12) pop. 100

KOOTENAY TROUT HATCHERY is 8 km (5 mi.) n. on the e. side of the Kootenay River at 4522 Fenwick Rd. The facility raises 3 million trout annually. An aquarium contains fish species raised at the hatchery, including the rare white sturgeon. Displays explain fish raising. An outside moat holds large rainbow trout. Allow 30 minutes minimum. Daily 8-4, May-Sept.; 8-3:30, rest of year. Donations. Phone (250) 429-3214.

WESTBANK—*see Okanagan Valley p. 146*

WEST VANCOUVER—*see Vancouver p. 180.*

WHISTLER (G-12)
pop. 8,896, elev. 640 m/2,009'

Whistler, a popular year-round resort village and skiing destination, is cradled by Whistler and Blackcomb mountains.

Walking trails start at Whistler Village for such destinations as Alta and Lost lakes, nearby alpine meadows and glacier regions. Mountain biking enthusiasts can test their mettle atop Whistler Mountain. Climbing to 6,000 feet, a gondola or chairlift ride up Whistler and Blackcomb mountains, respectively, affords a breathtaking view of the surround. The Valley Trail is available for roller skating, cycling and walking. Day excursions to the southern Cariboo region are available aboard the British Columbia Railway. This railway also makes daily runs to Whistler from North Vancouver; phone (604) 984-5246.

Several golf courses as well as tennis facilities and riding stables provide additional opportunities to enjoy the area in summer. The Whistler River is known for white-water rafting.

For information about the many private sightseeing companies, including float plane services, contact Whistler Resort Association, 4010 Whistler Way, Whistler, BC, Canada V0N 1B0; phone (604) 664-5625 or (800) 944-7853.

Tourism Whistler: 4010 Whistler Way, Whistler, BC V0N 1B4; phone (604) 938-2769 or (877) 991-9988, ext. 17.

Shopping areas: Whistler Village features more than 150 specialty shops in a pedestrian enclave.

BLACKCOMB HORSEDRAWN SLEIGH RIDES depart from Base II on Blackcomb Mountain, at the end of Glacier Dr. Tours of the wooded countryside stop at a warming cabin, where musical entertainment is provided. Lunch and dinner sleigh rides also are available by reservation. Trips daily on the hour 5-8, Nov. 25-Mar. 31. Fare $55; $45 (ages 13-18); $35 (ages 3-12). Phone (604) 932-7631.

WHISTLER AIR SERVICES is 3 km (1.9 mi.) n. on Hwy. 99, following signs. The company offers 30- to 70-minute floatplane tours over glaciers, ice caps

or alpine lakes. Trips depart daily Apr.-Nov. (weather permitting). Fare $129-$229; half-price (ages 0-11 with two adults). Reservations are required. MC, VI. Phone (604) 932-6615 or (888) 806-2299.

RECREATIONAL ACTIVITIES
Mountain Biking

• **Whistler Mountain Bike Park** is at the base of Whistler Mountain. Other activities are offered. Daily 10-8, June-early Sept.; 10-5, early Sept.- early Oct. Phone (604) 932-3434 or (866) 218-9690.

Skiing

• **Whistler/Blackcomb Mountain** is on Hwy. 99. Write 4545 Blackcomb Way, Whistler, BC, Canada V0N 1B4. Other activities are offered. Whistler daily mid-Nov. to early June. Blackcomb mid-Nov. to early Apr. Phone (604) 932-3434 or (800) 766-0449.

White-water Rafting

• **Canadian Outback Adventures** departs from various locations in Whistler. Write 332 East Esplanade, Suite 200, North Vancouver, BC, Canada V7L 1A4. Other activities are available. Tours daily 9-5, May-Sept. Shuttles depart at 7:30, 10:15 and 1. Phone (604) 924-9191 or (800) 565-8735.

• [SAVE] **Whistler River Adventures** departs from 4165 Springs Ln. at the base of the Whistler Mountain gondola in Whistler Village. Write P.O. Box 202, Whistler, BC, Canada V0N 1B0. Other activities are offered. Trips depart daily 8-8, May 17-Sept. 1. Phone (604) 932-3532 or (888) 932-3532 within British Columbia.

Winter Activities

• **Cougar Mountain Wilderness Adventures** is at 18-4314 Main St., Whistler, BC, Canada V0N 1B6. Other activities are offered. Daily 8:30-8, Dec.-Mar.; 8:30-7, June-Sept.; 9-5, rest of year. Phone (604) 932-4086 or (888) 297-2222.

WILLIAMS LAKE (G-5) pop. 11,153

The rush for gold brought prospectors to the heart of the Cariboo in the 1860s, but it was the 1920s Canadian Railway push that put Williams Lake on the map. Cattle ranching and timber production now are the economic mainstays. Twenty kilometres (12 mi.) north of Williams Lake, Bull Mountain Trails offers 30 kilometres (19 mi.) of trails for cross-country skiing, hiking and mountain biking.

Williams Lake and District Chamber of Commerce: 1660 S. Broadway, Williams Lake, BC, Canada V2G 2W4; phone (250) 392-5025 or (877) 967-5253.

MUSEUM OF THE CARIBOO CHILCOTIN is at 113 N. Fourth Ave. Highlights include the BC Cowboys Hall of Fame and displays portraying the ranching and rodeo history of the Cariboo Chilcotin. Artifacts and photographs depict the lifestyles of cowboys and ranchers as well as First Nations peoples. Allow 30 minutes minimum. Mon.-Sat. 10-4, June-Aug.; Tues.-Sat. 11-4, rest of year. Closed Jan. 1, Good Friday and Dec. 25. Admission $2; free (ages 0-12). Phone (250) 392-7404.

SCOUT ISLAND NATURE CENTER is off Hwy. 97 just e. of jct. Hwy. 20, s. on McKenzie Ave., then e. on Borland Rd. Nature trails lead to views of Williams Lake. The island and marsh are prime nesting grounds for migratory birds. A nature house offers interactive displays, a marsh aquarium and a beehive. A viewing platform on the roof provides a vista of the marsh and valley. Walking trails, interpretive signs and an arboretum are on-site.

Grounds daily 8-dusk. Nature house Mon.-Wed. 9-5, Thurs.-Fri. 9-6, Sat.-Sun. 1-4, May-Aug. Hours may vary; phone ahead. Donations.

YALE (C-7) pop. 171

Settled at the southern entrance to Fraser Canyon, Yale was a major steamship port during the gold rush. The town was established in 1848 as a Hudson's Bay Co. fort, taking its name from the commander of Fort Langley. After gold was discovered on Hill's Bar in 1858, Yale's population swelled to 30,000. In later years the number dwindled to 200. Several buildings from the mid-1800s still stand, and a pioneer cemetery contains Victorian monuments to early settlers.

The Alexandra Suspension Bridge, 22 kilometres (14 mi.) north of town, was constructed in 1863 to ferry miners across the Fraser River. From the bridge, which was rebuilt in 1926 with the original foundations, the original wagon road to the Cariboo goldfields is visible. A hiking trail leading to the nearby Spirit Caves offers views of the canyon.

YALE HISTORIC SITE is at 31187 Douglas St. The museum displays artifacts about mining, paddlewheelers, the Canadian Pacific Railway, early settlers and the First Nations. The Church of St. John the Divine has served the area since it was built in 1863. Guided walking tours of the old townsite are offered in the summer. Gold panning instructions and trips also are available.

Picnicking is permitted. Daily 10-5, Apr. 15-Oct. 15. Museum admission $5; $4.50 (senior citizens); $3 (ages 6-18); $15 (family, two adults and two children ages 0-17). Walking tour (includes museum) $10; $9.50 (senior citizens); $8 (ages 6-18). Gold panning (includes museum) $12; $11 (senior citizens); $10 (ages 6-18). MC, VI. Phone (604) 863-2324.

RECREATIONAL ACTIVITIES
White-water Rafting

• **Fraser River Raft Expeditions** is 1 km (.6 mi.) w. on Hwy. 1. Write P.O. Box 10, Yale, BC,

Canada V0K 2S0. Daily early May-late Sept.; departure times vary with trip. Phone (604) 863-2336 or (800) 363-7238.

▼ YOHO NATIONAL PARK OF CANADA (A-11)

Elevations in the park range from 1,098 metres (3,600 ft.) at the West Gate of the park to 3,562 metres (11,686 ft.) on Mount Goodsir at the South Tower. Refer to CAA/AAA maps for additional elevation information.

Reached by hwys. 1 and 93, Yoho National Park of Canada covers 1,310 square kilometres (507 sq. mi.) just west of the Great Divide and Banff National Park of Canada. The word *yoho* is an exclamation of wonder or astonishment in the language of the Cree Indians.

In 1884 the Canadian Pacific Railway laid tracks through Kicking Horse Pass, discovered by Sir James Hector during his search for the best transportation route through the Rockies. The Trans-Canada Hwy. later was built along this same route.

Open mid-June through September as weather permits, the 13-kilometre-long (7.8-mi.) Yoho Valley Road winds up a narrow valley between high, wooded mountain slopes. Takakkaw Falls ("magnificent" in the Cree language) drops 380 metres (1,265 ft.) in all, its highest sheer fall being 254 metres (833 ft.), making it one of the highest falls in Canada.

Other sights in the park include Natural Bridge, Emerald Lake, Wapta Falls and the Spiral Tunnels of the Canadian Pacific Railway. The lower Spiral Tunnel can be viewed from the Trans-Canada Hwy., 7 kilometres (4 mi.) east of Field. The upper Spiral Tunnel can be viewed from the Yoho Valley Road.

The park also contains the Burgess Shale fossil beds, which have preserved fossils of more than 120 species, including rare soft-bodied creatures dating back 515 million years to the Cambrian period.

Specimens from the beds are displayed at the park's visitor information center.

General Information and Activities

Although the park is open all year, most facilities and interpretive programs operate only during July and August. However, a park information center on Hwy. 1 at Field is open year-round. The Trans-Canada Hwy. traverses the park and provides access to most of its roads and trails.

Access to the Burgess Shale fossil beds is limited to guided tours during July and August; fees range from $25-$70. Full-day round trips cover 19 kilometres (12 mi.) and are considered strenuous. Reservations are required; phone (800) 343-3006 Mon.-Fri. 10-3 in season.

There are several campgrounds in the park. Prices range from $16-$30 for sites and $7.90 for firewood. A wilderness pass is required to stay overnight in the backcountry. Passes are $9 per person each night and are available from the visitor information center.

Hiking trails range from nature walks to extended back-country trips; travelers on overnight outings should register at the visitor information center or with a park warden. Fishing, particularly rewarding to those in search of char and many other varieties of trout, requires a $29.70 annual permit, or an $8.90 1-day permit.

Horses, canoes and rowboats are available for rent at Emerald Lake. Winter activities include cross-country skiing, snowshoeing, ice climbing, back-country ski touring and winter camping. *See the Recreation Chart and the AAA/CAA Western Canada & Alaska CampBook.*

ADMISSION to the park is $8.90; $7.65 (ages 65+); $4.45 (ages 6-16); $17.80 (all occupants of a private vehicle with up to seven people). AX, MC, VI.

ADDRESS inquiries to the Superintendent, Yoho National Park of Canada, P.O. Box 99, Field, BC, Canada V0A 1G0; phone (250) 343-6783.

Manitoba

Location is Everything
Winnipeg's position at the junction of two rivers led to its prominence as a trading post

Nature Made
Lakes, forests, rolling prairies and subarctic tundra are part of Manitoba's landscape

Polar Bears and Beluga Whales
Churchill is the place for viewing these magnificent creatures of the wild

The Water's Fine
Myriad lakes and rivers are popular with anglers, canoeists and boaters

Interpretive Sites
Manitoba's history is remembered at restored forts and trading posts

Churchill
© Milse / age fotostock

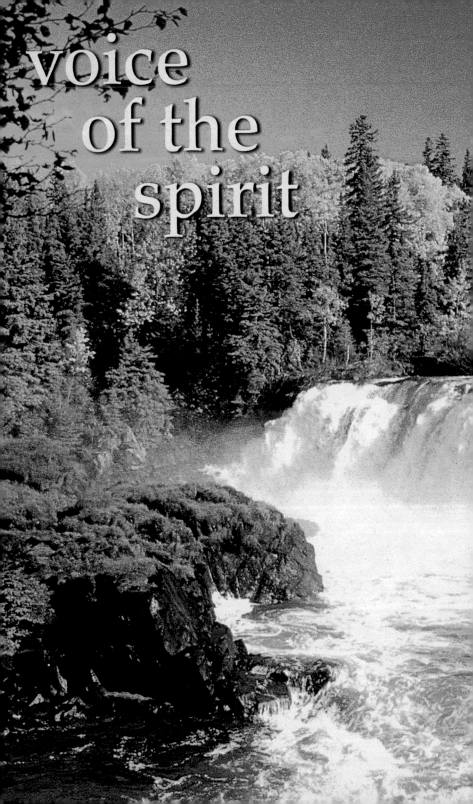

voice
of the
spirit

Pisew Falls Provincial Park,
south of Thompson
Travel Manitoba

Waves pound a rock-strewn shore at the narrows of Lake Manitoba, producing a noise oddly like a beating drum. To the Cree Indians, this sound was the great spirit Manitou, whose name was given to the lake and, in 1870, the entire province.

From clear water lapping in giant lakes— Winnipeg, Winnipegosis and Manitoba—to the rustling sigh of wind across golden seas of wheat, the great spirit of this province speaks with many voices and conveys many moods.

It echoes in the plaintive cry of migrating geese winging south and the hoarse chuffing of a protective mother polar bear herding her cubs along Hudson Bay's icy shore.

The spirit sings within a chorus of steel wheels as trains carry freight across the prairies from west to east and back again. It proclaims itself in the bustling streets of Winnipeg, where sundry languages—French, English, Ukrainian, Chinese and others—blend into a rich, evocative murmur, and laughs amid the joyous din of the city's various celebrations.

Even the silence deep within Manitoba's immense evergreen forests seems heavy with something left unsaid.

A province this vast has a lot to say; make the journey and let it speak to you.

Look north into the night sky. There. See it? A faint glow high above the horizon. . . .

Watch as an arc of yellow light gradually forms. As it drifts upward, shimmering yellow-green streamers rise from it, rippling like a breeze-blown curtain. New arcs appear lined with bright amber streaks that curl like wisps of smoke. Eventually the swirls of color fade and darkness returns, ending your encounter with the aurora borealis.

In Manitoba you won't have to wait long for a repeat performance. This far north you can count on basking in the aurora's eerie luminescence nearly 90 nights a year. Even citizens of Winnipeg, the capital, are often treated to this celestial light show, despite living in the province's extreme south.

Gem of the Prairies

Sky-obscuring pollution may be the bane of many cities, but Winnipeg's clean air isn't likely to spoil your auroral view. And while multihued lights dance overhead, visitors to the "Gem of the Prairies" can enjoy an equally colorful cultural spectrum spread out before them. Home to more than half of all Manitobans, Winnipeg is a city of surprising diversity; the Ellice-Sargent neighborhood alone boasts 43 resident nationalities. Here it's not unusual to find a German butcher shop sandwiched between an Italian clothing store and a Vietnamese restaurant, all within a few steps of a Portuguese cafe.

Finding the cuisine you crave is a snap in this polyglot town. For Italian, follow your nose to the source of the garlic-tinged scents wafting from Corydon Avenue, Winnipeg's Little Italy. Here you'll find delicious pastas galore—from agnolotti to tufoli—and a table at a sidewalk bistro is perfect for people-watching while you nibble on a biscotti.

Those desiring a bit of Gallic flavor should saunter over to St. Boniface, home to Canada's largest French community west of the province of Québec. Restaurants serving French dishes are easy to find here, especially along Provencher Boulevard. And in winter St. Boniface comes alive during Le Festival du Voyageur, when Winnipegers turn out to celebrate the *joie de vivre* of the French fur traders who explored the area.

Red northern lights were once regarded as omens of war. If so, the skies must have shone red fairly often during the 18th century

Manitoba Historical Timeline

Capt. Thomas Button winters at Port Nelson on Hudson Bay and claims the land for England.
1612

Travel Manitoba

Henry Kelsey of the Hudson's Bay Co. spends 2 years exploring the province to find new sources of fur.
1690-92

The Red River Colony, Manitoba's first permanent settlement, is established with a land grant from the Hudson's Bay Co.
1812

1738
French fur-trader Pierre Gaultier de la Vérendrye arrives at the site now known as Winnipeg.

1869-70
The Métis, native people of mixed European and Indian ancestry, are led by Louis Riel in the Red River Rebellion to protect their language and property rights.

as conflicts escalated between French *voyageurs* and their English rivals. During this strife-ridden period, Fort Rouge—site of modern Winnipeg—was established where the Red and Assiniboine rivers meet.

. Now known as The Forks, this riverfront area is a park where you can take a tree-shaded stroll past splashing fountains and vibrantly hued flower beds. During warm weather, people flock to the numerous festivals held here, including Winnipeg's International Children's Festival in early June.

Nearby, The Manitoba Museum invites visitors to take a whirlwind tour of the entire province by way of seven main galleries. And to learn more about auroras, stop by the museum's planetarium.

The Great White North

Follow your compass farther north and the chances of seeing Mother Nature's silent fireworks multiply. The northern lights not only occur more frequently in Manitoba's subarctic areas, but are brighter, too. In towns like Churchill, the lights are a major attraction.

But the real stars in this small community are its big, furry neighbors: polar bears. Sightings of the great white animals are common in October, when they migrate onto rapidly freezing Hudson Bay to fish, and late June, when thawing ice forces a return to shore.

The best way to meet these deceptively cuddly looking carnivores is safely ensconced in a specially designed, balloon-tired tundra vehicle. Climb aboard one for an unforgettable in-the-wild encounter. And when you're ready to thaw out, visit Churchill's Eskimo Museum, which is filled with ancient Inuit tools and other artifacts, as well as the recent, burnished wildlife sculptures carved in serpentine that are prized by international collectors.

Well-acquainted with the aurora's haunting glow, the Inuits crafted stories as elaborate as their carvings to explain what they saw. According to one tale, the lights are torches lit by spirits to guide those who will follow across the narrow bridge to heaven.

But you don't have to study Inuit mythology to appreciate the northern lights' otherworldly beauty, nor must you understand the scientific principles behind the phenomenon. All you really need to know is that the skies in Manitoba are perfect for admiring them.

Manitoba becomes the fifth Canadian province.
1870

Manitoba's boundary is extended north to Hudson Bay.
1912

Manitoba's French speakers win an important victory when the Supreme Court rules that all provincial laws passed since 1870 are invalid because they were written only in English.
1986

1900-13
Manitoba's grain production increases dramatically, and Winnipeg becomes the trade center for the prairie region.

© PhotoDisc

1997
More than 25,000 residents between the U.S. border and Winnipeg are forced to evacuate as Red River flood waters surge north.

1999
The Pan Am Games are held in Winnipeg.

Recreation

The overwhelming bulk of Manitoba's populace resides in a thin strip just above the U.S. border, which leaves a vast region of unspoiled territory farther north that's prime for exploration.

Much of the province's outdoor fun involves its 100,000 lakes and the many rivers that link them.

Colorful sails glide across the surface of Lake Winnipeg as **windsurfing** enthusiasts take advantage of breezy days. Put in at Grand Beach Provincial Park, at the far southeast end of the lake. **Canoeing** down the Grass River, near the junction of hwys. 10 and 39, gives you the opportunity to see the beauty of the northern frontier.

Manitoba's lakes are home to dozens of species of fish, including walleye, northern pike, smallmouth bass, trout, arctic grayling, sturgeon and channel catfish. Fly-in fishing—at such isolated spots as Aikens and Dogskin lakes, northeast of Bissett in Atikaki Provincial Park; Gods Lake, Gods River, Knee Lake, and Island Lake, all in northeast Manitoba; and Big Sand, Egenolf, and Nueltin lakes in the northwest region—attracts anglers of all skill levels. Contact Manitoba Conservation for information about licensing and regulations; phone (204) 945-6784.

Chilling Out

When the lakes freeze over, **ice fishing** and **ice skating** warm up as favored pursuits. Smooth blankets of snow—at such places as Assiniboine Park in Winnipeg—are irresistible for **snowshoeing** and **cross-country skiing.**

Many adventurers, too, have a hard time resisting the many **snowmobiling** trails that criss-cross the province. Kick up some powder in Duck Mountain and Turtle Mountain provincial parks.

Although **downhill skiing** is hard to come by in a province that's known mostly for its lowlands, skiers can take on 21 runs at Asessippi and Winter Park ski areas.

For **tobogganing** fun, head for the slides at Kildonan Park in Winnipeg.

Riding Mountain National Park of Canada rises from the flat prairie to provide a wealth of opportunity for activity. Self-guiding **hiking** trails range from the easy Beach Ridges Trail to the difficult Bald Hill Trail, named for the barren hill towering over scores of lush, green trees. Most memorable is the grueling but beautiful Ochre River Trail, which entices both trekkers and cross-country skiers.

The park's Clear Lake Trail is a challenging **cycling** route that traverses part of an unmaintained Indian reserve. Before tackling the entire 25-kilometre (16-mile) trail, obtain permission from the reserve; phone (204) 625-2004. **Mountain bikers** favor the exhilarating J.E.T. Trail, which rewards risk-takers with great views from the ridge. The multiuse Central Trail, the longest at 73 kilometres (45 miles), is especially popular for **horseback riding.**

Taking A Dive

Even **scuba divers** can indulge their passion in the crystal waters of Clear Lake. Register with the park before heading to facilities at Glen Beag day-use area. Divers also frequent West Hawk Lake, Manitoba's deepest. Formed by a meteorite, the lake is near the eastern entrance to Whiteshell Provincial Park.

Cree for "white bear," Wapusk National Park of Canada fittingly lives up to its name as a hot spot for polar bear viewing.

Black bears, whitetail deer, caribou and moose are among the big game species that contribute to the province's excellent rifle and bow **hunting** reputation.

An abundance of specimens draws **rockhounders** to Flin Flon, Souris, Thompson and Bissett, a former gold-mining town northwest of Nopiming Provincial Park. Contact the Deputy Office of Government Services for maps and information about rocks and minerals; phone (204) 945-1119.

Recreational Activities

Throughout the TourBook, you may notice a Recreational Activities heading with bulleted listings of recreation-oriented establishments listed underneath. Similar operations also may be mentioned in Destination City recreation sections. Since normal AAA inspection criteria cannot be applied, these establishments are presented only for information. Age, height and weight restrictions may apply. Reservations often are recommended and sometimes are required. Addresses and/or phone numbers are provided so visitors can contact the attraction for additional information.

Fast Facts

POPULATION: 1,148,401.

AREA: 552,370 sq km (213,270 sq mi); ranks 8th.

CAPITAL: Winnipeg.

HIGHEST POINT: 831 m/2,727 ft., Baldy Mountain.

LOWEST POINT: Sea level, Churchill.

TIME ZONE(S): Central. DST.

MINIMUM AGE FOR UNRESTRICTED DRIVER'S LICENSE: 17 years, 6 months.

MINIMUM AGE FOR GAMBLING: 18.

SEAT BELT/CHILD RESTRAINT LAWS: Seat belts required for driver and all passengers age 5 and over. Child restraints required for under age 5 and under 23 kg. (50 lbs.). Ages 5-17 and over 23 kg. (50 lbs.) are required to be in a child restraint or seat belt.

HELMETS FOR MOTORCYCLISTS: Required for all riders.

RADAR DETECTORS: Not permitted.

FIREARMS LAWS: By federal law, all nonresidents entering Canada with a firearm must declare their weapon in writing and pay a fee of $25 (Canadian). Contact the Canadian Firearms Centre at (800) 731-4000 to receive a declaration form or for additional information.

HOLIDAYS: Jan. 1; Good Friday; Easter; Easter Monday; Victoria Day, May 24 (if a Mon.) or the closest prior Mon.; Canada Day, July 1; Civic Holiday, Aug. (1st Mon.); Labour Day, Sept. (1st Mon.); Thanksgiving, Oct. (2nd Mon.); Remembrance Day, Nov. 11; Christmas, Dec. 25; Boxing Day, Dec. 26.

TAXES: In addition to Manitoba's provincial sales tax of 7 percent, there is a national 6 percent Goods and Services Tax (GST).

INFORMATION CENTERS: Free travel literature and information are available at the following locations: Canada/United States border, Hwy. 75 at Emerson (daily 8 a.m.-9 p.m., mid-May to early Sept.; Thurs.-Mon. 9-5, rest of year); Canada/United States border, Hwy. 10 at the International Peace Garden (daily 8 a.m.-9 p.m., mid-May to early Sept.); Manitoba/Ontario boundary, Hwy. 1E just east of West Hawk Lake (daily 8 a.m.-9 p.m., mid-May through Labour Day; Tues.-Sat. 9-4, day after Labour Day-second Mon. in Oct.); Manitoba/Saskatchewan boundaries on Hwy. 1W west of Kirkella, and Hwy. 16W near Russell (daily 8 a.m.-9 p.m., mid-May to early Sept.); and the Explore Manitoba Centre at The Forks National Historic Site of Canada in Winnipeg (daily 10-6).

FURTHER INFORMATION FOR VISITORS:

Travel Manitoba
155 Carlton St., 7th Floor
Winnipeg, MB, Canada R3C 3H8
(204) 927-7838
(800) 665-0040, ext. RM5

Explore Manitoba Centre
The Forks National Historic Site of Canada
21 Forks Market Rd.
Winnipeg, MB, Canada R3C 4T7
(204) 927-7838
(800) 665-0040

RECREATION INFORMATION:

Manitoba Conservation
Parks and Natural Areas
200 Saulteaux Crescent
Winnipeg, MB, Canada R3J 3W3
(204) 945-6784
(800) 214-6497

ALCOHOL CONSUMPTION: Legal age 18.

SPECIAL REGULATIONS: Dogs and cats transported from the United States must have proof of rabies vaccination.

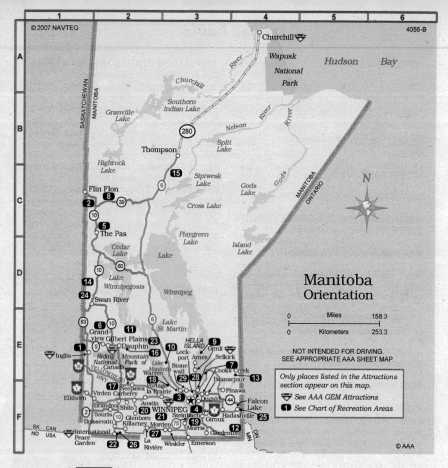

Manitoba
Orientation

	Miles	158.3
0		
0	Kilometers	253.3

NOT INTENDED FOR DRIVING.
SEE APPROPRIATE AAA SHEET MAP.

Only places listed in the Attractions
section appear on this map.

▼ See AAA GEM Attractions
❶ See Chart of Recreation Areas

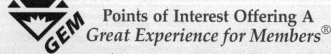

Points of Interest Offering A
Great Experience for Members®

Churchill (A-4)

ESKIMO MUSEUM—The museum's collections of
Inuit artifacts are among the finest in the world.
See p. 212.

Inglis (E-1)

**INGLIS GRAIN ELEVATORS NATIONAL HISTORIC
SITE**—These five restored wooden grain elevators
are the sole survivors of what once was a common sight on Canadian prairies. See p. 215.

International Peace
Garden (F-2)

INTERNATIONAL PEACE GARDEN—The friendship
shared by Canada and the United States along

the world's longest unfortified border is celebrated at this park that straddles the Manitoba/
North Dakota border. See p. 215.

Riding Mountain National
Park of Canada (E-2)

**RIDING MOUNTAIN NATIONAL PARK OF
CANADA**—The park's grasslands, forests and
lakes are home to a diverse population that includes elk, bears and moose as well as pike and
several varieties of trout. See p. 218.

Selkirk (E-3)

**LOWER FORT GARRY NATIONAL HISTORIC SITE
OF CANADA**—Costumed interpreters re-create

daily life during the 1850s at this restored stone fur-trading outpost. See p. 219.

Winnipeg (F-3)

DALNAVERT MUSEUM—The 1895 home of a prominent lawyer and politician is furnished with Victorian antiques. See p. 229.

THE FORKS—People meet today at The Forks just as they have for over 6,000 years; a national historic site, a marketplace and a children's museum currently occupy the area at the confluence of the Red and Assiniboine rivers. See p. 229.

MANITOBA CHILDREN'S MUSEUM—Fun and learning go hand-in-hand in this museum's six galleries. See p. 229.

THE MANITOBA MUSEUM—The museum's exhibits, audiovisual presentations and dioramas all center on a common theme—the historical relationship of Manitoba's citizens and the environment of the province. See p. 231.

ROYAL CANADIAN MINT—A production facility for Canadian and foreign coins, the facility is considered one of the world's most modern; a viewing gallery provides an observation point. See p. 231.

RECREATION AREAS

	MAP LOCATION	CAMPING	PICNICKING	HIKING TRAILS	BOATING	BOAT RAMP	BOAT RENTAL	FISHING	SWIMMING	PETS ON LEASH	BICYCLE TRAILS	WINTER SPORTS	VISITOR CENTER	LODGE/CABINS	FOOD SERVICE
NATIONAL PARKS *(See place listings)*															
Riding Mountain (E-2) 2,978 square kilometres. Backpacking, cross-country skiing, golf, hiking, horseback riding, scuba diving, tennis, water skiing, wind surfing; boat cruises, paddleboats.		•	•	•	•	•	•	•	•	•	•	•	•	•	•
Wapusk (A-5) 11,475 square kilometres. Polar bear viewing.										•					
PROVINCIAL															
Asessippi (E-1) 2,330 hectares 13 km from Shellmouth Dam on Hwy. 83. Fishing, snowmobiling; nature trail.	**1**	•	•	•	•	•		•	•	•		•	•		•
Bakers Narrows (C-1) 145 hectares 27 km s. of Flin Flon on Hwy. 10. Board sailing, canoeing; playground, wildlife watching.	**2**	•	•		•	•		•	•			•	•	•	
Beaudry (F-3) 939 hectares 10 km w. of Winnipeg on Roblin Blvd./Hwy. 241.	**3**		•	•	•			•		•					
Birds Hill (F-3) 3,550 hectares 24 km n.e. of Winnipeg on Hwy. 59. Cross-country skiing, horseback riding, snowmobiling; interpretive programs, playground, wildlife watching.	**4**	•	•	•					•		•	•			
Clearwater Lake (C-2) 59,265 hectares 19 km n. of The Pas on Hwy. 10, then 2.5 km e. on Hwy. 287. Cross-country skiing, snowmobiling; interpretive trail.	**5**	•	•	•	•	•		•	•	•		•		•	•
Duck Mountain (E-2) 142,430 hectares 56 km n. of Roblin off Hwy. 83. Canoeing, cross-country skiing, snowmobiling.	**6**	•	•	•	•	•		•	•	•		•		•	•
Grand Beach (E-4) 2,490 hectares 80 km n.e. of Winnipeg on Hwy. 59, then 6 km w. on Hwy 12. Cross-country skiing, sailing, snowmobiling, tennis, windsurfing; interpretive programs, sand beaches.	**7**	•	•	•	•	•		•	•	•		•	•		•
Grass River (C-2) 228,018 hectares at Cranberry Portage off Hwy. 10. Canoeing; interpretive trail.	**8**	•	•	•	•	•		•	•	•				•	•
Hecla/Grindstone (E-3) 108,440 hectares 165 km n. of Winnipeg via Hwy. 8. Cross-country skiing, golf, sailing, snowmobiling, tennis, windsurfing; interpretive programs. *(See Hecla Island p. 215)*	**9**	•	•	•	•	•		•	•	•		•	•	•	•
Lundar Beach (E-3) 23 hectares 18 km w. of Lundar on Hwy. 419.	**10**	•	•		•	•		•	•	•			•		
Manipogo (E-2) 61 hectares 47 km n. of Dauphin on Hwy. 20. Board sailing; playground, wildlife watching.	**11**	•	•		•	•		•	•						
Moose Lake (F-4) 956 hectares 30 km n.e. of Sprague on Hwy. 308. Board sailing, canoeing, snowmobiling; playground, wildlife watching.	**12**	•	•		•			•	•				•	•	•
Nopiming (E-4) 142,910 hectares 70 km n.e. of Lac du Bonnet. Canoeing; interpretive trail.	**13**	•	•					•	•	•				•	
North Steeprock Lake (D-1) 13 hectares 3 km n. of Birch River on Hwy. 10, then 40 km w. on Hwy. 365.	**14**	•	•		•	•		•	•						
Paint Lake (C-3) 8,848 hectares 32 km s. of Thompson on Hwy. 6. Canoeing, cross-country skiing, ice skating, snowmobiling, tobogganing, windsurfing.	**15**	•	•		•	•		•	•	•		•	•		•	•

RECREATION AREAS

	MAP LOCATION	CAMPING	PICNICKING	HIKING TRAILS	BOATING	BOAT RAMP	BOAT RENTAL	FISHING	SWIMMING	PETS ON LEASH	BICYCLE TRAILS	WINTER SPORTS	VISITOR CENTER	LODGE/CABINS	FOOD SERVICE
Rainbow Beach (E-2) 52 hectares 17 km e. of Dauphin on Hwy. 20. Board sailing, golfing; playground, wildlife watching.	16	•	•	•	•	•		•	•		•				
Rivers (F-2) 37 hectares 14 km n. of Brandon on Hwy. 10, then 26 km w. on Hwy. 25. Playground.	17	•	•		•	•	•		•						
St. Ambroise Beach (F-2) 46 hectares 47 km w. of Winnipeg on Hwy. 1, then 35 km n. on Hwy. 430. Windsurfing; interpretive trail.	18	•	•		•	•		•	•	•					
St. Malo (F-3) 148 hectares 64 km s. of Winnipeg on Hwy. 59. Motorized boats not allowed.	19	•	•	•	•			•	•	•					
Spruce Woods (F-2) 26,950 hectares 20 km s.e. of Carberry on Hwy. 5. Canoeing, cross-country skiing, ice skating, snowmobiling, tobogganing; horseback riding trails, interpretive programs. *(See Carberry p. 210)*	20	•	•	•	•	•		•	•	•	•	•	•		
Stephenfield (F-2) 94 hectares 10 km w. of Carman on Hwy. 245. Board sailing, golfing; playground.	21	•	•	•	•	•	•	•	•	•					
Turtle Mountain (F-2) 18,570 hectares 23 km s. of Boissevain off Hwy. 10. Cross-country skiing, ice skating, snowmobiling, tobogganing; interpretive trail, horse trails. *(See Boissevain p. 209)*	22	•	•	•	•	•	•	•	•	•	•	•	•		
Watchorn (E-2) 10 hectares 11 km w. of Moosehorn on Hwy. 237. Playground.	23	•	•		•	•		•	•	•					
Whitefish Lake (D-1) 24 hectares 13 km n. of Swan River, then 28 km w. on Hwy. 279. Playground.	24	•	•		•	•		•	•	•					
Whiteshell (F-4) 272,090 hectares off Hwy. 1 at Falcon lake, near the Ontario border. Cross-country skiing, downhill skiing, golf, horseback riding, sailing, snowmobiling, tennis, tobogganing, windsurfing; interpretive programs, museum. *(See Falcon Lake p. 213)*	25	•	•	•	•	•	•	•	•	•	•	•	•	•	•
William Lake (F-2) 199 hectares 7 km e. of Horton, then 8 km s. Amphitheater, playground.	26	•	•	•	•	•		•	•	•					
OTHER															
Kildonan (F-3) 40 hectares at 2021 Main St. in Winnipeg. Cross-country skiing, ice skating, tobogganing; pool. *(See Winnipeg p. 230)*			•	•					•	•		•	•		
La Barriere (F-3) 21 hectares 6 km s. of jct. Waverley St. and Perimeter Hwy. in Winnipeg. Canoeing, cross-country skiing, naturalist-guided hikes, snowshoeing.			•	•				•		•		•			
Lake Minnewasta (F-2) 125 hectares 2 km w. of Morden on Hwy. 3, then 1 km s. on Hwy. 434.	27	•	•	•	•	•		•	•	•		•			•
Selkirk Park (E-3) 81 hectares on the banks of the Red River at Eveline St. in Selkirk. Cross-country skiing, ice fishing; bird sanctuary.	28	•	•	•	•			•	•	•					
Stonewall Quarry (F-3) 30 hectares 4 blks. n. on Main St. in Stonewall. Nature programs. Cross-country skiing, ice skating, tobogganing. *(See Stonewall p. 220)*	29	•	•	•					•	•		•	•	•	•

Manitoba Temperature Averages
Maximum/Minimum (Celsius)
From the records of The Weather Channel Interactive, Inc.

	JAN	FEB	MAR	APR	MAY	JUNE	JULY	AUG	SEPT	OCT	NOV	DEC
The Pas	-17 / -26	-12 / -23	-4 / -17	6 / -6	15 / 2	21 / 9	23 / 12	22 / 11	14 / 5	7 / -1	-4 / -12	-14 / -22
Winnipeg	-13 / -23	-10 / -21	-2 / -13	9 / -3	18 / 4	23 / 10	26 / 13	24 / 12	18 / 6	11 / 0	-1 / -9	-10 / -19

Points of Interest

ARNES (E-3) elev. 225 m/739'

An old fishing village, Arnes today offers sandy beaches, a marina and a nine-hole golf course. A monument to writer and explorer Vilhjalmur Stefansson is inscribed "I know what I have experienced, and I know what it has meant to me," a statement from his autobiography. Born in 1879, Stefansson traveled by boat and dog sled across the Arctic, mapping large areas of the archipelago and collecting ethnological data from the central Arctic coast. He proved through his explorations that it was possible to live off the land in this forbidding area.

Lake Winnipeg Visitor Centre—Arnes: P.O. Box 1246, Gimli, MB, Canada R0C 1B0; phone (204) 642-7974.

AUSTIN (F-2) elev. 262 m/860'

MANITOBA AGRICULTURAL MUSEUM, 2.5 km (1.6 mi.) s. of Hwy. 1 on Hwy. 34, displays a large collection of steam engines, gasoline tractors, farm equipment and artifacts of pioneer farmers. The location also is home of the Manitoba Amateur Radio Museum. Mon.-Sat. 9-5, Sun. 12:30-5, mid-May through Sept. 30. Admission $5; $4 (students with ID and senior citizens); free (ages 0-5); $15 (family). MC. Phone (204) 637-2354.

Homesteaders' Village, at the museum, depicts pioneer life in the late 19th century through furnished buildings of the period. Included are log cabins, an 1883 schoolhouse, two churches, a printing office, blacksmith's shop, grain elevator, pioneer-style store and gristmill. Daily 9-5, mid-May through Sept. 30. Admission included with Manitoba Agricultural Museum.

BEAUSEJOUR (E-3)
pop. 2,823, elev. 247 m/810'

Just 46 kilometres (29 mi.) northeast of Winnipeg, Beausejour is on one of the main roads to Whiteshell Provincial Park (see attraction listing p. 213). Nature enthusiasts take advantage of the walking, hiking and cross-country ski trails available at Wally Chryplywy Nature Park on First Street.

Beausejour and District Chamber of Commerce: P.O. Box 224, Beausejour, MB, Canada R0E 0C0; phone (204) 268-3502 or (204) 268-7550.

BROKEN BEAU HISTORICAL SOCIETY PIONEER VILLAGE MUSEUM, 1 blk. n. of Park Ave. and Seventh St. N., features a reassembled pioneer village with a restored railroad station, a blacksmith shop, a school, an old church, a community hall, a general store, a tailor's shop, a harness shop and a house, as well as pioneer artifacts and farm implements. Allow 1 hour minimum. Mon.-Fri. 1-5, July-Aug.; by appointment rest of year. Admission $4; free (ages 0-14). Phone (204) 268-3048.

BOISSEVAIN (F-1) pop. 1,497

Nearby Turtle Mountain Provincial Park (see Recreation Chart) is named for the western painted turtle, which lives in the park's many shallow lakes. The park is the year-round home of a large number of waterfowl and of migratory birds in spring and fall. A wildlife center also is available.

As a connection to the park, the town has adopted as its symbol an 8.5-metre-tall (28-ft.) statue known as Tommy Turtle, which can be seen beside the visitor center on Hwy. 10.

An outdoor art gallery throughout the town depicts area history by way of more than 20 colorful wall-size murals, including a large scene painted on a grain elevator in downtown Boissevain. Scenic Hwy. 10 leads south to the North Dakota border and the International Peace Garden (see place listing p. 215).

Boissevain & District Tourism Office: P.O. Box 368, Boissevain, MB, Canada R0K 0E0; phone (204) 534-6303 or (800) 497-2393.

Self-guiding tours: Literature for a self-guiding walking tour of the city's historic buildings is available at the Boissevain Visitors Centre on Hwy. 10S.

BECKONING HILLS MUSEUM is at 425 Mill Rd. S. The museum exhibits pioneer artifacts, mementos such as uniforms from World Wars I and II, farming equipment, early photographs and items relating to culture, education and literature. Allow 1 hour minimum. Daily 1-5, June-Sept.; other times by appointment. Donations. Phone (204) 534-6544.

IRVIN GOODON INTERNATIONAL WILDLIFE MUSEUM is at 298 Mountain St. (Hwy. 10). Visitors can gain a better understanding of wildlife through the mounted animals displayed in natural-like dioramas. Each setting provides information about the animals and their behavior. An audiovisual presentation about wildlife is offered.

Guided tours are available. Allow 30 minutes minimum. Mon.-Sat. 10-6, Sun. noon-6, May-Oct.; by appointment rest of year. Admission $7; $6 (ages 60+); $5 (ages 13-16); $3 (ages 6-12). MC, VI. Phone (204) 534-6662.

MONCUR GALLERY & MUSEUM, in the Civic Centre/Library Complex at 420 S. Railway St., contains 10,000 years of archeological history of early southwestern Manitoba. Included in the collection are projectile points, scrapers, ceremonial items and food preparation utensils. Allow 30 minutes minimum. Tues.-Sat. 10-5. Admission $2; $1 (ages 12-17). Phone (204) 534-6478.

BRANDON (F-2)
pop. 41,511, elev. 409 m/1,300'

An agricultural and industrial center, Brandon is the second largest city in the province after Winnipeg and is known for its small-town warmth and big-city amenities.

The Riverbank Discovery Centre, in addition to providing information about Brandon and the surrounding region, is the starting point for the Assiniboine Riverbank Trail System, 17 kilometres (10.5 mi.) of trails that wind throughout Brandon, linking the downtown area with parks, picnic spots and sports venues.

The Keystone Centre, with more than 3.5 hectares (9 acres) under one roof, plays host to some of Manitoba's larger events, concerts and sports competitions; phone (204) 726-3500. The Canada Games Sportsplex offers both winter and summer recreational activities. Built for the 1979 Canada Winter Games, the structure houses racquetball courts, an ice arena, Olympic-size swimming pool, indoor water slide and an outdoor running track; phone (204) 729-2475.

The Brandon Hills Wildlife Management Area, just a short drive south of the city on Hwy. 10 and east along Beresford Road, provides a setting for a variety of recreational pursuits such as hiking, mountain bicycling and cross-country skiing.

Regional Tourism Centre/Riverbank Discovery Centre: #1-545 Conservation Dr., Brandon, MB, Canada R7A 7L8; phone (204) 729-2141 or (888) 799-1111.

Self-guiding tours: A historical walking tour of the residential area between 10th and 18th streets offers interesting architecture and turn-of-the-20th-century homes; a booklet describing the tour is available for $3 from the tourism center.

ART GALLERY OF SOUTHWESTERN MANITOBA, 710 Rosser Ave., features changing exhibits with an emphasis on contemporary Manitoba artists; displays change every 6-7 weeks. Workshops and art classes are offered for a fee. Allow 1 hour minimum. Mon.-Sat. 10-6 (also Thurs. 6-9 p.m., Sept.-June); closed major holidays. Donations. Phone (204) 727-1036.

B.J. HALES MUSEUM OF NATURAL HISTORY is at 270 18th St., on the lower level of the Richardson Library Complex at Brandon University. The museum features a collection of more than 500 mounted Manitoba birds and mammals. Allow 45 minutes minimum. Mon.-Fri. 1:30-4:30 or by appointment; closed major holidays. Donations. Phone (204) 727-7307.

COMMONWEALTH AIR TRAINING PLAN MUSEUM, in Hangar 1 at Brandon Airport, is dedicated to preserving the history of the British Commonwealth Air Training Plan of 1939-45. It has many of the aircraft used for training, photographs, artifacts and memorabilia. Three of the 11 aircraft displayed are in flying condition. A chapel has a book with names of more than 18,000 Canadian Air Force personnel who died during World War II.

Guided tours are available by appointment. Daily 10-4, May-Sept.; 1-4, rest of year. Closed Dec. 25. Admission $5; $3 (ages 6-18). MC, VI. Phone (204) 727-2444.

DALY HOUSE MUSEUM, 122 18th St., was built in 1882 as the home of Brandon's first mayor, Thomas Mayne Daly. It is furnished with late 19th-century upper middle-class pieces and houses photographs and artifacts that relate the city's history. Also featured are a general store and Brandon's old city hall council chambers. A research center on the third floor is available by appointment.

Guided tours are available. Allow 1 hour minimum. Mon.-Sat. 10-noon and 1-5, Sun. 1-4, July-Aug.; Tues.-Sat. 10-noon and 1-5, rest of year. Closed major holidays. Admission $5; $4 (ages 0-17 and 66+); $10 (family, two adults and two children). Phone (204) 727-1722.

WESTMAN REPTILE GARDENS is 19 km (12 mi.) e. on PR 457 to the end of the road, 1.6 km (1 mi.) s. on Wagglesprings Rd. (gravel) to Thompson Rd., then just w. following signs. One of Canada's largest reptile exhibits, the museum has more than 150 displays. Visitors can see rattlesnakes, crocodiles, a giant tarantula, monitors and turtles. Mon.-Sat. 10-8, Sun. and holidays noon-5, Mar.-Oct. Admission $5; $3 (ages 3-15). MC, VI. Phone (204) 763-4030.

CARBERRY (F-2)
pop. 1,502, elev. 369 m/1,210'

The forests and sand dunes of nearby Spruce Woods Provincial Park *(see attraction listing)* inspired many of the works of artist, naturalist and writer Ernest Thompson Seton, including his stories "The Trail of the Sandhill Stag" and "Wild Animals I Have Known." He was appointed naturalist to the Manitoba government in 1892. A small highway park 15 kilometres (9 mi.) east of Carberry on Hwy. 1 has been dedicated to Seton.

Carberry Municipal Offices: P.O. Box 130, Carberry, MB, Canada R0K 0H0; phone (204) 834-6600.

CARBERRY PLAINS MUSEUM, at 520 James White Way, contains pioneer artifacts relating to the area, including period clothing, pictures and furniture as well as displays of original 19th-century art, a schoolroom, a church, a store, a bedroom and a kitchen. Military memorabilia from World Wars I and II also are displayed. Allow 30 minutes minimum. Daily 1-6, June-Sept. Admission $2; $1 (students with ID); $5 (family). Phone (204) 834-6609, or (204) 834-2439 in the off-season.

THE SETON CENTRE, 116 Main St., features artwork and photographs depicting the life and philosophies of writer, artist, naturalist and early conservationist Ernest Thompson Seton. Allow 30 minutes minimum. Tues.-Sat. 9-5, June-Aug.; by appointment rest of year. Donations. Phone (204) 834-2509.

SPRUCE WOODS PROVINCIAL PARK is 25 km (16 mi.) s. on Hwy. 5. The 26,950-hectare (66,593-acre) park, a mosaic of geographic features, includes deciduous forests, creeping sand dunes, white spruce-covered sand hills, pots of quicksand and mixed grass prairie. The Assiniboine River winds through the park. Spirit Sands, rainwater trapped beneath the sandy surface that has emerged to create springs and quicksand, and Devil's Punch Bowl, a bowl-shaped depression, are highlights.

Comfortable walking shoes, a hat and drinking water are recommended. Allow 2 hours minimum. Park open daily 24 hours. Entrance fee $5.95 per vehicle (3-day pass); $24.55 (annual provincial park pass). Phone the visitor center at (204) 827-8850 May-Sept. or (204) 834-8800 rest of year. *See Recreation Chart and Glenboro in the AAA/CAA Western Canada & Alaska CampBook.*

Spirit Sands Wagon Outfitters, 27 km (17 mi.) s.e. on Hwy. 5 in Spruce Woods Provincial Park, offers 90-minute covered wagon rides through the Spirit Sands and Devil's Punch Bowl, providing views of sand dunes, cactuses, rare snakes and lizards, rolling grasslands and marshes. Trips depart daily mid-May through Labour Day. Fare $10; $6 (ages 3-16). Phone (204) 827-2800 for wagon office or (204) 526-2764 off-season.

CHURCHILL (A-4) pop. 923, elev. 29 m/100′

Churchill, on the shore of Hudson Bay, is Canada's northernmost subarctic sea port. It also is the site of the Hudson's Bay Co.'s Prince of Wales Fort National Historic Site of Canada *(see attraction listing),* a partially restored ruin across from Churchill and Cape Merry Battery at the mouth of the Churchill River. Built over a period of 40 years during the 1700s to hold as many as 400 soldiers, the impressive stone fortress housed only 39 untrained men when three French warships mounted a surprise attack in 1782. The fort's governor wisely surrendered without engaging in battle.

After spending 3 unsuccessful days trying to demolish the 12-metre-thick (40-ft.) outer walls, the French abandoned the fort; it was never occupied again. The site is accessible by boat July through August (weather and tides permitting).

The area around Churchill holds an attraction for two giant mammals: the polar bear and the beluga whale. In fact the Churchill region is said to have the greatest concentration of accessible polar bears in the world. Having spent the winter hunting on the frozen bay, the bears come to shore south of Churchill as the ice melts, scatter along the coast and up to 50 kilometres (31 mi.) inland, and then return to the ice in autumn when the bay refreezes. Beluga whales are often sighted off the coast of Cape Merry during July and August.

Other natural features include flowers, arctic plant life, various wildlife and some 200 species of birds, which nest or pass through Churchill on their annual migrations. An excellent spot for bird-watching is Bird Cove, on the coast 16 kilometres (9 mi.) east of Churchill. The aurora borealis (northern lights) seen from Churchill during the fall and winter months are among the most brilliant in the world.

Churchill can be reached only by train or airplane. Via Rail Canada trains run from Winnipeg and Thompson to Churchill; phone (888) 842-7245. Calm Air offers flights from Winnipeg to Churchill; phone (800) 839-2256.

The Parks Canada Visitor Reception Centre offers information, interpretive displays and programs, historical exhibits and videotaped presentations June though November; by appointment rest of year. Phone (204) 675-8863.

Churchill Chamber of Commerce: P.O. Box 176, Churchill, MB, Canada R0B 0E0; phone (204) 675-2022 or (888) 389-2327.

CAPE MERRY NATIONAL HISTORIC SITE, accessible via the Cape Merry Centennial Pkwy., 3 km (1.9 mi.) w. to the e. shore of the Churchill River, is marked by a stone cannon battery built in 1746 to complement the defenses of the Prince of Wales Fort. An original cannon and powder magazine remain. A cairn commemorating Capt. Jens Munk, the first European to enter the Churchill River in 1619, is displayed. The cape offers views of harbor activity as well as whales, waterfowl and the Prince of Wales Fort.

Allow 30 minutes minimum. Daily 24 hours. Parks Canada offers guided tours June-Aug. Donations. Phone (204) 675-8863.

ESKIMO MUSEUM, 242 La Verendrye Ave., contains exhibits that depict the history and culture of the northern region of Canada. Founded in 1944 by Roman Catholic missionaries, it pays tribute to the creativity of the Canadian Inuit people. Highlights of the museum are Inuit carvings in bone, ivory, stone and antler as well as wildlife specimens, artifacts, and tools dating from 1700 B.C. Mon. 1-5, Tues.-Sat. 9-noon and 1-5, June-Nov.; Mon.-Sat. 1-4:30, rest of year. Closed holidays. Donations. Phone (204) 675-2030.

FRONTIERS NORTH'S TUNDRA BUGGY ADVENTURE is at 124 Kelsey Blvd. Specially designed vehicles called Tundra Buggies carry guests on full-day fall tours across the tundra to view polar bears in the Churchill Wildlife Management Area. Half-and full-day summer wildlife and nature tours, also on Tundra Buggies, venture along area shorelines. Multiday beluga whale-watching and ecological boat tours off the coast of Cape Merry also are offered; phone for information.

Full-day Tundra Buggy tours are offered most days, early Oct. to mid-Nov. Half-day wildlife and nature tours are available Tues., Thurs. and Sat., early July-late Sept. Full-day wildlife and nature tours are offered Wed. and Fri., early July-late Sept.

Tundra Buggy fare early Oct. to mid-Oct. $279; $209 (ages 0-11). Tundra Buggy fare mid-Oct. to mid-Nov. $349; $269 (ages 0-11). Half-day wildlife and nature tour fare $109; $79 (ages 0-11). Full-day sightseeing tour fare $189; $139 (ages 0-11). Reservations are required. MC, VI. Phone (204) 675-2121 or (800) 663-9832. *See color ad p. 211.*

SAVE **NORTH STAR TOURS,** 203 La Verendrye St., conducts historical and land-based cultural tours of the Churchill area by bus. Allow 4 hours minimum. Daily 8-1, mid-June to mid-Nov. Fare $93.50; free (children). AX, MC, VI. Phone (204) 675-2356 or (800) 665-0690.

PRINCE OF WALES FORT NATIONAL HISTORIC SITE OF CANADA, at the mouth of the Churchill River, is accessible by boat only. A huge stone fortress built 1731-71 by the Hudson's Bay Co., the fort fell to the French without incident in 1782. Independent whale-watching boat tours, including those offered by Sea North Tours Ltd. *(see attraction listing)* and Lazy Bear Lodge, usually include the fort on their itineraries.

Allow 2 hours minimum. Access is possible on the changing tides 6 hours daily, July-Aug. (weather permitting); by appointment in Sept. Boat fare (site admission included) $80-$86. Phone Parks Canada at (204) 675-8863 for historic site information, or Sea North Tours at (204) 675-2195 or (888) 348-7591 for tour information, or Lazy Bear Lodge at (204) 675-2969.

SEA NORTH TOURS LTD., 39 Franklin St., offers boat tours to Prince of Wales Fort National Historic Site of Canada *(see attraction listing)* in craft ranging in size up to the 30-passenger *Sea North II.* This vessel is equipped with stereo hydrophones so that passengers can listen to the sounds made by the beluga whales that swim within feet of the boat. Tours also offer chances of sighting polar bears, ice formations and indigenous birds. Kayak tours and snorkeling also are available.

Allow 3 hours minimum. Daily dawn-dusk (times may vary depending on tides), mid-June to late Aug. Fare $86; $43 (ages 0-11). AX, MC, VI. Phone (204) 675-2195 or (888) 348-7591.

YORK FACTORY NATIONAL HISTORIC SITE OF CANADA is 250 km (150 mi.) s.e. near the mouth of the Hayes River; access to the site is limited to charter plane or boat. The site was established by the Hudson's Bay Co. as part of a series of fur trading posts. The 1832 depot is the oldest wooden structure still standing on permafrost. Interpretive tours of the site feature reconstructed buildings containing area artifacts.

Visitors should contact Parks Canada for transportation and safety information. Facilities at the site are limited; camping is not permitted. Allow 4 hours minimum. Daily 8-5, June 15-Sept. 1 (weather permitting). Site free. Guided tour $7.90; free (ages 0-4). Phone (204) 675-8863.

COOKS CREEK (E-3) elev. 238 m/780′

COOK'S CREEK HERITAGE MUSEUM, jct. Hwy. 212 and Sapton Rd., houses artifacts pertaining to the life of the early settlers from Poland, Ukraine and other eastern European countries. Highlights include religious artifacts, folk art, clothing, a blacksmith shop, pioneer houses furnished in period and farm machines. Allow 1 hour minimum. Thurs.-Tues. 11-5, mid-May through Aug. 31. Admission $3; $2 (ages 0-18 and 66+). Phone (204) 444-4448.

IMMACULATE CONCEPTION CHURCH AND THE GROTTO OF OUR LADY OF LOURDES is 3 km (1.9 mi.) n. on Hwy. 212 (Cooks Creek Rd.) from jct. Hwy. 213 (Garvin Rd.). The Ukrainian Catholic church, built by Father Philip Ruh 1930-52, features onion domes and the Icon of Our Lady of Perpetual Help, a replica of the Miraculous Icon in Rome. The grotto adjacent to the church is a replica of the original Grotto of Lourdes in France.

Guided tours are available. Allow 1 hour minimum. Daily noon-6, July 1-Labour Day; Sat.-Sun. noon-6 in June and day after Labour Day-Sept. 30. Admission $1. Phone (204) 444-2478.

DAUPHIN (E-2) pop. 7,906, elev. 293 m/960′

Dauphin (DAW-fin) lies in a fertile farming valley between Duck Mountain Provincial Park *(see Recreation Chart)* and Riding Mountain National Park of Canada *(see place listing p. 218).* Lake Dauphin, 15 kilometres (9 mi.) east of Dauphin, offers fishing.

The nation's rich Ukrainian culture and heritage are celebrated each year during ⬇ Canada's National Ukrainian Festival, a 3-day event held in early

August. Ukrainian music, food and dance take center stage at Selo Ukraina, a heritage village 12 kilometres (7.5 mi.) south of Dauphin near Riding Mountain National Park of Canada.

Dauphin Economic Development: 100 Main St. S., Dauphin, MB, Canada R7N 1K3; phone (204) 622-3229 or (877) 566-5669.

FORT DAUPHIN MUSEUM, 140 Jackson St., is surrounded by a wooden palisade suggestive of an 18th-century fur trading fort of the North West Co. A trapper's cabin, schoolhouse, church, blacksmith shop, trading post and pioneer house inside the fort are furnished in the style of the early settlers. Archeological, fur trade and pioneer artifacts also are featured.

Allow 1 hour minimum. Daily 9-5, mid-June through Aug. 31; Mon.-Fri. 9-5, May 1 to mid-June and Sept. 1 to mid-Oct. Admission $4; $3 (students with ID); free (ages 0-11 with adult). Phone (204) 638-6630.

ELKHORN (F-1) pop. 461, elev. 526 m/1,700′

SAVE **THE MANITOBA ANTIQUE AUTOMOBILE MUSEUM** is on Hwy. 1W. The museum displays some 100 vintage automobiles dating from 1908 to the mid-1960s; several are in operating condition. Also exhibited are steam engines, gas tractors and other farm machinery as well as aboriginal, household and pioneer artifacts. Allow 1 hour minimum. Daily 9-6, May-Sept. Admission $5; $2 (ages 5-16). Phone (204) 845-2604, or (204) 845-2161 Oct.-Apr.

EMERSON (F-3) pop. 689

Emerson was named after American poet Ralph Waldo Emerson. When Manitoba became a province in 1870, this town on the border of the United States and Canada was the site of the province's first customs house. The original log buildings still stand just north of the Customs Port of Entry.

In 1874 the North West Mounted Police, later renamed the Royal Canadian Mounted Police, organized at Fort Dufferin, thus beginning their career of maintaining law and order in the untamed western areas of Canada. A 5-metre (15-ft.) bronze statue of a North West Mounted Police Officer and his horse is located next to the Tourist Information Centre on Hwy. 75. The statue is a tribute to the members of the force who made the historic "Trek West" from Emerson to Fort McLeod, Alberta.

The Boundary Commission Trail provides 3 kilometres (1.9 mi.) of hiking along the Red River north to the Historic Fort Dufferin Site. At the fort are the remains of old buildings, grave sites and a memorial to the North West Mounted Police.

Town of Emerson: P.O. Box 340, Emerson, MB, Canada R0A 0L0; phone (204) 373-2002.

FALCON LAKE (F-4) elev. 305 m/1,001′

As it winds its way across the country, the Trans Canada Trail enters Manitoba from Ontario at West Hawk Lake in Whiteshell Provincial Park *(see attraction listing)*, crossing the park diagonally as it heads westward to Pinawa. Incorporating many existing trails and utilizing abandoned railway lines, the trail offers hikers a diverse sampling of the province's topography.

WHITESHELL PROVINCIAL PARK is accessible via an especially scenic stretch of Hwy. 1E. The park's four districts encompass both wilderness and developed resort areas, more than 200 lakes and 12 rivers.

Alfred Hole Goose Sanctuary, east of Rennie on Hwy. 44, is a nesting ground for giant Canada geese, which can be seen from the interpretive center's observation deck. Rocks found throughout the park are part of the Precambrian Shield, the oldest geological formation in the world.

Park open daily 24 hours. An interpretive center at Whiteshell Fish Hatchery is open daily 9:30-4:30, June 1-Labour Day. One-hour tours of the center are given daily at 11 and 2. Entrance fee $5.95 per private vehicle (3-day pass); $24.75 (annual provincial park pass). Phone the Falcon Lake District at (204) 349-2201, West Hawk District at (204) 349-2245, Rennie District at (204) 369-5246, Seven Sisters District at (204) 348-4004, or the interpretive center at the fish hatchery at (204) 349-8204. *See Recreation Chart and the AAA/CAA Western Canada & Alaska CampBook.*

Whiteshell Natural History Museum is deep within Whiteshell Provincial Park near Seven Sisters Falls on PR 307 at Nutimik Lake, opposite the boat launch. Mounted animals within the log cabin museum depict the wildlife residing within the provincial park. Other exhibits include displays about the boreal forest, native peoples, wild rice, sturgeon and the Winnipeg River.

Picnicking is permitted. Allow 30 minutes minimum. Daily 9-noon and 1-5, Victoria Day weekend-Labour Day weekend. Museum free. Park entrance fee $5.95 per private vehicle (3-day pass); $24.75 (annual provincial park pass). Phone (204) 348-2846.

RECREATIONAL ACTIVITIES
Horseback Riding

• **Falcon Beach Riding Stables and Guest Ranch** is off Hwy. 1 Falcon Lake exit. Write Falcon Beach Ranch, P.O. Box 179, Falcon Lake, MB, Canada R0E 0N0. Daily 9-5, July-Aug.; by appointment rest of year. Phone (204) 349-2410, or (877) 949-2410 in Canada.

FLIN FLON (C-2)
pop. 5,836, elev. 304 m/1,000′

Flin Flon was founded in 1915 when Tom Creighton, one of six prospectors, discovered an ore body which led to the development of Flin Flon as a mining town.

The community owes its name to Josiah Flintabbatey Flonatin, the major character of "The Sunless

City," a dime novel found in the area by the discoverers of the mineral deposits. Off Hwy. 10 is a humorous 7.5-metre (25-ft.) statue of Flintabbatey Flonatin ("Flinty" for short) designed by the American cartoonist Al Capp, of "L'il Abner" fame. A boardwalk around Ross Lake, a walking trail and a park also remember the city's namesake; the park features a smaller statue of Flinty.

The Flin Flon Station Museum, north on Hwy. 10A, is open seasonally and displays artifacts collected from mining, transportation and cultural sources; phone (204) 687-2946. Bordering Saskatchewan, Flin Flon is the northern terminus of the Manitoba stretch of scenic Hwy. 10.

Flin Flon and District Chamber of Commerce: 228-35 Main St., Flin Flon, MB, Canada R8A 1J7; phone (204) 687-4518.

GARDENTON (F-3) elev. 298 m/979′

Some of the earliest Ukrainian settlers in Manitoba came to Gardenton in 1896. St. Michael's Ukrainian Orthodox Historical Church, 4 kilometres (2.5 mi.) west, is purportedly North America's first Ukrainian Orthodox church; the church was built 1897-99. Lithographed icons from St. Petersburg, Moscow and Kiev ornament the sanctuary. A pilgrimage is held the third Sunday in August. Phone (204) 425-3595 for an appointment to tour the church.

The Ukrainian Museum contains articles of clothing and hand tools depicting life in the late 1800s and early 1900s, a one-room schoolhouse and a thatched roof house. Also in the area is a tallgrass prairie. For further information about the museum phone (204) 425-3072 in summer, or (204) 425-3501 rest of year.

GILBERT PLAINS (E-2) pop. 760

WASYL NEGRYCH PIONEER HOMESTEAD is 17.3 km (10.8 mi.) n. on PR 274, then 3.2 km (2 mi.) e. on Negrych Rd. (gravel). The homestead's 10 log buildings, built in 1899, are said to be the province's most complete set of period farmyard buildings and the oldest Ukrainian-style house in Manitoba. The buildings reflect the architectural style of the Carpathian Mountain region. Picnicking is permitted. Allow 1 hour minimum. Daily 10-5, July-Aug. Admission $3; free (ages 0-5). Phone (204) 548-2326.

GIMLI (E-3) pop. 1,891, elev. 220 m/723′

Established in 1875, Gimli was the site of Canada's first permanent Icelandic settlement, the largest outside Iceland. The town's name, derived from Norse mythology, means "home of the gods." A Viking statue designed by Gissur Eliasson and the oldest Icelandic cemetery in Canada testify to Gimli's Nordic heritage. Gimli is located on the western shore of Lake Winnipeg, one of the largest freshwater lakes in the world.

Lake Winnipeg Visitor Centre—Gimli: P.O. Box 1246, Gimli, MB, Canada R0C 1B0; phone (204) 642-7974.

SAVE **NEW ICELAND HERITAGE MUSEUM** is at 94 1st Ave. Displayed in three buildings are exhibits that focus on the area's Icelandic roots, the fishing industry and Lake Winnipeg's natural history. Multimedia exhibits at the Waterfront Centre examine area history, while displays at the visitor center feature the fishing industry and the lake's natural history. A classroom typical of early 1900s rural Manitoba can be seen at the 1915 Gimli Public School.

Food is available. Allow 30 minutes minimum. Waterfront Centre open daily 10-4, Victoria Day weekend-Labour Day; Mon.-Fri. 10-4, Sat.-Sun. 1-4, rest of year. Visitor center and school open daily 10-4, Victoria Day weekend-Labour Day. Admission $5; $4 (ages 61+ and students with ID); free (ages 0-6); $15 (family). AX, MC, VI. Phone (204) 642-4001.

GIROUX (F-3) elev. 271 m/888′

PHILIP'S MAGICAL PARADISE: MUSEUM OF MAGIC AND ILLUSION, 39 Municipal Rd. at jct. Hwy. 311, houses a variety of items donated by magicians from around the world. Allow 30 minutes minimum. Mon.-Fri. 7 p.m.-9 p.m., Sat.-Sun. 1-8, mid-May to late Sept. Donations. Phone (204) 326-1219.

GLENBORO (F-2) pop. 633, elev. 375 m/1,230′

Glenboro is known as the gateway to Spruce Woods Provincial Park *(see Carberry p. 210)* and the Manitoba Desert. At the junction of Hwys. 2 and 5 in Camel Park stands Sara the Camel, a 7-metre-high (24-ft.) symbol of the Spirit Sands. A portion of the SS *Alpha,* a steamship that ran aground on the Assiniboine River in 1885, also is displayed in the park.

Slightly northwest of Glenboro on Hwy. 2 is what is purported to be the last cable river ferry in southern Manitoba; phone (204) 827-2252.

GRANDVIEW (E-2)
pop. 839, elev. 434 m/1,425′

WATSON CROSSLEY COMMUNITY MUSEUM is on the w. side of town at the sports grounds on Railway Ave. The museum displays regional pioneer items including automobiles, horsedrawn equipment, tractors, farm machinery and other artifacts. A restored 1896 homesteader's cabin, a pioneer church with a free-standing bell tower, a rural schoolhouse and a three-story 1918 pioneer house are furnished in their respective periods.

Allow 2 hours minimum. Daily 10-6, late June-early Sept.; by appointment rest of year. Admission $2; free (ages 0-11). Phone (204) 546-2040 late June-early Sept., or (204) 546-2661 or (204) 546-2764 rest of year.

HADASHVILLE (F-3) elev. 297 m/975′

SANDILANDS FOREST CENTRE, about 2 km (1.2 mi.) s. of jct. Hwys. 1 and 11, tells visitors about forest conservation, reforestation and fire prevention. A train car used 1919-74 to promote the nationwide planting of trees is shown, an electronic display tests tree species knowledge and a museum has area plants and animals. The Old Beaver Dam Trail, reached by a suspension bridge over the Whitemouth River, penetrates aspen parkland and a boreal forest.

Guided tours of the center are available. Allow 1 hour minimum. Daily 10-5, July-Aug.; by appointment May-June and in Sept. Hours may vary; phone ahead. Donations. Guided tours $3. Reservations are required for guided tours. Phone (204) 453-3182.

HECLA ISLAND (E-4) elev. 210 m/690′

HECLA/GRINDSTONE PROVINCIAL PARK, 165 km (103 mi.) n. of Winnipeg, or 54 km (34 mi.) n. of Riverton, on Hwy. 8, is comprised of several islands in Lake Winnipeg, the largest of which is Hecla Island. The original settlers were Icelanders displaced from their homeland in 1876, fleeing poverty and Danish rule. Guided walks through the restored buildings of Hecla Village—a church, school, community hall, period house, dockside fish station, a tool display and a partially completed boarding house—are offered.

Park open daily 24 hours. Entrance fee $5.95 per private vehicle (3-day pass); $24.75 (annual provincial park pass). Phone (204) 279-2056 May-Sept., or (204) 378-2261 rest of year. *See Recreation Chart.*

Grassy Narrows Marsh and Wildlife Viewing Tower, at Hecla/Grindstone Provincial Park, offers wildlife viewing from trails and boardwalks along the marsh as well as from towers along the trails. Some trails are designated bicycling trails. The marsh, a nesting area for Canada geese and other waterfowl, is named after the Narrows, a channel between Hecla Island and the mainland. The tower was built for viewing moose as they feed in the marsh. **Note:** Visitors should bring drinking water and wear comfortable walking shoes. Daily 24 hours. Admission included with park.

Hecla Fish Station, at Hecla/Grindstone Provincial Park, is in an old ice house, or "fish station." The site provides a look at the commercial fishing industry of Lake Winnipeg through artifacts, wall plaques and a small museum. During fishing season visitors may view fishermen bringing in the day's catch. Daily 11:30-4:30, June 10-Aug. 30. Free.

Hecla Island Heritage Home Museum, at Hecla/Grindstone Provincial Park, depicts the lifestyle of an Icelandic family from the 1920s to the 1940s. The restored 1928 house is furnished in period with items donated by descendants of the original owners and by other islanders. Walking tours are available. Wed.-Sun. 10-4, June 15-Aug. 30. Schedule may vary; phone ahead. Donations.

INGLIS (E-1)

INGLIS GRAIN ELEVATORS NATIONAL HISTORIC SITE is along Railway Ave. These five vintage grain elevators, once a common sight on western Canadian prairies, have been restored and are now the last remaining row of standard wooden grain elevators in Canada. Dating to the 1920s, similar rows of elevators, built by grain companies and agricultural cooperatives, once stood along rail lines in most small Canadian communities.

An interpretive center in the Paterson elevator explains the importance of these structures to the nation's agricultural history. Exhibits and displays complement a videotape presentation, which shows how the elevators operated, transporting wheat into storage bins. A walking tour of the grounds provides further insights into the development of Canada's grain industry.

Picnicking is permitted. Allow 1 hour minimum. Mon.-Fri. 8:30-4:30, Sat. 9-5, Sun. 1-5, July-Aug.; otherwise by appointment. Admission $4; $2 (students with ID); free (ages 0-10). Phone (204) 564-2243.

INTERNATIONAL PEACE GARDEN (F-2)

On US 281 and scenic Hwy. 10, the International Peace Garden consists of 586 hectares (1,451 acres) in Canada and an adjoining 360 hectares (888 acres) in North Dakota. Set among the lakes and streams of the wooded Turtle Mountains, the botanical garden and park commemorates the friendship between these two countries on the longest unfortified border in the world.

Centers of attraction include the Peace Tower, which represents people from the four corners of the world coming together for the common purpose of peace; an interpretive center depicting the history and development of the park; the Peace Chapel, which includes quotations etched in limestone walls; more than 150,000 annual flowers in the formal gardens that line the boundary; a floral clock; the Carillon Bell Tower, which chimes every 15 minutes; and a memorial cairn, constructed of steel salvaged from the destruction of the World Trade Center, commemorating the tragic events of September 11, 2001.

Other facilities include campgrounds, hiking and bicycling trails and picnic areas. Walking tours of the garden, nature hikes and arts and crafts classes are offered daily. Self-guiding walking and driving tours also are available. Flowers are in full bloom mid-July to early September (weather permitting).

The International Music Camp Summer School of Fine Arts is held at the garden June through July. The Canadian Legion Sports Camp, held during July through August, attracts coaches and athletes from many countries.

Allow 1 hour minimum. The garden and port of entry offices are open daily 24 hours. Daily vehicle permits $10; season permits $25; pedestrian permits $5. Visitors are required to go through customs when leaving the garden. Phone (204) 534-2510 in Canada, (701) 263-4390 in the United States, or (888) 432-6733.

KILLARNEY (F-2)
pop. 2,199, elev. 495 m/1,625'

The area's resemblance to Ireland's Killarney Lakes prompted John Sidney O'Brien to change the name of the town of Oak Lake to Killarney. Green fire engines and a replica of the Blarney Stone are further evidence of the town's Irish heritage.

Killarney and District Chamber of Commerce: P.O. Box 809, Killarney, MB, Canada R0K 1G0; phone (204) 523-4202.

J.A.V. DAVID MUSEUM, 414 Williams Ave., displays Indian and pioneer artifacts, local memorabilia, quilts and collections of birds, butterflies and animals. Also featured are an early 1900s schoolroom, a Ninette Sanitorium display, a post office display and a country store. Allow 1 hour minimum. Tues.-Sat. 10-noon and 1-5, July-Aug.; by appointment rest of year. Closed holidays. Admission $2; $1 (students); free (ages 0-9); $5 (family). Phone (204) 523-7325, or (204) 523-8836 during the off-season.

LA RIVIÈRE (F-2)

ARCHIBALD HISTORICAL MUSEUM is 3 km (2 mi.) e. on Hwy. 3, then 6 km (4 mi.) n. on a dirt road, following signs. The museum consists of buildings moved to the site from neighboring areas. Two homes lived in by social activist and author Nellie McClung in the late 19th and early 20th centuries are included, both furnished in period, as are the mansard-roofed former CPR train station (with a 1913 wooden caboose in front), a house with tin siding and a three-story barn with a country store, tools, buggies, household artifacts and tractors.

Native artifacts and vintage cars, trucks and gas pumps also can be seen. Picnicking is permitted. Allow 1 hour minimum. Fri.-Mon. noon-8, mid-May through Labour Day. Phone ahead to verify schedule. Admission $6; $2 (ages 5-11). Phone (204) 242-2825.

LOCKPORT (E-3) elev. 313 m/1,000'

At Lockport Provincial Heritage Park (see attraction listing), on Hwy. 44 just east of the Lockport bridge, is St. Andrews Lock and Dam. This rare structure on Canada's flat prairies was completed in 1910 to allow access and permit navigation on the Red River from Lake Winnipeg to the city of Winnipeg; it is purportedly the only lock and dam of its kind still standing in North America. Picnic sites and footpaths overlook the dam.

Red River North Tourism—Lockport: 18 Main St., 2nd floor, Selkirk, MB, Canada R1A 1P5; phone (204) 482-2022 or (800) 894-2621.

LOCKPORT PROVINCIAL HERITAGE PARK is on Hwy. 44 just e. of the Lockport Bridge. Archeological digs at the park have established the site as the location where Manitoba's aboriginal "first farmers" worked the land along the banks of the

Red River. In addition to a display about the St. Andrews Lock and Dam, the park also has a fish ladder and a large colony of white pelicans.

A .7-kilometre (.4-mi.) trail along the river has interpretive signs explaining the resources that brought native peoples to the area. Picnicking is permitted. Daily dawn-dusk, mid-May to mid-Oct. Free. Phone (204) 757-2902.

Kenosewun Interpretive Centre is in Lockport Provincial Heritage Park. One of the province's most important archeological sites, Kenosewun (the Cree word for "there are many fishes") interprets the history of the area's aboriginal cultures. The center has displays featuring early artifacts, a 10-minute videotape presentation and a crafts room for children. Allow 30 minutes minimum. Wed.-Sun. 9-5, mid-May through Labour Day weekend. Free. Phone (204) 757-2902.

ST. ANDREW'S CHURCH is 2 km (1.2 mi.) s. on Hwy. 9, then e. on St. Andrews Rd. (Hwy. 410) to jct. River Rd. (Hwy. 238) at 374 River Rd. Designed by its first rector 1844-49, this stone Gothic-Revival Anglican church is the oldest house of worship in continuous use in western Canada. It retains many of its original fixtures, such as buffalo-hide-covered kneeling benches. The church's cemetery is adjacent. Allow 30 minutes minimum. Tours daily 10-6, mid-May through Labour Day. Donations. Phone (204) 334-6405.

St. Andrew's Rectory National Historic Site of Canada is across from St. Andrew's Church. The two-story stone building, constructed in 1854 for the church's rectors, has exhibits on the ground floor about the building's architecture, the work of the early missionaries and life in the Red River Settlement. The building is home to the current church rector. Daily 10-6, mid-May through Labour Day. Donations. Phone (204) 334-6405.

MORDEN (F-2) pop. 6,571, elev. 302 m/990'

Named after the area's first settler, Alvey Morden, the town grew almost overnight when the Canadian Pacific Railroad arrived in 1882. Located near the Boundary Commission-NWMP Trail in the Boundary Trail Heritage Region, Morden has a progressive industrial and business sector. Abundant recreational activities at Lake Minnewasta (see Recreation Chart) and Colert Beach include camping, swimming, fishing, water skiing, canoeing, sailing, bicycling and hiking in the summer. Winter activities include cross-country skiing, snowmobiling and ice fishing.

The Agriculture and Agri-Food Canada Research Station on Hwy. 100 develops field crops, fruits and ornamentals on 254 hectares (627 acres). Tours of the Morden area and the research station are offered May through September. For further information phone (204) 822-4471.

A mural on the corner of Stephen and Nelson streets is a re-creation of one of the earliest known photographs taken in the area. The scene depicts the supply train for Her Majesty's British North American Boundary Commission at Dead Horse Creek in June 1873.

Another mural, at the corner of Stephen and 7th streets, remembers the visit of Canada's first prime minister, Sir John A. MacDonald, to the town on July 15, 1886. The depiction features Sir John speaking from the rear of his railcar and Philip Locke presenting him with a bouquet of prairie flowers; a version of an Indian war dance also is depicted.

A third mural, at 306 N. Railway St., depicts the original uniform of the North West Mounted Police and provides a history of the force, now known as the Royal Canadian Mounted Police.

Morden and District Chamber of Commerce: 311 N. Railway St., Morden, MB, Canada R6M 1S9; phone (204) 822-5630.

Self-guiding tours: The Morden Mansion pamphlet describes a self-guiding architectural/historical walking tour of Morden's turn-of-the-20th-century homes and buildings; it is available for $2 from the chamber of commerce.

CANADIAN FOSSIL DISCOVERY CENTRE is in the lower level of the recreation center at 111-B Gilmour St. Fossil displays chronicle regional archeology and paleontology. Marine reptile fossils, such as mosasaurs and plesiosaurs, date from 80 million years ago when the Colorado Sea covered much of North America. The process of finding, excavating and displaying the fossils is depicted. Other exhibits deal with First Nations and pioneer life. Paleo Tours offer a chance to excavate fossils at a site nearby.

Allow 1 hour minimum. Daily 1-5; closed Dec. 25. Admission $6; $3 (ages 6-17); $12 (family, two adults and up to three children). A fee is charged for Paleo Tours. Phone (204) 822-3406.

MORRIS (F-3) pop. 1,643, elev. 236 m/775′

Two rival fur-trading companies—the North West Co. and the Hudson's Bay Co.—set up shop on the Morris River in 1801. Not until 1874 did a permanent settlement take hold; incorporation took place in 1883. Both the town and the river on which it grew were named for Alexander Morris, the second lieutenant governor of Manitoba during the 1870s.

Morris & District Chamber of Commerce: P.O. Box 98, Morris, MB, Canada R0G 1K0; phone (204) 746-6275.

MORRIS & DISTRICT CENTENNIAL MUSEUM, on Main St. at jct. Hwys. 75 and 23, consists of two buildings. The main building is the original Carleton School, which contains pioneer era displays of farm tools and a laundry and dairy section. The second building contains five rooms featuring furniture and artifacts from the turn of the 20th century. A mural depicts the history of the Red River Valley. Daily noon-5, June-Sept. Donations. Phone (204) 746-2169.

NEEPAWA (E-2) pop. 3,298, elev. 400 m/1,300′

Neepawa, whose name derives from a native word for plenty, is a service center for the surrounding grain and livestock farms on the fertile plains northwest of Winnipeg. This community of tree-lined streets, well-known as the birthplace of author Margaret Laurence, offers many pleasant diversions for residents and travelers alike, including Riverbend Park, a fitness trail and camping area.

The city calls itself the World Lily Capital. This claim is bolstered by the annual 🌸 Neepawa & Area Lily Festival held the third week in July. More than 2,000 varieties of lilies are grown in the Neepawa area, and the community celebrates their beauty with live entertainment, music, street vendors and food kiosks, a quilt show, a parade, tours by bus and horse-drawn vehicles and a photography contest.

Neepawa and District Chamber of Commerce: 282 Hamilton St., P.O. Box 726, Neepawa, MB, Canada R0J 1H0; phone (204) 476-5292.

BEAUTIFUL PLAINS MUSEUM, 91 Hamilton St. W., is housed in a former CNR station. The museum features several rooms of historical items. A children's room contains antique toys and books, and a military room has uniforms and pictures of local residents involved in World Wars I and II. Other rooms include items dedicated to nature, stores, Masonic lodges, sports and vintage clothing. An extensive doll collection also is displayed.

Allow 30 minutes minimum. Mon.-Fri. 9-5, Sat.-Sun. 1-5, July 1-early Sept.; Mon.-Fri. 9-5, late May-June 30. Donations. Phone (204) 476-3896.

MARGARET LAURENCE HOME, 312 First Ave., contains photographs, memorabilia, autographed books and research materials of the award-winning Canadian author, born here in 1926. Guided tours are available. Daily 10-4, mid-May through Sept. 30; by appointment rest of year. Admission $3; $2 (students); free (ages 0-5); $6 (family). Phone (204) 476-3612.

PINAWA (F-3) pop. 1,450, elev. 282 m/925′

Named "Pinnawak," meaning calm waters, by the aboriginal people, Pinawa was first settled by families who operated one of the earliest hydroelectric power dams built between Sault Ste. Marie, Ontario, and the Rockies. The townsite was abandoned in 1951, and the historic site is now Pinawa Dam Provincial Heritage Park. The new Pinawa was built in 1963 when the Federal Crown Corp., Atomic Energy of Canada Limited (AECL) built its research center near the old townsite.

PORTAGE LA PRAIRIE (F-2)
pop. 12,728, elev. 332 m/1,100′

The city's name is derived from the prairie portage between the Red and Assiniboine rivers and Lake Manitoba. In the heart of the city at Crescent Road and Royal Road S. is Island Park. Surrounded by horseshoe-shaped Crescent Lake, this scenic park has a deer sanctuary, a large captive flock of Canada geese and offers opportunities for other bird-watching. Park features include exhibition grounds, seasonal harness racing, a golf course, an arboretum, tennis courts, picnic areas and bicycling and hiking trails.

Portage la Prairie City Hall, built in 1898, was designed by one of Canada's foremost architects, Thomas Fuller.

Portage and District Chamber of Commerce: 11 Second St. N.E., Portage la Prairie, MB, Canada R1N 1R8; phone (204) 857-7778.

Self-guiding tours: A brochure detailing a self-guiding historic tour of Portage la Prairie is available at the chamber of commerce.

FORT LA REINE MUSEUM, PIONEER VILLAGE AND TOURIST BUREAU is at jct. Hwys. 26 and 1A E. The central museum includes pioneer household articles and implements, a log fort, school, doctor's office, trading post, furnished homestead and church as well as railway, farming and military displays. Canadian railway official Sir William Van Horne's business car also is displayed. A tourist bureau is available.

Picnicking is permitted. Allow 1 hour minimum. Mon.-Sat. 9-6, Sun. noon-6, mid-May to mid-Sept. Admission $8; $6 (ages 60+); $3 (ages 6-12). Phone (204) 857-3259.

◤GEM RIDING MOUNTAIN NATIONAL PARK OF CANADA (E-2)

Elevations in the park range from 230 metres (755 ft.) at Henderson Creek in the northeastern area to 756 metres (2,480 ft.) at Bald Hill in the eastern side of the park. Refer to CAA/AAA maps for additional elevation information.

Accessible from the north and south via scenic Hwy. 10, or from the east via Hwy. 19, Riding Mountain National Park of Canada lies on the plateau of the Manitoba escarpment, 197 kilometres (123 mi.) north of the U.S. border and 259 kilometres (162 mi.) northwest of Winnipeg. This 2,978-square-kilometre (1,150-sq.-mi.) area is blanketed with forests, lakes and meadows. The park is home to elk, moose, deer, bears and a wide variety of birds and vegetation. Waterfowl and beavers populate the waterways, and a herd of bison grazes in a large enclosure near Lake Audy.

General Information and Activities

Although the park is open year-round, complete facilities are available only from mid-May to mid-October. The park also encompasses the historic resort town of Wasagaming on Clear Lake, which offers the amenities of a resort destination.

Recreational activities available within the park include tennis, golfing, lawn bowling, swimming, hiking, fishing, canoeing, sailing, cross-country skiing, horseback riding, bicycling, camping and snowshoeing. More than 400 kilometres (250 mi.) of hiking, bicycling and horseback trails lead to lakes, meadows and evergreen forests. Bicycle and boat rentals are available.

Several forms of recreation can be pursued nearby. Guides and outfitters offer horseback riding and wagon excursions along with other wilderness activities. Located at Lake Katherine, the Native Cultural Anishinabe Village, or "Shawenequanape Kipichewin," offers cultural tours, interpretation programs and powwows. There are boat launching facilities at Clear Lake. Snowshoeing and dog sledding are other popular activities. *See Recreation Chart and the AAA/CAA Western Canada & Alaska CampBook.*

ADMISSION is $6.90; over 64, $5.90; family rate (up to seven people) $16.80. Annual pass $34.65; over 64, $29.70; family rate $87.15. AX, MC, VI .

PETS are allowed in the park. Dogs must be leashed at all times.

ADDRESS inquiries to Visitor Information, Riding Mountain National Park of Canada, Wasagaming, MB, Canada R0J 2H0; phone (204) 848-7275 or (204) 848-7272.

VISITOR INFORMATION CENTRE OF WASAGAMING is on the s. shore of Clear Lake. The center maintains exhibits and displays about the natural and human history of the area. Interpretive programs include nature walks, campfires, theater programs and guided hikes. A campground is available. Daily 9-8, Victoria Day weekend-early Sept. Phone (204) 848-7275 or (204) 848-7272.

SELKIRK (E-3) pop. 9,515, elev. 231 m/800'

Selkirk's name honors Lord Selkirk, the Scottish philanthropist whose 1803 settlement in the Red River Valley to the south laid the foundation for Winnipeg. During the late 19th and early 20th centuries, Selkirk's position on the Red River made it a base for trade and communication with the more isolated settlements around Lake Winnipeg.

Chuck the Channel Catfish, a 9-metre (30-ft.) fiberglass statue, greets visitors on Main Street. The oversized catfish is an apt representation of the live version: Catfish weighing more than 9 kilograms (20 lbs.) abound in the Red River between Selkirk and Lockport.

St. Peter's Dynevor Church, 6.5 kilometres (4 mi.) northeast off Hwy. 59, was built in 1853. The original church, erected in 1836, was the center for Anglican missionary work among the Saulteaux Indians.

Red River North Tourism—Selkirk: 18 Main St., 2nd floor, Selkirk, MB, Canada R1A 1P5; phone (204) 482-2022 or (800) 894-2621.

LOWER FORT GARRY NATIONAL HISTORIC SITE OF CANADA, 5 km (3 mi.) s. on Hwy. 9, is purportedly the oldest intact stone fur-trading post in North America. The 19th-century buildings are restored and furnished as they might have been in their early days. Costumed staff members perform tasks and re-enact events that re-create the early 1850s atmosphere of the fort in its heyday. The Visitor Reception Centre offers exhibits and a slide presentation about the fort's history.

Picnic facilities and food are available. Allow 2 hours minimum. Daily 9-5, mid-May through Labour Day. Admission $7.15; $5.90 (ages 65+); $3.45 (ages 6-16); $17.80 (family, maximum two adults and five children). MC, VI. Phone (204) 785-6055 or (888) 773-8888.

MARINE MUSEUM OF MANITOBA, at the entrance to Selkirk Park at Eveline St. and Queen Ave., reflects Selkirk's nautical past through displays of outboard motors, tools used for early 1900s shipbuilding, two lighthouses and six restored ships. The 1897 passenger steamship SS *Keenora* houses nautical artifacts and photographs.

Other displays include early 1900s underwater diving and a graphite exhibit representing the species of fish caught in Lake Winnipeg and the Red River. Allow 1 hour minimum. Mon.-Fri. 9-5, Sat.-Sun. and holidays 10-6, mid-May through Labour Day. Admission $5; $4 (ages 66+); $3 (ages 6-17). Phone (204) 482-7761.

SHILO (F-2)

THE ROYAL REGIMENT OF CANADIAN ARTILLERY MUSEUM is on the Canadian Forces Base via Hwy. 340. This indoor-outdoor museum exhibits more than 10,000 articles of dress, technical instruments, ammunition, small arms, guns and World War II vehicles. Among the more than 150 pieces of major military equipment dating to 1796 are German, Russian and French guns.

Guided tours are available by appointment. Allow 1 hour minimum. Mon.-Fri. 9-5, Sat.-Sun. and holidays 1-5, Victoria Day-second Mon. in Oct.; Mon.-Fri. 9-5, rest of year. Donations. Phone (204) 765-3000, ext. 3531.

SOURIS (F-2) pop. 1,772, elev. 396 m/1,300′

The free-swinging 177-metre (581-ft.) footbridge built in 1904 over the Souris (SIR-iss) River is considered the longest free-suspension foot bridge in Canada. The bridge was reconstructed after being destroyed by a flood in 1976. Victoria Park has more than 6 kilometres (4 mi.) of walking trails, a viewing tower and a bird sanctuary containing geese, peacocks and swans *(see the AAA/CAA Western Canada & Alaska CampBook).*

Rockhounding in nearby agate pits yields agate, dendrite, jasper, petrified wood and epidote; the area offers one of the largest varieties of semi-precious stones found in North America. Permits are required and cost $10 per private vehicle. Contact the Rock

Bison

The Europeans who explored Canada in the 18th century were awed by the throngs of huge furry cattle that swarmed across the plains. Then, as many as 60 million North American bison, or plains buffalo, roamed the Canadian flatlands. They were the main food source for the Plains Indians, who had mastered the art of harvesting bison for food and clothing: Scaring the animals into a stampede, the Indians then ran them into corrals, where the bison could be killed as they were needed.

Later, the Métis, people of French and Indian heritage, became expert bison hunters as well. Hides were transformed into heavy robes that became the fashion in Europe; tongues were cooked and prized as delicacies; and bison meat, dried and pounded and mixed with fat and sometimes berries, was used to make pemmican, a Canadian aboriginal food which was packed in bags and stored.

As the Europeans fought the Indians and each other, the bison fell victim to reckless slaughter, the repeating rifle and politics. Carcasses of animals killed solely for their tongues or hides littered the plains. When the white settlers realized they could starve the natives by killing the bison, they set fire to the plains, killing thousands of the animals and driving others into what is now the United States. By 1885 the bison faced extinction in Canada.

Around 1900 a handful of conservation-minded cattlemen convinced the Canadian government to protect the bison, and the killing stopped. Manitoba acknowledges its debt to the bison by placing its image on the province's crest.

Shop, 8 First St. S., Souris, MB, Canada R0K 2C0; phone (204) 483-2561.

HILLCREST MUSEUM, Crescent Ave. and Sowden St. next to the swinging bridge, is a restored late 19th-century residence furnished with settler artifacts and antiques. Highlights include an agricultural display with a covered wagon, tractor and farm tools as well as a printing press, a collection of more than 5,000 butterflies and a caboose. Allow 30 minutes minimum. Daily 10-6, July 1-Labour Day. Admission $2; $1 (ages 6-15). Phone (204) 483-2008.

STEINBACH (F-3)
pop. 11,066, elev. 261 m/900'

[SAVE] **MENNONITE HERITAGE VILLAGE,** 3 km (1.9 mi.) n. on Hwy. 12, centers on a replica of a Mennonite village with more than 20 completely furnished buildings that were moved to the site. On the 16-hectare (40-acre) grounds are a fruit garden, stock pens, a steam engine, gas tractors and other machinery. The village windmill is said to be the only one of its kind in Canada. A museum displays antiques and manuscripts.

Allow 1 hour minimum. Mon.-Sat. 10-6, Sun. noon-6, July-Aug.; Mon.-Sat. 10-5, Sun. noon-5, May-June and in Sept.; Tues.-Fri. 10-4 or by appointment, rest of year. Admission $8; $6 (ages 13-22 and 66+); $2 (ages 6-12); $20 (family). Admission may be increased during special events. MC, VI. Phone (204) 326-9661.

STONEWALL (E-3) pop. 4,376

Nobody knows for sure if Stonewall was named after founding father S.J. "Stonewall" Jackson or the limestone ridge on which the town is built. The name fits well, though, since limestone quarrying sustained the area's economy from the early 1880s until 1967. Stonewall's past is captured through the old stone buildings dotting its streets.

Stonewall and District Chamber of Commerce: P.O. Box 762, Stonewall, MB, Canada R0C 2Z0; phone (204) 467-8377.

[SAVE] **OAK HAMMOCK MARSH INTERPRETIVE CENTRE** is 13 km (8 mi.) e. on Hwy. 67, then 4 km (2.5 mi.) n. on Hwy. 220. This 3,600-hectare (9,000-acre) restored prairie wetland is home to more than 295 species of birds, 25 species of mammals and thousands of other plant and animal species. Scores of migrating birds and waterfowl can be seen in the spring and fall.

Hikers can explore 30 kilometres (19 mi.) of trails over a system of boardwalks and dikes. The interpretive center has displays, films and interpretive programs.

Picnicking is permitted. Food is available. Allow 2 hours minimum. Area open daily 24 hours. Interpretive center open daily 10-dusk, Sept.-May; 10-8, rest of year. Closed Dec. 25. Admission to interpretive center (includes guided tours of the center and the wetlands) $5; $4 (ages 3-17 and 56+); $18 (family). AX, MC, VI. Phone (204) 467-3300 or (800) 665-3825.

STONEWALL QUARRY PARK, on the n. end of Main St., commemorates the important role limestone played in the town's development. The interpretive center has a museum, videotape presentations and exhibits; an observation tower affords a panorama of the area. Self-guiding tours around the 30-hectare (75 acre) grounds offer a closer look at kilns, fossil deposits in rock and wildlife. Kinsmen Lake has a sandy beach and swimming; tobogganing is a winter option.

Guided tours are available. Picnicking is permitted. Food and camping facilities are available. Allow 1 hour minimum. Interpretive center daily 11-5, May 1-Labour Day. Hours vary rest of year; phone ahead. Park, museum and observation tower free. Admission to the lake area for swimming $5; $4 (ages 66+ and students); free (ages 0-1). Reservations are required for guided tours. DC, MC, VI. Phone (204) 467-7980. *See Recreation Chart.*

SWAN RIVER (D-2)
pop. 3,859, elev. 340 m/1,116'

During the last 13 years of the 18th century, control of the Swan River Valley was sought by both the North West Co. and the Hudson's Bay Co. Each company built fur-trading posts in the area, but by 1800 the concentrated trapping generated by the rivalry had depleted the number of fur-bearing animals. The Hudson's Bay Co. abandoned the area until the two companies joined in 1821.

The Swan River Valley, nestled between the Duck and Porcupine mountains, offers fishing, hunting, boating, camping, swimming and picnicking. Scenic Hwy. 10 passes just east of town.

Swan River Chamber of Commerce: P.O. Box 1540, Swan River, MB, Canada R0L 1Z0; phone (204) 734-3102.

SWAN VALLEY HISTORICAL MUSEUM, 1.5 km (1 mi.) n. on Hwy. 10, reflects life in Manitoba's pioneer era through artifacts and restored buildings. Highlights include two machine sheds, two log cabins, a CN railroad station, a telephone station, a blacksmith shop, a pioneer store, two churches and a 1900s one-room schoolhouse.

Allow 1 hour minimum. Mon.-Fri. 9-5, Sat.-Sun. and holidays 1-5, May-Sept.; by appointment rest of year. Admission $2; free (ages 0-11). Phone (204) 734-3585 or (204) 734-2713.

THE PAS (C-2) pop. 5,589, elev. 274 m/900'

A cairn in Devon Park at The Pas (pronounced "the paw") honors Henry Kelsey, the first known European to see the northern prairies in 1690. It is rumored that the first wheat on the prairies was planted in the area in 1734. Natural history exhibits, local historical materials and Indian and fur-trading artifacts are displayed in the Sam Waller Museum at 306 Fischer Ave. The museum also offers historic walking tours of the downtown and riverfront areas; phone (204) 623-3802.

Family Values

The safety and security of AAA is something every member of your family can value.

To purchase a AAA Associate Membership for someone in your family, contact your local AAA office, visit AAA.com, or call 1-800-Join-AAA.

Christ Church (Anglican), on Edwards Avenue, was founded in 1840 by Henry Budd, the first native Indian ordained to the Anglican ministry. The church contains hand-hewn furnishings made by ships' carpenters in 1847. Tours are offered by appointment; phone (204) 623-2119 or (204) 624-5433.

The Town of The Pas Tourism Commission: P.O. Box 870, The Pas, MB, Canada R9A 1K8; phone (204) 627-1134.

THOMPSON (B-3)
pop. 13,446, elev. 206 m/675'

Thompson sprang up after the discovery of one of the world's largest nickel deposits and is a major mining, communications, transportation, medical and retailing center. Inco Limited (Thompson Division) offers 90-minute walking tours of its nickel mining and processing complex; phone (204) 677-2216 for information.

Lakes and rivers abound in this rugged, picturesque area. Paint Lake Provincial Recreation Park *(see Recreation Chart and the AAA/CAA Western Canada & Alaska CampBook)* is 32 kilometres (20 mi.) south on Hwy. 6.

Also south of Thompson on Hwy. 6 is the starting point for a 10 kilometre (6-mi.) hiking trail that will take you over a bridge to Kwasitchewan Falls, the highest waterfall in the province. Between Wabowden and Thompson, within Pisew Falls Provincial Park, is Pisew Falls, the second-highest waterfall in Manitoba accessible by road. A 1.3-kilometre (.8-mi.) trail leads from the highway through the dense foliage to a platform overlooking the 12.8-metre (42-ft.) falls. Twelve site plaques describe the flora and fauna of this boreal forest. Picnic facilities are available.

Thompson Chamber of Commerce: 4 Nelson Rd., Thompson, MB, Canada R8N 1M2; phone (204) 677-4155 or (888) 307-0103.

HERITAGE NORTH MUSEUM, in a log cabin at jct. Princeton Dr. and Mystery Lake Rd., also serves as the tourist information center. Displayed are an assortment of stuffed and mounted animals native to the area, fossils, a mining exhibit, a woolly mammoth tusk found near Thompson, a boreal forest exhibit which includes a caribou-hide tepee, and changing exhibits. A second log building houses a mining exhibit. Archives are available.

Daily 9-5, in summer; Mon.-Sat. 1-5, rest of year. Admission $3.25; $2 (ages 13-18 and 60+); $1 (ages 6-12). Phone (204) 677-2216.

VIRDEN (F-2) pop. 3,010, elev. 439 m/1,440'

About 1,200 oil wells dot the landscape in and around Virden—the richest source of petroleum in Manitoba. The first oil-producing well was sunk in the 1950s in the Rosalee field northwest of Virden.

Many original fieldstone buildings, such as the 1892 St. Mary's Anglican Church at the corner of Queen Street and 9th Avenue, are still in use today. The site of Fort Montagne à la Bosse, built by the North West Co. in 1790, is northeast of Virden on the old Trans-Canada Highway. To help cool things off in the summer, the fairgrounds has a public pool and waterslides.

Virden and District Chamber of Commerce: P.O. Box 899, Virden, MB, Canada R0M 2C0; phone (204) 748-3955.

VIRDEN PIONEER HOME MUSEUM INC. is at 390 King St. W. The museum, in a large brick house, is a living memorial to the pioneers who came to the region. Built in 1888, it is furnished with family pieces donated by descendants of the pioneers. Allow 30 minutes minimum. Mon.-Sat. 9-6, Sun. 1-6, May-Aug.; by appointment rest of year. Admission $3; $1 (ages 0-16). Phone (204) 748-1659, (204) 748-1897 or (204) 748-2740.

WAPUSK NATIONAL PARK OF CANADA (A-4)

Elevations in the park range from sea level along the Hudson Bay coastal areas to 94 metres (308 ft.) at Silcox Creek. Refer to CAA/AAA maps for additional elevation information.

South and east of Churchill on the shore of Hudson Bay, Wapusk (pronounced to rhyme with tusk) was established in 1996. The park consists of 11,475 square kilometres (7,119 sq. mi.). Translated from the Cree language, Wapusk means "white bear," a fitting name for a park that has an area where polar bears den and produce offspring.

Much of the national park, part of the Hudson Bay and James Bay lowlands, is a flat plain covered by an extensive layer of peat; a layer of permafrost lies underneath. The treeless tundra consists mainly of wetlands—lakes, streams, bogs and rivers.

Polar bears congregate in the northern part of the park near Churchill around October, as they wait for freezing weather and the time when they can return to the ice in search of seals, their main food. The females dig their dens, and their young are born in late November and in December. The area around Churchill *(see place listing p. 211)* is one of the world's best places for viewing polar bears in their native habitat. Specialized tundra vehicles take visitors for close-up encounters.

The park, along a migratory flyway, also is a popular spring and fall feeding spot for waterfowl and shorebirds, including such rare species as the king eider, Ross' gull and gyrfalcon. Many build their nests here on the coast of Hudson Bay during the summer.

Churchill, in a somewhat remote location in northern Manitoba, can be reached by air and rail from Winnipeg. Since Wapusk is a wilderness park, it has no roads or trails. In order to visit the park, it is necessary to be part of an organized tour group, and several commercial operators provide tours into the park by plane, helicopter or tundra vehicle. The park office can provide a list. Park admission is free. For additional information contact Wapusk National Park of Canada, P.O. Box 127, Churchill, MB, Canada R0B 0E0; phone (204) 675-8863.

WARREN (E-2) elev. 248 m/815′

[SAVE] **V. GROSS' DOLL MUSEUM,** on Hwy. 3W, 3 km (1.9 mi.) n. of jct. Hwys. 6 and 67, displays some 3,500 dolls, ranging from those of the late 1890s to the present. Allow 30 minutes minimum. Sun.-Fri. 10-5 (also Sat. and evenings by appointment), May-Oct.; by appointment rest of year. Admission $4; free (ages 0-5). MC, VI. Phone (204) 322-5346.

WINKLER (F-3) pop. 9,106, elev. 271 m/890′

PEMBINA THRESHERMAN'S MUSEUM, 5 km (3 mi.) w. on Hwy. 3, features guided tours through displays of agricultural machinery, tools and household items as well as a steam threshing unit and a working sawmill. Allow 1 hour minimum. Mon.-Fri. 9-5, Sat.-Sun. and holidays 1-5, May-Sept. Admission $3; free (ages 0-11). Phone (204) 325-7497.

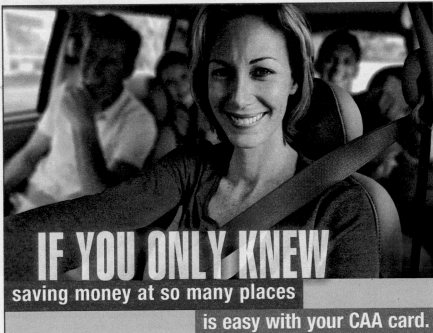

Winnipeg

City Population: 633,451
Elevation: 229 m/763 ft.

Editor's Picks:

Dalnavert Museum ....(see p. 229)

The Forks............................(see p. 229)

The Manitoba Museum...........(see p. 231)

Manitoba Legislative Building / Travel Manitoba

The real estate agent's cry of "Location!" could have been invented in Winnipeg; the position of Manitoba's capital has determined both the city's past and present. Archeological evidence shows that Winnipeg has been an important place of settlement for more than 6,000 years.

The confluence of the Red River, which flows from south to north, and the Assiniboine River, whose eastward flowing waters were a main route of Western exploration, led to the founding of fur-trading posts in the early 18th century near the present site of Winnipeg. The fertile lands created by the rivers later drew farmers and other settlers.

Still later, the area's position south of the peaks of the Canadian Shield meant that roads and railroads were forced to converge at Winnipeg, making it the point through which the eastbound raw materials of the West and the westbound manufactured goods of the East passed. Profiting by the hydroelectric power generated from its rivers, the city emerged in the 20th century as a manufacturing center in its own right.

French Canadian explorer and trader Pierre Gaultier de la Vérendrye founded Fort Rouge at the confluence of the rivers in 1738. This fur-trading post was succeeded by Fort Gibraltar, built by the North West Co. in 1804, and Fort Garry, founded by the Hudson's Bay Co. in 1821. In the same year, Lord Selkirk brought a party of Scottish settlers to these fertile lands, a move that greatly disturbed the trappers and voyageurs who feared their livelihoods would be destroyed.

The small settlement managed to survive, and the shift from trapping and hunting to agriculture began. Because of aggressive Canadian advertising campaigns in Europe and a homestead policy similar to that being used to settle the plains of the United States, large numbers of immigrants began to flow into the area in the 1860s.

In 1873 the village that had grown about a half mile north of Fort Garry was incorporated and named for the Cree Indian words *win* ("muddy") and *nipee* ("water"). The railroad aided Winnipeg's growth still further: In 1876 the city began to ship wheat east, and when the Canadian Pacific Railway connected the coasts in 1885, freight and passengers began to flow through the city in both directions.

The diversity of today's Winnipeg mirrors the many nationalities who settled it, some drawn by agriculture, some by the railroad, some by industry. From countries throughout Great Britain and Europe they came, creating a cultural mix that is reflected in the city's skyline, which includes the neoclassical splendor of the Manitoba Legislative Building *(see attraction listing p. 230)*, the century-old buildings of Old Market Square and the rounded spires of the Ukrainian Greek Orthodox Cathedral.

The Golden Boy, sculpted by Charles Gardet of Paris, is a 5.25-metre-tall (17.2-ft.), 1,650-kilogram (3,638-lb.) statue sheathed in 24 karat gold leaf atop the dome of the Legislative Building. In many ways it symbolizes both the past and the future of the residents of Winnipeg. The statue was diverted on its journey from a French foundry during World War

Getting There — starting on p. 225

Getting Around — starting on p. 225

What To See — starting on p. 227

What To Do — starting on p. 232

Where To Stay — starting on p. 691

Where To Dine — starting on p. 694

I, while the vessel that was carrying it served as a troop transport for 2 years.

After crossing the Atlantic many times, the golden immigrant was finally placed where he stands today, one hand holding aloft the torch of progress, the other cradling a symbolic sheaf of wheat. High above the city, he strides toward the increasingly important natural resources of the north, his color echoing the golden hue of the rolling fields of grain that brought the city below both population and prosperity.

Evidence has been uncovered through archeological digs that the current site of The Forks (see attraction listing p. 229) was a seasonal meeting place for aboriginal peoples more than 6,000 years ago. Tools, bones, footprints and pottery have been unearthed at the site located at the confluence of the Red and Assiniboine rivers.

Getting There

By Car

Forming a circle around Winnipeg is a perimeter highway. To the north of the Trans-Canada Highway, the major approach from the east and west, this perimeter road is designated Hwy. 101. To the south of the Trans-Canada Highway it is numbered Hwy. 100.

There are three major approaches to the perimeter highway: the Trans-Canada Highway, which approaches from both the east and west, and Hwy. 75, which approaches from the south. To the west of the city the Trans-Canada Highway is posted Hwy. 1W; from the east, Hwy. 1E.

Within the perimeter highway all three major approaches change designation: Hwy. 1W becomes Metro Rte. 85, Hwy. 1E becomes Metro Rte. 135, and Hwy. 75 becomes Metro Rte. 42.

© Dave Reede

Getting Around

Generally, rush hour in Winnipeg is from 7 to 9 a.m. and 3:30 to 5:30 p.m. As in most cities, stress can be alleviated if driving during rush hour is avoided. If driving during these times, be careful and be patient; the city's speed limit is 50 kilometres per hour (30 mph) unless otherwise posted.

Note the pedestrian crosswalks marked by pavement stripes and illuminated overhead signs. All vehicles must stop if the crosswalk is occupied by a pedestrian or if a pedestrian on the curb indicates an intention to cross. No vehicle may pass another that is stopped or slowing to yield to a pedestrian. Right turns on red are permitted after a stop, unless otherwise posted.

Street System

Winnipeg's streets are laid out in a number of grids, but each is oriented to a different compass direction. Visitors will find it easiest to orient themselves to the major thoroughfares, which have signs

The Informed Traveler

Sales Tax: Manitoba's provincial sales tax is 7 percent. A 6 percent Goods and Services Tax (GST) also is levied in Canada on most sales and services. There is no additional local sales tax or tax on hotel/motel rooms or car rentals.

WHOM TO CALL

Emergency: 911

Police (non-emergency): (204) 986-6222

Time and Temperature: (204) 784-9000

Weather: (204) 983-2050

Hospitals: Concordia Hospital, (204) 667-1560; Health Sciences Centre, (204) 774-6511; St. Boniface General Hospital, (204) 233-8563; Seven Oaks General Hospital, (204) 632-7133; Victoria General Hospital, (204) 269-3570.

WHERE TO LOOK

Newspapers

Winnipeg has two daily newspapers, the *Free Press* and *The Sun*, both distributed in the morning.

Radio

The Canadian Broadcasting Corporation (CBC) has both AM (990) and FM (98.3) stations in Winnipeg as well as an AM (1050) station broadcasting in French.

Visitor Information

Destination Winnipeg: 259 Portage Ave., Winnipeg, MB, Canada R3B 2B4; phone (204) 943-1970 or (800) 665-0204.

Destination Winnipeg is open Mon.-Fri. 8:30-4:30. A second branch, at Winnipeg International Airport, is open daily 8 a.m.-9:45 p.m.; phone (204) 982-7543.

Travel Manitoba's Explore Manitoba Centre at The Forks: 21 Forks Market Rd., Winnipeg, MB, Canada R3C 4T7; phone (204) 927-7838 or (800) 665-0040.

Explore Manitoba Centre is staffed with on-site travel counselors daily 9-6. The telephones are manned daily 8:30-4:30. The 24-hour Forks Hot Line, (204) 957-7618, also provides information. The center features dioramas depicting the various regions of the province.

TRANSPORTATION

Air Travel

Winnipeg International Airport is about 8 kilometres (5 mi.) northwest of downtown off Metro Rte. 90. Daily bus service between the airport and downtown is provided by Winnipeg Transit between 5:58 a.m. and 12:17 a.m. The one-way fare is $2; passengers must have exact change. Phone (204) 986-5700 for information. Major hotels offer limousine service to and from the airport.

Rental Cars

Hertz, (204) 925-6600, (800) 263-0600 in Canada, or (800) 654-3080 out of Canada, offers discounts to AAA and CAA members. Winnipeg locations are at Winnipeg International Airport, 1577 Erin St. and 830 Waverly St.

Rail Service

The VIA Rail Canada depot is downtown at 123 Main St.; phone (888) 842-7245.

Taxis

Cab companies include Blueline, (204) 925-8888; Duffy's, (204) 775-0101; and Unicity, (204) 925-3131. Base fare is $3.30, plus a charge of 10c for each additional 80 metres (263 ft.) or 14 seconds of metered waiting time.

Public Transport

Winnipeg Transit, the public bus system, serves downtown Winnipeg and its suburbs. Route maps and route information are available by phoning (204) 986-5700. The average bus fare is $2; riders must have exact change.

carrying the word "Route" and a number. Routes ending in even numbers designate north-south thoroughfares, and those ending in odd numbers designate major east-west arteries.

The primary north-south routes that cross the downtown area are 42, 52 and 62. The major east-west highways include 105, 115, 57 and 85. A good street map will enable drivers to see how the various grids of named streets connect with the main numbered routes.

Parking

Visitors will do best to park in a commercial lot, where rates average about $1.10 to $1.35 for the first hour and $1.10 to $1.60 for subsequent hours. Daily rates are about $4 to $7. Parking meters downtown cost $1 an hour, but most carry a 1- or 2-hour limit. Some parking in downtown is free in designated metered areas.

Parking is strictly controlled along major downtown streets. Cars parked between signs reading "No Parking Between" from 7 to 9 a.m. and 3:30 to 5:30 p.m. will be towed.

What To See

AIR FORCE HERITAGE PARK AND MUSEUM is off Ness Ave. at n. end of Sharpe Blvd. (Air Force Way). The museum, in Air Force Headquarters, includes two Victoria Crosses, the highest medal awarded to British Commonwealth service personnel. Historical Canadian Air Force aircraft and memorabilia are displayed in an outdoor setting; highlights include a Garden of Memories as well as military fighters, helicopters and transport aircraft.

Note: Due to security regulations, visitors must phone ahead for an appointment prior to visiting the museum. Allow 1 hour minimum. Museum open Mon.-Fri. 8-4. Guided tours are given by request. Air park open daily 24 hours. Donations. Phone (204) 833-2500, ext. 6532.

ASSINIBOINE PARK is at jct. Park Blvd. and Wellington Crescent; it also may be accessed from Portage Ave. via a footbridge over the Assiniboine River. The 153-hectare (378-acre) park has a zoo, miniature railway, duck pond, walking and biking paths, a conservatory, sculpture garden, a pavilion, Citizens Hall of Fame, gardens and an outdoor theater where concerts are held in summer. Tobogganing, cross-country skiing and ice skating are available in the winter.

Assiniboine Forest, south of the park off Grant Avenue, is one of the largest urban nature parks in Canada. Daily dawn-dusk. Free. Phone (204) 986-7234.

Assiniboine Park Conservatory, in Assiniboine Park, features indoor gardens, changing floral and plant displays and art work by local artists. A tropical palm house contains orchids, ferns and banana plants. Food is available. Daily 9-8, mid-Apr. to early Sept.; 9-4:30, rest of year. Free. Phone (204) 986-5537.

Assiniboine Park Zoo, in Assiniboine Park, has more than 1,600 different animals in naturalistic settings. The zoo specializes in animals found in cooler climates from around the world as well as native North American species. Siberian tigers, snow leopards, polar bears, lynxes, elk, bison, and many other hardy species can be seen outside throughout the year. Large indoor facilities provide warm-weather viewing of many tropical animals.

Food is available. Daily 9-7, July 1-Labour Day; 9-6, Victoria Day weekend-June 30; 10-4, rest of year. Closed mornings of Nov. 11 and Dec. 25. Admission (Mar.-Oct.) $4.25; $4 (ages 65+); $2.75 (ages 13-17); $2.25 (ages 2-12); $15 (family, two adults and children ages 0-17 living in the same household). Admission (rest of year) $3.75; $3.50 (ages 65+); $2.25 (ages 13-17); $1.75 (ages 2-12); $12 (family, two adults and children ages 0-17 living in the same household). AX, MC, VI. Phone (204) 986-2327.

Leo Mol Sculpture Garden, in Assiniboine Park, is said to be the first sculpture garden in North America dedicated to the works of a single artist. The garden and gallery feature bronze sculptures, porcelains, paintings and sketches by the Winnipeg artist. The gardens also are home to the Leo Mol Schoolhouse Studio. A reflecting pool and fountain are located in front of the gallery. Grounds open daily 7 a.m.-dusk. Gallery and studio open Tues.-Sun. 10-6, May-Aug.; Sat.-Sun. 11-5, in Sept. Donations. Phone (204) 895-7554.

Pavilion Gallery Museum is in Assiniboine Park at 55 Pavilion Crescent. Housed in a restored 1929 pavilion, the museum contains a permanent collection featuring the work of three prominent artists: Ivan Eyre, Walter Phillips and Clarence Tillenius. Allow 1 hour minimum. Tues.-Sun. 10-5, Victoria Day-Labour Day; Tues.-Sun. 11-5, rest of year. Free. Phone (204) 888-5466.

[SAVE] **COSTUME MUSEUM OF CANADA,** 109 Pacific Ave., features a 35,000-piece collection of textiles, clothing and accessories dating from 1565. The museum's exhibitions are presented in a *tableau vivant,* or living-picture style; each year a new exhibition is displayed. A visual storage room offers a close-up view of accessories.

Allow 1 hour minimum. Mon.-Sat. 10-5 (also Thurs. 5-8), Sun. noon-4, May-Aug. Admission $5; $4.50 (senior citizens and students with ID); $3.50 (ages 0-11); $14 (family). AX, MC, VI. Phone (204) 989-0072.

DALNAVERT MUSEUM, .5 blk. s. of Broadway at 61 Carlton St., is the former home of Sir Hugh John Macdonald, prominent lawyer and politician. Built in 1895, it was one of the first houses in Winnipeg to have hot-water heating, electric lighting and indoor plumbing.

Named after the Scottish birthplace of Macdonald's grandmother, the red brick Queen Anne Revival-style house features stained glass windows and a wraparound porch. The restored house, which was saved from demolition, is opulently furnished with Victorian antiques. Guided tours provide a glimpse into the lifestyles of early 20th-century Winnipeg society.

The visitor center behind the museum has been designed to be a "green" building, incorporating reclaimed and recycled materials during its construction and utilizing geothermal energy to heat and cool the building.

Allow 1 hour minimum. Guided tours are given Wed.-Fri. 10-5, Sat. 11-6, Sun. noon-4, July 1-Labour Day; Wed.-Fri. 11-4, Sat. 11-6, Sun. noon-4, rest of year. Closed holidays. Admission $5; $4 (ages 65+); $3 (ages 5-17); $12 (family, maximum two adults and three children). VI. Phone (204) 943-2835.

THE FORKS, at the confluence of the Red and Assiniboine rivers, has been a meeting place for more than 6,000 years, beginning with the aboriginal peoples. By virtue of location the 23-hectare (56-acre) site evolved into the center of the European fur trade in the 1730s. Métis, natives and eventually European settlers created a community along the rivers. More than a century later, the area became a transportation center as the railways laid tracks of steel across the prairie.

Now Winnipeg's main gathering spot, The Forks is a favorite place for shopping, dining and entertainment. The Riverwalk follows the water's edge from the Manitoba Legislature to The Forks through downtown Winnipeg, and the Wall Through Time chronicles area history from glacial Lake Agassiz to the present.

A water bus service offers historical tours of the Red and Assiniboine rivers as well as transportation *(see attraction listing p. 233).* Concerts and special events take place at The Forks throughout the year *(see Special Events p. 235).* Phone (800) 665-0040, or (204) 957-7618 for an events hotline.

The Forks Market is at the confluence of the Red and Assiniboine rivers. Housed in refurbished stable buildings, the market contains shops that offer jewelry and crafts; fresh, specialty and ethnic foods; produce; and baked goods. A six-story glass tower affords a view of the rivers and the downtown area. Mon.-Sat. 9:30-9, Sun. 9:30-6:30, July-Aug.; daily 9:30-6:30 (also Fri. 6:30-9 p.m.), rest of year. Free. Phone (204) 942-6302.

The Forks National Historic Site of Canada, at the confluence of the Red and Assiniboine rivers, is a 3.5-hectare (9-acre) park that offers an outdoor playground and a riverside amphitheater with a view of historic St. Boniface. Interpretive programs and festivals are held Victoria Day through Labour Day. A variety of guided tours and theatrical presentations are available July through August. Daily 24 hours. Free. Phone (204) 983-6757.

Johnston Terminal, in the heart of The Forks, is a renovated railway cold storage warehouse. The four-story structure now features shops, boutiques and restaurants. Allow 1 hour minimum. Mon.-Sat. 10-9, Sun. 10-6. Free. Phone (204) 956-5593.

Manitoba Children's Museum, in the Kinsmen Building at 45 Forks Market Rd., is in western Canada's oldest train repair facility. The museum houses six galleries offering a wide variety of hands-on activities. At All Aboard children can pretend to be an engineer or conductor on the diesel train or Pullman car that are inside the museum.

They can climb into and slide down a 5-metre-tall (17-ft.) oak tree and see what life is in a beaver lodge at The Tree & Me, or play with the latest technology in the Livewire gallery. They can be the star anchor in their own newscast at Our TV, then move on to Wonderworks and use child-size heavy equipment to design and build their own cities.

Picnicking is permitted. Allow 1 hour minimum. Daily 9:30-6, July 1-Labour Day; Sun.-Thurs. 9:30-4:30, Fri.-Sat. 9:30-6, rest of year. Closed Easter, 4 days following Labour Day and Dec. 24-26. Admission $6.75 (ages 2-17); $6.25 (adults); $5.75 (ages 65+). MC, VI. Phone (204) 924-4000.

FORTWHYTE ALIVE is at 1961 McCreary Rd. Bison on their own prairie, deer, foxes, prairie dogs, waterfowl and songbirds can be seen at this 259-hectare (640-acre) nature and recreational center.

There also are trails, floating boardwalks, birdfeeding stations, a bison-viewing mound, a family treehouse, fishing, boat and canoe rentals, snowshoeing, skating, tobogganing, a sod house, a tipi encampment and an interpretive center.

Picnic facilities and food are available. Allow 1 hour minimum. Mon.-Fri. 9-7, Sat.-Sun. and holidays 9-5; closed Dec. 25. Schedule varies summer and fall; phone for hours. Evening hours are extended Sept.-Oct. for viewing migrating Canada geese. Admission $5; $4 (ages 66+); $3 (ages 3-17). MC, VI. Phone (204) 989-8364.

FUN MOUNTAIN WATER SLIDE PARK, off Hwy. 1E on Murdock Rd., offers 10 waterslides, a swimming area, a hot tub, bumper boats, miniature golf, picnic areas and locker and changing facilities. Food is available. Open daily at 10, June-Aug. (weather permitting). Closing hours vary; phone ahead. Admission $14.50; $11.50 (ages 4-12); $6 (observers and ages 55+). Twilight rate $9. AX, MC, VI. Phone (204) 255-3910.

GRANT'S OLD MILL is at Portage Ave. and Booth Dr. This operational, reconstructed log flour mill—the original was built in 1829—marks the first use of water power in the Western provinces. Guided tours are available. Allow 30 minutes minimum. Daily 10-6, mid-May through Labour Day. Donations. Phone (204) 986-5613.

HISTORICAL MUSEUM OF ST. JAMES-ASSINIBOIA, 3180 Portage Ave., houses a collection of artifacts relating to the history of the St. James-Assiniboia area and a display building of pioneer activities. Guided interpretive tours through the mid-19th-century William Brown Red River Log House offer a glimpse of the pioneer lifestyle. Allow 1 hour minimum. Daily 10-4:30, mid-May through Labour Day; Mon.-Fri. 10-5, rest of year. Donations. Phone (204) 888-8706.

JEWISH HERITAGE CENTRE OF WESTERN CANADA, 123 Doncaster St., site of the Fort Osborne Barracks, shares the history, experiences, achievements and culture of Jewish people in Western Canada. The museum's permanent exhibit depicts the settlement of Jews in Western Canada through artifacts, photographs and archival material. The education center features items from the Holocaust. Changing exhibits and a library also are available.

Allow 30 minutes minimum. Mon.-Thurs. 9-5, Fri. 9-3. Donations. Phone (204) 477-7466, or (204) 477-7460 for tours or appointments.

KILDONAN PARK is at 2021 Main St. In its 40 hectares (99 acres) along the Red River the park has some of the province's oldest and largest trees, flower and rock gardens, and a model of the witch's hut from "Hansel and Gretel."

Summer options include swimming; boating; bicycling; walking; in-line skating; and Rainbow Stage, Winnipeg's outdoor theater. Tobogganing, ice skating and cross-country skiing are winter sports.

Food is available. Daily 8-dusk. Free. Phone (204) 986-7623. *See Recreation Chart.*

LA MAISON GABRIELLE-ROY, 375 Deschambault St. in St. Boniface, is the birthplace and childhood home of Gabrielle Roy, one of Canada's most famous 20th-century authors, known for her works about the underprivileged and poverty-stricken. The 1905 house contains furnishings and artifacts indicative of the early 20th-century period when the author lived here. Tours are given in English and French.

Allow 30 minutes minimum. Mon.-Fri. 10-5, Sat.-Sun. 1-5, June-Aug.; Wed.-Sun. 1-4, rest of year. Closed Jan. 1 and Dec. 25. Last tour begins 30 minutes before closing. Admission $4; $3 (ages 66+); $2 (ages 12-18). VI. Phone (204) 231-3853 or (866) 808-8338.

LIVING PRAIRIE MUSEUM is at 2795 Ness Ave. This 12-hectare (30-acre) unplowed tract supports more than 160 native plant species and is a remnant of the prairie that once covered much of North America. An interpretive center features displays of plants and animals of the tall grass prairie. Nature talks and hikes are offered, and a self-guiding trail brochure is available.

Allow 1 hour minimum. Interpretive center open daily 10-5, July-Aug.; Sun. 10-5, May-June; by appointment rest of year. Donations. Phone (204) 832-0167.

THE MANITOBA CRAFTS MUSEUM AND LIBRARY, downtown at 183 Kennedy St., has a permanent collection of approximately 5,000 traditional Manitoba crafts, including embroidery, knitting, quilting, weaving, lace, pottery, beadwork and basketry. The library has books, patterns and scrapbooks about many forms of craftwork. Allow 30 minutes minimum. Tues.-Wed. 10-4, Sat. noon-4 or by appointment; closed major holidays. Summer hours may vary; phone ahead. Donations. Phone (204) 487-6117.

MANITOBA ELECTRICAL MUSEUM & EDUCATION CENTRE is 1 blk. w. of jct. Pembina Hwy. and Stafford St. at 680 Harrow St. The museum's six galleries tell the story of electricity in the province beginning in the 1870s.

Themed areas such as The Light Goes On 1882-1900, Energizing Manitoba 1900-1960 and Powering up the Farm 1942-1960 provide an idea of the museum's offerings. A yellow turbine runner from one of the oldest hydroelectric stations in Manitoba is outside the 1931 building. Allow 1 hour minimum. Mon.-Thurs. 1-4; closed major holidays. Free. Phone (204) 477-7905.

MANITOBA LEGISLATIVE BUILDING, bordered by Broadway Ave., Kennedy and Osborne sts. and the Assiniboine River, reflects neoclassical design in native Tyndall limestone. The Italian marble grand staircase is guarded at its base by two life-size bronze bison, the emblems of Manitoba.

Atop the dome is Golden Boy by Parisian sculptor Charles Gardet. The torch, in the right hand, points to economic development and progress in the north; the sheaf of wheat in the left arm represents agriculture.

Guided tours are conducted daily on the hour 9-4, July 1-Labour Day; by appointment rest of year. Self-guiding tours are available daily 8-8, year-round. Free. Phone (204) 945-5813.

THE MANITOBA MUSEUM, Main St. and Rupert Ave., illustrates the relationship of people and their environment in Manitoba's history. The Earth History Gallery shows geologic and organic evolution, the Arctic/Sub-Arctic Gallery explores Inuit culture and the zone's flora and fauna, and the Boreal Forest Gallery features a diorama of a granite cliff, waterfall, marsh, Cree family and a wandering moose. A bat cave, snake pit and a Ukrainian rye farm can be seen at the Parklands/Mixed Woods Gallery.

Visitors can see a replica of the ketch *Nonsuch;* the ship's 1668 voyage to Hudson Bay opened western Canada to commerce. The Hudson's Bay Company Gallery highlights fur trading and early exploration. A teepee and a sod house are part of the Grasslands Gallery, and the Urban Gallery shows a 1920s boom-town Winnipeg.

Allow 1 hour minimum. Daily 10-5, Victoria Day-Labour Day; Tues.-Fri. 10-4, Sat.-Sun. and holidays 11-5, rest of year. Admission $8; $6.50 (ages 3-17, ages 60+ and students with ID); $26.50 (family, up to six people with no more than two adults). Combination ticket including museum, The Planetarium and The Science Gallery $18; $12.50 (ages 3-17, ages 60+ and students with ID); $60 (family, up to six people with no more than two adults). AX, MC, VI. Phone (204) 956-2830 or (204) 943-3139.

The Planetarium, on the lower level of The Manitoba Museum, presents interactive and multimedia shows about our universe. Allow 1 hour minimum. Shows are presented daily, Victoria Day-second Mon. in Oct.; Tues.-Sun., rest of year. Schedule varies; phone ahead.

Admission $6.50; $5 (ages 3-17, ages 60+ and students with ID); $20 (family, up to six people with no more than two adults). Combination ticket including The Manitoba Museum, The Planetarium and The Science Gallery $18; $12.50 (ages 3-17, ages 60+ and students with ID); $60 (family, up to six people with no more than two adults). AX, MC, VI. Phone (204) 956-2830, or (204) 943-3139 for show times.

The Science Gallery, on the lower level of The Manitoba Museum, has more than 100 hands-on exhibits. Allow 1 hour minimum. Daily 10-5, July 1-Labour Day; Tues.-Fri. 10-4, Sat.-Sun. and holidays 11-5, rest of year.

Admission $6.50; $5 (ages 3-17, ages 60+ and students with ID); $20 (family, up to six people with no more than two adults). Combination ticket including The Manitoba Museum, The Planetarium

and The Science Gallery $18; $12.50 (ages 3-17, ages 60+ and students with ID); $60 (family, up to six people with no more than two adults). AX, MC, VI. Phone (204) 956-2830 or (204) 943-3139.

MANITOBA SPORTS HALL OF FAME AND MUSEUM, on the fifth floor of The Bay, 450 Portage Ave., focuses on sports history and legendary athletes and teams. Interactive exhibits change every few months. Allow 1 hour minimum. Tues.-Sat. 10-5, in summer; Wed.-Sat. 10-5, rest of year. Closed major holidays. Donations. Phone (204) 774-0002.

RIEL HOUSE NATIONAL HISTORIC SITE OF CANADA, 330 River Rd., was the home of the mother of Louis Riel. Although this leader of the Métis and founder of the provisional government of Manitoba never lived in the house, his body lay in state for several days after his execution in 1885. The small log building with board siding is furnished in period.

The walkway to the house has signs explaining the history of the Métis and of the Riel family. Allow 30 minutes minimum. Guided tours daily 10-6, mid-May through Labour Day. Admission $3.95; $3.45 (ages 65+); $1.95 (ages 6-16). Phone (204) 257-1783.

ROSS HOUSE MUSEUM, 140 Meade St. N. in Joe Zuken Heritage Park, was the first post office in western Canada in 1854. Displays reflect the life of the Ross family when their home served as the post office. Allow 30 minutes minimum. Wed.-Sun. 10-4:30, June-Aug. Free. Phone (204) 943-3958.

ROYAL CANADIAN MINT is at 520 Lagimodière Blvd. at jct. Trans-Canada Hwy. and Hwy. 59. This high-tech, high-volume manufacturing facility is considered one of the world's most modern mints; its high-speed coining presses can each strike 750 coins per minute. The Winnipeg Plant produces all of the circulation coinage for Canada as well as coinage for more than 60 foreign countries.

The building includes a landscaped interior courtyard, a glass tower and a horseshoe-shaped tour route overlooking the manufacturing plant. At the mint's interactive museum visitors can lift a gold bar worth more than $200,000.

Guided tours are available. Mon.-Sat. 9-5, June-Aug. and in Dec.; Mon.-Fri. 9-5, rest of year. Last tour begins 1 hour before closing. Schedule may vary; phone ahead. Museum free. Guided tour (Mon.-Fri.) $5; $3 (ages 4-15); $13 (family, two adults and up to four children). Guided tour (Sat.) $3.50; $2 (ages 4-15); $10 (family, two adults and up to four children). Phone (204) 983-6429 or (888) 974-6468.

SAINT BONIFACE MUSEUM, s.e. on Main St. (Hwy. 1), then n. to 494 Taché Ave., was built 1846-51 as the first convent and hospital in western Canada. Displays depict the Red River Settlement and early French and Métis Manitoba; an exhibit is dedicated to Louis Riel, leader of the Red

River Resistance. Visitors also can view the nearby ruins of the cathedral as well as the cemetery where Riel is buried.

Allow 30 minutes minimum. Mon.-Fri. 9-5 (also Thurs. 5-8), Sat.-Sun. and holidays noon-4, May-Sept.; Mon.-Fri. 9-5, Sun. noon-4, rest of year. Closed Dec. 24-25 and 31. Admission $5; $3 (ages 61+, physically impaired and students with ID); free (ages 0-5); $12 (family). AX, MC, VI. Phone (204) 237-4500.

SAINT NORBERT PROVINCIAL HERITAGE PARK is at 40 Turnbull Dr. at the fork of the Red and La Salle rivers. Near the former village of St. Norbert, this 7-hectare (17-acre) park is rich in history and linked to Manitoba's entry into the Confederation. A restored 19th-century farmhouse and village house are decorated in period.

A walking trail with information about native inhabitants and Manitoba history and a house belonging to a member of Louis Riel's provisional government are available. Guided tours are available. Picnicking and fishing are permitted. Allow 1 hour minimum. Daily 10:30-5, Victoria Day-Labour Day. Donations. Phone (204) 945-4236, or (204) 945-4375 Sept.-Apr.

SEVEN OAKS HOUSE MUSEUM, 1.5 blks. e. of Main St. off Rupertsland Blvd. and Jones St. in W. Kildonan, is said to be the oldest habitable house in Manitoba. This sturdy building, with its stone foundation, hand-hewn oak timbers, hand-split shingles and buffalo hair-bound plaster, was built 1851-53. The house displays belongings of the original occupants and other period furnishings. Guided tours are available. Allow 30 minutes minimum. Daily 10-5, last weekend in May-Labour Day. Donations. Phone (204) 339-7429.

TRANSCONA HISTORICAL MUSEUM is at 141 Regent Ave. W. In a 1925 bank building, the museum explores the origins of Transcona, a railroad town amalgamated into Winnipeg, and the accomplishments of its residents. In addition to displays about the town's railroad heritage, veterans and community leaders, there also are archeology and butterfly exhibits.

Allow 30 minutes minimum. Mon.-Sat. 10-4, June-Aug.; Tues.-Fri. noon-4, Feb.-May and Sept.-Dec. Donations. Phone (204) 222-0423.

UKRAINIAN CULTURAL AND EDUCATIONAL CENTRE (OSEREDOK), 184 Alexander Ave. E., at Main St. and Disraeli Frwy., is dedicated to the preservation of Canadian-Ukrainian culture. Highlights include a museum, an art gallery, a library and archives. Interpretive exhibits relate to the Ukrainian heritage around the world and include a wide range of artifacts, from fine art to farm implements to rare 16th-century maps.

Guided tours are available by appointment. Allow 30 minutes minimum. Mon.-Sat. 10-4; July-Aug.; Mon.-Sat. 10-4, rest of year. Donations. Phone (204) 942-0218.

SAVE **WESTERN CANADA AVIATION MUSEUM,** in an aircraft hangar off Ellice Ave. at 958 Ferry Rd., displays 23 vintage aircraft. All aspects of aviation are exhibited, from bush planes to commercial airliners to combat planes and homemade aircraft. Children can explore the interactive Skyways exhibit. Videotaped presentations about historical aircraft are offered. A research library and archives can be seen by appointment.

Guided tours are available by appointment. Allow 1 hour minimum. Mon.-Fri. 9:30-4:30, Sat. 10-5, Sun. and holidays noon-5; closed Jan. 1, Good Friday and Dec. 25-26. Admission $7.50; $5 (students with ID and senior citizens); $3 (ages 3-12); $18 (family, two adults and three children). AX, MC, VI. Phone (204) 786-5503.

WINNIPEG ART GALLERY is at 300 Memorial Blvd. Eight galleries contain contemporary and historical works by Manitoba, Canadian and international artists. The Inuit art collection is reputed to be the largest public collection of contemporary Inuit art in the world. Guided tours are offered; reservations must be made 2 weeks in advance.

Food is available. Allow 1 hour minimum. Tues.-Sun. 11-5 (also Thurs. 5-9). Admission $6; $4 (ages 60+ and students with ID); $3 (ages 6-12); $15 (family); free (Sat.). AX, MC, VI. Phone (204) 786-6641, or (204) 789-1760 for recorded information.

GAMBLING ESTABLISHMENTS

- **Club Regent** is at 1425 Regent Ave. Mon.-Sat. 10 a.m.-3 a.m., Sun. noon-3 a.m.; closed Jan. 1, Easter, Nov. 11 and Dec. 24-25. Phone (204) 957-2500.

- **McPhillips Street Station** is at 484 McPhillips St. Mon.-Sat. 10 a.m.-3 a.m., Sun. noon-3 a.m.; closed Jan. 1, Easter, Nov. 11 and Dec. 24-25. Phone (204) 957-2500.

What To Do

Sightseeing

The intersection of Portage Avenue and Main Street, a few blocks from the juncture of Winnipeg's two rivers, has been the major crossroads since the city's earliest days and is a good place to start a sightseeing foray.

Although now part of Winnipeg, the early settlement of St. Boniface has retained its French Canadian identity. A monument honoring the explorer Pierre Gaultier de la Vérendrye is on Taché Avenue opposite St. Boniface Hospital. Also in St. Boniface is the grave of Louis Riel, leader of the Métis and of the provisional government 1869-70. The grave is at Taché and Cathedral avenues in the churchyard of the St. Boniface Basilica.

Boat Tours

PADDLEWHEEL RIVER BOATS LTD. departs from the Alexander Docks at jct. Alexander Ave. and Waterfront Dr. The company offers 2-hour daytime sightseeing tours of Winnipeg aboard the MS *Paddlewheel Queen*, MS *Paddlewheel Princess* and the MS *River Rouge* as well as evening dinner and dance cruises on the Assiniboine and Red rivers.

Food is available. Sightseeing cruise departs daily at 1, May-Oct. Sightseeing fare $16.75; $14.75 (ages 65+); $8.25 (ages 0-11). Reservations are recommended. MC, VI. Phone (204) 942-4500 or (204) 944-8000.

RIVER INTERPRETIVE BOAT TOURS departs from The Forks National Historic Site of Canada boat dock at 25 Forks Market Rd. Ninety-minute tours on an all-weather pontoon boat explore the Assiniboine, Red and Seine rivers. Passengers learn about the importance these waterways played in Winnipeg's history, including their relationship to the fur trade and the early forts.

Allow 1 hour, 30 minutes minimum. Departures require a minimum of four people, with a maximum of 10. Departures Tues.-Fri. at 10, noon, 2, 5:30 and 7, Sat.-Sun. at noon, 2 and 4, June 15-Sept. 15. Fare $8. Reservations are required. AX, MC, VI. Phone (204) 986-5663.

SPLASH DASH WATER BUS departs from the bottom of the river walk at The Forks. The boats provide 30-minute guided historical tours of a section of the Red and Assiniboine rivers. Points of interest are noted along the way. Allow 30 minutes minimum. Departures every 15 minutes daily 10-dusk (weather permitting), mid-June through Aug. 31; noon-6, Sept.-Oct. Fare $10; $9 (ages 4-18 and 55+). MC, VI. Phone (204) 783-6633.

Plane Tours

The Winnipeg Flying Club, (204) 338-7927, 16 kilometres (10 mi.) north of the perimeter on Hwy. 9 at St. Andrews Airport, offers scenic flights over Winnipeg, the Red River and the Lake Winnipeg area. Phone for information and reservations.

Train Tours

Antique rail cars pulled by a vintage locomotive take passengers on 2.5-hour trips departing from a 1910 station at Inkster Junction, 3 kilometres (1.9 mi.) west of Hwy. 90 and Inkster Boulevard. The Prairie Dog Central Railway makes stops at country markets in Grosse Isle and Warren. The scenic ride operates weekends May through September; phone (204) 832-5259.

Walking Tours

Guided walking tours of the 20-block Historic Winnipeg area near Portage Avenue and Main Street in the Exchange District are available June through Labour Day weekend. Departing from the Exchange District Information Booth on the east corner of King Street and Bannatyne in Old Market Square, these tours visit many of Manitoba's finest historical buildings; for schedule information phone (204) 942-6716.

One of the city's original ethnic neighborhoods, Selkirk Avenue is a mini-city that grew with the development of the railway in the 1880s. One-hour historic walking tours of the area are available from June to August; for information phone (204) 586-3445.

Walking tours of the old St. Boniface area are available; phone (204) 233-8343 or (866) 808-8338 for information and reservations. A self-guiding walking tour of Osborne Village, a densely populated area with many shops and restaurants, includes more than 33 buildings; for information phone (204) 474-1008. Crescentwood, an area of stately homes, can be seen on a self-guiding tour; pamphlets are available at the McNally Robinson bookstore at Grant Park Shopping Centre, 1120 Grant Ave.

Sports and Recreation

Devotees of organized sports will find many opportunities to indulge themselves in Winnipeg. Canadians love **hockey,** and those who fancy flying sticks and flashing skates will find the American Hockey League's Manitoba Moose locking horns with their opponents downtown at the MTS Centre at Donald Street and Portage Avenue.

Football fans can watch the Canadian Football League's Winnipeg Blue Bombers playing at the Canad Inns Stadium from June to November. The Northern **Baseball** League's Winnipeg Goldeyes play at CanWest Global Park at The Forks from May to August.

To obtain additional information and tickets for sports and recreation events listed above, phone (204) 780-3333.

Sports car racing enthusiasts converge at the Red River Speedway, (204) 582-0527, on Hwy. 75, 4 kilometres (2.5 mi.) south of St. Norbert, from April through October (weather permitting).

Assiniboia Downs, 3975 Portage Ave. at the Perimeter Highway, offers **Thoroughbred racing** early May to mid-October. Simulcast races are offered year-round; phone (204) 885-3330.

Note: Policies concerning admittance of children to pari-mutuel betting facilities vary. Phone for information.

Other spectator sports include minor league hockey, **curling** and **ringette** games, held at municipal skating rinks, and **cricket** played in Assiniboine Park. Ringette, similar to hockey, is a popular women's sport developed in Canada.

There are 33 **golf** courses in Winnipeg. Nine-hole public courses include Crescent Drive, 781 Crescent Dr., (204) 986-5911, and Harbour View, 1867 Springfield Rd., (204) 222-2751. Among the 18-hole public courses are Kildonan Park, 2021 Main St., (204) 986-5679; Tuxedo, 400 Shaftesbury Blvd., (204) 888-2867; and Windsor Park, 10 Rue des Meurons, (204) 986-3006. John Blumberg, 4540 Portage Ave., (204) 986-3490, offers both nine- and 18-hole layouts.

Winnipeg has more than 280 **tennis** courts, some lighted for night matches. Many courts are at community centers. Championship matches are held during the summer at various locations throughout the city. **Squash, handball** and **racquetball** players can avail themselves of courts at a number of athletic clubs and local universities. For information contact Sport Manitoba; phone (204) 925-5600.

Fans of **bicycling** and **in-line skating** take to the marked paths in Winnipeg's city parks. Bicycle trails along less-traveled side streets in and around Winnipeg also have been established. **Cross-country skiing, tobogganing** and **ice skating** facilities are available at Assiniboine, Kildonan and St. Vital parks; facilities for ice skating also are found at numerous schools and community clubs.

Downhill skiing is available at Spring Hill Winter Park Ski Area, (204) 224-3051, near Birds Hill Provincial Park at the junction of Hwy. 59N at the Floodway; and Stony Mountain Winter Park, (204) 344-5977, 10 kilometres (6 mi.) north of the perimeter of Hwy. 7. Birds Hill Provincial Park, (204) 222-9151, also is a site for **snowmobiling** and cross-country skiing.

Swimming can be pursued all year in Winnipeg, where numerous indoor pools include those at four YM-YWCAs; phone (204) 947-3044. The Pan-Am Pool, 25 Poseidon Bay, is one of the largest indoor bodies of water in Canada and is open all year; phone (204) 986-5890.

Many recreational activities are available at the Harbour View Recreation Complex in the northeastern section of Winnipeg in Kil-Cona Park, 1867 Springfield Rd. At this 162-hectare (400-acre) park are facilities for **miniature golf, lawn bowling, shuffleboard** and **horseshoes** as well as tennis courts, a golf course, a driving range and pedal boats during the summer. Golf and tennis lessons are available April to October. Ice skating, tobogganing and cross-country skiing are available during the winter. Phone (204) 222-2766.

Shopping

The intersection of Portage Avenue and Main Street is a good starting point for a shopping excursion. Winnipeg Square and the underground Lombard Concourse offer shops ranging from boutiques to bookstores. Portage Avenue also is the site of the city's largest department stores. Portage Place connects The Bay (The Hudson's Bay Co.) to other department stores with an extensive system of skywalks.

Winnipeg has a historic area where shoppers can browse through merchandise of today amid structures of the past. The Forks Market (see attraction listing p. 229) is behind Union Station, off Main Street (near Portage and Main). The shops and restaurants are located in an indoor market with more than 80 vendors selling everything from fresh fish and baked goods to arts and crafts items. The Johnston Terminal (see attraction listing p. 229), across from the market, offers specialty boutiques and eateries.

Shopping for Western wear and accessories is possible at such factory outlet stores as Canada West Boots, 2188 McPhillips St., or MWG Factory Outlet, 1147 Notre Dame Ave.

More than 125 shops and restaurants can be found at Osborne Village, between River and Wardlaw avenues 2 blocks south of the Manitoba Legislative Building. Travelers in search of a truly representative souvenir may want to examine the native arts and crafts and western wear available at Winnipeg Outfitters Inc. at 250 McPhillips St.

Finally, visitors who like their shopping climate-controlled and under one roof can visit the malls at Cityplace, 333 St. Mary Ave. at Hargrave Street; Garden City, 2305 McPhillips St., with Sears and Winners as its anchor stores; Grant Park, 1120 Grant Ave., with Zellers; Kildonan Place, 1555 Regent Ave. W., with anchors Sears and Zellers; Polo Park, 1485 Portage Ave., which has The Bay and Sears for anchors; Portage Place, 393 Portage Ave.; or St. Vital Centre, 1225 St. Mary's Rd., with The Bay and Sears as its anchor stores.

Performing Arts

Canada's Royal Winnipeg Ballet, Winnipeg Symphony Orchestra and Manitoba Opera perform in Centennial Concert Hall, 555 Main St., opposite City Hall. The oldest company in Canada and the second oldest in North America, Canada's Royal Winnipeg Ballet is known for its versatile style and performs an eclectic mix of classical and contemporary ballets. At home performances are from October through May. For ticket information phone (204) 956-2792 or (800) 667-4792.

The Winnipeg Symphony Orchestra performs September to May and offers classical, contemporary and popular orchestral music; for concert information phone (204) 949-3999. The Manitoba Opera performs October through May; phone (204) 942-7479, or (204) 780-3333 for tickets.

Modern dance is presented by Winnipeg's Contemporary Dancers from December through April at the Centennial Concert Hall; for information phone (204) 452-0229.

Theater lovers can enjoy performances of the classics, comedies and modern dramas at the Manitoba Theatre Centre Mainstage, 174 Market St., from October to May; for general information or tickets phone (204) 942-6537. The MTC Warehouse Theatre, 140 Rupert Ave., (204) 942-6537, features alternative theater performances from November to April. The Lyric Theatre, just east of the Pavilion in Assiniboine Park, (204) 885-9742, is an outdoor theater showcasing drama festivals as well as performances by the Royal Winnipeg Ballet, the Winnipeg Symphony Orchestra and other musical groups.

For both adults and young people, the Prairie Theatre Exchange, at Portage Place, 393 Portage Ave., (204) 942-7291, or (204) 942-5483 for ticket information, presents a season of modern Canadian plays from October to April. Rainbow Stage in Kildonan Park offers musicals in a covered outdoor theater from July through August; phone (204) 989-5261 or (888) 989-0888. Celebrations Dinner Theatre, 1824 Pembina Hwy. in the Canad Inn Fort

Garry, combines an original, three-act musical comedy with a four-course dinner for a one-stop evening out; phone (204) 982-8282.

The IMAX Theatre, Portage Place, 393 Portage Ave. in downtown Winnipeg, features a five-and-one-half-story-high by 22-metre-wide (72-ft.) screen; phone (204) 956-4629 for information or (204) 780-7328 to reserve tickets.

A variety of theatrical productions for children of all ages is presented at The Forks by the Manitoba Theatre for Young People; for information phone (204) 942-8898.

The French Canadian heritage of St. Boniface, in the heart of the French district, is remembered through the support of the Centre Culturel Franco-Manitobain at 340 Provencher Blvd.; phone (204) 233-8972. The center is the home of such cultural groups as Le Cercle Molière theater company (Canada's oldest active theater group), the dance group L'Ensemble Folklorique de la Rivière Rouge, and the choral groups L'Alliance Chorale Manitoba and La Chorale des Intrépides; phone (204) 233-8053 for more information.

Special Events

Winnipeg's calendar of events, with more than 130 days of festivals, reflects more than 43 nationalities that have made the city home. The *joie de vivre* spirit of the French voyageurs is revived each February during ◈ Le Festival du Voyageur, a 10-day-long celebration including winter sports, ice-sculpting contests, music and food. With the 18th-century fur trade as its theme, the event takes place in St. Boniface, Winnipeg's French quarter.

The city plays host to the 4-day Winnipeg International Children's Festival at The Forks in early June. Music, theater, dance and comedy performances are offered as well as hands-on workshops and evening shows.

The weeklong Jazz Winnipeg Festival in late June features jazz performers on an outdoor stage. The ◈ Red River Exhibition, known locally as the "The Ex" is held during late June. The Ex's many rides, midway activities and games of chance as well as nightly concerts take place at Red River Exhibition Park off Perimeter Highway behind Assiniboia Downs.

In mid-July is the 10-day Winnipeg Fringe Festival, with various theater performances in the Exchange District. Mid-July also brings the 4-day ◈ Winnipeg Folk Festival to nearby Birds Hill Provincial Park, where more than 200 concerts, children's activities, music workshops and food are highlighted.

Early August brings the 2-week ◈ Folklorama multicultural celebration, Winnipeg's largest event and reputedly the largest multicultural festival of its kind.

Travel the world...

...get more for your money.

Show your AAA membership card
at these participating international partners —
museums, hotels, attractions and dining
locations around the world ... *and SAVE*.

Northwest Territories and Nunavut

Northern Lights

Paint the late summer and autumn sky in anticipation of winter holidays

"Long Day's Journey into Night"

Above the Arctic Circle, the June sun doesn't set until late July

A Hike on the Wild Side

Beluga whales, bison, musk oxen, caribou, moose, polar bears, wolves and falcons

Winter Wanderings

By airplane, snowmobile, dogsled or on a highway of ice

Sundry Scenery

Tundra, alpine plains, mountains, spruce forests, pristine lakes and rivers

Hood River, near Bathurst Inlet, Arctic Circle
© Brian Sytnyk
Masterfile

head
north

Nunavut
© John Foster
Masterfile

T ake a journey into northern Canada and you may be surprised at your options for enjoyment.

Residents joke that the four seasons in the Northwest Territories and Nunavut—June, July, August and winter—are a bit unlike seasons in the rest of the world. The absence of a "real" spring or fall leaves busy summers and extra-long winters.

Arrive in June, July or August and you can dip your toes in the Arctic Ocean and marvel at the wildflower-dotted tundra under a midnight sun.

Or visit during the 6 months of winter and you can choose from myriad activities that involve snow and ice: snowmobiling, building an igloo, ice fishing, riding on a paw-powered sled or simply driving on an "ice highway," made of hard-packed snow piled on frozen lakes.

Celebrate the end of a long, dark winter by living it up at Inuvik's Sunrise Festival—held in January in honor of the sun's appearance after months of hiding.

Other diversions do not depend on snow or sun: Try a musk ox burger or dine on arctic char. Shop for such treasures as whalebone or soapstone carvings. Stay at a remote wilderness lodge and discover the specialized flora and fauna of the Arctic Circle. Learn about the traditions of the Inuit and Dene cultures. Set your sights on beluga whales or polar bears. See a shaggy musk-ox up close or listen to the roar of hooves from a migrating herd of caribou.

Whatever the season, the Northwest Territories and Nunavut invite you to refresh your senses in the north.

On April Fools' Day, 1999, in the eastern Northwest Territories, very few Inuit people were worried about such practical jokes as sugar in the salt shaker.

Instead the focus was on celebrating the birth of Nunavut, Canada's newest territory. On this night Inuit eyes were toward the heavens, watching as a grand display of colorful explosions lit up the black sky. Matching the glow of the fireworks were the sparks in the hearts of the Inuit, whose hopes are high for a bright future.

Twenty-four years after a separation was proposed, Nunavut (meaning "our land" in the Inuktitut language) officially seceded from the expansive Northwest Territories to form its own territory. A new line on the Canadian map allows its approximately 29,474 residents—85 percent of whom are Inuit—the chance to reclaim and govern what they have always believed to be their own.

Where the Streets Have No Name

Nunavut, a giant chunk of arctic earth stretching so far northeast it almost tickles the shores of Greenland, contains only one road within its nearly 2 million square kilometres

(772,204 sq. mi.). Above the tree line it's a place where animals outnumber humans; where brightly colored rhododendron, lupines, yellow buttercups and mountain avens sprinkle treeless tundra; and where it may be easier to hook a trout for dinner than pick up a cheeseburger at a drive-thru.

The capital city of Iqaluit rests at the southern tip of mountainous Baffin Island, from which steep cliffs drop about 610 metres (2,001 ft.) to the sea. It's no surprise to see caribou wandering just outside the city limits along the Road to Nowhere. But don't worry; there are plenty of folks who can show you around, and during summer the midnight sun shines bright to light your way.

Even farther north is Quttinirpaaq National Park of Canada, which extends above the 80th parallel, just a snowball's throw from Santa's workshop. In this globe-top world of snow-capped peaks and glaciers, ice simply does not melt.

Despite the recent division of Nunavut and Northwest Territories, the two still share similar features. Take light, for example. During summer above the Arctic Circle, days have no end. A shining sun never dips below the horizon, and the sky is illuminated 24 hours a

Sir Martin Frobisher, searching for the Northwest Passage to the Orient, arrives.
1576

The Treaty of Paris grants Canada to the British.
1763

Alexander Mackenzie leads an expedition along a westward-flowing river, unearthing another route to the Arctic Ocean.

1789

1771
Hudson's Bay Co. explorer-trader Samuel Hearne arrives at Great Slave Lake.

NW Territories Historical Timeline

1850
Capt. Robert John Le Mesurier McClure discovers the Northwest Passage.

day. In winter the opposite occurs as days and nights melt together under a cold, dark sky.

Sound dismal and depressing? Well, picture the sight of a black sky pin-pricked with stars surrounding a full, glowing moon, its light sprawling across wide, snow-covered tundra and frozen lakes. On such a clear winter night the flat, stark-white landscape glistens and appears endless.

Bright Lights, Small Cities

The northern lights, or "aurora borealis," painting the winter sky are no less impressive. A faint glow slightly above the horizon serves as the show's opening act. When the lights rise, they resemble curtains in shades of red, lavender and green. Feather-shaped and stretching across the night sky, the lights ripple and curl, forming watercolor waves.

In the Northwest Territories you'll have a good chance to catch this dazzling display October through March. A spot void of city lights is best; try giant Great Slave Lake near Yellowknife. Frozen in winter, this fifth largest freshwater lake in North America provides a fine view of the vivid night sky.

Then visit Yellowknife, on the lake's north arm. Once glittering with gold, this former 1930s mining camp now flaunts its colorful past in Old Town, where shops and quaint neighborhoods nestle against the shore.

West of the city is Nahanni National Park Reserve of Canada, where Virginia Falls plummets 90 metres (295 ft.) into South Nahanni River. The falls, arguably more spectacular than Niagara, form a pool of eddies and perilous rapids surrounded by cliffs taller than Toronto's CN Tower.

Roads are in short supply here, but sparkling falls and rivers await you on scenic drives. Mackenzie Hwy., the Territories' only paved highway, crosses the Mackenzie River near Fort Providence. Continue east along the Waterfalls Route (Hwy. 1) to Sambaa Deh Falls Territorial Park, where trails lead to two cascades.

Some ice roads mid-December through April allow drives as far north as Tuktoyaktuk and Aklavik. Many motorists also choose to navigate the Dempster Hwy., which begins in Dawson City, Yukon Territory, and dead-ends at Inuvik, the continent's farthest point north accessible by road.

In fact visiting the lands north of the 60th parallel may be the brightest idea you've ever had.

Hudson's Bay Co. cedes the region to Canada. **1870**

Northwest Territories divides into two territories; the eastern, Inuit-governed territory becomes Nunavut. **1999**

A Soviet nuclear-powered satellite crashes into the Great Slave Lake area; debris is spread over 124,000 square kilometres. **1978**

1920 Oil is discovered at Norman Wells.

1993 The Nunavut Land Claims Agreement, under which the Inuit give up any future aboriginal rights to their traditional land in return for the power to govern their own territory, is passed.

T. Macintosh/GNWT

1934 Gold is discovered at Yellowknife on Great Slave Lake.

Recreation

Welcome to the top of the world. The vast Northwest Territories and Nunavut boast an area filled with wild rivers, icy seas, lofty mountains and Arctic tundra. Recreational diversions for both the adventure seeker and casual traveler are numerous.

Summer days, typically June through August, are long and surprisingly mild. With an average temperature of 21 C (70 F), visitors can enjoy the outdoors without the gear that winter demands. **Hikers** can check out a wide variety of topography, from steep mountain trails to Arctic tundra. The Canol Heritage Trail, en route to the Yukon, offers some challenging terrain.

Snowmobiling, snowshoeing, dogsledding and **cross-country skiing** are a way of life that has been known to extend into May—the warmer air and long days make this the perfect time for such outdoor pursuits. Recreational activities also can be combined with viewing the spectacular northern lights. Many outfitters offer snowmobile tours or flights to remote areas to observe this brilliant display. Hint: The best time for viewing these dancing lights is October through March.

Getting There is Half the Fun

Travel anywhere in the territories can include aircraft, boat, automobile, snowmobile, Inuit qomatiq (sled) and even dogsled. Of the Northwest Territories' four national parks, only Wood Buffalo can be reached by road. Nahanni's rugged beauty is accessible solely by air. Only the hardy recreationalist should fly to the extremely remote Aklavik, where craggy badlands include thousands of archeological sites. The newest park, Tuktut Nogait, is a hiker's paradise where float planes begin landing on the Homaday River in mid-June.

High in Canada's eastern Arctic is Nunavut's Baffin Island. Auyuittuq National Park of Canada, reached by dogsled in winter and boat in summer, draws avid hikers and **climbers** to its lofty peaks. The sheer cliffs and arctic fiords of Quttinirpaaq National Park of Canada (formerly Ellesmere Island National Park Reserve), the northernmost national park in North America, can be explored by guided tour; outfitters are available in Grise Fiord, Iqaluit and Resolute.

Land of Adventure

Water challenges come in varying degrees of difficulty. **Canoeing** and **kayaking** conditions depend on the weather. Arctic rivers, while dangerous, can offer the ultimate thrill if explored cautiously. Sea kayakers can flow beside towering icebergs, while the many rivers stemming off the meandering Mackenzie are a canoeist's dream. Paddlers will be dazzled by the breathtaking scenery on the Nahanni. Hoist your sails on Great Slave Lake, where the wind is just right for **sailing,** or if you are brave enough, **scuba dive** in the frigid waters. Slave River rapids await **whitewater rafting** enthusiasts.

Cold northern waters yield excellent **fishing.** Plenty of lakes, streams and rivers are full of prize catches, from the feisty arctic char to the fierce northern pike. Some of the territories' waters are ranked the best in the world for angling, including Great Slave, Great Bear and Murky lakes and the Stark and Snowdrift rivers. **Ice fishing** is another way to reel in the big one. Don't forget your fishing license.

The land's beauty, combined with unspoiled wilderness and vast game selections, makes **hunting** quite a rewarding experience. For the ultimate hunt, sports enthusiasts can track down one of the world's largest predators—the polar bear—by dogsled. Hunting for caribou or musk ox are additional options. Hunts are strictly controlled; licensed guides and permits are required.

For those who like to shoot with a camera, **wildlife viewing** is rewarding. **Bird-watchers** flock to the Mackenzie River delta, one of the world's biggest nesting grounds.

Whether you are seeking adventure for a few hours or several days, an outfitter will help. Northwest Territories Tourism, (867) 873-5007 or (800) 661-0788, or Nunavut Tourism, (866) 686-2888, can offer information about tour companies and outfitters.

Recreational Activities

Throughout the TourBook, you may notice a Recreational Activities heading with bulleted listings of recreation-oriented establishments listed underneath. Similar operations also may be mentioned in Destination City recreation sections. Since normal AAA inspection criteria cannot be applied, these establishments are presented only for information. Age, height and weight restrictions may apply. Reservations often are recommended and sometimes are required. Addresses and/or phone numbers are provided so visitors can contact the attraction for additional information.

Fast Facts

POPULATION: Northwest Territories 41,464. Nunavut 29,474.

AREA: Northwest Territories 1,140,835 sq km (440,479 sq mi); ranks 3rd. Nunavut 1,932,255 sq km (746,048 sq mi); ranks 1st.

CAPITAL: Yellowknife, Northwest Territories; Iqaluit, Nunavut.

HIGHEST POINT: 2,762 m/9,062 ft., Cirque of the Unclimbables Mountain northwest of Nahanni National Park Reserve of Canada.

LOWEST POINT: Sea level, Beaufort Sea.

TIME ZONE(S): Mountain/Central/Eastern/Atlantic. DST.

MINIMUM AGE FOR UNRESTRICTED DRIVER'S LICENSE: 17.

SEAT BELT/CHILD RESTRAINT LAWS: Seat belts required for driver and all passengers 18 kg (40 lbs.) and over; children under 18 kg (40 lbs.) required to be in a child restraint.

HELMETS FOR MOTORCYCLISTS: Required for all riders.

RADAR DETECTORS: Not permitted.

FIREARMS LAWS: By federal law, all nonresidents entering Canada with a firearm must declare their weapon in writing and pay a fee of $25 (Canadian).

HOLIDAYS: Jan. 1; Good Friday; Easter Monday; Victoria Day, May 24 (if a Mon.) or the closest prior Mon.; Aboriginal Day, June 21; Canada Day, July 1; Nunavut Day, July 9; Civic Holiday, Aug. (1st Mon.); Labour Day, Sept. (1st Mon.); Thanksgiving, Oct. (2nd Mon.); Remembrance Day, Nov. 11; Christmas, Dec. 25; Boxing Day, Dec. 26.

TAXES: The Northwest Territories and Nunavut have no territorial sales tax. However, a 6 percent Goods and Services Tax (GST) is levied.

INFORMATION CENTERS: Territorial welcome centers in the Northwest Territories include an office on Hwy. 1 at the Alberta border (on the 60th parallel) near Enterprise; it is open 8:30-8:30, mid-May to mid-Sept. Dempster/Delta Visitor Information Centre at Km-post 77 on Hwy. 8 near Fort McPherson is open 10-10, mid-May to mid-Sept. The Western Arctic Regional Visitor Information Centre at the termination of the Dempster Hwy. in Inuvik is open daily 9-8, mid-May to mid-Sept. The Northern Frontier Visitor's Centre in Yellowknife is open daily 8:30-6, June-Sept.; Mon.-Fri. 9-5, Sat.-Sun. and holidays noon-4, rest of year. Phone (867) 873-4262 or (877) 881-4262.

In Nunavut the Unikkaarvik Visitor Centre in Iqaluit is open Mon.-Fri. 9-6, Sat.-Sun. 1-4, June-Aug.; Mon.-Fri. 9-6, rest of year. Phone (867) 979-4636 or (866) 686-2888.

FURTHER INFORMATION FOR VISITORS:
Northwest Territories Tourism
P.O. Box 610
Yellowknife, NT, Canada X1A 2N5
(867) 873-7200
(800) 661-0788

Nunavut Tourism
P.O. Box 1450
Iqaluit, NU, Canada X0A 0H0
(866) 686-2888

FISHING AND HUNTING REGULATIONS:
Northwest Territories Environment and
    Natural Resources
P.O. Box 2668
Yellowknife, NT, Canada X1A 2P9
(867) 873-7184
(800) 661-0788

FERRY AND ROAD INFORMATION: (800) 661-0750 (valid only in Canada)

ALCOHOL CONSUMPTION: Legal age 19.

Northwest Territories Temperature Averages Maximum/Minimum (Celsius)
From the records of The Weather Channel Interactive, Inc.

	JAN	FEB	MAR	APR	MAY	JUNE	JULY	AUG	SEPT	OCT	NOV	DEC
Yellowknife	-24	-19	-13	-1	10	18	21	18	10	1	-11	-20
	-32	-29	-24	-12	-1	8	12	10	3	-4	-19	-28

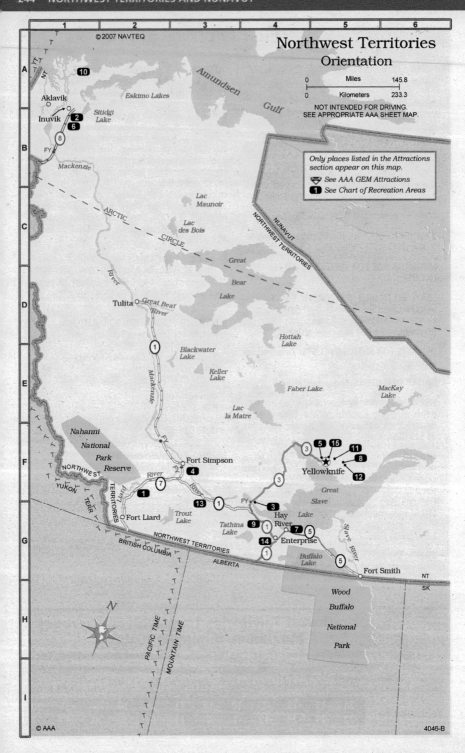

© 2007 NAVTEQ

Northwest Territories
Orientation

Miles		
0		145.8
0		233.3
Kilometers		

NOT INTENDED FOR DRIVING.
SEE APPROPRIATE AAA SHEET MAP.

Only places listed in the Attractions
section appear on this map.
▽ See AAA GEM Attractions
① See Chart of Recreation Areas

Amundsen Gulf

Eskimo Lakes

Aklavik
Inuvik
Sitidgi Lake

Mackenzie

ARCTIC CIRCLE

NUNAVUT
NORTHWEST TERRITORIES

Lac Maunoir

Lac des Bois

Great Bear Lake

Tulita
Great Bear River

Blackwater Lake

Keller Lake

Hottah Lake

Faber Lake

MacKay Lake

Lac la Matre

Mackenzie

Nahanni National Park Reserve

NORTHWEST

YUKON

TERRITORIES

Fort Simpson

Yellowknife

Great Slave Lake

River

Fort Liard

Trout Lake

Tathina Lake

Hay River

Enterprise

Buffalo Lake

Slave River

Fort Smith

NT
SK

NORTHWEST TERRITORIES

BRITISH COLUMBIA

ALBERTA

Wood Buffalo National Park

N

PACIFIC TIME

MOUNTAIN TIME

© AAA

4046-B

Nunavut
Orientation

NOT INTENDED FOR DRIVING.
SEE APPROPRIATE AAA SHEET MAP.

© 2007 NAVTEQ

RECREATION AREAS

	MAP LOCATION	CAMPING	PICNICKING	HIKING TRAILS	BOATING	BOAT RAMP	BOAT RENTAL	FISHING	SWIMMING	PETS ON LEASH	BICYCLE TRAILS	WINTER SPORTS	VISITOR CENTER	LODGE/CABINS	FOOD SERVICE
NATIONAL PARKS *(See place listings)*															
Nahanni (F-1) 4,766 square kilometres 145 km w. of Fort Simpson. The park is not accessible by road; no motor boats allowed.		•	•	•	•	•		•	•	•			•		
Wood Buffalo (G-5) 44,807 square kilometres on Hwy. 5.		•	•	•	•	•		•	•	•			•	•	
TERRITORIAL															
Blackstone (F-2) 166 km s. of Fort Simpson. on Hwy. 7 or 115 km n. of Fort Liard on Hwy. 7.	**1**	•	•	•	•	•		•		•			•		
Chuk (B-1) s. of Inuvik on Hwy. 8.	**2**	•	•	•				•		•			•		
Fort Providence (G-4) at Fort Providence on Hwy. 3.	**3**	•	•					•		•			•		
Fort Simpson (F-3) in Fort Simpson on Hwy. 1.	**4**	•	•							•			•		
Fred Henne (F-5) on Hwy. 3 across from Yellowknife airport. *(See Yellowknife p. 250)*	**5**	•	•	•	•			•	•	•			•		•
Gwich'in Reserve (B-1) s. of Inuvik on Hwy. 8.	**6**	•	•							•			•		
Hay River (G-4) on Vale Island in Hay River.	**7**	•	•		•			•		•			•		
Hidden Lake (F-5) 3,000 hectares 45 km e. of Yellowknife along Hwy. 4. Scenic. Canoeing, golf; interpretive displays.	**8**	•							•	•					
Lady Evelyn Falls (G-4) 6.5 km off Hwy. 1 near Kakisa.	**9**	•	•	•				•		•			•		
Paniksak (A-1) w. of Tuktoyaktuk.	**10**	•	•							•				•	•
Prelude Lake (F-5) 29 km w. of Yellowknife on Hwy. 4. *(See Yellowknife p. 250)*	**11**	•	•	•	•	•		•	•	•					
Reid Lake (FG-5) 60 km e. of Yellowknife on Hwy. 4.	**12**	•	•	•	•			•	•	•					
Sambaa Deh Falls (G-3) s. of Fort Simpson on Hwy. 1.	**13**	•	•					•		•			•		
Twin Falls Gorge (G-4) at Km-post 75 on Hwy. 1.	**14**	•	•	•				•		•			•		
Yellowknife River (F-5) 9 km. e. of Yellowknife on Hwy. 4.	**15**		•		•	•	•	•		•					

Points of Interest

AKLAVIK (A-1)

Aklavik, which means "the place of the Barrenland grizzly," was founded in 1912 as the Mackenzie River delta outpost of Hudson's Bay Co. A thriving company base in addition to a trading and trapping center, the town became the administrative center of the Western Arctic region.

However, since the community rested in the middle of the largest delta in Canada, it faced constant change as the powerful Mackenzie River built up new land and flooded the old. These conditions prevented the construction of major roads and airstrips. As a result, the newer town of Inuvik *(see place listing p. 248)* absorbed Aklavik's administrative role. There are no roads into Aklavik; it is accessible by air from Inuvik or by ice roads during winter.

Many Aklavik residents refuse to move. The descendants of the early traders and trappers work on oil rigs in the Beaufort Sea or trap muskrat in the delta, which is rich in wildlife. A museum, the original company store and restored log cabins serve as reminders of the past.

Just off Main Street is a tree stump in which Albert Johnson, the suspected "Mad Trapper of Rat River," carved his initials. The town also contains his grave. Johnson, who allegedly killed prospectors and trappers for the gold in their teeth, was shot in 1932 after one of the most intensive manhunts in Canadian history. Whether he actually was the "mad trapper" has been a subject explored in both books and film.

BAFFIN ISLAND

High in Nunavut's Eastern Arctic is Baffin Island, the homeland of the Inuit. It is a land of majestic fiords, icebergs, bountiful wildlife and the midnight sun, which shines until 3 a.m. from March to June. Although Baffin Island is not accessible by car, Iqaluit *(see place listing p. 248)*, Nunavut's capital city, is served by two airlines.

Qaummaarviit Territorial Park, 12 kilometres (7 mi.) west of Iqaluit, can be reached by boat in summer or by dogsled and snowmobile in spring. An easy-to-follow trail links the island's ruins with signs depicting aspects of prehistoric life and culture.

Auyuittuq National Park of Canada, 32 kilometres (20 mi.) from Pangnirtung, is accessible by dogsled, snowmobile or boat. The park is notable for its fiords and glaciated valleys and mountains and for being the first national park established above the Arctic Circle. Polar bears, arctic foxes, caribou, seals, walruses, whales and narwhals inhabit the region.

Included in the approximately 40 bird species spotted in the park are the rare gyrfalcon and whistling swan. Remains of the 1,000-year-old Thule Eskimo culture have been found in Cumberland Sound. Hikers and mountain campers traversing Auyuittuq's Akshayuk Pass—commonly known as the "Pang Pass"—will find challenging trails, abundant wildlife and spectacular scenery.

Quttinirpaaq National Park of Canada (formerly known as Ellesmere Island National Park Reserve) is the most northerly land mass in Canada and contains 2,604-metre (8,544-ft.) Mount Barbeau, the highest mountain in eastern North America, and Lake Hazen, one of the largest lakes north of the Arctic Circle. The reserve is primarily a polar desert encompassing 39,500 square kilometres (15,250 sq. mi.) of mountain ranges, glaciers, ice shelves and fiords. Remains of buildings from European expeditions can be found on the rocky terrain. Outfitters in Grise Fiord, Iqaluit and Resolute Bay can arrange trips into the park.

Katannilik Territorial Park, between Kimmirut and Iqaluit, is rich with wildlife and unique flora. River tours, hiking and northern survival challenge even the hardiest adventurers. Information can be obtained from Nunavut Tourism; phone (866) 686-2888.

In spring and summer licensed guides from Angmarlik Visitors Centre lead expeditions into Kekerten Territorial Park, 50 kilometres (32 mi.) south of Pangnirtung; phone (867) 473-8737. Visitors can see remains of whale lookouts, blubber vats, whalers' houses and Inuit homes. A self-guiding trail connects dozens of ruins.

In the northeasternmost part of Baffin Island is Sirmilik National Park of Canada, approximately 22,000 square kilometres (8,494 sq. mi.) of rugged mountains, glaciers, ice fields, ocean fiords and coastal lowlands. In fact Sirmilik translates to "the place of glaciers." Pond Inlet, the closest community to the park, is 25 kilometres (16 mi.) south. Travel to the park—by boat, dogsled or snowmobile (depending on the season)—can be arranged through outfitters in Pond Inlet or Arctic Bay.

The park is accessible year-round, except in October and November when the ice freezes up and in July during ice break up. Popular with mountain climbers, Sirmilik is also a haven for bird-watchers. Colonies of seabirds, including thick-billed murres, black-legged kittiwakes and greater snow geese, inhabit Bylot Island. For additional information contact the park office in Pond Inlet; phone (867) 899-8092.

ENTERPRISE (G-4) pop. 100

Enterprise is the first Northwest Territories community encountered by travelers heading north on

Mackenzie Hwy. A major service center for commercial traffic, the town is best known for its spectacular view of Hay River Gorge near the local Esso station.

Scenic 33-metre (108-ft.) Alexandra Falls and 15-metre (50-ft.) Louise Falls in Twin Falls Gorge Territorial Park *(see Recreation Chart)* are about 9 kilometres (6 mi.) south on Mackenzie Hwy. Camping and picnicking are permitted.

FORT LIARD (G-2) pop. 500

Fort Liard is in the Territories' southwest corner. Nearby archeological digs have revealed strata showing 9,000 years of human occupancy. Prior to 1807 Northwest Co. founded a post that was taken over by Hudson's Bay Co. in 1821 when the companies merged. An earnest fur trade continues.

The opening of Liard Hwy. in the early 1980s put the quiet village on the map. The community is characterized by lush growth and a relatively mild climate, despite its northern location. Bird-watchers will find many songbirds during spring and summer. A small lakefront campground is nearby.

Boat launching is possible on the Petitot and Liard rivers, where visitors can see interesting rock formations and fish for pickerel at the rivers' mouth. Fort Liard is a good jumping-off point for exploring the surrounding mountains or Nahanni National Park Reserve of Canada *(see place listing p. 248)*. Chartered flights and a forestry office are available in town.

FORT SIMPSON (F-3) pop. 1,300

Established in 1804 at the fork of the Mackenzie and Liard rivers, Fort Simpson is the oldest continuously occupied trading post in the Mackenzie River Valley. Once a district headquarters for Hudson's Bay Co., the town developed into a center of river trade. Originally Fort of the Forks, the town was renamed to honor Thomas Simpson, first governor of the merged Northwest and Hudson's Bay companies.

Fort Simpson has always been a gathering place for people. It serves as a center for territorial government administration and oil and mining exploration. It also serves as a departure point for air, raft and canoe trips into Nahanni National Park Reserve of Canada *(see place listing p. 248)*. A visitor center offers interpretive films, historical walking tours and a native crafts display; phone (867) 695-3182.

The Village of Fort Simpson Tourist Information Centre: P.O. Box 438, Fort Simpson, NT, Canada X0E 0N0; phone (867) 695-3182.

FORT SMITH (G-5) pop. 2,400

Initially a link in a strategic chain of 19th-century trading posts along the Mackenzie portage route to the Arctic, Fort Smith became an autonomous town in 1966. It is regional headquarters for the government of the Northwest Territories and contains several governmental offices. The town also is the site

Permafrost

Permafrost, or permanently frozen ground, is a fact of life in most of the Northwest Territories and Nunavut. In his "Observations on Hudson's Bay 1743," James Isham wrote "the shortness of the summers is not sufficient to thaw the ice...therefore it gathers more and more every year." The permafrost layer is estimated to be as deep as 500 metres (1,640 ft.) in some areas.

Settlers found that attempts to build on the ice-filled ground were

© PhotoDisc

thwarted when heat from their structures melted the permafrost's top layer, causing foundations to crack and buildings to sink. Nearby Yukon Territory gold miners had to thaw and remove permafrost before they could extract the gold that lay beneath it.

In the 20th century Canadians began to work with permafrost. They found they could maintain its frozen state by insulating or preserving the top layer, making a surface strong enough to support any construction. Gravel pads 1 to 2 metres (4 to 6 ft.) thick were used beneath smaller structures; pilings driven into the permafrost elevated larger buildings, preventing heat from penetrating the ground beneath them. In some instances permafrost was excavated and replaced with various forms of fill.

In 1954 the Canadian government spent $34 million to build the new town of Inuvik on stilts. Pilings support buildings and connecting "utilidors," insulated corridors that house heating, water and sewage pipes.

Although the number of successful settlements built on top of permafrost is growing, mining is still a problem. To prevent shaft collapses resulting from a permafrost thaw, miners must shore open their holes with timbers or concrete.

of the Thebacha Campus of Aurora College. Nearby Wood Buffalo National Park of Canada *(see place listing p. 249)* is home to one of the largest buffalo herds in the world.

Fort Smith Visitor Information Centre: 108 King St., P.O. Box 147, Fort Smith, NT, Canada X0E 0P0; phone (867) 872-3065 or (867) 872-8400.

NORTHERN LIFE MUSEUM is at 110 King St. The museum examines area history through collections of native artifacts, tools, crafts, manuscripts and paintings. Exhibits cover the history of the fur trade, aboriginal culture and the unique aspects of transportation in the north. Traveling exhibits from other Canadian museums are occasionally featured. Mon.-Fri. 10-7, Sat.-Sun. 10-5, late May-early Sept.; Mon.-Fri. 10-5, rest of year. Donations. Phone (867) 872-2859.

HAY RIVER (G-4) pop. 3,600

Recent archeological finds show that the Slavey Dene have used the area around Hay River for thousands of years, but the first buildings did not appear until 1868 when Hudson's Bay Co. established a trading post. The town's strategic location prompts its occasional reference as the "Hub of the North."

Hay River is the southernmost port of the Mackenzie River system. During the 5-month shipping season barges, fishing boats and Coast Guard craft clog the protected river channels. The town serves as headquarters of the Great Slave Lake commercial fishing industry, which supplies the demand for Great Slave Lake whitefish. Dene Cultural Institute, on the Hay River Dene Reserve, is open for tours mid-May to mid-September. A visitor center on Mackenzie Hwy. is open 9-9, mid-May to mid-September; phone (867) 874-3180.

Hay River Chamber of Commerce: 10 Gagnier St., Suite K, Hay River, NT, Canada X0E 1G1; phone (867) 874-2565.

INUVIK (B-1) pop. 3,300

Inuvik, meaning "place of man," was erected in 1958 to replace nearby Aklavik *(see place listing p. 246)*, which appeared to be sinking into the Mackenzie River delta. The town boomed in the 1970s as the center of the Beaufort Sea oil exploration, which since has shifted to other areas. As well as being the communications, commerce and government center for the Western Arctic, the town was the site of a Canadian Forces station until 1986.

Accessible via Dempster Hwy., Inuvik is one of the northernmost points on the North American continent that can be reached by public road. During June and most of July there are 24 hours of daylight. The town also serves as a departure point for plane trips to the Arctic Ocean and the Mackenzie River delta system.

Western Arctic Regional Visitors Centre: P.O. Box 1160, Inuvik, NT, Canada X0E 0T0; phone (867) 777-8608.

IQALUIT, NUNAVUT (C-12)

In 1576 British explorer Martin Frobisher arrived at Iqaluit's bay in present-day Nunavut and assumed that he had discovered the Northwest Passage. A discovery he had believed to be gold proved to be iron pyrite, or "fools gold." The Baffin Island town honored his memory in its name—Frobisher Bay—until 1987, when its name officially was changed back to the traditional Inuit name, Iqaluit (ih-KA-loo-it), which means "place of many fish."

Iqaluit, now the capital of Nunavut, began as a small trading post. During the 19th century European and American whalers frequented the bay waters hoping to supply their home ports with whalebone for women's corsets and blubber for lamp oil. Hiking opportunities are plentiful on the outskirts of town or through the nearby mountains. Inaccessible by car, Iqaluit can be reached by air from Calgary and Edmonton via Yellowknife, Winnipeg via Rankin Inlet, Montréal and Ottawa.

With the construction of the Distant Early Warning (DEW) Line in 1954, the town became an important defense site and a major refueling station for both commercial and military aircraft. Iqaluit is the largest community in Nunavut and the educational, administrative, transportation and economic center for the Baffin region. A focal point for Inuit art, the town boasts numerous galleries.

In 1971 the Astro Hill Complex, which includes retail stores, a hotel, movie theater, high-rise apartments, offices and a swimming pool, was completed using modular precast concrete units. Of architectural interest at the time, the complex was designed to withstand northern climatic extremes.

Nunavut Tourism: P.O. Box 1450, Iqaluit, NU, Canada X0A 0H0; phone (866) 686-2888.

NUNATTA SUNAKKUTAANGIT is at 212 Sinnani. The museum's name translates to "things of the land." Exhibits of various art forms and artifacts, housed in a renovated Hudson's Bay Co. warehouse, focus on the Inuit culture of the Baffin region through displays. Daily 1-5, June-Aug.; Tues.-Sun. 1-5, rest of year. Closed July 1, Nov. 11 and Dec. 25. Donations. Phone (867) 979-5537.

NAHANNI NATIONAL PARK RESERVE OF CANADA (F-1)

Elevations in the park range from 1,853 metres (6,079 ft.) at the South Nahanni River to 2,652 metres (8,700 ft.) on the north end of the park near Hole-in-the-Wall Lake. Refer to CAA/AAA maps for additional elevation information.

About 145 kilometres (90 mi.) west of Fort Simpson and accessible only by air, the park uses Fort Liard and Fort Simpson in the Territories, Muncho Lake in British Columbia, and Watson Lake and

Whitehorse in the Yukon Territory as its major supply and jumping-off points. Steeped in myth, mystery and adventure, Nahanni National Park Reserve of Canada covers 4,766 square kilometres (1,840 sq. mi.) of wilderness in the South Nahanni country.

Liard Hwy., linking Fort Nelson and Fort Simpson *(see place listing p. 247)*, passes Blackstone Territorial Park, east of Nahanni National Park Reserve of Canada, providing access to Liard River and Nahanni Butte, 30 kilometres (19 mi.) upriver.

A land of rivers, ragged peaks, more than 30 species of mammals and a waterfall twice the height of Niagara Falls, Nahanni National Park Reserve of Canada was created in 1972. It was placed on the UNESCO (United Nations Educational, Scientific and Cultural Organization) World Heritage list 6 years later and cited as an "exceptional natural site forming part of the heritage of mankind."

In the early 1900s the area received a reputation for myth and adventure. Gold prospectors, drawn by rumors of placer deposits, began to arrive. When the decapitated bodies of the two MacLeod brothers were found, stories of huge mountain men proliferated.

Although no real mountain men ever were seen, the park remains a place of rugged beauty with little development, including accommodations for visitors. Those who come to raft and canoe on the rivers and hike the forests, alpine tundra and canyons of Nahanni will find it a bracing experience. Travel by water is an excellent way to enjoy the park; however, it can be dangerous and should be attempted only by those experienced in canoeing and rafting. Reservations are required for river trips. Due to the trips' popularity, reservations should be made well in advance; phone the park office for information.

Less experienced river travelers should hire a licensed outfitter for guided river trips down the South Nahanni River. Tours pass Virginia Falls, where the South Nahanni River plunges more than 90 metres (295 ft.); the Gate, a 90-degree river bend below 213-metre (700-ft.) vertical cliffs; and hot springs such as those at First Canyon and Rabbitkettle. Visitors to Rabbitkettle **must** register at the warden's cabin and have park staff accompany them to the springs. Daytime air trips to Virginia Falls should be prearranged through an air charter company in Fort Simpson, Fort Liard, Watson Lake, Whitehorse or Muncho Lake.

Fishing for arctic grayling, lake and bull trout and northern pike is permitted with a national park fishing license (annual pass $29.70), which can be obtained at the Fort Simpson Administration Office or at the warden's cabin at Rabbitkettle Lake. All national park regulations apply. Firearms are not permitted.

Wildlife species include moose, beavers, woodland caribou, Dall sheep, grizzly and black bears, white-tailed deer and mountain goats. Visitors should take particular care when traveling in areas where they are likely to encounter bears.

The park is open year-round. The park administration office at Fort Simpson is open daily 8-noon and 1-5, mid-June to mid-Sept.; Mon.-Fri. 8:30-noon

and 1-5, rest of year. Overnight visitors and those planning river rafting or canoe trips must register before entering the park and upon leaving.

One-day admission to the park is $19.80 per person. For route information, park regulations, weather conditions and park activities write to the Superintendent, Nahanni National Park Reserve of Canada, P.O. Box 348, Fort Simpson, NT, Canada X0E 0N0; phone (867) 695-3151. *See Recreation Chart.*

TULITA (D-2)

Because of the lack of roads on the frontier, most towns were founded along rivers. Originally called Fort Norman, Tulita was established in 1810 when Northwest Co. built a trading post at the confluence of the Great Bear and Mackenzie rivers. The town's name means "where two rivers meet."

Later years brought additional industries. In 1920 pitchblende—the chief ore-mineral source of uranium—was discovered, and the early 1980s brought the construction of the Wells-Zama oil pipeline.

Tulita is accessible via air service from Norman Wells. No all-weather roads lead into the community, but a winter road—open from late January to mid-March—connects Tulita to surrounding communities. Nearby is one of the Northwest Territories' oldest Anglican churches, built of squared logs in the 1860s. The restored church can be visited.

About 20 kilometres (12 mi.) away is a bed of low-grade coal that has been burning for centuries. Although the fire likely was ignited by lightning, Dene legend attributes it to a giant's campfire. During the summer the surface of the bed sometimes rises and coals are exposed. Firefighters' attempts to extinguish the smoldering coals have failed.

Hamlet Office: P.O. Box 91, Tulita, NT, Canada X0E 0K0; phone (867) 588-4471.

WOOD BUFFALO NATIONAL PARK OF CANADA (G-5)

Elevations in the park range from 183 metres (600 ft.) at the Little Buffalo River to 945 metres (3,100 ft.) in the Caribou Mountains. Refer to CAA/AAA maps for additional elevation information.

Accessible by Hwy. 5, which connects with Mackenzie Hwy. at Hay River, Wood Buffalo National Park of Canada is the second largest park in the world. Covering about the same area as the states of Maryland and New Jersey combined, the national park straddles the border between the Northwest Territories and Alberta.

This vast subarctic wilderness contains such remarkable geological features as the Salt Plains, Alberta Plateau, the deltas and lowlands of the Peace and Athabasca rivers, and extensive gypsum karst formations. The park was established in 1922 to protect one of the world's largest free-roaming herds of wood bison; approximately 4,300 of these animals now live there. Moose, caribou, muskrats, beavers and black bears are among other park residents.

The Peace Athabasca Delta is an important stopover for North America's four major waterfowl flyways. A large variety of waterfowl as well as hawks, eagles and pelicans, are present for part of the year. The northeastern corner of the park is one of the last nesting grounds in the world for the endangered whooping crane. Some of the park's lakes and rivers contain pike, pickerel, trout, whitefish and goldeye. Wildflowers and berries abound in the rolling meadows.

The 508-kilometre (316-mi.) Fort Chipewyan Winter Road is open mid-December to mid-March (weather permitting). The road runs from Fort McMurray, Alberta, to Fort Smith; part of the road is formed by ice. To check road conditions between Fort Chipewyan and Fort Smith, phone the park office or (867) 872-7962 for recorded information. To check road conditions between Fort Chipewyan and Fort McMurray, phone the Regional Municipality of Wood Buffalo at (780) 697-3600.

Visitors can see such magnificent snow-covered scenery as boreal forest, lakes and wide-open meadows. Before departure travelers should contact the park office for a list of driving regulations and recommended travel supplies.

Boating, picnicking and camping are permitted at Pine Lake. The park has hiking trails, which can be used for snowshoeing and cross-country skiing in winter. Contact the park for information about guided nature hikes and other interpretive events.

The park is open year-round; however, campgrounds and facilities are open Victoria Day weekend through Labour Day. The Fort Smith Visitor Reception Centre at 126 McDougal Rd. is open Mon.-Fri. 9-noon and 1-5, Sat.-Sun. 1-5, mid-June through Labour Day; Mon.-Fri. 9-noon and 1-5, rest of year. Phone (867) 872-7960, or TTY (867) 872-7961. The Fort Chipewyan Visitor Reception Centre on MacKenzie Avenue is open Mon.-Fri. 8:30-noon and 1-5, Sat.-Sun. 1-5, mid-June through Labour Day; Mon.-Fri. 8:30-noon and 1-5, rest of year. Phone (780) 697-3662.

Admission to the park is free. For route information, road conditions or details about park activities contact the Superintendent, Wood Buffalo National Park of Canada, P.O. Box 750, Fort Smith, NT, Canada X0E 0P0; phone (867) 872-7900. *See Recreation Chart and the AAA/CAA Western Canada & Alaska CampBook.*

YELLOWKNIFE (F-5) pop. 18,700

Although the Dene hunted the Yellowknife region for thousands of years and Europeans explored it in 1771, a permanent settlement was not established until the discovery of gold in 1934. Taking the name of the copper knives carried by the Chipewyan Indians, the town is now the capital of the Northwest Territories and the site of a functioning gold mine and a booming diamond industry.

In 1967 Yellowknife replaced Ottawa as the seat of government for the Northwest Territories. Tours of the Legislative Assembly are available Mon.-Fri. at 10:30, 1:30 and 3:30, Sun. at 1:30, June-Aug.;

Mon.-Fri. at 10:30, rest of year. Phone (867) 669-2200. On the northern shore of Great Slave Lake, this "metropolis" of the north lies less than 500 kilometres (311 mi.) from the Arctic Circle and is an excellent place to shop for Northern arts.

The city's historic Old Town retains the gold rush excitement of the 1930s with quaint restaurants, art galleries, shops, and boat, kayak, canoe and yacht rentals. Planes are available for sightseeing and fishing trips. The visitor center on 49th Street can provide information about rentals and excursions. The visitor center also is the starting point for guided tours of the Capital Park area, conducted in July and August.

Best viewed October through March, the aurora borealis, or northern lights, is produced when atomic particles from outside the atmosphere strike and excite atoms within the upper atmosphere. The lights sweep mysteriously across the clear night sky as luminescent curtains of red, green, pink and purple light in patterns called rayed bands. Guided viewing trips are available.

The scenic 71-kilometre (44-mi.) Ingraham Trail (Hwy. 4) to Tibbett Lake allows year-round access to several chains of lakes and streams. Seven boat launches and two campgrounds lie along the road. Prelude Nature Trail runs 3 kilometres (1.8 mi.) from Prelude Lake Territorial Park *(see Recreation Chart)* through the wilderness to several lookout points, while another trail leads to Cameron Falls.

Prospector's Trail is in Fred Henne Territorial Park *(see Recreation Chart)*, west near Long Lake. The 4-kilometre (2.5-mi.) loop points out the region's varied geological features and is of interest to rock hounds; sturdy footwear and insect repellent are necessary. Other hiking trails lead from Ingraham Trail; information and brochures are available at the visitor center.

Easily accessible area lakes include Prosperous, Pontoon, Prelude, Reid and Tibbett. Walsh Lake has good trout fishing, but is accessible only by going through Reid Lake.

The scenic portion of Hwy. 3 runs north from Mackenzie Bison Sanctuary to Edzo, then parallels the northern shore of Great Slave Lake. Driving anywhere in the area, or throughout the Northwest Territories, demands that a vehicle be in top mechanical condition.

Northern Frontier Regional Visitor Center: 4807 49th St., Yellowknife, NT, Canada X1A 3T5; phone (867) 873-4262 or (877) 881-4262.

Self-guiding tours: The visitor center provides brochures for a walking tour of Old Town and New Town.

THE PRINCE OF WALES NORTHERN HERITAGE CENTRE is .4 km (.25 mi.) w. on Hwy. 4 at 4750 48th St. The center preserves area history through exhibits depicting aspects of Dene and Inuit cultures. Displays pertain to geology, archeology, exploration, fur trading, transportation, aviation and bush pilots, natural history, artwork and handicrafts. Daily 10:30-5:30, June-Aug.; Mon.-Fri. 10:30-5, Sat.-Sun. noon-5, rest of year. Closed Jan. 1 and Dec. 25. Donations. Phone (867) 873-7551.

Saskatchewan

The Last Frontier

Rolling grasslands and evergreen forests create an unspoiled paradise

Big Muddy Badlands

Trace Butch Cassidy's Outlaw Trail through this colorfully rugged terrain

Call of the Wild

Whistling swans and white-tailed deer are among the many wilderness residents

Qu'Appelle Valley

The sun seems a little brighter as it shines upon this region's golden farmland

The Mounties

Explore the history of those who brought law and order to the Canadian West

North Saskatchewan
Canadian Tourism
Commission

a pastoral portrait

A visit to Saskatchewan is a perfect escape from the hustle and bustle.

Named after the Plains Indian term *kisiskatchewan,* meaning "the river that flows swiftly," Saskatchewan boasts more than just a great river with an unusual name.

Along country roads, you'll encounter prairies, mountains, grasslands and even sand dunes. While approximately half the province is covered in pine, white spruce and other trees, a good portion is blanketed with fields of wheat.

Look for signs marked with a barn symbol; they designate bed and breakfast inns and vacation farms, where you can take part in milking cows and—if you're lucky—enjoy homemade berry preserves or baked goods.

Take a dip into one of more than 100,000 freshwater lakes, some of which can be found in the Qu'Appelle Valley. Nestled among the water holes in this region are resorts and golf courses with rolling fairways.

For history, head to towns that preserve the origin of the Mounted Police, the heritage of Métis culture or the rough-and-tumble cowboy lifestyle.

Or visit the Beaver Lodge Cabin on Ajawaan Lake in Prince Albert National Park of Canada, residence of naturalist author Grey Owl, who coined the now-popular belief that "you belong to nature, not it to you."

The hues of Saskatchewan's palette were determined both with and without man's help. Painted by nature and the history of the plains, vibrant gold, green and red are the prominent colors in the province's scheme.

Sheaves of Golden Wheat

Shimmering fields of grain, glinting gold in the sunlight, are probably the image most associated with Saskatchewan. Captured on innumerable postcards and snapshots, the plains seem to stretch to the horizon in a never-ending series of undulating waves, interrupted only by an occasional silo. And the fields are certainly productive—more than 50 percent of Canada's wheat crop comes from this land.

Proof of the grain's economic importance to the province are the three golden wheat sheaves on its coat of arms. Saskatchewan's flag provides further evidence; its lower half, a solid band of gold, represents the grain fields dominating the province's southern portion.

You can experience early 20th-century pioneer prairie life at Motherwell Homestead National Historic Site, near Abernethy. Costumed interpreters busily carry out typical daily tasks of the period at the 1912 farmstead of William Richard Motherwell, farmer, politician and agricultural innovator. Motherwell developed techniques enabling early settlers to overcome the region's dry soil and short growing season.

If a more modern approach to rural life appeals to you, spend a few days at one of Saskatchewan's vacation farms. Helping with chores can offset the pounds you might gain from the hearty meals provided by your hosts. More than 70 Saskatchewan families offer visitors a chance to experience what living on a farm is all about.

Landscapes of Green

Color Regina green—the city is known for having more than 350,000 trees. A particularly verdant section of town is Wascana Centre, a 930-hectare urban park that is truly the heart of Saskatchewan's capital.

The center, lining the rambling shoreline of Wascana Lake, is home to cultural and educational institutions as well as the architecturally impressive Legislative Building, the seat of provincial government. Works by Canadian artists grace the building's walls. Galleries at the nearby Royal Saskatchewan Museum are devoted to earth and life sciences and the First Nations People. Young guests will have fun

Henry Kelsey, an English fur trader, explores Saskatchewan.
1690

The first permanent settlement is built by the Hudson's Bay Company.
1774

The massacre of a band of Assiniboine Indians by U.S. wolf hunters prompts the creation of the Mounted Police.
1873

Tourism Saskatchewan
Douglas E.Walker

1870
Canada acquires present-day Saskatchewan as part of the Northwest Territories.

Saskatchewan Historical Timeline

1885
Louis Riel leads the Métis tribe's battle for land rights in the Northwest Rebellion.

visiting a robotic dinosaur and digging into the hands-on exhibits in the Paleo Pit.

Initially known as Pile-O-Bones (the translation of the Cree word *Oscana*), Regina's early name is a reference to the buffalo remains left behind when the site served as a hunters' camp. Its present name was adopted in honor of Queen Victoria—Regina being Latin for queen. And the good monarch's husband was not forgotten when provincial town names were assigned—the city of Prince Albert was named for Victoria's consort in 1886.

The nearly 1 million acres of nearby Prince Albert National Park of Canada encompass other shades of green, primarily those of aspens and evergreens. Its woodlands, boreal landscapes and grasslands form just a small portion of the forests covering half the province.

Within the park is the simple lakeside cabin of Grey Owl, the Indian name assumed by Englishman Archibald Belaney. This early environmentalist, writer and lecturer, accepted into the Ojibwa tribe in the 1930s, was dedicated to the preservation of the Canadian wilderness and its wildlife. His gravesite is close by on a wooded hill.

Red Coats of the Canadian West

The Royal Canadian Mounted Police are immediately recognizable by their scarlet tunics. In fact, the route they took across the prairie in 1874 to establish law and order in western Canada is retraced along Hwy. 13, the Red Coat Trail. Many of their early posts are now national historic sites, including Fort Battleford, off Hwy. 4 near Battleford, and Fort Walsh, southwest of Maple Creek.

Regina is home to the RCMP's only training academy. Visitors are welcomed at the RCMP Heritage Centre, which tells the story of the force through interactive exhibits and the stirring sculptural procession "March of the Mounties." If your timing is right, you can watch the cadets drill at the Sergeant Major's Parade, usually held Monday through Friday at 12:45 p.m.

If you're in town in July or early August and truly want to be inspired by the colors of the province, try to catch the Sunset Retreat Ceremony. Culminating in the lowering of the Canadian flag at dusk, the golden glow cast by the fading sun seems a fitting background as the cadets, in traditional red jackets, proudly march against the backdrop of lush greenery bordering the parade grounds.

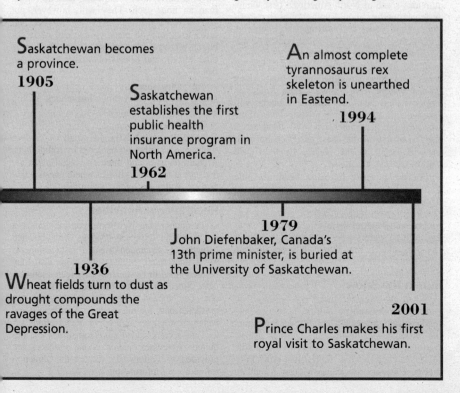

Saskatchewan becomes a province.
1905

Saskatchewan establishes the first public health insurance program in North America.
1962

An almost complete tyrannosaurus rex skeleton is unearthed in Eastend.
1994

1979
John Diefenbaker, Canada's 13th prime minister, is buried at the University of Saskatchewan.

1936
Wheat fields turn to dust as drought compounds the ravages of the Great Depression.

2001
Prince Charles makes his first royal visit to Saskatchewan.

Recreation

Contrary to popular belief, Saskatchewan is not all prairie. Even in the southern half, where farming is predominant, lakes and parks abound with recreational options.

Angling Heaven

With more than 100,000 lakes, rivers and streams to choose from, you're never really far from a good freshwater **fishing** spot. While northern pike, rainbow trout and walleye will take your bait at fishin' holes throughout the province, you'll have to head for northern waters to land trophy-size lake trout, Arctic grayling and other sport fish.

Lake Diefenbaker, south of Outlook, is a favorite fishing destination with both locals and visitors; this is the place to go if you're after walleye or northern pike. The Precambrian Shield, in the northern third of the province, is just about as good as it gets for anglers, with almost 40 percent of its area consisting of H20. Try Lac la Ronge if you're a trout fishing devotee. Outfitters will be happy to fly you to some of the more remote northern fishing lakes.

Tumbling east to west across the province north of the 55th parallel, the Churchill River provides some of North America's best whitewater **canoeing.** Should you choose to experience white water by **rafting,** check out the Clearwater River. Both of these bodies of water flow in northern Saskatchewan.

If the rush of white-water action is too intense, consider paddling your boat along calmer waters. The Bagwa Canoe Route, in Prince Albert National Park of Canada, will take you through several pristine lakes. Late May through September, when the lakes are at their warmest, is the best time to dip your oars. A bonus is the chance to sight bald eagles, ospreys and loons.

For the ultimate in calm, head to Little Manitou Lake, near the resort community of Manitou Beach. Indians knew about the lake's curative powers long before the arrival of European settlers. And there's no danger of sinking in these waters—the high concentration of minerals makes this impossible, so float to your heart's content.

Fun in the Snow

When the weather turns cold, bundle up and try **cross-country skiing.** Groomed and marked trails are easily accessible throughout the province—even in cities. Prince Albert National Park of Canada, almost in the middle of Saskatchewan, has more than 100 kilometres (60 mi.) of trails. Moose Mountain

Provincial Park, north of Carlyle, adds another 50 kilometres (30 mi.) to explore, while the forests, lakes and valleys of Duck Mountain Provincial Park, east of Kamsack, provide a picturesque backdrop for cross-country excursions.

If you prefer to stay within city limits, the Meewasin Valley Trail follows the Saskatchewan River through the middle of Saskatoon, the province's largest city.

Snowmobiling enthusiasts love the thousands of kilometres of interconnected, groomed trails linking towns and parks along Canada's version of Route 66, in this case a cross-country snowmobile route. Popular put-in points include Hudson Bay, Nipawin, North Battleford and Yorkton. Trail permits are mandatory; phone Tourism Saskatchewan, (877) 237-2273, for a provincial snowmobile trail map.

Warm Weather Choices

When the weather turns warm, everyone flocks to Prince Albert National Park of Canada. You don't even need **hiking** boots on a few of the park's short trails. Boundary Bog, Mud Creek and Treebeard, all loop trails, traverse fairly level terrain and take no longer than an hour each. They will, however, put you in touch with a variety of Mother Nature's creations—a black spruce and tamarack bog; sightings of beavers, otters and great blue herons; and forests of aspens and balsam firs.

An abundance of lakes and trails also makes **boating, bicycling, horseback riding** and fishing popular choices.

Another popular summer playground is the Qu'Appelle Valley, a broad swath of land in southern Saskatchewan bordered by rolling hills. A chain of lakes and three provincial parks are the setting for resort villages where guests enjoy boating, **water skiing** and **swimming.**

Recreational Activities

Throughout the TourBook, you may notice a Recreational Activities heading with bulleted listings of recreation-oriented establishments listed underneath. Similar operations also may be mentioned in Destination City recreation sections. Since normal AAA inspection criteria cannot be applied, these establishments are presented only for information. Age, height and weight restrictions may apply. Reservations often are recommended and sometimes are required. Addresses and/or phone numbers are provided so visitors can contact the attraction for additional information.

Fast Facts

POPULATION: 978,933.

AREA: 651,036 sq km (251,365 sq mi); ranks 7th.

CAPITAL: Regina.

HIGHEST POINT: 1,392 m/4,566 ft., Cypress Hills.

LOWEST POINT: 65 m/213 ft., Lake Athabasca.

TIME ZONE(S): Central and Mountain.

MINIMUM AGE FOR UNRESTRICTED DRIVER'S LICENSE: 17 years, 6 months.

MINIMUM AGE FOR GAMBLING: 19.

SEAT BELT/CHILD RESTRAINT LAWS: Seat belts are required for the driver and all passengers 16 and older. Children under 16 and weighing more than 18 kilograms (40 lbs.) are required to wear a seat belt; child restraints are required for children weighing less than 18 kilograms.

HELMETS FOR MOTORCYCLISTS: Required for all riders.

RADAR DETECTORS: Permitted.

FIREARMS LAWS: By federal law, all nonresidents entering Canada with a firearm must declare their weapon in writing and pay a fee of $25 (Canadian). Contact the Canadian Firearms Centre at (800) 731-4000 for additional information or to receive a declaration form.

HOLIDAYS: Jan. 1; Family Day, Feb. (3rd Mon.); Good Friday; Victoria Day, May 24 (if a Mon.) or the closest prior Mon.; Canada Day, July 1; Saskatchewan Day, Aug. (1st Mon.); Labour Day, Sept. (1st Mon.); Thanksgiving, Oct. (2nd Mon.); Remembrance Day, Nov. 11; Christmas, Dec. 25; Boxing Day, Dec. 26.

TAXES: Saskatchewan's provincial sales tax is 5 percent.

INFORMATION CENTERS: Provincial welcome centers are along Hwy. 1 east of Fleming; at 1922 Park St. in Regina; near Maple Creek on Hwy. 1; Hwy. 16 at Langenburg and Lloydminster; and Hwy. 39 at North Portal. All information centers are open daily mid-May to early September except the center in Regina, which is open Mon.-Fri. 8-5.

FURTHER INFORMATION FOR VISITORS:

Tourism Saskatchewan
1922 Park St.
Regina, SK, Canada S4N 7M4
(306) 787-2300 or (877) 237-2273

FISHING AND HUNTING REGULATIONS:

Saskatchewan Environment
3211 Albert St.
Regina, SK, Canada S4S 5W6
(306) 953-3750

ALCOHOL CONSUMPTION: Legal age 19.

Saskatchewan Temperature Averages Maximum/Minimum (Celsius)

From the records of The Weather Channel Interactive, Inc.

	JAN	FEB	MAR	APR	MAY	JUNE	JULY	AUG	SEPT	OCT	NOV	DEC
Prince Albert	-14 / -26	-9 / -22	-3 / -16	9 / -4	18 / 3	22 / 8	24 / 11	23 / 9	16 / 3	9 / -3	-3 / -13	-12 / -22
Regina	-11 / -22	-8 / -18	-1 / -12	10 / -3	18 / 4	23 / 9	26 / 12	26 / 11	18 / 4	12 / -2	0 / -11	-9 / -19

Saskatchewan
Orientation

NOT INTENDED FOR DRIVING.
SEE APPROPRIATE AAA SHEET MAP.

Only places listed in the Attractions section appear on this map.

See AAA GEM Attractions

See Chart of Recreation Areas

4056-B © 2007 NAVTEQ

© AAA

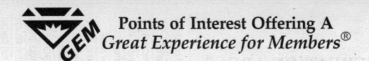

Points of Interest Offering A *Great Experience for Members*®

Prince Albert National Park of Canada (B-3)

PRINCE ALBERT NATIONAL PARK OF CANADA— This wilderness area is a beautiful example of Saskatchewan's transition from poplar bluffs and prairie lands to the evergreen forests and spruce bogs of the north. See p. 272.

Regina (E-4)

GOVERNMENT HOUSE MUSEUM AND HERITAGE PROPERTY—The elegance of the Victorian era and the power and prestige of former lieutenant governors, occupants from 1891-1945, are reflected in this Italianate-style mansion. See p. 273.

RCMP HERITAGE CENTRE—The history of the Royal Canadian Mounted Police unfolds at the RCMP Heritage Centre, a combination museum and educational facility that employs state-of-the-art exhibits and multimedia technologies to tell the story of this distinctly Canadian institution. See p. 273.

ROYAL SASKATCHEWAN MUSEUM—The museum comprises galleries that focus on the evolution of the province, such as geology and paleontology, culture and heritage, and natural history and environment. See p. 274.

Saskatoon (D-2)

WANUSKEWIN HERITAGE PARK—The Cree word for "seeking peace of mind," Wanuskewin is a fitting name for this park, once a center of spiritual renewal used by the Northern Plains Indians. See p. 276.

RECREATION AREAS

	MAP LOCATION	CAMPING	PICNICKING	HIKING TRAILS	BOATING	BOAT RAMP	BOAT RENTAL	FISHING	SWIMMING	PETS ON LEASH	BICYCLE TRAILS	WINTER SPORTS	VISITOR CENTER	LODGE/CABINS	FOOD SERVICE
NATIONAL PARKS *(See place listings)*															
Grasslands 906 square kilometres.		•	•	•						•			•		
Prince Albert 3,875 square kilometres. Horse rental.		•	•	•	•	•	•	•	•	•	•	•	•	•	•
PROVINCIAL															
The Battlefords (C-2) 600 hectares 4.75 km n. of Cochin off Hwy. 4. Cross-country skiing, golf.	❶	•	•	•	•	•	•	•	•	•	•	•	•	•	•
Blackstrap (D-3) 530 hectares 8 km e. of Dundurn via Hwy. 211. Cross-country and downhill skiing; sailboard rental.	❷	•	•		•	•	•	•	•	•		•	•		•
Buffalo Pound (E-4) 1,930 hectares 19 km n. of Moose Jaw on Hwy. 2, then 13 km e. on Hwy. 202. Cross-country and downhill skiing, tennis; pool.	❸	•	•	•	•	•		•	•	•		•	•		•
Candle Lake (C-4) 1,270 hectares 60 km n.e. of Prince Albert on hwys. 55 and 120. Cross-country skiing.	❹	•	•	•	•	•	•	•	•	•		•	•	•	•
Clearwater River 224,040 hectares 50 km n.e. of La Loche on Hwy. 955 (north of area shown on map). Canoeing.		•	•	•				•		•					
Crooked Lake (E-5) 190 hectares 30 km n. of Broadview on Hwy. 605. Golf.	❺	•	•		•	•		•	•	•			•	•	•
Cypress Hills (F-2) 18,410 hectares 30 km s. of Maple Creek on Hwy. 21. Cross-country skiing, golf, tennis; horse rental, pool. Five horsepower limit for boats.	❻	•	•	•	•	•	•	•	•	•		•	•	•	•
Danielson (E-3) 2,910 hectares on n. end of Lake Diefenbaker via hwys. 44, 45 or 219.	❼	•	•		•	•		•	•	•				•	•
Douglas (E-3) 4,430 hectares 11 km s.e. of Elbow on Hwy. 19. Houseboat rental.	❽	•	•	•	•	•	•	•	•	•		•	•		•
Duck Mountain (D-6) 26,160 hectares 25 km e. of Kamsack on Hwy. 57. Cross-country and downhill skiing, golf, tennis; horse rental.	❾	•	•	•	•	•	•	•	•	•	•	•	•	•	•

RECREATION AREAS

RECREATION AREAS	MAP LOCATION	CAMPING	PICNICKING	HIKING TRAILS	BOATING	BOAT RAMP	BOAT RENTAL	FISHING	SWIMMING	PETS ON LEASH	BICYCLE TRAILS	WINTER SPORTS	VISITOR CENTER	LODGE/CABINS	FOOD SERVICE
Echo Valley (E-4) 640 hectares 8 km w. of Fort Qu'Appelle off Hwy. 10. Cross-country skiing; horse rental.	10	•	•	•	•	•			•	•	•		•	•	•
Good Spirit Lake (D-5) 1,900 hectares 24 km n.e. of Springside via Hwy. 47. Cross-country skiing, tennis.	11	•	•	•	•	•	•	•	•	•			•		•
Greenwater Lake (D-4) 20,720 hectares 38 km n. of Kelvington on Hwy. 38. Cross-country skiing, golf, tennis.	12	•	•	•	•	•	•	•	•	•		•	•	•	•
Katepwa Point (E-5) 8 hectares 10 km s.e. of Lebret on Hwy. 56.	13		•		•	•	•	•	•	•					•
Lac la Ronge (A-4) 344,470 hectares 48.25 km n. of La Ronge on Hwy. 102. Cross-country skiing; houseboat rental.	14	•	•	•	•	•	•	•	•	•		•	•	•	•
Makwa Lake (B-2) 2,560 hectares n.w. of Loon Lake off Hwy. 26. Cross-country skiing; horse rental.	15	•	•	•	•	•	•	•	•	•			•	•	•
Meadow Lake (B-2) 156,970 hectares 5 km n. of Goodsoil via Hwy. 26. Cross-country skiing, tennis; horse rental, sailboat rental.	16	•	•	•	•	•	•	•	•	•		•	•	•	•
Moose Mountain (F-5) 40,060 hectares 22.5 km n. of Carlyle on Hwy. 9. Cross-country skiing, golf (18 holes), tennis; horse rental.	17	•	•	•	•	•		•	•	•	•	•	•	•	•
Narrow Hills (B-4) 53,610 hectares 64.25 km n. of Smeaton on Hwy. 106. Canoeing, cross-country skiing, snowmobiling; playground.	18	•	•	•	•	•	•	•	•	•		•	•	•	•
Pike Lake (D-3) 500 hectares 30.5 km s. of Saskatoon on Hwy. 60. Golf, tennis; pool. Ten horsepower limit for boats.	19	•	•		•	•	•	•	•	•			•		•
Rowan's Ravine (E-4) 270 hectares 22.5 km w. of Bulyea on Hwy. 220.	20	•	•	•	•	•	•	•	•	•			•		•
Saskatchewan Landing (E-3) 5,600 hectares 45 km n. of Swift Current via Hwy. 4. Horse rental, windsurfing rental.	21	•	•	•	•	•	•	•	•	•		•	•	•	•
OTHER															
Bright Sand Lake (C-2) 648 hectares 27 km e. of St. Walburg off Hwy. 26 on a gravel road. Bird-watching, canoeing, cross-country skiing, golf, miniature golf, mountain biking, snowmobiling; beach, canoe rental, nature trails with interpretive signs, playground.	22	•	•	•	•	•	•	•	•	•		•	•		•
Dunnet (E-4) 50 hectares 7 km s. of Avonlea on Hwy. 334. Cross-country skiing, ice fishing, snowmobiling.	23	•	•	•	•	•		•	•	•	•	•			•
Kipabiskau (D-4) 16 hectares 35 km s.w. of Tisdale off Hwy. 3 or Hwy. 35. Cross-country skiing, ice fishing, snowmobiling; beach, canoe and kayak rental, nature trails, playground.	24	•	•	•	•	•	•	•	•	•	•	•	•		•
Last Mountain Lake (D-4) 65 hectares 20 km n.w. of Govan off Hwy. 20 on a gravel road. Bird-watching, ice fishing; pool. (See Simpson p. 276).	25	•	•	•				•	•	•		•			•
Macklin Lake (D-2) 154 hectares .4 km s. of Macklin on Hwy. 31. Golf; beach, playground, wildlife preserve.	26	•	•	•	•			•	•	•		•			•
Nipawin and District (C-4) 121 hectares 3 km n.w. of Nipawin on Hwy. 55. Cross-country skiing, golf, snowmobiling; petting zoo, playground, spray pool.	27	•	•	•	•	•		•	•	•	•	•	•		•
Pasquia (C-4) 65 hectares 12 km n. of Arborfield on Hwy. 23. Cross-country and downhill skiing, golf; Andy Jamault nature trail to the Pasquia paleontological site, pool.	28	•	•	•					•	•		•	•		•
Redberry Lake (D-3) 5,600 hectares 12.8 km e. of Hafford on Hwy. 40. Cross-country skiing, golf.	29	•	•	•	•			•	•	•		•	•	•	•
St. Brieux (D-4) 65 hectares 1 km w. of St. Brieux on Hwy. 368. Historic. Cross-country skiing, golf, miniature golf; beach, playground.	30	•	•	•	•	•		•	•	•	•	•	•		•
Whitesand (D-5) 49 hectares 9 km n.e. of Theodore off Hwy. 16. Golf, miniature golf; playground.	31	•	•	•				•		•	•	•			•

Points of Interest

ABERNETHY (E-5) pop. 213

In 1882, about 2 decades before he began his distinguished career in Canadian politics, William Richard Motherwell arrived in southeastern Saskatchewan from his Ontario birthplace and acquired a 64-hectare (160-acre) homestead grant near Abernethy. He farmed the land using several techniques of scientific agriculture then considered revolutionary.

Motherwell was later instrumental in launching the Territorial Grain Growers Association. His knowledge of the land groomed him for later roles as Saskatchewan's minister of agriculture 1905-18 and federal minister of agriculture during the 1920s.

MOTHERWELL HOMESTEAD NATIONAL HISTORIC SITE is 8 km (5 mi.) s. on Hwy. 22. The site commemorates William Richard Motherwell and his contributions to Canadian agriculture. Motherwell's farmstead, including 8 acres of landscaped grounds, Ontarian-style barn and six-bedroom fieldstone house, have been restored to the pre-World War I era. Guided tours are available. Allow 1 hour minimum. Daily 9-5, Victoria Day-Labour Day. Admission $7.90; $6.65 (ages 65+); $3.95 (ages 6-16); $19.80 (family). AX, MC, VI. Phone (306) 333-2116.

ASSINIBOIA (F-3) pop. 2,483

Assiniboia is an Ojibwa Indian word meaning "one who cooks with stones." Southeast of town off Hwy. 2 is St. Victor Petroglyphs Provincial Historic Park, the site of a sandstone cliff etched with prehistoric Indian carvings. The carvings at the top of the cliff depict human faces, footprints and animal tracks. Since they have faded with time, the designs are best seen late in the afternoon or on a cloudy day. There is a picnic site near the base of the cliff that is open June 1-Labour Day. Phone (306) 694-3659 for more information.

The Prince of Wales Cultural and Recreation Centre, 201 3rd Ave. W., was built through volunteer effort; Charles, Prince of Wales turned the sod for the groundbreaking during a visit to Saskatchewan. It houses an auditorium where performing arts, trade shows and other events take place, and the Assiniboia & District Public Library, which presents monthly displays featuring the work of local artists in the Kay Cristo Room. The grounds feature xerioscaping, landscaping with plants that require little water. For information phone (306) 642-3634.

The Visitor Information Centre at 501 Hwy. 2 N. houses the Prentice African Safari Exhibit, a collection of 24 mounted animals hunted during three 1970s safaris. The center is open Mon.-Fri. 10-6, Sat.-Sun. 1-5, May-Aug.; Wed. and Sat. 1-5, rest of year.

The Shurniak Art Gallery, 122 3rd Ave. W., has a permanent collection that includes works by noted Canadian and Saskatchewan artists as well as examples of contemporary Chinese and Australian art; phone (306) 642-5292.

ASSINIBOIA AND DISTRICT MUSEUM is at 506 3rd Ave. W. The museum depicts the growth of Assiniboia from 1913 to the present. A guided tour includes exhibits such as a collection of antique cars dating from 1916-50 as well as vintage heavy farm equipment. Picnicking is permitted. Allow 30 minutes minimum. Daily 9-5, July-Aug.; Mon.-Fri. 9-noon and 1-5, rest of year. Closed major holidays. Admission $4; $1 (ages 13-18). Phone (306) 642-5353 or (306) 642-4216 (after hours).

BATOCHE (C-3)

Having had their lands in Manitoba's Red River Valley divided and bought out from under them by swelling numbers of homesteaders, the Métis—a people of mixed Indian and French heritage—migrated to the area around Batoche, in the valley of the South Saskatchewan River, about 1870. Building a settlement along the riverbank, they farmed and hunted, but conflict arose with the Canadian government, which was bent on settling the country's western reaches. Although the Métis set up a provisional government to give voice to their concerns and petitioned for rights to the land, their requests were ignored.

Batoche National Historic Site (see attraction listing) chronicles the history behind the events that led to armed conflict in 1885. It also presents the culture and traditions of Métis descendants who continue to prosper in Saskatchewan today.

BATOCHE NATIONAL HISTORIC SITE is w. on Hwy. 225. The decisive battle of the Northwest Rebellion/Métis Resistance of 1885 was fought at this site, which covers 1,080 hectares (1,650 acres). Features include the ruins of a Batoche village, the St. Antoine de Padoue church, a rectory and a Visitor Reception Centre, with an audiovisual presentation. There are interpretive signs and costumed interpreters at key locations throughout the park.

Daily 9-5, May 8-Sept. 30. Admission $7.15; $5.90 (ages 65+); $3.45 (ages 6-16); $17.80 (family). Phone (306) 423-6227 or (306) 423-6228.

BATTLEFORD (D-2) pop. 3,820

Once capital of the Northwest Territories, Battleford is one of Saskatchewan's oldest communities. As soon as the Canadian Pacific Railway began construction, citizens made plans for their town to become a western metropolis. But the railroad took a more southerly route, and in 1883 the capital was moved to Regina.

Battleford's hopes revived in 1905 when the Canadian Northern Railway proposed a westward route, but the line was built north of town on the other side of the Saskatchewan River, spawning the new town of North Battleford *(see place listing p. 270)*. Battleford and its sister city have continued to grow as the province's vast northwest region has become more developed.

FORT BATTLEFORD NATIONAL HISTORIC SITE is 2 km (1.2 mi.) off Hwy. 4. The North West Mounted Police district headquarters was established here in 1876 to enforce law and order. The fort became the site of armed confrontations between the First Nations and federal troops in 1885. Five buildings have been preserved; various illustrative exhibits are featured. Costumed staff members provide interpretive information. Historic weapons demonstrations are given, and historic trails also are on site.

Guided tours are available. Picnicking is permitted. Allow 1 hour, 30 minutes minimum. Daily 9-5, Victoria Day weekend-Labour Day. Tours are offered every 30 minutes. Admission $7.25; $6 (ages 65+); $3.50 (ages 6-16); $18 (family). Phone (306) 937-2621.

BIGGAR (D-2) pop. 2,243

Named after W.H. Biggar, General Counsel for the Grand Trunk Pacific Railroad, Biggar was incorporated as a village in 1909 and as a town in 1911. In 1910 the GTPR established a divisional point. A construction boom resulted, and so did an increase in population. The town became one of the home terminals where train crews changed: The station was one of the largest in the West. During the years that followed the population remained stable, and it wasn't until the 1950s that Biggar experienced renewed growth.

The name Sandra Schmirler is synonymous with Biggar. A three-time world curling champion (1993, 1994 and 1997) and 1998 Olympic gold medalist for the sport of curling, Schmirler was born and schooled in Biggar. Sandra Schmirler Olympic Gold Park was opened in her honor on Aug. 6, 2000.

BIGGAR MUSEUM AND GALLERY is at 105 3rd Ave. W. Highlighting the story of settlement in Biggar, the museum features two outdoor murals; a plesiosaur diorama; the Earl of Saskesk exhibit; replicas of a CN railway station, the Hanson Buck, and a silent film theater; and a Ku Klux Klan exhibit. Also included is an art gallery. Changing exhibits are presented regularly in the museum and art gallery. Allow 30 minutes minimum. Mon.-Sat. 9-5, June-Sept.; 1-5, rest of year. Closed holidays. Donations. Phone (306) 948-3451.

HOMESTEAD MUSEUM is 1.6 km (1 mi.) w. on Hwy. 51. The museum houses an early 20th-century wooden home, a replica of a sod house, a store with a barbershop, a school, a restored 1913 homestead with a collection of character dolls, a bunkhouse, a church, a barn and a general display building. Allow 2 hours minimum. Mon.-Sat. 9-9, Sun. noon-9, Victoria Day weekend-second Mon. in Oct. Free. Phone (306) 948-3427.

BROADVIEW (E-5) pop. 669

Broadview began as a division point on the Canadian Pacific Railway. A marker in a park on the west side of town marks the location of the original tracks laid in 1882. Also in town is a sanctuary for Canada geese.

Broadview Chamber of Commerce: P.O. Box 119, Broadview, SK, Canada S0G 0K0; phone (306) 696-2533.

BROADVIEW MUSEUM is 1 blk. s. of Hwy. 1 on N. Front St. An Indian log house, an 1897 rural school and a Canadian Pacific Railroad station and caboose are displayed at the museum. Exhibits include Indian and pioneer artifacts, old photographs, and maps of early homesteads and trails. Daily 9:30-5:30, June-Aug. Donations. Phone (306) 696-3244.

CARLYLE (F-5) pop. 1,260

North of Carlyle is Moose Mountain Provincial Park *(see Recreation Chart and the AAA/CAA Western Canada & Alaska CampBook)*, which began as a resort beach on Lake Kenosee in 1906. The park is home to herds of moose and elk and is a nesting place for geese and other birds. There also are more than 450 beaver lodges.

Recreational facilities include an 18-hole golf course, hiking and equestrian trails, riding stables, a clubhouse and a swimming beach. Across from the entrance is Kenosee Superslide, a water park.

CANNINGTON MANOR PROVINCIAL HISTORIC PARK is e. on Hwy. 13 to Grid Rd. 603, then 2 km (1.2 mi.) n. on gravel roads. The village of Cannington Manor, founded in 1882, was an attempt to duplicate the upper-middle-class English way of life, including cricket matches and fox hunts. The museum and seven buildings contain antiques, artifacts and farming implements used by the settlers.

Guides in period costumes demonstrate activities typical of the settlement in the last 2 decades of the 19th century. Picnicking is permitted. Wed.-Mon. 10-5, Victoria Day-Labour Day. Admission $2; $1 (students with ID); free (ages 0-5); $5 (family). Phone (306) 577-2600 or (306) 739-5251.

CARLYLE RUSTY RELIC MUSEUM AND TOURIST INFORMATION CENTRE is at Railway Ave. and 3rd St. W. Housed in the former Canadian National Railway Station, the museum features historical items from the area. Thirteen rooms contain such exhibits as a dentistry collection, farm equipment, World War II military uniforms, medical equipment, a restored kitchen and photographs. A restored one-room schoolhouse and a tourist information center also are on the grounds.

Allow 1 hour minimum. Mon.-Fri. 9-5, mid-June through Labour Day. Admission $2; $1 (ages 6-18). Phone (306) 453-2266.

GAMBLING ESTABLISHMENTS

- **Bear Claw Casino**, Hwy. 9. Mon.-Thurs. 9 a.m.-midnight, Fri.-Sat. 9 a.m.-2 a.m.; closed Dec. 25. Phone (306) 577-4577.

CHAPLIN (E-3) pop. 292, elev. 674 m/2,214′

CHAPLIN NATURE CENTRE is at the western approach to town via Hwy. 1. The center is in the midst of the Chaplin Lake area, which encompasses some 6,000 hectares (15,000 acres) of inland saline water. More than 30 species of shorebirds, some endangered, either rest and refuel here during migratory journeys or nest and raise their young in the summer, feasting on brine shrimp that teem in the salty, shallow water.

Guided bus tours are available; binoculars are provided. Allow 1 hour, 30 minutes minimum. Tues.-Sun. 10-5, Victoria Day weekend-Labour Day. Center displays free. Guided tour $10; $5 (students with ID). Reservations are recommended. MC, VI. Phone (306) 395-2770 or (877) 746-7273.

CLAYBANK (F-4) pop. 20

CLAYBANK BRICK PLANT NATIONAL HISTORIC SITE is 1 km (.6 mi.) e. on Hwy. 339. This plant is said to be North America's most intact early 20th-century brick factory and was active 1914-89. Visitors may tour the large site, which comprises more than 20 structures. The plant also is open on special event days to afford visitors an opportunity to see the brick-making process.

Picnicking is permitted. Food is available. Allow 1 hour minimum. Tours daily at 11:30, 1, 2:30 and 4, July-Aug.; by appointment rest of year. Admission $8; $20 (family). Phone (306) 868-4474.

CORONACH (F-4) pop. 822

POPLAR RIVER POWER STATION AND STRIP MINE is 10 km (6 mi.) s.e. Two-hour bus tours depart from the information center at jct. Centre St. and Railway Ave. (Hwy. 18). Guides provide interpretive explanations during a walking tour of the power plant and the bus tour of the strip-mining site. Durable clothing and flat-heeled shoes are recommended. Tours are given daily at 9:30 and 1, Mar.-Dec. (weather permitting). Free. Phone (306) 267-2078, or (306) 267-2157 Sat.-Sun.

CRAVEN (E-4) pop. 264

Last Mountain House Provincial Historic Park, 8 kilometres (5 mi.) north of town on Hwy. 20, preserves the site of a fur-trade outpost that operated 1869-71. Park interpreters offer guided tours of the site's three reconstructed buildings Thurs.-Sun. 10-5, July 1-Labour Day; phone (306) 731-4409 or (306) 787-0731.

CUT KNIFE (D-2) pop. 556

In 1885 Cut Knife was the site of several Indian uprisings that were inspired by the Métis rebellion

(*see Batoche p. 261*). The Battle of Cut Knife Hill, between the Cree tribe led by Chief Poundmaker and the North West Mounted Police under Col. W.D. Otter, ended in the retreat of the Mounties to Battleford.

Poundmaker, who stopped his warriors from pursuing and ambushing Otter's troops, later surrendered to the authorities to help restore peace between the Indians and settlers. A national historic plaque and a framework of tepee poles mark the chief's grave at the Poundmaker Reserve.

Dominating Cut Knife's horizon is the massive tomahawk in Tomahawk Park. The handle is a pipe donated by steel manufacturer Ipsco; it is 36 inches in diameter, 57 feet long and weighs 8,660 pounds.

Cut Knife Chamber of Commerce: P.O. Box 504, Cut Knife, SK, Canada S0M 0N0; phone (306) 398-2363.

CLAYTON McLAIN MEMORIAL MUSEUM is 3 blks. w. on Hill Ave. in Tomahawk Park. First Nations artifacts, local historical records and articles used by early settlers are exhibited at the museum, which also includes several buildings depicting an early pioneer settlement. A trout pond is on the grounds. Allow 1 hour minimum. Mon.-Sat. 9-5, Sun. 1-4, July-Aug.; by appointment rest of year. Admission $2; $1 (ages 0-11); $5 (family). Phone (306) 398-2345.

DUCK LAKE (C-3) pop. 624

The town of Duck Lake lies between the North Saskatchewan and South Saskatchewan rivers. The actual lake is a few kilometres west of town. A nearby cairn marks the site of the Battle of Duck Lake, in which the Métis Indians defeated the North West Mounted Police on Mar. 26, 1885.

DUCK LAKE REGIONAL INTERPRETIVE CENTRE is at the jct. of hwys. 11 and 212. The center focuses on the historical contributions made by Indian, Métis and pioneer populations in the area's development. A museum features collections ranging from traditional clothing to tools used in buffalo hunts. The history and cultures of the area are presented in a 15-minute video, and a tower provides panoramic views.

Allow 30 minutes minimum. Daily 10-5:30, Victoria Day weekend-Labour Day weekend. Admission $4.50; $3.50 (senior citizens); $2.50 (students with ID); free (ages 0-5); $12 (family). MC, VI. Phone (306) 467-2057 or (866) 467-2057.

FORT CARLTON PROVINCIAL HISTORIC PARK is 26 km (16 mi.) w. on Hwy. 212. The fort that played a part in the settlement of north-central Saskatchewan has been reconstructed at the site, which features three tepees depicting the Plains Cree culture as it existed 1860-70. A replica of the Hudson's Bay Store is a museum of fur-trading history. The visitor center is a reconstruction of the 1879 home of the trading post overseer.

Camping is available. Allow 30 minutes minimum. Daily 10-6, Victoria Day-Labour Day. Admission $2.50; $1 (ages 6-17); free (ages 66+); $6 (family). MC, VI. Phone (306) 467-5205.

EASTEND (F-2) pop. 576

EASTEND MUSEUM-CULTURAL CENTRE is downtown at 306 Redcoat Dr. Items of local interest are displayed, including early settler, business and Indian artifacts and a collection of dinosaur bones found in the area. Adjoining the museum is a rancher's restored log house dating from around 1911. Allow 30 minutes minimum. Daily 10-7, Victoria Day-Labour Day; by appointment rest of year. Admission $3; free (ages 0-11). Phone (306) 295-3375.

T.REX DISCOVERY CENTRE is at 1 T-rex Dr. In partnership with the Royal Saskatchewan Museum, the center houses fossils and replicas of dinosaurs, a 98-seat theater and interpretive displays. Educational activities also are offered. A nearly complete T-rex skeleton was discovered in the area in 1991.

Guided tours are available. Allow 1 hour minimum. Daily 9-9, Jul.-Aug.; 9-5 rest of year. Admission $7.50; $5 (ages 6-18). Reservations are suggested. MC, VI. Phone (306) 295-4009.

ELBOW (E-3) pop. 298

ELBOW MUSEUM is at 239 Saskatchewan St. The area's history is depicted from 1905 to the present. Items displayed include arrowheads, photographs and maps. A replica of a sod house, furnished in pioneer style, also is on-site. The house reflects the ingenuity of early settlers in surviving the harsh environment with a scarcity of building materials. Allow 30 minutes minimum. Daily 1-5, July-Aug.; by appointment rest of year. Donations. Phone (306) 854-2277.

ESTEVAN (F-5)
pop. 10,242, elev. 570 m/1,870′

Estevan, founded in 1892 just north of the Souris River, is one of Saskatchewan's major centers for coal and oil. The sun shines an average of 2,540 hours annually, making the town among the sunniest spots in Canada.

Southeast of town off Hwy. 39 is Roche Percée, a group of strangely eroded rock formations that were once venerated by local Indians. Although most of the animals and initials carved on the rocks can no longer be seen, the site is still supposedly visited by spirits whose murmurs can be heard when the wind blows.

On Hwy. 39 at 118 4th St. is the Estevan Art Gallery & Museum. The facility provides information about local events and also presents changing exhibitions and occasional interpretive programs or tours; phone (306) 634-7644.

The Wood End Building, next to the center, was the 1893 barracks for the North West Mounted Police and contains artifacts that relate to the organization's early days. Also nearby is Eli Mandel Heritage Park, which contains an oil field display.

Tours to Shand Power Station and Luscar Boundary Mine can be arranged June through August through the Estevan Tourism Booth; phone (306) 634-6044.

Estevan Chamber of Commerce: 303-1133 4th St., Estevan, SK, Canada S4A 0W6; phone (306) 634-2828.

BOUNDARY DAM POWER STATION is 5 km (3 mi.) w. on Hwy. 18. This power station, which contains one of the largest lignite-burning plants in Canada, utilizes southeast Saskatchewan's vast coal reserves to produce more kilowatts than any other dam in the province. Swimming and boating are permitted. Allow 2 hours minimum. Guided tours are given Tues.-Sat. at 9 and 1, June-Aug. Tour schedule may vary; phone ahead. Free. Phone (306) 634-6044.

RECREATIONAL ACTIVITIES
Recreational Complex

• **Souris Valley Aquatic and Leisure Center**, 701 Souris Ave., Estevan, SK, Canada S4A 2T1. Mon.-Fri. 6 a.m.-9:30 p.m., Sat. 8 a.m.-9:30 p.m., Sun. noon-9:30. Phone (306) 634-1888.

ESTON (E-2) pop. 1,048, elev. 682 m/2,240′

Founded in 1916, Eston is a major grain center; more than one million bushels of grain are produced annually.

PRAIRIE WEST HISTORICAL CENTRE is at 946 2nd St. S.E. The restored 1910 Evans house contains more than 3,000 artifacts that include period furnishings and photographs, agricultural displays, a homesteader shack and the Heritage Art Gallery. A pioneer schoolroom is depicted at the Lovedale school. A wildflower garden is on the grounds. Allow 30 minutes minimum. Mon.-Sat. 9-noon and 1-5, Sun. 1-5, July-Aug.; daily 1:30-4:30, in June and Sept. Free. Phone (306) 962-3772.

FORT QU'APPELLE (E-4) pop. 1,940

With the 1874 signing of Treaty Number IV, representatives of the Cree and Saulteaux Indians gave away their legal right to vast tracts of southern Saskatchewan; near the center of Fort Qu'Appelle (kwah-PELL) a cairn marks the site of the signing. The fort for which the town is named was built in 1864 mainly for use as a trading post.

Fort Qu'Appelle is on the Qu'Appelle River in a broad valley of lush farmland. The area is known for the wide variety of berries growing on the moist, north-facing slopes. The dry, south-facing slopes are carpeted with wildflowers. Several kinds of hawks soar above this peaceful valley, and pelicans, herons, ducks and geese nest in the marshes. Near Fort Qu'Appelle the river widens into a chain of lakes.

The river's unusual name is the French translation of the Cree word *catabuysepu*, or "the river that calls." According to Indian legend, the river was haunted by a spirit that could be heard crying as it moved up and down the water.

Also taking its name from this Cree expression is nearby Katepwa Point Provincial Park, a lakeside recreation area offering day-use facilities. Another provincial park, Echo Valley, is west of town. *See Recreation Chart and the AAA/CAA Western Canada & Alaska CampBook.*

Fort Qu'Appelle Chamber of Commerce: P.O. Box 1273, Fort Qu'Appelle, SK, Canada S0G 1S0.

FISH CULTURE STATION is 6 km (4 mi.) w. on Hwy. 210. The station raises such fish as northern pike, whitefish, walleye, sturgeon and rainbow, brown, lake, tiger and brook trout through their life cycle from the egg stage to adult, then distributes them to various lakes and rivers to bolster fish population. Guided tours are available. Allow 30 minutes minimum. Daily 9-noon and 1-4, May 1-Labour Day. Free. Phone (306) 332-3200.

FORT QU'APPELLE MUSEUM is at Bay Ave. and 3rd St. A small log building remaining from the original 1864 Hudson's Bay Co. trading post adjoins a modern structure displaying relics of the past, Indian crafts and a model of Fort Qu'Appelle. Daily 10-noon and 1-5, June 1-Labour Day; other times by appointment. Admission $2; $1 (children); $5 (family). Phone (306) 332-6033.

GRASSLANDS NATIONAL PARK (F-3)

Elevations in the park range from 747 metres (2,450 ft.) at the Frenchman River to 998 metres (3,275 ft.) at Horse Creek. Refer to CAA/AAA maps for additional elevation information.

Grasslands National Park of Canada encompasses the grasslands in two separate blocks between Val Marie and Killdeer in the southern part of the province. When completed, the park will preserve 900 square kilometres (350 sq. mi.) of Saskatchewan's original mixed-grass prairie, including such topographic features as buttes, badlands and coulees. Among the wildlife species found in the park are black-tailed prairie dogs, golden eagles, rattlesnakes, short-horned lizards, pronghorn antelopes, mule deer and most recently, reintroduced plains bison.

These grasslands also claim a rich history. The first recorded discovery of dinosaur remains in western Canada was made in the badlands in 1875. Proof of early habitation includes remnants of tepee rings, ranch buildings, corrals and old homestead shacks.

Ranching operations exist in the area, and some of the proposed parkland is still under private ownership. Before entering the park, visitors are invited to contact or stop at the visitor center located in Val Marie, which offers park information, maps and permits as well as interpretive programs, guided hikes and special events. Park open year-round. Visitor center daily 8-5, Victoria Day weekend-Labour Day weekend; 8-noon and 1-4:30, Apr. 1-Victoria Day weekend and Labour Day weekend-Oct. 31. Write Grasslands National Park, P.O. Box 150, Val Marie,

SK, Canada S0N 2T0; phone (306) 298-2257. *See Recreation Chart.*

GRAVELBOURG (F-3) pop. 1,187

CATHÉDRALE NOTRE-DAME DE L'ASSOMPTION is at 1st Ave. and Main St. The 1918 Cathedral of Our Lady of the Assumption is noted for the beauty of its interior murals, painted 1921-31 by founding pastor Monsignor Charles Maillard, as well as its stained-glass windows. Guided tours are available in English and French. Open daily 9-5, July-Aug.; by appointment rest of year. Donations. Phone (306) 648-3322, or (306) 648-3105 to schedule a guided tour.

GRENFELL (E-5) pop. 1,067

Grenfell is located about 124 kilometres (77 mi.) east of Regina at the junction of Hwys. 1 and 47. Hwy. 47 north from town leads to scenic Hwy. 247, which runs east along the northern shores of Crooked and Round lakes to the junction with Hwy. 9; from there, Hwy. 9 offers another scenic stretch of roadway south to Whitewood.

GRENFELL MUSEUM is at Wolseley Ave. and Stella St. Adare, the former home of the editor/publisher of Grenfell's first newspaper, is furnished in period. The 1904 house contains a brass bed, a wood-burning kitchen range, an icebox, a hand-operated vacuum cleaner and a dining table set with china. A separate building houses antiques, pioneer artifacts and military displays. Allow 2 hours minimum. Fri.-Sun. 2-8, early July-Aug. 31; other times by appointment. Donations. Phone (306) 697-2998.

HERSCHEL (D-2) pop. 35

ANCIENT ECHOES INTERPRETIVE CENTRE is on 1st Ave. The first part of this attraction—the interpretive center—depicts the area's natural history. Items include fossils, aboriginal artifacts and examples of taxidermy. The second part leads visitors on a guided tour, using their own vehicle, to 1,800-year-old petroglyphs located 3.2 kilometres (2 mi.) away. At the destination, a hiking trail reveals glacial ravines, freshwater springs and a variety of flora and fauna. A video of the hike is available for viewing.

Food is available. Picnicking is permitted. Allow 1 hour, 30 minutes minimum. Daily 9-5, May 15-Sept. 1; by appointment rest of year. Interpretive center $3; $2 (ages 5-12 and 65+). Guided tour to the petroglyphs $5; $3 (ages 5-12). Reservations are required for archeological site tours. Phone (306) 377-2045.

HUMBOLDT (D-3) pop. 5,161

Humboldt is located on Hwy. 5 about an hour's drive east of Saskatoon. It was named for author, explorer and scientist Baron Friedrich Heinrich Alexander von Humboldt. The town's German heritage is reflected through its architecture, festivals, downtown murals and folk art, a cottage industry. Annual events include the Summer Sizzler & Rodeo in June, Polkafest in July and Oktoberfest in November.

There are hiking trails at Waldsea Lake Regional Park, about 6 kilometres (4 mi.) north of town via Hwy. 20, then west about 4 kilometres (2.5 mi.). The semi-saline lake is excellent for boating, sailing and swimming. The Willkommen Centre has information about Humboldt's history and area sightseeing.

Willkommen Centre/Humboldt Tourism: 601 Main St., P.O. Box 1598, Humboldt, SK, Canada S0K 2A0; phone (306) 682-3444 or (877) 277-6748.

HUMBOLDT AND DISTRICT MUSEUM AND GALLERY is at Main St. and Sixth Ave. Housed in a restored, early 20th-century post office (a national historic site), the museum features a Humboldt Telegraph Station exhibit, a Sports Hall of Fame and local history displays. It also showcases the work of regional artists. Allow 30 minutes minimum. Tues.-Sat. 10-5, Sun. 1-5, July-Aug.; Tues.-Sat. 1-5, rest of year. Donations. Phone (306) 682-5226.

INDIAN HEAD (E-5) pop. 1,758

INDIAN HEAD MUSEUM is at 610 Otterloo St. Housed in an old fire hall, this museum displays an extensive collection of artifacts dating back to the district's pioneer beginnings. Also on the grounds is an 1883 cottage that farm laborers lived in, as well as a 1926 school. A 1952 Pontiac in mint condition resides in a replicated 1930s village garage. A large assortment of farm machinery also is on display.

Guided tours are available by appointment. Allow 1 hour minimum. Daily 1-4, July-Aug.; by appointment rest of year. Admission $2; 50c (ages 12-19). Phone (306) 695-3908.

PFRA SHELTERBELT CENTRE is 1.6 km (1 mi.) s. of jct. hwys. 1 and 56. A short, self-guiding nature trail and picnic areas are part of the Prairie Farm Rehabilitation Administration (PFRA). Outdoor areas open daily dawn-dusk. Free. Phone (306) 695-2284.

KAMSACK (D-5) pop. 2,009

KAMSACK POWERHOUSE MUSEUM is 1.5 km (1 mi.) w. of Hwy. 5 to the Riverside Golf Course, following signs. Housed in a 1914 power plant, the museum features a 1914 generator, old farm equipment, household artifacts, a printing press, vintage clothing and replicas of an early 1900s doctor's office, hospital room, kitchen, bedroom and barbershop. Daily 1-5, June 1-Labour Day; by appointment rest of year. Admission $3; free (ages 0-17). Phone (306) 542-4415.

KINDERSLEY (D-2) pop. 4,548

Kindersley is a popular stop for bird watchers. The surrounding region annually attracts thousands of migrating geese, more than 10 species of ducks, and a few whistling swans and whooping cranes.

Kindersley celebrates the annual Goose Festival in September.

Kindersley Chamber of Commerce: 305 Main St., Box 1537, Kindersley, SK, Canada S0L 1S0; phone (306) 463-2320.

KINDERSLEY PLAINS MUSEUM is 1 km (.6 mi.) e. on Hwy. 7 to 903 11th Ave. Geological displays, Indian artifacts and farming and military items are featured. Guided tours are available. Allow 30 minutes minimum. Daily 9-5, May 13-Aug. 31. Admission $3; $2 (ages 12-18); $7 (family). Phone (306) 463-6620 or (306) 463-2971.

KINISTINO (C-4) pop. 702

One of the oldest purely agricultural settlements in the province, Kinistino takes its name from *kinistineaux*, meaning "they who were the first to arrive." The allusion refers to the Cree Indians, who lived in the area before the arrival of homesteaders.

KINISTINO DISTRICT PIONEER MUSEUM is on Main St. The museum displays pioneer and aboriginal artifacts. Allow 30 minutes minimum. Mon., Wed. and Fri. 1-7, Jul.-Aug. Donations. Phone (306) 864-2838.

LLOYDMINSTER (C-1) pop. 18,900

Lloydminster is the province's only city with one foot planted in Saskatchewan and the other in Alberta. Four 100-foot-tall border markers—shaped like the survey stakes used during the original survey of the border between the two provinces, represent four themes: oil and gas, agriculture, the Barr Colonists and native North Americans. The downtown monument, erected in 1994, denotes the city's bi-provincial status.

Many nearby lakes, regional parks and campgrounds offer opportunities for fishing, birdwatching and other pursuits. Other recreational opportunities include an 18-hole golf course and an aquatic leisure center with a wave pool and a water slide.

The Border City Petting Zoo, 8 kilometres (5 mi.) east of Lloydminster on Hwy. 16, is home to such species as deer, exotic cattle, chickens, ducks, sheep, pigs and a large collection of reptiles including zoo mascot Peanut, a royal ball python. One of the zoo's newest members is Minka, a lioness cub born in 2006. Phone (306) 825-4472.

Summer events include Colonial Days, a 4-day fair with a parade, agricultural exhibits and grandstand entertainment held in mid-July, and racing action at the Canadian Professional Chuckwagon Finals in mid-August. Canada Day celebrations are held July 1 in Weaver Park.

Lloydminster Tourism: 4420 50th Ave., Lloydminster, AB, Canada T9V 0W2; phone (780) 871-8333 or (800) 825-6180.

BARR COLONY HERITAGE CULTURAL CENTRE is on Hwy. 16E at 45th Ave. This complex of museums, galleries and changing exhibits chronicles the history of one of North America's largest organized colonizations, led by Rev. Isaac Barr. It is next to Weaver Park, where the English colonists built their first settlement in 1903. The facilities and exhibits include The Richard Larsen Museum, The Fuchs Wildlife Exhibit, The Imhoff Art Collection and The Oilfield Technical Society Heavy Oil Science Centre.

Cultural center open daily 9-8, Victoria Day weekend-Labour Day; Wed.-Fri. 9-5, Sat.-Sun. 1-5, rest of year. Admission $6.25; $5.25 (students with ID and senior citizens); $3.50 (ages 6-12); $2.25 (ages 2-5). MC, VI. Phone (306) 825-5655.

BUD MILLER ALL SEASONS PARK is at 2902 59th Ave. The park consists of 81 hectares (200 acres) of walking and bicycling trails, gardens, picnic areas, playgrounds, sports facilities and a skateboard park. Fishing, tennis, beach volleyball, lawn bowling and miniature golf are among the activities offered. An aquatic complex offers a wave pool, waterslide, whirlpool, steam room and sauna. Self-guiding interpretive trails are available.

Picnicking is permitted. Park open daily 7 a.m.-11 p.m. Aquatic complex hours vary with seasons and events; phone ahead. Park admission free. Aquatic complex $6.25; $5.25 (ages 13-17 and 61+); $3.75 (ages 6-12); $2.50 (ages 2-5). Phone (780) 875-4497, (780) 875-4499 or (800) 825-6180.

MANITOU BEACH (D-3) pop. 212

The resort community of Manitou Beach is on the shore of Little Manitou Lake. The mineral waters of this lake were believed by the First Nations people to possess curative powers, and the sick of the tribe were brought for treatment long before Europeans knew of the land. Akin to the Dead Sea, the 19-kilometre-long (12-mi.) lake is three times saltier than the ocean and perfectly buoyant, allowing swimmers to float effortlessly. The village has a nine-hole golf course, spa hotel, convention center, mini-mall, tennis courts, drive-in movie theater, cross-country ski trails, an indoor heated mineral pool and a 212-site, full-service campground.

Along the lake lies Camp Easter Seal, which provides summer recreation for the physically impaired; visitors are welcome. At the east end of town on Hwy. 365 is Danceland, a dance hall with a 5,000-square-foot maple hardwood dance floor. On Friday and Saturday evenings couples take to the floor for old-fashioned ballroom and rousing square dancing to live music; gospel shows take place on Sunday. For tourism information phone (866) 756-6665.

MAPLE CREEK (F-2) pop. 2,270

The town of Maple Creek was named by the Canadian Pacific Railway workers who spent the winter of 1882 on the banks of Maple Creek. Livestock, grain, tourism, natural gas and oil development provide the area with a stable economy. Maple Creek also has a golf course and campgrounds.

South of town on Hwy. 21 is Cypress Hills Interprovincial Park (see attraction listing in Alberta p.

78, Recreation Chart and the AAA/CAA Western Canada & Alaska CampBook). The lofty hills are characterized by forest-covered buttes, plateaus and ridges interspersed with large areas of ranchland.

The Great Sand Hills region is located about 150 kilometres (93 mi.) north of Maple Creek via Hwy. 21. Occupying approximately 1,900 square kilometres (190,000 hectares), this area in southwestern Saskatchewan is characterized by fragile native grasslands and open sand dunes, the largest some 25 metres (82 ft.) high. The dunes are fringed by small clumps of aspen, birch and willow trees, rose bushes, sagebrush and choke cherry. Subjected to strong winds blowing from the northwest, the dunes are moving east at a rate of almost 4 metres per year.

Cypress Hills Regional Economic Development Authority: 124 Jasper St., P.O. Box 428, Maple Creek, SK, Canada S0N 1N0; phone (306) 662-4299.

FORT WALSH NATIONAL HISTORIC SITE is 55 km (34 mi.) s.w. on Hwy. 271. The site preserves an early North West Mounted Police fort. Reconstructed period buildings house exhibits of original post artifacts. Tours include trips to a reconstructed whiskey trading post and the fort. Visitors also can bird watch, walk a self-guiding nature trail and participate in geocaching.

A bus trip around the park includes an interpretive commentary. Allow 2 hours minimum. Daily 9:30-5:30, Victoria Day weekend-Labour Day. Admission (includes bus tour) $9.15; $7.90 (ages 66+); $4.45 (ages 6-16); $20.30 (family). MC, VI. Phone (306) 662-3590.

THE JASPER CULTURAL AND HISTORICAL CENTRE is at 311 Jasper St. Several rooms of historical displays and art are housed in a 1913 two-story brick school building. Exhibits include ranching, railroad, rodeo and school memorabilia. Allow 30 minutes minimum. Mon.-Fri. 9-5, Sat.-Sun. and holidays noon-5. Admission $5; $2 (students with ID); $1 (ages 6-12); $10 (family). Phone (306) 662-2434.

OLDTIMER'S MUSEUM is at 218 Jasper St. The museum contains collections of photographs, artifacts and archival material relating to the First Nations people, the North West Mounted Police, ranching and early settlement. Daily 9-5:30, Victoria Day weekend-Labour Day. Admission $5; $4 (students with ID); $2 (ages 0-11). Phone (306) 662-2474.

MEADOW LAKE (B-2) pop. 4,582

Meadow Lake functions as a retail, service and distribution center for northwestern Saskatchewan's major industries as well as a shopping destination for communities in the region. Pastimes include fishing and hunting for big game, ducks and geese as well as snowmobiling, cross-country skiing and other recreational activities.

With 25 sparkling lakes, Meadow Lake Provincial Park *(see Recreation Chart and the AAA/CAA Western Canada & Alaska CampBook)* is a haven for fishing, swimming, boating and camping. The park offers hiking trails, beaches, interpretive and recreational programs, cabins, a miniature golf course and a 179-kilometre (111-mi.) canoe route stretching along the Waterhen and Beaver rivers. The town's recreational facilities include the Lions Regional Campground and RV Park, an aquatic center and an 18-hole golf course.

Of historical interest is Steele Narrows Provincial Historic Park, 72 kilometres (45 mi.) southwest via hwys. 304 and 26. The last armed conflict on Canadian soil occurred between Big Bear and his band of Cree Indians and Maj. Sam Steele of the North West Mounted Police. The defeat of Big Bear on June 3, 1885, was the end of the Métis and Indian rebellion that began in March 1885 *(see Batoche p. 261).*

Meadow Lake & District Chamber of Commerce: P.O. Box 1168, Meadow Lake, SK, Canada S9X 1Y8; phone (306) 236-4447.

MEADOW LAKE & DISTRICT INFORMATION CENTRE & MUSEUM is at Hwy. 4 and 9th St. W. Local pioneer artifacts and antiques are displayed. Mon.-Sat. 8-6, Sun. noon-6, Victoria Day-Labour Day; by appointment rest of year. Donations. Phone (306) 236-3622.

MELFORT (C-4) pop. 5,559, elev. 457 m/1,500′

Known as the City of Northern Lights due to the visibility of the aurora borealis in the night sky for much of the year, Melfort is in the Carrot River Valley, an area known for its fertile black loam. Agriculture has been the major industry in the area since the days of early settlement in the late 19th century. Melfort was incorporated as a village in 1903, as a town in 1907 and as the province's twelfth city on Sept. 2, 1980.

Melfort & District Chamber of Commerce: Box 2002, Melfort, SK, Canada S0E 1A0; phone (306) 752-4636.

MELFORT & DISTRICT MUSEUM is at 401 Melfort St. W. Historic buildings include a 1912 power house, reconstructed log farmhouse, general store and post office, barbershop, schoolhouse, blacksmith shop and real estate office. The museum also features farm machinery, equipment and tools used in the development of the local agricultural industry.

Guided tours are available. Allow 1 hour minimum. Mon.-Fri. 9-4, Sat. 10-3, mid-May to early Sept.; closed holidays. Admission $4; $3 (ages 13-17); $2 (ages 6-12); $12 (family). Phone (306) 752-5870.

MELVILLE (E-5) pop. 4,453, elev. 555 m/1,820′

Situated on the east-west main line of the Canadian National Railway and also on an important north-south line of that company, Melville is known as "The Rail Centre." It came to provincial prominence when it was selected as a major railway service center early in the 20th century. The railway is still the city's largest employer, and its facilities are essential in marketing agricultural products as well as potash from nearby Esterhazy.

Melville & District Chamber of Commerce: P.O. Box 429, Melville, SK, Canada S0A 2P0; phone (306) 728-4177.

MELVILLE HERITAGE MUSEUM is at 100 Heritage Dr. Formerly the Luther Academy, the restored 1913 building now houses this regional museum. Exhibits include artifacts from various churches and denominations; sports, recreation and railway exhibits; military memorabilia; and more than 100 original photographs depicting Melville's early 20th-century progress. The oldest artifact, a German pulpit Bible, dates to 1721. A chapel and library are here as well.

Guided tours are available. Allow 1 hour minimum. Tues.-Sun. 10-noon and 1-4, mid-May to mid-Oct.; by appointment rest of year. Donations. Phone (306) 728-2070.

MOOSE JAW (E-3)
pop. 32,131, elev. 542 m/1,778′

Moose Jaw's unusual name is probably derived from the big bend in Moose Jaw Creek. The Indians called this creek *moosichappishannissippi,* or "the creek that bends like a moose's jaw." Another popular theory is that an early traveler through the area fixed his cart wheel with a moose's jawbone found in the vicinity. Today's visitors are greeted by "Mac," a 30-foot-tall statue said to be the world's largest moose.

During Prohibition in the United States Moose Jaw was the home of an industrious band of bootleggers and American gangsters, earning the town the nickname "Little Chicago of the Prairies." Moose Jaw is an important western Canadian industrial city, and hard spring wheat also is grown in the area. The Canadian Forces base just south of the city is home to one of Canada's busiest airports and headquarters of the Snowbirds, the Canadian armed forces aerobatic team.

The Murals of Moose Jaw, painted on several downtown buildings, are a collection of more than 40 scenes depicting the town's history. Tours of the murals and heritage buildings can be arranged at Trudy's Gift Shop, in the lobby of the Temple Gardens Mineral Spa Resort Hotel, 24 Fairford St. E.; phone (306) 694-5055. The Yvette Moore Gallery, downtown at 76 Fairford St. W., exhibits the work of local artist Yvette Moore, whose paintings also can be seen in Moose Jaw hotels and businesses; phone (306) 693-7600.

A historic landmark south of town is Hwy. 2, once part of the Powder River Trail used by freighters and ranchers to reach Denver before the advent of the railroad. About 42 kilometres (26 mi.) north on Hwy. 2 is Buffalo Pound Provincial Park *(see*

Recreation Chart and the AAA/CAA Western Canada & Alaska CampBook), where 350 hectares (865 acres) are set aside as grazing land for a herd of buffaloes.

Wakamow Valley, in Moose Jaw, is a recreational development that includes Plaxton's Lake, North River Park, Kiwanis River Park, Kinsmen Wellesley Park, Connor Park and the Devonian Trail, a pedestrian and bicycle trail system. Visitors can enjoy picnicking, camping, bird-watching, hiking, jogging and bicycling.

Moose Jaw Chamber of Commerce: 88 Saskatchewan St. E., Box 1359, Moose Jaw, SK, Canada S6H 4R3; phone (306) 692-6414.

Self-guiding tours: Brochures outlining a self-guiding tour of some of downtown Moose Jaw's most significant historic sites are available at the Moose Jaw Art Museum and National Exhibits in Crescent Park (*see attraction listing*).

CRESCENT PARK is at Fairford and Athabasca sts. An outdoor swimming pool, war memorial gardens and recreational facilities are contained on 11 hectares (27 acres). Free entertainment is presented Wednesday evenings July through August. The Moose Jaw Art Museum and National Exhibits, next to the public library, displays historical items of local, regional and national interest.

Museum open Tues.-Sun. noon-5 (also Tues. and Thurs. 7-9 p.m.); closed Good Friday, Easter and Dec. 25. Outdoor pool open daily 1-4 and 7-8:30, June 1-Labour Day. Museum free. Admission to pool $3.47; $2.48 (ages 13-17); $2.25 (ages 3-12); $7.93 (family). Phone (306) 692-4471, or (306) 694-4500 for the pool.

MOOSE JAW TROLLEY COMPANY tours depart from the spa at 24 Fairford St. E. Visitors are led on a guided tour of the city's quaint streets and can experience its rich history while riding on board a replicated electric streetcar that operated 1911-32. Allow 1 hour minimum. Tours depart daily (weather permitting), May-Oct. Phone ahead for tour schedule. Fare $12; $10 (ages 65+); $7 (ages 13-17); $5 (ages 6-12). Tickets can be purchased at Tourism Moose Jaw, 450 Diefenbaker Dr. MC, VI. Phone (306) 693-8091.

SUKANEN SHIP, PIONEER VILLAGE AND MUSEUM is 13 km (8 mi.) s. on Hwy. 2. The large, unfinished ship was built by Tom Sukanen, a Finnish settler who had planned to sail the boat home to his native country by way of the South Saskatchewan River, Hudson Bay, Greenland and Iceland. A village preserves an old post office, blacksmith shop, school, church, railroad station, a general store and the Diefenbaker homestead as well as a collection of antique tractors, trucks and cars.

Mon.-Sat. 9-5, Sun. noon-6, mid-May to mid-Sept. Admission $6; $5 (students with ID and ages 66+); $2 (ages 8-12). Phone (306) 693-7315.

TUNNELS OF MOOSE JAW is at 18 N. Main St. Two themed 50-minute tours take visitors under the streets of Moose Jaw. Miss Fanny and Gus are the guides for the Chicago Connection tour, which explores gangster Al Capone's bootlegging operation and the tunnels he is said to have used to escape American authorities. The Passage to Fortune tour depicts the story of early Chinese immigrants who came to build the Canadian Pacific Railway and their footsteps through adversity and persecution to eventual success.

Guided tours are offered daily 10-8, July-Aug.; 10-5:30, rest of year. Closed Dec. 25. Schedule may vary; phone ahead. Individual tour fare $13; $10 (ages 66+); $9.50 (ages 13-17); $6.50 (ages 5-12). Combination ticket $21; $17 (ages 66+); $16 (ages 13-17); $10 (ages 5-12). Reservations are recommended. AX, MC, VI. Phone (306) 693-5261. *See color ad inside front cover.*

WESTERN DEVELOPMENT MUSEUM'S HISTORY OF TRANSPORTATION is at 50 Diefenbaker Dr. Displays illustrate air, water, rail and land transportation. The museum also houses an observatory. The Snowbird Gallery contains aircraft and memorabilia from the Canadian armed forces aerobatic team. Trips aboard the Short Line, a miniature steam locomotive, are available on weekends.

Picnicking is permitted. Allow 1 hour minimum. Museum open daily 9-5 (closed Mon., Jan.-Mar.); closed Jan. 1 and Dec. 25-26. Train rides Sat.-Sun., Victoria Day-Labour Day (weather permitting); phone to confirm schedule. Museum $8.50; $7.50 (ages 65+); $5.75 (students with ID); $2 (ages 6-12); $18.50 (family). Train rides $2. AX, MC, VI. Phone (306) 693-5989.

GAMBLING ESTABLISHMENTS

- **Casino Moose Jaw**, 21 Fairford St. E. Sun.-Thurs. 9 a.m.-2 a.m., Fri.-Sat. 9 a.m.-3 a.m.; closed Dec. 25. Phone (306) 694-3888.

RECREATIONAL ACTIVITIES

Recreational Complex

- **Kinsmen Sportsplex**, 855 McDonald St. W., Moose Jaw, SK, Canada S6H 2W3. Daily 1-4 and 7-9, mid-Mar. to mid-Oct.; Sat. 2-3, Sun. 7-8, rest of year. Closed Jan. 1, Good Friday and Dec. 25. Phone (306) 694-4483.

MORSE (E-3) pop. 248

MORSE MUSEUM & CULTURAL CENTRE is at 410 McKenzie St. Housed in a brick school built in 1912, the exhibits focus on the town's development from the time of the early settlers to the 1970s. The displays include nine themed rooms, a Victorian-style parlor and an art gallery featuring works by local, regional and provincial artists. Tea is served at the end of the guided tour.

Allow 1 hour minimum. Mon.-Sat. 9-5, May-Oct.; Mon.-Fri. 9-5, rest of year. Closed holidays. Donations. Phone (306) 629-3230 or (306) 629-3626.

MUENSTER (D-4) pop. 379

ST. PETER'S ABBEY is 1 km (.6 mi.) e. off Muenster access rd. on Hwy. 5. A self-guiding walking tour of the abbey complex enables visitors to learn about monastic life. Brochures are available at Severin Hall. Sts. Peter and Paul Church, recreational facilities, a farm, gardens, an orchard, trails, print shop, workshops, a cemetery and a greenhouse are points of interest. Allow 1 hour minimum. Daily 8-dusk. Free. Phone (306) 682-1777.

ST. PETER'S CATHEDRAL is 1 km (.6 mi.) n. of Hwy. 5 on the Muenster access rd. The cathedral's walls and ceiling are lined with paintings by Berthold von Imhoff, who created the 80 life-size figures as a gift to the abbot of St. Peter's Abbey. Allow 30 minutes minimum. Daily 9-9, Mar.-Dec. Free. Phone (306) 682-1777 or (306) 682-1789.

NIPAWIN (C-4) pop. 4,275

The Nipawin Hydroelectric Station, northwest of town, uses water impounded in Codette Lake by the Francois-Finlay Dam to generate 1.1 billion kilowatt hours of electricity annually. Guided tours of the facility are conducted by the chamber of commerce on Fridays, June through August; phone ahead to confirm tour availability. SaskPower also conducts tours, but requires 2 weeks' advance notice; phone (306) 862-3148.

Nipawin & District Chamber of Commerce: Box 177, Nipawin, SK, Canada S0E 1E0; phone (306) 862-5252.

LIVING FORESTRY MUSEUM is just w. on Hwy. 35N. The museum contains rotating exhibits that describe the history of the area. Several historic buildings have been relocated to the vicinity, including a sawmill, schoolhouse, shingle mill, church and the 1924 Hornseth House. Demonstrations of the saw and shingle mills and a steam engine are provided during the summer months. Allow 1 hour minimum. Daily 9-5, May-Aug. Admission $3; free (ages 0-12). Phone (306) 862-9299.

NOKOMIS (D-4) pop. 436

First named Blakemore and then Blaikie by railroad officials, Nokomis began as the junction of the Old Grand Trunk Railway and the Canadian Provincial Railway. Arriving from England, Mrs. Thomas Halstead, the town's postmistress, was intrigued by the West and the romantic domain of the Indians and chose the name Nokomis, from Henry Wadsworth Longfellow's poem "Hiawatha," for the young town.

NOKOMIS AND DISTRICT MUSEUM is at 3rd Ave. and Queen St. Housed in the former railway station, the museum features re-creations of a post office, schoolhouse, dentist's office, hospital room and equipment, hardware store, a garage with a 1930 Chevrolet and a church. Photographs, vintage clothing and antiques are displayed. Junction City 1907, behind the museum, is a replica of a small

town. Allow 1 hour minimum. Daily 10-5, June 1-Labour Day. Admission $2; $5 (family). Phone (306) 528-2979.

NORTH BATTLEFORD (C-2) pop. 13,692

On the bank of the North Saskatchewan River, North Battleford is a gateway to the province's northwest parkland area. Agriculture is the backbone of the area's economy, with farms producing cereal grains, oil seeds and hay crops as well as cattle, hogs, poultry and bison. Forestry, manufacturing and heavy crude oil development also are important industries.

The Battlefords Provincial Park *(see Recreation Chart and Cochin in the AAA/CAA Western Canada & Alaska CampBook)* is approximately 42 kilometres (26 mi.) north off Hwy. 4 and offers fishing, water skiing, boating and hiking trails. Cross-country skiing and ice fishing are popular winter activities at the park.

Battlefords Chamber of Commerce: Junction hwys. 16 and 40E, P.O. Box 1000, North Battleford, SK, Canada S9A 3E6; phone (306) 445-6226.

ALLEN SAPP GALLERY is at 1 Railway Ave. This award-winning public gallery features powerful and sensitive images of the Northern Plains Cree by renowned Cree artist Allen Sapp. Sapp's works capture the life and history of the Cree at the turn of the 20th century. Other exhibits include large-screen videos and historical artifacts.

Daily 11-5, June-Sept.; Wed.-Sun. noon-4, rest of year. Donations. Phone (306) 445-1760.

THE CHAPEL GALLERY is at 891 99th St., just e. of S. Railway Ave., at the s. end of the Don Ross Centre. Formerly a chapel, the building was converted to a gallery in 1986. The collection includes local, regional and provincial works; exhibits change regularly. Guided tours are available. Allow 30 minutes minimum. Daily noon-5, June-Aug.; Wed.-Sun. noon-4, rest of year. Closed Jan. 1 and Dec. 25. Donations. Phone (306) 445-1757.

WESTERN DEVELOPMENT MUSEUM'S HERITAGE FARM AND VILLAGE is at jct. hwys. 16 and 40. The story of agriculture and pioneer life is the focus of the museum, which preserves a 1920s pioneer village and features the exhibit Winning the Prairie Gamble. A working farm offers demonstrations of early agricultural equipment and techniques.

Picnicking is permitted. Allow 2 hours minimum. Daily 9-5, May-Sept.; Mon.-Fri. 10-4, rest of year. Closed provincial holidays. Admission (good for 2 consecutive days) $8.50; $7.50 (ages 66+); $5.75 (students with ID); $2 (ages 6-12); $18.50 (family). AX, MC, VI. Phone (306) 445-8033.

GAMBLING ESTABLISHMENTS

- **Gold Eagle Casino**, 11902 Railway Ave. E. Thurs.-Sat. 9 a.m.-4 a.m., Sun.-Wed. 9 a.m.-3 a.m.; closed Dec. 24-25. Phone (306) 446-3833 or (877) 446-3833.

OUTLOOK (D-3) pop. 2,129

Agriculture has traditionally sustained Outlook, where such crops as corn, potatoes, vegetables and sunflowers are grown. The town came upon its name in an unusual way. As two Canadian Pacific Railway officials stood quietly on the edge of an expansive valley, intensely watching the raging South Saskatchewan River gushing below them, the silence was broken when one uttered the words, "What a wonderful outlook!"

Outlook and District Regional Park, located along the South Saskatchewan River on the west edge of town, covers of 40 hectares (100 acres) and features a golf course, swimming pool, campgrounds and hiking trails. Nature enthusiasts will especially appreciate the many species of birds as well as the venerable elm trees. Phone (306) 867-8846.

A large salt and pepper shaker collection is the highlight of the Outlook & District Heritage Museum, in the center of town at 100 Railway Ave. E. Skytrail, just northwest of the center of town following signs, is one of Canada's longest pedestrian bridges, spanning the South Saskatchewan River 150 above the water and running for a distance of 3,000 feet. Side rails and a safe walking surface allow users to focus their attention on the views.

The South Saskatchewan River Project, on the South Saskatchewan and Qu'Appelle rivers, consists of two dams. Gardiner Dam, midway between Elbow and Outlook, is 5 kilometres (3 mi.) long, 64 metres (210 ft.) high and 1,615 metres (5,300 ft.) wide at its base. The impounded water forms Lake Diefenbaker, about 225 kilometres (140 mi.) long, up to 5 kilometres (3 mi.) wide and 56 metres (184 ft.) deep. The second, smaller structure is Qu'Appelle Dam. The visitor center at Gardiner Dam is open daily 9-5, Victoria Day weekend-Labour Day; phone (306) 857-5500.

Town of Outlook: 400 Saskatchewan Ave., Box 518, Outlook, SK, Canada S0L 2N0; phone (306) 867-8663.

PONTEIX (F-2) pop. 550

NOTUKEU HERITAGE MUSEUM is at 110 Railway Ave. An extensive collection of First Nations artifacts, including arrowheads, is displayed. Guided tours are available in French or English. Picnicking is permitted. Allow 30 minutes minimum. Mon.-Fri. 9-noon and 1-5, Sat.-Sun. by appointment; closed major holidays. Admission $3; $2 (ages 8-12); $10 (family). Phone (306) 625-3340.

PRINCE ALBERT (C-4) pop. 34,291

The gateway to Saskatchewan's north country, Prince Albert is one of the province's oldest communities. Trapper Peter Pond built a trading post on the north side of the North Saskatchewan River in 1776. Credited with founding the town, the Rev. James Nisbet settled on the south shore in 1866.

The log Presbyterian church that Nisbet built that year is now in Kinsmen Park. A blockhouse next to the church dates from the Northwest Rebellion/Métis Resistance of 1885. The Prince Albert Historical Museum *(see attraction listing)* occupies the site of the church built by Nisbet.

Prince Albert Tourism & Convention Bureau: 3700 2nd Ave. W., Prince Albert, SK, Canada S6W 1A2; phone (306) 953-4386.

ART GALLERY OF PRINCE ALBERT is at 142 12th St. W., at the jct. with Hwy. 2 North. The spacious gallery area displays paintings and other works, with a focus on contemporary art. Temporary exhibitions also are presented. Allow 30 minutes minimum. Daily noon-5; closed holidays. Free. Phone (306) 763-7080.

DIEFENBAKER HOUSE MUSEUM is at 246 19th St. W. The 1947-75 home of the Right Honourable John G. Diefenbaker contains furniture and other possessions of the prime minister of Canada 1957-63. Allow 30 minutes minimum. Daily 9-5, Victoria Day-Labour Day. Donations. Phone (306) 953-4863.

EVOLUTION OF EDUCATION MUSEUM is at the corner of Marquis Rd. and Hwy. 2 at 3700 2nd Ave. W. The one-room, 1920 schoolhouse was designed to provide maximum warmth and light, with all large windows on the building's east side and desks facing south. Exhibits relate to area education and include pencil boxes, Dick and Jane readers and chalk clamps once used to draw lines on a blackboard. An interpreter is available to answer questions; a visitor information center also is in the building.

Allow 30 minutes minimum. Daily 10-6, Victoria Day weekend-Labour Day; by appointment rest of year. Free. Phone (306) 763-3506 Victoria Day weekend-Aug. 31, or (306) 764-2999 rest of year.

LITTLE RED RIVER PARK is at the confluence of the North Saskatchewan and Little Red rivers on Hwy. 55. A scenic drive follows the north bank of the North Saskatchewan River. Picnic facilities and winter sports are available. Swimming in the river is not recommended. Free.

PRINCE ALBERT HISTORICAL MUSEUM is at 10 River St. E. at Central Ave. The museum is housed in an old fire hall that overlooks the North Saskatchewan River. Featured is the first fire engine pumper used in the territory. Other displays include Indian, fur trade and pioneer artifacts as well as a table and benches carved by the Rev. James Nisbet. A tearoom provides a view of the river. Allow 1 hour minimum. Daily 9-5, Victoria Day-Labour Day weekend. Admission $2; $1 (ages 6-12). Phone (306) 764-2992.

ROTARY MUSEUM OF POLICE AND CORRECTIONS is at the corner of Marquis Rd. and Hwy. 2 at 3700 2nd Ave. W. Displays pertain to the Royal Canadian Mounted Police, local police, provincial police and corrections services. Exhibits include corporal punishment items, police uniforms and weapons. The museum is in a landscaped park with a visitor center; an interpreter is available to answer questions. Allow 30 minutes minimum. Daily 10-6, Victoria Day weekend-Labour Day; by appointment rest of year. Free. Phone (306) 922-3313.

GAMBLING ESTABLISHMENTS

• **Northern Lights Casino**, 44 Marquis Rd. Thurs.-Sat. 9 a.m.-4 a.m., Sun.-Wed. 9 a.m.-3 a.m.; closed Dec. 25. Phone (306) 764-4777.

PRINCE ALBERT NATIONAL PARK OF CANADA (B-3)

Elevations in the park range from 488 metres (1,600 ft.) on the western side of the park to 724 metres (2,375 ft.) on the southern side of the park. Refer to CAA/AAA maps for additional elevation information.

The main entrance to Prince Albert National Park of Canada is 81 kilometres (50 mi.) north of the city of Prince Albert via hwys. 2 and 264.

The park covers 3,875 square kilometres (1,496 sq. mi.) of wilderness in central Saskatchewan. Its lakes, ponds, streams, bogs and rolling hills are a legacy of the glacial epoch. Notable are Sandy, Waskesiu, Kingsmere, Namekus, Crean and the Hanging Heart lakes. There also are several hundred smaller lakes and ponds and many sand beaches.

Heavy growths of conifers and several species of hardwoods surround the lakes, along with numerous shrubs and wildflowers. Fall foliage is especially colorful. Such wild animals as elk, deer, moose and bears are plentiful. A herd of bison roams the southwest corner of the park.

Early morning and evening provide the best chances of seeing wildlife along park roads, especially the Narrows and Kingsmere roads along Waskesiu Lake. Although some animals may seem tame, they are wild and should be observed only from a safe distance.

The park also preserves the legacy of Grey Owl. Born as Archibald Stansfeld Belaney, this controversial Englishman arrived in Canada in 1905. Adopted by the Ojibwa Indians and later married into the tribe, Grey Owl turned his love of nature to the re-establishment of the region's beaver population, which had been decimated by hunters and trappers. For 7 years he lived at Beaver Lodge on Ajawaan Lake, where he continued his restoration and conservation efforts.

General Information and Activities

Although the park is open throughout the year, complete facilities are provided Victoria Day-Labour Day only. Information is available from the information bureau in the Waskesiu Lake Visitor Services Centre, 8 kilometres (5 mi.) from the park's main gate on Hwy. 264.

Roads traverse the park and lead to Waskesiu, Namekus, Sandy and the Hanging Heart lakes and to the Kingsmere River. Although no roads lead directly to Kingsmere and Crean lakes, access is possible by boat. A light railway with handcars assists in portaging around the unnavigable stretch of the Kingsmere River.

There are more than 100 kilometres (60 mi.) of hiking trails traversing the park. Some are suitable for day walks, while others require an overnight stop. Pamphlets outlining self-guiding tours are available for the Mud Creek and Boundary Bog nature trails. From the boat dock on the north shore of Kingsmere Lake a 3-kilometre (1.9-mi.) trail leads to the home and grave of Grey Owl.

Park facilities include boat launching and berthing areas at the Hanging Heart Lakes, the Narrows and the main marina on Waskesiu Lake. Boats, canoes and outboard motors can be rented at all three marinas; paddle-wheeler tours are offered daily in summer. There are bicycle rentals, tennis and volleyball courts and bowling greens at the Waskesiu Lake Visitor Services Centre.

Waskesiu Lake's 18-hole golf course ranks among the finest in Canada. A 150-kilometre (93-mi.) network of groomed cross-country ski trails is open in winter. Snowshoeing and ice fishing also are permitted. Fishing licenses are required and can be obtained at the park information center, park entrances and campground offices.

Park naturalists offer a free summer interpretive program that includes car caravans on park roadways and special daily events. Interpretive programs are regularly presented at the outdoor theaters at the Narrows and Beaver Glen campgrounds.

At the Waskesiu Lake Visitor Services Centre is the Park Nature Centre, which has natural history exhibits, a bookstore and a theater; the nature center is open in July and August. *See Recreation Chart and the AAA/CAA Western Canada & Alaska Camp-Book.*

ADMISSION to the park is $6.90 per day; over 65, $5.90; ages 6-16, $3.45. Admission $17.30 per day per group of up to seven adults.

PETS (dogs and cats) are permitted in the park as long as they are on leashes.

ADDRESS inquiries to the Superintendent, Prince Albert National Park of Canada, P.O. Box 100, Waskesiu Lake, SK, Canada S0J 2Y0; phone (306) 663-4522.

QU'APPELLE (E-4) pop. 648

CREEKSIDE GARDENS is .4 km (.25 mi.) e. of town on Hwy. 1, following signs (about 35 minutes east of Regina). The gardens encompass approximately 2 hectares (5 acres) and feature lawns, shrubs, trees, perennials and more than 50,000 annuals. Picnicking is permitted. Allow 30 minutes minimum. Daily 9-9, mid-June to mid-Sept. Admission $2; free (ages 0-11). Phone (306) 699-2375 or (306) 924-2204.

REGINA (E-4) pop. 178,225, elev. 578 m/1,896'

Indians once used the banks of Wascana Creek for drying buffalo meat and cleaning and stretching the hides. Thus the area became known as *Oscana*, a Cree word meaning "pile of bones." In 1882 the Canadian Pacific Railway completed its track across the plains, and the settlement of Pile-O-Bones sprang up at the rail terminal on Wascana Creek.

The seat of government of the Northwest Territories and the headquarters of the North West Mounted Police were established the same year. A few years later Princess Louise, the wife of Canada's governor-general, renamed the city Regina (Latin for queen) to honor her mother, Queen Victoria. In 1905 Saskatchewan became a province, with Regina as its capital.

In the heart of downtown is City Centre, the site of such buildings as the municipal government offices and the public library. The Prairie History Room, which documents local history, and the Dunlop Art Gallery, which displays works by regional artists, are both housed in the library. A glockenspiel chimes at the corner of 12th Avenue and Scarth Street in tribute to the city's ethnic vitality.

The Globe Theatre in the old City Hall is the home of Regina's professional acting company. Another restored building is Union Station, a transportation hub in the early years of rail travel that is now occupied by Casino Regina. Guided historical tours explore parts of a tunnel system that once stretched beneath downtown streets and also offer a behind-the-scenes look at casino operations. Under 19 are not permitted. For ticket information phone (800) 555-3189.

Following Wascana Creek for about 8 kilometres (5 mi.) is the Devonian Pathway, a paved bicycle trail that passes through six city parks and is used for jogging and walking as well as other activities; in winter it is groomed and lighted for cross-country skiing. The Condie Nature Refuge, just north of the city on Hwy. 11, offers nature trails that afford views of the refuge's grassland and marsh animals. For spectators the No. 1 sport is summer football, played by the Canadian Football League's Saskatchewan Roughriders at Mosaic Stadium at Taylor Field.

Further information is available from Tourism Saskatchewan, 1922 Park St., Regina, SK, Canada S4P 3V7; phone (306) 787-9600 or (877) 237-2273.

Regina Convention and Visitors Bureau: Hwy. 1 E., P.O. Box 3355, Regina, SK, Canada S4P 3H1; phone (306) 789-5099 or (800) 661-5099.

Shopping areas: Regina's major shopping mall is Cornwall Centre, 2101 11th Ave. It has 87 stores, including The Bay and Sears. The specialty shops and eateries of Scarth Street Mall, downtown between 11th and 12th avenues, line a pedestrian-only street. The Cathedral Village shopping district, another downtown cluster of shops, is centered around 13th Avenue from Albert to Argyle streets and from Saskatchewan Drive to College Avenue.

GOVERNMENT HOUSE MUSEUM AND HERITAGE PROPERTY is at 4607 Dewdney Ave. This Italianate-style mansion was the home of the lieutenant governors of the Northwest Territories 1891-1905 and the lieutenant governors of Saskatchewan 1905-45. Flanked by 2.5 hectares (6 acres) of gardens and orchards, the official residence has been restored to its Victorian elegance. Picnicking is permitted. Allow 1 hour minimum. Tues.-Sun. 10-4; closed Good Friday and Dec. 25. Guided tours depart every 30 minutes. Free. Phone (306) 787-5773.

HOLY ROSARY CATHEDRAL is at 3125 13th Ave., just w. of jct. with Albert St. This Cruciform/Romanesque structure, built in 1912, features 43 stained-glass windows installed in 1951 by French artisan Andre Rault, who designed windows for more than 50 other Canadian churches. Their artistry is best appreciated on a sunny day. A Casavant pipe organ, known for its exceptional sound quality, plays during Sunday services.

Guided tours are available. Allow 30 minutes minimum. Tues.-Fri. 9-1, July-Aug.; Mon.-Fri. 8:30-noon and 1-4:30, rest of year. The cathedral is kept locked for security purposes; phone ahead. Donations. Phone (306) 565-0909.

LEGISLATIVE BUILDING (Capitol) is off Albert St. in Wascana Centre. Surrounded by 67 hectares (165 acres) of landscaped grounds, the imposing landmark is the seat of provincial government. Completed in 1912, the building reflects the architecture of the English Renaissance and Louis XIV of France. The building houses several art galleries, including the Cumberland Gallery, a showcase for works of the Native Heritage Foundation of Canada.

Tours in French are available. Allow 30 minutes minimum. Daily 8 a.m.-8:30 p.m., Victoria Day-Labour Day; 8-4:30, rest of year. Closed Jan. 1, Good Friday and Dec. 25. Guided tours of the building are offered. Tours depart every 30 minutes. Free. Phone (306) 787-5358.

REGINA PLAINS MUSEUM is on the second floor at 1835 Scarth St. It features Saskatchewan artist Jacqueline Berting's sculpture "The Glass Wheatfield," consisting of 14,000 waist-high stalks of hand-crafted glass. Also on display is a mural by aboriginal artist Sherry Farrell Racette. Rotating exhibitions focus on the city's history. Mon.-Fri. 10-4. Free. Phone (306) 780-9435.

RCMP HERITAGE CENTRE is on Dewdney Ave. at the entrance to the RCMP Academy, "Depot" Division. The center tells the story of the Royal Canadian Mounted Police (RCMP), created by an act of Parliament in 1873 to maintain law and order on the Canadian frontier and pave the way for westward settlement. Stretching the length of the main exhibition hall, the sculptural procession "March of the Mounties" anchors the core exhibit areas; graphics trace Canada's geography from west to east and depict the historical evolution of the RCMP from its inception to the present day.

Interactive educational exhibits include Maintaining Law and Order in the West, which chronicles the force's late 19th-century efforts to suppress the whisky trade, establish amicable relations with Native tribes and ensure the safety of settlers and rail workers; Serving All of Canada, an overview of the RCMP's 20th-century evolution; and Cracking the Case, a hands-on look at the high-tech side of contemporary policing. The 27-minute multimedia presentation "Tour of Duty" is shown in the center's SGI CANADA Theatre.

Food is available. Allow 2 hours minimum. Daily 10-6 (also Thurs. 6-8 p.m.), May 20-Sept. 3; Tues.-Sun. 10-4:30, rest of year. A colorful Sergeant Major's Parade is usually held Mon.-Fri. at 12:45 p.m. (except Fridays preceding a holiday weekend). Sunset Ceremonies are held Tues. at 6:30 p.m., July 1-first week in Aug. Closed Dec. 25. Admission $12; $10 (ages 13-17 and 65+); $6 (ages 6-12); $3 (ages 3-5). AX, MC, VI. Phone (306) 522-7333 or (866) 567-7267.

ST. PAUL'S CATHEDRAL is at 1861 McIntyre St. This Gothic Revival-style church is said to be the oldest in Regina; its cornerstone was laid in 1894. A columbarium (housing the ashes of the deceased) and museum are located under the church and are open by appointment; the museum houses books and artifacts dating to the 1600s. Guided tours are available. Allow 30 minutes minimum. Mon.-Fri. 9-4, Sun. 9-noon. Donations. Phone (306) 522-6439.

[SAVE] **SASKATCHEWAN SCIENCE CENTRE** is on Winnipeg St. at Wascana Dr. in Wascana Centre. The Powerhouse of Discovery houses more than 100 permanent hands-on science exhibits and features live stage shows and demonstrations. Visitors who want to test their physical skills can tackle one of the tallest climbing walls in Canada. The 165-seat Kramer IMAX Theatre uses a five-story screen and four-way sound system to present science and nature films in a giant format.

Allow 2 hours minimum. Mon.-Fri. 9-6, Sat.-Sun. noon-6, Victoria Day-Labour Day; Tues.-Fri. and Mon. holidays 9-5, Sat.-Sun. noon-6, rest of year. Admission $7; $5 (ages 6-13 and 61+); $3 (ages 3-5). IMAX shows $7; $5 (ages 6-13 and 61+); $3.75 (ages 3-5). Combination tickets are available. MC, VI. Phone (306) 522-4629, or (800) 667-6300 in Canada.

SASKATCHEWAN SPORTS HALL OF FAME is at 2205 Victoria Ave. Photographs, trophies, records and other memorabilia represent noted athletes and teams from Saskatchewan. Mon.-Fri. 9-5, Sat.-Sun. and holidays 1-5, Victoria Day-Labour Day; Mon.-Fri. 9-5, rest of year. Free. Phone (306) 780-9232.

WASCANA CENTRE surrounds Wascana Lake. The 930-hectare (2,300-acre) park is the center of recreational and cultural activity in Regina and includes the Conexus Centre of the Arts. Wascana Place is

both a departure point for sightseeing tours and a reservation office for special events. Ferry boat rides to the Willow Island picnic area are available. Wascana Waterfowl Park and Speakers' Corner also are in the area.

Ferry boat rides Mon.-Fri. noon-4:30, Sat.-Sun. noon-9. Ferry boat fare $4. Phone (306) 522-3661 daily 5-9 p.m. for reservation information.

MacKenzie Art Gallery is in the T.C. Douglas Building at the s.w. corner of Wascana Centre at Albert St. and 23rd Ave. A major exhibition center for Saskatchewan, it contains permanent and changing exhibits of Canadian and international art. Guided tours are available. Allow 1 hour minimum. Mon.-Sat. 10-5:30 (also Thurs.-Fri. 5:30-9 p.m.), Sun. and holidays 11-5:30. Donations. Phone (306) 584-4250.

▼[GEM] **Royal Saskatchewan Museum** is at College Ave. and Albert St. in Wascana Centre.

The Earth Sciences Gallery focuses on the geological and paleontological evolution of Saskatchewan and includes Canada's only resident robotic dinosaur. The Paleo Pit features hands-on exhibits. The First Nations Gallery portrays the culture and heritage of the province's aboriginal population through artwork and artifacts.

The Life Sciences Gallery explores Saskatchewan's natural history and current environmental issues. Exhibits depict life in a beaver pond, a Costa Rican rain forest and human actions that are disturbing the global ecosystem.

Allow 1 hour minimum. Daily 9-5:30; closed Dec. 25. Donations. Phone (306) 787-2815.

GAMBLING ESTABLISHMENTS

- **Casino Regina**, 1880 Saskatchewan Dr. Daily 9 a.m.-4 a.m.; closed Dec. 24-25. Phone (306) 565-3000 or (800) 555-3189.

ROCANVILLE (E-5) pop. 887

ROCANVILLE AND DISTRICT MUSEUM is at Qu'Appelle Ave. and Saint Albert St. A variety of local artifacts include steam tractors, a train station, blacksmith shop and schoolhouse. Allow 2 hours minimum. Wed.-Sun. 10-5, July-Aug.; by appointment rest of year. Donations. Phone (306) 645-2113 or (306) 645-2164.

ROSTHERN (D-3) pop. 1,504

[SAVE] **SEAGER WHEELER FARM** is 7 km (4 mi.) e. on Hwy. 312, following signs. One of the most noted farmers in Canada, Wheeler won five international wheat championships 1911-18 and was a prominent educator in progressive agricultural techniques. The farm features restored buildings and equipment. Also on the grounds are English flower gardens, orchards, a 24-hectare (60-acre) bird sanctuary, a tearoom and a visitor center with interpretive displays.

Guided tours are available. Picnicking is permitted. Allow 1 hour minimum. Tues.-Sun. 9-5 (also Thurs. 7-9 p.m.), May-Aug. Admission $5; free (ages 0-12 when accompanied by an adult). Guided tour $1. MC, VI. Phone (306) 232-5959.

ST. BRIEUX (D-4)
pop. 505, elev. 547 m/1,797'

ST. BRIEUX MUSEUM is at 300 Barbier Dr., the main access road to the village. Originally a Roman Catholic rectory, it displays pioneer tools, furniture, period clothing and other artifacts and memorabilia related to the early 20th-century settlement of the St. Brieux district. Guided tours are available. Mon.-Fri. 10-5, Victoria Day-Aug. 31; by appointment rest of year. Guided tour fee $2; free (ages 0-18). Phone (306) 275-2229, or (306) 752-3707 off season.

SASKATOON (D-2)
pop. 196,811, elev. 487 m/1,598'

Saskatoon was founded in 1882 as a temperance colony under leader John Lake. According to legend a Cree Indian brought Lake a handful of the purple berries that grew in abundance alongside the river. Lake was so taken with the fruit he named his settlement Saskatoon, after *misaskquatoomina*, the Indian name for the wild berries. Today a slice of Saskatoon pie is a traditional treat recalling the city's past.

Straddling the South Saskatchewan River, Saskatoon is known as "The City of Bridges" because of the seven spans connecting its banks. It also is home to the University of Saskatchewan, which is building a reputation for research and development in science, medicine and agriculture. The Diefenbaker Canada Centre on campus showcases memorabilia of Canada's 13th prime minister.

The Local History Room on the second floor of the Frances Morrison Library, 311-23rd St. E., serves as a research facility for information that focuses on prairie history relating to Saskatoon in particular and western Canada in general. Collections include more than 60,000 historic photographs, thousands of books, pamphlets, maps, artifacts and periodicals. An art gallery is next to the room. Phone (306) 975-7578.

The Saskatchewan Railway Museum, 6 kilometres (4 mi.) west on Hwy. 7, then 2 kilometres (1.2 mi.) south on Hwy. 60, is operated by the Saskatchewan Railroad Historical Association and displays old railroad buildings and artifacts, including locomotives, cabooses and streetcars; phone (306) 382-9855 June-Sept.

TCU Place—Saskatoon's Art & Convention Centre, 35 22nd St., is home to the Saskatoon Symphony and the site of traveling shows throughout the year. The Meewasin Valley Centre, 402 3rd Ave. S., features interpretive displays pertaining to the area's history. Credit Union Centre features rock concerts, trade shows, and hockey and other sporting events. The facility is on the north side of the city next to hwys. 2 and 16.

The Meewasin Valley Trail, following the South Saskatchewan River through the heart of the city, has bicycle and jogging trails, picnic areas and playgrounds and provides opportunities for cross-country

skiing and ice skating. Recreational activities are available at nearby Pike Lake and Blackstrap provincial parks *(see Recreation Chart and the AAA/CAA Western Canada & Alaska CampBook).*

Queen Elizabeth Power Station, 3 kilometres (1.9 mi.) south of the junction of 11th Street W. and Avenue H S. at 2211 Spadina Crescent W., is a thermal power station originally named the South Saskatchewan River Generating Station but renamed and commissioned in 1959 by Queen Elizabeth II. Guided tours are available with 24 hours' advance notice; phone (306) 934-7994.

Racing fans can enjoy horse racing at Marquis Downs from late May to early September. Races are held Fri.-Sat. 7-10 p.m.; phone (306) 242-6100. Drag racing heats up the Saskatchewan International Raceway from early May to mid-September; phone (306) 955-3724. Stock car racing takes place at the Auto Clearing Motor Speedway from May through September; phone (306) 651-3278.

Note: Policies concerning admittance of children to pari-mutuel betting facilities vary. Phone for information.

Tourism Saskatoon: 6-305 Idylwyld Dr. N., Saskatoon, SK, Canada S7L 0Z1; phone (306) 242-1206 or (800) 567-2444.

BEAVER CREEK CONSERVATION AREA is 13 km (8 mi.) s. on Hwy. 219 (Lorne Ave.). Self-guiding nature trails and interpretive displays are offered. Allow 2 hours minimum. Daily 9-9, July-Aug.; daily 9-5, May-June; Mon.-Fri. 9-5, Sat.-Sun. and holidays noon-5, Sept.-Oct.; Mon.-Fri. 9-5, Sat.-Sun. noon-5, rest of year. Free. Phone (306) 374-2474 or (306) 665-6887.

DIEFENBAKER CANADA CENTRE is at 101 Diefenbaker Pl. on the University of Saskatchewan campus. The archives and personal belongings of prime minister John Diefenbaker are housed at the center; his grave site is on the grounds. The museum also offers changing exhibits about Canadian history, art, politics, science, culture and current affairs.

Mon.-Fri. 9:30-4:30, Sat.-Sun. and holidays noon-4:30; closed Jan. 1, Good Friday, Nov. 11 and Dec. 25-26. Admission $5; $12.50 (family, parents and dependent children). Phone (306) 966-8384.

MENDEL ART GALLERY AND CIVIC CONSERVATORY is at 950 Spadina Crescent E. in a park between Queen and 25th sts. This attractive complex overlooks the South Saskatchewan River. In the art gallery are exhibitions of international, national and regional works, including historical and contemporary art. Visitors may view the display of tropical and native plants in the conservatory. Programs and activities are presented in combination with each series of exhibitions. Allow 30 minutes minimum. Daily 9-9; closed Dec. 25. Free. Phone (306) 975-7610.

SASKATCHEWAN INDIAN CULTURAL CENTRE is at 120 33rd St. E. The center is dedicated to preserving First Nations cultures in Saskatchewan such as the Woodland, Swampy and Plains Cree; Dene; Nakawe; Dakota; Lakota; and Nakota. Exhibits include historic artifacts as well as contemporary arts and crafts. Allow 30 minutes minimum. Mon.-Thurs. 8:30-5, Fri. 8:30-4. Tours are given by appointment. Free. Phone (306) 244-1146 to schedule a guided tour.

SASKATOON FORESTRY FARM PARK AND ZOO is n.e. off Attridge Dr., following signs. Displayed in settings resembling their natural habitats are 350 species of birds and animals native to Saskatchewan and western Canada. The park offers a children's zoo, a reptile and tropical fish display, stocked fishing pond and nature walkways. The Kinsmen Express train provides a tour around the park and zoo.

Allow 1 hour, 30 minutes minimum. Zoo and park open daily 9-9, May 1-Labour Day; 10-4, rest of year. Admission $7.10; $4.25 (ages 6-18); $14.20 (family). An additional $2 fee per vehicle is charged May 1-Labour Day. Fishing pond $2; $1 (ages 6-16). Phone (306) 975-3382.

SHEARWATER BOAT CRUISES is off Spadina Crescent opposite Kinsmen Park, at the Mendel Art Gallery dock. Scenic 1-hour cruises aboard the *Saskatoon Princess* take in the downtown waterfront. The 49-passenger vessel is equipped with restrooms and a heated cabin and has a licensed bar. Cruises depart daily at 1:30, 3 and 4:30, Victoria Day weekend-Labour Day. Schedule may vary; phone ahead. Fare $14; $12 (ages 7-19 and 61+); $9 (ages 0-5). AX, MC, VI. Phone (888) 747-7572.

UKRAINIAN MUSEUM OF CANADA is at 910 Spadina Crescent E. Displays include folk and fine art, domestic and agricultural tools, and documents and photographs of Ukrainian immigrants. Two galleries feature changing exhibits. Guided tours are available. Allow 30 minutes minimum. Tues.-Sat. 10-5, Sun. 1-5; closed Canadian holidays, Orthodox Christmas (early Jan.) and Good Friday. Admission $4; $3 (ages 65+); $2 (ages 6-16). Phone (306) 244-3800.

WANUSKEWIN HERITAGE PARK is 5 km (3.1 mi.) n. on Hwy. 11, 3 km (1.9 mi.) s. on Warman Rd., then 2 km (1.2 mi.) e. on Penner Rd., following signs. This 760-acre First Nations heritage park traces more than 6,000 years of area history. It showcases 19 sites representing the Northern Plains peoples, including summer and winter campsites, bison kill sites, tipi rings and a boulder alignment known as a medicine wheel.

The park's interpretive center contains a DVD theater and features state-of-the-art exhibits pertaining to Northern Plains culture. Self-guiding trails take visitors through the park, with interpretive signs explaining past uses of the land.

Food is available. Allow 2 hours minimum. Daily 9-8, Victoria Day-Labour Day; 9-5, rest of year. Closed Good Friday and Dec. 25-Jan. 1. Admission $8.50; $7.50 (ages 65+); $6.50 (ages 6-18); $25 (family). AX, MC, VI. Phone (306) 931-6767 or (877) 547-6546. *See color ad inside front cover.*

WESTERN DEVELOPMENT MUSEUM'S 1910 BOOMTOWN is at 2610 Lorne Ave. This indoor representation of a typical prairie town features more than 30 buildings. Displays include transportation artifacts and vintage agricultural equipment. Food is available. Allow 2 hours minimum. Daily 9-5, Apr.-Dec.; Tues.-Sun. 9-5, rest of year. Closed Jan. 1, Nov. 11 and Dec. 25-26. Admission $8.50; $7.50 (ages 66+); $5.75 (students with ID); $2 (ages 6-12); $18 (family). Phone (306) 931-1910. *See color ad inside front cover.*

SCEPTRE (E-2) pop. 136, elev. 671 m/2,200'

GREAT SANDHILLS MUSEUM is off Hwy. 32. Rooms represent historic buildings in the community, including a boarding house, library, hospital, blacksmith shop, dentist office, schoolhouse, general store display, barn and church. An interpretive center provides information about the great sandhills. Allow 30 minutes minimum. Mon.-Sat. 10-noon and 12:30-4, Sun. 1-5, May 15-Sept. 2; by appointment rest of year. Admission $3; $2 (ages 6-18). Phone (306) 623-4345.

SHAUNAVON (F-2) pop. 1,775

GRAND COTEAU HERITAGE AND CULTURAL CENTRE, 2 blks. n. of Third Ave. at 440 Centre St., houses a museum with displays depicting local and natural history. The building also mounts exhibitions of contemporary art and serves as a tourist information center. Picnicking is permitted. Allow 30 minutes minimum. Mon.-Sat. 9-5, May 1-Oct. 1; Tues.-Sat. 1:30-5, rest of year. Free. Phone (306) 297-3882.

SIMPSON (D-3) pop. 194

LAST MOUNTAIN LAKE SANCTUARY is at the n. end of Last Mountain Lake; access is via a grid road branching off Hwy. 2 at Simpson (watch for signs). Said to be the oldest bird sanctuary in North America, the wildlife refuge was established in 1887 and covers 1,012 hectares (2,500 acres). The area's favorable habitats and location make it a haven for more than 280 species of birds. Each year during May and between mid-August and mid-September more than 20,000 sandhill cranes stop at the sanctuary during their seasonal migration.

Picnicking is permitted. Allow 1 hour minimum. Daily dawn-dusk. Free. Phone (306) 836-2022. *See Recreation Chart.*

STRASBOURG (E-4) pop. 760

STRASBOURG AND DISTRICT MUSEUM is at Mountain St. and Railway Ave. Nature displays, handicrafts and pioneer artifacts are exhibited. Tues.-Sat. 10-4, Sun. 1-5, July-Sept. Donations. Phone (306) 725-3443.

SWIFT CURRENT (E-3) pop. 14,821

Once the site of transient Indian and fur trader camps, Swift Current began as a North West

Mounted Police encampment on Swift Current Creek in 1874. Soon after, the Canadian Pacific Railway built a depot, and the settlement became the freight terminus for western Canada. From this point goods were hauled by wagon on overland trails; deep ruts can still be seen on the old North Battleford Trail north of Swift Current.

With the turn of the 20th century came the farmers and ranchers whose trades formed the backbone of the city's economy. Oil was discovered in this area in 1952, and in the decades since Swift Current has not only developed into a business hub for the oil, gas and agricultural industries but has become the major health care center for southwestern Saskatchewan.

Swift Current Creek runs through town, and two nearby lakes offer recreational facilities. At Saskatchewan Landing Provincial Park *(see Recreation Chart)*, a plaque marks the spot where pioneers once forded the South Saskatchewan River on their way into the wilds of the northern province. In the park's hills are several Indian grave sites and tepee rings.

Doc's Heritage Village, 17th Avenue S.E. and S. Railway Street in Kinetic Exhibition Park, has a collection of buildings typical of early 20th-century prairie towns, including a blacksmith shop, church and school. Costumed staff are on hand to answer questions; phone (306) 773-2944.

Swift Current Chamber of Commerce: 1703 22nd Ave. N.E., Swift Current, SK, Canada S9H 5B7; phone (306) 773-7268.

ART GALLERY OF SWIFT CURRENT is at 411 Herbert St. E. This public art gallery offers exhibitions of local, provincial and national artwork. Cultural events and festivals are scheduled throughout the year. Guided tours are given upon request. Mon.-Thurs. 2-5 and 7-9 p.m., Fri.-Sat. 1-5, Sun. 1-4:30 (closed Sun., July-Aug.); closed major holidays and during exhibition changes. Free. Phone (306) 778-2736.

SWIFT CURRENT MUSEUM is at 44 Robert St. W. Exhibits depict the natural and human history of southwest Saskatchewan. Mon.-Fri. 10-5, Sat.-Sun. 1-5, June-Aug.; Mon.-Fri. 1:30-4:30, rest of year. Closed holidays. Free. Phone (306) 778-2775.

TISDALE (C-4) pop. 3,063

This rural community in northeastern Saskatchewan provides easy access to several provincial parks offering recreational activities from fishing and boating in summer to skiing in winter. A roadside attraction, claimed to be the world's largest honeybee, stands on the south side of Hwy. 3 in town.

Greville Jones Wildlife Sanctuary is reached by a gravel access road about 6.4 kilometres (4 mi.) southwest of Tisdale off Hwy. 3, following signs. The site of an old farmstead, it is a pleasant place for a summer picnic or hike along one of several nature trails. Another scenic route is the Doghide River Trail, a system of walking, cycling and skiing

trails that run along several sections of the riverbank. The trail can be accessed from the junction of Hwys. 3 and 35; proceed east .8 kilometre (.5 mi.), then north .5 kilometre (.3 mi.) and turn right into Kinsmen McKay Park.

TISDALE & DISTRICT MUSEUM, HERITAGE CENTRE AND DOGHIDE VILLAGE, at jct. Hwy. 3 and Heritage Rd. at the western approach to town, comprises three main areas. The Station houses a bee farming display, while Doghide Village features the furnished 1920 Pearse House, a log barn and milk house and a fire hall complete with antique water wagon. The Heritage Centre contains the Dagg Collection of vintage automobiles, which range from standard Fords and Chevrolets to such unusual makes as Star, Whippet and Essex.

Guided tours are available. Picnicking is permitted. Allow 30 minutes minimum. Daily 9-5, Victoria Day-Labour Day. Admission $2; $5 (family). Phone (306) 873-4999.

VEREGIN (D-5) pop. 83

Emigrating from Russia in 1899 due to persecution, the Doukhobours named their village after their theocratic leader, Peter Vasilovich Veregin. The Doukhobour way of life centers on communal living and renounces violence and war. Its followers do not eat meat or use alcohol or tobacco. The community flourished for 2 decades before a majority of the sect relocated to British Columbia. A prayer house built by Veregin and a machine shed are all that remain of the original Doukhobour colony.

NATIONAL DOUKHOBOUR HERITAGE VILLAGE is across the tracks s. of Hwy. 5. The village is composed of the original Doukhobour prayer home and several reconstructed buildings typical of Veregin's Doukhobour dwellings at the turn of the 20th century. A museum displays Doukhobour handicrafts, clothing, hand tools, a collection of Leo Tolstoy's works and other artifacts.

Allow 30 minutes minimum. Daily 10-6, mid-May to mid-Sept.; by appointment rest of year. Admission $5; $3 (students with ID); $1 (ages 5-12). Phone (306) 542-4441.

WADENA (D-4) pop. 1,412, elev. 488 m/1,600'

WADENA & DISTRICT MUSEUM is at 302 Main St. S. Housed in a 1904 train station, the museum preserves items relating to the history of the pioneers who settled the area in the early 20th century. Exhibits include antique farm equipment, a 1914 farm house, a country schoolhouse, general store, blacksmith shop and a Royal Canadian Mounted Police barracks. A caboose is adjacent to the station. Allow 30 minutes minimum. Tues.-Sat. 9-5, Sun. 10-5, mid-May to Labour Day; closed holidays. Admission $3; $10 (family). Phone (306) 338-3454.

WAKAW (D-4) pop. 884

WAKAW HERITAGE MUSEUM is in the center of town at 300 1st St. S. Exhibits include Ukrainian artworks and implements, mementos from both world wars, homestead displays and a wide assortment of items dating from the early to late 1900s. Allow 1 hour minimum. Fri.-Mon. 1-4, July 1-Labour Day. Donations. Phone (306) 233-4223.

John Diefenbaker's Law Office is off 1st St. S. at 3rd Ave. S. The site is a replica of the original office where the 13th prime minister of Canada practiced law 1919-25. Guides are available at the Wakaw Heritage Museum. Fri.-Mon. 1-4, July-Aug. Phone (306) 233-4223.

WEYBURN (F-4) pop. 9,534

Weyburn's name was coined in 1893 by Scottish railroad workers, who called this marshy area at the headwaters of the Souris River "wee burn." From these humble beginnings the town has grown into a major marketing center for the surrounding agricultural area. Weyburn is the southeastern terminus of scenic Hwy. 39, which continues to Moose Jaw.

The town was immortalized as "Crocus, Saskatchewan" in the works of W.O. Mitchell, who was born and reared in Weyburn and penned the book "Who Has Seen the Wind." A summary of Weyburn's history since its earliest days is depicted on the "Wheel of Progress" at the Weyburn Library. Between the spokes of the brass-rimmed mahogany wheel, which weighs 909 kilograms (2,000 lbs.) and has a diameter of 3.9 metres (13 ft.), are 10 mosaic panels showing highlights of the city's past.

Weyburn Chamber of Commerce: 405 Coteau Ave., Weyburn, SK, Canada S4H 3G5; phone (306) 842-4738.

Shopping areas: A major outlet mall in the Weyburn area is City Centre Mall, off Hwy. 39 at 110 Souris Ave.; it contains 28 stores.

[SAVE] **SOO LINE HISTORICAL MUSEUM** is e. on Hwy. 39 at 411 Industrial Ln. Local pioneer artifacts trace the area's early history. The museum houses more than 5,000 pieces of silver, glass and antique furniture dating 1750-1970. Donated by Charles Wilson, the exhibit is reputed to be one of the country's largest private collections. Allow 30 minutes minimum. Mon.-Sat. 9-7:30, Sun. 11:30-7:30, June-Aug.; Mon.-Fri. 1-5, rest of year. Admission $5; $4 (students with ID); $2 (ages 0-11). Phone (306) 842-2922.

[SAVE] **WEYBURN HERITAGE VILLAGE** is 1 km (.6 mi.) s. from jct. Hwys. 35 and 39, then 1 km (.6 mi.) e. on 10th Ave. S.E. This historical village has been replicated to depict community life from the turn of the 20th century to the 1940s. All the buildings have been restored. Farm machinery is on display and visitors also may view a one-room school, rural municipality office, country church and blacksmith shop.

Guided tours are available. Picnicking is permitted. Allow 1 hour minimum. Daily 1-8, May-Aug.; closed Victoria Day, July 1 and first weekend in Aug. Admission $3; $2 (ages 13-19); $1 (ages 5-12); $10 (family). Phone (306) 842-6377.

WHITEWOOD (E-5) pop. 947

OLD GEORGE'S HIDDEN VILLAGE MUSEUM AND ANTIQUES is on Hwy. 1 just w. of town. On this 11-acre property, a 30-room brick dwelling houses such collectibles as oil lamps, clocks, crocks and jugs, Indian artifacts, antique bottles and spinning wheels. Hidden Village consists of 30 buildings representative of pioneer life, including four log cabins, a saloon, a trapper's cabin, a post office and a general store.

Guided tours are available. Allow 1 hour minimum. Daily 10-6, mid-May to mid-Oct.; by appointment rest of year. Reservations are required for tour buses; phone ahead. Admission $5; $1 (ages 0-11). Phone (306) 735-2255.

WOLSELEY (E-4) pop. 766

Incorporated in 1898, Wolseley earned the nickname "The Town With the Swinging Bridge" when just such a contraption was built over man-made Fairly Lake in the center of town—itself created by damming Wolf Creek to provide the Canadian Pacific Railway with a badly needed reservoir for its steam engines. The bridge, which connected homes on the north side of the lake with the business section on the south side, has had a checkered history: It was destroyed by a storm in 1954, rebuilt 10 years later, collapsed in 1993 during repairs and reopened again in 2004 thanks to the fund-raising efforts of the Heritage Canada Foundation.

The Romanesque-style Town Hall & Opera House, at the corner of Richmond and Varennes streets, was completed in 1907. The two-tone brick building (brick was imported from Manitoba when the local supply ran out) housed the town's administrative offices, fire hall, library, jail cell and community hall—commonly known as an Opera House—where touring vaudeville, theatrical and opera companies would perform. The building was extensively refurbished in the early 1990s.

WOLSELEY & DISTRICT MUSEUM is at 101 Blanchard St., n. of the post office. A collection of locally obtained artifacts reflecting life in the area circa 1880-1950 is displayed in a two-story boarding house built in 1901. Exhibits include medical, real estate and lumber offices as well as clothing from the various eras. Guided tours are available. Allow 30 minutes minimum. Thurs.-Sun. 2-4, July-Aug.; by appointment rest of year. Donations. Phone (306) 698-2360.

WOOD MOUNTAIN (F-3) pop. 100

RODEO RANCH MUSEUM is 6 km (4 mi.) s. on Hwy. 18 at Wood Mountain Post Provincial Historic Park. The museum features exhibits about local ranching, Indians and saddle making. An adjacent adobe and log building houses blacksmithing tools. A rodeo is held on the grounds during the second weekend in July. Camping and picnic facilities are available. Allow 1 hour minimum. Daily 10-noon and 1-5, mid-May through Labour Day. Admission

$2; $1 (students with ID); free (ages 0-9 with adult). Phone (306) 266-4953 or (306) 266-4205.

WOOD MOUNTAIN POST PROVINCIAL HISTORIC PARK is 8 km (5 mi.) s. on Hwy. 18. Two buildings are on the site of the North West Mounted Police post that stood 1874-1918; small stumps outline the rest of the post. Inside the buildings are displays on the Mounted Police, Sioux Indians and local history. An interpretive staff is on duty to answer questions. Allow 1 hour minimum. Thurs.-Mon. 10-5, June 1 to mid-Aug. Donations. Phone (306) 266-5525.

YORKTON (E-5) pop. 15,107

In 1882 some 200 settlers from Ontario bought land in the Northwest Territories in what is now southeastern Saskatchewan. They called the community around their trading post York City. In 1890 the railroad arrived in the area 5 kilometres (3 mi.) to the south. The York City colonists relocated to be near the railroad and named the new settlement Yorkton. A plaque marks the site of York City; nearby are millstones from the original colony's gristmill.

Recreation is available at nearby Good Spirit Lake Provincial Park *(see Recreation Chart and the AAA/CAA Western Canada & Alaska CampBook).* The park, originally a Hudson's Bay Co. post in the 1880s, is noted for its miles of sandy beaches and fine dunes.

Tourism Yorkton Visitor Information Centre: Hwy. 9, Box 460, Yorkton, SK, Canada S3N 2W4; phone (306) 783-8707.

Self-guiding tours: The Yorkton Heritage Walking Tour affords visitors the opportunity to view gardens and historic buildings. The City Cemetery Walking Tour features the grave sites of many of the city's early pioneers. Materials outlining each tour are available at the information center.

GODFREY DEAN ART GALLERY is in the Godfrey Dean Centre at 49 Smith St. E. Assorted art forms are displayed, along with works by contemporary Canadian artists. Exhibits change monthly. Mon.-Fri. 11-5, Sun. 1-4; closed holidays. Free. Phone (306) 786-2992.

WESTERN DEVELOPMENT MUSEUM'S STORY OF PEOPLE is .4 km (.25 mi.) w. on Hwy. 16A. The museum focuses on the cultural roots of the settlers of western Canada. Picnic facilities are on the grounds. Allow 1 hour minimum. Daily 9-5, May-Aug.; Mon.-Wed. 2-5, rest of year. Admission $5; $4 (ages 65+); $3 (students with ID); $1 (ages 6-12); $10 (family). Phone (306) 783-8361.

GAMBLING ESTABLISHMENTS

- **Painted Hand Casino**, 30 3rd Ave. N. Mon.-Wed. 9 a.m.-3 a.m., Thurs.-Sat. 9 a.m.-4 a.m., Sun. 10 a.m.-3 a.m.; closed Dec. 25. Phone (306) 786-6777.

Yukon Territory

A Panful of Nuggets

Miners still find gold a century after the great Klondike Gold Rush

Spirit of Adventure

Wild waterways, rugged mountains and unexplored wilderness await

All That Glitters

Black diamond jade, amber, topaz, malachite, obsidian and gold bejewel the territory

Lofty Mount Logan

Canada's highest peak rises from the icy St. Elias Mountains

The Northern Lights

Aurora borealis offers nature's nightly light show

Kluane National Park and Reserve of Canada
© 2007 Michael DeYoung
AlaskaStock

unspoiled majesty

Klondike Hwy / © Gina Bringman / AlaskaStock

To find gleaming gifts of topaz in outcroppings of rock. To wander trails once trodden by miners and trappers. To cry "Mush!" behind a stalwart team of sturdy Alaskan huskies.

To do any of these is to begin to understand the majestic allure of the endless Yukon.

The roughly triangular territory is a land of adventure, a lonely wilderness, a rugged and pristine land of splendor and beauty.

Turbulent rivers of splashing white water weave through soaring mountain ranges. Soft blankets of white pull up snugly over a serene countryside.

The very essence of the sprawling territory is aptly captured in one moving stanza from poet Robert Service's homage, "The Spell of the Yukon":

There's gold, and
it's haunting and haunting;
It's luring me on as of old;
Yet it isn't the gold that I'm wanting
so much as just finding the gold.

It's the great, big, broad
land 'way up yonder,
It's the forests
where silence has lease;
It's the beauty
that thrills me with wonder,
It's the stillness
that fills me with peace.

"Thick between the flaky slabs, like cheese sandwiches"—this was how prospector George Washington Carmack described the gold he saw glimmering between rocks in Bonanza Creek near Dawson City on August 16, 1896.

On July 14, 1897, the steamship *Excelsior* arrived in San Francisco carrying a treasure worth more than $500,000; a few days later the *Portland* docked in Seattle with one ton of gold piled on its deck. News of these recently discovered riches spread like wildfire, and thousands of get-rich-quick hopefuls began to head for the wealth that lay in Yukon Territory.

Klondike or Bust

That following winter, some 100,000 prospectors began a long, arduous journey to the Yukon to seek their fortunes. While the rush only lasted about 5 years, history was left in its trampled tracks. Following the Yukon River from Marsh Lake, near British Columbia's border, to Dawson City, you can explore the past on a course pursued by gold diggers more than 100 years ago.

If stampeders survived the trek through Chilkoot Pass—a climb over frozen mountains with heavy packs full of supplies strapped to their backs—they crossed the border into the Yukon Territory at Bennett Lake.

The lake, surrounded by mighty peaks and woodlands, links to the Yukon River. Most fortune seekers waited out the harsh winter at the southern shore, which quickly transformed into a crowded tent city. Transients built boats, temporary shelter and a little log church out of timber hewn from the forest. In late May of 1898, the lake's ice broke and 7,000 handmade vessels headed across its waters, leaving memories of a bitter season behind.

Today, original miners' cabins still line Bennett Lake's northern shore at Carcross, a town chock full of gold rush history. Graves of such early pioneers as Kate Carmack, Skookum Jim Mason and Tagish Charlie dot the city's cemetery.

From Carcross the gold route followed the Yukon River to Miles Canyon, just south of Whitehorse. Currents here were so dangerous that hundreds of boats capsized, and licensed

---

The Hudson's Bay Co. sets up trading posts in the Yukon.
1800

Yukon Territory becomes a provisional district of the Northwest Territories.
1895

Gold rush veteran Martha Black is elected to the House of Commons.
1935

1898-1904
More than $100 million in gold is mined in the region.

Government of Yukon

1942
The Alaska Highway is constructed, creating a new overland transportation route.

Yukon Territory Historical Timeline

guides were a must for piloting would-be miners with smaller vessels through the rocks and whirlpools.

Cheechakos, or newcomers, relied upon their own floating devices until stern-wheelers became a popular means of travel; by the early 1950s, more than 250 steamboats plied the Yukon. Boats were specifically designed for the river, employing flat bottoms that allowed for docking on sandbars. Nevertheless, many ran aground or were smashed by rapids or rocks on the Yukon's perilous waters.

A few stout vessels remain from this turbulent time. The restored steamer SS *Klondike II* resides in Whitehorse, while Dawson City is home to the dry-docked SS *Keno*.

The River to Riches

After stopping to relax and dry out in Whitehorse, miners pressed on, traversing Lake Laberge to enter a stretch of the Yukon called Thirty Mile. Due to swift currents and rocks, it was perhaps the most dangerous portion of the entire route. Historical sites along Thirty Mile—which is designated a Historic River—include abandoned Northwest Mounted Police posts, simple grave markers, woodcutters' cabins, telegraph stations, old log buildings and remains of beached paddlewheelers. They all bring yesteryear into focus.

More dangerous eddies had to be negotiated at Five Finger Rapids, just outside Carmacks, before exhausted voyagers passed Fort Selkirk and reached Dawson City—the golden ticket.

Downtown Dawson City remains much as it was when prospectors arrived, thanks to codes requiring new buildings to sport fronts reminiscent of the gold rush era. And old buildings have been restored: Cancan dancing takes place at Diamond Tooth Gertie's Casino and the log cabins once inhabited by author Jack London and poet Robert Service remain as examples of gold rush housing. A 1912 dredge can be seen along a tributary of the Klondike, and placer mining still occurs at nearby creeks such as the Eldorado.

And don't forget to stop by where it all began—a brass plaque on Bonanza Creek Road marks the spot that caused a great many to risk life and limb for a golden nugget that promised a change of fate.

Yukon's capital is moved from Dawson City to Whitehorse.
1953

Government of Yukon

Kluane National Park is declared a Natural World Heritage Site.
1979

The Council for Yukon Indians and the Canadian and Yukon Territory governments sign an agreement stating the terms for final land claim settlements in the territory.
1993

1959
At a cost of $1 million, a large fish ladder is built at the Whitehorse Rapids for migrating chinook salmon.

1997
Yukon spends $37 million on mining exploration.

1999
Yukon signs an accord with the Vuntut Gwitchin people, thereby recognizing a First Nation tribe as a legitimate government for the first time in the territory's history.

Recreation

Through its pristine waterways, rugged mountains and unexplored wilderness, the Yukon evokes a spirit of adventure in visitors.

Highways to Adventure

There is no better place than the Chilkoot Trail to understand the challenges faced by early pilgrims—the gold-rush stampeders—coming into Yukon Territory. The Yukon's original inroad, with its trail head in Dyea, Alaska, affords today's experienced **hiking** enthusiasts a 53-kilometre (33-mi.), one-way walk through history that can take 3 to 5 days to complete.

Preparation—proper gear, provisions, permits and registration—is key to enjoying this demanding trip through boreal forests and over alpine tundra and snow-patched mountains. You must reserve a campsite for each night you plan to spend on the trail. The Trail Centre in Skagway, Alaska, is the official registration point and offers maps, safety tips and a few words about bears during the Chilkoot hiking season, May through early September. For information phone Parks Canada year-round at (800) 661-0486.

At trail's end in Bennett, British Columbia, reward yourself with a railroad ride back to Skagway aboard the White Pass & Yukon Route, which shuttles returning Chilkoot hikers regularly. Reservations are a must; phone (907) 983-2217 or (800) 343-7373. Another return option is to hop a bus at Log Cabin, British Columbia.

Camping in summer, June through mid-September, truly is a wilderness experience. While you won't have to chop firewood (it's there and it's free), you will have to pump your own water. Government campgrounds are spread throughout the Yukon roughly 81-121 kilometres (50-75 mi.) apart. Many are beside lakes, rivers or streams, where you might hook a few Arctic graylings for dinner. Of the 10 campgrounds along the Alaska Hwy. (Hwy. 1), Watson Lake is one of the first you'll find as you enter the Yukon from British Columbia; it has 55 campsites. Farther west bordering the Kluane region is Congdon Creek; with 78 campsites, it's one of the largest in the territory. Both areas offer **fishing, swimming** and hiking.

Take scenic Dempster Hwy. (Hwy. 5) from Dawson City to Rock River Campground, the northernmost public facility at Km-post 447. Congratulate yourself upon arriving: You've crossed the Continental Divide—twice—*and* the Arctic Circle! There is no well water for the 14 sites at Rock River, so be sure to stock up on supplies in Dawson City or when you get to Eagle Plains—your last chance—at Km-post 371.

The Klondike Hwy. (Hwy. 2), open all year, is dotted with roadside respites for camping and **picnicking.** You also can camp just off the Robert Campbell and Silver Trail hwys. (hwys. 4 and 11, respectively). Travelers can access daily road condition reports by dialing the Department of Highways and Public Works hotline; phone (877) 456-7623 within the Yukon or (867) 456-7623 outside the Yukon. Wherever the road leads, watch for wildlife, especially around viewing areas identified with a sign picturing binoculars.

The Other Extremes

With almost 7 months of winter (October through April), **snow skiing** is a way of life in the Yukon. Near Whitehorse, a chalet and night lighting attract cross-country skiers to Mount McIntyre's world-class trails, while Mount Sima, one of the largest ski areas in the Yukon, appeals to downhill skiers with its nine runs and one chairlift. **Snowboarding,** too, is a favorite at Mount Sima's snowpark. Power up a snowmobile and glide on groomed trails around Whitehorse, or venture over more rugged terrain out of Dawson City, said to be the **snowmobiling** capital of the Yukon.

The territory's rich "veins"—its wild rivers—yield excitement other than gold finds. Outfitters are available in Whitehorse to take you **kayaking** or **white-water rafting** on the Tatshenshini's class three and four rapids, or through Kluane National Park and Reserve of Canada on the Alsek, a designated heritage river. Many sections of the Yukon River, which once ushered fortune seekers north to the Klondike goldfields, are easily navigated by canoe. And there are tons more nuggets of adventure to be discovered in the Yukon Territory.

Recreational Activities

Throughout the TourBook, you may notice a Recreational Activities heading with bulleted listings of recreation-oriented establishments listed underneath. Similar operations also may be mentioned in Destination City recreation sections. Since normal AAA inspection criteria cannot be applied, these establishments are presented only for information. Age, height and weight restrictions may apply. Reservations often are recommended and sometimes are required. Addresses and/or phone numbers are provided so visitors can contact the attraction for additional information.

Fast Facts

POPULATION: 28,674.

AREA: 482,443 sq km (186,271 sq mi); ranks 9th.

CAPITAL: Whitehorse.

HIGHEST POINT: 5,959 m/19,545 ft., Mount Logan.

LOWEST POINT: Sea level, Beaufort Sea.

TIME ZONE(S): Pacific.

MINIMUM AGE FOR UNRESTRICTED DRIVER'S LICENSE: 17 years, 6 months.

MINIMUM AGE FOR GAMBLING: 19.

SEAT BELT/CHILD RESTRAINT LAWS: Seat belts required for driver and all passengers ages 6 and older. Child restraints required for under age 7 and under 22 kg (48 lbs).

HELMETS FOR MOTORCYCLISTS: Required for all riders.

RADAR DETECTORS: Not permitted.

FIREARMS LAWS: By federal law, all nonresidents entering Canada with a firearm must declare their weapon in writing and pay a fee of $25 (Canadian). Contact the Canadian Firearms Centre at (800) 731-4000 to receive a declaration form or for additional information.

HOLIDAYS: Jan. 1; Heritage Day, Feb. 25; Good Friday; Easter Monday; Victoria Day, May 24 or the closest prior Mon.; Canada Day, July 1; Discovery Day, Aug. (3rd Mon.); Labour Day, Sept. (1st Mon.); Thanksgiving, Oct. (2nd Mon.); Remembrance Day, Nov. 11; Christmas, Dec. 25; Boxing Day, Dec. 26.

TAXES: The Yukon Territory has no territorial sales tax.

FERRY SCHEDULES AND INFORMATION: The Department of Highways runs ferries along Dempster Hwy. and at Dawson City. Phone (867) 667-3710.

ROAD CONDITIONS: Through its Yukon Network the Canadian Broadcasting Corporation reports road conditions on the Alaska Hwy. and all other Yukon highways. Major participating stations, with their frequencies in kilohertz (kHz), are listed from south to north: Watson Lake, 990; Swift River, 970; Teslin, 940; Whitehorse, 570; Haines Junction, 860; Destruction Bay, 940; Beaver Creek, 690; Carmacks, 990; Mayo, 1230; Elsa, 560; Dawson City, 560; Faro, 105.1 FM; and Ross River, 990.

For changes on Yukon road conditions, phone (867) 456-7623 or (877) 456-7623 within the Yukon Territory.

INFORMATION CENTERS: Territorial information centers in Beaver Creek, Carcross, Dawson City, Haines Junction, Watson Lake and Whitehorse are open 12 hours a day, mid-May to mid-September. The Whitehorse Visitor Information Center also is open Mon.-Fri. 8:30-5, in winter.

FURTHER INFORMATION FOR VISITORS:
Department of Tourism & Culture
P.O. Box 2703
Whitehorse, YT, Canada Y1A 2C6
(867) 667-5430

FISHING AND HUNTING REGULATIONS:
Yukon Government Fish and Wildlife Branch
P.O. Box 2703
Whitehorse, YT, Canada Y1A 2C6
(867) 667-5221

ALCOHOL CONSUMPTION: Legal age 19.

Yukon Territories Temperature Averages Maximum/Minimum (Celsius)
From the records of The Weather Channel Interactive, Inc.

	JAN	FEB	MAR	APR	MAY	JUNE	JULY	AUG	SEPT	OCT	NOV	DEC
Watson Lake	-19	-12	-3	6	13	19	21	19	13	4	-11	-18
	-30	-25	-18	-7	0	6	8	7	2	-5	-20	-28
Whitehorse	-14	-8	-2	6	12	18	20	18	12	4	-7	-12
	-23	-18	-13	-6	0	5	7	6	2	-3	-14	-20

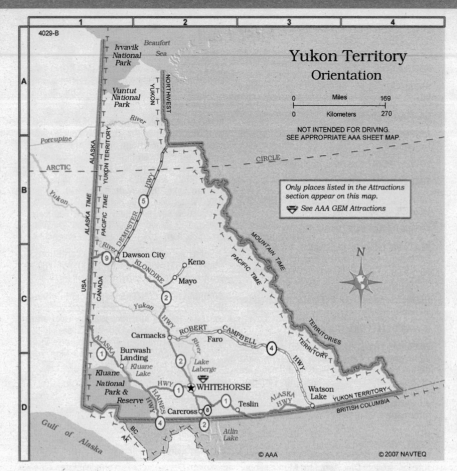

4029-B

Yukon Territory
Orientation

Miles 0 — 169
Kilometers 0 — 270

NOT INTENDED FOR DRIVING.
SEE APPROPRIATE AAA SHEET MAP.

Only places listed in the Attractions
section appear on this map.

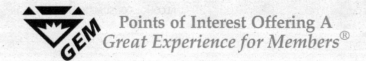 See AAA GEM Attractions

© AAA   © 2007 NAVTEQ

Points of Interest Offering A
Great Experience for Members ®

Whitehorse (F-10)

THE *SS KLONDIKE II* **NATIONAL HISTORIC SITE—** More than 7,000 artifacts represent the period 1937-40 and provide insights into the lives of the people who lived along the Whitehorse and Dawson city route. See p. 294.

YUKON BERINGIA INTERPRETIVE CENTRE— Life-size fossils of woolly mammoths, giant beavers and scimitar cats as well as First Nations exhibits are showcased in this centre that depicts the Yukon Beringia from the ice age to the present. See p. 295.

YUKON RIVER CRUISE— Narrated trips on the Yukon River travel through Miles Canyon and pass the remains of a wooden tramway, the site of Canyon City and the ruins of the Camp McCrae laundry. See p. 295.

Points of Interest

Map coordinates relate to the map on page 304.

BURWASH LANDING (D-1)

In 1904, a year after gold was discovered in Fourth of July Creek, Morley Bones staked a discovery claim on Burwash Creek. Soon after the small community of Burwash sprang up around a trading post. Burwash Landing, with an airstrip and a resort, lies between the Kluane Lake and Kluane Game Sanctuary.

KLUANE MUSEUM OF NATURAL HISTORY is at Historic Mile 1093 on the Alaska Hwy. The museum contains a nature and taxidermy display, handmade First Nations crafts and costumes, a mineral and fossil collection and a large topographical map of the surrounding area. Allow 1 hour minimum. Daily 9-7, May 15-Sept. 15. Admission $3.95; $2.95 (ages 61+); $2.25 (ages 6-16); $9.75 (family). Phone (867) 841-5561.

CARCROSS (D-2) pop. 152

Carcross, 74 kilometres (46 mi.) from Whitehorse on the S. Klondike Hwy., originally was called Caribou Crossing. The town's current name is a combination of the first syllable of each word. From this settlement George Carmack's party set out on the prospecting trip that began the gold rush of 1898. On July 29, 1900, the railroad's final spike was driven, marking the completion of the White Pass & Yukon Route, which linked Alaska and the Yukon Territory by rail.

Today the White Pass & Yukon Route *(see attraction listing in Alaska p. 351)* transports passengers between Carcross and Bennett, British Columbia; phone (907) 983-2217 or (800) 343-7373 for schedule and reservations.

Near the town's train depot is the "Duchess," a tiny locomotive that ran the 6.4-kilometre (4-mi.) line from Taku Arm on Tagish Lake to Atlin Lake in the early 1900s. It supposedly was the shortest and most expensive rail trip in the world—one-way fare was $2—and passengers had to sit on their baggage in the cramped compartment.

The Carcross Visitor Information Centre on the Klondike Hwy. at Km-post 106 is in the historic White Pass and Yukon Route train depot. The center provides extensive information about Carcross—one of the Yukon's most picturesque areas; phone (867) 821-4431.

Just north of town along the Klondike Hwy. lies the Carcross Desert, considered the smallest desert in the world. The 260-hectare (650-acre) area was created by retreating glaciers that left a sandy lake bottom; today winds from Lake Bennett constantly shift the sand, limiting vegetation to such plants as kinnikinnick and lodgepole pine.

CARIBOU CROSSING TRADING POST is 3.2 km (2 mi.) n. on S. Klondike Hwy. to Km-post 109. At this 12-hectare (30-acre) park, visitors can view mounted animals in dioramas representing their natural habitats, explore an outdoor heritage area depicting the region's frontier days and climb to a lookout that provides a view of Lake Bennett, Carcross and surrounding mountains. The park includes a nature trail, petting farm and miniature golf.

Food is available. Allow 1 hour, 30 minutes minimum. Daily 9-5, mid-May to mid-Sept. Admission $7.25; $5.25 (ages 3-12). Miniature golf tickets $12; $9 (ages 3-12). Phone (867) 821-4055.

CARMACKS (C-2) pop. 500

Carmacks, named for George Washington Carmack, one of the discoverers of gold in the Klondike, was an important stopover point on the Overland Trail that linked Whitehorse and Dawson City before the Klondike Hwy. was built. Items from early travelers still can be found along the trail near town.

About 22 kilometres (14 mi.) north of Carmacks are the Five Fingers Rapids, which claimed the lives of many prospectors trying to reach Dawson City by way of the Yukon River.

TAGE CHO HUDAN INTERPRETIVE CENTRE is .4 km (.25 mi.) n. on the Klondike Hwy. The culture of the Northern Tutchone people, Yukon's oldest inhabitants, is explored through dioramas including a dugout and moose skin boats, moose skin clothing as well as a collection of traditional tools. Outside displays such as a pole house, a moose skin tanning camp and a winter moose skin home are featured. A garden with medicinal plants and a trail also are on-site.

Guided tours are available. Picnicking is permitted. Allow 30 minutes minimum. Daily 9-6, mid-May to mid-Sept. Donations. Phone (867) 863-5830.

DAWSON CITY (C-1) pop. 1,251

Dawson City was the center of the excitement caused by one of the world's most fabulous gold strikes. On Aug. 16, 1896, George Washington Carmack and his companions Skookum Jim and Tagish Charlie made the first strike on Bonanza Creek, a tributary of the Klondike River.

In the summer of 1897 miners from Dawson City arrived in Seattle and San Francisco with nearly $2 million as they carried word of the discovery to the United States, then in the midst of a depression. By the next spring more than 60,000 men and women had passed through Seattle and Alaska's Chilkoot and White passes on their way to the Klondike.

The Dawson settlement, which sprang up at the confluence of the Yukon and Klondike rivers, became a thriving city with some 30,000 inhabitants by the summer of 1898, making it the largest city west of Winnipeg and north of San Francisco.

All the creeks in the area had been staked by the spring of 1899. Hillside and bench claims were made, some yielding rich gold finds in the White Channel gravels. Between 1896 and 1904 Klondike creeks brought in more than $100 million in gold.

This period of Dawson City's history has been preserved by Rex Beach, Jack London, Robert W. Service and others who wrote colorful tales of personal experiences.

It was in Dawson City that London became acquainted with a large dog that he named Buck, a cross between a St. Bernard and a German shepherd that became the prototype for the dog in "Call of the Wild." Daily readings from the works of Jack London are given 10-6, mid-May to mid-Sept. at his cabin on Eighth Avenue.

Many historic buildings, some still in use, survive from the days when Dawson City was the gold capital of the world. The Midnight Sun and Eldorado hotels conjure memories of a lively past.

Harrington's Store, Princess Street and Third Avenue, has a free photographic exhibit titled "Dawson as They Saw It." The 1901 Post Office, King Street and Third Avenue, offers a visitor information exhibit; phone (867) 993-7200. Both are open June through September.

The SS *Keno*, in dry-dock on First Avenue between King and Queen streets, is typical of the stern-wheelers of the gold rush era. Built in 1922, it was one of the last riverboats to run between Dawson City and Whitehorse.

The summit of Midnight Dome, 7 kilometres (4 mi.) southeast via Front Street, offers a panorama of Dawson City, the Yukon and Klondike rivers and the gold fields. Many Dawson City pioneers are buried in cemeteries on the hillsides flanking the dome.

South on Bonanza Creek Road is the Discovery Claim, which started the great rush. Panning for gold is possible at several locations along the Klondike Hwy.: Claim 33, Guggieville RV Park, Dawson City RV Park, Gold Bottom Mines and Eureka Mines.

Yukon Queen River Cruises has one-way and round-trip cruises to Eagle, Alaska; for schedule and information phone (867) 993-5599.

The Dawson City Visitor Information Centre features exhibits about Klondike history. The center is open daily 8-8, mid-May to late Sept.

Dawson City Visitor Information Centre: Front and King streets, Dawson City, YT, Canada Y0B 1G0; phone (867) 993-5566.

Self-guiding tours: A brochure describing walking tours of historic sites is available at the visitor reception center.

BONANZA CREEK DISCOVERY CLAIM is 14.8 km (9.3 mi.) s. on Bonanza Creek Rd. Signs portray the story of gold mining along this famous creek. Discovery Claim #1 is the spot where gold first was discovered. A historical marker at Km-post 17.71 identifies the town of Grand Forks, which had a population of 5,000 during its prime. Dredge #4 at Km-post 12.3 was used to recover gold from creekbeds.

A trailer with exhibits about the dredge is open daily 9-5, mid-June to mid-Sept. Free. Phone (867) 993-7200.

DANOJA ZHO CULTURAL CENTRE is on Front St., across from the Visitor Information Centre. Guided tours, exhibits, video presentations, dance performances and hands-on activities give visitors an interesting perspective into the culture of the Tr'ondek Hwech'in First Nations peoples. Displays include archeological artifacts, traditional costumes and reproduction tools. Special events also are featured. Allow 30 minutes minimum. Daily 10-6, June-Sept. Admission $5; $2.50 (ages 12-18). Phone (867) 993-6768.

SAVE **DAWSON CITY MUSEUM** is on Fifth Ave. Gold rush items are displayed at the museum, which contains a smithy, a general store, an old miner's cabin, a saloon and Chilkoot Hall. First Nations artifacts and an outdoor transportation exhibit with locomotives from the Klondike Mines railway also are featured. Daily 10-6, Victoria Day weekend-Labour Day; limited hours in May and day after Labour Day-Sept. 30. Admission $7; $5 (senior citizens and students with ID); free (ages 0-6); $16 (family). Phone (867) 993-5291.

ROBERT SERVICE CABIN is 1 blk. s. of Church St. on Eighth Ave. The restored 1898 log cabin of the Bard of the Yukon is furnished as it was 1909-12 when Service was a resident and wrote many of his ballads and poems. Guided tours are available. Allow 30 minutes minimum. Daily 10-noon and 1-4:30, late May to mid-Sept. Admission $6; free (children). Rates may vary; phone ahead. Phone (867) 993-7200.

TOMBSTONE TERRITORIAL PARK is 71 km (44 mi.) n. of jct. Dempster and Klondike hwys. This park spans an area of more than 2,164 square kilometres (836 sq. mi.) and features a diversity of wildlife and bird species as well as a variety of vegetation. Although there are no established hiking trails within the park, there are accessible portions off the highway that offer short hikes and challenging backpacking and mountain climbing excursions. The park's Arctic Tundra environment creates a landscape with spectacular views. The interpretive center has natural history displays and provides interpretive programs and nature walks.

Note: When traveling to the park have enough gas and spare tires since there are no roadside services available until Eagle Plains, which is 369 kilometres (229 mi.) north of the Klondike Hwy. Once in the park, be aware that it is an isolated and potentially hazardous environment. Rough terrain, drastic weather changes and encounters with wildlife are factors to consider. Allow 3 hours minimum. Interpretive center open daily 9-9, mid-June to mid-Sept.

Park daily 9-dusk year-round. Hours may vary; phone ahead. Free. Phone (867) 667-5648.

GAMBLING ESTABLISHMENTS

- **Diamond Tooth Gertie's Casino**, Queen St. and Fourth Ave. Daily 7 p.m.-2 a.m., May 12-Sept. 17 (opens at 2 p.m. Sat.-Sun., mid-June through Labour Day). Phone (867) 993-5575.

FARO (C-2) pop. 313, elev. 2,352'

CAMPBELL REGION INTERPRETIVE CENTRE is at Campbell Street. A spruce log building houses a permanent exhibit about the history, geology and wildlife of the Faro area. Allow 1 hour minimum. Daily 8-6, June-Aug.; 10-5, May 5-31 and Sept. 1-29. Donations. Phone (867) 994-2288.

IVVAVIK NATIONAL PARK OF CANADA (A-1)

Ivvavik National Park of Canada is in the extreme northwestern corner of the Yukon. Virtually untouched by humans, the Arctic wilderness is of great geologic interest; it is one of the few regions in Canada that contains areas never covered by glaciers.

Every spring it becomes the calving grounds of Porcupine caribou that arrive after a long, difficult migration from the south and west. The park provides an important nesting area for North American waterfowl and a home to grizzly, black and polar bears. The only access to the park is by air.

KENO (C-2) pop. 20, elev. 3,120'

In 1919, silver and lead ore were discovered in Keno Hill, and by 1920 Keno became a busy community with cabins, a stable and a hotel. The following year, the city was the center of a thriving mining district. The town's name comes from the popular gambling game played at casinos. Today, Keno is home to artists who are inspired by the area's natural beauty.

No matter the season, outdoor recreational opportunities abound and include hiking, bicycling, cross-country skiing, snowmobiling, fishing and canoeing. The awe-inspiring northern lights may be seen from late August through April. A must-see is the often-photographed signpost at the top of Keno Hill, showing mileage to such cities as London, Paris and Rome. The 1,829-metre (6,000-ft.) hill also plays host to a breathtaking view.

Self-guiding tours: This historic walking tour starts from Tolmie Cabin on Duncan Creek Road and includes the Beer Bottle House, Keno City Mining Museum and the All Saints Anglican Church. Brochures are available from the Keno City Mining Museum. Phone (867) 995-2792 or (867) 995-2730.

KENO CITY MINING MUSEUM is on Silver Tr. Hwy. Housed in a dance hall, the museum depicts the history of the local community and gold and silver mining through exhibits, photographs, equipment and tools. Allow 30 minutes minimum. Daily

Sourdoughs and Cheechakos

To distinguish between the fortune seekers who entered the Yukon Territory during the 1897-98 Klondike Gold Rush, veterans of the '49 California Rush labeled the seasoned arrivals "Sourdoughs" and the greenhorns "Cheechakos" (CHE-cha-kos). Named after the staple bread of the frontier, Sourdoughs were prospectors who had survived a Yukon winter. The term Cheechako came from the Chinook Indian word for "new to come."

© PhotoDisc

Once off the steamer at Skagway, Alaska, these newcomers had to transport thousands of pounds of survival gear—the Northwest Mounted Police wisely required each prospector to bring a year's supply of food—over the precipitous Chilkoot Pass. After that they had to float their unwieldy cargo over the treacherous rapids of the Yukon River.

More obstacles awaited the greenhorns at the gold sites. By the time the Cheechakos arrived, much of the gold field already was depleted or staked. To make things worse, Cheechakos were often directed to the hills by unscrupulous Sourdoughs who knew the gold nuggets tended to settle in creek beds. Nonetheless, some did tap into a channel of an ancient gold-bearing stream on Cheechako Hill.

Those who had survived to see the ice melt were dubbed Sourdoughs; the graveyards of those who had not succeeded dotted the route all the way back to Skagway. As one cynical Sourdough put it: "We were SOUR on the Yukon and didn't have enough DOUGH to get out."

10-6, mid-May to mid-Sept. Admission $3.50; $2.50 (ages 66+); free (ages 0-12). Phone (867) 995-2792.

KLUANE NATIONAL PARK AND RESERVE OF CANADA (D-1)

Elevations in the park range from 400 metres (1,300 ft.) in the Alsek River to 5,959 metres (19,545 ft.) at Mount Logan. Refer to CAA/AAA maps for additional elevation information.

Kluane (kloo-AH-nee) National Park and Reserve of Canada is bounded by the Haines (Hwy. 3) and Alaska (Hwy. 1) hwys. along its northeastern border. The park covers 22,015 square kilometres (8,500 sq. mi.) of wilderness.

Near its southeastern boundary was the Dalton Trail, a route used during the Klondike Rush of 1898. In 1904 a North West Mounted Police post was established on the south shore of Kluane Lake, and in 1942 the lake became a meeting place for crews building the Alaska Hwy.

During the building of the highway the wilderness area was preserved as the Kluane Game Sanctuary. In 1979 Kluane was declared a World Heritage Site for its impressive topographical features and its massive nonpolar ice fields.

The park is dominated by the Saint Elias Mountains, which run through the park in a southeasterly direction. Mount Logan, Canada's highest peak at 5,959 metres (19,545 ft.), and Mount St. Elias at 5,489 metres (18,008 ft.) dominate the range. The Saint Elias Mountains hold extensive ice fields that date from the last ice age and constitute the largest nonpolar glacier systems in the world.

An extensive network of glaciers, together with the ice fields, covers more than half of the park's area throughout the year. Notable are the Steele Glacier, which moves sporadically at a relatively rapid rate, and the Kaskawulsh and Lowell glaciers, which are flanked by moraines—accumulations of earth and stones carried and deposited by the glaciers. The movement and debris of the glaciers contribute to such park features as sand dunes and dust storms.

The park has a variety of flora. Such coniferous species as white spruce characterize the boreal forest of the river valleys. Lichens, dwarf birch trees and low shrubs distinguish the tundra uplands in the northern section, and colorful Arctic flowers cling to the crevices and ledges of the mountains. In the southeastern section where the Pacific Ocean's moderating influence is felt in the climate, the vegetation is more luxuriant.

Arctic grayling, lake trout, northern pike and kokanee salmon are found in lakes and streams. Other park species include golden eagles, ptarmigans, Dall sheep, mountain goats, caribou, moose and wolves. Kluane has one of the largest populations of grizzly bears and subspecies of moose in the world.

General Information and Activities

The park is open all year, but access may be limited in the winter, depending on weather conditions.

The Kluane National Park and Reserve of Canada headquarters, at Km-post 1635 in Haines Junction, is open year-round. The Sheep Mountain Visitor Centre at Km-post 1707 is open mid-May to early September.

The park primarily is a wilderness area, so there are no roads except on the eastern and northern perimeters, traversed by Hwy. 3 and Hwy. 1, respectively. Hiking is the most popular activity in the park, with approximately 250 kilometres (155 mi.) of hiking trails. Hiking is possible along a few old mining roads, creekside paths and marked trails. Some trails are self-guiding. All overnight hikers must register at one of the information centers or with a park warden before and after hikes.

Mountain climbing should be done only by well-trained climbers, who must obtain a climbing permit and register with the Warden Service before and after climbs.

Other recreational pursuits include fishing, backpacking, boating, cross-country skiing and ice fishing. All anglers within the park must obtain a national park fishing license, available at the park visitor centers and from area stores and lodges. Camping, fishing and picnic facilities are available at Kathleen Lake, 27 kilometres (17 mi.) south of Haines Junction.

During the summer the Kluane National Park and Reserve of Canada headquarters sponsors interpretive activities including campfire talks and guided walks. A relief map and an interactive computer touch screen are available. Information about recreational opportunities, sightseeing by small aircraft and other guided tours is available.

ADMISSION to the park is free.

PETS are permitted in the park if kept on a leash, but visitors are advised not to bring them.

ADDRESS inquiries about the park to Kluane National Park and Reserve of Canada, P.O. Box 5495, Haines Junction, YT, Canada Y0B 1L0; phone (867) 634-7250.

MAYO (C-2) pop. 400

Mayo lies 53 kilometres (33 mi.) northeast of the Klondike Hwy. at the confluence of the Stewart and Mayo rivers. Both the town and the river were named for the pioneer prospector and trader Alfred Mayo. In the early 1900s Mayo Landing became a shipping point for the gold and silver that was mined farther north in Elsa.

Mayo Lake to the northeast provides excellent fishing. The summit of nearby 1,890-metre (6,200-ft.) Keno Mountain provides a scenic view of the mining village of Keno. This once bustling community has a mining museum.

Further details about the silver mining towns of Mayo, Elsa and Keno, known collectively as the Silver Trail, are available at the information booth at Stewart Crossing.

BINET HOUSE INTERPRETIVE CENTRE is at jct. 2nd Ave. and Centre St. The two-story building features exhibits that include a collection of historic photographs, artifacts and a 3-D relief map of the region identifying the location of mineral deposits. Guided tours are available. Picnicking is permitted. Allow 30 minutes minimum. Daily 10-6, June-Aug. Admission $2; free (ages 0-11). Phone (867) 996-2926.

TESLIN (D-3) pop. 189

The Nisutlin Bay Bridge, the longest water span on the Alaska Hwy., crosses an arm of Teslin Lake at Teslin. The highway parallels the 116-kilometre (72-mi.) lake for about 55 kilometres (34 mi.), providing a scenic drive bordered on both sides by mountains. The area is noted for abundant game, and the fjord-like lake provides excellent fishing. The economy of the community depends heavily on hunting, fishing and trapping.

Teslin has one of the largest First Nations populations in the Yukon, with many of its residents descended from the coastal Tlingit tribe. The original First Nations settlement is reached by a loop road. In the old village are Catholic and Anglican missions as well as a Royal Canadian Mounted Police station.

GEORGE JOHNSTON MUSEUM is 1 km (.6 mi.) w. of the Alaska Hwy. at Km-post 296. George Johnston, a Tlingit Indian, recorded his culture through his camera. A selection of Johnston's work, displays of the Tlingit tribe's rich and colorful history, Tlingit dancing costumes and pioneer items are exhibited. Daily 9-5, mid-May through Aug. 31. Admission $5; $4 (ages 61+ and college students with ID); $3 (ages 6-17); $15 (family). Phone (867) 390-2550.

TESLIN TLINGIT HERITAGE CENTRE is 4 km (2.5 mi.) w. on Hwy. 1. Totem poles, hand-carved masks, crafts, artifacts and photographs relay the life and culture of the Teslin Tlingit people. Picnicking is permitted. Allow 30 minutes minimum. Mon.-Sat. 9-5, Sun. 11-5, June-Aug. Admission $4; $3 (ages 55+ and students with ID); $3 (ages 6-17); $15 (family). MC, VI. Phone (867) 390-2532.

WATSON LAKE (D-3) pop. 1,000

At Km-post 1016.8 on the Alaska Hwy., Watson Lake is an important transportation, distribution and communication center for the southern Yukon. The town was named for Frank Watson, a trapper from England who settled there in 1898.

Watson Lake is known for the signpost collection that was begun by a homesick soldier during construction of the Alaska Hwy. in 1942. Over the years, tourists have continued adding signs showing the names of their hometowns, and now the collection includes more than 60,000 signs.

From Watson Lake the historic Robert Campbell Hwy. loops north and west through the wilderness of southeastern Yukon.

NORTHERN LIGHTS CENTRE is at 807 Frank Tr. Images of the aurora borealis are displayed in a planetarium-like dome theater. Narration details the myths and science behind the luminous phenomena. Allow 1 hour minimum. Daily 12:30-9:30, mid-May to mid-Sept. Admission $10; $9 (ages 66+ and students with ID); $6 (ages 6-12); $24 (family, two adults and three children). AX, MC, VI. Phone (867) 536-7827.

WATSON LAKE VISITOR INFORMATION CENTRE is at jct. Alaska and Robert Campbell hwys. A DVD presentation explains the history and hardship surrounding the construction of the Alaska Hwy. Allow 30 minutes minimum. Daily 8-8, mid-May to late Sept. Free. Phone (867) 536-7469.

WHITEHORSE (D-2)
pop. 19,058, elev. 689 m/2,260′

Whitehorse began during the Klondike gold rush when thousands of prospectors journeyed by ship to Skagway, Alaska, then climbed the rugged mountain passes to the headwaters of the Yukon River. They constructed nearly anything floatable for the more than 900-kilometre (559-mi.) trip to Dawson City via Whitehorse. Above Whitehorse many prospectors died in the dangerous Whitehorse Rapids.

When stern-wheeler service to Dawson became available, the trip from Whitehorse took 2.5 days; the return trip against the current took 5 days. The first rails of the White Pass and Yukon Route railway were laid at Skagway in May 1898, and the line to Whitehorse opened in July 1900.

During World War II Canadian and United States Army personnel building the Alaska Hwy. moved to Whitehorse, which became the capital of the Yukon Territory in 1953.

Evolving into the transportation, communication and distribution center of the Yukon, Whitehorse also became the territorial headquarters of the Royal Canadian Mounted Police as well as the heart of the territorial government and federal departments.

Attractions on a much larger scale include Lake Laberge, the setting for Robert W. Service's "The Cremation of Sam McGee," and the Robert Lowe Suspension Bridge across Miles Canyon.

The Whitehorse Power Dam features one of the world's longest wooden fish ladders; the salmon, running in late July or early August, can be seen from viewing windows. Lake Schwatka, impounded by the power dam, was named after Frederick Schwatka, the first U.S. army lieutenant to navigate the entire length of the Yukon River.

Visible from the Alaska Hwy., 24 kilometres (15 mi.) south of Whitehorse, is Marsh Lake Lock, the northernmost lock in the Western Hemisphere. It is used by small craft navigating the upper Yukon River.

Several guided tours of the town and surrounding area are available. [SAVE] Gray Line/Yukon offers guided bus tours of Whitehorse and Miles Canyon as well as cruises from Lake Schwatka through Miles Canyon. Several companies provide Yukon River cruises, guided hikes, and canoe, boat and raft trips on area rivers. The Yukon Conservation Society gives guided nature walks in the summer.

The Swan Haven Interpretive Centre, on the shores of M'Clintock Bay, affords bird enthusiasts the opportunity to learn about migratory birds, in particular Trumpeter swans. The center is open Mon.-Fri. 5-8 p.m., Sat.-Sun. noon-7, Apr. 1-early May. Phone (867) 667-8291.

Whitehorse Visitor Information Centre, on 2nd Avenue and Hanson Street, features exhibits and audiovisual presentations about the Yukon. The center is open daily 8-8, mid-May to late Sept.; Mon.-Fri. 8:30-5, rest of year. Phone (867) 667-3084.

City of Whitehorse: 2121 Second Ave., Whitehorse, YT, Canada Y1A 1C2; phone (867) 668-8660. *See color ad.*

Self-guiding tours: Books detailing walking tours are available for $8.95 plus postage from the Yukon Historical and Museums Association, 3126 Third Ave., P.O. Box 4357, Whitehorse, YT, Canada Y1A 3T5; phone (867) 667-4704.

"FRANTIC FOLLIES" is presented in the Village Square room of the Westmark Whitehorse Hotel at 201 Wood St. The Gay '90s vaudeville revue has a cast of professional actors, dancers and musicians and recaptures the spirit and enthusiasm of the Klondike gold rush. The 1.7-hour family-style show includes music, comedy, magic, dancing and the poetry of Robert W. Service, Bard of the Yukon.

Performances are given nightly at 7 and 9:15, June 14-July 25; at 8:30, May 26-June 13 and June 26-Sept. 5. Phone to verify schedule. Admission $19; $9.50 (ages 0-11). Phone (867) 668-2042.

SAVE **THE GRAY LINE YUKON WHITEHORSE CITY TOUR** leaves from the Westmark Whitehorse Hotel, 201 Wood St. The narrated tour acquaints visitors with the city by calling upon such landmarks as the stern-wheeler SS *Klondike II*, the Whitehorse Power Dam and the Miles Canyon lookout. Other places of interest include museums, the longest wooden fish ladder in North America and a log skyscraper. Bus tours depart daily at 9, May 22-Sept. 9. Fare $25; $13 (ages 2-12). Phone (867) 668-3225.

SAVE **MACBRIDE MUSEUM** is at 1124 First Ave. The museum offers an in-depth look at the Yukon heritage with exhibits ranging from prehistoric mammals to the 1898 gold rush. Displays include Sam McGee's 1899 cabin, First Nations relics and sample minerals of the territory. On the grounds are an old steam locomotive, a sleigh wagon and a giant nugget of copper weighing about 1,170 kilograms (2,580 lbs.).

Daily 10-6, June 1-Labour Day; daily noon-4, Apr.-May; Mon.-Sat. 10-4, day after Labour Day-Sept. 30; Thurs.-Sat. noon-4, rest of year. Admission $7; $6 (ages 61+); $3.50 (ages 6-12). Phone (867) 667-2709.

OLD LOG CHURCH MUSEUM is at Third Ave. and Elliott St. Built in 1900, the church houses many missionary, First Nations and Inuit items as well as an audiovisual presentation about the history of the Anglican church in the Yukon. Guided tours are available. Allow 30 minutes minimum. Daily 10-6, mid-May through Labour Day. Admission $3; $2.50 (ages 56+ and students with ID); free (ages 0-11); $6 (family). Phone (867) 668-2555.

GEM **THE SS *KLONDIKE II* NATIONAL HISTORIC SITE** is next to the river at Second Ave. and Robert Campbell Bridge. One of the largest stern-wheelers on the Yukon River, the

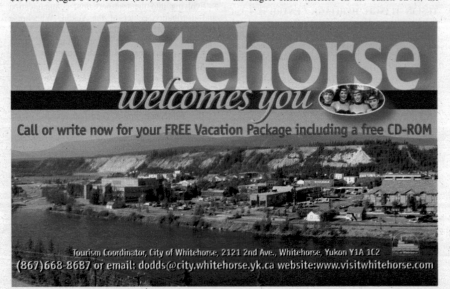

Klondike II ran its route 1937-55. The original *Klondike* struck a reef in 1936; a replacement was built the same year.

Tours are available. A videotape, "In the Days of the Riverboat," is presented prior to each tour. Allow 30 minutes minimum. Daily 10-6, mid-May to mid-Sept. Last tour begins 30 minutes before closing. Admission $6; free (ages 0-5). Phone (867) 667-4511.

TAKHINI HOT SPRINGS is 10 km (6 mi.) w. off Klondike Hwy. at Km-post 10. Natural mineral hot spring pools are maintained at 36 degrees C (96.8 degrees F) for year-round swimming. Other activities include horseback riding, hiking, camping and cross-country skiing. Pool open daily 8 a.m.-10 p.m., July 1 through mid-Sept. Admission $7; $6.50 (ages 13-18); $5.25 (ages 5-12); $5.50 (ages 66+). Phone (867) 633-2706.

WHITEHORSE FISHWAY is at the end of Nisutlin Dr. via Lewes Blvd. Said to be the longest wooden fish ladder in the world, the fishway enables chinook salmon and other fish to bypass the Whitehorse Rapids Dam during their 3,000-kilometre (1,860-mi.) migration between the Bering Sea and their freshwater spawning grounds in southern Yukon. Underwater windows provide a close-up view of the migrating fish. Allow 30 minutes minimum. Daily 9-9, June 1-early Sept. Donations. Phone (867) 633-5965.

YUKON ARTS CENTRE is at 80 Range Rd. An art gallery features contemporary revolving exhibits and a theater presents concerts, dramas and musicals throughout the year. Phone for schedules and show information. Allow 1 hour minimum. Tues.-Fri. noon-6, Sat.-Sun. noon-5; closed major holidays. Donations. Phone (867) 667-8578.

YUKON BERINGIA INTERPRETIVE CENTRE is 2 km (1.2 mi.) e. on the Alaska Hwy. to Km-post 1473 (mi. 914) by Whitehorse Airport. An area of the Yukon, Alaska and Siberia never covered by glaciers during the ice age, Beringia is believed to be the route traveled by the first people who entered the Americas from Asia.

Fossils, life-size animal and First Nations exhibits, interactive computer kiosks, and murals and dioramas of Beringia's landscape illustrate the area's history, geographical events and culture, from the ice age to the present. Highlights include fossils of woolly mammoths, scimitar cats, giant beavers, short-faced bears and steppe bison. A diorama depicts the Bluefish Caves, an important North American archeological site.

Daily 8:30-7, June-Aug.; 9-6, May and Sept. Mon.-Sat. by appointment and Sun. 1-5, rest of year. Hours may vary; phone to confirm. Admission $6; $5 (ages 56+); $25 (family). Combination ticket with Yukon Transportation Museum $9. MC, VI. Phone (867) 667-8855.

YUKON HISTORICAL AND MUSEUMS ASSOCIATION GUIDED TOURS depart from the Donnenworth House, 3126 Third Ave. Guides in period costume describe the architecture, history and local color of Whitehorse on 1-hour walking tours. Historic sights include the 1901 telegraph office, the log church and rectory, the city fire station, the Klondike Airways building, the Royal Canadian Mounted Police compound, the Mast house and Sam McGee's cabin.

Self-guiding walking tour brochures also are available. Allow 1 hour minimum. Tours depart Mon.-Sat. at 9, 11, 1 and 3, June-Aug. Fee $2; free (ages 0-11). Self-guiding walking tour brochure $8.95. Phone (867) 667-4704.

YUKON RIVER CRUISE docks 3.2 km (2 mi.) s. of downtown at 68 Miles Canyon Rd. Two-hour narrated excursions of the Yukon River through Miles Canyon are offered aboard the MV *Schwatka*. The boat passes the remains of a wooden tramway built to carry freight around the rapids, the site of Canyon City and the ruins of the Camp McCrae laundry, which served 30,000 troops stationed nearby during the construction of the Alaska Hwy.

SAVE Gray Line/Yukon provides shuttle service to the departure site from downtown hotels. Cruises depart daily at 2 and 7, mid-June to mid-Aug.; at 2, early June to mid-June and mid Aug. to mid-Sept. Hours may vary; phone ahead. Shuttle departs hotels about 30 minutes before cruise time. Cruise fare $35. A fee is charged for shuttle. Fare may vary; phone ahead. Phone (867) 668-4716 or (866) 417-7365 for reservations or (867) 668-3225 for the shuttle service.

YUKON TRANSPORTATION MUSEUM is off Alaska Hwy. at Km-post 1475.7 by Whitehorse Airport. Exhibits highlight various modes of transportation, including snowshoes, dog sleds, stage coaches, boats, aircraft and military vehicles used during the construction of the Alaska Hwy. The *Queen of the Yukon*, the sister plane of Charles A. Lindbergh's *Spirit of St. Louis*, also is displayed.

Allow 30 minutes minimum. Daily 10-6, mid-May through Aug. 31. Hours may vary; phone ahead. Admission $6; $5 (ages 56+); $4 (ages 13-17 and students with ID); $3 (ages 6-12). Phone (867) 668-4792.

THE YUKON WILDLIFE PRESERVE is 40 km (25 mi.) n. on Takhini Hot Springs Rd. Guided 1-hour interpretive tours depart from the log gatehouse every 90 minutes. The more than 283-hectare (700-acre) site is home to 10 major species of Northern mammals, including moose, muskox, mountain goats and caribou. Allow 1 hour minimum. Daily 8-5, June-Sept. Admission $22; $20 (senior citizens); $12 (ages 6-17); $55 (family, two adults and up to three children). AX, MC, VI. Phone (867) 633-2922.

RECREATIONAL ACTIVITIES
White-water Rafting

- **Tatshenshini Expeditions**, 17 Koidern Ave., Whitehorse, YT, Canada Y1A 3N7. Daily mid-June to early Sept. Phone (867) 633-2742.

Alaska

Batter-up at Midnight
Fairbanks hosts late-night baseball as the Arctic Circle is blanketed with continuous sunshine

Dancing Northern Lights
Brilliant bands of yellow, green and red quietly jump across night skies

"The Mountain"
Mount McKinley, North America's tallest mountain, towers over Denali National Park

Seward's Folly
Bought at just 2 cents per acre, Alaska surprised the world with its wealth of natural resources

Pacific Ring of Fire
Erupting volcanoes are commonplace in the Valley of Ten Thousand Smokes

sounds of
The Great Land

Glacier Bay National Park and Preserve
© age fotostock / SuperStock

While the sights of The Last Frontier can be described as splendid, its sounds are no less spectacular.

A breathy blow accompanied by a geyserlike spray of seawater alerts you to the presence of a humpback whale. It's hard to ignore the loud, slapping sound associated with tail lobbing or breaching—when a whale will throw itself completely out of the water and smack the sea upon return—and it's usually followed by hoots and hollers from observers.

Sea lions make music all their own. Their squawky barking can be heard as you approach a rock packed with the huge creatures.

Drop anchor in ice-filled waters to experience the most spectacular sounds: A popping noise similar to a firecracker signals a calving, when ice separates from a glacier. As chunks detach and fall, a thunderous roar echoes against the mountains, followed by a crash as they hit the sea. The show ends with the soft hiss of settling water.

Alaskan sounds identify the state's history and culture: Drumbeats, clapping, rattle-shaking, foot-tapping and rhythmic chanting resonate from native performances. A sharp cry of "Mush!" or "All right!" from a musher gets a team of sled dogs moving; a command of "Come gee!" alerts the huskies to a right turn.

And just when a hush falls over The Great Land, the low hum of a floatplane is heard from the clouds, ready to take you to another adventure.

Totem poles—slender cedar logs with intricately carved and brightly painted bears, eagles, fish, whales, ravens or frogs—are true artistic works representing the history and customs of native Alaskans. Features of these poles give insight to the blessings of the 49th state.

When visiting Alaska, a stop at a totem pole park should be high on your list of things to do. To get the full effect, choose a tall, colorful totem and stand about 2 feet from it. After admiring the details, look up. Your first impression? Massive. At 85 feet tall and too big to hug, you may have to step back just to be able to catch a glimpse of the figure at the top of the pole. A glance at an Alaska state map also may elicit amazement—it's *huge*, and there's much to see and do.

Natives didn't call this state *Alyeska*—the Great Land—for nothing. It looms larger than life. There are approximately 3 million lakes, 3,000 rivers, 1,800 islands and 100,000 glaciers in Alaska's 586,000 square miles of untamed wilderness. And if that isn't enough, nine national parks and preserves and two expansive national forests total about 66 million acres of undisturbed land. Don't be upset when you find that little of this grandiose scenery fits nicely into your camera lens.

Tales from The Last Frontier

When examined in sequence, the array of symbolic figures on totem poles describe native tales. Likewise, Alaska's diversity is illustrated through its distinct natural features, which leave most anyone speechless. The state is home to towering Mount McKinley—so high that it's cloaked in clouds most of the time. Long, bright days are typical during the summer solstice, when the sun accompanies your every move and never completely disappears.

Options for excitement in The Land of the Midnight Sun seem endless. You can walk on an ice field and feel the crunch of ice under your boots; explore muted, willow-covered desert tundra; peer over chunky glaciers and sweeping mountain ranges from the seat of a helicopter; gaze at a sky painted with watercolored northern lights; enjoy a ride on a boat navigating through blue-green waters packed with bobbing icebergs; marvel at 25-foot-tall sand dunes; or board a bush plane to catch a glimpse of steam from an active volcano.

Library of Congress

U.S. Secretary of State William H. Seward purchases Alaska from Russia for less than 2 cents per acre; the unpopular deal becomes known as "Seward's Folly."

1867

Russian explorer Vitus Bering, sent by Peter the Great to explore the North Pacific, is the first European to set foot on Alaskan soil.

1725

A submarine cable links Seattle to Sitka and Sitka to Valdez, increasing communication between Alaska and the rest of the world.

1903

1880

"**S**eward's Folly" becomes a gold mine as vast deposits of precious metals are discovered in Juneau, followed by discoveries in Skagway in 1897, Nome in 1898 and Fairbanks in 1903.

Alaska Historical Timeline

© Natalie Fobes/Corbis

1942

Japan attacks Dutch Harbour and consequently occupies the Aleutian Islands for nearly a year during World War II.

Tribe members, ingenious at adapting to their variable and sometimes hostile surroundings, made the most of the state's natural offerings, which included the creatures portrayed in their art.

Salmon and orcas are just a couple of animals that appear on totems. Used for sustenance, they were often depicted in oral tales; today animals remain the focus of many pictures and the subjects of travelogues. Visitors relish the opportunity to snap a photograph of a moose cow nibbling grass alongside her twins or grizzly cubs wrestling under the protective watch of mama bear.

Affluent Alaska

For many residents Alaska's riches are liquid: The creation of the Trans-Alaska Pipeline made it possible to transport crude oil almost 800 miles from Prudhoe Bay south to Valdez. The pipeline, an amazing engineering feat crossing three mountain ranges and three fault lines, is able to withstand an earthquake measuring up to 8.5 on the Richter scale as well as temperatures as low as minus 80 F.

Oil isn't Alaska's only rich resource. Discoveries of gold in Fairbanks, Fort Yukon, Juneau, Nome, Skagway and Wrangell lured prospectors from the "Lower 48" to seek their fortune. Visit abandoned gold dredges, camps and mines scattered throughout the state and imagine the fervor that once pervaded these sites, many of which now serve as attractions.

And there was more money to be made. Russian trappers came in search of valuable sea otter pelts, placing the term "fur trade" in Alaskan history books. The first capital of Russian America, Kodiak is graced by the onion-shaped domes of a historic Russian Orthodox church.

But Alaska's native tribes have left the most enduring impact. Traditions of the Aleut, Alutiiq, Athabascan, Cup'ik, Haida, Inupiaq, Tlingit, Tsimshian and Yup'ik tribes can be appreciated through the acts of proud dancers and storytellers who keep family legacies alive. And artisans create soapstone and whalebone carvings, clothing adorned with intricate beading and baskets made from white birch bark—all coveted by visitors.

And totem poles, Alaska's silent, symbolic sentries, are just one reminder of what makes this land truly great.

A Good Friday earthquake destroys Anchorage, the Northwest Panhandle and Cook Inlet and sends a tsunami that wipes out the town of Valdez.
1964

International efforts to rescue two whales trapped in ice off the Barrow coast captures worldwide attention.
1988

Alaska Dept. of Commerce

One of the most devastating fires in state history destroys homes and property in the south central area near Big Lake.
1996

1968
"Black Gold" is discovered on Prudhoe Bay, spurring the construction of an 800-mile pipeline to transport the oil to an ice-free port at Valdez.

1989
The worst oil spill in U.S. history occurs when the *Exxon Valdez* spills some 11 million gallons of crude oil into Prince William Sound.
Alaska Dept. of Commerce

1977
Construction of the Trans-Alaska Pipeline is complete.

Recreation

In the Land of the Midnight Sun, it's a far better idea to set your itinerary by "sight" rather than time. While there are lots of activities to keep your blood pumping, most people visit Alaska for what there is to *see:* Chances for **wildlife viewing** are as plentiful as snowflakes during winter.

Oh, *Another* Bald Eagle?

This phrase, overheard on a small boat weaving through the watery inlets of the Tongass National Forest, testifies to the fact that Alaska has one of the largest bald eagle populations in the world. If you know what to look for—white dots on dark spruce tree branches—you may lose count of all these stately birds. They aren't difficult to spot at the Chilkat Bald Eagle Preserve near Haines; more than 3,500 visit the area to feed.

Many **wildlife cruises** headed for the Inside Passage depart from Juneau. Arm yourself with some good binoculars, a camera and a journal to record your sightings. Entries might include descriptions of huge, barking Stellar sea lions lounging on top of each other; Dall's porpoises frolicking in a boat's wake; Sitka black- or white-tailed deer sipping from a stream; soaring peregrine falcons; or furry otters doing the backstroke.

Black bears fish for salmon in Anan Creek near Wrangell Island, and the west coast of Prince of Wales Island (near Ketchikan) is a great spot for watching tufted puffins. It's no "fluke" to see a whale tail—humpbacks often make appearances in Prince William Sound, and wherever there's an iceberg, you can be sure to find harbor seals resting upon floating ice chunks.

Day cruises depart from Seward and Whittier to explore Prince William Sound and Kenai Fjords National Park, home to sea mammals galore. Along the Kenai Peninsula, both humpback and beluga whales perform aquatic acrobatics near the Turnagain Arm. Nearby, Dall sheep can be seen grazing atop steep cliffs that grace Cook Inlet.

Looking for bears? The Kodiak National Wildlife Refuge is home to some 3,000 Kodiak bears, and Brooks Camp in Katmai National Park and Preserve safeguards one of the world's largest brown bear populations.

Grizzlies as well as caribou and moose roam the desertlike tundra of Denali National Park; take a narrated bus tour into the interior to catch a glimpse. Near the park entrance, forest rangers give a demonstration of sled dogs at work, which is a howling good show.

Even better, hang on tight for a **sled ride** pulled by Iditarod huskies in Seward.

And a View, Too

Seward Highway, connecting Seward and Anchorage, is Alaska's most traveled scenic byway, and it's easy to see why. Snaking along the coast of Turnagain Arm, scenes from the road include the lush Kenai Mountains, saltwater bays, jagged ridges and green alpine meadows. **Rock climbers** dangle from cliffs between Potters Marsh and Bird Creek.

As a matter of fact, any activity in Alaska includes a magnificent view: Try **rafting** in Denali on the Nenana River Gorge or **canoeing** near Admiralty Island National Monument. **Kayakers** also enjoy the Sarkar Lake Canoe Route in Tongass National Forest. Winter options include **cross-country skiing, dog sledding** or **snowmobiling** on the Twin Ridge or Upper Twin ski trails in Tongass National Forest, or **downhill skiing** at Mount Alyeska in Girdwood.

Want to stand on a glacier? **Hikers** in Kenai Fjords National Park follow rangers on **nature walks** to a nearby ice field. For a bit of history, try **bicycling** or **walking** the first mile of the original Iditarod Trail, now a paved beach path in Seward. Horseshoe Lake Trail provides a leisurely walk through the woods of Denali National Park.

Floatplane or **helicopter sightseeing** is an excellent way to see glaciers, ice fields, mountain ranges, waterfalls, lakes or stark tundra. Nearly every city has **flightseeing** tour operators.

A **fishing** charter from one of various harbors is a good way to hook steelhead, grayling or rainbow trout. **Sport fishing** yields red snapper or cod—and Resurrection Bay (near Seward), Sitka and Wrangell are home to world-class halibut and salmon.

Recreational Activities

Throughout the TourBook, you may notice a Recreational Activities heading with bulleted listings of recreation-oriented establishments listed underneath. Similar operations also may be mentioned in Destination City recreation sections. Since normal AAA inspection criteria cannot be applied, these establishments are presented only for information. Age, height and weight restrictions may apply. Reservations often are recommended and sometimes are required. Addresses and/or phone numbers are provided so visitors can contact the attraction for additional information.

Fast Facts

POPULATION: 626,932.

AREA: 586,412 square miles; ranks 1st.

CAPITAL: Juneau.

HIGHEST POINT: 20,320 ft., Mount McKinley.

LOWEST POINT: Sea level, Pacific Ocean.

TIME ZONE(S): Alaska for most of the state; Hawaii-Aleutian for the extreme western portion of the Aleutian Islands. DST.

MINIMUM AGE FOR UNRESTRICTED DRIVER'S LICENSE: 16 years and 6 months.

SEAT BELT/CHILD RESTRAINT LAWS: Seat belts required for driver and all passengers 16 and older. Children ages 6 until 16 are required to be in a child restraint or seat belt; child restraints required for ages 0-5.

HELMETS FOR MOTORCY-CLISTS: Required for drivers under 18 years old and all passengers.

RADAR DETECTORS: Permitted.

FIREARMS LAWS: Vary by state and/or county. Contact the Division of State Troopers, Headquarters, 5700 E. Tudor Rd., Dept. P, Anchorage, AK 99507; phone (907) 269-5511.

HOLIDAYS: Jan. 1; Martin Luther King Jr. Day, Jan. (3rd Mon.); Presidents Day, Feb. (3rd Mon.); Seward's Day, Mar. (last Mon.); Memorial Day, May (last Mon.); July 4; Labor Day, Sept. (1st Mon.); Columbus Day, Oct. (2nd Mon.); Alaska Day, Oct. 18; Veterans Day, Nov. 11; Thanksgiving; Christmas, Dec. 25.

TAXES: Alaska does not have a statewide sales tax, but cities and boroughs may levy a sales tax of up to 7 percent, plus special taxes on goods and services.

INFORMATION CENTERS: Tok Information Center, jct. SR 2 (Alaska Hwy.) and SR 1, provides general tourist literature as well as reports on highway and weather conditions. The center is open daily 8-7, early May to mid-Sept.

FURTHER INFORMATION FOR VISITORS:

> Alaska Travel Industry Association
> 2600 Cordova St., Suite 201
> Anchorage, AK 99503
> (907) 929-2200

FISHING AND HUNTING REGULATIONS:

> Alaska Department of Fish and Game
> P.O. Box 115526
> Juneau, AK 99811-5526
> (907) 465-4180 (Division of Sport Fishing) (907) 465-4190 (Division of Wildlife Conservation)

ALASKA FERRY INFORMATION:
> Alaska Marine Highway
> P.O. Box 112505
> Juneau, AK 99811-2505
> (800) 642-0066

NATIONAL FOREST INFORMATION:
> U.S. Forest Service
> 8510 Mendenhall Loop Rd.
> Juneau, AK 99801
> (907) 586-8800
> (877) 444-6777 (reservations)

NATIONAL PARK INFORMATION:
> Alaska Public Lands
> 250 Cushman St., Suite 1A
> Fairbanks, AK 99701
> (907) 456-0527

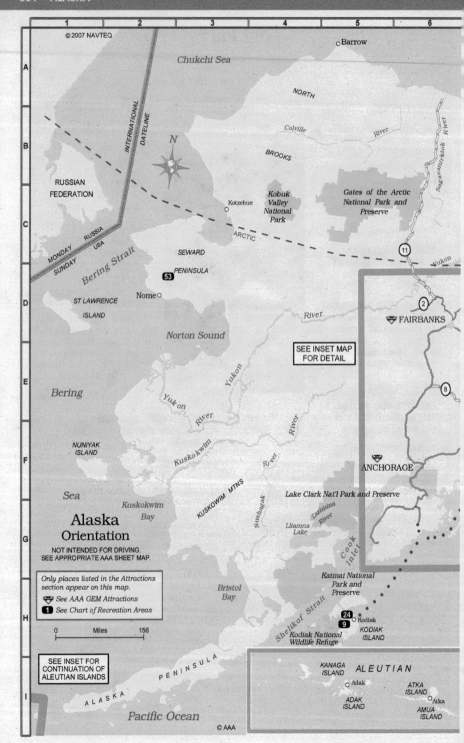

© 2007 NAVTEQ

Chukchi Sea

A

Barrow

NORTH

Colville   River

B

**RUSSIAN
FEDERATION**

BROOKS

Kobuk
Valley
National
Park

Gates of the Arctic
National Park and
Preserve

Kotzebue

ARCTIC

C

MONDAY   RUSSIA
SUNDAY   USA

Bering Strait

SEWARD

53

PENINSULA

(11)

Yukon

Yukon

D

ST LAWRENCE

ISLAND

Nome

Norton Sound

River

(2)

FAIRBANKS

SEE INSET MAP
FOR DETAIL

E

Bering

Yukon

River

Yukon

River

(8)

NUNIYAK
ISLAND

F

Sea

Kuskokwim
Bay

Kuskokwim

River

KUSKOKWIM MTNS

Nushagak

ANCHORAGE

Alaska
Orientation

NOT INTENDED FOR DRIVING.
SEE APPROPRIATE AAA SHEET MAP.

Lake Clark Nat'l Park and Preserve

Tadmina
River

Lliamna
Lake

Cook
Inlet

G

Only places listed in the Attractions
section appear on this map.
▼ See AAA GEM Attractions
1 See Chart of Recreation Areas

*Bristol
Bay*

Katmai National
Park and
Preserve

0   Miles   156

H

Shelikof Strait

24
9

Kodiak

KODIAK
ISLAND

SEE INSET FOR
CONTINUATION OF
ALEUTIAN ISLANDS

Kodiak National
Wildlife Refuge

KANAGA
ISLAND

ALEUTIAN

ATKA
ISLAND

ALASKA

PENINSULA

Adak

ADAK
ISLAND

Atka

AMUA
ISLAND

I

Pacific Ocean

© AAA

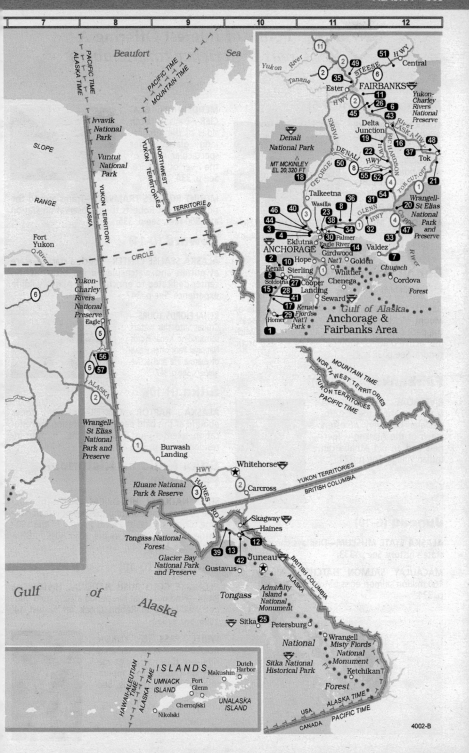

Anchorage & Fairbanks Area

ISLANDS

Points of Interest Offering A
Great Experience for Members®

Anchorage (C-10, F-5)

ALASKA NATIVE HERITAGE CENTER—Why did Tlingit tribe members carve totem poles? Learn about this and other traditions of native Alaskans. See p. 317.

ANCHORAGE MUSEUM AT RASMUSON CENTER—The art, history and culture of the 49th state are presented in various exhibits. See p. 317.

Denali National Park & Preserve (B-10)

DENALI NATIONAL PARK & PRESERVE—Home of Mount McKinley, North America's highest peak, the park covers 9,419 square miles of native wildlife, active glaciers, snowcapped peaks and arctic tundra. See p. 321.

Fairbanks (A-11, D-6)

RIVERBOAT DISCOVERY—A trip aboard the sternwheeler *Discovery III* offers views of the Alaskan wilderness and an old Athabascan Indian village. See p. 329.

Juneau (G-10)

ALASKA STATE MUSEUM—Displays chronicle the state's history. See p. 333.

MACAULAY SALMON HATCHERY—More than 160 million salmon eggs hatch here annually. See p. 334.

MENDENHALL GLACIER—Trails on both sides of the 13-mile-long glacier offer spectacular views of the river of blue ice. See p. 334.

MOUNT ROBERTS TRAMWAY—Trams ascend the side of Mount Roberts to an observation station at 1,800 feet. See p. 335.

Seward (D-11)

ALASKA SEALIFE CENTER—Touch a starfish, stare at puffins and watch playful sea otters at this center dedicated to enriching the Alaska wildlife experience. See p. 347.

KENAI FJORDS TOURS—Cruises into the waters surrounding Kenai Fjords National Park offer views of marine life and active glaciers. See p. 347.

Sitka (H-10)

ALASKA RAPTOR CENTER—Success stories abound at this bald eagle rehabilitation and education center—just watch the raptors-in-residence. See p. 349.

Sitka National Historical Park (H-10)

SITKA NATIONAL HISTORICAL PARK—This 107-acre park commemorating the Tlingit Indian heritage contains a fort that was the site of the 1804 Battle of Sitka as well as the 1853 Russian Bishop's House. See p. 349.

Skagway (G-10)

KLONDIKE GOLD RUSH NATIONAL HISTORICAL PARK—Find out what happened after a gold nugget was found in Rabbit Creek on August 14, 1896. See p. 350.

WHITE PASS & YUKON ROUTE—A 3-hour narrated ride on this narrow-gauge railroad chugs across mountain rivers and chasms. See p. 351.

RECREATION AREAS

	MAP LOCATION	CAMPING	PICNICKING	HIKING TRAILS	BOATING	BOAT RAMP	BOAT RENTAL	FISHING	SWIMMING	PETS ON LEASH	BICYCLE TRAILS	WINTER SPORTS	VISITOR CENTER	LODGE/CABINS	FOOD SERVICE
NATIONAL PARKS AND PRESERVES *(See place listings)*															
Denali (B-10) 6,028,203 acres.		•	•	•				•		•			•	•	•
Gates of the Arctic (C-6) 8,500,000 acres.		•			•			•					•	•	
Glacier Bay (G-9) 3,283,168 acres.		•			•	•	•	•		•			•	•	•
Katmai (G-5) 4,159,097 acres.		•	•	•	•	•	•	•					•	•	•
Kenai Fjords (D-11) 600,000 acres.		•	•	•	•			•		•			•	•	
Kobuk Valley (C-5) 1,710,000 acres.		•		•	•			•							
Lake Clark (F-5) 4,000,000 acres.		•			•			•		•			•	•	
Wrangell-St. Elias (C-12, F-8) 3,000,000 acres.		•	•	•				•		•			•	•	•
Yukon-Charley Rivers (B-12, D-8) 500,000 acres.		•			•								•		
NATIONAL FORESTS *(See place listings)*															
Chugach (D-12) 5,500,000 acres in south-central Alaska.		•	•	•	•	•		•		•			•	•	
Tongass (G-9) 17,000,000 acres in southeastern Alaska.		•	•	•	•			•		•			•	•	
STATE															
Anchor River (D-10) 264 acres near Anchor Point on Sterling Hwy., Milepost 157.	❶	•	•	•				•		•					
Bernice Lake (C-10) 152 acres 10 mi. n. of Kenai on N. Kenai Rd.	❷	•	•		•	•		•	•	•					
Big Lake (North) (C-10) 19 acres 10 mi. w. of Wasilla on Parks Hwy., then 6 mi. s.w. on Big Lake Rd.	❸	•	•		•	•		•	•	•		•			
Big Lake (South) (C-10) 16 acres 10 mi. w. of Wasilla on Parks Hwy., then 4 mi. s.w. on Big Lake Rd. and 2 mi. s.	❹	•	•		•	•		•	•	•		•			
Bings Landing (D-10) 126 acres e. of Soldotna on Sterling Hwy., Milepost 79.	❺	•	•	•	•	•		•		•					
Birch Lake (A-12) 191 acres n.e. of Delta Junction on Richardson Hwy., Milepost 305.5.	❻	•			•	•		•	•	•					
Blueberry Lake (C-12) 192 acres e. of Valdez on Richardson Hwy., Milepost 23.	❼	•	•	•				•		•					
Bonnie Lake (C-11) 129 acres e. of Palmer on Glenn Hwy., Milepost 83. Canoeing.	❽	•			•	•		•		•					
Buskin River (H-5) 168 acres 4 mi. s.e. on Base-Town Rd. in Kodiak.	❾	•	•	•				•		•					
Captain Cook (C-10) 3,466 acres 24 mi. n. of Kenai on N. Kenai Rd.	❿	•	•	•	•	•		•	•	•			•		
Chena River (A-12) 254,000 acres 27 mi. e. of Fairbanks on Chena Hot Springs Rd.	⓫	•	•	•	•			•		•		•	•	•	
Chilkat (G-10) 9,837 acres 7 mi. s. of Haines on Haines Hwy.	⓬	•	•	•	•	•		•					•		
Chilkoot Lake (G-10) 80 acres 11 mi. n. of Haines on Lutak Rd., Milepost 10.	⓭	•	•		•	•		•	•	•					
Chugach (C-11) 495,204 acres just e. of Eagle River on Glenn Hwy. Numerous access points. Horse rental. *(See Eagle River p. 324)*	⓮	•	•	•				•		•	•	•			
Clam Gulch (D-10) 129 acres s. of Soldotna on Sterling Hwy., Milepost 117.	⓯	•	•					•		•					
Clearwater (B-12) 27 acres 11 mi. s.e. of Delta Junction on Alaska Hwy., Milepost 1415, then 8 mi. n.e. on side road.	⓰	•			•	•		•		•					
Deep Creek (D-10) 155 acres near Ninilchik on Sterling Hwy., Milepost 138.	⓱	•	•		•			•		•					
Denali (B-11) 324,240 acres n. of Talkeetna on Parks Hwy., Milepost 135-164.	⓲	•	•	•	•	•		•		•					

RECREATION AREAS

	MAP LOCATION	CAMPING	PICNICKING	HIKING TRAILS	BOATING	BOAT RAMP	BOAT RENTAL	FISHING	SWIMMING	PETS ON LEASH	BICYCLE TRAILS	WINTER SPORTS	VISITOR CENTER	LODGE/CABINS	FOOD SERVICE
Donnelly Creek (B-11) 42 acres s. of Delta Junction on Richardson Hwy., Milepost 238.	19	•	•					•		•					
Dry Creek (C-12) 372 acres n. of Glennallen on Richardson Hwy., Milepost 117.5.	20	•	•	•				•		•					
Eagle Trail (B-12) 280 acres 16 mi. s. of Tok on Tok Cut-off, Milepost 109.5.	21	•	•	•						•					
Fielding Lake (B-11) 300 acres s. of Delta Junction on Richardson Hwy., Milepost 201.	22	•			•	•		•		•					
Finger Lake (C-11) 47 acres 4 mi. w. of Palmer on Palmer-Wasilla Rd., then 1 mi. n. and .5 mi. w.	23	•	•	•	•			•	•	•		•			
Fort Abercrombie (H-5) 183 acres 4.5 mi. s.e. of Kodiak on Miller Point. Historic. *(See Kodiak p. 340)*	24	•	•	•				•	•	•			•		
Halibut Point (H-10) 40 acres 4 mi. n.e. of Sitka on Halibut Rd.	25		•	•				•		•					
Harding Lake (A-12) 169 acres .5 mi. n.e. from Milepost 321 on the Richardson Hwy.	26	•	•		•	•		•	•	•		•			
Izaak Walton (D-10) 8 acres e. of Soldotna off Glenn Hwy.	27	•	•		•	•		•		•					
Johnson Lake (D-10) 332 acres 16 mi. s. of Soldotna on Glenn Hwy.	28	•	•		•	•		•	•	•					
Kachemak Bay (D-10) 368,290 acres near Seldovia, at the end of Sterling Hwy., then by boat or plane across Kachemak Bay.	29	•	•	•	•			•		•					
Kepler-Bradley Lakes (C-11) 344 acres e. of Palmer on Glenn Hwy., Milepost 36.4.	30	•	•	•				•		•					
Lake Louise (C-11) 90 acres n.w. of Glennallen on Glenn Hwy., Milepost 160.	31	•	•		•	•		•	•	•					
Little Nelchina (C-11) 22 acres s.e. of Glennallen on Glenn Hwy., Milepost 137.4.	32	•		•	•			•		•					
Little Tonsina (C-12) 103 acres near Copper Center on Richardson Hwy., Milepost 65.	33	•						•		•					
Long Lake (C-11) 480 acres 7 mi. e. of Sutton on Glenn Hwy.	34	•	•		•	•		•	•	•					
Lower Chatanika River (A-11) 120 acres n.w. of Fairbanks off SR 2, Milepost 9.	35	•	•		•	•		•		•					
Matanuska Glacier (C-11) 229 acres e. of Palmer on Glenn Hwy., Milepost 101.	36	•	•	•						•					
Moon Lake (B-12) 22 acres 18 mi. w. of Tok on Alaska Hwy.	37	•	•		•	•		•	•	•					
Moose Creek (C-11) 40 acres near Palmer on Glenn Hwy., Milepost 54.4.	38	•	•	•						•					
Mosquito Lake (G-9) 10 acres 27.5 mi. w. of Haines on Haines Hwy., then 2.5 mi. on Mosquito Lake Rd.	39	•	•		•			•	•	•		•			
Nancy Lake, South (C-11) 22,685 acres 3.5 mi. s. of Willow on Parks Hwy., then 7 mi. w. on side road.	34	•	•	•	•	•		•		•		•	•		•
Ninilchik (D-10) 97 acres n. of Homer on Sterling Hwy., Milepost 135.	58	•	•					•		•					
Portage Cove (G-10) 7 acres s. of Haines at 1 Beach Rd.	59	•	•					•		•					
Quartz Lake (B-11) 600 acres 2 mi. n.w. of Delta Junction on Alaska Hwy.	36	•	•		•	•	•	•	•	•		•			•
Rocky Lake (C-10) 48 acres 28 mi. w. of Palmer via Wasilla off Parks Hwy. at Milepost 3.5 of Big Lake Rd.	37	•	•		•	•		•		•					
Salcha River (B-12) 61 acres s.e. of North Pole on Alaska Hwy., Milepost 323. Canoeing.	38		•		•	•		•		•					
South Rolly Lake (C-10) 200 acres just w. of Wasilla off Parks Hwy. at Milepost 6.5 of Nancy Lake Pkwy.	39	•	•		•	•		•	•	•		•			

RECREATION AREAS

	MAP LOCATION	CAMPING	PICNICKING	HIKING TRAILS	BOATING	BOAT RAMP	BOAT RENTAL	FISHING	SWIMMING	PETS ON LEASH	BICYCLE TRAILS	WINTER SPORTS	VISITOR CENTER	LODGE/CABINS	FOOD SERVICE
Squirrel Creek (C-12) 350 acres near Copper Center on Richardson Hwy., Milepost 79.5.	40	•	•					•		•					
Tok River (B-12) 9 acres 5 mi. e. of Tok Junction on Alaska Hwy., Milepost 1309.	41	•			•	•		•	•	•			•		
Upper Chatanika River (A-11) 73 acres n.e. of Fairbanks off Steese Hwy.	7	•	•		•			•		•					
OTHER															
Brushkana (B-11) 15 acres 30 mi. e. of Cantwell on Denali Hwy., Milepost 104.	51	•	•					•		•					
Cripple Creek (A-12) 5 acres 50 mi. n.e. of Fairbanks on Steese Hwy., Milepost 60.	60	•	•					•		•					
Paxson Lake (C-12) 80 acres 10 mi. s. of Paxson on Richardson Hwy., Milepost 175.	43	•	•		•	•		•		•					
Salmon Lake (C-3) 20 acres 40 mi. n. of Nome.	61	•	•		•			•		•					
Sourdough (C-12) 140 acres 35 mi. n. of Glennallen on the Richardson Hwy., Milepost 148.	44	•	•		•	•		•		•					
Tangle Lakes (B-12) 100 acres 22 mi. w. of Paxson on Denali Hwy., Milepost 22.	45	•	•		•	•		•		•					
Walker Fork (E-8) 10 acres 80 mi. n.e. of Tok on Taylor Hwy., Milepost 82.	62	•	•	•				•		•					
West Fork (E-8) 10 acres 65 mi. n.e. of Tok on Taylor Hwy., Milepost 49.	63	•	•					•		•					

Alaska Temperature Averages
Maximum/Minimum (Fahrenheit)
From the records of The Weather Channel Interactive, Inc.

	JAN	FEB	MAR	APR	MAY	JUNE	JULY	AUG	SEPT	OCT	NOV	DEC
Anchorage	22 / 9	26 / 12	34 / 18	44 / 29	55 / 39	62 / 47	65 / 52	63 / 49	55 / 41	40 / 28	28 / 16	24 / 11
Barrow	-8 / -20	-10 / -224	-7 / -20	6 / -7	25 / 15	40 / 30	47 / 34	44 / 34	35 / 28	19 / 10	5 / -6	-5 / -16
Fairbanks	2 / -13	10 / -10	26 / 01	44 / 19	61 / 35	71 / 47	73 / 50	67 / 45	55 / 34	32 / 16	12 / -2	5 / -9
Juneau	31 / 21	34 / 24	39 / 28	48 / 33	56 / 40	62 / 46	64 / 49	63 / 48	56 / 44	47 / 38	38 / 29	33 / 24
Kotzebue	4 / -9	3 / -10	7 / -8	20 / 3	38 / 25	51 / 39	60 / 49	57 / 47	46 / 37	28 / 19	13 / 3	6 / -6
Nome	13 / -2	14 / -2	18 / 1	27 / 12	43 / 31	54 / 41	59 / 47	56 / 45	49 / 37	34 / 23	23 / 11	16 / 1

Points of Interest

ADMIRALTY ISLAND NATIONAL MONUMENT (H-11)

Accessible by floatplane from Juneau and Sitka or via ferries of the Alaska Marine Highway to Angoon, Admiralty Island is part of Tongass National Forest *(see place listing p. 352).* Between the rocky beaches and high mountain peaks lie a million acres of coastal rain forests, freshwater lakes and streams, alpine meadows and dense thickets of wild currants and other berries.

Alaskan brown bears outnumber human beings, and the greatest concentration of bald eagles in North America nests along the coast. Beavers, martens, minks, river otters, Sitka black-tailed deer and weasels share the island with Vancouver Canada geese and trumpeter and whistling swans. Offshore are harbor seals, sea lions and whales.

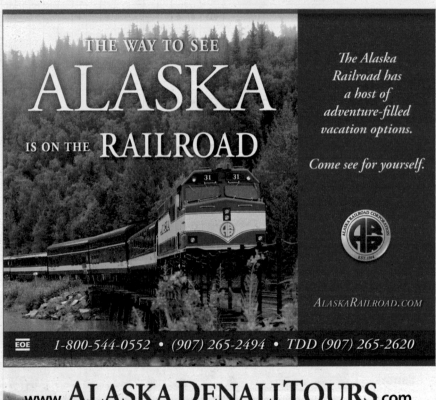

Motorboating and sea kayaking are popular in protected saltwater bays, and a canoe portage trail connects nine interior lakes to bays on the east and west shores. Rustic cabins can be reserved, and campsites and open shelters are available on a first-come-first-served basis. Most of the island is a wilderness area; be prepared for rain and follow no-trace camping practices.

For more information write the U.S. Forest Service (see Fast Facts).

ANCHORAGE (C-10, F-5)
pop. 260,283, elev. 118'

See map page 312.

Anchorage, on a high bluff enfolded by the two branches of Cook Inlet, lies as far west as the Hawaiian Islands and as far north as Helsinki, Finland. The tides in the inlet rise from 30 to 33 feet, and the surrounding mountains loom several thousand feet overhead. The protective mountain barrier and the proximity of the ocean afford Anchorage a surprisingly moderate climate, relative to most of Alaska.

Anchorage is Alaska's largest city and is home to almost half of the state's residents. While not a dazzling metropolis, each summer the city is beautifully decorated with almost 100,000 hanging flower baskets brimming with brightly-colored blooms.

Established in 1915 as the construction headquarters for the Alaska Railroad (see attraction listing),

it is the transportation and business center of south-central Alaska and a major winter recreation area. Anchorage's heritage as a road town is recalled by a number of historic buildings, notably the Pioneer Schoolhouse in Ben Crawford Memorial Park and two nearby one-room log cabins. As well, landmarks denote both Russian and American Indian heritage.

Anchorage suffered from the effects of the 1964 Good Friday earthquake, one of the strongest in history, which destroyed much of downtown. Earthquake Park, at the west end of Northern Lights Boulevard, has a walking trail and interpretive signs that provide information about the massive temblor. The park also provides a stunning vista of Cook Inlet.

The dramatic beauty of the nearby mountains, inlets and glaciers offers an easily accessible sampling of Alaska's natural splendors. Two roads affording beautiful views link to Anchorage; scenic SR 1/9 extends south to Seward, and SR 1 extends north to Glennallen.

From Anchorage visitors also can take various sightseeing tours of the area, including the Kenai Peninsula and places of interest inaccessible by road. Trolley, flightseeing and other types of tours given by Anchorage City Trolley Tours depart daily May through September from 612 W. Fourth Ave. between F and G streets; phone (907) 276-5603. Among the more novel sightseeing trips are dog sled tours, which leave from the Alyeska Resort and

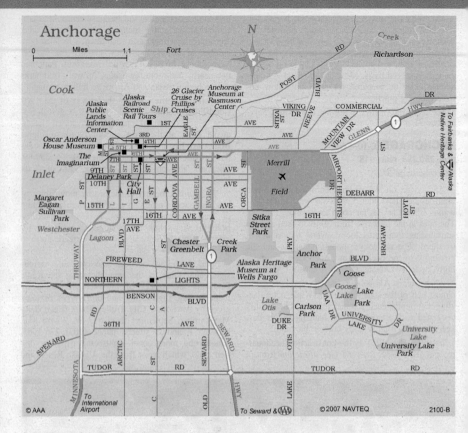

Anchorage

N

0   Miles   1.1

Cook

Inlet

Alaska Public Lands Information Center

Oscar Anderson House Museum

The Imaginarium

Delaney Park

City Hall

Margaret Eagan Sullivan Park

Westchester Lagoon

Alaska Railroad Scenic Rail Tours

26 Glacier Cruise by Phillips Cruises

Anchorage Museum at Rasmuson Center

Ship Creek

Merrill Field

Chester Greenbelt

Creek Park

Sitka Street Park

Alaska Heritage Museum at Wells Fargo

Anchor Park

Goose Lake Park

Lake Otis

Carlson Park

University Lake

University Lake Park

Fort Richardson

To Fairbanks & Alaska Native Heritage Center

To International Airport

To Seward &

© AAA   © 2007 NAVTEQ   2100-B

Ski Area *(see Girdwood p. 330)* December through March.

The Alaska Backpacker Shuttle offers daily shuttle service from Anchorage to Denali National Park and Fairbanks mid-May to mid-September; phone (907) 344-8775.

One-hour float trips on the Matanuska River depart by van from Anchorage to the launch point. Panning for gold is available an hour from downtown. For a different perspective, try flightseeing—operators can be found at the airport and Lake Hood.

Alaska Sightseeing Tours, Gray Line of Alaska *(see color ad p. 314 & p. 327)* and Princess Tours offer a float adventure on Eagle River; tours to Barrow, Kodiak Island, Kotzebue, Matanuska Valley, Nome, Portage Glacier and Prudhoe Bay; fishing on the Kenai River; cruises on Prince William Sound to Columbia Glacier; and a tour of Anchorage.

These agencies also offer 2-, 3- and 4-day round trips between Anchorage and Denali National Park. The trips include travel in railway cars equipped with glass ceiling panels. These same three companies also offer longer excursions to the interior and cruises up the Inside Passage.

The Alaska Center for the Performing Arts Discovery Theatre, at 621 W. 6th Ave., presents a large-screen slide show called "Sky Song" that displays a series of stunning images of the aurora borealis synchronized to classical music. Also shown is a narrated film titled "Alaska: Spirit of the Wild," which introduces visitors to the state through dramatic aerial footage. Phone (907) 263-2900.

Anchorage serves as the starting line for the 1,049-mile Iditarod Trail Race, which begins the first Saturday in March. The actual mileage of the race is 1,161 miles; however, 1,049 is often used as a symbolic figure because the distance is always more than 1,000 miles, and 49 was added to signify Alaska's rank as the 49th state. Dogs and mushers travel over the Alaska Range and across frozen Norton Bay, arriving in Nome nearly 2 weeks later.

Anchorage Convention and Visitors Bureau: 524 W. Fourth Ave., Anchorage, AK 99501-2212; phone (907) 276-4118, or (800) 478-1255 to request a visitors guide.

Self-guiding tours: A guide outlining a walking tour and driving tours north and south of the city is available at Log Cabin Visitor Information Center, Fourth Avenue and F Street; phone (907) 274-3531.

26 GLACIER CRUISE BY PHILLIPS CRUISES— *see Whittier p. 355.*

SAVE **ALASKA AVIATION HERITAGE MUSEUM,** on Lake Hood at 4721 Aircraft Dr., displays 24 vintage aircraft and a flight simulator. Visitors also can observe restorations in progress. Memorabilia and photographs chronicle the history of civilian and military aviation in Alaska; films are shown continuously. Allow 30 minutes minimum. Daily 9-5, mid-May to mid-Sept.; Wed.-Sun. 9-5, rest of year. Closed major holidays in winter. Admission $10; $8 (ages 65+ and students with ID); $6 (ages 5-12). Phone (907) 248-5325.

ALASKA BOTANICAL GARDEN is 3 mi. e. of New Seward Hwy. on Tudor Rd., then just s. on Campbell Airstrip Rd. Arctic horticulture is showcased in a 110-acre birch and spruce woodland replete with more than 900 varieties of plants in demonstration, herb, perennial and alpine rock gardens. The park includes a wildflower walk, an interpretive nature trail and a creek where salmon spawn in the summer. Peak blooming season is late May to mid-September.

Allow 1 hour, 30 minutes minimum. Daily 9-9. Admission $5; $10 (family). MC, VI. Phone (907) 770-3692.

minimal

At 100 kph, if you reach down
to change the radio station
you can travel the length
of a football field.

Stay Focused
Keep your mind on the road.

ALASKA HERITAGE MUSEUM AT WELLS FARGO, at Northern Lights Blvd. and C St. in the Wells Fargo Bank Building, displays more than 900 Eskimo and other native artifacts, an extensive collection of walrus ivory carvings and paintings by Alaskan artists. Allow 30 minutes minimum. Mon.-Fri. noon-5 in summer; noon-4, rest of year. Free. Phone (907) 265-2834.

 ALASKA NATIVE HERITAGE CENTER is about 3 mi. e. on Glenn Hwy. to N. Muldoon Rd. exit, then 1 mi. e. on Heritage Center Dr. Situated on 26 wooded acres, the center presents information about the five regional, native groups that inhabit Alaska: the Aleut and Alutiiq; Athabascan; Eyak, Tlingit, Haida and Tsimshian; Inupiaq and St. Lawrence Island Yup'ik; and Yup'ik and Cup'ik cultures.

The main building offers the Gathering Place for storytelling, dance, native games and musical performances as well as a theater for cultural films. The Hall of Cultures exhibit is divided into five areas with changing multimedia displays about the ways of life of native cultures. Artisans create and display their crafts in adjacent studios.

Outside, five village sites surround Lake Tiulana, and site hosts are available to explain each dwelling, aspects of daily life and customs. Allow 2 hours minimum. Daily 9-5, mid-May to mid-Sept. Admission $23.50; $21.15 (ages 62+); $15.95 (ages 7-16). AX, MC, VI. Phone (907) 330-8000. *See color ad p. 311.*

ALASKA PUBLIC LANDS INFORMATION CENTER, 605 W. Fourth Ave., offers information about Alaska's state and federal public lands, including forests, parks and refuges. Exhibits include displays about Alaska's native culture, history and wildlife; films and interpretive programs are offered during the summer season. Visitors can plan their own trips with assistance from the staff as well as free brochures and maps. State and federal passes also are available. Daily 9-5, June-Aug.; Mon.-Fri. 10-5, rest of year. Closed winter holidays. Free. Phone (907) 644-3661 or (866) 869-6887.

ALASKA RAILROAD SCENIC RAIL TOURS departs from 411 W. First Ave. Narrated sightseeing tours are offered northward between Anchorage and Fairbanks with stops at Wasilla, Talkeetna and Denali National Park. Southbound trips from Anchorage to Whittier follow the Turnagain Arm of Cook Inlet and stop at Girdwood and Portage.

Domed cars with glass-covered viewing platforms allow for 180-degree views. Excursions and connections to air, rail and boat tours also are available. Trips depart three times daily, mid-May through mid-Sept.; trains depart Sat.-Sun., rest of year. Schedules vary; phone ahead. One-way fares $41-$185 (an extra fee applies for first-class seating on northbound trains). Reservations are recommended. DS, MC, VI. Phone (907) 265-2494 or (800) 544-0552. *See color ad p. 310.*

ALASKA ZOO is 7.5 mi. s. on SR 1 (Seward Hwy.), then 2 mi. e. on O'Malley Rd.; a shuttle provides transportation from some local hotels. The grounds encompass a 20-acre wooded area with many arctic and Alaskan native animals, including Amur (Siberian) tigers, snow leopards, Tibetan yaks and several bear species. Allow 1 hour, 30 minutes minimum. Daily 9-6 (also Tues. and Fri. 6-9), May 1-Labor Day; 10-5, rest of year. Closed Thanksgiving and Dec. 25. Admission $9; $8 (senior citizens); $5 (ages 12-17); $4 (ages 3-11). MC, VI. Phone (907) 346-3242.

ALYESKA RESORT AND SKI AREA—
see Girdwood p. 330.

 ANCHORAGE MUSEUM AT RASMUSON CENTER, 121 W. Seventh Ave., has exhibits focusing on the art, history and cultures of Alaska. The Alaska Gallery includes objects dating from prehistoric times through European exploration, Russian settlement, the gold rush era, World War II and statehood. Full-scale dioramas of an Athabascan tent; Yupik Eskimo, Tlingit and Aleut houses; a gold miner's cabin; an early Anchorage house; and Quonset huts (in use during World War II) provide insight to early Alaskan life.

In addition, a display about the Alaska Pipeline features a sample of the 4-foot-tall pipe. "Art of the Far North" contains drawings and paintings by Alaska's first explorers to current artists. Other highlights include summer films, a children's gallery and traveling exhibitions.

Moments *that* Matter

Bonus SPEED OFFERS** FOR CAA/AAA MEMBERS

For details, visit **offers.holidayinn.com**

Holiday Inn
HOTELS · RESORTS

- Cozy, Comfortable Rooms • Full-Service Restaurants • Pools
- FREE High Speed Internet Access • Kids Eat & Stay Free*
- Warm, Friendly Service

1-800-HOLIDAY   holidayinn.com

Alberta
Calgary-Airport
Grande Prairie ▼
British Columbia
North Vancouver ▼
Vancouver-Centre (Broadway)
Vancouver-Downtown Tower & Suites ▼
Whistler Village Centre ✦
Manitoba
Winnipeg-Airport West
Winnipeg-South
New Brunswick
Fredericton
Ontario
Barrie-Hotel & Conference Centre
Brantford
Burlington-Hotel & Conference Center

Cambridge-Hespeler Galt
Guelph
Kingston-Waterfront
Kitchener-Waterloo Conf. Ctr.
Mississauga ■
Oakville (Centre)
Oakville @ Bronte ✦
Oshawa
Ottawa-Downtown ▼
Ottawa-Kanata ✦
Peterborough-Waterfront
Sault Ste. Marie-Waterfront
St. Catharines-Niagara
Toronto-Airport East
Toronto-Brampton ■
Toronto-Int'l Airport ■
Toronto-Markham ▼
Toronto-Midtown
Toronto-Mississauga

Toronto-On King (Downtown)
Toronto-West
Toronto-Yorkdale
Windsor (Ambassador Bridge) ■
Quebec
Gatineau-Ottawa Plz Chaudière
Montreal-Airport
Montreal-Centre Ville
  (Dwtn Conv Ctr) ■
Montreal-Longueuil
Montreal-Midtown
Pointe Claire-Montreal Airport
Saguenay (Convention Centre)

Holiday Inn
EXPRESS

- FREE Express Start® Breakfast Bar
- SimplySmart™ Guest Bathroom with Guest Preferred Showerhead
- FREE Local and Toll-Free Calls • FREE High Speed Internet Access
- Wake up feeling RESTED and REFRESHED with our NEW Simply Smart™ Bedding Collection

1-800-HOLIDAY   hiexpress.com

Alberta
Airdrie-Calgary North ▲
Edmonton Downtown
Medicine Hat ▲
Red Deer
Rocky Mountain House
British Columbia
Kelowna
Langley ▲
Surrey ▲
Vancouver
Vernon ▲

New Brunswick
Saint John Harbour Side ▲
Nova Scotia
Halifax (Bedford)
Ontario
Barrie ▲
Belleville ▲
Collingwood - Blue Mountain ▲
Dryden
1000 Islands - Gananoque ▲
Guelph ▲
Hamilton-Stoney Creek

North Bay ▲
Toronto-Downtown
Toronto-East
Toronto-North York
Whitby
Prince Edward Island
Charlottetown ▲
Quebec
Montreal Centre-Ville ▲
Saskatchewan
Regina ▲

Food is available. Allow 1 hour minimum. Daily 9-6 (also Thurs. 6-9), May 15-Sept. 15; Tues.-Sat. 10-6, Sun. noon-5, rest of year. Closed Jan. 1, Thanksgiving and Dec. 25. Admission $8; $7 (ages 65+, military and students with ID); free (ages 0-17). Phone (907) 343-4326.

ANCHORAGE TRAIL SYSTEM , found throughout and near the city, consists of 120 miles of paved trails and 300 miles of unpaved and wilderness trails. The 11-mile Tony Knowles Coastal Trail stretches from downtown and winds along the scenic coastline; Flattop Mountain is a popular 3-mile day hike with spectacular views of the Alaska Range and Anchorage; and Williwaw Valley contains a 14-mile-long trail with views of emerald lakes, wildflowers and Dali sheep. Phone (907) 276-4118.

THE IMAGINARIUM, Fifth Ave. and G St., is a hands-on science discovery center offering exhibits that explore nature, science and technology. Highlights include a marine wildlife area, reptile exhibits, a bubble lab and a planetarium. Allow 1 hour minimum. Mon.-Sat. 10-6, Sun. noon-5; closed major holidays. Admission $5.50; $5 (ages 2-12 and 66+). MC, VI. Phone (907) 276-3179.

MAJOR MARINE TOURS—*see Whittier p. 355.*

OSCAR ANDERSON HOUSE MUSEUM, 420 M St. in Elderberry Park, was built by Swedish immigrant and businessman Oscar Anderson in 1915 on one of the first townsite lots in Anchorage. The small wood-frame house has been restored and furnished in period and offers a fine view of Cook Inlet. An operational 1909 Hallet & Davis player piano is demonstrated during tours. Swedish Christmas decorations and holiday traditions are featured during Swedish Christmas tours the first two weekends of December.

Guided tours are available. Allow 30 minutes minimum. Mon.-Fri. 1-5, June 1 to mid-Sept. Admission $3; $1 (ages 5-12). Phone (907) 274-2336.

PORTAGE GLACIER RECREATION AREA—*see Chugach National Forest p. 320.*

RENOWN TOURS—*see Seward p. 348.*

RUST'S FLYING SERVICE departs from the south shore of Lake Hood off International Airport Rd. at Anchorage International Airport. The service provides narrated sightseeing tours by seaplane of Denali National Park, Knik Glacier, Mount McKinley and Prince William Sound. Tours to Brooks Falls and Redoubt Bay Lodge provide opportunities to view such wildlife as brown bears and marine animals. Glacier landings, river float trips and one-day and three-night fishing trips also are available.

Inquire about weather policies. Allow 1 hour, 30 minutes minimum. Departures require a minimum of 2 people. Singles are accommodated on a space-available basis. Daily by appointment; closed Jan. 1, Thanksgiving and Dec. 25. Fare $95-$695. AX, MC, VI. Phone (907) 243-1595, or (800) 544-2299 out of Alaska.

TRANS ARCTIC CIRCLE TREKS AND GLACIER BLUE TOURS—*see Fairbanks p. 329.*

BARROW (A-5) pop. 4,581, elev. 2′

The northernmost settlement in Alaska, Barrow is 340 miles north of the Arctic Circle on the edge of the omnipresent Arctic icepack. The sun does not go below the horizon for 82 days from early May to early August or rise above the horizon for 51 days between November and January. The town is reached by daily scheduled flights from Anchorage and Fairbanks. Husky sled dogs still are used, but snowmobiles have become more popular.

Barrow is one of the world's largest Eskimo settlements. Although to some extent the people continue to follow their old traditions, the trend is toward a more modern way of life: The North Slope oil discovery created great wealth in the area.

The Post-Rogers Memorial, at the airport, commemorates the deaths of Will Rogers and his pilot, Wiley Post, who were killed in a 1935 plane crash 12 miles down the coast.

CENTRAL (D-7)

Named Central House in the 1890s, the mining community officially became known as Central in the 1930s following the completion of the nearby Steese Highway. The town's mining industry has experienced great fluctuation, reaching lows during and after World War II and peaking in the 1970s as gold rose in value.

An eight-mile trip southeast via the gravel Circle Hot Springs Road culminates at Circle Hot Springs. The town was discovered when George Crowe, a prospector on Deadwood Creek, wounded and trailed a moose across an unusually warm creek. Crowe traced the heat to the hot springs, which run 140 degrees Fahrenheit at the source.

The Circle District Historical Society Museum, Steese Highway Milepost 128, features artifacts, mining equipment and a miner's cabin; phone (907) 520-1893.

CHUGACH NATIONAL FOREST (D-12, G-6)

Elevations in the forest range from sea level at the Pacific Ocean at Prince William Sound to 13,176 ft. at Mount Marcus Baker. Refer to AAA maps for additional elevation information.

Extending along the Gulf of Alaska from Cape Suckling to Seward, Chugach (CHEW-gatch) National Forest covers 5,500,000 acres, roughly as large as New Hampshire. It is second in size only to the Tongass National Forest (see place listing p. 352) and includes many of the islands and much of the land bordering Prince William Sound and the northeastern portion of the Kenai Peninsula.

Within the 700,000-acre Copper River Delta Wildlife Management Area just east of Cordova is one of the largest concentrations of trumpeter swans in North America. Also in abundance are dusky Canada geese, short-billed dowitchers, red-throated loons and green-winged teal. Prince William Sound has spectacular scenic opportunities with its 3,500 miles of coastline as well as dramatic tidewater glaciers and marine life that includes many species of whales.

Both saltwater and freshwater fishing are available in abundance in the forest. Halibut, red snapper, salmon and crabs are plentiful along the more than 3,500 miles of saltwater shoreline. Popular spots are Resurrection Bay at Seward and in Prince William Sound around Valdez and Cordova. Freshwater lakes and streams provide red salmon, Dolly Varden char and rainbow trout. A sportfishing license is required for all types of fishing within the forest.

For photographers and sport hunters, the forest offers a variety of big game, including black and brown bears, moose and Dall sheep. Hunting is subject to Alaska's fish and game management laws, seasons and bag limits.

Seward Highway offers 127 miles of scenic driving along saltwater bays, ice-blue glaciers and valleys dotted with native wildlife. The highway connects the cities of Anchorage and Seward. Bordering the forest on the northwest is SR 4; its scenic portion extends from Valdez to the junction of SR 10 west of Chitina. Portions of one of the most famous trails, The Historic Iditarod Trail, can be hiked, skied, dog sledded or explored on snowmobile.

In addition to 14 road-accessible campgrounds and 200 miles of hiking trails, the Forest Service operates 42 cabins in remote areas near lakes, bays and streams. Accessible by trail, boat or floatplane, the cabins are equipped with bunks, tables, chairs, wood or oil stoves and outdoor sanitary facilities, but not electricity.

The fee is $25-$45 per night per party. Reservations are required and can be made up to six months in advance. Further information also can be obtained from the Chugach National Forest, 3301 C St., Suite 300, Anchorage, AK 99503, phone (907) 743-9500, (877) 444-6777 for reservations or the U.S. Forest Service in Juneau (see Fast Facts). Also see Recreation Chart and the AAA Western Canada & Alaska CampBook.

ALASKA WILDLIFE CONSERVATION CENTER, Seward Hwy. Milepost 79, is a 140-acre, drive-through wild animal park. Among the animals to be seen are musk oxen, red foxes, lynx, buffaloes, Sitka blacktail deer, caribous, eagles, moose, reindeer, elk and bears. Allow 30 minutes minimum. Daily 10-6, early Apr. to mid-May; 8-8, mid-May to mid-Sept.; 10-5, rest of year. Last admission is 30 minutes before closing. Admission $7.50; $5 (ages 4-12, ages 56+ and active military with ID). The maximum fee is $25 per carload. Pets are not permitted. MC, VI. Phone (907) 783-2025.

PORTAGE GLACIER CRUISES depart 1.5 mi. s. of the Begich-Boggs Visitor Center in the Portage Glacier Recreation Area (see attraction listing). A 1-hour narrated cruise takes passengers to the face of Portage Glacier. Sections of the glacier "calving" or breaking away into the lake below often can be seen. The 200-passenger ship has a climate-controlled cabin with oversize windows and an open-air observation deck. Shuttle and tour packages from Anchorage also are available.

Inquire about weather policies. Cruises depart daily at 10:30, noon, 1:30, 3 and 4:30, mid-May to late Sept. Fare $29; $14.50 (ages 3-11). MC, VI. Phone (907) 277-5581.

PORTAGE GLACIER RECREATION AREA is 5.5 mi. e. from Milepost 79 of the Seward-Anchorage Hwy. Large icebergs calve off the face of the glacier into 650-foot-deep Portage Lake. An observation platform and a wayside exhibit are at the entrance to Williwaw Campground. Wayside exhibits also are available at Explorer Glacier. Iceworm safaris are offered. Guided tours and food are available. Picnicking is permitted. The road to and within the area is open all year. Phone (907) 783-3242.

Begich-Boggs Visitor Center, off the Seward-Anchorage Hwy. on Portage Valley Rd., contains an observatory, orientation area and exhibit hall. A 20-minute film titled "Voices from the Ice" is shown

20 minutes past every hour. Daily 9-6, Memorial Day-Labor Day; Sat.-Sun. 10-5, rest of year. Film $1. Phone (907) 783-2326.

COOPER LANDING (D-10) pop. 369

RECREATIONAL ACTIVITIES
Boating

- **Alaska Wildland Adventures** departs for Kenai River trips from the launch site on Sterling Hwy. (SR 1) Milepost 50.1. Write 16520 Sterling Hwy., Cooper Landing, AK 99572. Other activities are offered. Daily May-Sept. Phone (907) 783-2928, (800) 478-4100 or (800) 334-8730.

CORDOVA (D-12) pop. 2,454, elev. 100′

Cordova is located on the eastern shores of Prince William Sound and is surrounded by the Chugach Mountain Range and the Chugach National Forest. The town can be reached by air from Juneau and Anchorage or via the Alaska Marine Highway from Valdez and Whittier. In the early 1900s, Cordova was the terminus of the Copper River Northwest Railroad that carried copper ore from the Kennecott Mines in McCarthy. Today the town's industry focuses on commercial fishing.

Cordova Chamber of Commerce: P.O. Box 99, Cordova, AK 99574; phone (907) 424-7260.

DELTA JUNCTION (B-11) pop. 840

The official northern terminus of the Alaska Highway, Delta Junction is one of the state's strongest agricultural producers. The town offers panoramic views of the Alaska Range as well as the Trans-Alaska Pipeline, the Delta Bison Range and glaciers.

BIG DELTA STATE HISTORICAL PARK AND RIKA'S ROADHOUSE AND LANDING, at Milepost 275 on Richardson Hwy., is a restored 10-acre homestead with a museum, historic cabins, a roadhouse, a garden and livestock and poultry pens. Guided tours are available. Food is available. Daily 9-5, May 15-Sept. 15; by appointment rest of year. Free. Phone (907) 895-4201 May 15-Sept. 15, or (907) 895-4938 rest of year.

DENALI NATIONAL PARK AND PRESERVE (B-10)

Elevations in the park and preserve range from 626 ft. at the northwest corner of the park at Chilcukabena Lake to the 20,320 ft. Mount McKinley. Refer to AAA maps for additional elevation information.

In the interior of Alaska, primitive and wild Denali National Park and Preserve covers 9,419 square miles and offers spectacular views of quiet lakes, snowcapped peaks and varicolored tundra. In addition to 20,320-foot Mount McKinley, the highest peak in North America, the park encompasses 17,400-foot Mount Foraker, 13,220-foot Silverthrone and 11,670-foot Mount Russell.

Mount McKinley, known to the early Athabascan Indians as Denali, "the high one," has two peaks: South Peak, the true summit, and 2 miles away, 19,470-foot North Peak. Most of the mountain is covered by ice and snow all year. Excellent views of Mount McKinley are possible along the park road (weather permitting); clouds hide the summit about 75 percent of the time in summer and 60 percent the rest of the year.

The park's many glaciers originate on the slopes of the Alaska Range. Muldrow Glacier, the largest northward-flowing glacier in Alaska, stretches from between Mount McKinley's twin peaks to within a few miles of the park road; it can be seen from several vantage points.

More than 167 species of birds and 39 kinds of mammals inhabit the park; grizzly bears, moose, Dall sheep, wolves and caribou are some of the larger mammals. Equally varied is the vegetation. The chief conifers are black and white spruce, while dwarf birch grow in thickets on the lower slopes and along the intermountain valleys. Low, boggy meadows are the habitat of stunted, twisted black spruce.

Above the river valleys, forests give way to vast stretches of wet tundra supporting shrubby plants and often underlain by permafrost. Dry alpine tundra blankets the slopes and ridges at the higher elevations.

General Information and Activities

From Anchorage and Fairbanks, the George Parks Highway (SR 3) provides access to the park all year, and SR 8 from Paxson is usually open from early June to mid-October. The park also is accessible from Anchorage or Fairbanks via the Alaska Railroad; there is daily service from late May to mid-September. Trains run northbound to Fairbanks on Saturday and southbound to Anchorage on Sunday the rest of the year. Charter flights are available from principal airports.

Denali Park Road, beginning at SR 3 at the park's eastern boundary, runs about 90 miles westward through the park, terminating at a partly abandoned mining town, Kantishna. Only the first 14.8 miles to Savage River are paved, and most of the road is narrow with many sharp curves. It is usually open from early June to mid-September. The George Parks Highway (SR 3) runs along the eastern border of the park and offers sweeping views of the park's alpine scenery from Willow to Nenana.

Private vehicles may be used only on the first 14.8 miles of Denali Park Road unless you have a registered campsite at Teklanika Campground. Transportation beyond Savage River or to Sanctuary, Igloo and Wonder Lake campgrounds is provided by shuttle buses that operate to Toklat, Wonder Lake and other points in the park.

Fare for the shuttle varies with destination. Fare to Wonder Lake $32.50; $16.25 (ages 15-17). Fare to Toklat and Polychrome $18; $9 (ages 15-17). Three- and 6-day trip passes are available; prices vary by destination. These fares do not include the $4 registration fee or the park admission fees.

More than half of the shuttle seats are available for telephone reservation; phone (907) 272-7275 or (800) 622-7275 in advance. The rest of the spaces can be reserved only in person within 2 days of departure. Buses depart approximately every half-hour beginning at 5 a.m. from the Wilderness Access Center near the entrance at Milepost 0.6 on Denali Park Road. The bus stops to view wildlife when conditions are safe. Shuttle buses also drop off and pick up passengers along the park road on a space-available basis. The center houses a small theater.

The Denali Visitor Center, Milepost 1.2 on Denali Park Road, contains an information desk, exhibits, a slide show and interpretive programs. It is open daily 9-9, late May to mid-September. The Murie Science and Learning Center, at Milepost 1.3 on Denali Park Road, is dedicated to research and education about America's eight northernmost national parks and offers field seminars and educational programs. It is open daily 8:30-4, late May to mid-September; 10-4, rest of year. Phone (907) 683-1269 or (888) 688-1269.

The Talkeetna Ranger Station, Milepost 98 on George Parks Highway, also offers interpretive programs and is open daily 8-6, mid-April through late July; 9-6, late July through Labor Day; Mon.-Fri. 8-4:30, rest of year.

To camp outside the established campgrounds, stop at the Wilderness Access Center for a backcountry permit. Reservations for all campgrounds may be made here.

Sled dog demonstrations are given by rangers at the park kennels, Milepost 3 on Denali Park Road. The 40-minute presentations are offered daily at 10, 2 and 4, June through August; phone ahead for availability. Ranger-naturalists also present various lectures, hikes and other activities daily at various campgrounds. Information about activities is available at the park Visitor Center and ranger stations, or pick up a copy of the park's informational newspaper, *Denali Alpenglow.*

Guided and self-guiding hikes are available along several nature trails with trailheads along the paved portion of the park road. Throughout the rest of the park, hiking is generally cross-country. The Spruce Forest Trail loop takes about 15 minutes, while the Morino Trail takes 30 minutes to complete. Backcountry permits are available from the Backcountry Information Center, adjacent to the Wilderness Access Center. Five- and 8-hour guided hikes depart from the Denali Visitor Center and range from $24-$74, depending on the tour.

Do not feed or disturb wildlife. Grizzly bears in particular can be dangerous; inquire at the Visitor Center about how to avoid close encounters with grizzlies. Firearms must be declared and made inoperative when you enter the park; hunting and shooting are forbidden.

Most fishing is poor in the park; only streams that are free of glacial silt are good fishing spots. No license is required within the national park; the daily creel limit is 10 fish, only two of which may be lake trout. An Alaska fishing license is required in the national preserve areas. Check at a ranger station for further information.

Temperatures during the park season can vary from 40 to 80 degrees Fahrenheit, with an average of 50 to 54 degrees June through August. Daylight generally lasts for more than 18 hours during the summer months.

A store near the park entrance contains supplies, but no gas is available; the store is open approximately 7 a.m.-9 p.m. during peak season, shorter hours at other times. A gas station north of the park entrance on George Parks Highway is open in the summer. Food and supplies also are available at Riley Creek campground just inside the park boundaries. *See Recreation Chart and the AAA Western Canada & Alaska CampBook.*

ADMISSION is $10 per person or $20 per family.

PETS are permitted in the park only if they are leashed or otherwise physically restrained; they are not allowed on trails, shuttle buses or in the backcountry.

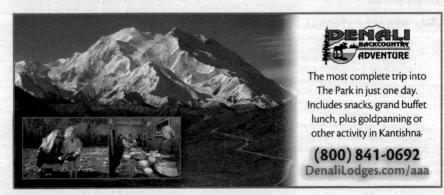

ADDRESS inquiries to the Superintendent, Denali National Park and Preserve, P.O. Box 9, Denali Park, AK 99755; phone (907) 683-2294 or (800) 622-7275 for reservations.

ALASKA CABIN NIGHT DINNER THEATRE is 1.7 mi. n. of the park entrance on George Parks Hwy. at Milepost 239. The theater presents a 1915-style dinner show that highlights Alaska's gold-mining history. A pre-show dinner is served. Allow 2 hours minimum. Shows daily at 5:30 and 8:30 p.m., mid-May to mid-Sept. Admission $52; $25 (ages 0-11). Reservations are recommended. AX, DS, MC, VI. Phone (907) 683-8200 or (800) 276-7234 for reservations.

DENALI AIR is 10 mi. s. on George Parks Hwy. (SR 3) at Milepost 229.5. Commentary about history, scenery and topography complements an hour-long flight along the Alaska Range and around Mount McKinley. Allow 1 hour minimum. Flights depart every even hour daily 8-8 (weather permitting). Fare $287; $145 (ages 2-12). AX, DS, MC, VI. Phone (907) 683-2261.

DENALI BACKCOUNTRY ADVENTURE departs from Denali Cabins, Milepost 229, George Parks Hwy., 9 mi. s. of park entrance. This narrated bus tour travels along the 90-mile Denali Park Road to Denali Backcountry Lodge in Kantishna. Along the route, the guide points out wildlife such as moose and caribou, and makes stops at various times for photography. The complete trip lasts 13 hours and includes either goldpanning or a guided nature walk to a historic pioneer cabin. Lunch and snacks are provided.

Allow 13 hours minimum. Tours depart daily at 6:30 a.m., June 5-Sept. 11. Fee $135 (includes park entrance fee). AX, MC, VI. Phone (907) 376-1992 or (877) 233-6254.

DENALI WILDERNESS SAFARIS, at Milepost 215 on George Parks Hwy., offers 3-hour heated jet boat rides to a camp in the Alaskan "bush" country, where locals share their methods of hunting, prospecting and trapping. Gold panning opportunities are presented. Free transportation is provided from all area hotels. Wilderness trips depart daily at 7:30, 8:30, 2, 5 and 6. Wilderness trip fare (includes a snack) $95; $55 (ages 0-11). Reservations are recommended. MC, VI. Phone (907) 768-2550.

ERA HELICOPTERS FLIGHTSEEING TOURS is at 1 Glacier Way. The company offers a narrated, 50-minute aerial tour of North America's highest mountain, Mount McKinley, as well as 75-minute glacier landing tours. Four-hour heli-hiking excursions also are available. Caribous, moose and Dall sheep can be seen in the valleys. Free transportation is provided from area hotels. Daily 7-7, May-Sept. Tours range from $299-$399. Tours subject to passenger minimums. AX, MC, VI. Phone (907) 683-2574 or (800) 843-1947.

NATURAL HISTORY TOUR, departing from area hotels, takes visitors on a bus tour across sections of the park where they can enjoy views of the Alaska Range from Mount McKinley to Mount Deborah. Driver-guides explain the region's natural history, unusual geological formations and local flora and fauna. A stop at the Wilderness Access Center allows time to view the film "Across Time and Tundra."

The 5-hour trip departs two times daily, mid-May to mid-Sept. Hours vary; phone ahead. Fare (includes a snack) $75; $50 (ages 0-13). AX, DS, MC, VI. Phone (907) 276-7234 or (800) 276-7234.

TUNDRA WILDERNESS TOURS picks up visitors at local hotels. Buses travel to Toklat River, making frequent stops en route for photography. Driver-guides explain in detail the region's geology, flora and fauna on the 6- to 8-hour tours. Binoculars are recommended for spotting moose, caribou, bears and other wildlife.

Inquire about weather policies. Trips depart daily 5:30-7 a.m. and 1:30-3:30 p.m., mid-May to mid-Sept. Fare (includes a box lunch) $90; $51 (ages 0-14). Reservations are recommended. AX, MC, VI. Phone (907) 276-7234, (907) 683-8200 or (800) 276-7234.

RECREATIONAL ACTIVITIES
White-water Rafting
- **Alaska Raft Adventures** departs from the McKinley Chalet at Milepost 238 on George Parks

Hwy. (SR 3). Write 241 W. Ship Creek Ave., Anchorage, AK 99501. Trips depart daily at 8, noon, 1:30 and 6. Phone (907) 276-7234 or (800) 276-7234

- **SAVE** **Denali Raft Adventures, Inc.** is .5 mi. n. of the park entrance. Write Drawer 190, Denali National Park, AK 99755. Trips depart daily mid-May to mid-Sept.; check-in at 7:30, 9, 10, 12:30, 3 and 6:30. Phone (907) 683-2234 or (888) 683-2234.

EAGLE (D-8) pop. 129

Eagle was settled in 1897 by 28 miners who named the town after the bald eagles that nested on the nearby bluff. In 1899, the Army established Fort Egbert and within several years, some 37 military buildings were constructed. Founded along the Yukon River near the Canadian border, Eagle is the only planned town of the gold rush.

Eagle Historical Society: P.O. Box 23, Eagle, AK 99738; phone (907) 547-2325.

EAGLE MUSEUMS are all within 1 sq. mi. of town. Tours depart from the courthouse at First and Berry sts. Visitors can join a walking tour that includes six restored buildings, including James Wickersham's original courthouse, the Army Mule Barn, Redman Lodge, Customs House, St. Paul's Log Church and the Waterwagon Shed. Each building contains memorabilia portraying the small town's history. Allow 3 hours minimum. Tours depart daily at 9, Memorial Day-Labor Day. Admission $5; free (ages 0-11). DS, MC, VI. Phone (907) 547-2325.

EAGLE RIVER (C-11)

CHUGACH STATE PARK is e. on Glenn Hwy. Wildlife populations flourish within the park's 700 square miles of mountains, rivers, lakes and glaciers, providing many opportunities for viewing moose and beavers as well as the occasional bear or wolf. Major areas are Eklutna Lake, Eagle River, Anchorage Hillside and Turnagain Arm. A number of recreational activities are available. The park's headquarters is in the historic Potter Section House, at Milepost 115 of the Seward Highway.

Headquarters open Mon.-Fri. 10-4:30. Free. Parking $5 at many trailheads. Phone (907) 345-5014. *See Recreation Chart and the AAA Western Canada & Alaska CampBook.*

EAGLE RIVER NATURE CENTER is 12 mi. s.e. on Eagle River Rd. to its end at 32750 Eagle River Rd. The center sponsors interpretive programs including guided hikes along the four trails it maintains. A hands-on area allows visitors to touch antlers, bones, pelts and other collected items. Allow 30 minutes minimum. Daily 10-5 (also Fri.-Sat. 5-7), June-Aug.; Fri.-Sun. 10-5, Oct.-Apr.; Tues.-Sun. 10-5, rest of year. Free. Parking $5. Phone (907) 694-2108.

EKLUTNA (C-10)

More than 150 years ago Russian missionaries came to Eklutna to convert the Athabascan Indians. Originally built in the 1830s, the St. Nicholas Russian Orthodox Church was reconstructed in the 1970s. The church is at the site of the former Eklutna Historical Park. Adjacent to the church is the Eklutna Cemetery, which dates to the 1650s and remains in use.

ESTER (G-9) pop. 1,680

ESTER GOLD CAMP is at 3660 Main St. The site contains buildings that date back to the Ester townsite of 1904 and Fairbanks Exploration Co., which operated a gold camp there until 1958. Transportation is available from many local hotels. Food is available. Allow 1 hour minimum. Daily 24 hours, mid-May to mid-Sept. Free. Phone (907) 479-2500 or (800) 676-6925.

"Photosymphony" is at Firehouse Theater. "The Crown of Light," an audiovisual re-creation of the aurora borealis, or northern lights, is presented. The show is offered nightly at 6:45 and 7:45, mid-May to mid-Sept. Admission $8; $4 (ages 3-12). Reservations are recommended. The show is not recommended for infants and young children. AX, DS, MC, VI .

"Service with a Smile" is in the Malemute Saloon. The 1.5-hour performance recounts the gold rush days in story and song. The poetry of Robert Service, author of "The Shooting of Dan McGrew," is featured. The saloon, with swinging doors and sawdust-covered floors, is filled with historical relics. Shows nightly at 9, mid-May to mid-Sept. Admission $18; $9 (ages 3-12). Reservations are recommended. AX, DS, MC, VI.

DID YOU KNOW

The northernmost region of Alaska receives almost 3 months of continuous sunlight.

© AAA

Fairbanks

0   Miles   0.9

© 2007 NAVTEQ

2101-B

FAIRBANKS (A-11, D-6)
pop. 30,224, elev. 432'

Fairbanks, near the geographical center of Alaska, is a major visitor center and the northern terminus of the Alaska Railroad. The military, transportation and market nucleus of the Alaskan interior, Fairbanks is a supply point for arctic oil operations and a departure point for airlines statewide.

In 1901 Capt. E.T. Barnette founded a trading post where Fairbanks now stands—a riverboat captain refused to ferry him any farther up the Chena River due to the low water level. Gold was discovered nearby a year later, and the first wave of prospectors flooded up the river. The settlement was named for Charles Warren Fairbanks of Indiana, a U.S. senator who later became vice president to Theodore Roosevelt.

The construction of the Alaska Highway and the influx of the military into Fairbanks heralded a second boom. And in 1968 the discovery of oil in Prudhoe Bay, 390 miles north, triggered a third wave of development. Of interest is Pioneer Park, a frontier theme park at Airport and Peger roads.

Fairbanks offers a variety of winter sports and other activities, including aurora viewing, cross-country and downhill skiing, curling, ice hockey and dog mushing. The city's geographical location allows the semiprofessional Alaska Goldpanners baseball team to play its Midnight Sun Game at 10:30 p.m. on June 18 without using artificial lighting.

Local sightseeing tours to Alaska's arctic zone and other remote places are available from Fairbanks. Using railway cars with skylights, Alaska Sightseeing Tours, Gray Line of Alaska and Princess Tours offer trips between Anchorage and Fairbanks via Denali National Park. Canoes for trips on the Chena River can be rented from several outfitters.

Interesting drives include visits to Chena Hot Springs and the town of Ester. Abandoned gold dredges can be seen outside of Fairbanks along the roads to Chatanika and Ester. The Alaska Public Lands Information Center, on the lower level of Courthouse Square at Third Avenue and Cushman Street, shows free movies and has information about public lands and parks; phone (907) 456-0531.

Fairbanks Log Cabin Visitor Information Center: 550 First Ave., Fairbanks, AK 99701; phone (907) 456-5774 or (800) 327-5774. *See color ad p. 326.*

FAIRBANKS

is the gateway to your authentic Alaskan adventure.

FAIRBANKS
CONVENTION & VISITORS BUREAU

For your free *Visitors Guide* or *Winter Guide* on Fairbanks and Interior Alaska contact

1-800-327-5774
www.explorefairbanks.com

FAIRBANKS' PREMIER ATTRACTIONS
Call Toll Free 1-866-479-6673

•Riverboat Discovery•

AAA GEM Attraction

Daily Sailing 8:45am & 2pm
www.riverboatdiscovery.com

Join the Binkley family aboard the authentic sternwheeler Riverboat Discovery

reservations@riverboatdiscovery.com

•El Dorado Gold Mine•

Featured nationally on NBC!

Daily Tours
www.eldoradogoldmine.com

Join the Binkley family for an adventure into Fairbanks' gold mining history

reservations@eldoradogoldmine.com

Call for reservations   **Local Calls 907-479-6673**

Self-guiding tours: Information about a historical walking and driving tour is available from the Fairbanks Log Cabin Visitor Information Center.

EL DORADO GOLD MINE is 9 mi. n. off Old Steese Hwy. to Elliott Hwy. at Milepost 1.3. A 2-hour narrated trip aboard a replica of a Tanana Valley Railroad train passes through a permafrost tunnel into a working gold mine where mining techniques are demonstrated. Passengers have the opportunity to pan for gold. *See color ad p. 326.*

Allow 2 hours minimum. Tours depart Mon.-Fri. and Sun. at 9:45 and 3, Sat. at 3, mid-May to mid-Sept. Fare $29.95; $19.95 (ages 3-12). Rates may vary; phone ahead. Reservations are required. AX, DS, MC, VI. Phone (907) 479-6673 or (866) 479-6673.

GOLD DREDGE NUMBER 8 is n. on SR 2 (Old Steese Hwy.) to Goldstream Rd. following signs. The five-deck, 250-foot-long ship was built in 1928 to ply Goldstream and Engineer creeks for the precious metal. Following a 90-minute tour, visitors can pan for gold and search for bison and mammoth bones. Food is available. Tours depart on the half-hour daily 9:30-3:30, mid-May to mid-Sept. Admission $25; $12.50 (ages 6-12). MC, VI. Phone (907) 457-6058. *See color ad.*

NORTHERN ALASKA TOUR COMPANY departs from the e. ramp of the Fairbanks International Airport. Tours highlight the natural and cultural aspects of Alaska's arctic region. Excursions, which last a

IF YOU ONLY KNEW

saving money at so many places
is easy with your CAA card.

Shopping. Playing. Traveling. Dining. Living life to its fullest and with savings galore! It's what the CAA membership card is all about!

With special deals on everything from shoes and school supplies to hotel rooms and theme park tickets. You'll receive immediate savings, or at some locations in Canada, will earn CAA Dollars - simply by presenting your CAA membership card.

Save at more than 150,000 merchant locations worldwide. CAA is your shopping source for living the good life. It pays to belong to CAA.

Discover your savings at **caa.ca/save** or visit one of **148 CAA locations.**

full day to multiple days, explore the arctic circle by plane, or bus along the Dalton Highway. Other trips visit the Brooks Range, Barrow and Prudhoe Bay. Guides offer insight along the route. Allow 1 hour minimum. Tours depart daily, mid-May to mid-Sept.; Mon.-Sat., rest of year. Hours vary by trip. Fare $139-$749. MC, VI. Phone (907) 474-8600 or (800) 474-1986. *See color ad p. 327.*

RIVERBOAT DISCOVERY, departing from a pier on Discovery Rd. off Airport Way, provides 3.5-hour trips on the Chena and Tanana rivers aboard the stern-wheeler *Discovery III.* Guides discuss area wildlife, history, anthropology, geology and customs. Views vary from wilderness to elegant houses, and the trip includes a guided walking tour of the Chena Indian village. Trips depart daily at 8:45 and 2, late May to mid-Sept. Fare $46.95; $31.95 (ages 3-12). Reservations are required. Phone (907) 479-6673 or (866) 479-6673. *See color ad p. 326.*

TRANS ARCTIC CIRCLE TREKS AND GLACIER BLUE TOURS is at 4825 Glasgow Dr., with pick-up service available from area hotels and RV parks. This tour company offers a variety of guided excursions including day trips to the Arctic Circle and multi-day trips to the Arctic Ocean, Prudhoe Bay and Point Barrow. Visitors on the 1-day tour can enjoy mountain scenery, a walk through alpine tundra and a hands-on Trans-Alaska Pipeline demonstration. Add-on land and air excursions are available.

One-day tour departs daily mid-May to mid-Sept. Other tours depart throughout the year. Fare for 1-day tour $139. Rates vary according to tour; phone ahead. Reservations are required. AX, DS, MC, VI. Phone (907) 479-5451 or (800) 336-8735.

UNIVERSITY OF ALASKA MUSEUM OF THE NORTH, on the West Ridge of the University of Alaska campus, contains natural and cultural history exhibits. One wing is dedicated to Alaskan art. Also on display are an extensive gold collection and a steppe bison killed by a lion 36,000 years ago and preserved in the permafrost. "Dynamic Aurora," which explains the northern lights, and "Winter," which documents Alaska's longest season, are 50-minute multimedia presentations offered during summer months.

Allow 30 minutes minimum. Daily 9-7, May 15-Sept. 15; Mon.-Fri. 9-5, Sat.-Sun. noon-5, rest of year. "Dynamic Aurora" daily at 10 and 2, "Winter" daily at 11 and 3 during summer months. Closed Jan. 1, Thanksgiving and Dec. 25. Admission $10; $9 (ages 60+); $6 (ages 7-17). Multimedia shows $5. MC, VI. Phone (907) 474-7505.

Student-guided Walking Tours of the University of Alaska Fairbanks depart across the street from the University of Alaska Museum of the North. Tours of the campus last 1.5 to 2 hours. Comfortable shoes are recommended. Other activities include the Arctic Region Supercomputing tour; the International Arctic Research Center tour; the Poker Flat Research Range tour; and the Georgeson Botanical Garden tour. Campus walking tour Mon.-Fri. at 10, June-Aug.; closed July 3-4. Phone (907) 474-7581.

FORT YUKON (C-7) pop. 595

Just north of the Arctic Circle at a point where the Yukon River is almost 3 miles wide, the Athabascan Indian village of Fort Yukon was established as a trading post by the Hudson's Bay Co. in 1847. The village was an important port during the gold rush days, and the post office has remained popular for those who wish to mail from above the Arctic Circle.

Fort Yukon is reached by daily air service from Fairbanks. Visitors can see fish wheels in operation and purchase craftwork and fine furs. Temperatures have ranged as high as 100 degrees Fahrenheit in the summer and as low as minus 78 Fahrenheit in winter.

GATES OF THE ARCTIC NATIONAL PARK AND PRESERVE (C-5)

Elevations in the park and preserve range from 300 ft. along the Kobuk River to 8,510 ft. at Mount Igikpak. Refer to AAA maps for additional elevation information.

Lying north of the Arctic Circle, Gates of the Arctic National Park and Preserve's 8.5 million acres features a raw, austere landscape of sparse vegetation and jagged spires. The rocky spine of the Brooks Range forms the park's backbone, and a boreal forest, or taiga, of spruce, birch and poplar meets the almost treeless tundra that rolls uninterrupted to the Arctic Ocean.

Despite being four times the size of Yellowstone National Park, Gates of the Arctic is a meager larder for the caribous, moose, wolves and bears that roam the park in search of food. Fortunately much of their arctic range is protected, as Gates of the Arctic is joined on either side by Noatak National Preserve and nearby Arctic National Wildlife Refuge.

It was a forester on leave, Bob Marshall, who, in exploring this uncharted region in the late 1930s, christened this land Gates of the Arctic. The term both describes and evokes the grandeur of this wilderness—the soaring immensity of sky and mountains, the burst of wildflowers in summer and the cyclical abundance of wildlife.

But as Marshall remarked, the greatest pleasure is its undeveloped and wild character, which gives the visitor the sense of being the first to visit the tundra foothills or one of the park's nameless peaks. Today a good way to enjoy the park is to follow Marshall's example and hike the park's rugged terrain, which offers challenging backpacking. A popular alternative is to canoe or raft the network of rivers and lakes.

Most visitors use various air charter services from Fairbanks and Bettles Field to reach the park's interior. The Dalton Highway skirts the park's eastern edge and is the only road that approaches the park. Because of Gates of the Arctic's fragile ecology, there are no park facilities, trails or campgrounds within the park. For trip planning assistance and a list of outfitters, guides and air taxi operators, write Gates of the Arctic National Park and Preserve, P.O. Box 26030, Bettles, AK 99726; phone (907) 692-5494. *See Recreation Chart.*

GIRDWOOD (C-11) elev. 23′

Initially called Glacier City, Girdwood was established at the turn of the 20th century as a gold mining town. The community prospered until mine closures in the 1930s reduced it to a virtual ghost town. Misfortune struck again when the 1964 Good

Friday earthquake caused massive destruction along the coast, forcing residents to move the town 2.5 miles inland to its present location. Today Girdwood thrives as a year-round recreation destination.

Girdwood is on Turnagain Arm, a fjord carved by glaciers and known for its dramatic bore tides, which can be 6 feet high and travel at speeds of up to 15 miles an hour. The town also is located at the base of 3,939-foot Mount Alyeska; a 60-passenger tramway ascends to the 2,300-foot level and offers a panorama of the valley and Turnagain Arm.

RECREATIONAL ACTIVITIES
Skiing

- **Alyeska Resort and Ski Area** is on SR 1 (Seward Hwy.). Write P.O. Box 249, Girdwood, AK 99587. Other activities are offered. Mid-Nov. to mid-Apr., weather permitting. Phone (907) 754-1111.

GLACIER BAY NATIONAL PARK AND PRESERVE (G-9)

Elevations in the park and preserve range from sea level at Glacier Bay to 15,320 ft. at Mount Fairweather. Refer to AAA maps for additional elevation information.

Stretching northward from Cross Sound to the Canadian border, Glacier Bay National Park is one of the most scenic spots in Alaska. In this 3,283,168-acre park, blue-white glaciers flow from the snow-clad peaks of the Fairweather Range to fiordlike inlets.

The park features 15,320-foot Mount Fairweather and Glacier Bay. The bay, about 65 miles long and 2.5 to 10 miles wide, was filled with ice 5,000 feet thick as recently as 200 years ago. The park contains some of the world's most impressive tidewater glaciers. Icebergs that crack off, or calve, from the nearly vertical ice cliffs dot the waters of the upper bay. Boaters are likely to encounter numerous harbor seals and an occasional whale.

This spectacular region is accessible only by plane or boat. Alaska Airlines offers flights from Juneau daily June through early September. A 10-mile road connects the park headquarters with the small community of Gustavus, where charter vessels and air and boat service to Juneau are available.

A boat tour of the bay departs from Glacier Bay Lodge each morning, late May to mid-September; phone (888) 229-8687.

Due to concern for the endangered humpback whale, permits are required from June through August for private vessels to enter Glacier Bay. An Alaska fishing license is required for fishing. Boaters should contact the National Park Service for current regulations; phone (907) 697-2627. For further information about the park contact the Superintendent, Glacier Bay National Park and Preserve, P.O. Box 140, Gustavus, AK 99826; phone (907) 697-2230. *See Recreation Chart.*

GUSTAVUS (G-9) pop. 429

FOUR SEASONS TOURS departs from Gustavus dock. During a 3-hour whale watch tour, passengers view a variety of local wildlife, including bald eagles, humpback whales, seals, sea otters, orca whales and Stellar sea lions. An on-board naturalist provides background about these animals and their environment. Allow 4 hours minimum. Daily departures at 2, late May to early Sept. Fare $79; $49 (ages 3-12). MC, VI. Phone (877) 774-8687.

HAINES (G-10) pop. 1,811, elev. 66'

Haines lies in a spectacular setting on the Chilkat Peninsula near the northern end of Lynn Canal between the waters of the Inside Passage and the Chilkat River. The Alaska Marine Highway links Haines with Prince Rupert, British Columbia, and Bellingham, Wash., and enables visitors to connect with the Alaska Highway at Haines Junction, Milepost 1016, via SRs 7 and 4. For information about the Alaska Marine Highway phone (907) 766-2111 or (800) 642-0066, ext. 9604.

The 40-acre Kroschel Wildlife Park, 27 miles north on scenic Haines Highway, is home to reindeer, wolverines, bears, falcons and other native species. Reservations are required for tours; phone (907) 767-5464.

Nearby, from late October through February the 48,000-acre Chilkat Bald Eagle Preserve, between Mileposts 9 and 31 on Haines Highway, harbors one of the largest congregations of bald eagles in the world. More than 3,500 of the birds gather to feed on the salmon in the Chilkat River; sometimes as many as 30 eagles roost in a tree during this time. Use roadside pull-offs for viewing; stopping on the road is prohibited. Tour information is available at Haines Visitor Center.

Other interesting drives near Haines include Lutak Road, leading to Chilkoot Lake, and Mud Bay Road, which passes Pyramid Harbor and an old cannery with its salmon boats before approaching Chilkat State Park *(see Recreation Chart and the AAA Western Canada & Alaska CampBook)*. Davidson and Rainbow glaciers also are visible from this route.

The fishing industry that once was so vital to Alaska's economy sustained several area salmon canneries in the early part of the 20th century. Tsirku Canning Co. at Fifth and Main streets offers demonstrations of the only known working three-piece canning machinery. A museum contains photographs, a videotape and exhibits about the packing process; phone (907) 766-3474.

Buildings that once comprised Fort William H. Seward, the site of the first permanent Army post in Alaska, have been restored and contain inns, hotels and galleries. A historic area at the south end of Haines Highway, the fort also contains a replica of a tribal house, where Chilkat Dancers Storytelling Theater Shows are performed most weekdays. The old hospital houses carvers who use traditional Tlingit Indian methods. Phone (907) 766-2234 for fort

information, or (907) 766-2540 for performance information.

Fjord Express, (800) 320-0146, and Chilkat Cruises Fast Ferry, (888) 766-2103, provide efficient transportation between Haines, Skagway and Juneau.

Haines Convention & Visitors Bureau: 122 Second Ave., P.O. Box 530, Haines, AK 99827; phone (907) 766-2234 or (800) 458-3579. *See color ad.*

Self-guiding tours: Brochures featuring walking tours of Haines and Fort William H. Seward are available from Haines Visitor Center and Hotel Halsingland.

CHILKAT BALD EAGLE PRESERVE FLOAT TRIPS, on Sawmill Rd., pass through the Bald Eagle Preserve on the Chilkat River and offer views of the Chilkat Mountains and bald eagles in their natural habitat. Transportation to and from the river is provided. Bring warm clothes, binoculars, camera, sunglasses and rain gear. Inquire about weather policies. The 4-hour float trip departs daily, May-Sept. Departure times vary; phone ahead. Fare $79; $62.50 (ages 7-14). Reservations are recommended. MC, VI. Phone (907) 766-2491.

CHILKOOT LAKE TOURS, 1069 Haines Hwy., offers sightseeing and fishing cruises of Chilkoot Lake. Brown bears, bald eagles and spawning

Haines
All you dreamed Alaska Would Be

Plan to make your dream come true.
For a free vacation planner
907-766-2234 • 800-458-3579
www.haines.ak.us • hcvb@haines.ak.us

salmon often are seen. Inquire about weather policies. Allow 3 hours minimum. Daily at 9 and 2, May 1-Sept. 15; other times by appointment. Fare for sightseeing cruise $85; fishing cruise $99. AX, CB, MC, VI. Phone (907) 766-3779.

SHELDON MUSEUM AND CULTURAL CENTER, on Main St. above the boat harbor, allows visitors to experience the art and culture of the Tlingit native people and to learn about the early pioneer history of Haines Mission, the Porcupine gold rush and Fort Seward, a frontier army post. Allow 1 hour, 30 minutes minimum. Mon.-Fri. 10-5, Sat.-Sun. 1-4, mid-May to mid-Sept.; Mon.-Fri. 1-4, rest of year. Admission $3; free (ages 0-12). MC, VI. Phone (907) 766-2366.

HOMER (D-10) pop. 3,946, elev. 67'

Homer Pennock landed a party of gold and coal prospectors in the schooner *Excelsior* in 1896 and established Homer. Gold was not found, but an abundance of coal was and the settlement remained.

Healthy fishing and tourism industries support Homer's economy. Kachemak Bay, a 30-mile arm of lower Cook Inlet, provides a usually ice-free deep-water harbor for Homer. A small boat harbor has launching facilities and charter boats. Charter planes are available in town for hunting, fishing, wildlife viewing and sightseeing expeditions. Cross-country skiing is popular in winter. The city is linked by daily air service with Anchorage, and by the Alaska Marine Highway with Seward, Kodiak and Seldovia.

Skyline Drive, accessible from West and East Hill roads, follows the rim of the plateau behind the town and offers access to ski slopes and views of the bay, Homer Spit and the Kenai Mountains. Chartered bush flights afford panoramas of the bay, open coal seams and Harding Icefield to the southeast.

Homer Chamber of Commerce: P.O. Box 541, Homer, AK 99603; phone (907) 235-7740.

ALASKA ISLANDS & OCEAN VISITOR CENTER is at 95 Sterling Hwy. The center presents an overview of the area through interpretive exhibits about Kachemak Bay; local estuaries; research ships; and the seabird and marine inhabitants of the Alaska Maritime National Wildlife Refuge. Outdoor nature trails link the 60-acre site with Bishop's Beach Park on Kachemak Bay. Naturalist-led tours are offered, and a short movie about the Aleutian Islands is shown.

Allow 2 hours minimum. Daily 9-6, Memorial Day-Labor Day; hours vary rest of year. Closed holidays. Donations. Phone (907) 226-4619.

PRATT MUSEUM is .5 blks. n. of Pioneer Ave. at 3779 Bartlett St. Highlights at the community museum include a botanical garden; a marine gallery;

fishing boat models; sea birds and marine mammals; a forest trail; an exhibit detailing the impact of the *Exxon Valdez* oil spill; and cultural displays, which feature artifacts left by Russian and native cultures of the Kachemak Bay. Alaskan art from the Kenai Peninsula also is exhibited.

Allow 1 hour minimum. Daily 10-6, Memorial Day-Labor Day; Tues.-Sun. noon-5, mid-Sept. to mid-May. Closed Thanksgiving and Dec. 25. Admission $6; $5.50 (ages 66+ and students with ID); $3 (ages 6-18); $20 (family). Phone (907) 235-8635.

RECREATIONAL ACTIVITIES

Fishing

- **Homer Ocean Charters** is at Cannery Row boardwalk on Homer Spit Rd. Write P.O. Box 2543, Homer, AK 99603. Trips depart daily by appointment. Phone (907) 235-6212 or (800) 426-6212.

HOPE (C-10) pop. 137, elev. 32'

RECREATIONAL ACTIVITIES

White-water Rafting

- **Chugach Outdoor Center** departs from Milepost 7.5, Hope Hwy. Write P.O. Box 28, Hope, AK 99605. Other activities are offered. Trips depart daily at 9 and 2, May-Sept. Phone (907) 277-7238 or (866) 277-7238.

JUNEAU (G-10) pop. 30,711, elev. 12'

Juneau, Alaska's capital city, lies along the beautiful Gastineau Channel at the foot of snowcapped mounts Roberts and Juneau. The borough of Juneau covers 3,108 square miles of towering mountains, islands, saltwater bays, forested valleys and residential flatlands. Its road system extends from Thane, 6 miles southeast of downtown, northwest to Echo Cove at Milepost 40.2 on the Glacier Highway. The city is accessible by air or by sea.

When Joe Juneau and Richard Harris discovered gold in 1880, they started the first rush in American Alaska. At one time the Alaska-Juneau and Treadwell mines were producing about 20,000 tons of ore daily. Not until 1944, when the low price of gold and the high cost of extraction rendered it impractical, did mining operations cease.

The Alaska State Capitol, Fourth and Main streets, offers free 30-minute tours in summer. One block west of the capitol is the State Office Building, which contains a century-old totem pole and a Kimball Theatre pipe organ equipped with such accessories as a glockenspiel, sleigh bells and bird whistles. Free concerts are held Friday at noon in the eighth-floor atrium. Also on the eighth floor, a terrace affords panoramas of the harbor and the surrounding mountains.

Juneau

© 2007 NAVTEQ

To Mendenhall Glacier & Macaulay Salmon Hatchery

Tours of one of the oldest churches in southeastern Alaska are available mid-May to mid-September. Built in 1894, St. Nicholas Russian Orthodox Church is at Fifth and Gold streets. The Shrine of St. Therese, near Milepost 23 on the Glacier Highway, is a stone chapel on an island connected to shore by a gravel causeway.

There are many ways to tour Juneau. Nearby hiking trails, which vary in length and difficulty, lead to fishing spots, scenic mountain areas, old mine ruins and points near Mendenhall Glacier. Bus tours circle points of interest in Juneau and visit Mendenhall Glacier and the log Chapel-by-the-Lake at Auke Lake. Tours depart from the cruise ship docks during the summer. Visitors also can charter boats for sightseeing or fishing.

A good way to see the ice field is to take a charter flight. Companies that offer flightseeing tours from Juneau are Alaska Fly 'n' Fish Charters, (907) 790-2120; Alaska Seaplane Service, (907) 789-3331; L.A.B. Flying, (907) 789-9160; Ward Air, (907) 789-9150; and Wings of Alaska, (907) 789-0790. Helicopter tours, float trips, gold-panning excursions and several tours of nearby and more distant points of interest are available through Alaska Sightseeing,

(907) 586-6300; Gray Line of Alaska, (907) 586-3773; and Princess Tours, (907) 463-3900.

Salmon bakes are held in Salmon Creek and at Thane Ore House daily in summer.

Juneau Convention and Visitors Bureau: 101 Egan Dr., Juneau, AK 99801; phone (907) 586-2201 or (888) 581-2201. *See color ad p. 334.*

Self-guiding tours: Free walking tour maps of the historical and governmental districts are available at Juneau Visitor Information Center in Centennial Hall, 101 Egan Dr.

ALASKA STATE MUSEUM, w. of Egan Dr. at 395 Whittier St., chronicles the state's history and preserves and exhibits Tlingit and Athabascan Indian, Eskimo and Aleut culture. Wildlife and mining displays, Russian-American historical exhibits and art of Alaska are featured. Highlights include a bald eagle nesting tree.

Guided tours are available in summer. Allow 1 hour minimum. Daily 8:30-5:30, mid-May to mid-Sept.; Tues.-Sat. 10-4, rest of year. Closed Memorial Day, July 4 and Labor Day. Admission (mid-May to mid-Sept.) $5; free (ages 0-18). Admission (rest of year) $3; free (ages 0-18 and first Fri. of Oct.-Apr. 4-6:30). Phone (907) 465-2901.

DOLPHIN WHALE WATCH TOURS provides pick-up service from various downtown locations. Three-hour tours on a jet boat offer the opportunity to view humpback and killer whales, porpoises, sea lions, seals and eagles. Daily 7-7, May 1-Sept. 20. Fare $105; $84 (ages 2-12). AX, MC, VI. Phone (907) 463-3422.

ERA HELICOPTERS FLIGHTSEEING TOURS depart from the North Douglas Heliport. Narrated, 1-hour tours offer views of the capital city, abandoned mines and four glaciers in the Juneau Icefield. Highlights include a glacier landing to explore the blue ice. A 1.75-hour flight to visit dog sled camps near Anchorage also is available. Allow 2 hours minimum. Daily 8-6. Fare $229-$410. Flights require a minimum of four passengers. AX, DS, MC, VI. Phone (800) 843-1947.

FOREST SERVICE INFORMATION CENTER is at 8510 Mendenhall Loop Rd. Trail guides, maps, current conditions and recreation and cabin reservation information about Tongass National Forest and Glacier Bay National Park are available. Mon.-Fri. 8-5. Free. Phone (907) 586-8800.

GLACIER GARDENS RAINFOREST ADVENTURE is at 7600 Glacier Hwy. A motorized shuttle takes passengers up Thunder Mountain through botanical gardens nestled in a lush Alaskan rain forest. Guests travel past streams, ponds, waterfalls and such flora as rhododendrons, Japanese maples and ferns. A scenic overlook at the 580-foot marker offers a spectacular view of the Mendenhall Valley and Chilkat Mountains. Allow 1 hour minimum. Daily 9-6, May-Sept. Admission $21.95; $15.95 (ages 6-12). AX, MC, VI. Phone (907) 790-3377.

HOUSE OF WICKERSHAM, 213 Seventh St., was the residence of Judge James Wickersham, noted Alaskan statesman, historian and pioneer judge. Built 1898-99 on "Chicken Ridge," this large Victorian house offers panoramic views of Gastineau Channel. Wherever the judge traveled in Alaska he

collected ivory pieces, basketry and carvings, which are on display.

Thurs.-Tues. 10-noon and 1-5, mid-May to late Sept.; by appointment rest of year. Donations. Phone (907) 586-9001.

JUNEAU-DOUGLAS CITY MUSEUM is at Fourth and Main sts. Visitors can view exhibits about the area's early gold mining days, Tlingit culture and life in the Juneau-Douglas areas. Special exhibits about the greater Juneau area change annually. A relief map of the city's topography and a video presentation titled "Juneau: City Built on Gold" are other features. Free maps outlining a historic walking tour are available.

Mon.-Fri. 9-5, Sat.-Sun. 10-5, mid-May through Sept. 30; Tues.-Sat. 10-4 and by appointment, rest of year. Closed July 4 and winter holidays. Admission $4; free (ages 0-17). MC, VI. Phone (907) 586-3572.

MACAULAY SALMON HATCHERY, 2697 Channel Dr., hatches more than 122 million salmon eggs annually, including chum, coho and king. The hatchery features many exhibits and saltwater aquariums that contain live adult salmon and more than 100 species of southeast Alaska sea life. Guided tours are available. Allow 30 minutes minimum. Daily 8-5, May-Sept.; by appointment rest of year. Admission $3.25; $1.75 (ages 3-12). AX, MC, VI. Phone (907) 463-4810.

MENDENHALL GLACIER, 13 mi. n.w. via SR 7 and Mendenhall Loop Rd., is an impressive river of blue ice, 13 miles long and 1.5 miles wide at its widest point. The glacier is fed by the 1,500-square-mile Juneau Icefield, part of the Tongass National Forest *(see place listing p. 352).*

Trails on either side of the glacial valley afford scenic views. To the east are Mendenhall Lake and Nugget Creek Falls; the west trail ascends above the glacier. Camping and picnic facilities are available at Mendenhall Lake. An easily traversable .5-mile nature trail begins near the visitor center; brochures are available.

The Steep Creek viewing platform near the visitor center parking lot is a good vantage point from which to see spawning sockeye salmon mid-July through mid-September. The salmon run attracts bald eagles and black bears mid-September through November.

Mendenhall Glacier Visitor Center, at the end of Glacial Spur Rd., contains a model depicting glacier dynamics, dioramas and display cases that interpret five evolving ecosystems at the glacier and a naturalistic salmon-filled stream that tumbles over rocks. A film is shown three times every hour during the summer, otherwise by request. Interpretive talks and nature hikes also are offered. Daily 8-7:30, May-Sept.; Thurs.-Sun. 10-4, rest of year. Admission $3 (May-Sept.); free (ages 0-15 and rest of year). MC, VI. Phone (907) 789-0097 or (907) 789-6640.

MENDENHALL GLACIER TRANSPORT LTD., departing from the cruise ship dock downtown, provides sightseeing excursions of Juneau by bus. The tour stops at the Chapel by the Lake and Mendenhall Glacier. Other tours are available. Allow 2 hours, 30 minutes minimum. Daily 9-3:30, May-Sept. Fare $25. MC, VI. Phone (907) 789-5460. *See color ad.*

MOUNT ROBERTS TRAMWAY, 490 S. Franklin St. on the cruise ship dock, offers a 6-minute ride to the 1,800-foot level of Mount Roberts. At the top, visitors can stop at the nature center, see a live bald eagle displayed by the Juneau Raptor Center, take wildlife or nature walks and view the spectacular scenery. "Seeing Daylight," a movie about Alaska's native Tlingit, is presented in the Chilkat Theater. Food is available. Allow 1 hour, 30 minutes minimum. Daily 9-9, May 5-Sept. 25. Fare $24.95; $13.50 (ages 6-12). AX, CB, MC, VI. Phone (907) 463-3412 or (888) 461-8726.

TAKU GLACIER LODGE FLIGHTSEEING ADVENTURE departs from the wharf near the cruise ship docks. A floatplane takes passengers to a 1923 fishing and hunting lodge in the Taku River Valley for a salmon feast. Aerial views include mountains, Taku Inlet, waterfalls and five glaciers. Walking trails explore the area surrounding the historic lodge, which is across the river from the Hole-in-the-Wall Glacier. Allow 3 hours minimum. Trips depart daily at 9, 11, 1 and 3, May-Sept. Fare $210; $170 (ages 0-11). AX, MC, VI. Phone (907) 586-6275.

TRACY ARM FJORD GLACIER CRUISE departs the Goldbelt Tour Center Dock at 76 Egan Dr. The boat traverses iceberg-laden fjords that larger ships cannot. Visitors come in close proximity to glaciers, cliffs and cascading waterfalls. Food is available. Allow 8 hours minimum. Daily 8-5, May 17-Sept. 11. Fare $148; $102 (ages 3-12). Alaska residents $119; $70 (ages 3-12). AX, MC, VI. Phone (907) 586-8687 or (800) 820-2628.

RECREATIONAL ACTIVITIES

Fishing

- **Juneau Sportfishing** offers round-trip transportation from local hotels and ships. Write P.O. Box 20438, Juneau, AK 99802. Trips depart daily. Reservations are required. Phone (907) 586-1887.

- **Salmon Guaranteed Charters**, 4510 Prospect Way, Juneau, AK 99801. Daily May-Oct. Reservations are required. Phone (907) 364-3474.

Skiing

- **Eaglecrest Ski Area** is 12 mi. n.w. off the N. Douglas Hwy. Write 155 S. Seward St., Juneau,

Mountains of Ice

Glaciers—blue-white in color, with long frozen tongues reaching into the water—cover more than 75,000 square miles in the United States, and most are found in Alaska.

If you've explored the waters of the Inside Passage or Prince William Sound, you've certainly seen them.

But how is a glacier formed? Here are the basics: Glaciers are created when more snow falls each winter than melts the following summer. As areas receive snowfall year after year, new snow layers create pressure on existing layers of snow and ice. This creates firn, small granules of compacted snow. Firn from previous years is buried and turns to ice through crystallization. The process continues, increasing the pressure on the ice field until air diminishes, and solid crystalline ice is formed.

As the layers of snow, firn and ice thicken, the lower ice can no longer support the weight of the mass, and it moves downward, smoothing surrounding mountain walls and floors and leaving grooves in a U-shaped valley.

You may be wondering why glacial ice is blue. It's actually not. Glacial ice is so concentrated that it absorbs all colors in the light spectrum except blue, which is reflected back at the viewer—making the ice *appear* blue. The lack of oxygen in the ice causes it to melt much more slowly than ice created in your freezer.

Some of the more popular glaciers to visit are Columbia, Exit, Hubbard, LeConte, Mendenhall and Portage. But while you're gazing at these giant frozen wonders, keep in mind that almost 90 percent of an iceberg is below water!

AK 99801. Thurs.-Mon. 9-4, Dec.-Mar. (also Thurs. 4-9, early Jan. to mid-Mar.). Phone (907) 790-2000.

KATMAI NATIONAL PARK AND PRESERVE (G-4)

Elevations in the park and preserve range from sea level at the Shelikof Strait to 7,606 ft. at Mount Dennison. Refer to AAA maps for additional elevation information.

On the northern portion of the Alaska Peninsula, 4.1-million-acre Katmai National Park and Preserve displays an outstanding example of volcanism. In 1912 one of the greatest volcanic explosions in recorded history turned a nameless green valley into what became known as the Valley of Ten Thousand Smokes. For more than 45 years the eruption was attributed to Mount Katmai, but recent studies indicate that the source was a new volcanic vent called Novarupta, some 6 miles distant.

During or shortly after the eruption, the peak of Mount Katmai collapsed, forming a caldera that subsequently filled with water. Molten material released from Novarupta and surrounding vents flowed down the valley, and thousands of holes from which smoke and gases arose formed as gases and vaporized surface water percolated through the volcanic deposits. These fumaroles, which gave the valley its name, lasted only about 20 years.

Although nearly all of the "smokes" have died out, steam columns from nearby volcanoes sometimes can be seen. By air it is possible to see the jade-green lake in the crater of Mount Katmai and to circle over still-active mounts Trident, Mageik and Martin.

In addition to its superlative scenery—large lakes, rivers, glaciers and active volcanoes—the park is noted for its abundant wildlife. The most prominent mammal is the Alaskan brown bear, the world's largest carnivore, averaging 500 pounds with some reaching 1,200 pounds. It is recommended that visitors maintain at least 50 yards from individual bears and 100 yards from sows with young. Visitors also should make noises while walking or hiking.

Katmai National Park can be reached only by boat or plane. A boat ramp is at Lake Camp, 10 miles by dirt road from King Salmon. Commercial airlines serve King Salmon, 35 miles from Brooks Camp. Amphibious aircraft make daily scheduled flights between King Salmon and Brooks Camp. Bush planes can be chartered.

Daily 1-hour tours to the Valley of Ten Thousand Smokes begin at Brooks Camp. Fare $145. Departures require a minimum of 2 people. Other tours are available; for more information phone Katmailand, Inc., (800) 544-0551. *See Recreation Chart.*

KENAI (D-10) pop. 6,942, elev. 86'

Established as Fort St. Nicholas by Russian fur traders in 1791, Kenai (KEEN-eye) is one of the oldest permanent settlements in Alaska. Until 1953 the town grew under a squatters' rights policy. Kenai is the closest settlement to the south-central region's most promising oil-development fields and is the site of major petrochemical plants.

Kenai's Russian Orthodox Church, established in 1894, contains religious and art objects brought from Russia in 1841.

A popular, colorful pastime during the summer months in Kenai is berry picking. Such berries as Alaska blueberries (a smaller version of its common cousin), nagoonberries (reddish purple in color), cloudberries and salmonberries (both peach in color), crowberries (black in color), northern red currants, wild raspberries and cranberries grow on the peninsula.

Kenai Visitors and Convention Bureau: 11471 Kenai Spur Hwy., Kenai, AK 99611; phone (907) 283-1991.

KENAI NATIONAL WILDLIFE REFUGE— *see Soldotna p. 351.*

KENAI VISITORS & CULTURAL CENTER, 11471 Kenai Spur Hwy., offers visitor information as well as displays about Kenai's history and culture. Exhibit rooms showcase Dena'ina Athabascan art and artifacts, Russian relics and educational displays describing Alaskan wildlife. The center also hosts traveling and temporary exhibitions of photography, art, crafts, native culture and Alaska history throughout the year.

Allow 30 minutes minimum. Mon.-Fri. 9-7, Sat.-Sun. 10-6, mid-May to mid-Sept.; Mon.-Fri. 9-5, rest of year. Admission $3; free (ages 0-18). MC, VI. Phone (907) 283-1991.

KENAI FJORDS NATIONAL PARK (D-11)

Elevations in the park range from sea level at Nuka Bay to 6,400 ft. at a peak on the Harding Icefield. Refer to AAA maps for additional elevation information.

On the southeastern side of the Kenai Peninsula, Kenai Fjords National Park covers more than 600,000 acres. Access to the park is by private vehicle, plane or boat from Seward. Air charters also are available from other communities on the Kenai Peninsula. Scheduled bus service is available between Seward and Anchorage. Several tour companies offer trips to Exit Glacier and boat trips to the fjords.

The park encompasses a coastal mountain range that includes most of Harding Icefield, one of the four largest ice fields in the United States. A remnant of the ice age, it blankets all but the top of the Kenai Mountains. Along the coast is the rugged shoreline of the glacier-carved Kenai Fjords. Seals, porpoises, whales and sea otters are some of the 23 marine mammal species that inhabit the coastal waters.

Exit Glacier is the most accessible of the glaciers that flow from Harding Icefield. Three miles north of Seward via the Seward Highway and Exit Glacier Road, the glacier is reached by a .7-mile trail that begins at the Exit Glacier parking area. A strenuous 7-mile round-trip journey from the base of Exit Glacier to Harding Icefield departs from the visitor center at 9, July through August. Bald eagles, bears, moose, mountain goats and Stellar sea lions inhabit the area.

Picnicking and backcountry camping are permitted; a 12-site walk-in tent campground is available.

Hikes to the glacier and nature walks are conducted daily at Exit Glacier by park rangers on duty, Memorial Day through Labor Day. Winter activities at Exit Glacier include skiing, snowmobiling, snowshoeing and dog sledding. Boat and air charters provide access to the coast during the summer.

Both park headquarters and a visitor center are in Seward. Park headquarters is at 500 Adams St., Suite 103, and the visitor center is at 1212 4th Ave. next to the harbormaster's office. Slide shows, exhibits and information about ranger-conducted activities are available.

Headquarters and visitor center open daily 9-6, Memorial Day-Labor Day; Mon.-Fri. 8-5, rest of year. Admission to Exit Glacier is $5 per vehicle. For information write the Superintendent, Kenai Fjords National Park, P.O. Box 1727, Seward, AK 99664; phone (907) 224-7500 or (907) 224-2132 for mailing information. *See Recreation Chart.*

KETCHIKAN (I-11) pop. 7,922

Alaska's southernmost city sits on stilts at the base of the Tongass National Forest *(see place listing p. 352).* On Revillagigedo Island, separated from the mainland by Behm Canal, Ketchikan claims to be the salmon capital of the world. An average annual rainfall of 156 to 162 inches makes it the wettest community in North America. The city's economic base relies on fishing, canning, mineral exploration, tourism and logging and cold-storage operations.

The town is populated with native culture and contains the largest concentration of Tlingit (KLINK-it), Haida (HY-dah), and Tsimshian (SIMP-shee-ane) people in Alaska. This heritage can be seen in the many totem poles that populate the area. Totem poles—tall cedar logs carved with eagles, ravens, wolves, bears, whales and other figures—depict stories or designate clans or lineage, and Ketchikan is reputed to contain the most in the world.

Creek Street is a relic of Ketchikan's rough-and-tumble past. Built on stilts over Ketchikan Creek, the street was once the site of a thriving red-light district. Highlights include art galleries, shops and a museum. The creek is a spawning ground for salmon.

Gray Line of Alaska, (907) 225-6260, and Princess Tours, (800) 774-6237, are among the companies that offer tours of the city. Ketchikan Visitors Center can provide a more complete list. Charter aircraft, boats, rental cars, buses and taxis are available at the Ketchikan Visitors Bureau, the airport and the ferry terminal.

Southeast Alaska Discovery Center: 50 Main St., Ketchikan, AK 99901; phone (907) 228-6220 or TTY (907) 228-6237.

Self-guiding tours: Maps of a 2-hour walking tour of downtown are available at Ketchikan Visitors Bureau, 131 Front St., Ketchikan, AK 99901; phone (907) 225-6166 or (800) 770-3300.

Shopping areas: The Creek Street boardwalk area in downtown contains a number of specialty shops and boutiques.

CLASSIC TOURS picks up passengers at the downtown cruise ship dock or local accommodation. Up to five passengers may ride in a restored 1955 Chevy driven by a retired schoolteacher clad in a poodle skirt and saddle shoes. Narrated tours, which focus on the natural and cultural history of Ketchikan, include visits to Saxman Totem Pole Park, the Creek Street boardwalk area, a bald eagle's nest and a king salmon site (in season). Wildlife viewing is possible. Private tours can be arranged.

Daily 8-6, early May-Sept. 30. Fare $99 (3-hour tour); $84 (2-hour tour). Fare includes admission to area museums and parks. Reservations are recommended. Phone (907) 225-3091.

DEER MOUNTAIN TRIBAL HATCHERY AND EAGLE CENTER, .5 mi. n.e. at 1158 Salmon Rd. across the bridge from the Totem Heritage Center, raises king (chinook) and coho (silver) salmon, and steelhead and rainbow trout. Bald eagles also are featured in a landscaped enclosure. Allow 30 minutes minimum. Daily 8-4:30, May-Sept. Guided tour $9; free (ages 0-12). MC, VI. Phone (907) 228-5530.

SAXMAN NATIVE VILLAGE, 2.5 mi. s. on S. Tongass Hwy., is a Tlingit (KLINK-it) Indian village of about 350 residents. The totem park contains 30 totem poles, and master carvers can be seen at work in the carving center. Other highlights include the Beaver Tribal House and the Old School House. Tickets for Cape Fox Dancers performances can be purchased at the village store.

Guided tours are available. Allow 30 minutes minimum. Daily 8-5, mid-May through Sept. 30; hours vary rest of year. Cape Fox Dancers performance schedule varies; phone ahead. Free. Tour fee $35; $17.50 (ages 0-11). MC, VI. Phone (907) 225-4846, ext. 100.

TONGASS HISTORICAL MUSEUM, 629 Dock St. in Ketchikan's Centennial Building, displays pioneer items as well as art and artifacts from northwest cultures. Historical and changing exhibits are offered. Allow 30 minutes minimum. Daily 8-5, early May-Sept. 30; Wed.-Fri. 1-5, Sat.-Sun. 1-4, rest of year. Closed winter holidays. Admission $2. Phone (907) 225-5600.

TOTEM BIGHT STATE HISTORIC PARK, 10 mi. n. on N. Tongass Hwy., displays 14 poles by Haida and Tlingit clans and a model of a Tlingit clan house. The site is reached by a short trail through a forest from the parking area. A brochure describes typical totem characters and gives insight to the art of totem carving. More totem poles are in Saxman Native Village, 2.5 miles south on S. Tongass Highway. Allow 30 minutes minimum. Daily 6 a.m.-10 p.m. Donations. Phone (907) 247-8574.

TOTEM HERITAGE CENTER, 601 Deermount St., displays original 19th-century totem poles retrieved from native villages and emphasizes traditional Tlingit, Haida and Tsimshian art. Guided tours are available. Allow 30 minutes minimum. Daily 8-5, mid-May through Sept. 30; Mon.-Fri. 1-5 and during classes, rest of year. Closed winter holidays. Admission $5 (mid-May through Sept. 30); free (rest of year). Phone (907) 225-5900.

KLONDIKE GOLD RUSH NATIONAL HISTORICAL PARK—*see Skagway p. 350.*

KOBUK VALLEY NATIONAL PARK (C-5)

Elevations in the park range from 100 ft. at the point where the Kobuk River flows out of the southwest corner of the park to 4,700 ft. in the Brooks Range, which forms the park's northern border. Refer to AAA maps for additional elevation information.

Some 25 miles north of the Arctic Circle, Kobuk Valley National Park covers 1,710,000 acres in the heart of the arctic wildlands, where the boreal forest gives way to the frozen tundra. The broad Kobuk Valley is enclosed almost completely by the Baird Mountains to the north and the Waring Mountains to the south. Traversing the valley from east to west, the wide and placid Kobuk River offers good fishing and idyllic float trips. The swifter Salmon River, a designated Wild and Scenic River, flows south from the Baird Mountains.

Preserved within the park are the 25-square-mile Great Kobuk Sand Dunes, the largest active dunes in the Arctic. Created by the grinding action of ancient glaciers, the sand was carried by wind and water to a wide area south of the Kobuk River. The 100-foot dunes are accessible by a difficult hike from the river along Kavet Creek.

Home to seminomadic tribes for more than 12,500 years, the region still supports the native Inupiats; they are granted by law the right to continue subsistence hunting, trapping and other practices. Important to their survival is North America's largest caribou herd, numbering some 500,000. Many can be seen crossing the Kobuk River in September during their migration southward.

Other wildlife common to the region include moose, grizzly and black bears, wolves, red foxes, lynxes, wolverines and martens. Golden eagles can be seen in the northern latitudes; other birds include sandhill cranes, arctic loons, American golden plovers and arctic terns.

The park attracts experienced backpackers, campers and river travelers. Though the park is open year-round, the elements limit most visits to June through September. Fishing is good when the rivers are clear of silt; catches include salmon, pike, arctic char, whitefish and grayling. An Alaska fishing license is required. Hunting is not permitted, but it is legal to carry a firearm for protection from bears.

Access to the region is by daily commercial flights from Anchorage and Fairbanks to Kotzebue (*see place listing p. 340*), where connections to the villages of Kiana and Ambler can be made. Air taxi service into the park is available from Kotzebue, Kiana and Ambler. There are no facilities, services, trails or campgrounds in the park; a ranger station near Onion Portage is open June through September. The park headquarters in Kotzebue is open late May through September.

Due to its location, the area is subject to harsh weather and high winds. It is advisable to carry protection against hypothermia, mosquitoes and biting flies.

For trip planning assistance and a list of authorized outfitters, guides and air taxi operators, write the Superintendent, Western Arctic National Parklands, P.O. Box 1029, Kotzebue, AK 99752; phone (907) 442-3760 or (907) 442-3890. *See Recreation Chart.*

KODIAK (H-5) pop. 6,334

A Russian explorer-trader's quest for sea otter pelts led to the European settlement of Kodiak Island in 1784. The community of Kodiak was established about 1792 when Alexander Baranov moved his headquarters from the original 1784 settlement at Three Saints Bay, making Kodiak the first capital of Russian America. The blue, onion-shaped domes of the Holy Resurrection Russian Orthodox Church recall the days when the Russian Empire in the North Pacific was administered from Kodiak.

One of the oldest communities in Alaska, Kodiak also is a leading commercial fishing port. The town is on the northeastern tip of Kodiak Island, which is home to the Kodiak brown bear.

Kodiak was nearly destroyed twice; in June 1912, an eruption from Mount Novarupta covered the town with ash. On Good Friday in 1964 an earthquake in south central Alaska created tsunamis that enveloped the islands. Citizens found refuge on nearby Pillar Mountain and returned with the task of rebuilding the city.

Kodiak can be reached by air service from Anchorage or by the Alaska Marine Highway, a passenger/vehicle ferry, from Homer and Seward. Reservations are required well in advance for the ferry; write Alaska Marine Highway, P.O. Box 703, Kodiak, AK 99615, or phone (907) 486-3800 or (800) 526-6731.

Kodiak Island Convention and Visitors Bureau: 100-AAA Marine Way, Suite 200, Kodiak, AK 99615; phone (907) 486-4782 or (800) 789-4782.

BARANOV MUSEUM, in the Erskine House on the harbor front, has collections of early Russian and Alaskan artifacts as well as American household furnishings from the early 20th century. The building, which dates from 1808, was used by Alexander Baranov as a warehouse for storing furs. Original log construction methods can be examined inside. Allow 1 hour minimum. Mon.-Sat. 10-4, Sun. noon-4, Memorial Day-Labor Day; Tues.-Sat. 10-3, rest of year. Closed major holidays. Admission $3; free (ages 0-11). AX, DS, MC, VI. Phone (907) 486-5920.

FORT ABERCROMBIE STATE HISTORICAL PARK, 4.5 mi. n.e. on Miller Point, is a World War II fortification. The 183-acre park offers a view of the rocky coastline and nearby islands. Interpretive programs are given, and hiking trails are available. World War II artifacts remain; the visitor center offers natural-history displays and information about Alaska's participation in World War II. Tidal pools are within walking distance of the visitor center.

Picnicking is permitted. Daily 24 hours. Free. Phone (907) 486-6339. *See Recreation Chart and the AAA Western Canada & Alaska CampBook.*

KODIAK ALUTIIQ DANCERS perform at 312 W. Marine Way. Traditional Alutiiq dances are performed by elaborately costumed dancers, who express cultural and spiritual values that have survived for thousands of years. Narration is provided. Allow 30 minutes minimum. Performances daily at 10, June-Sept.; by appointment rest of year. Times may vary; phone ahead. Closed legal holidays. Admission $12; $10 (ages 55+); $7 (ages 0-8). Reservations are recommended. Phone (907) 486-4449.

KODIAK NATIONAL WILDLIFE REFUGE occupies the southwestern two-thirds of Kodiak Island and 50,000 acres on Ban Island and the northwestern tip of Afognak Island. The 1,865,000 acres were set aside to preserve the habitat of the Kodiak bear, some of which weigh up to 1,500 pounds. Among other inhabitants are Sitka black-tailed deer, sea lions, sea otters and bald eagles. The refuge is accessible only by plane and boat. Cabins and a number of recreational activities are available. Phone (907) 487-2600 or (888) 408-3514.

Visitor Center, .2 mi. n. of the state airport, offers displays, videotapes, audiovisual presentations and information about the refuge. Allow 1 hour minimum. Mon.-Fri. 8-4:30, Sat.-Sun. noon-4; closed holidays.

KODIAK TOURS depart from the lobby of the Kodiak Inn. Narrated historic tours of the island are tailored to the interests of the visitor. The U.S. Coast Guard Base, Cannery Row, boat harbors, Fisheries Research Center and Pillar Mountain are among the sites. The tour stops to view the island's wildlife and scenery. Half-day tours last 4 hours, while full-day tours last 8 hours.

Inquire about weather policies. Full-day tours depart daily at 9. Half-day tours depart daily at 9 and 1. Full-day fare (includes all attraction admission fees) $90. Half-day fare $50. Reservations are required. MC, VI. Phone (907) 486-3920.

KOTZEBUE (C-3) pop. 3,082, elev. 20'

Kotzebue, on the Baldwin Peninsula, sits on glacial moraine on the eastern edge of Kotzebue Sound. It was named after Otto Von Kotzebue, a German sailor exploring for Russia around 1818. Inhabited by the Kikiktagruk Inupiat Eskimos since the early 19th century, the area later became a seasonal trading center for the various Eskimo tribes due to its position at the confluence of the Noatak and Kobuk rivers. Its establishment as a permanent city began in 1899 with a Quaker mission.

Kotzebue is situated 33 miles above the Arctic Circle in the treeless tundra; the sun rises each year in early June and remains above the horizon for only 38 days. A spectacular ice breakup takes place for 2 weeks between mid-May and mid-June.

The second-largest Eskimo village in Alaska, Kotzebue is reached only by daily air service from Anchorage, Nome and Fairbanks. Arrangements for bush plane flights over the surrounding tundra and to the Kobuk River for hunting and fishing expeditions can be made at the airport. Short air and boat excursions to most of the surrounding villages also are available through independent operators. Nana Museum of the Arctic, near the airport, offers a slide show and a tour.

LAKE CLARK NATIONAL PARK AND PRESERVE (F-5)

Elevations in the park and preserve range from sea level along Cook Inlet to 10,197 ft. at Mount Redoubt. Refer to AAA maps for additional elevation information.

West of Cook Inlet, Lake Clark National Park and Preserve is an almost 4-million-acre mountainous crossroads where ice and fire meet. The Pacific crust grinds beneath the North American plate, creating the Chigmit Mountains, a jagged array of spires and two steaming volcanoes, Mount Redoubt and Mount Iliamna. Mount Redoubt, the more active, last erupted in December 1989; it continues to emit steam and, less frequently, ash.

Covered by massive ice fields, the seemingly impenetrable Chigmit Mountains are formed by the linkage of two great ranges, the Alaska and the Aleutian. Together the ranges divide the park into distinct areas: the eastern flank's coastal plain bordering Cook Inlet and the lake and tundra region on the western flank. Lake Clark, 50 miles long, juts in from the southwest.

Moisture abounds along the park's coastal area, which is characterized by rocky cliffs along its southern portion, giving way to tidal marshes and grasslands in the north. In contrast to the luxuriant alder thickets and Sitka spruce along Cook Inlet, lakes, boreal forests and rolling tundra highlands distinguish the park's western landscape.

Numerous glacier-fed rivers and creeks are channeled through Lake Clark, creating one of the richest sockeye salmon spawning grounds in the world.

The park was created primarily to protect this fruitful breeding area.

Although the park is open all year, most people visit during the peak of the summer season, late June through August. Even in summer months, weather conditions vary in the interior; it is advisable to bring protection against insects as well as clothing for sunny, wet or freezing weather. Visitors should outfit themselves in Kenai, Homer or Anchorage, as the communities closer to the park have limited supplies.

For anglers the rivers and lakes on the park's western side provide a variety of trophy-size fish, including salmon, arctic grayling and trout. A 2- to 3-mile trail to Tanalian Falls and Kontrashibuna Lake is accessible from Port Alsworth, near Lake Clark. The open foothills are ideal for backpacking. River-running also is popular on the Mulchatna, Tlikakila and Chilikadrotna rivers, all federally designated wild and scenic rivers.

As there are no roads in the park, access is almost exclusively by air. Most travelers charter aircraft; the closest airport is south of the park in Iliamna. A 1- to 2-hour flight from Anchorage, Homer or Kenai will provide access to most points within the park and preserve.

The National Park Service facility is at Port Alsworth and contains a visitor center with displays regarding natural history topics. While there are minimal National Park facilities—staffed patrol cabins at Telaquana Lake, Twin Lakes, Crescent Lake and Chinitna Bay—there are a number of private lodges and cabins in the park.

For information about accommodations as well as a list of outfitters and maps, write the Superintendent, Lake Clark National Park and Preserve, 4230 University Dr., Suite 311, Anchorage, AK 99508; phone (907) 644-3626. *See Recreation Chart.*

MISTY FIORDS NATIONAL MONUMENT (H-12)

East of Ketchikan and within the Tongass National Forest *(see place listing p. 352)*, Misty Fiords National Monument covers about 3,580 square miles of wilderness. The area is accessible by float plane from Ketchikan and other communities near the national forest. An information center and cruises to the monument are available in Ketchikan *(see place listing p. 338)*.

Behm Canal, a deep inlet of the Pacific Ocean, leads to the interior of the monument, where rock walls that rise 3,000 feet surround Walker Cove and Rudyerd Bay. Geological features include mineral springs, 237-foot-tall New Eddystone Rock, 3,150-foot-tall Punchbowl Face, lava flows, five major rivers and hundreds of small streams. The region receives more than 120 inches of precipitation each year. Bald eagles, brown and black bears, wolves and mountain goats inhabit the area; whales, porpoises, seals and sea lions can be sighted in Behm Canal or in the ocean nearby.

Stories in Cedar

The art of totem pole carving in Alaska originated with the Tlingit, Haida and Tsimshian native tribes. Abundant food supplies along the Inside Passage allowed the natives the leisure time necessary to develop their elaborate craft.

Cedar totem poles served many purposes. Each figure on the pole represented an element in a story, and together the figures recorded the legends and histories of the

tribes, who have no written language.

Genealogy poles, erected in front of an owner's house, identified a clan, told a family story or conveyed the family's status. Crests (usually in the shapes of eagles or ravens) denoted the clans of the husband and wife. Mortuary poles included a compartment for the ashes of a deceased clan member or chief and were carved in honor of that individual. Shame poles were created to chastise someone who wronged the clan or village—the pole remained standing until the debt was repaid tenfold. Other totem poles conveyed mythological or legendary stories, or commemorated a notable event, such as a birth or a good deed.

Colors were limited to natural pigments made from salmon eggs or hematite. Black was the primary color; red was used for secondary elements; and blue-green was used for highlighting.

An intimate knowledge of native traditions is necessary to fully interpret the totem poles, but there are common figures that are relatively easy to identify: the raven, a symbol of the creator, who changes form at will; the eagle, representing peace and friendship; the killer whale, a symbol of strength; and the beaver, bear and wolf.

Recreational activities include backpacking, picnicking, birdwatching, hunting, fishing and crabbing. Rustic cabins are available for $25-$45 per day; reservations may be made by calling Reserve America, (877) 444-6777. For further information contact the Southeast Alaska Discovery Center, 50 Main St., Ketchikan, AK 99901; phone (907) 228-6220.

NOME (D-2) pop. 3,505, elev. 13′

Placer gold washed from the hillsides to the beaches at Nome lured thousands to the remote shores of the Bering Sea in 1898. At the height of the gold rush, 20,000 people lived in Nome, once the largest settlement in Alaska.

On the Seward Peninsula, Nome is the judicial and commercial center of northwestern Alaska and the main supply point for nearby mining districts and Eskimo villages. The city is accessible daily by plane from Anchorage. Regularly scheduled and charter flights are available to various Eskimo villages.

Cruise ships serve Nome during the summer, and rental cars provide visitors with opportunities for self-guiding trips to nearby villages.

When a diphtheria epidemic threatened the town in 1925, the necessary serum was delivered by dog team. The annual Iditarod Trail Race commemorates this emergency mission. The race, which begins in Anchorage *(see place listing p. 311)* in early March, encompasses treacherous climbs, river passages and bone-chilling blizzards. Mushers cross the finish line in Nome after traveling roughly 1,100 miles, exhausted but invigorated by cheers from supporters lining the chute on Front Street.

One of the activities during the final week of the race is the Bering Sea Ice Classic, a six-hole golf tournament played on frozen Norton Sound.

The Midnight Sun Festival celebrates the summer solstice, the longest day of the year with almost 24 hours of sunlight. The mid-June festival lasts several days and includes a parade and The Nome River Raft Race.

Nome Convention and Visitors Bureau: P.O. Box 240-AAA, Nome, AK 99762; phone (907) 443-6624.

CARRIE M. McLAIN MEMORIAL MUSEUM is at 223 Front St. The museum showcases the history of the Nome gold rush, the lifestyles of Bering Strait Eskimos and the early days of sled dog racing. Daily 9:30-5:30, June-Sept.; Tues.-Sat. noon-6, rest of year. Closed holidays. Hours may vary; phone ahead. Donations. Phone (907) 443-6630.

PALMER (C-11) pop. 4,533, elev. 240′

The peaks of the Chugach and Talkeetna mountains rise above Palmer, a city surrounded by the lush pastures and dairy and vegetable farms of the fertile Matanuska Valley, where cabbages can grow to weigh more than 70 pounds. A drive to Wasilla *(see place listing p. 355)* provides a good view of the valley and its farms. The Matanuska Agricultural Experimental Farm, 7 miles southwest, welcomes visitors.

Palmer lies near the intersection of the Glenn and George Parks highways (SRs 1 and 3), both of which are scenic highways. An interesting drive is along a narrow, rough, winding road that follows Willow Creek through formerly rich gold areas. The road crosses Hatcher Pass en route to Willow.

The Palmer Visitor and Information Center, 723 S. Valley Way, contains a historical museum featuring items from the city's pioneer era. The 2-acre Agricultural Showcase Garden is on the center's grounds and features a variety of perennials; phone (907) 745-2880.

Mat-Su Convention & Visitors Bureau: Milepost 35.5, Parks Hwy., 7744 E. Visitors View Ct., Palmer, AK 99645; phone (907) 746-5000.

Self-guiding tours: Brochures describing a walking tour of downtown Palmer are available at the Visitor and Information Center.

INDEPENDENCE MINE STATE HISTORICAL PARK, 19 mi. n. on Hatcher Pass Rd., is a 761-acre park in the 221,000-acre Hatcher Pass region. The park preserves 15 buildings and numerous artifacts from its heyday as a gold boom town in the 1930s and 1940s. The history of the mine is chronicled in a museum and at the visitor center. Walking trails

lead visitors past many of the mine camp's buildings, including bunkhouses, warehouses, the com-
missary and mess halls.

Guided tours are available. Park open daily. Visitor center open daily 10-7, June 15-Labor Day; Sat.-
Sun. 11-7, day after Labor Day-Sept. 15. Tours are
given Mon.-Fri. at 1 and 3, Sat.-Sun. at 1, 3 and
4:30, second week of June-Labor Day. Admission
$5 per private vehicle. Tour fee $5. Phone (907)
745-2827 or (907) 745-3975.

MUSK OX FARM, 2 mi. n. at Milepost 50 on Glenn
Hwy., is said to be the only musk ox domestication
project in the world. The shaggy creatures are valued for their fine underwool called "qiviut." Eskimos knit the hair, eight times warmer by weight
than wool, into hats and scarves. Hands-on exhibits
are available. Guided tours offer insight into the animal's history and behavior and allow observation
from fenced walkways.

Picnicking is permitted. Daily 10-6, mid-May to
late Sept. Admission $8; $7 (ages 66+ and military
with ID); $6 (ages 5-12). MC, VI. Phone (907)
745-4151.

PETERSBURG (H-10) pop. 3,224, elev. 28´

Petersburg, at the north end of Mitkof Island, is
an Alaska Marine Highway port. In 1897 Norwegian
Peter Buschmann decided to build a cannery on
Mitkof Island at the head of picturesque Wrangell
Narrows. The facility at the north end of Nordic
Drive was completed in 1900 and packed 32,750
cases of salmon during its first production year.
Now Petersburg Fisheries, the firm is a pioneer in
Alaska's expanding bottom-fishing and salmon
industries.

Nicknamed "Little Norway," Petersburg boasts
brightly painted wooden houses decorated with
hand-painted floral designs, a traditional craft called
rosemaling.

Among the nearby points of interest is LeConte
Glacier, the southernmost of its kind in the northern
hemisphere; just south of Petersburg; it can be
reached via chartered plane, helicopter or boat. In
nearby Frederick Sound whale-watching is popular;
the area is home to orca and humpback whales as
well as other sea mammals.

Petersburg Visitor Information Center: First
and Fram sts., P.O. Box 649, Petersburg, AK 99833;
phone (907) 772-4636 or (866) 484-4700.

CLAUSEN MEMORIAL MUSEUM, 203 Fram St.,
features exhibits about commercial fishing and canning, a dugout Tlingit Indian canoe, tools and artifacts. A "Fisk" fountain and a 126.5-pound king
salmon, said to be a world record catch, also are on
display. Guided tours are available. Mon.-Fri. 10-5,
May 1-Sept. 6; Sat. 10-5, rest of year. Closed holidays. Winter hours may vary; phone ahead. Admission $3; free (ages 0-11). MC, VI. Phone (907)
772-3598.

The Last Great Race

To commemorate the 1925 event in
which 20 mushers relayed serum to
Nome to save children who contracted
diphtheria, the first Iditarod Race took
place on Mar. 3, 1973.

Beginning in Anchorage and culminating in Nome, the race trail covers some
1,000 miles of rugged terrain, takes between 9-17 days to complete and can
reach temperatures of minus 60 F.

In preparation for the great race,
the trail is broken and marked with

© PhotoDisc

reflector
tape, and
checkpoints
are chosen
where
teams stop
to eat and
rest. Since
it's not fea-
sible for
mushers to
carry all of
their provi-
sions in
their sleds, the bulk of food and supplies is shipped to the checkpoints
prior to the race.

To aid in endurance, dogs ingest
5,000 calories or more each day, gob-
bling such delicacies as moose, caribou
or even seal meat. Concern for the
dogs' health is strong: Booties are
worn for paw protection, and about
25 veterinarians man the checkpoints
to examine each dog.

While teams may begin the race
with as many as 16 dogs, some drop
from the race. "Dropped dogs"—dogs
that do not finish the race due to de-
hydration, flu or fatigue—are carried
to the nearest checkpoint and flown
back to Anchorage. A musher must
finish the race with at least five dogs.

Teams travel at night as well as during the day, and dogs rest about 10-12
hours per 24-hour period. But mushers
don't enjoy that luxury: Responsible
for feeding and caring for the dogs
(including changing their booties every
100 miles), they rarely sleep more than
2 hours per night.

The goal? Nome's Burled Arch on
Front Street. At this finish line, teams
are greeted by cheering crowds and
the sounding of the city's fire siren.

SEWARD (D-11) pop. 2,830, elev. 70'

Named for William H. Seward, who negotiated the purchase of Alaska, Seward is an ice-free port in a setting of great beauty. At the northeast end of a bay named Resurrection by Russians who arrived in its waters on Easter, the city is surrounded by lush, tall mountains and ice fields.

Charter boats and planes can be hired for fishing, hunting and sightseeing trips. Seward is the southern terminus of the Seward Highway, a national scenic byway extending north to Anchorage through an alpine terrain of glaciers and lakes. Seward also is the main access point to Kenai Fjords National Park

(see place listing p. 337), which includes Exit Glacier, one of the few accessible glaciers.

Seward Community Library, 238 5th Ave., shows movies and slides of the havoc wreaked by the 1964 Good Friday earthquake. Phone (907) 224-4082 for information and reservations.

Seward Chamber of Commerce: P.O. Box 749, Seward, AK 99664; phone (907) 224-8051. *See color ad.*

Self-guiding tours: Guides containing information about a walking tour are available at the chamber of commerce's visitor information center, 2001 Seward Hwy.; phone (907) 224-8051 for details.

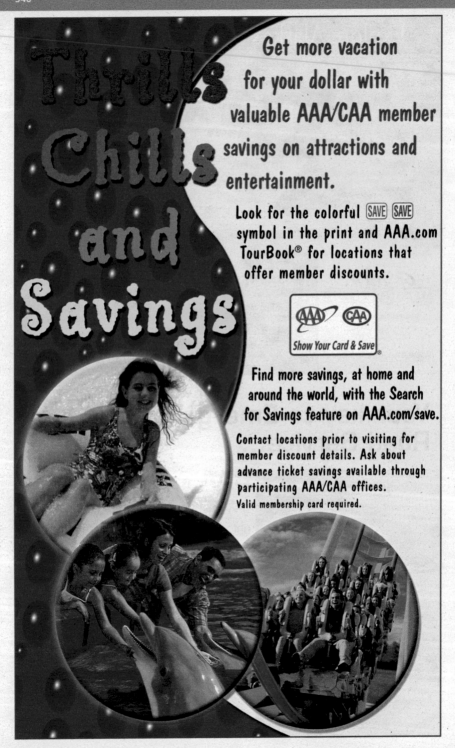

ALASKA SEALIFE CENTER, on Seward Hwy. (SR 9) at Milepost 0, is dedicated to understanding and maintaining the integrity of Alaska's marine ecosystem through research, rehabilitation, conservation and public education. Highlights include Steller sea lions, harbor seals, Giant Pacific octopus and a sea bird habitat that allows visitors to get up close to puffins, kittiwakes and other Alaskan avian wonders.

Exhibits also include a jellyfish display, the hands-on Discovery touch pool and the Lifecycles of Pacific Salmon, which examines the life stages of all five species of Pacific Salmon. More than 300 of the fish may be observed in 2,200- to 6,000-gallon tanks.

Guided behind-the-scenes tours are available, including octopus and puffin encounters. Reservations for behind-the-scenes and encounter tours are recommended. Allow 1 hour, 30 minutes minimum. Daily 8-7, Apr. 15-Sept. 15; 10-5, rest of year. Closed Thanksgiving and Dec. 25. Admission $15; $12 (ages 7-12). Inquire about pricing for tours. AX, DS, MC, VI. Phone (907) 224-6300 or (800) 224-2525, or (888) 378-2525 for reservations. *See color ad p. 344.*

GODWIN GLACIER DOG SLED TOURS offers excursions departing from the Seward Airport off Seward Hwy. Beginning with a helicopter flight to Godwin Glacier, the guided tour includes a 2.5-mile dog sled ride traversing the glacier's ancient snowfield. During the round-trip flight, passengers may spot mountain goats, bears, moose and eagles. Allow 2 hours minimum. Mon.-Sat. 8-6, May 20 to late Aug. (weather permitting). Fare $430; $390 (ages 0-12). MC, VI. Phone (907) 224-8239 or (888) 989-8239.

IDIDARIDE SLED DOG TOURS is off Seward Hwy. (SR 9) Milepost 3.6, 1 mi. w. on Exit Glacier Rd., .4 mi. n. on Old Exit Glacier Rd. (gravel road) following signs. An Iditarod champion offers a summer version of a sled dog ride aboard a wheeled sled during a 2-mile trip through Box Canyon. Visitors can tour the dog kennel to socialize with the husky puppies and witness a sled dog training demonstration.

Allow 1 hour, 30 minutes minimum. Daily 8-8, May-Sept. Fare $49; $24 (ages 2-11). Fare may vary; phone ahead. MC, VI. Phone (907) 224-8607 or (800) 478-3139.

KENAI FJORDS TOURS depart from the Seward Small Boat Harbor. The company offers glacier and wildlife cruises into the waters that surround Kenai Fjords National Park. Cruises also explore Resurrection Bay and the northwestern fjords, where active tidewater glaciers are a highlight. A variety of marine mammals can be seen; gray whales often are spotted on whale-watching tours. Six-hour Kenai Fjords National Park tours; 9.5-hour Northwestern Fjords tours; 3-hour Resurrection Bay wildlife tours and Fox Island Salmon Bake cruises, which last 4, 5 or 8.5 hours, are available.

Inquire about weather policies. Tours depart daily, late Mar.-Oct. 31. Kenai Fjords National Park tours depart at 8, 11:30 and 3. Northwestern Fjords tours depart at 9. Resurrection Bay wildlife tours depart at 2:30. Fox Island Salmon Bake cruises depart at noon, 10 and 5:30. Park tour $115; $57.50 (ages 0-11). Fjord tour $149; $74.50 (ages 0-11). Bay tour $59; $29.50 (ages 0-11). Salmon bake cruise $79; $39.50 (ages 0-11). Reservations are recommended. AX, DS, MC, VI. Phone (907) 224-8068 or (800) 478-8068. *See color ad & p. 311.*

MAJOR MARINE TOURS depart from the Seward Small Boat Harbor, 1 blk. e. of Seward Hwy. Narrated glacier and wildlife sightseeing cruises visit Kenai Fjords National Park. Passengers may spot bald eagles, otters, porpoises, puffins, sea lions and whales.

Food is available. Inquire about weather policies. Cruises depart daily, early May to late Sept. Half-day cruise departs at 12:30 (also at 6:15, mid-June to mid-Aug.), full-day cruise departs at 11:45. Half-day fare $44-$54; $22-$27 (ages 2-11). Full-day fare $125; $62 (ages 0-11). AX, DS, MC, VI. Phone (907) 274-7300 or (800) 764-7300. *See color ad p. 314 & p. 345.*

SAVE **RENOWN TOURS** depart from the Seward Small Boat Harbor. Six-hour catamaran cruises into Kenai Fjords National Park and 3-hour Resurrection Bay cruises are guided by local, experienced captains. In addition to glaciers, humpback whales, orcas, sea otters, Stellar sea lions, Dall's porpoises, bald eagles and puffins can be spotted.

National park cruise departs daily at 11:30, May-Sept. Resurrection Bay cruise departs daily at noon and 3:30, Mar.-Sept. Check-in is 30 minutes before departure. National park cruise $129; $65 (ages 0-12). Resurrection Bay cruise $69; $35 (ages 0-12). Reservations are recommended. AX, DS, MC, VI. Phone (907) 224-3806 or (888) 514-8687. *See color ad & p. 313.*

SAVE **SCENIC MOUNTAIN AIR (FLIGHTSEEING)** operates wheeled planes from Seward Airport and float planes from Trail Lake in Moose Pass. Sights on the varied tours include Harding Icefield, Kenai Fjords and wildlife. Fly-in fishing tours also are available. Flights depart daily 8 a.m.-7 p.m., May 1-Sept. 15 (weather permitting). Fares $100-$320, depending on length of tour. DS, MC, VI. Phone (907) 288-3646.

SEWARD MUSEUM, 336 Third Ave., is operated by the Resurrection Bay Historical Society and has exhibits about the main events in Seward's history. A collection of native baskets and ivory carvings is displayed. Daily 10-5, Memorial Day-Labor Day; otherwise varies. Admission $3; 50c (ages 5-18). Phone (907) 224-3902.

RECREATIONAL ACTIVITIES
Kayaking

• **Sunny Cove Sea Kayaking** offers tours departing 2 mi. from downtown at Lowell's Point on Resurrection Bay, and Fox Island. Write P.O. Box 3332, Seward, AK 99664. Other activities are offered. Daily 7:30-7:30, May-Sept.; by appointment, rest of year. Closed winter holidays. Phone (907) 224-8810, or (800) 770-9119 for reservations.

SITKA (H-10) pop. 8,835

Surrounded by high peaks and small wooded islands, historic Sitka is accessible by air or the Alaska Marine Highway.

In 1804 Russians led by Alexander Baranov established a settlement on the site of an ancient Tlingit (KLINK-it) village; that settlement became the capital of Russian America. Originally named New Archangel, it was a thriving port of nearly 3,000 when San Francisco was just a mission village. Castle Hill marks the site of Baranov's headquarters and commemorates the 1867 ceremony that transferred ownership of Alaska from Russia to the United States. St. Michael's Cathedral, a restored Russian church with an onion-shaped dome, contains a collection of religious icons and artwork.

The colorfully costumed New Archangel Dancers perform Russian dances in the Harrigan Centennial Hall auditorium during summer when large ships are in port. Performances by the Sheet'ka Kwaan Naa Kahadi Native Dancers are given at the Tribal Community House on Katlian Street.

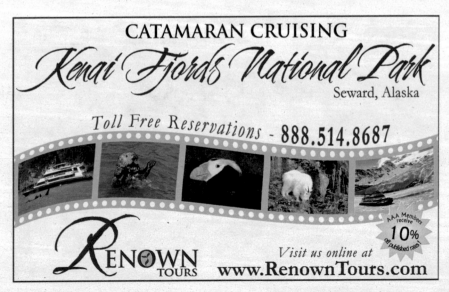

For cruise ship and ferry passengers, Sitka Tours offers a short bus tour of Sitka, which includes guide service and round-trip transportation from the port. Boat tours to view wildlife and the surrounding area also are available.

Sitka Convention and Visitors Bureau: Dept. A, Box 1226, Sitka, AK 99835; phone (907) 747-5940.

 ALASKA RAPTOR CENTER, .8 mi. e. of Lake St. at 1000 Raptor Way, is home to 25 "raptors in residence," including bald and golden eagles, hawks, falcons and owls. The 17-acre rehabilitation center, surrounded by muskeg, mountains and the Indian River, provides medical treatment to more than 100 eagles and other birds of prey each year. A stage presentation, a videotape, live demonstrations of birds in flight training and a .25-mile nature trail are available.

Raptors unable to be released into the wild help educate visitors and travel to schools nationwide to raise awareness of wild birds and their habitats. Feathers, bones, photographs and a national map indicating where birds have been released are displayed. Visitors can view raptors in their natural habitats outside the center as well as in the clinic's treatment room and recuperation areas.

Guide tours are available. Allow 1 hour, 30 minutes minimum. Daily 8-4, May-Sept. Admission $12; $6 (ages 0-11). AX, DS, MC, VI. Phone (907) 747-8662 or (800) 643-9425.

ISABEL MILLER MUSEUM is in Harrigan Centennial Building. The museum features exhibits depicting the history of Sitka, including the area's earliest inhabitants and the legacy of World War II. Displays illustrate the lifestyles of the Tlingit along with the town's Russian, Finish, Asian and American settlers. An 8-square-foot diorama shows Sitka as it appeared in 1867, the year Alaska was transferred to the United States from Russia.

Allow 30 minutes minimum. Mon.-Sat. 8:30-5:30, Sun. noon-4, early May to late Sept.; Tues.-Sat. 10-4, rest of year. Hours may vary; phone ahead. Donations. Phone (907) 747-6455.

SHELDON JACKSON MUSEUM is at 104 College Dr. Housed in one of the first concrete structures built in Alaska, it is reputed to be the oldest continuing museum in Alaska. Displays of Eskimo, Aleut and Northwest Coast and Athabaskan Indian artifacts include pelts, sleds, kayaks, ceremonial masks, and tools and utensils of wood, bone and ivory.

Allow 30 minutes minimum. Daily 9-5, mid-May to mid-Sept.; Tues.-Sat. 10-4, rest of year. Closed holidays. Admission $4 (mid-May to mid-Sept.); $3 (rest of year); free (ages 0-18). Phone (907) 747-8981.

SITKA NATIONAL HISTORICAL PARK (H-10)

Near downtown Sitka on Lincoln Street, this urban park commemorates the Battle of Sitka, fought in 1804 between the Kiksadi Tlingit Indians and the fur hunters and Aleut natives of the Russian-American Co. The battle marked the last major resistance by Alaskan natives to European domination. The 113-acre park preserves the Tlingit fort site, the battlefield and the 1842 Russian Bishop's House.

A fine collection of Tlingit (KLINK-it) and Haida (HY-dah) totem poles, some more than a century old, is displayed along a 2-mile trail through the park's temperate rain forest and coastal intertidal area. During August and September visitors may view salmon spawning in the Indian River.

The visitor center contains exhibits and audiovisual presentations about the area's Tlingit Indian heritage as well as its Russian legacy. Within the visitor center skilled native artisans demonstrate traditional crafts at the Southeast Alaska Indian Cultural Center, which is open daily.

Visitor center open daily 8-5, mid-May through Sept. 30; Mon.-Sat. 8-5, rest of year. Park free. Visitor center $4. AX, DS, MC, VI. Address inquiries to the Superintendent, Sitka National Historical Park, 103 Monastery St., Sitka, AK 99835; phone (907) 747-0110.

THE RUSSIAN BISHOP'S HOUSE, 501 Lincoln St. across from Crescent Harbor, is a two-story log structure completed in 1843. It is one of the last surviving colonial Russian buildings in North America. Restored to its 1853 appearance, the building reflects the influence of the Russian Orthodox Church and the traders of the Russian-American Co., who made Sitka the capital of colonial Russian America.

Allow 30 minutes minimum. Daily and holidays 9-5, May 15-late Sept.; by appointment rest of year. Admission $4; free (ages 0-11); $15 (family). Phone (907) 747-0110.

SKAGWAY (G-10) pop. 862, elev. 2′

During the icy winter of 1897-98 hordes of enthusiastic would-be prospectors who had heard of the Klondike gold strike swarmed ashore at Dyea. They assembled their gear and began the trek over treacherous mountains and down raging rivers to the Klondike. Within 3 months of the first gold strike, the settlement at Skagway grew from one cabin into a thriving city of more than 20,000 people. But the gold rush ended suddenly, and those who had come to Skagway moved on.

The notorious outlaw Jefferson R. "Soapy" Smith and Frank Reid, who represented the outraged citizenry, shot it out in a battle that cost both men their lives. Gold Rush Cemetery, 1.5 miles from town, contains the graves of both "Soapy" Smith and Frank Reid.

A stop on many summer cruises along the Inside Passage, Skagway is the northern terminus of the Alaska Marine Highway. Sightseeing opportunities include visits to Reid Falls and flower gardens; tours of the city and the harbor; flightseeing tours to Glacier Bay, gold rush trails and the Juneau Ice Cap; bus excursions to Dyea and Carcross, Yukon Territory; and hiking trips to AB Mountain and the Dewey Lakes.

Gray Line of Alaska offers historical points-of-interest tours daily; phone (907) 983-2241 or (800) 544-2206.

Skagway Convention & Visitors Bureau: P.O. Box 1029, Skagway, AK 99840; phone (907) 983-2854 or (888) 762-1898. *See color ad.*

THE DAYS OF '98 SHOW WITH SOAPY SMITH, presented at Eagles' Hall, 6th Ave. and Broadway, includes a stage show with original songs, a cancan line, a historic shoot-out and mock gambling. Mock gambling nightly at 7. Stage shows daily at 10:30, 12:30, 2:30 and 8, mid-May to late Sept. Shows $16; $8 (ages 3-15). MC, VI. Phone (907) 983-2545.

KLONDIKE GOLD RUSH NATIONAL HISTORICAL PARK includes the Skagway Historic District and Chilkoot and White Pass trails, over which each prospector was required to haul nearly a ton of supplies during the gold rush of 1897-98. It was during this stampede that Skagway's population boomed from 5 to more than 10,000.

The park visitor center is in the original White Pass and Yukon Route Railroad Depot, one of Alaska's oldest. At Broadway and Second Avenue, it contains exhibits and interpretive programs about the era. Two films are shown: an orientation film about the gold rush, and a film about hiking the Chilkoot Trail. Walking tours led by a park ranger explore the Skagway Historic District, where many restored buildings represent a colorful history. The Trail Center provides information about day hikes and backpacking on the Chilkoot Trail.

Visitor center daily 8-6, early May-late Sept. Orientation film is shown on the hour at 8, 9 and 11-5. Walking tours depart the visitor center daily on the hour 9-11 and at 2 and 3, early May-late Sept. Trail Center daily 8-5, June-Labor Day weekend. Visitor and trail centers free. Fees apply and reservations are recommended for Chilkoot Trail backpacking. Phone (907) 983-2921 for the visitor center, or (907) 983-9234 for trail information June-Aug., or (800) 661-0486 for trail information rest of year.

SKAGWAY MUSEUM is at Seventh Ave. and Spring St. in the McCabe College Building. Displays pertain to Alaskan history and native cultures, including a Tlingit war canoe, photographs, documents, gold rush relics and native artifacts. Mon.-Fri. 9-5, Sat. 10-5, Sun. 10-4, May-Sept.; hours vary, rest of year. Admission $2; $1 (senior citizens and students with ID); free (ages 0-12). MC, VI. Phone (907) 983-2420.

GEM WHITE PASS & YUKON ROUTE is at Second Ave. and Spring St. A vintage train chugs across mountain rivers and chasms during full-day and half-day fully narrated narrow-gauge rides. The rail line was built in 1898 to carry people and supplies to the Klondike gold rush. Passengers travel round-trip in a period parlor car to the summit of White Pass, past granite gulches, cascading waterfalls and spectacular scenery. A narrator tells the story of the stampede north into the gold fields through some of the most rugged terrain in the United States and Canada.

The 4-hour summit excursion to Fraser Meadows rises from tidewater elevation to 3,000 feet in 26 miles. The full-day tour includes a layover with a 2-hour walking tour and a box lunch.

Ticket office open daily 7:30-4:30, May-Sept. Three-hour trips depart Mon.-Thurs. at 8:15, 12:45 and 4:30, Fri.-Sun. at 8:15 and 12:45 (weather permitting), May 1-Sept. 3. Full-day trips depart Sat. at 8, Sun.-Mon. at 7:45. Fraser Meadows summit excursions depart Sat.-Sun. at noon, mid-May to mid-Sept. Inquire about additional excursions. Three-hour fare $98; $49 (ages 3-12). Fraser Meadows full-day fare Sat. $180; $90 (ages 3-12). Fraser Meadows summit fare Sun.-Mon. $150; $75 (ages 3-12). Summit excursion $125; $62.50 (ages 3-12). AX, DS, MC, VI. Phone (800) 343-7373. *See color ad p. 350.*

SOLDOTNA (D-10) pop. 3,759

Soldotna's location on the Kenai Peninsula at the junction of Sterling and Kenai Spur highways has ensured its steady growth since homesteading began in 1947. World War II veterans were among the first homesteaders; they were given a 90-day preference right in choosing and filing for land.

The area is rich with opportunities for year-round recreation—hiking, fishing, camping, canoeing and ice fishing are favored activities. Nearby Kenai River yields record catches of salmon and rainbow trout.

Soldotna Chamber of Commerce and Visitor Information Center: 44790 Sterling Hwy., Soldotna, AK 99669; phone (907) 262-9814.

KENAI NATIONAL WILDLIFE REFUGE, with its headquarters in Soldotna, covers about 1,920,000 acres. The refuge was established in 1941 by President Franklin D. Roosevelt to preserve the area's large moose population. Other wildlife include Dall sheep, coyotes, black bears and bald eagles. Fishing and hunting are subject to state and federal regulations. Boat ramps, trails and camping are available.

The refuge is open all year, except when roads are impassable. Phone (907) 262-7021. *See the AAA Western Canada & Alaska CampBook.*

Visitor Center, 1 mi. s.e. of the Kenai River Bridge on Ski Hill Rd., exhibits wildlife dioramas and presents films. Mon.-Fri. 8-4:30, Sat.-Sun. 9-5, June 1-Labor Day; Mon.-Fri. 8-4:30, Sat.-Sun. 10-5, rest of year.

STERLING (D-10) pop. 4,705, elev. 198'

RECREATIONAL ACTIVITIES

Fishing

- **Great Alaska Fish Camp**, 33881 Sterling Hwy., Sterling, AK 99672. Other activities are offered. Trips are offered mid-May through Sept. 30. Phone (800) 544-2261.

TALKEETNA (C-11) pop. 772, elev. 355'

Situated at the confluence of the Talkeetna, Susitna and Chulitna rivers, Talkeetna takes its name from the Tanaina Indian word for "river of plenty." The village was an important supply station for gold prospectors from the late 1800s to 1940, but is now a popular staging area for outdoors enthusiasts.

Mat-Su Convention & Visitors Bureau: Milepost 35.5, Parks Hwy., 7744 E. Visitors View Ct., Palmer, AK 99645; phone (907) 746-5000. *See color ad p. 315.*

Self-guiding tours: A map of a downtown walking tour is available at Talkeetna Historical Society Museum *(see attraction listing)* and the visitor center next to Village Park on Main Street.

K-2 AVIATION is at Talkeetna State Airport off Talkeetna Spur Rd. Flightseeing tours of varying types and lengths include a 1-hour flight to the summit of Mount McKinley; extended tours that encircle the mountain; and mountain tours with a glacier landing. Daily 7 a.m.-9 p.m. Fare for 1-hour tour $165. Rates vary according to tour. Reservations are recommended. AX, MC, VI. Phone (907) 733-2291 or (800) 764-2291.

MAHAY'S RIVERBOAT SERVICE departs from Milepost 14 on Talkeetna Spur Rd. The company offers three excursions: a 2-hour, 20-mile Wilderness Jetboat Adventure; a 3.5-hour, 60-mile three-river tour on the Chulitna, Susitna and Talkeetna rivers; and a 5-hour Devil's Canyon tour. Tours offer a leisurely .25-mile nature walk to a native Indian encampment and a view into the lives of turn-of-the-century trappers.

Allow 2 hours minimum. Office open daily 7 a.m.-9 p.m., mid-May to mid-Sept. Wilderness Jetboat Adventure departs daily at 8:45, noon, 2:30 and 6:30, mid-May to mid-Sept. Three-river tour departs daily at 3:15, mid-May to mid-Sept. Canyon tour departs daily at 9:30, mid-May to mid-Sept. Wilderness Jetboat Adventure $55; $27.50 (ages 0-5). Three-river tour $95; $47.50 (ages 0-5). Canyon tour $145; $72.50 (ages 0-12). MC, VI. Phone (907) 733-2223 or (800) 736-2210.

MUSEUM OF NORTHERN ADVENTURE, on Main St. across from the post office, recounts the eras, lore and natural history of northern Alaska through dioramas, life-size wax figures, sound effects, photographs and newspaper articles. A trophy room contains big game and other wildlife taxidermy. Allow 30 minutes minimum. Daily 10-6, May 1 to mid-Sept. Admission $2; $1 (ages 0-11 and 66+); $5 (family). AX, MC, VI. Phone (907) 733-3999.

TALKEETNA AERO SERVICES/FLY DENALI departs from Talkeetna State Airport, off Talkeetna Spur Rd., and Healy Denali Airport. Passengers are treated to views of Mt. McKinley, Denali Park or the Kahiltna Glacier from 20,000 feet as well as glacier landings on Mt. McKinley. Flights from Anchorage and Talkeetna to Denali National Park are available. Allow 2 hours minimum. Daily 7 a.m.-8 p.m., mid-May to mid-Sept.; 9-5, rest of year (weather permitting). Fare $150-$295 (depending on tour). AX, DS, MC, VI. Phone (907) 733-2899 or (888) 733-2899.

TALKEETNA AIR TAXI is at Talkeetna State Airport off Talkeetna Spur Rd. Flightseeing tours of the area are offered. Scenic views from the air include Mount McKinley and nearby glaciers. Other activities such as mountain climbing, glacier landings and support and wilderness tours also are offered. Daily 7 a.m.-10 p.m., May-Sept.; 9-4, rest of year. Fare $140-$265. DS, MC, VI. Phone (907) 733-2218 or (800) 533-2219.

TALKEETNA HISTORICAL SOCIETY MUSEUM, in five buildings at the corner of First Alley and Village Airstrip Rd., displays a wealth of local history memorabilia within re-creations of a log cabin, a one-room schoolhouse, a railroad depot and section house. Of interest is a large-scale model of Mount McKinley and the surrounding area.

Allow 30 minutes minimum. Daily 10-6, May-Sept.; Fri.-Sat. 11-4, Oct.-Dec. Hours may vary; phone ahead. Admission $3; free (ages 0-11 and students with ID). MC, VI. Phone (907) 733-2487.

TOK (B-12) pop. 1,393

On the Alaska Highway 93 miles from the Canadian border, Tok is a trade center for nearby Athabascan villages. Some claim that Tok's name derives from the native word meaning "peace crossing"; others say Tok was the name of a survey crew's dog.

A center for dog breeding, training and mushing, Tok claims the title "Dog Capital of Alaska."

Tok Chamber of Commerce: P.O. Box 389, Tok, AK 99780; phone (907) 883-5775.

ALASKA PUBLIC LANDS INFORMATION CENTER, Milepost 1314 on Alaska Hwy., includes displays, state and federal information, a trip planning room and interpretive programs. Daily 8-7, Memorial Day-Labor Day; Mon.-Fri. 8-5, rest of year. Free. Phone (907) 883-5666 or (907) 883-5667.

TETLIN NATIONAL WILDLIFE REFUGE is in e. central Alaska, directly s. of the Alaska Hwy. and n. of Wrangell-St. Elias National Park and Preserve; the visitor center is at Milepost 1229 on Alaska Hwy. The gateway to Alaska, the refuge occupies 730,000 acres along a major bird migration corridor. At least 115 of the 186 bird species stay to nest. Black and grizzly bears, moose, wolves and caribou are year-round residents.

Hunting and fishing are permitted. The refuge operates two seasonal, public campgrounds. Refuge open daily 24 hours. Visitor center open daily 8-4:30, May 15-Sept. 15. Free. Phone (907) 883-5312.

TONGASS NATIONAL FOREST (G-9)

Elevations in the forest range from sea level at the Pacific Ocean to 10,290 ft. at Mount Ratz. Refer to AAA maps for additional elevation information.

In southeastern Alaska, Tongass National Forest covers about 17 million acres, making it the largest national forest. In 1907 Teddy Roosevelt created the forest, taking the name from the "Tongass" clan of Tlingit Indians that lived along the southern edge of the forest's present-day boundaries. It boasts more than 5 million acres of preserved wilderness, including Misty Fiords National Monument *(see place listing p. 341)* and Admiralty Island National Monument *(see place listing p. 310).*

Consisting mostly of islands, the forest also includes a mountainous mainland strip deeply cleft by rock-walled fiords, bays, inlets and channels with glaciers, ice fields and waterfalls. The abundant wildlife includes trumpeter swans, bald eagles and Alaskan brown (grizzly) and black bears. Licenses are required for hunting and fishing.

The largest island within the National Forest and one of the largest islands in the United States is Prince of Wales Island. Long inlets and deep bays mark its 1,000-mile coastline, while U-shaped valleys and low mountains rising up to 3,800 feet distinguish its interior. Thanks to a moist climate, a dense forest of spruce and hemlock blankets the landscape.

One of the most interesting features of the island is its caves, including El Capitan, a large limestone cave system with 11,000 feet of mapped passages. Grizzly bear bones more than 12,000 years old have been found inside. The Forest Service provides free 2-hour tours of El Capitan from mid-May to early September; reservations are required. Access to the cave entrance is via a steep 1,300-foot-long trail and visitors need to bring their own equipment for the tour, including flashlights and sturdy footgear.

Phone (907) 828-3304 for information and reservations.

The Forest Service provides cabins at several locations within Tongass National Forest. Many rental cabins are near lakes and streams or high in alpine meadows. Although a few can be reached by boat or trail, most are accessible only by charter plane from Craig, Hoonah, Juneau, Ketchikan, Petersburg, Sitka, Wrangell and Yakutat. Charter planes seating two to five people cost about $325-$550 an hour.

A $25-$45 per-party, per-night fee is charged for cabins. There is a 7-night limit May through September; a 10-night limit the rest of the year. Cabin permits are necessary and can be requested up to 180 days prior to use; full payment is required at the time the reservation is made. Forest information centers with exhibits, films and cabin reservation information are in Juneau *(see place listing p. 332),* Ketchikan *(see place listing p. 338)* and Petersburg *(see place listing p. 343);* phone (877) 444-6777 for information.

For further information write Southeast Alaska Discovery Center, 50 Main St., Ketchikan, AK 99901; phone (907) 228-6220 or (877) 444-6777 for camping reservations. *See Recreation Chart and the AAA Western Canada & Alaska CampBook.*

 MENDENHALL GLACIER— *see Juneau p. 334.*

VALDEZ (C-11) pop. 4,036, elev. 15′

Called the "Switzerland of Alaska," Valdez (val-DEEZ) is ringed by snowcapped mountains. As the northernmost ice-free port, the town was established in 1898 as an outfitting point for miners taking the hazardous pack trail over Valdez Glacier to the northern gold fields.

In addition to the gold rush, Valdez's rich history includes a 5-minute, 9.2-magnitude earthquake in 1964; construction of the Trans-Alaska Pipeline and Marine Terminal in the 1970s; and the 1989 *Exxon Valdez* oil spill and cleanup.

Access into Valdez is by scheduled air service, ferry or via the scenic Richardson Highway. Near Milepost 16 are Bridal Veil and Horsetail falls and the Historic 1899 Trans-Alaska Military Trail & Wagon Road. Thompson Pass, Milepost 26, offers a spectacular view of the Chugach Mountains, valley rivers and historic Keystone Canyon. At Milepost 29 is Worthington Glacier State Park, which has walking trails.

Nearby glaciers in Prince William Sound include Mears, Shoup and Columbia, the second largest tidewater glacier in North America. Cruises are available to Mears and Columbia.

Valdez Convention and Visitors Bureau: P.O. Box 1603-3A, Valdez, AK 99686; phone (907) 835-2984. *See color ad.*

[SAVE] **STAN STEPHENS GLACIER & WILDLIFE CRUISES** departs from 112 N. Harbor Dr., 3 blks. e. of jct. Richardson Hwy. and Meals St. The outfit offers 6- to 9-hour narrated sightseeing cruises on Prince William Sound to Columbia and Meares glaciers. Along the way, guests might glimpse bald eagles, Dall's porpoises, black bears, sea otters, Stellar sea lions, puffins, mountain goats and humpback, minke and orca whales. A narrator details area history and information about the Trans-Alaska Pipeline. A light meal is included.

Trips depart daily, mid-May to mid-Sept. Fare $95-$130; $47-$65 (ages 3-12). Reservations are recommended. MC, VI. Phone (907) 835-4731 or (866) 867-1297. *See color ad.*

VALDEZ MUSEUM & HISTORICAL ARCHIVE is at 217 Egan Dr. The museum documents the complete history of Valdez. Interpretive exhibits explain the impact of the gold rush, the 1964 earthquake, the construction of the Trans-Alaska Pipeline and the 1989 *Exxon Valdez* oil spill. The Remembering Old Valdez exhibit, 436 S. Hazelet Ave., focuses on the years 1957-67. A 1907 Ahrens fire truck and a Fresnel lighthouse lens also are featured.

Allow 30 minutes minimum. Museum daily 9-6, May 15-Labor Day; Mon.-Fri. 1-5, Sat. noon-4, rest of year. Remembering Old Valdez daily 9-6, May 16-Labor Day; by appointment rest of year. Admission $6; $5.50 (ages 65+); $5 (ages 14-17); free (ages 0-13). Phone (907) 835-2764.

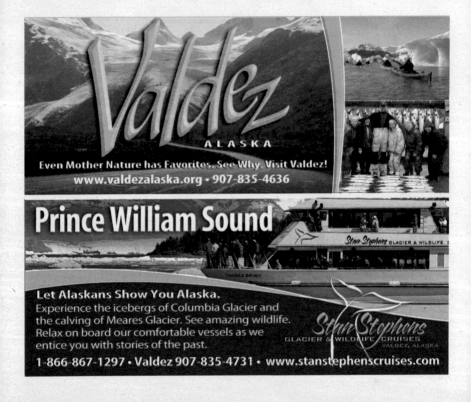

WORTHINGTON GLACIER, about 30 mi. e. on the Richardson Hwy., is Alaska's most accessible glacier. Milepost 28.7 provides an excellent viewpoint; a road leads to the glacier. Camping at the foot of the glacier is permitted.

RECREATIONAL ACTIVITIES
Kayaking

- **Anadyr Adventures** departs from 225 N. Harbor Dr. Daily 8 a.m.-10 p.m., May-Oct.; call ahead for specific excursion times and dates. Phone (907) 835-2814.

WASILLA (C-11) pop. 5,469

Founded in 1917, Wasilla is a growing community in the Matanuska-Susitna Valley named after a respected Athabascan Indian chief. Home to the Iditarod Trail Committee headquarters, the town has two warm-water lakes. Dorothy G. Page Museum on Main Street contains historical artifacts; the Old Wasilla Town Site behind the museum preserves Wasilla's first school, two log cabins, a smithy and the town's first public bath. Wasilla lies near the intersection of SRs 1 and 3, both of which are scenic highways.

Greater Wasilla Chamber of Commerce: 415 E. Railroad Ave., Wasilla, AK 99654; phone (907) 376-1299.

MUSEUM OF ALASKA TRANSPORTATION AND INDUSTRY, Milepost 47 on Parks Hwy., displays various items relating to Alaska's transportation and industrial history. Fifteen acres of outdoor exhibits include aircraft, boats, tractors, dog sleds, snowmobiles, farm implements, railroad cars, fire trucks, antique automobiles and memorabilia from early railroading days. Also featured are aviation photographs, vintage farm equipment and engines.

Picnicking is permitted. Daily 10-5, May-Sept. Admission $8; $5 (ages 3-18 and 66+); $18 (family). AX, DS, MC, VI. Phone (907) 376-1211.

WHITTIER (D-11) pop. 1,658

Nearly surrounded by mountains and perched at the edge of beautiful Prince William Sound, Whittier

remained relatively isolated until June 2000 when a 2.5-mile railroad tunnel was converted to accommodate automobile traffic. The unusual Anton Anderson Memorial Tunnel is a single-lane combination highway and railway that enables cars and trains to take turns passing through the tunnel. Because the tunnel has only one lane, the direction of traffic alternates, ceasing altogether while trains travel through.

Phone (877) 611-2586 for the tunnel's traffic schedule. Tunnel information also is broadcast by radio on 530 AM in Whittier and 1610 AM in Portage and Bear Valley. A toll of $12 per car is charged at the tunnel's western entrance; toll increases with size of vehicle.

26 GLACIER CRUISE BY PHILLIPS CRUISES departs from the port of Whittier. Cruises explore the calm, protected waters of Prince William Sound. Passengers aboard the company's high-speed catamaran can see tidewater glaciers plus an array of wildlife on this 4.5-hour tour.

Cruises depart daily at 1 early May-Sept. 30. Fare $139; $79 (ages 2-11). Bus or rail service is offered from Anchorage at an additional cost. Reservations are recommended. AX, DC, DS, MC, VI. Phone (907) 276-8023 or (800) 544-0529. *See color ad p. 317.*

MAJOR MARINE TOURS depart from the marina day-cruise dock. A 5-hour sightseeing cruise narrated by a Chugach forest ranger takes passengers to see spectacular 1,700-foot-tall active tidewater glaciers and picturesque waterfalls in Prince William Sound. Eagles, otters and shorebirds may be spotted.

Food is available. Inquire about weather policies. Allow 5 hours minimum. Departures daily at 1:15, mid-May to mid-Sept. Reservations are recommended. Fare $105; $52 (ages 2-11). Rates may vary; phone ahead. AX, DS, MC, VI. Phone (907) 274-7300 or (800) 764-7300. *See color ad p. 345.*

PRINCE WILLIAM SOUND CRUISES AND TOURS, departing from the foot of Pier 1 at the Whittier Boat Harbor, offers two cruises. The 4-hour Glacier Adventure Cruise brings passengers close to two active tidewater glaciers and waterfalls. The 6-hour Wilderness Explorer Glacier Cruise plies the calm waters of Prince William Sound, passes glaciers in Esther Passage, Harriman Fjord and Barry Arm, and stops at a working fish hatchery. Both trips include lunch and opportunities for spotting wildlife.

Allow 4 hours minimum. Glacier Adventure Cruise departs daily at 1:30, early June-early Sept. Wilderness Explorer Glacier Cruise departs daily at 11, mid-May to mid-Sept. Glacier Adventure Cruise $89; $44.50 (ages 2-11). Wilderness Explorer Glacier Cruise $119; $59.50 (ages 2-11). MC, VI. Phone (907) 777-2805, (800) 992-1297 or (877) 777-2805. *See color ad p. 355.*

RECREATIONAL ACTIVITIES
Kayaking

- **Alaska Sea Kayakers** depart from the Whittier Boat Harbor. Daily 8-7, May-Sept. Phone (877) 472-2534.

WRANGELL (H-11) pop. 2,308, elev. 37'

Petroglyphs pecked into shale rock and elaborately carved totem poles, cedar monuments of the Stikine (STIK-een) and Tlingit (KLINK-it) Indians, are interesting aspects of Wrangell. Although European and American explorers visited the area in the late 1700s, Russians began trading here by 1811 and established a redoubt in Wrangell in 1834. The only Alaskan town to have existed under Russian, British and American rule, it also survived three gold rushes—In 1861, 1872 and 1898 the lure of riches brought a rush of miners and settlers.

Petroglyphs can be seen on a beach at the north end of Wrangell Island. Of undetermined age, some carvings face the water, others the shore or sky. They are best viewed at low tide. Nearby Anan Creek allows the opportunity to observe sea lions and seals and watch black bear fish for salmon.

Other attractions include the nine totem poles (some are replicas carved by the Civilian Conservation Corps in the late 1930s) on Shakes Island in Wrangell Harbor, as well as the four totem poles in Kiksadi Totem Park at Front and Episcopal streets. Artifacts are displayed in Chief Shakes Tribal House, also on the island. A large concentration of bald eagles gather in Wrangell from January to mid-April waiting for smelt to run up the Stikine River. A visitor center is in the Stikine Inn, at Front Street and Stikine Avenue.

Wrangell Chamber of Commerce: P.O. Box 49, Wrangell, AK 99929; phone (907) 874-3901 or (800) 367-9745.

WRANGELL MUSEUM is at 296 Outer Dr. The collection describes the colorful history of the Wrangell area. Of note are four beautiful Tlingit houseposts—carved in the 1700s, they are believed to be the oldest in existence. A variety of displays detail early Russian and English settlement and the city's role in the 1861 Stikine gold rush. Spruceroot and cedar-bark baskets, beadwork, stone tools and other artifacts crafted by Alaskan natives are shown.

Allow 30 minutes minimum. Mon.-Sat. 10-5, May-Sept.; Tues.-Sat. 1-5, rest of year. Closed holidays. Admission $5; $3 (ages 65+); $2 (ages 6-12); $12 (family). MC, VI. Phone (907) 874-3770.

WRANGELL-ST. ELIAS NATIONAL PARK AND PRESERVE (C-12, F-8)

Elevations in the park and preserve range from sea level at the Gulf of Alaska to 18,008 ft. at Mount St. Elias. Refer to AAA maps for additional elevation information.

In south central Alaska bordering Canada's Yukon Territory, Wrangell-St. Elias National Park and Preserve is the country's largest national park. It is a place of overpowering dimensions, embracing an area larger than Massachusetts, Rhode Island and Connecticut combined; glaciers five times the size of Manhattan; and nine of the 16 highest peaks in North America.

In this 13-million-acre park, the collision of two continental plates has produced some of the world's highest coastal ranges. Forming a barrier along the Gulf of Alaska are the Chugach Mountains, and paralleling them to the north are the Wrangell Mountains.

Between these two ranges are the St. Elias Mountains, extending like the stem of the letter "Y" into Canada's Kluane National Park. Atop these towering peaks are ice fields so immense that they act as a natural cooling system, affecting areas as far south as Chicago and the Central Plains.

As imposing as its ice fields are, it was another commodity traded by the Ahtna Dene or "people of the Copper River" that caught the world's attention. These and other tribes forged tools of locally mined copper. The first person of European descent to verify the source of the copper trading was Lt. Henry Allen, who in 1885 explored much of Alaska's interior.

Fifteen years later two miners discovered the malachite cliffs above the Kennicott Glacier, which became one of the world's richest sources of copper. The subsequent founding of the Kennecott Mine became one of the most significant events in Alaska's history: The great wealth and development it spawned affected not only Alaska but the entire nation. Currently the ruined mine is all that remains of this immense enterprise.

Legacies of the Kennecott Mine and the Yukon gold fields are some of the area's roads, which provide limited access to the park. One of Alaska's oldest roadways is the Richardson Highway, which was completed in 1919 and was the first all-Alaska route to the Yukon gold fields. Both the Richardson and Glenn highways follow the curve of the park's western boundary and offer several spectacular views of 12,010-foot Mount Drum, 14,163-foot Mount Wrangell and 16,237-foot Mount Sanford.

Two other roads penetrate the park's interior—the Chitina-McCarthy and the Nabesna. Both of these gravel roads offer good views of the mountains and are convenient jumping-off places for hiking and river-running. The 60-mile McCarthy Road follows an abandoned railroad bed. Visitors should allow a minimum of 3 hours to drive between Chitina and McCarthy. Before using either of these routes, check with the ranger stations in Slana and Chitina.

The park's visitor center, 3 miles north of Copper Center on Richardson Highway, provides trip-planning assistance and information about park activities.

Fishing, hiking, rafting and wildlife- viewing, especially of the park's large population of Dall sheep, are just some of the activities pursued in the park.

On the southeastern edge of the park and accessible only by sea is Hubbard Glacier on Disenchantment Bay. In 1986 this vast, active tidewater glacier advanced so quickly that for several months it blocked the entrance to Russell Fjord behind a dam of ice, briefly turning it into a lake.

For more information write the Superintendent, Wrangell-St. Elias National Park and Preserve, P.O. Box 439, Copper Center, AK 99573; phone (907) 822-5234. *See Recreation Chart.*

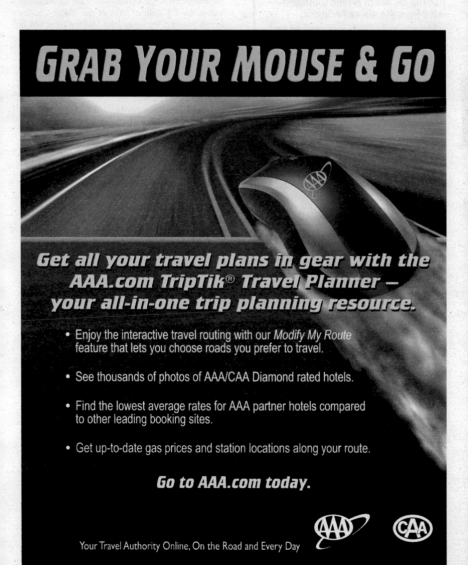

The Alaska Highway

On March 9, 1942, the U.S. Army Corps of Engineers began bulldozing its way through mountains and forests to create a direct land route linking the United States to the Alaska Territory. The Alaska Highway originated as an emergency passage for American troops during World War II following the Japanese occupation of the Aleutian Islands, which extend southwestward from the Alaska Peninsula.

More than 11,000 troops worked on the road, and American Indians, trappers and prospectors were hired to help. Canada supplied the right of way and materials in exchange for use of the road following the war. The workers built 133 log and pontoon bridges and dug more than 8,000 culverts. Despite untold hardships and the worst winter in recorded history, the highway was completed in just 8 months. In 1943 the highway became public, and for the next 7 years more than 70 companies and 16,000 civilian workers labored to turn it into a year-round, all-weather road.

Alaska Dept. of Commerce

The 1,523-mile Alaska Highway takes its travelers on a wilderness tour starting at Dawson Creek, British Columbia, through the Yukon Territory and on through Delta Junction to Fairbanks. The scenery is picture perfect, with an abundance of spruce forests, magnificent mountain passes, lakes, rivers and glacial ice formations. Bears, moose and other wildlife can appear at any time.

The road is maintained daily, but be aware that conditions often change depending on the weather. Take your time, drive with your headlights on and drive defensively. Always be alert for bumps and holes in the road. Gas, food and lodging are conveniently found every 20 to 50 miles.

YUKON-CHARLEY RIVERS NATIONAL PRESERVE (C-12, F-7)

Elevations in the preserve range from 600 ft. on the Yukon River where it leaves the preserve near Circle to 6,435 ft. in the Cirque Lakes area on the Charley River drainage. Refer to AAA maps for additional elevation information.

Near the Canadian border in east central Alaska, more than 140 miles of the Yukon River and the entire watershed of the Charley River are encompassed within the 2.5 million acres of the Yukon-Charley Rivers National Preserve. John McPhee remarked in his book "Coming into the Country" that New Jersey could easily fit into this vast emptiness between Eagle and Circle.

Although only 10 year-round residents now live within the preserve's boundaries, it was not always so sparsely populated. During the gold rush, the Yukon—a summer waterway and winter highway—was thronged with people who briefly transformed such communities as Circle and Dawson City, Canada into the "Paris of the North." This rough-and-tumble gold rush region was the grist of Robert Service's poetry and Jack London's stories.

Now quiet has returned, and where riverboats once departed from Eagle, river runners make the 5- to 7-day float down the river to Circle. One of the pleasures of this trip is the opportunity to see Peregrine falcons, a threatened species that makes its home in the bluffs along the river. Hikers can catch a glimpse of caribou and Dall sheep in the preserve's upland regions and moose in the lowlands.

The Taylor and Steese highways are the primary summer access routes to the national preserve, terminating respectively in Eagle and Circle just outside the preserve's boundaries. The scenic portion of the Taylor Highway from Chicken to Eagle runs through mountains, rolling tundra and river valleys. Most people, however, reach the park by boat or float on the Yukon River and its tributaries.

The preserve has no roads and no established trails or maintained public airstrips. Seven public-use cabins are available on a first-come, first-served basis. Food service, basic supplies, lodgings and charter boat and air service are available during the summer months in nearby Eagle and Circle. A list of authorized guides can be obtained from the preserve headquarters and visitor center in Eagle.

In addition, the Bureau of Land Management administers Fort Egbert and a campground in Eagle (see the AAA Western Canada & Alaska Camp-Book). A visitor center, open Mon.-Fri. 8-5, Memorial Day-Labor Day, can be contacted at P.O. Box 167, Eagle, AK 99738; phone (907) 547-2233. For more information write the Superintendent, Yukon-Charley Rivers National Preserve, P.O. Box 74718, Fairbanks, AK 99707-4718. See Recreation Chart.

DISCOVER THE KEY TO EASY HOTEL AND RESTAURANT SELECTION

Use the trusted AAA/CAA Diamonds to choose the right hotel or restaurant for your needs, every time.

Approved

Quality Assurance
Every AAA/CAA Diamond rated hotel and restaurant has been AAA/CAA Approved by a professional inspector to ensure it offers the cleanliness and comfort members expect.

Easy Selection
AAA/CAA Approved hotels and restaurants receive a rating of One Diamond to Five Diamonds to indicate the level of hospitality — from no-frills hotels and restaurants to full-service resorts and world-class dining.

For more details, go to pages 20-21 or AAA.com/Diamonds

No matter the Disney destination,
the smiles are always the same.

Let a AAA/CAA Travel professional help you get there.

A Disney vacation can take you to the world's greatest Theme
Parks, *Walt Disney World*® Resort in Florida and *Disneyland*®
Resort in California, and much, much more. Chart a course for
magic on *Disney Cruise Line*, featuring fun for every member
of the family. Or immerse your family in the stories of some of
the world's greatest destinations with *Adventures by Disney*.
A brand-new way for you to travel the globe.

Whatever you choose, make sure you book
through your AAA/CAA Travel professional to
receive exclusive benefits.

Where dreams come true

*A*lberta

Abraham Lake,
near Cline River
Travel Alberta

AIRDRIE —See Calgary p. 420.

Banff

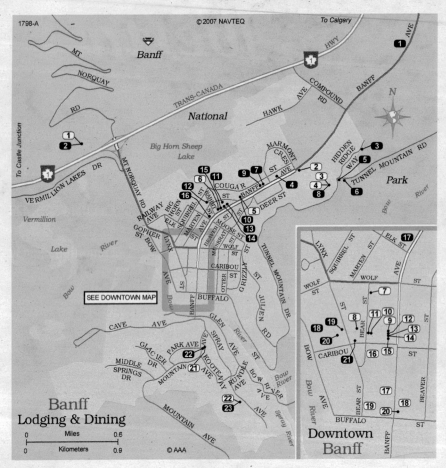

1798-A   © 2007 NAVTEQ

SEE DOWNTOWN MAP

Banff
Lodging & Dining

Miles 0.6
Kilometers 0.9

© AAA

Downtown
Banff

This index helps you "spot" where approved lodgings and restaurants are located on the corresponding detailed maps. Lodging daily rate range is for comparison only and show the property's high season. Restaurant rate range is a combination of lunch and/or dinner. Turn to the listing page for more detailed rate information and consult display ads for special promotions.

Spotter/Map Page Number	OA	BANFF - Lodgings	Diamond Rating	Rate Range High Season	Listing Page
❶ / above		Banff Rocky Mountain Resort	▽▽	$165-$380	369
❷ / above	AAA	**The Juniper**	▽▽▽	$165-$385 SAVE	376
❸ / above		Hidden Ridge Resort - see color ad p 367	▽▽	$149-$499	373
❹ / above	AAA	**Rundlestone Lodge** - see color ad p 374	▽▽▽	$109-$279 SAVE	377
❺ / above	AAA	**Douglas Fir Resort & Chalets** - see color ad p 371	▽▽▽	$177-$459 SAVE	371
❻ / above		Tunnel Mountain Resort	▽▽	$233-$294	379
❼ / above		Banff Caribou Lodge - see color ad p 367	▽▽	$169-$475	366

Spotter/Map Page Number	OA	**BANFF - Lodgings (continued)**	Diamond Rating	Rate Range High Season	Listing Page
8 / p. 364		Buffalo Mountain Lodge	◈◈◈	$159-$329	370
9 / p. 364		Charlton's Cedar Court - see color ad p 370	◈◈◈	$129-$248	370
10 / p. 364		Delta Banff Royal Canadian Lodge - see color ad p 371	◈◈◈	$208-$414	370
11 / p. 364	CAA	**Best Western Siding 29 Lodge**	◈◈	$99-$349 SAVE	369
12 / p. 364		Buffaloberry Bed and Breakfast	◈◈◈	$235-$325	370
13 / p. 364	CAA	**Irwin's Mountain Inn**	◈◈	$110-$165 SAVE	373
14 / p. 364	CAA	**Red Carpet Inn**	◈◈	$75-$169 SAVE	376
15 / p. 364	CAA	**High Country Inn** - see color ad p 374	◈◈	$99-$289 SAVE	373
16 / p. 364	CAA	**Banff Aspen Lodge**	◈◈	$116-$238 SAVE	366
17 / p. 364		Banff Ptarmigan Inn - see color ad p 367	◈◈	$159-$289	368
18 / p. 364		Bow View Lodge	◈◈	$119-$320	369
19 / p. 364		Banff Park Lodge Resort Hotel & Conference Centre - see color ad p 366	◈◈◈	$175-$400	366
20 / p. 364		Homestead Inn	◈	$85-$149	373
21 / p. 364	CAA	**Brewster's Mountain Lodge** - see color ad p 369	◈◈	$109-$409 SAVE	369
22 / p. 364	CAA	**The Rimrock Resort Hotel** - see color ad p 377	◈◈◈◈	$215-$575 SAVE	376
23 / p. 364	CAA	**The Fairmont Banff Springs** - see color ad p 372	◈◈◈◈	$233-$593 SAVE	372
		BANFF - Restaurants			
① / p. 364	CAA	**Muk a Muk Bistro & Lounge**	◈◈	$10-$44	380
② / p. 364		Bumper's The Beef House	◈◈	$15-$40	379
③ / p. 364		Cilantro Mountain Cafe	◈◈	$14-$30	379
④ / p. 364		Sleeping Buffalo Restaurant & Lounge	◈◈	$9-$37	380
⑤ / p. 364		The Evergreen	◈◈◈	$10-$37	379
⑥ / p. 364	CAA	**Ticino Swiss-Italian Restaurant**	◈◈◈	$14-$38	381
⑦ / p. 364		St James's Gate Olde Irish Pub	◈◈	$9-$25	380
⑧ / p. 364		Saltlik A Rare Steakhouse	◈◈◈	$10-$30	380
⑨ / p. 364		Giorgio's Trattoria	◈◈	$15-$40	379
⑩ / p. 364		Cafe Soleil	◈◈	$8-$35	379
⑪ / p. 364		Coyotes Deli & Grill	◈◈	$8-$22	379
⑫ / p. 364		Sunfood Cafe	◈◈	$5-$15	381
⑬ / p. 364		Sukiyaki House	◈◈	$8-$27	380
⑭ / p. 364	CAA	**Silver Dragon Restaurant**	◈◈	$6-$15	380
⑮ / p. 364		Grizzly House	◈◈	$10-$50	380
⑯ / p. 364		Typhoon	◈◈	$6-$22	381
⑰ / p. 364	CAA	**The Maple Leaf Grille & Spirits**	◈◈◈	$13-$50	380
⑱ / p. 364		Tommy's Neighbourhood Pub	◈	$8-$18	381
⑲ / p. 364	CAA	**Le Beaujolais**	◈◈◈◈	$25-$95	380
⑳ / p. 364		Fuze Finer Dining	◈◈◈	$11-$35	379
㉑ / p. 364	CAA	**Eden**	◈◈◈◈◈	$90-$150	379
㉒ / p. 364	CAA	**The Banffshire Club**	◈◈◈◈◈	$90-$130	379

BANFF pop. 6,700   (See map and index starting on p. 364)

———— WHERE TO STAY ————

BANFF ASPEN LODGE   *Book great rates at AAA.com*   Phone: (403)762-4401 **16**

Small-scale Hotel
$116-$238 All Year

Address: 401 Banff Ave T1L 1A9 **Location:** At Moose St; centre. **Facility:** Smoke free premises. 89 units. 69 one- and 20 two-bedroom standard units. 3 stories, interior/exterior corridors. **Parking:** on-site, winter plug-ins. **Terms:** cancellation fee imposed. **Amenities:** hair dryers. *Some:* irons. **Leisure Activities:** sauna, whirlpool, steamroom, ski locker. **Guest Services:** valet and coin laundry, area transportation (fee)-ski hills, wireless Internet. **Business Services:** meeting rooms, PC (fee). **Cards:** AX, MC, VI. **Free Special Amenities: expanded continental breakfast and early check-in/late check-out.**

BANFF CARIBOU LODGE   *Book great rates at AAA.com*   Phone: (403)762-5887 **7**

Small-scale Hotel
$169-$475 All Year

Address: 521 Banff Ave T1L 1A4 **Location:** Banff Ave and Marmot St. Located opposite Rotary Park. **Facility:** Smoke free premises. 197 one-bedroom standard units, some with whirlpools. 4 stories, interior corridors. **Parking:** on-site. **Terms:** check-in 4 pm, 3 day cancellation notice-fee imposed. **Amenities:** voice mail, irons, hair dryers. **Fee:** video games, high-speed Internet. **Leisure Activities:** sauna, whirlpools, steamroom, exercise room, spa. **Guest Services:** valet and coin laundry, area transportation (fee). **Business Services:** meeting rooms, PC (fee). **Cards:** AX, DC, DS, JC, MC, VI. *(See color ad p 367)*

BANFF PARK LODGE RESORT HOTEL & CONFERENCE CENTRE   *Book great rates at AAA.com*   Phone: (403)762-4433 **19**

Large-scale Hotel
$175-$400 All Year

Address: 222 Lynx St T1L 1K5 **Location:** Between Caribou and Wolf sts; downtown. **Facility:** Designated smoking area. 211 units. 208 one-bedroom standard units, some with whirlpools. 3 one-bedroom suites with whirlpools. 3 stories, interior corridors. **Parking:** on-site (fee) and valet. **Terms:** 3 day cancellation notice. **Amenities:** voice mail, safes, irons, hair dryers. *Some:* high-speed Internet (fee). **Pool(s):** heated indoor. **Leisure Activities:** whirlpool, steamroom, hiking trails. **Fee:** bicycles. **Guest Services:** valet and coin laundry, area transportation (fee), wireless Internet. **Business Services:** conference facilities, PC (fee). **Cards:** AX, DC, MC, VI. *(See color ad below)*

(See map and index starting on p. 364)

BANFF PTARMIGAN INN   *Book great rates at AAA.com*   Phone: (403)762-2207   ❶❼

Small-scale Hotel
$159-$289 All Year

Address: 337 Banff Ave T1L 1H8 **Location:** Sw of Moose St; centre. **Facility:** Smoke free premises. 134 one-bedroom standard units, some with whirlpools. 2-3 stories, interior corridors. **Parking:** on-site, winter plug-ins. **Terms:** check-in 4 pm, 3 day cancellation notice-fee imposed. **Amenities:** hair dryers. **Leisure Activities:** sauna, whirlpools, steamroom, limited exercise equipment. *Fee:* massage. **Guest Services:** valet laundry, area transportation (fee), wireless Internet. **Business Services:** meeting rooms, PC (fee). **Cards:** AX, DC, DS, JC, MC, VI. *(See color ad p 367)*

       / SOME UNITS

(See map and index starting on p. 364)

BANFF ROCKY MOUNTAIN RESORT   *Book at AAA.com*   Phone: (403)762-5531   ❶

Resort Condominium
$165-$380 All Year

Address: 1029 Banff Ave T1L 1A2 **Location:** Banff Ave and Tunnel Mountain Rd; just s of Trans-Canada Hwy 1. **Facility:** Just outside of downtown, this condo-style resort is nestled at the base of the Rundle and Cascade mountains; all rooms have gas fireplaces. 171 units. 54 one-bedroom standard units, some with kitchens. 52 one- and 65 two-bedroom suites with kitchens, some with whirlpools. 2 stories (no elevator), exterior corridors. **Parking:** on-site, winter plug-ins. **Terms:** check-in 5 pm, 3 day cancellation notice-fee imposed. **Amenities:** video games, voice mail, irons, hair dryers. **Pool(s):** heated indoor. **Leisure Activities:** sauna, whirlpools, 2 tennis courts, recreation programs, playground, exercise room, basketball, volleyball. *Fee:* bicycles, massage. **Guest Services:** valet and coin laundry, area transportation. **Business Services:** meeting rooms, PC (fee). **Cards:** AX, MC, VI.

BEST WESTERN SIDING 29 LODGE   *Book great rates at AAA.com*   Phone: (403)762-5575   ⓫

Small-scale Hotel
$99-$349 All Year

Address: 453 Marten St T1L 1B3 **Location:** 0.6 mi (1 km) ne, just off Banff Ave. Located in a residential area. **Facility:** 57 units. 54 one- and 1 two-bedroom standard units, some with kitchens and/or whirlpools. 2 one-bedroom suites with whirlpools. 3 stories, interior corridors. **Parking:** on-site. **Terms:** 2 night minimum stay - seasonal, cancellation fee imposed. **Amenities:** high-speed Internet, irons, hair dryers. **Pool(s):** heated indoor. **Leisure Activities:** whirlpool. **Business Services:** PC (fee). **Cards:** AX, DC, DS, JC, MC, VI. **Free Special Amenities:** local telephone calls and high-speed Internet.

AAA Benefit:
Members save 10% everyday, plus an exclusive frequent stay program.

BOW VIEW LODGE   *Book at AAA.com*   Phone: (403)762-2261   ⓳

Motel
$119-$320 All Year

Address: 228 Bow Ave T1L 1A5 **Location:** Between Lynx St and Bow Ave; on Wolf St. **Facility:** Smoke free premises. 57 units. 54 one- and 3 two-bedroom standard units. 3 stories, interior corridors. **Parking:** on-site, winter plug-ins. **Terms:** check-in 4 pm, 3 day cancellation notice. **Amenities:** voice mail. **Cards:** AX, DC, MC, VI.

BREWSTER'S MOUNTAIN LODGE   *Book great rates at AAA.com*   Phone: (403)762-2900   ㉑

Small-scale Hotel
$109-$409 3/1-1/2
$119-$369 1/3-2/28

Address: 208 Caribou St T1L 1C1 **Location:** Just w off Banff Ave; centre. **Facility:** Smoke free premises. 77 one-bedroom standard units, some with whirlpools. 3 stories, interior corridors. **Parking:** on-site (fee). **Terms:** check-in 4 pm, 2-3 night minimum stay - seasonal and/or weekends, 3 day cancellation notice. **Amenities:** irons, hair dryers. **Dining:** Cafe Soleil, see separate listing. **Leisure Activities:** sauna, whirlpool, exercise room. **Guest Services:** valet and coin laundry, area transportation (fee), wireless Internet. **Business Services:** meeting rooms, PC (fee). **Cards:** AX, MC, VI. **Free Special Amenities:** continental breakfast and high-speed Internet. *(See color ad below)*

(See map and Index starting on p. 364)

BUFFALOBERRY BED AND BREAKFAST

Bed & Breakfast
$235-$325 All Year

Phone: (403)762-3750   **12**

Address: 417 Marten St T1L 1G5 **Location:** Just e of jct Rabbit St. Located in a residential area. **Facility:** Each room at this B&B offers its own unique, attractive decor, and secure underground parking is available. Smoke free premises. 4 one-bedroom standard units. 2 stories, interior corridors. **Bath:** combo or shower only. **Parking:** on-site. **Terms:** check-in 4 pm, 21 day cancellation notice-fee imposed. **Amenities:** high-speed Internet, hair dryers. **Cards:** MC, VI.

[ASK] [S▯] [X] [K] [▯]

BUFFALO MOUNTAIN LODGE

Small-scale Hotel
$159-$329 All Year

Phone: (403)762-2400   **8**

Address: 700 Tunnel Mountain Rd T1L 1B3 **Location:** 1 mi (1.6 km) ne. **Facility:** 108 units. 92 one-bedroom standard units, some with efficiencies. 16 one-bedroom suites with efficiencies. 2 stories (no elevator), exterior corridors. **Parking:** on-site, winter plug-ins. **Terms:** check-in 4 pm, 3 day cancellation notice-fee imposed. **Amenities:** video library, high-speed Internet, voice mail, irons, hair dryers. **Dining:** Cilantro Mountain Cafe, Sleeping Buffalo Restaurant & Lounge, see separate listings. **Leisure Activities:** whirlpool, steamroom, recreation programs, exercise room. **Guest Services:** valet laundry, area transportation (fee). **Business Services:** conference facilities, business center. **Cards:** AX, MC, VI.

[ASK] [S▯] [†1] [▯] [X] [K] [▯] / SOME UNITS [X] [VCR] [▯] [▯]

CASTLE MOUNTAIN CHALETS   *Book great rates at AAA.com*

[CAA] [SAVE]

Cabin
$150-$345 All Year

Phone: (403)762-3868

Address: Bow Valley Pkwy (Hwy 1A) T1L 1B5 **Location:** 20 mi (32 km) w on Trans-Canada Hwy 1, jct Castle, 0.6 mi (1 km) ne on Hwy 1A (Bow Valley Pkwy). **Facility:** Smoke free premises. 23 units. 2 one-bedroom standard units. 21 cabins. 1 story, exterior corridors. **Bath:** combo or shower only. **Parking:** on-site, winter plug-ins. **Terms:** office hours 7 am-10 pm, 2 night minimum stay, 14 day cancellation notice-fee imposed. **Amenities:** video library, hair dryers. **Leisure Activities:** steamroom, cross country skiing, recreation programs, telephone & library in central recreation building, exercise room. *Fee:* fishing rods, bicycles. **Guest Services:** coin laundry. **Cards:** AX, MC, VI.

[S▯] CALL [M] [X] [X] [K] [VCR] [▯] [Z] [▯] [▯] / SOME UNITS FEE [▯] [▯]

CHARLTON'S CEDAR COURT   *Book great rates at AAA.com*

Motel
$129-$248 All Year

Phone: (403)762-4485   **9**

Address: 513 Banff Ave T1L 1B4 **Location:** 0.6 mi (1 km) ne. **Facility:** Smoke free premises. 57 units. 41 one- and 16 two-bedroom standard units, some with efficiencies. 2-3 stories, exterior corridors. **Parking:** on-site, winter plug-ins. **Terms:** office hours 7 am-11 pm, check-in 4 pm, cancellation fee imposed. **Amenities:** video games (fee), voice mail, irons, hair dryers. **Pool(s):** heated indoor. **Leisure Activities:** whirlpool, steamroom. **Guest Services:** valet laundry, area transportation (fee), wireless Internet. **Business Services:** meeting rooms, PC (fee). **Cards:** AX, DC, MC, VI. *(See color ad below)*

[ASK] [S▯] [†1•] [≈] [X] [▯] [▯] [▯] / SOME UNITS [▯]

DELTA BANFF ROYAL CANADIAN LODGE   *Book great rates at AAA.com*

[image: diamond rating]

Small-scale Hotel
$208-$414 All Year

Phone: (403)762-3307   **10**

Address: 459 Banff Ave T1L 1B4 **Location:** 0.6 mi (1 km) ne. **Facility:** Designated smoking area. 99 one-bedroom standard units, some with whirlpools. 3 stories, interior corridors. **Parking:** on-site (fee) and valet. **Terms:** check-in 4 pm, 5 day cancellation notice-fee imposed. **Amenities:** video games, high-speed Internet, voice mail, safes, irons, hair dryers. **Dining:** The Evergreen, see separate listing. **Pool(s):** heated indoor. **Leisure Activities:** whirlpool, steamroom, exercise room. *Fee:* massage. **Guest Services:** valet laundry, area transportation (fee). **Business Services:** meeting rooms. **Cards:** AX, DC, MC, VI. *(See color ad p 371)*

[ASK] [S▯] [†1] [24†] [▯] [≈] [X] [X] [▯] [▯] [▯]

(See map and index starting on p. 364)

DOUGLAS FIR RESORT & CHALETS *Book great rates at AAA.com*   Phone: (403)762-5591

Condominium
$177-$459 All Year

Address: 525 Tunnel Mountain Rd T1L 1B2 **Location:** From centre, 1 mi (1.6 km) ne. **Facility:** On a wooded hillside with scenic mountain views, the resort offers a mix of chalets and condos featuring upscale decor. Smoke free premises. 133 units. 34 one-bedroom standard units with kitchens. 56 one-, 33 two- and 1 three-bedroom suites with kitchens, some with whirlpools. 9 cottages. 2-3 stories, interior/exterior corridors. **Parking:** on-site, winter plug-ins. **Terms:** check-in 4 pm, 2-3 night minimum stay - seasonal, cancellation fee imposed. **Amenities:** high-speed Internet, dual phone lines, voice mail, safes, irons, hair dryers. **Pool(s):** heated indoor. **Leisure Activities:** saunas, whirlpools, waterslide, tennis court, playground, exercise room. **Guest Services:** coin laundry. **Business Services:** PC (fee). **Cards:** AX, DC, MC, VI. **Free Special Amenities:** local telephone calls and high-speed Internet. *(See color ad below)*

▼ See AAA listing above ▼

▼ See AAA listing p 370 ▼

(See map and index starting on p. 364)

THE FAIRMONT BANFF SPRINGS   *Book great rates at AAA.com*   Phone: (403)762-2211   **23**

Resort
Large-scale Hotel
$233-$593 All Year

Address: 405 Spray Ave T1L 1J4 **Location:** Just s on Banff Ave over the bridge, 0.3 mi (0.5 km) e. **Facility:** With a distinctive design that brings to mind a castle, this engaging hotel offers impressive public areas that serve to offset its small guest rooms. 770 units. 720 one-bedroom standard units, some with whirlpools. 39 one- and 11 two-bedroom suites, some with whirlpools. 3-9 stories, interior corridors. **Parking:** on-site (fee) and valet, winter plug-ins. **Terms:** check-in 4 pm, 3 day cancellation notice-fee imposed. **Amenities:** voice mail, honor bars, irons, hair dryers. *Fee:* video games, high-speed Internet. *Some:* CD players, safes. **Dining:** 7 restaurants, also, The Banffshire Club, see separate listing. **Pool(s):** heated outdoor, heated indoor. **Leisure Activities:** saunas, whirlpools, steamrooms, 5 tennis courts, ice skating, recreation programs, audio visual theatre, hiking trails, jogging, spa. *Fee:* golf-27 holes, tobogganing, bowling, bicycles, horseback riding. **Guest Services:** valet laundry, beauty salon. **Business Services:** conference facilities, business center. **Cards:** AX, CB, DC, DS, JC, MC, VI. *(See color ad below)*

▼ See AAA listing above ▼

MAKE ROYAL MEMORIES AT FAIRMONT'S CASTLE IN THE ROCKIES

(See map and index starting on p. 364)

HIDDEN RIDGE RESORT *Book great rates at AAA.com* Phone: (403)762-3544   **3**

Condominium
$149-$499 All Year

Address: 901 Hidden Ridge Way T1L 1B7 **Location:** 1.5 mi (2.4 km) ne at Tunnel Mountain Rd. **Facility:** Smoke free premises. 94 units. 40 one- and 44 two-bedroom suites with kitchens, some with whirlpools. 10 cottages. 2 stories (no elevator), exterior corridors. **Parking:** on-site, winter plug-ins. **Terms:** check-in 4 pm, 3 day cancellation notice-fee imposed. **Amenities:** hair dryers. **Leisure Activities:** whirlpool, recreation programs. **Guest Services:** area transportation. **Business Services:** meeting rooms, PC (fee). **Cards:** AX, DC, DS, JC, MC, VI. *(See color ad p 367)*

HIGH COUNTRY INN *Book great rates at AAA.com* Phone: (403)762-2236 **15**

Small-scale Hotel
$99-$289 All Year

Address: 419 Banff Ave T1L 1A7 **Location:** N of Rabbit St. **Facility:** Smoke free premises. 70 units. 62 one-bedroom standard units, some with whirlpools. 7 one- and 1 two-bedroom suites. 3 stories, interior corridors. **Bath:** combo or shower only. **Parking:** on-site, winter plug-ins. **Terms:** check-in 4 pm, cancellation fee imposed. **Amenities:** voice mail, hair dryers. *Some: Fee:* DVD players, video games. **Dining:** Ticino Swiss-Italian Restaurant, see separate listing. **Pool(s):** heated indoor. **Leisure Activities:** sauna, whirlpools. **Guest Services:** valet and coin laundry, area transportation (fee)-ski areas, wireless Internet. **Business Services:** meeting rooms, PC (fee). **Cards:** AX, MC, VI. *(See color ad p 374)*

HOMESTEAD INN Phone: 403/762-4471 **20**

Motel
$85-$149 All Year

Address: 217 Lynx St T1L 1A7 **Location:** Between Caribou and Wolf sts; downtown. **Facility:** 27 one-bedroom standard units. 3 stories (no elevator), exterior corridors. **Parking:** on-site, winter plug-ins. **Terms:** office hours 7 am-11 pm. **Amenities:** hair dryers. **Guest Services:** area transportation (fee). **Cards:** AX, MC, VI.

IRWIN'S MOUNTAIN INN *Book great rates at AAA.com* Phone: (403)762-4566 **13**

Small-scale Hotel
$110-$165 All Year

Address: 429 Banff Ave T1L 1B2 **Location:** N of Rabbit St. **Facility:** 65 units. 59 one- and 6 two-bedroom standard units, some with whirlpools. 3 stories, interior corridors. **Parking:** on-site, winter plug-ins. **Terms:** check-in 4 pm, 2 night minimum stay - weekends, cancellation fee imposed. **Amenities:** voice mail, hair dryers. **Leisure Activities:** sauna, whirlpool, steamroom, ski lockers, exercise room. *Fee:* game room. **Guest Services:** coin laundry, area transportation (fee)-ski areas, wireless Internet. **Business Services:** meeting rooms, PC (fee). **Cards:** AX, MC, VI. **Free Special Amenities:** continental breakfast and high-speed Internet.

▼ See AAA listing p 424 ▼

(See map and index starting on p. 364)

JOHNSTON CANYON RESORT   Phone: 403/762-2971

Cabin
$149-$318 6/20-10/13
$119-$268 5/16-6/19

Address: Hwy 1A T1L 1A9 **Location:** 15 mi (24 km) nw on Hwy 1A (Bow Valley Pkwy). Located at Johnston Canyon. **Facility:** Designated smoking area. 42 cabins. 1 story, exterior corridors. *Bath:* combo or shower only. **Parking:** on-site. **Terms:** open 5/16-10/13, office hours 8 am-10 pm, check-in 4 pm, 3 day cancellation notice. **Amenities:** video library (fee). **Leisure Activities:** tennis court, bicycles, hiking trails. **Cards:** MC, VI. *(See color ad below)*

THE JUNIPER   Phone: (403)762-2281   **2**

Small-scale Hotel
$165-$385 All Year

Address: 1 Juniper Way T1L 1E1 **Location:** Trans-Canada Hwy 1A, exit Mt. Norquay Rd. **Facility:** Smoke free premises. 52 units. 50 one-bedroom standard units, some with kitchens and/or whirlpools. 2 cabins. 3 stories (no elevator), interior corridors. *Bath:* combo or shower only. **Parking:** on-site, winter plug-ins. **Terms:** 3 day cancellation notice-fee imposed. **Amenities:** CD players, high-speed Internet, voice mail, irons, hair dryers. *Some:* safes. **Dining:** Muk a Muk Bistro & Lounge, see separate listing. **Leisure Activities:** whirlpool. **Business Services:** meeting rooms, business center. **Cards:** AX, DC, MC, VI. **Free Special Amenities:** local telephone calls and high-speed Internet.

RED CARPET INN   *Book great rates at AAA.com*   Phone: (403)762-4184   **14**

Small-scale Hotel
$75-$169 All Year

Address: 425 Banff Ave T1L 1B6 **Location:** N of Rabbit St. **Facility:** 52 one-bedroom standard units, some with whirlpools. 3 stories, interior/exterior corridors. **Parking:** on-site, winter plug-ins. **Terms:** check-in 4 pm. **Amenities:** safes, hair dryers. **Leisure Activities:** whirlpool. **Guest Services:** valet laundry, area transportation (fee)-ski shuttle, wireless Internet. **Business Services:** PC (fee). **Cards:** AX, MC, VI.

THE RIMROCK RESORT HOTEL   *Book great rates at AAA.com*   Phone: (403)762-3356   **22**

Large-scale Hotel
$215-$575 All Year

Address: 300 Mountain Ave T1L 1J2 **Location:** 2.4 mi (4 km) s via Sulphur Mountain Rd; adjacent to Upper Hot Springs Pool. Located in a quiet secluded area. **Facility:** Tucked away in the mountains just on the outside of town, this luxurious resort hotel features elegant rooms and upscale dining. 346 one-bedroom standard units. 9 stories, interior corridors. **Parking:** on-site and valet, winter plug-ins. **Terms:** 3 day cancellation notice. **Amenities:** video games (fee), dual phone lines, voice mail, honor bars, irons, hair dryers. **Dining:** Eden, see separate listing, entertainment. **Pool(s):** heated indoor. **Leisure Activities:** sauna, whirlpool, steamrooms, ice skating, hiking trails, spa, aerobics, sports court. *Fee:* ski shuttle. **Guest Services:** valet laundry, area transportation-downtown, wireless Internet. **Business Services:** conference facilities, business center. **Cards:** AX, DC, DS, JC, MC, VI. **Free Special Amenities:** local telephone calls. *(See color ad p 377)*

(See map and index starting on p. 364)

RUNDLESTONE LODGE *Book great rates at AAA.com* **Phone:** (403)762-2201 **4**

Small-scale Hotel
$109-$279 All Year

Address: 537 Banff Ave T1L 1A6 **Location:** 0.9 km ne. **Facility:** 96 units. 94 one-bedroom standard units, some with whirlpools. 2 one-bedroom suites with kitchens and whirlpools. 3 stories, interior corridors. **Parking:** on-site. **Terms:** cancellation fee imposed. **Amenities:** high-speed Internet, hair dryers. **Pool(s):** heated indoor. **Leisure Activities:** whirlpool, ski locker, exercise room. **Guest Services:** valet and coin laundry, area transportation (fee)-ski shuttle. **Business Services:** meeting rooms, PC (fee). **Cards:** AX, DC, DS, MC, VI.
(See color ad p 374)

▼ See AAA listing p 376 ▼

(See map and index starting on p. 364)

TUNNEL MOUNTAIN RESORT　*Book great rates at AAA.com*　Phone: (403)762-4515　**6**

Condominium
$233-$294 1/7-2/28
$195-$294 3/1-1/6

Address: Tunnel Mountain Rd T1L 1B1 **Location:** From centre, 1 mi (1.6 km) ne. **Facility:** 94 units. 24 one-bedroom standard units with whirlpools. 15 one- and 55 two-bedroom suites, some with whirlpools. 2 stories, exterior corridors. **Parking:** on-site, winter plug-ins. **Terms:** check-in 4 pm, cancellation fee imposed. **Amenities:** voice mail, hair dryers. *Some:* DVD players, high-speed Internet (fee), dual phone lines. **Pool(s):** heated indoor. **Leisure Activities:** sauna, whirlpools, steamroom, playground, exercise room. *Fee:* massage. **Guest Services:** valet and coin laundry. **Business Services:** meeting rooms, PC (fee). **Cards:** AX, DC, DS, JC, MC, VI.

── WHERE TO DINE ──

THE BANFFSHIRE CLUB　Phone: 403/762-6860　**22**

Continental
$90-$130

A meal at the sophisticated, exquisite restaurant likely will be remembered for a lifetime. Harp music permeates the air and sets the tone for an evening of fine dining, where meals are as pleasant as a finely tuned orchestra. Scottish furnishings are plentiful, and the servers don kilts. Each dish is a work of art and almost too beautiful to eat. Guests should be prepared for fine food, fine wine and fine service. Dressy casual. **Bar:** Full bar. **Reservations:** required. **Hours:** 6 pm-10 pm, Tues-Thurs to 9 pm. Closed: Sun & Mon. **Address:** 405 Spray Ave T1L 1J4 **Location:** Just s on Banff Ave over the bridge, 0.3 mi (0.5 km) e; in The Fairmont Banff Springs. **Parking:** on-site and valet. **Cards:** AX, DC, DS, JC, MC, VI.

BUMPER'S THE BEEF HOUSE　Phone: 403/762-2622　**2**

Steak House
$15-$40

Established in 1975, the restaurant occupies an A-frame building. The decor is a blend of the Old West and a mountain chalet, with the loft-lounge overlooking the dining room. Patrons can enjoy the all-you-can-eat salad bar with each entree. Although the succulent hamburgers are a favorite, the menu also features prime rib and steaks, all served by the friendly staff. Casual dress. **Bar:** Full bar. **Reservations:** accepted. **Hours:** 5 pm-10 pm. Closed: 12/24, 12/25. **Address:** 603 Banff Ave T1L 1A9 **Location:** 0.8 mi (1.2 km) ne on Banff Ave at Marmot St; in Bumper's Inn. **Parking:** on-site. **Cards:** AX, DC, MC, VI.

CAFE SOLEIL　Phone: 403/762-2090　**10**

Mediterranean
$8-$35

The Mediterranean-style bistro is owned by the same folks who run Typhoon and is fast becoming a popular spot in Banff. Guests can sit for hours sampling and sharing the distinctive tapas, including lamb lollipops, eggplant and homemade soup. Casual dress. **Bar:** Full bar. **Hours:** 7 am-2 & 6-10:30 pm. Closed major holidays. **Address:** 208 Caribou St T1L 1C1 **Location:** Just w off Banff Ave; centre; in Brewster's Mountain Lodge. **Parking:** street. **Cards:** AX, DC, MC, VI.

CILANTRO MOUNTAIN CAFE　Phone: 403/760-4488　**3**

Southwest
California
$14-$30

The seasonal restaurant treats patrons to fine, friendly service in a casual atmosphere. However, the food— an eclectic mix of designer wood-fired pizzas, pasta dishes and fantastic desserts, all relying heavily on regional ingredients—is anything but casual. On summer days, locals often congregate on the patio. Casual dress. **Bar:** Full bar. **Hours:** Open 3/1-9/10 & 12/13-2/28; 5 pm-10 pm. Closed: Mon & Tues 12/13-5/31. **Address:** 700 Tunnel Mountain Rd T1L 1B3 **Location:** 1 mi (1.6 km) ne; in Buffalo Mountain Lodge. **Parking:** on-site. **Cards:** AX, DC, MC, VI.

COYOTES DELI & GRILL　Phone: 403/762-3963　**11**

Regional
Canadian
$8-$22

Set in a relaxed yet lively deli-bistro, Coyotes focuses on contemporary Southwest cuisine with an accent on creativity and color. A large open kitchen allows you to watch your food being prepared. Casual dress. **Bar:** Full bar. **Reservations:** suggested, for dinner. **Hours:** 7:30-11 am, 11:30-4 & 5-11 pm. Closed: 12/25. **Address:** 206 Caribou St T1L 1A2 **Location:** Just w of Banff Ave; centre. **Parking:** street. **Cards:** AX, DC, MC, VI.

EDEN　*Menu on AAA.com*　Phone: 403/762-1840　**21**

French
$90-$150

Tastes, textures, creativity and imagination mingle to produce an exquisite meal from beginning to end. A touch of something magical is evident at the intimate restaurant, where hours pass unnoticed as diners unwind in plush wingback chairs, gazing out at the spectacular mountains. The finest crystal touches guests' lips, and the finest food teases their taste buds. A team of professional servers will provide attentive and knowledgeable service, creating a memorable experience. Dressy casual. **Bar:** Full bar. **Reservations:** suggested. **Hours:** 6 pm-10 pm. **Address:** 100 Mountain Ave T1L 1J2 **Location:** 2.4 mi (4 km) s via Sulphur Mountain Rd; adjacent to Upper Hot Springs Pool; in The Rimrock Resort Hotel. **Parking:** on-site and valet. **Cards:** AX, DC, DS, JC, MC, VI.

THE EVERGREEN　Phone: 403/762-3307　**5**

International
$10-$37

An open-concept kitchen, innovative Continental menu and comfortable yet elegant ambience make the restaurant a popular choice. Dishes highlight fresh local and regional ingredients. This place is within easy walking distance of the town center. Casual dress. **Bar:** Full bar. **Reservations:** suggested. **Hours:** 6:30 am-10 pm; seasonal hours may vary. **Address:** 459 Banff Ave T1L 1B4 **Location:** 0.6 mi (1 km) ne; in Delta Banff Royal Canadian Lodge. **Parking:** valet and street. **Cards:** AX, DC, DS, JC, MC, VI.

FUZE FINER DINING　Phone: 403/760-0853　**20**

International
$11-$35

This chic, sexy restaurant has distinctive display cases filled with wines that professionally trained sommeliers know well. Global dishes integrate the accents and ingredients of France, Asia and India. Casual dress. **Bar:** Full bar. **Reservations:** accepted. **Hours:** 11:30 am-2 & 5-9 pm. Closed major holidays. **Address:** 110 Banff Ave, 2nd Floor T1L 1C9 **Location:** Centre; 2nd floor of Clock Tower Village Mall. **Parking:** street. **Cards:** AX, DC, MC, VI.

GIORGIO'S TRATTORIA　Phone: 403/762-5114　**9**

Italian
$15-$40

This restaurant's Southern and Mediterranean decor offers a warm, relaxed ambience. The dishes include fresh pasta made in-house, meat and seafood specialties, and pizza cooked in a traditional wood-burning oven. Casual dress. **Bar:** Full bar. **Reservations:** suggested. **Hours:** 5 pm-10:30 pm; to 10 pm off season. **Address:** 219 Banff Ave T0L 0C0 **Location:** Centre. **Parking:** street. **Cards:** AX, MC, VI.

(See map and index starting on p. 364)

GRIZZLY HOUSE   **Phone:** 403/762-4055

Fondue

$10-$50

The eclectic and rustic downtown restaurant treats patrons to a distinctive fondue experience. Beef, buffalo, chicken, ostrich, rattlesnake, lobster and shark are among meats available for dipping. Finish the meal with a decadent chocolate fondue. Hot rock fondues are a particularly memorable experience. The bustling atmosphere is fun and lively. Casual dress. **Bar:** Full bar. **Reservations:** suggested. **Hours:** 11:30 am-midnight. **Address:** 207 Banff Ave T1L 1B4 **Location:** Between Caribou and Wolf sts. **Parking:** street. **Cards:** AX, MC, VI.

LE BEAUJOLAIS   *Menu on AAA.com*   **Phone:** 403/762-2712   ⑲

French

$25-$95

Guests ascend the stairs to the elegant dining room, which overlooks one of the main streets. The restaurant offers an experience, not just a meal. Professional servers ensure a memorable event from beginning to end. The cuisine, a harmony of traditional elements prepared with a contemporary flair, is available as a prix fixe menu or a la carte. The wine list is among the most impressive in town. Dressy casual. **Bar:** Full bar. **Reservations:** suggested. **Hours:** Open 3/1-10/31 & 12/1-2/28; 6 pm-11 pm. **Address:** 212 Buffalo St T1L 1B5 **Location:** Northwest corner of Banff Ave and Buffalo St; upstairs; near bridge. **Parking:** street. **Cards:** AX, MC, VI.

THE MAPLE LEAF GRILLE & SPIRITS   **Phone:** 403/760-7680   ⑰

Canadian

$13-$50

The restaurant is a favorite for a truly Canadian experience, both in food and decor. The cozy, rock-and-wood interior displays Canadian art, as well as a canoe on the ceiling and snowshoes on the walls. The chef creates artistic regional dishes, using organic, free-range, locally grown ingredients when possible. Among selections are preparations of elk, venison, salmon and char, all made to complement the season. **Bar:** Full bar. **Reservations:** suggested. **Hours:** 11 am-10 pm. Closed: for lunch 12/25. **Address:** 137 Banff Ave T1L 1C8 **Location:** Corner of Banff Ave and Caribou St. **Parking:** street. **Cards:** AX, DC, MC, VI.

MUK A MUK BISTRO & LOUNGE   *Menu on AAA.com*   **Phone:** 403/763-6205   ①

Canadian

$10-$44

CALL ♿ M

Offering an unparallel view of Mt. Rundle, the Vermillion Lakes and the Banff town site, this upscale restaurant with its semi-open kitchen features a creative Canadian menu and a variety of Native dishes designed to be shared as a group. Casual dress. **Bar:** Full bar. **Reservations:** accepted. **Hours:** 7 am-10 pm. **Address:** 1 Juniper Way T1L 1E1 **Location:** Trans-Canada Hwy 1A, exit Mt. Norquey Rd; in The Juniper. **Parking:** on-site. **Cards:** AX, MC, VI.

ST JAMES'S GATE OLDE IRISH PUB   **Phone:** 403/762-9355   ⑦

Irish

$9-$25

For a casual place to kick back in the typical Irish way, look no further. The modern-day version of a rustic pub serves traditional food, such as shepherd's pie, steak and Guinness pie. Lamb stew is a fantastic, hearty choice, served with a chunk of soda bread. Guests can savor a pint of locally brewed beer or try some of the ales from overseas. Also on hand is an impressive selection of single-malt scotches, local and imported draft beers and cigars. Entertainment. **Bar:** Full bar. **Reservations:** accepted. **Hours:** 11 am-1 am, Fri & Sat-2 am. **Address:** 207 Wolf St T1L 1C2 **Location:** Just w of Banff Ave; centre. **Parking:** street. **Cards:** AX, MC, VI.

SALTLIK A RARE STEAKHOUSE   **Phone:** 403/762-2467   ⑧

Steak House

$10-$30

CALL ♿ M

True to its name, the restaurant truly is a "rare steak house" and a superb place. From the moment guests ascend the stairs to the upscale, contemporary dining room, they're impressed by the atmosphere. Also praiseworthy is the incredibly friendly, attentive service. Servers take the time to explain the different cuts of meat and accompanying sauces. All entrees are a la carte, and the side orders are large enough to split. Casual dress. **Bar:** Full bar. **Reservations:** accepted. **Hours:** 11 am-11 pm. Closed: 12/25. **Address:** 221 Bear St T1L 1B3 **Location:** Jct Caribou and Bear sts. **Parking:** street. **Cards:** AX, MC, VI.

SILVER DRAGON RESTAURANT   **Phone:** 403/762-3939   ⑭

Chinese

$6-$15

Two flights up from street level, the restaurant is a definite stop for those who crave Chinese food. Portions of seafood, pork, noodles and beef are certain to satisfy any appetite. Patrons discover a contemporary decor, complete with a fish tank that the kids will enjoy. Casual dress. **Bar:** Full bar. **Reservations:** accepted. **Hours:** 11:30 am-10 pm. **Address:** 211 Banff Ave T1L 1E4 **Location:** Centre. **Parking:** street. **Cards:** AX, DC, JC, MC, VI.

SLEEPING BUFFALO RESTAURANT & LOUNGE   **Phone:** 403/760-4484   ④

Regional Canadian

$9-$37

You'll appreciate the casual elegance in this restaurant's mountain setting. Its Rocky Mountain cuisine features wild-game meat, robust flavors and an excellent wine list. After-dinner drinks and a cigar menu are offered fireside in the lounge. Casual dress. **Bar:** Full bar. **Reservations:** suggested. **Hours:** 7 am-10 pm. **Address:** 700 Tunnel Mountain Rd T1L 1B3 **Location:** 1 mi (1.6 km) ne; in Buffalo Mountain Lodge. **Parking:** on-site. **Cards:** AX, DC, MC, VI.

SUKIYAKI HOUSE   **Phone:** 403/762-2002   ⑬

Japanese

$8-$27

Diners who crave sushi might try the modest eatery, upstairs along the city's main avenue. The traditional sushi house decor includes an open-concept sushi bar, where guests can choose from love boat platters, varied sushi and sashimi and traditional miso soup. Casual dress. **Bar:** Full bar. **Reservations:** suggested. **Hours:** 4:30 pm-10 pm; also noon-2:30 pm 6/1-9/30. Closed: 12/24, 12/25. **Address:** 211 Banff Ave T1L 1B8 **Location:** Downtown; in Park Avenue Mall, 2nd floor. **Parking:** street. **Cards:** AX, MC, VI.

(See map and index starting on p. 364)

SUNFOOD CAFE
Phone: 403/760-3933 ⑫

Vegetarian
$5-$15

Upon arrival at the small, intimate bistro, tucked upstairs off the beaten path, guests most likely will be greeted by Christian, the energetic owner of the city's only vegetarian restaurant. He has cultivated a reputation for hearty and healthy options, ranging from curry to soups to daily specials. Casual dress. **Bar:** Full bar. **Reservations:** not accepted. **Hours:** 11 am-9 pm; 10 am-10 pm 6/1-9/15. Closed: Sun. **Address:** 215 Banff Ave T1L 1B4 **Location:** Downtown; 2nd level of Sundance Mall. **Parking:** on-site. **Cards:** MC, VI.

TICINO SWISS-ITALIAN RESTAURANT
Phone: 403/762-3848 ⑥

Swiss
$14-$38

Set amongst the spectacular mountain peaks of Banff, this Swiss restaurant, which has been serving customers for over 30 years, has developed a solid reputation with locals and repeat visitors alike for its contemporary "Cucina Nostrana." Using local ingredients, whenever possible, the restaurant also features a number of traditional Swiss dishes including Medallions of Venison, roasted duck breasts and their famous fondues including a superb chocolate fondue for desert. Casual dress. **Bar:** Full bar. **Reservations:** suggested. **Hours:** Open 3/1-11/9 & 12/8-2/28; 5:30 pm-10 pm. **Address:** 415 Banff Ave T1L 1B5 **Location:** N of Rabbit St; in High Country Inn. **Parking:** on-site. **Cards:** AX, DC, JC, MC, VI.

TOMMY'S NEIGHBOURHOOD PUB
Phone: 403/762-8888 ⑱

American
$8-$18

After a day on the ski hills or hiking in the mountains, the restaurant is a good stop for a great burger and a pint of ale. Locals frequent the place not only for its food but also for its casual, pub-style atmosphere. Menu offerings also include soups, salads and sandwiches. Guests can settle into a booth or belly up to the bar for great conversation and good times. Casual dress. **Bar:** Full bar. **Hours:** 11 am-2 am. Closed: 12/25. **Address:** 120 Banff Ave T1L 1A4 **Location:** Downtown. **Parking:** street. **Cards:** AX, MC, VI.

TYPHOON
Phone: 403/762-2000 ⑯

International
$6-$22

Funky, eclectic, chic and upbeat all are words that describe the atmosphere at the laid-back, intimate bistro, where the food is anything but casual. The owners label the fare as "eclectic Asian," and the menu proves it, with Thai, Vietnamese, Japanese and other Asian influences. Fast becoming a popular spot with the locals, this place prepares innovative food in an eclectic environment. Bright and bold, the decor features artwork by one of the owners. Casual dress. **Bar:** Full bar. **Reservations:** suggested. **Hours:** 10 am-11 pm. Closed major holidays. **Address:** 211 Caribou St T1L 1B5 **Location:** Downtown. **Parking:** street. **Cards:** AX, CB, DS, JC, MC, VI.

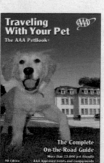

BEAVER MINES pop. 71

—————— WHERE TO STAY ——————

ASPEN GROVE B & B

Bed & Breakfast
$80 All Year

Phone: 403/627-2928

Address: Buckhord Rd T0K 1W0 **Location:** Hwy 6, 11.8 mi (19 km) w on SR 507, 4.3 mi (7 km) s on SR 744, then 1.2 mi (2 km) w; Hwy 3, 12.5 mi (20 km) s on SR 744, then 1.2 mi (2 km) w at Buckhorn Rd. **Facility:** Nestled in a spectacular mountain setting, this upscale B&B offers sweeping views and proximity to skiing. Smoke free premises. 4 one-bedroom standard units. 2 stories (no elevator), interior corridors. *Bath:* combo or shower only. **Parking:** on-site, winter plug-ins. **Terms:** 7 day cancellation notice. **Amenities:** *Some:* hair dryers. **Leisure Activities:** whirlpool, fishing, hiking trails. *Fee:* horseback riding. **Guest Services:** complimentary laundry. **Business Services:** meeting rooms. **Cards:** VI.

⊠ ⊠ 🄺 🄿 ☎

BROOKS pop. 12,498

—————— WHERE TO STAY ——————

BEST WESTERN BROOKS INN   *Book great rates at AAA.com*

ⒸⒶⒶ 🆂🅰🆅🅴

Small-scale Hotel
Rates not provided

Phone: 403/363-0080

Address: 115 Fifteenth Ave W T1R 1C4 **Location:** Just s off Trans-Canada Hwy 1. **Facility:** 94 units. 89 one-bedroom standard units, some with efficiencies and/or whirlpools. 5 one-bedroom suites. 3 stories, interior/exterior corridors. *Bath:* combo or shower only. **Parking:** on-site, winter plug-ins. **Amenities:** high-speed Internet, voice mail, safes, irons, hair dryers. *Some:* video games (fee). **Pool(s):** heated indoor. **Leisure Activities:** whirlpool, waterslide, exercise room. **Guest Services:** coin laundry. **Business Services:** meeting rooms. **Free Special Amenities:** expanded continental breakfast and high-speed Internet.

[Best Western logo]
AAA Benefit:
Members save 10% everyday, plus an exclusive frequent stay program.

🍴 CALL 🅼 🏊 ⊠ 📷 🎞 🖥 🖵 ☕ / SOME UNITS FEE 🐾 ⊠ 🆅🅲🆁

HERITAGE INN

Small-scale Hotel
$105-$120 All Year

Phone: (403)362-6666

Address: 1217 2nd St W T1R 1B8 **Location:** Trans-Canada Hwy 1, exit Hwy 873, 0.5 mi (0.8 km) s. **Facility:** 106 units. 103 one-bedroom standard units. 3 one-bedroom suites, some with efficiencies. 2 stories (no elevator), interior corridors. **Parking:** on-site, winter plug-ins. **Amenities:** voice mail. *Some:* high-speed Internet (fee). **Leisure Activities:** sauna, whirlpool, exercise room. **Guest Services:** valet laundry. **Business Services:** meeting rooms. **Cards:** AX, MC, VI.

🄰🅂🄺 🆂🄳 🍴 🍸 ⊠ 📷 🖵 / SOME UNITS FEE 🐾 ⊠ 🆅🅲🆁 🖥 🖵

HERITAGE INN & SUITES

🔽🔽🔽

Small-scale Hotel
$124-$245 12/1-2/28
$119-$239 3/1-11/30

Phone: (403)362-8579

Address: 1239 2nd St W T1R 1B8 **Location:** Trans-Canada Hwy 1, exit Hwy 873, 0.5 mi (0.8 km) s. **Facility:** 61 units. 52 one- and 6 two-bedroom standard units, some with whirlpools. 2 one- and 1 two-bedroom suites, some with efficiencies and/or whirlpools. 3 stories, interior corridors. *Bath:* combo or shower only. **Parking:** on-site, winter plug-ins. **Amenities:** high-speed Internet, voice mail, irons, hair dryers. *Some:* DVD players (fee), CD players. **Pool(s):** heated indoor. **Leisure Activities:** whirlpool, exercise room. **Guest Services:** coin laundry. **Business Services:** meeting rooms, business center. **Cards:** AX, DS, MC, VI.

🄰🅂🄺 🆂🄳 🍴 CALL 🅼 🏊 🎞 🖥 🖵 ☕ / SOME UNITS ⊠ FEE 🆅🅲🆁

LAKEVIEW INN & SUITES   *Book great rates at AAA.com*

🔽🔽🔽🔽

Small-scale Hotel
$139-$179 All Year

Phone: (403)362-7440

Address: 1307 2nd St W T1R 1B7 **Location:** Trans-Canada Hwy 1, exit Hwy 873, 0.5 mi (0.8 km) s. **Facility:** 78 units. 63 one-bedroom standard units, some with whirlpools. 15 one-bedroom suites. 3 stories, interior corridors. **Parking:** on-site, winter plug-ins. **Amenities:** high-speed Internet, dual phone lines, irons, hair dryers. **Pool(s):** heated indoor. **Leisure Activities:** whirlpool, exercise room. **Guest Services:** valet and coin laundry. **Business Services:** meeting rooms. **Cards:** AX, MC, VI.

🄰🅂🄺 🆂🄳 🍴 CALL 🅼 🏊 📷 🖥 🖵 🖵 / SOME UNITS FEE 🐾 ⊠

TRAVELODGE BROOKS   *Book at AAA.com*

🔽🔽

Small-scale Hotel
$96-$119 3/1-12/31
$92-$114 1/1-2/28

Phone: (403)362-8000

Address: 1240 Cassils Rd E T1R 1C3 **Location:** Trans-Canada Hwy 1, just sw on SR 542, exit E Brooks. **Facility:** 61 one-bedroom standard units. 2 stories (no elevator), interior/exterior corridors. **Parking:** on-site, winter plug-ins. **Terms:** check-in 4 pm, cancellation fee imposed. **Amenities:** video games (fee). **Guest Services:** coin laundry. **Business Services:** meeting rooms. **Cards:** AX, MC, VI.

🄰🅂🄺 🆂🄳 🍴 CALL 🅼 📷 🖥 🖵 🖵 / SOME UNITS FEE 🐾 ⊠

—————— WHERE TO DINE ——————

LUIGI'S PIZZA AND STEAKHOUSE

Steak House
$5-$25

Phone: 403/501-5995

The simple family restaurant serves a variety of options sure to satisfy even the pickiest of eaters. Whether ordering pizza, a Greek specialty or a steak, patrons can anticipate fast service and a hearty meal. Casual dress. **Bar:** Full bar. **Hours:** 11 am-midnight, Fri & Sat-1 am, Sun 11:30 am-midnight. Closed: 12/25. **Address:** 1020 2nd St W T1R 0C3 **Location:** Trans-Canada Hwy 1, 1.2 mi (2 km) s. **Parking:** on-site. **Cards:** AX, MC, VI.

Destination Calgary

pop. 988,193

A versatile city with an abundance of theaters and shopping malls, Calgary seems to have something for everyone.

Y ou can attend a horse show, join in a rousing celebration of the Wild West or browse through unique marketplaces. Want to ride down a rushing river? Calgary won't leave you high and dry.

Travel Alberta

Spruce Meadows, Calgary.
Show jumping horses are a common sight at this equestrian center. (See mention page 58)

Tourism Calgary

Taste of Calgary.
The menus of Calgary's restaurants range from four-diamond *haute cuisine* to chuck wagon plain.

Tourism Calgary

Airdrie●
② **See Vicinity map page 388**

●Cochrane

†

(1A)

See Downtown map page 384

Calgary

Strathmore

Okotoks●
②

Pengrowth Saddledome, Calgary.
The area's Wild West legacy is reflected in the saddle shape of this premier venue for concerts and sporting events. (See mention page 58)

© Gibson Stock Photography

Stephen Avenue Walk, Calgary.
Strollers and cyclists soak up summer sunshine in this downtown pedestrian mall with benches for people-watching, shops for browsing and eateries for grazing. (See mention page 58)

P laces included in this AAA Destination City:

Airdrie................420   Okotoks..............421
Cochrane...........420   Strathmore.........422

Downtown
Calgary
Lodging and Dining

Downtown Calgary

This index helps you "spot" where approved lodgings and restaurants are located on the corresponding detailed maps. Lodging daily rate range is for comparison only and show the property's high season. Restaurant rate range is a combination of lunch and/or dinner. Turn to the listing page for more detailed rate information and consult display ads for special promotions.

Spotter/Map Page Number	OA	DOWNTOWN CALGARY - Lodgings	Diamond Rating	Rate Range High Season	Listing Page
1 / p. 384	CAA	Sheraton Suites Calgary Eau Claire	◆◆◆◆	Rates not provided SAVE	396
2 / p. 384	CAA	Kensington Riverside Inn	◆◆◆◆	$339-$439 SAVE	395
3 / p. 384	CAA	The Westin Calgary	◆◆◆◆	$129-$489 SAVE	396
4 / p. 384		International Hotel of Calgary	◆◆	Rates not provided	395
5 / p. 384		5 Calgary Downtown Suites	◆◆	$99-$369	393
6 / p. 384	CAA	Delta Bow Valley	◆◆◆	$139-$469 SAVE	394
7 / p. 384	CAA	Best Western Suites Downtown - see color ad p 393	◆◆	$142-$161 SAVE	393
8 / p. 384		Sandman Hotel Downtown Calgary	◆◆◆	$179-$199	395
9 / p. 384		Holiday Inn Express Hotel & Suites Calgary Downtown	◆◆◆	$199-$259	394
10 / p. 384	CAA	Hyatt Regency Calgary - see color ad p 395	◆◆◆◆	$149-$439 SAVE	395
11 / p. 384	CAA	Calgary Marriott Hotel - see color ad p 394	◆◆◆	$318-$340 SAVE	393
12 / p. 384		The Fairmont Palliser	◆◆◆◆	$179-$449	394
13 / p. 384		Hotel Arts	◆◆◆	$139-$309	394
		DOWNTOWN CALGARY - Restaurants			
1 / p. 384		Broken Plate Kitchen & Bar	◆◆	$10-$24	397
2 / p. 384		La Brezza	◆◆	$9-$25	400
3 / p. 384	CAA	La Dolce Vita Ristorante Italiano	◆◆◆	$9-$25	401
4 / p. 384		Charly Chan's Rice House	◆◆	$8-$16	398
5 / p. 384		Maurya	◆◆	$8-$16	401
6 / p. 384		Barclay's	◆◆◆	$10-$25	397
7 / p. 384		Julio's Barrio Mexican Restaurant	◆◆	$12-$19	400
8 / p. 384		Pulcinella	◆◆	$11-$21	403
9 / p. 384	CAA	Il Sogno	◆◆◆	$10-$40	400
10 / p. 384		Muse Restaurant & Lounge	◆◆◆	$25-$40	402
11 / p. 384		Sakana Grill	◆◆	$7-$17	403
12 / p. 384		The Belvedere	◆◆◆	$18-$35	397
13 / p. 384		Don Quijote	◆◆	$9-$22	399
14 / p. 384	CAA	Silver Dragon Restaurant	◆◆	$6-$17	404
15 / p. 384	CAA	Caesar's Steakhouse	◆◆◆	$10-$70	397
16 / p. 384		Oriental Phoenix	◆◆◆	$6-$15	402
17 / p. 384		The Glory Of India	◆◆	$16-$23	399
18 / p. 384		The Chophouse	◆◆◆	$15-$38	398
19 / p. 384		Metropolitian Grill	◆◆◆	$9-$25	401
20 / p. 384	CAA	Catch Dining Room	◆◆◆	$10-$40	398
21 / p. 384	CAA	Centini Restaurant and Lounge	◆◆◆	$7-$45	398
22 / p. 384	CAA	Teatro	◆◆◆	$15-$120	404

Spotter/Map Page Number	OA	DOWNTOWN CALGARY - Restaurants (continued)	Diamond Rating	Rate Range High Season	Listing Page
23 / p. 384		Murrieta's Westcoast Grill	◆◆◆	$10-$35	402
24 / p. 384		Thomson's Restaurant	◆◆◆	$10-$35	404
25 / p. 384		River Cafe	◆◆◆	$7-$40	403
26 / p. 384		Tribune Restaurant	◆◆◆	$12-$50	404
27 / p. 384		Prairie Ink Restaurant & Bakery	◆◆	$6-$13	403
28 / p. 384		The Orchid Room Fusion Cuisine	◆◆	$14-$30	402
29 / p. 384		Rose Garden Thai Restaurant	◆◆	$8-$15	403
30 / p. 384		Divino Wine & Cheese Bistro	◆◆◆	$12-$35	399
31 / p. 384		Saltlik, A Rare Steakhouse	◆◆◆	$12-$40	403
32 / p. 384		Avenue Diner	◆◆	$6-$13	397
33 / p. 384	CAA	**Catch Restaurant**	◆◆◆◆	$16-$40	398
34 / p. 384		The Rimrock Dining Room	◆◆◆	$11-$34	403
35 / p. 384		The Panorama Dining Room	◆◆◆	$11-$38	402
36 / p. 384		Deane House Historic Site Restaurant at Fort Calgary	◆◆	$8-$14	398
37 / p. 384		Bonterra Trattoria	◆◆◆	$12-$38	397
38 / p. 384		The Holy Grill	◆	$8-$12	400
39 / p. 384		Pegasus	◆	$8-$18	403
40 / p. 384		Thai Sa-On Restaurant	◆◆	$6-$18	404
41 / p. 384		The King & I	◆◆◆	$8-$25	400
42 / p. 384		Vintage Chophouse & Tavern	◆◆◆	$10-$50	404
43 / p. 384		Gnocchi's Ristorante	◆◆◆	$8-$23	399
44 / p. 384		Mescalero	◆◆◆	$7-$24	401
45 / p. 384		Galaxie Diner	◆	$6-$10	399
46 / p. 384		Palace of Eats	◆	$9-$12	402
47 / p. 384		Manuel Latruwe Belgian Patisserie & Bread Shop	◆◆	$4-$7	401
48 / p. 384		Ric's Grill	◆◆◆	$10-$30	403
49 / p. 384		Good Earth Coffeehouse & Bakery	◆	$5-$8	400
50 / p. 384		Steeps The Urban Teahouse	◆	$3-$6	404
51 / p. 384		Restaurant Indonesia	◆◆	$8-$15	403
52 / p. 384		Cilantro	◆◆◆	$12-$40	398
53 / p. 384		El Sombrero Restaurant	◆◆	$11-$20	399
54 / p. 384		Nellie's Kitchen	◆	$4-$9	402
55 / p. 384		Wrapture	◆	$5-$8	405
56 / p. 384		The Living Room	◆◆◆	$15-$40	401
57 / p. 384		Kyoto 17	◆◆	$6-$20	400
58 / p. 384		Mt. Everest's Kitchen	◆◆	$10-$22	401
59 / p. 384		Moti Mahal	◆◆	$10-$20	401
60 / p. 384		Da Paolo Ristorante	◆◆◆	$8-$29	398
61 / p. 384		La Chaumiere Restaurant	◆◆◆◆	$9-$33	400

Spotter/Map Page Number	OA	DOWNTOWN CALGARY - Restaurants (continued)	Diamond Rating	Rate Range High Season	Listing Page
62 / p. 384		Brava Bistro	◆◆◆	$8-$32	397
63 / p. 384		Sultan's Tent	◆◆	$14-$23	404
64 / p. 384		Codo Vietnamese Restaurant	◆	$5-$15	398
65 / p. 384		Hana Sushi	◆◆	$5-$20	400
66 / p. 384		Peking Dragon	◆◆	$7-$12	403
67 / p. 384		Fleur de Sel	◆◆	$12-$38	399
68 / p. 384		Le Chien Chaud	◆	$6-$8	401
69 / p. 384		Ouzo Greek Taverna	◆◆	$6-$16	402
70 / p. 384		Sushi Kawa	◆◆	$6-$20	404
71 / p. 384		Aida's	◆◆	$5-$12	397
72 / p. 384		Bistro Twenty Two Ten	◆◆◆	$12-$28	397
73 / p. 384		Mercato	◆◆◆	$12-$35	401
74 / p. 384		The Joyce on 4th Irish Pub	◆◆	$6-$18	400
75 / p. 384		Wildwood	◆◆◆	$10-$30	404

Calgary
Lodging & Dining

✈ Airport Accommodations

Spotter/Map Page Number	OA	CALGARY INTERNATIONAL AIRPORT	Diamond Rating	Rate Range High Season	Listing Page
18 / p. 388	CAA	Best Western Airport Inn, 10 km s of airport	▽▽	$120-$260 SAVE	405
4 / p. 388	CAA	Best Western Port O'Call Hotel, 3.8 mi (6 km) s of airport	▽▽▽	$139-$199 SAVE	406
26 / p. 388		Coast Plaza Hotel & Conference Centre, 12 km s of airport	▽▽▽	$139-$249	406
10 / p. 388	CAA	Comfort Inn And Suites-Airport, 8 km s of airport	▽▽▽	$129-$299 SAVE	406
6 / p. 388	CAA	Country Inn & Suites By Carlson, 4.1 mi (6.5 km) s of airport	▽▽▽	$164-$208 SAVE	407
15 / p. 388		Days Inn Calgary Airport, 8 km s of airport	▽▽▽	$129-$159	407
1 / p. 388	CAA	Delta Calgary Airport, at airport	▽▽▽	$159-$550 SAVE	407
12 / p. 388		Executive Royal Inn North Calgary, 8.2 km s of airport	▽▽▽	$144-$205	408
7 / p. 388		Hampton Inn & Suites-Calgary Airport, 5.8 km s of airport	▽▽▽	Rates not provided	409
3 / p. 388		Hilton Garden Inn-Calgary Airport, 4.2 mi (7 km) s of airport	▽▽▽	$189-$269	411
25 / p. 388	CAA	Holiday Inn Calgary-Airport, 10 km s of airport	▽▽▽	$139-$259 SAVE	411
5 / p. 388	CAA	Lakeview Signature Inn, 6 km s of airport	▽▽▽	$139-$199 SAVE	411
23 / p. 388		Radisson Hotel Calgary Airport, 10 km s of airport	▽▽▽	$240	411
2 / p. 388		Sandman Hotel Suites & Spa Calgary Airport, 7 km s of airport	▽▽▽	$189	411
9 / p. 388		Sheraton Cavalier Hotel, 7.5 km s of airport	▽▽▽	$469	412
11 / p. 388	CAA	Super 8 Motel Calgary Airport, 8 km s of airport	▽▽	$130-$240 SAVE	412
13 / p. 388	CAA	Travelodge Hotel Calgary Airport, 8 km s of airport	▽▽	$179-$229 SAVE	412

Calgary

This index helps you "spot" where approved lodgings and restaurants are located on the corresponding detailed maps. Lodging daily rate range is for comparison only and show the property's high season. Restaurant rate range is a combination of lunch and/or dinner. Turn to the listing page for more detailed rate information and consult display ads for special promotions.

Spotter/Map Page Number	OA	CALGARY - Lodgings	Diamond Rating	Rate Range High Season	Listing Page
1 / p. 388	CAA	Delta Calgary Airport	▽▽▽	$159-$550 SAVE	407
2 / p. 388		Sandman Hotel Suites & Spa Calgary Airport	▽▽▽	$189	411
3 / p. 388		Hilton Garden Inn-Calgary Airport	▽▽▽	$189-$269	411
4 / p. 388	CAA	Best Western Port O'Call Hotel - see color ad p 405	▽▽▽	$139-$199 SAVE	406
5 / p. 388	CAA	Lakeview Signature Inn	▽▽▽	$139-$199 SAVE	411
6 / p. 388	CAA	Country Inn & Suites By Carlson - see color ad p 407	▽▽▽	$164-$208 SAVE	407
7 / p. 388		Hampton Inn & Suites-Calgary Airport	▽▽▽	Rates not provided	409
8 / p. 388	CAA	Four Points by Sheraton Hotel and Suites, Calgary West	▽▽▽	$200-$280 SAVE	409
9 / p. 388		Sheraton Cavalier Hotel	▽▽▽	$469	412
10 / p. 388	CAA	Comfort Inn And Suites-Airport - see color ad on insert	▽▽▽	$129-$299 SAVE	406

Spotter/Map Page Number	OA	CALGARY - Lodgings (continued)	Diamond Rating	Rate Range High Season	Listing Page
11 / p. 388	CAA	**Super 8 Motel Calgary Airport**	◆◆	$130-$240 SAVE	412
12 / p. 388		Executive Royal Inn North Calgary	◆◆◆	$144-$205	408
13 / p. 388	CAA	**Travelodge Hotel Calgary Airport - see color ad p 413**	◆◆	$179-$229 SAVE	412
14 / p. 388		Staybridge Suites Calgary Airport	◆◆◆	Rates not provided	412
15 / p. 388		Days Inn Calgary Airport	◆◆◆	$129-$159	407
16 / p. 388	CAA	**Comfort Inn & Suites-Motel Village - see color ad on insert**	◆◆◆	$119-$399 SAVE	407
17 / p. 388	CAA	**Quality Inn University - see color ad on insert**	◆◆	$119-$299 SAVE	411
18 / p. 388	CAA	**Best Western Airport Inn**	◆◆	$120-$260 SAVE	405
19 / p. 388	CAA	**Best Western Village Park Inn**	◆◆	$119-$229 SAVE	406
20 / p. 388	CAA	**Hampton Inn & Suites Calgary-University - see color ad p 409**	◆◆◆	$159-$329 SAVE	409
21 / p. 388	CAA	**Econo Lodge Inn & Suites University - see color ad on insert, p 408**	◆◆	$89-$299 SAVE	408
22 / p. 388	CAA	**Travelodge Calgary-University**	◆◆	$98-$187 SAVE	412
23 / p. 388		Radisson Hotel Calgary Airport	◆◆◆	$240	411
24 / p. 388	CAA	**Econo Lodge Motel Village - see color ad on insert**	◆◆	Rates not provided SAVE	408
25 / p. 388	CAA	**Holiday Inn Calgary-Airport - see color ad on insert**	◆◆◆	$139-$259 SAVE	411
26 / p. 388		Coast Plaza Hotel & Conference Centre	◆◆◆	$139-$249	406
27 / p. 388	CAA	**Calgary Westways Guest House**	◆◆◆	$110-$170 SAVE	406
28 / p. 388	CAA	**Best Western Calgary Centre Inn**	◆◆◆	$169-$259 SAVE	405
29 / p. 388	CAA	**Comfort Inn & Suites-South - see color ad on insert**	◆◆◆	$109-$329 SAVE	407
30 / p. 388		Blackfoot Inn	◆◆◆	$195-$325	406
31 / p. 388	CAA	**Econo Lodge South - see color ad on insert**	◆◆	$89-$209 SAVE	408
32 / p. 388		Carriage House Inn	◆◆	$145-$225	406
33 / p. 388	CAA	**Travelodge Calgary Macleod Trail - see color ad p 413**	◆◆	$131-$167 SAVE	412
34 / p. 388	CAA	**Delta Calgary South**	◆◆◆	$399 SAVE	408
35 / p. 388		Holiday Inn Express Hotel & Suites Calgary-South	◆◆◆	Rates not provided	411
36 / p. 388		Wingate Inn	◆◆◆	$147-$169	412
		CALGARY - Restaurants			
1 / p. 388		Buffet Yangtze	◆	$8-$16	415
2 / p. 388		Captain Scott's Fish & Chips	◆	$5-$12	415
3 / p. 388		Alberta King of Subs	◆	$4-$10	414
4 / p. 388		Madisons Cafe & Bar	◆◆	$8-$25	417
5 / p. 388		Nick's Steakhouse & Pizza	◆◆	$8-$30	418
6 / p. 388		Carver's Steakhouse	◆◆◆	$28-$35	415
7 / p. 388		Misai Japanese Restaurant	◆◆	$9-$15	417
8 / p. 388		Thai Boat	◆◆	$4-$13	419
9 / p. 388		Clay Oven	◆◆	$10-$20	415
10 / p. 388		Earl's Barlow Trail	◆◆	$8-$25	416

Spotter/Map Page Number	OA	CALGARY - Restaurants (continued)	Diamond Rating	Rate Range High Season	Listing Page
⑪ / p. 388		Samosa Grill	◆◆	$8-$24	419
⑫ / p. 388		Big T's BBQ	◆◆	$12-$40	414
⑬ / p. 388		Oriental Phoenix	◆◆◆	$6-$15	418
⑭ / p. 388		Lina's Italian Market	◆	$5-$10	417
⑮ / p. 388		Jamesons Irish Pub	◆◆	$8-$15	416
⑯ / p. 388		The Cheesecake Cafe	◆◆	$10-$26	415
⑰ / p. 388		Thai Place Restaurant	◆◆	$9-$20	419
⑱ / p. 388		Gus's Cafe & Pizzeria	◆◆	$5-$15	416
⑲ / p. 388		Santorini Greek Taverna	◆◆	$10-$30	419
⑳ / p. 388		Forbidden City Seafood & Dim Sum Restaurant	◆	$4-$15	416
㉑ / p. 388		Open Range	◆◆	$21-$30	418
㉒ / p. 388		Boogie's Burgers	◆	$5-$10	414
㉓ / p. 388		Diner Deluxe	◆◆	$4-$15	416
㉔ / p. 388		Heartland Cafe	◆	$5-$10	416
㉕ / p. 388		Rouge	◆◆◆	$16-$44	419
㉖ / p. 388		Sugo Caffe Italia	◆◆◆	$15-$40	419
㉗ / p. 388		Kane's Harley Diner	◆	$4-$10	417
㉘ / p. 388		Spolumbo's Deli	◆	$6-$10	419
㉙ / p. 388		Capo Restaurant	◆◆◆	$13-$35	415
㉚ / p. 388		Crete Souvlaki	◆	$5-$10	416
㉛ / p. 388		Rajdoot Restaurant	◆◆	$9-$17	418
㉜ / p. 388		Belmont Diner	◆	$5-$8	414
㉝ / p. 388		Nellie's in the Loop	◆◆	$5-$9	417
㉞ / p. 388		Janine's Bistro	◆◆	$5-$14	416
㉟ / p. 388		Rocky's Burger Bus	◆	$3-$6	418
㊱ / p. 388		Alexis Bistro and Lounge	◆◆	$14-$36	414
㊲ / p. 388		Boyd's Seafood Restaurant	◆◆	$10-$37	414
㊳ / p. 388	CAA	**Pfanntastic Pannenkoek Haus**	◆◆	$7-$13	418
㊴ / p. 388		Oriental Phoenix	◆◆◆	$6-$15	418
㊵ / p. 388		Bagolac Saigon Restaurant	◆◆	$6-$12	414
㊶ / p. 388		Open Sesame	◆◆	$7-$28	418
㊷ / p. 388		Smuggler's Inn	◆◆	$9-$30	419
㊸ / p. 388		The Cheesecake Cafe	◆◆	$10-$26	415
㊹ / p. 388		Big T's BBQ	◆◆	$7-$40	414
㊺ / p. 388		Emperor Buffet & Restaurant	◆	$8-$14	416
㊻ / p. 388		Cannery Row	◆◆	$8-$55	415
㊼ / p. 388	CAA	**Newport Grill on Lake Bonavista**	◆◆◆	$14-$39	417

DOWNTOWN CALGARY (See map and index starting on p. 384)

—— WHERE TO STAY ——

5 CALGARY DOWNTOWN SUITES
Book at AAA.com **Phone:** (403)263-0520 **5**

Large-scale Hotel
$99-$369 All Year

Address: 618 5th Ave SW T2P 0M7 **Location:** Corner of 5th Ave SW and 5th St SW. **Facility:** 304 units. 44 one-bedroom standard units with kitchens. 194 one- and 66 two-bedroom suites with kitchens. 28 stories, interior corridors. **Parking:** on-site (fee), winter plug-ins. **Terms:** cancellation fee imposed. **Amenities:** voice mail, irons, hair dryers. *Fee:* video games, high-speed Internet. **Pool(s):** heated outdoor. **Leisure Activities:** sauna, steamroom, exercise room. **Guest Services:** valet and coin laundry. **Business Services:** meeting rooms, business center. **Cards:** AX, CB, DC, MC, VI.

BEST WESTERN SUITES DOWNTOWN
Book great rates at AAA.com **Phone:** (403)228-6900 **7**

Small-scale Hotel
$142-$161 All Year

Address: 1330 8th St SW T2R 1B6 **Location:** Corner of 8th St and 13th Ave SW. **Facility:** 123 units. 82 one-bedroom standard units, some with efficiencies and/or whirlpools. 17 one- and 24 two-bedroom suites, some with kitchens and/or whirlpools. 16 stories, interior corridors. **Parking:** on-site, winter plug-ins. **Terms:** 30 day cancellation notice-fee imposed. **Amenities:** high-speed Internet (fee), voice mail, irons, hair dryers. *Some:* dual phone lines. **Leisure Activities:** sauna, exercise room. **Guest Services:** valet and coin laundry. **Business Services:** meeting rooms, PC. **Cards:** AX, CB, DC, DS, JC, MC, VI. **Free Special Amenities:** continental breakfast and local telephone calls. *(See color ad below)*

AAA Benefit:
Members save 10% everyday, plus an exclusive frequent stay program.

CALGARY MARRIOTT HOTEL
Book great rates at AAA.com **Phone:** 403/266-7331 **11**

Large-scale Hotel
$318-$340 All Year

Address: 110 9th Ave SE T2G 5A6 **Location:** Jct 9th Ave and Centre St; adjacent to Telus Convention Centre. Located across from Calgary Tower. **Facility:** Smoke free premises. 384 units. 374 one-bedroom standard units. 10 one-bedroom suites. 22 stories, interior corridors. *Bath:* combo or shower only. **Parking:** on-site (fee) and valet, winter plug-ins. **Amenities:** voice mail, irons, hair dryers. *Fee:* video games, high-speed Internet. **Pool(s):** heated indoor. **Leisure Activities:** sauna, whirlpool, exercise room. *Fee:* massage. **Guest Services:** valet laundry. **Business Services:** meeting rooms, business center. **Cards:** AX, DC, DS, JC, MC, VI. *(See color ad p 394)*

AAA Benefit:
Members save 5% off of the best available rate.

(See map and index starting on p. 384)

DELTA BOW VALLEY
Book great rates at AAA.com Phone: 403-266-1980 **6**

(CAA) (SAVE)

Large-scale Hotel
$139-$469 1/1-2/28
$139-$399 3/1-12/31

Address: 209 4th Ave SE T2G 0C6 **Location:** 1st St SE and 4th Ave SE. **Facility:** 398 one-bedroom standard units, some with whirlpools. 25 stories, interior corridors. **Parking:** on-site (fee) and valet. **Amenities:** dual phone lines, voice mail, irons, hair dryers. *Fee:* video games, high-speed Internet. *Some:* honor bars. **Pool(s):** heated indoor. **Leisure Activities:** saunas, whirlpool, exercise room. **Guest Services:** valet laundry, area transportation-downtown. **Business Services:** conference facilities, business center. **Cards:** AX, CB, DC, DS, JC, MC, VI.

THE FAIRMONT PALLISER
Book at AAA.com Phone: (403)262-1234 **12**

Large-scale Hotel
$179-$449 All Year

Address: 133 9th Ave SW T2P 2M3 **Location:** 9th Ave SW and 1st St SW. **Facility:** A sense of history and nostalgia reigns at this grand hotel, which features an imperial theme throughout its luxurious and upscale guest rooms. 405 units. 385 one-bedroom standard units. 20 one-bedroom suites. 12 stories, interior corridors. **Parking:** on-site (fee) and valet, winter plug-ins. **Terms:** check-in 4 pm, cancellation fee imposed. **Amenities:** dual phone lines, voice mail, honor bars, irons, hair dryers. *Fee:* video games, high-speed Internet. *Some:* DVD players, CD players, safes. **Dining:** The Rimrock Dining Room, see separate listing. **Pool(s):** heated indoor. **Leisure Activities:** whirlpool, steamroom. *Fee:* massage, esthetics. **Guest Services:** valet laundry, beauty salon. **Business Services:** conference facilities, business center. **Cards:** AX, DC, DS, MC, VI.

HOLIDAY INN EXPRESS HOTEL & SUITES
CALGARY DOWNTOWN
Book at AAA.com Phone: (403)269-8262 **9**

Small-scale Hotel
$199-$259 3/1-10/31
$189-$249 11/1-2/28

Address: 1020 8th Ave SW T2P 1J2 **Location:** 8th Ave at 10th St SW. **Facility:** 56 units. 49 one-bedroom standard units. 7 one-bedroom suites with whirlpools. 9 stories, interior corridors. **Parking:** on-site, winter plug-ins. **Amenities:** high-speed Internet, dual phone lines, voice mail, irons, hair dryers. **Leisure Activities:** exercise room. **Guest Services:** valet and coin laundry. **Business Services:** meeting rooms, PC. **Cards:** AX, CB, DC, DS, JC, MC, VI.

HOTEL ARTS
Book at AAA.com Phone: (403)266-4611 **13**

Small-scale Hotel
$139-$309 1/1-2/28
$129-$299 3/1-12/31

Address: 119 12th Ave SW T2R 0G8 **Location:** At 1st St SW; centre. **Facility:** 185 one-bedroom standard units, some with whirlpools. 11 stories, interior corridors. *Bath:* combo or shower only. **Parking:** on-site (fee), winter plug-ins. *Fee:* video games, high-speed Internet. **Pool(s):** heated outdoor. **Leisure Activities:** exercise room. **Guest Services:** valet laundry. **Business Services:** meeting rooms, business center. **Cards:** AX, DC, DS, MC, VI.

(See map and index starting on p. 384)

HYATT REGENCY CALGARY
Book great rates at AAA.com
Phone: (403)717-1234 🔟

CAA SAVE
▼▼▼▼ ▼▼▼▼
Large-scale Hotel
$149-$439 All Year

Address: 700 Centre St SE T2G 5P6 **Location:** Corner of Centre St and 7th Ave SW. Located adjacent to Telus Convention Centre. **Facility:** Featuring a Canadian theme throughout, this downtown hotel with a luxurious ambience offers attentive service, upscale rooms and a new spa. 355 units. 342 one-bedroom standard units. 13 one-bedroom suites, some with whirlpools. 22 stories, interior corridors. *Bath:* combo or shower only. **Parking:** on-site (fee) and valet. **Terms:** cancellation fee imposed. **Amenities:** high-speed Internet (fee), dual phone lines, voice mail, safes, honor bars, irons, hair dryers. *Some:* DVD players, CD players. **Dining:** Thomson's Restaurant, see separate listing. **Pool(s):** heated indoor. **Leisure Activities:** sauna, whirlpool, exercise room, spa. **Guest Services:** valet laundry, wireless Internet. **Business Services:** conference facilities, business center. **Cards:** AX, CB, DC, DS, JC, MC, VI. *(See color ad below)*

HYATT HOTELS & RESORTS ®

AAA Benefit:
Ask for the AAA rate
and save 10%.

🍴 🍷 CALL ⓜ 🏊 ✕ 📷 💻 / SOME UNITS ✕ FEE VCR 🖥

INTERNATIONAL HOTEL OF CALGARY
Book at AAA.com
Phone: 403/265-9600 4️⃣

▼▼ ▼▼
Large-scale Hotel
Rates not provided

Address: 220 4th Ave SW T2P 0H5 **Location:** Corner of 4th Ave and 2nd St SW. **Facility:** 248 one-bedroom suites, some with kitchens. 35 stories, interior corridors. **Parking:** on-site (fee) and valet. **Amenities:** voice mail, honor bars, irons, hair dryers. *Fee:* video games, high-speed Internet. *Some:* CD players. **Pool(s):** heated indoor. **Leisure Activities:** saunas, whirlpool, exercise room. **Guest Services:** area transportation (fee). **Business Services:** meeting rooms.

FEE ✈ 🍴 🍷 🏊 ✕ 📷 💻 / SOME UNITS FEE 🛏 ✕ 🖥

KENSINGTON RIVERSIDE INN
Book great rates at AAA.com
Phone: (403)228-4442 2️⃣

CAA SAVE
▼▼▼▼ ▼▼▼▼
Bed & Breakfast
$339-$439 All Year

Address: 1126 Memorial Dr NW T2N 3E3 **Location:** Just w of 10th St NW; downtown. Located in Kensington area. **Facility:** Upscale and exquisite, this high-end B&B features original artwork, gourmet breakfasts and rooms well equipped for business travelers. Smoke free premises. 19 one-bedroom standard units, some with whirlpools. 2 stories, interior corridors. **Parking:** on-site. **Terms:** cancellation fee imposed. **Amenities:** video library, DVD players, CD players, high-speed Internet, dual phone lines, voice mail, irons, hair dryers. **Leisure Activities:** jogging. **Guest Services:** valet laundry, wireless Internet. **Business Services:** meeting rooms. **Cards:** AX, MC, VI. **Free Special Amenities: full breakfast and high-speed Internet.**

🍴 FEE 📺 ✕ VCR 📷

SANDMAN HOTEL DOWNTOWN CALGARY
Book at AAA.com
Phone: (403)237-8626 8️⃣

▼▼▼
Large-scale Hotel
$179-$199 All Year

Address: 888 7th Ave SW T2P 3J3 **Location:** Corner of 7th Ave SW and 8th St SW. **Facility:** 301 one-bedroom standard units. 23 stories, interior corridors. **Parking:** on-site (fee). **Terms:** cancellation fee imposed. **Amenities:** video games (fee), dual phone lines, voice mail, irons, hair dryers. *Some:* high-speed Internet. **Dining:** Moxie's Classic Grill, see separate listing. **Pool(s):** heated indoor. **Leisure Activities:** whirlpool, exercise room. **Guest Services:** valet laundry. **Business Services:** meeting rooms, administrative services, PC. **Cards:** AX, DS, MC, VI.

ASK S🅳 🍴 🍷 🏊 📷 💻 / SOME UNITS FEE 🛏 ✕ 🖥 🖥

▼ *See AAA listing above* ▼

(See map and index starting on p. 384)

SHERATON SUITES CALGARY EAU CLAIRE *Book great rates at AAA.com* Phone: 403/266-7200

(CAA) (SAVE)

▼▼▼ ▼▼▼

Large-scale Hotel
Rates not provided

Address: 255 Barclay Parade SW T2P 5C2 **Location:** At 3rd St SW and 2nd Ave SW. Located adjacent to Eau Claire Market. **Facility:** Set along the river's edge, and with a prime location next to the Eau Claire market, this all-suite hotel offers upscale rooms and attentive service. 323 units. 313 one- and 10 two-bedroom suites, some with whirlpools. 15 stories, interior corridors. *Bath:* combo or shower only. **Parking:** on-site (fee) and valet. **Amenities:** dual phone lines, voice mail, honor bars, irons, hair dryers. *Fee:* video games, high-speed Internet. *Some:* DVD players, CD players, fax, safes. **Dining:** 2 restaurants, also, Barclay's, see separate listing. **Pool(s):** heated indoor. **Leisure Activities:** sauna, whirlpool, waterslide, jogging, exercise room. *Fee:* bicycles, massage. **Guest Services:** valet and coin laundry, wireless Internet. **Business Services:** conference facilities, business center.

(S) Sheraton

AAA Benefit:
Members get up to 15% off, plus Starwood Preferred Guest® bonuses.

THE WESTIN CALGARY *Book great rates at AAA.com* Phone: (403)266-1611

(CAA) (SAVE)

▼▼▼ ▼▼▼

Large-scale Hotel
$129-$489 All Year

Address: 320 4th Ave SW T2P 2S6 **Location:** Corner of 4th Ave SW and 3rd St. **Facility:** Refinement can be found in both towers of this upscale hotel; one side features contemporary decor, the other a more plush, royal atmosphere. Smoke free premises. 525 units. 467 one-bedroom standard units. 58 one-bedroom suites. 20 stories, interior corridors. *Bath:* combo or shower only. **Parking:** on-site (fee) and valet. **Terms:** cancellation fee imposed. **Amenities:** dual phone lines, voice mail, safes, honor bars, irons, hair dryers. *Fee:* video games, high-speed Internet. **Pool(s):** heated indoor. **Leisure Activities:** saunas, whirlpool, exercise room, spa. **Guest Services:** valet laundry, wireless Internet. **Business Services:** conference facilities, business center. **Cards:** AX, CB, DC, DS, JC, MC, VI.

WESTIN
HOTELS & RESORTS

AAA Benefit:
Members get up to 15% off, plus Starwood Preferred Guest® bonuses.

(See map and index starting on p. 384)

———— WHERE TO DINE ————

AIDA'S

Lebanese
$5-$12

Phone: 403/541-1189 [71]

Hearty portions of tasty, traditional Lebanese food await patrons of the cozy, bistro-style restaurant. A taste of Lebanon infuses such dishes as falafel and flavorful tabbouleh salad. Save room for dessert, particularly the delicious layali loubnan, a Lebanese version of tiramisu. Casual dress. **Bar:** Full bar. **Reservations:** suggested, weekends. **Hours:** 11 am-10 pm, Mon-9 pm, Fri & Sat-11 pm, Sun 4 pm-9 pm. Closed major holidays. **Address:** 2208 4th St SW T2S 1W9 **Location:** At 4th St and 23rd Ave. **Parking:** street. Cards: AX, MC, VI.

CALL 🔊M

AVENUE DINER

Canadian
$6-$13

Phone: 403/263-2673 [32]

The quiet but welcoming exterior overlooking the Stephen Street pedestrian mall hints at things to come. Inside this comfortable and slightly upscale restaurant, tables near the back, which look over to the open kitchen, are in high demand. The menu is limited to breakfast and lunch items, and the kitchen uses some of the finest quality and local ingredients in its creative twists on standard French toast and fried egg sandwiches. Casual dress. **Bar:** Full bar. **Reservations:** not accepted. **Hours:** 7 am-3 pm, Sat & Sun from 8 am. Closed major holidays. **Address:** 105 8th Ave SW T2P 1B4 **Location:** Jct Centre St S; along Stephen Ave walk. **Parking:** street. Cards: MC, VI.

BARCLAY'S

International
$10-$25

Phone: 403/517-6666 [6]

Patrons can choose from the regular a la carte menu or share selections from the new fondue menu. The casually upscale eatery offers fine service and good value for the dollar. Casual dress. **Bar:** Full bar. **Reservations:** suggested. **Hours:** 6 am-10 pm, Fri & Sat-11 pm. Closed major holidays. **Address:** 255 Barclay Parade SW T2P 5C2 **Location:** At 3rd St SW and 2nd Ave SW; in Sheraton Suites Calgary Eau Claire. **Parking:** on-site (fee) and valet. **Cards:** AX, DC, MC, VI.

CALL 🔊M

THE BELVEDERE

Continental
$18-$35

Phone: 403/265-9595 [12]

New York meets Calgary at the upscale, intimate restaurant, tucked amid the shops and restaurants of Stephen Avenue. The decor is all New York, a long, narrow space with exposed brick walls, mirrors, walnut trim and exposed lighting. The menu changes every few months but might list such innovative creations as gingered ahi tuna, venison or duck. The romantic setting is fitting for special occasions. Dressy casual. **Bar:** Full bar. **Reservations:** suggested. **Hours:** 11:30 am-2 & 4:30-10 pm, Fri-11 pm, Sat 4:30 pm-11 pm. Closed: Sun & Mon. **Address:** 107 8th St SW T2P 1B4 **Location:** Just e of 1st St SW. **Parking:** street. Cards: AX, DC, MC, VI.

CALL 🔊M

BISTRO TWENTY TWO TEN

Canadian
$12-$28

Phone: 403/228-4528 [72]

Casual dress. **Bar:** Full bar. **Reservations:** accepted. **Hours:** 11 am-2 & 5-10 pm, Sat from 5 pm. Closed major holidays; also Sun. **Address:** 2210 4th St SW T2S 1W9 **Location:** Just n of 22nd Ave. **Parking:** street. Cards: AX, MC, VI.

BONTERRA TRATTORIA

Nouvelle Italian
$12-$38

Phone: 403/262-8480 [37]

For an upscale, Italian dining experience, look no further than Bonterra. Sumptuous smells waft from the open concept kitchen, where contemporary Italian dishes are created. The romantic dining room is a great place for a special occasion, and in the summer a garden oasis patio awaits in the back. With an extensive wine list, and superb professional service, this is one fine place for a great meal. Casual dress. **Bar:** Full bar. **Reservations:** suggested. **Hours:** 11:30 am-2:30 & 5-10 pm, Fri-11 pm, Sat 5 pm-11 pm, Sun 5 pm-10 pm. Closed major holidays. **Address:** 1016 8th St SW T2R 1K2 **Location:** 10th Ave and 8th St SW. **Parking:** on-site. Cards: AX, DC, MC, VI.

BRAVA BISTRO

Canadian
$8-$32

Phone: 403/228-1854 [62]

Old World inspiration combines with New World ingredients at the upscale, trendy addition to the dining options on 17th Avenue. The restaurant is an ideal place for a first date or special occasion. Artistic and creative dishes—ranging from risotto with squash and duck confit to linguine with saffron and seafood—emphasize freshness, simplicity and seasonality. Diners can complete their meal with a selection from the award-winning wine list. Dressy casual. **Bar:** Full bar. **Reservations:** suggested. **Hours:** 11:30 am-10 pm, Fri & Sat-midnight, Sun 5 pm-10 pm. Closed: 12/25. **Address:** 723 17th Ave SW T2S 0B6 **Location:** Just e of 7th St. **Parking:** on-site and street. Cards: AX, MC, VI.

BROKEN PLATE KITCHEN & BAR

Greek
$10-$24

Phone: 403/283-6300 [1]

Casual dress. **Bar:** Full bar. **Reservations:** accepted. **Hours:** 11:30 am-10 pm, Fri & Sat-11 pm, Sun 5 pm-10 pm. Closed major holidays. **Address:** 302 10th St NW T2N 1V8 **Location:** 0.6 mi (1 km) n of Memorial Dr. **Parking:** street. Cards: AX, MC, VI.

CAESAR'S STEAKHOUSE
(AAA)

Steak House
$10-$70

Phone: 403/264-1222 [15]

One of the city's original steakhouses, the dark, dimly lit restaurant speaks to years gone by, with professionally dressed servers, intimate corners and a booming lunch business. A trip to the West is not complete without a stop at the popular restaurant. An extensive selection of Alberta AAA beef is prepared to the diner's liking from the glassed-in barbecue area. This place buzzes at lunch, as many corporate types nosh on a Caesar alongside their steak. Dressy casual. **Bar:** Full bar. **Reservations:** suggested. **Hours:** 11 am-2 & 4:30-midnight, Sat from 4:30 pm. Closed major holidays; also Sun. **Address:** 512 4th Ave SW T2P 0J6 **Location:** Just e of 5th St. **Parking:** valet and street. Cards: AX, DC, MC, VI.

(See map and index starting on p. 384)

CATCH DINING ROOM   *Menu on AAA.com*   Phone: 403/206-0000   ⑳

Seafood
$10-$40

Down the stairs from Catch, which offers a more upscale experience, the oyster bar is more casual yet still boasts the same fine food. The bustling, nautical place prepares an extensive selection of fresh seafood, flown in each day. Guests can enjoy not only oysters but also other distinctive choices, including salmon, traditional fish and chips and the catch of the day. Casual dress. **Bar:** Full bar. **Reservations:** suggested. **Hours:** 11:30 am-2 & 5-11 pm. Closed major holidays; also for dinner Sun. **Address:** 100 8th Ave SE T2P 1B3 **Location:** Corner of 8th Ave SE (Stephen Ave) and Centre St SE; main level. **Parking:** street. **Cards:** AX, DC, MC, VI.

CATCH RESTAURANT   Phone: 403/206-0000   ㉝

Seafood
$16-$40

There are three levels to this restaurant. On the first floor, you'll find a fun, casual oyster bar. On the third level, an atrium and nestled in the middle, a stunning, upscale dining room, with lofty ceilings, warm wood tones, and exquisite table presentations. If you have a craving for seafood, this is the place to go. With an impressive selection of seafood from around the world, including Alaskan sablefish, Atlantic halibut cheeks, and Pacific salmon, seafood lovers will be in heaven. Dressy casual. **Bar:** Full bar. **Reservations:** suggested. **Hours:** 11:30 am-2 & 5-11 pm. Closed major holidays; also Sun. **Address:** 100 8th Ave SE T2P 1B3 **Location:** Corner of 8th Ave SE (Stephen Ave) and Centre St SE; second level. **Parking:** street. **Cards:** AX, DC, MC, VI.

CENTINI RESTAURANT AND LOUNGE   Phone: 403/269-1600   ㉑

Italian
$7-$45

An upscale dining room with an informal atmosphere. Seasonal menus feature new Italian cuisines incorporating Asian and French influences combined with more local ingredients. Must-try entrees include the stuffed roast quail and housemade pasta dishes. Dressy casual. **Bar:** Full bar. **Reservations:** suggested. **Hours:** 11 am-11 pm, Fri-midnight, Sat 5 pm-midnight. Closed major holidays; also Sun. **Address:** 160 8th Ave SE T2G 0K6 **Location:** Corner of 8th Ave SE (Stephen Ave) and 1st St SE; in Telus Convention Centre. **Parking:** street. **Cards:** AX, DC, MC, VI.

CHARLY CHAN'S RICE HOUSE   Phone: 403/283-6165   ④

Sichuan
$9-$16

In the heart of Kensington and just below street level, the simple restaurant serves Szechuan food. Dishes are hearty and tasty, and the service pleasant and friendly. Those seeking good value for the dollar will like this place. Casual dress. **Bar:** Full bar. **Reservations:** accepted. **Hours:** 11 am-11 pm, Fri & Sat-midnight. Closed: 12/25. **Address:** 1140 Kensington Rd NW T2N 3P3 **Location:** From 10th St NW, just w at Kensington Rd. **Cards:** AX, DC, DS, JC, MC, VI.

THE CHOPHOUSE   Phone: 403/265-3000   ⑱

Steak House
$15-$38

Guests can see and be seen at the ultra-modern, contemporary steakhouse, in the heart of the city. Efficient, professional servers help make this place popular with the business crowd at lunchtime. The menu blends a wide selection of top-quality cuts of beef with sandwiches and meal-size salads. The chic, lofty interior has an open-concept kitchen, and the selection of by-the-glass wines is one of the best in the city. Casual dress. **Bar:** Full bar. **Reservations:** required, for lunch. **Hours:** 11 am-11 pm, Fri-midnight, Sat 5 pm-midnight, Sun 5 pm-10 pm. Closed major holidays. **Address:** 604 8th Ave SW T2P 1G4 **Location:** Corner of 8th Ave SW and 5th St SW. **Parking:** street. **Cards:** AX, DC, MC, VI.

CALL Ⓖ🅜

CILANTRO   Phone: 403/229-1177   �52

Southwest
California
$12-$40

The dark wood interior and lovely stained-glass windows combine to create an intimate atmosphere in the small dining room, where guests can enjoy an interesting selection of California-inspired cuisine. Good choices include melts-in-the-mouth sea bass, various pastas and salads and any of the delectable desserts. Service is professional and friendly. Casual dress. **Bar:** Full bar. **Reservations:** suggested. **Hours:** 11 am-10 pm, Sat 5 pm-11 pm, Sun 5 pm-10 pm. Closed major holidays. **Address:** 338 17th Ave SW T2S 0A8 **Location:** Just e of 4th St SW. **Parking:** on-site and street. **Cards:** AX, MC, VI.

Ⓐ🅒

CODO VIETNAMESE RESTAURANT   Phone: 403/228-7798   ㉔

Vietnamese
$5-$15

A favorite among locals, the simple restaurant is one of the city's best-kept secrets. Huge portions of fresh Vietnamese food mean great value for the dollar. Representative of traditional fare are spring rolls, vermicelli rice dishes and a variety of curries. Although it can often be busy, especially on weekends, the restaurant's service is quick and attentive. Casual dress. **Bar:** Full bar. **Hours:** 11 am-10 pm, Sun noon-9 pm. Closed major holidays. **Address:** 1411 17th Ave SW T2T 0L4 **Location:** Just e of jct 14th St and 17th Ave SW. **Parking:** street. **Cards:** MC, VI.

DA PAOLO RISTORANTE   Phone: 403/228-5556   �60

Italian
$8-$29

The popular restaurant serves traditional fare with a warm, welcoming attitude. Dozens of fresh pasta and seafood dishes are complemented by chicken and veal entrees. The wine list includes well-chosen Italian selections. Formal service is the standard. Semi-formal attire. **Bar:** Full bar. **Reservations:** suggested. **Hours:** 11:30 am-2 & 5-10 pm, Sat from 5 pm. Closed major holidays; also Sun & 7/15-7/28. **Address:** 121 17th Ave SE T2G 1H3 **Location:** Just w on 17th Ave SE from MacLeod Trail S (which becomes Hwy 2A S). **Parking:** on-site. **Cards:** AX, DC, MC, VI.

DEANE HOUSE HISTORIC SITE RESTAURANT AT
FORT CALGARY   Phone: 403/269-7747   ㊱

Canadian
$8-$14

The glassed-in, veranda dining room offers a lovely view of the Elbow River. Menu offerings include fresh scones, homemade soup, eggs Benedict, French toast, quiche, bacon and eggs and gingerbread cake. On Friday from 6:30 pm to 10:30 pm, the Mystery from History dinner theater takes the stage. Casual dress. **Bar:** Full bar. **Reservations:** suggested. **Hours:** 11 am-3 pm, Sat & Sun from 10 am. Closed major holidays. **Address:** 806 9th Ave SE T2P 2M5 **Location:** Corner of 8th St. **Parking:** on-site. **Cards:** AX, MC, VI. **Historic**

CALL Ⓖ🅜

(See map and index starting on p. 384)

DIVINO WINE & CHEESE BISTRO
Phone: 403/410-5555 **30**

International
$12-$35

There is more than just wine and cheese at the upscale bistro, and the variety makes it a good reason to come. Cheese from around the world, including Alberta varieties, is paired with fresh artisan bread. Those in the mood for something more can expect decadent, beautiful food, ranging from mushroom risotto appetizers to roasted halibut to lobster cannelloni. Upscale decor and professional service complete the experience. Casual dress. **Bar:** Full bar. **Reservations:** suggested. **Hours:** 11:30 am-10 pm, Fri & Sat-midnight. Closed major holidays. **Address:** 113 8th Ave SW T2P 1B4 **Location:** On 8th Ave (Stephen Ave). **Parking:** street. **Cards:** AX, MC, VI.

DON QUIJOTE
Phone: 403/205-4244 **13**

Spanish
$9-$22

This restaurant is a great place to have tapas and dance the salsa. Focusing on the seafood of the Spanish ports, it relies heavily on the tradition of butter, garlic and lemon. For a decadent finish, try the rich custard-filled cake soaked in cinzano. Dressy casual. Entertainment. **Bar:** Full bar. **Reservations:** suggested. **Hours:** 11:30 am-2 & 5-10 pm, Sat & Sun from 5 pm. Closed major holidays; also for dinner Mon. **Address:** 309 2nd Ave SW T2P 0C5 **Location:** Across from Eau Claire Market. **Parking:** street. **Cards:** AX, DC, MC, VI.

EARL'S BANKERS HALL
Phone: 403/265-3275

Canadian
$8-$25

Offering an experience that falls between fast food and fine dining, the fun, relaxed restaurant prepares great food at a great price. Choices range from juicy burgers, hearty sandwiches, fresh salads, wings and pizza to full entrees of steak, chops and seafood. Made-from-scratch soups and assorted breads, as well as a nice choice of wines and beers, round out the offerings. This is a fitting spot for impromptu get-togethers and festive occasions. Casual dress. **Bar:** Full bar. **Hours:** 11:30 am-11 pm, Fri & Sat-1 am. Closed major holidays. **Address:** 315 8th Ave SW, A1, Level 1 T2P 1C4 **Location:** In Bankers Hall. **Parking:** street. **Cards:** AX, DC, MC, VI.

CALL

EARL'S ON FOURTH
Phone: 403/228-4141

Canadian
$8-$25

Offering an experience that falls between fast food and fine dining, the fun, relaxed restaurant prepares great food at a great price. Choices range from juicy burgers, hearty sandwiches, fresh salads, wings and pizza to full entrees of steak, chops and seafood. Made-from-scratch soups and assorted breads, as well as a nice choice of wines and beers, round out the offerings. This is a fitting spot for impromptu get-togethers and festive occasions. Casual dress. **Bar:** Full bar. **Hours:** 11 am-midnight, Fri & Sat-1 am. Closed major holidays. **Address:** 2401 4th St SW T2S 1X5 **Location:** Corner of 4th St SW and 24th Ave. **Parking:** on-site and street. **Cards:** AX, DC, MC, VI.

CALL

EL SOMBRERO RESTAURANT
Phone: 403/228-0332 **53**

Mexican
$11-$20

A taste of Mexico awaits at the cozy bistro-style restaurant, one staircase up from street level in the trendy 17th Avenue district. A guitarist adds ambience to the evening, strumming and singing in the background as guests enjoy hearty Mexican fare. Casual dress. **Bar:** Full bar. **Hours:** 11:30 am-2 & 5-10 pm, Sat 5 pm-11 pm, Sun 5 pm-9 pm. Closed: 12/25, 12/26. **Address:** 520 17th Ave SW T2S 0B1 **Location:** Between 5th and 4th sts SW; upper level. **Parking:** street. **Cards:** AX, DC, MC, VI.

FLEUR DE SEL
Phone: 403/228-9764 **67**

Nouvelle French
$12-$38

Elegantly funky describes the atmosphere at this small brasserie, where diners appreciate nouveau French cuisine and a fine wine selection. The memorable experience here is about more than just the creative, sophisticated food, encompassing the inviting atmosphere and charming decor. **Bar:** Full bar. **Reservations:** suggested. **Hours:** 11 am-2 & 5-midnight, Sat-Mon from 5 pm. Closed: 1/1, 12/25. **Address:** 2015 4th St SW, #2 T2S 1W6 **Location:** 4th St and 21st Ave SW; in Tivoli Theatre Building. **Parking:** street. **Cards:** AX, DC, MC, VI.

GALAXIE DINER
Phone: 403/228-0001 **45**

Canadian
$6-$10

Decorated with a few Elvis posters, this unassuming diner often has locals waiting in lengthy lines on the weekend in hopes of grabbing a spot at one of the few crowded tables. It would be fair to say the atmosphere is intimate, very intimate, but it's worth it for the simple, uncomplicated home cooking and comfort foods. Casual dress. **Hours:** 7 am-3 pm, Sat & Sun-4 pm. Closed: 1/1, 12/25. **Address:** 1413 11th St SW T3C 0M9 **Location:** Just n of 17th Ave SW. **Parking:** street. **Cards:** AX, MC, VI.

THE GLORY OF INDIA
Phone: 403/263-8804 **17**

Indian
$16-$23

The casual Indian restaurant serves tasty portions of traditional Indian cuisine. The lunch buffet is popular, and reservations are recommended. A la carte dinner items are best enjoyed with several people to allow for sampling of the varied dishes, including ali goobi, lamb and beef curries and chicken tikka. Casual dress. **Bar:** Full bar. **Reservations:** accepted. **Hours:** 11:30 am-2 & 5-10 pm, Sat from 5 pm. Closed major holidays; also Sun. **Address:** 515 4th Ave SW T2P 0J8 **Location:** Jct 5th St and 4th Ave SW; on ground floor of apartment building. **Parking:** street. **Cards:** AX, DC, JC, MC, VI.

GNOCCHI'S RISTORANTE
Phone: 403/262-2887 **43**

Italian
$8-$23

An elegant, upscale dining room awaits guests of the bistro, which prepares a wide array of traditional Italian cuisine. Hearty portions of minestrone soup, pasta, veal and the namesake gnocchi are sure to please. Casual dress. **Bar:** Full bar. **Reservations:** suggested. **Hours:** 11:30 am-10 pm, Sat & Sun from 5 pm. Closed major holidays. **Address:** 1238 8th St SW T2R 1A9 **Location:** Corner of 8th St SW and 13th Ave SW. **Parking:** on-site. **Cards:** AX, MC, VI.

CALL

(See map and index starting on p. 384)

GOOD EARTH COFFEEHOUSE & BAKERY
Phone: 403/228-9543   49

Deli/Subs
Sandwiches
$5-$8

One of several locations in Calgary, this casual restaurant offers a variety of take-out items, including garden salads and soups. Also on the menu are sweet and savory baked goods, freshly made sandwiches and a limited selection of hot entrees that can be enjoyed over a lingering cup of coffee at one of the comfortable tables. Casual dress. **Reservations:** not accepted. **Hours:** 6 am-10 pm. Closed major holidays. **Address:** 1502 11th St SW T3C 0M9 **Location:** Just n of 17th Ave. **Parking:** street. **Cards:** MC, VI.

HANA SUSHI
Phone: 403/229-1499   65

Japanese
$5-$20

The small, traditional restaurant is a great spot for good sushi at a great value. In addition to a wide variety of sushi and sashimi, the menu lists full dinners that include miso soup, salad and a selection of sushi. Casual dress. **Bar:** Full bar. **Reservations:** suggested. **Hours:** 11:30 am-2 & 5-10 pm, Sun-9 pm. Closed major holidays. **Address:** 1803 4th St SW T2S 1W2 **Location:** Corner of 18th Ave SW. **Parking:** street. **Cards:** AX, MC, VI.

THE HOLY GRILL
Phone: 430/261-9759   38

Deli/Subs
Sandwiches
$8-$12

The casual restaurant serves exciting and interesting soups, sandwiches and salads that are made to order while guests wait. Casual dress. **Reservations:** not accepted. **Hours:** 10 am-4 pm. Closed major holidays; also Sun. **Address:** 827 10th Ave SW T2R 0B4 **Location:** Jct 8th St SW; across from MEC. **Parking:** street. **Cards:** MC, VI.

IL SOGNO   *Menu on AAA.com*
Phone: 403/232-8901   9

Italian
$10-$40

Italian for "the dream," Il Sogno is a simply elegant restaurant with an upscale decor and sumptuous Italian food. Classically prepared dishes on the seasonally inspired menu include some new twists on old favorites. Ravioli with walnut-cream sauce, veal and a trilogy of surprise desserts are among choices that might be found. The building originally was used as a rooming house, and the owners have maintained the history and integrity in the decor. Casual dress. **Bar:** Full bar. **Reservations:** suggested. **Hours:** 11:30 am-2 & 5-10 pm. Closed major holidays; also Mon. **Address:** 24 4th St NE T2E 3R7 **Location:** Just n of Memorial Dr; at Edmonton Trail and 4th St NE. **Parking:** on-site. **Cards:** AX, MC, VI. **Historic**

JOEY TOMATO'S
Phone: 403/263-6336

Mediterranean
$10-$29

The cuisine blends Mediterranean and Asian cooking styles and emphasizes finger foods for sharing. Those who aren't big fans of tapas can consider full meal offerings centered on steaks and chops. Casual dress. **Bar:** Full bar. **Hours:** 11:30 am-1 am, Sun-midnight. Closed: 12/25. **Address:** 200 Barclay Parade SW T2P 4R5 **Location:** At 208 Eau Claire Market. **Parking:** on-site. **Cards:** AX, MC, VI.

THE JOYCE ON 4TH IRISH PUB
Phone: 403/541-9168   74

Irish
$6-$18

A wide selection of ales and whiskeys complements traditional fare, including boxty, an Irish dish made with a potato pancake and various fillings, and Guinness and beef pie. Saturday visitors can expect live music and Celtic dancers. The rich decor incorporates oversized couches and a long bar. The mood is lively and upbeat. Casual dress. **Bar:** Full bar. **Reservations:** suggested. **Hours:** 11 am-1 am, Thurs-Sat to 2 am, Sun-midnight. Closed: 12/25. **Address:** 506 24th Ave SW T2S 0K4 **Location:** Jct 24th Ave SW and 4th St SW. **Parking:** on-site. **Cards:** AX, MC, VI.

JULIO'S BARRIO MEXICAN RESTAURANT
Phone: 403/203-3066   7

Mexican
$12-$19

The upbeat, casual and boisterous restaurant is a fun place to visit for hearty helpings of Mexican cuisine. Casual dress. **Bar:** Full bar. **Reservations:** accepted. **Hours:** 11:30 am-11 pm, Fri & Sat-midnight. Closed: 1/1, 10/13, 12/24, 12/25. **Address:** Kensington Gate NW T5J 0G6 **Location:** Corner of Memorial Dr and Kensington Rd NW. **Parking:** on-site (fee) and street. **Cards:** AX, DC, MC, VI.
CALL ♿M

THE KING & I
Phone: 403/264-7241   41

Thai
$8-$25

An upscale, contemporary atmosphere awaits you at the King & I, where modern furnishings and decor set the scene for authentic, tasty Thai dishes. The menu features a wide variety of appetizers, including calamari and fresh spring rolls. Arrive with an appetite, as the main dishes are heaping, and you can choose from traditional Pad Thai to various curry dishes. If you are looking for a taste of Thailand in modern surroundings, look no further. Casual dress. **Bar:** Full bar. **Reservations:** suggested. **Hours:** 11:30 am-10:30 pm, Fri-11:30 pm, Sat 4:30 pm-11:30 pm, Sun 4:30 pm-9:30 pm. Closed major holidays. **Address:** 822 11th Ave SW T2R 0E5 **Location:** Corner of 11th Ave SW and 8th St SW. **Parking:** street. **Cards:** AX, DC, MC, VI.

KYOTO 17
Phone: 403/245-3188   57

Japanese
$6-$20

The restaurant features a sushi bar, rice, curry, Japanese noodles and full dinners with teriyaki chicken and steak. The decor is contemporary in the smoke-free main dining room, while the traditional private rooms offer a more authentic experience. Metered parking is available during the day. **Bar:** Full bar. **Reservations:** accepted. **Hours:** 11:30 am-2 & 5-10 pm, Fri-11 pm, Sat 5 pm-11 pm, Sun 5 pm-9 pm. Closed major holidays. **Address:** 908 17th Ave SW T2T 0A3 **Location:** Corner of 17th Ave SW and 8th St SW; basement level of the Devenish Building. **Parking:** street. **Cards:** AX, DC, JC, MC, VI.

LA BREZZA
Phone: 403/262-6230   2

Italian
$9-$25

In a small house, the physical setting enhances the warm, relaxed atmosphere. Funky lighting crisscrosses the ceiling. Whether for a first date or a reunion of old friends, the restaurant's eclectic atmosphere, refined service and creative Italian cuisine will create a lingering memory. Casual dress. **Bar:** Full bar. **Reservations:** suggested. **Hours:** 11:30 am-2:30 & 5-11 pm, Sat & Sun from 5 pm. **Address:** 990 1st Ave NE T2E 4J9 **Location:** 9th St NE; in Bridgeland. **Parking:** on-site. **Cards:** AX, MC, VI.

LA CHAUMIERE RESTAURANT
Phone: 403/228-5690   61

Continental
$9-$33

The upscale restaurant's impressive, almost castle-like building has a peaked roof and elegant exterior, making it an ideal spot for fine French dining. Patrons cross the threshold over polished granite floors into an exquisitely appointed dining room, where servers dressed in formal attire await. Superb entrees range from various seafood dishes to mouthwatering preparations of beef. Semi-formal attire. **Bar:** Full bar. **Reservations:** required. **Hours:** 11:30 am-2 & 5-10 pm, Sat 5:30 pm-midnight. Closed major holidays; also Sun. **Address:** 139 17th Ave SW T2S 0A1 **Location:** Corner of 1st St SW and 17th Ave SW. **Parking:** on-site. **Cards:** AX, DC, MC, VI.

(See map and index starting on p. 384)

LA DOLCE VITA RISTORANTE
ITALIANO
ⒸⒶⒶ

▼▼▼▼

Italian
$9-$25

Phone: 403/263-3445 ③

In the city's "Little Italy" area, the restaurant features casual dining upstairs and more formal dining downstairs. Fresh pasta, seafood and veal are prepared with a balance of traditions and imaginative presentations. Vine-covered, lemon walls, warm terra cotta tiles and Mediterranean decor will make patrons think they are in a small villa in Italy. Semi-formal attire. **Bar:** Full bar. **Reservations:** suggested. **Hours:** 11:30 am-2 & 5:30-10:30 pm, Sat 5:30 pm-11 pm. Closed major holidays; also Sun. **Address:** 916 1st Ave NE T2E 0C5 **Location:** At 9th St NE; in Bridgeland. **Parking:** street. **Cards:** AX, DC, MC, VI.

LE CHIEN CHAUD
▼

Deli/Subs
Sandwiches
$6-$8

Phone: 403/229-3041 ⑥⑧

Casual dress. **Reservations:** not accepted. **Hours:** 11 am-9 pm, Sun noon-6 pm. Closed major holidays. **Address:** #3 2015 4th St SW T2S 1W6 **Location:** Jct 20th Ave. **Parking:** street. **Cards:** MC, VI.

THE LIVING ROOM
▼▼▼

Canadian
$15-$40

Phone: 403/228-9830 ⑤⑥

The contemporary restaurant serves imaginative Canadian fare, including a five-course menu surprise. As the name suggests, the decor—including oversize couchlike chairs—contributes to a cozy and comfortable dining environment. Casual dress. **Bar:** Full bar. **Hours:** 11:30 am-2 & 5-11 pm. Closed major holidays. **Address:** 514 17th Ave SW T5W 4X6 **Location:** Just e of 5th St SW. **Parking:** on-site and street. **Cards:** AX, MC, VI.

MANUEL LATRUWE BELGIAN PATISSERIE &
BREAD SHOP
▼ ▼

Bakery/Desserts
$4-$7

Phone: 403/261-1092 ④⑦

Elegance and refinement characterize the upscale bakery, which features the divine dessert creations of Manuel Latruwe. The display case is filled with gorgeous mousses, cheesecakes, tarts and pastries, as well as artisan breads. Although there are three small cafe tables, most people, including business folks en route to work and skiers headed to the mountains, get their selections to go. Ice creams and sorbets also are concocted here. Casual dress. **Hours:** 7:30 am-5 pm. Closed major holidays; also Sun & Mon. **Address:** 1333 1st St SE T2G 5L1 **Location:** 1st St SE at 13th Ave. **Parking:** on-site. **Cards:** MC, VI.

CALL Ⓜ

MAURYA
▼▼ ▼

East Indian
$8-$16

Phone: 403/270-3133 ⑤

You'll find excellent and tasty East Indian cuisine at Maurya's, with a menu that specializes in tandoori and includes many vegetarian dishes. The extensive lunch buffet has more than a dozen items, and you can spend hours dining in this relaxing, simple ambience. Casual dress. **Bar:** Full bar. **Reservations:** suggested. **Hours:** 11:30 am-2 & 5-10 pm, Fri & Sat-11 pm. Closed major holidays. **Address:** #100, 1204 Kensington Rd NW T2N 3P5 **Location:** At 12th St NW. **Parking:** street. **Cards:** AX, DC, MC, VI.

MERCATO
▼▼▼

Italian
$12-$35

Phone: 403/263-5535 ⑦③

Casual dress. **Bar:** Full bar. **Reservations:** suggested. **Hours:** 11 am-2:30 & 5-10 pm. Closed major holidays; also Sun. **Address:** 2224 4 St SW T2S 1W9 **Location:** Just s of 22 Ave SW. **Parking:** street. **Cards:** AX, MC, VI.

MESCALERO
▼▼▼

Southwest
Mexican
$7-$24

Phone: 403/266-3339 ④④

A charming, rustic Mexican decor and warm, lively atmosphere greet diners. The restaurant has an appealing menu of lamb, beef, veal, chicken and seafood dishes, many of which are grilled over an applewood fire and creatively presented. Casual dress. **Bar:** Full bar. **Reservations:** suggested. **Hours:** 11:30 am-2 & 5-10 pm, Thurs-11 pm, Fri & Sat-midnight. Closed: 12/24-12/26. **Address:** 1315 1st St SW T2R 0V5 **Location:** Corner of 1st St SW and 13th Ave SW. **Parking:** street. **Cards:** AX, MC, VI.

METROPOLITIAN GRILL
▼▼▼

Canadian
$9-$25

Phone: 403/263-5432 ⑲

Across from Banker's Hall, the Stephen Street location is the place to be for a power lunch. The upscale restaurant is known for its creative takes on classic comfort food, ranging from lobster macaroni and cheese to great AAA Alberta steaks. Casual dress. **Bar:** Full bar. **Hours:** 11 am-10 pm, Fri & Sat-1 am. Closed major holidays. **Address:** 318 8th Ave SW T2P 1C4 **Location:** In TD Square. **Parking:** street. **Cards:** AX, DS, MC, VI.

CALL Ⓜ

MOTI MAHAL
▼▼ ▼

Northern Indian
$10-$20

Phone: 403/228-9990 ⑤⑨

Based on the cuisine of Northern India, the varied menu lists such dishes as buttery masalas, curries and the specialty chicken tikka with spicy yogurt and tomato sauce. Tapestries hang around the dining room, creating a royal environment. Casual dress. **Bar:** Full bar. **Reservations:** suggested. **Hours:** 11:30 am-1:30 & 5:30-9 pm, Thurs-9:30 pm, Fri-10:30 pm, Sat 5:30 pm-10:30 pm, Sun 11:30 am-2 & 5:30-9 pm. Closed major holidays. **Address:** 1805 14th St SW T2T 3P1 **Location:** Just s of jct 17th Ave SW and 14th St SW; in small strip mall. **Parking:** on-site. **Cards:** AX, DC, MC, VI.

MT. EVEREST'S KITCHEN
▼▼ ▼▼

Nepali
$10-$22

Phone: 403/806-2337 ⑤⑧

The distinct cuisine of the Himalayas merges influences of both Indian and Tibetan cultures. The rare cuisine, prepared in only a handful of Nepali restaurants in North America, is simple and subtle in flavor. In addition to vegetarian preparations are several dishes that incorporate meat (excluding beef). Nepali cuisine makes extensive use of common ingredients and a variety of unique spices. Casual dress. **Bar:** Full bar. **Reservations:** accepted. **Hours:** 11:30 am-2 & 5:30-9:30 pm, Fri & Sat-10 pm, Sun noon-2 & 5:30-9:30 pm. Closed: major holidays, 12/26; also Mon. **Address:** 1448 A 17th Ave SW T2T 0C8 **Location:** 17th Ave SW and 14th St SW, just w. **Parking:** street. **Cards:** AX, DC, MC, VI.

(See map and index starting on p. 384)

MOXIE'S CLASSIC GRILL
Phone: 403/234-7507

Canadian
$10-$30

This sleek, funky and popular restaurant presents an extensive menu of creatively prepared dishes, including pizza, pasta, rice, noodles, signature salads and burgers. Other menus include one for children and one for Sunday brunch. Lending to the upbeat, stylish decor are dark wood appointments and river rock fireplaces. Casual dress. **Bar:** Full bar. **Reservations:** accepted. **Hours:** 6 am-midnight. **Address:** 888 7th Ave SW T2P 3J3 **Location:** Corner of 7th Ave SW and 8th St SW; in Sandman Hotel Downtown Calgary. **Parking:** on-site (fee). **Cards:** AX, MC, VI.

CALL

MURRIETA'S WESTCOAST GRILL
Phone: 403/269-7707　[23]

West Pacific Rim
$10-$35

The lively, airy dining room buzzes with sounds from the open-concept kitchen and animated conversations. The bustling restaurant has an energy and liveliness that makes it a popular spot for a gathering of friends. For a more intimate experience, smaller areas are tucked away from the main dining room. Among offerings are mussels, ahi tuna, salmon and various pasta dishes. Casual dress. **Bar:** Full bar. **Reservations:** suggested. **Hours:** 11 am-11 pm, Sun 4 pm-10 pm. Closed major holidays. **Address:** 200-808 1st St SW T2P 1M9 **Location:** Corner of 8th Ave SW and 1st St SW; 2nd floor. **Parking:** street. **Cards:** AX, DC, DS, MC, VI.

CALL

MUSE RESTAURANT & LOUNGE
Phone: 403/670-6873　[10]

International
$25-$40

As one of the city's best new restaurants, the establishment presents a dazzling, innovative menu. The decor sets the scene for an upscale evening. The chef emphasizes regional items in the imaginative dishes. Desserts are delicious. Dressy casual. **Bar:** Full bar. **Reservations:** suggested. **Hours:** 5 pm-midnight. Closed major holidays. **Address:** 107-10A St NW T2N 4M7 **Location:** From Memorial Dr, just n on 10th St, just w on Kensington Rd, then just s at 10A St NW. **Parking:** street. **Cards:** AX, MC, VI.

NELLIE'S KITCHEN
Phone: 403/244-4616　[54]

Canadian
$4-$9

Particularly popular on weekends, the bustling, cozy diner is a favorite for fabulous home-cooked breakfast. In addition to all-day breakfasts, ranging from omelets to French toast to pancakes, the menu also lists some lunch options. Homemade banana bread is well worth a splurge. Casual dress. **Hours:** 7:30 am-3:30 pm, Sat & Sun from 8:30 am. Closed: 12/25. **Address:** 738B 17th Ave SW T2S 0B7 **Location:** Corner of 7th St and 17th Ave SW. **Parking:** street. **Cards:** MC, VI.

THE ORCHID ROOM FUSION CUISINE
Phone: 403/263-4457　[28]

Vietnamese
$14-$30

A combination of Vietnamese and French cuisine makes for an eclectic menu with an accent on healthy choices. Colorful plate presentations include banana leaves, yellow daisies and orchids. Among choices are many unusual vegan dishes. The cozy setting has an open annex. Casual dress. **Bar:** Full bar. **Reservations:** suggested, for lunch. **Hours:** 10 am-8 pm, Thurs-Sat to 9 pm. Closed major holidays; also Sun. **Address:** 315 8th Ave SW T2P 4K1 **Location:** Corner of 2nd St SW; in Bankers Hall, 2nd Floor. **Parking:** on-site (fee) and street. **Cards:** AX, MC, VI.

ORIENTAL PHOENIX
Phone: 403/262-3633　[16]

Vietnamese
$6-$15

Traditional Vietnamese food is served simply, but the service and decor is anything but. Upscale and sleek, the modern dining room is a busy place at lunch and around the dinner hour. Guests can sample tasty food in fine surroundings characterized by bold, contemporary colors and art. Among the varied choices are salad rolls, rice vermicelli dishes and noodle soups. Semi-formal attire. **Bar:** Full bar. **Hours:** 11 am-8:30 pm, Fri-9:30 pm, Sat noon-9:30 pm. Closed major holidays; also Sun & 2 weeks during Christmas. **Address:** 401 9th Ave SW, #105 T2P 3C5 **Location:** Jct 4th St SW. **Parking:** street. **Cards:** AX, DC, MC, VI.

CALL

OUZO GREEK TAVERNA
Phone: 403/229-1400　[69]

Greek
$6-$16

One of the newest additions to the Fourth Street restaurant scene, the family-owned Greek restaurant serves hearty, delicious fare prepared in the traditional sense. This spot is popular with the locals for its large seasonal patio, healthy portions and friendly service. Casual dress. **Bar:** Full bar. **Reservations:** suggested. **Hours:** 11:30 am-9 pm, Fri & Sat-10 pm. Closed major holidays. **Address:** 2005 B 4th St SW T2S 1W6 **Location:** Corner of 20th Ave and 4th St SW. **Parking:** street. **Cards:** AX, MC, VI.

PALACE OF EATS
Phone: 403/244-6602　[46]

Deli/Subs
Sandwiches
$9-$12

The funky, table-free eatery takes its name from a restaurant that stood in downtown Calgary from 1920 to the mid-60s. A true gem, this place specializes in Montreal-style bagels, creamy milkshakes and hand-sliced, stacked Montreal smoked meat sandwiches on Winnipeg rye. Check out the original mahogany paneling and benches, which give the restaurant an antique feel. Casual dress. **Hours:** 11 am-4 pm. Closed major holidays. **Address:** 1411 11th St SW T2R 1G7 **Location:** Just n of 17th Ave SW. **Parking:** street. **Cards:** MC, VI.

THE PANORAMA DINING ROOM
Phone: 403/266-7171　[35]

Continental
$11-$38

Mouthwatering selections of regional Canadian cuisine range from pan-seared Atlantic salmon to grilled strip loin of New Zealand venison to grilled tenderloin of Alberta beef. The revolving room atop the city's tallest building offers a spectacular view of the city and Rocky Mountains. An elevation fee is charged. Casual dress. **Bar:** Full bar. **Reservations:** suggested. **Hours:** 7 am-2:30 & 5-9:30 pm, Sun 9:30 am-1:30 & 5-9:30 pm; Sunday brunch; winter hours vary. **Address:** 101 9th Ave SW T2P 1J9 **Location:** At top of Calgary Tower; in Palliser Square. **Parking:** no self-parking. **Cards:** AX, DC, MC, VI.

(See map and Index starting on p. 384)

PEGASUS
Phone: 403/229-1231   39

Greek
$8-$18

A favorite among the locals, the homey, traditional restaurant features a wide selection of Greek dishes, such as souvlaki and moussaka. Patrons who visit on the weekend may enjoy traditional Greek dancing and entertainment. Casual dress. **Bar:** Full bar. **Reservations:** suggested. **Hours:** 11:30 am-2 & 5-10 pm, Fri-11 pm, Sat 5 pm-11 pm, Sun 5 pm-10 pm. Closed: 1/1, 12/24-12/26. **Address:** 1101 14th St SW T3C 1C2 **Location:** At 11th Ave SW. **Parking:** on-site. **Cards:** AX, DC, MC, VI.

PEKING DRAGON
Phone: 403/228-1205   66

Chinese
$7-$12

A popular spot with the locals, the casual Chinese restaurant prepares traditional selections and offers fine, friendly service. Among choices are egg rolls, Peking duck and egg foo yong. Casual dress. **Bar:** Full bar. **Hours:** 11 am-1 pm, Fri-midnight, Sat 4:30 pm-midnight, Sun 4:30 pm-10 pm. Closed major holidays. **Address:** 1904 4th St SW T2S 1W3 **Location:** At 19th Ave SW. **Parking:** on-site. **Cards:** AX, MC, VI.

CALL [M]

PRAIRIE INK RESTAURANT & BAKERY
Phone: 403/538-1798   27

Canadian
$6-$13

The tranquil setting is a superb spot for a great meal. Guests can sit by the window overlooking the street below and enjoy heaping portions of food, ranging from crab cakes to pear and goat cheese salad to pizza and pasta cooked in a wood-burning oven. The bakery generates mouthwatering dessert creations. Bookshelves offer literary inspiration. Casual dress. **Hours:** 9 am-9 pm, Fri & Sat-10 pm, Sun 11 am-6 pm. Closed major holidays. **Address:** 120 8th Ave SW T2P 1B3 **Location:** Between Centre and 1st sts SW; in McNally Robinson bookstore, top floor. **Parking:** street. **Cards:** AX, MC, VI.

PULCINELLA
Phone: 403/283-7793   8

Pizza
$11-$21

Casual dress. **Bar:** Full bar. **Reservations:** accepted. **Hours:** 11:30 am-11 pm, Fri & Sat-midnight. Closed major holidays. **Address:** 1147 Kensington Crescent NW T2N 1X7 **Location:** 0.3 mi (0.4 km) e of jct 14th St NW. **Parking:** street. **Cards:** AX, MC, VI.

RESTAURANT INDONESIA
Phone: 403/244-0645   51

Indonesian
$8-$15

Choices such as satay, chili-basil chicken and gado-gado are among palate-pleasing offerings that tease with rich, intense flavors. Fresh, colorful food jumps with memories of the Spice Islands. Try the favourite aduk-aduk tempeh. Dressy casual. **Bar:** Full bar. **Reservations:** suggested. **Hours:** 11:30 am-2:30 & 5-11 pm, Sat 5 pm-11:30 pm, Sun 5 pm-9 pm. Closed major holidays; also Mon. **Address:** 1604 14th St SW T3C 1E2 **Location:** Corner of 16th Ave SW and 14th St SW. **Parking:** street. **Cards:** AX, MC, VI.

RIC'S GRILL
Phone: 403/269-7427   48

Steak & Seafood
$10-$30

"Funky and modern" describes the decor and the food at the upscale steakhouse, which bustles with activity. Reservations are definitely recommended. Steaks are well worth it, but then again, so are the salmon, chicken and pasta dishes. A wide variety of distinctive appetizers rounds out the menu. Servers are friendly and attentive. Dressy casual. **Bar:** Full bar. **Reservations:** suggested. **Hours:** 11 am-10 pm, Fri & Sat-midnight, Sun 4 pm-10 pm. Closed major holidays. **Address:** 1436 8th St SW T2R 1R7 **Location:** Just n of jct 17th Ave SW. **Parking:** on-site (fee) and street. **Cards:** AX, MC, VI.

THE RIMROCK DINING ROOM
Phone: 403/260-1219   34

Continental
$11-$34

Tucked in a corner of the Palliser Hotel, the fine dining room has a reputation for steaks and fine service. Patrons celebrating anniversaries or other special occasions are treated by attentive servers. In addition to quality beef, the menu also lists seafood dishes and exquisite desserts. Dressy casual. **Bar:** Full bar. **Reservations:** suggested. **Hours:** 6:30 am-2 & 5:30-10 pm, Sun from 7 am. **Address:** 133 9th Ave SW T2P 2M3 **Location:** 9th Ave SW and 1st St SW; in The Fairmont Palliser. **Parking:** on-site (fee) and valet. **Cards:** AX, CB, DC, DS, JC, MC, VI.

RIVER CAFE
Phone: 403/261-7670   25

Regional Canadian
$7-$40

In the heart of Prince's Island Park, the enchanting, tree house-like restaurant features a decor that includes natural wood accents and a large fireplace. The focus of the menu is on Canadian Rocky Mountain cuisine. During summer, seating is available on the patio, and in winter, the atmosphere is cozy inside. Parking is not available on the island, but city lots are just a short walk away. Casual dress. **Bar:** Full bar. **Reservations:** suggested. **Hours:** Open 3/1-12/31 & 2/1-2/28; 11 am-11 pm, Sat & Sun from 10 am. Closed: 12/25. **Location:** On Prince's Island; on Bow River. **Parking:** no self-parking. **Cards:** AX, DC, MC, VI.

ROSE GARDEN THAI RESTAURANT
Phone: 403/263-1900   29

Thai
$8-$15

The family-owned restaurant in the heart of downtown serves Thai favorites. The menu includes pad Thai, savory curries and salad rolls. Servers are friendly. Casual dress. **Bar:** Full bar. **Hours:** 11:30 am-9 pm, Fri & Sat-10 pm. Closed major holidays. **Address:** 207 8th Ave SW T2P 1B7 **Location:** At 8th Ave SW and 2nd St SW. **Parking:** street. **Cards:** AX, MC, VI.

SAKANA GRILL
Phone: 403/290-1118   11

Japanese
$7-$17

On the fringe of Chinatown near the Eau Claire market, the bustling Japanese restaurant has many distinctive features, including a sushi bar, teppanyaki grill and private dining rooms. Business folks frequent the place at lunch time, grabbing seats at the sushi bar and making selections from the boat that floats by. Fantastic sushi and sashimi options offer exceptional value for the dollar. Casual dress. **Bar:** Full bar. **Reservations:** suggested. **Hours:** 11 am-2 & 5-11 pm. Closed: 1/1, 12/25. **Address:** 116 2nd Ave SW T2P 0B9 **Location:** Corner of 1st St and 2nd Ave SW; in Chinatown. **Parking:** on-site (fee) and street. **Cards:** AX, DC, MC, VI.

SALTLIK, A RARE STEAKHOUSE
Phone: 403/537-1160   31

Steak House
$12-$40

True to its name, the restaurant is a "rare steakhouse" and a superb one at that. In the heart of downtown along the trendy Stephen Avenue pedestrian shopping district, the upscale, contemporary dining room and atmosphere is impressive. Also praiseworthy is the incredibly friendly, attentive service. Servers take time to explain the different cuts of meat and accompanying sauces. All entrees are a la carte, and side orders are large enough to split. Casual dress. **Bar:** Full bar. **Reservations:** suggested. **Hours:** 11 am-10 pm, Fri & Sat-midnight. Closed: 12/25, 12/26. **Address:** 101 8th Ave SW T6E 1H1 **Location:** Corner of 8th Ave SW and 1st St SW. **Parking:** street. **Cards:** AX, DC, DS, MC, VI.

CALL

(See map and index starting on p. 384)

SILVER DRAGON RESTAURANT   *Menu on AAA.com*   Phone: 403/264-5326   ⑭

Chinese
$6-$17

The restaurant specializes in Cantonese and Szechuan cuisine, including excellent ginger beef. A delicious dim sum selection is served each day. The contemporary decor comprises nouveau Oriental artwork. Servers are cordial. Casual dress. **Bar:** Full bar. **Reservations:** suggested. **Hours:** 10 am-midnight, Fri & Sat-2 am, Sun 9:30 am-10 pm. **Address:** 106 3rd Ave SE T2G 0B6 **Location:** In Chinatown. **Parking:** street. **Cards:** AX, DC, JC, MC, VI.

STEEPS THE URBAN TEAHOUSE   Phone: 403/209-0076   ㊿

Deli/Subs
Sandwiches
$3-$6
CALL

The teahouse lures those who yearn for a pot of tea. It's a little-known fact that the Americanization of tea involved the creation of the tea bag, but loose teas—150 types, ranging from the rare and exotic to more common varieties—are the preference at the urban spot. Guests can take their time choosing from one of the many tins, which can be paired with soup and a sandwich, a samosa or wrap or one of the homemade desserts. Casual dress. **Reservations:** not accepted. **Hours:** 10 am-11 pm, Fri & Sat-midnight. Closed major holidays. **Address:** 880 16th Ave SW T2T 0A3 **Location:** At 8th St SW; in Mount Royal Shops. **Parking:** street. **Cards:** MC, VI.

SULTAN'S TENT   Phone: 403/244-2333   ㊿63

Traditional
Moroccan
$14-$23

Eating is a communal event at the cozy Moroccan restaurant. Representative of the food are such delicacies as couscous, merguez, lamb, a five-course sultan's feast and other traditional dishes. And the traditional method of eating such creations is with the hands. The decor, which is inspired by the Berber culture of North Africa, offers intimate seating. Casual dress. **Bar:** Full bar. **Reservations:** suggested. **Hours:** 5:30 pm-10:30 pm, Fri & Sat 5 pm-11 pm. Closed major holidays; also Sun. **Address:** 909 17th Ave SW T2T 0A4 **Location:** Just w of 8th St SW. **Parking:** on-site. **Cards:** AX, DC, MC, VI.

SUSHI KAWA   Phone: 403/802-0058   ⑦0

Japanese
$6-$20

Fourth Street is a popular area for sushi restaurants, but what sets this one apart is the incredible and imaginative variety of appetizers and sushi platters. Patrons might try a vegetable sushi bowl—fresh vegetables atop sushi rice. Sushi pizzas, vegetable gyozas and an incredible variety of other appetizers are pictured on the colorful menu, making decisions difficult. Sumo wrestling often is shown on the large-screen TV, and the decor is simple and contemporary. Casual dress. **Bar:** Full bar. **Reservations:** suggested. **Hours:** 11:30 am-2 & 5-9:30 pm, Thurs & Fri-10:30 pm, Sat 5 pm-10:30 pm, Sun 5 pm-9 pm. Closed major holidays. **Address:** 2204 4th St SW T2S 1W9 **Location:** Jct 4th St SW and 22nd Ave. **Parking:** street. **Cards:** AX, MC, VI.

TEATRO   Phone: 403/290-1012   ㉒

Nouvelle Italian
$15-$120

Located in the theatre district, this upsale Italian tratorria is a great place to dine before the show. Featured several times on the Food Network, the chef will surprise and delight you with many inventive creations. Whether you're in the mood for seafood, pasta or meat dishes, you'll find something exquisite to satisfy your appetite. A perfect place for a special occasion or a first date. Dressy casual. **Bar:** Full bar. **Reservations:** suggested. **Hours:** 11:30 am-2 & 5-10:30 pm. Closed major holidays. **Address:** 200 8th Ave SE T2G 0K7 **Location:** Corner of 8th Ave SE and 1st St SE. **Parking:** street. **Cards:** AX, DC, MC, VI.

THAI SA-ON RESTAURANT   Phone: 403/264-3526   ㊵

Thai
$6-$18

Decorative presentation and good use of spices and condiments characterize offerings of well-prepared cuisine, including many vegetarian items. The quiet, casual ambience is enhanced by music and artwork from Thailand. Casual dress. **Bar:** Full bar. **Reservations:** suggested. **Hours:** 11:30 am-2 & 5-10 pm, Fri & Sat-10:30 pm. Closed major holidays; also Sun. **Address:** 351 10th Ave SW T2R 0A5 **Location:** At 4th St SW; behind Gulf Canada Parkade. **Parking:** street. **Cards:** AX, MC, VI.

THOMSON'S RESTAURANT   Phone: 403/537-4449   ㉔

Canadian
$10-$35
CALL

The restaurant presents a varied menu of seafood, steaks and other regional meats. Thursday prime rib nights pack the place with locals. Guests can expect casual yet attentive service in the upscale dining room. Casual dress. **Bar:** Full bar. **Reservations:** suggested. **Hours:** 6:30 am-2 & 5-11 pm, Fri & Sat-midnight. **Address:** 700 Centre St SE T2G 5P6 **Location:** Corner of Centre St and 7th Ave SW; in Hyatt Regency Calgary. **Parking:** on-site. **Cards:** AX, CB, DC, DS, MC, VI.

TRIBUNE RESTAURANT   Phone: 403/269-3160   ㉖

Continental
$12-$50
CALL

Dressy casual. **Bar:** Full bar. **Reservations:** suggested. **Hours:** 11 am-11 pm, Sat from 4 pm. Closed: Sun. **Address:** 118 8 Ave (Stephen Ave) T2E 0P5 **Location:** Just w of Centre Ave; centre. **Parking:** street. **Cards:** AX, MC, VI.

VINTAGE CHOPHOUSE & TAVERN   Phone: 403/262-7262   ㊷

Steak House
$10-$50

An upscale and elegant experience awaits at the fine steakhouse, which is in a historic building. Inside, the atmosphere is anything but historic. A large lounge caters to the after-work crowd, and the dining room allows for a more leisurely and romantic meal. Steaks feature prominently on the menu, but diners also will find salmon, pasta dishes and ribs. Finely executed service, including tableside preparation of Caesar salad, adds to the overall experience. Dressy casual. Entertainment. **Bar:** Full bar. **Reservations:** suggested. **Hours:** 11:30 am-close, Sat & Sun from 5 pm. Closed: 12/25. **Address:** 322 11th Ave SW T2R 0C5 **Location:** Corner of 3rd St and 11th Ave SW. **Parking:** street. **Cards:** AX, DC, MC, VI.

WILDWOOD   Phone: 403/228-0100   ㊆5

Regional
Canadian
$10-$30
CALL

Rocky Mountain cuisine is the specialty at the upscale brew pub and dining room. Upstairs, diners enter into a beautiful loft-like dining room done in rich, warm tones and where sounds and smells float from the open-concept kitchen. The food, including Arctic char, flatbreads and chicken, is beautiful and imaginative. Guests can expect to enjoy some regional dishes in a warm, cozy atmosphere. Casual dress. **Bar:** Full bar. **Reservations:** suggested, weekends. **Hours:** 11:30 am-3 & 5-10 pm, Fri & Sat-11 pm, Sun 5 pm-9 pm. Closed: 12/25. **Address:** 2417 4th St SW T2S 1X5 **Location:** Corner of 4th St SW and 25th Ave. **Parking:** on-site and street. **Cards:** AX, MC, VI.

(See map and index starting on p. 384)

WRAPTURE

Deli/Subs
Sandwiches
$5-$8

CALL [&][M]

Phone: 403/228-5777 (55)

If you're looking for something a little different, try Wrapture, where everything is made fresh to order. Located in the trendy 17th Ave district, this small fast food restaurant specializes in healthy choices, with a variety of wraps, salads and smoothies on the menu. For a quick, healthy inexpensive meal, this is an ideal choice. **Hours:** 11 am-10 pm. Closed major holidays. **Address:** 1208 17th Ave SW T2T 0L2 **Location:** 17th Ave at 11th St. **Parking:** on-site. **Cards:** AX, MC, VI.

CALGARY pop. 988,193 (See map and index starting on p. 388, 392)

——— **WHERE TO STAY** ———

BEST WESTERN AIRPORT INN *Book great rates at AAA.com*

Phone: (403)250-5015 ⑱

Small-scale Hotel
$120-$260 3/1-9/15
$110-$240 9/16-2/28

Address: 1947 18th Ave NE T2E 7T8 **Location:** 0.6 mi (1 km) e of jct Hwy 2 (Deerfoot Trail) and 16th Ave NE (Trans-Canada Hwy 1). **Facility:** Smoke free premises. 76 one-bedroom standard units, some with whirlpools. 3 stories, interior corridors. **Parking:** on-site, winter plug-ins. **Terms:** cancellation fee imposed. **Amenities:** voice mail, irons, hair dryers. *Some:* high-speed Internet. **Dining:** Thai Place Restaurant, see separate listing. **Pool(s):** heated indoor. **Leisure Activities:** whirlpool, exercise room. **Guest Services:** valet and coin laundry, wireless Internet. **Business Services:** PC (fee). **Cards:** AX, DC, DS, MC, VI. **Free Special Amenities:** continental breakfast and high-speed Internet.

AAA Benefit:
Members save 10% everyday, plus an exclusive frequent stay program.

BEST WESTERN CALGARY CENTRE INN *Book great rates at AAA.com*

Phone: (403)287-3900 ㉘

Small-scale Hotel
$169-$259 All Year

Address: 3630 MacLeod Tr S T2G 2P9 **Location:** East side of Hwy 2A (MacLeod Trail) at 36th Ave SE. **Facility:** 71 units. 69 one-bedroom standard units, some with whirlpools. 2 one-bedroom suites with whirlpools. 4 stories, interior corridors. **Parking:** on-site, winter plug-ins. **Amenities:** video games (fee), high-speed Internet, dual phone lines, voice mail, irons, hair dryers. **Pool(s):** heated indoor. **Leisure Activities:** whirlpool, exercise room. **Guest Services:** valet and coin laundry, wireless Internet. **Cards:** AX, DC, DS, MC, VI. **Free Special Amenities:** continental breakfast and newspaper.

AAA Benefit:
Members save 10% everyday, plus an exclusive frequent stay program.

▼ See AAA listing p 406 ▼

(See map and index starting on p. 388)

BEST WESTERN PORT O'CALL HOTEL   *Book great rates at AAA.com*   Phone: (403)291-4600   **4**

Small-scale Hotel
$139-$199 All Year

Address: 1935 McKnight Blvd NE T2E 6V4 **Location:** 1.6 mi (2.5 km) ne of jct Hwy 2 (Deerfoot Trail); at 19th St NE. **Facility:** 201 units. 198 one-bedroom standard units, some with whirlpools. 3 one-bedroom suites with whirlpools. 6-7 stories, interior corridors. *Bath:* combo or shower only. **Parking:** on-site. **Terms:** check-in 4 pm. **Amenities:** voice mail, irons, hair dryers. *Some:* high-speed Internet, dual phone lines, safes. **Dining:** 2 restaurants. **Pool(s):** heated indoor. **Leisure Activities:** whirlpool, steamrooms, racquetball court, exercise room. *Fee:* massage. **Guest Services:** valet laundry, wireless Internet. **Business Services:** conference facilities, PC. **Cards:** AX, DC, DS, JC, MC, VI. **Free Special Amenities:** early check-in/late check-out and high-speed Internet.
(See color ad p 405)

AAA Benefit:
Members save 10% everyday, plus an exclusive frequent stay program.

BEST WESTERN VILLAGE PARK INN   *Book great rates at AAA.com*   Phone: (403)289-0241   **19**

Small-scale Hotel
$119-$229 All Year

Address: 1804 Crowchild Tr NW T2M 3Y7 **Location:** Just ne of jct Trans-Canada Hwy 1 and Crowchild Trail. Located in Motel Village. **Facility:** 159 units. 156 one-bedroom standard units. 3 one-bedroom suites with whirlpools. 5 stories, interior corridors. **Parking:** on-site. **Terms:** cancellation fee imposed. **Amenities:** video games (fee), voice mail, irons, hair dryers. *Some:* DVD players, CD players, safes. **Pool(s):** heated indoor. **Leisure Activities:** whirlpool. **Guest Services:** valet and coin laundry, wireless Internet. **Business Services:** meeting rooms, business center. **Cards:** AX, DC, MC, VI. **Free Special Amenities:** local telephone calls and high-speed Internet.

AAA Benefit:
Members save 10% everyday, plus an exclusive frequent stay program.

BLACKFOOT INN   *Book at AAA.com*   Phone: (403)252-2253   **30**

Small-scale Hotel
$195-$325 All Year

Address: 5940 Blackfoot Tr SE T2H 2B5 **Location:** At 58th Ave SE; access to property from 58th Ave only. **Facility:** 200 units. 199 one-bedroom standard units. 1 one-bedroom suite. 7 stories, interior corridors. **Parking:** on-site, winter plug-ins. **Terms:** cancellation fee imposed. **Amenities:** voice mail, irons, hair dryers. *Fee:* video games, high-speed Internet. *Some:* CD players, fax, safes. **Pool(s):** heated outdoor. **Leisure Activities:** whirlpool, steamroom, exercise room. **Guest Services:** valet laundry, wireless Internet. **Business Services:** conference facilities, business center. **Cards:** AX, MC, VI.

CALGARY WESTWAYS GUEST HOUSE   *Book great rates at AAA.com*   Phone: 403/229-1758   **27**

Historic Bed & Breakfast
$110-$170 3/1-10/31
$110-$140 11/1-2/28

Address: 216 25th Ave SW T2S 0L1 **Location:** 1.1 mi (1.7 km) s on Hwy 2A (MacLeod Trail S), 0.2 mi (0.5 km) w. Located in a residential area. **Facility:** This unassuming 1912 house offers a variety of upscale lodgings ranging from smaller original units to deluxe, designer rooms. Smoke free premises. 5 one-bedroom standard units, some with whirlpools. 3 stories (no elevator), interior corridors. *Bath:* combo or shower only. **Parking:** on-site, winter plug-ins. **Terms:** 2 night minimum stay, 4 day cancellation notice-fee imposed. **Amenities:** video library, DVD players, CD players, high-speed Internet, voice mail, irons, hair dryers. **Leisure Activities:** bicycles, hiking trails. **Guest Services:** complimentary laundry, area transportation (fee). **Business Services:** PC. **Cards:** AX, DC, JC, MC, VI. **Free Special Amenities:** local telephone calls and high-speed Internet.

CARRIAGE HOUSE INN   *Book at AAA.com*   Phone: (403)253-1101   **32**

Small-scale Hotel
$145-$225 All Year

Address: 9030 MacLeod Tr S T2H 0M4 **Location:** On Hwy 2A (MacLeod Trail); corner of 90th Ave SW. **Facility:** 157 one-bedroom standard units, some with whirlpools. 4-10 stories, interior corridors. **Parking:** on-site, winter plug-ins. **Amenities:** voice mail, irons, hair dryers. *Some:* dual phone lines. **Pool(s):** heated outdoor. **Leisure Activities:** saunas, whirlpool, exercise room. **Guest Services:** valet laundry, wireless Internet. **Business Services:** conference facilities. **Cards:** AX, CB, DC, DS, JC, MC, VI.

COAST PLAZA HOTEL & CONFERENCE CENTRE   *Book at AAA.com*   Phone: (403)248-8888   **26**

Large-scale Hotel
$139-$249 All Year

Address: 1316 33rd St NE T2A 6B6 **Location:** Just s of jct 16th Ave (Trans-Canada Hwy 1) and 36th St NE, just w on 12th Ave NE. Located adjacent to Pacific Place Mall. **Facility:** 248 units. 245 one-bedroom standard units. 3 one-bedroom suites with whirlpools. 6-12 stories, interior corridors. *Bath:* combo or shower only. **Parking:** on-site, winter plug-ins. **Amenities:** video games (fee), high-speed Internet, voice mail, irons, hair dryers. *Some:* CD players. **Pool(s):** heated indoor. **Leisure Activities:** sauna, whirlpool, exercise room. *Fee:* massage. **Guest Services:** valet laundry. **Business Services:** conference facilities, business center. **Cards:** AX, CB, DC, DS, JC, MC, VI.

COMFORT INN AND SUITES-AIRPORT   *Book great rates at AAA.com*   Phone: (403)735-1966   **10**

Small-scale Hotel
$129-$299 3/1-9/30
$119-$189 10/1-2/28

Address: 3111 26th St NE T1Y 7E4 **Location:** Just se of jct 32nd Ave NE and Barlow Trail NE. **Facility:** 74 units. 56 one-bedroom standard units, some with whirlpools. 18 one-bedroom suites. 3 stories, interior corridors. **Parking:** on-site, winter plug-ins. **Amenities:** high-speed Internet, voice mail, safes (fee), irons, hair dryers. **Pool(s):** heated indoor. **Leisure Activities:** whirlpool, steamroom, waterslide, limited exercise equipment. **Guest Services:** valet and coin laundry. **Business Services:** meeting rooms, PC (fee). **Cards:** AX, DC, DS, MC, VI. **Free Special Amenities:** expanded continental breakfast and high-speed Internet. *(See color ad on insert)*

(See map and index starting on p. 388)

COMFORT INN & SUITES-MOTEL VILLAGE

 Book great rates at AAA.com   Phone: (403)289-2581   **16**

CAA **SAVE**

Small-scale Hotel
$119-$399 All Year

Address: 2369 Banff Tr NW T2M 4L2 **Location:** Just n of jct Trans-Canada Hwy 1 and Crowchild Trail. Located in Motel Village. **Facility:** 82 units. 58 one-bedroom standard units, some with whirlpools. 24 one-bedroom suites. 4 stories, interior corridors. **Parking:** on-site, winter plug-ins. **Amenities:** voice mail, safes (fee), irons, hair dryers. **Pool(s):** heated indoor. **Leisure Activities:** whirlpool, waterslide, limited exercise equipment. **Guest Services:** valet and coin laundry, wireless Internet. **Business Services:** meeting rooms. **Cards:** AX, CB, DC, DS, MC, VI. **Free Special Amenities: expanded continental breakfast and high-speed Internet.** *(See color ad on insert)*

COMFORT INN & SUITES-SOUTH

 Book great rates at AAA.com   Phone: (403)287-7070   **29**

CAA **SAVE**

Small-scale Hotel
$109-$329 All Year

Address: 4611 MacLeod Tr SW T2G 0A6 **Location:** Hwy 2A (MacLeod Trail), w on 45th Ave. **Facility:** 93 units. 68 one-bedroom standard units, some with whirlpools. 25 one-bedroom suites. 4 stories, interior corridors. **Parking:** on-site, winter plug-ins. **Terms:** cancellation fee imposed. **Amenities:** video games (fee), high-speed Internet, voice mail, safes, irons, hair dryers. **Pool(s):** heated indoor. **Leisure Activities:** whirlpool, waterslide, limited exercise equipment. *Fee:* massage. **Guest Services:** valet and coin laundry. **Business Services:** meeting rooms, business center. **Cards:** AX, CB, DC, DS, MC, VI. **Free Special Amenities: expanded continental breakfast and high-speed Internet.** *(See color ad on insert)*

COUNTRY INN & SUITES BY CARLSON

 Book great rates at AAA.com   Phone: (403)250-1800   **6**

CAA **SAVE**

Small-scale Hotel
$164-$208 All Year

Address: 2481 39th Ave NE T2E 8V8 **Location:** Barlow Trail and 39th Ave NE. **Facility:** 106 units. 54 one-bedroom standard units, some with whirlpools. 52 one-bedroom suites. 3 stories, interior corridors. *Bath:* combo or shower only. **Parking:** on-site, winter plug-ins. **Amenities:** high-speed Internet, dual phone lines, voice mail, irons, hair dryers. **Pool(s):** heated indoor. **Leisure Activities:** whirlpool, exercise room. **Guest Services:** valet and coin laundry. **Business Services:** meeting rooms. **Cards:** AX, DC, DS, JC, MC, VI. **Free Special Amenities: expanded continental breakfast and local telephone calls.** *(See color ad below)*

DAYS INN CALGARY AIRPORT

 Book at AAA.com   Phone: (403)250-3297   **15**

Small-scale Hotel
$129-$159 All Year

Address: 2799 Sunridge Way NE T1Y 7K7 **Location:** Barlow Trail, just e of Sunridge Way NE. **Facility:** 76 units. 60 one-bedroom standard units, some with whirlpools. 16 one-bedroom suites, some with whirlpools. 4 stories, interior corridors. **Parking:** on-site, winter plug-ins. **Terms:** cancellation fee imposed. **Amenities:** voice mail, irons, hair dryers. *Some:* high-speed Internet, dual phone lines. **Pool(s):** heated indoor. **Leisure Activities:** whirlpool, waterslide, exercise room. **Guest Services:** valet and coin laundry, wireless Internet. **Business Services:** PC (fee). **Cards:** AX, MC, VI.

DELTA CALGARY AIRPORT

Book great rates at AAA.com   Phone: 403/291-2600   **1**

CAA **SAVE**

Large-scale Hotel
$159-$550 6/1-2/28
$209-$428 3/1-5/31

Address: 2001 Airport Rd NE T2E 6Z8 **Location:** At Calgary International Airport. **Facility:** 296 units. 284 one-bedroom standard units. 12 one-bedroom suites, some with whirlpools. 3-8 stories, interior corridors. **Parking:** on-site (fee) and valet. **Terms:** check-in 4 pm. **Amenities:** voice mail, irons, hair dryers. *Fee:* video games, high-speed Internet. **Dining:** 2 restaurants. **Pool(s):** heated indoor. **Leisure Activities:** whirlpool, exercise room. **Guest Services:** valet laundry. **Business Services:** conference facilities, business center. **Cards:** AX, DC, DS, JC, MC, VI.

(See map and index starting on p. 388)

DELTA CALGARY SOUTH   *Book great rates at AAA.com*   Phone: (403)278-5050   **34**

(CAA) (SAVE)

▼▼▼▼
Small-scale Hotel
$399 3/1-10/31
$389 11/1-2/28

Address: 135 Southland Dr SE T2J 5X5 **Location:** On Hwy 2A (MacLeod Trail); corner of Southland Dr. **Facility:** 260 units. 251 one-bedroom standard units. 9 one-bedroom suites, some with whirlpools. 3-8 stories, interior corridors. *Bath:* combo or shower only. **Parking:** on-site, winter plug-ins. **Terms:** cancellation fee imposed. **Amenities:** video games (fee), voice mail, irons, hair dryers. **Pool(s):** 2 heated indoor. **Leisure Activities:** whirlpool, waterslide, limited exercise equipment. **Guest Services:** valet laundry, wireless Internet. **Business Services:** conference facilities, business center. **Cards:** AX, MC, VI. **Free Special Amenities: high-speed Internet.**

[icons]

ECONO LODGE INN & SUITES UNIVERSITY   *Book great rates at AAA.com*   Phone: (403)289-1921   **21**

(CAA) (SAVE)

▼▼▼
Motel
$89-$299 All Year

Address: 2231 Banff Tr NW T2M 4L2 **Location:** Just n of jct 16th Ave NW (Trans-Canada Hwy 1) and Banff Trail NW. Located in Motel Village. **Facility:** 82 units. 78 one- and 4 two-bedroom standard units, some with efficiencies or kitchens. 2-5 stories, exterior corridors. **Parking:** on-site, winter plug-ins. **Terms:** cancellation fee imposed. **Amenities:** voice mail, irons, hair dryers. *Some:* high-speed Internet. **Pool(s):** heated indoor. **Leisure Activities:** whirlpool, exercise room. **Guest Services:** coin laundry. **Cards:** AX, CB, DC, DS, JC, MC, VI. **Free Special Amenities: continental breakfast and local telephone calls.** *(See color ad on insert & below)*

[icons]

ECONO LODGE MOTEL VILLAGE   *Book great rates at AAA.com*   Phone: 403/289-2561   **24**

(CAA) (SAVE)

▼▼▼
Motel
Rates not provided

Address: 2440 16th Ave NW T2M 0M5 **Location:** Jct 16th Ave NW (Trans-Canada Hwy 1) and Banff Trail NW. Located in Motel Village. **Facility:** 56 units. 54 one-bedroom standard units, some with efficiencies. 2 one-bedroom suites with efficiencies. 2 stories (no elevator), interior/exterior corridors. **Parking:** on-site, winter plug-ins. **Amenities:** irons, hair dryers. **Leisure Activities:** sauna, exercise room. **Guest Services:** valet and coin laundry. **Free Special Amenities: local telephone calls and newspaper.** *(See color ad on insert)*

[icons]

ECONO LODGE SOUTH   *Book great rates at AAA.com*   Phone: (403)252-4401   **31**

(CAA) (SAVE)

▼▼▼
Motel
$89-$209 All Year

Address: 7505 MacLeod Tr S T2H 0L8 **Location:** Corner of MacLeod Tr and 75th Ave. **Facility:** 72 units. 70 one-bedroom standard units, some with efficiencies or kitchens. 2 one-bedroom suites with efficiencies. 2 stories (no elevator), interior/exterior corridors. **Parking:** on-site, winter plug-ins. **Amenities:** voice mail, hair dryers. *Some:* irons. **Pool(s):** heated indoor. **Leisure Activities:** whirlpool, limited exercise equipment. **Guest Services:** valet and coin laundry, wireless Internet. **Cards:** AX, DC, DS, MC, VI. **Free Special Amenities: continental breakfast and high-speed Internet.** *(See color ad on insert)*

[icons]

EXECUTIVE ROYAL INN NORTH CALGARY   *Book at AAA.com*   Phone: (403)291-2003   **12**

▼▼▼
Small-scale Hotel
$144-$205 All Year

Address: 2828 23rd St NE T2E 8T4 **Location:** 27th Ave NE and Barlow Trail. **Facility:** 201 units. 191 one-bedroom standard units. 10 one-bedroom suites with whirlpools. 6 stories, interior corridors. **Parking:** on-site, winter plug-ins. **Terms:** check-in 4 pm. **Amenities:** video games (fee), high-speed Internet, dual phone lines, voice mail, irons, hair dryers. **Leisure Activities:** whirlpools, steamrooms, exercise room. **Guest Services:** valet laundry. **Business Services:** conference facilities, administrative services (fee). **Cards:** AX, MC, VI.

[icons]

▼ *See AAA listing above* ▼

(See map and index starting on p. 388)

FOUR POINTS BY SHERATON HOTEL AND SUITES, CALGARY WEST *Book great rates at AAA.com* Phone: (403)288-4441   **8**

Large-scale Hotel
$200-$280 3/1-10/15
$155-$250 10/16-2/28

Address: 8220 Bowridge Cres NW T3B 2V1 **Location:** Opposite Canada Olympic Park. **Facility:** 150 units. 100 one-bedroom standard units, some with whirlpools. 50 one-bedroom suites. 4 stories, interior corridors. **Parking:** on-site, winter plug-ins. **Terms:** cancellation fee imposed. **Amenities:** high-speed Internet, dual phone lines, voice mail, irons, hair dryers. **Pool(s):** heated indoor. **Leisure Activities:** whirlpool, steamroom, waterslide, exercise room, spa. **Guest Services:** valet and coin laundry, wireless Internet. **Business Services:** conference facilities, business center. **Cards:** AX, DC, DS, MC, VI.

FOUR POINTS
BY SHERATON

AAA Benefit:
Members get up to 15% off, plus Starwood Preferred Guest® bonuses.

HAMPTON INN & SUITES-CALGARY AIRPORT *Book great rates at AAA.com* Phone: 403/250-4667 **7**

Small-scale Hotel
Rates not provided

Address: 2420 37th Ave NE T2E 8S6 **Location:** Barlow Trail at 37th Ave NE. **Facility:** 103 units. 72 one-bedroom standard units. 31 one-bedroom suites, some with efficiencies. 4 stories, interior corridors. **Parking:** on-site, winter plug-ins. **Amenities:** video games (fee), high-speed Internet, dual phone lines, voice mail, irons, hair dryers. **Pool(s):** heated indoor. **Leisure Activities:** exercise room. **Guest Services:** valet and coin laundry, area transportation. **Business Services:** meeting rooms.

HAMPTON INN & SUITES CALGARY-UNIVERSITY *Book great rates at AAA.com* Phone: (403)289-9800 **20**

Small-scale Hotel
$159-$329 All Year

Address: 2231 Banff Tr NW T2M 4L2 **Location:** Just n of jct 16th Ave NW (Trans-Canada Hwy 1). **Facility:** 96 units. 72 one-bedroom standard units, some with whirlpools. 24 one-bedroom suites with efficiencies. 4 stories, interior corridors. **Parking:** on-site, winter plug-ins. **Terms:** cancellation fee imposed. **Amenities:** high-speed Internet, irons, hair dryers. *Some:* DVD players. **Pool(s):** heated indoor. **Leisure Activities:** whirlpool, waterslide, exercise room. **Guest Services:** valet and coin laundry. **Business Services:** meeting rooms, business center. **Cards:** AX, DC, DS, MC, VI. **Free Special Amenities:** expanded continental breakfast and high-speed Internet. *(See color ad below)*

▼ See AAA listing above ▼

Hertz NEVERL⊖ST

Navigate Like a Pro Wherever You Go

Get exclusive member savings on select Hertz vehicles with the NeverLost in-car navigation system.

Just start your engine, enter your destination, and go! While you focus on the road, NeverLost announces your upcoming turns and displays your progress on the map screen — even when you change course or make stops.

Hertz NeverLost features:

- **CAA/AAA Diamond rated hotels and restaurants**
- **CAA/AAA member discount locations**
- **CAA/AAA GEM attractions**
- **7 language options**
- **Available at most Hertz airport locations in US, Canada, and Puerto Rico with a 25% discount for CAA/AAA members.**

Show Your Card & Save

(See map and index starting on p. 388)

HILTON GARDEN INN-CALGARY AIRPORT   *Book great rates at AAA.com*   Phone: (403)717-1999   **3**

▽▽▽▽

Small-scale Hotel
$189-$269 All Year

Address: 2335 Pegasus Rd NE T2E 8C3 **Location:** Jct Barlow Tr and McKnight Blvd, just w, n on 19th St NE, then just e. **Facility:** 135 units. 131 one-bedroom standard units. 4 one-bedroom suites with whirlpools. 5 stories, interior corridors. **Parking:** on-site, winter plug-ins. **Terms:** 7 day cancellation notice-fee imposed. **Amenities:** video games (fee), high-speed Internet, dual phone lines, voice mail, irons, hair dryers. **Pool(s):** heated indoor. **Leisure Activities:** whirlpool, exercise room. **Guest Services:** valet and coin laundry, area transportation, wireless Internet. **Business Services:** meeting rooms, business center. **Cards:** AX, DC, DS, MC, VI.

HOLIDAY INN CALGARY-AIRPORT   *Book great rates at AAA.com*   Phone: (403)230-1999   **25**

(CAA) (SAVE)
▽▽▽▽
Small-scale Hotel
$139-$259 All Year

Address: 1250 McKinnon Dr NE T2E 7T7 **Location:** 0.6 mi (1 km) e of jct Hwy 2 (Deerfoot Trail) and 16th Ave NE (Trans-Canada Hwy 1). **Facility:** 168 units. 164 one-bedroom standard units. 4 one-bedroom suites with whirlpools. 5 stories, interior corridors. **Parking:** on-site, winter plug-ins. **Terms:** cancellation fee imposed. **Amenities:** video games (fee), high-speed Internet, dual phone lines, voice mail, irons, hair dryers. **Pool(s):** heated indoor. **Leisure Activities:** saunas, exercise room. **Guest Services:** valet and coin laundry, area transportation. **Business Services:** meeting rooms, business center. **Cards:** AX, DC, DS, JC, MC, VI. **Free Special Amenities:** local telephone calls and high-speed Internet. *(See color ad on insert)*

HOLIDAY INN EXPRESS HOTEL & SUITES CALGARY-SOUTH   *Book at AAA.com*   Phone: 403-225-3000   **35**

▽▽▽▽
Small-scale Hotel
Rates not provided

Address: 12025 Lake Fraser Dr SE (MacLeod Trail S) T2J 7G5 **Location:** Hwy 2 (Deerfoot Trail), exit Anderson Rd W, then just s on MacLeod Trail. **Facility:** 106 units. 63 one-bedroom standard units. 43 one-bedroom suites, some with whirlpools. 4 stories, interior corridors. **Parking:** on-site, winter plug-ins. **Amenities:** video games (fee), high-speed Internet, dual phone lines, voice mail, irons, hair dryers. **Pool(s):** heated indoor. **Leisure Activities:** whirlpool, waterslide, exercise room. **Guest Services:** valet and coin laundry. **Business Services:** meeting rooms, business center.

LAKEVIEW SIGNATURE INN   *Book great rates at AAA.com*   Phone: (403)735-3336   **5**

(CAA) (SAVE)
▽▽▽▽
Small-scale Hotel
$139-$199 All Year

Address: 2622 39th Ave NE T1Y 7J9 **Location:** Corner of Barlow Trail and 39th Ave NE. **Facility:** Smoke free premises. 120 units. 48 one-bedroom standard units, some with efficiencies or kitchens. 48 one- and 24 two-bedroom suites, some with efficiencies or kitchens. 4 stories, interior corridors. *Bath:* combo or shower only. **Parking:** on-site, winter plug-ins. **Terms:** cancellation fee imposed. **Amenities:** video games (fee), CD players, high-speed Internet, voice mail, irons, hair dryers. *Some:* dual phone lines. **Pool(s):** heated indoor. **Leisure Activities:** whirlpool, limited exercise equipment, sports court. **Guest Services:** valet and coin laundry, area transportation-within 3 km. **Business Services:** meeting rooms, PC. **Cards:** AX, CB, DC, JC, MC, VI.

QUALITY INN UNIVERSITY   *Book great rates at AAA.com*   Phone: (403)289-1973   **17**

(CAA) (SAVE)
▽▽▽▽
Small-scale Hotel
$119-$299 3/1-9/15
$99-$139 9/16-2/28

Address: 2359 Banff Tr NW T2M 4L2 **Location:** Just n of jct Trans-Canada Hwy 1 and Crowchild Trail. Located in Motel Village. **Facility:** 105 units. 104 one-bedroom standard units, some with whirlpools. 1 one-bedroom suite with whirlpool. 2 stories, interior/exterior corridors. *Bath:* combo or shower only. **Parking:** on-site, winter plug-ins. **Terms:** check-in 4 pm, 2 night minimum stay - weekends, cancellation fee imposed. **Amenities:** voice mail, irons, hair dryers. *Some:* high-speed Internet. **Pool(s):** heated indoor. **Leisure Activities:** steamroom, exercise room, spa. *Fee:* game room. **Guest Services:** valet and coin laundry, wireless Internet. **Business Services:** meeting rooms, business center. **Cards:** AX, DC, DS, MC, VI. **Free Special Amenities: continental breakfast and high-speed Internet.** *(See color ad on insert)*

RADISSON HOTEL CALGARY AIRPORT   *Book at AAA.com*   Phone: (403)291-4666   **23**

▽▽▽▽
Small-scale Hotel
$240 All Year

Address: 2120 16th Ave NE T2E 1L4 **Location:** Just e of jct 16th Ave NE (Trans-Canada Hwy 1) and Hwy 2 (Deerfoot Trail). **Facility:** Smoke free premises. 185 units. 177 one-bedroom standard units, some with whirlpools. 8 one-bedroom suites. 10 stories, interior corridors. *Bath:* combo or shower only. **Parking:** on-site, winter plug-ins. **Terms:** cancellation fee imposed. **Amenities:** video games (fee), high-speed Internet, dual phone lines, voice mail, irons, hair dryers. **Pool(s):** heated indoor. **Leisure Activities:** whirlpool, exercise room. **Guest Services:** valet laundry. **Business Services:** conference facilities, PC (fee). **Cards:** AX, CB, DC, DS, JC, MC, VI.

SANDMAN HOTEL SUITES & SPA CALGARY AIRPORT   *Book at AAA.com*   Phone: (403)219-2475   **2**

▽▽▽▽
Small-scale Hotel
$189 All Year

Address: 25 Hopewell Way NE T3J 4V7 **Location:** Just n of jct Barlow Trail and McKnight Blvd. **Facility:** 177 units. 113 one-bedroom standard units. 64 one-bedroom suites, some with whirlpools. 4 stories (no elevator), interior corridors. **Parking:** on-site, winter plug-ins. **Amenities:** video games (fee), high-speed Internet, dual phone lines, voice mail, irons, hair dryers. **Pool(s):** heated indoor. **Leisure Activities:** saunas, whirlpool, exercise room. *Fee:* massage. **Guest Services:** valet laundry. **Business Services:** meeting rooms, PC. **Cards:** AX, DC, DS, MC, VI.

(See map and index starting on p. 388)

SHERATON CAVALIER HOTEL   *Book great rates at AAA.com*   Phone: (403)291-0107   **9**

Large-scale Hotel
$469 All Year

Address: 2620 32nd Ave NE T1Y 6B8 **Location:** Barlow Trail at 32nd Ave NE. **Facility:** 306 units. 286 one-bedroom standard units. 20 one-bedroom suites with whirlpools. 7 stories, interior corridors. **Parking:** on-site and valet, winter plug-ins. **Terms:** cancellation fee imposed. **Amenities:** dual phone lines, voice mail, honor bars, irons, hair dryers. *Fee:* video games, high-speed Internet. *Some:* fax. **Dining:** Carver's Steakhouse, see separate listing. **Pool(s):** heated indoor. **Leisure Activities:** sauna, whirlpools, waterslide, exercise room. **Guest Services:** valet laundry. **Business Services:** conference facilities, business center. **Cards:** AX, DC, DS, MC, VI.

Sheraton
HOTELS & RESORTS

AAA Benefit:
Members get up to 15% off, plus Starwood Preferred Guest® bonuses.

ASK SD FEE 🛏 🍴 24📶 🍸 🏊 ✂ 🎥 💻 / SOME UNITS 🐾 ✗

STAYBRIDGE SUITES CALGARY AIRPORT   *Book at AAA.com*   Phone: 403/204-7829   **14**

Small-scale Hotel
Rates not provided

Address: 2825 Sunridge Way NE T1Y 7K7 **Location:** Trans-Canada Hwy 1, exit Barlow Trail NE, just n, then just e. **Facility:** 96 units. 43 one-bedroom standard units with efficiencies. 42 one- and 11 two-bedroom suites. 4 stories, interior corridors. *Bath:* combo or shower only. **Parking:** on-site, winter plug-ins. **Amenities:** video library (fee), DVD players, high-speed Internet, voice mail, irons, hair dryers. **Pool(s):** heated indoor. **Leisure Activities:** whirlpool, waterslide, exercise room. **Guest Services:** complimentary and valet laundry, wireless Internet. **Business Services:** meeting rooms, business center.

FEE 🛏 CALL 🔊M 🏊 ✂ 🎥 🖥 🖥 💻 / SOME UNITS ✗

SUPER 8 MOTEL CALGARY AIRPORT   *Book great rates at AAA.com*   Phone: (403)291-9888   **11**

CAA SAVE

Small-scale Hotel
$130-$240 6/2-2/28
$120-$180 3/1-6/1

Address: 3030 Barlow Tr NE T1Y 1A2 **Location:** Corner of 32nd Ave and Barlow Trail NE. **Facility:** 61 one-bedroom standard units. 4 stories, interior corridors. **Parking:** on-site, winter plug-ins. **Amenities:** irons, hair dryers. *Fee:* high-speed Internet, safes. **Guest Services:** coin laundry. **Business Services:** meeting rooms. **Cards:** AX, DC, DS, MC, VI. **Free Special Amenities:** continental breakfast and local telephone calls.

SD 🛏 🍴 🖥 / SOME UNITS FEE 🐾 ✗

TRAVELODGE CALGARY MACLEOD TRAIL   *Book great rates at AAA.com*   Phone: (403)253-7070   **33**

CAA SAVE

Small-scale Hotel
$131-$167 All Year

Address: 9206 MacLeod Tr S T2J 0P5 **Location:** On MacLeod Tr just s of 90th Ave SW. **Facility:** 254 units. 253 one-bedroom standard units. 1 one-bedroom suite. 6 stories, interior corridors. **Parking:** on-site, winter plug-ins. **Amenities:** video games (fee), voice mail, irons, hair dryers. *Some:* high-speed Internet. **Dining:** entertainment. **Pool(s):** heated indoor. **Leisure Activities:** whirlpool, limited exercise equipment. **Guest Services:** coin laundry, wireless Internet. **Business Services:** meeting rooms, PC (fee). **Cards:** AX, DC, DS, JC, MC, VI. *(See color ad p 413)*

SD 🍴 🍸 🏊 🎥 / SOME UNITS FEE 🐾 ✗ 🖥 🖥

TRAVELODGE CALGARY-UNIVERSITY   *Book great rates at AAA.com*   Phone: (403)289-6600   **22**

CAA SAVE

Small-scale Hotel
$98-$187 All Year

Address: 2227 Banff Tr NW T2M 4L2 **Location:** 16th Ave NW (Trans-Canada Hwy 1) and Banff Trail NW. Located in Motel Village across from McMahon Stadium. **Facility:** 64 one-bedroom standard units. 3 stories, interior corridors. *Bath:* combo or shower only. **Parking:** on-site, winter plug-ins. **Terms:** check-in 4 pm. **Amenities:** dual phone lines, voice mail, irons, hair dryers. **Leisure Activities:** pool privileges, exercise room. **Guest Services:** valet laundry, wireless Internet. **Business Services:** meeting rooms. **Cards:** AX, CB, DC, DS, JC, MC, VI. **Free Special Amenities:** expanded continental breakfast and high-speed Internet.

SD 🍴 CALL 🔊M 🎥 🖥 💻 / SOME UNITS 🐾 ✗

TRAVELODGE HOTEL CALGARY AIRPORT   *Book great rates at AAA.com*   Phone: (403)291-1260   **13**

CAA SAVE

Small-scale Hotel
$179-$229 6/1-2/28
$129-$199 3/1-5/31

Address: 2750 Sunridge Blvd NE T1Y 3C2 **Location:** Just se of jct 32nd Ave NE and Barlow Trail NE. **Facility:** 203 one-bedroom standard units. 6 stories, interior corridors. **Parking:** on-site, winter plug-ins. **Amenities:** video games (fee), voice mail, irons, hair dryers. *Some:* high-speed Internet. **Pool(s):** heated indoor. **Leisure Activities:** whirlpool, limited exercise equipment. **Guest Services:** valet and coin laundry. **Business Services:** meeting rooms, PC. **Cards:** AX, DC, MC, VI. *(See color ad p 413)*

SD 🛏 🍴 🍸 🏃 🏊 🎥 💻 / SOME UNITS 🐾 ✗ VCR 🖥 🖥

WINGATE INN   *Book at AAA.com*   Phone: (403)514-0099   **36**

Small-scale Hotel
$147-$169 All Year

Address: 400 Midpark Way T2X 3S4 **Location:** Hwy 2A (MacLeod Trail), 0.3 mi (0.5 km) e on Sun Valley, just n on Midpark Way, then just s. **Facility:** 103 units. 87 one-bedroom standard units, some with whirlpools. 16 one-bedroom suites, some with whirlpools. 4 stories, interior corridors. *Bath:* combo or shower only. **Parking:** on-site, winter plug-ins. **Terms:** 4 day cancellation notice-fee imposed. **Amenities:** video games (fee), high-speed Internet, dual phone lines, voice mail, safes, irons, hair dryers. **Pool(s):** heated indoor. **Leisure Activities:** whirlpool, waterslide, exercise room. **Guest Services:** valet and coin laundry, area transportation. **Business Services:** meeting rooms, business center. **Cards:** AX, DC, DS, MC, VI.

ASK SD 🍴 CALL 🔊M 🏊 ✂ 🎥 🖥 🖥 💻 / SOME UNITS FEE 🐾 ✗

(See map and index starting on p. 388)

——————— WHERE TO DINE ———————

ALBERTA KING OF SUBS
Phone: 403/293-5809   ③

Canadian
$4-$10

Montreal-style smoked-meat sandwiches and hot grilled subs are specialties at the strip-mall eatery, which has only nine tables and a counter. French fries, coleslaw and sugar pie also are on the menu. Service is friendly and polite. Casual dress. **Bar:** Beer only. **Reservations:** not accepted. **Hours:** 10 am-9 pm, Thurs-Sat to 10 pm. Closed: 3/24, 12/25. **Address:** 7196 Temple Dr NE, #22 T1Y 4E8 **Location:** McKnight Blvd and 52nd St NE, just s on 52nd St NE. **Parking:** on-site. **Cards:** VI.

ALEXIS BISTRO AND LOUNGE
Phone: 403/214-3616   ㊱

French
$14-$36

Dressy casual. **Bar:** Full bar. **Reservations:** suggested. **Hours:** 5 pm-10 pm. Closed major holidays; also Sun. **Address:** 4824 16th St SW T2T 4J5 **Location:** Just n of 50th Ave. **Parking:** on-site. **Cards:** AX, MC, VI.

BAGOLAC SAIGON RESTAURANT
Phone: 403/252-5588   ㊵

Vietnamese
$6-$12

Upscale decor awaits at this fancy Vietnamese restaurant, where a mixture of Thai and Vietnamese dishes are available. The selection on the menu is so outstanding that you may have a hard time selecting. It is best to order a variety of dishes to truly experience the tastes and flavors of this cuisine, starting with salad rolls, a traditional bun or noodle soup. Casual dress. **Bar:** Full bar. **Hours:** 11 am-9:30 pm. Closed major holidays; also Sun. **Address:** #8, 6130-1A St SW T2H 0G3 **Location:** Just e off MacLeod Trail near Chinook Centre. **Parking:** on-site. **Cards:** AX, MC, VI.

BEARS DEN
Phone: 403/241-7611

Regional
Canadian
$25-$42

A bit of a drive from downtown, the bunker-looking complex at the edge of the city limits offers a number of surprises. The restaurant follows in the tradition of legendary steakhouses with a rich and warmly luxurious set of dining rooms reminiscent of old gentlemen's clubs. Accents include dark wood paneling, hand-crafted relief murals and beautiful fireplaces. In addition to preparing some of the finest cuts of AAA Alberta beef, this place also puts together satisfying non-steak dishes. Semi-formal attire. **Bar:** Full bar. **Reservations:** suggested. **Hours:** 5 pm-10 pm, Fri & Sat 4 pm-midnight. Closed major holidays. **Address:** 254028 Bearspaw Rd NW T3L 2P7 **Location:** 1.2 mi (2 km) w of jct Stoney Tr; along Hwy IA Crowchild Trail. **Parking:** on-site. **Cards:** AX, DS, MC, VI.

CALL ♿ M

BELMONT DINER
Phone: 403/242-6782   ㉜

Canadian
$5-$8

Diners in search of a hearty breakfast need look no further than this Marda Loop diner. At lunchtime, sandwiches and milk shakes are popular choices. Casual dress. **Hours:** 7 am-3 pm, Sat & Sun from 8 am. Closed major holidays. **Address:** 2008 33rd Ave SW T2T 1Z6 **Location:** At 33rd Ave and 20th St; in Marda Loop. **Parking:** street.

BIG T'S BBQ
Phone: 403/252-5550   ㊹

Barbecue
$7-$40

Southern barbecue at its messiest is the name of the game at this casual restaurant, which piles up enormous portions that satisfy even the hungriest diner. Casual dress. **Bar:** Full bar. **Reservations:** not accepted. **Hours:** 11 am-10 pm, Fri & Sat-11 pm. Closed major holidays; also Sun. **Address:** 8330 Macleod Tr SE T2H 2V2 **Location:** Just s of Anderson Rd; in Heritage Plaza. **Parking:** on-site. **Cards:** AX, MC, VI.

CALL ♿ M

BIG T'S BBQ
Phone: 403/284-5959   ⑫

Barbecue
$12-$40

Southern barbecue at its messiest is the name of the game at this casual restaurant, where enormous portions will satisfy even the hungriest diner. Casual dress. **Bar:** Full bar. **Hours:** 11:30 am-10 pm, Fri & Sat-11 pm. Closed major holidays; also Sun. **Address:** 2138 Crowchild Tr NW T2M 3Y7 **Location:** Jct 23 Ave NW; across from McMann Stadium. **Parking:** on-site. **Cards:** AX, MC, VI.

BOOGIE'S BURGERS
Phone: 403/230-7070   ㉒

American
$5-$10

A favorite neighborhood haunt, the burger joint whips up creamy milkshakes, huge burgers and crispy fries. Guests can grab a seat at the counter and chat with the friendly owners, or in the summer, enjoy a shake at a picnic table. Casual dress. **Bar:** Beer & wine. **Hours:** 9 am-9 pm, Sat 10 am-8 pm. Closed major holidays; also Sun. **Address:** 908 Edmonton Tr NE T2E 3K1 **Location:** Corner of 8th Ave NE. **Parking:** on-site.

BOYD'S SEAFOOD RESTAURANT
Phone: 403/253-7575   ㊲

Seafood
$10-$37

A long and varied menu of seafood is presented at the casual family restaurant, which transports guests to the east coast of Nova Scotia for a taste of the maritime. Fish and chips, mussels, Alaskan halibut, clams and more are dished in heaping portions. Most selections are flown in fresh daily, and there is something for everyone. This place offers a great value for the dollar. Service is friendly. Casual dress. **Bar:** Full bar. **Reservations:** suggested. **Hours:** 11:30 am-9 pm, Fri & Sat-10 pm. Closed major holidays. **Address:** 5211 MacLeod Tr T2H 0J3 **Location:** Corner of 52nd and MacLeod Trail. **Parking:** on-site. **Cards:** MC, VI.

CALL ♿ M

BROKEN PLATE KITCHEN & BAR
Phone: 403/225-9650

Greek
$10-$24

While guests are not encouraged to actually throw plates on to the ground after eating, it is not unusual to throw hands up in the air and shout "opa!" after enjoying Greek dishes made from fresh and authentic ingredients. One of three Calgary locations, this restaurant seems to have been imported directly from Greece. While service can be a little relaxed, the menu is serious about showcasing both comfortable and traditional selections. Casual dress. **Bar:** Full bar. **Reservations:** accepted. **Hours:** 11:30 am-10 pm, Fri & Sat-11 pm, Sun 5 pm-10 pm. Closed major holidays. **Address:** 590-10816 MacLeod Tr SE T2J 5N8 **Location:** Just n of Anderson Rd; west side of Willow Park Shopping Plaza. **Parking:** on-site. **Cards:** MC, VI.

CALL ♿ M

(See map and index starting on p. 388)

BUFFET YANGTZE

Chinese
$8-$16

Phone: 403-275-3337 ①

In the Deerfoot Crossing outlet mall, this unassuming restaurant is a bit of a drive from most hotels, especially during rush hour. However, the navigation skills that come in handy on the Deerfoot Expressway also prove useful in negotiating your way around the vast Chinese buffet. Food is refreshed regularly for the hungry patrons who loyally frequent this place. Casual dress. **Bar:** Full bar. **Reservations:** not accepted. **Hours:** 11 am-10 pm. Closed major holidays. **Address:** 901 64th Ave NW T2E 7P4 **Location:** At north entrance of Deerfoot Mall. **Parking:** on-site. **Cards:** AX, MC, VI.

CACTUS CLUB CAFE

International
$9-$29

Phone: 403-255-1088

This bustling, casual restaurant serves huge burgers, sandwiches, pasta, salads, soups, quesadillas, fajitas, vegetarian dishes, steak, ribs, chicken and fish. Featured are certified Angus beef and fresh wild British Columbia salmon. The thick and creamy milk shakes come highly recommended. Casual dress. **Bar:** Full bar. **Reservations:** accepted. **Hours:** 11 am-midnight, Fri & Sat-1 am. Closed: 12/25. **Address:** 7010 MacLeod Tr SE T2H 0L3 **Location:** Jct Glenmore Trail SW, just s. **Parking:** on-site. **Cards:** AX, MC, VI.

CALL

CACTUS CLUB CAFE

International
$9-$29

Phone: 403/250-1120

This bustling, casual restaurant serves huge burgers, sandwiches, pasta, salads, soups, quesadillas, fajitas, vegetarian dishes, steak, ribs, chicken and fish. Featured are certified Angus beef and fresh wild British Columbia salmon. The thick and creamy milk shakes come highly recommended. Casual dress. **Bar:** Full bar. **Reservations:** accepted. **Hours:** 11 am-midnight, Fri & Sat-1 am. Closed: 12/25. **Address:** 2612 39th Ave NE T1Y 7S9 **Location:** Barlow Trail at 39th Ave NE. **Parking:** on-site. **Cards:** AX, MC, VI.

CALL

CANNERY ROW

Seafood
$8-$55

Phone: 403-225-1273 ㊼

The restaurant, which includes an open kitchen and oyster bar, nurtures a fun, exciting atmosphere. On the menu are superb seafood and pasta entrees, as well as noteworthy appetizers. The attractive wine list includes several by-the-glass selections. Wood beams and a restrained nautical vibe give the fast-paced spot an almost rustic feel. Patrons can watch the team of chefs preparing meals in the open kitchen. Attentive and friendly servers lend to enjoyable experiences. Casual dress. **Bar:** Full bar. **Reservations:** accepted. **Hours:** 11:30 am-midnight. Closed: 12/25; also Sun. **Address:** 12101 Lake Fraser Dr SE, #500 T2J 7G3 **Location:** Hwy 2 (Deerfoot Trail), exit Anderson Rd W, just s on MacLeod Trail; in Lake Bonavista Square. **Parking:** on-site. **Cards:** AX, DC, DS, MC, VI.

CALL

CAPO RESTAURANT

Nouvelle Italian
$13-$35

Phone: 403-264-2276 ㉙

Dressy casual. **Bar:** Full bar. **Reservations:** suggested. **Hours:** 11:30 am-2 & 5:30-10 pm. Closed major holidays; also Sun for lunch, Mon & Tues. **Address:** 1420 9th Ave SE, Suite 4 T2G 0T5 **Location:** Just e of 12th St SE; in Inglewood. **Parking:** street. **Cards:** AX, MC, VI.

CAPTAIN SCOTT'S FISH & CHIPS

Seafood
$5-$12

Phone: 408/280-0009 ②

With its location in the far northeast of landlocked Calgary, Captain Scott's does a pretty good imitation of an East Coast fish and chips shop. While the fish isn't wrapped in newspaper for take-out, most guests regardless enjoy a good selection of deep-fried fish with a tasty batter in the modest, nautically themed restaurant. Casual dress. **Reservations:** not accepted. **Hours:** 11 am-9 pm. Closed major holidays; also Sun. **Address:** 55 Castleridge Blvd NE, #76 T3J 1Y9 **Location:** Jct 52nd St NE (Falconridge Blvd NE) and McKnight Blvd NE; in Castleridge Plaza. **Parking:** on-site. **Cards:** MC, VI.

CARVER'S STEAKHOUSE

Steak House
$28-$35

Phone: 403/250-6327 ⑥

One of Calgary's finest steak houses, the formal restaurant is the place to go for beef. The contemporary, upscale dining room features superb steaks and decadent desserts. Made-to-order steaks are mouthwatering. Casual dress. **Bar:** Full bar. **Reservations:** required. **Hours:** 5:30 pm-10:30 pm, Sun 5 pm-9 pm. Closed major holidays. **Address:** 2620 32nd Ave NE T1Y 6B8 **Location:** Barlow Trail at 32nd Ave NE; in Sheraton Cavalier Hotel. **Parking:** on-site and valet. **Cards:** AX, DC, DS, MC, VI.

THE CHEESECAKE CAFE

Canadian
$10-$26

Phone: 403/255-7443 ㊸

As might be expected, cheesecake is the cafe's signature item, and lip-smacking varieties are made on the premises. A huge dessert display case greets guests upon arrival. Offerings on the extensive lunch and dinner menu range from sandwiches and entree salads to pasta, pizza and seafood selections. It takes a while to get through the menu. Casual dress. **Bar:** Full bar. **Reservations:** not accepted. **Hours:** 11 am-11 pm, Fri & Sat-1 am, Sun 10 am-11 pm; Sunday brunch. Closed major holidays. **Address:** 7600 MacLeod Tr SE T2H 0L9 **Location:** Just s of jct Glenmore Trail. **Parking:** on-site. **Cards:** AX, MC, VI.

THE CHEESECAKE CAFE

Canadian
$10-$26

Phone: 403/280-7798 ⑯

As might be expected, cheesecake is the cafe's signature item, and lip-smacking varieties are made on the premises. A huge dessert display case greets guests upon arrival. Offerings on the extensive lunch and dinner menu range from sandwiches and entree salads to pasta, pizza and seafood selections. It takes a while to get through the menu. Casual dress. **Bar:** Full bar. **Reservations:** not accepted. **Hours:** 11 am-11 pm, Fri & Sat-1 am, Sun 10 am-11 pm; Sunday brunch. Closed: 12/24, 12/25. **Address:** 2121 36th St NE T1Y 5S3 **Location:** Just n of jct 16th Ave; adjacent to Sunridge Shopping Centre. **Parking:** on-site. **Cards:** AX, MC, VI.

CLAY OVEN

East Indian
$10-$20

Phone: 403/250-2161 ⑨

Casual dress. **Bar:** Full bar. **Reservations:** suggested. **Hours:** 11:30 am-2 & 5-9 pm, Sat-10 pm. Closed major holidays; also Sun. **Address:** 3132 26 St NE, #349 T1Y 6Z1 **Location:** Just n of 32 Ave; in small strip plaza. **Parking:** on-site. **Cards:** AX, MC, VI.

(See map and index starting on p. 388)

CRETE SOUVLAKI
Greek
$5-$10

Phone: 403/246-4777   ③⓪

Fast, fresh and cheap are all words to describe the distinctive eatery. Heaping portions of Greek food are dished at the quick-serve eatery, which is attached to the OK gas station on 17th Avenue. Most people get their food to go, but there are a few tables available. Casual dress. **Hours:** 9 am-10 pm, Sat & Sun 11:30 am-9:30 pm. Closed: 12/25. **Address:** 2623 17th Ave SW T3E 0A5 **Location:** Jct 26th St SW. **Parking:** on-site. **Cards:** AX, MC, VI.

DINER DELUXE
Canadian
$4-$15

Phone: 403/276-5499   ②③

Everything old is new again, and such is the case at this funky retro diner, where you can find all day breakfasts made with gourmet and specialty ingredients. If you're looking for a nostalgic atmosphere, this is the place. You can enjoy a taste of the fifties, including formica countertops, boldly coloured vinyl chairs, tall milkshakes and hearty burgers. Friendly servers are quick and knowledgeable, and can offer great detail about the various dishes. Casual dress. **Bar:** Full bar. **Hours:** 7:30 am-9 pm, Sat 8 am-3 & 5-9 pm, Sun 8 am-3 pm. Closed: 12/25. **Address:** 804 Edmonton Tr NE T2E 3J6 **Location:** Corner of Edmonton Trail NE and 7th Ave NE. **Parking:** street. **Cards:** AX, MC, VI.

EARL'S 16TH AVE
Canadian
$8-$25

Phone: 403/289-2566

Offering an experience that falls between fast food and fine dining, the fun, relaxed restaurant prepares great food at a great price. Choices range from juicy burgers, hearty sandwiches, fresh salads, wings and pizza to full entrees of steak, chops and seafood. Made-from-scratch soups and assorted breads, as well as a nice choice of wines and beers, round out the offerings. This is a fitting spot for impromptu get-togethers and festive occasions. Casual dress. **Bar:** Full bar. **Hours:** 11 am-midnight, Fri & Sat-1 am. Closed major holidays. **Address:** 1110 16th Ave T2M 0K8 **Location:** Jct 11th St NW. **Parking:** on-site. **Cards:** AX, DC, MC, VI.

EARL'S BARLOW TRAIL
Canadian
$8-$25

Phone: 403/291-6700   ①⓪

Offering an experience that falls between fast food and fine dining, the fun, relaxed restaurant prepares great food at a great price. Choices range from juicy burgers, hearty sandwiches, fresh salads, wings and pizza to full entrees of steak, chops and seafood. Made-from-scratch soups and assorted breads, as well as a nice choice of wines and beers, round out the offerings. This is a fitting spot for impromptu get-togethers and festive occasions. Casual dress. **Bar:** Full bar. **Hours:** 11 am-midnight, Fri & Sat-1 am. Closed major holidays. **Address:** 3030 23rd St NE T2E 8R7 **Location:** Jct 32nd Ave NE and Barlow Tr NE. **Parking:** on-site. **Cards:** AX, DC, MC, VI.

EMPEROR BUFFET & RESTAURANT
Chinese
$8-$14

Phone: 403/252-8250   ④⑤

Overlooking the parking lot of a strip mall, this second-floor restaurant isn't known for its views. However, the owners of this attractive buffet restaurant have garnered extensive experience in various restaurants in Calgary's Chinatown and bring their touches to this place's extensive spread of Chinese and Western dishes. Casual dress. **Bar:** Full bar. **Hours:** 11 am-2 & 5-9 pm. Closed: 12/25. **Address:** 9737 MacLeod Trail SW, #100 T2J 0P6 **Location:** Jct Southland Dr at Southland Crossing. **Parking:** on-site. **Cards:** MC, VI.

CALL 🚻♿M

FORBIDDEN CITY SEAFOOD & DIM SUM RESTAURANT
Chinese
$4-$15

Phone: 403/250-1848   ②⓪

In the Northeast, the large, contemporary restaurant serves wonton soup, ginger beef, Peking-style sesame prawns and the specialty, dim sum. Best enjoyed with a group of people, dim sum items include steamed shrimp dumplings and onion cakes. Service is quick and efficient, and the atmosphere is bustling. Casual dress. **Bar:** Full bar. **Hours:** 10 am-10 pm, Fri & Sat-11 pm. **Address:** 220 Pacific Pl, 999 36th St NE T2A 7X6 **Location:** 16th Ave NE (Trans-Canada Hwy 1), exit 36th St S; in Pacific Place Shopping Plaza. **Parking:** on-site. **Cards:** AX, MC, VI.

GUS'S CAFE & PIZZERIA
Pizza
$5-$15

Phone: 403/282-4005   ①⑧

Ideally located just off Trans-Canada Highway 1 and near the hospital, this family-run restaurant serves simply good food. Though they specialize in pizza, you'll also find a variety of other items on the menu including soups, salads and sandwiches. Service is quick and prompt, and if you become a regular, don't be surprised to see the owner sit and chat with you! Casual dress. **Bar:** Full bar. **Hours:** 9 am-10 pm, Thurs & Fri-11 pm, Sat 4 pm-10 pm. Closed major holidays; also Sun. **Address:** 1620 29th St NW, #180 T2W 4L7 **Location:** 16th Ave (Trans-Canada Hwy 1), just s at 29th St NW. **Parking:** on-site. **Cards:** MC, VI.

HEARTLAND CAFE
Deli/Subs
Sandwiches
$5-$10

Phone: 403/270-4541   ②④

Casual dress. **Reservations:** not accepted. **Hours:** 7 am-11 pm. Closed major holidays. **Address:** 940 2nd Ave NW T2M 0E7 **Location:** Just n of Memorial Dr NW; in Kensington. **Parking:** street. **Cards:** AX, MC, VI.

JAMESONS IRISH PUB
Irish
$8-$15

Phone: 403/285-1608   ①⑤

Just across from Sunridge Mall, the Irish pub welcomes travelers from around the globe. The restaurant offers a lively atmosphere, friendly service and live entertainment, as well as an extensive menu of both pub and Irish favorites. The selection of on-tap Irish beers is excellent. Casual dress. **Bar:** Full bar. **Hours:** 11 am-midnight. Closed major holidays. **Address:** 3575 20th Ave NE T1Y 6R3 **Location:** Jct 36th St NE; across from Sunridge Mall. **Parking:** on-site. **Cards:** AX, MC, VI.

CALL 🚻♿M

JANINE'S BISTRO
Polish
$5-$14

Phone: 403/233-0995   ③④

Eastern European is the way Janine describes her fare, and her menu boasts such specialties as pierogies, pork schnitzel, cabbage rolls and, on Fridays, borscht for those who arrive early enough. Burgers are another good choice. Only 12 tables are available at the cozy, family-run restaurant, which serves huge portions of tasty food. In a small plaza, this little place is easy to miss, but it's well worth the drive. Casual dress. **Bar:** Full bar. **Hours:** 8 am-8 pm, Thurs-Sat to 9 pm. Closed major holidays; also Sun & holiday weekends. **Address:** #6, 3919 Richmond Rd SW T3E 4P2 **Location:** From Sarcee Trail, just e at Richmond Rd; in Glamorgan Shopping Centre. **Parking:** on-site. **Cards:** VI.

CALL 🚻♿M

(See map and index starting on p. 388)

JOEY TOMATO'S

Mediterranean
$10-$29

Phone: 403/692-6626

The cuisine blends Mediterranean and Asian cooking styles and emphasizes finger foods for sharing. Those who aren't big fans of tapas can consider full meal offerings centered on steaks and chops. Casual dress. **Bar:** Full bar. **Hours:** 11:30 am-1 am, Sun-midnight. Closed: 12/25. **Address:** 6455 MacLeod Trail SW, 100A T2H 0K8 **Location:** At Chinook Centre Mall. **Parking:** on-site. **Cards:** AX, MC, VI.

JOEY TOMATO'S

Mediterranean
$10-$29

Phone: 403/547-5639

The cuisine blends Mediterranean and Asian cooking styles and emphasizes finger foods for sharing. Those who aren't big fans of tapas can consider full meal offerings centered on steaks and chops. Casual dress. **Bar:** Full bar. **Hours:** 11:30 am-1 am, Sun-midnight. Closed: 12/25. **Address:** 50 Crowfoot Way T3G 4C8 **Location:** Just nw of Nose Hill Dr NW and Ranchlands Blvd NW. **Parking:** on-site. **Cards:** AX, MC, VI.

JOEY TOMATO'S

Mediterranean
$10-$29

Phone: 403/219-8465

The cuisine blends Mediterranean and Asian cooking styles and emphasizes finger foods for sharing. Those who aren't big fans of tapas can consider full meal offerings centered on steaks and chops. Casual dress. **Bar:** Full bar. **Hours:** 11:30 am-1 am, Sun-midnight. Closed: 12/25. **Address:** 3026 23rd St NE T2E 8R7 **Location:** At Barlow Tr, just w of 26th St NE. **Parking:** on-site. **Cards:** AX, MC, VI.

KANE'S HARLEY DINER

Canadian
$4-$10

Phone: 403/269-7311   27

Orange and brown retro decor sets the scene at the popular diner in the town's heart. Guests seat themselves in booths and admire Harley motorcycles as they peruse the menu, which is laden with comfort foods. Among choices are grilled cheese and ham sandwiches, poutine, hearty hamburgers and even liver and onions. Breakfast is served all day, and service always comes with a smile. Casual dress. **Bar:** Full bar. **Reservations:** not accepted. **Hours:** 7 am-10 pm. Closed: 12/25. **Address:** 1209 9th Ave SE T2G 3E8 **Location:** 9th Ave SE at 12th St; in Inglewood. **Parking:** street. **Cards:** MC, VI.

LINA'S ITALIAN MARKET

Deli/Subs
Sandwiches
$5-$10

Phone: 403/277-9166   14

The family-owned, coffee-bar-style restaurant has eight tables and over-the-counter ordering. Big food comes at small prices. On the menu are homemade pizzas, pasta dishes, soups, salads and Italian pastries. Check out the family-size tiramisu in the cooler. Service is casual and friendly. Casual dress. **Bar:** Full bar. **Reservations:** not accepted. **Hours:** 9 am-7 pm, Sat & Sun-5 pm. Closed major holidays. **Address:** 2202 Centre St NE T2E 2T4 **Location:** 0.5 km n of jct 16th Ave (Trans-Canada Hwy 1). **Parking:** on-site. **Cards:** MC, VI.

MADISONS CAFE & BAR

West Canadian
$8-$25

Phone: 403/220-9888   4

The restaurant's atmosphere is cheerful, upbeat and funky, providing something for everyone. West Coast and Asian influences are reflected in imaginative versions of popular dishes, including brie and mango quesadillas, vermicelli salad rolls and traditional crust pizza. **Bar:** Full bar. **Reservations:** suggested. **Hours:** 10 am-11 pm, Fri & Sat-midnight, Sun-10 pm. Closed: 1/1, 12/25. **Address:** 17-3802 Brentwood Rd NW T2L 1K8 **Location:** Just nw of Crowchild Trail and 32nd Ave NW; in Brentwood Village Mall. **Parking:** on-site. **Cards:** AX, MC, VI.

MISAI JAPANESE RESTAURANT

Japanese
$9-$15

Phone: 403/250-1688   7

Traditional decor awaits at the Northeast establishment, which is near many hotels and not far from the airport. The restaurant offers shuttle service to and from local hotels. Japanese art decorates individual booths, as well as rooms, in the dark-wood interior. The selection of sushi, sashimi, tempura and stir-fries offers good value for the dollar. Casual dress. **Bar:** Full bar. **Reservations:** suggested. **Hours:** 11 am-10 pm, Fri & Sat-11 pm. Closed: for dinner on holidays. **Address:** #7 1915-32 Ave NE T2E 7C8 **Location:** From Barlow Trail, 0.6 mi (1 km) w at 32nd Ave. **Parking:** on-site. **Cards:** AX, DC, MC, VI.

CALL

MOXIE'S CLASSIC GRILL

Canadian
$10-$30

Phone: 403/291-4636

This sleek, funky and popular restaurant presents an extensive menu of creatively prepared dishes, including pizza, pasta, rice, noodles, signature salads and burgers. Other menus include one for children and one for Sunday brunch. Lending to the upbeat, stylish decor are dark wood appointments and river rock fireplaces. Casual dress. **Bar:** Full bar. **Reservations:** accepted. **Hours:** 6 am-midnight. Closed: 12/24, 12/25. **Address:** 29 Hopewell Way NE T3J 4V7 **Location:** Just n of jct Barlow Trail and McKnight Blvd; adjacent to Sandman Hotel Suites & Spa Calgary Airport. **Parking:** on-site. **Cards:** AX, MC, VI.

CALL

NELLIE'S IN THE LOOP

Canadian
$5-$9

Phone: 403/802-2174   33

Particularly popular on weekends, this Marda Loop outpost of the Nellie's chain is particularly popular on weekends. Not surprisingly, the bustling, cozy diner is a favorite for its fabulous home-cooked breakfasts, which are available all day. In addition to omelets, French toast and pancakes, the menu also lists some lunch options. The moist and tasty homemade banana bread is well worth the indulgence. Friendly, chatty servers keep things moving swiftly. Casual dress. **Hours:** 7:30 am-4 pm, Sat & Sun from 8:30 am. Closed: 12/25. **Address:** 2015 33rd Ave SW T2T 1Z5 **Location:** 0.6 mi (1 km) e of jct Crowchild Trail SW; in Marda Loop. **Parking:** street. **Cards:** AX, MC, VI.

NEWPORT GRILL ON LAKE BONAVISTA

Continental
$14-$39

Phone: 403/271-6711   47

Lovely views of Lake Bonavista can be had from almost every table at the upscale restaurant. Among interesting and eclectic entrees are preparations of salmon, linguine and buffalo. Formerly called the Inn on Lake Bonavista, the restaurant has undergone a complete renovation and now boasts good food in fine surroundings. Casual dress. **Bar:** Full bar. **Reservations:** suggested. **Hours:** 11:30 am-close, Sat from 5 pm, Sun from 11 am. Closed: 5/19, 9/1. **Address:** 205-747 Lake Bonavista Dr SE T2J 0N2 **Location:** 6.7 mi (11.2 km) se via MacLeod Trail, 0.5 mi (0.8 km) e on Anderson Rd to Bonaventure Dr, just s to Lake Bonavista Dr, then 0.7 mi (1.2 km) e to Lake Bonavista Shopping Centre. **Parking:** on-site. **Cards:** AX, MC, VI.

(See map and index starting on p. 388)

NICK'S STEAKHOUSE & PIZZA
Phone: 403/282-9278 ⑤

Steak House
$8-$30

A favorite with families, the restaurant has been a local fixture for more than 20 years. Steaks are grilled to perfection, and pizza is prepared with a variety of unusual toppings. The cozy decor and simple menu suit the tastes of all kinds of patrons. Casual dress. **Bar:** Full bar. **Hours:** 11 am-midnight. Closed: 12/24, 12/25. **Address:** 2430 Crowchild Tr NW T2M 4N5 **Location:** Just nw of Motel Village. **Parking:** on-site. **Cards:** AX, MC, VI.

OPEN RANGE
Phone: 403/277-3408 ㉑

Canadian
$21-$30

Boasting a menu of nouveau Greek cuisine, the sophisticated restaurant features fine service and upscale, modern decor. Casual dress. **Bar:** Full bar. **Reservations:** suggested. **Hours:** 5 pm-10 pm. Closed major holidays. **Address:** 1114 Edmonton Trail NE T2E 3K4 **Location:** Just s of Jct 16 Ave (Trans-Canada Hwy 1). **Parking:** on-site. **Cards:** AX, MC, VI.

OPEN SESAME
Phone: 403/259-0123 ㊶

Asian
$7-$28

Guests must descend the stairs to discover the restaurant's treasures. The Pan Asian noodle house features a do-it-yourself stir-fry station, as well as a full menu. Made-to-order dishes include sumptuous pot sticker appetizers and varied stir-fried noodle preparations. The rich decor of mahogany woods and dark, intimate corners sets the stage for a memorable meal. Casual dress. **Bar:** Full bar. **Reservations:** suggested. **Hours:** 11:30 am-10 pm, Fri & Sat-11 pm, Sun 4:30 pm-10 pm. Closed major holidays. **Address:** 6920 MacLeod Tr S T2H 0L3 **Location:** Just s of Hwy 8 (Glenmore Trail). **Parking:** on-site. **Cards:** AX, CB, DC, DS, MC, VI.

ORIENTAL PHOENIX
Phone: 403/253-8383 ㊴

Vietnamese
$6-$15

Traditional Vietnamese food is served simply, but the service and decor is anything but. Upscale and sleek, the modern dining room is a busy place at lunch and around the dinner hour. Guests can sample tasty food in fine surroundings characterized by bold, contemporary colors and art. Among the varied choices are salad rolls, rice vermicelli dishes and noodle soups. Semi-formal attire. **Bar:** Full bar. **Hours:** 11 am-8:30 pm, Fri-9:30 pm, Sat noon-9:30 pm. Closed major holidays; also Sun & 10 days during Christmas. **Address:** 104 58th Ave SW, #80 T2H 0N7 **Location:** Jct MacLeod Trail SW, 0.2 mi (0.4 km) e. **Parking:** on-site. **Cards:** AX, DC, MC, VI.

CALL 🆑M

ORIENTAL PHOENIX
Phone: 403/250-8813 ⑬

Vietnamese
$6-$15

Traditional Vietnamese food is served simply, but the service and decor is anything but. Upscale and sleek, the modern dining room is a busy place at lunch and around the dinner hour. Guests can sample tasty food in fine surroundings characterized by bold, contemporary colors and art. Among the varied choices are salad rolls, rice vermicelli dishes and noodle soups. Casual dress. **Bar:** Full bar. **Reservations:** accepted. **Hours:** 11 am-8:30 pm, Fri-9:30 pm, Sat 5 pm-9:30 pm. Closed major holidays; also Sun; 10 days during Christmas. **Address:** 2493 27th Ave NE T2E 8M1 **Location:** Corner of 27th Ave NE and Barlow Tr. **Parking:** on-site. **Cards:** AX, DC, MC, VI.

CALL 🆑M

PFANNTASTIC PANNENKOEK HAUS   *Menu on AAA.com*
Phone: 403/243-7757 ㊳

Dutch
$7-$13

The restaurant prepares 75 varieties of meal-size Dutch crepes served with various toppings. A savory selection for dinner and a sweet choice for dessert make for a tasty meal. Diners should come with an appetite since servings are huge. Soups and salads are also offered. Casual dress. **Bar:** Full bar. **Reservations:** accepted, except Sun. **Hours:** 10 am-8 pm, Sat from 8 am, Sun 8 am-3 pm. Closed: Mon & Tues. **Address:** 2439 54th Ave SW T3E 1M4 **Location:** Just ne of jct Hwy 8 (Glenmore Tr) and Crowchild Tr; in small strip mall. **Parking:** on-site. **Cards:** AX, MC, VI.

RAJDOOT RESTAURANT
Phone: 403/245-0181 ㉛

Indian
$9-$17

The casual Indian restaurant lures locals and celebrities alike for its fantastic all-you-can-eat lunch buffet. Casual dress. **Bar:** Full bar. **Reservations:** suggested. **Hours:** 11:30 am-2 & 5-10 pm, Fri-11 pm, Sat 5 pm-11 pm. Closed: 12/25. **Address:** 2424 4th St SW T2S 2T4 **Location:** 4th St at 24th Ave SW. **Parking:** on-site and street. **Cards:** AX, DC, MC, VI.

THE RANCHE RESTAURANT
Phone: 403/225-3939

Regional
Canadian
$12-$40

Originally built more than 100 years ago as a wealthy gent's mansion that lapsed into disuse, the house has been restored to its former grandeur. Creative, well-executed preparations draw on a variety of prairie ingredients and flavours. In a park in the southern part of Calgary, the restaurant offers a superb setting and experience. Casual dress. **Bar:** Full bar. **Reservations:** required. **Hours:** 11:30 am-3 & 5-9 pm, Fri & Sat-10 pm, Sun 10:30 am-2:30 & 5-9 pm. Closed major holidays. **Address:** 9005 15979 Bow Bottom Trail SE T2P 0Y8 **Location:** Off Bow Bottom Trail; in Fish Creek Provincial Park. **Parking:** on-site. **Cards:** AX, DC, MC, VI. **Historic**

RICKY'S ALL DAY GRILL
Phone: 403/571-3220

Continental
$8-$15

The comfortable eatery, which employs friendly servers, presents a varied menu that includes pasta dishes, wraps, omelets, stir-fry preparations and burgers. Portions are generous. Children's and senior selections are offered. Guests can request seating in a booth or at a table. Casual dress. **Bar:** Full bar. **Hours:** 7 am-9 pm, Fri & Sat-10 pm. Closed: 1/1, 12/25. **Address:** 3321 20th Ave NE T1Y 7A8 **Location:** Just w of 36th St NE; across from Sunridge Mall. **Parking:** on-site. **Cards:** AX, MC, VI.

CALL 🆑M

ROCKY'S BURGER BUS
Phone: 403/243-0405 ㉟

Canadian
$3-$6

Inside an old transit bus in an industrial section of the city are some of the best hamburgers in the province. Hand-made beef burgers, hand-cut fries and creamy milkshakes make this spot popular and distinctive. Plus, the food is cheap. Casual dress. **Hours:** 9 am-4 pm, Sat from 10 am; hours may vary. Closed major holidays; also Sun. **Address:** 4645 12th St SE T3E 4R7 **Location:** From MacLeod Trail, 1.2 mi (2 km) e at 46th Ave to 12th St. **Parking:** on-site.

(See map and index starting on p. 388)

ROUGE

French
$16-$44

Phone: 403/531-2767 ㉕

In a residential area near the zoo, the historic house has been converted into a quaint restaurant featuring contemporary French cuisine. Seasonally inspired dishes range from ricotta ravioli to salmon and specialty soups. Each dish is a work of art, and servers are highly attentive. The home maintains its historic roots with Victorian decor in each of its small dining rooms. Casual dress. **Bar:** Full bar. **Reservations:** suggested. **Hours:** 11:30 am-2 & 5:30-10 pm, Sat from 5:30 pm. Closed major holidays; also Sun. **Address:** 1240 8th Ave SE T2G 0M7 **Location:** Corner of 12th St and 8th Ave SE. **Parking:** on-site. **Cards:** AX, DC, MC, VI. **Historic**

SAMOSA GRILL
East Indian
$8-$24

Phone: 403/250-2515 ⑪

Located across the street from the Peter Lougheed Hospital, this second floor walk-up restaurant offers a unique mix of East Indian and East African cuisine. Surrounded by lots of greenery and African tribal masks, diners will enjoy tasty and exotic dishes such as the house specialties of crispy samosas and tandoori chicken. Casual dress. **Bar:** Full bar. **Hours:** 11:30 am-2:30 & 5-9 pm, Fri & Sat-10 pm. Closed major holidays. **Address:** 210-3393 26th Ave NE T1Y 6L4 **Location:** Jct 36th St NE; across from Peter Longhead Hospital. **Parking:** on-site. **Cards:** AX, MC, VI.

SANTORINI GREEK TAVERNA
Greek
$10-$30

Phone: 403/276-8363 ⑲

Hearty Greek food, friendly service and a bustling, festive atmosphere define the cozy taverna, which makes guests feel as though they've stepped into small town Greece. The menu features traditional dishes, including mouthwatering moussaka, sumptuous souvlaki and spanakopita. Save some room for bougasta, a distinctive custard dessert. Casual dress. **Bar:** Full bar. **Reservations:** suggested, weekends. **Hours:** 11 am-11 pm, Fri-midnight, Sat 1 pm-midnight, Sun 4 pm-10 pm. Closed: major holidays, 12/26; also Mon. **Address:** 1502 Centre St N T2E 2R9 **Location:** Just s of 16th Ave and Centre St N. **Parking:** on-site. **Cards:** AX, DC, MC, VI.

SMUGGLER'S INN
Steak House
$9-$30

Phone: 403/253-5355 ㊷

One of the city's oldest steak and prime rib houses, this place lets guests sample the all-you-can-eat soup and salad bar with any entree. The menu centers on steak, prime rib and chicken. The dark, cozy interior is a favorite with the business-lunch crowd. Casual dress. **Bar:** Full bar. **Reservations:** suggested. **Hours:** 11 am-10 pm, Fri & Sat-11 pm, Sun 9:30 am-2 & 4:30-10 pm. Closed: 12/25. **Address:** 6920 MacLeod Tr T2H 0L3 **Location:** Just s of Glenmore Trail; attached to Open Sesame. **Parking:** on-site. **Cards:** AX, DC, DS, MC, VI.

SPOLUMBO'S DELI

Deli/Subs
Sandwiches
$6-$10

Phone: 403/264-6452 ㉘

Owned by a group of former Canadian Football League Stampeders players, the bustling, energetic deli serves varied meats, including outstanding, high-quality sausage. This is a popular place at lunch, when patrons order at the counter and have their basket of food delivered to them. Casual dress. **Bar:** Beer & wine. **Reservations:** not accepted. **Hours:** 8 am-5:30 pm. Closed major holidays; also Sun. **Address:** 1308 9th Ave SE T2G 0T3 **Location:** Corner of 9th Ave SE and 13th St SE; in Inglewood. **Parking:** on-site. **Cards:** AX, MC, VI.

SUGO CAFFE ITALIA

Italian
$15-$40

Phone: 403/263-1115 ㉖

In the funky Inglewood area, the upscale Italian eatery has a cozy decor to complement its innovative menu. Although the ingredients are not classically Italian, guests still can find daily selections of pasta and traditionally prepared food. The service is fine, and the atmosphere is casually elegant. Casual dress. **Bar:** Full bar. **Reservations:** suggested. **Hours:** 5 pm-11 pm. Closed: 12/25, 12/26; also Sun. **Address:** 1214 9th Ave SE T2G 0S9 **Location:** Corner of 9th Ave SE and 12th St; in Inglewood. **Parking:** street. **Cards:** AX, DC, MC, VI.

THAI BOAT
Thai
$4-$13

Phone: 403/291-9887 ⑧

The restaurant is a must-stop for folks staying out by the airport. A sister property to Thai SaOn downtown, this place displays casual Thai decor inside, but the food—an array of traditional items—is anything but casual. Thai salad rolls wow the taste buds. This place is affordable and enjoyable at lunch, and the service is friendly and efficient. Casual dress. **Bar:** Full bar. **Reservations:** suggested. **Hours:** 11 am-2 & 5-9:30 pm, Fri-10:30 pm, Sat 5 pm-10:30 pm, Sun 5 pm-9 pm. Closed major holidays. **Address:** 2323 32 Ave NE, #108 T2E 6Z3 **Location:** Just w of Barlow Tr at 32nd Ave. **Parking:** on-site. **Cards:** MC, VI.

THAI PLACE RESTAURANT
Thai
$9-$20

Phone: 403/291-4148 ⑰

The restaurant employs a Thai chef who creates a variety of hearty and delicious dishes. Locals and visitors alike fill the small restaurant each night. Casual dress. **Bar:** Full bar. **Reservations:** suggested. **Hours:** 5 pm-10 pm. Closed major holidays. **Address:** 1947 18th Ave NE T2E 2T8 **Location:** 0.6 mi (1 km) e of jct Hwy 2 (Deerfoot Trail) and 16th Ave NE (Trans-Canada Hwy 1); in Best Western Airport Inn. **Parking:** on-site. **Cards:** MC, VI.

WHITE SPOT CENTURY PLAZA
Canadian
$8-$15

Phone: 403/278-8212

Open for three meals a day, the popular casual restaurant prepares offerings such as sandwiches and burgers, fresh salads, pastas and stir-fries, fish and chips, chargrilled sirloin steaks and chicken, in addition to a selection of yummy desserts. Casual dress. **Bar:** Full bar. **Hours:** 7:30 am-10 pm, Fri-11 pm. Closed major holidays. **Address:** 10440 MacLeod Tr SE T2J 0P8 **Location:** 0.3 mi (0.5 km) s of jct Southland Dr SE. **Parking:** on-site. **Cards:** AX, DS, MC, VI.

The Calgary Vicinity

AIRDRIE pop. 28,927

——— WHERE TO STAY ———

HOLIDAY INN EXPRESS HOTEL & SUITES
AIRDRIE-CALGARY NORTH *Book great rates at AAA.com*

Phone: (403)912-1952

Small-scale Hotel
$160-$220 6/1-2/28
$150-$210 3/1-5/31

Address: 64 E Lake Ave NE T4A 2G8 **Location:** Hwy 2, exit E Lake Crescent, 0.6 mi (1 km) n. **Facility:** Smoke free premises. 79 one-bedroom standard units, some with whirlpools. 4 stories, interior corridors. *Bath:* combo or shower only. **Parking:** on-site. **Terms:** cancellation fee imposed. **Amenities:** high-speed Internet, voice mail, irons, hair dryers. **Pool(s):** heated indoor. **Leisure Activities:** whirlpool, waterslide, exercise room. **Guest Services:** valet and coin laundry. **Business Services:** meeting rooms. **Cards:** AX, DC, DS, JC, MC, VI. *(See color ad on insert)*

RAMADA INN & SUITES *Book great rates at AAA.com*

Phone: (403)945-1288

Small-scale Hotel
$149-$289 All Year

Address: 191 E Lake Crescent T4B 2B8 **Location:** Hwy 2, exit E Airdrie. **Facility:** 59 units. 37 one-bedroom standard units, some with kitchens. 20 one- and 2 two-bedroom suites, some with kitchens and/or whirlpools. 4 stories, interior corridors. *Bath:* combo or shower only. **Parking:** on-site, winter plug-ins. **Terms:** cancellation fee imposed. **Amenities:** high-speed Internet, voice mail, irons, hair dryers. **Pool(s):** heated indoor. **Leisure Activities:** waterslide, exercise room. **Guest Services:** valet and coin laundry. **Business Services:** meeting rooms, business center. **Cards:** AX, MC, VI. **Free Special Amenities: local telephone calls and high-speed Internet.**

SUPER 8 MOTEL-AIRDRIE *Book at AAA.com*

Phone: 403/948-4188

Small-scale Hotel
Rates not provided

Address: 815 E Lake Blvd T4A 2G4 **Location:** Hwy 2, exit E Airdrie, 0.5 mi (0.8 km) e on Hwy 587 E. **Facility:** 49 units. 47 one- and 2 two-bedroom standard units. 3 stories, interior corridors. **Parking:** on-site, winter plug-ins. **Amenities:** hair dryers. **Guest Services:** coin laundry, wireless Internet.

——— WHERE TO DINE ———

SMITTY'S

Phone: 403/945-1225

International
$6-$15

The family-oriented restaurant satisfies patrons with its ever-popular all-day breakfast items, as well as tasty and wholesome soups and salads at lunchtime. A relaxed mood characterizes the dining space. Casual dress. **Reservations:** not accepted. **Hours:** 6 am-9 pm, Fri-10 pm, Sat 7 am-10 pm, Sun 7 am-9 pm. Closed major holidays. **Address:** 191 E Lake Crescent T4A 1H3 **Location:** Hwy 2, exit E Lake Cresent; beside Ramada Inn & Suites. **Parking:** on-site. **Cards:** AX, MC, VI.

COCHRANE pop. 13,760

——— WHERE TO STAY ———

BEST WESTERN HARVEST COUNTRY INN *Book great rates at AAA.com*

Phone: (403)932-1410

Small-scale Hotel
$139-$149 3/1-10/31
$129-$139 11/1-2/28

Address: 11 West Side Dr T4C 1M1 **Location:** Hwy 1A, 0.6 mi (1 km) sw on Hwy 22. **Facility:** 49 one-bedroom standard units, some with whirlpools. 3 stories (no elevator), interior/exterior corridors. **Parking:** on-site, winter plug-ins. **Amenities:** voice mail, irons, hair dryers. *Some:* high-speed Internet. **Leisure Activities:** sauna, exercise room. **Guest Services:** valet and coin laundry, wireless Internet. **Business Services:** PC (fee). **Cards:** AX, MC, VI. **Free Special Amenities: continental breakfast and high-speed Internet.**

AAA Benefit:
Members save 10% everyday, plus an exclusive frequent stay program.

SUPER 8 MOTEL-COCHRANE *Book at AAA.com*

Phone: (403)932-6355

Small-scale Hotel
$165-$175 3/1-9/30
$155-$165 10/1-2/28

Address: 10 Westside Dr T4C 1M1 **Location:** Hwy 1A, 0.6 mi (1 km) sw on Hwy 22. **Facility:** 72 units. 71 one- and 1 two-bedroom standard units, some with efficiencies and/or whirlpools. 4 stories, interior corridors. *Bath:* combo or shower only. **Parking:** on-site, winter plug-ins. **Amenities:** high-speed Internet, voice mail, irons, hair dryers. *Some:* video games (fee). **Pool(s):** heated indoor. **Leisure Activities:** whirlpool, waterslide, exercise room. **Guest Services:** valet and coin laundry. **Business Services:** meeting rooms, PC (fee). **Cards:** AX, DC, DS, MC, VI.

TRAVELODGE COCHRANE *Book at AAA.com*

Phone: (403)932-5588

Small-scale Hotel
$117-$129 3/1-9/15
$99-$109 9/16-2/28

Address: 5 West Side Dr T4C 1M1 **Location:** Hwy 1A, 0.6 mi (1 km) sw on Hwy 22. **Facility:** 61 units. 55 one-bedroom standard units, some with efficiencies, kitchens and/or whirlpools. 6 one-bedroom suites. 4 stories, interior corridors. *Bath:* combo or shower only. **Parking:** on-site, winter plug-ins. **Amenities:** high-speed Internet, voice mail, irons, hair dryers. **Pool(s):** heated indoor. **Leisure Activities:** whirlpool, limited exercise equipment. **Guest Services:** valet and coin laundry. **Business Services:** PC. **Cards:** AX, DC, DS, MC, VI.

——— WHERE TO DINE ———

BLUE DOG CAFE

Cajun
$6-$18

Phone: 403/932-4282

With a touch of jazz and a taste of funk, the eclectic cafe offers an intimate, memorable dining experience in this small town. The dining room has a mere 15 tables. On the menu are Cajun specialty dishes, including jambalaya and catfish. Casual dress. **Bar:** Full bar. **Reservations:** suggested. **Hours:** 11 am-10 pm, Fri & Sat-midnight. **Closed:** 12/25, 12/26. **Address:** 110 Third Ave W T0L 0W0 **Location:** Hwy 1A, 2 blks w. **Parking:** on-site. **Cards:** AX, MC, VI.

HOME QUARTER RESTAURANT & PIE SHOPPE
Continental
$6-$17

Phone: 403/932-2111

A cozy, country atmosphere awaits at the restaurant, known throughout the province for its "splurgeworthy" homemade pies, of which there are usually more than 45 varieties. Homemade comfort foods range from quiches to soups to sandwiches. Also available are afternoon tea and an extensive breakfast menu. Casual dress. **Bar:** Full bar. **Reservations:** suggested. **Hours:** 10 am-9 pm, Sat & Sun from 9 am. **Closed:** 12/25. **Address:** 216 1st St W T4C 1B3 **Location:** Downtown. **Parking:** on-site. **Cards:** DC, MC, VI.

PRAIRIE SMOKE RESTAURANT
Canadian
$7-$24

Phone: 403/932-9001

Located a few steps away from the hotels, this stylish restaurant offers diners a comfortable setting to enjoy its extensive menu. Featuring Alberta beef, many items ranging from steaks, shish kebabs, shrimps and chicken are charbroiled to order. The restaurant also offers a full range of hamburgers and chicken dishes. Casual dress. **Bar:** Full bar. **Hours:** 11 am-10 pm. **Address:** 19 Westside Dr T4C 1M1 **Location:** Hwy 1A, 0.6 mi (1 km) sw on Hwy 22. **Parking:** on-site. **Cards:** AX, MC, VI.

OKOTOKS pop. 17,145

——— WHERE TO STAY ———

LAKEVIEW INNS & SUITES   *Book great rates at AAA.com*

Phone: (403)938-7400

Small-scale Hotel
$129-$149 All Year

Address: 22 Southridge Dr T1S 1N1 **Location:** Hwy 2, exit 2A, 2.5 mi (4 km) s to Southridge Dr. **Facility:** 64 units. 41 one-bedroom standard units. 23 one-bedroom suites, some with whirlpools. 2 stories, interior corridors. **Parking:** on-site. **Terms:** check-in 4 pm. **Amenities:** DVD players, dual phone lines, irons, hair dryers. *Some:* high-speed Internet. **Leisure Activities:** whirlpool, limited exercise equipment. **Guest Services:** complimentary laundry. **Business Services:** meeting rooms, PC (fee). **Cards:** AX, MC, VI. *(See color ad p 362)*

STRATHMORE pop. 10,225

—— **WHERE TO STAY** ——

BEST WESTERN STRATHMORE INN   *Book great rates at AAA.com*   Phone: 403/934-5777

Small-scale Hotel
Rates not provided

Address: 550 Hwy 1 T1P 1M6 **Location:** Trans-Canada Hwy 1, jct SR 817; centre. **Facility:** 81 units. 54 one- and 14 two-bedroom standard units. 11 one- and 2 two-bedroom suites, some with whirlpools. 3 stories (no elevator), interior corridors. **Parking:** on-site, winter plug-ins. **Terms:** check-in 4 pm. **Amenities:** high-speed Internet (fee), voice mail, irons, hair dryers. **Pool(s):** heated indoor. **Leisure Activities:** whirlpool, barbecue area, exercise room. **Guest Services:** valet and coin laundry. **Business Services:** meeting rooms, PC. **Free Special Amenities: continental breakfast and high-speed Internet.**

AAA Benefit:
Members save 10% everyday, plus an exclusive frequent stay program.

TRAVELODGE STRATHMORE   *Book at AAA.com*   Phone: (403)901-0000

Small-scale Hotel
$144-$154 6/1-2/28
$134-$144 3/1-5/31

Address: 350 Ridge Rd T1P 1B5 **Location:** Just n of Trans-Canada Hwy 1 at Ridge Rd. **Facility:** 121 units. 116 one-bedroom standard units, some with whirlpools. 2 one- and 3 two-bedroom suites, some with whirlpools. 3 stories, interior corridors. **Parking:** on-site, winter plug-ins. **Terms:** check-in 4 pm, cancellation fee imposed. **Amenities:** high-speed Internet, dual phone lines, voice mail, irons, hair dryers. **Pool(s):** heated indoor. **Leisure Activities:** whirlpool, waterslide, exercise room. **Guest Services:** valet and coin laundry. **Business Services:** conference facilities, business center. **Cards:** AX, MC, VI.

—— **WHERE TO DINE** ——

STRATHMORE STATION RESTAURANT & PUB   Phone: 403/934-0000

International
$6-$16

Families and groups alike will enjoy the nostalgia of the Strathmore Station, which has a medley of comfort foods, including pizza, steak, pasta and oversize salad. Railway enthusiasts will enjoy the railway decor, complete with black and white photos from the railway days, large colourful murals and a special caboose dining car. Casual dress. **Bar:** Full bar. **Hours:** 8 am-1 am, Sun & Mon-midnight. Closed: 12/25. **Address:** 380 Ridge Rd T1P 1B5 **Location:** Trans-Canada Hwy 1, just w of jct SR 817. **Parking:** on-site. **Cards:** AX, MC, VI.

The Calgary Stampede / © Hans-Peter Merten / age fotostock

This ends listings for the Calgary Vicinity.
The following page resumes the alphabetical listings of cities in Alberta.

CAMROSE pop. 15,620

─── WHERE TO STAY ───

NORSEMEN INN

Small-scale Hotel
$95 All Year

Phone: (780)672-9171
Address: 6505 48th Ave T4V 3K3 **Location:** Hwy 13 (48th Ave) at 65th St; west end of town. **Facility:** 76 one-bedroom standard units. 4 stories, interior corridors. *Bath:* combo or shower only. **Parking:** on-site, winter plug-ins. **Amenities:** high-speed Internet, irons, hair dryers. **Leisure Activities:** *Fee:* game room. **Guest Services:** valet laundry. **Business Services:** conference facilities, PC (fee). **Cards:** AX, DC, MC, VI.

R & R INN AND SUITES CAMROSE

Small-scale Hotel
Rates not provided

Phone: 780/672-2292
Address: 6508 48th Ave (Hwy 13) T4V 3A3 **Location:** Hwy 13 (48th Ave) at 66th St. **Facility:** 44 one-bedroom standard units, some with whirlpools. 2 stories (no elevator), interior/exterior corridors. **Parking:** on-site, winter plug-ins. **Amenities:** high-speed Internet, voice mail, hair dryers. **Leisure Activities:** sauna, whirlpool. **Guest Services:** coin laundry. **Business Services:** meeting rooms, PC (fee).

─── WHERE TO DINE ───

MONTE CARLO RESTAURANT

Continental
$9-$33

Phone: 780/672-1040
One of the most popular places in town, the restaurant draws flocks of locals for lunch. Among menu choices are steaks, pizzas, pasta dishes and entree-size salads. Service is fast and friendly, and the atmosphere is casual. Casual dress. **Bar:** Full bar. **Hours:** 11 am-9 pm, Fri-10 pm, Sat 11:30 am-10 pm, Sun 11:30 am-8 pm, Mon 11 am-8 pm. Closed major holidays. **Address:** 4907 48th Ave T4V 0J4 **Location:** Corner of 49th St and 48th Ave (Hwy 13). **Parking:** on-site. **Cards:** MC, VI.

CALL

CANMORE pop. 12,039

─── WHERE TO STAY ───

BANFF BOUNDARY LODGE   *Book great rates at AAA.com*

Condominium
$89-$239 All Year

Phone: (403)678-9555
Address: 1000 Harvie Heights Rd T1W 2W2 **Location:** Just e of Banff National Park east gate, parallel to Trans-Canada Hwy 1, exit Harvie Heights Rd. **Facility:** Smoke free premises. 42 units. 4 one- and 38 two-bedroom suites with kitchens. 1-2 stories (no elevator), exterior corridors. **Parking:** on-site, winter plug-ins. **Terms:** office hours 8 am-8 pm, check-in 4 pm, 3 day cancellation notice-fee imposed. **Amenities:** video library (fee), hair dryers. **Leisure Activities:** whirlpool, childern's play area, picnic area with gas barbecue. **Guest Services:** coin laundry. **Business Services:** meeting rooms. **Cards:** AX, MC, VI. **Free Special Amenities:** local telephone calls and high-speed Internet.

BEST WESTERN POCATERRA INN   *Book great rates at AAA.com*

Small-scale Hotel
Rates not provided

Phone: 403/678-4334
Address: 1725 Mountain Ave T1W 2W1 **Location:** 3.6 mi (5.8 km) e of Banff National Park east gate on Hwy 1A (Bow Valley Trail). **Facility:** Smoke free premises. 83 units. 81 one-bedroom standard units, some with whirlpools. 2 one-bedroom suites with whirlpools. 4 stories, interior corridors. **Parking:** on-site, winter plug-ins. **Terms:** check-in 4 pm. **Amenities:** high-speed Internet, dual phone lines, voice mail, irons, hair dryers. **Pool(s):** heated indoor. **Leisure Activities:** sauna, whirlpool, steamroom, waterslide, exercise room. *Fee:* game room. **Guest Services:** valet and coin laundry, wireless Internet. **Business Services:** meeting rooms, PC (fee). **Free Special Amenities:** continental breakfast and high-speed Internet.

AAA Benefit:
Members save 10% everyday, plus an exclusive frequent stay program.

BOW VALLEY MOTEL

Motel
$115-$125 3/1-9/30
$85-$95 10/1-2/28

Phone: 403/678-5085
Address: 610 8th St T1W 2B5 **Location:** Downtown. **Facility:** 25 one-bedroom standard units, some with efficiencies. 1-3 stories (no elevator), exterior corridors. **Parking:** on-site, winter plug-ins. **Terms:** office hours 8 am-11 pm, cancellation fee imposed. **Amenities:** voice mail, hair dryers. **Leisure Activities:** whirlpool. **Guest Services:** coin laundry. **Cards:** DS, MC, VI.

CANMORE INN & SUITES   *Book great rates at AAA.com*

Small-scale Hotel
Rates not provided

Phone: 403/609-4656
Address: 1402 Bow Valley Tr T1W 1N5 **Location:** 3.5 mi (5.6 km) e of Banff National Park east gate on Hwy 1A (Bow Valley Trail); Trans-Canada Hwy 1, exit Canmore. Located next to railway tracks. **Facility:** 189 units. 187 one-bedroom standard units, some with efficiencies and/or whirlpools. 1 one- and 2-bedroom suites with kitchens and whirlpools. 3 stories, interior corridors. *Bath:* combo or shower only. **Parking:** on-site, winter plug-ins. **Terms:** check-in 4 pm. **Amenities:** voice mail, irons, hair dryers. *Fee:* video games, safes. **Pool(s):** heated indoor. **Leisure Activities:** whirlpool, waterslide, exercise room. **Guest Services:** valet and coin laundry, wireless Internet. **Free Special Amenities:** continental breakfast and high-speed Internet.

CANMORE MOUNTAIN LODGE

Small-scale Hotel
$120-$240 All Year

Phone: (403)678-5488

Address: 1602 2nd Ave T1W 1M8 **Location:** 3.5 mi (5.6 km) e of Banff National Park east gate on Hwy 1A (Bow Valley Trail); Trans-Canada Hwy 1, exit Canmore. **Facility:** 61 one-bedroom standard units, some with efficiencies. 2 stories (no elevator), interior corridors. **Parking:** on-site, winter plug-ins. **Terms:** check-in 4 pm, cancellation fee imposed. **Amenities:** voice mail, irons, hair dryers. **Dining:** Chez Francois, see separate listing. **Leisure Activities:** whirlpool, steamroom, limited exercise equipment. **Guest Services:** valet laundry, area transportation (fee)-ski hills. **Business Services:** meeting rooms, PC (fee). **Cards:** AX, DS, MC, VI.

FALCON CREST LODGE   *Book great rates at AAA.com*

Cottage
$159-$299 All Year

Phone: (403)678-6150

Address: 190 Kananaskis Way T1W 3K5 **Location:** From Trans-Canada Hwy 1, exit Canmore, 0.8 mi (1.9 km) e. **Facility:** Located a short walk from the downtown, many units in this family-friendly property feature full kitchens, fireplaces and in-suite laundry facilities. Smoke free premises. 69 units. 23 one-bedroom standard units, some with efficiencies or kitchens. 38 one- and 8 two-bedroom suites, some with kitchens. 4 stories, interior corridors. **Parking:** on-site. **Terms:** 3 day cancellation notice. **Amenities:** hair dryers. **Leisure Activities:** whirlpools, limited exercise equipment. **Guest Services:** complimentary and valet laundry, wireless Internet. **Cards:** AX, MC, VI. **Free Special Amenities:** room upgrade (subject to availability with advance reservations) and high-speed Internet. *(See color ad p 373)*

FIRE MOUNTAIN LODGE   *Book at AAA.com*

Condominium
$209-$429 All Year

Phone: (403)609-9949

Address: 121 Kananaskis Way T1W 2X2 **Location:** Trans-Canada Hwy 1, exit 1A (Bow Valley Trail), 0.6 mi (1 km) w, then just n. **Facility:** Smoke free premises. 24 units. 12 two- and 12 three-bedroom suites with kitchens. 2 stories (no elevator), exterior corridors. **Parking:** on-site. **Terms:** off-site registration, 1-2 night minimum stay - seasonal and/or weekends, cancellation fee imposed. **Amenities:** voice mail, irons, hair dryers. **Guest Services:** complimentary and valet laundry, wireless Internet. **Cards:** AX, MC, VI.

FOUR POINTS BY SHERATON CANMORE   *Book great rates at AAA.com*

Small-scale Hotel
Rates not provided

Phone: 403/609-4422

Address: #1 Silver Tip Tr T1W 2Z7 **Location:** Trans-Canada Hwy 1, exit 2nd St westbound; exit 3rd St eastbound; on north side of Trans-Canada Hwy 1. **Facility:** 99 units. 94 one-bedroom standard units, some with whirlpools. 5 one-bedroom suites. 3 stories, interior corridors. *Bath:* combo or shower only. **Parking:** on-site, winter plug-ins. **Amenities:** video games (fee), high-speed Internet, voice mail, irons, hair dryers. **Leisure Activities:** whirlpool, hiking trails, exercise room. **Guest Services:** valet laundry, area transportation. **Business Services:** meeting rooms, business center.

FOUR POINTS
BY SHERATON

AAA Benefit:
Members get up to 15% off, plus Starwood Preferred Guest® bonuses.

THE LADY MACDONALD COUNTRY INN

Country Inn
$110-$250 All Year

Phone: (403)678-3665

Address: 1201 Bow Valley Tr T1W 1P5 **Location:** Trans-Canada Hwy 1, exit Canmore; 3.6 mi (5.7 km) e of Banff National Park east gate on Hwy 1A (Bow Valley Trail). **Facility:** A retreatlike ambience enhances this upscale country inn, which features individually decorated rooms and a Victorian-style dining room. Designated smoking area. 12 units. 11 one- and 1 two-bedroom standard units, some with whirlpools. 2 stories (no elevator), interior corridors. *Bath:* combo or shower only. **Parking:** on-site, winter plug-ins. **Terms:** office hours 9 am-5 pm. **Amenities:** voice mail, hair dryers. **Leisure Activities:** *Fee:* massage. **Guest Services:** coin laundry, area transportation (fee)-ski shuttle. **Cards:** MC, VI. **Free Special Amenities:** full breakfast.

THE LODGES AT CANMORE   *Book at AAA.com*

Small-scale Hotel
$175-$339 All Year

Phone: (403)678-9350

Address: 107 Montane Rd T1W 3J2 **Location:** Trans-Canada Hwy 1, exit 1A (Bow Valley Trail), 0.6 mi (1.6 km) w to Montane Rd. **Facility:** Smoke free premises. 41 units. 6 one-bedroom standard units with kitchens. 35 two-bedroom suites with kitchens. 3 stories, interior corridors. **Parking:** on-site. **Terms:** office hours 7 am-11 pm, 1-2 night minimum stay - weekends, cancellation fee imposed. **Amenities:** voice mail, irons, hair dryers. *Some:* DVD players. **Pool(s):** heated outdoor. **Leisure Activities:** whirlpool. **Guest Services:** complimentary and valet laundry, wireless Internet. **Business Services:** meeting rooms, PC (fee). **Cards:** AX, MC, VI.

MYSTIC SPRINGS CHALETS & HOT POOLS   *Book great rates at AAA.com*

Condominium
$245-$369 All Year

Phone: (403)609-0333

Address: 140 Kananaskis Way T1W 2X2 **Location:** Trans-Canada Hwy 1, exit 1A (Bow Valley Trail), 0.6 mi (1 km) w, then n at Montane Dr. **Facility:** Featuring an outdoor saltwater pool, a barbecue area and upscale accommodations, this property offers amenities from martini glasses to DVD players. Smoke free premises. 44 two-bedroom suites with kitchens. 2 stories (no elevator), exterior corridors. **Parking:** on-site. **Terms:** office hours 7 am-11 pm, check-in 4 pm, 2 night minimum stay - weekends. **Amenities:** DVD players, CD players, high-speed Internet, voice mail, irons, hair dryers. **Pool(s):** heated outdoor. **Leisure Activities:** whirlpool, limited exercise equipment. *Fee:* massage. **Guest Services:** valet and coin laundry. **Business Services:** meeting rooms. **Cards:** AX, MC, VI.

QUALITY RESORT-CHATEAU CANMORE *Book great rates at AAA.com* Phone: (403)678-6699

CAA SAVE

Small-scale Hotel
$50-$220 All Year

Address: 1720 Bow Valley Tr T1W 2X3 **Location:** Trans-Canada Hwy 1, exit Canmore; 3 mi (4.8 km) e of·Banff National Park east gate on Hwy 1A (Bow Valley Trail). **Facility:** 93 units. 26 one-bedroom standard units. 67 one-bedroom suites, some with whirlpools. 4 stories, interior/exterior corridors. **Parking:** on-site, winter plug-ins. **Terms:** check-in 4 pm. **Amenities:** video library (fee), voice mail, hair dryers. *Some:* DVD players. **Pool(s):** heated indoor. **Leisure Activities:** sauna, hot tub, lighted tennis court, ice skating, sports court. *Fee:* bicycles, massage. **Guest Services:** valet and coin laundry, tanning facilities, wireless Internet. **Business Services:** meeting rooms, PC (fee). **Cards:** AX, DC, DS, JC, MC, VI. *(See color ad on insert)*

RADISSON HOTEL & CONFERENCE CENTRE *Book great rates at AAA.com* Phone: (403)678-3625

CAA SAVE

Small-scale Hotel
$169-$249 All Year

Address: 511 Bow Valley Tr T1W 1N7 **Location:** Trans-Canada Hwy 1, exit Canmore, just e. **Facility:** 224 units. 214 one-bedroom standard units, some with efficiencies. 2 one- and 8 two-bedroom suites, some with kitchens and/or whirlpools. 2-3 stories, interior/exterior corridors. **Parking:** on-site, winter plug-ins. **Terms:** check-in 4 pm, cancellation fee imposed. **Amenities:** voice mail, irons, hair dryers. *Some:* high-speed Internet. **Pool(s):** heated indoor. **Leisure Activities:** whirlpool, steamroom, picnic area, playground, exercise room. *Fee:* massage. **Guest Services:** valet and coin laundry, area transportation (fee)-ski hills. **Business Services:** conference facilities, PC (fee). **Cards:** AX, DC, DS, JC, MC, VI. **Free Special Amenities: local telephone calls and high-speed Internet.**

ROCKY MOUNTAIN SKI LODGE Phone: (403)678-5445

CAA SAVE

Motel
$120-$205 All Year

Address: 1711 Bow Valley Tr T1W 2T8 **Location:** Trans-Canada Hwy 1, exit Canmore; 3 mi (4.8 km) e of Banff National Park east gate on Hwy 1A (Bow Valley Trail). Located in a commercial area. **Facility:** 82 units. 59 one- and 23 two-bedroom standard units, some with efficiencies or kitchens. 1-2 stories (no elevator), exterior corridors. **Parking:** on-site, winter plug-ins. **Terms:** office hours 7 am-11 pm, 1-30 night minimum stay - seasonal, cancellation fee imposed. **Amenities:** voice mail, hair dryers. **Leisure Activities:** sauna, whirlpool, ski & bike storage, playground. **Guest Services:** coin laundry. **Business Services:** meeting rooms, PC (fee). **Cards:** AX, MC, VI. **Free Special Amenities: newspaper and high-speed Internet.**

RUNDLE MOUNTAIN LODGE Phone: (403)678-5322

CAA SAVE

Motel
$75-$125 All Year

Address: 1723 Bow Valley Tr T1W 1L7 **Location:** Trans-Canada Hwy 1, exit Canmore; 3 mi (4.8 km) e of Banff National Park east gate on Hwy 1A (Bow Valley Trail). **Facility:** 61 units. 47 one- and 6 two-bedroom standard units, some with efficiencies, kitchens and/or whirlpools. 8 one-bedroom suites with kitchens. 1-2 stories (no elevator), exterior corridors. **Parking:** on-site, winter plug-ins. **Terms:** office hours 7 am-11 pm, check-in 4 pm, 7 day cancellation notice-fee imposed. **Amenities:** *Some:* DVD players, hair dryers. **Pool(s):** heated indoor. **Leisure Activities:** whirlpool, playground. **Guest Services:** coin laundry. **Business Services:** meeting rooms. **Cards:** AX, MC, VI.

WINDTOWER LODGE & SUITES *Book great rates at AAA.com* Phone: (403)609-6600

CAA SAVE

Condominium
$139-$399 All Year

Address: 160 Kananaskis Way T1W 3E2 **Location:** Trans-Canada Hwy 1, exit 1A (Bow Valley Trail), 0.6 mi (1 km) w, then n at Montane Dr. **Facility:** Designated smoking area. 105 units. 49 one-bedroom standard units. 56 one-bedroom suites with kitchens. 2 stories, interior corridors. *Bath:* combo or shower only. **Parking:** on-site (fee) and street. **Terms:** check-in 4 pm, 3 day cancellation notice-fee imposed. **Amenities:** voice mail, hair dryers. **Leisure Activities:** whirlpool, exercise room. **Guest Services:** wireless Internet. **Business Services:** meeting rooms, PC (fee). **Cards:** AX, MC, VI. **Free Special Amenities: local telephone calls and newspaper.**

——— WHERE TO DINE ———

BEAMER'S COFFEE BAR
Phone: 403/678-3988

Coffee/Espresso
$3-$7

In a convenient spot, the contemporary coffeehouse draws both locals and those en route to the ski hills. Among healthy offerings are magnificent muffins, soups, breakfast bagels and, of course, Beamer's coffee. Big boy sandwiches are built on the premises with fresh, multigrain bread and a choice of toppings. For those with a sweet tooth, the display case features some tempting choices. Casual dress. **Bar:** Full bar. **Hours:** 6 am-9 pm. Closed: 12/25. **Address:** 1702A Bow Valley Tr T1W 1N5 **Location:** Trans-Canada Hwy 1, exit Canmore, 0.6 mi (1 km) w. **Parking:** on-site. **Cards:** AX, MC, VI.

CHEZ FRANCOIS
Phone: 403/678-6111

French
$8-$26

This fine-dining establishment features classic French cuisine, seafood and pasta. This is a popular place with locals. Dressy casual. **Bar:** Full bar. **Reservations:** suggested. **Hours:** 7 am-2:30 & 5-10 pm, Sat & Sun 7 am-3 & 5-10 pm. **Address:** 1602 2nd Ave T1W 1P7 **Location:** 3.2 mi (5.2 km) e of Banff National Park east gate on Hwy 1A (Bow Valley Trail); Trans-Canada Hwy 1, exit Canmore; in Canmore Mountain Lodge. **Parking:** on-site. **Cards:** AX, DC, MC, VI.

CALL

CRAZY WEED KITCHEN
Phone: 403/609-2530

Canadian
$10-$25

First-timers who aren't careful might pass by this gem. There are but 10 tables in the bright, airy, lemon-yellow interior, which has a casual bistro feel to it. The food, however, is anything but casual. The artistic chef mixes distinctive and flavorful ingredients to create delicious dishes. Choose the mixed green salad with lemon grass vinaigrette or any of the specials of the day, which might include tea-smoked salmon or pomegranate chicken. Service is friendly and casual. Casual dress. **Bar:** Beer & wine. **Hours:** 11:30 am-3:30 & 5:30-10:30 pm. **Address:** 626 8th St T1W 2B5 **Location:** Centre. **Parking:** street. **Cards:** MC, VI.

THE GRIZZLY PAW BREWING COMPANY
Phone: 403/678-9983

Canadian
$8-$12

A taste of local ales awaits at the popular brew pub, where beer is made on site. The menu features a variety of hearty pub fare, ranging from hamburgers to fish and chips, jalapeno poppers, soups and salads. For a casual meal, this is a popular spot. Casual dress. **Bar:** Full bar. **Hours:** 11 am-midnight, Fri & Sat-1 am. Closed: 12/25. **Address:** 622 Main St T1W 2B5 **Location:** Downtown. **Parking:** on-site. **Cards:** AX, MC, VI.

LUNA BLUE RESTAURANT
Phone: 403/609-3221

Italian
$8-$20

Almost every pasta dish on the extensive menu contains fresh pasta made locally every day. On the main drag, the casual eatery serves hearty and healthy options in a cozy environment. Casual dress. **Bar:** Full bar. **Reservations:** suggested. **Hours:** noon-3 & 5-9 pm, Fri & Sat-10 pm. Closed: 12/25. **Address:** 107-721 Main St T1W 2B2 **Location:** Jct 7th Ave; downtown. **Parking:** street. **Cards:** MC, VI.

MURRIETA'S BAR & GRILL
Phone: 403/609-9500

West Pacific Rim
$8-$35

Upstairs from street level, the classy, upbeat restaurant boasts West Coast cuisine, including a variety of sandwiches and salads at lunch and heartier dishes at dinner. Reservations are recommended at the popular spot in this mountain town, especially for the dinner hour. Lending to the restaurant's atmosphere are cozy mountain decor, wooden accents, a lounge and a fireplace. Dressy casual. **Bar:** Full bar. **Reservations:** suggested. **Hours:** 11 am-11 pm, Fri & Sat-1 am, Sun-10 pm. Closed major holidays. **Address:** 200, 737 Main St T1W 2B2 **Location:** Corner of 7th and Main sts; downtown, on 2nd level. **Parking:** street. **Cards:** AX, DC, MC, VI.

PATRINOS STEAKHOUSE & PUB
Phone: 403/678-4060

Continental
$7-$23

The simple, family-run, roadside restaurant features a good selection of comfort foods, ranging from pizza and pasta to steaks. Guests can eat in the casual dining room or grab something in the lounge next door. Expect friendly, attentive service. Casual dress. **Bar:** Full bar. **Hours:** 11 am-11 pm, Sun from 10 am. Closed: 12/25. **Address:** 1602 Bow Valley Tr T1W 1N5 **Location:** At 15th St. **Parking:** on-site. **Cards:** AX, MC, VI.

QUARRY BISTRO
Phone: 403/678-6088

Provincial French
$8-$28

Along the city's main street, the restaurant shows a contemporary, simple and chic decor. Guests find comfortable surroundings and outdoor seating in the warmer months. The menu, a collection of locally and seasonally inspired dishes, is rooted in the classic French and Italian Provincial style. On the menu might be macaroni and cheese with three cheeses, veal saltimbocca and cranberry-ricotta ravioli. Servers are efficient and extremely friendly. Casual dress. **Bar:** Full bar. **Reservations:** suggested. **Hours:** noon-2:30 & 5-10 pm, Sat & Sun from 9 am; Saturday & Sunday brunch. Closed major holidays; also Tues & Wed in winter. **Address:** 718 Main St T1W 2B6 **Location:** Downtown. **Parking:** street. **Cards:** AX, MC, VI.

ROCKY MOUNTAIN FLATBREAD CO
Phone: 403/609-5508

Pizza
$8-$15

The comfortable, casual restaurant offers diners a wide selection of thin-crust pizzas and a few daily specials, many of which are cooked in the hand-built masonry oven. Casual dress. **Bar:** Full bar. **Hours:** 11:30 am-10 pm. Closed major holidays. **Address:** 838 10th St, Unit 101 T1W 2A8 **Location:** Corner of 8th Ave and 10th St. **Parking:** on-site and street. **Cards:** MC, VI.

CALL

SAGE BISTRO
Phone: 403/678-4878

Canadian
$10-$22

On its own by the gas station, the log cabin-like roadhouse would be easy to drive by. Inside this rustic space, the kitchen elevates Canadian comfort food to new levels by using local products, including produce and game. Casual dress. **Bar:** Full bar. **Hours:** 5 pm-9 pm, Fri-10 pm, Sat 9 am-10 pm, Sun 9 am-9 pm. Closed major holidays. **Address:** 1712 Bow Valley Tr T1W 1P2 **Location:** 3.1 mi (5.2 km) e of Banff National Park east gate on Hwy 1A (Bow Valley Trail); jct 17th St. **Parking:** on-site. **Cards:** AX, MC, VI.

TAPAS RESTAURANT

Mediterranean
$9-$35

CALL 🔊M

Phone: 403/609-0583

Diners should come in groups to sample and savor the widest variety of memorable tapas preparations. Drawing on influences from both Spain and Portugal, selections are mouthwatering. Delicious favorites include fiery sweet potato tapas, eggplant and paella for two. A relatively new addition to the city scene, the casual spot is popular with locals and visitors alike for its comfortable surroundings and superb food. Casual dress. **Bar:** Full bar. **Reservations:** suggested. **Hours:** 8 am-11 pm; from 5 pm in winter. Closed major holidays. **Address:** 633 10th St T1W 2A2 **Location:** Downtown; next to Paintbox Lodge. **Parking:** street.
Cards: MC, VI.

ZONA'S LATE NIGHT BISTRO

Canadian
$15-$21

Phone: 403/609-2000

The small bistro's cozy wooden interior sets the stage for a memorable meal. Among hearty, healthy menu options are vegetarian lasagna and curry. Each dish is served on a one-of-a-kind piece of pottery, created by the owner. A favorite with the locals, this place often bustles on weekends. Casual dress. **Bar:** Full bar. **Reservations:** suggested. **Hours:** 5 pm-10 pm. Closed: 1/1, 12/25. **Address:** 710 9th St T1W 2V7 **Location:** Corner of 7th Ave and 9th St. **Parking:** street. **Cards:** AX, MC, VI.

CARDSTON pop. 3,452

———— WHERE TO STAY ————

SOUTH COUNTRY INN

CAA SAVE

Small-scale Hotel
$79-$135 All Year

Phone: 403/653-8000

Address: 404 Main St T0K 0K0 **Location:** On Hwy 2; centre. **Facility:** 45 units. 40 one- and 5 two-bedroom standard units, some with whirlpools. 2 stories (no elevator), interior corridors. **Parking:** on-site, winter plug-ins. **Pool(s):** indoor. **Leisure Activities:** whirlpool. **Guest Services:** coin laundry, tanning facilities. **Business Services:** meeting rooms. **Cards:** AX, MC, VI. **Free Special Amenities:** local telephone calls and high-speed Internet.

S🔊D 🍴 🏊 📺 / SOME UNITS ✕

———— WHERE TO DINE ————

PIZZAS & CREAM

Pizza
$3-$7

Phone: 403/653-4143

A play on words, the retro diner's name aptly describes its food: pizza and ice cream. Guests seat themselves in a red and silver booth and phone orders to the front. Whimsical, nostalgic memorabilia ranges from Trivial Pursuit to Lite Brite. Piping-hot pizza delivered atop an old-fashioned pizza stand tastes great with a frothy milkshake. Casual dress. **Hours:** 11 am-10 pm, Fri-midnight, Sat-11 pm. Closed: Sun. **Address:** 325 Main St T0K 0K0 **Location:** Downtown. **Parking:** street. **Cards:** AX, MC, VI.

CLAIRMONT pop. 1,508

———— WHERE TO STAY ————

RAMADA INN & SUITES   *Book great rates at AAA.com*

CAA SAVE

Small-scale Hotel
$169-$299 All Year

Phone: (780)814-7448

Address: 7201 99 St T0H 0W0 **Location:** Jct Hwy 43 and 2, just n. **Facility:** 98 units. 70 one-bedroom standard units. 28 one-bedroom suites, some with whirlpools. 4 stories, interior corridors. **Parking:** on-site, winter plug-ins. **Terms:** cancellation fee imposed. **Amenities:** high-speed Internet, voice mail, irons, hair dryers. **Leisure Activities:** whirlpool, exercise room. **Guest Services:** valet and coin laundry. **Business Services:** meeting rooms, PC. **Cards:** AX, DC, MC, VI. **Free Special Amenities:** local telephone calls and high-speed Internet.

S🔊D 🍴 📺 📶 📷 💻 / SOME UNITS FEE 🐾 ✕

CLARESHOLM pop. 3,700

—— WHERE TO STAY ——

BLUEBIRD MOTEL

Motel
$80-$90 All Year

Phone: 403/625-3395

Address: 5505 1st St W T0L 0T0 **Location:** 0.3 mi (0.5 km) n on Hwy 2. **Facility:** 22 units. 14 one-bedroom standard units, some with efficiencies or kitchens. 7 one- and 1 two-bedroom suites, some with efficiencies or kitchens. 1 story, exterior corridors. *Bath:* combo or shower only. **Parking:** on-site, winter plug-ins. **Terms:** office hours 7 am-11 pm. **Amenities:** high-speed Internet, voice mail, hair dryers. *Some:* irons. **Cards:** AX, MC, VI.

MOTEL 6 CLARESHOLM

[fyi]
Small-scale Hotel
Rates not provided

Phone: 403/625-4646

Too new to rate, opening scheduled for December 2007. **Address:** 11 Alberta Rd (Hwy #2) T0L 0T0 **Amenities:** 69 units, pets, restaurant. *(See color ad p 368)*

COCHRANE —See Calgary p. 420.

DEAD MAN'S FLATS

—— WHERE TO STAY ——

PIGEON MOUNTAIN MOTEL

Motel
$75-$135 All Year

Phone: 403/678-5756

Address: 250 1st Ave T1W 2T8 **Location:** On Trans-Canada Hwy 1. Located at Dead Man's Flats Service Centre. **Facility:** 16 units. 8 one- and 8 two-bedroom standard units. 2 stories (no elevator), exterior corridors. **Parking:** on-site, winter plug-ins. **Terms:** 3 day cancellation notice-fee imposed. **Cards:** AX, MC, VI. **Free Special Amenities: local telephone calls and early check-in/late check-out.**

DRAYTON VALLEY pop. 6,893

—— WHERE TO STAY ——

LAKEVIEW INNS & SUITES   *Book great rates at AAA.com*

Small-scale Hotel
Rates not provided

Phone: 780/542-3200

Address: 4302 50th St T7A 1M4 **Location:** Hwy 22, exit Drayton Valley, just n. **Facility:** 91 units. 82 one-bedroom standard units, some with whirlpools. 9 one-bedroom suites. 3 stories (no elevator), interior corridors. **Parking:** on-site, winter plug-ins. **Amenities:** video library (fee), DVD players, irons, hair dryers. **Leisure Activities:** sauna, whirlpool, exercise room. **Guest Services:** coin laundry, wireless Internet. **Business Services:** meeting rooms, PC (fee). *(See color ad p 362)*

DRUMHELLER pop. 7,932

—— WHERE TO STAY ——

BEST WESTERN JURASSIC INN   *Book great rates at AAA.com*

Small-scale Hotel
$114-$153 All Year

Phone: (403)823-7700

Address: 1103 Hwy 9 S T0J 0Y0 **Location:** Hwy 9, southeast access to town. **Facility:** 48 units. 45 one-bedroom standard units, some with efficiencies. 3 one-bedroom suites with efficiencies, some with whirlpools. 2 stories (no elevator), interior/exterior corridors. **Parking:** on-site, winter plug-ins. **Terms:** check-in 4 pm. **Amenities:** voice mail, irons, hair dryers. **Pool(s):** heated indoor. **Leisure Activities:** whirlpool, exercise room. **Guest Services:** valet and coin laundry, wireless Internet. **Business Services:** meeting rooms, PC (fee). **Cards:** AX, CB, DC, DS, JC, MC, VI. **Free Special Amenities: room upgrade (subject to availability with advance reservations) and high-speed Internet.**

AAA Benefit:
Members save 10% everyday, plus an exclusive frequent stay program.

INN AND SPA AT HEARTWOOD

Bed & Breakfast
$99-$280 All Year

Phone: 403/823-6495

Address: 320 N Railway Ave E T0J 0Y4 **Location:** Downtown. **Facility:** Classic old-fashioned touches like high beds with step stools distinguish this commercial-district inn, skillfully renovated to modern standards. Smoke free premises. 10 units. 8 one-bedroom standard units with whirlpools. 1 vacation home and 1 cottage with whirlpools. 2 stories (no elevator), interior/exterior corridors. **Parking:** on-site, winter plug-ins. **Terms:** office hours 8 am-11 pm, check-in 4 pm, age restrictions may apply, 3 day cancellation notice. **Amenities:** video library, irons, hair dryers. *Some:* DVD players (fee). **Leisure Activities:** spa. **Guest Services:** wireless Internet. **Cards:** AX, MC, VI. **Free Special Amenities: local telephone calls and high-speed Internet.**

RAMADA INN & SUITES   *Book at AAA.com*   Phone: 403/823-2028

▽▽▽

Small-scale Hotel
Rates not provided

Address: 680 2nd St SE T0J 0Y0 **Location:** Off Hwy 9. **Facility:** 74 units. 68 one-bedroom standard units, some with whirlpools. 6 one-bedroom suites. 4 stories, interior/exterior corridors. *Bath:* combo or shower only. **Parking:** on-site, winter plug-ins. **Amenities:** high-speed Internet, voice mail, irons, hair dryers. **Pool(s):** heated indoor. **Leisure Activities:** whirlpool, waterslide, exercise room. **Guest Services:** coin laundry. **Business Services:** meeting rooms, business center.

[icons] CALL &M ⨀ ⨂ ✦ ▯ ▭ ▭ / SOME UNITS FEE 🐕 ⨂

SUPER 8 MOTEL   *Book at AAA.com*   Phone: 403/823-8887

▽▽▽ ▽▽

Small-scale Hotel
Rates not provided

Address: 600-680 2nd St SE T0J 0Y0 **Location:** Off Hwy 9. **Facility:** 70 units. 66 one-bedroom standard units, some with kitchens (no utensils) and/or whirlpools. 4 one-bedroom suites, some with whirlpools. 2 stories, interior/exterior corridors. **Parking:** on-site, winter plug-ins. **Amenities:** voice mail, irons, hair dryers. *Some:* DVD players (fee), high-speed Internet. **Pool(s):** heated indoor. **Leisure Activities:** whirlpool, waterslide, exercise room. **Guest Services:** valet and coin laundry, wireless Internet. **Business Services:** business center.

[icons] ⨀ ⨂ ✦ ▯ ▭ ▭ / SOME UNITS FEE 🐕 ⨂

TASTE THE PAST BED & BREAKFAST   Phone: 403/823-5889

▽▽ ▽▽

Historic Bed
& Breakfast
$100-$115 All Year

Address: 281 2nd St W T0J 0Y0 **Location:** Hwy 9, exit 2nd St W; centre. **Facility:** This large home was built by a coal baron in 1910. Smoke free premises. 3 one-bedroom standard units. 3 stories (no elevator), interior corridors. *Bath:* combo or shower only. **Parking:** on-site, winter plug-ins. **Terms:** check-in 4 pm. **Guest Services:** TV in common area. **Cards:** MC, VI.

[icons] ⨂ 🅰 🄿 🆉

------- WHERE TO DINE -------

CAFE ITALIANO   Phone: 403/823-4443

▽▽

Coffee/Espresso
$4-$8

The upscale, downtown cafe is best known for panini and dessert, not to mention a good cup of coffee. Casual dress. **Hours:** 7 am-6 pm. Closed major holidays. **Address:** 35 3rd Ave W T0J 0Y0 **Location:** Downtown. **Parking:** street. **Cards:** MC, VI.

SIZZLING HOUSE   Phone: 403/823-8098

(CAA)

▽▽

Chinese
$7-$16

This is the place for Chinese food with Thai and Szechuan twists. The decor is simple, the service is friendly, and the food is delicious. The lunch buffet is a great value, but diners also can opt to order a la carte from the menu. Casual dress. **Bar:** Full bar. **Hours:** 11 am-9 pm, Fri & Sat-10 pm. Closed: 12/25, 12/26. **Address:** 160 Centre St T0J 0Y0 **Location:** Downtown. **Parking:** street. **Cards:** AX, MC, VI.

THAT'S CRAFTY CRAFT BARN & TEA ROOM   Phone: 403/677-2207

▽▽ ▽▽

Canadian
$5-$8

Just outside of town, the tea room is a lovely place for fresh tea biscuits and a good bowl of soup. Casual dress. **Hours:** Open 3/15-12/31; 10 am-5 pm. Closed major holidays; also Sun. **Address:** Box 1477 T0J 0Y0 **Location:** 16 mi (26 km) w on Hwy 9. **Parking:** on-site. **Cards:** AX, MC, VI.

CALL &M

THE WHISTLING KETTLE   Phone: 403/823-9997

▽▽

Coffee/Espresso
$3-$6

Across from the visitor information center, the simple cafe serves homemade soups and sandwiches with assorted teas. Casual dress. **Hours:** 7:30 am-4 pm. Closed: 12/25-1/2. **Address:** 109 Centre St T0J 0Y0 **Location:** Downtown; across from Tourist Information Centre. **Parking:** street. **Cards:** MC, VI.

🅰

Destination Edmonton

pop. 730,372

*E*dmonton, nicknamed "Gateway to the North," was once a place for gold miners to stop and gather provisions for their rough journey into the icy Klondike.

*D*isappointed prospectors who eventually returned to help build Edmonton indeed struck gold: Today the shining city is a mecca of culture and recreation with its lovely theaters, parks and gardens.

Ukrainian Cultural Heritage Village, Edmonton.
With costumes and more than 30 buildings, this village re-creates the lives of early 20th-century Ukrainian immigrants. (See listing page 72)

Travel Alberta

Old Strathcona dining, Edmonton.
Shoppers dine *al fresco* along Whyte Avenue in Old Strathcona after browsing the boutiques and specialty shops. (See mention page 75)

The Saskatchewan River, Edmonton.
In warmer months enjoy picturesque Edmonton with a boat ride down the North Saskatchewan River. (See mention page 91)

Edmonton

See Downtown map page 431

St. Albert

Stony Plain

Fort Saskatchewan

Sherwood Park

See Vicinity map page 434

Nisku

Leduc

William Hawrelak Park, Edmonton.
When the mercury dips, old and young alike experience the fun of ice skating outdoors at Hawrelak Park. (See mention page 76)

*P*laces included in this AAA Destination City:

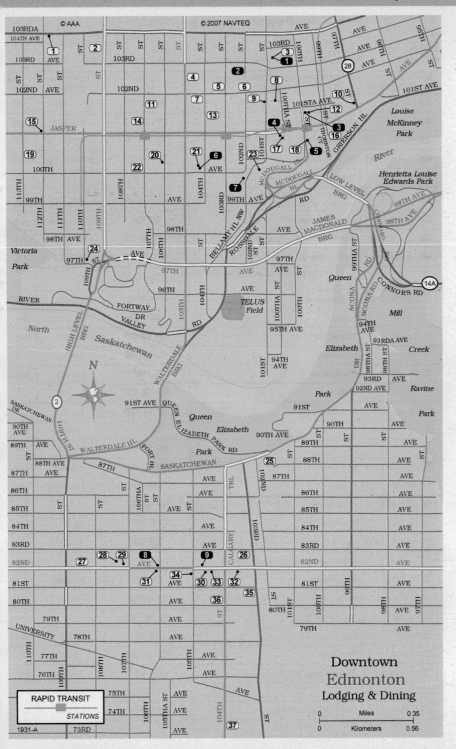

Downtown
Edmonton
Lodging & Dining

RAPID TRANSIT
STATIONS

1931-A

© AAA   © 2007 NAVTEQ

Downtown Edmonton

This index helps you "spot" where approved lodgings and restaurants are located on the corresponding detailed maps. Lodging daily rate range is for comparison only and show the property's high season. Restaurant rate range is a combination of lunch and/or dinner. Turn to the listing page for more detailed rate information and consult display ads for special promotions.

Spotter/Map Page Number	OA	DOWNTOWN EDMONTON - Lodgings	Diamond Rating	Rate Range High Season	Listing Page
1 / p. 431		The Sutton Place Hotel, Edmonton	◆◆◆	$325-$355	438
2 / p. 431		Delta Edmonton Centre Suite Hotel	◆◆◆	$99-$389	438
3 / p. 431	CAA	The Westin Edmonton	◆◆◆	$119-$399 SAVE	439
4 / p. 431	CAA	Union Bank Inn	◆◆◆	$99-$409 SAVE	438
5 / p. 431	CAA	The Fairmont Hotel Macdonald	◆◆◆◆	$159-$465 SAVE	438
6 / p. 431	CAA	Holiday Inn Express Edmonton-Downtown - see color ad on insert	◆◆◆	$128 SAVE	438
7 / p. 431		Coast Edmonton House	◆◆	$105-$245	438
8 / p. 431		Varscona Hotel on Whyte	◆◆◆	$150-$300	439
9 / p. 431		Metterra Hotel on Whyte	◆◆◆	$170-$350	438
		DOWNTOWN EDMONTON - Restaurants			
1 / p. 431		Wild Tangerine	◆◆◆	$13-$20	442
2 / p. 431		Mikado	◆◆	$6-$16	441
3 / p. 431		Capitals Restaurant	◆◆◆	$12-$30	440
4 / p. 431		Characters	◆◆◆	$14-$39	440
5 / p. 431		The Creperie	◆◆	$10-$23	440
6 / p. 431		L'azia	◆◆◆	$10-$25	441
7 / p. 431		Ric's Grill	◆◆◆	$15-$37	442
8 / p. 431		Bistro Praha	◆◆	$6-$20	439
9 / p. 431		Chance	◆◆◆	$9-$40	440
10 / p. 431		Hardware Grill	◆◆◆	$28-$49	441
11 / p. 431		Khazana	◆◆	$10-$20	441
12 / p. 431		Pradera Cafe	◆◆◆	$9-$35	442
13 / p. 431		Blue Plate Diner	◆◆	$8-$12	439
14 / p. 431	CAA	Doan's Restaurant	◆◆	$7-$18	440
15 / p. 431		French Meadow Artisan Bakery Cafe	◆	$5-$10	440
16 / p. 431		Riverside Bistro	◆◆	$10-$25	442
17 / p. 431		Madison's Grill	◆◆◆	$11-$39	441
18 / p. 431		The Harvest Room	◆◆◆	$16-$42	441
19 / p. 431		Bua Thai Restaurant	◆◆	$9-$18	439
20 / p. 431		Cafe Select	◆◆◆	$8-$20	440
21 / p. 431		The Free Press Bistro	◆◆	$8-$22	440
22 / p. 431	CAA	Il Portico	◆◆◆	$10-$30	441
23 / p. 431		La Ronde Revolving Restaurant	◆◆◆	$26-$70	441

Spotter/Map Page Number	OA	DOWNTOWN EDMONTON - Restaurants (continued)	Diamond Rating	Rate Range High Season	Listing Page
(24) / p. 431		The Copper Pot Restaurant	▽▽▽	$8-$42	440
(25) / p. 431		New Asian Village	▽▽▽	$8-$25	442
(26) / p. 431		Packrat Louie's Kitchen & Bar	▽▽▽	$9-$30	442
(27) / p. 431		Cafe Mosaics	▽	$5-$11	439
(28) / p. 431		Tokyo Noodle Shop	▽	$8-$10	442
(29) / p. 431		The King & I	▽▽	$7-$17	441
(30) / p. 431		Yiannis Taverna	▽▽	$6-$21	442
(31) / p. 431		O'Byrne's Irish Pub	▽	$8-$15	442
(32) / p. 431		Block 1912	▽	$8-$12	439
(33) / p. 431		The Funky Pickle Pizza Co	▽	$4-$18	440
(34) / p. 431		Chianti	▽▽	$7-$19	440
(35) / p. 431		Von's Steak & Fish House	▽▽	$19-$40	442
(36) / p. 431		Bee-Bell Health Bakery	▽	$2-$9	439
(37) / p. 431		Billingsgate Seafood Market Lighthouse Cafe	▽▽	$8-$40	439

Edmonton
Lodging & Dining

RAPID TRANSIT
STATIONS

✈ Airport Accommodations

Spotter/Map Page Number	OA	EDMONTON MUNICIPAL AIRPORT	Diamond Rating	Rate Range High Season	Listing Page
4 / p. 434	CAA	Chateau Louis Hotel & Conference Centre, 0.3 mi (0.4 km) se of airport	◆◆	$119-$209 SAVE	444
		EDMONTON INTERNATIONAL AIRPORT			
N/A	CAA	Best Western Denham Inn and Suites, 5 mi (8 km) se of airport	◆◆◆	$116-$230 SAVE	453
N/A	CAA	Edmonton International Airport-Super 8 Motel, 3.8 mi (6 km) se of airport	◆◆	Rates not provided	453
N/A	CAA	Holiday Inn Express Edmonton Int'l Airport, 2.3 mi (3.7 km) e of airport	◆◆◆	$150-$160 SAVE	454
N/A		Quality Inn & Suites-Airport, 2.3 mi (3.7 km) e of airport	◆◆◆	$120-$160	454

Edmonton and Vicinity

This index helps you "spot" where approved lodgings and restaurants are located on the corresponding detailed maps. Lodging daily rate range is for comparison only and show the property's high season. Restaurant rate range is a combination of lunch and/or dinner. Turn to the listing page for more detailed rate information and consult display ads for special promotions.

Spotter/Map Page Number	OA	EDMONTON - Lodgings	Diamond Rating	Rate Range High Season	Listing Page
1 / p. 434	CAA	Best Western North Edmonton Inn & Suites	◆◆	$119-$210 SAVE	443
2 / p. 434	CAA	Rosslyn Inn & Suites	◆◆	$111 SAVE	447
3 / p. 434	CAA	Travelodge Edmonton East	◆◆	$89-$129 SAVE	447
4 / p. 434	CAA	Chateau Louis Hotel & Conference Centre - see color ad p 444	◆◆	$119-$209 SAVE	444
5 / p. 434	CAA	Mayfield Inn & Suites at West Edmonton	◆◆◆	$150-$225 SAVE	447
6 / p. 434		Glenora Bed & Breakfast Inn	◆◆◆	$90-$175	446
7 / p. 434		Hilton Garden Inn-West Edmonton	◆◆◆	$169-$249	446
8 / p. 434	CAA	Travelodge Edmonton West - see color ad p 413	◆◆	$109-$159 SAVE	449
9 / p. 434	CAA	Best Western Westwood Inn - see color ad p 443	◆◆	Rates not provided SAVE	443
10 / p. 434	CAA	Continental Inn	◆◆	$110-$135 SAVE	444
11 / p. 434		West Harvest Inn	◆◆	Rates not provided	449
12 / p. 434	CAA	Comfort Inn West - see color ad on insert	◆◆	$109-$154 SAVE	444
13 / p. 434		Executive Royal Inn West Edmonton	◆◆	$105	445
14 / p. 434	CAA	Holiday Inn Express Hotel & Suites Edmonton - see color ad p 447	◆◆◆	Rates not provided SAVE	447
15 / p. 434	CAA	Days Inn & Suites West Edmonton - see color ad p 447, p 445	◆◆◆	$129-$144 SAVE	444
16 / p. 434		Wingate Inn Edmonton West	◆◆◆	$135-$150	449
17 / p. 434		West Edmonton Mall Inn	◆◆	$149	449
18 / p. 434		Campus Tower Suite Hotel	◆◆	$119-$249	443
19 / p. 434	CAA	Holiday Inn Convention Centre (S.E. Edmonton)	◆◆◆	$145-$175 SAVE	446
20 / p. 434	CAA	Four Points by Sheraton Edmonton South - see color ad p 446	◆◆◆	$205-$225 SAVE	445
21 / p. 434		Hotel Selkirk	◆◆◆	$175-$225	447
22 / p. 434	CAA	Best Western Cedar Park Inn	◆◆	Rates not provided SAVE	443

Spotter/Map Page Number	OA	EDMONTON - Lodgings (continued)	Diamond Rating	Rate Range High Season	Listing Page
23 / p. 434		Greenwood Hotel & Suites	◆◆◆	$129-$249	446
24 / p. 434	CAA	**Delta Edmonton South Hotel and Conference Centre**	◆◆◆	$160-$270 [SAVE]	445
25 / p. 434		Holiday Inn Edmonton-The Palace	◆◆◆	Rates not provided	446
26 / p. 434	CAA	**Super 8 Hotel**	◆◆	$129-$149 [SAVE]	447
		EDMONTON - Restaurants			
1 / p. 434		Fife N' Dekel	◆	$6-$10	450
2 / p. 434		The Blue Pear	◆◆◆	$59	449
3 / p. 434		The Dish Bistro	◆◆	$6-$15	450
4 / p. 434		Glenora Grill	◆◆◆	$15-$25	450
5 / p. 434		Dante's Bistro	◆◆◆	$7-$22	450
6 / p. 434		Urban Diner	◆◆	$8-$15	452
7 / p. 434		La Favorite Pastry Shop	◆	$4-$8	451
8 / p. 434		La Spiga	◆◆◆	$15-$35	451
9 / p. 434		Manor Cafe	◆◆	$14-$39	451
10 / p. 434		Il Pasticcion Trattoria	◆◆	$10-$34	450
11 / p. 434		The Cheesecake Cafe	◆◆	$10-$25	449
12 / p. 434		ConYac's Bar & Grill	◆◆	$8-$18	450
13 / p. 434		Homefire Bar & Grill	◆◆	$10-$26	450
14 / p. 434		Delux Burger Bar	◆◆	$9-$13	450
15 / p. 434		The Funky Pickle Pizza Co	◆	$4-$10	450
16 / p. 434		T & T Supermarket Cafe	◆	$5-$7	452
17 / p. 434		Fantasy Grill Dining Room	◆◆◆	$18-$30	450
18 / p. 434		Unheardof Restaurant	◆◆◆	$32-$42	452
19 / p. 434		Barb & Ernie's	◆	$8-$15	449
20 / p. 434		Parkallen Restaurant	◆◆◆	$8-$20	451
21 / p. 434		Jack's Grill	◆◆◆	$28-$39	451
22 / p. 434		Seasons Grill	◆◆	$8-$20	452
23 / p. 434		Lemongrass Cafe	◆◆	$6-$17	451
24 / p. 434		Koutouki Taverna	◆◆	$20-$40	451
25 / p. 434		Tom Goodchilds Moose Factory	◆◆	$9-$50	452
26 / p. 434		Century Grill	◆◆◆	$11-$35	449
27 / p. 434		OPM Asian Bistro & Lounge	◆◆	$8-$14	451
		ST. ALBERT - Restaurants			
30 / p. 434		River House Grill	◆◆◆	$19-$29	454
31 / p. 434		Ric's Grill	◆◆◆	$9-$30	454

DOWNTOWN EDMONTON   (See map and index starting on p. 431)

──────── **WHERE TO STAY** ────────

COAST EDMONTON HOUSE   *Book at AAA.com*
Phone: (780)420-4000   **7**

Condominium
$105-$245 All Year

Address: 10205 100th Ave T5J 4B5 **Location:** Just se of jct 102nd St and 100th Ave. **Facility:** 305 units. 289 one- and 16 two-bedroom suites with kitchens. 35 stories, interior corridors. **Parking:** on-site, winter plug-ins. **Amenities:** irons, hair dryers. *Some:* voice mail. **Pool(s):** heated indoor. **Leisure Activities:** exercise room. *Fee:* massage, game room. **Guest Services:** valet and coin laundry. **Business Services:** meeting rooms. **Cards:** AX, DC, MC, VI.

DELTA EDMONTON CENTRE SUITE HOTEL   *Book at AAA.com*
Phone: 780/429-3900   **2**

Large-scale Hotel
$99-$389 All Year

Address: 10222 102nd St T5J 4C5 **Location:** At 102nd St at 103rd Ave. **Facility:** 169 units. 63 one-bedroom standard units with whirlpools. 106 one-bedroom suites, some with whirlpools. 7 stories, interior corridors. **Parking:** on-site (fee) and valet, winter plug-ins. **Terms:** cancellation fee imposed. **Amenities:** video games (fee), high-speed Internet, dual phone lines, voice mail, honor bars, irons, hair dryers. **Leisure Activities:** whirlpool, steamroom, exercise room. **Guest Services:** valet laundry. **Business Services:** conference facilities, business center. **Cards:** AX, CB, DC, DS, JC, MC, VI.

THE FAIRMONT HOTEL MACDONALD   *Book great rates at AAA.com*
Phone: (780)424-5181   **5**

(CAA) (SAVE)

Large-scale Hotel
$159-$465 All Year

Address: 10065 100th St T5J 0N6 **Location:** Just s of Jasper Ave. **Facility:** Perched atop the river valley, this historic hotel with a majestic ambience offers attentive service and upscale rooms, some with a view. 198 units. 189 one-bedroom standard units. 9 one-bedroom suites with whirlpools. 9 stories, interior corridors. **Parking:** on-site (fee) and valet, winter plug-ins. **Amenities:** voice mail, honor bars, irons, hair dryers. *Fee:* video games, high-speed Internet. *Some:* CD players. **Dining:** The Harvest Room, see separate listing. **Pool(s):** heated indoor. **Leisure Activities:** sauna, whirlpool, steamroom, 2 squash courts. *Fee:* massage. **Guest Services:** valet laundry. **Business Services:** conference facilities, business center. **Cards:** AX, DC, DS, MC, VI. **Free Special Amenities:** early check-in/late check-out and room upgrade (subject to availability with advance reservations).

HOLIDAY INN EXPRESS EDMONTON-DOWNTOWN   *Book great rates at AAA.com*
Phone: 780/423-2450   **6**

(CAA) (SAVE)

Small-scale Hotel
$128 All Year

Address: 10010 104th St T5J 0Z1 **Location:** Corner of 100th Ave; centre. **Facility:** 140 one-bedroom standard units. 7 stories, interior corridors. **Parking:** on-site (fee). **Terms:** cancellation fee imposed. **Amenities:** video games (fee), high-speed Internet, dual phone lines, voice mail, irons, hair dryers. *Some:* CD players. **Pool(s):** heated indoor. **Leisure Activities:** whirlpool, steamrooms, exercise room. **Guest Services:** valet and coin laundry, beauty salon. **Business Services:** conference facilities, business center. **Cards:** AX, MC, VI. **Free Special Amenities:** continental breakfast and local telephone calls. *(See color ad on insert)*

METTERRA HOTEL ON WHYTE   *Book at AAA.com*
Phone: (780)465-8150   **9**

Small-scale Hotel
$170-$350 All Year

Address: 10454 82nd Ave (Whyte Ave) T6E 4Z7 **Location:** Just e of 105th St. **Facility:** 98 units. 92 one-bedroom standard units. 6 one-bedroom suites with whirlpools. 8 stories, interior corridors. **Bath:** combo or shower only. **Parking:** valet and street. **Terms:** cancellation fee imposed. **Amenities:** CD players, high-speed Internet, voice mail, honor bars, irons, hair dryers. *Some:* safes. **Leisure Activities:** exercise room. **Guest Services:** valet laundry. **Business Services:** meeting rooms, PC. **Cards:** AX, MC, VI.

THE SUTTON PLACE HOTEL, EDMONTON   *Book at AAA.com*
Phone: (780)428-7111   **1**

Large-scale Hotel
$325-$355 All Year

Address: 10235 101st St T5J 3E9 **Location:** 102nd Ave at 101st St. **Facility:** 313 one-bedroom standard units. 26 stories, interior corridors. **Parking:** on-site (fee) and valet. **Terms:** cancellation fee imposed. **Amenities:** video games (fee), voice mail, irons, hair dryers. *Some:* CD players, high-speed Internet, dual phone lines, safes. **Dining:** Capitals Restaurant, see separate listing. **Pool(s):** heated indoor. **Leisure Activities:** saunas, whirlpool, wireless Internet. **Guest Services:** valet laundry. **Business Services:** conference facilities, business center. **Cards:** AX, DC, MC, VI.

UNION BANK INN   *Book great rates at AAA.com*
Phone: (780)423-3600   **4**

(CAA) (SAVE)

Small-scale Hotel
$99-$409 All Year

Address: 10053 Jasper Ave T5J 1S5 **Location:** Corner of 101st St. **Facility:** Smoke free premises. 34 units. 33 one-bedroom standard units, some with whirlpools. 1 one-bedroom suite with whirlpool. 3-5 stories, interior corridors. **Parking:** on-site. **Terms:** cancellation fee imposed. **Amenities:** high-speed Internet, voice mail, irons, hair dryers. **Dining:** Madison's Grill, see separate listing. **Leisure Activities:** limited exercise equipment. **Guest Services:** valet laundry. **Business Services:** meeting rooms, PC. **Cards:** AX, DC, DS, MC, VI. **Free Special Amenities:** full breakfast and high-speed Internet.

(See map and index starting on p. 431)

VARSCONA HOTEL ON WHYTE   *Book at AAA.com*   Phone: (780)434-6111   **8**

Small-scale Hotel
$150-$300 All Year

Address: 8208 106th St T6E 6R9 **Location:** Corner of 82nd Ave (Whyte Ave) and 106th St. **Facility:** Smoke free premises. 89 units. 85 one-bedroom standard units. 4 one-bedroom suites. 6 stories, interior corridors. *Bath:* combo or shower only. **Parking:** on-site and valet, winter plug-ins. **Terms:** cancellation fee imposed. **Amenities:** CD players, high-speed Internet, voice mail, irons, hair dryers. *Some:* DVD players, dual phone lines. **Leisure Activities:** exercise room. **Guest Services:** valet laundry, wireless Internet. **Business Services:** meeting rooms, PC. **Cards:** AX, CB, DC, MC, VI.

THE WESTIN EDMONTON   *Book great rates at AAA.com*   Phone: (780)426-3636   **3**

Large-scale Hotel
$119-$399 All Year

Address: 10135 100th St T5J 0N7 **Location:** 101st Ave at 100th St. **Facility:** Smoke free premises. 413 units. 402 one-bedroom standard units. 8 one- and 3 two-bedroom suites. 20 stories, interior corridors. **Parking:** on-site (fee) and valet. **Terms:** cancellation fee imposed. **Amenities:** video games (fee), dual phone lines, voice mail, honor bars, irons, hair dryers. *Some:* fax. **Dining:** Pradera Cafe, see separate listing. **Pool(s):** heated indoor. **Leisure Activities:** saunas, whirlpool, exercise room. **Guest Services:** valet laundry, wireless Internet. **Business Services:** conference facilities, business center. **Cards:** AX, CB, DC, DS, JC, MC, VI. **Free Special Amenities:** newspaper.

WESTIN
HOTELS & RESORTS

AAA Benefit:
Members get up to 15% off, plus Starwood Preferred Guest® bonuses.

— WHERE TO DINE —

BEE-BELL HEALTH BAKERY   Phone: 780/439-3247   **36**

Bakery/Desserts
$2-$9

Although there are no places to sit and eat, the bakery is a favorite for those planning a picnic in the park or a festival outing. Patrons step up to the counter to order a variety of breads, quiches and delectable desserts. **Reservations:** not accepted. **Hours:** 9 am-5:30 pm, Sat from 8 am. Closed major holidays; also Sun. **Address:** 10416 80th Ave T6E 5T7 **Location:** E at 80th Ave to 104th St. **Parking:** street. **Cards:** MC, VI.

BILLINGSGATE SEAFOOD MARKET LIGHTHOUSE CAFE   Phone: 780/433-0091   **37**

Seafood
$8-$40

Patrons walk past displays of fresh seafood to the lively, bright restaurant, where seafood lovers indulge in jewels from the ocean. Fresh halibut, salmon, trout and a catch of the day are sure to delight, as does traditional fish and chips. Desserts made on the premises are well worth saving room for. The cafe-style restaurant bustles at lunchtime, and a distinctive East Coast flair characterizes the decor. Casual dress. **Bar:** Full bar. **Reservations:** suggested. **Hours:** 11:30 am-9 pm, Fri & Sat-10 pm, Sun 11 am-8 pm. Closed: 12/25. **Address:** 7331 104th St T6E 4B9 **Location:** Corner of 73rd Ave and 104th St. **Parking:** on-site. **Cards:** MC, VI.

BISTRO PRAHA   Phone: 780/424-4218   **8**

Czechoslovak
$6-$20

Guests can enjoy meals at a leisurely pace, while relaxing in antique furniture and appreciating the sounds of classical music. The warm, inviting decor creates a pleasant atmosphere. On the menu are hearty portions of steak tartare, various schnitzels and a selection of crepes for dessert. Casual dress. **Bar:** Full bar. **Reservations:** suggested. **Hours:** 11 am-1 am, Sat noon-2 am, Sun 4 pm-midnight. Closed major holidays. **Address:** 10168 100A St T5J 0R6 **Location:** Just n of Jasper Ave. **Parking:** street. **Cards:** AX, DC, MC, VI.

BLOCK 1912   Phone: 780/433-6575   **32**

Bakery/Desserts
$8-$12

There's a bit of an interesting mix to the decor of this European feeling dining room, and it could be the decidedly Indian artwork that hangs on the walls. Primarily a coffee shop, the large space is perfectly placed as a pit stop among the shops of Whyte Avenue. Offerings include a decent selection of sandwiches, in-house-made gelato and freshly baked sweet and savory baked goods. Casual dress. **Reservations:** not accepted. **Hours:** 9 am-11 pm, Fri & Sat-midnight, Sun 10 am-11 pm. Closed: 12/25. **Address:** 10361 82nd Ave NW T6E 1Z9 **Location:** Jct Calgary Tr NW; on historic Whyte Ave. **Parking:** street. **Cards:** AX, MC, VI.

BLUE PLATE DINER   Phone: 780/429-0740   **13**

Vegetarian
$8-$12

In the heart of downtown, the eatery, which sports comfortable but eclectic decor, including exposed brick walls and bright paint, is as far from a classic diner as it gets. Offering an ever-changing menu, the kitchen produces a good selection of vegetarian dishes, as well as a variety of creative takes on down-home comfort food. Casual dress. **Bar:** Full bar. **Reservations:** not accepted. **Hours:** 11 am-10 pm, Sat from 9 am, Sun 9 am-2 pm. Closed major holidays. **Address:** 10145 104th St T5J 0Z9 **Location:** Just s of Jasper Ave. **Parking:** street. **Cards:** AX, MC, VI.

BUA THAI RESTAURANT   Phone: 780/482-2277   **19**

Thai
$9-$18

For fantastic Thai food, diners need look no further than this family-run restaurant just south of Jasper Avenue. Because locals frequent this place, it's a good idea to make a reservation. Dishes range from pad thai to various curries, and all are sure to please. Casual dress. **Bar:** Full bar. **Reservations:** suggested. **Hours:** 11 am-9:30 pm, Sat 10 am-5 pm. Closed major holidays; also Sun. **Address:** 10049 113th St NW T5K 1N9 **Location:** Just s of Jasper Ave at 113th St. **Parking:** on-site. **Cards:** AX, MC, VI.

CAFE MOSAICS   Phone: 780/433-9702   **27**

Vegetarian
$5-$11

An eclectic and funky respite for vegetarians, the small cafe is along trendy Whyte Avenue. Home-cooked meals, including a large selection of vegetarian entrees, are served in a cozy setting. Whether a hearty bowl of soup, a distinctive pizza or an entree-size spinach salad, the servings are large and a good value for the dollar. This place is nice for spending hours catching up with a friend over a cup of tea. Casual dress. **Bar:** Full bar. **Reservations:** not accepted. **Hours:** 9 am-9 pm, Sun 11 am-2:30 pm. Closed major holidays. **Address:** 10844 82nd Ave T6E 2B3 **Location:** 82nd Ave (Whyte Ave), just e of 109th St. **Parking:** street. **Cards:** AX, DC, DS, MC, VI.

(See map and index starting on p. 431)

CAFE SELECT

Continental
$8-$20

Phone: 780/428-1629   ⑳

Patrons unwind in a comfortable, intimate atmosphere while contemplating a menu of traditional favorites, such as rack of lamb and beef tenderloin, as well as lighter fare ranging from salads to fondue. Patio dining is available in season. **Bar:** Full bar. **Reservations:** suggested. **Hours:** 11:30 am-midnight, Thurs & Fri-2 am, Sat 5 pm-2 am, Sun 5 pm-midnight. Closed: 1/1, 12/25. **Address:** 10018-106 St T5J 1G1 **Location:** Just s of Jasper Ave. **Parking:** street. **Cards:** AX, CB, DC, MC, VI.

CAPITALS RESTAURANT

Canadian
$12-$30

Phone: 780/428-7111   ③

The upscale restaurant prepares selections of regional cuisine. Service is fine and friendly. Casual dress. **Bar:** Full bar. **Reservations:** suggested. **Hours:** 6-10:30 am, 11:30-2:30 & 5:30-11 pm. **Address:** 10235 101st St T5J 3E9 **Location:** 102nd Ave at 101st St; in The Sutton Place Hotel, Edmonton. **Parking:** on-site (fee) and valet. **Cards:** AX, CB, DC, DS, JC, MC, VI.

CHANCE

Regional
Continental
$9-$40

Phone: 780/424-0400   ⑨

In the heart of downtown, the upscale, contemporary restaurant prepares a good selection of entrees with a regional flair. The intimate atmosphere incorporates booths, as well as a New York-style long bar. The dedicated staff provides attentive service and delivers tasty entrees ranging from salmon to risotto to maybe even venison. **Bar:** Full bar. **Reservations:** suggested. **Hours:** 11 am-10 pm, Sat from 5 pm. Closed major holidays; also Sun. **Address:** 10155 101st St, Commerce Place T5J 4G8 **Location:** Just n of Jasper Ave at 101st St. **Parking:** on-site (fee). **Cards:** AX, DC, MC, VI.

CHARACTERS

Canadian
$14-$39

Phone: 780/421-4100   ④

Polished hardwood floors, brick walls and a glimmering open concept kitchen set the tone for this fresh contemporary restaurant. The seasonally inspired menu changes, but can include a variety of offerings including duck, lamb, Alberta pork and beef. An impressive wine list will ensure a memorable experience. Dressy casual. **Bar:** Full bar. **Reservations:** suggested. **Hours:** 11 am-2 & 5:30-10 pm, Sat from 5:30 pm, Mon 11 am-2 pm. Closed major holidays; also Sun. **Address:** 10257 105th St T5J 1E3 **Location:** Just n of jct 102nd Ave and 105th St. **Parking:** on-site. **Cards:** AX, DC, MC, VI.

CALL 🚻Ⓜ

CHIANTI

Italian
$7-$19

Phone: 780/439-9829   ㉞

In a former post office building on trendy Whyte Avenue, the lively, long-established restaurant serves entrees of pasta, veal, seafood and chicken, and most menu items can be served in half portions. This place is ideal for large gatherings or an evening out in a festive atmosphere. Casual dress. **Bar:** Full bar. **Reservations:** accepted. **Hours:** 11 am-11 pm, Fri & Sat-midnight. Closed: 1/1, 12/25. **Address:** 10501 82nd Ave NW T6E 2A3 **Location:** Corner of 105th St. **Parking:** street. **Cards:** AX, DC, DS, MC, VI.

THE COPPER POT RESTAURANT

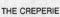
International
$8-$42

Phone: 780/452-7800   ㉔

Near the legislative buildings and overlooking the river valley, the intimate restaurant is tucked away on the ground floor of an office tower. The innovative and eclectic menu lists several pasta dishes, Alberta bison and seafood selections, all plated in hearty portions. Service is relaxed yet professional. Casual dress. **Bar:** Full bar. **Reservations:** suggested. **Hours:** 11 am-2:30 & 4-close, Sat from 4 pm. Closed: Sun. **Address:** #101, 9707-110th St T5K 2L9 **Location:** From 109th St, just w at 97th Ave (one way street), then just n. **Parking:** on-site. **Cards:** AX, DC, MC, VI.

THE CREPERIE

French
$10-$23

Phone: 780/420-6656   ⑤

Patrons can prepare themselves for delectable French cuisine—including outstanding stuffed crepes—in the cozy restaurant, just below street level. Menu options, such as seafood and vegetarian dishes, are varied enough to tempt any palate. Casual dress. **Bar:** Full bar. **Reservations:** suggested. **Hours:** 11:30 am-10 pm, Fri-11 pm, Sat 5 pm-11 pm, Sun 5 pm-9 pm. Closed: 12/25, 12/26; also Mon. **Address:** 10220 103rd St T5J 0Y8 **Location:** Just n of 102nd Ave. **Parking:** on-site (fee) and street. **Cards:** AX, DC, MC, VI.

DOAN'S RESTAURANT

Vietnamese
$7-$18

Phone: 780/424-3034   ⑭

Visitors to the simple, neatly furnished and spacious dining room can enjoy classic Vietnamese dishes, such as hearty rice and noodle soup. Several meat dishes are expertly spiced by the restaurant's signature sauces. **Bar:** Full bar. **Reservations:** suggested. **Hours:** 11 am-10 pm, Fri & Sat-11 pm. Closed: 12/25. **Address:** 10130 107th St NW T5J 1J4 **Location:** Just n of Jasper Ave at 107th St. **Parking:** on-site. **Cards:** AX, DC, MC, VI.

THE FREE PRESS BISTRO

Deli/Subs
Sandwiches
$8-$22

Phone: 780/497-7784   ㉑

On the back end of the Holiday Inn Express hotel, this quiet and casual restaurant seems miles away from the hustle and bustle of nearby Jasper Avenue. Offerings include a good selection of paninis and in-house-made soups. A throwback to the days when newspapers were the kings of media, this place imports syrups for its delicious egg custards directly from New York. Casual dress. **Bar:** Full bar. **Reservations:** accepted. **Hours:** 11 am-10 pm, Sun-9 pm. Closed major holidays. **Address:** 10014 104th St, #80 T5J 0Z1 **Location:** Centre; attached to Holiday Inn Express Edmonton-Downtown. **Parking:** street. **Cards:** MC, VI.

CALL 🚻Ⓜ

FRENCH MEADOW ARTISAN BAKERY CAFE

Bakery/Desserts
$5-$10

Phone: 780/414-6089   ⑮

After a relaxing stroll along Jasper Avenue, one of the comfortable chairs at this neighborhood-style bakery is a welcomed change. This place is well known among local office workers for its soups and sandwiches, which are made with varied artisan breads. Casual dress. **Reservations:** not accepted. **Hours:** 7 am-midnight, Sat & Sun from 7:30 am. Closed major holidays. **Address:** 11212 Jasper Ave T5K 2V2 **Location:** Jct 112th St NW. **Parking:** street. **Cards:** AX, MC, VI.

THE FUNKY PICKLE PIZZA CO

Pizza
$4-$18

Phone: 780/433-3865   ㉝

This small pizza bar will do the trick for hungry folks looking for a quick bite to eat. Guests can order eclectic and designer pizza toppings on whole wheat crust; the large slices are sure to satisfy any appetite. Seating here is limited, so many opt to get their meal to go. Casual dress. **Reservations:** not accepted. **Hours:** 11 am-midnight, Thurs-Sat to 3:30 am. Closed: 12/25. **Address:** 10440 82nd Ave NW T6E 1Z9 **Location:** Jct 104th St; on historic Whyte Ave. **Parking:** street. **Cards:** AX, MC, VI.

(See map and index starting on p. 431)

HARDWARE GRILL

Regional
Canadian
$28-$49

Phone: 780/423-0969 ⑩

Superb service, fine surroundings and a wonderful menu combine to create a truly memorable dining experience in the former hardware store. The warehouse-like dining room is open and airy, and there are hints of history throughout. Representative of seasonally inspired Canadian cuisine are such choices as bison, duck sausage and cedar-planked salmon. But the grand finale—exceptional desserts, including warm gingerbread cake—will make guests want to come back again. Dressy casual. **Bar:** Full bar. **Reservations:** suggested. **Hours:** 5 pm-9:30 pm, Fri & Sat-10 pm. Closed major holidays; also Sun. **Address:** 9698 Jasper Ave T5H 3V5 **Location:** Corner of 97th St. **Parking:** street. **Cards:** AX, DC, MC, VI.

THE HARVEST ROOM

Canadian
$16-$42

Phone: 780/424-5181 ⑱

The atmosphere is warm and vibrant in the elegant surroundings of this restaurant. Views of the North Saskatchewan River are beautiful. Creative Canadian Prairie cuisine is prepared in the open-concept kitchen. Among tempting entrees are preparations of Alberta beef and venison. Professional, upscale service complements the delicious, upscale food presentations. Dressy casual. **Bar:** Full bar. **Reservations:** suggested. **Hours:** 6:30 am-10 pm, Sat & Sun from 7 am. **Address:** 10065 100th St T5J 0N6 **Location:** Just s of Jasper Ave; in The Fairmont Hotel Macdonald. **Parking:** valet. **Cards:** AX, DC, DS, JC, MC, VI.

CALL ♿M

IL PORTICO

Italian
$10-$30

Menu on AAA.com   **Phone: 780/424-0707** ㉒

A popular spot with the business crowd, the innovative downtown restaurant has been recognized for its notable wine selection. Among offerings on the seasonally inspired menus are beef tenderloin and various creative pasta dishes. Downstairs is a large wine cellar, suitable for small dinner gatherings. Casual dress. **Bar:** Full bar. **Reservations:** suggested. **Hours:** 11:30 am-2:30 & 5:30-10:30 pm, Sat from 5:30 pm. Closed major holidays; also Sun. **Address:** 10012 107th St T5J 1J2 **Location:** Corner of 100th Ave and 107th St. **Parking:** on-site. **Cards:** AX, DC, MC, VI.

JOEY TOMATO'S

Mediterranean
$10-$29

Phone: 780/420-1996

The cuisine blends Mediterranean and Asian cooking styles and emphasizes finger foods for sharing. Those who aren't big fans of tapas can consider full meal offerings centered on steaks and chops. Casual dress. **Bar:** Full bar. **Hours:** 11:30 am-1 am, Sun-midnight. Closed: 12/25. **Address:** 11228 Jasper Ave T5K 2V2 **Location:** At 112th St NW. **Parking:** on-site. **Cards:** AX, MC, VI.

KHAZANA

Indian
$10-$20

Phone: 780/702-0330 ⑪

Khazana's features an authentic, tasty tandoori cuisine of papadams, fresh Nan bread, peshawari kebab (lamb), boti kebab (prime beef) and murgh tandoori (chicken). The inviting, upscale decor includes original artwork from New Delhi and costumed servers. Casual dress. **Bar:** Full bar. **Reservations:** suggested. **Hours:** 11:30 am-2 & 5-9:30 pm, Fri-10:30 pm, Sat 5 pm-10:30 pm, Sun 5 pm-9:30 pm. Closed major holidays. **Address:** 10177 107 St T5J 1J5 **Location:** Corner of 102nd Ave. **Parking:** street. **Cards:** AX, DC, MC, VI.

THE KING & I

Thai
$7-$17

Phone: 780/433-2222 ㉙

Zesty vegetarian, meat, seafood and poultry dishes provide sensational, savory variety at the pleasant southside curry house, just off Whyte Avenue. Steaming regional Thai curries are an aromatic and tasty choice to enjoy with friends. Casual dress. **Bar:** Full bar. **Reservations:** suggested. **Hours:** 11:30 am-10:30 pm, Fri-11:30 pm, Sat 4:30 pm-11:30 pm. Closed: 12/25, 12/26; also Sun. **Address:** 8208 107th St T6E 6P4 **Location:** Corner of 107th St, just n of 82nd Ave (Whyte Ave). **Parking:** street. **Cards:** AX, DC, MC, VI.

LA RONDE REVOLVING RESTAURANT

Canadian
$26-$70

Phone: 780/428-6611 ㉓

The revolving rooftop restaurant offers a panoramic view of the city. The atmosphere is elegant, yet casual, and classic European cuisine reflects Asian influences. Prix fixe selections cater to couples and include aperitifs and champagnes. Dressy casual. **Bar:** Full bar. **Reservations:** suggested. **Hours:** 5:30 pm-10:30 pm, Sun also 10:30 am-2 pm. **Address:** 10111 Bellamy Hill T5J 1N7 **Location:** Jct 101st St, MacDonald Dr and Bellamy Hill; in Crowne Plaza Edmonton-Chateau Lacombe. **Parking:** on-site. **Cards:** AX, CB, DC, DS, JC, MC, VI.

L'AZIA

Asian
$10-$25

Phone: 780/990-0188 ⑥

Inside a downtown shopping center, the restaurant entices hordes of office workers on their lunch hours. Upscale Asian fusion dishes exhibit creative and unusual twists on the foods of China, Korea, Thailand and Vietnam. Dressy casual. **Bar:** Full bar. **Reservations:** accepted. **Hours:** 11 am-10 pm, Fri & Sat-11 pm. Closed major holidays. **Address:** 10200 102nd Ave T5J 4B7 **Location:** Centre; in Edmonton City Centre; beside the Bay. **Parking:** on-site (fee) and street. **Cards:** AX, MC, VI.

CALL ♿M

MADISON'S GRILL

Continental
$11-$39

Phone: 780/401-2222 ⑰

The popular, trendy restaurant features food flavored with contemporary touches. Patrons can tempt their taste buds with crab cakes prepared in tempura batter. Among the wide selection of main courses are preparations of halibut, snapper and lamb chops. After dinner, guests can relax in the small library lounge with a sumptuous dessert. Dressy casual. **Bar:** Full bar. **Reservations:** suggested. **Hours:** 7 am-10 pm, Fri-11 pm, Sat 8 am-11 & 5-11 pm, Sun 8 am-11 & 5-9 pm. **Address:** 10053 Jasper Ave T5J 1S5 **Location:** Corner of 101st St; in Union Bank Inn. **Parking:** on-site and street. **Cards:** AX, DC, DS, MC, VI.

MIKADO

Japanese
$6-$16

Phone: 780/425-8096 ②

The eatery is a hot spot for sushi in the capital city. As they enter, patrons are greeted with a warm towel and a friendly smile. The bright, contemporary dining room offers a variety of seating options—in private dining rooms, in the main restaurant or at the sushi bar. The chef is a master, creating a wide variety of sushi and sashimi. Casual dress. **Bar:** Full bar. **Reservations:** suggested. **Hours:** 11 am-10 pm, Fri & Sat-11 pm, Sun 4 pm-9 pm. Closed: 12/25. **Address:** 10350 109th St T5J 4X9 **Location:** Jct 103rd Ave and 109th St; in shopping plaza. **Parking:** on-site. **Cards:** AX, MC, VI.

CALL ♿M

(See map and index starting on p. 431)

NEW ASIAN VILLAGE
East Indian
$8-$25

Phone: 780/433-3804 ㉕

East Indian cuisine is served in a cozy maharajah room or in the main dining room, which affords views of the city. Sounds of Indian music and scents of curry pique the senses, arousing an appetite for dishes such as tasty tandoori chicken, goat, lamb and vegetarian specialties. Casual dress. **Bar:** Full bar. **Reservations:** suggested. **Hours:** 11 am-2 & 5-10 pm, Fri & Sat-11 pm, Sun 5 pm-10 pm. Closed: 12/25. **Address:** 10143 Saskatchewan Dr T2E 1V6 **Location:** From 109th St, just e. **Parking:** on-site. **Cards:** AX, DS, MC, VI.

O'BYRNE'S IRISH PUB
Irish
$8-$15

Phone: 780/414-6766 ㉛

In a trendy area, the Irish pub welcomes travelers from around the globe. The restaurant offers a lively atmosphere, friendly service and live entertainment, as well as all-day Irish breakfast and an excellent selection of Irish beers on tap. Casual dress. **Bar:** Full bar. **Hours:** 11 am-2 am. Closed: 12/25. **Address:** 10616 82nd Ave (Whyte Ave) T6E 2A7 **Location:** Corner of 106th St. **Parking:** on-site (fee) and street. **Cards:** AX, DC, MC, VI.

PACKRAT LOUIE'S KITCHEN & BAR
Continental
$9-$30

Phone: 780/433-0123 ㉖

In the heart of Old Strathcona, the bistro-style restaurant prepares fresh market cuisine. Guests can choose from pizza made in a wood-burning oven, organic chicken breasts or fresh fish and weekly specials. Dessert is a must. The Swiss owner is known for his fine desserts and Swiss chocolate truffles. Casual dress. **Bar:** Full bar. **Reservations:** suggested. **Hours:** 11:30 am-10 pm, Fri & Sat-11 pm. Closed major holidays; also Sun & Mon. **Address:** 10335 83rd Ave T6E 2C6 **Location:** Jct 103rd St and 83rd Ave, just 1 blk n of Jasper Ave. **Parking:** on-site. **Cards:** AX, DC, MC, VI.

PRADERA CAFE
Canadian
$9-$35

Phone: 780/493-8994 ⑫

The elegant dining room invites diners to peruse an excellent menu, which blends International influences with regional ingredients. Among dishes to satisfy any appetite are superbly presented English-cut prime rib, fresh lake trout and chateaubriand. Casual dress. **Bar:** Full bar. **Reservations:** suggested. **Hours:** 6:30 am-10 pm, Sat & Sun from 7 am. **Address:** 10135 100th St T5J 0N7 **Location:** 101st St at 100th St; in The Westin Edmonton. **Parking:** on-site (fee) and valet. **Cards:** AX, DC, MC, VI.

RIC'S GRILL
Steak & Seafood
$15-$37

Phone: 780/429-4333 ⑦

"Funky and modern" describes the decor and the food at the upscale steakhouse, which bustles with activity. Reservations are definitely recommended. Steaks are well worth it, but then again, so are the salmon, chicken and pasta dishes. A wide variety of distinctive appetizers rounds out the menu. Servers are friendly and attentive. Casual dress. **Bar:** Full bar. **Reservations:** suggested. **Hours:** 11 am-10 pm, Fri & Sat-11 pm, Sun 4 pm-10 pm. Closed major holidays. **Address:** 10190 104th St T5J 1A7 **Location:** Corner of 104th St and 102nd Ave; in historic Metals Building. **Parking:** street. **Cards:** AX, MC, VI. **Historic**

CALL

RIVERSIDE BISTRO
Canadian
$10-$25

Phone: 780/945-4747 ⑯

The restaurant affords spectacular views. Guests can sit on one of the city's best and largest patios to take in sights along the river valley while savoring a glass of wine with contemporary Canadian cuisine. Inside, an upscale lobby lounge adjoins the restaurant, and the decor and service are just as upscale. Casual dress. **Bar:** Full bar. **Reservations:** suggested. **Hours:** 6:30 am-10 & 11-11 pm, Sat & Sun from 7 am. **Address:** One Thornton Ct T5J 2E7 **Location:** Just s of Jasper Ave at Thornton Ct and 99th St; in Courtyard by Marriott Edmonton. **Parking:** on-site (fee) and valet. **Cards:** AX, DC, MC, VI.

CALL

TOKYO NOODLE SHOP
Japanese
$8-$10

Phone: 780/430-0838 ㉘

On Whyte Avenue, the popular restaurant gives diners a choice of good, affordable sushi selections. Casual dress. **Bar:** Full bar. **Hours:** 11:30 am-10 pm, Thurs-Sat to 2 am. Closed: 12/25. **Address:** 10736 82nd Ave T6E 6P4 **Location:** On 82nd Ave (Whyte Ave) at 107th St. **Parking:** street. **Cards:** AX, MC, VI.

VON'S STEAK & FISH HOUSE
Steak & Seafood
$19-$40

Phone: 780/439-0041 ㉟

In Strathcona, an old part of town south of the river, the restaurant offers casual dining in a warm, quiet atmosphere. The dining room sports wood beams and a large riverstone fireplace. Beef and seafood are mainstays on a menu of choices that display Louisiana and Mediterranean influences. Casual dress. **Bar:** Full bar. **Reservations:** suggested. **Hours:** 4:30 pm-10 pm. Closed: 1/1, 12/25. **Address:** 10309 81st Ave T6E 1X3 **Location:** Just s of 82nd Ave (Whyte Ave) at 103rd St. **Parking:** street. **Cards:** AX, DC, MC, VI.

WILD TANGERINE
Asian
$13-$20

Phone: 780/429-3131 ①

Casual dress. **Bar:** Full bar. **Reservations:** not accepted. **Hours:** 11:30 am-10 pm, Fri-11:30 pm, Sat 5 pm-11:30 pm. Closed major holidays; also Sun. **Address:** 10383 112 St T5K 1M9 **Location:** Jct 104 Ave; at Coinfield Shopping Center. **Parking:** on-site. **Cards:** AX, MC, VI.

YIANNIS TAVERNA
Greek
$6-$21

Phone: 780/433-6768 ㉚

The lively, traditional restaurant is reminiscent of a cozy tavern in Greece, complete with a quaint sidewalk patio. Music, art and atmosphere combine to provide an enjoyable experience. Weekend entertainment features the hasapiko dance, belly dancing at 8:30 pm and later in the evening, the Zorba dance, in which patrons are encouraged to participate. Casual dress. **Bar:** Full bar. **Reservations:** suggested. **Hours:** 11:30 am-11 pm, Sun & Mon from 5 pm. Closed: 1/1, 3/24, 12/25. **Address:** 10444 82nd Ave NW (Whyte Ave) T6E 2A2 **Location:** Corner of 104th St. **Parking:** street. **Cards:** AX, DC, MC, VI.

EDMONTON pop. 730,372 (See map and index starting on p. 434)

──────── WHERE TO STAY ────────

BEST WESTERN CEDAR PARK INN   *Book great rates at AAA.com*

Phone: 780/434-7411

Small-scale Hotel
Rates not provided

Address: 5116 Gateway Blvd T6H 2H4 **Location:** Hwy 2 (Gateway Blvd) at 51st Ave. **Facility:** 190 units. 187 one-bedroom standard units, some with whirlpools. 3 one-bedroom suites, some with whirlpools. 5 stories, interior corridors. **Parking:** on-site, winter plug-ins. **Amenities:** video games (fee), high-speed Internet, voice mail, irons, hair dryers. *Some:* CD players, safes. **Dining:** Seasons Grill, see separate listing. **Pool(s):** heated indoor. **Leisure Activities:** limited exercise equipment. **Guest Services:** valet laundry, area transportation-West Edmonton Mall. **Business Services:** meeting rooms. **Free Special Amenities:** newspaper and high-speed Internet.

AAA Benefit:
Members save 10% everyday, plus an exclusive frequent stay program.

 / SOME UNITS FEE

BEST WESTERN NORTH EDMONTON INN & SUITES   *Book great rates at AAA.com*

Phone: (780)476-9898

Small-scale Hotel
$119-$210 All Year

Address: 13742 50th St NW T5A 4Y3 **Location:** Hwy 16 (Yellowhead Trail); 1 mi (1.6 km) n on 50th St (SR 15). **Facility:** Smoke free premises. 95 units. 56 one-bedroom standard units, some with whirlpools. 39 one-bedroom suites. 6 stories, interior corridors. *Bath:* combo or shower only. **Parking:** on-site. **Terms:** cancellation fee imposed. **Amenities:** high-speed Internet, irons, hair dryers. **Pool(s):** heated indoor. **Leisure Activities:** whirlpool. **Cards:** AX, DS, MC, VI. **Free Special Amenities: continental breakfast and high-speed Internet.**

AAA Benefit:
Members save 10% everyday, plus an exclusive frequent stay program.

CALL   / SOME UNITS

BEST WESTERN WESTWOOD INN   *Book great rates at AAA.com*

Phone: 780/483-7770   9

Small-scale Hotel
Rates not provided

Address: 18035 Stony Plain Rd T5S 1B2 **Location:** Hwy 16A (Stony Plain Rd) at 180th St. **Facility:** 169 one-bedroom standard units, some with whirlpools. 3-6 stories, interior corridors. **Parking:** on-site, winter plug-ins. **Amenities:** video games (fee), voice mail, safes, irons, hair dryers. *Some:* high-speed Internet. **Pool(s):** heated indoor. **Leisure Activities:** whirlpool, steamroom, squash court, exercise room. *Fee:* game room. **Guest Services:** valet and coin laundry, beauty salon. **Business Services:** conference facilities, business center. **Free Special Amenities: room upgrade (subject to availability with advance reservations) and high-speed Internet.** *(See color ad below)*

AAA Benefit:
Members save 10% everyday, plus an exclusive frequent stay program.

  CALL   / SOME UNITS

CAMPUS TOWER SUITE HOTEL   *Book at AAA.com*

Phone: (780)439-6060   18

Condominium
$119-$249 All Year

Address: 11145 87th Ave T6G 0Y1 **Location:** At 111th St and 87th Ave. Located near University and Hospital campuses. **Facility:** 90 units. 74 one- and 16 two-bedroom suites, some with efficiencies or kitchens. 16 stories, interior corridors. **Parking:** on-site, winter plug-ins. **Terms:** cancellation fee imposed. **Amenities:** voice mail, irons, hair dryers. *Some:* CD players, high-speed Internet, dual phone lines. **Leisure Activities:** exercise room. **Guest Services:** valet and coin laundry, area transportation. **Business Services:** meeting rooms. *Fee:* administrative services, PC. **Cards:** AX, MC, VI.

 / SOME UNITS

──── ▼ *See AAA listing above* ▼ ────

(See map and index starting on p. 434)

CHATEAU LOUIS HOTEL & CONFERENCE CENTRE
Phone: (780)452-7770   **4**

 CAA SAVE

◆◆ ◆◆

Small-scale Hotel
$119-$209 All Year

Address: 11727 Kingsway T5G 3A1 **Location:** On Kingsway and 117th St. **Facility:** 141 units. 139 one-bedroom standard units, some with whirlpools. 2 one-bedroom suites, some with whirlpools. 3 stories, interior corridors. *Bath:* combo or shower only. **Parking:** on-site, winter plug-ins. **Amenities:** high-speed Internet, voice mail. *Some:* CD players, irons, hair dryers. **Dining:** nightclub. **Leisure Activities:** pool tables, gazebo, exercise room. **Guest Services:** valet laundry, airport transportation-City Centre Airport, area transportation-train station. **Business Services:** conference facilities, PC (fee). **Cards:** AX, DC, MC, VI. **Free Special Amenities: full breakfast and high-speed Internet.** *(See color ad below)*

COMFORT INN WEST
Book great rates at AAA.com   Phone: (780)484-4415   **12**

CAA SAVE

◆◆ ◆◆

Small-scale Hotel
$109-$154 All Year

Address: 17610 100th Ave T5S 1S9 **Location:** At 176th St. **Facility:** 100 one-bedroom standard units. 2 stories (no elevator), interior corridors. **Parking:** on-site, winter plug-ins. **Terms:** cancellation fee imposed. **Amenities:** irons, hair dryers. **Guest Services:** valet laundry, wireless Internet. **Business Services:** meeting rooms. **Cards:** AX, DC, DS, MC, VI. *(See color ad on insert)*

CONTINENTAL INN
Phone: (780)484-7751   **10**

CAA SAVE

◆◆ ◆◆

Small-scale Hotel
$110-$135 All Year

Address: 16625 Stony Plain Rd T5P 4A8 **Location:** On Hwy 16A (Stony Plain Rd) at 166th St. **Facility:** 100 one-bedroom standard units, some with whirlpools. 6 stories, interior corridors. **Parking:** on-site, winter plug-ins. **Terms:** 6 day cancellation notice-fee imposed. **Amenities:** high-speed Internet (fee), voice mail, hair dryers. *Some:* irons. **Dining:** 2 restaurants. **Guest Services:** valet and coin laundry. **Business Services:** meeting rooms, PC (fee). **Cards:** AX, CB, DC, DS, JC, MC, VI. **Free Special Amenities: local telephone calls and high-speed Internet.**

DAYS INN & SUITES WEST EDMONTON
Book great rates at AAA.com   Phone: (780)444-4440   **15**

CAA SAVE

◆◆ ◆◆

Small-scale Hotel
$129-$144 All Year

Address: 10010 179A St T5S 2T1 **Location:** On 100th Ave, just w of 178th St. **Facility:** Smoke free premises. 108 units. 84 one-bedroom standard units. 24 one-bedroom suites with efficiencies, some with whirlpools. 4 stories, interior corridors. **Parking:** on-site, winter plug-ins. **Terms:** check-in 4 pm. **Amenities:** high-speed Internet, dual phone lines, voice mail, irons, hair dryers. *Some:* CD players. **Dining:** ConYac's Bar & Grill, see separate listing. **Leisure Activities:** whirlpool, exercise room. **Guest Services:** valet laundry, area transportation-West Edmonton Mall. **Business Services:** meeting rooms, business center. **Cards:** AX, CB, MC, VI. *(See color ad p 447 & p 445)*

▼ See AAA listing above ▼

(See map and index starting on p. 434)

DELTA EDMONTON SOUTH HOTEL AND CONFERENCE CENTRE   *Book great rates at AAA.com*   **Phone:** (780)434-6415   **24**

Large-scale Hotel
$160-$270 All Year

Address: 4404 Gateway Blvd T6H 5C2 **Location:** Jct Calgary Trail (Hwy 2) and Whitemud Dr. **Facility:** 237 units. 229 one-bedroom standard units. 8 one-bedroom suites, some with whirlpools. 11 stories, interior corridors. **Parking:** on-site and valet, winter plug-ins. **Terms:** cancellation fee imposed. **Amenities:** video games (fee), high-speed Internet, voice mail, irons, hair dryers. **Pool(s):** heated indoor. **Leisure Activities:** whirlpool, exercise room. **Guest Services:** valet laundry. **Business Services:** conference facilities, business center. **Cards:** AX, DC, DS, JC, MC, VI.

EDMONTON MARRIOTT AT RIVER CREE RESORT   *Book great rates at AAA.com*   **Phone:** 780/484-2121

Large-scale Hotel
$176-$196 All Year

Address: 300 E Lapotac Blvd T7X 3Y3 **Location:** 1 mi (1.6 km) w of jct Hwy 216 (Anthony Hendoy) and Whitemud Dr W. **Facility:** Smoke free premises. 255 units. 247 one-bedroom standard units. 8 one-bedroom suites. 9 stories, interior corridors. *Bath:* combo or shower only. **Parking:** on-site and valet. **Amenities:** high-speed Internet (fee), voice mail, irons, hair dryers. **Dining:** Sage Restaurant, see separate listing. **Pool(s):** outdoor. **Leisure Activities:** whirlpool, exercise room. **Guest Services:** valet laundry, area transportation. **Business Services:** conference facilities, business center. **Cards:** AX, DC, MC, VI.

Marriott
HOTELS & RESORTS

AAA Benefit:
Members save 5% off of the best available rate.

EXECUTIVE ROYAL INN WEST EDMONTON   *Book at AAA.com*   **Phone:** (780)484-6000   **13**

Small-scale Hotel
$105 All Year

Address: 10010 178th St T5S 1T3 **Location:** Corner of 178th St and 100th Ave. **Facility:** 238 units. 233 one-bedroom standard units, some with whirlpools. 5 one-bedroom suites with whirlpools. 4 stories, interior corridors. *Bath:* combo or shower only. **Parking:** on-site, winter plug-ins. **Terms:** check-in 4 pm. **Amenities:** video games (fee), voice mail, irons, hair dryers. *Some:* high-speed Internet. **Leisure Activities:** whirlpools, exercise room. **Fee:** game room. **Guest Services:** valet laundry, wireless Internet. **Business Services:** conference facilities, PC. **Cards:** AX, DC, MC, VI.

FOUR POINTS BY SHERATON EDMONTON SOUTH   *Book great rates at AAA.com*   **Phone:** (780)465-7931   **20**

Large-scale Hotel
$205-$225 All Year

Address: 7230 Argyll Rd T6C 4A6 **Location:** Hwy 2 (Gateway Blvd), 2.3 mi (3.7 km) e at 63rd Ave (which becomes Argyll Rd); at 75th St. **Facility:** 139 units. 109 one-bedroom standard units, some with whirlpools. 30 one-bedroom suites. 7 stories, interior corridors. **Parking:** on-site, winter plug-ins. **Amenities:** high-speed Internet, voice mail, irons, hair dryers. **Dining:** 2 restaurants. **Pool(s):** heated indoor. **Leisure Activities:** whirlpool, exercise room. **Guest Services:** valet laundry. **Business Services:** conference facilities, business center. **Cards:** AX, DC, DS, MC, VI. *(See color ad p 446)*

FOUR POINTS
BY SHERATON

AAA Benefit:
Members get up to 15% off, plus Starwood Preferred Guest® bonuses.

▼ See AAA listing p 444 ▼

(See map and index starting on p. 434)

GLENORA BED & BREAKFAST INN

▼▼▼▼
Bed & Breakfast
$90-$175 All Year

Phone: 780/488-6766 [6]

Address: 12327 102nd Ave T5N 0L8 **Location:** At 124th St. Located in the Glenora District (art gallery district). **Facility:** Built in 1912, this restored B&B is partly furnished with antiques and offers a variety of guest rooms ranging from apartment-style to traditional. Smoke free premises. 25 units. 17 one-bedroom standard units. 8 one-bedroom suites, some with kitchens. 3 stories (no elevator), interior corridors. *Bath:* some shared or private, combo or shower only. **Parking:** on-site, winter plug-ins. **Terms:** office hours 7 am-9 pm. **Amenities:** video library, hair dryers. *Some:* high-speed Internet, irons. **Dining:** Glenora Grill, see separate listing. **Guest Services:** coin laundry. **Cards:** AX, MC, VI.

⏶ ✕ / SOME UNITS VCR 🕿 🖥 📼

GREENWOOD HOTEL & SUITES   *Book great rates at AAA.com*

▼▼▼
Small-scale Hotel
$129-$249 All Year

Phone: (780)431-1100 [23]

Address: 4485 Gateway Blvd T6H 5C3 **Location:** Hwy 2 (Gateway Blvd), just n of Whitemud Dr. **Facility:** 224 units. 221 one-bedroom standard units. 3 one-bedroom suites, some with whirlpools. 6 stories, interior corridors. *Bath:* combo or shower only. **Parking:** on-site, winter plug-ins. **Amenities:** voice mail, irons, hair dryers. *Fee:* video games, high-speed Internet. **Leisure Activities:** whirlpool, steamroom, exercise room. **Business Services:** valet laundry. **Business Services:** conference facilities, PC (fee). **Cards:** AX, CB, DC, DS, JC, MC, VI.

(ASK) S🔊 ⏶ 🍽 🍷 CALL 🅼 ✕ 🎥 🖥 / SOME UNITS FEE 🐾 ✕ 🖥 📼

HILTON GARDEN INN-WEST EDMONTON   *Book great rates at AAA.com*

▼▼▼
Small-scale Hotel
$169-$249 All Year

Phone: (780)443-2233 [7]

Address: 17610 Stony Plain Rd T5S 1A2 **Location:** From 176th St, just w. **Facility:** Smoke free premises. 160 units. 155 one-bedroom standard units. 5 one-bedroom suites with whirlpools. 6 stories, interior corridors. **Parking:** on-site, winter plug-ins. **Amenities:** video games (fee), high-speed Internet, dual phone lines, voice mail, irons, hair dryers. **Pool(s):** heated indoor. **Leisure Activities:** whirlpool, exercise room. **Guest Services:** valet and coin laundry. **Business Services:** meeting rooms, business center. **Cards:** AX, DC, DS, JC, MC, VI.

(ASK) ⏶ 🍽 🍷 🏊 ✕ 🎥 🖥 📼 ☕

HOLIDAY INN CONVENTION CENTRE (S.E. EDMONTON)   *Book great rates at AAA.com*

(AAA) (SAVE)
▼▼▼
Small-scale Hotel
$145-$175 All Year

Phone: (780)468-5400 [19]

Address: 4520 76th Ave T6B 0A5 **Location:** Hwy 14, just s via 50th St exit, then just e. **Facility:** 93 one-bedroom standard units, some with whirlpools. 6 stories, interior corridors. **Parking:** on-site, winter plug-ins. **Amenities:** high-speed Internet (fee), dual phone lines, voice mail, irons, hair dryers. **Pool(s):** heated indoor. **Leisure Activities:** whirlpool, steamroom, exercise room. **Guest Services:** valet laundry, area transportation-West Edmonton Mall. **Business Services:** conference facilities, PC. **Cards:** AX, DC, DS, MC, VI. **Free Special Amenities:** newspaper and room upgrade (subject to availability with advance reservations).

S🔊 ✈ ⏶ 🍷 CALL 🅼 🏊 🐾 ✕ 🎥 🖥 / SOME UNITS FEE 🐾 ✕ 🖥 📼

HOLIDAY INN EDMONTON-THE PALACE   *Book great rates at AAA.com*

▼▼▼
Small-scale Hotel
Rates not provided

Phone: 780/438-1222 [25]

Address: 4235 Gateway Blvd T6J 5H2 **Location:** Just s of Whitemud Dr. **Facility:** 137 units. 110 one- and 14 two-bedroom standard units, some with whirlpools. 13 one-bedroom suites. 5 stories, interior corridors. *Bath:* combo or shower only. **Parking:** on-site, winter plug-ins. **Amenities:** video games (fee), high-speed Internet, dual phone lines, voice mail, irons, hair dryers. **Leisure Activities:** whirlpools, exercise room. **Guest Services:** valet laundry, area transportation, beauty salon, wireless Internet. **Business Services:** conference facilities.

✈ ⏶ 🍷 🎥 🖥 / SOME UNITS FEE 🐾 ✕ 🖥 📼

▼ See AAA listing p 445 ▼

(See map and index starting on p. 434)

HOLIDAY INN EXPRESS HOTEL & SUITES EDMONTON
Book great rates at AAA.com **Phone:** 780/483-4000 **14**

CAA SAVE

Small-scale Hotel
Rates not provided

Address: 10017 179A St T5S 2L4 **Location:** On 100th Ave, just w of 178th St. **Facility:** 102 units. 68 one-bedroom standard units, some with whirlpools. 34 one-bedroom suites, some with whirlpools. 4 stories, interior corridors. **Parking:** on-site, winter plug-ins. **Terms:** check-in 4 pm. **Amenities:** video games (fee), dual phone lines, voice mail, irons, hair dryers. *Some:* CD players. **Pool(s):** heated indoor. **Leisure Activities:** whirlpool, steamroom, exercise room. *Fee:* game room. **Guest Services:** valet and coin laundry, area transportation (fee)-West Edmonton Mall, wireless Internet. **Business Services:** meeting rooms. *(See color ad below)*

HOTEL SELKIRK
Phone: (780)496-7227 **21**

Small-scale Hotel
$175-$225 5/16-9/1

Address: 7000 143rd St T5J 2R7 **Location:** From Whitemud Dr, exit Fox Dr, follow signs. Located in Fort Edmonton Park. **Facility:** Smoke free premises. 30 units. 28 one-bedroom standard units. 2 one-bedroom suites. 2 stories, interior corridors. **Parking:** on-site and valet. **Terms:** open 5/16-9/1, office hours 7 am-11 pm, check-in 4 pm, 3 day cancellation notice. **Amenities:** voice mail, hair dryers. **Leisure Activities:** hiking trails. **Cards:** AX, MC, VI.

MAYFIELD INN & SUITES AT WEST EDMONTON
Book great rates at AAA.com **Phone:** 780/484-0821 **5**

CAA SAVE

Large-scale Hotel
$150-$225 All Year

Address: 16615 109th Ave T5P 4K8 **Location:** 1 mi (1.6 km) n of jct Hwy 2 (Gateway Blvd) and 16A on Mayfield Rd. **Facility:** 327 units. 219 one-bedroom standard units, some with kitchens and/or whirlpools. 108 one-bedroom suites, some with whirlpools. 10 stories, interior corridors. **Parking:** on-site, winter plug-ins. **Amenities:** video games (fee), high-speed Internet, voice mail, irons, hair dryers. *Some:* dual phone lines, safes. **Dining:** 2 restaurants, nightclub. **Pool(s):** heated indoor. **Leisure Activities:** saunas, whirlpool, steamroom, racquetball courts, 5 squash courts, spa. *Fee:* esthetics, game room. **Guest Services:** valet and coin laundry. **Business Services:** conference facilities, business center. **Cards:** AX, CB, DC, DS, JC, MC, VI. **Free Special Amenities: full breakfast and high-speed Internet.**

ROSSLYN INN & SUITES
Book great rates at AAA.com **Phone:** (780)476-6241 **2**

CAA SAVE

Small-scale Hotel
$111 All Year

Address: 13620 97 St T5E 4E2 **Location:** Hwy 16 (Yellowhead Hwy), exit 97th St, 1 mi (1.6 km) n. **Facility:** 93 units. 77 one-bedroom standard units, some with whirlpools. 16 one-bedroom suites. 2-5 stories, interior corridors. *Bath:* combo or shower only. **Parking:** on-site, winter plug-ins. **Terms:** cancellation fee imposed. **Amenities:** video games (fee), high-speed Internet, voice mail. *Some:* dual phone lines, irons, hair dryers. **Leisure Activities:** exercise room. **Guest Services:** valet and coin laundry. **Business Services:** meeting rooms. **Cards:** AX, DC, JC, MC, VI. **Free Special Amenities: local telephone calls and high-speed Internet.**

SUPER 8 HOTEL
Book great rates at AAA.com **Phone:** (780)433-8688 **26**

CAA SAVE

Small-scale Hotel
$129-$149 All Year

Address: 3610 Gateway Blvd T6J 7H8 **Location:** Jct 36th Ave. **Facility:** 104 units. 69 one-bedroom standard units, some with whirlpools. 35 one-bedroom suites. 4 stories, interior corridors. *Bath:* combo or shower only. **Parking:** on-site, winter plug-ins. **Amenities:** high-speed Internet, dual phone lines, voice mail, irons, hair dryers. **Pool(s):** heated indoor. **Leisure Activities:** whirlpool, waterslide. **Guest Services:** valet and coin laundry. **Cards:** AX, DC, JC, MC, VI. **Free Special Amenities: continental breakfast and high-speed Internet.**

TRAVELODGE EDMONTON EAST
Book great rates at AAA.com **Phone:** (780)474-0456 **3**

CAA SAVE

Small-scale Hotel
$89-$129 All Year

Address: 3414 118th Ave T5W 0Z4 **Location:** 5 mi (8 km) e of Capilano Dr, 0.6 mi (1 km) s from W Hwy 16 (Yellowhead Trail) on Victoria Trail exit. **Facility:** 86 one-bedroom standard units. 2 stories (no elevator), interior corridors. **Parking:** on-site, winter plug-ins. **Amenities:** voice mail, hair dryers. **Dining:** 2 restaurants, nightclub. **Guest Services:** valet laundry, barber shop. **Business Services:** meeting rooms, administrative services (fee). **Cards:** AX, MC, VI. **Free Special Amenities: continental breakfast and high-speed Internet.**

(See map and index starting on p. 434)

TRAVELODGE EDMONTON WEST   *Book great rates at AAA.com*   Phone: (780)483-6031

 CAA SAVE

Small-scale Hotel
$109-$159 All Year

Address: 18320 Stony Plain Rd T5S 1A7 **Location:** Hwy 16A (Stony Plain Rd) at 184th St. **Facility:** 220 one-bedroom standard units. 5 stories, interior corridors. **Parking:** on-site. **Amenities:** video games (fee), voice mail, irons, hair dryers. *Some:* high-speed Internet. **Pool(s):** heated indoor. **Leisure Activities:** whirlpool, waterslide. *Fee:* game room. **Guest Services:** valet and coin laundry. **Business Services:** meeting rooms. **Cards:** AX, DC, DS, MC, VI.
(See color ad p 413)

WEST EDMONTON MALL INN   *Book at AAA.com*   Phone: (780)444-9378   **17**

Small-scale Hotel
$149 All Year

Address: 17504 90th Ave T5T 6L6 **Location:** Whitemud Dr, exit 170th St N, just w on 90th Ave. Located next to the mall. **Facility:** 88 one-bedroom standard units. 3 stories, interior corridors. **Parking:** on-site, winter plug-ins. **Terms:** check-in 4 pm, cancellation fee imposed. **Amenities:** voice mail, hair dryers. *Fee:* video games, high-speed Internet. **Guest Services:** valet laundry. **Business Services:** meeting rooms. **Cards:** AX, MC, VI.

WEST HARVEST INN   *Book great rates at AAA.com*   Phone: 780/484-8000   **11**

Small-scale Hotel
Rates not provided

Address: 17803 Stony Plain Rd NW T5S 1B4 **Location:** Hwy 16A (Stony Plain Rd) at 178th St. **Facility:** 160 one-bedroom standard units, some with whirlpools. 3 stories, interior corridors. *Bath:* combo or shower only. **Parking:** on-site, winter plug-ins. **Terms:** check-in 4 pm. **Amenities:** voice mail, irons, hair dryers. **Guest Services:** valet laundry, wireless Internet. **Business Services:** meeting rooms, PC.

WINGATE INN EDMONTON WEST   *Book at AAA.com*   Phone: (780)443-1000   **16**

Small-scale Hotel
$135-$150 All Year

Address: 18220 100th Ave T5S 2V2 **Location:** 100th Ave at 182nd St. **Facility:** 106 units. 82 one-bedroom standard units. 24 one-bedroom suites, some with whirlpools. 4 stories, interior corridors. **Parking:** on-site, winter plug-ins. **Amenities:** video games (fee), high-speed Internet, dual phone lines, voice mail, safes, irons, hair dryers. **Pool(s):** heated indoor. **Leisure Activities:** whirlpool, waterslide, exercise room. **Guest Services:** valet and coin laundry, area transportation. **Business Services:** meeting rooms, business center. **Cards:** AX, DC, DS, MC, VI.

——— WHERE TO DINE ———

BARB & ERNIE'S   Phone: 780-433-3242   **19**

German
$8-$15

Ask any local for a favorite breakfast place, and this is often mentioned. Lunch and dinner are popular as well. Ernie himself often greets guests as they enter. Among the homey restaurant's pleasing array of Bavarian dishes are sauerkraut and sausages. Casual dress. **Bar:** Full bar. **Reservations:** accepted. **Hours:** 7 am-8 pm, Sat from 8 am, Sun 8 am-7 pm. Closed major holidays; also Mon. **Address:** 9906 72nd Ave NW T6E 0Z3 **Location:** 99th St S, w at 72nd Ave. **Parking:** on-site. **Cards:** AX, DC, DS, MC, VI.

THE BLUE PEAR   Phone: 780/482-7178   **2**

French
$59

The distinctive name of the upscale restaurant is derived from its previous name, D'Anjou. After ringing the doorbell, guests enter the small dining room, where there are but 12 tables. The five-course prix fixe menu changes monthly, and the chef marries French cooking techniques with regional ingredients. Representative of typical menu fare are such creations as Arctic char with peppercorns, lamb or salmon. Service is exceptional. **Bar:** Full bar. **Reservations:** required. **Hours:** 5 pm-10 pm. Closed major holidays; also Mon & Tues. **Address:** 10643 123rd St T5N 1P3 **Location:** Southeast corner of 123rd St and 7th Ave. **Parking:** on-site. **Cards:** AX, MC, VI.

CENTURY GRILL   Phone: 780/431-0303   **26**

Northern Pacific Rim
$11-$35

Chic and contemporary, the upscale restaurant features a lovely open-concept dining room with black and gray decor. Patrons can dine in the restaurant or the more casual lounge. Creative cuisine boldly pairs varied tastes and sensations. The menu focuses heavily on regional ingredients and also exhibits a Californian flair. Casual dress. **Bar:** Full bar. **Reservations:** suggested. **Hours:** 11 am-10 pm, Fri-11 pm, Sat & Sun 5 pm-10 pm. Closed major holidays. **Address:** 3975 Calgary Tr T6J 6S6 **Location:** Calgary Trail S at 39th Ave. **Parking:** on-site. **Cards:** AX, MC, VI.

CALL

THE CHEESECAKE CAFE   Phone: 780/486-0440   **11**

American
$10-$25

As might be expected, cheesecake is the signature item, and it's worth saving room for one of the lip-smacking varieties made on the premises. A huge dessert display case greets guests upon arrival. Offerings on the extensive lunch and dinner menu range from sandwiches and entree salads to pasta, pizza and seafood selections. It takes a while to get through the menu. Casual dress. **Bar:** Full bar. **Hours:** 11 am-11 pm, Fri & Sat-1 am, Sun 10 am-11 pm. Closed: 12/24. **Address:** 17011 100th Ave T5S 1T9 **Location:** Jct 100th Ave and 170th St. **Parking:** on-site. **Cards:** AX, MC, VI.

CALL

(See map and index starting on p. 434)

CONYAC'S BAR & GRILL
Canadian
$8-$18

Phone: 780/483-2255 12

As far as hotel restaurants go, this place doesn't fit into the conventional mold. Seats and booths in the comfortably decorated dining room are designed to be comfortable for longer visits. While the menu does not take any risks, diners will find all of the classic dishes to be solidly executed and tasty. Casual dress. **Bar:** Full bar. **Hours:** 6:30 am-midnight, Sun-10 pm. **Address:** 10010 179A St T5S 2T1 **Location:** On 100th Ave, just w of 178th St; in Days Inn & Suites West Edmonton. **Parking:** on-site. **Cards:** AX, MC, VI.

CALL ⑤M

DANTE'S BISTRO
International
$7-$22

Phone: 780/486-4448 5

Although it's difficult to classify the restaurant's cuisine, a possible description might be "food without borders." The eclectic, International menu features a huge range of options, with Asian, Mexican, French and fusion influences to name a few. Offerings include sushi, oven-fired pizza, entree salads and creative pasta dishes. The bustling atmosphere in the lofty, airy dining room creates a festive environment. Casual dress. **Bar:** Full bar. **Reservations:** suggested. **Hours:** 11:30 am-10 pm, Thurs-midnight, Fri & Sat-1 am, Sun-9 pm. **Closed:** 12/25. **Address:** 17328 Stony Plain Rd T5S 1K6 **Location:** At 173rd St. **Parking:** on-site. **Cards:** AX, DC, MC, VI.

DELUX BURGER BAR
American
$9-$13

Phone: 780/420-0101 14

Casual dress. **Bar:** Full bar. **Reservations:** not accepted. **Hours:** 11 am-midnight. Closed major holidays. **Address:** 9682 142 St T5N 4B2 **Location:** Jct 97 Ave NW; in shopping plaza. **Parking:** on-site. **Cards:** AX, MC, VI.

THE DISH BISTRO
International
$6-$15

Phone: 780/488-6181 3

In the art district, the little bistro is a cozy place for a healthy quick bite or quaint, leisurely meal. Among interesting creations are curried egg sandwiches, crab cakes and sumptuous pastas. The dining room has original artwork, hardwood floors and large, street-view windows. Casual dress. **Bar:** Full bar. **Reservations:** suggested. **Hours:** 11 am-9 pm. Closed major holidays; also Sun. **Address:** 12417 Stony Plain Rd T5N 3N3 **Location:** Just w of jct Hwy 16A (Stony Plain Rd) and 124th St. **Parking:** street. **Cards:** AX, MC, VI.

FANTASY GRILL DINING ROOM
Continental
$18-$30

Phone: 780/444-3000 17

Located on the second floor of the West Edmonton Mall, this quiet and subtly upscale restaurant is set well back from the crowded mall corridors. Drawing inspiration from around the globe, the well executed menu offers a few very pleasant surprises such as pan fried alligator and imaginative pastas and steaks. While servers are anything but stuffy, they specialize in tableside presentations of Caesar salad for two, flambes and Chateaubriand. Casual dress. **Bar:** Full bar. **Reservations:** suggested. **Hours:** 5:30 pm-10 pm, Fri & Sat-11 pm, Sun 9:30 am-1:30 pm; Sunday brunch. Closed major holidays. **Address:** 17700 87th Ave T5T 4V4 **Location:** At 178th St; in Fantasyland Hotel, 2nd floor. **Parking:** on-site and valet. **Cards:** AX, MC, VI.

CALL ⑤M

FIFE N' DEKEL
Deli/Subs
Sandwiches
$6-$10

Phone: 780/489-6436 1

Quick, healthy lunch options are plentiful at the cafeteria-style eatery. Guests order at the counter and watch their sandwich being made. In addition to such sandwiches as roasted turkey, beef, ham and vegetarian, the menu lists soups, salads and tempting selections from a dessert case full of sumptuous options. Because this place draws a good crowd at lunch, patrons should arrive early to avoid lines. Casual dress. **Reservations:** not accepted. **Hours:** 7 am-4:30 pm, Sat 10 am-3 pm. Closed major holidays; also Sun. **Address:** 10646 170th St T5S 1P3 **Location:** At 106th Ave; in industrial shopping plaza; on west side of road. **Parking:** on-site. **Cards:** AX, MC, VI.

THE FUNKY PICKLE PIZZA CO
Pizza
$4-$10

Phone: 780/423-3865 15

The small pizza bar might do the trick for hungry folks looking for a quick bite to eat. Guests can order eclectic and designer pizza toppings on whole-wheat crust, and the large slices are sure to satisfy any appetite. Seating here is limited so many opt to get their food to go. Casual dress. **Reservations:** not accepted. **Hours:** 11 am-11:30 pm, Fri & Sat-2:30 am, Sun 4 pm-11:30 pm. Closed: 1/1, 12/25. **Address:** 17104 90th Ave T5T 4C8 **Location:** At 171st St, just n of West Edmonton Mall. **Parking:** on-site. **Cards:** AX, DC, MC, VI.

GLENORA GRILL
Canadian
$15-$25

Phone: 780/482-3531 4

On the ground floor of a bed and breakfast, this European-feeling restaurant serves up food that's anything but quaint. Taking a contemporary international approach, the chef sources out the best of local and seasonal ingredients to create classic dishes that have clean, distinct and exciting flavors and truly express what good food is all about. Dressy casual. **Bar:** Full bar. **Reservations:** accepted. **Hours:** 9 am-10 pm. **Address:** 12327 102nd Ave NW T5N 0L8 **Location:** At 124th St; in Glenora Bed & Breakfast Inn. **Parking:** street. **Cards:** MC, VI.

HOMEFIRE BAR & GRILL
Canadian
$10-$26

Phone: 780/489-8086 13

Right across from the Wingate hotel, this upscale yet comfortable restaurant features a large central fireplace that serves to remind guests that this place specializes in forno-style dishes. In addition to oven-baked pasta, pizzas, rotisserie chicken and other comfort foods, the menu also take a few detours into Vietnamese and Thai cooking. Casual dress. **Bar:** Full bar. **Hours:** 11 am-10 pm, Fri & Sat-11 pm. Closed major holidays. **Address:** 18210 100th Ave T5S 2V2 **Location:** Jct 184th St and 100th Ave; next to Wingate Inn Edmonton West. **Parking:** on-site. **Cards:** AX, MC, VI.

CALL ⑤M

IL PASTICCION TRATTORIA
Italian
$10-$34

Phone: 780/488-9543 10

Just a block south of Jasper Avenue, the funky little trattoria has a light and lively dining room, complete with an open concept kitchen. Boldly painted walls and checkered tablecloths set the scene. Guests can choose from homemade pastas and traditional Italian meat dishes. Servers are prompt and friendly. Casual dress. **Bar:** Full bar. **Hours:** 11 am-2 & 5-10 pm. Closed major holidays; also Sun. **Address:** 11520 100th Ave T5K 0J7 **Location:** Corner of 115th St and 100th Ave. **Parking:** on-site (fee). **Cards:** AX, MC, VI.

(See map and index starting on p. 434)

JACK'S GRILL

Regional
Canadian
$28-$39

Phone: 780/434-1113 21

The chef is an architect who builds unusual, inventive cuisine with fresh ingredients, bold flavors and French and West Coast influences. The relaxed, casual atmosphere sustains a feel of upscale elegance. Regardless of whether diners choose seating in the dining room or on the seasonal patio, they can expect superb service. Dressy casual. **Bar:** Full bar. **Reservations:** suggested. **Hours:** 5 pm-10 pm. Closed: 12/25, 12/26; also 1st week of Jan. **Address:** 5842 111th St T6H 3G1 **Location:** Whitemud Dr, exit 111th St, 0.5 mi (0.8 km) n, then just w on 57th Ave; in a strip mall. **Parking:** on-site. **Cards:** AX, DC, MC, VI.

JOEY TOMATO'S
Mediterranean
$10-$29

Phone: 780/465-1880

The cuisine blends Mediterranean and Asian cooking styles and emphasizes finger foods for sharing. Those who aren't big fans of tapas can consider full meal offerings centered on steaks and chops. Casual dress. **Bar:** Full bar. **Hours:** 11:30 am-1 am, Sun-midnight. Closed: 12/25. **Address:** 9911 19th Ave NW T6N 1M4 **Location:** South Edmonton Commons. **Parking:** on-site. **Cards:** AX, MC, VI.

KOUTOUKI TAVERNA
Greek
$20-$40

Phone: 780/432-3660 24

Casual dress. **Bar:** Full bar. **Hours:** 4:30 pm-10 pm. Closed major holidays. **Address:** 10310 45 Ave T6H 5K3 **Location:** Jct Gateway Blvd NW; just n of Whitemud Dr. **Parking:** on-site. **Cards:** AX, MC, VI.

LA FAVORITE PASTRY SHOP

Bakery/Desserts
$4-$8

Phone: 780/482-7024 7

Opening into a bookstore, the pastry shop generates the smells of chocolate and sugar that tend to waft through both. The cute little chocolate shop has several small tables and chairs at which to enjoy a fresh cup of coffee and a slice (or more) of any of the beautiful cakes the store makes fresh each day. Casual dress. **Hours:** 10 am-5:30 pm, Sun noon-4 pm. Closed major holidays. **Address:** 12431 102nd Ave NW T5N 0M2 **Location:** Just w of jct 124th St W. **Parking:** on-site. **Cards:** AX, MC, VI.

LA SPIGA

Italian
$15-$35

Phone: 780/482-3100 8

Dining is intimate, elegant and formal dining in the charming, two-story 1913 mansion. The menu centers on Northern Italian cuisine, with dishes ranging from creamy pasta to succulent veal. The exquisite tiramisu could rival even some created in Italy. The semi-casual atmosphere accents the superb food. Service is professional. Dressy casual. **Bar:** Full bar. **Reservations:** suggested. **Hours:** 5 pm-10 pm, Fri & Sat-11 pm. Closed major holidays; also Sun. **Address:** 10133 125th St T5N 1S7 **Location:** Just s of 102nd Ave. **Parking:** on-site. **Cards:** AX, DC, MC, VI. **Historic**

LEMONGRASS CAFE

Vietnamese
$6-$17

Phone: 780/413-0088 23

This restaurant has a deceptively unassuming exterior. Just behind the doors is a bright, cheerful, airy cafe, offering exciting, fresh, healthy entrees. Traditional Vietnamese fare includes salad rolls, curries and the house specialty: spiced salmon wrapped in banana leaf with vermicelli. Guests can finish off the meal with a single malt scotch or innovative dessert. Casual dress. **Bar:** Full bar. **Reservations:** suggested, weekends. **Hours:** 11 am-9 pm, Fri & Sat-10 pm, Sun 4 pm-9 pm. Closed major holidays; also Mon. **Address:** 10417 51st Ave T6H 0K4 **Location:** Just w of 104th St on Allard Way; in small strip mall. **Parking:** on-site. **Cards:** AX, MC, VI.

MANOR CAFE

International
$14-$39

Phone: 780/482-7577 9

The cafe occupies the beautifully restored home of one of Alberta's former Attorney Generals. Decor is charming, warm and intimate, with a casual feel. The bistro-style menu includes progressive and innovative international dishes. Casual dress. **Bar:** Full bar. **Reservations:** suggested. **Hours:** 11 am-10 pm, Fri & Sat-midnight, Sun 11 am-2 & 5-10 pm. Closed major holidays; also Sun in winter. **Address:** 10109 125th St T5N 1S7 **Location:** Just s of 102nd Ave. **Parking:** on-site. **Cards:** AX, MC, VI.

MOXIE'S CLASSIC GRILL

Canadian
$10-$30

Phone: 780/484-2040

This sleek, funky and popular restaurant presents an extensive menu of creatively prepared dishes, including pizza, pasta, rice, noodles, signature salads and burgers. Other menus include one for children and one for Sunday brunch. Lending to the upbeat, stylish decor are dark wood appointments and river rock fireplaces. Casual dress. **Bar:** Full bar. **Reservations:** accepted. **Hours:** 11 am-midnight. Closed major holidays. **Address:** 17109 100th Ave NW T5S 2G5 **Location:** Jct 170th St NW and 100 Ave NW. **Parking:** on-site. **Cards:** AX, MC, VI.

CALL

MOXIE'S CLASSIC GRILL

Canadian
$10-$30

Phone: 780/484-6669

This sleek, funky and popular restaurant presents an extensive menu of creatively prepared dishes, including pizza, pasta, rice, noodles, signature salads and burgers. Other menus include one for children and one for Sunday brunch. Lending to the upbeat, stylish decor are dark wood appointments and river rock fireplaces. Casual dress. **Bar:** Full bar. **Reservations:** accepted. **Hours:** 9:30 am-11 pm. Closed major holidays. **Address:** 1670 8882-170 St T5T 4M2 **Location:** In West Edmonton Mall; in Bourbon Street District. **Parking:** on-site. **Cards:** AX, MC, VI.

OPM ASIAN BISTRO & LOUNGE

Asian
$8-$14

Phone: 780/989-5898 27

In among the retail outlets and big box stores, this sleek Asian-inspired bistro is a popular gathering spot for those looking for creative interpretations of nouveau Asian cuisine. Casual dress. **Bar:** Full bar. **Reservations:** accepted. **Hours:** 11 am-midnight. Closed: 12/25. **Address:** 1820 99th St T6N 1M5 **Location:** On southside of South Edmonton Commons. **Parking:** on-site. **Cards:** AX, MC, VI.

PARKALLEN RESTAURANT
Lebanese
$8-$20

Phone: 780/436-8080 20

A popular spot with the locals, the family-run restaurant is considered to be one of the city's best ethnic restaurants. The menu centers on selections of traditional Lebanese fare, including fatouche salad, baba ghanoush and marinated kebabs. Those not in the mood for Lebanese cuisine also can try award-winning pizza. The wine list is extensive. The casually elegant dining room displays traditional art. Servers are friendly and knowledgeable. Casual dress. **Bar:** Full bar. **Reservations:** suggested. **Hours:** 11 am-11 pm. Closed: Sun. **Address:** 7018 109th St NW T6H 3C1 **Location:** Corner of 70th Ave and 109th St. **Parking:** on-site. **Cards:** AX, MC, VI.

(See map and index starting on p. 434)

RICKY'S ALL DAY GRILL
Phone: 780/486-7109

Continental
$8-$15

The comfortable eatery, which employs friendly servers, presents a varied menu that includes pasta dishes, wraps, omelets, stir-fry preparations and burgers. Portions are generous. Children's and senior selections are offered. Guests can request seating in a booth or at a table. Casual dress. **Bar:** Full bar. **Hours:** 7 am-9 pm, Fri & Sat-10 pm. Closed: 1/1, 12/25. **Address:** 9917 170th St T5P 4S2 **Location:** Just s of jct 100th Ave NW. **Parking:** on-site. **Cards:** AX, MC, VI.

CALL

ROYAL FORK BUFFET RESTAURANT
Phone: 780/484-7025

American
$10-$14

The Royal Fork features buffet-style dining with a wide variety of freshly made choices, including sugar-free desserts. Families can be fed for an excellent value. Dinner prices are in effect starting at 4 p.m. Monday through Saturday and all day on Sunday and major holidays. Casual dress. **Reservations:** not accepted. **Hours:** 11 am-8:30 pm, Fri & Sat-9 pm, Sun 10 am-8 pm; Sunday brunch. Closed: 12/25. **Address:** 15061 Stony Plain Rd NW T5P 4W1 **Location:** Hwy 16A (Stony Plain Rd) at 150th St. **Parking:** on-site. **Cards:** CB, MC, VI.

SAGE RESTAURANT
Phone: 780/930-2626

Steak & Seafood
$25-$45

Casual dress. **Bar:** Full bar. **Reservations:** suggested. **Hours:** 5 pm-10 pm. **Address:** 300 E Lapotac Blvd T7X 3Y3 **Location:** 1 mi (1.6 km) w of jct Hwy 216 (Anthony Hendoy and Whitemud Dr W); in Edmonton Marriott At River Cree Resort. **Parking:** on-site. **Cards:** AX, MC, VI.

CALL

SEASONS GRILL
Phone: 780/437-7011   ㉒

Canadian
$8-$20

The recently renovated restaurant lets patrons peruse a seasonally inspired menu amid cozy, contemporary surroundings. Ranging from prime rib to pumpkin seed-encrusted sole, the menu variety is surprising and delightful. Casual dress. **Bar:** Full bar. **Reservations:** suggested. **Hours:** 6:30 am-10 pm, Sat & Sun from 7 am. **Address:** 5116 Gateway Blvd T6H 2H4 **Location:** Hwy 2 (Gateway Blvd) at 51st Ave; in Best Western Cedar Park Inn. **Parking:** on-site. **Cards:** AX, DC, DS, JC, MC, VI.

T & T SUPERMARKET CAFE
Phone: 780/484-6638   ⑯

Chinese
$5-$7

Casual dress. **Hours:** 9:30 am-9:30 pm, Sun-9 pm. Closed major holidays. **Address:** 2580-8882 170th St T5T 4M2 **Location:** In West Edmonton Mall; 2nd Floor above Bourbon St. **Parking:** on-site. **Cards:** AX, MC, VI.

TOM GOODCHILDS MOOSE FACTORY
Phone: 780/437-5616   ㉕

Steak & Seafood
$9-$50

The restaurant doesn't look big from the outside, but inside the formal yet comfortable dining area, guests have the choice of being seated in one of several differently decorated rooms. Tuxedoed servers have a casual edge that makes everyone feel at home. Known for its steaks, the menu is a carnivore's dream come true. Casual dress. **Bar:** Full bar. **Reservations:** accepted. **Hours:** 11 am-2 & 4-11 pm, Sat 11 am-11:30 pm, Sun 10 am-10 pm. Closed major holidays. **Address:** 4810 Calgary Tr S T6H 5H5 **Location:** Just n of Whitemud Dr NW. **Parking:** on-site. **Cards:** AX, MC, VI.

CALL

UNHEARDOF RESTAURANT
Phone: 780/432-0480   ⑱

Canadian
$32-$42

Where? Never heard of it! The owners and servers have heard the joke time and time again, yet regardless, the restaurant remains a must. In an old house along the east end of Whyte Avenue, the cozy eatery draws patrons for its fine food and splendid service. Food made from regional ingredients is offered from a prix fixe menu or a la carte. The wine list is fantastic. This place is a favorite for special occasions. Casual dress. **Bar:** Full bar. **Reservations:** suggested. **Hours:** 5:30 pm-close. Closed major holidays; also Mon. **Address:** 9602 82nd Ave T6C 1A1 **Location:** Corner of 82nd Ave (Whyte Ave) and 96th St. **Parking:** street. **Cards:** AX, DC, MC, VI.

URBAN DINER
Phone: 780/488-7274   ⑥

Canadian
$8-$15

We should be so lucky as to have such a classic neighborhood restaurant in our neck of the woods. While there is a definite upscale diner feel to this place, the kitchen presents a tight little menu of comfort food and regularly, sometimes daily, changing specials. Using top-notch ingredients, much of them sourced locally, the chefs displays their talents in the partially open kitchen and evoke clean and distinct flavors from even the simplest of dishes. Casual dress. **Bar:** Full bar. **Reservations:** not accepted. **Hours:** 7 am-9 pm, Sat from 9 am, Sun 9 am-3 pm. Closed major holidays. **Address:** 12427 102nd Ave T5N 0M2 **Location:** Just w of jct 124th St W. **Parking:** on-site. **Cards:** AX, MC, VI.

CALL

WHITE SPOT
Phone: 780/432-9153

Canadian
$8-$15

Open for three meals a day, the popular casual restaurant prepares offerings such as sandwiches and burgers, fresh salads, pastas and stir-fries, fish and chips, chargrilled sirloin steaks and chicken, in addition to a selection of yummy desserts. Casual dress. **Bar:** Full bar. **Hours:** 7:30 am-10 pm, Fri-11 pm. Closed major holidays. **Address:** 3921 Calvary Tr T6J 5M8 **Location:** Just s of jct Whitemud Dr NW. **Parking:** on-site. **Cards:** AX, DC, MC, VI.

The Edmonton Vicinity

FORT SASKATCHEWAN pop. 14,957

------ WHERE TO STAY ------

LAKEVIEW INNS & SUITES   **Phone:** 780/998-7888

vvvvv
Small-scale Hotel
Rates not provided

Address: 10115 88th Ave T8L 2T3 **Location:** Just w of Hwy 15/21 and 101st St. **Facility:** 70 units. 63 one-bedroom standard units, some with whirlpools. 7 one-bedroom suites, some with whirlpools. 4 stories, interior corridors. **Parking:** on-site, winter plug-ins. **Terms:** check-in 4 pm. **Amenities:** video library (fee), DVD players, dual phone lines, irons, hair dryers. *Some:* high-speed Internet. **Leisure Activities:** exercise room. **Guest Services:** coin laundry, wireless Internet. *(See color ad p 362)*

🍴 🎬 💻 / SOME UNITS 🐕 ✕ FEE VCR 🔌 🖨

SUPER 8 HOTEL-FORT SASKATCHEWAN   *Book at AAA.com*   **Phone:** 780/998-2898

vvvv
Small-scale Hotel
Rates not provided

Address: 8750 84th St T8L 4P5 **Location:** Just e of jct Hwy 15/21. **Facility:** 86 units. 80 one- and 6 two-bedroom standard units, some with whirlpools. 3 stories, interior corridors. *Bath:* combo or shower only. **Parking:** on-site, winter plug-ins. **Amenities:** high-speed Internet, hair dryers. **Pool(s):** heated indoor. **Leisure Activities:** whirlpool, limited exercise equipment. **Guest Services:** coin laundry, wireless Internet. **Business Services:** PC (fee).

🏊 🎬 🔌 💻 / SOME UNITS ✕ 🖨

LEDUC pop. 16,967

------ WHERE TO STAY ------

BEST WESTERN DENHAM INN AND SUITES   *Book great rates at AAA.com*   **Phone:** (780)986-2241

(AAA) (SAVE)
vvvvv
Small-scale Hotel
$116-$230 All Year

Address: 5207 50th Ave T9E 6V3 **Location:** Hwy 2, exit Leduc/City Centre, just e. **Facility:** 95 one-bedroom standard units, some with whirlpools. 2-5 stories, interior corridors. **Parking:** on-site, winter plug-ins. **Terms:** check-in 4 pm, 7 day cancellation notice. **Amenities:** video games (fee), voice mail, irons, hair dryers. *Some:* high-speed Internet. **Leisure Activities:** whirlpool, exercise room. **Guest Services:** valet and coin laundry, airport transportation-Edmonton International Airport, wireless Internet. **Business Services:** meeting rooms, PC. **Cards:** AX, CB, DC, DS, JC, MC, VI. **Free Special Amenities:** continental breakfast and high-speed Internet. *(See color ad below)*

AAA Benefit:
Members save 10% everyday, plus an exclusive frequent stay program.

💲 ✈ 🍴 🍷 CALL (5M) 🎬 💻 / SOME UNITS ✕ 🔌 🖨

EDMONTON INTERNATIONAL AIRPORT-SUPER 8 MOTEL   *Book at AAA.com*   **Phone:** 780/986-8898

vvvv
Small-scale Hotel
Rates not provided

Address: 8004 Sparrow Crescent T9E 7G1 **Location:** Hwy 2, exit N Business Section. **Facility:** Smoke free premises. 64 units. 52 one-bedroom standard units. 12 one-bedroom suites, some with whirlpools. 4 stories, interior corridors. **Parking:** on-site, winter plug-ins. **Amenities:** high-speed Internet, hair dryers. **Guest Services:** valet and coin laundry. **Business Services:** PC (fee).

✈ ✕ 🎬 🔌 🖨 💻

——— WHERE TO DINE ———

RUTH'S DELI

Deli/Subs
Sandwiches
$3-$8

Phone: 780/986-0433

The delicatessen appeals to hurried diners looking for a quick, healthy bite to eat. Guests can get a sandwich and soup to go or eat in at one of the small dinner tables. Check out the sandwich board for day specials and order at the counter for a meal that's ready in minutes. Casual dress. **Hours:** 8 am-5 pm. Closed major holidays; also Sat & Sun. **Address:** #26, 5201 50th St T9E 6T4 **Location:** Just n at 50th St; in City Centre Mall. **Parking:** on-site. **Cards:** MC, VI.

ZAMBELLIS RESTAURANT

International
$8-$33

Phone: 780/980-9669

Although it's described as a steak and pizza place, the restaurant presents a much more diverse menu. Greek food is a highlight, as are child- and senior-size portions. The large, bustling dining room features an open-concept kitchen and small sports lounge. Expect generous portions and friendly service. Casual dress. **Bar:** Full bar. **Hours:** 11 am-10 pm. Closed major holidays. **Address:** 6210 50th St T9E 7G9 **Location:** Hwy 2, exit Leduc Business Centre (50th St). **Parking:** on-site. **Cards:** AX, DC, MC, VI.

NISKU

——— WHERE TO STAY ———

HOLIDAY INN EXPRESS EDMONTON INT'L AIRPORT   *Book great rates at AAA.com*

(CAA) (SAVE)

Small-scale Hotel
$150-$160 All Year

Phone: (780)955-1000

Address: 1102 4th St T9E 8E2 **Location:** Hwy 2, exit Edmonton International Airport/Nisku Business Park (10th Ave), 0.5 mi (0.8 km) e. **Facility:** 120 units. 118 one-bedroom standard units. 2 one-bedroom suites with whirlpools. 4 stories, interior corridors. *Bath:* combo or shower only. **Parking:** on-site, winter plug-ins. **Amenities:** video games (fee), high-speed Internet, dual phone lines, voice mail, irons, hair dryers. **Pool(s):** heated indoor. **Leisure Activities:** whirlpool, waterslide, exercise room. **Guest Services:** valet and coin laundry, airport transportation-Edmunton International Airport, wireless Internet. **Business Services:** meeting rooms, PC (fee). **Cards:** AX, DC, DS, MC, VI. **Free Special Amenities:** continental breakfast and high-speed Internet.

QUALITY INN & SUITES-AIRPORT   *Book at AAA.com*

Small-scale Hotel
$120-$160 All Year

Phone: (780)955-3001

Address: 501 11th Ave T9E 7N5 **Location:** Hwy 2, exit Edmonton International Airport/Nisku Business Park (10th Ave), 0.5 mi (0.8 km) e. **Facility:** 73 units. 64 one-bedroom standard units, some with whirlpools. 9 one-bedroom suites. 2-4 stories (no elevator), interior corridors. **Parking:** on-site, winter plug-ins. **Terms:** cancellation fee imposed. **Amenities:** voice mail, irons, hair dryers. **Guest Services:** valet laundry. **Business Services:** meeting rooms, PC. **Cards:** AX, MC, VI. *(See color ad on insert)*

ST. ALBERT pop. 57,719   (See map and index starting on p. 434)

——— WHERE TO DINE ———

RIC'S GRILL

Steak & Seafood
$9-$30

Phone: 780/460-6602   [31]

"Funky and modern" describes the decor and the food at the upscale steakhouse, which bustles with activity. Reservations are definitely recommended. Steaks are well worth it, but then again, so are the salmon, chicken and pasta dishes. A wide variety of distinctive appetizers rounds out the menu. Servers are friendly and attentive. Dressy casual. **Bar:** Full bar. **Reservations:** accepted. **Hours:** 11:30 am-10 pm, Fri & Sat-11 pm, Sun 4:30 pm-10 pm. Closed major holidays. **Address:** 24 Perron St T8N 1E7 **Location:** Hwy 2 N, just e at St. Anne St; corner of St. Anne and Perron sts. **Parking:** on-site. **Cards:** AX, MC, VI.

RIVER HOUSE GRILL

Canadian
$19-$29

Phone: 780/458-2232   [30]

Dressy casual. **Reservations:** accepted. **Hours:** 5 pm-9 pm, Fri-10 pm, Sat & Sun 4:30 pm-8 pm. Closed major holidays; also Mon. **Address:** 8 Mission Ave T8N 1H4 **Location:** Jct Hwy 2 (St Albert Rd); downtown. **Parking:** on-site. **Cards:** AX, MC, VI.

SHERWOOD PARK

——— WHERE TO STAY ———

BEST WESTERN SHERWOOD HOTEL & CONFERENCE CENTRE   *Book great rates at AAA.com*

(CAA) (SAVE)

Small-scale Hotel
Rates not provided

Phone: 780/464-4900

Address: 2100 Premier Way T8H 2G4 **Location:** Hwy 16, exit Broadmoor Blvd, 0.6 mi (1 km) sw. Located next to Millenium Place Recreation Centre. **Facility:** 125 units. 119 one- and 6 two-bedroom standard units, some with whirlpools. 5 stories, interior corridors. *Bath:* combo or shower only. **Parking:** on-site, winter plug-ins. **Terms:** check-in 4 pm. **Amenities:** video games (fee), high-speed Internet, dual phone lines, voice mail, irons, hair dryers. **Leisure Activities:** exercise room. **Guest Services:** valet and coin laundry. **Business Services:** conference facilities. **Free Special Amenities:** local telephone calls and high-speed Internet.

AAA Benefit:
Members save 10% everyday, plus an exclusive frequent stay program.

FRANKLIN'S INN

(CAA) (SAVE)

Small-scale Hotel
$105-$149 All Year

Phone: (780)467-1234

Address: 2016 Sherwood Dr T8A 3X3 **Location:** At Granada Blvd. Located next to a shopping complex. **Facility:** 40 one-bedroom standard units, some with whirlpools. 3 stories, interior corridors. **Parking:** on-site, winter plug-ins. **Amenities:** voice mail. *Some:* irons, hair dryers. **Leisure Activities:** *Fee:* esthetics. **Guest Services:** valet laundry, beauty salon. **Business Services:** conference facilities. **Cards:** AX, DC, MC, VI.

HOLIDAY INN EXPRESS   *Book great rates at AAA.com*   Phone: (780)417-3388

Small-scale Hotel
$144-$299 1/1-2/28
$134-$279 3/1-12/31

Address: 11 Portage Ln T8H 2R7 **Location:** Hwy 16, exit Broadmoor Blvd, 0.6 mi (1 km) s. **Facility:** 90 one-bedroom standard units, some with whirlpools. 4 stories, interior corridors. *Bath:* combo or shower only. **Parking:** on-site. **Amenities:** high-speed Internet, voice mail, irons. *Some:* CD players. **Leisure Activities:** whirlpool, exercise room. **Guest Services:** valet laundry. **Business Services:** meeting rooms, business center. **Cards:** AX, DC, DS, MC, VI. **Free Special Amenities:** expanded continental breakfast and high-speed Internet.

RAMADA LIMITED-EDMONTON EAST/SHERWOOD
PARK   *Book great rates at AAA.com*   Phone: 780/467-6727

Small-scale Hotel
Rates not provided

Address: 30 Broadway Blvd T8H 2A2 **Location:** Hwy 16, exit Broadmoor Blvd, 1.2 mi (2 km) s. **Facility:** 63 one-bedroom standard units. 4 stories, interior corridors. **Parking:** on-site, winter plug-ins. **Amenities:** voice mail, irons, hair dryers. **Leisure Activities:** whirlpool, exercise room. **Guest Services:** valet and coin laundry, wireless Internet. **Business Services:** meeting rooms. **Free Special Amenities:** expanded continental breakfast.

ROADKING INNS   Phone: (780)464-1000

Small-scale Hotel
$129-$149 All Year

Address: 26 Strathmoor Dr T8H 2B6 **Location:** Just sw of Hwy 16, exit Broadmoor Blvd. Located next to a truck stop facility. **Facility:** 88 one-bedroom standard units. 2 stories, interior corridors. **Parking:** on-site. **Terms:** cancellation fee imposed. **Amenities:** voice mail, irons, hair dryers. *Some:* high-speed Internet. **Dining:** 2 restaurants. **Leisure Activities:** exercise room. *Fee:* game room. **Guest Services:** valet and coin laundry. **Business Services:** meeting rooms. **Cards:** AX, MC, VI. **Free Special Amenities:** local telephone calls and newspaper.

────── **WHERE TO DINE** ──────

JOEY TOMATO'S   Phone: 780/449-1161

Mediterranean
$10-$29

The cuisine blends Mediterranean and Asian cooking styles and emphasizes finger foods for sharing. Those who aren't big fans of tapas can consider full meal offerings centered on steaks and chops. Casual dress. **Bar:** Full bar. **Hours:** 11:30 am-1 am, Sun-midnight. Closed: 12/25. **Address:** 360-222 Baseline Rd T8H 1S8 **Location:** Between 17th St NE and Sherwood Dr. **Parking:** on-site. **Cards:** AX, MC, VI.

SORRENTINO'S BISTRO BAR   Phone: 780/449-1384

Italian
$8-$18

Italian ambience and cuisine await at the cozy restaurant, which prepares pizza, calzones and, of course, pasta dishes. There are daily specials, and the service is friendly and attentive. **Bar:** Full bar. **Reservations:** suggested. **Hours:** 11 am-2:30 & 5-10 pm, Fri 11 am-2:30 & 4-11 pm, Sat 4 pm-10 pm, Sun 4 pm-10 pm. Closed: 1/1, 12/25. **Address:** 1020 Sherwood Dr T8A 2G4 **Location:** Hwy 16, exit Broadmoor Blvd S, 3.1 mi (5 km) to Wye Rd; northeast corner of Sherwood Dr and Wye Rd. **Parking:** on-site. **Cards:** AX, MC, VI.

THE SOUP & SANDWICH CO.   Phone: 780/467-8530

Deli/Subs
Sandwiches
$5-$6

Crowds often line out the front door in this cozy little restaurant, which seems lost in the generic-looking commercial plaza near the Holiday Inn Express. Patrons get good value for the dollar in the varied homemade soups, made-to-order sandwiches and hot, freshly made daily entrees. Casual dress. **Hours:** 8 am-3 pm. Closed major holidays; also Sat & Sun. **Address:** 2833 Broadmoor Blvd, #144 T8H 2H3 **Location:** Hwy 16, exit Broadmoor Blvd, 0.6 mi (1 km) s. **Parking:** on-site. **Cards:** MC, VI.

SUMO SUMO SUSHI BAR & GRILL   Phone: 780/416-7866

Sushi
$5-$13

In a small shopping plaza, this gem of a restaurant appeals to those with sumo appetites but who don't want to pay sumo prices. A wonderful selection of traditional and nouveau sushi is available, as is a teppanyaki bar. Locals frequent this place. Casual dress. **Bar:** Full bar. **Hours:** 11:30 am-9 pm, Fri & Sat-9:30 pm, Sun noon-9 pm. Closed: 12/25. **Address:** #390, 222 Baseline Rd T8H 1S8 **Location:** Corner of Baseline Rd and Broadmoor Blvd; in Baseline Village Shopping Plaza. **Parking:** on-site. **Cards:** MC, VI.

VICKY'S RESTAURANT   Phone: 780/417-1750

International
$7-$20

A well-known spot in the Sherwood Park community, the family-run restaurant has been serving excellent homemade food for many years. Patrons can choose from such Greek specialties as spanakopita and souvlaki or try one of the other International dishes. A visit is not complete without a trip to the restroom, where an eclectic mix of interesting trinkets is on display. Casual dress. **Bar:** Full bar. **Hours:** 11 am-10 pm, Sat from 5 pm, Sun from 4 pm. Closed: 12/25, 12/26. **Address:** #86, 993 Fir St T8A 4N5 **Location:** Corner of Broadmoor Blvd and Wye Rd; accessible from Broadmoor Blvd. **Parking:** on-site. **Cards:** AX, MC, VI.

STONY PLAIN pop. 12,363

────── **WHERE TO STAY** ──────

MOTEL 6 STONY PLAIN   Phone: 780/968-5123

Small-scale Hotel
Rates not provided

Too new to rate, opening scheduled for November 2007. **Address:** 66 Boulder Blvd T7Z 1V7 **Location:** 16A. **Amenities:** 78 units, pets. *(See color ad p 368)*

RAMADA INN & SUITES   Phone: (780)963-0222

Small-scale Hotel
$64-$115 All Year

Address: 3301 43rd Ave T7Z 1L1 **Location:** Hwy 16A, exit Dunmore Rd, just s. **Facility:** 88 units. 70 one- and 2 two-bedroom standard units, some with efficiencies and/or whirlpools. 16 one-bedroom suites, some with efficiencies, kitchens and/or whirlpools. 2 stories (no elevator), interior/exterior corridors. **Parking:** on-site, winter plug-ins. **Terms:** check-in 4 pm. **Amenities:** irons, hair dryers. **Pool(s):** heated indoor. **Leisure Activities:** sauna, whirlpool. **Guest Services:** valet and coin laundry, area transportation (fee)-West Edmonton Mall, wireless Internet. **Business Services:** meeting rooms. **Cards:** AX, DC, DS, JC, MC, VI. **Free Special Amenities:** local telephone calls and high-speed Internet.

Santa Maria, Deep Sea Adventure, West Edmonton Mall / Travel Alberta

This ends listings for the Edmonton Vicinity.
The following page resumes the alphabetical listings of cities in Alberta.

EDSON pop. 8,098

-------- WHERE TO STAY --------

BEST WESTERN HIGH ROAD INN   *Book great rates at AAA.com*

Phone: (780)712-2378

Small-scale Hotel
$133-$229 All Year

Address: 300 52nd St T7E 1V8 **Location:** On 2nd Ave; centre. **Facility:** 114 units. 107 one-bedroom standard units. 7 one-bedroom suites, some with whirlpools. 4 stories, interior corridors. **Parking:** on-site, winter plug-ins. **Terms:** check-in 4 pm. **Amenities:** high-speed Internet, voice mail, irons, hair dryers. *Some:* dual phone lines. **Pool(s):** heated indoor. **Leisure Activities:** whirlpool, waterslide, exercise room. **Guest Services:** valet laundry. **Business Services:** meeting rooms. **Cards:** AX, DC, DS, JC, MC, VI.

AAA Benefit:
Members save 10% everyday, plus an exclusive frequent stay program.

GUEST HOUSE INN & SUITES

Phone: (780)723-4486

Motel
$101-$122 All Year

Address: 4411 4th Ave T7E 1B8 **Location:** 0.6 mi (1 km) e on Hwy 16. **Facility:** 108 units. 89 one-bedroom standard units, some with kitchens and/or whirlpools. 18 one- and 1 two-bedroom suites with kitchens. 1-3 stories (no elevator), interior/exterior corridors. **Parking:** on-site, winter plug-ins. **Amenities:** high-speed Internet, voice mail, hair dryers. **Leisure Activities:** sauna, steamroom, exercise room. **Guest Services:** coin laundry. **Business Services:** meeting rooms, PC. **Cards:** AX, MC, VI. **Free Special Amenities:** full breakfast and high-speed Internet.

LAKEVIEW INNS & SUITES   *Book great rates at AAA.com*

Phone: (780)723-2500

Small-scale Hotel
$120 All Year

Address: 4300 2nd Ave T7E 1B8 **Location:** 0.6 mi (1.1 km) e on Hwy 16. **Facility:** 45 one-bedroom standard units. 2 stories (no elevator), interior corridors. **Parking:** on-site, winter plug-ins. **Terms:** cancellation fee imposed. **Guest Services:** coin laundry. **Business Services:** PC. **Cards:** AX, DC, DS, MC, VI. *(See color ad p 362)*

FORT MACLEOD pop. 3,072

-------- WHERE TO STAY --------

SUNSET MOTEL

Phone: 403-553-4448

Motel
$54-$74 All Year

Address: 104 Hwy 3 W T0L 0Z0 **Location:** 0.6 mi (1 km) w on Hwy 2 and 3. **Facility:** 22 units. 13 one- and 8 two-bedroom standard units, some with kitchens. 1 two-bedroom suite with kitchen. 1 story, exterior corridors. *Bath:* combo or shower only. **Parking:** on-site, winter plug-ins. **Terms:** office hours 7 am-11 pm. **Guest Services:** wireless Internet. **Business Services:** meeting rooms. **Cards:** AX, MC, VI. **Free Special Amenities:** continental breakfast and high-speed Internet.

-------- WHERE TO DINE --------

AUNTY LYNDA'S CAFE & GRILL

Phone: 403-553-2655

Canadian
$6-$17

The charming restaurant's menu lists a good selection of seafood, veal, beef and pasta dishes, as well as creative burgers and home-baked pies and cheesecake. The clean, bright, homey decor has a country flair. Casual dress. **Bar:** Full bar. **Hours:** 7 am-9 pm. Closed: 12/25. **Address:** 2323 7th Ave T0L 0Z0 **Location:** East end of town. **Parking:** on-site. **Cards:** AX, MC, VI.

JOHNNY'S RESTAURANT

Phone: 403-553-3939

Chinese
$6-$17

The highly trained chef/owner prepares an extensive selection of Western and Chinese dishes. Fresh ingredients, generous portions and unsurpassed friendliness make this a gem of a place. Entrees include selections of salmon, veal, prawns, ribs and steak, as well as fresh pasta and lighter sandwiches. Casual dress. **Bar:** Full bar. **Reservations:** suggested. **Hours:** 10 am-9 pm, Sun 11 am-8 pm. Closed: 1/1, 12/25. **Address:** 225 24th St (Main St) T0L 0Z0 **Location:** Centre; next to Empress Theatre. **Parking:** street. **Cards:** AX, MC, VI.

FORT MCMURRAY pop. 47,705

-------- WHERE TO STAY --------

ADVANTAGE WEST INNS & SUITES   *Book great rates at AAA.com*

Phone: (780)713-4111

Small-scale Hotel
$169-$209 All Year

Address: 200 Parent Way T9H 5E6 **Location:** 3.1 mi (5 km) s on Hwy 63. **Facility:** 83 one-bedroom standard units. 4 stories, interior corridors. **Parking:** on-site, winter plug-ins. **Terms:** cancellation fee imposed. **Amenities:** video library (fee), DVD players, CD players, high-speed Internet, voice mail, hair dryers. **Guest Services:** coin laundry. **Cards:** AX, DS, MC, VI. **Free Special Amenities:** expanded continental breakfast and high-speed Internet.

MERIT HOTEL
Book great rates at AAA.com

Small-scale Hotel
Rates not provided

Phone: 780/714-9444

Address: 8200 Franklin Ave T9H 2H9 **Location:** Hwy 63, exit Hospital St, just e to Franklin Ave, then 1 km se. **Facility:** 92 units. 62 one-bedroom standard units, some with whirlpools. 30 one-bedroom suites. 3 stories, interior corridors. **Parking:** on-site. **Amenities:** high-speed Internet, dual phone lines, voice mail, irons, hair dryers. **Pool(s):** heated indoor. **Leisure Activities:** whirlpool, exercise room. **Guest Services:** valet laundry. **Business Services:** meeting rooms, PC.

RADISSON HOTEL & SUITES
Book at AAA.com

Small-scale Hotel
$199-$319 All Year

Phone: (780)743-2400

Address: 435 Gregoire Dr T9H 4K7 **Location:** From Hwy 63, 0.6 mi (1 km) e. **Facility:** 134 units. 123 one-bedroom standard units. 11 one-bedroom suites, some with whirlpools. 5 stories, interior corridors. **Bath:** combo or shower only. **Parking:** on-site. **Terms:** check-in 4 pm, cancellation fee imposed. **Amenities:** video games (fee), high-speed Internet, voice mail, safes, irons, hair dryers. *Some:* dual phone lines. **Pool(s):** heated indoor. **Leisure Activities:** whirlpool, waterslide, exercise room. **Guest Services:** valet and coin laundry. **Business Services:** meeting rooms. **Cards:** AX, DC, DS, MC, VI.

SUPER 8 MOTEL
Book at AAA.com

Small-scale Hotel
$144-$185 All Year

Phone: 780/799-8450

Address: 321 Sakitawaw Tr T9H 5E7 **Location:** Just w of Hwy 63, 3.1 mi (5 km) s. **Facility:** 100 one-bedroom standard units, some with whirlpools. 2 stories (no elevator), interior corridors. **Parking:** on-site, winter plug-ins. **Terms:** cancellation fee imposed. **Amenities:** high-speed Internet, voice mail. *Some:* irons, hair dryers. **Leisure Activities:** whirlpool, exercise room. **Guest Services:** valet and coin laundry. **Business Services:** meeting rooms, PC. **Cards:** AX, MC, VI.

------- **WHERE TO DINE** -------

THE FISH PLACE

Seafood
$9-$40

Phone: 780/791-4040

A well-known fact about Fort McMurray is that the largest population of Newfoundlanders outside of Newfoundland is found here. As a result, the superb fish restaurant was established to accommodate that population. Seven days a week, the nautical, cozy restaurant is busy serving seafood and evening specials. Seafood lovers looking for a hearty meal with speedy service should look no further. Casual dress. **Bar:** Full bar. **Reservations:** accepted. **Hours:** 11 am-11 pm, Sun-10 pm. Closed major holidays. **Address:** 412 Thickwood Blvd T9K 1P1 **Location:** Hwy 63, exit Thickwood Blvd, 1.8 km w; in small shopping plaza. **Parking:** on-site. **Cards:** AX, DC, MC, VI.

FORT SASKATCHEWAN —*See Edmonton p. 453.*

GRANDE PRAIRIE pop. 47,076

------- **WHERE TO STAY** -------

BEST WESTERN GRANDE PRAIRIE HOTEL & SUITES
Book great rates at AAA.com

Small-scale Hotel
Rates not provided

Phone: 780/402-2378

Address: 10745 117th Ave T8V 7N6 **Location:** Corner of Hwy 43 and 117th Ave. **Facility:** 100 units. 63 one-bedroom standard units and whirlpools. 37 one-bedroom suites. 4 stories, interior corridors. **Parking:** on-site, winter plug-ins. **Amenities:** video games (fee), high-speed Internet, dual phone lines, voice mail, irons, hair dryers. **Dining:** Sorrentino's, see separate listing. **Pool(s):** heated indoor. **Leisure Activities:** whirlpool, exercise room. **Guest Services:** tanning facilities, wireless Internet. **Business Services:** meeting rooms, business center. **Free Special Amenities:** continental breakfast and local telephone calls.

Best Western

AAA Benefit:
Members save 10% everyday, plus an exclusive frequent stay program.

POMEROY INN & SUITES
Book great rates at AAA.com

Small-scale Hotel
$179-$189 All Year

Phone: (780)831-2999

Address: 11710 102nd St T8V 7S7 **Location:** 102nd St at 117th Ave. **Facility:** 152 units. 112 one-bedroom standard units, some with kitchens and/or whirlpools. 37 one- and 3 two-bedroom suites with kitchens, some with whirlpools. 3-4 stories, interior corridors. *Bath:* combo or shower only. **Parking:** on-site, winter plug-ins. **Amenities:** high-speed Internet, voice mail, irons, hair dryers. *Some:* video games (fee). **Pool(s):** heated indoor. **Leisure Activities:** whirlpool, waterslide, exercise room. **Guest Services:** valet and coin laundry. **Business Services:** meeting rooms, business center. **Cards:** AX, DS, MC, VI. **Free Special Amenities:** expanded continental breakfast and high-speed Internet.

QUALITY HOTEL & CONFERENCE CENTRE GRANDE PRAIRIE
Book great rates at AAA.com

Large-scale Hotel
$254-$300 3/1-8/31
$203-$250 9/1-2/28

Phone: 780/539-6000

Address: 11201 100th Ave T8V 5M6 **Location:** 1.8 mi (2.9 km) w on Hwy 2. **Facility:** 102 units. 98 one-bedroom standard units. 4 one-bedroom suites with efficiencies. 10 stories, interior corridors. **Parking:** on-site, winter plug-ins. **Terms:** cancellation fee imposed. **Amenities:** voice mail, irons, hair dryers. *Fee:* video games, high-speed Internet. **Dining:** nightclub. **Leisure Activities:** exercise room, game room. **Guest Services:** valet laundry. **Cards:** AX, DC, MC, VI. **Free Special Amenities:** full breakfast and high-speed Internet. *(See color ad on insert)*

SERVICE PLUS INNS AND SUITES *Book at AAA.com* Phone: (780)538-3900

Small-scale Hotel
$159-$300 All Year

Address: 10810 107th A Ave T8V 7A9 **Location:** 1.4 mi (2.2 km) w on Hwy 2, just n. Located adjacent to a casino. **Facility:** 123 units. 120 one- and 2 two-bedroom standard units. 1 one-bedroom suite with whirlpool. 4 stories, interior corridors. *Bath:* combo or shower only. **Parking:** on-site, winter plug-ins. **Amenities:** video games (fee), voice mail, irons, hair dryers. *Some:* dual phone lines, fax. **Pool(s):** heated indoor. **Leisure Activities:** whirlpool, waterslide, limited exercise equipment. **Guest Services:** valet laundry, wireless Internet. **Business Services:** meeting rooms, PC. **Cards:** AX, DC, MC, VI.

STANFORD INN *Book great rates at AAA.com* Phone: (780)539-5678

Small-scale Hotel
$139-$149 All Year

Address: 11401 100th Ave T8V 5M6 **Location:** 1.8 mi (2.8 km) w on Hwy 2. **Facility:** 204 units. 202 one-bedroom standard units, some with efficiencies, kitchens and/or whirlpools. 2 two-bedroom suites with kitchens and whirlpools. 2 stories (no elevator), interior/exterior corridors. **Parking:** on-site, winter plug-ins. **Amenities:** video library, voice mail, irons, hair dryers. *Some:* high-speed Internet. **Leisure Activities:** whirlpool, steamroom, exercise room. **Guest Services:** coin laundry. **Business Services:** meeting rooms. **Cards:** AX, MC, VI. **Free Special Amenities: local telephone calls and high-speed Internet.**

SUPER 8 MOTEL *Book great rates at AAA.com* Phone: (780)532-8288

Small-scale Hotel
$129-$169 All Year

Address: 10050 116 Ave T8V 4K5 **Location:** 102nd St at 117th Ave. **Facility:** 103 units. 67 one-bedroom standard units, some with whirlpools. 28 one- and 8 two-bedroom suites. 4 stories, interior corridors. *Bath:* combo or shower only. **Parking:** on-site, winter plug-ins. **Amenities:** video games (fee), voice mail, irons, hair dryers. *Some:* high-speed Internet (fee). **Pool(s):** heated indoor. **Leisure Activities:** whirlpool, waterslide, exercise room. **Guest Services:** valet and coin laundry. **Business Services:** business center. **Cards:** AX, DC, JC, MC, VI. **Free Special Amenities: continental breakfast and high-speed Internet.**

TRUMPETER HOTEL & MEETING CENTRE Phone: 780/539-5561

Small-scale Hotel
Rates not provided

Address: 12102 100th St T8V 5P1 **Location:** 100th St at 121st Ave. **Facility:** 122 units. 120 one-bedroom standard units, some with whirlpools. 2 one-bedroom suites with whirlpools. 3 stories, interior corridors. **Parking:** on-site, winter plug-ins. **Amenities:** voice mail, hair dryers. *Some:* high-speed Internet, irons. **Leisure Activities:** exercise room. **Guest Services:** valet laundry, wireless Internet. **Business Services:** meeting rooms, PC.

——— WHERE TO DINE ———

ACROPOLIS Phone: 780/538-4424

Greek
$8-$21

A taste of Greece is found at the downtown eatery, where diners find fare ranging from spanakopita and souvlaki to moussaka and baklava. Portions are not skimpy and are served by friendly, attentive staff members. Casual dress. **Bar:** Full bar. **Reservations:** suggested. **Hours:** 11 am-2 & 5-10 pm, Sat from 5 pm. Closed major holidays; also Sun & Mon. **Address:** 10011 101st Ave T8V 0X9 **Location:** Corner of 100th St and 101st Ave; downtown. **Parking:** street. **Cards:** AX, DC, MC, VI.

BARCELONA STEAKHOUSE & GRILL Phone: 780/532-4201

Steak House
$10-$28

In the Holiday Inn Grande Prairie, the upscale steakhouse offers both an a la carte menu and a fantastic buffet at lunch. With fine surroundings, friendly service and great AAA Alberta beef, this is a great place to dine. Casual dress. **Reservations:** suggested. **Hours:** 11 am-2 & 4:30-10 pm. Closed: 12/25. **Address:** 9816 107th St T8V 1L4 **Location:** Corner of Hwy 40 and 98th Ave; in Holiday Inn. **Parking:** on-site. **Cards:** MC, VI.

THE GOLDEN STAR Phone: 780/532-7549

Chinese
$6-$14

Patrons can expect a friendly atmosphere and a contemporary setting. A few Western dishes show up on a menu that's predominantly Chinese. Dim sum is served on weekends. Service is prompt and cordial. Casual dress. **Bar:** Full bar. **Reservations:** accepted. **Hours:** 11 am-11 pm, Sun-9 pm. Closed: 12/25. **Address:** 10112 101st Ave T8V 0Y2 **Location:** Centre. **Parking:** street. **Cards:** AX, CB, DC, MC, VI.

SORRENTINO'S Phone: 780/814-7171

Italian
$15-$26

This Italian eatery is intimately lit and employs an efficient staff. Representative of traditional dishes are risotto, lasagna, fettuccine and lamb. The decadent desserts shouldn't be overlooked. Casual dress. **Bar:** Full bar. **Hours:** 4:30 pm-11 pm. Closed major holidays. **Address:** 10745 117th Ave T8V 7N6 **Location:** Corner of Hwy 43 and 117th Ave; in Best Western Grande Prairie Hotel & Suites. **Parking:** on-site. **Cards:** AX, DC, MC, VI.

HIGH RIVER pop. 10,716

——— WHERE TO STAY ———

HERITAGE INN *Book at AAA.com* Phone: (403)652-3834

Small-scale Hotel
$119-$225 All Year

Address: 1104 11th Ave SE T1V 1M4 **Location:** Trans-Canada Hwy 2, exit 23, 0.5 mi (0.8 km) w of Hwy 2. **Facility:** 73 units. 72 one-bedroom standard units, some with whirlpools. 1 one-bedroom suite with whirlpool. 2 stories (no elevator), interior corridors. **Parking:** on-site, winter plug-ins. **Amenities:** *Some:* high-speed Internet. **Pool(s):** heated indoor. **Leisure Activities:** whirlpool, limited exercise equipment. **Business Services:** meeting rooms. **Cards:** AX, DS, MC, VI.

SUPER 8 MOTEL

Small-scale Hotel
$150-$200 3/1-9/30
$140-$200 10/1-2/28

Phone: (403)652-4448

Address: 1601 13th Ave SE T1V 2B1 **Location:** Trans-Canada Hwy 2, exit High River, just w. **Facility:** 60 one-bedroom standard units, some with efficiencies and/or whirlpools. 3 stories, interior corridors. *Bath:* combo or shower only. **Parking:** on-site, winter plug-ins. **Amenities:** high-speed Internet, voice mail, irons, hair dryers. *Some:* video games. **Pool(s):** heated indoor. **Leisure Activities:** whirlpool, waterslide, exercise room. **Guest Services:** valet and coin laundry. **Business Services:** meeting rooms. **Cards:** AX, DC, DS, MC, VI.

WHERE TO DINE

WHISTLESTOP CAFE

Canadian
$5-$8

Phone: 403/652-7026

Simple, well-prepared food is one of the reasons to come to the distinctive eatery. Its location in a 1947 Canadian Pacific rail coach car, complete with CP memorabilia, is another. On the menu is a wide variety of comfort foods, including sandwiches, quiche, quesadillas and fried green tomatoes. The dessert selection is extensive. Guests can enjoy lunch or afternoon tea and imagine the car swaying gently along the tracks as it did long ago. Casual dress. **Hours:** 8 am-5 pm; 10 am-4 pm in winter. Closed major holidays. **Address:** 406 lst St SW T1V 1S2 **Location:** 0.6 mi (1 km) n at 3rd Ave; next to museum. **Parking:** on-site. **Cards:** MC, VI.

HINTON pop. 9,738

WHERE TO STAY

BEST WESTERN WHITE WOLF INN

Small-scale Hotel
$126-$160 All Year

Phone: (780)865-7777

Address: 828 Carmichael Ln T7V 1T1 **Location:** At west end of town; just off Hwy 16. **Facility:** 42 units. 39 one- and 2 two-bedroom standard units, some with whirlpools. 1 one-bedroom suite. 2 stories (no elevator), exterior corridors. **Parking:** on-site, winter plug-ins. **Terms:** cancellation fee imposed. **Amenities:** irons, hair dryers. *Some:* high-speed Internet. **Leisure Activities:** whirlpool, interpretative trail, limited exercise equipment. **Guest Services:** valet laundry, wireless Internet. **Cards:** AX, CB, DC, DS, MC, VI. **Free Special Amenities:** expanded continental breakfast and high-speed Internet.

AAA Benefit:
Members save 10% everyday, plus an exclusive frequent stay program.

HOLIDAY INN HINTON

Small-scale Hotel
$149-$159 All Year

Phone: (780)865-3321

Address: 393 Gregg Ave T7V 1N1 **Location:** 0.3 mi (0.5 km) w on Hwy 16. **Facility:** 104 units. 102 one-bedroom standard units. 1 one- and 1 two-bedroom suites, some with whirlpools. 2 stories (no elevator), interior corridors. **Parking:** on-site, winter plug-ins. **Amenities:** video games (fee), dual phone lines, voice mail, irons, hair dryers. **Pool(s):** heated indoor. **Leisure Activities:** sauna, whirlpool, waterslide, exercise room. **Guest Services:** valet and coin laundry, wireless Internet. **Business Services:** meeting rooms, PC (fee). **Cards:** AX, DC, DS, MC, VI. **Free Special Amenities:** newspaper and high-speed Internet.

LAKEVIEW INNS & SUITES

Small-scale Hotel
Rates not provided

Phone: 780/865-2575

Address: 500 Smith St T7V 2A1 **Location:** 1.1 mi (1.7 km) e on Hwy 16. **Facility:** 55 units. 46 one-bedroom standard units. 9 one-bedroom suites, some with kitchens and/or whirlpools. 2 stories (no elevator), interior/exterior corridors. *Bath:* combo or shower only. **Parking:** on-site, winter plug-ins. **Amenities:** DVD players, voice mail, irons, hair dryers. **Leisure Activities:** whirlpool, limited exercise equipment. **Guest Services:** coin laundry. **Business Services:** meeting rooms, PC (fee). *(See color ad p 362)*

OVERLANDER MOUNTAIN LODGE

Country Inn
$145-$255 All Year

Phone: 780/866-2330

Address: Hwy 16 T7V 1X5 **Location:** Hwy 16, 15 mi (24 km) w; just outside Jasper National Park Gates. **Facility:** 40 units. 24 one-bedroom standard units, some with kitchens and/or whirlpools. 12 one-bedroom suites. 4 cottages. 1-2 stories (no elevator), interior/exterior corridors. *Bath:* combo or shower only. **Parking:** on-site, winter plug-ins. **Terms:** office hours 7 am-11 pm, check-in 4 pm, 3 day cancellation notice. **Amenities:** hair dryers. *Some:* irons. **Dining:** Stone Peak Restaurant & Lounge, see separate listing. **Leisure Activities:** hiking trails. *Fee:* horseback riding. **Guest Services:** valet laundry, wireless Internet. **Business Services:** meeting rooms. **Cards:** AX, DC, MC, VI. **Free Special Amenities:** newspaper and room upgrade (subject to availability with advance reservations).

SUPER 8 MOTEL

Small-scale Hotel
$139-$159 3/1-9/1
$129-$139 9/2-2/28

Phone: (780)817-2228

Address: 284 Smith St T7V 2A1 **Location:** 1 mi (1.6 km) e on Hwy 16. **Facility:** 48 units. 46 one-bedroom standard units. 2 one-bedroom suites. 2 stories (no elevator), interior corridors. **Parking:** on-site, winter plug-ins. **Amenities:** hair dryers. *Some:* high-speed Internet. **Pool(s):** heated indoor. **Leisure Activities:** whirlpool. **Guest Services:** coin laundry, wireless Internet. **Cards:** AX, DC, DS, MC, VI.

WHERE TO DINE

L & W FAMILY RESTAURANT

Canadian
$5-$16

Phone: 780/865-4892

Ask any local in town for a good place to eat, and the diner-style restaurant is mentioned time and time again. Guests order at the counter and pick up their food when their number is called. Among offerings are Greek specialties, such as souvlaki and spanakopita, and hamburgers, pizzas and steaks, which are served in ample portions. Casual dress. **Bar:** Full bar. **Hours:** 10:30 am-1 am. Closed: 1/1, 12/25, 12/26. **Address:** 414 Carmichael Ln T7V 1X7 **Location:** West end of city on Hwy 16; across from Holiday Inn Hinton. **Parking:** on-site. **Cards:** MC, VI.

SMITTY'S

International
$6-$15

Phone: 780/865-6151

The family-oriented restaurant satisfies patrons with its ever-popular all-day breakfast items, as well as tasty and wholesome soups and salads at lunchtime. A relaxed mood characterizes the dining space. Casual dress. **Reservations:** not accepted. **Hours:** 5:30 am-10 pm. Closed major holidays. **Address:** 445 Gregg Ave T7V 1X8 **Location:** 0.7 km w on Hwy 16. **Parking:** on-site. **Cards:** AX, MC, VI.

STONE PEAK RESTAURANT & LOUNGE *Menu on AAA.com*

(CAA)

International
$5-$31

Phone: 780/866-2330

Just outside of town, the restaurant is worth the drive. Diners can enjoy seasonally inspired cuisine in the log interior, which features a cozy decor. Chocolate pecan pie, created from a recipe so secret that the chef won't allow his staff to see him make it, is a great way to finish a fine meal. The cozy surroundings afford views of the mountains in the distance. Casual dress. **Bar:** Full bar. **Reservations:** suggested. **Hours:** 7 am-9:30 pm; 7 am-10:30 & 5-9 pm in winter. Closed: 12/25, 12/26; also 1st week of Jan. **Address:** Hwy 16 T7V 1X5 **Location:** Hwy 16, 15 mi (24 km) w; just outside Jasper National Park Gates; in Overlander Mountain Lodge. **Parking:** on-site. **Cards:** AX, DC, MC, VI.

JASPER pop. 4,265

WHERE TO STAY

ALPINE VILLAGE

(CAA) (SAVE)

Cabin
$180-$310 6/6-10/14
$110-$250 5/2-6/5

Phone: 780/852-3285

Address: Hwy 93A T0E 1E0 **Location:** Jct Hwy 16 and 93, 0.9 mi (1.4 km) s on Hwy 93, then just n. **Facility:** These upscale cabins, which range in size and decor, are in a wooded, riverfront setting outside of town; a 16-foot outdoor hot pool is on site. Designated smoking area. 41 units. 12 one-bedroom standard units. 29 cabins. 1 story, exterior corridors. *Bath:* combo or shower only. **Parking:** on-site. **Terms:** open 5/2-10/14, office hours 8 am-10 pm, check-in 4 pm, 14 day cancellation notice-fee imposed. **Amenities:** *Some:* hair dryers. **Leisure Activities:** large outdoor hot tub, bocci, board games, hiking trails, playground. **Guest Services:** valet laundry. **Cards:** MC, VI.
(See color ad below)

[icons] / SOME UNITS FEE (VCR)

AMETHYST LODGE

(CAA) (SAVE)

Small-scale Hotel
$85-$285 All Year

Phone: (780)852-3394

Book great rates at AAA.com

Address: 200 Connaught Dr T0E 1E0 **Location:** 0.3 mi (0.5 km) e. **Facility:** 97 units. 91 one-bedroom standard units. 6 one-bedroom suites. 3 stories, interior/exterior corridors. **Parking:** on-site, winter plug-ins. **Terms:** check-in 4 pm. **Amenities:** voice mail, hair dryers. *Some:* high-speed Internet. **Leisure Activities:** whirlpools. **Guest Services:** valet laundry, area transportation-train station. **Business Services:** meeting rooms. **Cards:** AX, CB, DC, DS, JC, MC, VI. **Free Special Amenities:** local telephone calls and high-speed Internet.

[icons] / SOME UNITS

BECKER'S CHALETS

(CAA) (SAVE)

[icons]
Cabin
$130-$185 5/2-10/13

Phone: 780/852-3779

Address: Hwy 93 S T0E 1E0 **Location:** 4.25 mi (6.8 km) s. Located in a quiet rustic area. **Facility:** Smoke free premises. 118 units. 5 one-bedroom standard units. 52 one-, 14 two- and 2 three-bedroom suites with kitchens. 45 cabins. 2 stories (no elevator). *Bath:* combo or shower only. **Parking:** on-site. **Terms:** open 5/2-10/13, office hours 7 am-11 pm, 7 day cancellation notice. **Amenities:** irons, hair dryers. **Leisure Activities:** fishing, hiking trails, playground. *Fee:* bicycles. **Guest Services:** coin laundry. **Cards:** AX, MC, VI.

[icons]

CHATEAU JASPER

Phone: (780)852-5644

Small-scale Hotel
$109-$295 All Year

Address: 96 Geikie St T0E 1E0 **Location:** Corner of Juniper and Geikie sts. Located in a residential area. **Facility:** Designated smoking area. 119 units. 115 one-bedroom standard units, some with whirlpools. 4 one-bedroom suites. 3 stories, interior corridors. **Parking:** on-site, winter plug-ins. **Terms:** check-in 4 pm. **Amenities:** video games, voice mail, safes, irons, hair dryers. **Pool(s):** heated indoor. **Leisure Activities:** whirlpool, exercise room. **Guest Services:** valet laundry, area transportation-train & bus station, wireless Internet. **Business Services:** conference facilities. **Cards:** AX, CB, DC, DS, JC, MC, VI. **Free Special Amenities:** local telephone calls and high-speed Internet.

THE COAST PYRAMID LAKE RESORT

Phone: (780)852-4900

Small-scale Hotel
$209-$364 4/24-10/26

Address: Pyramid Lake Rd T0E 1E0 **Location:** Jct Connaught Dr and Cedar St, 3.75 mi (6 km) nw via Pyramid Lake Rd. Located in a quiet area. **Facility:** Smoke free premises. 62 units. 34 one-bedroom standard units. 26 one- and 2 two-bedroom suites with efficiencies. 2 stories (no elevator), exterior corridors. **Parking:** on-site, winter plug-ins. **Terms:** open 4/24-10/26, check-in 4 pm, 2-3 night minimum stay - weekends, 3 day cancellation notice. **Amenities:** voice mail, hair dryers. **Dining:** The Pines, see separate listing. **Leisure Activities:** whirlpool, steamroom, rental boats, rental canoes, rental paddleboats, boat ramp, cross country skiing, hiking trails, exercise room. *Fee:* fishing, 2 person kayaks, ice skating, barbecue patio, bicycles. **Business Services:** meeting rooms. **Cards:** AX, DC, DS, MC, VI. **Free Special Amenities:** local telephone calls and newspaper. *(See color ad below)*

THE FAIRMONT JASPER PARK LODGE

Phone: (780)852-3301

Resort
Large-scale Hotel
$169-$629 All Year

Address: Lodge Rd T0E 1E0 **Location:** 3 mi (4.8 km) ne via Hwy 16; 2 mi (3.2 km) se off highway via Maligne Rd, follow signs. **Facility:** It's said that at one time, Marilyn Monroe frequented this resort set along two lakes just outside of town; activities and scenic grounds await. 446 units. 331 one-bedroom standard units. 115 one-bedroom suites, some with whirlpools. 1-2 stories (no elevator), exterior corridors. **Parking:** on-site and valet, winter plug-ins. **Terms:** check-in 4 pm, 3 day cancellation notice-fee imposed. **Amenities:** video games (fee), voice mail, irons, hair dryers. *Some:* CD players, high-speed Internet (fee), dual phone lines, safes. **Dining:** 5 restaurants, also, The Edith Cavell, Moose's Nook, see separate listings, entertainment. **Pool(s):** heated outdoor. **Leisure Activities:** saunas, whirlpool, steamroom, rental boats, rental canoes, rental paddleboats, 4 tennis courts, cross country skiing, ice skating, tobogganing, recreation programs, hiking trails, playground, exercise room, horseshoes, shuffleboard. *Fee:* fishing, guided fishing trips, white-water rafting, canoe rides, golf-18 holes, wagon rides, snowshoeing, canyon tours, guided mountain hikes, trail rides, bicycles, horseback riding, massage, game room. **Guest Services:** valet laundry. *Fee:* airport transportation-Edmonton, Calgary & Hinton airports, area transportation-ski hills. **Business Services:** conference facilities, business center. **Cards:** AX, DC, DS, JC, MC, VI. **Free Special Amenities:** newspaper.

JASPER HOUSE BUNGALOWS   Phone: 780/852-4535

🔶🔶🔶
Cabin
$160-$265 6/10-10/15
$75-$150 5/1-6/9

Address: Hwy 93 S T0E 1E0 **Location:** 2.5 mi (4 km) s on Hwy 93. Located in a quiet rustic area. **Facility:** Smoke free premises. 56 cabins, some with whirlpools. 1 story, exterior corridors. *Bath:* combo or shower only. **Parking:** on-site. **Terms:** open 5/1-10/15, office hours 8 am-10 pm, 2 night minimum stay, 7 day cancellation notice. **Amenities:** hair dryers. **Leisure Activities:** hiking trails, horseshoes. **Guest Services:** coin laundry. **Cards:** AX, MC, VI.

🍽 ✕ 🆓 🚫 🖥 / SOME UNITS 📶 🖨

JASPER INN ALPINE RESORT   *Book great rates at AAA.com*   Phone: (780)852-4461

CAA SAVE
🔶🔶🔶
Small-scale Hotel
$243-$413 6/1-2/28
$118-$310 3/1-5/31

Address: 98 Geikie St T0E 1E0 **Location:** Corner of Geikie and Bonhomme sts. Located in a residential area. **Facility:** 143 units. 101 one- and 26 two-bedroom standard units, some with kitchens and/or whirlpools. 16 one-bedroom suites. 2-3 stories (no elevator), interior/exterior corridors. **Parking:** on-site, winter plug-ins. **Terms:** check-in 4 pm, 3 day cancellation notice-fee imposed. **Amenities:** irons, hair dryers. **Pool(s):** heated indoor. **Leisure Activities:** sauna, whirlpool, steamroom, ski lockers. **Guest Services:** coin laundry. **Business Services:** meeting rooms, PC. **Cards:** AX, MC, VI. **Free Special Amenities:** local telephone calls. *(See color ad below)*

SD 🍽 🍸 🏊 ✕ 🆓 🖥 📶 / SOME UNITS FEE 📶 ✕ VCR 🖨 🖨

LOBSTICK LODGE   *Book great rates at AAA.com*   Phone: (780)852-4431

CAA SAVE
🔶🔶🔶🔶
Small-scale Hotel
$99-$255 All Year

Address: 94 Geikie St T0E 1E0 **Location:** Corner of Geikie and Juniper sts. **Facility:** 139 units. 134 one-bedroom standard units, some with kitchens. 5 one-bedroom suites with kitchens. 3 stories, interior corridors. **Amenities:** voice mail, irons, hair dryers. **Leisure Activities:** sauna, whirlpools, steamroom, sun deck. **Guest Services:** valet and coin laundry, area transportation-train station, wireless Internet. **Business Services:** meeting rooms, PC (fee). **Cards:** AX, CB, DC, DS, JC, MC, VI. **Free Special Amenities:** local telephone calls and high-speed Internet.

SD 🍽 🍸 ✕ 🆓 🖨 🖥 / SOME UNITS 📶 ✕ FEE VCR 🖨

MALIGNE LODGE   *Book great rates at AAA.com*   Phone: (780)852-3143

CAA SAVE
🔶🔶🔶
Motel
$99-$400 All Year

Address: 900 Connaught T0E 1E0 **Location:** 0.6 mi (1 km) sw. **Facility:** 98 units. 79 one-bedroom standard units. 19 two-bedroom suites with kitchens, some with whirlpools. 2 stories (no elevator), interior/exterior corridors. **Parking:** on-site, winter plug-ins. **Terms:** check-in 4 pm. **Amenities:** hair dryers. **Pool(s):** heated indoor. **Leisure Activities:** saunas, whirlpool. **Guest Services:** wireless Internet. **Cards:** AX, MC, VI.

SD 🍽 🍸 🏊 📷 🖥 / SOME UNITS FEE 📶 ✕ 🆓 🖨 🖨

MARMOT LODGE   *Book great rates at AAA.com*   Phone: (780)852-4471

CAA SAVE
🔶🔶🔶
Motel
$89-$255 All Year

Address: 86 Connaught Dr T0E 1E0 **Location:** 1 mi (1.6 km) ne. **Facility:** 107 units. 81 one-bedroom standard units, some with kitchens. 25 one- and 1 two-bedroom suites with kitchens, some with whirlpools. 2 stories (no elevator), exterior corridors. *Bath:* combo or shower only. **Parking:** on-site, winter plug-ins. **Terms:** check-in 4 pm. **Amenities:** voice mail, hair dryers. **Pool(s):** heated indoor. **Leisure Activities:** sauna, whirlpools. **Guest Services:** coin laundry, area transportation-train station. **Business Services:** meeting rooms. **Cards:** AX, CB, DC, DS, JC, MC, VI. **Free Special Amenities:** local telephone calls and high-speed Internet.

SD 🍽 🍸 🏊 🖥 / SOME UNITS 📶 ✕ 🆓 🖨 🖨

▼ *See AAA listing above* ▼

MOUNT ROBSON INN
Book great rates at AAA.com

Phone: (780)852-3327

 CAA SAVE
◆◆◆◆ ◆◆
Motel
$99-$309 All Year

Address: 902 Connaught Dr T0E 1E0 **Location:** 0.6 mi (1 km) sw. **Facility:** 80 units. 74 one-bedroom standard units, some with whirlpools. 6 one-bedroom suites. 2 stories (no elevator), exterior corridors. **Parking:** on-site, winter plug-ins. **Terms:** cancellation fee imposed. **Amenities:** video library (fee), hair dryers. *Some:* video games, irons. **Leisure Activities:** whirlpools. **Guest Services:** coin laundry, area transportation-train station, wireless Internet. **Business Services:** PC (fee). **Cards:** AX, DC, JC, MC, VI. **Free Special Amenities:** local telephone calls and high-speed Internet. *(See color ad below)*

[icons]

PARK PLACE INN

Phone: 780/852-9770

CAA SAVE
◆◆◆◆ ◆◆◆
Small-scale Hotel
$129-$265 All Year

Address: 623 Patricia St T0E 1E0 **Location:** Downtown. **Facility:** Smoke free premises. 14 units. 12 one-bedroom standard units, some with whirlpools. 2 one-bedroom suites with whirlpools. 2 stories, interior corridors. **Parking:** on-site. **Terms:** 5 day cancellation notice. **Amenities:** hair dryers. *Some:* DVD players. **Guest Services:** wireless Internet. **Cards:** AX, MC, VI. **Free Special Amenities:** local telephone calls.

[icons]

PATRICIA LAKE BUNGALOWS

Phone: 780/852-3560

◆◆◆◆ ◆◆◆◆
Cabin
$75-$325 5/2-10/15

Address: Pyramid Lake Rd T0E 1E0 **Location:** 3 mi (4.8 km) nw via Pyramid Lake Rd. **Facility:** Designated smoking area. 47 units. 9 one-bedroom standard units. 11 one- and 8 two-bedroom suites with kitchens. 19 cabins. 1 story, exterior corridors. *Bath:* combo or shower only. **Parking:** on-site. **Terms:** open 5/2-10/15, office hours 8 am-10 pm, check-in 3:30 pm, 7 day cancellation notice. **Amenities:** *Some:* hair dryers. **Leisure Activities:** whirlpool, rental boats, rental canoes, rental paddleboats, boat dock, fishing, playground. *Fee:* bicycles, horseback riding. **Guest Services:** coin laundry. **Cards:** MC, VI.

[icons]

THE SAWRIDGE INN AND CONFERENCE CENTRE
Book great rates at AAA.com

Phone: (780)852-5111

CAA SAVE
◆◆◆ ◆◆◆
Small-scale Hotel
$139-$289 All Year

Address: 82 Connaught Dr T0E 1E0 **Location:** 1.1 mi (1.7 km) e. **Facility:** 153 units. 149 one-bedroom standard units. 4 one-bedroom suites with whirlpools. 3 stories, interior corridors. **Parking:** on-site, winter plug-ins. **Terms:** check-in 4 pm, 3 day cancellation notice-fee imposed. **Amenities:** voice mail, irons, hair dryers. *Fee:* video games, high-speed Internet. *Some:* CD players. **Dining:** nightclub. **Pool(s):** heated indoor. **Leisure Activities:** sauna, whirlpools, exercise room, spa. **Guest Services:** valet and coin laundry, area transportation-within Jasper, wireless Internet. **Business Services:** conference facilities, PC (fee). **Cards:** AX, DC, DS, JC, MC, VI. **Free Special Amenities:** local telephone calls and high-speed Internet.

[icons]

SUNWAPTA FALLS RESORT
Book great rates at AAA.com

Phone: (780)852-4852

CAA SAVE
◆◆◆ ◆◆◆
Motel
$89-$389 5/8-10/10

Address: Hwy 93 T0E 1E0 **Location:** 34.75 mi (55 km) s on Icefields Pkwy (Hwy 93). Located in a quiet secluded setting. **Facility:** Smoke free premises. 53 one-bedroom standard units. 1-2 stories (no elevator), exterior corridors. **Parking:** on-site. **Terms:** open 5/8-10/10, check-in 4 pm, 7 day cancellation notice. **Leisure Activities:** hiking trails. *Fee:* fishing, fishing equipment, whitewater rafting, bicycles. **Guest Services:** wireless Internet. **Business Services:** meeting rooms, PC. **Cards:** AX, MC, VI. **Free Special Amenities:** local telephone calls and high-speed Internet. *(See color ad p 466)*

[icons]

―――― ▼ See AAA listing above ▼ ――――

TONQUIN INN *Book great rates at AAA.com*   Phone: 780/852-4987

Motel
$135-$260 All Year

Address: 100 Juniper St T0E 1E0 **Location:** Corner of Juniper and Geikie sts. **Facility:** 137 units. 107 one- and 20 two-bedroom standard units, some with kitchens. 4 one- and 6 two-bedroom suites with kitchens. 2-3 stories, interior/exterior corridors. **Parking:** on-site, winter plug-ins. **Terms:** check-in 4 pm, cancellation fee imposed. **Amenities:** hair dryers. *Some:* irons. **Pool(s):** heated indoor. **Leisure Activities:** whirlpools, exercise room. **Guest Services:** coin laundry. **Business Services:** meeting rooms. **Cards:** AX, DC, MC, VI.

▼ See AAA listing p 465 ▼

SUNWAPTA FALLS RESORT

Call Us First!

- COMPLIMENTARY DAY PLANNING
- HERITAGE DAY LODGE IN A WILDERNESS SETTING
  - CABIN STYLE ACCOMMODATIONS
  - FIREPLACES/DUVETS
  - HOMESTYLE BREAKFAST & DELI
  - RENOWNED FINE DINING
  - COURTESY INTERNET
  - STOP & SHOP TRADING POST
- RIVER RAFTING
- BICYCLE & FISHING RENTALS
- ANIMAL SIGHTINGS

TOLL FREE:1-888-828-5777 PH: (780) 852-4852 FAX: (780) 852-5353
LOCATED 52 KM (34 MI) SOUTH OF JASPER ON THE ICEFIELDS PARKWAY (HWY 93)
VISIT OUR WEBSITE PHOTO GALLERY @ WWW.SUNWAPTA.COM

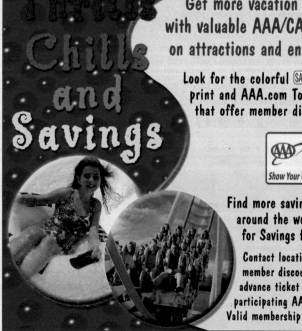

Thrills Chills and Savings

Get more vacation for your dollar with valuable AAA/CAA member savings on attractions and entertainment.

Look for the colorful SAVE SAVE symbol in the print and AAA.com TourBook® for locations that offer member discounts.

Show Your Card & Save®

Find more savings, at home and around the world, with the Search for Savings feature on AAA.com/save.

Contact locations prior to visiting for member discount details. Ask about advance ticket savings available through participating AAA/CAA offices.
Valid membership card required.

——— WHERE TO DINE ———

ANDY'S BISTRO

International
$18-$32

Phone: 780/852-4559

It is difficult to choose one word to define the fine cuisine, as the International menu reflects influences from around the world. Guests might find salmon, veal, spaetzle or chicken, all prepared a la minute. The bistro nurtures a casual atmosphere. Casual dress. **Bar:** Full bar. **Reservations:** suggested. **Hours:** 5 pm-9 pm. Closed major holidays; also 12/23-12/26. **Address:** 606 Patricia St T0E 1E0 **Location:** Centre. **Parking:** street. **Cards:** MC, VI.

BEAR'S PAW BAKERY

Bakery/Desserts
$2-$10

Phone: 780/852-3233

Guests can savor the aroma of freshly baked goods at the cozy hideaway bakery. Eyes feast on European-style pastries, artisan breads and Vienna pastries. Beware: Standing too long in front of the display case will cause mouths to water. Representative of the many temptations are trail cookies, Bear's Paw cinnamon buns, carrot cake and date squares. Only one table is available, so most patrons grab a sweet and a cup of coffee and head out into the mountain air. Casual dress. **Hours:** Open 3/1-10/31 & 12/1-2/28; 6 am-8 pm. Closed: 1/1, 12/25. **Address:** 4 Cedar Ave T0E 1E0 **Location:** Just w off Connaught Dr at Cedar Ave. **Parking:** street. **Cards:** AX, MC, VI.

BECKER'S GOURMET RESTAURANT

Continental
$16-$30

Phone: 780/852-3535

Along the river just south of the city, the restaurant is a favorite among Jasper residents. The dining room's warm oak and fir decor is distinctly Canadian and, set against the backdrop of the river, provides an idyllic setting. Regionally inspired Continental cuisine ranges from salmon and scallops to beef tenderloin and lamb. Casual dress. **Bar:** Full bar. **Reservations:** suggested. **Hours:** Open 5/1-10/15; 8 am-11 & 5:30-9:30 pm. **Address:** Hwy 93 T0E 1E0 **Location:** On Hwy 93, 4.3 mi (6.8 km) s. **Parking:** on-site. **Cards:** AX, DS, MC, VI.

CAFE MONDO
Deli/Subs
Sandwiches
$5-$7

Phone: 780/852-9676

Under the same ownership as the former Truffles and Trout, this casual eatery has a subtle European feel that just begs customers to sit and relax for a while. A good variety of baked goods, soups and sandwiches can be enjoyed with a freshly made cup of coffee or cold beverage. Casual dress. **Hours:** 8 am-9 pm; to 8 pm in winter. Closed major holidays. **Address:** 616 Patricia St T0E 1E0 **Location:** Centre. **Parking:** street. **Cards:** MC, VI.

THE EDITH CAVELL
Canadian
$34-$42

Phone: 780/852-6052

The sounds of the harp, views of Lac Beauvert and Mount Edith Cavell, and the rich, mahogany woodwork of the elegant dining room set the scene for a truly enchanting experience. The restaurant's delightful, complex nouvelle cuisine draws inspiration from the Northwest. Among delicacies are preparations of Arctic char, salmon and venison. In season, guests can savor a weekly changing tasting menu. Dressy casual. Entertainment. **Bar:** Full bar. **Reservations:** required. **Hours:** 6 pm-10 pm; seasonal hours may vary. **Address:** Lodge Rd T0E 1E0 **Location:** 3 mi (4.8 km) ne via Hwy 16; 2 mi (3.2 km) se off highway via Maligne Rd, follow signs; in The Fairmont Jasper Park Lodge. **Parking:** on-site and valet. **Cards:** AX, DC, DS, JC, MC, VI.

FIDDLE RIVER RESTAURANT

Seafood
$15-$35

Phone: 780/852-3032

An ever-changing seafood menu is the highlight of the casual yet cozy restaurant, upstairs from street level. Fresh is the operative word, and patrons might find salmon, trout, sole, king crab, cod or blackened shrimp on the menu. For a view of the mountains, request a window seat. Service is friendly and attentive. Semiformal attire. **Bar:** Full bar. **Hours:** 5 pm-10 pm. Closed: 12/25, 12/26. **Address:** 620 Connaught Dr T0E 1E0 **Location:** At Hazel Ave; upstairs. **Parking:** street. **Cards:** AX, MC, VI.

JASPER BREWING CO

Continental
$8-$25

Phone: 780/852-4111

Casual dress. **Bar:** Full bar. **Reservations:** not accepted. **Hours:** 11:30 am-10 pm. **Address:** 624 Connaught Dr T0E 1E0 **Location:** Centre. **Parking:** street. **Cards:** AX, MC, VI.

JASPER PIZZA PLACE

Pizza
$4-$15

Phone: 780/852-3225

Those looking for pizza need search no further. Whether guests choose to eat in the restaurant, order at the counter or get it to go, they can anticipate great pizza, served with thick or thin crust. Unusual toppings—such as spinach, asparagus and artichokes—are available. Service is friendly and attentive. Casual dress. **Bar:** Full bar. **Hours:** 11 am-11 pm. Closed: 12/25. **Address:** 402 Connaugt Dr T0E 1E0 **Location:** Centre. **Parking:** street. **Cards:** MC, VI.

KAROUZO'S STEAKHOUSE
Steak House
$7-$60

Phone: 780/852-4640

On the main street leading into town, the family-run steak and seafood restaurant features a wide variety of entrees, including some pasta dishes. Casual dress. **Bar:** Full bar. **Hours:** Open 4/1-10/31; 11 am-11 pm. **Address:** 628 Connaught Dr T0E 1E0 **Location:** Between Spruce and Hazel aves. **Parking:** street. **Cards:** MC, VI.

LA FIESTA

Spanish
$8-$23

Phone: 780/852-0404

An oasis of Spanish cuisine awaits in the cozy restaurant, a new addition to the city scene. Inside, guests can experience the wonders of tapas (Spanish appetizers) that range from lamb and chorizo sausage meatballs to goat cheese and artichoke dip. Group of friends often linger over a pitcher of sangria, especially the owner's specialty, made with white wine. The simple decor of white walls and dark woods is nonetheless festive and evocative of Spain. Semi-formal attire. **Bar:** Full bar. **Hours:** 11:30 am-11 pm; noon-2:30 & 4:30-10 pm 11/1-5/31. Closed: 12/25; also Sun in winter. **Address:** 504 Patricia St T0E 1E0 **Location:** Between Elm and Miette aves; across from Information Centre. **Parking:** street. **Cards:** MC, VI.

L & W FAMILY RESTAURANT

Phone: 780/852-4114

International
$8-$19

Those looking for good value for the dollar will find the family-run restaurant at the corner of Patricia and Hazel a good choice. There is something for everyone on the menu, including Greek dishes, burgers, pizza and sandwiches. Casual dress. **Bar:** Full bar. **Hours:** 11 am-midnight. Closed major holidays. **Location:** Corner of Hazel Ave and Patricia St. **Parking:** street. **Cards:** AX, MC, VI.

MOOSE'S NOOK

Phone: 780/852-6052

Regional
Canadian
$27-$40

This "nook" of a restaurant is casual, but the food is anything but. Representative of creative, inventive regional cuisine are Alberta beef and pork entrees, seasonal greens and tempting desserts. The service and ambience are upscale without being pretentious and laid-back yet classy. This spot shouldn't be missed for those looking for a taste of Canada. Casual dress. **Bar:** Full bar. **Reservations:** suggested. **Hours:** Open 5/15-10/31; 6 pm-10 pm. **Address:** Lodge Rd T0E 1E0 **Location:** 3 mi (4.8 km) ne via Hwy 16; 2 mi (3.2 km) se off highway via Maligne Rd, follow signs; in The Fairmont Jasper Park Lodge. **Parking:** on-site and valet. **Cards:** AX, CB, DC, DS, MC, VI.

PAPA GEORGE'S RESTAURANT

Phone: 780/852-3351

Continental
$6-$35

You'll enjoy the family dining in Papa George's bistro setting. They have a varied menu with International flavour and specialize in hearty sandwiches, freshly baked bread and pastry, duck a l'orange, lamb, fresh seafood, pork and Alberta steak. Casual dress. **Bar:** Full bar. **Reservations:** suggested. **Hours:** 7 am-2:30 & 5-10 pm. **Address:** 404 Connaught Dr T0E 1E0 **Location:** Centre; in Astoria Hotel. **Parking:** on-site. **Cards:** AX, MC, VI.

PATRICIA STREET DELI

Phone: 780/852-4814

Deli/Subs
Sandwiches
$5-$7

It would be easy to walk past the small, unassuming entrance to the subtly decorated delicatessen. However, it's worth seeking this place out for freshly made sandwiches, which can be eaten at one of the limited tables or in a multitude of green spaces within a short walk. Casual dress. **Hours:** 10 am-6 pm; seasonal hours may vary. Closed: 12/25. **Address:** 606 Patricia St T0E 1E0 **Location:** Centre. **Parking:** street. **Cards:** MC, VI.

THE PINES

Phone: 780/852-3810

Canadian
$9-$28

The cozy yet upscale dining room makes guests feel as through they are dining in a lodge, with wooden beams overhead and lovely views of the lake. Each preparation of regional cuisine is an artistic creation. The atmosphere and service are sure to please. Casual dress. **Bar:** Full bar. **Reservations:** suggested, in summer. **Hours:** 8 am-9 pm. **Location:** Jct Connaught Dr and Cedar St, 3.8 mi (6 km) nw via Pyramid Lake Rd; in The Coast Pyramid Lake Resort. **Parking:** on-site. **Cards:** AX, DC, JC, MC, VI. *(See color ad p 462)*

SOFT ROCK CAFE'

Phone: 780/852-5850

Deli/Subs
Sandwiches
$4-$10

The cafe is a popular spot for a quick bite while surfing the 'net. Breakfast is available until 4 pm, but patrons also may choose a hearty soup, sandwich, baked good or croque monsieur/madame. Casual dress. **Bar:** Full bar. **Hours:** 7:30 am-10 pm; 7 am-4 pm in winter. Closed: 12/25. **Address:** 632 Connaught Dr T0E 1E0 **Location:** Just n of Hazel Ave. **Parking:** street. **Cards:** MC, VI.

SOMETHING ELSE RESTAURANT

Phone: 780/852-3850

Greek
$6-$23

The menu lists large portions of lamb and chicken dishes and pizza. Preparations show a tasty mix of International flavor. The staff provides friendly, cheerful and prompt service in a modest, casual atmosphere. Casual dress. **Bar:** Full bar. **Hours:** 11 am-11 pm. Closed: 12/25. **Address:** 621 Patricia St T0E 1E0 **Location:** Just w of Connaught Dr; centre. **Parking:** on-site. **Cards:** AX, DC, DS, MC, VI.

TREELINE RESTAURANT

Phone: 780/852-3093

Canadian
$4-$8

A spectacular view awaits above the trees in the tundra just south of town. A $20 tram ride whisks guests up past the tree line and affords views of five mountain ranges, lakes and the town. Diners can work up an appetite climbing to the summit of Whistler's Mountain and then enter the cafeteria-style restaurant for burgers, sandwiches and salads or perhaps a beer or glass of wine. A full menu is available only in high season; the early season offers light meals. Casual dress. **Bar:** Beer & wine. **Reservations:** accepted. **Hours:** Open 4/30-10/31; 9:30 am-5:30 pm; to 6:30 pm 6/1-6/30; 8:30 am-10 pm 7/1-8/20; 9:30 am-4:30 pm 8/21-10/1. **Location:** 1.8 mi (3 km) s on Hwy 93, 2.5 mi (4 km) w at Whistlers Campground; train ride to restaurant for an additional charge. **Parking:** on-site. **Cards:** AX, DC, MC, VI.

VILLA CARUSO

Steak House
$8-$30

Phone: 780/852-3920

Established in 1977, the longstanding steakhouse sits above street level but is accessible via elevator. The spacious lodge-like setting has wood beams and hardwood floors, and guests seated near the windows are treated to a great view of the mountains. Alberta beef is the house specialty, but other Canadian specialties, including salmon, also find their way onto the menu. Casual dress. **Bar:** Full bar. **Hours:** 11 am-midnight; 3 pm-11 pm 11/1-4/30. Closed major holidays. **Address:** Connaught Dr & Hazel Ave T0E 1E0 **Location:** Connaught Dr and Hazel Ave; 2nd level. **Parking:** street. **Cards:** AX, DC, MC, VI.

KANANASKIS pop. 429

------ **WHERE TO STAY** ------

DELTA LODGE AT KANANASKIS   *Book great rates at AAA.com*

Resort
Large-scale Hotel
Rates not provided

Phone: 403/591-7711

Address: Kananaskis Village T0L 2H0 **Location:** Trans-Canada Hwy 1, 14.7 mi (23.5 km) s on Hwy 40 (Kananaskis Trail), then 1.8 mi (3 km) on Kananaskis Village access road, follow signs. Located in a quiet area. **Facility:** This attractive resort, nestled in a tranquil mountain village, is near recreation areas and offers a mix of room styles. 321 units. 281 one- and 14 two-bedroom standard units, some with whirlpools. 26 one-bedroom suites, some with whirlpools. 3 stories, interior corridors. **Parking:** on-site (fee) and valet, winter plug-ins. **Terms:** check-in 4 pm. **Amenities:** video games (fee), high-speed Internet, voice mail, irons, hair dryers. *Some:* CD players. **Pool(s):** heated indoor. **Leisure Activities:** whirlpool, steamroom, 6 lighted tennis courts, cross country skiing, ice skating, tobogganing, recreation programs, hiking trails, playground, sports court. *Fee:* bicycles, horseback riding, massage, game room. **Guest Services:** valet and coin laundry, area transportation. **Business Services:** conference facilities, business center. *(See color ad below)*

EXECUTIVE RESORT AT KANANASKIS   *Book at AAA.com*

Small-scale Hotel
Rates not provided

Phone: 403/591-7500

Address: 2 Terrace Dr, Box 10 T0L 2H0 **Location:** Trans-Canada Hwy 1, 14.7 mi (23.5 km) s on Hwy 40 (Kananaskis Trail), then 1.8 mi (3 km) on Kananaskis Village access road, follow signs. **Facility:** Smoke free premises. 90 units. 84 one- and 2 two-bedroom standard units, some with whirlpools. 3 one- and 1 two-bedroom suites. 3 stories, interior corridors. **Parking:** on-site, winter plug-ins. **Terms:** check-in 4 pm. **Amenities:** high-speed Internet, dual phone lines, voice mail, irons, hair dryers. **Leisure Activities:** whirlpool, 3 lighted tennis courts, downhill skiing, rental bicycles, hiking trails, exercise room. **Guest Services:** coin laundry. **Business Services:** conference facilities, PC (fee).

------ **WHERE TO DINE** ------

THE FIREWEED GRILL

Canadian
$8-$20

Phone: 403/591-7711

This comfortably casual restaurant is a popular pick for both hotel guests and day-trippers. Casual dress. **Bar:** Full bar. **Hours:** 11 am-9 pm. **Address:** Kananaskis Village T0L 2H0 **Location:** Trans-Canada Hwy 1, 14.7 mi (23.5 km) s on Hwy 40 (Kananaskis Trail), then 1.8 mi (3 km) on Kananaskis Village access road, follow signs; in Delta Lodge at Kananaskis. **Parking:** on-site (fee) and valet. **Cards:** MC, VI. *(See color ad below)*

CALL

------ ▼ *See AAA listing above* ▼ ------

LAKE LOUISE

THE FAIRMONT CHATEAU LAKE LOUISE   *Book great rates at AAA.com*   **Phone:** (403)522-3511

Ⓐ SAVE

▼▼▼▼ ▼▼▼▼
Resort
Large-scale Hotel
$249-$659 All Year

Address: 111 Lake Louise Dr T0L 1E0 **Location:** 1.8 mi (3 km) up the hill from the village. Located in a mountain area. **Facility:** Surrounded by mountains and set alongside Lake Louise, the property features a grand lobby; some rooms offer views of the Victoria Glacier. 550 units. 533 one-bedroom standard units, some with whirlpools. 17 one-bedroom suites with whirlpools. 8 stories, interior corridors. **Parking:** on-site (fee) and valet, winter plug-ins. **Terms:** check-in 4 pm, 3 day cancellation notice-fee imposed. **Amenities:** voice mail, honor bars, irons, hair dryers. *Fee:* video games, high-speed Internet. *Some:* CD players, dual phone lines, safes. **Dining:** 7 restaurants, also, Chateau Deli, Fairview Dining Room, see separate listings. **Pool(s):** heated indoor. **Leisure Activities:** whirlpool, steamroom, rental canoes, recreation programs, hiking trails, exercise room, spa. *Fee:* cross country skiing, ice skating, horseback riding. **Guest Services:** valet laundry, area transportation-ski hill, beauty salon. **Business Services:** conference facilities, business center. **Cards:** AX, DC, DS, JC, MC, VI. *(See color ad p 471)*

ⓈⒹ FEE 🛬 🍽 24🕐 🍷 🛗 🏊 🎿 📷 💻 / SOME UNITS FEE 🐕 🚫 ✗

▼ See AAA listing p 470 ▼

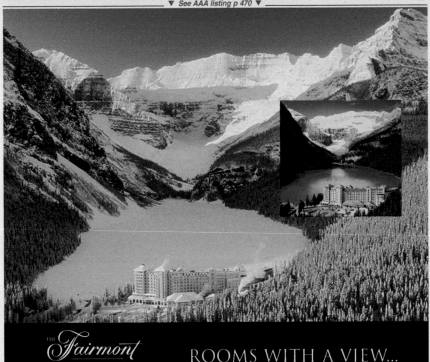

THE Fairmont
CHATEAU LAKE LOUISE

ROOMS WITH A VIEW...

Fall into bed tonight and wake up tomorrow in a world of adventure that is yours to discover.

The Fairmont Chateau Lake Louise has everything from the serene to the extreme for your next mountain adventure.

Reservations 1 800 441 1414
www.fairmont.com/lakelouise

LAKE LOUISE INN

Small-scale Hotel
Rates not provided

Book at AAA.com

Address: 210 Village Rd T0L 1E0 **Location:** Just w of 4-way stop. **Facility:** 232 units. 214 one-bedroom standard units, some with efficiencies. 18 one-bedroom suites. 2-3 stories, interior/exterior corridors. **Parking:** on-site, winter plug-ins. **Terms:** check-in 4 pm. **Amenities:** voice mail, hair dryers. *Some:* irons. **Pool(s):** heated indoor. **Leisure Activities:** whirlpools, steamroom, ice skating, recreation programs, exercise room. *Fee:* massage. **Guest Services:** coin laundry, area transportation. **Business Services:** meeting rooms, PC (fee).

Phone: 403/522-3791

MOUNTAINEER LODGE

Small-scale Hotel
$169-$339 6/24-10/15
$109-$229 5/15-6/23

Address: 101 Village Rd T0L 1E0 **Location:** Just e of 4-way stop. **Facility:** Smoke free premises. 78 units. 74 one- and 4 two-bedroom standard units. 2 stories (no elevator), interior/exterior corridors. *Bath:* combo or shower only. **Parking:** on-site. **Terms:** open 5/15-10/15, office hours 7 am-midnight, check-in 4 pm, 7 day cancellation notice-fee imposed. **Amenities:** irons, hair dryers. **Leisure Activities:** whirlpool, steamroom. **Business Services:** PC (fee). **Cards:** MC, VI. *(See color ad p 470)*

Phone: (403)522-3844

POST HOTEL & SPA

Small-scale Hotel
$320-$715 6/20-2/28
$250-$545 3/1-6/19

Book great rates at AAA.com

Address: 200 Pipestone Rd T0L 1E0 **Location:** Just w of main intersection; in village. **Facility:** Mountain decor, luxurious bathrooms, upscale rooms and fine service await at this cozy hotel, located in the heart of Lake Louise village. Designated smoking area. 96 units. 65 one-bedroom standard units. 27 one-bedroom suites with whirlpools. 4 cabins. 3 stories, interior corridors. **Parking:** on-site. **Terms:** check-in 3:30 pm, 14 day cancellation notice-fee imposed. **Amenities:** video library, voice mail, safes, hair dryers. *Some:* irons. **Dining:** Post Hotel Dining Room, see separate listing. **Pool(s):** heated indoor. **Leisure Activities:** whirlpool, steamroom, exercise room, spa. **Guest Services:** valet laundry, wireless Internet. **Business Services:** meeting rooms, PC. **Cards:** AX, MC, VI. *(See color ad p 470)*

Phone: (403)522-3989

——— **WHERE TO DINE** ———

BAKER CREEK BISTRO   Phone: 403/522-2182

Canadian

$8-$35

The bistro's cozy, log-cabin setting sustains a warm-spirited ambience. Among regional dishes are lamb chops, baked chicken and beef tenderloin, with an accent on fresh herbs and spices and hearty portions. **Bar:** Full bar. **Reservations:** suggested. **Hours:** 7 am-10, noon-2 & 5-10 pm; seasonal hours vary. Closed major holidays. **Address:** Bow Valley Pkwy T0L 1E0 **Location:** 6.8 mi (11 km) e on Hwy 1A (Bow Valley Pkwy). **Parking:** on-site. **Cards:** MC, VI.

CHATEAU DELI   Phone: 403/522-3511

Deli/Subs
Sandwiches

$5-$9

Long lines are not uncommon at this delicatessen, which is open 24 hours. Selections from the limited wine list complement custom-made sandwiches and hot entrees. Desserts have good eye appeal. Casual dress. **Bar:** Wine only. **Hours:** 24 hours. **Address:** 111 Lake Louise Dr T0L 1E0 **Location:** 1.8 mi (3 km) up the hill from the village; in The Fairmont Chateau Lake Louise. **Parking:** on-site (fee) and valet. **Cards:** AX, MC, VI.

CALL

DEER LODGE DINING ROOM   Phone: 403/552-3941

Regional
Canadian

$20-$45

The restaurant is behind the lounge in this historic hotel deep in the heart of the Rockies. With windows on three sides, the dining room affords commanding views of the mountain scenery and the nearby Chateau hotel from every seat. An extraordinary wine list includes selections perfectly matched to the creative and artistic food, which blends the best seasonal and local ingredients. This place is well known for its preparations of game, most of which is raised in a ranch outside of Calgary. Dressy casual. **Bar:** Full bar. **Reservations:** suggested. **Hours:** 5 pm-10 pm. **Address:** 80 Lake Louise Dr T0L 1E0 **Location:** 1.8 mi (3 km) up hill from village; in Deer Lodge Hotel. **Parking:** on-site. **Cards:** AX, DC, MC, VI.

ELKHORN DINING ROOM   Phone: 403/522-2167

Regional
Canadian

$15-$32

The cozy dining room features a creative and fine selection of regional cuisine, ranging from sea bass to venison to salmon. The wood interior has high ceilings and a large fireplace. Friendly, attentive service and a cozy, alpine atmosphere add to the experience. Casual dress. **Bar:** Full bar. **Reservations:** required, for dinner. **Hours:** Open 3/1-10/1 & 2/1-2/28; 7:30 am-9:30 pm. **Address:** Mile 22, Bow Lake, Icefields Pkwy T0L 1E0 **Location:** Hwy 93, (40 km) n; in Num-Ti-Jah Lodge. **Parking:** on-site. **Cards;** MC, VI.

FAIRVIEW DINING ROOM   Phone: 403/522-3511

CAA

Canadian

$25-$37

Ask for a seat by the oversized windows and be rewarded with commanding views of Lake Louise and the Victoria Glacier. From start to finish, diners can expect professional and knowledgeable service amid exquisite surroundings. The menu explores a diverse selection of Canadian cuisine, ranging from venison to organic chicken, and decadent desserts. A trip to Lake Louise would be remiss without a meal in this elegant restaurant. Dressy casual. **Bar:** Full bar. **Reservations:** required. **Hours:** 5:30 pm-9:30 pm; hours may vary off season. **Address:** 111 Lake Louise Dr T0L 1E0 **Location:** 1.8 mi (3 km) up the hill from the village; in The Fairmont Chateau Lake Louise. **Parking:** on-site (fee) and valet. **Cards:** AX, DC, DS, JC, MC, VI. **Historic**

LAGGAN'S MOUNTAIN BAKERY   Phone: 403/522-2017

Deli/Subs
Sandwiches

$6-$7

One of the few village restaurants not located in a hotel, the popular bakery serves an extensive range of baked goods and freshly made sandwiches, as well as several soups of the day. Casual dress. **Hours:** 6 am-7 pm. Closed: 1/1, 12/25. **Address:** 101 Lake Louise Dr T0L 1E0 **Location:** Centre; in Samson Mall. **Parking:** on-site.

LAKE LOUISE STATION   Phone: 403/522-2600

Canadian

$7-$28

This restaurant is located in a beautifully restored heritage railway station that includes a 1925 dining car. The progressive Continental cuisine offers lasagna, chicken, pork ribs, stuffed halibut, salmon, rack of lamb and even build-your-own pizza. Casual dress. **Bar:** Full bar. **Reservations:** suggested. **Hours:** 11:30 am-10 pm; to 6 pm 10/1-5/15. Closed: 12/25. **Address:** 200 Sentinel Rd T0L 1E0 **Location:** From 4-way stop, just s via underpass, 0.6 mi (1 km) w. **Parking:** on-site. **Cards:** MC, VI.

POST HOTEL DINING ROOM   Phone: 403/522-3989

CAA

Continental

$9-$46

Delicious food lends to the restaurant's exceptional reputation. European classics are wonderfully flavorful and colorfully presented. A less extensive menu is offered at lunch. A cigar room is available. Dressy casual. **Bar:** Full bar. **Reservations:** suggested, for dinner. **Hours:** Open 3/1-10/17 & 12/9-2/28; 7-11 am, 11:30-2 & 5-10 pm. Closed: 12/25. **Address:** 200 Pipestone Rd T0L 1E0 **Location:** Just w of main intersection; in village; in Post Hotel & Spa. **Parking:** on-site. **Cards:** AX, MC, VI.

LEDUC —*See Edmonton p. 453.*

LETHBRIDGE pop. 74,637

—— **WHERE TO STAY** ——

BEST WESTERN HEIDELBERG INN
Book great rates at AAA.com
Phone: (403)329-0555

Small-scale Hotel
$119-$139 6/1-2/28
$109-$129 3/1-5/31

Address: 1303 Mayor Magrath Dr T1K 2R1 **Location:** 2.4 mi (4 km) se on Hwy 4 and 5. **Facility:** 66 one-bedroom standard units. 9 stories, interior corridors. **Parking:** on-site, winter plug-ins. **Amenities:** voice mail, irons, hair dryers. *Some:* high-speed Internet, dual phone lines. **Leisure Activities:** sauna, limited exercise equipment. **Guest Services:** valet laundry. **Business Services:** PC. **Cards:** AX, CB, DC, DS, JC, MC, VI. **Free Special Amenities:** local telephone calls and newspaper.

AAA Benefit:
Members save 10% everyday, plus an exclusive frequent stay program.

🛇 🍴 🍽 💻 / SOME UNITS ✕ FEE VCR 🔌

COMFORT INN
Book at AAA.com
Phone: 403/320-8874

Small-scale Hotel
Rates not provided

Address: 3226 Fairway Plaza Rd S T1K 7T5 **Location:** Southeast end of city; Mayor Magrath Dr, exit n at Scenic Dr. **Facility:** 58 units. 55 one-bedroom standard units. 3 one-bedroom suites. 4 stories, interior corridors. **Bath:** combo or shower only. **Parking:** on-site, winter plug-ins. **Amenities:** high-speed Internet, voice mail, irons, hair dryers. **Pool(s):** heated indoor. **Leisure Activities:** whirlpool, exercise room. **Guest Services:** valet and coin laundry. **Business Services:** PC.
(See color ad on insert)

🍴 🏊 ♿ 🔌 🖨 💻 / SOME UNITS FEE 🐾 ✕

DAYS INN LETHBRIDGE
Book at AAA.com
Phone: (403)327-6000

Small-scale Hotel
$100-$180 3/1-8/31
$90-$165 9/1-2/28

Address: 100 3rd Ave S T1J 4L2 **Location:** Corner of 3rd Ave and Scenic Dr; centre. **Facility:** 91 units. 90 one-bedroom standard units, some with whirlpools. 1 one-bedroom suite with kitchen. 2 stories (no elevator), interior/exterior corridors. **Parking:** on-site, winter plug-ins. **Terms:** cancellation fee imposed. **Amenities:** video library (fee), hair dryers. *Some:* irons. **Pool(s):** heated indoor. **Leisure Activities:** whirlpool, exercise room. **Guest Services:** coin laundry. **Business Services:** PC. **Cards:** AX, DC, DS, MC, VI.

🍴 🏊 ♿ 💻 / SOME UNITS 🐾 ✕ VCR 🔌 🖨

HOLIDAY INN EXPRESS HOTEL & SUITES LETHBRIDGE
Book great rates at AAA.com
Phone: (403)394-9292

Small-scale Hotel
$129-$229 All Year

Address: 120 Stafford Dr S T1J 4W4 **Location:** Hwy 3, exit Stafford Dr, just s; downtown. **Facility:** 102 units. 82 one-bedroom standard units, some with whirlpools. 20 one-bedroom suites. 4 stories, interior corridors. **Parking:** on-site, winter plug-ins. **Amenities:** high-speed Internet, dual phone lines, voice mail, irons, hair dryers. **Pool(s):** heated indoor. **Leisure Activities:** whirlpool, waterslide, limited exercise equipment. **Guest Services:** valet and coin laundry. **Business Services:** meeting rooms, PC. **Cards:** AX, CB, DC, DS, MC, VI.

ASK 🛇 ♿ 🍴 🏊 ✕ ♿ 🔌 🖨 💻 / SOME UNITS FEE 🐾 ✕

LETHBRIDGE LODGE HOTEL AND CONFERENCE CENTRE
Book great rates at AAA.com
Phone: (403)328-1123

Large-scale Hotel
$109-$189 All Year

Address: 320 Scenic Dr T1J 4B4 **Location:** Scenic Dr at 4th Ave S; centre. **Facility:** 190 units. 154 one-bedroom standard units. 36 one-bedroom suites, some with whirlpools. 4 stories, interior corridors. **Parking:** on-site, winter plug-ins. **Terms:** check-in 4 pm, cancellation fee imposed. **Amenities:** video games (fee), high-speed Internet, voice mail, irons, hair dryers. **Dining:** nightclub. **Pool(s):** heated indoor. **Leisure Activities:** whirlpool, exercise room. **Guest Services:** valet laundry. **Business Services:** conference facilities. **Cards:** AX, DC, DS, JC, MC, VI. **Free Special Amenities:** local telephone calls and high-speed Internet.

🛇 🍴 🍽 🏊 ♿ 💻 / SOME UNITS FEE 🐾 ✕ 🔌 🖨

PEPPER TREE INN
Phone: (403)328-4436

Motel
$65-$90 3/1-10/31
$55-$80 11/1-2/28

Address: 1142 Mayor Magrath Dr S T1K 2P8 **Location:** 2.5 mi (4 km) se on Hwy 4 and 5, exit Mayor Magrath Dr S. **Facility:** 56 one-bedroom standard units, some with efficiencies. 2 stories (no elevator), exterior corridors. **Parking:** on-site, winter plug-ins. **Terms:** cancellation fee imposed. **Amenities:** video library (fee), voice mail. **Pool(s):** outdoor. **Leisure Activities:** whirlpool. **Guest Services:** coin laundry. **Cards:** AX, CB, DC, DS, MC, VI.

🛇 🍴 🏊 VCR ♿ 🔌 / SOME UNITS FEE 🐾 ✕ 🖨

PREMIER INN & SUITES
Book great rates at AAA.com
Phone: (403)380-6677

Small-scale Hotel
$90-$130 3/1-9/30
$80-$115 10/1-2/28

Address: 2225 Mayor Magrath Dr T1K 7M1 **Location:** 2.6 mi (4.5 km) se on Hwy 4 and 5, exit Mayor Magrath Dr, then just w. **Facility:** 50 units. 43 one- and 7 two-bedroom standard units. 4 stories, interior corridors. **Bath:** combo or shower only. **Parking:** on-site, winter plug-ins. **Terms:** cancellation fee imposed. **Amenities:** high-speed Internet. **Leisure Activities:** whirlpool, exercise room. **Guest Services:** valet and coin laundry, wireless Internet. **Business Services:** meeting rooms, PC. **Cards:** AX, DC, DS, MC, VI. **Free Special Amenities:** expanded continental breakfast and high-speed Internet.

🛇 ♿ 🍴 CALL 🛎 / SOME UNITS 🐾 ✕ 🔌 🖨

RAMADA HOTEL & SUITES *Book at AAA.com* Phone: (403)380-5050

Large-scale Hotel
$140-$150 All Year

Address: 2375 Mayor Magrath Dr S T1K 7M1 **Location:** 2.6 mi (4.5 km) se on Hwy 4 and 5, exit Mayor Magrath Dr S. **Facility:** 119 units. 97 one- and 10 two-bedroom standard units. 12 one-bedroom suites, some with whirlpools. 4 stories, interior corridors. **Parking:** on-site, winter plug-ins. **Terms:** check-in 4 pm, cancellation fee imposed. **Amenities:** video games (fee), dual phone lines, voice mail, irons, hair dryers. *Some:* high-speed Internet. **Pool(s):** heated indoor. **Leisure Activities:** whirlpool, waterslide, exercise room. *Fee:* game room. **Guest Services:** valet and coin laundry. **Business Services:** meeting rooms, business center. **Cards:** AX, DC, DS, MC, VI.

SANDMAN HOTEL LETHBRIDGE *Book at AAA.com* Phone: (403)328-1111

Small-scale Hotel
$129 All Year

Address: 421 Mayor Magrath Dr T1J 3L8 **Location:** Hwy 3, exit Mayor Magrath Dr, just s. **Facility:** 138 units. 136 one-bedroom standard units, some with whirlpools. 2 one-bedroom suites. 8 stories, interior corridors. **Parking:** on-site, winter plug-ins. **Terms:** cancellation fee imposed. **Amenities:** high-speed Internet, irons, hair dryers. **Pool(s):** heated indoor. **Leisure Activities:** saunas, limited exercise equipment. **Guest Services:** valet laundry. **Business Services:** conference facilities, business center. **Cards:** AX, DS, MC, VI.

——— **WHERE TO DINE** ———

THE CHEESECAKE CAFE RESTAURANT Phone: 403/394-2253

American
$8-$15

As might be expected, cheesecake is the signature item, and it's worth saving room for one of the lip-smacking varieties made on the premises. A huge dessert display case greets guests upon arrival. Offerings on the extensive lunch and dinner menu range from sandwiches and entree salads to pasta, pizza and seafood selections. It takes a while to get through the menu. Casual dress. **Bar:** Full bar. **Reservations:** not accepted. **Hours:** 11 am-11 pm, Fri & Sat-1 am, Sun 10 am-11 pm. Closed: 12/24, 12/25. **Address:** 904 2nd Ave S T1J 0C6 **Location:** At Stafford Dr and 2nd Ave S; downtown. **Parking:** on-site. **Cards:** AX, MC, VI.

CALL

COCO PAZZO Phone: 403/329-8979

Italian
$8-$27

The cozy Italian cafe has a fun, casual atmosphere. Finely tuned, guest-oriented service enhances the meals, which range from wood-fired-oven pizzas and fresh pasta to seafood and other nicely prepared meat and poultry dishes. Casual dress. **Bar:** Full bar. **Hours:** 11 am-11 pm, Fri & Sat-midnight, Sun 5 pm-9 pm. Closed: 1/1, 12/25, 12/26. **Address:** 1264 3rd Ave S T1J 0J9 **Location:** Corner of 12th St. **Parking:** on-site. **Cards:** AX, MC, VI.

DOURO'S PIZZA & STEAKHOUSE Phone: 403/327-3067

Steak House
$6-$18

A great place for families, the casual restaurant serves a wide range of pizzas and steaks, as well as other dishes, including large sandwiches, oversize salads and nachos. Patrons get great value for the dollar, and there's something for everyone. Casual dress. **Bar:** Full bar. **Reservations:** suggested. **Hours:** 11 am-midnight, Fri & Sat-1 am. Closed: 12/25. **Address:** 2433 Fairway Plaza Rd S T1K 6Z2 **Location:** From Mayor Magrath Dr, exit n at Scenic Dr to Fairway Plaza; southeast end of town. **Parking:** on-site. **Cards:** AX, MC, VI.

PENNY COFFEE HOUSE Phone: 403/320-5282

Deli/Subs
Sandwiches
$7-$10

Street signs and local artwork cover the walls of this local coffee shop which features a wide range of soups, salads and sandwiches; many of the pastries are made on the premises. Casual dress. **Hours:** 7:30-10:01 am, Sun 9:01 am-5:01 pm. Closed: 1/1, 12/25. **Address:** 331 5th St S T1J 2B4 **Location:** Jct 3rd Ave; centre. **Parking:** street. **Cards:** MC, VI.

STREATSIDE EATERY Phone: 403/328-8085

Canadian
$8-$23

A favorite among the locals, the casual downtown eatery prepares homemade comfort food from fresh ingredients. Although this place is known for its quiche of the day, guests also can also try entree-size salads and sandwiches. The red brick interior and outdoor patio contribute to a pleasant atmosphere. Casual dress. **Bar:** Full bar. **Reservations:** accepted. **Hours:** 11 am-close. Closed: 1/1, 3/24, 12/25. **Address:** 317 8th St S T1J 2J5 **Location:** At 3rd Ave and 8th St; downtown. **Parking:** street. **Cards:** AX, MC.

TREATS EATERY Phone: 403/380-4880

American
$7-$16

Although the fun, casual establishment has an unusual Western theme, it doesn't offer Western-style dishes. On the menu are deli-style burgers, sandwiches and quiche, as well as health-conscious dishes and more elaborate dinner items. **Bar:** Full bar. **Reservations:** suggested. **Hours:** 11 am-10 pm, Fri & Sat-11 pm, Sun noon-10 pm. Closed: 1/1, 12/25. **Address:** 1104 Mayor Magrath Dr T1K 2P9 **Location:** 2 mi (3.2 km) se on Hwy 4 and 5, exit Mayor Magrath Dr, at 10th Ave S. **Parking:** on-site. **Cards:** AX, DC, MC, VI.

LLOYDMINSTER pop. 15,910—*See also LLOYDMINSTER, SK*

———— WHERE TO STAY ————

BEST WESTERN WAYSIDE INN & SUITES   *Book great rates at AAA.com*   Phone: (780)875-4404

Small-scale Hotel
$160-$290 All Year

Address: 5411 44th St T9V 0A9 **Location:** 0.5 mi (0.8 km) w on Hwy 16 from jct Hwy 17. **Facility:** 128 units. 96 one-bedroom standard units. 32 one-bedroom suites, some with whirlpools. 6 stories, interior corridors. **Parking:** on-site, winter plug-ins. **Terms:** 7 day cancellation notice. **Amenities:** high-speed Internet, voice mail, irons, hair dryers. **Pool(s):** heated indoor. **Leisure Activities:** exercise room. *Fee:* massage. **Guest Services:** valet laundry. **Business Services:** conference facilities, administrative services (fee). **Cards:** AX, DS, MC, VI. **Free Special Amenities:** local telephone calls and high-speed Internet.

AAA Benefit:
Members save 10% everyday, plus an exclusive frequent stay program.

WEST HARVEST INN   *Book at AAA.com*   Phone: (780)875-6113

Small-scale Hotel
$129-$169 All Year

Address: 5620 44th St T9V 0B6 **Location:** Jct Hwy 16 and 17, 0.6 mi (1 km) w. **Facility:** 97 one-bedroom standard units, some with whirlpools. 2 stories (no elevator), interior/exterior corridors. **Parking:** on-site, winter plug-ins. **Amenities:** video games (fee), high-speed Internet, voice mail, hair dryers. *Some:* irons. **Pool(s):** heated indoor. **Leisure Activities:** steamrooms, exercise room. **Guest Services:** valet laundry. **Business Services:** meeting rooms, administrative services, PC (fee). **Cards:** AX, MC, VI.

———— WHERE TO DINE ————

MR BILL'S FAMILY RESTAURANT   Phone: 780/875-3388

Continental
$5-$19

In a border town that features predominantly chain eateries, the excellent family restaurant serves burgers, sandwiches, pasta and a few Greek dishes. Popular with the locals, this spot offers fast, friendly service amid comfortable, trendy decor. For a delicious, hearty lunch, try the superb Greek avgolemono soup. Casual dress. **Bar:** Full bar. **Reservations:** suggested. **Hours:** 10 am-10 pm. Closed major holidays; also Sun. **Address:** 10 5405 44th St T9V 0A9 **Location:** Corner of Hwy 16 and 54th Ave. **Parking:** on-site. **Cards:** AX, MC, VI.

MEDICINE HAT pop. 56,997

———— WHERE TO STAY ————

BEST WESTERN INN   *Book great rates at AAA.com*   Phone: (403)527-3700

Small-scale Hotel
$99-$249 All Year

Address: 722 Redcliff Dr T1A 5E3 **Location:** On Trans-Canada Hwy 1, 0.3 mi (0.4 km) w of jct Hwy 3, access 7th St SW. **Facility:** 122 units. 115 one-bedroom standard units, some with efficiencies and/or whirlpools. 7 one-bedroom suites, some with whirlpools. 2 stories (no elevator), interior/exterior corridors. **Parking:** on-site, winter plug-ins. **Terms:** cancellation fee imposed. **Amenities:** video games (fee), voice mail, irons, hair dryers. *Some:* high-speed Internet, dual phone lines. **Pool(s):** 2 heated indoor. **Leisure Activities:** sauna, whirlpools, steamroom, exercise room. **Guest Services:** valet and coin laundry. **Business Services:** meeting rooms, PC. **Cards:** AX, DC, DS, MC, VI. **Free Special Amenities:** continental breakfast and high-speed Internet.

AAA Benefit:
Members save 10% everyday, plus an exclusive frequent stay program.

COMFORT INN & SUITES   *Book great rates at AAA.com*   Phone: (403)504-1700

Small-scale Hotel
$79-$109 All Year

Address: 2317 Trans-Canada Way SE T1B 4E9 **Location:** 3.1 mi (5 km) se; just n off Trans-Canada Hwy 1; corner of Dunmore Rd. Located opposite Medicine Hat Mall. **Facility:** 100 units. 71 one-bedroom standard units, some with whirlpools. 29 one-bedroom suites, some with whirlpools. 3 stories, interior corridors. **Parking:** on-site, winter plug-ins. **Terms:** check-in 4 pm. **Amenities:** high-speed Internet, voice mail, irons, hair dryers. **Pool(s):** heated indoor. **Leisure Activities:** whirlpool, exercise room. **Guest Services:** valet and coin laundry, wireless Internet. **Business Services:** meeting rooms, PC (fee). **Cards:** AX, DC, DS, MC, VI. **Free Special Amenities:** expanded continental breakfast and high-speed Internet. *(See color ad on insert)*

DAYS INN-MEDICINE HAT   *Book at AAA.com*   Phone: (403)580-3297

Small-scale Hotel
$115-$145 3/1-5/31
$109-$140 6/1-2/28

Address: 24 Strachan Ct SE T1B 4R7 **Location:** Trans-Canada Hwy 1, exit Dunmore Rd, just sw. **Facility:** 76 units. 61 one-bedroom standard units, some with whirlpools. 15 one-bedroom suites, some with whirlpools. 4 stories, interior corridors. **Parking:** on-site, winter plug-ins. **Terms:** check-in 4 pm. **Amenities:** voice mail, irons, hair dryers. *Some:* video games, high-speed Internet. **Pool(s):** heated indoor. **Leisure Activities:** whirlpool, waterslide. **Guest Services:** valet and coin laundry, wireless Internet. **Business Services:** PC (fee). **Cards:** AX, DC, MC, VI.

HOLIDAY INN EXPRESS HOTEL & SUITES   *Book great rates at AAA.com*   Phone: (403)504-5151

Small-scale Hotel
$109-$249 All Year

Address: 9 Strachan Bay SE T1B 4Y2 **Location:** Trans-Canada Hwy 1, exit Dunmore Rd, just se. **Facility:** 93 units. 90 one- and 3 two-bedroom standard units, some with whirlpools. 4 stories, interior corridors. *Bath:* combo or shower only. **Parking:** on-site, winter plug-ins. **Amenities:** high-speed Internet, voice mail, irons, hair dryers. **Pool(s):** heated indoor. **Leisure Activities:** whirlpool, waterslide, exercise room. **Guest Services:** valet and coin laundry. **Business Services:** meeting rooms, business center. **Cards:** AX, DC, DS, MC, VI. *(See color ad on insert)*

MEDICINE HAT LODGE HOTEL CASINO
CONVENTION CENTRE HEALTH SPA & INDOOR *Book at AAA.com* Phone: (403)529-2222

Large-scale Hotel
$119-$136 1/2-2/28
$119-$134 3/1-12/30

Address: 1051 Ross Glen Dr SE T1B 3T8 **Location:** East end approach to city on Trans-Canada Hwy 1, at Dunmore Rd. **Facility:** Some rooms with pool view balconies are offered at this casino hotel; indoor waterslides are featured for children. 221 units. 187 one-bedroom standard units, some with whirlpools. 34 one-bedroom suites, some with whirlpools. 4 stories, interior corridors. **Bath:** combo or shower only. **Parking:** on-site, winter plug-ins. **Terms:** open 3/1-12/30 & 1/2-2/28, check-in 4 pm. **Amenities:** video games (fee), voice mail, irons, hair dryers. *Some:* high-speed Internet. **Dining:** Mamma's Ristorante, see separate listing. **Pool(s):** heated indoor. **Leisure Activities:** whirlpool, waterslide, rental bicycles, exercise room, spa. *Fee:* game room. **Guest Services:** valet and coin laundry, hair salon, wireless Internet. **Business Services:** conference facilities, PC. **Cards:** AX, DC, DS, MC, VI.

🎲 (ASK) ⑤D ✈ ⑪ 🍸 ⤳ ✕ 🧍 🛢 💻 / SOME UNITS FEE 🐾 ✕ 🖥

MOTEL 6-MEDICINE HAT *Book great rates at AAA.com* Phone: 403-527-1749

Small-scale Hotel
Rates not provided

Address: 20 Strochon Ct SE T1B 4R7 **Location:** Trans-Canada Hwy 1, exit Dunmore Rd, just sw. **Facility:** 79 one-bedroom standard units. 3 stories, interior corridors. **Bath:** combo or shower only. **Parking:** on-site, winter plug-ins. **Terms:** check-in 4 pm. **Amenities:** *Some:* irons, hair dryers. **Guest Services:** coin laundry, wireless Internet. **Business Services:** PC (fee). *(See color ad p 368)*

⑪ CALL ⑤M / SOME UNITS 🐾 ✕ FEE 🛢 FEE 🖥

SUPER 8 MOTEL *Book at AAA.com* Phone: (403)528-8888

Small-scale Hotel
$82-$89 All Year

Address: 1280 Trans-Canada Way SE T1B 1J5 **Location:** Trans-Canada Hwy 1 at 13 Ave SE; just n off Trans-Canada Hwy 1. **Facility:** 70 units. 69 one-bedroom standard units, some with kitchens. 1 one-bedroom suite with kitchen. 2-3 stories (no elevator), interior/exterior corridors. **Parking:** on-site, winter plug-ins. **Terms:** check-in 4 pm. **Amenities:** voice mail, hair dryers. **Pool(s):** heated indoor. **Leisure Activities:** whirlpool, limited exercise equipment. **Guest Services:** valet laundry, wireless Internet. **Cards:** AX, CB, DC, DS, JC, MC, VI.

(ASK) ⑤D ⑪ ⤳ 🛢 🖥 💻 / SOME UNITS FEE 🐾 ✕ FEE (VCR)

──────── **WHERE TO DINE** ────────

BEEFEATER STEAKHOUSE Phone: 403-526-6925

(CAA)

Steak & Seafood
$7-$30

Patrons appreciate the good value they receive at the restaurant, which offers relaxed dining in an attractive library-like setting. The menu specializes in prime rib and seafood, with a good selection of sandwiches at lunch. Service is good and efficient. Casual dress. **Bar:** Full bar. **Reservations:** suggested. **Hours:** 11 am-midnight, Sat from 4:30 pm, Sun 4:30 pm-10 pm. Closed: 12/25, 12/26. **Address:** 3286 13th Ave SE T1B 1H8 **Location:** 2.25 mi (3.6 km) se; just n off Trans-Canada Hwy 1; in Imperial Inn. **Parking:** on-site. **Cards:** AX, DC, MC, VI.

HAT'S RESTAURANT Phone: 403-529-9739

Chinese
$7-$15

Locals claim the wonderful Chinese restaurant as a favorite for its flavorful, reasonably priced food. Traditional foods line the all-you-can-eat buffet, as well as the a la carte menu. Also offered is a smattering of Western cuisine. Casual dress. **Bar:** Full bar. **Reservations:** suggested, weekends. **Hours:** 4 pm-10 pm, Fri & Sat-11 pm. Closed major holidays; also Mon. **Address:** 1701 Dunmore Rd SE T1A 1Z8 **Location:** In Crestwood Shopping Centre. **Parking:** on-site. **Cards:** AX, MC, VI.

MAD HATTER COFFEE ROASTERY

Coffee/Espresso
$3-$5

Phone: 403/529-2344

You know a restaurant takes its coffee seriously when it has a coffee roaster in the middle of its space, as is the case with this downtown eatery. A limited variety of baked goods are available at the front counter. Casual dress. **Hours:** 7:30 am-5:30 pm, Sat from 8 am, Sun 10 am-5 pm. Closed major holidays. **Address:** 513 3rd St SE T1A 0H2 **Location:** Jct 5th Ave; downtown. **Parking:** street. **Cards:** AX, MC, VI.

MAMMA'S RISTORANTE

Continental
$15-$23

Phone: 403/529-2222

The varied menu includes preparations of pasta, seafood, veal and Alberta beef. The restaurant's elegant garden setting lends to a casual, relaxed atmosphere. Service is efficient and friendly. Dressy casual. **Bar:** Full bar. **Reservations:** accepted. **Hours:** 5 pm-10 pm. **Address:** 1051 Ross Glen Dr SE T1B 3T8 **Location:** East end approach to city on Trans-Canada Hwy 1, at Dunmore Rd; in Medicine Hat Lodge Hotel Casino Convention Centre Health Spa & Indoor. **Parking:** on-site. **Cards:** AX, DC, DS, MC, VI.

MOUNTAIN VIEW pop. 20

——— WHERE TO STAY ———

ROCKY RIDGE COUNTRY RESORT

Bed & Breakfast
$60-$200 All Year

Phone: (403)653-2350

Address: Hwy 5 T0K 1N0 **Location:** 0.6 mi (1 km) n, follow signs; by Village Church. **Facility:** Smoke free premises. 7 units. 6 one-bedroom standard units. 1 cabin. 2 stories (no elevator), interior corridors. **Bath:** some shared or private, combo or shower only. **Parking:** on-site, winter plug-ins. **Terms:** check-in 4 pm, cancellation fee imposed. **Amenities:** hair dryers. **Leisure Activities:** sauna, whirlpool, game room. **Guest Services:** TV in common area. **Cards:** AX, MC, VI.

NISKU —See Edmonton p. 454.

OKOTOKS —See Calgary p. 421.

PINCHER CREEK pop. 3,625

——— WHERE TO STAY ———

HERITAGE INN   Book at AAA.com

Small-scale Hotel
$99-$149 11/1-2/28
$95-$145 3/1-10/31

Phone: (403)627-5000

Address: 919 Waterton Ave (Hwy 6) T0K 1W0 **Location:** SR 3, 2.9 mi (4.7 km) s. **Facility:** 42 one-bedroom standard units. 2 stories (no elevator), interior corridors. **Parking:** on-site, winter plug-ins. **Amenities:** Some: irons. **Guest Services:** coin laundry, wireless Internet. **Business Services:** meeting rooms. **Cards:** AX, DS, MC, VI.

——— WHERE TO DINE ———

SWISS ALPINE RESTAURANT

Continental
$8-$22

Phone: 403/627-5079

This popular restaurant features Swiss croute, crepes, lamb, Alberta beef, sandwiches, pasta and stir-fry dishes, which are prepared with fresh ingredients and a Swiss flair. Sunday night has a prime rib special. The rustic decor displays art for sale. **Bar:** Full bar. **Reservations:** suggested, in summer. **Hours:** 11 am-10 pm. Closed: 1/1, 12/25; also Sun & Mon. **Address:** 988 Main St T0K 1W0 **Location:** Jct Hwy 6 and Main St. **Parking:** on-site. **Cards:** AX, DC, MC, VI.

RED DEER pop. 82,772

——— WHERE TO STAY ———

BEST WESTERN RED DEER INN & SUITES   Book great rates at AAA.com

Small-scale Hotel
$115-$135 All Year

Phone: (403)346-3555

Address: 6839 66th St T4P 3T5 **Location:** Hwy 2, exit 67th St, just e. **Facility:** 92 units. 86 one- and 6 two-bedroom standard units, some with whirlpools. 4 stories, interior corridors. **Bath:** combo or shower only. **Parking:** on-site. **Amenities:** high-speed Internet, voice mail, irons, hair dryers. **Pool(s):** heated indoor. **Leisure Activities:** whirlpool. **Guest Services:** valet and coin laundry, wireless Internet. **Business Services:** PC. **Cards:** AX, DS, MC, VI. **Free Special Amenities:** room upgrade (subject to availability with advance reservations).

AAA Benefit:
Members save 10% everyday, plus an exclusive frequent stay program.

CAPRI HOTEL TRADE & CONVENTION CENTRE   Book great rates at AAA.com

Large-scale Hotel
Rates not provided

Phone: 403/346-2091

Address: 3310 50th Ave T4N 3X9 **Location:** 1.3 mi (2 km) n on Hwy 2A (Gaetz Ave). **Facility:** 220 units. 196 one-bedroom standard units. 16 one- and 8 two-bedroom suites, some with whirlpools. 2-14 stories, interior corridors. **Parking:** on-site, winter plug-ins. **Amenities:** video games (fee), voice mail, irons, hair dryers. Some: high-speed Internet (fee). **Dining:** 3 restaurants, also, Barbero's, see separate listing. **Pool(s):** heated outdoor. Fee: massage. **Leisure Activities:** sauna, whirlpool, exercise room. Fee: massage. **Guest Services:** valet laundry, area transportation (fee), beauty salon. **Business Services:** conference facilities, business center. **Free Special Amenities:** newspaper and high-speed Internet.

COMFORT INN & SUITES   *Book great rates at AAA.com*   Phone: (403)348-0025

Small-scale Hotel
$99-$149 All Year

Address: 6846 66th St T4P 3T5 **Location:** Hwy 2, exit 67th St, just e. Located in a commercial area. **Facility:** 88 units. 82 one-bedroom standard units, some with whirlpools. 6 one-bedroom suites. 4 stories, interior corridors. **Bath:** combo or shower only. **Parking:** on-site, winter plug-ins. **Amenities:** high-speed Internet, voice mail, irons, hair dryers. **Pool(s):** heated indoor. **Leisure Activities:** whirlpool, waterslide, exercise room. **Guest Services:** valet and coin laundry. **Business Services:** meeting rooms, business center. **Free Special Amenities: expanded continental breakfast and high-speed Internet.** *(See color ad on insert)*

HOLIDAY INN 67TH STREET   *Book great rates at AAA.com*   Phone: (403)342-6567

Small-scale Hotel
$130 All Year

Address: 6500 67th St T4P 1A2 **Location:** Hwy 2, exit 67th St, 0.5 mi (0.8 km) e. **Facility:** 142 units. 140 one-bedroom standard units, some with whirlpools. 2 one-bedroom suites with whirlpools. 4 stories, interior corridors. **Bath:** combo or shower only. **Parking:** on-site, winter plug-ins. **Amenities:** video games (fee), high-speed Internet, dual phone lines, voice mail, irons, hair dryers. **Pool(s):** heated indoor. **Leisure Activities:** sauna, whirlpool, game room. *Fee:* massage. **Guest Services:** valet laundry, tanning facilities. **Business Services:** conference facilities, business center. **Cards:** AX, DC, DS, JC, MC, VI. **Free Special Amenities: continental breakfast and local telephone calls.**

HOLIDAY INN EXPRESS RED DEER   *Book great rates at AAA.com*   Phone: 403-343-2112

Small-scale Hotel
$119-$129 All Year

Address: 2803 50th Ave T4R 1H1 **Location:** 1.1 mi (1.8 km) e on Hwy 2A (Gaetz Ave). **Facility:** 92 one-bedroom standard units, some with whirlpools. 2 stories (no elevator), interior corridors. **Parking:** on-site, winter plug-ins. **Amenities:** video games (fee), dual phone lines, voice mail, irons, hair dryers. *Some:* high-speed Internet. **Pool(s):** heated indoor. **Leisure Activities:** whirlpool, steamroom, exercise room. **Guest Services:** valet and coin laundry, wireless Internet. **Business Services:** PC (fee). **Cards:** AX, CB, DC, DS, JC, MC, VI. **Free Special Amenities: expanded continental breakfast and high-speed Internet.** *(See color ad on insert)*

MOTEL 6 - RED DEER   Phone: 403/340-1749

Small-scale Hotel
Rates not provided

Address: 900-5001 19th St T4R 3R1 **Location:** Hwy 2, exit 394 (Gaetz Ave), just n, then just w; in Southpointe Common Shopping District. Located in a commerical area. **Facility:** 79 one-bedroom standard units. 3 stories, interior corridors. **Bath:** combo or shower only. **Parking:** on-site, winter plug-ins. **Amenities:** high-speed Internet, voice mail. **Guest Services:** coin laundry. *(See color ad on p 368)*

RED DEER RAMADA INN   *Book at AAA.com*   Phone: 403/358-7722

Small-scale Hotel
$129 All Year

Address: 4217 50th Ave T4N 3Z4 **Location:** At 42nd St; centre. **Facility:** 86 units. 62 one-bedroom standard units, some with whirlpools. 24 one-bedroom suites. 4 stories, interior corridors. **Parking:** on-site, winter plug-ins. **Terms:** cancellation fee imposed. **Amenities:** voice mail, irons, hair dryers. **Leisure Activities:** limited exercise equipment. **Guest Services:** coin laundry, wireless Internet. **Business Services:** PC (fee). **Cards:** AX, MC, VI.

SANDMAN HOTEL RED DEER   *Book at AAA.com*   Phone: (403)343-7400

Small-scale Hotel
$124-$179 All Year

Address: 2818 Gaetz Ave T4R 1M4 **Location:** 1 mi (1.6 km) n on Hwy 2A (Gaetz Ave). **Facility:** 143 units. 94 one-bedroom standard units, some with whirlpools. 49 one-bedroom suites. 4 stories, interior corridors. **Parking:** on-site, winter plug-ins. **Terms:** check-in 4 pm, cancellation fee imposed. **Amenities:** video games, high-speed Internet, dual phone lines, voice mail, irons, hair dryers. **Pool(s):** heated indoor. **Leisure Activities:** whirlpool, exercise room. **Guest Services:** valet laundry. **Business Services:** meeting rooms, PC (fee). **Cards:** AX, DC, MC, VI.

------- **WHERE TO DINE** -------

BARBERO'S   Phone: (403)346-2091

Canadian
$8-$25

Tucked off the hotel lobby, this quietly upscale restaurant is too often overlooked. Exposed brick and dark wood accents create an intimate feeling, and the large display kitchen is exciting to watch as the restaurant gets busier and busier. In the midst of the controlled chaos, the kitchen continues to create a menu consisting of both international favorites and regional specialties. Casual dress. **Bar:** Full bar. **Hours:** 7 am-10 pm. **Address:** 3310 50th Ave T4N 3X9 **Location:** 1.3 mi (2 km) n on Hwy 2A (Gaetz Ave); in Capri Hotel Trade & Convention Centre. **Parking:** on-site. **Cards:** AX, MC, VI.

EARL'S   Phone: 403/342-4055

Canadian
$10-$28

Offering an experience that falls between fast food and fine dining, the fun, relaxed restaurant prepares great food at a great price. Choices range from juicy burgers, hearty sandwiches, fresh salads, wings and pizza to full entrees of steak, chops and seafood. Made-from-scratch soups and assorted breads, as well a nice choice of wines and beers, round out the offerings. This is a fitting spot for impromptu get-togethers and festive occasions. Casual dress. **Bar:** Full bar. **Hours:** 11 am-midnight, Fri & Sat-1 am. Closed major holidays. **Address:** 2111 Gaetz Ave T4R 1Z4 **Location:** 0.9 mi (1.5) km e on Hwy 2A (Gaetz Ave). **Parking:** on-site. **Cards:** AX, DC, MC, VI.

MOHAVE GRILL

Southwestern
$9-$20

Phone: 403/340-3463

Diners will find mainly Mexican food at the funky, festive restaurant, just off the highway. However, the eclectic menu takes some chances by delving into Cajun, Southwestern and Jamaican influences. Each dish is sure to please, and the servings are plentiful. Casual dress. **Bar:** Full bar. **Hours:** 11 am-11 pm, Fri & Sat-midnight, Sun-10 pm. Closed: 12/25. **Address:** 6608 Orr Dr T4P 3T5 **Location:** Hwy 2, exit 67th St, 0.3 mi (0.5 km) e; next to Service Plus Inns & Suites. **Parking:** on-site. **Cards:** AX, MC, VI.

MONTANA'S COOKHOUSE

Canadian
$8-$16

Phone: 403/352-0030

Pine boards, exposed beams, a fireplace and Western gear displayed about the dining room give the feeling of a back-country setting. The menu lists hearty portions of comfort fare, such as Yankee pot roast. While the focus is on steaks, ribs and chicken, some seafood entrees also are among offerings. Service is efficient and friendly. Casual dress. **Bar:** Full bar. **Hours:** 11 am-11 pm. Closed: 12/25. **Address:** 2004 50th Ave T4R 3A2 **Location:** On Hwy 2A (Gaetz Ave). **Parking:** on-site. **Cards:** MC, VI.

RUSTY PELICAN

Continental
$7-$30

Phone: 403/347-1414

Ask any local for a great place to eat, and this place is mentioned often. The large, loft-like dining room creates a casual atmosphere, and most tables feature a large umbrella. Many entrees amid the menu's eclectic array exhibit Asian influences. Among selections are lettuce wraps, sumptuous salmon, pasta and assorted sandwiches. **Bar:** Full bar. **Reservations:** suggested. **Hours:** 11 am-midnight. Closed: 12/25. **Address:** 2079 50th Ave T4R 1Z4 **Location:** 1.6 mi (2 km) n on Hwy 2A (Gaetz Ave). **Parking:** on-site. **Cards:** AX, DC, MC, VI.

CALL ⟨Ⓜ⟩

ROCKY MOUNTAIN HOUSE pop. 6,874

——— **WHERE TO STAY** ———

CHINOOK INN

Ⓒ SAVE

Motel
$70-$90 All Year

Phone: 403/845-2833

Address: 5321 59th Ave T4T 1J4 **Location:** 0.8 mi (1.3 km) w on Hwy 11, then s. **Facility:** 19 one-bedroom standard units, some with whirlpools. 1 story, interior corridors. **Parking:** on-site, winter plug-ins. **Amenities:** high-speed Internet (fee), voice mail, hair dryers. **Leisure Activities:** barbecue area, bicycles. **Guest Services:** valet laundry. **Business Services:** PC (fee). **Cards:** MC, VI. **Free Special Amenities:** continental breakfast and high-speed Internet.

HOLIDAY INN EXPRESS ROCKY MOUNTAIN HOUSE   *Book great rates at AAA.com*

Ⓒ SAVE

Small-scale Hotel
$119-$129 All Year

Phone: 403/845-2871

Address: 4715 45th St T4T 1B1 **Location:** Just nw of jct 47th Ave and 45th St. **Facility:** 40 units. 39 one-bedroom standard units. 1 one-bedroom suite with kitchen. 2 stories (no elevator), interior corridors. **Parking:** on-site, winter plug-ins. **Terms:** cancellation fee imposed. **Amenities:** dual phone lines, voice mail, irons, hair dryers. **Guest Services:** valet laundry, wireless Internet. **Business Services:** PC (fee). **Cards:** AX, CB, DC, DS, JC, MC, VI. **Free Special Amenities:** expanded continental breakfast and high-speed Internet. *(See color ad on insert)*

SUPER 8 MOTEL   *Book at AAA.com*

Small-scale Hotel
Rates not provided

Phone: 403/846-0088

Address: 4406 41st Ave T4T 1J6 **Location:** Just off Hwy 11 at east end of town. **Facility:** 59 units. 54 one-bedroom standard units, some with efficiencies and/or whirlpools. 5 one-bedroom suites. 3 stories, interior corridors. **Bath:** combo or shower only. **Parking:** on-site, winter plug-ins. **Amenities:** high-speed Internet, voice mail, irons, hair dryers. *Some:* video games. **Pool(s):** heated indoor. **Leisure Activities:** whirlpool, waterslide, exercise room. **Guest Services:** coin laundry. **Business Services:** meeting rooms.

ST. ALBERT —See Edmonton p. 454.

SASKATCHEWAN RIVER CROSSING

——— **WHERE TO STAY** ———

COLUMBIA ICEFIELD CHALET AT COLUMBIA ICEFIELD

Small-scale Hotel
$110-$260 5/1-10/1

Phone: 780/852-6550

Address: Hwy 93 N T1L 1J3 **Location:** 31.25 mi (50 km) n on Hwy 93 (Icefield Pkwy). **Facility:** Smoke free premises. 32 units. 10 one- and 22 two-bedroom standard units. 3 stories, interior corridors. **Parking:** on-site. **Terms:** open 5/1-10/1, check-in 4 pm. **Amenities:** hair dryers. **Leisure Activities:** hiking trails. **Cards:** AX, MC, VI.

SHERWOOD PARK —See Edmonton p. 454.

STONY PLAIN —See Edmonton p. 455.

STRATHMORE —See Calgary p. 422.

TABER pop. 7,591

——— WHERE TO STAY ———

HERITAGE INN

 Book at AAA.com

◆◆ ◆◆

Small-scale Hotel
$91-$125 1/1-2/28
$89-$123 3/1-12/31

Phone: (403)223-4424
Address: 4830 46th Ave T1G 2A4 **Location:** 0.6 mi (1 km) e of jct Hwy 3 and 36 S, on Hwy 3. **Facility:** 74 units. 72 one-bedroom standard units. 2 one-bedroom suites, some with whirlpools. 2 stories (no elevator), interior corridors. **Parking:** on-site, winter plug-ins. **Amenities:** high-speed Internet. *Some:* CD players. **Leisure Activities:** sauna, whirlpool. *Fee:* game room. **Guest Services:** valet laundry. **Business Services:** conference facilities. **Cards:** AX, DS, MC, VI.

ASK 🛏️ 🍽️ 🍸 ⊗ 🎥 💻 / SOME UNITS FEE 🐾 ⊗ 🖥️ 📷

SUPER 8 MOTEL, TABER *Book at AAA.com*

◆◆◆ ◆◆◆

Small-scale Hotel
Rates not provided

Phone: 403/223-8181
Address: 5700 46th Ave T1G 2B1 **Location:** Hwy 3, west end of town. **Facility:** 48 one-bedroom standard units. 2 stories (no elevator), interior/exterior corridors. **Parking:** on-site, winter plug-ins. **Guest Services:** coin laundry, wireless Internet.

🎥 🖥️ / SOME UNITS ⊗

TWIN BUTTE pop. 10

——— WHERE TO DINE ———

TWIN BUTTE COUNTRY GENERAL STORE

◆◆◆

Mexican
$5-$10

Phone: 403/627-4035
Halfway between Pincher Creek and Waterton on the Cowboy Trail, this small but cheerful Mexican-themed diner is located at the back of the country store and features a menu of simple but tasty Western and Mexican dishes. Casual dress. **Bar:** Full bar. **Hours:** 10 am-8 pm. Closed major holidays. **Address:** Box 461 T0K 2J0 **Location:** 16.9 mi (27 km) s of Dinchis Creek, on Hwy 6 (Cowboy Trail). **Parking:** on-site. **Cards:** AX, MC, VI.

WAINWRIGHT pop. 5,426

——— WHERE TO DINE ———

THE HONEY POT EATERY & PUB

◆◆◆ ◆◆◆

American
$5-$18

Phone: 780/842-4094
Diners receive a good meal and excellent value at the tucked-away restaurant. Its friendly, casual ambience enhances the country charm of its Western-style barnwood exterior. The extensive menu lists homemade bread, pies, soup and sandwiches. Casual dress. **Bar:** Full bar. **Reservations:** suggested. **Hours:** 11 am-9:30 pm, Wed-Sat to 10 pm. Closed major holidays; also Sun. **Address:** 823 2nd Ave T9W 1C5 **Location:** 0.6 mi (1 km) s on Main St from jct Hwy 14, just w at clock tower. **Parking:** street. **Cards:** AX, DC, MC, VI.

WATERTON PARK pop. 160

——— WHERE TO STAY ———

ASPEN VILLAGE INN

(AAA) SAVE

◆◆ ◆◆

Motel
$154-$270 5/1-10/10

Phone: (403)859-2255
Address: 111 Windflower Ave T0K 2M0 **Location:** Centre. **Facility:** 51 units. 38 one- and 1 two-bedroom standard units, some with kitchens. 11 one- and 1 two-bedroom suites, some with kitchens. 1-2 stories (no elevator), exterior corridors. **Parking:** on-site. **Terms:** open 5/1-10/10, office hours 7 am-11 pm. **Amenities:** hair dryers. **Leisure Activities:** whirlpool, recreation programs, barbecues, playground. **Cards:** AX, DC, DS, MC, VI.

🛏️⁺ ⊗ 🐾 💻 / SOME UNITS ⊗ VCR 🖥️ 📷

BAYSHORE INN *Book great rates at AAA.com*

(AAA) SAVE

◆◆◆ ◆◆◆

Motel
$119-$249 4/30-10/12

Phone: (403)859-2211
Address: 111 Waterton Ave T0K 2M0 **Location:** Centre. **Facility:** 70 units. 64 one- and 4 two-bedroom standard units, some with whirlpools. 2 one-bedroom suites. 2 stories (no elevator), exterior corridors. *Bath:* combo or shower only. **Parking:** on-site. **Terms:** open 4/30-10/12, 3 day cancellation notice. **Amenities:** hair dryers. **Dining:** 2 restaurants, nightclub. **Leisure Activities:** live theatre, hiking trails. *Fee:* massage. **Guest Services:** coin laundry. **Business Services:** meeting rooms, PC (fee). **Cards:** AX, MC, VI. **Free Special Amenities:** local telephone calls and early check-in/late check-out. *(See color ad p 482)*

🍽️ 🍸 ⊗ 🐾 💻 / SOME UNITS FEE 🐾 ⊗ FEE VCR 🖥️ 📷

CRANDELL MOUNTAIN LODGE

(AAA) SAVE

◆◆ ◆◆

Small-scale Hotel
$89-$209 All Year

Phone: (403)859-2288
Address: 102 Mt. View Rd T0K 2M0 **Location:** Centre. **Facility:** Designated smoking area. 17 units. 13 one-bedroom standard units, some with efficiencies. 4 one-bedroom suites with kitchens, some with whirlpools. 2 stories (no elevator), interior corridors. *Bath:* combo or shower only. **Parking:** on-site. **Terms:** office hours 8 am-10 pm, 3 day cancellation notice. **Amenities:** video library, hair dryers. **Leisure Activities:** hiking trails. **Cards:** AX, DS, MC, VI.

🍽️⁺ ⊗ 🐾 🎥 💻 / SOME UNITS FEE VCR 🖥️ 📷

KILMOREY LODGE

Historic
Country Inn
$129-$252 3/1-10/15
$99-$196 10/16-2/28

Phone: (403)859-2334
Address: 117 Evergreen Ave T0K 2M0 **Location:** Centre. **Facility:** As one of the original buildings in town, this quaint, historic country inn has cozy rooms that contribute to its retreat-like ambience. 23 units. 20 one- and 2 two-bedroom standard units, some with whirlpools. 1 one-bedroom suite. 3 stories (no elevator), interior corridors. *Bath:* combo or shower only. **Parking:** on-site, winter plug-ins. **Terms:** office hours 7 am-11 pm. **Amenities:** hair dryers. **Dining:** The Lamp Post Dining Room, see separate listing. **Leisure Activities:** Nordic ski trails, hiking trails. *Fee:* snowshoes, Canadian wilderness tours. **Guest Services:** TV in common area. **Business Services:** PC (fee). **Cards:** AX, DC, DS, MC, VI.

SHINTANGLE SPRING BED & BREAKFAST INN

Phone: 403/627-5751

Bed & Breakfast
Rates not provided

Address: Hwy #6 T0K 2M0 **Location:** 4.6 mi (7.4 km) n of park entrance, then just w at Nixon Rd. **Facility:** Smoke free premises. 4 one-bedroom standard units. 1 story, interior corridors. **Parking:** on-site, winter plug-ins. **Terms:** check-in 3:30 pm.

⊠ 𝒲 ☎

WATERTON GLACIER SUITES   *Book great rates at AAA.com*

Phone: (403)859-2004

CAA SAVE

Small-scale Hotel
$139-$249 All Year

Address: 107 Windflower Ave T0K 2M0 **Location:** Centre. **Facility:** Designated smoking area. 26 one-bedroom suites with whirlpools. 2 stories (no elevator), exterior corridors. **Parking:** on-site. **Terms:** office hours 7 am-midnight, 3 day cancellation notice. **Amenities:** voice mail, irons, hair dryers. **Business Services:** PC (fee). **Cards:** AX, MC, VI. **Free Special Amenities: local telephone calls and early check-in/late check-out.** *(See color ad p 482)*

╫ ⊠ 🔋 🖸 💻 / SOME UNITS FEE VCR

WATERTON LAKES RESORT

Phone: 403/859-2150

CAA SAVE

Large-scale Hotel
$114-$219 5/15-9/30

Address: 101 Clematis Ave T0K 2M0 **Location:** Centre. **Facility:** Smoke free premises. 80 units. 75 one-bedroom standard units, some with efficiencies and/or whirlpools. 5 one-bedroom suites with efficiencies. 2 stories (no elevator), interior/exterior corridors. *Bath:* combo or shower only. **Parking:** on-site, winter plug-ins. **Terms:** open 5/15-9/30, check-in 4 pm, 3 day cancellation notice-fee imposed. **Amenities:** video library (fee), voice mail, hair dryers. *Some:* CD players. **Pool(s):** heated indoor. **Leisure Activities:** sauna, whirlpool, steamroom, recreation programs, hiking trails. *Fee:* massage, aerobic facilities. **Guest Services:** coin laundry. **Business Services:** meeting rooms, PC (fee). **Cards:** AX, MC, VI.

🍸 CALL ⌂M 🛏 📺 ⊠ ⊠ VCR 💻 / SOME UNITS FEE 🐾 🔋 🖸

The following lodging was either not evaluated or did not meet AAA rating requirements but is listed for your information only.

PRINCE OF WALES HOTEL

Phone: 403/859-2231

fyi

Not evaluated. **Address:** Waterton Lakes National Park T0K 2M0 **Location:** Through park gates, about 5 mi (8 km), then just se. Facilities, services, and decor characterize a mid-range property. *(See color ad p 482)*

--- WHERE TO DINE ---

THE LAMP POST DINING ROOM

Phone: 403/859-2334

Canadian
$8-$28

This charming country-inn-style restaurant features an exciting, appealing lunch menu and more extensive dinner selections. Specialties include Alberta beef, wild game and fresh British Columbia salmon. Casual dress. **Bar:** Full bar. **Reservations:** required, for dinner. **Hours:** 7:30 am-10 pm. Closed: 12/25. **Address:** 117 Evergreen Ave T0K 2M0 **Location:** Centre; in Kilmorey Lodge. **Parking:** on-site. **Cards:** AX, DC, DS, MC, VI. **Country Inn**

WESTEROSE

--- WHERE TO STAY ---

VILLAGE CREEK COUNTRY INN

Phone: 780/586-0006

Motel
Rates not provided

Address: 9 Village Dr T0C 2V0 **Location:** Hwy 2, exit 482, 17.5 mi (28 km) w on Hwy 13. **Facility:** 35 one-bedroom standard units, some with whirlpools. 2 stories, interior/exterior corridors. **Parking:** on-site, winter plug-ins. **Terms:** check-in 4 pm. **Amenities:** irons, hair dryers. **Leisure Activities:** whirlpool, recreation programs, spa. **Business Services:** meeting rooms, PC.

╫ ⊠ VCR 🔋 🖸 💻 / SOME UNITS FEE 🐾 ⊠

--- WHERE TO DINE ---

ECO CAFE

Phone: 780/586-2622

Canadian
$5-$10

Bar: Wine only. **Hours:** 6:30 am-8 pm. Closed major holidays; also Mon. **Address:** 10 Village Dr T0C 2V0 **Location:** Hwy 2, exit 482, 17.5 mi (28 km) w on Hwy 13. **Parking:** on-site. **Cards:** AX, MC, VI.

WETASKIWIN pop. 11,673

—— **WHERE TO STAY** ——

BEST WESTERN WAYSIDE INN
Phone: (780)352-6681

Small-scale Hotel
$120-$130 All Year

Address: 4103 56 St T9A 1V2 **Location:** Just n of Hwy 13 W, on Hwy 2A. **Facility:** 28 one-bedroom standard units. 2 stories (no elevator), interior corridors. **Parking:** on-site, winter plug-ins. **Terms:** check-in 4 pm, cancellation fee imposed. **Amenities:** irons, hair dryers. *Some:* high-speed Internet. **Dining:** nightclub. **Leisure Activities:** exercise room. **Guest Services:** wireless Internet. **Business Services:** meeting rooms, PC (fee). **Cards:** AX, DC, MC, VI. **Free Special Amenities:** newspaper and high-speed Internet.

AAA Benefit:
Members save 10% everyday, plus an exclusive frequent stay program.

SUPER 8 MOTEL
Book at AAA.com
Phone: 780/361-3808

Small-scale Hotel
Rates not provided

Address: 3820 56th St T9A 2B2 **Location:** On Hwy 2A, just s of jct Hwy 13 W. **Facility:** 49 one-bedroom standard units. 2 stories (no elevator), interior/exterior corridors. **Parking:** on-site, winter plug-ins. **Terms:** check-in 4 pm. **Guest Services:** coin laundry. **Business Services:** meeting rooms.

—— **WHERE TO DINE** ——

HUCKLEBERRY'S CAFE
Phone: 780/352-3111

Continental
$7-$23

For a taste of the Wild West, the bustling restaurant fits the bill. Friendly servers are dressed in typical Western wear, and the decor follows suit. On the menu is a wide variety of burgers, pasta dishes and sandwiches that emphasize local ingredients, such as Alberta turkey and beef, as well as the famous huckleberry, a berry from the mountains. Not surprisingly, the berry, which is plumper and juicier than the blueberry, found its way into the cafe's name and desserts. **Bar:** Full bar. **Reservations:** suggested. **Hours:** 9:30 am-9 pm. **Closed:** 12/25, 12/26. **Address:** 103-3840 St T9A 2B2 **Location:** Just e of Hwy 2A; s of jct Hwy 13 W. **Parking:** on-site. **Cards:** AX, MC, VI.

WHITECOURT pop. 8,971

—— **WHERE TO STAY** ——

LAKEVIEW INNS & SUITES
Phone: 780/706-3349

Small-scale Hotel
$130 All Year

Address: 3325 Laxton St T7S 1N8 **Location:** Hwy 43 (Kepler St), just n of Park Dr. **Facility:** Smoke free premises. 50 one-bedroom standard units, some with whirlpools. 2 stories (no elevator), interior corridors. **Parking:** on-site, winter plug-ins. **Terms:** cancellation fee imposed. **Amenities:** DVD players, high-speed Internet, irons, hair dryers. **Leisure Activities:** whirlpool, limited exercise equipment. **Guest Services:** coin laundry. **Business Services:** PC (fee). **Cards:** AX, DC, DS, MC, VI. *(See color ad p 362)*

SUPER 8 MOTEL
Book great rates at AAA.com
Phone: (780)778-8908

Small-scale Hotel
$129-$139 All Year

Address: 4121 Kepler St T7S 1P6 **Location:** On Hwy 43, just e of Hwy 32. **Facility:** 59 units. 57 one-bedroom standard units. 2 one-bedroom suites with whirlpools. 3 stories, interior corridors. **Parking:** on-site, winter plug-ins. **Terms:** cancellation fee imposed. **Amenities:** video games (fee), voice mail, hair dryers. *Some:* high-speed Internet, irons. **Leisure Activities:** exercise room. **Guest Services:** valet and coin laundry. **Business Services:** PC. **Cards:** AX, DC, DS, MC, VI.

British Columbia

Mayne Island, Gulf
Islands National Park
Reserve of Canada
© Michael J. Hipple
age fotostock

100 MILE HOUSE

——— WHERE TO STAY ———

100 MILE HOUSE SUPER 8

Motel
$120-$150 3/1-10/31
$100-$120 11/1-2/28

Address: 989 Alder Ave V0K 2E0 **Location:** 0.6 mi (1 km) s on Hwy 97. **Facility:** 28 one-bedroom standard units. 2 stories (no elevator), exterior corridors. **Parking:** on-site, winter plug-ins. **Terms:** office hours 7 am-11 pm, 2 night minimum stay - weekends, 7 day cancellation notice. **Amenities:** hair dryers. **Cards:** AX, MC, VI.

[ASK] [S/D] [📷] [🍴] [📶] [💻] / SOME UNITS FEE [🐕] [✕] [🎥]

RAMADA LIMITED   *Book at AAA.com*   **Phone:** (250)395-2777

Motel
$80-$179 All Year

Address: 917 Alder Ave V0K 2E0 **Location:** 0.6 mi (1 km) s on Hwy 97. **Facility:** 36 one-bedroom standard units, some with efficiencies and/or whirlpools. 3 stories, interior corridors. *Bath:* combo or shower only. **Parking:** on-site. **Terms:** office hours 6 am-11 pm. **Amenities:** voice mail, irons, hair dryers. **Leisure Activities:** sauna, whirlpool. **Guest Services:** coin laundry, wireless Internet. **Cards:** AX, MC, VI.

[ASK] [S/D] [💻] / SOME UNITS FEE [🐕] [✕] [🍴] [🎥]

RED COACH INN   **Phone:** 250/395-2266
Small-scale Hotel
Rates not provided

Address: 170 Cariboo Hwy N V0K 2E0 **Location:** On Hwy 97, on north end of town. **Facility:** 49 one-bedroom standard units. 2 stories (no elevator), interior/exterior corridors. *Bath:* combo or shower only. **Parking:** on-site, winter plug-ins. **Terms:** office hours 7 am-11 pm. **Pool(s):** heated indoor. **Leisure Activities:** whirlpool, limited exercise equipment. **Guest Services:** valet laundry, wireless Internet. **Business Services:** meeting rooms, business center.

[🍴] [🍸] CALL [📶M] [🏊] [📷] [💻] / SOME UNITS FEE [🐕] [✕] [🍴]

——— WHERE TO DINE ———

HAPPY LANDING RESTAURANT   **Phone:** 250/395-5359
Swiss
$6-$20

Behind the village restaurant's charming blue shutters, diners are welcomed to savor the flavors of traditional Swiss cuisine. Among choices are steak tartare, veal sausages with onions, schnitzels, roestis and other Continental favorites. Casual dress. **Bar:** Full bar. **Reservations:** suggested. **Hours:** 5 pm-9 pm, Tues, Wed & Fri also 11:30 am-2 pm. Closed major holidays; also Sun. **Address:** 725 Alder Ave V0K 2E0 **Location:** Hwy 97, 0.6 mi (1 km) s on Service Rd. **Parking:** on-site. **Cards:** MC, VI.

SMITTY'S FAMILY RESTAURANT   **Phone:** 250/395-4655
Canadian
$6-$18

The family-oriented restaurant satisfies patrons with its ever-popular all-day breakfast items, as well as tasty and wholesome soups and salads at lunchtime. A relaxed mood characterizes the dining space. Casual dress. **Bar:** Full bar. **Hours:** 5:30 am-9 pm. Closed: 12/25. **Address:** Box 1217, 451 Cariboo Hwy V0K 2E0 **Location:** On Hwy 97; by tourist information booth. **Parking:** on-site. **Cards:** AX, MC, VI.

108 MILE HOUSE

——— WHERE TO STAY ———

108 RESORT & CONFERENCE CENTRE   *Book great rates at AAA.com*   **Phone:** (250)791-5211
[CAA] [SAVE]

Resort
Small-scale Hotel
$80-$140 All Year

Address: 4816 Telqua Dr V0K 2Z0 **Location:** From Hwy 97, 1 mi (1.6 km) nw on access road, follow signs. Located on the 108 Recreational Ranch. **Facility:** Many activities are offered at this 600-acre resort, which features spacious guest rooms overlooking a golf course and lake. 62 units. 61 one-bedroom standard units. 1 one-bedroom suite. 2 stories (no elevator), exterior corridors. **Parking:** on-site. **Terms:** office hours 7 am-11 pm, cancellation fee imposed. **Amenities:** hair dryers. *Some:* irons. **Pool(s):** heated outdoor. **Leisure Activities:** saunas, whirlpool, beach access, rental canoes, 4 tennis courts (2 lighted), 5000 ft airstrip with hangar, rental bicycles, hiking trails, jogging, playground. *Fee:* golf-18 holes, horseback riding. **Guest Services:** coin laundry. **Business Services:** conference facilities, PC. **Cards:** AX, DC, DS, MC, VI. **Free Special Amenities:** local telephone calls and high-speed Internet.

[S/D] [🍴] [🍸] CALL [📶M] [🏊] [🏇] [✕] [💻] / SOME UNITS FEE [🐕] [✕] [🍴]

ABBOTSFORD pop. 115,463

——— WHERE TO STAY ———

BEST WESTERN BAKERVIEW INN   *Book great rates at AAA.com*   **Phone:** (604)859-1341
[CAA] [SAVE]

Motel
$109-$159 All Year

Address: 1821 Sumas Way V2S 4L5 **Location:** Trans-Canada Hwy 1, exit 92 (Town Centre), just n on Hwy 11. **Facility:** 61 one-bedroom standard units, some with efficiencies. 2 stories (no elevator), exterior corridors. **Parking:** on-site. **Amenities:** irons, hair dryers. **Pool(s):** heated indoor. **Leisure Activities:** whirlpool. **Guest Services:** valet and coin laundry, wireless Internet. **Business Services:** PC. **Cards:** AX, CB, DC, DS, JC, MC, VI. **Free Special Amenities:** local telephone calls and high-speed Internet.

[S/D] [🍴] [🏊] [🍴] [📷] [💻] / SOME UNITS [🐕] [✕]

BEST WESTERN REGENCY INN & CONFERENCE CENTRE *Book great rates at AAA.com*

Phone: 604/853-3111

Small-scale Hotel
Rates not provided

Address: 32110 Marshall Rd V2T 1A1 **Location:** Trans-Canada Hwy 1, exit 87 (Clearbrook Rd). Located behind an elementary school. **Facility:** 128 one-bedroom standard units, some with efficiencies and/or whirlpools. 2-3 stories, interior corridors. **Parking:** on-site. **Amenities:** video games (fee), voice mail, irons, hair dryers. *Some:* high-speed Internet. **Pool(s):** 2 heated indoor. **Leisure Activities:** whirlpools, limited exercise equipment. **Guest Services:** valet and coin laundry, wireless Internet. **Business Services:** conference facilities, business center. **Free Special Amenities: expanded continental breakfast and high-speed Internet.**

AAA Benefit:
Members save 10% everyday, plus an exclusive frequent stay program.

COAST ABBOTSFORD HOTEL & SUITES *Book at AAA.com*

Phone: (604)853-1880

Small-scale Hotel
$99-$260 All Year

Address: 2020 Sumas Way V2S 2C7 **Location:** Trans-Canada Hwy 1, exit 92 (Town Centre), just n on Hwy 11. **Facility:** 60 one-bedroom standard units, some with whirlpools. 4 stories, interior corridors. **Parking:** on-site. **Amenities:** high-speed Internet, irons, hair dryers. **Pool(s):** heated indoor. **Leisure Activities:** whirlpool, limited exercise equipment. **Guest Services:** valet laundry. **Business Services:** meeting rooms. **Cards:** AX, DC, DS, MC, VI.

RAMADA PLAZA & CONFERENCE CENTRE-ABBOTSFORD *Book at AAA.com*

Phone: (604)870-1050

Small-scale Hotel
$119-$149 3/1-9/30
$109-$149 10/1-2/28

Address: 36035 N Parallel Rd V3G 2C6 **Location:** Trans-Canada Hwy 1, exit 95 (Whatcom Rd). **Facility:** Smoke free premises. 116 one-bedroom standard units, some with whirlpools. 4 stories, interior corridors. **Parking:** on-site. **Amenities:** high-speed Internet, voice mail, irons, hair dryers. **Pool(s):** heated indoor. **Leisure Activities:** whirlpool, limited exercise equipment. **Guest Services:** valet and coin laundry, wireless Internet. **Business Services:** meeting rooms, business center. **Cards:** AX, CB, DC, DS, JC, MC, VI.

SUPER 8 MOTEL ABBOTSFORD *Book great rates at AAA.com*

Phone: (604)853-1141

Small-scale Hotel
$99-$229 All Year

Address: 1881 Sumas Way V2S 4L5 **Location:** Trans-Canada Hwy 1, exit 92 (Town Centre), just n on Hwy 11. **Facility:** 99 units. 82 one-bedroom standard units, some with kitchens. 17 one-bedroom suites with kitchens. 2-4 stories, interior/exterior corridors. **Parking:** on-site. **Terms:** check-in 4 pm. **Amenities:** voice mail, irons, hair dryers. *Some:* high-speed Internet. **Pool(s):** heated indoor. **Leisure Activities:** whirlpool, waterslide, exercise room. **Guest Services:** valet and coin laundry. **Business Services:** meeting rooms, business center. **Cards:** AX, DC, DS, MC, VI. **Free Special Amenities: expanded continental breakfast and high-speed Internet.** *(See color ad below)*

——— WHERE TO DINE ———

MILESTONE'S GRILL & BAR

Phone: 604/850-3826

Canadian
$12-$28

Popular with locals, the bustling eatery is a great gathering place. Diners enjoy the relaxed setting and casual menu featuring pasta, pizza, roasted chicken and a tasty choice of egg and brunch options. A nice wine list complements the food choices. Casual dress. **Bar:** Full bar. **Hours:** 11 am-10 pm, Fri-midnight, Sat 10 am-midnight, Sun 9:30 am-10 pm. Closed: 12/25. **Address:** 200-2070 Sumas Way V2S 2C7 **Location:** Corner of S Fraser Way and Sumas Way (Hwy 11); in Abbotsford Village Mall. **Parking:** on-site. **Cards:** AX, DC, MC, VI.

SMITTY'S FAMILY RESTAURANT

Phone: 604/853-1911

Canadian
$6-$18

The family-oriented restaurant satisfies patrons with its ever-popular all-day breakfast items, as well as tasty and wholesome soups and salads at lunchtime. A relaxed mood characterizes the dining space. Casual dress. **Hours:** 6 am-8 pm. Closed: 12/25. **Address:** 1965 Sumas Way V2S 4L5 **Location:** From Trans-Canada Hwy 1, exit 92, just n to Marshall Rd. **Parking:** on-site. **Cards:** AX, MC, VI.

▼ *See AAA listing above* ▼

SWISS CHALET

Phone: 604/864-4002

WWW WW
Canadian
$6-$18

The popular restaurant is known for its rotisserie chicken and ribs and the tangy Chalet sauce that gives food its special zip. Diners munch on a half or quarter chicken with sides such as steamed vegetables, fries, baked potatoes and salads. Lunch guests often go for the great soup and sandwich combination. Take-out and delivery service are popular options. Casual dress. **Bar:** Full bar. **Hours:** 11 am-9 pm, Fri & Sat-10 pm. Closed: 12/25. **Address:** 32470 S Fraser Way V2T 1X3 **Location:** S Fraser Way at Trethewey. **Parking:** on-site. **Cards:** AX, DC, MC, VI.

AINSWORTH HOT SPRINGS

———— **WHERE TO STAY** ————

AINSWORTH HOT SPRINGS RESORT

Phone: (250)229-4212

CAA SAVE
WWW WW
Small-scale Hotel
$123-$199 All Year

Address: 3609 Hwy 31 V0G 1A0 **Location:** On Hwy 31. **Facility:** Smoke free premises. 43 one-bedroom standard units, some with efficiencies and/or whirlpools. 4 stories, interior/exterior corridors. **Parking:** on-site. **Amenities:** hair dryers. **Leisure Activities:** hot springs pool, whirlpool & cave, cross country skiing, bicycles, hiking trails. *Fee:* helicopter tours, massage. **Guest Services:** complimentary laundry. **Business Services:** meeting rooms. **Cards:** AX, MC, VI. **Free Special Amenities: high-speed Internet.**

⬛ 🍴 🍷 ✂ ✕ 📷 💻 / SOME UNITS ♿

ALDERGROVE —*See Vancouver p. 612.*

ARMSTRONG —*See Okanagan Valley p. 526.*

BARRIERE

———— **WHERE TO STAY** ————

MOUNTAIN SPRINGS MOTEL & RV PARK

Phone: (250)672-0090

WWW WW
Motel
$80 All Year

Address: 4253 Yellowhead Hwy V0E 1E0 **Location:** 1 km s on Hwy 5 (Yellowhead Hwy). **Facility:** 12 one-bedroom standard units, some with efficiencies. 1 story, exterior corridors. **Parking:** on-site, winter plug-ins. **Terms:** office hours 7 am-midnight, 7 day cancellation notice-fee imposed. **Guest Services:** coin laundry, wireless Internet. **Cards:** AX, MC, VI.

ASK ⬛ 🍴 📷 ♿ 💻 / SOME UNITS ✕ 🛏

BIG WHITE

———— **WHERE TO STAY** ————

SUNDANCE RESORT

Book at AAA.com

Phone: 250/491-3272

WWW WW
Small-scale Hotel
Rates not provided

Address: 255 Feathertop Way V1Y 2E5 **Location:** From jct Hwy 33 and Big White Rd, 15 mi (24 km) n on Big White Rd. Located at Big White Ski Resort. **Facility:** Smoke free premises. 96 units. 50 one-bedroom standard units. 18 one- and 28 two-bedroom suites, some with kitchens. 3-4 stories, interior corridors. *Bath:* combo or shower only. **Parking:** on-site. **Terms:** open 11/23-2/28. **Amenities:** high-speed Internet, voice mail, hair dryers. *Some:* DVD players. **Pool(s):** heated outdoor. **Leisure Activities:** whirlpools, steamroom, waterslide, exercise room. *Fee:* downhill & cross country skiing, snowmobiling, tobogganing.

🏊 ✂ ✕ 🎿 📷 ♿ 🛏 💻

BLUE RIVER

———— **WHERE TO STAY** ————

GLACIER MOUNTAIN LODGE

Phone: (250)673-2393

WWW WW
Motel
$89-$159 All Year

Address: 869 Shell Rd V0E 1J0 **Location:** On Hwy 5 (Yellowhead Hwy) at Shell Rd, follow signs. **Facility:** Smoke free premises. 35 units. 34 one-bedroom standard units. 1 two-bedroom suite with kitchen. 2 stories (no elevator), interior corridors. **Parking:** on-site, winter plug-ins. **Terms:** cancellation fee imposed. **Amenities:** hair dryers. **Leisure Activities:** whirlpool. **Guest Services:** wireless Internet. **Cards:** AX, MC, VI.

ASK 🍴 ✕ 📷 ♿ / SOME UNITS FEE 🐕

BOSTON BAR pop. 188

———— **WHERE TO DINE** ————

HELL'S GATE RESTAURANT

Menu on AAA.com

Phone: 604/867-9277

CAA
WWW
Canadian
$8-$13

The restaurant is accessed via a thrilling Hell's Gate Airtram ride over the mighty Fraser River. Regular Airtram admission, which is discounted for CAA/AAA members, applies. On the menu are homemade salmon chowder, salmon lasagna, sandwiches and burgers. Casual dress. **Bar:** Full bar. **Hours:** Open 4/11-10/19; 10 am-5:30 pm; from 9:30 am 5/16-9/1. **Location:** 6.9 mi (11 km) s on Trans-Canada Hwy 1; at Hell's Gate Airtram. **Parking:** on-site. **Cards:** MC, VI.

BOWEN ISLAND   (See map and index starting on p. 568)

──────── WHERE TO STAY ────────

WILDWOOD LANE COTTAGES

Vacation Rental Cottage

Rates not provided

Phone: 604/947-2253

Address: 1291 Adams Rd V0N 1G0 **Location:** From ferry terminal, 3.5 mi (5.6 km) w on Grafton Rd, then 0.6 mi (1 km) n. **Facility:** Smoke free premises. 4 cottages. 1 story, exterior corridors. *Bath:* shower only. **Parking:** on-site. **Terms:** office hours 8 am-10 pm. **Amenities:** video library, DVD players, hair dryers. **Leisure Activities:** sauna, whirlpool.

[X] [K] [符] [符] / SOME UNITS FEE [符]

BRENTWOOD BAY —*See Victoria p. 663.*

BURNABY —*See Vancouver p. 612.*

CACHE CREEK pop. 1,037

──────── WHERE TO STAY ────────

BONAPARTE MOTEL

(CAA) [SAVE]

Motel
$69-$120 3/1-10/31
$49-$89 11/1-2/28

Phone: 250/457-9693

Address: 1395 Hwy 97 N V0K 1H0 **Location:** Just n of jct Trans-Canada Hwy 1. **Facility:** 24 units. 20 one- and 4 two-bedroom standard units, some with efficiencies or kitchens. 1 story, exterior corridors. **Parking:** on-site, winter plug-ins. **Terms:** office hours 7 am-midnight. **Pool(s):** heated outdoor. **Leisure Activities:** sauna, whirlpool. **Guest Services:** wireless Internet. **Cards:** AX, DS, MC, VI. **Free Special Amenities:** local telephone calls and high-speed Internet.

[符符] [符] [符] [符] / SOME UNITS FEE [符] [X]

──────── WHERE TO DINE ────────

WANDER INN RESTAURANT   *Menu on AAA.com*

(CAA)

Chinese
$7-$16

Phone: 250/457-6511

The cuisine features Cantonese dishes such as the emperor's plate with chicken, beef and stir-fry, as well as burgers, sandwiches, soup, steak and chops. Seniors and visitors like this place, which has a coffee shop and dining room section. Casual dress. **Bar:** Full bar. **Hours:** 11:30 am-9 pm. Closed: 12/25, 12/26. **Address:** Trans-Canada Hwy 1 V0K 1H0 **Location:** Just s of jct Hwy 97. **Parking:** on-site. **Cards:** AX, MC, VI.

CAMPBELL RIVER pop. 28,456

──────── WHERE TO STAY ────────

ANCHOR INN & SUITES   *Book great rates at AAA.com*

(CAA) [SAVE]

Small-scale Hotel
$119-$289 All Year

Phone: (250)286-1131

Address: 261 Island Hwy 19A V9W 2B3 **Location:** On Island Hwy 19A, 1.3 mi (2 km) s. **Facility:** 77 one-bedroom standard units, some with whirlpools. 7 stories, interior corridors. **Parking:** on-site. **Terms:** cancellation fee imposed. **Amenities:** voice mail, irons, hair dryers. *Some:* high-speed Internet. **Dining:** 2 restaurants. **Pool(s):** heated indoor. **Leisure Activities:** whirlpool, limited exercise equipment. **Guest Services:** valet and coin laundry, wireless Internet. **Business Services:** conference facilities, PC. **Cards:** AX, CB, DC, DS, MC, VI. **Free Special Amenities: continental breakfast and high-speed Internet.**

[S符] [符符] [符] [符] [K] [符] [符] [符] [符] / SOME UNITS FEE [符] [X]

ARBOUR'S GUEST HOUSE

Bed & Breakfast
$85-$115 All Year

Phone: 250/287-9873

Address: 375 S Murphy St V9W 1Y8 **Location:** 1.3 mi (2 km) s on Island Hwy 19A, just e on 1st Ave, then 0.5 mi (0.8 km) s on Murphy St; on water side of street. Located in a residential area. **Facility:** Smoke free premises. 4 one-bedroom standard units. 2 stories (no elevator), interior corridors. *Bath:* some shared or private. **Parking:** on-site. **Terms:** office hours 8 am-10 pm, age restrictions may apply, 14 day cancellation notice-fee imposed. **Amenities:** *Some:* hair dryers. **Cards:** AX, MC, VI.

[X] [K] [Z] / SOME UNITS [W]

BEST WESTERN AUSTRIAN CHALET   *Book great rates at AAA.com*

(CAA) [SAVE]

Motel
$114-$147 All Year

Phone: (250)923-4231

Address: 462 S Island Hwy V9W 1A5 **Location:** 2 mi (3.2 km) s on Island Hwy 19A. **Facility:** 59 one-bedroom standard units, some with efficiencies and/or whirlpools. 2-3 stories (no elevator), interior/exterior corridors. **Parking:** on-site. **Amenities:** voice mail, irons, hair dryers. *Some:* high-speed Internet. **Pool(s):** heated indoor. **Leisure Activities:** sauna, whirlpool, putting green, table tennis, barbecue, limited exercise equipment. **Guest Services:** valet and coin laundry, wireless Internet. **Business Services:** meeting rooms. **Cards:** AX, CB, DC, DS, JC, MC, VI. **Free Special Amenities:** continental breakfast and high-speed Internet. *(See color ad p 490)*

[S符] [符符] CALL [符M] [符] [X] [K] [符] [符]
/ SOME UNITS FEE [符] [X] [VCR] [符]

AAA Benefit:

Members save 10% everyday, plus an exclusive frequent stay program.

CAMPBELL RIVER LODGE FISHING & ADVENTURE RESORT

Motel

$75-$115 All Year

Phone: 250/287-7446

Address: 1760 N Island Hwy V9W 2E7 **Location:** On Island Hwy 19A, 1.3 mi (2 km) nw of downtown; just e from Hwy 19 and 28. **Facility:** 28 one-bedroom standard units, some with efficiencies. 2 stories (no elevator), interior/exterior corridors. *Bath:* combo or shower only. **Parking:** on-site. **Terms:** office hours 7:30 am-11:30 pm, 3 day cancellation notice-fee imposed. **Amenities:** hair dryers. **Leisure Activities:** whirlpool, saltwater & freshwater charter fishing with guides. *Fee:* custom fish canning, freezing & shipping. **Guest Services:** coin laundry, wireless Internet. **Business Services:** meeting rooms. **Cards:** AX, MC, VI. *(See color ad below)*

OCEAN RESORT

Book at AAA.com

Motel

Rates not provided

Phone: 250/923-4281

Address: 4834 S Island Hwy V9H 1E8 **Location:** 11 mi (18 km) s on Hwy 19A. **Facility:** Smoke free premises. 29 units. 28 one-bedroom standard units. 1 one-bedroom suite with kitchen. 2 stories (no elevator), interior corridors. **Parking:** on-site. **Terms:** office hours 7 am-9 pm. **Amenities:** voice mail. **Leisure Activities:** sauna.

TOWN CENTRE INN

Motel

$84-$89 3/1-10/31
$74-$79 11/1-2/28

Phone: (250)287-8866

Address: 1500 Dogwood St V9W 3A6 **Location:** Follow Island Hwy 19A through town, watch for signs, just e on Dogwood St; corner of 16th Ave. **Facility:** 34 one-bedroom standard units, some with efficiencies. 2 stories (no elevator), exterior corridors. **Parking:** on-site. **Terms:** office hours 7:30 am-midnight. **Amenities:** hair dryers. **Leisure Activities:** sauna. **Guest Services:** coin laundry. **Cards:** AX, MC, VI.

TRAVELODGE CAMPBELL RIVER

Book at AAA.com

Motel

$78-$145 3/1-9/30
$80-$115 10/1-2/28

Phone: 250/286-6622

Address: 340 S Island Hwy V9W 1A5 **Location:** 1.9 mi (3 km) s on Island Hwy 19A. **Facility:** 39 one-bedroom standard units. 2 stories (no elevator), interior corridors. **Parking:** on-site. **Amenities:** high-speed Internet, hair dryers. **Pool(s):** heated indoor. **Leisure Activities:** whirlpool. **Cards:** AX, JC, MC, VI.

The following lodging was either not evaluated or did not meet AAA rating requirements but is listed for your information only.

HERON'S LANDING, A BOUTIQUE HOTEL

Phone: 250/923-2848

Not evaluated. **Address:** 492 S Island Hwy V9W 1A5 **Location:** 2 mi (3.2 km) s on Island Hwy 19A. Facilities, services, and decor characterize a mid-range property.

WHERE TO DINE

BAAN THAI RESTAURANT
Phone: 250/286-4850

Thai
$8-$15

The traditional flavors and aromas of Thailand's distinctive cuisine are honored at the contemporary downtown restaurant. The second-floor spot also features a small rooftop patio. Casual dress. **Bar:** Full bar. **Reservations:** suggested, for dinner. **Hours:** 11:30 am-2 & 5-9 pm, Fri & Sat-9:30 pm. Closed major holidays; also Sun. **Address:** 1090B Shoppers Row V9W 2C6 **Location:** At 11th Ave; downtown. **Parking:** street. **Cards:** MC, VI.

BEST WOK
Phone: 250/287-2831

Chinese
$5-$16

Contemporary Chinese and Western food is on the menu at the downtown restaurant. Combination meals serve two, four, six or eight to 10 diners. Plenty of on-site parking is available, but for those who can't dine in, take-out and delivery also are offered. Casual dress. **Bar:** Full bar. **Reservations:** accepted. **Hours:** 11 am-9:30 pm. Closed: 10/13, 12/25. **Address:** 968 Alder St V9W 2P9 **Location:** From Shoppers Row, just e on 10th Ave, then just s. **Parking:** on-site. **Cards:** MC, VI.

FUSILLI GRILL
Phone: 250/830-0090

Mediterranean
$9-$26

Contemporary West Coast creations inspired by Italian cuisine highlight the menu of the youthful and casual bistro-restaurant. This place is in a small strip mall, away from the busy town center and highways. Daily specials and British Columbia wines are featured. Casual dress. **Bar:** Full bar. **Reservations:** suggested, for dinner Fri & Sat. **Hours:** 4:30 pm-10 pm, Sun & Mon 4:30 pm-9 pm. Closed: 1/1, 12/25. **Address:** 4-220 Dogwood St V9W 2X9 **Location:** Island Hwy 19A, 1.5 mi (2.4 km) se; in Dogwood Plaza. **Parking:** on-site. **Cards:** AX, MC, VI.

LOOKOUT WEST COAST GRILL & SEAFOOD HOUSE
Phone: 250/286-6812

Seafood
$8-$26

Near the start of the downtown shopping district, the waterfront restaurant offers views of Quadra Island just across the water. In addition to local seafood, such as oysters, mussels, salmon and halibut, the menu includes tapas and tidbits, gourmet soup and salads and pastas. All are priced reasonably. Casual dress. **Bar:** Full bar. **Hours:** 11 am-10 pm. Closed: 12/25. **Address:** 921 Island Hwy V9W 2C2 **Location:** Just s on Island Hwy 19A from downtown. **Parking:** on-site. **Cards:** MC, VI.

MOXIE'S CLASSIC GRILL
Phone: 250/830-1500

Canadian
$8-$18

This sleek, funky and popular restaurant presents an extensive menu of creatively prepared dishes, including pizza, pasta, rice, noodles, signature salads and burgers. Other menus include one for children and one for Sunday brunch. Lending to the upbeat, stylish decor are dark wood appointments and river rock fireplaces. Casual dress. **Bar:** Full bar. **Hours:** 9:30 am-midnight. **Address:** 1360 Island Hwy V9W 8C9 **Location:** From Island Hwy 19A, just n on Discovery Cres; in Discovery Harbour Mall. **Parking:** on-site. **Cards:** AX, MC, VI.

RICKY'S ALL DAY GRILL
Phone: 250/286-3448

Canadian
$6-$15

The comfortable eatery, which employs friendly servers, presents a varied menu that includes pasta dishes, wraps, omelets, stir-fry preparations and burgers. Portions are generous. Children's and senior selections are offered. Guests can request seating in a booth or at a table. Casual dress. **Bar:** Full bar. **Hours:** 6 am-8 pm, Sun from 7 am. **Address:** 811 13th Ave V9W 4G9 **Location:** Island Hwy 19A, just s on Dogwood St, then just e. **Parking:** on-site. **Cards:** MC, VI.

CASTLEGAR pop. 7,002

WHERE TO STAY

QUALITY INN CASTLEGAR *Book at AAA.com*
Phone: 250/365-2177

Motel
Rates not provided

Address: 1935 Columbia Ave V1N 2W8 **Location:** Jct Hwy 3A and 3B, just s. **Facility:** 48 units. 47 one-bedroom standard units. 1 two-bedroom suite with kitchen. 2 stories, interior/exterior corridors. **Parking:** on-site. **Terms:** office hours 7 am-11 pm. **Amenities:** voice mail, irons, hair dryers. *Some:* high-speed Internet. **Guest Services:** valet laundry, wireless Internet. **Business Services:** meeting rooms, PC. *(See color ad on insert)*

SUPER 8 MOTEL-CASTLEGAR *Book at AAA.com*
Phone: 250/365-2700

Small-scale Hotel
Rates not provided

Address: 651 18th St V1N 2N1 **Location:** Hwy 3, exit city centre. **Facility:** 56 units. 52 one-bedroom standard units, some with efficiencies and/or whirlpools. 4 one-bedroom suites with efficiencies. 3 stories, interior corridors. *Bath:* combo or shower only. **Parking:** on-site. **Amenities:** voice mail, hair dryers. *Some:* video games (fee), high-speed Internet, irons. **Leisure Activities:** whirlpool, waterslide. **Guest Services:** valet and coin laundry, wireless Internet. **Business Services:** meeting rooms, PC.

CHASE pop. 2,460

--------- **WHERE TO STAY** ---------

CHASE COUNTRY INN MOTEL
Phone: (250)679-3333

Motel
$69-$99 3/1-10/31
$59-$79 11/1-2/28

Address: 576 Coburn St V0E 1M0 **Location:** Trans-Canada Hwy 1 and Coburn St. **Facility:** 21 one-bedroom standard units, some with efficiencies or kitchens. 2 stories (no elevator), exterior corridors. **Parking:** on-site, winter plug-ins. **Terms:** office hours 8 am-11 pm, cancellation fee imposed. **Amenities:** hair dryers. **Guest Services:** coin laundry. **Cards:** AX, MC, VI.

TALKING ROCK AT QUAAOUT LODGE
Phone: 250/679-3090

Resort
Small-scale Hotel
$130-$219 3/1-10/31
$99-$139 11/1-2/28

Location: Trans-Canada Hwy 1, exit Squilax Bridge, 1.5 mi (2.5 km) w on Little Shuswap Rd. Located in a quiet secluded area. **Facility:** Native interpretative trails crisscross the grounds of this lakefront lodge offering brightly decorated guest rooms. 72 one-bedroom standard units, some with whirlpools. 3 stories, interior corridors. **Parking:** on-site. **Terms:** office hours 7 am-11 pm, check-in 4 pm. **Amenities:** high-speed Internet (fee), dual phone lines, hair dryers. **Pool(s):** heated indoor. **Leisure Activities:** whirlpool, steamroom, rental canoes, boat dock, fishing, rental bicycles, hiking trails, jogging, exercise room. **Guest Services:** coin laundry. **Business Services:** conference facilities. **Cards:** AX, MC, VI.

CHEMAINUS pop. 2,937

--------- **WHERE TO STAY** ---------

BEST WESTERN CHEMAINUS FESTIVAL INN
Book great rates at AAA.com
Phone: (250)246-4181

Small-scale Hotel
$128-$158 All Year

Address: 9573 Chemainus Rd V0R 1K5 **Location:** Trans-Canada Hwy 1, exit Henry Rd, 0.9 mi (1.4 km) e. **Facility:** Smoke free premises. 75 units. 24 one-bedroom standard units, some with efficiencies. 51 one-bedroom suites with efficiencies. 4 stories, interior corridors. **Parking:** on-site. **Terms:** 3 day cancellation notice. **Amenities:** high-speed Internet, dual phone lines, voice mail, safes, irons, hair dryers. **Pool(s):** heated indoor. **Leisure Activities:** whirlpool, exercise room. **Guest Services:** coin laundry. **Business Services:** meeting rooms, PC. **Cards:** AX, DS, MC, VI. **Free Special Amenities: continental breakfast and high-speed Internet.**

AAA Benefit:
Members save 10% everyday, plus an exclusive frequent stay program.

--------- **WHERE TO DINE** ---------

MANDOLINOS
Phone: 250/246-2848

Canadian
$8-$20

The pleasant all-day restaurant downtown serves wraps, sandwiches and homemade soups for lunch, while the dinner menu focuses on Mediterranean preparations of lamb and pork. After eating, diners can stroll the downtown area to view the city's famous murals. Casual dress. **Bar:** Full bar. **Hours:** 8 am-10 pm. Closed: 12/25. **Address:** 2976 Mill St V0R 1K0 **Location:** Between Chemainus Rd and Willow St. **Parking:** street. **Cards:** AX, MC, VI.

CHILLIWACK pop. 62,927

--------- **WHERE TO STAY** ---------

BEST WESTERN RAINBOW COUNTRY INN
Book great rates at AAA.com
Phone: (604)795-3828

Small-scale Hotel
$100-$130 All Year

Address: 43971 Industrial Way V2R 3A4 **Location:** Trans-Canada Hwy 1, exit 116 (Lickman Rd). **Facility:** 74 one-bedroom standard units, some with whirlpools. 2 stories (no elevator), interior corridors. **Parking:** on-site. **Amenities:** voice mail, irons, hair dryers. **Pool(s):** heated indoor. **Leisure Activities:** sauna, whirlpool. **Guest Services:** valet and coin laundry, wireless Internet. **Business Services:** meeting rooms, PC. **Cards:** AX, DC, DS, MC, VI. **Free Special Amenities: early check-in/late check-out and high-speed Internet.**

AAA Benefit:
Members save 10% everyday, plus an exclusive frequent stay program.

CHILLIWACK TRAVELODGE
Book great rates at AAA.com
Phone: (604)792-4240

Small-scale Hotel
$89-$99 3/1-9/30
$79-$89 10/1-2/28

Address: 45466 Yale Rd W V2R 3Z8 **Location:** Trans-Canada Hwy 1, exit 119, just n. **Facility:** 82 units. 81 one- and 1 two-bedroom standard units, some with efficiencies. 2 stories (no elevator), interior corridors. **Parking:** on-site. **Amenities:** voice mail, hair dryers. **Pool(s):** heated indoor. **Leisure Activities:** whirlpool. **Guest Services:** coin laundry, wireless Internet. **Business Services:** meeting rooms. **Cards:** AX, DC, DS, MC, VI. **Free Special Amenities: preferred room (subject to availability with advance reservations) and high-speed Internet.**

COMFORT INN *Book at AAA.com*   Phone: (604)858-0636

♦♦♦ ♦♦♦
Motel
$100-$145 All Year

Address: 45405 Luckakuck Way V2R 3C7 **Location:** Trans-Canada Hwy 1, exit 119, s on Vedder Rd, then 0.6 mi (1 km) w. **Facility:** 83 one-bedroom standard units. 2 stories (no elevator), interior corridors. **Parking:** on-site. **Amenities:** irons, hair dryers. **Guest Services:** valet laundry, wireless Internet. **Business Services:** PC (fee). **Cards:** AX, CB, DC, DS, JC, MC, VI.
(See color ad on insert)

DAYS INN CHILLIWACK *Book at AAA.com*   Phone: 604/792-1955

♦♦♦ ♦♦♦
Motel
Rates not provided

Address: 8583 Young Rd S V2P 4P3 **Location:** Hwy 1, exit 119 eastbound, 0.6 mi (1 km) n on Yale Rd, then just e on Hocking Ave; exit 120 (Young Rd) westbound, 0.6 mi (1 km) n. **Facility:** 29 one-bedroom standard units. 2 stories (no elevator), interior corridors. **Parking:** on-site. **Amenities:** voice mail, hair dryers. **Guest Services:** wireless Internet. **Business Services:** PC.

---- **WHERE TO DINE** ----

EARL'S   Phone: 604/858-3360

♦♦♦ ♦♦♦
Canadian
$10-$28

Offering an experience that falls between fast food and fine dining, the fun, relaxed restaurant prepares great food at a great price. Choices range from juicy burgers, hearty sandwiches, fresh salads, wings and pizza to full entrees of steak, chops and seafood. Made-from-scratch soups and assorted breads, as well as a nice choice of wines and beers, round out the offerings. This is a fitting spot for impromptu get-togethers and festive occasions. Casual dress. **Bar:** Full bar. **Hours:** 11:30 am-11 pm. Closed: 12/25. **Address:** 45585 Luckakuck Way V2R 1A1 **Location:** Trans-Canada Hwy 1, exit 119, just w on Vedder Rd; in Cottonwood Shopping Center. **Parking:** on-site. **Cards:** AX, DC, MC, VI.

RICKY'S ALL DAY GRILL   Phone: 604/858-5663

♦♦♦ ♦♦♦
Canadian
$6-$15

The comfortable eatery, which employs friendly servers, presents a varied menu that includes pasta dishes, wraps, omelets, stir-fry preparations and burgers. Portions are generous. Children's and senior selections are offered. Guests can request seating in a booth or at a table. Casual dress. **Bar:** Full bar. **Hours:** 6:30 am-9:30 pm. **Address:** 45389 Luckakuck Way V2R 3C7 **Location:** Trans-Canada Hwy 1, exit 119, just s on Vedder Rd, then 0.6 mi (1 km) n. **Parking:** on-site. **Cards:** MC, VI.

CHRISTINA LAKE pop. 986

---- **WHERE TO STAY** ----

NEW HORIZON MOTEL   Phone: (250)447-9312

♦♦♦♦ ♦♦♦♦
Motel
$95-$185 All Year

Address: 2037 Hwy 3 V0H 1E2 **Location:** Just e. **Facility:** 25 units. 19 one-bedroom standard units, some with kitchens and/or whirlpools. 6 one-bedroom suites with kitchens. 1-2 stories (no elevator), exterior corridors. *Bath:* combo or shower only. **Parking:** on-site. **Terms:** office hours 7 am-10 pm, 2-4 night minimum stay - seasonal and/or weekends, cancellation fee imposed. **Amenities:** irons, hair dryers. *Some:* high-speed Internet. **Leisure Activities:** basketball, volleyball. **Cards:** AX, DC, MC, VI.

CLEARWATER

---- **WHERE TO STAY** ----

CLEARWATER VALLEY RESORT & KOA
KAMPGROUND *Book great rates at AAA.com*   Phone: (250)674-3909

(CAA) (SAVE)

♦♦♦ ♦♦♦
Cottage
$85-$135 5/1-10/12

Address: 373 Clearwater Valley Rd V0E 1N0 **Location:** Jct Hwy 5 (Yellowhead Hwy) and Clearwater Valley Rd. **Facility:** 18 one-bedroom standard units. 1-2 stories (no elevator), exterior corridors. **Parking:** on-site. **Terms:** open 5/1-10/12, office hours 7:30 am-10 pm, cancellation fee imposed. **Pool(s):** heated outdoor. **Leisure Activities:** playground, horseshoes, volleyball, game room. *Fee:* miniature golf. **Guest Services:** coin laundry, wireless Internet. **Business Services:** PC. **Cards:** MC, VI. **Free Special Amenities:** high-speed Internet.

DUTCH LAKE MOTEL AND CAMPGROUND   Phone: (250)674-3325

♦♦♦ ♦♦♦
Motel
$60-$160 All Year

Address: 333 Roy Rd V0E 1N0 **Location:** Hwy 5 (Yellowhead Hwy) at Roy Rd. **Facility:** 27 units. 19 one- and 2 two-bedroom standard units, some with efficiencies. 6 one-bedroom suites with efficiencies (utensils extra charge). 2 stories (no elevator), exterior corridors. **Parking:** on-site, winter plug-ins. **Terms:** office hours 7 am-11 pm. **Amenities:** hair dryers. *Some:* high-speed Internet. **Leisure Activities:** rental boats, rental canoes, fishing. **Guest Services:** coin laundry, wireless Internet. **Cards:** MC, VI.

LOONS AT THE LAKESHORE MOTEL   Phone: (250)674-3345

(CAA) (SAVE)

♦♦♦
Motel
$65-$90 3/1-9/30
$50-$85 10/1-2/28

Address: 57 E Old N Thompson Hwy V0E 1N0 **Location:** 0.6 mi (1 km) w on Old N Thompson Hwy, just off Hwy 5 (Yellowhead Hwy). **Facility:** 16 units. 12 one- and 4 two-bedroom standard units, some with kitchens. 2 stories (no elevator), exterior corridors. *Bath:* combo or shower only. **Parking:** on-site, winter plug-ins. **Terms:** office hours 9 am-10 pm. **Leisure Activities:** rental boats, rental canoes, boat dock, fishing. **Cards:** DC, MC, VI. **Free Special Amenities:** local telephone calls.

COMOX pop. 11,172

——— WHERE TO STAY ———

PORT AUGUSTA INN & SUITES
Book great rates at AAA.com
Phone: (250)339-2277

Motel
$85-$165 All Year

Address: 2082 Comox Ave V9M 1P8 **Location:** From Hwy 19A (Cliffe Ave), follow signs to Comox Ave, then 2.5 mi (4 km) e. **Facility:** 69 one-bedroom standard units, some with efficiencies, kitchens and/or whirlpools. 2 stories (no elevator), interior/exterior corridors. *Bath:* combo or shower only. **Parking:** on-site. **Terms:** office hours 7:30 am-11 pm, cancellation fee imposed. **Amenities:** irons, hair dryers. *Some:* high-speed Internet. **Pool(s):** heated outdoor. **Guest Services:** valet laundry. **Cards:** AX, DS, MC, VI. **Free Special Amenities:** continental breakfast and high-speed Internet.

——— WHERE TO DINE ———

SANDBAR GRILL
Phone: 250/339-5570

Continental
$7-$22

Just two blocks from the marina, the charming and casual downtown restaurant prepares delicious tapas meant for sharing, as well as gourmet pizza, fresh seafood and tempting desserts. During warmer weather, the outdoor patio is a great place to unwind. Casual dress. **Bar:** Full bar. **Reservations:** accepted. **Hours:** 11 am-2 & 5-close, Sun from 8 am, Tues 11 am-2 pm; Sunday brunch. Closed: 12/25, 12/26; also Mon. **Address:** 1832 Comox Ave V9M 3M7 **Location:** From Hwy 19A (Cliffe Ave), follow signs to Comox Ave, then 3.1 mi (5 km) e. **Parking:** street. **Cards:** AX, DC, MC, VI.

SMITTY'S FAMILY RESTAURANT
Phone: 250/339-3911

Canadian
$6-$18

The family-oriented restaurant satisfies patrons with its ever-popular all-day breakfast items, as well as tasty and wholesome soups and salads at lunchtime. A relaxed mood characterizes the dining space. Casual dress. **Bar:** Full bar. **Hours:** 7:30 am-8 pm. Closed: 12/25, 12/26. **Address:** 1747 Comox Ave V9M 3M2 **Location:** Between Port Augusta and Nordin sts. **Parking:** on-site. **Cards:** AX, MC, VI.

COQUITLAM —*See Vancouver p. 614.*

COURTENAY pop. 18,304

——— WHERE TO STAY ———

THE ANCO MOTEL
Phone: 250/334-2451

Motel
$65-$85 All Year

Address: 1885 Cliffe Ave V9N 2K9 **Location:** Just s of Hwy 19 Connector. **Facility:** 67 one-bedroom standard units, some with efficiencies. 2 stories (no elevator), exterior corridors. *Bath:* combo or shower only. **Parking:** on-site. **Amenities:** *Some:* high-speed Internet, hair dryers. **Pool(s):** heated outdoor. **Guest Services:** coin laundry. **Cards:** AX, MC, VI.

BEST WESTERN THE WESTERLY HOTEL
Book great rates at AAA.com
Phone: (250)338-7741

Small-scale Hotel
$144-$289 All Year

Address: 1590 Cliffe Ave V9N 2K4 **Location:** Corner of Cliffe Ave and Island Hwy 19A N. **Facility:** 108 units. 105 one-bedroom standard units, some with whirlpools. 3 one-bedroom suites. 4 stories, interior corridors. **Parking:** on-site. **Terms:** cancellation fee imposed. **Amenities:** irons, hair dryers. **Pool(s):** heated indoor. **Leisure Activities:** saunas, whirlpool, exercise room. **Guest Services:** valet laundry, wireless Internet. **Business Services:** meeting rooms. **Cards:** AX, MC, VI. **Free Special Amenities:** local telephone calls and newspaper.

AAA Benefit:
Members save 10% everyday, plus an exclusive frequent stay program.

CROWN ISLE RESORT & GOLF COMMUNITY
Phone: 250/703-5050

Resort
Small-scale Hotel
Rates not provided

Address: 399 Clubhouse Dr V9N 9G3 **Location:** Island Hwy 19A N, 0.9 mi (1.5 km) n on Comox Ave, then 1.6 mi (2.5 km) ne on Ryan Rd, follow signs. **Facility:** World-class golfing awaits at the Crown Isle Resort, where many of the guest rooms overlook the golf course; also featured is an on-site car museum. Smoke free premises. 90 units. 83 one- and 7 two-bedroom standard units, some with efficiencies, kitchens and/or whirlpools. 2-3 stories (no elevator), exterior corridors. **Parking:** on-site. **Terms:** office hours 6 am-11 pm. **Amenities:** DVD players, high-speed Internet, voice mail, irons, hair dryers. *Some:* CD players. **Leisure Activities:** whirlpool, steamrooms, exercise room. *Fee:* golf-18 holes. **Guest Services:** complimentary laundry. **Business Services:** conference facilities.

GREYSTONE MANOR BED & BREAKFAST
Phone: 250/338-1422

Historic Bed
& Breakfast
$98 All Year

Address: 4014 Haas Rd V9N 9T4 **Location:** 2.5 mi (4 km) s on Island Hwy 19A S to Hilton Rd. Located in a quiet secluded area. **Facility:** This secluded B&B features a wonderful English-style garden, a common area with original hardwood floors, and cozy rooms with simple decor. Smoke free premises. 3 one-bedroom standard units. 2 stories (no elevator), interior corridors. *Bath:* combo or shower only. **Parking:** on-site. **Terms:** office hours 7:30 am-10 pm, check-in 4 pm, age restrictions may apply. **Amenities:** hair dryers. **Cards:** MC, VI.

KINGFISHER OCEANSIDE RESORT & SPA

Phone: 250-338-1323

WWWW
Small-scale Hotel
Rates not provided

Address: 4330 S Island Hwy V9N 9R9 **Location:** 3.8 mi (6 km) s on Island Hwy 19A S, watch for signs. **Facility:** Smoke free premises. 64 units. 44 one-bedroom standard units, some with efficiencies and/or whirlpools. 20 one-bedroom suites with efficiencies, some with whirlpools. 2 stories, exterior corridors. *Bath:* combo or shower only. **Parking:** on-site. **Terms:** office hours 7 am-11 pm. **Amenities:** video library (fee), irons, hair dryers. *Some:* DVD players, high-speed Internet (fee). **Pool(s):** heated outdoor. **Leisure Activities:** sauna, whirlpool, steamroom, tennis court, rental bicycles, exercise room, spa. **Guest Services:** valet laundry, wireless Internet. **Business Services:** meeting rooms, PC.

OLD HOUSE VILLAGE SUITES & HOTEL

Phone: 250/703-0202

WWWW
Condominium
Rates not provided

Address: 1800 Riverside Ln V9N 8C7 **Location:** Island Hwy 19A (Cliffe Ave), just n on 19th St. **Facility:** Located along the riverbank and near a large shopping complex, these condo-style accommodations provide separate bedrooms and a full kitchen. Smoke free premises. 34 one-bedroom suites with kitchens, some with whirlpools. 3 stories, interior corridors. *Bath:* combo or shower only. **Parking:** on-site. **Terms:** check-in 4 pm. **Amenities:** video library (fee), DVD players, high-speed Internet, voice mail, irons, hair dryers. **Leisure Activities:** sauna, whirlpool, limited exercise equipment. **Guest Services:** wireless Internet. **Business Services:** PC.

TRAVELODGE COURTENAY   *Book great rates at AAA.com*

Phone: (250)334-4491

(AAA) [SAVE]
WW
Motel
$93-$118 All Year

Address: 2605 Cliffe Ave V9N 2L8 **Location:** 0.8 mi (1.2 km) s on Island Hwy 19A S. Located adjacent to Driftwood Mall. **Facility:** 91 one-bedroom standard units, some with efficiencies. 2 stories (no elevator), exterior corridors. **Parking:** on-site. **Amenities:** voice mail, hair dryers. *Some:* high-speed Internet. **Pool(s):** heated outdoor. **Guest Services:** coin laundry. **Business Services:** meeting rooms. **Cards:** AX, CB, DC, DS, JC, MC, VI. **Free Special Amenities: expanded continental breakfast and high-speed Internet.**

———— WHERE TO DINE ————

MCSWIGGINS CAFE

Phone: 250/338-2966

WW
Canadian
$7-$10

The popular breakfast and lunch cafe professes: "We're not fast food. All food is freshly prepared and may take longer; your patience is appreciated." Wonderful aromas greet those who walk in the door. Casual dress. **Bar:** Full bar. **Hours:** 7 am-8 pm. Closed: 12/25. **Address:** 2270 Cliffe Ave V9N 2L4 **Location:** 1 km s on Island Hwy 19A (Cliffe Ave). **Parking:** on-site. **Cards:** AX, MC, VI.

MONTE CHRISTO ON THE RIVER

Phone: 250/338-1468

WWW
Continental
$9-$21

Along the river, the well-established restaurant presents a casual lunch menu with daily specials and homemade soups. At the heart of the dinner menu are steak, seafood, pasta and barbecue dishes. Also offered are many seniors' and children's choices. Casual dress. **Bar:** Full bar. **Hours:** 11:30 am-10 pm, Fri-11 pm, Sat 4 pm-11 pm, Sun 4 pm-10 pm. Closed: 1/1, 12/25, 12/26. **Address:** 975 Comox Rd V9N 3P7 **Location:** Island Hwy 19A N. **Parking:** on-site. **Cards:** AX, MC, VI.

RICKY'S ALL DAY GRILL

Phone: 250/334-9638

WWW
Canadian
$6-$15

The comfortable eatery, which employs friendly servers, presents a varied menu that includes pasta dishes, wraps, omelets, stir-fry preparations and burgers. Portions are generous. Children's and senior selections are offered. Guests can request seating in a booth or at a table. Casual dress. **Bar:** Full bar. **Hours:** 7 am-8:30 pm. **Address:** 795 Ryan Rd V9N 3R6 **Location:** Island Hwy 19A N, just ne; in Washington Park Centre Mall. **Parking:** on-site. **Cards:** MC, VI.

TOMATO TOMATO

Phone: 250/338-5406

WWW
Canadian
$9-$30

This locally popular dining spot is housed in a rustic 1938 home that has been renovated inside and now features very modern decor. Sitting alongside the river, the exterior still features an old farmhouse-like charm. Patrons will find friendly, attentive service and plenty of parking. Casual dress. **Bar:** Full bar. **Reservations:** accepted. **Hours:** 11:30 am-9:30 pm, Fri & Sat-10 pm. **Address:** 1760 Riverside Ln V9N 8C7 **Location:** Island Hwy 19A (Cliffe Ave), just n on 19th St. **Parking:** on-site. **Cards:** AX, DC, MC, VI.

CRANBROOK pop. 18,476

———— WHERE TO STAY ————

BEST WESTERN CRANBROOK HOTEL   *Book great rates at AAA.com*

Phone: 250/417-4002

(AAA) [SAVE]
WWW
Small-scale Hotel
Rates not provided

Address: 1019 Cranbrook St N V1C 3S4 **Location:** Hwy 3 and 95; centre. **Facility:** 94 units. 86 one-bedroom standard units. 4 one- and 4 two-bedroom suites, some with whirlpools. 4 stories, interior corridors. **Parking:** on-site. **Amenities:** high-speed Internet, voice mail, irons, hair dryers. **Pool(s):** indoor. **Leisure Activities:** waterslide, exercise room. **Guest Services:** wireless Internet. **Free Special Amenities: local telephone calls and early check-in/late check-out.**

AAA Benefit:
Members save 10% everyday, plus an exclusive frequent stay program.

HERITAGE INN

WWW WWW

Small-scale Hotel
$130-$229 1/1-2/28
$120-$199 3/1-12/31

Phone: (250)489-4301

Address: 803 Cranbrook St N V1C 3S2 **Location:** Hwy 3 and 95; centre. **Facility:** 100 units. 97 one-bedroom standard units. 2 one- and 1 two-bedroom suites. 3 stories (no elevator), interior corridors. **Parking:** on-site, winter plug-ins. **Amenities:** voice mail. *Some:* high-speed Internet (fee), safes, irons, hair dryers. **Pool(s):** heated indoor. **Leisure Activities:** whirlpool, limited exercise equipment. **Guest Services:** valet laundry, wireless Internet. **Business Services:** conference facilities. **Cards:** AX, DS, MC, VI.

[ASK] [S◇] FEE [✈] [↑↓] [⊋] [⊠] [※] [▭] / SOME UNITS FEE [☂] [✕] [VCR] [⊟] [▣]

ST. EUGENE GOLF RESORT & CASINO

WWWW WWWW

Historic Resort
Large-scale Hotel
$105-$179 All Year

Phone: 250/420-2000

Address: 7731 Mission Rd V1C 7E5 **Location:** Hwy 3, exit Kimberley/Airport (Hwy 95A) to Mission Rd, 2.8 mi (4.5 km) n. Spectacular mountain setting outside of town on golf course. **Facility:** This upscale hotel, in a picturesque setting, was built in an old mission school dating to the 1800s. Designated smoking area. 125 units. 122 one-bedroom standard units. 3 one-bedroom suites, some with whirlpools. 3 stories, interior corridors. **Parking:** on-site. **Terms:** check-in 4 pm, cancellation fee imposed. **Amenities:** video games (fee), high-speed Internet, dual phone lines, voice mail, irons, hair dryers. **Dining:** Purcell Grill, see separate listing. **Pool(s):** heated outdoor. **Leisure Activities:** sauna, whirlpools, steamrooms, fishing, cross country skiing, ice skating, hiking trails. *Fee:* golf-18 holes, horseback riding. **Guest Services:** valet laundry, area transportation, wireless Internet. **Business Services:** conference facilities, administrative services. **Cards:** AX, MC, VI.

[ASK] [S◇] [✈] [↑↓] [⊋] [🏋] [⊠] [🐴] [✕] [※] [▭] / SOME UNITS FEE [☂] [⊟]

SUPER 8 MOTEL

WWW WWW

Small-scale Hotel
$115 3/1-10/1
$95 10/2-2/28

Phone: (250)489-8028

Address: 2370 Cranbrook St N V1C 3T2 **Location:** Just w of jct Hwy 93 and 95. **Facility:** 48 one-bedroom standard units. 2 stories (no elevator), interior corridors. **Parking:** on-site, winter plug-ins. **Terms:** cancellation fee imposed. **Leisure Activities:** whirlpool. **Guest Services:** coin laundry. **Business Services:** PC (fee). **Cards:** AX, MC, VI.

[ASK] [S◇] [↑↓] CALL [&M] / SOME UNITS FEE [☂] [✕] [VCR] [⊟]

------ **WHERE TO DINE** ------

BAVARIAN CHALET

WWW WWW

Continental
$5-$25

Phone: 250/489-3305

The restaurant is a favorite for good, hearty food, a relaxing atmosphere and European touches. Among menu choices are ribs, chicken cordon bleu, schnitzels and German spaetzle, as well as excellent prime rib specials Thursday-Saturday nights. Save room for the delicious apple strudel. **Bar:** Full bar. **Reservations:** required. **Hours:** 11 am-3 & 5-10 pm. Closed major holidays; also Sun. **Address:** 1617 Cranbrook St N V1C 3S7 **Location:** 1.2 mi (2 km) n on Hwy 3 and 95. **Parking:** on-site. **Cards:** AX, MC, VI.

[✕]

HEIDI'S EUROPEAN & INTERNATIONAL CUISINE

(AAA)

WWW WWW

International
$7-$26

Phone: 250/426-7922

The cozy, comfortable, European-style restaurant serves an extensive menu of International fare, including rotisserie chicken, schnitzel, bratwurst and steak. Prime rib is offered Fridays and Saturdays. Dressy casual. **Bar:** Full bar. **Reservations:** suggested. **Hours:** 11 am-2:30 & 5-9 pm, Fri-10 pm, Sat 11:30 am-10 pm, Sun 5 pm-9 pm. **Address:** 821 C Baker St V1C 1A3 **Location:** On 9th Ave S; centre. **Parking:** street. **Cards:** AX, DC, MC, VI.

PURCELL GRILL

WWW WWW WWW

Regional
Canadian
$10-$26

Phone: 250/420-2025

Creative, artistic dishes are created with many regional ingredients at the delta St. Eugene Mission school, lends a sense of history. Exposed brick walls, heavy overhead beams and views of the golf course set the scene for a luxurious meal. Service is friendly and attentive. Casual dress. **Bar:** Full bar. **Reservations:** suggested. **Hours:** 6:30 am-11 pm, Sun 7 am-10 pm; hours vary off season. **Address:** 7731 Mission Rd V1C 7E5 **Location:** Hwy 3, exit Kimberley/Airport (Hwy 95A) to Mission Rd, 2.8 mi (4.5 km) n; in St. Eugene Golf Resort & Casino. **Parking:** on-site. **Cards:** AX, DC, MC, VI.

CALL [&M]

SMITTY'S FAMILY RESTAURANT

WWW WWW

Canadian
$6-$18

Phone: 250/426-6155

The family-oriented restaurant satisfies patrons with its ever-popular all-day breakfast items, as well as tasty and wholesome soups and salads at lunchtime. A relaxed mood characterizes the dining space. Casual dress. **Bar:** Full bar. **Hours:** 6:30 am-9 pm. Closed: 12/25. **Address:** 1028 Cranbrook St N V1C 3S3 **Location:** Between 6th St NW and Theatre Rd. **Parking:** on-site. **Cards:** MC, VI.

CRESTON pop. 4,826

------ **WHERE TO STAY** ------

DOWNTOWNER MOTOR INN

WWW

Small-scale Hotel
$59-$79 3/1-9/30
$48-$65 10/1-2/28

Phone: (250)428-2238

Address: 1218 Canyon St V0B 1G0 **Location:** Corner of 12th Ave N. **Facility:** 23 one-bedroom standard units. 2 stories (no elevator), interior corridors. **Parking:** on-site, winter plug-ins. **Terms:** office hours 7 am-11 pm, cancellation fee imposed. **Leisure Activities:** sauna, whirlpool. **Guest Services:** wireless Internet. **Business Services:** meeting rooms. **Cards:** AX, DC, DS, MC, VI.

[↑↓] / SOME UNITS FEE [☂] [✕] [⊟]

SKIMMERHORN INN

Phone: (250)428-4009

CAA SAVE

◈◈◈◈

Motel
$87-$157 All Year

Address: 2711 Hwy 3 V0B 1G0 **Location:** 0.5 mi (0.8 km) e on Hwy 3. **Facility:** 25 units. 16 one- and 5 two-bedroom standard units, some with kitchens. 4 two-bedroom suites with kitchens. 2 stories (no elevator), exterior corridors. **Parking:** on-site, winter plug-ins. **Pool(s):** heated outdoor. **Leisure Activities:** playground. **Guest Services:** wireless Internet. **Cards:** MC, VI. **Free Special Amenities: newspaper and high-speed Internet.**

⑪ 🏊 💻 / SOME UNITS FEE 🐾 ✖ FEE VCR 🔌 🖨

SUNSET MOTEL

Phone: (250)428-2229

CAA SAVE

◈◈◈

Motel
$63-$99 All Year

Address: 2705 Canyon St, Hwy 3 E V0B 1G0 **Location:** On Hwy 3, 0.6 mi (1 km) e. **Facility:** 24 one-bedroom standard units, some with efficiencies, kitchens and/or whirlpools. 2 stories (no elevator), exterior corridors. **Parking:** on-site, winter plug-ins. **Guest Services:** wireless Internet. **Cards:** AX, DS, MC, VI. **Free Special Amenities: local telephone calls and high-speed Internet.**

S/D ⑪ 🏊 📺 🔌 💻 / SOME UNITS FEE 🐾 ✖ 🖨

------- WHERE TO DINE -------

GRANNY'S PLACE

Phone: 250/428-3990

◈◈ ◈◈

Canadian
$5-$11

All day breakfasts can be found at this simple roadside restaurant, which is a favorite amongst the locals. Vinyl booths line one wall of the dining room, with an outdoor patio in season. You can choose from a variety of omelettes, salads and sandwiches, but a note of caution: the pies are known throughout the town to be the best, so save room! **Bar:** Full bar. **Hours:** 6 am-9 pm; 7 am-8 pm 10/31-5/24. Closed: 12/25. **Address:** 1230 Canyon St V0B 1G1 **Location:** On Hwy 3; centre. **Parking:** on-site. **Cards:** MC, VI.

DAWSON CREEK pop. 10,994

------- WHERE TO STAY -------

BEST WESTERN DAWSON CREEK HOTEL & SUITES   *Book great rates at AAA.com*

Phone: 250/782-6226

CAA SAVE

◈◈◈◈

Small-scale Hotel
Rates not provided

Address: 500 Hwy 2 V1G 0A4 **Location:** 1.8 mi (3 km) e of center. **Facility:** 100 units. 55 one-bedroom standard units, some with efficiencies and/or whirlpools. 45 one-bedroom suites, some with whirlpools. 3 stories, interior corridors. *Bath:* combo or shower only. **Parking:** on-site. **Amenities:** high-speed Internet, voice mail, irons, hair dryers. **Pool(s):** heated indoor. **Leisure Activities:** waterslide, exercise room. **Guest Services:** valet laundry, wireless Internet. **Business Services:** meeting rooms, business center. **Free Special Amenities: expanded continental breakfast and high-speed Internet.** *(See color ad below)*

CALL 🕭 ⟨M⟩ 🏊 📺 🔌 🖨 💻 / SOME UNITS ✖

AAA Benefit:

Members save 10% everyday, plus an exclusive frequent stay program.

▼ *See AAA listing above* ▼

Best Western

AAA Member

500 Highway #2 • Dawson Creek, BC
Toll Free 1-877-782-6008   www.pomeroygroup.ca

DAWSON CREEK SUPER 8

Phone: (250)782-8899

Small-scale Hotel
$133-$220 3/1-9/30
$140-$200 10/1-2/28

Address: 1440 Alaska Ave V1G 1Z5 **Location:** Just s of jct Hwy 97 S (Hart Hwy) and 97 N (Alaska Hwy). **Facility:** 66 one-bedroom standard units, some with whirlpools. 2 stories (no elevator), interior corridors. **Parking:** on-site, winter plug-ins. **Amenities:** irons, hair dryers. *Some:* high-speed Internet. **Leisure Activities:** limited exercise equipment. **Guest Services:** coin laundry. **Business Services:** meeting rooms, PC. **Cards:** AX, DC, DS, MC, VI. **Free Special Amenities: expanded continental breakfast and high-speed Internet.**

POMEROY INN & SUITES

Phone: 250/782-3700

Small-scale Hotel
Rates not provided

Address: 540 Hwy #2 V1G 0A4 **Location:** 1.8 mi (3 km) e of centre. **Facility:** 94 units. 41 one- and 8 two-bedroom standard units, some with whirlpools. 45 one-bedroom suites with kitchens, some with whirlpools. 4 stories, interior corridors. *Bath:* combo or shower only. **Parking:** on-site. **Amenities:** high-speed Internet, voice mail, irons, hair dryers. **Pool(s):** heated indoor. **Leisure Activities:** whirlpool, waterslide, exercise room. **Guest Services:** valet laundry, wireless Internet. **Business Services:** meeting rooms, business center.

DELTA —*See Vancouver p. 615.*

DUNCAN pop. 4,986

———— **WHERE TO STAY** ————

BEST WESTERN COWICHAN VALLEY INN

Phone: 250/748-2722

Small-scale Hotel
Rates not provided

Address: 6474 Trans-Canada Hwy 1 V9L 6C6 **Location:** 1.8 mi (3 km) n. **Facility:** 42 one-bedroom standard units. 2 stories (no elevator), interior corridors. **Parking:** on-site. **Amenities:** voice mail, irons, hair dryers. **Pool(s):** heated outdoor. **Leisure Activities:** limited exercise equipment. **Guest Services:** valet laundry, wireless Internet. **Business Services:** meeting rooms, PC. **Free Special Amenities: local telephone calls and high-speed Internet.**

AAA Benefit:
Members save 10% everyday, plus an exclusive frequent stay program.

FALCON NEST MOTEL

Phone: (250)748-8188

Motel
$58-$84 All Year

Address: 5867 Trans-Canada Hwy 1 V9L 3R9 **Location:** 0.9 mi (1.5 km) n. **Facility:** Smoke free premises. 24 one-bedroom standard units, some with efficiencies or kitchens. 2 stories (no elevator), exterior corridors. **Parking:** on-site. **Terms:** office hours 8 am-midnight. **Amenities:** hair dryers. **Pool(s):** heated outdoor. **Cards:** AX, MC, VI.

TRAVELODGE SILVER BRIDGE INN DUNCAN

Phone: (250)748-4311

Small-scale Hotel
$109-$199 All Year

Address: 140 Trans-Canada Hwy 1 V9L 3P7 **Location:** Just n of Silver Bridge. **Facility:** 33 one-bedroom standard units, some with efficiencies, kitchens and/or whirlpools. 2 stories (no elevator), exterior corridors. **Parking:** on-site. **Terms:** cancellation fee imposed. **Amenities:** high-speed Internet, irons, hair dryers. **Guest Services:** valet laundry, wireless Internet. **Business Services:** conference facilities, PC. **Cards:** AX, DC, MC, VI.

———— **WHERE TO DINE** ————

DOGHOUSE A FAMILY RESTAURANT

Phone: 250/746-4614

Canadian
$5-$17

You'll enjoy the quality home-style cooking, generous family servings and reasonable prices at this restaurant, which has been in business since 1955. Known locally for their special fish 'n' chips, they also offer veal cutlets and homemade desserts. Casual dress. **Bar:** Full bar. **Hours:** 6 am-10 pm. Closed: 12/25. **Address:** 271 Trans-Canada Hwy 1 V9L 3R1 **Location:** Corner of Trans-Canada Hwy 1 and Trunk Rd. **Parking:** on-site. **Cards:** AX, MC, VI.

ENDERBY —*See Okanagan Valley p. 526.*

ESQUIMALT —*See Victoria p. 663.*

FAIRMONT HOT SPRINGS pop. 489

———— **WHERE TO STAY** ————

FAIRMONT HOT SPRINGS RESORT

Phone: (250)345-6311

Resort
Large-scale Hotel
$114-$304 All Year

Address: 5225 Fairmont Resort Rd V0B 1L1 **Location:** 1 mi (1.6 km) n off Hwy 93 and 95. **Facility:** The resort's outstanding feature is an area with natural hot-spring pools on its landscaped grounds. Smoke free premises. 140 units. 125 one- and 4 two-bedroom standard units, some with efficiencies. 6 one-bedroom suites, some with whirlpools. 5 cottages. 3 stories, interior/exterior corridors. **Parking:** on-site, winter plug-ins. **Terms:** check-in 4 pm, 3 day cancellation notice. **Amenities:** high-speed Internet, voice mail, irons, hair dryers. **Leisure Activities:** saunas, fishing, 2 tennis courts, cross country skiing, recreation programs in summer, jogging, playground, spa. *Fee:* golf-36 holes, miniature golf, downhill skiing, horseback riding. **Guest Services:** coin laundry. **Business Services:** conference facilities. **Cards:** AX, DC, DS, MC, VI.

FANNY BAY pop. 766

---------- WHERE TO STAY ----------

SHIPS POINT INN B&B

Bed & Breakfast
Rates not provided

Phone: 250/335-1004

Address: 7584 Ships Point Rd V0R 1W0 **Location:** Hwy 19, exit 87 to Hwy 19A, 4.3 mi (7 km) n, then 1.8 mi (3 km) e, follow signs. **Facility:** The secluded property is at the edge of Fanny Bay, known for its clam farming and frequented by resident seals and otters; rooms are large and cozy. Smoke free premises. 6 one-bedroom standard units. 2 stories (no elevator), interior corridors. *Bath:* combo or shower only. **Parking:** on-site. **Terms:** office hours 8 am-10 pm, age restrictions may apply. **Amenities:** hair dryers. **Leisure Activities:** whirlpool.

FERNIE pop. 4,217

---------- WHERE TO STAY ----------

BEST WESTERN FERNIE MOUNTAIN LODGE   *Book great rates at AAA.com*

(CAA) [SAVE]

Small-scale Hotel
Rates not provided

Phone: 250/423-5500

Address: 1622 7th Ave V0B 1M0 **Location:** Jct Hwy 3 and 7th Ave; east end of town. **Facility:** 95 units. 85 one-bedroom standard units, some with efficiencies and/or whirlpools. 10 one-bedroom suites, some with efficiencies and/or whirlpools. 3 stories, interior corridors. **Parking:** on-site, winter plug-ins. **Amenities:** high-speed Internet, voice mail, irons, hair dryers. **Pool(s):** heated indoor. **Leisure Activities:** whirlpools, exercise room. **Guest Services:** valet and coin laundry. **Business Services:** meeting rooms, PC (fee). **Free Special Amenities:** local telephone calls and high-speed Internet.

AAA Benefit:
Members save 10% everyday, plus an exclusive frequent stay program.

CORNERSTONE LODGE

Condominium
$214-$378 12/14-2/28
$144-$292 3/1-12/13

Phone: (250)423-6855

Address: 5339 Ski Hill Rd V0B 1M6 **Location:** 6.5 km w on Hwy 3, then 1.4 km n. **Facility:** Smoke free premises. 26 units. 8 one- and 18 two-bedroom suites with kitchens. 3 stories, interior corridors. **Parking:** on-site, winter plug-ins. **Terms:** off-site registration, cancellation fee imposed. **Amenities:** high-speed Internet, hair dryers. *Some:* DVD players. **Leisure Activities:** whirlpool, downhill & cross country skiing, snowmobiling, bicycles, limited exercise equipment. **Guest Services:** complimentary laundry. **Cards:** AX, MC, VI.

LIZARD CREEK LODGE AND CONDOMINIUMS AT FERNIE ALPINE RESORT

(CAA) [SAVE]
Condominium
$310-$370 3/1-3/29
$120-$295 3/30-2/28

Phone: (250)423-2057

Address: 5346 Highline Dr V0B 1M6 **Location:** 4 mi (6.5 km) w on Hwy 3, 0.8 mi (1.4 km) on Ski Area Rd, follow signs. **Facility:** Featuring ski-in/ski-out access, this luxurious property offers a mix of lodge rooms in the main building as well as upscale, fully equipped condos. Designated smoking area. 99 units. 7 one-bedroom standard units with kitchens. 47 one-, 34 two- and 11 three-bedroom suites with kitchens. 3 stories, interior corridors. **Parking:** on-site. **Terms:** check-in 4 pm, 5 night minimum stay - seasonal, 30 day cancellation notice. **Amenities:** dual phone lines, voice mail, irons, hair dryers. *Some:* high-speed Internet. **Dining:** Lizard Creek Lodge Dining Room, see separate listing. **Pool(s):** heated outdoor. **Leisure Activities:** whirlpools, steamroom, cross country skiing, recreation programs, hiking trails, exercise room. *Fee:* downhill skiing, snowmobiling, bicycles, horseback riding, massage. **Guest Services:** valet and coin laundry, area transportation-Fernie townsite. **Business Services:** meeting rooms, PC (fee). **Cards:** AX, MC, VI.

PARK PLACE LODGE   *Book great rates at AAA.com*

(CAA) [SAVE]

Small-scale Hotel
$129-$249 12/12-2/28
$109-$229 3/1-12/11

Phone: (250)423-6871

Address: 742 Hwy 3 V0B 1M1 **Location:** At 7th St. **Facility:** 64 one-bedroom standard units, some with efficiencies or kitchens. 3 stories, interior corridors. **Parking:** on-site, winter plug-ins. **Terms:** check-in 4 pm, cancellation fee imposed. **Amenities:** DVD players, video games (fee), CD players, dual phone lines, voice mail, irons, hair dryers. *Some:* high-speed Internet. **Pool(s):** heated indoor. **Leisure Activities:** saunas, whirlpool, bicycles, hiking trails, exercise room. **Guest Services:** valet laundry, area transportation-within 1.2 mi (2 km). **Business Services:** meeting rooms. **Cards:** AX, DC, DS, MC, VI. **Free Special Amenities:** local telephone calls and high-speed Internet.

STANFORD HOTELS & RESORTS

Condominium
Rates not provided

Phone: 250/423-5000

Address: 100 Riverside Way V0B 1M1 **Location:** From centre, 1.2 mi (2 km) on Hwy 3. **Facility:** Set just outside of town along the river, this luxurious condo property offers many services found at full-scale hotels. Smoke free premises. 144 units. 57 one-bedroom standard units. 11 one-, 47 two- and 29 three-bedroom suites with kitchens, some with whirlpools. 3 stories, interior/exterior corridors. **Parking:** on-site, winter plug-ins. **Terms:** check-in 4 pm. **Amenities:** voice mail, irons. *Some:* CD players, high-speed Internet (fee). **Pool(s):** heated indoor. **Leisure Activities:** sauna, whirlpools, waterslide, fishing, downhill & cross country skiing, ice skating, hiking trails, playground, exercise room, spa. **Guest Services:** coin laundry, area transportation. **Business Services:** meeting rooms, PC (fee). *(See color ad on insert)*

SUPER 8 MOTEL-FERNIE   *Book at AAA.com*   Phone: 250/423-6788

Small-scale Hotel
Rates not provided

Address: 2021 Hwy 3 V0B 1M1 **Location:** On Hwy 3; west end of town. **Facility:** 43 one-bedroom standard units. 3 stories, interior corridors. **Parking:** on-site, winter plug-ins. **Leisure Activities:** whirlpool. *Fee:* game room. **Guest Services:** coin laundry, wireless Internet. **Business Services:** meeting rooms, PC (fee).

—————— WHERE TO DINE ——————

KELSEY'S   Phone: 250/423-2444

Canadian
$7-$21

A fun, relaxed atmosphere and tasty menu of casual fare make the restaurant a popular favorite with locals. Diners might start a meal with some tempting appetizers, such as wings, loaded potato skins or nachos, and follow them with an old-time favorite, such as a burger, wrap, pizza or pasta dish. For a heartier meal, it's hard to beat pork back ribs or a steak. The diverse menu has broad appeal. Casual dress. **Bar:** Full bar. **Hours:** 11 am-11 pm; to 9 pm 7/1-9/30. Closed: Mon & Tues 7/1-9/30. **Address:** 5339 Ski Hill Rd, Fernie Alpine Resort V0B 1M0 **Location:** At base of ski hill. **Parking:** on-site. **Cards:** AX, DC, DS, MC, VI.

LIZARD CREEK LODGE DINING ROOM   Phone: 250/423-2057

Canadian
$8-$42

Considered to be one of the best places in Fernie, this upscale dining room is a superb place for a fine meal. With a regional menu and creative dishes, you'll enjoy a great meal after a day on the ski hill. Casual dress. **Bar:** Full bar. **Reservations:** suggested, winter. **Hours:** 7 am-11 pm. **Address:** 5346 Highline Dr V0B 1M1 **Location:** 4 mi (6.5 km) w on Hwy 3, 0.8 mi (1.4 km) on Ski Area Rd, follow signs; in Lizard Creek Lodge and Condominiums at Fernie Alpine Resort. **Parking:** on-site. **Cards:** AX, MC, VI.

CALL

MUGSHOTS BISTRO   Phone: 250/423-8018

Coffee/Espresso
$4-$8

Quirky and eclectic best describes the funky coffeehouse, which prepares a wide selection of soups, sandwiches, ground coffees and sumptuous desserts. The downtown spot is popular with locals and visitors alike not only for its hearty, healthy food but also for the Internet cafe. Casual dress. **Hours:** 7 am-9 pm; to 6 pm 5/1-11/1. Closed: 10/13, 12/25; also Sun 5/1-11/1. **Address:** 592 3rd Ave V0B 1M0 **Location:** Corner of 5th St and 3rd Ave; downtown. **Parking:** street. **Cards:** MC, VI.

CALL

THE OLD ELEVATOR   Phone: 250/423-7115

Canadian
$22-$45

On the outskirts is the town's original grain elevator, which dates back to 1908. Today, it houses an intimate restaurant, which presents a menu with regional flair. Representative of taste bud-tempting choices are preparations of salmon, veal or even Alaskan cod. Selections change seasonally. Wood accents lend to an atmosphere of coziness, and guests can check out the original grain shaft. Casual dress. **Bar:** Full bar. **Reservations:** suggested. **Hours:** Open 3/1-4/7 & 6/15-2/28; 5 pm-10:30 pm; seasonal hours may vary. Closed: Mon 6/15-12/1. **Address:** 291 1st Ave V0B 1M0 **Location:** 1st Ave and 2nd St. **Parking:** street. **Cards:** AX, MC, VI. **Historic**

FIELD

—————— WHERE TO DINE ——————

TRUFFLE PIGS CAFE   Phone: 250/343-6462

Canadian
$6-$20

The funky cafe has a wonderful selection of home-cooked food, ranging from delicious baked goods to sandwiches to all-day breakfast items. Guests can enjoy a casual meal in the contemporary dining room, which features a light, airy decor. Casual dress. **Bar:** Beer & wine. **Hours:** 8 am-10 pm; 8:30 am-7 pm in winter. Closed: 12/25. **Address:** 318 Stephen Ave V0A 1G0 **Location:** Centre; across from hotel. **Parking:** street. **Cards:** AX, MC, VI.

FORT NELSON pop. 4,514

———— **WHERE TO STAY** ————

LAKEVIEW INN & SUITES *Book great rates at AAA.com* **Phone:** (250)233-5001
(AAA) (SAVE)
◆◆◆ ◆◆◆
Small-scale Hotel
$129-$149 All Year

Address: 4507-50th Ave S V0C 1R0 **Location:** Just off Hwy 97 (Alaska Hwy); at 44th St. **Facility:** 82 units. 70 one-bedroom standard units, some with efficiencies and/or whirlpools. 12 one-bedroom suites with efficiencies and whirlpools. 4 stories, interior corridors. *Bath:* combo or shower only. **Parking:** on-site. **Amenities:** video library (fee), DVD players, high-speed Internet, voice mail, irons, hair dryers. **Leisure Activities:** whirlpool, steamroom, limited exercise equipment. **Guest Services:** coin laundry. **Business Services:** meeting rooms, business center. **Cards:** AX, MC, VI. **Free Special Amenities:** expanded continental breakfast and high-speed Internet. *(See color ad p 362)*

[icons]

WOODLANDS INN *Book great rates at AAA.com* **Phone:** (250)774-6669
(AAA) (SAVE)
◆◆◆ ◆◆◆
Small-scale Hotel
$139-$159 All Year

Address: 3995 50th Ave S V0C 1R0 **Location:** On Hwy 97 (Alaskan Hwy). **Facility:** 131 units. 116 one-bedroom standard units. 15 one-bedroom suites, some with efficiencies or kitchens. 4 stories, interior corridors. **Parking:** on-site, winter plug-ins. **Terms:** cancellation fee imposed. **Amenities:** high-speed Internet, hair dryers. **Leisure Activities:** whirlpool, steamroom, exercise room. **Guest Services:** coin laundry. **Business Services:** meeting rooms, PC (fee). **Cards:** AX, DC, DS, MC, VI. **Free Special Amenities:** expanded continental breakfast and high-speed Internet. *(See color ad below)*

[icons]

FORT ST. JOHN pop. 16,034

———— **WHERE TO STAY** ————

BEST WESTERN COACHMAN INN *Book great rates at AAA.com* **Phone:** 250/787-0651
(AAA) (SAVE)
◆◆◆ ◆◆◆
Small-scale Hotel
Rates not provided

Address: 8540 Alaska Rd V1J 5L6 **Location:** 1.2 mi (2 km) s on Hwy 97. **Facility:** 70 one-bedroom standard units. 2 stories (no elevator), interior corridors. **Parking:** on-site, winter plug-ins. **Amenities:** irons, hair dryers. *Some:* DVD players. **Leisure Activities:** sauna, whirlpool, limited exercise equipment. **Guest Services:** wireless Internet. **Business Services:** meeting rooms, PC. **Free Special Amenities:** local telephone calls and high-speed Internet.

[icons]

AAA Benefit:
Members save 10% everyday, plus an exclusive frequent stay program.

LAKEVIEW INN & SUITES *Book great rates at AAA.com* **Phone:** (250)787-0779
(AAA) (SAVE)
◆◆◆ ◆◆◆
Small-scale Hotel
$96-$106 All Year

Address: 10103 98th Ave V1J 1P8 **Location:** Corner of 100th Ave; centre of downtown. **Facility:** 73 one-bedroom standard units, some with efficiencies and/or whirlpools. 3 stories (no elevator), interior corridors. *Bath:* combo or shower only. **Parking:** on-site, winter plug-ins. **Terms:** check-in 4 pm. **Amenities:** high-speed Internet, voice mail, irons, hair dryers. **Leisure Activities:** whirlpool, exercise room. **Guest Services:** valet and coin laundry. **Business Services:** meeting rooms. **Cards:** AX, DC, DS, MC, VI. *(See color ad p 362)*

[icons]

———— ▼ *See AAA listing above* ▼ ————

POMEROY INN & SUITES

▼▼▼
Small-scale Hotel
$179-$199 All Year

Phone: (250)262-3030

Address: 9304 Alaska Rd V1J 6Z5 **Location:** Just s on Hwy 97 (Alaska Hwy). **Facility:** 92 units. 60 one-bedroom standard units, some with whirlpools. 32 one-bedroom suites with kitchens. 4 stories, interior corridors. *Bath:* combo or shower only. **Parking:** on-site. **Terms:** cancellation fee imposed. **Amenities:** voice mail, irons, hair dryers. **Leisure Activities:** exercise room. **Guest Services:** valet laundry, wireless Internet. **Business Services:** business center. **Cards:** AX, MC, VI.

[ASK] [S/D] [¶↑+] [▦] [🖥] [🖩] [▣] / SOME UNITS FEE [🐾] [✕]

QUALITY INN NORTHERN GRAND   *Book great rates at AAA.com*

▼▼▼▼
Large-scale Hotel
$119-$159 All Year

Phone: (250)787-0521

Address: 9830 100th Ave V1J 1Y5 **Location:** Centre. **Facility:** 125 units. 124 one-bedroom standard units, some with whirlpools. 1 one-bedroom suite. 6 stories, interior corridors. **Parking:** on-site, winter plug-ins. **Terms:** 30 day cancellation notice. **Amenities:** voice mail, irons, hair dryers. *Some:* CD players. **Pool(s):** heated indoor. **Leisure Activities:** sauna, whirlpool, exercise room. **Guest Services:** valet laundry, wireless Internet. **Business Services:** conference facilities. **Cards:** AX, CB, DC, DS, JC, MC, VI. *(See color ad on insert)*

[ASK] [S/D] [¶↑] [Y] [≈] [✕] [🖥] [▣] / SOME UNITS FEE [🐾] [✕] [VCR] [▦]

SUPER 8 MOTEL-FORT ST. JOHN   *Book great rates at AAA.com*

(AAA) [SAVE]
▼▼▼▼
Small-scale Hotel
$180-$200 3/1-9/30
$160-$190 10/1-2/28

Phone: (250)785-7588

Address: 9500 Alaska Hwy V1J 6S7 **Location:** Just s on Hwy 97 (Alaska Hwy). **Facility:** 94 units. 86 one-bedroom standard units. 8 one-bedroom suites, some with whirlpools. 4 stories, interior corridors. *Bath:* combo or shower only. **Parking:** on-site, winter plug-ins. **Amenities:** high-speed Internet, voice mail, irons, hair dryers. **Dining:** 2 restaurants. **Pool(s):** heated indoor. **Leisure Activities:** whirlpool, waterslide, exercise room. **Guest Services:** valet and coin laundry. **Business Services:** meeting rooms, business center. **Cards:** AX, DC, MC, VI. **Free Special Amenities: continental breakfast and high-speed Internet.**

[S/D] [✈+] [¶↑] [Y] CALL [🔊M] [≈] [✕] [🖥] [▦] [▣] [🖩] / SOME UNITS FEE [🐾] [✕]

FORT STEELE

———— WHERE TO STAY ————

BULL RIVER GUEST RANCH

◆▼ ◆▼
Ranch
Rates not provided

Phone: 250/429-3760

Location: Hwy 95, 21.9 km se of town on Ft Steele-Wardner Rd, 12 km ne on gravel road, follow signs; Hwy 3 W, 41 km e of Cranbrook, use Ft Steele Rd. Located in a quiet rustic area. **Facility:** Smoke free premises. 7 cabins. 1 story, exterior corridors. *Bath:* shower only. **Parking:** on-site. **Terms:** open 5/1-12/31. **Leisure Activities:** sauna, whirlpool, boating, canoeing, fishing, bicycles, hiking trails, jogging, horseshoes, volleyball. *Fee:* horseback riding. **Guest Services:** coin laundry. **Business Services:** meeting rooms.

[✕] [✕] [🐾] [🏊] [🖼] [▦] [🖥] [▣] / SOME UNITS [🐾]

GALIANO ISLAND —*See Gulf Islands National Park Reserve p. 505.*

GIBSONS pop. 4,182

———— WHERE TO STAY ————

BONNIEBROOK LODGE BED & BREAKFAST

▼▼▼
Country Inn
Rates not provided

Phone: 604/886-2887

Address: 1532 Ocean Beach Esplanade V0N 1V5 **Location:** Hwy 101, 3.8 mi (6 km) s on Veterans Rd to Fichett St, just sw to King St, 0.6 mi (1 km) sw to Chaster, then 5 mi (8 km) sw to Gowers Pt Rd, follow signs. **Facility:** Renovated guest rooms in this 1922 lodge include hot tubs and gas fireplaces; suites overlook the ocean, and cottages are just behind the lodge. Smoke free premises. 7 units. 6 one-bedroom standard units with whirlpools. 1 three-bedroom suite with kitchen. 1-3 stories (no elevator), interior/exterior corridors. **Parking:** on-site. **Terms:** office hours 9 am-9 pm. **Amenities:** video library, CD players, hair dryers. **Leisure Activities:** beach access.

[✕] [🐾] [VCR] [☎] [▦] [▣] / SOME UNITS FEE [🐾]

CEDARS INN HOTEL & CONVENTION CENTRE

(AAA) [SAVE]
▼▼ ▼▼
Motel
$94-$156 All Year

Phone: (604)886-3008

Address: 895 Gibsons Way V0N 1V0 **Location:** Hwy 101 and Shaw Rd; 3.8 mi (6 km) n from ferry terminal. Located opposite Sunnycrest Mall. **Facility:** 45 one-bedroom standard units, some with efficiencies. 2 stories (no elevator), interior/exterior corridors. *Bath:* combo or shower only. **Parking:** on-site. **Terms:** office hours 7 am-11 pm, cancellation fee imposed. **Amenities:** irons, hair dryers. **Pool(s):** heated outdoor. **Leisure Activities:** sauna, whirlpool, limited exercise equipment. **Guest Services:** valet laundry, wireless Internet. **Business Services:** meeting rooms. **Cards:** AX, DC, MC, VI. **Free Special Amenities: local telephone calls and high-speed Internet.**

[S/D] [¶↑] [≈] [✕] [▦] [▣] / SOME UNITS FEE [🐾] [✕]

———— WHERE TO DINE ————

HAUS UROPA RESTAURANT   *Menu on AAA.com*

(AAA)
▼▼▼
Swiss
$19-$28

Phone: 604/886-8326

The charming Bavarian chalet-style restaurant serves a mix of Swiss and German dishes, along the lines of Wiener Schnitzel, bratwurst and weisswurst. Daily lunch specials are popular. The owner/chef makes sure everything served is of high quality. Casual dress. **Bar:** Full bar. **Reservations:** suggested. **Hours:** open 3/1-12/31 & 1/28-2/28; 5 pm-10 pm. Closed: 12/25, 12/26; also Tues & Wed. **Address:** 426 Gower Pointe Rd V0N 1V0 **Location:** Hwy 101, just s on School Rd (towards ocean), then just w. **Parking:** on-site. **Cards:** MC, VI.

[AC]

MOLLY'S REACH RESTAURANT

Canadian
$8-$18

Phone: 604/886-9710

The famous landmark originally was built as a set for "The Beachcombers," a popular CBC TV series of the late 70s and early 80s. Today, it's a family restaurant that serves a mix of seafood, steaks, sandwiches and soups. This place is well worth the stop for the memories alone. Casual dress. **Bar:** Full bar. **Reservations:** accepted. **Hours:** 8:30 am-9 pm. Closed: 12/25. **Location:** School Rd and Gibsons Way; on waterfront. **Parking:** on-site. **Cards:** MC, VI.

GOLD BRIDGE

——— **WHERE TO STAY** ———

MORROW CHALETS

Vacation Rental Cottage
$225-$350 All Year

Phone: 250/238-2462

Address: Tyaughton Lake V0K 1P0 **Location:** 5 mi (8 km) n from the Tyaughton Lake turnoff, follow signs. **Facility:** Fully self-contained log cabins on Tyaughton Lake, these lodgings can accommodate six or more persons; summer and winter activities are available. Smoke free premises. 4 cottages, some with whirlpools. 2 stories (no elevator), exterior corridors. **Parking:** on-site. **Terms:** office hours 8 am-8 pm, check-in 4 pm, cancellation fee imposed. **Amenities:** video library, DVD players, hair dryers. **Guest Services:** complimentary laundry. **Cards:** MC, VI.

TYAX MOUNTAIN LAKE RESORT

Resort
Small-scale Hotel
$118-$286 5/1-10/15

Phone: (250)238-2221

Address: Tyaughton Lake Rd V0K 1P0 **Location:** 5 mi (8 km) n from the Tyaughton Lake turnoff, follow signs. **Facility:** A log lodge and log chalets are featured at this resort offering family-oriented wilderness activities. Smoke free premises. 34 units. 30 one-bedroom standard units. 4 three-bedroom suites with kitchens, some with whirlpools. 2 stories (no elevator), interior corridors. **Parking:** on-site. **Terms:** open 5/1-10/15, office hours 8 am-11 pm, check-in 4 pm, cancellation fee imposed. **Amenities:** voice mail, hair dryers. **Leisure Activities:** sauna, whirlpool, rental boats, canoeing, paddleboats, fishing, tennis court, cross country skiing, ice skating, tobogganing, hiking trails, playground, limited exercise equipment. **Fee:** snowmobiling, bicycles, horseback riding. **Guest Services:** coin laundry. **Business Services:** meeting rooms. **Cards:** AX, MC, VI.

GOLDEN pop. 3,811

——— **WHERE TO STAY** ———

BEST WESTERN MOUNTAIN VIEW INN

Book great rates at AAA.com

(CAA) (SAVE)

Small-scale Hotel
$129-$179 All Year

Phone: (250)344-2333

Address: 1024 11th St N V0A 1H0 **Location:** Just w of jct Hwy 95 and Trans-Canada Hwy 1; on S Service Rd. **Facility:** 71 one-bedroom standard units. 3 stories, interior corridors. **Parking:** on-site, winter plug-ins. **Terms:** cancellation fee imposed. **Amenities:** video games (fee), irons, hair dryers. *Some:* high-speed Internet. **Pool(s):** heated indoor. **Leisure Activities:** ATV tours. **Fee:** whitewater rafting, snowmobile tours. **Guest Services:** valet and coin laundry, wireless Internet. **Cards:** AX, MC, VI. **Free Special Amenities:** local telephone calls and early check-in/late check-out.

AAA Benefit:
Members save 10% everyday, plus an exclusive frequent stay program.

COLUMBIA VALLEY B&B

Bed & Breakfast
$95-$135 All Year

Phone: 250/348-2508

Address: 2304 Hwy 95 S V0A 1H0 **Location:** On Hwy 95, 14.4 mi (23 km) s of jct Trans-Canada Hwy 1. **Facility:** Smoke free premises. 6 one-bedroom standard units. 2 stories (no elevator), interior/exterior corridors. *Bath:* combo or shower only. **Parking:** on-site, winter plug-ins. **Terms:** office hours 7 am-midnight, 2 night minimum stay, 3 day cancellation notice-fee imposed. **Leisure Activities:** rental canoes. **Business Services:** PC (fee). **Cards:** MC, VI.

GOLDEN RIM MOTOR INN

Motel
$69-$185 All Year

Phone: (250)344-2216

Address: 1416 Golden View Rd V0A 1H0 **Location:** On Trans-Canada Hwy 1, 1 mi (1.6 km) e of jct Hwy 95. **Facility:** 81 units. 78 one-bedroom standard units, some with kitchens. 3 two-bedroom suites with whirlpools. 2-3 stories (no elevator), exterior corridors. **Parking:** on-site, winter plug-ins. **Terms:** office hours 6 am-midnight, cancellation fee imposed. **Amenities:** hair dryers. **Pool(s):** heated indoor. **Leisure Activities:** sauna, whirlpool, waterslide. **Guest Services:** coin laundry, wireless Internet. **Business Services:** PC. **Cards:** AX, DC, MC, VI.

HILLSIDE LODGE & CHALETS

(CAA) (SAVE)

Cabin
$125-$165 All Year

Phone: (250)344-7281

Address: 1740 Seward Frontage Rd V0A 1H0 **Location:** 9.4 mi (15 km) w on Hwy 1, follow signs; n off highway. Located in a quiet area. **Facility:** Spectacular mountain scenery and the sound of moving water give this lodge's grounds a serene sense of place; offerings include cabins and B&B rooms. Smoke free premises. 12 units. 4 one-bedroom standard units. 8 cabins. 1-2 stories, exterior corridors. *Bath:* combo or shower only. **Parking:** on-site, winter plug-ins. **Terms:** 5 day cancellation notice. **Amenities:** *Some:* hair dryers. **Leisure Activities:** sauna, whirlpool, steamroom, cross country skiing, hiking trails, limited exercise equipment. **Fee:** massage. **Cards:** MC, VI. **Free Special Amenities:** preferred room (subject to availability with advance reservations).

KAPRISTO LODGE

Bed & Breakfast
Rates not provided

Phone: 250/344-6048

Address: 1297 Campbell Rd V0A 1H7 **Location:** Jct Trans-Canada Hwy 1, 8.8 mi (14 km) s on Hwy 95, 0.6 mi (1 km) se on Austin Rd, then 0.4 mi (0.7 km) se, follow signs. Located in a quiet secluded area. **Facility:** This B&B is in a picturesque mountain setting and features cozy, comfortable gathering spaces enhanced by sweeping views. Smoke free premises. 6 units. 3 one- and 1 two-bedroom standard units, some with kitchens and/or whirlpools. 2 one-bedroom suites. 2 stories (no elevator), interior corridors. **Parking:** on-site, winter plug-ins. **Amenities:** video library, hair dryers. *Some:* DVD players. **Leisure Activities:** sauna, hiking trails, basketball. **Fee:** horseback riding. **Guest Services:** TV in common area, area transportation (fee).

── WHERE TO DINE ──

CEDAR HOUSE CAFE & RESTAURANT

Canadian
$13-$38

Phone: 250/344-4679

Casual mountain dining is what's to be expected at the small, bistro-style restaurant. The cozy, comfortable dining room has many rustic features, yet a surprising elegance. Menu selections ranging from salmon to lamb to other Canadian specialties often incorporate produce grown in the chef's own garden. Service is laid-back and friendly, and even the owner has been known to come out and greet guests. Casual dress. **Bar:** Full bar. **Reservations:** suggested. **Hours:** Open 3/1-4/14 & 6/2-2/28; 5 pm-10:30 pm. Closed: 1/1. **Address:** 735 Hefti Rd V0A 1H2 **Location:** 4.6 mi (7.4 km) s of town, just e at Almberg Rd, follow signs. **Parking:** on-site. **Cards:** MC, VI.

ELEVEN 22 GRILL & LIQUIDS

West Canadian
$11-$25

Phone: 250/344-2443

The charming eatery's International menu lists health-conscious curries, pastas, salads, hummus, tzatziki, spanakopita and burgers, plus fondue is offered weekly in winter. The restored centennial home nurtures a warm, casual ambience. Casual dress. **Bar:** Full bar. **Reservations:** suggested. **Hours:** 5 pm-10 pm. Closed: call for days in spring & fall. **Address:** 1122 10th Ave S V0A 1H0 **Location:** Just e at 12th St; centre. **Parking:** on-site. **Cards:** MC, VI.

CALL

GOLDEN BAKERY & DELI

Deli/Subs
Sandwiches
$3-$7

Phone: 250/344-2928

One of the town's best-kept secrets, the simple delicatessen and bakery serves homemade soups, salads and sandwiches, along with a huge selection of sweets. Just off the highway, the eatery invites guests to dine in or get their food to go. Don't bypass the display case of treats. Casual dress. **Hours:** 6:30 am-6 pm. Closed major holidays; also Sun. **Address:** 415 9th St N V0A 1H0 **Location:** Just w off Hwy 95; downtown. **Parking:** street. **Cards:** MC, VI.

THE KICKING HORSE GRILL

International
$19-$38

Phone: 250/344-2330

The restaurant's small lodge-like interior is perfect for a casual meal with friends. Dark wood beams crisscross the ceiling and line the walls, creating a true Rocky Mountain feel. The food draws upon many influences, ranging from Asian to Swedish and even some Canadian elements, resulting in an interesting and eclectic menu. Casual dress. **Bar:** Full bar. **Reservations:** suggested. **Hours:** 4:30 pm-11 pm. Closed: 1/1. **Address:** 1105 9th St S V0A 1H0 **Location:** Hwy 95, just e; downtown. **Parking:** on-site. **Cards:** AX, MC, VI.

LEGENDZ DINER

Canadian
$5-$10

Phone: 250/344-5059

Appointed in a 1950s theme, the diner is a popular stopover for residents and those just passing through. In addition to an extensive list of diner classics, this place prepares burgers, steaks and some hot entrees. The homemade pies are legendary. Casual dress. **Bar:** Beer & wine. **Reservations:** not accepted. **Hours:** 7 am-10 pm. Closed major holidays. **Address:** 1405 N Trans-Canada Hwy V0A 1H0 **Location:** Jct Trans-Canada Hwy 1 and 95, 0.6 mi (1 km) n. **Parking:** on-site. **Cards:** MC, VI.

GRAND FORKS pop. 4,036

── WHERE TO STAY ──

RAMADA LIMITED

Book at AAA.com

Motel
Rates not provided

Phone: 250/442-2127

Address: 2729 Central Ave V0H 1H2 **Location:** West end of town on Hwy 3. **Facility:** 45 units. 38 one- and 6 two-bedroom standard units, some with kitchens (utensils extra charge) and/or whirlpools. 1 one-bedroom suite. 2 stories (no elevator), exterior corridors. **Parking:** on-site, winter plug-ins. **Amenities:** voice mail, irons, hair dryers. **Pool(s):** heated outdoor. **Guest Services:** coin laundry. **Business Services:** PC.

WESTERN TRAVELLER MOTEL

Motel
$64-$139 All Year

Phone: (250)442-5566

Address: 1591 Central Ave V0H 1H0 **Location:** West end of town on Hwy 3. **Facility:** 32 one-bedroom standard units, some with efficiencies. 2 stories (no elevator), exterior corridors. **Parking:** on-site, winter plug-ins. **Terms:** office hours 7 am-11 pm. **Amenities:** *Some:* irons, hair dryers. **Guest Services:** wireless Internet. **Business Services:** meeting rooms, PC. **Cards:** AX, MC, VI. **Free Special Amenities:** local telephone calls and high-speed Internet.

Gulf Islands
National Park Reserve

GALIANO ISLAND pop. 1,258

─────── WHERE TO STAY ───────

GALIANO OCEANFRONT INN & SPA

Small-scale Hotel
$249-$399 All Year

Phone: (250)539-3388

Address: 134 Madrona Dr V0N 1P0 **Location:** From Sturdies Bay ferry terminal, just ne on Sturdies Bay Rd. **Facility:** Smoke free premises. 20 units. 10 one-bedroom standard units, some with whirlpools. 10 one-bedroom suites with kitchens and whirlpools. 2 stories (no elevator), interior/exterior corridors. **Parking:** on-site. **Terms:** office hours 8 am-6 pm, 7 day cancellation notice-fee imposed. **Amenities:** DVD players, CD players, honor bars, irons, hair dryers. **Dining:** Atrevida Restaurant, see separate listing. **Leisure Activities:** whirlpool, exercise room, spa, yoga classes. **Guest Services:** wireless Internet. **Business Services:** meeting rooms. **Cards:** DC, MC, VI.

WOODSTONE COUNTRY INN

Country Inn
$129-$209 3/1-11/30
$129-$199 2/1-2/28

Phone: (250)539-2022

Address: 743 Georgeson Bay Rd V0N 1P0 **Location:** From Sturdies Bay ferry terminal, 2.2 mi (3.5 km) nw on Sturdies Bay Rd. **Facility:** A wood-burning fireplace in the common area sets the tone for this warm, modern inn with attractive rooms and country views. Smoke free premises. 12 one-bedroom standard units, some with whirlpools. 2 stories (no elevator), interior corridors. **Parking:** on-site. **Terms:** open 3/1-11/30 & 2/1-2/28, office hours 8 am-10 pm, 2 night minimum stay - weekends, age restrictions may apply, 7 day cancellation notice-fee imposed. **Amenities:** hair dryers. **Business Services:** meeting rooms. **Cards:** AX, MC, VI.

─────── WHERE TO DINE ───────

ATREVIDA RESTAURANT

Pacific Rim
$9-$30

Phone: 250/539-3388

The waterfront restaurant serves delightful West Coast cuisine prepared with fresh local ingredients, including Salt Spring Island organic goat cheese and West Coast seafood. A fine selection of British Columbia wines complements the fare. Hours vary in the off-season, so call ahead. Casual dress. **Bar:** Full bar. **Reservations:** required, for dinner. **Hours:** 6 pm-10 pm; also 9 am-3 & 6-10 pm 7/1-9/4. **Address:** 134 Madrona Dr V0N 1P0 **Location:** From Sturdies Bay ferry terminal, just ne on Sturdies Bay Rd; in Galiano Oceanfront Inn & Spa. **Parking:** on-site. **Cards:** MC, VI.

GALIANO GRAND CENTRAL EMPORIUM

Canadian
$7-$18

Phone: 250/539-9885

Not far from the Sturdies Bay ferry terminal, this simple restaurant is one of few open all year long. The building isn't much to look at, but the food is really good, and it's a great place to stop while waiting for the ferry. Order from the wall-mounted, blackboard-style menu, grab a seat and enjoy daily homemade soups, lunch sandwiches and morning breakfasts. Casual dress. **Bar:** Full bar. **Hours:** 7 am-1 am. Closed: 12/25. **Address:** 2740 Sturdies Bay Rd, S24 C31 V0N 1P0 **Location:** Just nw of Sturdies Bay Ferry Terminal. **Parking:** on-site. **Cards:** MC, VI.

─────── *The following restaurant has not been evaluated by AAA* ───────
but is listed for your information only.

HUMMINGBIRD INN PUB

[fyi]

Phone: 250/539-5472

Not evaluated. Dining choices on the island are limited, but those who visit the adult-oriented pub can expect pub-style food. **Address:** 47 Sturdies Bay Rd V0N 1P0 **Location:** From Sturdies Bay ferry terminal, 1.8 mi (3 km) nw.

PENDER ISLAND

─────── WHERE TO STAY ───────

POETS COVE RESORT & SPA

Small-scale Hotel
Rates not provided

Phone: 250/629-2100

Address: 9801 Spalding Rd, South Pender Island V0N 2M3 **Location:** From Otter Bay Ferry Terminal, follow signs to South Pender Island, then 10 mi (16 km) s; Otter Bay Rd to Bidwell Harbour Rd to Canal Rd. **Facility:** Smoke free premises. 46 units. 22 one-bedroom standard units. 24 cottages. 1-3 stories, interior/exterior corridors. **Parking:** on-site. **Amenities:** DVD players, high-speed Internet, voice mail, irons, hair dryers. **Dining:** Aurora Restaurant, see separate listing. **Pool(s):** 2 heated outdoor. **Leisure Activities:** whirlpools, exercise room, spa. **Fee:** marina. **Guest Services:** coin laundry. **Business Services:** meeting rooms, PC.

------- WHERE TO DINE -------

AURORA RESTAURANT
Phone: 250/629-2115

Canadian
$25-$35

You will find this restaurant inside Pender Island's newest upscale lodging; all tables overlook the marina. Enjoy a cuisine that uses only the highest quality ingredients specially brought in just for this restaurant. Dinner is very popular so reservations are a must. Casual dress. **Bar:** Full bar. **Reservations:** required. **Hours:** 7:30 am-10:30 & 5:30-9 pm. **Address:** 9801 Spalding Rd V0N 2M3 **Location:** From Otter Bay Ferry Terminal, follow signs to South Pender Island, then 10 mi (16 km) s; Otter Bay Rd to Bidwell Harbour Rd to Canal Rd; in Poets Cove Resort & Spa. **Parking:** on-site and valet. **Cards:** AX, MC, VI.

QUADRA ISLAND

------- WHERE TO STAY -------

TAKU RESORT & MARINA
Phone: (250)285-3031

Motel
$89-$295 All Year

Address: 616 Taku Rd V0P 1H0 **Location:** From Campbell River ferry terminal, 4.1 mi (6.6 km) n on West Rd, then just e on Heriot Bay Rd, follow signs to Heriot Bay. **Facility:** Smoke free premises. 14 units. 5 one- and 4 two-bedroom standard units, some with efficiencies, kitchens and/or whirlpools. 5 cabins. 1 story, exterior corridors. **Parking:** on-site. **Terms:** office hours 8 am-8 pm, check-in 4 pm, 2 night minimum stay - seasonal, 15 day cancellation notice-fee imposed. **Amenities:** hair dryers. **Leisure Activities:** whirlpool, rental canoes, fishing, tennis court, basketball, horseshoes, volleyball. *Fee:* sailboats, boat dock. **Guest Services:** coin laundry. **Business Services:** PC. **Cards:** AX, MC, VI.

TSA-KWA-LUTEN LODGE & RV PARK
Phone: (250)285-2042

Small-scale Hotel
$95-$380 4/1-10/13

Address: 1 Lighthouse Rd V0P 1N0 **Location:** From Campbell River ferry terminal, just se on Green Rd, 0.6 mi (1 km) e on Noble Rd, 1.8 mi (2.9 km) se on Cape Mudge Rd to Joyce Rd, 0.6 mi (1 km) sw, then 1.4 mi (2.2 km) s. **Facility:** Smoke free premises. 35 units. 30 one-bedroom standard units, some with whirlpools. 5 cottages, some with whirlpools. 1-2 stories (no elevator), interior/exterior corridors. **Parking:** on-site. **Terms:** open 4/1-10/13, 3 day cancellation notice. **Amenities:** irons, hair dryers. **Dining:** Hama Elas Dining Room, see separate listing. **Leisure Activities:** sauna, whirlpool, bicycles, limited exercise equipment, horseshoes. *Fee:* charter fishing. **Business Services:** meeting rooms, PC. **Cards:** AX, DC, DS, JC, MC, VI.

------- WHERE TO DINE -------

HAMA ELAS DINING ROOM
Phone: 250/285-2042

Seafood
$8-$23

The menu centers on a native theme and lists North American dishes familiar to many guests, such as steak, chicken and pasta. Casual dress. **Bar:** Full bar. **Reservations:** suggested. **Hours:** Open 5/3-10/31; 7:30 am-9 pm. **Address:** 1 Lighthouse Rd V0P 1N0 **Location:** From Campbell River ferry terminal, just se on Green Rd, 0.6 mi (1 km) e on Noble Rd, 1.8 mi (2.9 km) se on Cape Mudge Rd to Joyce Rd, 0.6 mi (1 km) sw, then 1.4 mi (2.2 km) s; in Tsa-Kwa-Luten Lodge & RV Park. **Parking:** on-site. **Cards:** AX, DC, DS, JC, MC, VI.

SALT SPRING ISLAND pop. 9,780

------- WHERE TO STAY -------

ANNE'S OCEANFRONT HIDEAWAY B & B
Phone: (250)537-0851

Bed & Breakfast
$210-$285 3/1-9/30
$195-$225 10/1-2/28

Address: 168 Simson Rd V8K 1E2 **Location:** From Ganges township, just n, 3 km w on Vesuvius Bay Rd, 6 km n on Sunset Dr. Located in a quiet secluded area. **Facility:** As the name suggests, this is truly a hideaway; on a hillside overlooking the ocean, the B&B offers a wrap-around veranda, perfect for boat watching. Smoke free premises. 4 one-bedroom standard units with whirlpools. 2 stories, interior corridors. **Parking:** on-site. **Terms:** office hours 6 am-11 pm, 2 night minimum stay - seasonal, 10 day cancellation notice-fee imposed. **Amenities:** CD players, hair dryers. **Cards:** AX, MC, VI.

HARBOUR HOUSE
Phone: (250)537-5571

Small-scale Hotel
$59-$295 All Year

Address: 121 Upper Ganges Rd V8K 2S2 **Location:** 0.6 mi (1 km) n on Lower Ganges Rd, then just e, towards Long Harbour ferry terminal. **Facility:** 37 one-bedroom standard units, some with whirlpools. 2 stories (no elevator), interior/exterior corridors. *Bath:* combo or shower only. **Parking:** on-site. **Amenities:** voice mail, hair dryers. *Some:* irons. **Dining:** restaurant, see separate listing. **Guest Services:** wireless Internet. **Business Services:** meeting rooms. **Cards:** AX, MC, VI.

OLD FARMHOUSE BED & BREAKFAST
Phone: 250/537-4113

Historic Bed
& Breakfast

Rates not provided

Address: 1077 North End Rd V8K 1L9 **Location:** From Ganges township, 2.5 mi (4 km) n on Lower Ganges North End Rd. **Facility:** This 100-year old heritage farmhouse is nestled among tall trees, orchards and lovely gardens. Smoke free premises. 4 one-bedroom standard units. 2 stories (no elevator), interior corridors. **Parking:** on-site. **Terms:** office hours 8 am-10 pm. **Leisure Activities:** whirlpool.

⊠ Ⓚ 🅿 🕿 / SOME UNITS 🐾

SALT SPRINGS SPA RESORT   *Book at AAA.com*
Phone: 250/537-4111

Vacation Rental
Cottage

$109-$299 All Year

Address: 1460 N Beach Rd V8K 1J4 **Location:** From Ganges township, 4.9 mi (8 km) n on North End Rd, 0.6 mi (1.1 km) ne on Fernwood Rd, then 0.6 mi (1.8 km) nw. **Facility:** Smoke free premises. 13 cottages with whirlpools. 1 story, exterior corridors. *Bath:* shower only. **Parking:** on-site. **Terms:** office hours 8 am-8 pm, check-in 4 pm, 7 day cancellation notice-fee imposed. **Amenities:** hair dryers. **Leisure Activities:** bicycles, spa. **Guest Services:** coin laundry. **Cards:** MC, VI.

⊠ Ⓚ 🅿 🕿 🛄 🖼 📷 📺

The following lodging was either not evaluated or did not
meet AAA rating requirements but is listed for your information only.

HASTINGS HOUSE COUNTRY HOUSE HOTEL
Phone: 250/537-2362

[fyi]

Not evaluated. **Address:** 160 Upper Ganges Rd V8K 2S2 **Location:** 0.6 mi (1 km) n on Lower Ganges Rd, then just e, towards Long Harbour ferry terminal. Facilities, services, and decor characterize an upscale property.

——— WHERE TO DINE ———

BARB'S BUNS/BAKERY & BISTRO
Phone: 250/537-4491

Bakery/Desserts
$9-$20

The mouthwatering aromas of fresh bread, pastries and coffee hang in the air at the vibrant and busy bohemian spot, where healthy vegetarian breakfasts and lunches are built around organic ingredients. Leaving without a bag of carry-out baked goods should be a crime. Casual dress. **Hours:** 7 am-10 pm. Closed: 1/1, 12/25, 12/26; also Sun. **Address:** #1, 121 McPhillips Ave V8K 2T6 **Location:** In Ganges township; from Lower Ganges Rd, just w; centre. **Parking:** street. **Cards:** MC, VI.

Ⓚ

CALVIN'S SALTSPRING ISLAND BISTRO
Phone: 250/538-5551

Canadian
$6-$28

Located in the heart of the Ganges township right near the water, this simple bistro type restaurant offers hearty meals like burgers, sandwiches and soups, as well as a number of hearty desserts. There's a choice of booth seating or tables that are set up near the large windows with a great view of the water. Casual dress. **Bar:** Full bar. **Reservations:** suggested. **Hours:** Open 3/1-12/31 & 2/1-2/28; 11:30 am-2 & 5-9 pm, Sun from 5 pm. Closed: Mon, Sun 10/1-4/30. **Address:** 133 Lower Ganges Rd V8K 2T2 **Location:** In Ganges township; corner of Hereford Ave. **Parking:** street. **Cards:** CB, DC, DS, JC, MC, VI.

Ⓚ

HARBOUR HOUSE RESTAURANT & LOUNGE
Phone: 250/537-4700

Canadian
$6-$22

Views of Ganges Harbour are excellent both from the nicely decorated dining room, which has tables set against the window, and the spacious garden patio. The menu focuses on down-home Canadian fare, including daily specials. Servers merit acknowledgement for their attentiveness. Casual dress. **Bar:** Full bar. **Reservations:** accepted. **Hours:** 7 am-11 pm. Closed major holidays. **Address:** 121 Upper Ganges Rd V8K 2S2 **Location:** 0.6 mi (1 km) n on Lower Ganges Rd, then just e, towards Long Harbour ferry terminal; in Harbour House. **Parking:** on-site. **Cards:** AX, MC, VI.

Ⓚ

HASTINGS HOUSE DINING ROOM
Phone: 250/537-2362

CAA

Pacific Rim
$36-$45

This restaurant holds a truly wonderful dining experience. There is only one sitting each night, so reservations are a must. Each dinner guest gets their own personalized menu which features your pre-set course meal along with the featured wines. Dressy casual. **Bar:** Full bar. **Reservations:** required. **Hours:** Open 3/15-11/15; 6 pm-8 pm. **Address:** 160 Upper Ganges Rd V8K 2S2 **Location:** 0.6 mi (1 km) n on Lower Ganges Rd, then just e, towards Long Harbour ferry terminal; in Hastings House Country House Hotel. **Parking:** on-site. **Cards:** AX, MC, VI.

Ⓚ

RESTAURANT HOUSE PICCOLO
Phone: 250/537-1844

Continental
$27-$36

Reservations are a must at the cozy restaurant, which has limited seating space in a setting nestled away from the busy shops of Ganges. Reasonably priced wines pair with Scandinavian and European standards and seafood preparations. Casual dress. **Bar:** Full bar. **Reservations:** required, 8/1-9/30. **Hours:** 5 pm-9:30 pm. Closed: 12/25, 12/26; also Sun & Mon. **Address:** 108 Hereford Ave V8K 2V9 **Location:** In Ganges township; cross street Lower Ganges Rd. **Parking:** street. **Cards:** MC, VI.

Ⓚ

The previous listings were for the Gulf Islands NP Reserve.
This page resumes the alphabetical listings of cities in British Columbia.

HALFMOON BAY pop. 417

──────── WHERE TO STAY ────────

──────── *The following lodging was either not evaluated or did not* ────────
meet AAA rating requirements but is listed for your information only.

ROCKWATER SECRET COVE RESORT   **Phone:** 604/885-7038

 Did not meet all AAA rating requirements for locking devices in some guest rooms at time of last
evaluation. **Address:** 5356 Ole Rd V0N 1Y2 **Location:** 4.4 mi (7 km) n on Hwy 101, follow signs.
Small-scale Hotel   Facilities, services, and decor characterize a basic property.

──────── WHERE TO DINE ────────

ROCKWATER SECRET COVE RESORT
  RESTAURANT   **Phone:** 604/885-7038
 Diners are treated to stunning water views from every table. Among offerings of wonderful West Coast
cuisine are a fish of the day, as well as rack of lamb and hearty steaks. The homemade chuck steak burger
Pacific Rim   is a good lunch choice. Casual dress. **Bar:** Full bar. **Reservations:** suggested, for dinner. **Hours:** 8 am-2 &
$12-$32   5:30-9:30 pm, Wed & Thurs 5:30 pm-8 pm, Fri-Sun 11:30 am-3 & 5:30-8 pm. **Address:** 5356 Ole's Cove Rd
V0N 1Y2 **Location:** 4.4 mi (7 km) n on Hwy 101, follow signs; in Rockwater Secret Cove Resort. **Parking:**
on-site. **Cards:** AX, MC, VI.

HARRISON HOT SPRINGS pop. 1,573

──────── WHERE TO STAY ────────

HARRISON BEACH HOTEL   *Book great rates at AAA.com*   **Phone:** (604)796-1111

 Address: 160 Esplanade Ave V0M 1K0 **Location:** Just w; on the lakefront. **Facility:** Smoke free
premises. 42 units. 39 one-bedroom standard units with efficiencies. 3 one-bedroom suites with
efficiencies and whirlpools. 4 stories, interior corridors. **Bath:** combo or shower only. **Parking:** on-site
(fee). **Terms:** cancellation fee imposed. **Amenities:** video library (fee), DVD players, high-speed
Small-scale Hotel   Internet, voice mail, irons, hair dryers. **Pool(s):** heated indoor. **Leisure Activities:** limited exercise
$145-$265 All Year   equipment. **Guest Services:** coin laundry. **Business Services:** meeting rooms. **Cards:** AX, MC, VI.

HARRISON HOT SPRINGS RESORT & SPA   *Book great rates at AAA.com*   **Phone:** (604)796-2244

Address: 100 Esplanade Ave V0M 1K0 **Location:** Just w; on lakefront.
Facility: Smoke free premises. 337 one-bedroom standard units. 8
stories, interior corridors. **Bath:** combo or shower only. **Parking:** on-site
(fee) and valet. **Terms:** check-in 4 pm, 1-2 night minimum stay -
Large-scale Hotel   seasonal and/or weekends, 3 day cancellation notice-fee imposed.
$139-$599 All Year   **Amenities:** voice mail, irons, hair dryers. *Some:* video games (fee), high-
speed Internet. **Dining:** The Copper Room, see separate listing,
entertainment. **Pool(s):** 3 heated outdoor, 2 heated indoor. **Leisure
Activities:** steamrooms, rental boats, indoor/outdoor hot therapeutic
mineral pools, 2 tennis courts, rental bicycles, hiking trails, jogging,
exercise room, spa. *Fee:* golf-9 holes. **Guest Services:** valet laundry.
Business Services: conference facilities. **Cards:** AX, DC, DS, MC, VI.
Free Special Amenities: newspaper. *(See color ad below)*

──────── ▼ *See AAA listing above* ▼ ────────

——— WHERE TO DINE ———

BLACK FOREST RESTAURANT
German
$8-$26

Phone: 604/796-9343

You'll enjoy the steak and West Coast salmon at the Black Forest, which also serves German specialties of beef rouladen and schnitzel. The Alpine decor features a central European flair in its paintings and murals. Visitors like the warm, cozy atmosphere. Casual dress. **Bar:** Full bar. **Reservations:** suggested, in summer. **Hours:** 5 pm-10 pm; from noon 6/1-9/30. Closed: 12/25. **Address:** 180 Esplanade Ave V0M 1K0 **Location:** Just w; on lakefront. **Parking:** street. **Cards:** AX, MC, VI.

THE COPPER ROOM
Pacific Rim
$25-$36

Phone: 604/796-2244

You'll appreciate The Copper Room for its popular evening dining and dancing. This restaurant is also known for its delicious prime rib and Fraser Valley local produce. Nightly entertainment is featured and a dress code is imposed. Dressy casual. Entertainment. **Bar:** Full bar. **Reservations:** required. **Hours:** 6 pm-10 pm, Fri & Sat-11 pm. **Address:** 100 Esplanade Ave V0M 1K0 **Location:** Just w; on lakefront; in Harrison Hot Springs Resort & Spa. **Cards:** AX, DC, DS, MC, VI.

HARRISON MILLS pop. 209

——— WHERE TO STAY ———

HISTORIC FENN LODGE BED & BREAKFAST
Historic Bed & Breakfast
Rates not provided

Phone: 604/796-9798

Address: 15500 Morris Valley Rd V0M 1L0 **Location:** Hwy 7, 2.5 mi (4 km) n of the Sasquatch Inn, follow signs. **Facility:** This distinctive hotel built in 1903 retains many of its original furnishings. Smoke free premises. 6 one-bedroom standard units. 2 stories (no elevator), interior corridors. *Bath:* shower or tub only. **Parking:** on-site. **Terms:** office hours 8:30 am-10 pm. **Pool(s):** outdoor.

HEDLEY pop. 256

——— WHERE TO STAY ———

——— *The following lodging was either not evaluated or did not* ———
meet AAA rating requirements but is listed for your information only.

COLONIAL INN
[fyi]

Phone: 250/292-8131

Not evaluated. **Address:** 608 Colonial Rd V0X 1K0 **Location:** Just e on Hwy 3. Facilities, services, and decor characterize a basic property.

HOPE pop. 6,185

——— WHERE TO STAY ———

ALPINE MOTEL
(CAA) [SAVE]
Motel
$95-$110 3/1-9/30
$78-$85 10/1-2/28

Phone: (604)869-9931

Address: 505 Old Hope-Princeton Way V0X 1L0 **Location:** Trans-Canada Hwy 1, exit 173 westbound; exit 170 eastbound, just n from lights. **Facility:** 14 one-bedroom standard units, some with efficiencies. 1 story, exterior corridors. **Parking:** on-site. **Terms:** office hours 7 am-midnight. **Amenities:** high-speed Internet. **Cards:** AX, MC, VI. **Free Special Amenities: local telephone calls and high-speed Internet.**

 / SOME UNITS FEE

BEST CONTINENTAL MOTEL
(CAA) [SAVE]
Motel
$59-$125 All Year

Phone: 604/869-9726

Address: 860 Fraser Ave V0X 1L0 **Location:** Trans-Canada Hwy 1, exit 170 to downtown; at Fort St. **Facility:** 15 one-bedroom standard units. 2 stories (no elevator), exterior corridors. **Parking:** on-site. **Terms:** office hours 8 am-midnight. **Guest Services:** wireless Internet. **Cards:** AX, MC, VI. **Free Special Amenities: local telephone calls and high-speed Internet.**

 / SOME UNITS FEE

BEST WESTERN HERITAGE INN   *Book great rates at AAA.com*

Phone: 604/869-7166

(CAA) [SAVE]
Motel
Rates not provided

Address: 570 Old Hope-Princeton Hwy V0X 1L0 **Location:** Trans-Canada Hwy 1, exit 173 westbound; exit 170 eastbound, just n from lights. **Facility:** Smoke free premises. 26 one-bedroom standard units, some with kitchens. 1-2 stories (no elevator), exterior corridors. **Parking:** on-site. **Terms:** office hours 6:30 am-midnight. **Amenities:** irons, hair dryers. *Some:* high-speed Internet. **Leisure Activities:** whirlpool, limited exercise equipment. **Guest Services:** coin laundry, wireless Internet. **Free Special Amenities: continental breakfast and high-speed Internet.**

AAA Benefit:

Members save 10% everyday, plus an exclusive frequent stay program.

COLONIAL '900' MOTEL

(AA) (SAVE)

▽▽▽▽
Motel
$95-$135 3/1-9/10
$75-$125 9/11-2/28

Phone: (604)869-5223

Address: 900 Old Hope-Princeton Way V0X 1L0 **Location:** Trans-Canada Hwy 1, exit 173 westbound; exit 170 eastbound, 0.6 mi (1 km) n from lights. **Facility:** Smoke free premises. 16 one-bedroom standard units, some with efficiencies or kitchens. 1 story, exterior corridors. **Parking:** on-site, winter plug-ins. **Terms:** office hours 8 am-11 pm. **Amenities:** hair dryers. **Guest Services:** wireless Internet. **Cards:** AX, MC, VI. **Free Special Amenities: local telephone calls and high-speed Internet.**

[icons] / SOME UNITS

QUALITY INN   *Book great rates at AAA.com*

(AA) (SAVE)

▽▽▽ ▽▽▽
Motel
$75-$145 All Year

Phone: (604)869-9951

Address: 350 Old Hope-Princeton Way V0X 1L0 **Location:** Trans-Canada Hwy 1, exit 173 westbound; exit 170 eastbound, just n from lights. **Facility:** 25 one-bedroom standard units, some with efficiencies. 2 stories (no elevator), interior corridors. **Parking:** on-site. **Terms:** office hours 8 am-midnight. **Amenities:** hair dryers. **Pool(s):** heated indoor. **Leisure Activities:** sauna, whirlpool. **Guest Services:** wireless Internet. **Business Services:** PC. **Cards:** AX, CB, DC, DS, JC, MC, VI. **Free Special Amenities: continental breakfast and high-speed Internet.** *(See color ad on insert)*

[icons] CALL [icons] / SOME UNITS

SKAGIT MOTOR INN

(AA) (SAVE)

▽▽▽ ▽▽▽
Motel
$88-$108 All Year

Phone: (604)869-5220

Address: 655 3rd Ave V0X 1L0 **Location:** Trans-Canada Hwy 1, exit 170 to downtown; just e of Water Ave. Located in a residential area. **Facility:** 31 one-bedroom standard units, some with efficiencies. 1 story, exterior corridors. **Parking:** on-site. **Terms:** office hours 7 am-11 pm, 3 day cancellation notice-fee imposed. **Amenities:** voice mail, hair dryers. **Leisure Activities:** whirlpool. **Guest Services:** coin laundry, wireless Internet. **Business Services:** meeting rooms. **Cards:** AX, DC, JC, MC, VI. **Free Special Amenities: room upgrade (subject to availability with advance reservations) and high-speed Internet.**

[icons] / SOME UNITS

──────── **WHERE TO DINE** ────────

THE GOLDRUSH PUB

◆◆◆
Canadian
$9-$16

Phone: 604/860-4333

Examples of the good pub food include burgers, sandwiches and many appetizers. Various beers on tap or in the bottle are available. Provincial liquor laws do not allow entry to those under age 19. Casual dress. **Bar:** Full bar. **Hours:** 11 am-11 am. **Address:** 629 Old Hope Princeton Hwy V0X 1L2 **Location:** Trans-Canada Hwy 1, exit 170 eastbound; exit 173 westbound. **Parking:** on-site. **Cards:** AX, MC, VI.

HOME RESTAURANT

◆◆◆
Canadian
$4-$12

Phone: 604/869-5558

You'll enjoy this very popular family-style eatery, which features all your favorites—burgers, meat loaf, club-house sandwiches, mountain-men breakfasts and homemade soup, sauce and pie. Food is king here, and you'll want to come back again and again. Casual dress. **Bar:** Beer & wine. **Hours:** 6 am-9 pm; to 11 pm 7/1-8/31. Closed: 12/25. **Address:** 665 Old Hope-Princeton Way V0X 1L4 **Location:** Trans-Canada Hwy 1, exit 173 westbound; exit 170 eastbound, just n from lights. **Parking:** on-site. **Cards:** MC, VI.

HOPE DRIVE-IN & RESTAURANT

◆◆◆
Canadian
$6-$15

Phone: 604/869-5380

The casual drive-in is a good stop for good food at reasonable prices. Guests can eat in or order from the take-out window. On the menu are freshly made sandwiches, burgers and homemade soups and desserts. Casual dress. **Bar:** Full bar. **Hours:** 6 am-10 pm. Closed: 1/1, 12/25, 12/26. **Address:** 590 Old Hope-Princeton Way V0X 1L0 **Location:** Trans-Canada Hwy 1, exit 173 westbound; exit 170 eastbound, just n from lights. **Parking:** on-site. **Cards:** MC, VI.

[icon]

PAPANDREAS GREEK TAVERNA

◆◆ ◆◆
Greek
$8-$18

Phone: 604/869-7218

On the north end of town next door to Colonial 900 Motel, this restaurant features fine Greek dishes along with steaks and some really good pizza. Guests can dine in or take out. Casual dress. **Bar:** Full bar. **Reservations:** accepted. **Hours:** 4 pm-10 pm; 11:30 am-11 pm 6/1-9/30. Closed: 12/25, 12/26. **Address:** 904 Old Hope-Princeton Way V0X 1L0 **Location:** Trans-Canada Hwy 1, exit 173 westbound; exit 170 eastbound, 0.6 mi (1 km) n from lights. **Parking:** on-site. **Cards:** MC, VI.

ROLLY'S RESTAURANT

◆◆◆
Canadian
$6-$15

Phone: 604/869-7448

Rolly's is a great casual, family-dining experience with breakfast served all day. Their home-style cooking menu features chicken teriyaki, halibut, salmon, pasta, Angus beef, fish 'n' chips and more. The open and casual atmosphere is very comfortable. Casual dress. **Bar:** Full bar. **Hours:** 6 am-8:30 pm, Fri & Sun-9 pm. Closed: 12/25. **Address:** 888 Fraser Ave V0X 1L0 **Location:** Trans-Canada Hwy 1, exit 170 to downtown; Hudson Bay St. **Parking:** on-site. **Cards:** AX, MC, VI.

INVERMERE pop. 3,002

──────── **WHERE TO STAY** ────────

BEST WESTERN INVERMERE INN   *Book great rates at AAA.com*

(AA) (SAVE)

▽▽▽ ▽▽▽
Small-scale Hotel
$119-$199 All Year

Phone: (250)342-9246

Address: 1310 7th Ave V0A 1K0 **Location:** 1.8 mi (3 km) w of Hwy 93 and 95 at Invermere exit; centre. **Facility:** 45 units. 43 one- and 1 two-bedroom standard units. 1 one-bedroom suite. 3 stories, interior corridors. **Parking:** on-site, winter plug-ins. **Terms:** check-in 4 pm, 3 day cancellation notice. **Amenities:** voice mail, irons, hair dryers. *Some:* high-speed Internet. **Dining:** nightclub. **Leisure Activities:** whirlpool, limited exercise equipment. **Guest Services:** wireless Internet. **Business Services:** meeting rooms, PC (fee). **Cards:** AX, DC, DS, MC, VI. **Free Special Amenities: continental breakfast and high-speed Internet.**

[icons] / SOME UNITS FEE

INVERMERE SUPER 8

Small-scale Hotel
$160-$180 3/1-9/30
$110-$150 10/1-2/28

Phone: (250)342-8888
Address: 8888 Arrow Rd V0A 1K0 **Location:** On Hwy 95. **Facility:** 49 one-bedroom standard units. 3 stories, interior corridors. **Parking:** on-site. **Amenities:** voice mail, hair dryers. *Some:* irons. **Leisure Activities:** whirlpool. **Guest Services:** coin laundry, wireless Internet. **Business Services:** PC (fee). **Cards:** AX, CB, DC, DS, JC, MC, VI.

ASK ⊞ 🎥 🖥 / SOME UNITS FEE 🛏 ✕ 📦 🖼

———— WHERE TO DINE ————

BLACK FOREST STEAK & SCHNITZEL HOUSE

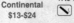

Continental
$13-$24

Phone: 250/342-9417
On the menu is a good selection of schnitzels, bratwurst, steak and seafood finely prepared with a respect for tradition. Table d'hotes are offered daily, and the decor and relaxed ambience are inspired by Europe. The restaurant is a favorite with birders, who can enjoy watching the owner's pets while dining. **Bar:** Full bar. **Reservations:** suggested. **Hours:** 5 pm-11 pm; to 10 pm off season. **Address:** 540 Hwy 93 & 95 V0A 1K0 **Location:** On Hwy 93 and 95. **Parking:** on-site. **Cards:** AX, DC, MC, VI.

🖊

PORTABELLA RESTAURANT

International
$15-$30

Phone: 250/342-0606
On a side street just off downtown, the small converted house decorated in a casual Mediterranean style can seem a little tight for elbow room. Regardless, the dining room is surprisingly intimate and moments of silence indicate guests are enjoying the creatively prepared dishes. It isn't hard to see the commitment to quality, as many things seem to be made in-house and the restaurant has built its reputation on using local, seasonal ingredients and merging them with Mediterranean accents. Dressy casual. **Bar:** Full bar. **Reservations:** accepted. **Hours:** 5 pm-10 pm. Closed major holidays; also Mon. **Address:** 722 13th Ave V0A 1K4 **Location:** Just e of Main St; downtown. **Parking:** street. **Cards:** AX, MC, VI.

STRAND'S OLD HOUSE RESTAURANT

Continental
$13-$30

Phone: 250/342-6344
The restaurant offers intimate dining in a restored historic house. The varied menu includes sumptuous venison in blackberry sauce, a selection of pastas and dinner-size salads. The covered porch provides a bright, airy alternative to the more secluded corners of the main dining room. Servers are friendly and courteous. Casual dress. **Bar:** Full bar. **Reservations:** suggested. **Hours:** 5 pm-10 pm; Mon-Fri to 10:30 pm in summer. Closed: 12/25. **Address:** 818 12th St V0A 1K0 **Location:** Centre. **Parking:** on-site. **Cards:** AX, MC, VI. **Historic**

CALL ♿

KAMLOOPS pop. 80,376

———— WHERE TO STAY ————

ACCENT INNS

Motel
$99-$169 All Year

Book great rates at AAA.com
Phone: (250)374-8877
Address: 1325 Columbia St W V2C 6P4 **Location:** Trans-Canada Hwy 1, exit 369 (Columbia St) eastbound, at Notre Dame Dr; exit 370 (Summit Dr) westbound, at Notre Dame Dr. **Facility:** 83 one-bedroom standard units, some with efficiencies. 3 stories, exterior corridors. **Parking:** on-site, winter plug-ins. **Amenities:** voice mail, irons, hair dryers. **Pool(s):** heated outdoor. **Leisure Activities:** sauna, whirlpool, limited exercise equipment. **Guest Services:** valet and coin laundry, wireless Internet. **Business Services:** meeting rooms. **Cards:** AX, CB, DC, DS, MC, VI. **Free Special Amenities:** newspaper and high-speed Internet. *(See color ad p 639)*

🅂ⓓ ⊞ CALL ♿ 🏊 ✕ 🎥 🖥 / SOME UNITS FEE 🛏 ✕ 🖼

BEST WESTERN KAMLOOPS

Large-scale Hotel
Rates not provided

Book great rates at AAA.com
Phone: 250/828-6660
Address: 1250 Rogers Way V1S 1N5 **Location:** Trans-Canada Hwy 1, exit 368 (Hillside Ave), just s. **Facility:** Smoke free premises. 203 units. 189 one-bedroom standard units. 8 one- and 6 two-bedroom suites, some with whirlpools. 3 stories, interior corridors. *Bath:* combo or shower only. **Parking:** on-site, winter plug-ins. **Amenities:** high-speed Internet, voice mail, irons, hair dryers. **Pool(s):** heated indoor. **Leisure Activities:** sauna, whirlpool, exercise room. **Guest Services:** valet laundry. **Business Services:** conference facilities, business center. **Free Special Amenities:** local telephone calls and high-speed Internet.

⊞ 🍸 CALL ♿ 🏊 ✕ 🎥 🖥 🖨 / SOME UNITS FEE 🛏 🖼

AAA Benefit:
Members save 10% everyday, plus an exclusive frequent stay program.

COMFORT INN & SUITES

Small-scale Hotel
$110-$169 All Year

Book great rates at AAA.com
Phone: (250)372-0987
Address: 1810 Rogers Pl V1S 1T7 **Location:** Trans-Canada Hwy 1, exit 368 (Hillside Ave), just w. **Facility:** 128 units. 118 one-bedroom standard units, some with efficiencies and/or whirlpools. 10 one-bedroom suites, some with efficiencies and/or whirlpools. 3 stories, interior corridors. **Parking:** on-site, winter plug-ins. **Amenities:** voice mail, irons, hair dryers. **Dining:** Vittorio's Italian Restaurant, see separate listing. **Pool(s):** heated outdoor, heated indoor. **Leisure Activities:** whirlpools, waterslide, limited exercise equipment. **Guest Services:** valet and coin laundry, wireless Internet. **Business Services:** meeting rooms, PC. **Cards:** AX, CB, DC, DS, JC, MC, VI. **Free Special Amenities:** expanded continental breakfast and high-speed Internet. *(See color ad on insert & p 512)*

🅂ⓓ ⊞ CALL ♿ 🏊 ✕ 🎥 🖥 / SOME UNITS ✕ 🖼

ECONO LODGE INN & SUITES

Book great rates at AAA.com

Phone: (250)372-8533

CAA **SAVE**

Motel

$79-$99 3/1-9/30
$69-$89 10/1-2/28

Address: 1773 Trans-Canada Hwy E V2C 3Z6 **Location:** 1.5 mi (2.4 km) e on Trans-Canada Hwy 1, south side of service access road. **Facility:** 45 one-bedroom standard units, some with kitchens. 2 stories (no elevator), exterior corridors. **Parking:** on-site, winter plug-ins. **Terms:** office hours 7 am-midnight. **Pool(s):** heated indoor. **Leisure Activities:** whirlpool. **Guest Services:** coin laundry, wireless Internet. **Cards:** AX, DC, DS, MC, VI. **Free Special Amenities:** local telephone calls and high-speed Internet. *(See color ad on insert)*

FOUR POINTS BY SHERATON

Book great rates at AAA.com

Phone: (250)374-4144

CAA **SAVE**

Small-scale Hotel

$110-$230 All Year

Address: 1175 Rogers Way V1S 1R5 **Location:** Trans-Canada Hwy 1, exit 368 (Hillside Ave), just s. **Facility:** Smoke free premises. 78 units. 77 one- and 1 two-bedroom standard units, some with efficiencies, kitchens and/or whirlpools. 4 stories, interior corridors. **Parking:** on-site, winter plug-ins. **Amenities:** dual phone lines, voice mail, irons, hair dryers. **Dining:** Ric's Grill Steak Seafood & Chop House, see separate listing. **Pool(s):** heated indoor. **Leisure Activities:** sauna, whirlpool, waterslide, limited exercise equipment. **Guest Services:** valet and coin laundry, wireless Internet. **Business Services:** meeting rooms, business center. **Cards:** AX, DC, JC, MC, VI. **Free Special Amenities:** local telephone calls and preferred room (subject to availability with advance reservations).

FOUR POINTS
BY SHERATON
AAA Benefit:
Members get up to 15% off, plus Starwood Preferred Guest® bonuses.

GRANDVIEW MOTEL

Phone: (250)372-1312

CAA **SAVE**

Motel

$55-$105 All Year

Address: 463 Grandview Terr V2C 3Z3 **Location:** Trans-Canada Hwy 1, exit 370 (Summit Dr) eastbound, 1.3 mi (2 km) n; exit 370 (Summit Dr) westbound to Columbia St, via City Centre. **Facility:** 26 one-bedroom standard units, some with efficiencies. 2 stories (no elevator), exterior corridors. **Parking:** on-site, winter plug-ins. **Terms:** office hours 8 am-11 pm, cancellation fee imposed. **Pool(s):** heated outdoor. **Leisure Activities:** gas barbecue area. **Cards:** AX, DC, JC, MC, VI. **Free Special Amenities:** local telephone calls and high-speed Internet. *(See color ad below)*

HAMPTON INN

Book great rates at AAA.com

Phone: (250)571-7897

CAA **SAVE**

Small-scale Hotel

$109-$179 All Year

Address: 1245 Rogers Way V1S 1R9 **Location:** Trans-Canada Hwy 1, exit 368 (Hillside Ave), just s via Hillside Way. **Facility:** 81 one-bedroom standard units, some with whirlpools. 3 stories, interior corridors. *Bath:* combo or shower only. **Parking:** on-site, winter plug-ins. **Terms:** cancellation fee imposed. **Amenities:** video games (fee), high-speed Internet, voice mail, irons, hair dryers. **Pool(s):** heated indoor. **Leisure Activities:** whirlpool, waterslide, limited exercise equipment. **Guest Services:** valet and coin laundry. **Business Services:** meeting rooms, business center. **Cards:** AX, CB, DC, DS, MC, VI. **Free Special Amenities:** expanded continental breakfast and high-speed Internet. *(See color ad p 512)*

HOLIDAY INN EXPRESS KAMLOOPS

Book great rates at AAA.com

Phone: (250)372-3474

CAA **SAVE**

Small-scale Hotel

$125-$145 3/1-9/30
$105-$125 10/1-2/28

Address: 1550 Versatile Dr V1S 1X4 **Location:** Trans-Canada Hwy 1, exit 367 (Pacific Way), just w. **Facility:** Smoke free premises. 80 units. 79 one-bedroom standard units. 1 one-bedroom suite with whirlpool. 4 stories, interior corridors. **Parking:** on-site, winter plug-ins. **Amenities:** high-speed Internet, dual phone lines, voice mail, irons, hair dryers. **Pool(s):** heated indoor. **Leisure Activities:** whirlpool, limited exercise equipment. **Guest Services:** valet laundry. **Business Services:** meeting rooms, business center. **Cards:** AX, DC, DS, MC, VI. **Free Special Amenities:** continental breakfast and high-speed Internet.

▼ See AAA listing above ▼

HOSPITALITY INN

Motel

$93-$101 3/1-10/15
$77-$85 10/16-2/28

Book at AAA.com

Phone: (250)374-4164

Address: 500 W Columbia St V2C 1K6 **Location:** Trans-Canada Hwy 1, exit 369 (Columbia St) eastbound, 1.3 mi (2 km) n; exit 370 (Summit Dr) westbound to Columbia St via City Centre. **Facility:** 76 one-bedroom standard units, some with efficiencies. 2 stories (no elevator), exterior corridors. **Parking:** on-site, winter plug-ins. **Terms:** office hours 7 am-11 pm. **Pool(s):** heated outdoor. **Leisure Activities:** whirlpool. **Cards:** AX, DC, DS, MC, VI.

KAMLOOPS SUPER 8 MOTEL

Motel

$135-$150 3/1-10/14
$100-$130 10/15-2/28

Book at AAA.com

Phone: (250)374-8688

Address: 1521 Hugh Allan Dr V1S 1P4 **Location:** Trans-Canada Hwy 1, exit 367 (Pacific Way). **Facility:** 47 one-bedroom standard units. 2 stories (no elevator), interior corridors. **Parking:** on-site. **Amenities:** hair dryers. **Cards:** AX, DC, DS, JC, MC, VI.

KAMLOOPS TRAVELODGE MOUNTVIEW

(CAA) SAVE

Motel

Rates not provided

Book great rates at AAA.com

Phone: 250/374-4788

Address: 1225 Rogers Way V1S 1R9 **Location:** Trans-Canada Hwy 1, exit 368 (Hillside Ave), just s. **Facility:** 53 units. 52 one-bedroom standard units, some with efficiencies and/or whirlpools. 1 two-bedroom suite. 3 stories, exterior corridors. **Parking:** on-site. **Terms:** office hours 7 am-midnight. **Amenities:** hair dryers. *Some:* high-speed Internet. **Pool(s):** heated outdoor. **Leisure Activities:** whirlpool. **Guest Services:** coin laundry, wireless Internet. **Business Services:** meeting rooms. **Free Special Amenities: continental breakfast and high-speed Internet.** *(See color ad below)*

MAVERICK MOTOR INN

Motel

$69-$199 All Year

Phone: (250)374-9666

Address: 1250 W Trans-Canada Hwy 1 V2C 6R3 **Location:** Trans-Canada Hwy 1, exit 368 (Hillside Ave). **Facility:** 42 one-bedroom standard units, some with efficiencies. 2 stories (no elevator), interior corridors. **Parking:** on-site. **Terms:** cancellation fee imposed. **Amenities:** video library (fee), voice mail; irons, hair dryers. **Pool(s):** heated indoor. **Leisure Activities:** whirlpool, waterslide. **Guest Services:** coin laundry, wireless Internet. **Business Services:** meeting rooms, PC. **Cards:** AX, MC, VI.

QUALITY INN   *Book at AAA.com*   **Phone:** 250/851-0111

Motel
Rates not provided

Address: 1860 Rogers Pl V1S 1T7 **Location:** Trans-Canada Hwy 1, exit 368 (Hillside Ave). **Facility:** 63 one-bedroom standard units, some with efficiencies and/or whirlpools. 2 stories (no elevator), interior corridors. **Parking:** on-site, winter plug-ins. **Amenities:** irons, hair dryers. **Pool(s):** heated outdoor. **Leisure Activities:** sauna, whirlpool, limited exercise equipment. **Guest Services:** coin laundry, wireless Internet. *(See color ad on insert)*

RAMADA INN-KAMLOOPS   *Book great rates at AAA.com*   **Phone:** (250)374-0358

Small-scale Hotel
$89-$189 All Year

Address: 555 W Columbia St V2C 1K7 **Location:** Trans-Canada Hwy 1, exit 369 (Columbia St) eastbound, 1.3 mi (2 km) n; exit 370 (Summit Dr) westbound to Columbia St via City Centre. **Facility:** 90 one-bedroom standard units, some with efficiencies. 2-3 stories, interior corridors. **Parking:** on-site, winter plug-ins. **Amenities:** video library (fee), voice mail, irons, hair dryers. **Pool(s):** heated outdoor. **Leisure Activities:** sauna, whirlpool. **Guest Services:** valet laundry, wireless Internet. **Business Services:** meeting rooms, PC. **Cards:** AX, CB, DC, DS, JC, MC, VI. **Free Special Amenities:** local telephone calls and high-speed Internet.

RANCHLAND MOTEL   **Phone:** (250)828-8787

Motel
$65-$89 All Year

Address: 2357 Trans-Canada Hwy E V2C 4A8 **Location:** 2.8 mi (4.5 km) e on Trans-Canada Hwy 1, exit River Rd, then just w along service access road. **Facility:** 36 one-bedroom standard units, some with efficiencies. 2 stories (no elevator), exterior corridors. **Parking:** on-site, winter plug-ins. **Terms:** office hours 7 am-11 pm. **Leisure Activities:** sauna, whirlpool. **Guest Services:** coin laundry, wireless Internet. **Cards:** AX, DS, MC, VI.

SCOTT'S INN & RESTAURANT   *Book great rates at AAA.com*   **Phone:** (250)372-8221

Motel
$90-$120 3/1-9/6
$80-$100 9/7-2/28

Address: 551 11th Ave V2C 3Y1 **Location:** Trans-Canada Hwy 1, exit 369 (Columbia St) eastbound, 3.1 mi (5 km) n; exit City Centre westbound, 1 mi (1.6) km s on Columbia St. Located in a residential area across from a playground. **Facility:** 51 units. 48 one- and 3 two-bedroom standard units, some with efficiencies or kitchens. 2 stories (no elevator), exterior corridors. *Bath:* combo or shower only. **Parking:** on-site, winter plug-ins. **Terms:** office hours 7 am-11 pm. **Amenities:** hair dryers. **Pool(s):** heated indoor. **Leisure Activities:** whirlpool. **Guest Services:** coin laundry, wireless Internet. **Business Services:** PC (fee). **Cards:** AX, MC, VI. **Free Special Amenities: continental breakfast and high-speed Internet.** *(See color ad p 514)*

————— WHERE TO DINE —————

CHAPTERS VIEWPOINT RESTAURANT & CATERING   **Phone:** 250/374-3224

Canadian
$8-$40

This restaurant's great location offers a spectacular view of the city and surrounding hills. The well-prepared menu features New Mexican cuisine, beef and prime rib, chicken and seafood. The decor is Pacific Northwest and makes use of the Douglas fir for beams. Casual dress. **Bar:** Full bar. **Reservations:** suggested. **Hours:** 8 am-9 pm. Closed: 12/25, 12/26. **Address:** 610 W Columbia St V2C 1L1 **Location:** Trans-Canada Hwy 1, exit 369 (Columbia St) eastbound, 1.2 mi (2 km) n; exit 370 (Summit Dr) westbound to Columbia St via City Centre; in Panorama/Howard Johnson Inn. **Parking:** on-site. **Cards:** AX, MC, VI.

MONTANA'S COOKHOUSE   **Phone: 250/314-0714**

Steak House
$7-$25

Pine boards, exposed beams, a fireplace and Western gear displayed about the dining room give the feeling of a back-country setting. The menu lists hearty portions of comfort fare, such as Yankee pot roast. While the focus is on steaks, ribs and chicken, some seafood entrees also are among offerings. Service is efficient and friendly. Casual dress. **Hours:** 11 am-11 pm, Fri & Sat-midnight. Closed: 12/25. **Address:** 600-1005 Hillside Dr V2E 2S5 **Location:** Trans-Canada Hwy 1, exit 367 (Pacific Way), just n to Hillside Dr, then 1 mi (1.6 km) ne. **Parking:** on-site. **Cards:** AX, MC, VI.

ON THE ROCKS PUB & GRILL   **Phone: 250/374-9761**

Canadian
$7-$18

The sports bar and grill features tons of appetizers, burgers, sandwiches, pitas and wraps, plus daily specials and lots of beers on tap. No one younger than 19 is permitted. The enclosed smoking room has a cozy fireplace. Casual dress. **Bar:** Full bar. **Reservations:** accepted. **Hours:** 11 am-11:30 pm. Closed: 12/25. **Address:** 1265 Rogers Way V1S 1R9 **Location:** Trans-Canada Hwy 1, exit 368 (Hillside Ave), just s. **Parking:** on-site and street. **Cards:** AX, MC, VI.

ORIENTAL GARDENS RESTAURANT   **Phone: 250/372-2344**

Chinese
$10-$20

Delicious Japanese and Chinese entrees are featured at this restaurant, where a full sushi bar and Japanese-style private dining booths are also offered. If you park in the lot to the side, ask the restaurant staff to validate your ticket stub. Casual dress. **Bar:** Full bar. **Reservations:** suggested. **Hours:** Open 3/1-12/23 & 1/23-2/28; 5 pm-10:30 pm, Fri & Sat-11:30 pm, Sun-10 pm. **Address:** 545 Victoria St V2C 2B1 **Location:** Victoria St at 5th Ave; downtown. **Parking:** on-site (fee). **Cards:** AX, MC, VI.

RICKY'S ALL DAY GRILL   **Phone: 250/851-9845**

Canadian
$6-$15

The comfortable eatery, which employs friendly servers, presents a varied menu that includes pasta dishes, wraps, omelets, stir-fry preparations and burgers. Portions are generous. Children's and senior selections are offered. Guests can request seating in a booth or at a table. Casual dress. **Bar:** Full bar. **Hours:** 6 am-9 pm. **Address:** 1967 E Trans-Canada Hwy, #90B V2C 4A4 **Location:** Between Robin and Oriole rds. **Parking:** on-site. **Cards:** MC, VI.

RIC'S GRILL STEAK SEAFOOD & CHOP HOUSE   **Phone: 250/377-3113**

Steak & Seafood
$12-$32

"Funky and modern" describes the decor and the food at the upscale steakhouse, which bustles with activity. Reservations are definitely recommended. Steaks are well worth it, but then again, so are the salmon, chicken and pasta dishes. A wide variety of distinctive appetizers rounds out the menu. Servers are friendly and attentive. Casual dress. **Bar:** Full bar. **Hours:** 6:30 am-10:30 pm. Closed: 12/25. **Address:** 1175 Rogers Way V1S 1R5 **Location:** Trans-Canada Hwy 1, exit 368 (Hillside Ave), just s; in Four Points by Sheraton. **Parking:** on-site. **Cards:** AX, MC, VI.

RIC'S MEDITERRANEAN GRILL   **Phone: 250/372-7771**

Steak & Seafood
$11-$30

A youthful and bustling ambience characterizes the popular downtown restaurant. The food blends Mediterranean ingredients with seafood, fish and steaks to create dishes that show sensitivity to International influences. The long list of appetizers and by-the-glass wine choices let diners turn dinner into a sampling event. Casual dress. **Bar:** Full bar. **Reservations:** suggested. **Hours:** 11 am-9:30 pm, Fri & Sat-10 pm, Sun 4 pm-9:30 pm. Closed: 12/25. **Address:** 227 Victoria St V2C 2A1 **Location:** Between 2nd and 3rd aves. **Parking:** street. **Cards:** AX, MC, VI.

TANDOORI GRILL   **Phone: 250/372-3418**

Indian
$9-$18

A fine East Indian restaurant featuring all the known and loved favorites like hot and tasty naan bread, butter chicken and, of course, lamb dishes. The hilltop location offers great views of the city. Casual dress. **Bar:** Full bar. **Reservations:** suggested. **Hours:** 11:30 am-2:30 & 5:30-9:30 pm, Sat from 12:30 pm. Closed: 12/25; also Sun. **Address:** 1550 Versatile Dr V1S 1X4 **Location:** Trans-Canada Hwy 1, exit 367 (Pacific Way); adjacent to Holiday Inn Express. **Parking:** on-site. **Cards:** AX, MC, VI.

VITTORIO'S ITALIAN RESTAURANT   **Phone: 250/851-2112**

Italian
$17-$30

"Come hungry, leave full!" is the motto of the family-friendly restaurant. Portions are huge, and the staff often sends diners on their way with doggie bags. Pizza dough is made from scratch, and the entree selection lists all the Italian favorites. Casual dress. **Bar:** Full bar. **Reservations:** suggested. **Hours:** 5 pm-10 pm. Closed: 1/1, 12/25. **Address:** 1820 Rogers Pl V1S 1T7 **Location:** Trans-Canada Hwy 1, exit 368 (Hillside Ave), just w; in Comfort Inn & Suites. **Parking:** on-site. **Cards:** AX, MC, VI.

KELOWNA —*See Okanagan Valley p. 526.*

KIMBERLEY pop. 6,139

———— WHERE TO STAY ————

INNWEST KIRKWOOD INN   **Phone: 250/427-7616**

Condominium
Rates not provided

Address: 880 North Star Dr V1A 2Y6 **Location:** From Gerry Sorensen Way, follow signs. **Facility:** 55 units. 7 one-bedroom standard units. 24 one- and 24 two-bedroom suites with kitchens, some with whirlpools. 2 stories (no elevator), exterior corridors. **Parking:** on-site. **Terms:** check-in 4 pm. **Amenities:** video library (fee), voice mail. *Some:* irons, hair dryers. **Pool(s):** heated outdoor. **Leisure Activities:** sauna, whirlpool, downhill & cross country skiing. **Guest Services:** coin laundry. **Business Services:** PC.

TRICKLE CREEK RESIDENCE INN BY MARRIOTT

Book great rates at AAA.com

Phone: 250/427-5175

Small-scale Hotel
$115-$135 All Year

Address: 500 Stemwinder Dr V1A 2Y6 **Location:** From Gerry Sorensen Way, follow signs. **Facility:** Smoke free premises. 80 units. 19 one-bedroom standard units with kitchens. 41 one- and 20 two-bedroom suites with kitchens. 3 stories, interior corridors. *Bath:* combo or shower only. **Parking:** on-site. **Terms:** check-in 4 pm. **Amenities:** high-speed Internet, dual phone lines, voice mail, irons, hair dryers. **Pool(s):** heated outdoor. **Leisure Activities:** whirlpools, downhill skiing, hiking trails, exercise room. *Fee:* golf-18 holes. **Guest Services:** valet and coin laundry. **Business Services:** meeting rooms, PC (fee). **Cards:** AX, DC, DS, MC, VI. **Free Special Amenities:** full breakfast and high-speed Internet.

AAA Benefit:
Members save 5% off of the best available rate.

––––––––– **WHERE TO DINE** –––––––––

KELSEY'S

Canadian
$7-$21

Phone: 250/427-1600

A fun, relaxed atmosphere and tasty menu of casual fare make the restaurant a popular favorite with locals. Diners might start a meal with some tempting appetizers, such as wings, loaded potato skins or nachos, and follow them with an old-time favorite, such as a burger, wrap, pizza or pasta dish. For a heartier meal, it's hard to beat pork back ribs or a steak. The diverse menu has broad appeal. Casual dress. **Bar:** Full bar. **Hours:** 11 am-midnight, Sun-11 pm. **Address:** 101-500 Stemwinder Dr V1A 2Y6 **Location:** Downtown. **Parking:** on-site. **Cards:** AX, MC, VI.

LANGLEY —*See Vancouver p. 616.*

LOGAN LAKE pop. 2,162

––––––––– **WHERE TO STAY** –––––––––

LOGAN LAKE LODGE

Motel
$70-$99 All Year

Phone: (250)523-9466

Address: 111 Chartrand Ave V0K 1W0 **Location:** At Meadow Creek Rd and Chartrand Cresent; centre. **Facility:** 21 one-bedroom standard units. 2 stories (no elevator), interior corridors. **Parking:** on-site, winter plug-ins. **Terms:** office hours 8 am-11 pm, 7 day cancellation notice. **Guest Services:** wireless Internet. **Business Services:** meeting rooms. **Cards:** AX, MC, VI.

LUND pop. 243

––––––––– **WHERE TO STAY** –––––––––

THE HISTORIC LUND HOTEL

Historic
Small-scale Hotel
$135-$250 3/1-9/30
$95-$165 10/1-2/28

Phone: (604)414-0474

Address: 1436 Hwy 101 V0N 2G0 **Location:** End of Hwy 101; on Sunshine Coast (Hwy 101). **Facility:** Simple and comfortable guest rooms offer cozy accommodations; for a more upscale unit, inquire about the newer suites. Smoke free premises. 27 one-bedroom standard units. 2 stories (no elevator), interior/exterior corridors. **Parking:** on-site. **Terms:** office hours 7 am-10 pm, 3 day cancellation notice. **Amenities:** video library, DVD players, voice mail, hair dryers. **Dining:** The Lund Hotel Restaurant, see separate listing. **Leisure Activities:** whirlpool. *Fee:* tours of Desolation Sound. **Guest Services:** coin laundry. **Business Services:** meeting rooms. **Cards:** AX, MC, VI.

––––––––– **WHERE TO DINE** –––––––––

THE LUND HOTEL RESTAURANT

Canadian
$8-$22

Phone: 604/414-0474

In the historic Lund Hotel—the gateway to Desolation Sound, an up-and-coming kayak and boating area on the Sunshine Coast—the restaurant presents a menu of fresh, creatively presented local seafood. Views of the water and distant mountains are breathtaking. Casual dress. **Bar:** Full bar. **Hours:** 11:30 am-10 pm; to 8 pm 10/1-4/30. Closed: 1/1, 12/25, 12/26. **Location:** End of Hwy 101; on Sunshine Coast (Hwy 101); in The Historic Lund Hotel. **Parking:** on-site. **Cards:** AX, DC, MC, VI.

MADEIRA PARK

––––––––– **WHERE TO STAY** –––––––––

SUNSHINE COAST RESORT & MARINA

Vacation Rental Condominium
$150-$495 3/1-9/21
$95-$295 9/22-2/28

Phone: 604/883-9177

Address: 12695 Sunshine Coast (Hwy 101) V0N 2H0 **Location:** Just n of Madeira Park Rd, follow signs. **Facility:** New condo units plus the original four self-contained cottage-style rooms all overlook the deep-water marina and surrounding mountains. Smoke free premises. 17 units. 3 one-bedroom standard units. 9 one- and 1 two-bedroom suites with kitchens, some with whirlpools. 4 cottages with whirlpools. 3 stories, interior/exterior corridors. *Bath:* combo or shower only. **Parking:** on-site. **Terms:** office hours 8 am-midnight, 2 night minimum stay - seasonal and/or weekends, 21 day cancellation notice. **Amenities:** video library, DVD players, high-speed Internet, voice mail, irons, hair dryers. **Leisure Activities:** whirlpool, rental boats, rental canoes, fishing. *Fee:* marina, charter fishing. **Guest Services:** coin laundry, wireless Internet. **Cards:** AX, MC, VI.

MALAHAT —*See Victoria p. 664.*

MANNING PARK

———— WHERE TO STAY ————

MANNING PARK RESORT

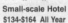

Small-scale Hotel
$134-$164 All Year

Phone: 250/840-8822

Address: 7500 Hwy 3 V0X 1R0 **Location:** Crowsnest Hwy 3; between Hope and Princeton. **Facility:** Smoke free premises. 73 units. 49 one-bedroom standard units. 24 cabins. 2 stories (no elevator), interior/exterior corridors. **Parking:** on-site. **Terms:** check-in 4 pm, 14 day cancellation notice. **Amenities:** video library (fee). *Some:* voice mail, hair dryers. **Pool(s):** heated indoor. **Leisure Activities:** sauna, whirlpools, steamroom, rental canoes, 2 lighted tennis courts, cross country skiing, ice skating, rental bicycles, playground, exercise room. *Fee:* ski rentals & instruction, game room. **Guest Services:** coin laundry. **Business Services:** meeting rooms. **Cards:** AX, MC, VI. **Free Special Amenities:** early check-in/late check-out and room upgrade (subject to availability with advance reservations).

🍴 🍸 🏊 ✂ ✕ 🐾 🎥 🛏 🖥 💻 / SOME UNITS FEE 🐕 FEE VCR ☎

MAPLE RIDGE —*See Vancouver p. 619.*

MCBRIDE pop. 660

———— WHERE TO STAY ————

NORTH COUNTRY LODGE

Motel
Rates not provided

Phone: 250/569-0001

Address: 868 Frontage Rd N V0J 2E0 **Location:** Just w of village main exit, on Hwy 16 north service road. **Facility:** 48 units. 44 one-bedroom standard units, some with efficiencies. 4 two-bedroom suites with efficiencies. 2 stories (no elevator), exterior corridors. **Parking:** on-site, winter plug-ins. **Terms:** office hours 7:30 am-11 pm. **Amenities:** hair dryers. **Leisure Activities:** whirlpool, limited exercise equipment. **Guest Services:** wireless Internet. **Business Services:** PC. **Free Special Amenities:** local telephone calls and high-speed Internet.

🍴 🍸 🎥 🛏 / SOME UNITS FEE 🐕 ✕ 💻

MERRITT pop. 6,998

———— WHERE TO STAY ————

BEST WESTERN NICOLA INN   *Book great rates at AAA.com*

Small-scale Hotel
$79-$179 All Year

Phone: 250/378-4253

Address: 4025 Walters St V1K 1K1 **Location:** Hwy 5, exit 290, 0.6 mi (1 km) w. **Facility:** 56 units. 52 one-bedroom standard units. 4 one-bedroom suites. 2 stories (no elevator), exterior corridors. **Parking:** on-site, winter plug-ins. **Amenities:** high-speed Internet, irons, hair dryers. **Pool(s):** heated indoor. **Leisure Activities:** whirlpool, limited exercise equipment. **Guest Services:** coin laundry. **Business Services:** meeting rooms, PC. **Cards:** AX, DC, DS, MC, VI. **Free Special Amenities:** preferred room (subject to availability with advance reservations) and high-speed Internet.

AAA Benefit:
Members save 10% everyday, plus an exclusive frequent stay program.

[S] 🍴 🏊 🛏 🖥 💻 / SOME UNITS FEE 🐕 ✕

SUPER 8 MOTEL   *Book at AAA.com*

Motel
$130 3/1-9/30
$95 10/1-2/28

Phone: 250/378-9422

Address: 3561 Voght St V1K 1C5 **Location:** Hwy 5, exit 290, just w. **Facility:** 35 one-bedroom standard units, some with efficiencies or kitchens. 2 stories (no elevator), exterior corridors. **Parking:** on-site. **Terms:** office hours 6 am-11 pm. **Amenities:** hair dryers. **Pool(s):** heated indoor. **Leisure Activities:** whirlpool. **Guest Services:** wireless Internet. **Cards:** DS, MC, VI.

ASK [S] 🍴 🏊 🛏 💻 / SOME UNITS FEE 🐕 ✕ 🖥

MISSION —*See Vancouver p. 620.*

NAKUSP pop. 1,524

———— WHERE TO STAY ————

THE SELKIRK INN

Small-scale Hotel
$52-$90 All Year

Phone: 250/265-3666

Address: 210 W 6th Ave V0G 1R0 **Location:** Centre. **Facility:** 39 one-bedroom standard units, some with efficiencies (utensils extra charge). 2 stories (no elevator), interior corridors. *Bath:* combo or shower only. **Parking:** on-site. **Terms:** office hours 7 am-11 pm. **Leisure Activities:** sauna. **Guest Services:** wireless Internet. **Business Services:** meeting rooms. **Cards:** AX, MC, VI.

NANAIMO pop. 78,692

—— **WHERE TO STAY** ——

BEST WESTERN DORCHESTER HOTEL   *Book great rates at AAA.com*   Phone: (250)754-6835

Small-scale Hotel
$135-$200 All Year

Address: 70 Church St V9R 5H4 **Location:** Island Hwy 19A to Comox Rd; downtown. **Facility:** Smoke free premises. 70 one-bedroom standard units. 4 stories, interior corridors. **Parking:** on-site. **Terms:** 30 day cancellation notice. **Amenities:** voice mail, safes, irons, hair dryers. *Some:* high-speed Internet. **Guest Services:** valet laundry, wireless Internet. **Business Services:** meeting rooms, PC (fee). **Cards:** AX, JC, MC, VI. **Free Special Amenities:** local telephone calls and high-speed Internet. *(See color ad below)*

AAA Benefit:
Members save 10% everyday, plus an exclusive frequent stay program.

     / SOME UNITS FEE

▼ *See AAA listing above* ▼

Nestled on the Inner Harbour in Downtown NANAIMO

- ◆ 70 guestrooms and suites with Harbour and City views
- ◆ Award winning Deep Blue Restaurant
- ◆ Only steps away from the Seawall, Old City Quarter, Nanaimo District Museum and the Great Canadian Casino
- ◆ 5 minutes from Departure Bay Ferry Terminal
- ◆ Complimentary High-speed Internet access
- ◆ 100% non-smoking ◆ Pet friendly rooms available

Call Toll Free: 1-800-661-2449 U.S. and Canada

Best Western Dorchester Hotel
70 Church Street, Nanaimo
Tel: (250) 754-6835 ◆ www.dorchesternanaimo.com

Approved

▼ *See AAA listing p 520* ▼

LOCATED BESIDE VANCOUVER ISLAND'S LARGEST SHOPPING MALL

- ◆ Newly Renovated Guestrooms
- ◆ Microwave and Fridge in all rooms
- ◆ Free Wireless Internet Access
- ◆ Restaurant, Pub & Meeting Rooms
- ◆ In Room Safe and Coffee Maker
- ◆ Complimentary bottle water
- ◆ Free Parking

Best Western Northgate Inn
6450 Metral Drive, Nanaimo, BC V9T 2L8 ● bestwesternnorthgate.com
Toll Free: 1-800-661-0061 U.S. and Canada
Each Best Western hotel is independently onwed and operated

THE WORLD'S LARGEST HOTEL CHAIN®

BEST WESTERN NORTHGATE INN

Small-scale Hotel
$112-$190 3/1-9/30
$102-$170 10/1-2/28

Book great rates at AAA.com

Phone: (250)390-2222

Address: 6450 Metral Dr V9T 2L8 **Location:** Hwy 19A (Island Hwy), just w on Aulds Rd, then just s. **Facility:** Smoke free premises. 72 one-bedroom standard units, some with efficiencies and/or whirlpools. 3 stories, interior corridors. **Parking:** on-site. **Terms:** cancellation fee imposed. **Amenities:** voice mail, safes, irons, hair dryers. **Leisure Activities:** sauna, whirlpool, limited exercise equipment. **Business Services:** meeting rooms, PC. **Cards:** AX, DS, JC, MC, VI. **Free Special Amenities:** preferred room (subject to availability with advance reservations). *(See color ad p 519)*

AAA Benefit:
Members save 10% everyday, plus an exclusive frequent stay program.

 / SOME UNITS FEE

BUCCANEER INN

Motel
$70-$199 All Year

Phone: 250/753-1246

Address: 1577 Stewart Ave V9S 4E3 **Location:** 1 mi (1.5 km) e; just before the ferry terminal. **Facility:** Smoke free premises. 13 units. 2 one-bedroom standard units. 11 one-bedroom suites with kitchens. 2 stories (no elevator), exterior corridors. *Bath:* combo or shower only. **Parking:** on-site. **Terms:** office hours 8:30 am-9 pm, 7 day cancellation notice-fee imposed. **Amenities:** irons, hair dryers. **Guest Services:** coin laundry, wireless Internet. **Cards:** MC, VI. **Free Special Amenities:** local telephone calls and high-speed Internet.

   / SOME UNITS

DAYS INN NANAIMO HARBOURVIEW

Small-scale Hotel
$139-$149 3/1-9/30
$114-$129 10/1-2/28

Book great rates at AAA.com

Phone: (250)754-8171

Address: 809 Island Hwy S V9R 5K1 **Location:** On Island Hwy 1, 1.3 mi (2 km) s. **Facility:** 79 one-bedroom standard units, some with efficiencies. 2 stories (no elevator), interior corridors. **Parking:** on-site. **Amenities:** hair dryers. *Some:* high-speed Internet, irons. **Pool(s):** heated indoor. **Leisure Activities:** whirlpool. **Guest Services:** valet and coin laundry, wireless Internet. **Business Services:** meeting rooms. **Cards:** AX, DC, DS, MC, VI.

 / SOME UNITS FEE

THE GRAND HOTEL NANAIMO *Book at AAA.com·*   Phone: 250/758-3000

Small-scale Hotel
$149-$350 All Year

Address: 4898 Rutherford Rd V9T 4Z4 **Location:** 3.8 mi (6 km) n on Hwy 19A (Island Hwy) from Departure Bay ferry terminal, then just e. **Facility:** Smoke free premises. 72 one-bedroom standard units, some with whirlpools. 4 stories, interior corridors. **Parking:** on-site. **Terms:** cancellation fee imposed. **Amenities:** high-speed Internet, voice mail, irons, hair dryers. **Pool(s):** heated indoor. **Leisure Activities:** limited exercise equipment. **Guest Services:** valet laundry. **Business Services:** meeting rooms, PC (fee). **Cards:** AX, VI.

INN ON LONG LAKE   *Book great rates at AAA.com*   Phone: (250)758-1144

Small-scale Hotel
$109-$189 All Year

Address: 4700 Island Hwy N V9T 1W6 **Location:** 3.1 mi (5 km) n on Hwy 19A (Island Hwy) from Departure Bay ferry terminal. **Facility:** 62 one-bedroom standard units, some with efficiencies, kitchens and/or whirlpools. 3 stories, exterior corridors. **Parking:** on-site. **Amenities:** high-speed Internet, voice mail, irons, hair dryers. **Leisure Activities:** sauna, whirlpool, rental canoes, rental paddleboats, boat dock, limited exercise equipment, horseshoes, volleyball. **Guest Services:** valet and coin laundry, wireless Internet. **Business Services:** meeting rooms, PC (fee). **Cards:** AX, CB, DC, DS, JC, MC, VI. **Free Special Amenities: continental breakfast and newspaper.**
(See color ad below)

TRAVELODGE NANAIMO   *Book great rates at AAA.com*   Phone: (250)754-6355

Motel
$133-$146 3/1-9/30
$120-$133 10/1-2/28

Address: 96 Terminal Ave N V9S 4J2 **Location:** Jct Terminal Ave and Island Hwy 19A. **Facility:** 78 one-bedroom standard units, some with efficiencies. 3 stories, interior corridors. **Parking:** on-site. **Amenities:** *Some:* high-speed Internet, hair dryers. **Leisure Activities:** sauna. **Guest Services:** valet and coin laundry, wireless Internet. **Business Services:** meeting rooms. **Cards:** AX, DC, MC, VI. **Free Special Amenities: continental breakfast and local telephone calls.** *(See color ad below)*

——— WHERE TO DINE ———

BLUE GINGER SUSHI BAR & SATAY GRILL
Phone: 250/751-8238

★★ ★★
Japanese
$6-$20

The restaurant represents an interesting idea: combining three Asian tastes—Japanese, Chinese and Thailand—on a single menu. Dishes reflect a melange of flavors and are a fun twist on the typical Asian dining experience. Casual dress. **Bar:** Full bar. **Hours:** 11:30 am-10 pm, Fri-11 pm, Sun noon-10 pm. Closed: 12/25. **Address:** 5769 Turner Rd, Unit 1 V9T 6L8 **Location:** Hwy 19A (Island Hwy), at Turner Rd; in Longwood Station. **Parking:** on-site. **Cards:** AX, MC, VI.

CACTUS CLUB CAFE
Phone: 250/729-0011

★★ ★★
Canadian
$9-$29

This bustling, casual restaurant serves huge burgers, sandwiches, pasta, salads, soups, quesadillas, fajitas, vegetarian dishes, steak, ribs, chicken and fish. Featured are certified Angus beef and fresh wild British Columbia salmon. The thick and creamy milk shakes come highly recommended. Casual dress. **Bar:** Full bar. **Hours:** 11 am-midnight, Fri & Sat-1 am. Closed: 12/25. **Address:** 801, 5800 Turner Rd V9T 6J4 **Location:** From Hwy 19A (Island Hwy) N, just e before Uplands Dr. **Parking:** on-site. **Cards:** AX, MC, VI.

DRIFT
Phone: 250/753-7438

★★★
Pacific Rim
$10-$29

Casual dress. **Bar:** Full bar. **Reservations:** suggested. **Hours:** 11:30 am-3 & 5-10 pm, Sat & Sun from 5 pm. Closed: 1/1, 12/25, 12/26. **Address:** 77 Skinner St V9R 5G9 **Location:** Island Hwy 19A, just e on Comox Rd, then just s on Chapel St. **Parking:** on-site. **Cards:** AX, JC, MC, VI.

EARLS
Phone: 250/756-4100

★★ ★★
Canadian
$9-$25

Offering an experience that falls between fast food and fine dining, the fun, relaxed restaurant prepares great food at a great price. Choices range from juicy burgers, hearty sandwiches, fresh salads, wings and pizza to full entrees of steak, chops and seafood. Made-from-scratch soups and assorted breads, as well as a nice choice of wines and beers, round out the offerings. This is a fitting spot for impromptu get-togethers and festive occasions. Casual dress. **Bar:** Full bar. **Hours:** 11 am-11 pm, Fri & Sat-midnight, Sun 10:30 am-10 pm. Closed: 12/25. **Address:** 100-2980 N Island Hwy V9T 5V4 **Location:** 2.5 mi (4 km) n on Hwy 19A (Island Hwy) from Departure Bay ferry terminal. **Parking:** on-site. **Cards:** AX, DC, MC, VI.

GINA'S A MEXICAN CAFE
Phone: 250/753-5411

★
Mexican
$8-$15

One of the busiest restaurants in downtown Nanaimo, Gina's has been serving Mexican food to hungry diners for more than 20 years in one of the gaudiest houses you'll ever see! Lines out the door are not uncommon, and the cramped interior and tacky Mexican decor add to its popularity. Nothing on the menu is more than $16, and portions are large so you won't go away hungry. Park at the street meters or in the nearby pay lot. Casual dress. **Bar:** Full bar. **Hours:** 11 am-9 pm, Fri-10 pm, Sat noon-10 pm, Sun noon-8 pm. Closed: 12/25, 12/26. **Address:** 47 Skinner St V9T 3C2 **Location:** Island Hwy 19A, just e on Comox Rd, then just s on Chapel St. **Parking:** street. **Cards:** AX, MC, VI.

🅜

KELSEY'S
Phone: 250/729-8882

★★ ★★
Canadian
$7-$21

A fun, relaxed atmosphere and tasty menu of casual fare make the restaurant a popular favorite with locals. Diners might start a meal with some tempting appetizers, such as wings, loaded potato skins or nachos, and follow them with an old-time favorite, such as a burger, wrap, pizza or pasta dish. For a heartier meal, it's hard to beat pork back ribs or a steak. The diverse menu has broad appeal. Casual dress. **Bar:** Full bar. **Hours:** 10:30 am-10 pm, Fri & Sat-midnight, Sun-11 pm. **Address:** 4711 Rutherford Rd V9T 4K6 **Location:** In Rutherford Mall. **Parking:** on-site. **Cards:** AX, DC, MC, VI.

LONGWOOD BREWPUB
Phone: 250/729-8225

★★ ★★
Canadian
$9-$27

Families are welcomed in the restaurant section, but the pub, which offers all the amenities of the restaurant, is strictly for adults. Patrons can sample hand-crafted lagers and ales, as well as hearty pub food, such as sandwiches, burgers, pastas and varied dinner entrees. Casual dress. **Bar:** Full bar. **Hours:** 11 am-11 pm, Sun 10 am-10 pm. Closed: 1/1, 12/25. **Address:** 5775 Turner Rd V9T 6L8 **Location:** Hwy 19A (Island Hwy) at Turner Rd; in Longwood Station. **Parking:** on-site. **Cards:** AX, DC, MC, VI.

MONTANA'S COOKHOUSE
Phone: 250/758-2388

★★ ★★
Steak House
$7-$25

Pine boards, exposed beams, a fireplace and Western gear displayed about the dining room give the feeling of a back-country setting. The menu lists hearty portions of comfort fare, such as Yankee pot roast. While the focus is on steaks, ribs and chicken, some seafood entrees also are among offerings. Service is efficient and friendly. Casual dress. **Bar:** Full bar. **Hours:** 11 am-11 pm, Fri & Sat-midnight. **Address:** 4715 Rutherford Rd V9T 5S5 **Location:** From Island Hwy 19A (Island Hwy), just e; in Rutherford Mall. **Parking:** on-site. **Cards:** AX, MC, VI.

MOXIE'S CLASSIC GRILL
Phone: 250/390-1079

★★ ★★
Canadian
$8-$18

This sleek, funky and popular restaurant presents an extensive menu of creatively prepared dishes, including pizza, pasta, rice, noodles, signature salads and burgers. Other menus include one for children and one for Sunday brunch. Lending to the upbeat, stylish decor are dark wood appointments and river rock fireplaces. Casual dress. **Bar:** Full bar. **Hours:** 11 am-11 pm, Fri & Sat-midnight. **Address:** 6750 Island Hwy N, #102 V9V 1S3 **Location:** Island Hwy 19A (Island Hwy); in Nored Plaza. **Parking:** on-site. **Cards:** AX, MC, VI.

RICKY'S ALL DAY GRILL
Phone: 250/390-1227

★★ ★★
Canadian
$6-$15

The comfortable eatery, which employs friendly servers, presents a varied menu that includes pasta dishes, wraps, omelets, stir-fry preparations and burgers. Portions are generous. Children's and senior selections are offered. Guests can request seating in a booth or at a table. Casual dress. **Bar:** Full bar. **Hours:** 6:30 am-9 pm. **Address:** 6550 Island Hwy N V9V 1K8 **Location:** Corner of Island Hwy 19A (Island Hwy) and Hammond Bay Rd. **Parking:** on-site. **Cards:** AX, MC, VI.

SMITTY'S FAMILY RESTAURANT
Phone: 250/716-8887

★★ ★★
Canadian
$6-$18

The family-oriented restaurant satisfies patrons with its ever-popular all-day breakfast items, as well as tasty and wholesome soups and salads at lunchtime. A relaxed mood characterizes the dining space. Casual dress. **Bar:** Full bar. **Hours:** 6:30 am-9 pm. Closed: 12/25. **Address:** 50 10th St V9R 6L1 **Location:** Just w from Hwy 19A (Island Hwy S). **Parking:** on-site. **Cards:** AX, MC, VI.

SWISS CHALET

Canadian
$6-$18

Phone: 250/729-7120

The popular restaurant is known for its rotisserie chicken and ribs and the tangy Chalet sauce that gives food its special zip. Diners munch on a half or quarter chicken with sides such as steamed vegetables, fries, baked potatoes and salads. Lunch guests often go for the great soup and sandwich combination. Take-out and delivery service are popular options. Casual dress. **Bar:** Full bar. **Hours:** 11 am-10 pm, Fri & Sat-11 pm. Closed: 12/25. **Address:** 3290 N Island Hwy V9T 1W1 **Location:** Hwy 19A (Island Hwy) at Bowen Rd. **Parking:** on-site. **Cards:** AX, MC, VI.

ZOUGLA

Mediterranean
$8-$30

Phone: 250/716-3233

You'll enjoy this restaurant's offerings of steak, seafood and Mediterranean specialties such as moussaka, spanakopita and souvlakia. Floor-to-ceiling windows offer a great view of the ocean and mountains. Couples and travellers like the relaxing ambience. Casual dress. **Bar:** Full bar. **Hours:** 11 am-10 pm, Fri & Sat-11 pm, Sun 4 pm-10 pm. Closed: 12/25, 12/26. **Address:** 2021 Estevan Rd V9S 3Y9 **Location:** Hwy 19A (Island Hwy) and Brechin Rd, on road to Departure Bay ferry terminal. **Parking:** on-site. **Cards:** AX, MC, VI.

NANOOSE BAY pop. 5,246

——— WHERE TO DINE ———

THE LANDING WEST COAST GRILL

Pacific Rim
$10-$35

Phone: 250/468-2400

Two large, 6,000-gallon saltwater aquariums dominate this restaurant, and each is stocked with local salmon, crab, sea urchins, herring, perch and abalone. The menu focuses on local ingredients with West Coast and Mediterranean influences. Casual dress. **Bar:** Full bar. **Reservations:** suggested. **Hours:** 11 am-10 pm, Sat & Sun from 10 am. **Address:** 1-1600 Stroulger Rd V9P 9B7 **Location:** Hwy 19, exit 46 (Parksville), 0.5 mi (0.8 km) n on Old Island Hwy (19A), just e on Franklin's Gull Rd, 1.5 mi (2.4 km) s on Northwest Bay Rd, then just e on Beaver Creek Wharf Rd; in Pacific Shores Resort & Spa. **Parking:** on-site. **Cards:** MC, VI.

NARAMATA —See Okanagan Valley p. 534.

NELSON pop. 9,298

——— WHERE TO STAY ———

BEST WESTERN BAKER STREET INN & CONVENTION CENTRE
Book great rates at AAA.com

Small-scale Hotel
$109-$259 All Year

Phone: (250)352-3525

Address: 153 Baker St V1L 4H1 **Location:** Jct Hwy 6 and 3A. **Facility:** 70 units. 69 one-bedroom standard units, some with whirlpools. 1 one-bedroom suite. 4 stories, interior corridors. **Parking:** on-site. **Terms:** check-in 4 pm. **Amenities:** high-speed Internet, voice mail, irons, hair dryers. **Leisure Activities:** whirlpool, exercise room. **Guest Services:** valet and coin laundry, area transportation (fee)-ski hill. **Business Services:** meeting rooms, PC. **Cards:** AX, DC, DS, MC, VI. **Free Special Amenities:** newspaper and high-speed Internet.

AAA Benefit:
Members save 10% everyday, plus an exclusive frequent stay program.

NORTH SHORE INN

Motel
$62-$85 All Year

Phone: (250)352-6606

Address: 687 Hwy 3A V1L 5P7 **Location:** 1.9 mi (3 km) n on Hwy 3A via Nelson Bridge. **Facility:** 30 units. 29 one-bedroom standard units, some with kitchens. 1 one-bedroom suite. 3 stories (no elevator), interior/exterior corridors. **Parking:** on-site. **Terms:** office hours 7:30 am-11 pm. **Leisure Activities:** whirlpool. **Business Services:** meeting rooms, PC (fee). **Cards:** AX, MC, VI.

——— WHERE TO DINE ———

ALL SEASONS CAFE

Canadian
$17-$28

Phone: 250/352-0101

True to its name, this funky restaurant features a regional and seasonal menu, incorporating the best of the area and time of year in terms of ingredients. Everything is made from scratch, and the dishes are quite beautiful. Located in a small house-like setting a block away from downtown, this is a true gem in the heart of Nelson. You can eat in the dimly lit romantic dining room or in the glass-enclosed veranda, with a view of the rock garden. Casual dress. **Bar:** Full bar. **Reservations:** suggested. **Hours:** 5 pm-10 pm. Closed: 12/25. **Address:** 620 Herridge Ln V1L 6A7 **Location:** Just e of Baker St; between Josephine and Hall sts. **Parking:** street. **Cards:** MC, VI.

MAZATLAN MEXICAN RESTAURANT

Mexican
$6-$12

Phone: 250/352-1388

Upbeat and funky describes the decor at the homey, family-run restaurant. Delicious dishes—including black bean soup, chimichangas, burritos and enchiladas—come from the Mazatlan area of Mexico. Portions are huge. The festive eatery is popular with longtime town residents. **Bar:** Full bar. **Hours:** 11 am-10 pm, Fri & Sat-11 pm. Closed: 12/25; also Mon. **Address:** 198 Baker St V1L 4H2 **Location:** Downtown; next to Savoy Hotel. **Parking:** street. **Cards:** AX, MC, VI.

RED FISH GRILL

International
$6-$19

Phone: 250/352-3456

Behind windows that overlook the town's main street, this deceptively large and eclectic restaurant has developed a reputation for itself. This place often touted as one of the more creative restaurants in town has a kitchen unafraid of taking chances in creating new interpretations of almost any global dish. The varied menu features a little bit of everything from all four corners of the world and uses fresh, local and homemade ingredients. Casual dress. **Bar:** Full bar. **Reservations:** not accepted. **Hours:** 8 am-8 pm, Fri & Sat-9 pm. Closed major holidays. **Address:** 479 Baker St V1L 4H7 **Location:** Jct Ward St; downtown. **Parking:** street. **Cards:** MC, VI.

THOR'S PIZZA

Pizza
$7-$25

Phone: 250/352-1212

Named after the owner's dog, the eatery uses the freshest quality ingredients and Italian-style bread crust. Surely the pooch has impeccable taste in pizza, what with a certified chef de cuisine in front of the oven. Most ingredients in the fabulous pizzas are sourced locally or made in house, so there is no wonder why customers line up out the door on weekends. Casual dress. **Reservations:** not accepted. **Hours:** 11 am-10 pm, Fri & Sat-midnight, Sun 4 pm-9 pm. Closed major holidays. **Address:** 303 Victoria St V1L 4H6 **Location:** Jct Kootenay St; downtown. **Parking:** street. **Cards:** MC, VI.

NEW DENVER pop. 512

——— WHERE TO STAY ———

SWEET DREAMS GUESTHOUSE

Country Inn
Rates not provided

Phone: 250/358-2415

Address: 702 Eldorado St V0G 1S0 **Location:** Just w of Hwy 6 on Slocan Ave. Located across the street from lake. **Facility:** Smoke free premises. 5 one-bedroom standard units. 2 stories (no elevator), interior corridors. **Bath:** some shared or private, shower only. **Parking:** on-site. **Terms:** check-in 5 pm. **Leisure Activities:** hiking trails.

NEW WESTMINSTER —See Vancouver p. 620.

NORTH VANCOUVER —See Vancouver p. 620.

OAK BAY —See Victoria p. 664.

Destination Okanagan Valley

The Okanagan Valley is a year-round recreation destination. Whether your pleasure is boating, biking, camping, fishing, golf, hiking or skiing, you'll find plenty of opportunities for outdoor pursuits.

The valley's cities offer all sorts of diversions for visitors, from museums to theater to casinos. Stroll around a farmers market or head out to one of the local wineries.

Okanagan Valley

Enderby
97A
Armstrong

97

Vernon
6

Okanagan Lake
97

Kelowna

Westbank

97

Summerland   Naramata

Penticton
33

3

3A

Oliver
3A
97
Osoyoos
3

CANADA

UNITED STATES

BRITISH COLUMBIA

WASHINGTON

Downtown Kelowna.
Kelowna, which boasts a scenic setting amid lush farmland and orchards on the eastern shore of Okanagan Lake, has several lovely waterfront parks.

A study in green and blue.
This scene near Osoyoos exemplifies what you'll see in the Okanagan Valley—the rich green of vineyards and fruit orchards set against the backdrop of a sparkling blue lake.

Places included in this AAA Destination Area:

© AAA / Ron Willis

© AAA / Ron Willis

Okanagan Valley

ARMSTRONG pop. 4,241

———— WHERE TO DINE ————

VILLAGE CHEESE COMPANY   **Phone:** 250/546-8651

Deli/Subs
Sandwiches
$5-$7

Casual dress. **Hours:** 8 am-5 pm, Sun from 10 am; seasonal hours vary. Closed major holidays. **Address:** 3475 Smith Dr V0E 1B0 **Location:** Centre. **Parking:** on-site. **Cards:** AX, MC, VI.

ENDERBY pop. 2,828

———— WHERE TO STAY ————

HOWARD JOHNSON INN FORTUNES LANDING   *Book great rates at AAA.com*   **Phone:** 250/838-6825

Motel
$109 3/1-9/16
$79 9/17-2/28

Address: 1510 George St V0E 1V0 **Location:** 0.6 mi (1 km) n on Hwy 974. **Facility:** 32 units. 31 one-bedroom standard units. 1 two-bedroom suite with kitchen. 2 stories (no elevator), exterior corridors. **Parking:** on-site. **Pool(s):** heated outdoor. **Leisure Activities:** whirlpool. **Business Services:** meeting rooms. **Cards:** AX, MC, VI. **Free Special Amenities:** local telephone calls and high-speed Internet.

KELOWNA pop. 106,707

———— WHERE TO STAY ————

ACCENT INNS   *Book great rates at AAA.com*   **Phone:** (250)862-8888

Small-scale Hotel
$99-$179 All Year

Address: 1140 Harvey Ave V1Y 6E7 **Location:** Corner of Hwy 97 N (Harvey Ave) and Gordon Dr. Located across from a shopping mall. **Facility:** 102 units. 89 one-bedroom standard units, some with efficiencies. 13 one-bedroom suites, some with efficiencies. 3 stories, exterior corridors. **Parking:** on-site, winter plug-ins. **Terms:** check-in 4 pm. **Amenities:** video games (fee), voice mail, hair dryers. *Some:* dual phone lines, irons. **Pool(s):** heated outdoor. **Leisure Activities:** sauna, whirlpool, limited exercise equipment. **Guest Services:** valet and coin laundry, wireless Internet. **Business Services:** meeting rooms, PC. **Cards:** AX, CB, DC, DS, MC, VI. **Free Special Amenities:** newspaper and high-speed Internet. *(See color ad p 639)*

A VISTA VILLA BED, BBQ & SPA   **Phone:** (250)762-7837

Bed & Breakfast
$289-$379 All Year

Address: 962 Ryder Dr V1Y 7T5 **Location:** Hwy 97 (Harvey Ave), 1.6 mi (2 km) n on Spall St to Summit Rd, just e to Valley Rd, follow Valley Rd (which becomes Ryder Dr). Located in a residential area. **Facility:** Though classified as a B&B, this is a decadent Bed & BBQ; a continental breakfast is in your room, and a BBQ dinner is served nightly on the deck. Designated smoking area. 4 one-bedroom standard units with whirlpools. 2 stories (no elevator), interior/exterior corridors. **Parking:** on-site, winter plug-ins. **Terms:** office hours 4 pm-8 pm, check-in 4 pm, 3 night minimum stay - seasonal, age restrictions may apply, 21 day cancellation notice-fee imposed. **Amenities:** video library, CD players, hair dryers. **Pool(s):** heated outdoor. **Leisure Activities:** limited exercise equipment, spa. **Guest Services:** complimentary laundry. **Business Services:** PC. **Cards:** AX, JC, MC, VI.

BEST WESTERN INN-KELOWNA   *Book great rates at AAA.com*   **Phone:** (250)860-1212

Small-scale Hotel
$129-$229 All Year

Address: 2402 Hwy 97 N V1X 4J1 **Location:** 0.6 mi (1 km) s of jct Hwy 33 and 97 N (Harvey Ave); corner of Leckie Rd. **Facility:** Smoke free premises. 154 units. 128 one-bedroom standard units, some with whirlpools. 26 one-bedroom suites, some with efficiencies or kitchens. 8 stories, interior/exterior corridors. *Bath:* combo or shower only. **Parking:** on-site. **Terms:** check-in 4 pm, cancellation fee imposed. **Amenities:** video games (fee), high-speed Internet, voice mail, irons, hair dryers. *Some:* honor bars. **Pool(s):** heated indoor. **Leisure Activities:** whirlpools, steamroom, exercise room, spa. **Guest Services:** valet and coin laundry. **Business Services:** conference facilities, PC (fee). **Cards:** AX, DC, DS, MC, VI. **Free Special Amenities:** expanded continental breakfast and high-speed Internet. *(See color ad p 527)*

AAA Benefit:
Members save 10% everyday, plus an exclusive frequent stay program.

COMFORT INN KELOWNA-WESTSIDE   *Book great rates at AAA.com*   Phone: 250/769-2355

Small-scale Hotel
Rates not provided

Address: 1655 Westgate Rd V1Z 3P1 **Location:** Jct Hwy 97 (Harvey Ave) and Bartley Rd, s to Ross Rd. **Facility:** 81 units. 80 one-bedroom standard units, some with kitchens and/or whirlpools. 1 one-bedroom suite with kitchen. 2 stories (no elevator), interior corridors. **Parking:** on-site. **Amenities:** irons, hair dryers. **Pool(s):** heated indoor. **Leisure Activities:** whirlpool, exercise room. **Guest Services:** valet and coin laundry, wireless Internet. **Business Services:** meeting rooms, PC (fee). **Free Special Amenities:** expanded continental breakfast and high-speed Internet.
(See color ad on insert)

🍴 🕭 📺 💻 / SOME UNITS   FEE 🐾 ✕ 📦 🖨

DAYS INN   *Book great rates at AAA.com*   Phone: (250)868-3297

Motel
$99-$174 All Year

Address: 2649 Hwy 97 N V1X 4J6 **Location:** Jct Hwy 97 (Harvey Ave) and 33, just n. **Facility:** 91 units. 68 one-bedroom standard units, some with efficiencies (utensils extra charge). 23 one-bedroom suites. 2 stories, interior/exterior corridors. *Bath:* combo or shower only. **Parking:** on-site. **Amenities:** voice mail, irons, hair dryers. **Pool(s):** heated outdoor. **Leisure Activities:** whirlpool. **Cards:** AX, MC, VI. **Free Special Amenities:** continental breakfast and room upgrade (subject to availability with advance reservations).** *(See color ad p 528)*

🆂 🍴 🕭 💻 / SOME UNITS   FEE 🐾 ✕ 📦

DILWORTH INN

Book great rates at AAA.com

Phone: (250)762-9666

CAA SAVE

Small-scale Hotel
$135-$195 All Year

Address: 1755 Dilworth Dr V1Y 8R1 **Location:** Hwy 97 N (Harvey Ave), just w. Located behind the White Spot Restaurant. **Facility:** Smoke free premises. 50 units. 48 one-bedroom standard units, some with efficiencies or kitchens. 2 one-bedroom suites with kitchens. 3 stories (no elevator), interior corridors. **Parking:** on-site. **Terms:** cancellation fee imposed. **Amenities:** voice mail, hair dryers. **Pool(s):** heated indoor. **Leisure Activities:** sauna, whirlpool, sun decks, sun decks; barbecue, limited exercise equipment. **Guest Services:** coin laundry. **Cards:** AX, MC, VI. **Free Special Amenities:** continental breakfast and high-speed Internet. *(See color ad below)*

Dilworth Inn
1-800-762-3881
1755 Dilworth Road, Kelowna, BC - Opposite Orchard Park Mall

WITMAR HOTELS - KELOWNA, BC

Recreation Inn & Suites
1-800-663-8603
1891 Parkinson Way, Kelowna, BC - Minutes from Orchard Park Mall & Downtown

▼ See AAA listing p 527 ▼

Mention this Ad to receive 15% off your stay*

*Off Published Rates. Double occupancy + 16% government taxes.

Days Inn Kelowna
2649 Highway 97 North
Kelowna, BC V1X 4J6

1-800-337-7177
250-868-3297 daysinnkelowna.com

The Best Value Under The Sun℠

7 Minutes From The Kelowna International Airport

High Speed Internet Access In Rooms

5 Minutes From Okanagan Lake

Tastefully Decorated In A Southwestern Motif

Seasonal Outdoor Pool

Year Round Hot Tub

Complimentary Deluxe Continental Breakfast

DAYS INN
The Best Value Under The Sun™

FAIRFIELD INN & SUITES BY MARRIOTT KELOWNA · *Book great rates at AAA.com* · Phone: 250/763-2800

Small-scale Hotel
Rates not provided

Address: 1655 Powick Rd V1X 4L1 **Location:** Just s of Jct Hwy 97 N and 33 W. **Facility:** Smoke free premises. 116 one-bedroom standard units. 4 stories, interior corridors. *Bath:* combo or shower only. **Parking:** on-site. **Amenities:** high-speed Internet, irons, hair dryers. **Pool(s):** heated outdoor. **Leisure Activities:** whirlpool, waterslide, limited exercise equipment. **Guest Services:** valet and coin laundry. **Business Services:** meeting rooms, PC (fee).

 CALL / SOME UNITS

AAA Benefit:
Members save 5% off of the best available rate.

THE GRAND OKANAGAN LAKEFRONT RESORT &
CONFERENCE CENTRE · *Book at AAA.com* · Phone: 250/763-4500

Resort
Large-scale Hotel
$189-$569 All Year

Address: 1310 Water St V1Y 9P3 **Location:** Hwy 97 (Harvey Ave), 0.6 mi (1 km) w along Water St. **Facility:** Featuring a spa, a casino and waterfront views, this luxurious, full-service, resort hotel has a retreat-like ambience. 391 units. 254 one-bedroom standard units, some with whirlpools. 30 one-, 101 two- and 6 three-bedroom suites with kitchens, some with whirlpools. 10 stories, interior corridors. *Bath:* combo or shower only. **Parking:** on-site (fee) and valet. **Terms:** check-in 4 pm, cancellation fee imposed. **Amenities:** video games (fee), voice mail, irons, hair dryers. *Some:* CD players, honor bars. **Dining:** Grand Bay Cafe, see separate listing. **Pool(s):** heated outdoor, heated indoor, heated indoor/outdoor. **Leisure Activities:** sauna, whirlpools, steamroom, rental boats, rental canoes, rental paddleboats, boat dock, fishing, rental bicycles, jogging, spa. *Fee:* waterskiing, game room. **Guest Services:** valet and coin laundry, wireless Internet. **Business Services:** conference facilities, business center. **Cards:** AX, DC, DS, MC, VI.

FEE   CALL / SOME UNITS FEE

THE GRAPEVINE BED & BREAKFAST · Phone: 250/860-5580

Bed & Breakfast
Rates not provided

Address: 2621 Longhill Rd V1V 2G5 **Location:** Hwy 97 N (Harvey Ave), 2.5 mi (4 km) w on Dilworth Dr, then just n. **Facility:** True to its name, the Grapevine is surrounded by vineyards and features a private garden, both of which add country charm to its near-city location. Designated smoking area. 4 one-bedroom standard units. 2 stories (no elevator), interior corridors. *Bath:* combo or shower only. **Parking:** on-site. **Terms:** check-in 4 pm, age restrictions may apply. **Amenities:** video library, hair dryers. *Some:* CD players. **Pool(s):** heated outdoor. **Leisure Activities:** whirlpool. **Guest Services:** coin laundry.

/ SOME UNITS VCR

HOLIDAY INN EXPRESS KELOWNA

Book great rates at AAA.com

Phone: (250)763-0500

Small-scale Hotel
$129-$209 3/1-10/31
$119-$149 11/1-2/28

Address: 2429 Hwy 97 N V1X 4J2 **Location:** 0.6 mi (1 km) s of jct Hwy 97 N (Harvey Ave) and 33. **Facility:** 120 one-bedroom standard units, some with whirlpools. 4 stories, interior corridors. *Bath:* combo or shower only. **Parking:** on-site. **Terms:** check-in 4 pm, 2 night minimum stay - seasonal and/or weekends, cancellation fee imposed. **Amenities:** video games (fee), high-speed Internet, voice mail, irons, hair dryers. *Some:* dual phone lines. **Pool(s):** heated indoor. **Leisure Activities:** whirlpool, exercise room. **Guest Services:** valet laundry. **Business Services:** meeting rooms, business center. **Cards:** AX, CB, DC, DS, JC, MC, VI.
(See color ad on insert)

THE HOTEL ELDORADO

Book at AAA.com

Phone: (250)763-7500

Small-scale Hotel
$109-$499 All Year

Address: 500 Cook Rd V1W 3G9 **Location:** Hwy 97 (Harvey Ave), 2.5 mi (4 km) s on Pandosy (which becomes Lakeshore Rd). **Facility:** Designated smoking area. 56 units. 50 one-bedroom standard units, some with whirlpools. 6 one-bedroom suites with whirlpools. 3 stories, interior corridors. *Bath:* combo or shower only. **Parking:** on-site. **Terms:** office hours 7 am-11 pm, 7 day cancellation notice-fee imposed. **Amenities:** video library (fee), high-speed Internet, voice mail, irons, hair dryers. **Dining:** Eldorado Dining Room & Bar, see separate listing. **Pool(s):** heated indoor. **Leisure Activities:** whirlpool, steamroom, rental boats, exercise room, spa. *Fee:* marina, waterskiing. **Guest Services:** valet laundry. **Business Services:** meeting rooms, PC (fee). **Cards:** AX, DC, MC, VI.

KELOWNA MOTOR INN

Phone: 250/762-2533

Motel
$95-$195 All Year

Address: 1070 Harvey Ave V1Y 8S4 **Location:** Corner of Hwy 97 N (Harvey Ave) and Gordon Dr. Located across from the mall. **Facility:** 112 units. 92 one- and 10 two-bedroom standard units, some with efficiencies, kitchens and/or whirlpools. 6 one- and 4 two-bedroom suites, some with efficiencies. 2 stories (no elevator), exterior corridors. **Parking:** on-site. **Amenities:** voice mail, hair dryers. **Dining:** Mekong Restaurant, see separate listing. **Pool(s):** heated indoor. **Leisure Activities:** whirlpool, steamroom, spa. **Guest Services:** coin laundry, wireless Internet. **Cards:** AX, MC, VI.

LAKE OKANAGAN RESORT

Book at AAA.com

Phone: (250)769-3511

Resort
Large-scale Hotel
$159-$399 All Year

Address: 2751 Westside Rd V1Z 3T1 **Location:** From floating bridge, 1.5 mi (2.5 km) sw on Hwy 97 (Harvey Ave), 10.6 mi (17 km) nw on Westside Rd (narrow winding road), then follow signs. **Facility:** Along the shores of Okanagan Lake, this older resort features a mix of unit styles and sizes, many with lake or golf course views in a quiet setting. 125 units. 12 one-bedroom standard units with efficiencies. 90 one-, 3 two- and 19 three-bedroom suites, some with efficiencies, kitchens and/or whirlpools. 1 vacation home. 3-6 stories, interior/exterior corridors. **Parking:** on-site. **Terms:** office hours 7 am-11 pm, check-in 4 pm, 14 day cancellation notice, in summer-fee imposed. **Amenities:** video library (fee), voice mail, irons, hair dryers. **Pool(s):** 4 heated outdoor. **Leisure Activities:** saunas, whirlpools, rental paddleboats, marina, fishing, 7 tennis courts (3 lighted), recreation programs, hiking trails, jogging, playground, exercise room. *Fee:* boats, waterskiing, bicycles, horseback riding. **Guest Services:** coin laundry. **Business Services:** conference facilities. **Cards:** AX, DC, MC, VI.

MANTEO RESORT-WATERFRONT HOTEL & VILLAS

Book at AAA.com

Phone: 250/860-1031

Resort Condominium
Rates not provided

Address: 3762 Lakeshore Rd V1W 3L4 **Location:** Hwy 97 N (Harvey Ave), 2.5 mi (4 km) s on Pandosy (which becomes Lakeshore Rd). **Facility:** Set along the lake, this resort offers extensive recreational facilities as well as large, upscale rooms ranging from studio to condo style. Designated smoking area. 102 units. 48 one-bedroom standard units. 30 one-, 17 two- and 7 three-bedroom suites with kitchens. 4 stories, interior/exterior corridors. **Parking:** on-site. **Terms:** check-in 4 pm. **Amenities:** voice mail, irons, hair dryers. *Some:* video games, CD players, high-speed Internet. **Dining:** Wild Apple Grill, see separate listing. **Pool(s):** 2 heated outdoor, heated indoor. **Leisure Activities:** saunas, whirlpools, steamrooms, waterslide, rental boats, rental canoes, rental paddleboats, boat dock, fishing, putting green, lighted tennis court, recreation programs, playground, exercise room. *Fee:* massage, game room. **Guest Services:** valet and coin laundry. **Business Services:** conference facilities, PC.

OTELLA'S WINE COUNTRY INN

Phone: 250/763-4922

Bed & Breakfast
$150-$200 All Year

Address: 42 Altura Rd V1V 1B6 **Location:** Hwy 97 (Harvey Ave), 1.2 mi (2 km) n on Spall/Glenmore rds, just w on High Summit Rd, 0.4 mi (0.8 km) on Clifton Rd, just ne on Caramillo, then just n. Located in a secluded residential area. **Facility:** The inn's owners are wine enthusiasts who have created picturesque gardens and serve up gourmet meals on a vine-covered patio. Smoke free premises. 4 one-bedroom standard units. 3 stories (no elevator), interior corridors. *Bath:* some shared or private, combo or shower only. **Parking:** on-site. **Terms:** check-in 3:30 pm, 2 night minimum stay - weekends, 14 day cancellation notice-fee imposed. **Amenities:** hair dryers. **Leisure Activities:** cross country skiing, hiking trails. **Guest Services:** coin laundry. **Cards:** VI.

RAMADA LODGE HOTEL

Book at AAA.com

Phone: (250)860-9711

Small-scale Hotel
$119-$189 3/1-9/30
$99-$189 10/1-2/28

Address: 2170 Harvey Ave V1Y 6G8 **Location:** Hwy 97 N (Harvey Ave) at Dilworth Dr. **Facility:** 135 units. 110 one-bedroom standard units, some with whirlpools. 25 one-bedroom suites, some with kitchens. 3 stories, interior/exterior corridors. **Parking:** on-site. **Terms:** check-in 4 pm. **Amenities:** voice mail, irons, hair dryers. **Pool(s):** heated indoor. **Leisure Activities:** whirlpool, exercise room. **Guest Services:** valet laundry. **Business Services:** conference facilities, business center. **Cards:** AX, DC, DS, MC, VI.

RECREATION INN & SUITES   *Book great rates at AAA.com*   Phone: (250)860-3982

Motel
$135-$175 3/1-9/30
$85-$120 10/1-2/28

Address: 1891 Parkinson Way V1Y 7V6 **Location:** From Hwy 97 N (Harvey Ave), just w on Spall Rd. **Facility:** 50 units. 31 one- and 8 two-bedroom standard units, some with efficiencies or kitchens. 11 one-bedroom suites with kitchens. 2 stories (no elevator), exterior corridors. **Parking:** on-site. **Terms:** cancellation fee imposed. **Amenities:** hair dryers. *Some:* irons. **Leisure Activities:** sauna, whirlpool. **Guest Services:** coin laundry. **Business Services:** PC (fee). **Cards:** AX, MC, VI. **Free Special Amenities: continental breakfast and high-speed Internet.** *(See color ad p 528)*

THE ROYAL ANNE HOTEL   *Book great rates at AAA.com*   Phone: (250)763-2277

Small-scale Hotel
$89-$189 All Year

Address: 348 Bernard Ave V1Y 6N5 **Location:** Corner of Pandosy and Bernard Ave; downtown. **Facility:** 64 one-bedroom standard units. 5 stories, interior corridors. **Parking:** on-site. **Terms:** cancellation fee imposed. **Amenities:** voice mail, irons, hair dryers. **Leisure Activities:** saunas, exercise room. **Guest Services:** valet laundry. **Business Services:** meeting rooms, PC. **Cards:** AX, DC, MC, VI. **Free Special Amenities: expanded continental breakfast and high-speed Internet.**

SIESTA MOTOR INN   Phone: (250)763-5013

Motel
$129-$279 3/1-9/20
$87-$182 9/21-2/28

Address: 3152 Lakeshore Rd V1W 3T1 **Location:** Hwy 97 (Harvey Ave), 1.8 mi (2.8 km) s on Pandosy (which becomes Lakeshore Rd). **Facility:** 96 units. 24 one-bedroom standard units, some with efficiencies. 68 one- and 4 two-bedroom suites with kitchens. 2 stories (no elevator), exterior corridors. **Parking:** on-site. **Terms:** cancellation fee imposed. **Amenities:** voice mail. *Some:* irons. **Pool(s):** heated outdoor, heated indoor. **Leisure Activities:** sauna, whirlpools, playground, exercise room. **Guest Services:** coin laundry, wireless Internet. **Business Services:** PC. **Cards:** AX, MC, VI.

SUPER 8 MOTEL   *Book at AAA.com*   Phone: (250)762-8222

Motel
$140 3/1-9/30
$110 10/1-2/28

Address: 2592 Hwy 97 N V1X 4J4 **Location:** From jct Hwy 33, just n on 97 N (Harvey Ave). **Facility:** 60 one-bedroom standard units. 2 stories (no elevator), interior corridors. **Parking:** on-site. **Terms:** cancellation fee imposed. **Amenities:** hair dryers. **Pool(s):** heated outdoor. **Leisure Activities:** whirlpool. **Guest Services:** wireless Internet. **Business Services:** PC. **Cards:** AX, DC, MC, VI.

TRAVELLER'S CHOICE MOTOR INN   Phone: 250/762-3221

Motel
$76-$174 All Year

Address: 1780 Gordon Dr V1Y 3H2 **Location:** Hwy 97 N (Harvey Ave), just e. Located across from the mall. **Facility:** 43 units. 34 one-bedroom standard units, some with kitchens. 7 one- and 2 two-bedroom suites, some with kitchens. 2 stories (no elevator), exterior corridors. **Parking:** on-site. **Terms:** office hours 7 am-midnight. **Amenities:** voice mail, hair dryers. *Some:* irons. **Pool(s):** heated indoor. **Leisure Activities:** whirlpool, barbecue. **Guest Services:** valet and coin laundry, wireless Internet. **Cards:** AX, CB, DC, DS, MC, VI. **Free Special Amenities: continental breakfast and local telephone calls.**

VINEYARD INN   Phone: (250)860-5703

Motel
$104-$184 3/1-9/30
$84-$144 10/1-2/28

Address: 2486 Hwy 97 N V1X 4J3 **Location:** Southwest corner of jct Hwy 97 (Harvey Ave) and 33. **Facility:** Smoke free premises. 26 units. 10 one-bedroom standard units. 14 one- and 2 two-bedroom suites, some with efficiencies or kitchens. Exterior corridors. **Parking:** on-site. **Terms:** office hours 7:30 am-11:30 pm. **Amenities:** voice mail, hair dryers. **Pool(s):** heated outdoor. **Leisure Activities:** whirlpool, putting green, playground, basketball, volleyball. **Guest Services:** coin laundry, wireless Internet. **Cards:** AX, CB, DC, DS, JC, MC, VI.

-------- WHERE TO DINE --------

BOUCHONS BISTRO   *Menu on AAA.com*   Phone: 250/763-6595

French
$19-$35

Dressy casual. **Bar:** Full bar. **Reservations:** suggested. **Hours:** Open 3/16-2/15; 5:30 pm-10 pm. Closed major holidays. **Address:** 105-1180 Sunset Dr V1Y 9W6 **Parking:** street. **Cards:** MC, VI.

CHRISTOPHER'S   Phone: 250/861-3464

Steak & Seafood
$15-$40

Patrons appreciate the restaurant's quaint dining room, personalized attention and fresh seafood. Selections also include steak, salad bar offerings and desserts. Large groups are accommodated at this local favorite, and the atmosphere can be boisterous. Casual dress. **Bar:** Full bar. **Reservations:** suggested. **Hours:** 4:30 pm-10 pm, Fri & Sat-11 pm. Closed: 1/1, 12/25, 12/26. **Address:** 242 Lawrence Ave V1Y 6L3 **Location:** Downtown. **Parking:** street. **Cards:** AX, DC, MC, VI.

COYOTE'S RESTAURANT UPSTAIRS   Phone: 250/860-1266

Mexican
$8-$23

Patrons can access the restaurant from the waterfront entrance or walk through the Grand Okanagan Hotel. Inside are a modern, upbeat atmosphere and a menu with preparations from around the world. Mexican, Pacific Rim and Japanese influences are all evident, but traditional steak and seafood entrees are every bit as satisfying. Casual dress. **Bar:** Full bar. **Hours:** 11:30 am-10 pm, Fri & Sat-11 pm. Closed: 12/25. **Address:** 1352 Water St V1Y 9P3 **Location:** 0.6 mi (1 km) w; at The Grand Okanagan Lakefront, above Rose's. **Parking:** street. **Cards:** AX, MC, VI.

DAWETT FINE INDIAN CUISINE
Phone: 250/717-1668

Indian
$4-$17

Considered one of the best Indian restaurants in the Okanagan, this place doesn't disappoint with its traditional ethnic cuisine. Guests can tantalize their taste buds with tandoori chicken, chicken masala, pakoras and samosas, all made with top-quality ingredients. Vegetarians will find many choices of fine food to enjoy in a simple, comfortable dining room. Semi-formal attire. **Bar:** Full bar. **Hours:** 11 am-2:30 & 4:30-9:45 pm, Fri-10:45 pm, Sat & Sun 1 pm-9:45 pm. **Closed:** 12/25. **Address:** 1435 Ellis St V1Y 2A3 **Location:** Downtown. **Parking:** on-site. **Cards:** AX, MC, VI.

ELDORADO DINING ROOM & BAR
Phone: 250/763-7500

Regional
Canadian
$10-$40

The casual yet elegant restaurant is right along the water and offers views of Lake Okanagan and the valley. Preparations of regionally diverse cuisine exceed expectations. In addition to seafood and pasta options, diners can select from several meat dishes. Known for its brunch, this place is a must stop for those visiting Kelowna. Dressy casual. **Bar:** Full bar. **Reservations:** suggested. **Hours:** 7 am-close. **Closed:** 12/25. **Address:** 500 Cook Rd V1W 3G9 **Location:** Hwy 97 (Harvey Ave), 2.5 mi (4 km) s on Pandosy (which becomes Lakeshore Rd); in The Hotel Eldorado. **Parking:** on-site. **Cards:** AX, MC, VI.

FRESCO RESTAURANT & LOUNGE
Phone: 250/868-8805

Regional
Canadian
$26-$37

In a historic brick building, the restaurant offers fine dining at its best in the heart of the Okanagan. The experience is memorable and lovely. Creative seasonal cuisine emphasizes the products of the area, as does the extensive list of regional wines. Artistic and delicious, each dish is prepared in an open kitchen and served by staff who are attentive and knowledgeable. Casual dress. **Bar:** Full bar. **Reservations:** suggested. **Hours:** Open 3/1-12/31 & 2/1-2/28; 5:30 pm-10 pm. **Closed:** 12/25, 12/26; also Sun & Mon 2/1-4/30. **Address:** 1560 Water St V1Y 1J7 **Location:** Hwy 97 (Harvey Ave), 3 blks n; jct Bernard and Water sts. **Parking:** street. **Cards:** AX, MC, VI.

CALL

GRAND BAY CAFE
Phone: 250/763-4500

Canadian
$10-$30

This restaurant's menu lines up a wide variety of fare, ranging from seafood to pasta to prime rib. Most tables offer a view overlooking the lake and river paths, and the service is attentive. Casual dress. **Bar:** Full bar. **Reservations:** suggested. **Hours:** 6:30 am-10 pm. **Address:** 1310 Water St V1Y 9P3 **Location:** Hwy 97 (Harvey Ave), 0.6 mi (1 km) w along Water St; in The Grand Okanagan Lakefront Resort & Conference Centre. **Parking:** on-site (fee) and valet. **Cards:** AX, CB, DC, DS, JC, MC, VI.

THE GRATEFUL FED PSYCHE DELI
Phone: 250/862-8621

Deli/Subs
Sandwiches
$5-$10

Popular with the late-night crowd, the small, unassuming delicatessen is a must stop for visiting rock stars and concertgoers. The menu comprises traditional deli fare. Casual dress. **Bar:** Full bar. **Reservations:** not accepted. **Hours:** 11 am-midnight. Closed major holidays. **Address:** 509 Bernard Ave V1Y 6N9 **Location:** Jct Ellis St; centre. **Parking:** street. **Cards:** MC, VI.

JAKX NEIGHBOURHOOD GRILL
Phone: 250/763-0773

Continental
$6-$20

A favorite among locals, the family-owned restaurant is on the second floor of a shopping center, with wheelchair access via an elevator. A wine list focused on bottles from area wineries matches with pizzas and pasta and meat entrees. Families are welcomed. Casual dress. **Bar:** Full bar. **Reservations:** suggested. **Hours:** 11 am-9 pm. Closed major holidays; also Sun. **Address:** 203-595 KLO Rd V1Y 8E7 **Location:** 1.9 mi (3 km) e on Pandosy (which becomes Lakeshore Rd); at Pandosy and Klo Rd; in shopping plaza. **Parking:** on-site. **Cards:** MC, VI.

CALL

THE JAMMERY
Phone: 250/766-1139

International
$6-$17

A play on the winery concept, the restaurant uses locally grown fruits in its creations. Guests can learn about the jam being made on site or just come for afternoon tea. The menu lays out an excellent selection of breakfast choices, many sandwiches and wraps, as well as afternoon tea items. **Reservations:** suggested. **Hours:** 8 am-4 pm; to 6 pm in summer. **Closed:** 1/1, 12/25, 12/26. **Address:** 8038 Hwy 97 N V1X 6A6 **Location:** Hwy 97 N (Harvey Ave), 7.4 mi (12 km) n. **Parking:** on-site. **Cards:** MC, VI.

CALL

JOEY TOMATO'S
Phone: 250/860-8999

Mediterranean
$10-$29

The cuisine blends Mediterranean and Asian cooking styles and emphasizes finger foods for sharing. Those who aren't big fans of tapas can consider full meal offerings centered on steaks and chops. Casual dress. **Bar:** Full bar. **Hours:** 11:30 am-1 am, Sun-midnight. **Closed:** 12/25. **Address:** 300-2475 Hwy 97 V1X 4J2 **Location:** Hwy 97; between Banks and Powick rds. **Parking:** on-site. **Cards:** AX, MC, VI.

KELSEY'S
Phone: 250/762-4774

Canadian
$7-$21

A fun, relaxed atmosphere and tasty menu of casual fare make the restaurant a popular favorite with locals. Diners might start a meal with some tempting appetizers, such as wings, loaded potato skins or nachos, and follow them with an old-time favorite, such as a burger, wrap, pizza or pasta dish. For a heartier meal, it's hard to beat pork back ribs or a steak. The diverse menu has broad appeal. Casual dress. **Bar:** Full bar. **Hours:** 11 am-11 pm. **Address:** 1755 Capri St V1Y 6E8 **Location:** Capri St and Gordon Ave. **Parking:** on-site. **Cards:** AX, MC, VI.

LAUGHING MOON RESTAURANT
Phone: 250/764-0674

Continental
$9-$13

The distinctive restaurant's simple dining room pipes with live local music on weekends. Although the menu is not extensive, its meals, which incorporate blends of Thai, Vietnamese and Canadian ingredients, are fantastic. The system of ordering is unusual, and servers are friendly. Casual dress. **Bar:** Beer & wine. **Hours:** 7:30 am-9:30 pm, Sun-Tues to 4 pm. **Closed:** 1/1, 12/25. **Address:** 4600 Lakeshore Rd V1W 1X4 **Location:** 4.4 mi (7 km) w at Pandosy (which becomes Lakeshore Rd). **Parking:** on-site. **Cards:** MC, VI.

MAMMA ROSA

Italian
$10-$20

Phone: 250/763-4114

As the name suggests, the restaurant is known for Italian food, just as Mama might have made it. The extensive menu lists homemade in various forms, ranging from cannelloni and lasagna to manicotti and penne. Also tempting is a fine selection of pizzas. Red- and white-checked tableclothes and Italian decor lend to a cozy atmosphere. The service is super. Casual dress. **Bar:** Full bar. **Reservations:** suggested. **Hours:** 5 pm-10 pm, Sun 5:30 pm-9 pm. Closed major holidays. **Address:** 561 Lawrence Ave V1Y 6L8 **Location:** Downtown. **Parking:** street. **Cards:** AX, MC, VI.

CALL

THE MARMALADE CAT CAFE

Vegetarian
$6-$7

Phone: 250/861-1312

Many people accidentally discover this cute and tiny restaurant as they wander through the aisles of the gift shop that seems to surround it. Guests line up to order choices from a good selection of hearty and creative sandwiches, hot daily specials that seem to sell out quickly, and assorted small tasty desserts. Casual dress. **Reservations:** not accepted. **Hours:** 6:30 am-5:30 pm, Sat from 7:30 am, Sun 8:30 am-4 pm. Closed major holidays. **Address:** 2903 Pansody St V1Y 1W1 **Location:** Jct West Ave. **Parking:** street. **Cards:** MC, VI.

MEKONG RESTAURANT

Traditional
Chinese
$6-$15

Phone: 250/763-8000

The restaurant prepares fresh, mouthwatering Szechuan cuisine. Ask about the signature deluxe meals for two to 10 people: ginger chicken and steak strips with black pepper sauce. The decor is bright, fresh and contemporary. Peak meal times can be busy. **Bar:** Full bar. **Reservations:** accepted. **Hours:** 11:30 am-10 pm. Closed: 12/25. **Address:** 1030 Harvey Ave V1Y 8S4 **Location:** Corner of Hwy 97 N (Harvey Ave) and Gordon Dr; in Kelowna Motor Inn. **Parking:** on-site. **Cards:** AX, DC, MC, VI.

MINI O-ZEKI JAPANESE RESTAURANT

Sushi
$8-$14

Phone: 250/862-8022

The eat-in/take-out eatery has but seven small tables, and diners can watch sushi and sashimi being made at the counter. Many locals patronize the popular, busy spot for take-out sushi. Regardless of where the food is eaten, patrons are tempted by artistic, traditional displays of delicious Japanese fare. Casual dress. **Reservations:** not accepted. **Hours:** 11:30 am-8:30 pm. Closed major holidays; also Mon. **Address:** 2684 Pandosy St V1Y 1V6 **Location:** Hwy 97 (Harvey Ave), 1.8 mi (3 km) s on Pandosy (which becomes Lakeshore Rd); in South Gate Plaza. **Parking:** on-site. **Cards:** MC, VI.

MINSTREL CAFE & BAR

International
$8-$40

Phone: 250/764-2301

A little off the beaten path, the distinctive cafe is considered to be one of Kelowna's best-kept secrets, especially for lunch. Upon entry, guests notice a large tree in the middle of the dining room, set against soft olive walls which boast original local art. The menu lists a wide range of soups, salads, frittatas and all-day breakfast items, which can be enjoyed in the open, airy dining room or on the patio outside. Live entertainment is featured on weekends. Dressy casual. **Bar:** Full bar. **Reservations:** suggested. **Hours:** 11:30 am-close. **Address:** 4638 Lakeshore Rd V1W 1X5 **Location:** Hwy 97 (Harvey Ave), 5.6 mi (9 km) s at Pandosy (which becomes Lakeshore Rd). **Parking:** on-site. **Cards:** MC, VI.

CALL

MOXIE'S CLASSIC GRILL

Canadian
$8-$18

Phone: 250/861-6110

This sleek, funky and popular restaurant presents an extensive menu of creatively prepared dishes, including pizza, pasta, rice, noodles, signature salads and burgers. Other menus include one for children and one for Sunday brunch. Lending to the upbeat, stylish decor are dark wood appointments and river rock fireplaces. Casual dress. **Bar:** Full bar. **Hours:** 11 am-midnight, Fri & Sat-1 am. **Address:** 1730 Cooper Rd V1Y 8V5 **Location:** From Hwy 97 (Harvey Ave), just e; corner of Enterprise Way. **Parking:** on-site. **Cards:** AX, MC, VI.

PEARSON'S EUROPEAN DELI

Deli/Subs
Sandwiches
$6-$12

Phone: 250/762-0800

As diners enter the small delicatessen, they are hit with the smell of fresh bread. Before them is a case of salads, ranging from pasta to curried chicken. Behind the counter is a chalkboard with several sandwich options, as well as such listings as cabbage rolls and pierogies. Made on thick slabs of fresh bread, sandwiches are incredible. This spot fits the bill for a healthy, quick meal. Casual dress. **Reservations:** not accepted. **Hours:** 6:30 am-6 pm, Sat 9 am-4 pm. Closed major holidays; also Sun. **Address:** #30-2070 Harvey Ave V1Y 8P8 **Location:** Hwy 95 S; at jct Cooper Ave; in strip mall. **Parking:** on-site. **Cards:** AX, MC, VI.

PHEASANT & QUAIL PUB

American
$8-$16

Phone: 250/860-1066

Modeled after an English ale house, the cozy restaurant invites patrons to drop in for a pint and some good pub food. Comfortable armchairs for lounging, a bar area and an enclosed smoking area encourage relaxing. Fish and chips, sandwiches, pastas and salads make up the menu, and the friendly servers share information about the local brews. Casual dress. **Bar:** Full bar. **Reservations:** accepted. **Hours:** 11 am-midnight. Closed: 12/25. **Address:** 3110 Lakeshore Rd V1W 3T1 **Location:** 1.8 mi (3 km) s on Pandosy (which becomes Lakeshore Rd). **Parking:** on-site. **Cards:** AX, MC, VI.

RICKY'S ALL DAY GRILL

Canadian
$6-$15

Phone: 250/763-4141

The comfortable eatery, which employs friendly servers, presents a varied menu that includes pasta dishes, wraps, omelets, stir-fry preparations and burgers. Portions are generous. Children's and senior selections are offered. Guests can request seating in a booth or at a table. Casual dress. **Bar:** Full bar. **Hours:** 6 am-8:30 pm. **Address:** 2435 Hwy 97 N V1X 4J2 **Location:** 0.6 mi (1 km) s of jct Hwy 97 N (Harvey Ave) and 33; in Holiday Inn Express. **Parking:** on-site. **Cards:** MC, VI.

RIC'S GRILL

Steak & Seafood
$14-$37

Phone: 250/869-1586

"Funky and modern" describes the decor and the food at the upscale steakhouse, which bustles with activity. Reservations are definitely recommended. Steaks are well worth it, but then again, so are the salmon, chicken and pasta dishes. A wide variety of distinctive appetizers rounds out the menu. Servers are friendly and attentive. Casual dress. **Bar:** Full bar. **Reservations:** suggested. **Hours:** 11 am-11 pm, Fri-midnight, Sat 4 pm-midnight, Sun 4 pm-11 pm. Closed major holidays. **Address:** 210 Lawrence Ave V1Y 6L3 **Location:** Corner of Lawrence Ave and Abbott St; downtown. **Parking:** street. **Cards:** AX, DC, MC, VI.

SUMMERHILL SUNSET BISTRO

Regional
Canadian
$9-$26

Phone: 250/764-8000

Overlooking the Okanagan Valley, the winery restaurant affords nice views. Food presentations are artistic. Guests can make their way to the eatery after a tour and tasting or come directly for a special meal. Several menu items incorporate regional ingredients and the Bavarian smokehouse cooking technique. Starters are large enough to share, and meals are exquisite. Casual dress. **Bar:** Full bar. **Reservations:** suggested. **Hours:** 11 am-9 pm. Closed: 12/25. **Address:** 4870 Chute Lake Rd V1W 4M3 **Location:** 9 mi (15 km) e at Pandosy (which becomes Lakeshore Rd), just s at Chute Lake Rd, follow signs. **Parking:** on-site. **Cards:** AX, DC, MC, VI.

CALL 🔊M

SWISS CHALET

Canadian
$6-$18

Phone: 250/762-6362

The popular restaurant is known for its rotisserie chicken and ribs and the tangy Chalet sauce that gives food its special zip. Diners munch on a half or quarter chicken with sides such as steamed vegetables, fries, baked potatoes and salads. Lunch guests often go for the great soup and sandwich combination. Take-out and delivery service are popular options. Casual dress. **Bar:** Full bar. **Hours:** 11 am-10 pm, Fri & Sat-11 pm. Closed: 12/25. **Address:** 1475 Harvey Ave V1Y 6E9 **Location:** Harvey Ave at Burtch. **Parking:** on-site. **Cards:** AX, MC, VI.

WILD APPLE GRILL   *Menu on AAA.com*

Regional
Canadian
$8-$30

Phone: 250/860-4488

A fresh, bright, contemporary dining room awaits guests of the restaurant along the waterfront. Featuring an open-concept kitchen and light, bright colors, the dining room transforms in the evening to become a bit more intimate. Upbeat, creative meals include pasta and sandwiches at lunch or creative seafood and meat preparations at dinner. Casual dress. **Bar:** Full bar. **Reservations:** suggested. **Hours:** 6 am-10 pm. **Address:** 3762 Lakeshore Rd V1W 3L4 **Location:** Hwy 97 N (Harvey Ave), 2.5 mi (4 km) s on Pandosy (which becomes Lakeshore Rd); in Manteo Resort-Waterfront Hotel & Villas. **Parking:** on-site. **Cards:** AX, DC, MC, VI.

YAMAS TAVERNA RESTAURANT

Greek
$8-$39

Phone: 250/763-5823

A typical and traditional Greek feel envelops the downtown restaurant, which is popular with the business crowd at lunch. Guests can choose from the all-you-can-eat lunch buffet or from delicious entrees on the menu. Casual dress. **Bar:** Full bar. **Hours:** 11 am-2 & 5-10 pm, Sat & Sun from 5 pm. **Address:** 1630 Ellis St V1Y 8L1 **Location:** From Hwy 97 (Harvey Ave), just w at Ellis St. **Parking:** street. **Cards:** AX, MC, VI.

NARAMATA pop. 1,787

——— **WHERE TO STAY** ———

THE VILLAGE MOTEL

Motel
$76-$145 3/1-12/31

Phone: (250)496-5535

Address: 244 Robinson Dr V0H 1N0 **Location:** 8.8 mi (14 km) n on Naramata Rd from Penticton. **Facility:** Designated smoking area. 9 units. 5 one-bedroom standard units, some with efficiencies. 4 one-bedroom suites with efficiencies. 1 story, exterior corridors. **Parking:** on-site. **Terms:** open 3/1-12/31, 2-3 night minimum stay - seasonal and/or weekends, 14 day cancellation notice. **Amenities:** hair dryers. **Leisure Activities:** bicycles. **Cards:** AX, JC, MC, VI.

[icons] 🛏️ 🍴 ✕ 🏋️ 📷 🈂️ 🛗 🖥️ / SOME UNITS FEE 🐕 🖼️

——— **WHERE TO DINE** ———

COBBLESTONE WINE BAR & RESTAURANT

Canadian
$8-$26

Phone: 250/496-5064

There is an intimate and cozy feel amongst the brick floors and walls of this restaurant, set in the basement of the Naramata Heritage Inn & Spa. This is casual dining at its best, with a menu that features many artistic dishes with regional ingredients. Your server will impress you with an extensive wine knowledge, helping to create a lovely and enjoyable meal. Semi-formal attire. **Bar:** Full bar. **Hours:** Open 3/1-12/31 & 2/7-2/28; 11 am-close. Closed: Mon-Thurs in winter. **Address:** 3625 First St V0H 1N0 **Location:** 11.4 mi (19 km) ne of Penticton; from Naramata Rd, w along Robinson to 1st St, just s; in Naramata Heritage Inn & Spa. **Parking:** on-site. **Cards:** AX, MC, VI.

CALL 🔊M

OLIVER pop. 4,370

——— **WHERE TO DINE** ———

TOASTED OAK WINE BAR & GRILL

Canadian
$9-$21

Phone: 250/498-4867

In the center of the self-proclaimed wine capital of Canada, this restored historic fire hall offers a comfortable place to sample one or more of the more than 280 British Columbia-produced wines from the cellar. The contemporary menu features wine-friendly dishes, such as savory onion and herb tart and beet risotto with roasted duck breast. Casual dress. **Bar:** Full bar. **Reservations:** accepted. **Hours:** 11 am-10 pm, Fri & Sat-11 pm. Closed major holidays. **Address:** 34881 - 97th St, Box 10 V0H 1T0 **Location:** Centre; in Wine Country Welcome Centre. **Parking:** on-site. **Cards:** AX, MC, VI.

CALL 🔊M

OSOYOOS pop. 4,752

─── WHERE TO STAY ───

BEST WESTERN SUNRISE INN

Book great rates at AAA.com

Small-scale Hotel
$90-$250 All Year

Address: 5506 Main St V0H 1V0 **Location:** Jct Hwy 97, 1.9 mi (3 km) on Hwy 3 (Main St). **Facility:** 66 units. 37 one-bedroom standard units, some with efficiencies and/or whirlpools. 29 one-bedroom suites with kitchens. 3 stories, interior corridors. *Bath:* combo or shower only. **Parking:** on-site, winter plug-ins. **Terms:** check-in 4 pm, 7 day cancellation notice-fee imposed. **Amenities:** high-speed Internet, voice mail, irons, hair dryers. **Pool(s):** heated indoor. **Leisure Activities:** whirlpool, exercise room. *Fee:* game room. **Guest Services:** coin laundry, wireless Internet. **Business Services:** meeting rooms, PC. **Cards:** AX, CB, DC, DS, JC, MC, VI.

AAA Benefit: Members save 10% everyday, plus an exclusive frequent stay program.

Phone: (250)495-4000

Free Special Amenities: continental breakfast and high-speed Internet. *(See color ad p 512)*

THE COAST OSOYOOS BEACH HOTEL

Book at AAA.com

Small-scale Hotel
Rates not provided

Phone: 250/495-6525

Address: 7702 Main St (Hwy 3 E) V0H 1V0 **Location:** Jct Hwy 97, 1.2 mi (2 km) e. **Facility:** 60 units. 47 one-bedroom standard units, some with kitchens. 9 one- and 4 two-bedroom suites with kitchens. 3 stories, interior/exterior corridors. **Parking:** on-site, winter plug-ins. **Terms:** office hours 7 am-11 pm, check-in 4 pm. **Amenities:** voice mail, hair dryers. **Pool(s):** heated indoor. **Leisure Activities:** whirlpool, waterslide. **Guest Services:** coin laundry. **Business Services:** meeting rooms, PC.

SPIRIT RIDGE VINEYARD RESORT & SPA

Condominium
$215-$429 All Year

Phone: 250/495-5445

Address: 1200 Rancher Creek Rd V0H 1V0 **Location:** Hwy 97 S, e on Hwy 3 (Main St), cross bridge, left on 45th St. **Facility:** This Tuscan-style, desert retreat bordering an award-winning winery is a short distance from a lake. Smoke free premises. 94 units. 74 one- and 20 two-bedroom suites with kitchens. 2-4 stories (no elevator), exterior corridors. **Parking:** on-site. **Terms:** office hours 8 am-8 pm, check-in 4 pm, 2 night minimum stay - weekends. **Amenities:** DVD players, video games (fee), high-speed Internet, voice mail, irons, hair dryers. **Pool(s):** heated outdoor. **Leisure Activities:** saunas, whirlpools, waterslide, beach access, exercise room, spa. *Fee:* boats, canoes, paddleboats, marina. **Guest Services:** complimentary laundry, area transportation, wireless Internet. **Cards:** AX, MC, VI.

▼ See AAA listing p 536 ▼

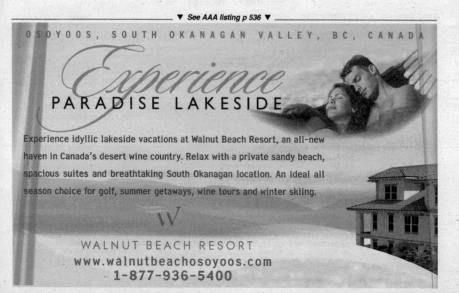

WALNUT BEACH RESORT

Phone: 250/495-5400

(fyi)
Small-scale Hotel

Under construction, scheduled to open April 2008. **Address:** 4200 Lakeshore Dr V0H 1V6 **Location:** S on Lakeshore Dr off Hwy 3. **Amenities:** pets, coffeemakers, microwaves, refrigerators, pool. *(See color ad p 535)*

——— **WHERE TO DINE** ———

CAMPO MARINA

Phone: 250/495-7650

Italian
$5-$15

The established, family-run restaurant is sure to please with its hearty Italian dishes. The cozy, comfortable dining room welcomes guests to linger over linguine, tantalize their taste buds with tiramisu and savor pan-seared scallops. Semi-formal attire. **Bar:** Full bar. **Hours:** 5 pm-9:30 pm. Closed major holidays. **Address:** 5907 Main St, RR 3 V0H 1V3 **Location:** East end of town on Hwy 3 (Main St). **Parking:** on-site. **Cards:** MC, VI.

CALL

THE CHALET HELVETIA

Phone: 250/495-7552

Continental
$10-$21

Just off Main Street in the center of town, the cozy, casual restaurant is a short distance from the lake. The cuisine is predominantly Swiss, offering several types of schnitzels, spaetzle and chicken and beef dishes. The owner and his wife make diners feel special by their desire to please. Casual dress. **Bar:** Full bar. **Reservations:** suggested, in summer. **Hours:** 11 am-2 & 5-9 pm; hours vary in winter. Closed major holidays; also Mon & Sun off season. **Address:** 8312 74th Ave V0H 1V0 **Location:** Just s off Hwy 3 (Main St) at 85th St. **Parking:** on-site. **Cards:** AX, DC, JC, MC, VI.

DIAMOND STEAK AND SEAFOOD HOUSE

Phone: 250/495-6223

Steak & Seafood
$10-$55

Tasty food and attentive service are hallmarks at the excellent family restaurant. The menu lists a nice selection of pasta, pizza and Greek specialties. Broiled chicken breast with peppercorn and brandy demi-glace sauce is simply delectable. Casual dress. **Bar:** Full bar. **Reservations:** suggested, in summer. **Hours:** 4 pm-10 pm. Closed: 12/25. **Address:** 8903 Main St V0H 1V0 **Location:** Hwy 3 (Main St) at 89th St; centre. **Parking:** street. **Cards:** AX, MC, VI.

WILDFIRE GRILL

Phone: 250/495-2215

Canadian
$8-$18

As patrons enter the downtown restaurant's small dining room, they are greeted by warm orange walls and tables that sparkle. The dining patio opens seasonally. "Globally inspired" is the motto of the contemporary bistro, which serves salmon, chicken and pasta dishes, as well as hearty salads. **Bar:** Full bar. **Hours:** 11 am-11 pm; 11 am-2 & 5-9 pm, Sat & Sun 5 pm-9 pm in winter. Closed: 12/25. **Address:** 8526 Main St V0H 1V0 **Location:** Just e of jct Hwy 97 and 3 (Main St), on Hwy 3 (Main St); downtown. **Parking:** street. **Cards:** AX, MC, VI.

PENTICTON pop. 31,909

——— **WHERE TO STAY** ———

BEST WESTERN INN AT PENTICTON

Book great rates at AAA.com   Phone: 250/493-0311

(CAA) (SAVE)

Small-scale Hotel
Rates not provided

Address: 3180 Skaha Lake Rd V2A 6G4 **Location:** 2.5 mi (4 km) s. **Facility:** 67 units. 55 one-bedroom standard units, some with whirlpools. 9 one- and 3 two-bedroom suites, some with efficiencies or kitchens. 2 stories (no elevator), exterior corridors. **Parking:** on-site. **Amenities:** voice mail, irons, hair dryers. *Some:* high-speed Internet. **Pool(s):** heated outdoor, heated indoor. **Leisure Activities:** whirlpool, playground. **Guest Services:** valet and coin laundry, wireless Internet. **Business Services:** meeting rooms, PC (fee). **Free Special Amenities: expanded continental breakfast and high-speed Internet.**

AAA Benefit:
Members save 10% everyday, plus an exclusive frequent stay program.

 SOME UNITS FEE

DAYS INN PENTICTON

Book at AAA.com   Phone: 250/493-6616

Small-scale Hotel
Rates not provided

Address: 152 Riverside Dr V2A 5Y4 **Location:** Hwy 97, just n. **Facility:** Smoke free premises. 105 one-bedroom standard units, some with whirlpools. 2 stories (no elevator), interior/exterior corridors. **Parking:** on-site. **Amenities:** voice mail, irons, hair dryers. *Some:* video games (fee), high-speed Internet. **Pool(s):** heated outdoor, heated indoor. **Leisure Activities:** whirlpool, limited exercise equipment. **Guest Services:** coin laundry, wireless Internet. **Business Services:** meeting rooms.

 SOME UNITS FEE

EMPIRE MOTEL

Phone: 250/493-2323

Motel
Rates not provided

Address: 3495 Skaha Lake Rd V2A 6G6 **Location:** From centre, 2.8 mi (4.5 km) s. **Facility:** Smoke free premises. 32 units. 17 one- and 5 two-bedroom standard units, some with efficiencies. 10 one-bedroom suites with kitchens. 2 stories (no elevator), exterior corridors. **Parking:** on-site. **Terms:** office hours 8 am-10 pm. **Amenities:** hair dryers. **Pool(s):** heated outdoor. **Leisure Activities:** playground. **Guest Services:** wireless Internet.

 / SOME UNITS

PENTICTON LAKESIDE RESORT, CONVENTION CENTRE & CASINO

 Book great rates at AAA.com

Phone: (250)493-8221

Large-scale Hotel
$165-$225 All Year

Address: 21 Lakeshore Dr W V2A 7M5 **Location:** Main St at Lakeshore Dr W. **Facility:** With an on-site casino, lakeside location and balconies in some rooms, this full-service, resort-style hotel is a destination property. 204 units. 197 one-bedroom standard units, some with whirlpools. 7 one-bedroom suites. 6 stories, interior corridors. **Parking:** on-site (fee) and valet. **Terms:** check-in 4 pm, 7 day cancellation notice. **Amenities:** video games, voice mail, irons, hair dryers. **Dining:** 2 restaurants. **Pool(s):** heated indoor. **Leisure Activities:** whirlpool, rental boats, rental canoes, rental paddleboats, boat dock, fishing, recreation programs in summer. *Fee:* massage. **Guest Services:** valet laundry, wireless Internet. **Business Services:** conference facilities, PC (fee). **Cards:** AX, DC, DS, MC, VI. *(See color ad below)*

RAMADA INN & SUITES   *Book at AAA.com*

Phone: (250)492-8926

Small-scale Hotel
$109-$269 3/1-10/13
$89-$269 10/14-2/28

Address: 1050 Eckhardt Ave W V2A 2C3 **Location:** 0.8 mi (1.2 km) w on Hwy 97. **Facility:** 125 units. 110 one-bedroom standard units, some with whirlpools. 15 one-bedroom suites with kitchens. 2-3 stories, exterior corridors. **Parking:** on-site, winter plug-ins. **Terms:** cancellation fee imposed. **Amenities:** voice mail, irons, hair dryers. *Some:* high-speed Internet. **Leisure Activities:** whirlpool, playground, limited exercise equipment, game room. **Guest Services:** valet and coin laundry, wireless Internet. **Business Services:** meeting rooms, PC. **Cards:** AX, CB, DC, DS, JC, MC, VI.

SPANISH VILLA RESORT

Phone: (250)492-2922

Motel
$68-$350 All Year

Address: 890 Lakeshore Dr W V2A 1C1 **Location:** Corner of Power St and Lakeshore Dr W. **Facility:** Smoke free premises. 60 units. 16 one-bedroom standard units. 38 one-, 5 two- and 1 three-bedroom suites (no elevator), exterior corridors. **Terms:** office hours 8 am-10 pm, 2-7 night minimum stay - seasonal and/or weekends, 14 day cancellation notice-fee imposed. **Amenities:** voice mail, hair dryers. *Some:* DVD players (fee). **Pool(s):** heated indoor. **Guest Services:** coin laundry, wireless Internet. **Cards:** AX, MC, VI. **Free Special Amenities:** newspaper and high-speed Internet.

SUPER 8 MOTEL PENTICTON   *Book at AAA.com*

Phone: 250/492-3829

Motel
Rates not provided

Address: 1706 Main St V2A 5G8 **Location:** Jct Main St and Industrial. **Facility:** 54 units. 43 one-bedroom standard units, some with efficiencies and/or whirlpools. 6 one- and 5 two-bedroom suites, some with efficiencies or kitchens. 2 stories (no elevator), interior/exterior corridors. **Bath:** combo or shower only. **Parking:** on-site. **Terms:** office hours 7 am-11 pm. **Amenities:** hair dryers. **Pool(s):** heated indoor. **Leisure Activities:** whirlpool. **Guest Services:** coin laundry. **Business Services:** PC (fee).

SWISS SUNSET INN

Phone: 250/492-8209

Motel
$59-$199 All Year

Address: 2604 Skaha Lake Rd V2A 6G1 **Location:** From centre; 2.1 mi (3.4 km) s. **Facility:** 25 units. 14 one- and 1 two-bedroom standard units. 10 one-bedroom suites, some with efficiencies or kitchens. 2 stories (no elevator), exterior corridors. **Parking:** on-site. **Terms:** office hours 7 am-11 pm, 10 day cancellation notice-fee imposed. **Amenities:** hair dryers. **Pool(s):** heated outdoor. **Guest Services:** coin laundry. **Cards:** MC, VI.

▼ See AAA listing above ▼

------ **WHERE TO DINE** ------

FIBONACCI ROASTERY & CAFE   Phone: 250/770-1913

Deli/Subs
Sandwiches
$7-$9

Casual dress. **Bar:** Beer & wine. **Reservations:** not accepted. **Hours:** 7:30 am-8 pm, Sun-6 pm. Closed major holidays. **Address:** 219 Main St V2A 5B1 **Location:** Centre. **Parking:** street. **Cards:** AX, MC, VI.

GRANNY BOGNER'S   Phone: 250/493-2711

Continental
$19-$30

For somewhere special to eat, the 100-year-old heritage mansion fits the bill. On a quiet residential street, the rustic restaurant has an elegant dining room and attentive servers. Guests can sit back and enjoy flavorful creations from the kitchen. Drawing largely on regional ingredients, the chef also chooses many local wines for the menu. Casual dress. **Bar:** Full bar. **Reservations:** accepted. **Hours:** Open 3/1-12/31 & 2/1-2/28; 5:30 pm-9:30 pm. Closed major holidays; also Sun & Mon. **Address:** 302 Eckhardt Ave W V2A 2A9 **Location:** 2 blks w of Main St; corner of Argyle St. **Parking:** on-site. **Cards:** AX, MC, VI.

LA CASA OUZERIA   Phone: 250/492-9144

Italian
$7-$43

A family-run operation, the homey restaurant satisfies those who can't decide what to have. The menu lists both Greek and Italian cuisine. The service and ambience merge to create a cozy, comfortable experience. Casual dress. **Bar:** Full bar. **Reservations:** suggested, weekends. **Hours:** 11:30 am-2 & 5-close, Sat & Sun from 5 pm. Closed: 1/1, 12/25, 12/26; also Mon. **Address:** 1090 Main St V2A 5E5 **Location:** Corner of Main St and Nelson Ave. **Parking:** on-site. **Cards:** MC, VI.

MON THONG THAI RESTAURANT   Phone: 250/770-9791

Thai
$5-$13

In the south end of town toward Skaha Lake, the friendly restaurant serves authentic Thai cuisine from an extensive menu that includes dishes from mild to hot and spicy. Bangkok-trained chefs prepare fresh, delicious food, while eschewing the use of monosodium glutamate. Casual dress. **Bar:** Full bar. **Hours:** 11:30 am-2:30 & 5-9 pm, Fri-Sun 5 pm-9:30 pm. Closed: 12/25. **Address:** 2985 Skaha Lake Rd V2A 5J6 **Location:** From centre, 2.2 mi (3.5 km) s. **Parking:** on-site. **Cards:** AX, DC, MC, VI.

RICKY'S ALL DAY GRILL   Phone: 250/490-0375

Canadian
$6-$15

The comfortable eatery, which employs friendly servers, presents a varied menu that includes pasta dishes, wraps, omelets, stir-fry preparations and burgers. Portions are generous. Children's and senior selections are offered. Guests can request seating in a booth or at a table. Casual dress. **Bar:** Full bar. **Hours:** 7 am-9 pm. **Address:** 2111 Main St V2A 6W6 **Location:** Between Warren and McDougall aves; in Cherry Lane Shopping Centre. **Parking:** on-site. **Cards:** MC, VI.

SHADES FAMILY RESTAURANT   Phone: 250/493-0465

American
$6-$12

For a quick, affordable meal that will please everyone in the family, the family-run restaurant hits the mark. On the menu is everything from grilled cheese sandwiches to burgers and fries. Guests shouldn't be surprised if the server addresses them as "honey" and knows almost all the regulars by name. **Bar:** Full bar. **Hours:** 6 am-9 pm, Fri & Sat-10 pm. Closed: 1/1, 12/25. **Address:** 1909 Main St V2A 5H5 **Location:** Corner of Main St and Okanagan Rd. **Parking:** on-site. **Cards:** AX, DC, MC, VI.

THEO'S RESTAURANT   Phone: 250/492-4019

Greek
$6-$30

The established downtown restaurant specializes in traditional Greek salads, souvlaki, moussaka and roast lamb, as well as steak and seafood. The Mediterranean decor is warm and family-oriented. Parking is available on the street or behind the restaurant. Casual dress. **Bar:** Full bar. **Reservations:** suggested. **Hours:** 11 am-midnight, Sun 4 pm-11 pm. Closed: 12/25. **Address:** 687 Main St V2A 5C9 **Location:** Main St at Eckhardt Ave. **Parking:** on-site. **Cards:** AX, DC, MC, VI.

SUMMERLAND pop. 10,713

------ **WHERE TO STAY** ------

SUMMERLAND MOTEL   Phone: 250/494-4444

Motel
$80-$150 All Year

Address: 2107 Tait St V0H 1Z4 **Location:** 3.1 mi (5 km) s on Hwy 97. **Facility:** Smoke free premises. 31 units. 26 one-bedroom standard units. 5 one-bedroom suites with kitchens, some with whirlpools. 2 stories (no elevator), exterior corridors. **Parking:** on-site. **Terms:** office hours 8 am-10 pm, 2 night minimum stay - seasonal and/or weekends, cancellation fee imposed. **Amenities:** voice mail. *Some:* hair dryers. **Pool(s):** heated outdoor. **Leisure Activities:** barbecues. **Guest Services:** coin laundry. **Business Services:** PC. **Cards:** AX, MC, VI. **Free Special Amenities:** local telephone calls and preferred room (subject to availability with advance reservations).

------ **WHERE TO DINE** ------

CELLAR DOOR BISTRO AT SUMAC
RIDGE ESTATE WINERY   Phone: 250/494-0451

Regional
Canadian
$9-$25

The restaurant at Sumac Ridge is perched atop the ridge. Some tables afford stunning views of the vineyard and valley below. After entering the wine and tasting shop, patrons notice the upscale, bistro-style eatery at the back. Local ingredients go into the marvelous, artistic dishes. The seasonal menu may feature a sandwich of the day, soup and a decadent dessert, and patrons also can opt to try a flight of wine. Casual dress. **Bar:** Full bar. **Reservations:** suggested. **Hours:** Open 3/1-12/31; 11:30 am-2:30 & 5:30-9 pm. **Address:** Hwy 97 V0H 1Z0 **Location:** On Hwy 97, follow signs for Sumac Ridge Estate Winery. **Parking:** on-site. **Cards:** AX, MC, VI.

CALL Ⓚ M

VANILLA POD RESTAURANT

Canadian
$8-$25

Phone: 250/494-8222

While traffic whizzes by on Highway 97, the pace slows down inside this small, slightly eclectic main street restaurant. The menu revolves around tapas dishes meant to be shared among friends, and along with some decided Spanish influences, many dishes employ some of the finest ingredients to be found in the surrounding Okanagan Valley. The smart wine list features only British Columbia-produced wines, many of which are produced within a stone's throw of the restaurant. Casual dress. **Bar:** Full bar. **Reservations:** accepted. **Hours:** 11:30 am-2 & 5:30-9:30 pm, Sat 5:30 pm-10 pm. Closed major holidays; also Sun & Mon. **Address:** 9917A Main St V0H 1Z8 **Location:** Jct Henry St; downtown. **Parking:** street. **Cards:** MC, VI.

VERNON pop. 33,494

--------- WHERE TO STAY ---------

BEST WESTERN VERNON LODGE & CONFERENCE
CENTRE *Book great rates at AAA.com*

Small-scale Hotel
$109-$193 All Year

Phone: (250)545-3385

Address: 3914 32nd St V1T 5P1 **Location:** 1 mi (1.5 km) n on Hwy 97 (32nd St). **Facility:** 127 units. 119 one-bedroom standard units. 8 one-bedroom suites, some with whirlpools. 3 stories (no elevator), interior corridors. **Parking:** on-site. **Amenities:** video games (fee), voice mail, irons, hair dryers. *Some:* high-speed Internet. **Pool(s):** heated indoor. **Leisure Activities:** whirlpool, exercise room. **Guest Services:** valet laundry, wireless Internet. **Business Services:** conference facilities, business center. **Cards:** AX, DC, DS, MC, VI. **Free Special Amenities:** room upgrade (subject to availability with advance reservations) and high-speed Internet. *(See color ad below)*

AAA Benefit:
Members save 10% everyday, plus an exclusive frequent stay program.

CASTLE ON THE MOUNTAIN B & B

Bed & Breakfast
$95-$250 All Year

Phone: (250)542-4593

Address: 8227 Silver Star Rd V1B 3M8 **Location:** Hwy 97A, exit 48th Ave (which becomes Silver Star Rd), 10 km e. **Facility:** Home to spectacular views and gracious hosts, this comfortable property overlooks the scenic Okanagan Valley. Smoke free premises. 7 units. 5 one-bedroom standard units, some with whirlpools. 1 one-bedroom suite with kitchen. 1 cottage. 3 stories (no elevator), interior corridors. *Bath:* combo or shower only. **Parking:** on-site, winter plug-ins. **Terms:** check-in 4 pm, 14 day cancellation notice. **Amenities:** video library, hair dryers. *Some:* CD players. **Leisure Activities:** whirlpool, hiking trails. *Fee:* massage. **Guest Services:** complimentary laundry. **Business Services:** meeting rooms. **Cards:** AX, MC, VI.

HOLIDAY INN EXPRESS HOTEL & SUITES VERNON

Book great rates at AAA.com

Phone: (250)550-7777

Small-scale Hotel
$159-$199 3/1-9/30
$119-$129 10/1-2/28

Address: 4716 34th St V1T 5Y9 **Location:** Hwy 97 (32nd St) northbound at 48th Ave. **Facility:** 85 one-bedroom standard units, some with whirlpools. 3 stories, interior corridors. *Bath:* combo or shower only. **Parking:** on-site. **Terms:** cancellation fee imposed. **Amenities:** high-speed Internet, dual phone lines, voice mail, irons, hair dryers. **Pool(s):** heated indoor. **Leisure Activities:** whirlpool, exercise room. **Guest Services:** valet and coin laundry. **Business Services:** meeting rooms, business center. **Cards:** AX, CB, DC, DS, JC, MC, VI. **Free Special Amenities:** continental breakfast and high-speed Internet. *(See color ad on insert & p 512)*

LAKESIDE ILLAHEE INN

Book at AAA.com

Phone: (250)260-7896

Bed & Breakfast
$169-$369 3/1-10/31
$129-$299 11/1-2/28

Address: 15010 Tamarack Dr V1B 2E1 **Location:** Hwy 97 (32nd St), s of town, 1.5 mi (2.5 km) se on College Way, 1.2 mi (2 km) e on Kalamalka Rd, then 1.8 mi (3 km) s on Kidston Rd, follow signs. Located in a quiet residential area. **Facility:** Luxurious rooms, all with balconies, and a lake setting give this upscale inn a relaxed atmosphere; a scenic provincial park is nearby. Designated smoking area. 6 one-bedroom standard units, some with whirlpools. 3 stories (no elevator), interior/exterior corridors. *Bath:* combo or shower only. **Parking:** on-site. **Terms:** 2 night minimum stay - seasonal, age restrictions may apply, 7 day cancellation notice-fee imposed. **Amenities:** video library, CD players, irons, hair dryers. **Leisure Activities:** whirlpool, canoeing. *Fee:* massage. **Business Services:** meeting rooms. **Cards:** MC, VI.

SUPER 8 VERNON

Book at AAA.com

Phone: (250)542-4434

Small-scale Hotel
$80-$175 All Year

Address: 4204 32nd St V1T 5P4 **Location:** Hwy 97 (32nd St); jct 43rd Ave. **Facility:** 62 units. 60 one- and 2 two-bedroom standard units. 2 stories (no elevator), interior corridors. **Parking:** on-site. **Amenities:** hair dryers. *Some:* irons. **Pool(s):** heated indoor. **Guest Services:** wireless Internet. **Business Services:** PC. **Cards:** AX, DC, DS, MC, VI.

VERNON TRAVELODGE

Book at AAA.com

Phone: (250)545-2161

Small-scale Hotel
$79-$159 All Year

Address: 3000 28th Ave V1T 1W1 **Location:** Hwy 97 (32nd St), just e on 28th Ave; near Polson Park. **Facility:** 39 one-bedroom standard units. 2 stories (no elevator), exterior corridors. *Bath:* combo or shower only. **Parking:** on-site. **Terms:** office hours 7:30 am-11 pm, cancellation fee imposed. **Pool(s):** heated outdoor. **Guest Services:** wireless Internet. **Cards:** AX, MC, VI.

——— WHERE TO DINE ———

AMARIN THAI RESTAURANT

Phone: 250/542-9300

Thai
$8-$19

Lining the extensive menu are many salads, some with meat, as well as beef, seafood, chicken and pork dishes. The stylish decor, including Thai artifacts and art, is warm and appealing. Service is fine. Parking is limited to the street. **Bar:** Full bar. **Reservations:** suggested. **Hours:** 11:30 am-2:30 & 5-10 pm, Sat & Sun from 5 pm. Closed major holidays; also Sun. **Address:** 2903 31st St V1T 5H6 **Location:** Between 29th and 30th aves. **Parking:** street. **Cards:** AX, MC, VI.

DIVINO'S ITALIANO RISTORANTE

Phone: 250/549-3463

Italian
$8-$20

The small, downtown, bistro-style restaurant serves a variety of homemade pastas, all made on the premises. Choices include fresh gnocchi, lasagna and spaghetti. Each table was painted by a local artist, which enables diners to enjoy art with their hearty, delicious meal. Casual dress. **Bar:** Full bar. **Hours:** 11 am-2 & 5-10 pm, Sat from 5 pm. Closed major holidays; also Sun & Mon. **Address:** 3224 30th Ave V1T 2C5 **Location:** Corner of 30th Ave and 33rd St; downtown. **Parking:** street. **Cards:** MC, VI.

THE ECLECTIC MED RESTAURANT INC

Phone: 250/558-4646

Mediterranean
$10-$32

In a word, the restaurant can be summed up as "funky," with a varied and eclectic menu of Mediterranean food. The many tempting food choices entice diners to return repeatedly. Appetizers are big enough to enjoy as a meal, and entrees incorporate everything from seafood to vegetarian staples. Throw in a superb wine list, a warm atmosphere and friendly service, and you've found the recipe for a fantastic evening. Dressy casual. **Bar:** Full bar. **Reservations:** suggested. **Hours:** 11 am-10 pm, Sat from 4 pm, Sun 5 pm-9 pm. Closed: 12/25, 12/26. **Address:** 2915 30th Ave V1T 5Z1 **Location:** Corner of Hwy 97 (32nd St) and 32nd Ave. **Parking:** street. **Cards:** AX, MC, VI.

EL PORTILLO COFFEE HOUSE

Phone: 250/545-9599

Deli/Subs
Sandwiches
$4-$10

It's an old adage that police officers know the best places in town to eat. This indeed may the safest spot in town. While the comfortably shabby space is well known for its coffee and baked goods, it also serves freshly made soups and sandwiches. Casual dress. **Bar:** Beer only. **Reservations:** not accepted. **Hours:** 7 am-10 pm, Sun 9 am-5 pm. Closed major holidays. **Address:** 2706 - 30th Ave V1T 2B6 **Location:** Jct 32nd St, 0.4 km e; centre. **Parking:** on-site. **Cards:** MC, VI.

INTERMEZZO RESTAURANT

Phone: 250/542-3853

Italian
$11-$25

You'll enjoy the wide variety of pasta, chicken, seafood, barbecue ribs and the specialty veal, prepared in six classic ways, at the Intermezzo, which is located downtown behind a small shopping complex. Meals are delicious and attractively presented. Casual dress. **Bar:** Full bar. **Reservations:** accepted. **Hours:** 5 pm-10 pm, Sun-9 pm. Closed: 12/24, 12/25. **Address:** 3206 34th Ave V1T 6M1 **Location:** Hwy 97 (32nd St), just w. **Parking:** street. **Cards:** AX, MC, VI.

THE ITALIAN KITCHEN COMPANY

Italian
$6-$17

Phone: 250/558-7899

Hearty, delicious food awaits at the funky, upbeat restaurant, along the main street downtown. Among offerings are traditional dishes, ranging from pastas to salads to savory soups. Hardwood floors and an exposed-brick wall are accentuated by large local art in a bright and cheery decor. Service is friendly and attentive. Casual dress. **Bar:** Full bar. **Hours:** 11 am-2 & 5-10 pm, Sat & Sun from 5 pm. Closed major holidays. **Address:** 2916 30th Ave V1T 2B7 **Location:** Downtown. **Parking:** street. **Cards:** AX, MC, VI.

SIDEWAY'S TAPAS & WINE

Canadian
$10-$15

Phone: 250/558-0202

At first glance, this sleek and sexy dining room in the heart of downtown might seem more at home in Vancouver or Calgary. In the company of friends, diners feel time slow right down, and it isn't out of the question for a couple of hours to slip by as they nibble off each others' plates. Spanish and locally sourced ingredients mingle in the kitchen's tapas-style dishes, which are perfect for sharing. Dressy casual. **Bar:** Full bar. **Reservations:** accepted. **Hours:** 5 pm-midnight. Closed major holidays. **Address:** 3006 30th Ave V1T 2B9 **Location:** Just e of jct 32nd St; centre. **Parking:** street. **Cards:** AX, MC, VI.

WESTBANK pop. 15,700

——— **WHERE TO STAY** ———

THE COVE LAKESIDE RESORT

Resort
Small-scale Hotel
$145-$300 All Year

Book great rates at AAA.com

Phone: (250)707-1800

Address: 4205 Gellatly Rd V4T 2K2 **Location:** Hwy 97, 1 mi (1.6 km) s. **Facility:** 150 units. 100 two- and 50 three-bedroom suites with kitchens. 4 stories, interior corridors. **Parking:** on-site. **Terms:** 3 day cancellation notice. **Amenities:** DVD players, voice mail, irons. **Pool(s):** 2 outdoor. **Leisure Activities:** whirlpools, waterslide, limited beach access, boat dock, putting green, tennis court, exercise room, spa. **Guest Services:** complimentary and valet laundry, wireless Internet. **Cards:** AX, MC, VI. **Free Special Amenities:** newspaper and early check-in/late check-out. *(See color ad p 527)*

     / SOME UNITS

HOLIDAY INN WESTBANK (KELOWNA)

Small-scale Hotel
$99-$275 3/1-10/14
$99-$225 10/15-2/28

Book great rates at AAA.com

Phone: (250)768-8879

Address: 2569 Dobbin Rd V4T 2J6 **Location:** Hwy 97 (Dobbin Rd) and Herbert Rd. **Facility:** 77 units. 75 one-bedroom standard units, some with whirlpools. 2 two-bedroom suites with kitchens and whirlpools. 3 stories, interior corridors. **Parking:** on-site. **Amenities:** high-speed Internet, voice mail, irons, hair dryers. **Pool(s):** heated indoor/outdoor. **Leisure Activities:** whirlpool, limited exercise equipment. **Guest Services:** valet laundry. **Business Services:** conference facilities, PC (fee). **Cards:** AX, DC, DS, MC, VI.

CALL / SOME UNITS   FEE   FEE   FEE

Art Gallery of the South Okanagan, Penticton / © AAA / Ron Willis

This ends listings for the Okanagan Valley.
The following page resumes the alphabetical listings of cities in British Columbia.

OLIVER —*See Okanagan Valley p. 534.*

OSOYOOS —*See Okanagan Valley p. 535.*

PARKSVILLE pop. 10,993

———— **WHERE TO STAY** ————

BEACH ACRES RESORT

Vacation Rental Cottage

$139-$399 All Year

Phone: (250)248-3424

Address: 1051 Resort Dr, #25 V9P 2E4 **Location:** Island Hwy 19, exit 46 (Parksville), 1.6 mi (2.5 km) n on Hwy 19A. **Facility:** This mix of condos is dispersed over several acres; some are set back and secluded, some sit on a cliff overlooking the ocean and some are beachfront. Smoke free premises. 57 units. 2 one- and 21 two-bedroom standard units with kitchens. 34 cottages. 1-2 stories (no elevator), exterior corridors. *Bath:* combo or shower only. **Parking:** on-site. **Terms:** office hours 8 am-9 pm, check-in 4 pm, 2-7 night minimum stay - seasonal and/or weekends, 30 day cancellation notice-fee imposed. **Amenities:** video library (fee), voice mail, irons. *Some:* DVD players (fee). **Pool(s):** heated indoor. **Leisure Activities:** sauna, whirlpool, 3 tennis courts, recreation programs, playground, basketball, horseshoes, shuffleboard, volleyball. **Guest Services:** coin laundry, wireless Internet. **Business Services:** meeting rooms, PC. **Cards:** AX, DS, MC, VI. *(See color ad below)*

OCEANSIDE VILLAGE RESORT

Cottage

$200-$295 6/29-2/28
$110-$180 3/1-6/28

Phone: 250/248-8961

Address: 1080 Resort Dr V9P 2E3 **Location:** Island Hwy 19, exit 46 (Parksville), 1.8 mi (2.5 km) n on Hwy 19A. **Facility:** Located within a short walk of beautiful Rathtrevor Park, these attractive cottages comfortably sleep six to eight people. Smoke free premises. 60 two-bedroom suites with kitchens. 1 story, exterior corridors. **Parking:** on-site. **Terms:** office hours 10 am-4 pm, check-in 4 pm, 2 night minimum stay, 30 day cancellation notice-fee imposed. **Amenities:** DVD players, CD players, voice mail, irons, hair dryers. **Pool(s):** heated indoor. **Leisure Activities:** whirlpool, limited exercise equipment. **Guest Services:** complimentary laundry, wireless Internet. **Cards:** MC, VI.

QUALITY RESORT BAYSIDE
Book great rates at AAA.com

Small-scale Hotel

$119-$259 All Year

Phone: (250)248-8333

Address: 240 Dogwood St V9P 2H5 **Location:** Island Hwy 19, exit 51 (Parksville/Coombs), 1.3 mi (2 km) e, then 0.6 mi (1 km) n on Hwy 19A. **Facility:** Smoke free premises. 59 one-bedroom standard units. 3 stories, interior corridors. **Parking:** on-site. **Amenities:** voice mail, irons, hair dryers. **Pool(s):** heated indoor. **Leisure Activities:** whirlpool, beach access, squash, exercise room, volleyball. **Guest Services:** valet laundry, area transportation-train & bus station, wireless Internet. **Business Services:** meeting rooms. **Cards:** AX, DC, MC, VI. **Free Special Amenities:** newspaper and high-speed Internet.** *(See color ad on insert)*

SANDCASTLE INN

Small-scale Hotel

$79-$139 All Year

Phone: 250/248-2334

Address: 374 W Island Hwy V9P 1K8 **Location:** Island Hwy 19, exit 51 (Parksville/Coombs), 1.3 mi (2 km) e, then just n on Hwy 19A. **Facility:** Smoke free premises. 36 one-bedroom standard units, some with efficiencies. 3 stories, interior corridors. *Bath:* combo or shower only. **Parking:** on-site. **Terms:** office hours 7 am-11 pm, 7 day cancellation notice-fee imposed. **Amenities:** voice mail. **Leisure Activities:** barbecue area. **Guest Services:** coin laundry, wireless Internet. **Business Services:** meeting rooms. **Cards:** AX, MC, VI.

SKYLITE MOTEL

Motel

$69-$129 All Year

Phone: (250)248-4271

Address: 459 E Island Hwy V9P 2G5 **Location:** Island Hwy 19, exit 46 (Parksville), 2.2 mi (3.5 km) n on Hwy 19A. **Facility:** 25 one-bedroom standard units, some with efficiencies or kitchens. 1-2 stories (no elevator), exterior corridors. **Parking:** on-site. **Terms:** office hours 7 am-11 pm. **Amenities:** irons, hair dryers. **Guest Services:** wireless Internet. **Cards:** AX, MC, VI.

▼ *See AAA listing above* ▼

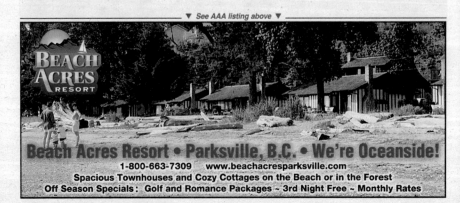

TIGH-NA-MARA SEASIDE SPA RESORT & CONFERENCE CENTER

Book great rates at AAA.com

Phone: (250)248-2072

Resort
Large-scale Hotel
$119-$359 All Year

Address: 1155 Resort Dr V9P 2E5 **Location:** Island Hwy 19, exit 46 (Parksville), 1.3 mi (2 km) n on Hwy 19A. **Facility:** This all-season resort features a cluster of lovely log cottages and deluxe condo-style units set in a forestlike setting or along a sandy beach. Smoke free premises. 192 units. 89 one-bedroom standard units, some with efficiencies and/or whirlpools. 66 one- and 4 two-bedroom suites, some with kitchens and/or whirlpools. 33 cottages. 1-3 stories (no elevator), exterior corridors. **Parking:** on-site. **Terms:** check-in 4 pm, 2 night minimum stay - seasonal and/or weekends, 5 day cancellation notice-fee imposed. **Amenities:** high-speed Internet (fee), voice mail, irons, hair dryers. **Dining:** Cedar Dining Room at Tigh-Na-Mara Seaside Spa Resort, see separate listing. **Pool(s):** heated indoor. **Leisure Activities:** sauna, whirlpool, tennis court, recreation programs, rental bicycles, playground, exercise room, spa, horseshoes, volleyball. **Guest Services:** coin laundry, airport transportation-Qualicum Airport, area transportation-bus & train station. **Business Services:** conference facilities, business center. **Cards:** AX, MC, VI.

⊕ 🍴 🍸 🏊 ⊠ ✕ 🏋 🎥 🔲 💻 / SOME UNITS FEE 🐾 🖥

TRAVELODGE PARKSVILLE

Book at AAA.com

Phone: (250)248-2232

Small-scale Hotel
$109-$189 3/1-9/30
$99-$179 10/1-2/28

Address: 424 W Island Hwy V9P 1K8 **Location:** Island Hwy 19, exit 51 (Parksville/Coombs), 1.3 mi (2 km) e, then just n on Hwy 19A. **Facility:** 84 one-bedroom standard units, some with whirlpools. 3 stories, interior corridors. **Parking:** on-site. **Amenities:** hair dryers. **Pool(s):** heated indoor. **Leisure Activities:** whirlpool, limited exercise equipment. **Guest Services:** coin laundry, wireless Internet. **Business Services:** meeting rooms. **Cards:** AX, JC, MC, VI.

🅂🄳 🍴 CALL 🅶🄼 🏊 💻 / SOME UNITS FEE 🐾 ✕

V.I.P. MOTEL

Phone: (250)248-3244

Motel
$69-$169 All Year

Address: 414 W Island Hwy V9P 1K8 **Location:** Island Hwy 19, exit 51 (Parksville/Coombs), 1.3 mi (2 km) e, then just n on Hwy 19A. **Facility:** 21 one-bedroom standard units, some with efficiencies. 1 story, exterior corridors. **Parking:** on-site. **Terms:** office hours 7 am-11 pm, cancellation fee imposed. **Amenities:** hair dryers. **Leisure Activities:** barbecue patio. **Guest Services:** coin laundry, wireless Internet. **Cards:** AX, MC, VI. **Free Special Amenities: continental breakfast and high-speed Internet.**

🅂🄳 🍴 🏋 🎥 🔲 💻 / SOME UNITS 🐾 ✕ 🖥

--------- **WHERE TO DINE** ---------

BUGSYS BAR & GRILL

Phone: 250/248-4545

Canadian
$8-$23

In gangster circles, the name Bugsy is a term of endearment or honor; here, Bugsy translates to pizza, calzones, ribs, chicken, pasta and burgers. A large bar features big screen TVs for all the sporting events you can handle, and the restaurant is open late. Casual dress. **Bar:** Full bar. **Hours:** 11 am-midnight. Closed: 12/25. **Address:** 332 W Island Hwy V9P 1K8 **Location:** Island Hwy 19, exit 51 (Parksville/Coombs), 1.3 mi (2 km) e, then just n on Hwy 19A. **Parking:** on-site. **Cards:** AX, MC, VI.

CEDAR DINING ROOM AT TIGH-NA-MARA SEASIDE SPA RESORT

Phone: 250/248-2333

Pacific Rim
$12-$36

Although the menu focuses on West Coast seafood, it also lists pasta and steak dishes and more casual breakfast and lunch offerings. Sunday brunch is popular. The authentic log restaurant is nestled in a forest by the sea. The country-elegant setting is informal, warm and friendly. Casual dress. **Bar:** Full bar. **Reservations:** suggested, for dinner & Sunday brunch. **Hours:** 7 am-9:30 pm. **Address:** 1155 Resort Dr V9P 2E5 **Location:** Island Hwy 19, exit 46 (Parksville), 1.3 mi (2 km) n on Hwy 19A; in Tigh-Na-Mara Seaside Spa Resort & Conference Center. **Parking:** on-site. **Cards:** AX, DC, MC, VI.

KALVAS RESTAURANT

Phone: 250/248-6933

Steak & Seafood
$12-$60

You'll surely enjoy the Alpine, log-cabin decor and high-quality, home cooking with fresh ingredients at this restaurant. It features an extensive menu of fresh seafood such as lobster, crab and oysters, as well as duck, pheasant and steak. Cozy setting. Casual dress. **Bar:** Full bar. **Reservations:** suggested. **Hours:** 5 pm-10 pm, Sat-11 pm. Closed: 12/25. **Address:** 180 Moilliet St, Island Hwy N V9P 2H4 **Location:** Island Hwy 19, exit 51 (Parksville/Coombs), 1.3 mi (2 km) e, then just n on Hwy 19A. **Parking:** on-site. **Cards:** MC, VI.

LEFTY'S FRESH FOOD RESTAURANT

Phone: 250/954-3886

Canadian
$7-$18

Three friends realized they all were left-handed, and a new restaurant was born. The kitchen is committed to fresh ingredients in such dishes as the signature "southpawtatoes," which are oven roasted in special seasoning, and the made-from-scratch desserts. The motto here: "Everyone is born right-handed; only the greatest overcome it". Casual dress. **Bar:** Full bar. **Reservations:** accepted. **Hours:** 8 am-8 pm, Fri-Sun to 9 pm. Closed: 12/25. **Address:** 101-280 E Island Hwy V9P 2G3 **Location:** Island Hwy 19, exit 46 (Parksville), 2.5 mi (4 km) n on Hwy 19A. **Parking:** on-site. **Cards:** MC, VI.

TRISKELL RESTAURANT

Phone: 250/248-2011

Regional French
$8-$35

Charming simplicity awaits guests at the restaurant, where traditional specialties of Brittany are featured. Savory, sweet crepes are offered alongside such dishes as coquille St. Jacques, lapin braise and veau aux poires. The owners themselves deliver warm and attentive service. Casual dress. **Bar:** Full bar. **Reservations:** suggested. **Hours:** Open 3/1-1/1 & 2/1-2/28; 4:30 pm-9:30 pm. Closed major holidays; also Sun. **Address:** 3-220 W Island Hwy V9P 2P3 **Location:** Island Hwy 19, exit 51 (Parksville/Coombs), 2 km e, then just n on Hwy 19A. **Parking:** on-site. **Cards:** MC, VI.

PARSON

---------- WHERE TO STAY ----------

ALEXA CHALETS-TIMBER INN & RESTAURANT

Phone: (250)348-2228

Small-scale Hotel
$75-$180 3/1-10/15 &
12/1-2/28

Address: 3483 Hwy 95 V0A 1L0 **Location:** Just off Hwy 95; 21.3 mi (34 km) s of Golden. **Facility:** Smoke free premises. 11 units. 5 one-bedroom standard units. 1 vacation home and 5 cabins. 2 stories (no elevator), interior/exterior corridors. *Bath:* combo or shower only. **Parking:** on-site. **Terms:** open 3/1-10/15 & 12/1-2/28, office hours 7 am-11 pm, check-in 4 pm, 30 day cancellation notice-fee imposed. **Amenities:** hair dryers. **Leisure Activities:** sauna, whirlpool, hiking trails, limited exercise equipment, basketball, horseshoes, volleyball. *Fee:* massage. **Guest Services:** TV in common area, complimentary laundry. **Business Services:** PC. **Cards:** MC, VI.

PEMBERTON pop. 1,637

---------- WHERE TO STAY ----------

PEMBERTON VALLEY LODGE   *Book great rates at AAA.com*

Phone: (604)894-2000

(CAA) (SAVE)

Small-scale Hotel
$129-$339 All Year

Address: 1490 Portage Rd V0N 2L1 **Location:** Just e on Hwy 99 from Pioneer Junction. **Facility:** Smoke free premises. 85 units. 43 one-bedroom standard units with efficiencies. 32 one- and 10 two-bedroom suites with kitchens. 3 stories, interior corridors. **Parking:** on-site. **Terms:** cancellation fee imposed. **Amenities:** DVD players, voice mail, irons, hair dryers. **Pool(s):** heated outdoor. **Leisure Activities:** whirlpool, limited exercise equipment. **Guest Services:** complimentary laundry, area transportation-Whistler Ski Hills, wireless Internet. **Business Services:** meeting rooms. **Cards:** AX, DC, DS, MC, VI. **Free Special Amenities:** local telephone calls and newspaper.
(See color ad p 672)

CALL

PENDER ISLAND —*See Gulf Islands National Park Reserve p. 505.*

PENTICTON —*See Okanagan Valley p. 536.*

PITT MEADOWS —*See Vancouver p. 622.*

PORT ALBERNI pop. 17,743

---------- WHERE TO STAY ----------

BEST WESTERN BARCLAY HOTEL   *Book great rates at AAA.com*

Phone: 250/724-7171

(CAA) (SAVE)

Small-scale Hotel
Rates not provided

Address: 4277 Stamp Ave V9Y 7X8 **Location:** Johnston Rd (Hwy 4), just s on Gertrude St. **Facility:** Smoke free premises. 86 one-bedroom standard units, some with whirlpools. 5 stories, interior corridors. **Parking:** on-site. **Amenities:** voice mail, irons, hair dryers. *Some:* high-speed Internet. **Pool(s):** heated outdoor. **Leisure Activities:** sauna, whirlpool, exercise room. **Guest Services:** valet laundry, wireless Internet. **Business Services:** meeting rooms. **Free Special Amenities:** local telephone calls and high-speed internet.

CEDAR WOOD LODGE BED AND BREAKFAST INN

Phone: (250)724-6800

Bed & Breakfast
$90-$149 All Year

Address: 5895 River Rd V9Y 6Z5 **Location:** 1.9 mi (3 km) w on River Rd (Hwy 4) from Johnston Rd. **Facility:** Smoke free premises. 8 one-bedroom standard units with whirlpools. 2 stories (no elevator), interior corridors. **Parking:** on-site. **Terms:** office hours 7 am-11 pm. **Amenities:** high-speed Internet. **Guest Services:** wireless Internet. **Business Services:** meeting rooms. **Cards:** AX, JC, MC, VI.

THE HOSPITALITY INN   *Book at AAA.com*

Phone: (250)723-8111

Small-scale Hotel
$129-$155 All Year

Address: 3835 Redford St V9Y 3S2 **Location:** 2 mi (3.2 km) sw of jct Hwy 4 via City Centre/Port Alberni South Route. **Facility:** 50 one-bedroom standard units. 2 stories (no elevator), interior corridors. **Parking:** on-site. **Terms:** cancellation fee imposed. **Amenities:** high-speed Internet, voice mail, irons, hair dryers. **Pool(s):** heated outdoor. **Leisure Activities:** whirlpool, limited exercise equipment. **Guest Services:** valet laundry, wireless Internet. **Business Services:** meeting rooms. **Cards:** AX, CB, DC, DS, JC, MC, VI.

RIVERSIDE MOTEL

Phone: (250)724-9916

(CAA) (SAVE)

Motel
$99 5/1-2/28
$79 3/1-4/30

Address: 5065 Roger St V9Y 3Y9 **Location:** Johnston Rd (Hwy 4), just s on Gertrude St, then just w. **Facility:** Smoke free premises. 10 one-bedroom standard units, some with efficiencies and kitchens. 1 story, exterior corridors. *Bath:* combo or shower only. **Parking:** on-site. **Terms:** office hours 7:30 am-11 pm. **Amenities:** voice mail, hair dryers. **Guest Services:** coin laundry, wireless Internet. **Cards:** AX, MC, VI. **Free Special Amenities:** local telephone calls and high-speed Internet.

───── WHERE TO DINE ─────

LITTLE BAVARIA RESTAURANT *Menu on AAA.com* Phone: 250/724-4242

German
$8-$20

This quaint restaurant features a pleasant Bavarian decor with an accent on good old-fashioned German food. Schnitzel, Hungarian goulash, cabbage rolls, steak, seafood, and fondue for two are on the menu. Couples and business people like this place. Casual dress. **Bar:** Full bar. **Reservations:** suggested. **Hours:** 11 am-2 & 5-10 pm, Sat & Sun from 5 pm. Closed: 12/24-12/29. **Address:** 3035 4th Ave V9Y 2B8 **Location:** Between Argyle and Angus. **Parking:** street. **Cards:** AX, MC, VI.

SMITTY'S FAMILY RESTAURANT Phone: 250/724-5022

Canadian
$6-$18

The family-oriented restaurant satisfies patrons with its ever-popular all-day breakfast items, as well as tasty and wholesome soups and salads at lunchtime. A relaxed mood characterizes the dining space. Casual dress. **Bar:** Full bar. **Hours:** 6:30 am-9 pm. Closed: 12/25. **Address:** 13426 3rd Ave V9Y 7M8 **Location:** Between Napier St and the Quadrant. **Parking:** on-site. **Cards:** AX, MC, VI.

PORT COQUITLAM —See Vancouver p. 623.

PORT HARDY pop. 3,822

───── WHERE TO STAY ─────

AIRPORT INN Phone: 250/949-9434

Small-scale Hotel
Rates not provided

Address: 4030 Byng Rd V0N 2P0 **Location:** Hwy 19, 3.1 mi (5 km) ne, follow signs. **Facility:** Smoke free premises. 45 one-bedroom standard units, some with efficiencies. 2 stories (no elevator), interior corridors. **Parking:** on-site. **Amenities:** voice mail, hair dryers. *Some:* irons. **Dining:** restaurant, see separate listing. **Guest Services:** coin laundry, wireless Internet. **Business Services:** meeting rooms, PC.

GLEN LYON INN Phone: 250/949-7115

Small-scale Hotel
$105-$180 All Year

Address: 6435 Hardy Bay Rd V0N 2P0 **Location:** Hwy 19, 0.9 mi (1.5 km) n, follow signs. **Facility:** 44 one-bedroom standard units, some with efficiencies and/or whirlpools. 3 stories, exterior corridors. **Parking:** on-site. **Terms:** 3 day cancellation notice. **Amenities:** voice mail, hair dryers. **Leisure Activities:** limited exercise equipment. **Guest Services:** coin laundry, wireless Internet. **Business Services:** meeting rooms, PC (fee). **Cards:** AX, MC, VI.

─────── *The following lodging was either not evaluated or did not* ───────
meet AAA rating requirements but is listed for your information only.

QUARTERDECK INN Phone: 250/902-0455

[fyi]

Not evaluated. **Address:** 6555 Hardy Bay Rd V0N 2P0 **Location:** Hwy 19, 0.9 mi (1.5 km) n. Facilities, services, and decor characterize a mid-range property.

───── WHERE TO DINE ─────

AIRPORT INN RESTAURANT Phone: 250/949-9434

Chinese
$7-$15

Locals and visitors alike enjoy the restaurant, near Port Hardy's airport. It prepares many Cantonese/Chinese selections, as well as some Western fare, including burgers, hot and cold sandwiches and appetizers. Families are welcomed. Casual dress. **Bar:** Full bar. **Hours:** 7 am-9:30 pm. Closed major holidays. **Address:** 4030 Byng Rd V0N 2P0 **Location:** Hwy 19, 3.1 mi (5 km) ne, follow signs; in Airport Inn. **Parking:** on-site. **Cards:** AX, MC, VI.

MALONE'S OCEANSIDE BISTRO Phone: 250/949-3050

Canadian
$10-$21

In a former shopping mall now housing North Island College, the popular family restaurant presents a menu of local seafood, steak, pizza and traditional Greek specialties. Casual dress. **Bar:** Full bar. **Reservations:** suggested. **Hours:** 11 am-9 pm. Closed major holidays; also Sun, 12/24-12/26. **Address:** 9300 Trustee Rd V0N 2P0 **Location:** 0.6 mi (1 km) se on Hwy 19, just sw; in The North Island Mall. **Parking:** on-site. **Cards:** AX, MC, VI.

MARKET CAFE Phone: 250/949-8110

Canadian
$5-$10

Serving homemade soup and sandwiches along with mouthwatering pastries, pie and muffins, the downtown cafe is in the heart of the business district. Find booth seating along the walls. **Hours:** 7 am-6 pm. Closed: 12/25. **Address:** 7030 Market St V0N 2P0 **Location:** Hwy 19, 0.6 mi (1 km) nw (towards water) on Granville St, then just ne. **Parking:** street. **Cards:** MC, VI.

TOUDAI RESTAURANT Phone: 250/949-8755

Japanese
$4-$13

Casual dress. **Bar:** Beer & wine. **Hours:** 11 am-2 & 5-9:30 pm, Sun from 5 pm. Closed: 12/25. **Address:** 7370 Market St V0N 2P0 **Location:** Corner of Market and Douglas sts; downtown; in Northshore Inn. **Parking:** on-site. **Cards:** AX, MC, VI.

PORT McNEILL pop. 2,623

BLACK BEAR RESORT

Motel
Rates not provided

Phone: 250/956-4900

Address: 1812 Campbell Pkwy V0N 2R0 **Location:** Hwy 19, 1.3 mi (2 km) e. **Facility:** Smoke free premises. 40 one-bedroom standard units, some with efficiencies. 2 stories (no elevator), exterior corridors. **Parking:** on-site. **Terms:** office hours 6 am-midnight. **Amenities:** high-speed Internet, voice mail, hair dryers. **Guest Services:** coin laundry, wireless Internet. **Business Services:** meeting rooms, PC.

HAIDA-WAY MOTOR INN

Motel
$85-$109 All Year

Phone: (250)956-3373

Address: 1817 Campbell Way V0N 2R0 **Location:** Hwy 19, 1.3 mi (2 km) e. **Facility:** 52 one-bedroom standard units, some with efficiencies or kitchens. 3 stories (no elevator), interior/exterior corridors. **Parking:** on-site. **Terms:** office hours 6 am-2 am, check-in 4 pm. **Dining:** Northern Lights Restaurant, see separate listing. **Guest Services:** coin laundry, wireless Internet. **Business Services:** meeting rooms, PC. **Cards:** AX, MC, VI.

——— WHERE TO DINE ———

NORTHERN LIGHTS RESTAURANT

Canadian
$15-$25

Phone: 250/956-3263

Popular among the locals for its tasty food, the restaurant offers summer choices that include fresh local seafood as well as some steak, chicken or pasta dishes. Save room for dessert, as there is always a nice selection. During summer, reservations are recommended. Casual dress. **Bar:** Full bar. **Reservations:** suggested, 6/15-9/15. **Hours:** 5 pm-10 pm. Closed: 12/23-1/3. **Address:** 1817 Campbell Way V0N 2R0 **Location:** Hwy 19, 1.3 mi (2 km) e; in Haida-Way Motor Inn. **Parking:** on-site. **Cards:** AX, MC, VI.

PORT RENFREW

——— WHERE TO DINE ———

LIGHTHOUSE PUB & RESTAURANT

Canadian
$8-$16

Phone: 250/647-5505

One of the best eating spots in town, the restaurant serves good pub food along with a wide selection of beers by the bottle or on tap. Casual dress. **Bar:** Full bar. **Hours:** 11 am-9 pm; hours vary off season. Closed: 1/1, 12/25. **Address:** General Delivery V0S 1K0 **Location:** 1.3 mi (2 km) w on Parkinson Rd. **Parking:** on-site. **Cards:** MC, VI.

POWELL RIVER pop. 12,957

——— WHERE TO STAY ———

POWELL RIVER TOWN CENTRE HOTEL *Book at AAA.com*

Small-scale Hotel
$135-$180 All Year

Phone: (604)485-3000

Address: 4660 Joyce Ave V8A 3B6 **Location:** 0.5 mi (0.8 km) e on Duncan St (BC ferry terminal), then 0.6 mi (1 km) n. **Facility:** 71 one-bedroom standard units, some with whirlpools. 2 stories, interior corridors. **Parking:** on-site. **Terms:** cancellation fee imposed. **Amenities:** video games (fee), high-speed Internet, voice mail, hair dryers. **Leisure Activities:** whirlpool. **Guest Services:** valet laundry, area transportation, wireless Internet. **Business Services:** meeting rooms, PC (fee). **Cards:** AX, DC, DS, MC, VI.

——— *The following lodging was either not evaluated or did not* ———
meet AAA rating requirements but is listed for your information only.

ISLAND VIEW MOTEL

[fyi]

Phone: 604/483-3113

Not evaluated. **Address:** 6255 Marine Ave V8A 4K6 **Location:** From Duncan St (BC ferry terminal), 2.2 mi (3.5 km) n. Facilities, services, and decor characterize a basic property.

——— WHERE TO DINE ———

THE SHINGLEMILL PUB & BISTRO

Canadian
$7-$24

Phone: 604/483-2001

The popular, longstanding pub and bistro sits on the shores of Powell Lake, and large bay windows overlook the marina. The view is best from the second floor. Food is typical bistro fare: burgers, sandwiches and soups. Although it's a bit of a drive to get here, it's worth the trip. Casual dress. **Bar:** Full bar. **Reservations:** accepted. **Hours:** 11 am-2:30 & 5-9 pm, Sat 11 am-9 pm, Sun 9 am-9 pm; 11 am-9 pm 7/1-9/5. Closed: 12/25. **Address:** 6233 Powell Pl V8A 4S6 **Location:** From Duncan St (BC ferry terminal), 2.2 mi (3.5 km) n on Marine Ave, 0.9 mi (1.5 km) e on Arbutus. **Parking:** on-site. **Cards:** AX, DC, MC, VI.

WESTVIEW RESTAURANT & PIZZA

Greek
$8-$20

Phone: 604/485-6162

The menu blends Greek dishes, such as souvlaki and moussaka, with Italian fare, including baked lasagna and many pizza varieties. Large bay windows overlook the ocean. Casual dress. **Bar:** Full bar. **Reservations:** accepted. **Hours:** 11 am-11 pm, Sat & Sun from 4 pm. Closed: 1/1, 12/25, 12/26. **Address:** 4553 Marine Ave V8A 2K5 **Location:** From Duncan St (BC ferry terminal), just n; between Burton and Courtney sts. **Parking:** on-site. **Cards:** MC, VI.

PRINCE GEORGE pop. 70,981

──── WHERE TO STAY ────

BEST WESTERN CITY CENTRE   *Book great rates at AAA.com*   Phone: 250/563-1267

Motel
Rates not provided

Address: 910 Victoria St V2L 2K8 **Location:** Just n of Victoria St (Hwy 16) and Patricia Blvd; downtown. **Facility:** 53 units. 49 one-bedroom standard units. 4 one-bedroom suites. 2 stories (no elevator), exterior corridors. **Parking:** on-site, winter plug-ins. **Terms:** office hours 6 am-11 pm. **Amenities:** irons, hair dryers. **Pool(s):** heated indoor. **Leisure Activities:** saunas, limited exercise equipment. **Guest Services:** valet and coin laundry, wireless Internet. **Free Special Amenities:** local telephone calls and high-speed Internet.

AAA Benefit:
Members save 10% everyday, plus an exclusive frequent stay program.

DAYS INN   *Book at AAA.com*   Phone: (250)562-7072

Small-scale Hotel
$110-$120 All Year

Address: 600 Quebec St V2L 1W7 **Location:** From Victoria St (Hwy 16), just n on 7th Ave. **Facility:** 75 units. 74 one-bedroom standard units. 1 one-bedroom suite with efficiency. 2 stories, interior corridors. **Parking:** on-site. **Amenities:** voice mail. *Some:* irons, hair dryers. **Leisure Activities:** limited exercise equipment. **Guest Services:** valet and coin laundry, wireless Internet. **Business Services:** meeting rooms. **Cards:** AX, CB, DC, MC, VI.

FOUR POINTS BY SHERATON PRINCE GEORGE   *Book great rates at AAA.com*   Phone: (250)564-7100

Small-scale Hotel
$129-$209 All Year

Address: 1790 Hwy 97 S V2L 5L3 **Location:** Hwy 97 N, exit Spruce; Hwy 97 S, exit city centre via Queensway. **Facility:** Smoke free premises. 74 units. 38 one-bedroom standard units. 36 one-bedroom suites, some with whirlpools. 3 stories, interior corridors. **Parking:** on-site, winter plug-ins. **Terms:** cancellation fee imposed. **Amenities:** high-speed Internet, voice mail, irons, hair dryers. **Leisure Activities:** exercise room. **Guest Services:** valet laundry. **Business Services:** meeting rooms, PC. **Cards:** AX, DC, DS, MC, VI. **Free Special Amenities:** newspaper and high-speed Internet.

FOUR POINTS BY SHERATON

AAA Benefit:
Members get up to 15% off, plus Starwood Preferred Guest® bonuses.

P.G. HI-WAY MOTEL   Phone: (250)564-6869

Motel
$60-$90 All Year

Address: 1737 20th Ave V2L 4B9 **Location:** Jct Hwy 97, 0.7 mi (1.2 km) e on Trans-Canada Hwy 16 (Yellowhead Hwy). **Facility:** 45 one-bedroom standard units, some with efficiencies. 2 stories (no elevator), exterior corridors. *Bath:* combo or shower only. **Parking:** on-site, winter plug-ins. **Terms:** office hours 7 am-midnight. **Guest Services:** wireless Internet. **Cards:** AX, MC, VI. **Free Special Amenities:** local telephone calls and high-speed Internet.

TREASURE COVE CASINO HOTEL   *Book at AAA.com*   Phone: (250)614-9111

Small-scale Hotel
$139-$189 All Year

Address: 2005 Hwy 97 S S V2N 7A3 **Location:** Corner of Hwy 97 and 16. **Facility:** Smoke free premises. 82 one-bedroom standard units, some with whirlpools. 4 stories, interior corridors. **Parking:** on-site. **Terms:** check-in 4 pm. **Amenities:** video games (fee), high-speed Internet, voice mail, irons, hair dryers. **Pool(s):** heated indoor. **Leisure Activities:** whirlpool, waterslide, exercise room, spa. **Guest Services:** valet laundry, wireless Internet. **Business Services:** meeting rooms, business center. **Cards:** AX, MC, VI.

──── WHERE TO DINE ────

CHINA SAIL RESTAURANT   Phone: 250/564-2828

Chinese
$9-$15

A local favorite for more than 20 years, this restaurant continues to serve delicious Chinese and Canadian dishes. You may select an individual meal, family dinner or combination plate; all are reasonably priced. Good food and good service. Casual dress. **Bar:** Full bar. **Hours:** 11:30 am-11 pm, Fri & Sat-midnight, Sun 2 pm-9 pm. Closed: 12/25, 12/26. **Address:** 4288 5th Ave V2M 7A2 **Location:** Hwy 97, 1.7 km w on 5th Ave; corner of 5th Ave and Tabor. **Parking:** on-site. **Cards:** AX, MC, VI.

EARLS PRINCE GEORGE   Phone: 250/562-1527

Canadian
$8-$19

Offering an experience that falls between fast food and fine dining, the fun, relaxed restaurant prepares great food at a great price. Choices range from juicy burgers, hearty sandwiches, fresh salads, wings and pizza to full entrees of steak, chops and seafood. Made-from-scratch soups and assorted breads, as well as a nice choice of wines and beers, round out the offerings. This is a fitting spot for impromptu get-togethers and festive occasions. Casual dress. **Bar:** Full bar. **Hours:** 11 am-midnight. Closed: 12/25. **Address:** 1440 E Central St V2M 3C1 **Location:** Corner of Hwy 97 and 15th Ave. **Parking:** on-site. **Cards:** AX, MC, VI.

MOXIE'S CLASSIC GRILL   Phone: 250/564-4700

Canadian
$8-$18

This sleek, funky and popular restaurant presents an extensive menu of creatively prepared dishes, including pizza, pasta, rice, noodles, signature salads and burgers. Other menus include one for children and one for Sunday brunch. Lending to the upbeat, stylish decor are dark wood appointments and river rock fireplaces. Casual dress. **Bar:** Full bar. **Hours:** 11 am-midnight, Sat & Sun from 10 am. **Address:** 1804 E Central St V2M 3C3 **Location:** Hwy 97 and 19th Ave. **Parking:** on-site. **Cards:** AX, MC, VI.

RIC'S GRILL, STEAK SEAFOOD & CHOP HOUSE *Menu on AAA.com*

Phone: 250/614-9096

(AAA)

Ric's is located downtown and close to the city's casino. Specializing in steak, this restaurant features Western Canadian beef known as "sterling silver," which is cooked any way you like it. Bustling atmosphere. Try a cozy booth for two. Casual dress. **Bar:** Full bar. **Reservations:** suggested. **Hours:** 4:30 pm-10 pm, Wed & Thurs 11:30 am-10 pm, Fri & Sat 11:30 am-11 pm. Closed: 12/25. **Address:** 547 George St V2L 1R8 **Location:** Between 5th and 6th aves; downtown. **Parking:** street. **Cards:** AX, MC, VI.

Steak & Seafood
$9-$45

PRINCE RUPERT pop. 12,815

──────── **WHERE TO STAY** ────────

ALEEDA MOTEL

Phone: (250)627-1367

(AAA) (SAVE)

Motel
$55-$110 All Year

Address: 900 3rd Ave W V8J 1M8 **Location:** Corner of 3rd Ave W and 8th St. **Facility:** 31 one-bedroom standard units, some with efficiencies. 2 stories (no elevator), interior corridors. **Parking:** on-site. **Cards:** AX, MC, VI. **Free Special Amenities:** continental breakfast and local telephone calls.

THE COAST PRINCE RUPERT HOTEL *Book at AAA.com*

Phone: (250)624-6711

Small-scale Hotel
$129-$189 3/1-9/30
$119-$179 10/1-2/28

Address: 118 6th St V8J 3L7 **Location:** Between 1st and 2nd aves W. **Facility:** 92 one-bedroom standard units. 8 stories, interior corridors. **Parking:** on-site. **Terms:** cancellation fee imposed. **Amenities:** high-speed Internet, voice mail, irons, hair dryers. **Guest Services:** valet laundry. **Business Services:** meeting rooms. **Cards:** AX, DS, MC, VI.

INN ON THE HARBOUR

Phone: 250/624-9107

Motel
$75-$135 All Year

Address: 720 1st Ave W V8J 3V6 **Location:** Corner of 6th St. **Facility:** 49 one-bedroom standard units. 3 stories (no elevator), interior corridors. *Bath:* combo or shower only. **Parking:** on-site. **Amenities:** hair dryers. **Guest Services:** valet laundry, wireless Internet. **Cards:** AX, MC, VI.

TOTEM LODGE MOTEL

Phone: 250/624-6761

(AAA) (SAVE)

Motel
$89-$99 3/1-10/1
$69-$79 10/2-2/28

Address: 1335 Park Ave V8J 1K3 **Location:** 1 mi (1.6 km) w on Hwy 16 (2nd Ave W) from downtown. **Facility:** 31 one-bedroom standard units, some with kitchens. 3 stories (no elevator), interior corridors. **Parking:** on-site. **Guest Services:** coin laundry, wireless Internet. **Cards:** AX, MC, VI. **Free Special Amenities:** continental breakfast and high-speed Internet.

──────── **WHERE TO DINE** ────────

OPA SUSHI

Phone: 250/627-4560

Japanese
$5-$30

The sushi restaurant occupies an old loft originally used for taking the main conk lines off the nets and putting them into a pot filled with tar that helped preserve the rope from rot and salt damage. The tar pot is still here, as is the tar on the floor. Seating is limited. Prices listed are for individual sushi rolls. Casual dress. **Bar:** Beer & wine. **Hours:** 11:30 am-2 & 5-9 pm. Closed major holidays; also Sun & Mon. **Address:** 34 Cow Bay Rd V8J 1A5 **Location:** From 3rd Ave E, 0.6 mi (1 km) n; in Cow Bay. **Parking:** street. **Cards:** AX, MC, VI.

RAIN DINING LOUNGE

Phone: 250/627-8272

Pacific Rim
$12-$25

Different for Prince Rupert, the restaurant offers a fine dining experience with a funky Vancouver feel. The decor incorporates bright colors, waterfalls and an open cocktail lounge and kitchen. Intense flavors and textures characterize dishes intended to share. Guests can try "small plates" from $4 to $12 or hearty "big boys" full entrees. Casual dress. **Bar:** Full bar. **Reservations:** suggested. **Hours:** 5 pm-1:30 am. Closed: 12/25, 12/26; also Sun. **Address:** 737 2nd Ave W V8J 1H4 **Location:** Between 8th and 7th sts. **Parking:** street. **Cards:** AX, MC, VI.

SMILES SEAFOOD CAFE

Phone: 250/624-3072

Seafood
$6-$20

In business since 1934, the distinctive diner-style restaurant serves locals and tourists alike with a variety of seafood, steaks, chops, sandwiches and salads. Any local can point the way to the cafe, in the city's Cow Bay area. Casual dress. **Bar:** Full bar. **Hours:** Open 3/1-12/25 & 2/1-2/28; 11 am-9 pm; 9 am-10 pm 6/1-9/6. Closed: 10/13, 12/25, 12/26. **Address:** 113 Cow Bay Rd V8J 1A4 **Location:** From 3rd Ave E, 0.6 mi (1 km) n; in Cow Bay. **Parking:** street. **Cards:** MC, VI.

STARDUST RESTAURANT

Phone: 250/627-1221

Chinese
$8-$20

Specializing in Mandarin and Western-style food, the downtown restaurant prepares combination plates for one person, as well as easy-to-share preparations of seafood, beef, pork, fried rice, chow mein, chop suey, chicken and duck. Casual dress. **Hours:** 11:30 am-9:30 pm. Closed: 1/1, 12/25, 12/26. **Address:** 627 3rd Ave W V8J 1M3 **Location:** Between 6th and 5th sts. **Parking:** street. **Cards:** MC, VI.

THE WATERFRONT RESTAURANT

 Canadian
$9-$34

Phone: 250/624-6771

This restaurant offers absolutely the best, most incredible view of the harbor and mountains as the hotel sits atop a cliff overlooking the strait. This all-day restaurant serves traditional dishes such as pasta, burgers, steak and specializes in seafood. Casual dress. **Bar:** Full bar. **Hours:** 6:30 am-10 pm. Closed: 12/25. **Address:** 222 1st Ave W V8J 3P6 **Location:** Hwy 16, just nw on 2nd St; in Crest Hotel. **Parking:** on-site. **Cards:** AX, DC, DS, MC, VI.

PRINCETON pop. 2,677

———— WHERE TO STAY ————

BEST WESTERN PRINCETON INN   *Book great rates at AAA.com*

CAA SAVE

Motel
$99-$139 All Year

Phone: (250)295-3537

Address: 169 Hwy 3 V0X 1W0 **Location:** On Hwy 3. **Facility:** 44 one-bedroom standard units, some with kitchens. 2 stories (no elevator), exterior corridors. **Parking:** on-site, winter plug-ins. **Amenities:** irons, hair dryers. **Pool(s):** heated outdoor. **Leisure Activities:** sauna, whirlpool. **Guest Services:** wireless Internet. **Business Services:** PC. **Cards:** AX, DC, DS, MC, VI. **Free Special Amenities:** room upgrade (subject to availability with advance reservations) and high-speed Internet.

AAA Benefit:
Members save 10% everyday, plus an exclusive frequent stay program.

VILLAGER INN   *Book great rates at AAA.com*

CAA SAVE
Motel
$65-$95 All Year

Phone: (250)295-6996

Address: 244 4th St V0X 1W0 **Location:** Just off Hwy 3. **Facility:** 26 one-bedroom standard units, some with efficiencies. 2 stories (no elevator), exterior corridors. **Parking:** on-site. **Terms:** office hours 7 am-11 pm. **Amenities:** hair dryers. **Pool(s):** heated outdoor. **Guest Services:** coin laundry, wireless Internet. **Cards:** MC, VI. **Free Special Amenities:** continental breakfast and high-speed Internet.

———— WHERE TO DINE ————

BELAIRE RESTAURANT

Canadian
$7-$15

Phone: 250/295-7711

Along one of the main downtown streets just off the highway and next door to the town museum, this simple diner housed the mine rescue training center, which served the area's nine underground coal mines during the 1930s, 40s and 50s. It's been a restaurant for more than 10 years. On the menu is good, old-fashioned Canadian food, including sandwiches, burgers and hearty steaks. Casual dress. **Bar:** Full bar. **Hours:** 7 am-9 pm; 8 am-8 pm 10/1-4/30. Closed major holidays; also 12/24-1/2. **Address:** 161 Vermilion Ave V0X 1W0 **Location:** Off Hwy 3, just e. **Parking:** street. **Cards:** AX, MC, VI.

QUADRA ISLAND —*See Gulf Islands National Park Reserve p. 506.*

QUALICUM BAY pop. 397

———— WHERE TO DINE ————

SANDBAR CAFE

Canadian
$6-$14

Phone: 250/757-9995

The Sandbar Cafe is a roadside-style diner and features a very nice view of the water. The traditional fare of very good food includes a daily selection of tasty sandwiches and homemade soup. The coffee is always fresh! Friendly and prompt service. Casual dress. **Bar:** Full bar. **Reservations:** accepted. **Hours:** 8 am-8 pm. Closed: 12/25, 12/26. **Address:** 6087 W Island Hwy V0R 1G0 **Location:** Hwy 19, exit 75 (Qualicum Bay/Bowser), 1.8 mi (3 km) e, follow Hwy 19A signs, then 1.2 mi (2.5 km) n on Hwy 19A. **Parking:** on-site. **Cards:** AX, MC, VI.

QUALICUM BEACH pop. 6,921

———— WHERE TO STAY ————

CASA GRANDE INN

Motel
Rates not provided

Phone: 250/752-4400

Address: 3080 W Island Hwy V9K 2C5 **Location:** Hwy 19, exit 60 (Qualicum Beach/Port Alberni), 2 mi (4 km) e on Memorial Ave, then 1.2 mi (2 km) n on Hwy 19A. **Facility:** Smoke free premises. 17 units. 15 one-bedroom standard units, some with efficiencies. 2 one-bedroom suites with kitchens. 3 stories, exterior corridors. *Bath:* combo or shower only. **Parking:** on-site. **Terms:** office hours 7 am-10 pm. **Amenities:** voice mail, hair dryers. **Guest Services:** coin laundry, wireless Internet.

OCEAN CREST MOTEL

Motel
$59-$104 All Year

Phone: 250/752-5518

Address: 3292 W Island Hwy V9K 2C6 **Location:** Hwy 19, exit 60 (Qualicum Beach/Port Alberni), 2.5 mi (4 km) e on Memorial Ave, then 1.9 mi (3 km) n on Hwy 19A. **Facility:** Smoke free premises. 19 one-bedroom standard units, some with efficiencies. 2 stories (no elevator), exterior corridors. **Parking:** on-site. **Terms:** office hours 8 am-10 pm. **Amenities:** hair dryers. **Guest Services:** wireless Internet. **Cards:** AX, MC, VI.

OLD DUTCH INN (BY THE SEA)

Small-scale Hotel
$80-$140 6/1-2/28
$80-$100 3/1-5/31

Phone: (250)752-6914

Address: 2690 Island Hwy W V9K 1G8 **Location:** Hwy 19, exit 60 (Qualicum Beach/Port Alberni), 2.5 mi (4 km) on Memorial Ave at jct Hwy 19A. **Facility:** 35 one-bedroom standard units. 2 stories (no elevator), interior corridors. *Bath:* combo or shower only. **Parking:** on-site. **Dining:** restaurant, see separate listing. **Pool(s):** heated indoor. **Leisure Activities:** sauna, whirlpool. **Guest Services:** wireless Internet. **Business Services:** meeting rooms. **Cards:** AX, DC, DS, MC, VI.

[ASK] [S⊘] [¶¶] [⊤] [⌖] [⅄] [▯] [▯] / SOME UNITS FEE [🐾] [✕]

WHERE TO DINE

GARY'S BISTRO

Canadian
$9-$18

Phone: 250/752-5800

Open for breakfast, lunch and dinner, the downtown bistro serves a host of burgers and a great selection of appetizers with great beers on tap. Casual dress. **Bar:** Full bar. **Hours:** 8 am-9 pm. Closed: 1/1, 12/25. **Address:** Box 145, 115 W Second Ave V9K 1S7 **Location:** Between Primrose St and Memorial Ave. **Parking:** street. **Cards:** MC, VI.

OLD DUTCH INN DINING ROOM

Dutch
$5-$25

Phone: 250/752-6914

You'll enjoy the wonderful ocean view at this restaurant, which offers creatively prepared, world-famous pastries as well as early bird specials and Dutch specialties. The servers dressed in Dutch costumes complete the Old Dutch atmosphere and decor. **Bar:** Full bar. **Reservations:** suggested, for dinner. **Hours:** 7 am-9:30 pm. **Address:** 2690 Island Hwy W V9K 1G8 **Location:** Hwy 19, exit 60 (Qualicum Beach/Port Alberni), 2.5 mi (4 km) on Memorial Ave at Hwy 19A; in Old Dutch Inn (By The Sea). **Parking:** on-site. **Cards:** AX, DC, DS, MC, VI.

THE SHADY REST WATERFRONT PUB RESTAURANT

Canadian
$12-$22

Phone: 250/752-9111

The waterfront restaurant and pub features all the usual favorites, like burgers and sandwiches for lunch and more hearty fare for dinner. The dining section directly overlooks the ocean. Casual dress. **Bar:** Full bar. **Hours:** 11 am-9 pm, Sat & Sun from 8 am. Closed: 12/25, 12/26. **Address:** 3109 Island Hwy W V9K 2C5 **Location:** Hwy 19, exit 60 (Qualicum Beach/Port Alberni), 2.4 mi (4 km) e on Memorial Ave, then 1.2 mi (2 km) n on Hwy 19A. **Parking:** on-site. **Cards:** MC, VI.

QUESNEL pop. 9,326

WHERE TO STAY

BEST WESTERN TOWER INN

Book great rates at AAA.com

(CAA) [SAVE]

Small-scale Hotel
$110 All Year

Phone: (250)992-2201

Address: 500 Reid St V2J 2M9 **Location:** Hwy 97, just e on Shepherd Ave; downtown. **Facility:** 63 units. 62 one- and 1 two-bedroom standard units, some with whirlpools. 4 stories, interior corridors. **Parking:** on-site. **Terms:** cancellation fee imposed. **Amenities:** high-speed Internet, irons, hair dryers. **Leisure Activities:** limited exercise equipment. **Guest Services:** valet laundry. **Business Services:** meeting rooms, business center. **Cards:** AX, DC, DS, MC, VI. **Free Special Amenities:** local telephone calls and high-speed Internet.

[S⊘] [¶¶] [⊤] [⌖] [▯] [▯] / SOME UNITS [✕]

AAA Benefit:
Members save 10% everyday, plus an exclusive frequent stay program.

TALISMAN INN

(CAA) [SAVE]

Motel
$79-$139 3/1-10/31
$69-$139 11/1-2/28

Phone: (250)992-7247

Address: 753 Front St V2J 2L2 **Location:** Hwy 97, 0.6 mi (1 km) n of Carson Ave. **Facility:** 85 one-bedroom standard units, some with efficiencies, kitchens and/or whirlpools. 2 stories, interior corridors. *Bath:* combo or shower only. **Parking:** on-site, winter plug-ins. **Terms:** office hours 6:30 am-11 pm, cancellation fee imposed. **Amenities:** voice mail, irons. *Some:* fax, hair dryers. **Leisure Activities:** whirlpool, limited exercise equipment. **Guest Services:** coin laundry, wireless Internet. **Business Services:** meeting rooms. **Cards:** AX, DC, MC, VI. **Free Special Amenities:** continental breakfast.

[S⊘] [▯] [▯] [▯] / SOME UNITS FEE [🐾] [✕]

WHERE TO DINE

GRANVILLE'S COFFEE

Canadian
$4-$7

Phone: 250/992-3667

Patrons easily can become too busy viewing the eatery's eclectically decorated walls to finish their coffee. Good choices include jumbo muffins, deli sandwiches and homemade soups. Fluent espresso is spoken here. **Hours:** 7 am-10 pm, Sun 9 am-5 pm. Closed: 12/25. **Address:** 383 Reid St V2J 2M5 **Location:** Reid St at St Laurent Ave; downtown. **Parking:** street. **Cards:** MC, VI.

RADIUM HOT SPRINGS pop. 735

WHERE TO STAY

CEDAR MOTEL

Motel
Rates not provided

Phone: 250/347-9463

Address: 7593 Main St W V0A 1M0 **Location:** Hwy 93 and 95, just s of jct Hwy 93, on service road (Main St). **Facility:** 17 units. 8 one- and 9 two-bedroom standard units, some with efficiencies. 2 stories (no elevator), exterior corridors. **Parking:** on-site, winter plug-ins. **Terms:** office hours 8 am-11 pm. **Amenities:** *Some:* hair dryers. **Guest Services:** wireless Internet.

[¶¶] [⌖] [▯] [▯] / SOME UNITS FEE [🐾] [✕] [▯]

CHALET EUROPE

▼▼▼ ▼▼▼
Motel
$89-$189 All Year

Phone: 250/347-9305

Address: 5063 Madsen Rd V0A 1M0 **Location:** 0.6 mi (1 km) off Hwy 93; up the hill. **Facility:** Smoke free premises. 17 one-bedroom suites. 3 stories (no elevator), exterior corridors. **Parking:** on-site. **Terms:** office hours 7 am-11 pm, 7 day cancellation notice-fee imposed. **Amenities:** hair dryers. *Some:* DVD players. **Leisure Activities:** sauna, whirlpool, cross country skiing, hiking trails, jogging, limited exercise equipment, game room. **Guest Services:** coin laundry. **Cards:** MC, VI.

[icons] / SOME UNITS FEE

LIDO MOTEL

▼▼▼
Motel
$55-$85 All Year

Phone: 250/347-9533

Address: 4876 McKay St V0A 1M0 **Location:** Jct Hwy 93 and 95, just w along Main St, then just s. **Facility:** Smoke free premises. 10 units. 2 one- and 8 two-bedroom standard units, some with efficiencies. 1 story, exterior corridors. *Bath:* combo or shower only. **Parking:** on-site, winter plug-ins. **Terms:** office hours 7:30 am-11 pm, 7 day cancellation notice. **Leisure Activities:** miniature golf, horseshoes. **Guest Services:** wireless Internet. **Cards:** MC, VI.

[icons] / SOME UNITS FEE

PRESTIGE RADIUM HOT SPRINGS

(CAA) (SAVE)
▼▼▼ ▼▼▼
Small-scale Hotel
$169-$209 3/1-9/30
$129-$189 10/1-2/28

Book great rates at AAA.com   **Phone:** (250)347-2300

Address: 7493 Main St W V0A 1M0 **Location:** Jct Hwy 93 and 95. **Facility:** 87 units. 82 one- and 2 two-bedroom standard units, some with efficiencies or kitchens. 3 one-bedroom suites with whirlpools, some with kitchens. 3 stories, interior corridors. **Parking:** on-site. **Terms:** cancellation fee imposed. **Amenities:** video games (fee), voice mail, irons, hair dryers. **Pool(s):** heated indoor. **Leisure Activities:** whirlpool, exercise room, spa. **Guest Services:** wireless Internet. **Business Services:** meeting rooms, PC (fee). **Cards:** AX, MC, VI. **Free Special Amenities:** newspaper and high-speed Internet.

[icons] / SOME UNITS

VILLAGE COUNTRY INN & TEA ROOM

(CAA) (SAVE)
▼▼▼ ▼▼▼
Country Inn
$85-$160 All Year

Phone: (250)347-9392

Address: 7557 Canyon Ave V0A 1M0 **Location:** Jct Hwy 93 and 95, just w along Main St, then just s on St Joseph St. Located in a residential area across from playground. **Facility:** From the luxurious duvets to the serene setting, this property is suitable for short- or long-term stays and offers a retreatlike ambience. Smoke free premises. 13 one-bedroom standard units. 2 stories (no elevator), interior corridors. *Bath:* combo or shower only. **Parking:** on-site, winter plug-ins. **Terms:** office hours 7 am-10 pm, check-in 4 pm, 7 day cancellation notice. **Amenities:** video library (fee), hair dryers. **Leisure Activities:** board games, chess and cards available in tea room, local art display. **Cards:** AX, MC, VI. **Free Special Amenities:** high-speed Internet.

CALL [icons]

———— WHERE TO DINE ————

THE OLD SALZBURG RESTAURANT

(CAA)
▼▼▼ ▼▼▼
Austrian
$8-$25

Phone: 250/347-6553

Prepared here are traditional Austrian and Continental dishes, such as schnitzel, hearty spaetzle, pasta, chicken and steak. The atmosphere is warm with a mountain village ambience. In the summer, patio seating is offered. Those who opt for a window seat in the dining room are treated to lovely mountain views. Casual dress. **Bar:** Full bar. **Reservations:** suggested, in summer. **Hours:** 11:30 am-4 & 5-11 pm; 5 pm-10 pm off season. Closed: Mon. **Address:** 4943 Hwy 93 V0A 1M0 **Location:** Hwy 93 and 95, just w; centre. **Parking:** on-site. **Cards:** AX, MC, VI.

REVELSTOKE pop. 7,230

——— WHERE TO STAY ———

BEST WESTERN WAYSIDE INN

Small-scale Hotel
$129-$169 3/1-9/30
$89-$139 10/1-2/28

Phone: (250)837-6161

Address: 1901 LaForme Blvd V0E 2S0 **Location:** North side of Trans-Canada Hwy 1, at intersection nearest east end of Columbia River Bridge. Located in a quiet area. **Facility:** Smoke free premises. 88 one-bedroom standard units, some with efficiencies. 2 stories (no elevator), interior/exterior corridors. **Parking:** on-site, winter plug-ins. **Terms:** 30 day cancellation notice. **Amenities:** irons, hair dryers. *Some:* high-speed Internet. **Pool(s):** heated indoor. **Leisure Activities:** whirlpool, exercise room. **Guest Services:** valet laundry, wireless Internet. **Business Services:** meeting rooms. **Cards:** AX, CB, DC, MC, VI. **Free Special Amenities:** local telephone calls and high-speed Internet.

AAA Benefit:
Members save 10% everyday, plus an exclusive frequent stay program.

[icons] SOME UNITS

THE COAST HILLCREST RESORT HOTEL

Book great rates at AAA.com

Large-scale Hotel
$155-$239 All Year

Phone: (250)837-3322

Address: 2100 Oak Dr V0E 2S0 **Location:** 2.7 mi (4.3 km) e on Trans-Canada Hwy 1, 0.6 mi (0.9 km) sw. **Facility:** Smoke free premises. 75 units. 74 one-bedroom standard units, some with whirlpools. 1 one-bedroom suite with whirlpool. 3 stories, interior corridors. **Parking:** on-site, winter plug-ins. **Terms:** cancellation fee imposed. **Amenities:** safes, irons, hair dryers. *Some:* CD players. **Leisure Activities:** sauna, whirlpools, steamroom, helicopter skiing, ATV tours, exercise room. *Fee:* white water rafting, massage, game room. **Guest Services:** wireless Internet. **Business Services:** meeting rooms, PC (fee). **Cards:** AX, DC, MC, VI. **Free Special Amenities:** local telephone calls.

[icons] SOME UNITS FEE

MONASHEE LODGE

Motel
$79-$89 All Year

Phone: 250/837-6778

Address: 1601 3rd St W V0E 2S0 **Location:** South side of Trans-Canada Hwy 1, just e of Columbia River Bridge at Victoria Rd, then just se on Wright Ave. **Facility:** Smoke free premises. 18 one-bedroom standard units, some with kitchens (utensils extra charge). 2 stories (no elevator), exterior corridors. **Parking:** on-site, winter plug-ins. **Terms:** office hours 7 am-11 pm. **Amenities:** voice mail. **Leisure Activities:** whirlpool. **Business Services:** PC. **Cards:** AX, MC, VI. **Free Special Amenities:** continental breakfast and high-speed Internet.

[icons] SOME UNITS FEE

SUPER 8 MOTEL REVELSTOKE

Book at AAA.com

Small-scale Hotel
Rates not provided

Phone: 250/837-0888

Address: 1700 W Victoria Rd V0E 2S0 **Location:** South side of Trans-Canada Hwy 1, just e of Columbia River Bridge at Victoria Rd (town centre exit). **Facility:** 44 units. 37 one-bedroom standard units. 7 one-bedroom suites. 2 stories (no elevator), interior corridors. **Parking:** on-site, winter plug-ins. **Terms:** office hours 7 am-midnight. **Amenities:** hair dryers. **Pool(s):** heated indoor. **Leisure Activities:** whirlpool. **Guest Services:** coin laundry, wireless Internet.

[icons] SOME UNITS

SWISS CHALET MOTEL

Motel
$74-$109 All Year

Phone: (250)837-4650

Address: 1101 Victoria Rd V0E 2S0 **Location:** 0.6 mi (1 km) s from Trans-Canada Hwy 1. **Facility:** Designated smoking area. 22 units. 20 one- and 2 two-bedroom standard units, some with efficiencies. 1-2 stories (no elevator), exterior corridors. *Bath:* combo or shower only. **Parking:** on-site, winter plug-ins. **Terms:** office hours 7:30 am-11 pm. **Amenities:** *Some:* hair dryers. **Guest Services:** wireless Internet. **Business Services:** PC (fee). **Free Special Amenities:** continental breakfast and high-speed Internet.

[icons] SOME UNITS FEE

——— WHERE TO DINE ———

THE ONE TWELVE RESTAURANT & LOUNGE

American
$9-$30

Phone: 250/837-2107

This restaurant maintains a cozy but elegant atmosphere with the help of subdued lighting, soft music, an antique fireplace and friendly service. Diners' taste buds are tempted with specialties such as Alberta steak, veal, lamb and seafood. Lunchtime offerings include a soup of the day, as well as quiche Lorraine and several chicken sandwiches. Casual dress. **Bar:** Full bar. **Reservations:** suggested. **Hours:** 11:45 am-2 & 5:30-9 pm. Closed major holidays. **Address:** 112 1st St E V0E 2S0 **Location:** 1.2 mi (2 km) s from Trans-Canada Hwy 1, at Victoria Rd; downtown; in The Regent Inn. **Parking:** on-site. **Cards:** AX, DC, MC, VI.

THREE VALLEY LAKE CHATEAU

Canadian
$6-$17

Phone: 250/837-2109

This easily accessible restaurant is a good place to stop for a rest and let the children browse. Fast, simple food is served in ample portions. A ghost town and antique train are next door. Casual dress. **Bar:** Full bar. **Hours:** Open 4/1-10/15; 7 am-close. **Address:** 8903 Trans-Canada Hwy 1 V0E 2S0 **Location:** 11.5 mi (19.2 km) w on Trans-Canada Hwy 1; on Three Valley Lake; in Three Valley Gap Lake Chateau. **Parking:** on-site. **Cards:** AX, DC, MC, VI.

RICHMOND —See Vancouver p. 623.

ROSSLAND pop. 3,278

───── WHERE TO STAY ─────

THRIFTLODGE ROSSLAND *Book at AAA.com*   Phone: (250)362-7364

Motel
$89-$99 12/1-2/28
$79-$89 3/1-11/30

Address: 1199 Nancy Green Hwy V0G 1Y0 **Location:** 0.6 mi (1 km) w on Hwy 3B, jct Hwy 22. **Facility:** 42 units. 40 one-bedroom standard units, some with efficiencies or kitchens. 2 one-bedroom suites with kitchens. 2 stories (no elevator), exterior corridors. **Parking:** on-site, winter plug-ins. **Terms:** office hours 6 am-11 pm, 2 night minimum stay - weekends, 3 day cancellation notice-fee imposed. **Leisure Activities:** whirlpool. *Fee:* bicycles. **Guest Services:** complimentary laundry, area transportation, wireless Internet. **Cards:** AX, MC, VI.

[ASK] [📷] [📶] / SOME UNITS FEE [🐕] [✕] [AC] [VCR] FEE [📠] [📷]

SAANICH —*See Victoria p. 665.*

SALMO pop. 1,007

───── WHERE TO DINE ─────

CHARLIE'S PIZZA & SPAGHETTI HOUSE   Phone: 250/357-9335

[💎]

Italian
$5-$18

In the small mountain town, the downtown restaurant enjoys great popularity. The food is a mixture of several types, with Italian being the main fare. Vinyl booths and some tables contribute to the "diner-style" feel. The warm greeting makes guests feel the staff is really glad to see them. Casual dress. **Bar:** Full bar. **Hours:** 5:30 am-8 pm. Closed: 12/25. **Address:** 205 4th St V0G 1Z0 **Location:** Just n of Hwy 6; centre. **Parking:** on-site. **Cards:** MC, VI.

TRAPPER JOHN'S RESTAURANT   Phone: 250/357-2296

[💎]

Canadian
$6-$21

Just outside town, this restaurant presents a menu of North American food to suit most tastes. Friendly service and large portions are the standard. The rustic log construction, with a large rock fireplace at one end of the room and beautiful stained-glass windows, adds to the ambience. Casual dress. **Bar:** Full bar. **Reservations:** accepted. **Hours:** 9 am-9 pm, Fri & Sat-10 pm, Sun-8 pm. Closed: 12/25. **Address:** 103 Motel Ave V0G 1Z0 **Location:** Jct Hwy 3 and 6, just w on Hwy 3. **Parking:** on-site. **Cards:** MC, VI.

SALMON ARM pop. 16,012

───── WHERE TO STAY ─────

BEST WESTERN SALMON ARM INN   *Book great rates at AAA.com*   Phone: 250/832-9793

[CAA] [SAVE]

Motel
$135-$169 3/1-9/30
$99-$129 10/1-2/28

Address: 61 10th St SW V1E 1E4 **Location:** From centre, 0.7 mi (1.1 km) w on Trans-Canada Hwy 1. **Facility:** 77 one-bedroom standard units, some with efficiencies. 2 stories (no elevator), exterior corridors. **Parking:** on-site. **Terms:** check-in 4 pm. **Amenities:** irons, hair dryers. *Some:* DVD players. **Pool(s):** heated outdoor. **Leisure Activities:** whirlpool. **Guest Services:** wireless Internet. **Business Services:** PC. **Cards:** AX, DC, DS, MC, VI. **Free Special Amenities:** continental breakfast and high-speed Internet.

AAA Benefit:
Members save 10% everyday, plus an exclusive frequent stay program.

[SD] [🍴] [♨] [📷] / SOME UNITS FEE [🐕] [✕] [📶] [📷]

HOLIDAY INN EXPRESS HOTEL & SUITES SALMON ARM   *Book at AAA.com*   Phone: (250)832-7711

Small-scale Hotel
$169-$299 3/1-9/10
$139-$199 9/11-2/28

Address: 1090 22nd St NE V1E 2V5 **Location:** 0.5 mi (0.8 km) on Trans-Canada Hwy 1. **Facility:** 115 units. 86 one-bedroom standard units, some with whirlpools. 29 one-bedroom suites. 5 stories, interior corridors. *Bath:* combo or shower only. **Parking:** on-site. **Amenities:** video games (fee), high-speed Internet, dual phone lines, voice mail, irons, hair dryers. **Pool(s):** heated indoor. **Leisure Activities:** whirlpool, waterslide, limited exercise equipment. **Guest Services:** valet and coin laundry. **Business Services:** meeting rooms, business center. **Cards:** AX, DC, DS, MC, VI.

[ASK] [SD] [🍴] CALL [&M] [♨] [✕] [📷] [📷] / SOME UNITS FEE [🐕] [✕] [📶] [📷]

SUPER 8 MOTEL   *Book at AAA.com*   Phone: 250/832-8812

[💎]

Small-scale Hotel
Rates not provided

Address: 2901 10th Ave NE V1E 2S3 **Location:** 0.6 mi (1 km) e on Trans-Canada Hwy 1. **Facility:** 40 units. 39 one-bedroom standard units, some with whirlpools. 1 one-bedroom suite with kitchen. 2 stories (no elevator), interior corridors. **Parking:** on-site. **Amenities:** video library (fee). **Guest Services:** coin laundry, wireless Internet. **Business Services:** PC.

[🍴] CALL [&M] [✕] [📷] [📶] / SOME UNITS [🐕] [VCR] [📷]

───── WHERE TO DINE ─────

CHIANG MAI ORCHID THAI RESTAURANT   Phone: 250/832-0699

[💎💎💎]

Thai
$6-$17

Bangkok-trained chefs prepare both spicy and mild dishes for the extensive menu. The entire family manages and staffs the simple dining room, and the chef often comes out to see how guests' meals are. Patrons need look no further for a tasty taste of Thailand in the middle of British Columbia. Casual dress. **Bar:** Full bar. **Hours:** 11:30 am-2:30 & 5-9:30 pm, Sat & Sun from 5 pm. Closed: 12/25, 12/26. **Address:** 131 Hudson Ave NE V1E 4N7 **Location:** From Trans-Canada Hwy 1, just sw at Alexander St to Hudson Ave, then just e. **Parking:** street. **Cards:** AX, MC, VI.

THE HERB GARDEN SMOKEHOUSE GRILL   Phone: 250/833-4983

Barbecue
$6-$19

The nostalgia of Mom's cuisine is evoked at the small country restaurant, where the owner proudly prepares wholesome food with an accent on freshness and sensitivity to the season's offerings. Dishes are creative yet comfortable. Weekend dinners feature roast beef with all the trimmings. Casual dress. **Bar:** Full bar. **Hours:** 11 am-9 pm. Closed major holidays; also Sun. **Address:** 111 Lakeshore Dr NE V1E 4N9 **Location:** At Alexander St NE; centre. **Parking:** on-site. **Cards:** MC, VI.

PRIMAVERA RISTORANTE ITALIANO

Italian
$7-$17

Phone: 250/833-0065

A small, authentic piece of Italy can be found just off the highway. Red-checkered tablecloths, vine-covered walls and Italian music create a cozy environment in which patrons can savor hearty dishes, ranging from veal to seafood fettuccine. The restaurant is busy on weekends and when entertainers perform several nights a week. Casual dress. Entertainment. **Bar:** Full bar. **Reservations:** suggested, weekends. **Hours:** 11 am-9 pm, Fri-10 pm, Sat 5 pm-10 pm. Closed major holidays; also Sun. **Address:** 260 Ross St NE V0E 1H1 **Location:** Trans-Canada Hwy 1, exit Ross St, just n. **Parking:** street. **Cards:** MC, VI.

SALT SPRING ISLAND —See Gulf Islands National Park Reserve p. 506.

SAVONA

——— WHERE TO STAY ———

LAKESIDE COUNTRY INN   *Book at AAA.com*

Motel
$80-$180 4/1-10/31

Phone: (250)373-2528

Address: 7001 Savona Access Rd V0K 2J0 **Location:** Trans-Canada Hwy 1, exit Savona; along business frontage road. **Facility:** Smoke free premises. 9 one-bedroom standard units, some with efficiencies or kitchens. 2 stories (no elevator), exterior corridors. *Bath:* combo or shower only. **Parking:** on-site, winter plug-ins. **Terms:** open 4/1-10/31, office hours 8 am-10 pm, age restrictions may apply, 3 day cancellation notice. **Amenities:** hair dryers. **Leisure Activities:** rental canoes, rental paddleboats, boat dock, bicycles. **Guest Services:** wireless Internet. **Cards:** AX, DC, DS, MC, VI.

SECHELT pop. 8,454

——— WHERE TO DINE ———

BLUE HERON INN   *Menu on AAA.com*

Seafood
$22-$30

Phone: 604/885-3847

Sitting on the shores of Porpoise Bay where the views are wonderful, this restaurant features some veal, chicken, lamb and steak dishes but mostly it's the wonderful, fresh seafood that keeps people coming back. All entrees include chef's soup or caesar salad. Casual dress. **Bar:** Full bar. **Reservations:** suggested. **Hours:** 5:30 pm-10 pm. Closed: 12/25; also Mon & Tues. **Address:** 5591 Delta Rd V0N 3A0 **Location:** From Sunshine Coast Hwy 101, just n on Wharf Rd, then 0.6 mi (4 km) ne on Porpoise Bay Rd. **Parking:** on-site. **Cards:** AX, MC, VI.

GEORGIA STRAIT CAFE

Continental
$10-$26

Phone: 604/885-1997

South of Sechelt toward Wilson Creek is this charming cafe that serves lunch and dinner during the week and breakfast on the weekend. The menu changes frequently, and daily drink specials are tempting. Casual dress. **Bar:** Full bar. **Hours:** 11 am-3 & 5-9 pm, Sat from 9 am, Sun 9 am-3 & 5-8 pm. Closed: 12/25, 12/26. **Address:** 4349 Sunshine Coast Hwy V0N 3A1 **Location:** 3.6 mi (5.8 km) s on Sunshine Coast Hwy 101. **Parking:** on-site. **Cards:** MC, VI.

SICAMOUS pop. 2,676

——— WHERE TO STAY ———

BEST WESTERN SICAMOUS INN   *Book great rates at AAA.com*

Motel
$109-$269 All Year

Phone: (250)836-4117

Address: 806 Trans-Canada Hwy 1 V0E 2V0 **Location:** Jct Trans-Canada Hwy 1 and 97; at east end of town. **Facility:** 65 units. 59 one- and 2 two-bedroom standard units. 4 one-bedroom suites, some with whirlpools. 2 stories (no elevator), exterior corridors. **Parking:** on-site. **Terms:** office hours 7 am-11 pm, 3 day cancellation notice. **Amenities:** irons, hair dryers. *Some:* high-speed Internet. **Pool(s):** heated indoor. **Leisure Activities:** whirlpools. **Guest Services:** coin laundry, wireless Internet. **Business Services:** PC. **Cards:** AX, DC, DS, MC, VI. **Free Special Amenities:** local telephone calls and high-speed Internet.

AAA Benefit:
Members save 10% everyday, plus an exclusive frequent stay program.

SICAMOUS SUPER 8 MOTEL   *Book at AAA.com*

Small-scale Hotel
$60-$150 All Year

Phone: 250/836-4988

Address: 1120 Riverside Ave V0E 2V0 **Location:** Trans-Canada Hwy 1, s on Hwy 97A, just w on Main St to traffic circle, then just s. **Facility:** 22 units. 18 one-bedroom standard units. 4 one-bedroom suites. 2 stories (no elevator), exterior corridors. **Parking:** on-site, winter plug-ins. **Terms:** office hours 7 am-10 pm. **Leisure Activities:** whirlpool. **Guest Services:** tanning facilities. **Cards:** AX, DS, MC, VI.

SIDNEY —See Victoria p. 666.

SILVERTON pop. 185

──── WHERE TO STAY ────

WILLIAM HUNTER CABINS

Cabin
Rates not provided

Phone: 250/358-2844

Address: 303 Lake Ave V0G 2B0 **Location:** Centre. **Facility:** Smoke free premises. 6 one-bedroom suites with efficiencies. 1 story, exterior corridors. **Parking:** on-site, winter plug-ins. **Amenities:** *Some:* CD players. **Leisure Activities:** canoeing, fishing, bicycles, hiking trails.

🍴 ❌ ✕ 🎣 🚲 🛢 📷 📼 / SOME UNITS 🐾 📶

SMITHERS pop. 5,217

──── WHERE TO STAY ────

ASPEN INN & SUITES
❤❤ ❤❤
Motel
Rates not provided

Phone: 250/847-4551

Address: 4628 Yellowhead Hwy V0J 2N0 **Location:** 0.9 mi (1.5 km) w on Hwy 16 (Yellowhead Hwy). **Facility:** 60 units. 55 one-bedroom standard units, some with efficiencies. 5 one-bedroom suites with efficiencies. 2 stories, exterior corridors. **Parking:** on-site, winter plug-ins. **Amenities:** voice mail, hair dryers.. **Pool(s):** heated indoor. **Leisure Activities:** saunas, whirlpool. **Guest Services:** wireless Internet. **Business Services:** meeting rooms.

🍴 🏊 📷 🛢 📼 / SOME UNITS FEE 🐾 ✕ 📶

SOOKE —*See Victoria p. 667.*

SORRENTO pop. 1,360

──── WHERE TO DINE ────

HOME RESTAURANT
❤
Canadian
$6-$12

Phone: 250/675-3552

The basic diner is good for delicious home-style cooking and large portions. Reasonable prices make eating here a good value. Scrumptious homemade desserts are the specialty. Servers are friendly. Casual dress. **Bar:** Beer & wine. **Hours:** 7 am-9 pm. **Closed:** 12/25. **Address:** 1235C Trans-Canada Hwy V0E 2W0 **Location:** Trans-Canada Hwy 1; in Petro Canada Gas Station. **Parking:** on-site. **Cards:** MC, VI.

SQUAMISH pop. 14,949

————— WHERE TO STAY —————

EXECUTIVE SUITES GARIBALDI SPRINGS GOLF RESORT

Phone: 604/815-0048

▼ See AAA listing p 557 ▼

MOUNTAIN RETREAT HOTEL & SUITES   *Book great rates at AAA.com*   Phone: (604)815-0883

(CAA) (SAVE)

▼▼▼

Small-scale Hotel
$129 All Year

Address: 38922 Progress Way V0N 3G0 **Location:** 0.9 mi (1.5 km) n on Hwy 99 at Industrial Way. **Facility:** 87 one-bedroom standard units, some with efficiencies. 4 stories, interior corridors. **Parking:** on-site. **Terms:** check-in 4 pm, cancellation fee imposed. **Amenities:** video games (fee), irons, hair dryers. **Pool(s):** heated indoor. **Leisure Activities:** whirlpool, waterslide, limited exercise equipment. **Guest Services:** coin laundry, wireless Internet. **Business Services:** meeting rooms, PC (fee). **Cards:** AX, DC, DS, MC, VI. **Free Special Amenities: local telephone calls and high-speed Internet.**

(S/D) CALL (M) ⛵ (X) (🎿) (📶) (💻) / SOME UNITS FEE (🐾) (X) (📷)

SEA TO SKY HOTEL   *Book great rates at AAA.com*   Phone: 604/898-4874

(CAA) (SAVE)

▼▼▼

Small-scale Hotel
$99-$189 All Year

Address: 40330 Tantalus Way V0N 1T0 **Location:** 2.9 mi (4.5 km) n on Hwy 99 at Garibaldi Way. **Facility:** Smoke free premises. 52 one-bedroom standard units. 3 stories, interior corridors. **Parking:** on-site. **Terms:** cancellation fee imposed. **Amenities:** irons, hair dryers. **Leisure Activities:** sauna, whirlpool, limited exercise equipment. **Guest Services:** valet and coin laundry, wireless Internet. **Business Services:** meeting rooms, PC. **Cards:** AX, DC, DS, MC, VI. **Free Special Amenities: local telephone calls and high-speed Internet.** *(See color ad p 556)*

(S/D) (🍴) (🍸) CALL (M) (X) (X) (📶) (💻) (📷) / SOME UNITS FEE (🐾)

——— WHERE TO DINE ———

PARKSIDE RESTAURANT   Phone: 604/892-2273

▼▼▼

Canadian
$8-$28

The cozy restaurant serves breakfast, lunch and dinner, including salads, tapas, sandwiches, wraps, pasta and such hearty dinner entrees as chicken Marsala, prosciutto halibut and grilled salmon. The motto is, "Fresh ingredients made to order. Please be patient; the best things are worth waiting for!". Casual dress. **Bar:** Full bar. **Hours:** 10 am-3 & 5:30-11 pm. Closed: 12/25. **Address:** 37996 Cleveland Rd V0N 3G0 **Location:** From Hwy 99, 0.6 mi (1 km) w on Cleveland Ave; corner of Victoria St. **Parking:** on-site. **Cards:** MC, VI.

(AC)

SUMMERLAND —*See Okanagan Valley p. 538.*

SUN PEAKS

——— WHERE TO STAY ———

COAST SUNDANCE LODGE   *Book great rates at AAA.com*   Phone: (250)578-0200

(CAA) (SAVE)

▼▼▼

Condominium
$89-$409 11/20-2/28
$75-$199 3/1-11/19

Address: 3160 Creekside Way V0E 5N0 **Location:** Hwy 5, 19.4 mi (31 km) ne on Todd Mountain Rd, follow signs to village. **Facility:** Smoke free premises. 84 units. 64 one-bedroom standard units, some with efficiencies. 15 one- and 5 two-bedroom suites, some with efficiencies or kitchens. 4 stories, interior corridors. **Parking:** on-site. **Terms:** cancellation fee imposed. **Amenities:** irons, hair dryers. **Leisure Activities:** whirlpool, ski locker rooms, hiking trails, exercise room. *Fee:* downhill & cross country skiing, snowmobiling, ice skating. **Guest Services:** coin laundry. **Business Services:** meeting rooms. **Cards:** AX, DS, MC, VI. **Free Special Amenities: local telephone calls and high-speed Internet.**

(S/D) (🍴) (X) (X) (AC) (🎿) (📶) (💻) / SOME UNITS (VCR)

DELTA SUN PEAKS RESORT   *Book great rates at AAA.com*   Phone: (250)578-6000

(CAA) (SAVE)

▼▼ ▼▼

Large-scale Hotel
$99-$329 All Year

Address: 3240 Village Way V0E 1Z1 **Location:** Hwy 5, 19.4 mi (31 km) ne on Todd Mountain Rd, follow signs to village. **Facility:** Set within the Sun Peaks Village, this resort hotel strives for superb service and offers ritzy accommodations done up in a Rocky Mountain theme. 220 units. 205 one-bedroom standard units. 15 one-bedroom suites. 5 stories, interior corridors. **Parking:** on-site (fee) and valet. **Terms:** check-in 4 pm. **Amenities:** dual phone lines, voice mail, irons, hair dryers. *Fee:* video games, high-speed Internet. *Some:* CD players. **Dining:** Mantles Restaurant, see separate listing. **Pool(s):** heated outdoor. **Leisure Activities:** sauna, whirlpools, steamroom, ski valet & storage, recreation programs, children's play area, hiking trails, jogging, exercise room, game room. *Fee:* downhill & cross country skiing, snowmobiling, ice skating, massage. **Guest Services:** valet and coin laundry. **Business Services:** conference facilities, business center. **Cards:** AX, DS, MC, VI.

(S/D) (🍴) (X) (🛎️) CALL (M) ⛵ (X) (🎿) (📶) (💻) / SOME UNITS FEE (🐾) (X)

NANCY GREENE'S CAHILTY LODGE   Phone: (250)578-7454

(CAA) (SAVE)

▼▼▼

Condominium
$139-$219 11/15-2/28
$109-$199 3/1-11/14

Address: 3220 Village Way V0E 5N0 **Location:** Hwy 5, 19.4 mi (31 km) ne on Todd Mountain Rd, follow signs to village. **Facility:** Olympic gold and silver medals are displayed in the lobby of this activity-oriented lodge, which offers ski-in/ski-out access to the slopes. Smoke free premises. 192 units. 147 one-bedroom standard units, some with efficiencies or kitchens. 38 one-, 6 two- and 1 three-bedroom suites, some with kitchens. 4 stories, interior corridors. **Parking:** on-site, winter plug-ins. **Terms:** check-in 4 pm, cancellation fee imposed. **Amenities:** video library (fee), voice mail, hair dryers. **Leisure Activities:** whirlpool, hiking trails, exercise room. *Fee:* downhill & cross country skiing, snowmobiling, ice skating. **Guest Services:** coin laundry. **Business Services:** meeting rooms, PC. **Cards:** AX, DC, MC, VI.

(🍴) (X) (X) (AC) (VCR) / SOME UNITS (📶) (📷)

——— WHERE TO DINE ———

MANTLES RESTAURANT   Phone: 250/578-6060

▼▼▼

Pacific Rim
$12-$30

Pacific Northwest fare is made in the vibrant family restaurant. The funky, upscale dining room, complete with an open-concept demonstration kitchen, sets the scene after a day on the ski hills. Among tempting starters are varied distinctive appetizers, ranging from scallops and portobello mushrooms to Caesar salad. The entrees are a piece of art. Good choices include salmon woven on a stalk of lemongrass, rack of lamb and oven-fired pizzas. Casual dress. **Bar:** Full bar. **Reservations:** suggested. **Hours:** 6:30 am-10 pm. **Address:** 3240 Village Way V0E 1Z1 **Location:** Hwy 5, 19.4 mi (31 km) ne on Todd Mountain Rd, follow signs to village; in Delta Sun Peaks Resort. **Parking:** on-site and valet. **Cards:** AX, DC, JC, MC, VI.

CALL (M)

TELEGRAPH COVE

―――― **WHERE TO STAY** ――――

TELEGRAPH COVE MARINA

Motel
$85-$135 All Year

Phone: 250/928-3163

Address: 1642B Telegraph Cove Rd V0N 3J0 **Location:** 9 mi (15 km) e on Beaver Cove Rd. **Facility:** Smoke free premises. 22 one-bedroom standard units with efficiencies. 2 stories (no elevator), exterior corridors. *Bath:* shower only. **Parking:** on-site. **Terms:** office hours 8 am-9 pm, 30 day cancellation notice-fee imposed. **Guest Services:** coin laundry, wireless Internet. **Cards:** MC, VI.

TERRACE pop. 11,320

―――― **WHERE TO STAY** ――――

BEST WESTERN TERRACE INN

 Book great rates at AAA.com

Phone: (250)635-0083

CAA SAVE

Small-scale Hotel
$90-$208 All Year

Address: 4553 Greig Ave V8G 1M7 **Location:** Hwy 16, just e on Greig Ave, follow City Centre signs. **Facility:** 68 one-bedroom standard units, some with whirlpools. 5 stories, interior corridors. **Parking:** on-site. **Terms:** cancellation fee imposed. **Amenities:** high-speed Internet, voice mail, irons, hair dryers. **Leisure Activities:** limited exercise equipment. **Guest Services:** valet laundry. **Business Services:** meeting rooms, PC. **Cards:** AX, CB, DC, DS, JC, MC, VI. **Free Special Amenities:** continental breakfast and high-speed Internet.

AAA Benefit:
Members save 10% everyday, plus an exclusive frequent stay program.

―――― **WHERE TO DINE** ――――

THE BAVARIAN INN STEAK & SEAFOOD GRILL

Steak & Seafood
$20-$35

Phone: 250/635-9161

Downstairs is The Black Eddy Pub, while the more formal dining room, which offers great views, is upstairs. In addition to the expected German specialties, the menu lists seafood, steaks and pasta. This place is just east of the downtown mall. Casual dress. **Bar:** Full bar. **Reservations:** suggested. **Hours:** 4:30 pm-10 pm. Closed major holidays. **Address:** 4332 Lakelse Ave V8G 1N8 **Location:** Hwy 16 to City Centre, 0.6 mi (1 km) e. **Parking:** on-site. **Cards:** AX, MC, VI.

BISTRO L'AMBIANCE

French
$9-$20

Phone: 250/615-0486

The little French bistro is next to the Coast Inn of the West, and parking is anywhere on the street. A French flair punctuates the food offerings, which range from fondues and appetizers to seafood, lunch sandwiches, children's choices and desserts. Casual dress. **Bar:** Full bar. **Hours:** 11 am-9 pm. Closed major holidays; also Sun. **Address:** 4608 Lakelse Ave V8G 1R1 **Location:** Hwy 16 to City Centre, just n on Emerson, then just e. **Parking:** street. **Cards:** MC, VI.

HOT HOUSE FLAVOURFUL FOOD

Indian
$7-$16

Phone: 250/615-5800

In a small strip mall, the simple eat-in-or-take-out restaurant presents a menu with worldwide influences, ranging from East Indian and Mexican to Asian and Cajun. Something extra distinguishes the flavorful food. Ask about the signature dishes. Casual dress. **Bar:** Beer & wine. **Hours:** 11:30 am-9 pm. Closed major holidays; also Sun. **Address:** 107-4717 Lakelse Ave V8G 1R5 **Location:** Corner of Spark St and Lakelse Ave; in small shopping complex. **Parking:** on-site. **Cards:** AX, MC, VI.

TOFINO pop. 1,655

―――― **WHERE TO STAY** ――――

BEST WESTERN TIN WIS RESORT LODGE

 Book great rates at AAA.com

Phone: (250)725-4445

CAA SAVE

Small-scale Hotel
$116-$420 All Year

Address: 1119 Pacific Rim Hwy V0R 2Z0 **Location:** 1.8 mi (3.5 km) s on Hwy 4. **Facility:** 85 units. 82 one-bedroom standard units, some with efficiencies. 3 one-bedroom suites with efficiencies and whirlpools. 2-3 stories, exterior corridors. **Parking:** on-site. **Terms:** cancellation fee imposed. **Amenities:** voice mail, irons, hair dryers. *Some:* high-speed Internet. **Leisure Activities:** whirlpool, exercise room. **Guest Services:** coin laundry, wireless Internet. **Business Services:** meeting rooms. **Cards:** AX, CB, DC, DS, JC, MC, VI.

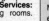

AAA Benefit:
Members save 10% everyday, plus an exclusive frequent stay program.

HIMWITSA LODGE

Small-scale Hotel
$175-$280 All Year

Phone: 250/725-2017

Address: 300 Main St V0R 2Z0 **Location:** Just n of centre via First St. **Facility:** Smoke free premises. 4 one-bedroom standard units, some with whirlpools. 2 stories (no elevator), interior corridors. **Parking:** on-site. **Terms:** office hours 8:30 am-9:30 pm, 14 day cancellation notice-fee imposed. **Amenities:** video library, DVD players, irons, hair dryers. **Cards:** MC, VI.

LONG BEACH LODGE RESORT

Small-scale Hotel
$299-$569 All Year

Phone: (250)725-2442

Address: 1441 Pacific Rim Hwy V0R 2Z0 **Location:** 4.7 mi (7.5 km) s on Hwy 4. **Facility:** Smoke free premises. 60 units. 40 one-bedroom standard units, some with whirlpools. 20 cottages with whirlpools. 2-3 stories, interior/exterior corridors. **Parking:** on-site. **Terms:** check-in 4 pm, cancellation fee imposed. **Amenities:** video library, DVD players, high-speed Internet, voice mail, irons, hair dryers. **Dining:** restaurant, see separate listing. **Leisure Activities:** exercise room. **Guest Services:** wireless Internet. **Business Services:** meeting rooms. **Cards:** AX, JC, MC, VI.

ASK ⁙ ⚲ ⊠ 🄰 🛗 ▯ / SOME UNITS FEE 🐾 🖥

PACIFIC SANDS BEACH RESORT

CAA SAVE

Small-scale Hotel
$170-$585 All Year

Phone: 250/725-3322

Address: 1421 Pacific Rim Hwy V0R 2Z0 **Location:** 4.7 mi (7.5 km) s on Hwy 4. Located next to Pacific Rim National Park. **Facility:** Smoke free premises. 77 units. 50 one-bedroom standard units with kitchens, some with whirlpools. 26 two- and 1 three-bedroom suites with kitchens, some with whirlpools. 1-3 stories (no elevator), exterior corridors. **Parking:** on-site. **Terms:** office hours 8 am-10 pm, 2-3 night minimum stay - seasonal and/or weekends, cancellation fee imposed. **Amenities:** video library (fee), DVD players, hair dryers. *Some:* voice mail. **Leisure Activities:** recreation programs in summer, barbecue, hiking trails. **Guest Services:** coin laundry. **Business Services:** PC. **Cards:** AX, DC, MC, VI. **Free Special Amenities:** newspaper and high-speed Internet.

SD CALL 🅂M ⊠ ⊠ 🄰 🐾 🛗 🖥 ▯ / SOME UNITS FEE 🐾 🄯

SCHOONER MOTEL

CAA SAVE

Motel
$85-$245 All Year

Phone: 250/725-3478

Address: 311-321 Campbell St V0R 2Z0 **Location:** Campbell and 2nd sts; downtown. **Facility:** Smoke free premises. 18 one-bedroom standard units, some with efficiencies. 2 stories, exterior corridors. *Bath:* combo or shower only. **Parking:** on-site. **Terms:** office hours 8 am-9 pm, 14 day cancellation notice-fee imposed. **Amenities:** hair dryers. **Guest Services:** coin laundry, wireless Internet. **Cards:** MC, VI.

⁙ ⊠ 🄰 🐾 🛗

TOFINO MOTEL

Motel
Rates not provided

Phone: 250/725-2055

Address: 542 Campbell St V0R 2Z0 **Location:** Campbell and 4th sts; downtown. **Facility:** Smoke free premises. 13 units. 12 one- and 1 two-bedroom standard units. 2 stories (no elevator), exterior corridors. **Parking:** on-site. **Terms:** office hours 8:30 am-10 pm. **Amenities:** hair dryers.

⁙ ⊠ 🄰 🐾 🛗 🖥

WICKANINNISH INN

CAA SAVE

Small-scale Hotel
$280-$1500 All Year

Book great rates at AAA.com   **Phone:** 250/725-3100

Address: Osprey Ln at Chesterman Beach V0R 2Z0 **Location:** 2.7 mi (4.3 km) e on Hwy 4. Located in a quiet area. **Facility:** The inn is on an oceanfront rock outcropping in an area known for its wild winter storms; rooms feature ocean views, fireplaces and soaker tubs. Closed 1/3-1/6. Smoke free premises. 75 units. 64 one-bedroom standard units, some with whirlpools. 11 one-bedroom suites, some with kitchens. 3 stories, interior corridors. **Parking:** on-site and valet. **Terms:** check-in 4 pm, 2 night minimum stay - seasonal and/or weekends, 14 day cancellation notice-fee imposed. **Amenities:** video library, DVD players, CD players, high-speed Internet, dual phone lines, voice mail, safes, honor bars, irons, hair dryers. **Dining:** Pointe Restaurant, see separate listing. **Leisure Activities:** steamroom, exercise room, spa. **Business Services:** meeting rooms, PC. **Cards:** AX, MC, VI. **Free Special Amenities:** local telephone calls and high-speed Internet.

⁙ ⚲ CALL 🅂M ⊠ ⊠ 🄰 🐾 🖥 ▯ / SOME UNITS FEE 🐾

The following lodging was either not evaluated or did not meet AAA rating requirements but is listed for your information only.

DAYS INN TOFINO WEIGH WEST MARINE
ADVENTURE RESORT

fyi

Small-scale Hotel

Phone: 250/725-3277

Did not meet all AAA rating requirements for some property operations at time of last evaluation on 06/13/2007. **Address:** 634 Campbell St V0R 2Z0 **Location:** 0.6 mi (1 km) s from downtown. Located in Inner Harbour Marina.

WHERE TO DINE

BLUE HERON RESTAURANT

Canadian
$9-$23

Phone: 250/725-3277

On the shores of Porpoise Bay, the restaurant treats patrons to wonderful views. On the menu are the excellent fresh seafood dishes that keep people coming back, along with some veal, chicken, lamb and steak. Entrees include the chef's soup or Caesar salad. Casual dress. **Bar:** Full bar. **Hours:** 7 am-9 pm. **Address:** 634 Campbell St V0R 2Z0 **Location:** 0.6 mi (1 km) s from downtown; in Days Inn Tofino Weigh West Marine Adventure Resort. **Parking:** on-site. **Cards:** AX, MC, VI.

POINTE RESTAURANT

CAA

Regional
Canadian
$18-$40

Phone: 250/725-3100

Built above the rocks and jutting out into the ocean, this restaurant offers breathtaking scenery of wild waves in the winter. The Canadian West Coast cuisine features fresh seafood and a good selection of wines. Walk-ins welcome for breakfast and lunch. Casual dress. **Bar:** Full bar. **Reservations:** required, for dinner. **Hours:** 7:30-11 am, 11:30-2:30 & 5-9 pm. **Address:** Osprey Ln/Chesterman Bch V0R 2Z0 **Location:** 2.7 mi (4.3 km) e on Hwy 4; in Wickaninnish Inn. **Parking:** on-site. **Cards:** AX, DC, MC, VI.

RAINCOAST CAFE

Phone: 250/725-2215

Pacific Rim
$19-$32

In a shopping complex, the small, intimate bistro prepares wonderfully distinctive Pacific Rim cuisine from fresh ingredients, including local seafood, pasta, vegetarian dishes and such red meats as veal and lamb. An open kitchen adds interest in the dining room, which displays local artwork. Due to limited seating, reservations are a must. Casual dress. **Bar:** Full bar. **Reservations:** required. **Hours:** 5:30 pm-10 pm; to 9 pm in winter. Closed: 12/25. **Address:** 101-120 Fourth St V0R 2Z0 **Location:** Fourth and Campbell sts; downtown. **Parking:** on-site and street. **Cards:** AX, MC, VI.

RESTAURANT AT LONG BEACH LODGE RESORT

Phone: 250/725-2442

Pacific Rim
$8-$42

This restaurant is located in a new lodge situated right along the beach, each table offering wonderful views of the waves and sand. The menu offers a wide range of items, and many ingredients are found locally or are strictly from the province, such as salmon, Salt Spring Island goat cheese, free range chickens and locally grown beef. **Bar:** Full bar. **Reservations:** required, for dinner. **Hours:** noon-9 pm. **Address:** 1441 Pacific Rim Hwy V0R 2Z0 **Location:** 4.7 mi (7.5 km) s on Hwy 4; in Long Beach Lodge Resort. **Parking:** on-site. **Cards:** AX, MC, VI.

SCHOONER RESTAURANT

Phone: 250/725-3444

Regional
Canadian
$10-$30

Great food has been a part of this building since 1949. Ask about "Morris the Ghost," who lived here in the early 70s and always made the chowder. Open for breakfast, lunch and dinner, the downtown restaurant prepares "out to sea" and "land ho" entrees. Casual dress. **Bar:** Full bar. **Reservations:** suggested, for dinner. **Hours:** 9 am-3 & 5-9 pm. Closed: 12/25. **Address:** 331 Campbell St V0R 2Z0 **Location:** Corner of 2nd St; downtown. **Parking:** on-site. **Cards:** AX, MC, VI.

SHELTER RESTAURANT

Phone: 250/725-3353

Pacific Rim
$20-$45

On the edge of town, the tastefully renovated old village house welcomes diners with regional cuisine featuring market produce and local seafood. Seating is offered by the stone fireplace in the lounge or in the candlelit upstairs loft. Casual dress. **Bar:** Full bar. **Reservations:** required, 6/15-10/15. **Hours:** 5 pm-11 pm; 5:30 pm-9:30 pm 11/15-4/30. Closed: 1/1, 12/25, 12/26. **Address:** 601 Campbell St V0R 2Z0 **Location:** Campbell and Gibson sts; downtown. **Parking:** on-site. **Cards:** AX, DC, MC, VI.

SOBO RESTAURANT

Phone: 250/725-2341

Pacific Rim
$6-$26

Locals are quick to rave about the food, which is prepared from an old catering truck parked in the Tofino Botanical Gardens. Diners can order seasonal specials, which are displayed on a colorful chalkboard, or such daily features as killer fish tacos, organic bean tostadas, crispy shrimp cakes, soba noodle salad and Caesar salad. Casual dress. **Hours:** Open 3/1-12/31 & 2/1-2/28; 11 am-9 pm. **Address:** 1184 Pacific Rim Hwy V0R 2Z0 **Location:** 1.8 mi (2.9 km) s on Pacific Rim Hwy; in Tofino Botanical Gardens. **Parking:** on-site. **Cards:** MC, VI.

TRAIL pop. 7,237

------ WHERE TO DINE ------

COLANDER RESTAURANT (1999) LTD   *Menu on AAA.com*

Phone: 250/364-1816

Italian
$5-$15

The Colander offers a nice selection of items at a self-service buffet. Lunch includes items such as pasta, chicken, burgers, subs and sandwiches; dinner is more extensive. Regional beers are served also. Pleasant atmosphere. Fee for to-go container. Casual dress. **Bar:** Full bar. **Reservations:** suggested. **Hours:** 11:30 am-2 & 4:30-8:30 pm, Sat & Sun from 4:30 pm. Closed: 12/25. **Address:** 1475 Cedar Ave V1R 4C5 **Location:** Centre. **Parking:** street. **Cards:** MC, VI.

UCLUELET pop. 1,487

------ WHERE TO STAY ------

THORNTON MOTEL

Phone: 250/726-7725

Motel
$79-$139 All Year

Address: 1861 Peninsula Rd V0R 3A0 **Location:** E on Peninsula Rd at Bay St. **Facility:** Smoke free premises. 17 units. 13 one- and 4 two-bedroom standard units, some with efficiencies. 2 stories (no elevator). **Parking:** on-site. **Terms:** office hours 8 am-10 pm, 5 day cancellation notice-fee imposed. **Cards:** AX, MC, VI.

------ ***The following lodgings were either not evaluated or did not*** ------
meet AAA rating requirements but are listed for your information only.

A SNUG HARBOUR INN

Phone: 250/726-2686

Bed & Breakfast

Did not meet all AAA rating requirements for locking devices in some guest rooms at time of last evaluation on 02/06/2004. **Address:** 460 Marine Dr V0R 3A0 **Location:** 1 mi (1.6 km) e on Peninsula Rd, just s. Facilities, services, and decor characterize a mid-range property.

TAUCA LEA BY THE SEA

fyi

Vacation Rental Condominium

Phone: 250/726-4625

Did not meet all AAA rating requirements for locking devices in some guest rooms at time of last evaluation on 06/02/2003. **Address:** 1971 Harbour Dr V0R 3A0 **Location:** From Peninsula Rd, just n on Sea Plane Base Rd, then just e. Facilities, services, and decor characterize a mid-range property.

─────── **WHERE TO DINE** ───────

BLUEBERRIES BAKERY CAFE

▽

Canadian
$8-$20

Phone: 250/726-7707

Known for eggs Benny, the quaint restaurant serves full breakfast, lunch and dinner. An outdoor patio is open during warmer months. Try the fresh seafood, wraps, fish and chips and burgers. Casual dress. **Hours:** 7:30 am-9 pm; hours vary in winter. Closed: 12/25, 12/26; also Mon & Tues. **Address:** 1627 Peninsula Rd V0R 3A0 **Location:** Peninsula Rd and Main St, just e. **Parking:** on-site. **Cards:** AX, MC, VI.

BOAT BASIN RESTAURANT

▽▽▽

Pacific Rim
$20-$35

Phone: 250/726-4644

Open for dinner only, this restaurant is located on the marina with both outdoor patio seating or fireside dining available. The menu features fresh Pacific cuisine, and the menu itself changes weekly. Sample locally caught fish and market fresh vegetables. Casual dress. **Bar:** Full bar. **Reservations:** required, in summer. **Hours:** 5:30 pm-9 pm; to 9:30 pm 7/1-9/15. **Address:** 1971 Harbour Crescent V0R 3A0 **Location:** From Peninsula Rd, just n on Sea Plane Base Rd, then just e on Harbour Rd; in Tauca Lea by the Sea. **Parking:** on-site. **Cards:** AX, MC, VI.

DELICADO'S SURFSIDE CAFE

▽

Southwestern
$6-$11

Phone: 250/726-4246

Near the township's entryway, the newer restaurant serves fresh, daily made dishes, such as roll-ups, Southwestern burritos, enchiladas, homemade soups and salads. Those seeking healthy alternatives should seek out the menu's low-carbohydrate and dairy- and wheat-free dishes. Casual dress. **Bar:** Beer & wine. **Hours:** 11 am-7 pm; to 9 pm 5/1-9/30. Closed: 1/1, 12/24, 12/26; also Wed. **Address:** 2082 Peninsula Rd V0R 3A0 **Location:** At Forbes Rd; west end of town. **Parking:** on-site. **Cards:** AX, MC, VI.

MATTERSON HOUSE RESTAURANT

▽

Canadian
$5-$19

Phone: 250/726-2200

This casual style restaurant is in a converted house located along the main road through town. Open for breakfast, lunch and dinner, the restaurant offers a menu that features regular Canadian type fare, such as soups and sandwiches for lunch, and more complex dinner entrees. Casual dress. **Bar:** Full bar. **Reservations:** required, for dinner. **Hours:** 11 am-8:30 pm, Fri-Sun from 9 am. Closed: 12/25, 12/26; also Mon. **Address:** 1682 Peninsula Rd V0R 3A0 **Location:** Just e. **Parking:** on-site. **Cards:** MC, VI.

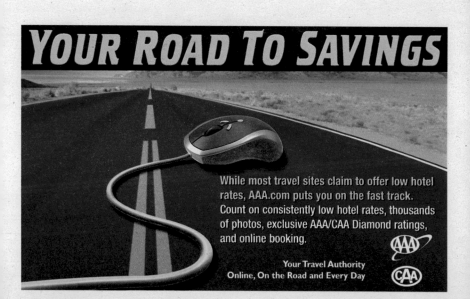

VALEMOUNT pop. 1,195

———— **WHERE TO STAY** ————

BEST WESTERN VALEMOUNT INN & SUITES *Book great rates at AAA.com*   Phone: 250/566-0086

Small-scale Hotel
Rates not provided

Address: 1950 Hwy 5 S V0E 2Z0 **Location:** 0.9 mi (1.5 km) s on Hwy 5 (Yellowhead Hwy). Located near wildlife sanctuary. **Facility:** 77 units. 49 one- and 2 two-bedroom standard units, some with whirlpools. 26 one-bedroom suites. 2 stories, interior corridors. *Bath:* combo or shower only. **Parking:** on-site, winter plug-ins. **Amenities:** dual phone lines, voice mail, irons, hair dryers. *Some:* DVD players, video games. **Pool(s):** heated indoor. **Leisure Activities:** whirlpool, waterslide, cross country skiing, bird-watching, hiking trails, exercise room. **Guest Services:** coin laundry, area transportation, wireless Internet. **Business Services:** meeting rooms, PC (fee). **Free Special Amenities:** local telephone calls and high-speed Internet. *(See color ad below)*

AAA Benefit:
Members save 10% everyday, plus an exclusive frequent stay program.

CANOE MOUNTAIN LODGE   Phone: (250)566-9171

Small-scale Hotel
$72-$124 All Year

Address: 1465 5th Ave V0E 2Z0 **Location:** Just e of Hwy 5 (Yellowhead Hwy). **Facility:** 47 one-bedroom standard units. 2 stories (no elevator), interior corridors. *Bath:* combo or shower only. **Parking:** on-site, winter plug-ins. **Terms:** office hours 7 am-11 pm, cancellation fee imposed. **Amenities:** hair dryers. *Some:* irons. **Leisure Activities:** steamroom. **Guest Services:** coin laundry, wireless Internet. **Cards:** AX, MC, VI. **Free Special Amenities: newspaper and high-speed Internet.**

CHALET CONTINENTAL MOTEL   Phone: (250)566-9787

Small-scale Hotel
$79-$135 All Year

Address: 1450 5th Ave V0E 2Z0 **Location:** Off Hwy 5 (Yellowhead Hwy), just e. **Facility:** 37 units. 35 one-bedroom standard units, some with kitchens and/or whirlpools. 2 one-bedroom suites. 2 stories (no elevator), interior corridors. **Parking:** on-site, winter plug-ins. **Terms:** office hours 7 am-11 pm, cancellation fee imposed. **Amenities:** high-speed Internet, hair dryers. *Some:* DVD players (fee), irons. **Pool(s):** heated indoor. **Leisure Activities:** sauna, whirlpool, steamroom, sun deck, barbecue area, exercise room. **Guest Services:** area transportation, beauty salon. **Cards:** AX, DC, MC, VI. **Free Special Amenities: room upgrade (subject to availability with advance reservations) and high-speed Internet.**

———— **WHERE TO DINE** ————

CARIBOU GRILL   Phone: 250/566-8244

Canadian
$10-$30

About five blocks off Highway 97 in a beautiful log cabin toward the end of the main street, the restaurant prepares casual fare. The menu centers on Canadian cuisine, from traditional pasta and meat dishes to the namesake caribou. Expect attentive, friendly service and original log house decor. Casual dress. **Bar:** Full bar. **Reservations:** not accepted. **Hours:** Open 3/1-10/31 & 12/1-2/28; 4:30 pm-10 pm. Closed: 12/25. **Address:** 1002 5th Ave V0C 2Z0 **Location:** Hwy 5 (Yellowhead Hwy), 0.6 mi (1 km) e at 5th Ave. **Parking:** on-site. **Cards:** AX, DC, MC, VI.

———— ▼ *See AAA listing above* ▼ ————

Destination Vancouver
pop. 545,671

*L*ose yourself in Vancouver. There's much to do, and getting there is half the fun.

*Y*ou can walk to downtown attractions, parks and shops; let SkyTrain whisk you to suburban destinations; or ride a ferry to the outer limits for recreation.

Waterfront dining, Vancouver.
Ocean breezes, wine and delicious fare marry well, making these aspects a superlative combination for alfresco dining.

Bicycling, Stanley Park.
A leisurely bicycle ride affords splendid views of the waterfront. (See listing page 167)

Granville Island Market, Vancouver.
Fresh fruits and vegetables are among the offerings at this open market. (See mention page 172)

See Downtown map page 564

Vancouver

West Vancouver

North Vancouver

Port Moody

Burnaby

Port Coquitlam

Coquitlam

New Westminster

Maple Ridge

Richmond

Delta

Surrey

Langley

Mission

Aldergrove

BRITISH COLUMBIA
WASHINGTON

UNITED STATES
CANADA

See Vicinity map page 568

*P*laces included in this AAA Destination City:

Chinatown, Vancouver.
Elaborately carved structures line the streets of the second largest area of its kind in North America. (See listing page 173)

Downtown Vancouver
Lodging & Dining

© 2007 NAVTEQ

RAPID TRANSIT
■ STATIONS

Miles
0   0.4   0.6
Kilometers

© AAA

1804-B

Downtown Vancouver

This index helps you "spot" where approved lodgings and restaurants are located on the corresponding detailed maps. Lodging daily rate range is for comparison only and show the property's high season. Restaurant rate range is a combination of lunch and/or dinner. Turn to the listing page for more detailed rate information and consult display ads for special promotions.

Spotter/Map Page Number	OA	DOWNTOWN VANCOUVER - Lodgings	Diamond Rating	Rate Range High Season	Listing Page
1 / p. 564	AAA	The Westin Bayshore Vancouver - see color ad p 591	◆◆◆◆	$460 SAVE	593
2 / p. 564		Sylvia Hotel	◆◆	$115-$200	590
3 / p. 564	AAA	Renaissance Vancouver Hotel Harbourside - see color ad p 588	fyi	$219-$329 SAVE	587
4 / p. 564	AAA	Pan Pacific Vancouver - see color ad p 586	◆◆◆◆	$269-$449 SAVE	585
5 / p. 564	AAA	Vancouver Marriott Pinnacle Downtown	◆◆◆◆	$219-$340 SAVE	590
6 / p. 564	AAA	The Fairmont Waterfront	◆◆◆◆	$249-$429 SAVE	580
7 / p. 564	AAA	The Listel Hotel	◆◆◆	$149-$399 SAVE	584
8 / p. 564	AAA	Pacific Palisades Hotel - see color ad p 579	◆◆◆	$370-$420 SAVE	585
9 / p. 564	AAA	Best Western Sands - see color ad p 576	◆◆◆	$119-$259 SAVE	576
10 / p. 564	AAA	West End Guest House	◆◆◆	$160-$285 SAVE	590
11 / p. 564		Terminal City Tower Hotel	◆◆◆	Rates not provided	590
12 / p. 564	AAA	Blue Horizon Hotel - see color ad p 578	◆◆◆	$99-$319 SAVE	576
13 / p. 564	AAA	Days Inn Vancouver Downtown - see color ad p 578	◆◆◆	$115-$295 SAVE	578
14 / p. 564		Barclay House in the West End	◆◆◆	Rates not provided	575
15 / p. 564	AAA	Hyatt Regency Vancouver - see color ad p 584	◆◆◆◆	$159-$439 SAVE	584
16 / p. 564	AAA	Hotel Le Soleil - see color ad p 582	◆◆◆◆	$365-$465 SAVE	583
17 / p. 564	AAA	Delta Vancouver Suites	◆◆◆	$174-$234 SAVE	580
18 / p. 564	AAA	The Fairmont Hotel Vancouver	◆◆◆◆	$229-$429 SAVE	580
19 / p. 564		Ramada Limited Downtown Vancouver - see color ad p 587	◆◆	$129-$229	587
20 / p. 564	AAA	The Sutton Place Hotel - see color ad p 590	◆◆◆◆◆	$209-$599 SAVE	589
21 / p. 564	AAA	Four Seasons Hotel Vancouver	◆◆◆◆	$240-$815 SAVE	581
22 / p. 564		'O Canada' House B&B	◆◆◆	Rates not provided	584
23 / p. 564	AAA	St Regis Hotel	◆◆	$129-$199 SAVE	588
24 / p. 564	AAA	The Wedgewood Hotel & Spa	◆◆◆◆	$450-$600 SAVE	590
25 / p. 564	AAA	Sheraton Vancouver Wall Centre Hotel - see color ad p 589	◆◆◆◆	$459 SAVE	588
26 / p. 564	AAA	The Westin Grand, Vancouver	◆◆◆◆	$429-$749 SAVE	593
27 / p. 564	AAA	Sunset Inn & Suites - see color ad p 575	◆◆◆	$99-$475 SAVE	589
28 / p. 564		Sandman Hotel Vancouver City Center	◆◆	Rates not provided	588
29 / p. 564	AAA	Holiday Inn Hotel & Suites Vancouver-Downtown - see color ad on insert	◆◆◆	$199-$379 SAVE	582
30 / p. 564	AAA	Landis Hotel & Suites - see color ad p 585	◆◆◆	$169-$349 SAVE	584
31 / p. 564	AAA	Best Western Chateau Granville	◆◆◆	$99-$249 SAVE	575
32 / p. 564	AAA	The Georgian Court Hotel	◆◆◆	$189-$359 SAVE	581
33 / p. 564	AAA	Residence Inn by Marriott Vancouver	◆◆◆	$252-$384 SAVE	587

Spotter/Map Page Number	OA	DOWNTOWN VANCOUVER - Lodgings (continued)	Diamond Rating	Rate Range High Season	Listing Page
34 / p. 564	◈	**Hampton Inn & Suites by Hilton, Downtown Vancouver** - see color ad p 577	◇◇◇	$159-$269 (SAVE)	581
35 / p. 564	◈	**Howard Johnson Hotel** - see color ad p 583	◇◇	$149-$259 (SAVE)	583
36 / p. 564	◈	**Ramada Inn & Suites Downtown Vancouver** - see color ad p 586	◇◇	$129-$259 (SAVE)	586
37 / p. 564		Quality Hotel Downtown-The Inn at False Creek - see color ad on insert	◇◇	$89-$209	585
38 / p. 564	◈	**Best Western Downtown Vancouver** - see color ad p 577	◇◇◇	$103-$206 (SAVE)	576
39 / p. 564	◈	**Granville Island Hotel** - see color ad p 581	◇◇◇	$160-$475 (SAVE)	581
		DOWNTOWN VANCOUVER - Restaurants			
1 / p. 564	◈	**The Fish House in Stanley Park**	◇◇◇	$10-$30	596
2 / p. 564	◈	**Ciao Bella Ristorante**	◇◇	$8-$29	594
3 / p. 564		Cafe de Paris	◇◇	$13-$30	594
4 / p. 564		Cardero's Restaurant	◇◇	$9-$25	594
5 / p. 564		Parkside on Haro Street	◇◇◇	$45-$52	598
6 / p. 564		Le Gavroche Restaurant Francais	◇◇◇	$13-$45	597
7 / p. 564		Delilah's	◇◇	$29-$39	595
8 / p. 564		Vistas Revolving Restaurant - see color ad p 588	◇◇◇	$28-$40	600
9 / p. 564		Five Sails Restaurant	◇◇◇◇	$32-$42	596
10 / p. 564		Show Case Restaurant	◇◇◇	$15-$30	599
11 / p. 564		Rain City Grill	◇◇◇	$22-$32	598
12 / p. 564		Imperial Chinese Seafood Restaurant	◇◇	$15-$58	596
13 / p. 564		Ezogiku Noodle Cafe	◇	$6-$9	595
14 / p. 564		Won More Szechuan Cuisine	◇◇	$7-$16	600
15 / p. 564		Herons Restaurant	◇◇◇	$12-$35	596
16 / p. 564		Pacific Crab Company Oyster Bar & Grill	◇◇	$9-$40	598
17 / p. 564	◈	**Zin**	◇◇	$10-$28	601
18 / p. 564		Rex Rotisserie & Grill	◇◇◇	$11-$30	599
19 / p. 564		Balthazar	◇◇	$13-$24	593
20 / p. 564		Aqua Riva	◇◇◇	$12-$35	593
21 / p. 564		Oysi Oysi Japanese Restaurant	◇◇	$7-$19	598
22 / p. 564		Copper Chimney	◇◇◇	$14-$30	595
23 / p. 564	◈	**The Hermitage**	◇◇◇	$12-$36	596
24 / p. 564		CINCIN	◇◇◇	$18-$45	595
25 / p. 564		Savory Coast	◇◇◇	$13-$35	599
26 / p. 564		Zefferelli's Restaurant	◇◇	$8-$25	601
27 / p. 564	◈	**Tropika Malaysian & Thai Cuisine**	◇◇	$8-$20	599
28 / p. 564	◈	**Joe Fortes Seafood & Chop House**	◇◇	$9-$35	597
29 / p. 564		Al Porto Ristorante	◇◇	$12-$27	593
30 / p. 564		Kobe Japanese Steak House	◇◇	$30-$56	597
31 / p. 564		Water St. Cafe	◇◇	$11-$24	600
32 / p. 564		Diva at the Met	◇◇◇◇	$12-$42	595

Spotter/Map Page Number	OA	DOWNTOWN VANCOUVER - Restaurants (continued)	Diamond Rating	Rate Range High Season	Listing Page
33 / p. 564		Cafe de Medici	◈◈◈	$15-$40	594
34 / p. 564		Saveur	◈◈◈	$9-$38	599
35 / p. 564		Fleuri Restaurant - see color ad p 590	◈◈◈◈	$16-$46	596
36 / p. 564	CAA	**Don Francesco Ristorante**	◈◈◈	$14-$40	595
37 / p. 564	CAA	**Bacchus Restaurant**	◈◈◈◈	$9-$35	593
38 / p. 564		Le Crocodile	◈◈◈◈	$15-$36	597
39 / p. 564	CAA	**Cafe Presto Panini**	◈	$9-$10	594
40 / p. 564		Wild Rice	◈◈	$10-$19	600
41 / p. 564		India Bistro	◈◈	$8-$13	597
42 / p. 564		Kingston Taphouse & Grille	◈◈	$10-$19	597
43 / p. 564		Stepho's Souvlaki Greek Taverna	◈◈	$7-$10	599
44 / p. 564		Relish-The Restaurant & Lounge	◈◈	$12-$25	598
45 / p. 564		Kam's Place Singaporean Cuisine	◈◈	$9-$15	597
46 / p. 564		Lucy Mae Brown Restaurant and Lounge	◈◈◈	$20-$30	597
47 / p. 564		Subeez Cafe	◈◈	$10-$23	599
48 / p. 564		Lickerish	◈◈◈	$15-$25	597
49 / p. 564		Villa de Lupo Restaurant	◈◈◈	$20-$36	600
50 / p. 564	CAA	**The William Tell**	◈◈◈	$23-$38	600
51 / p. 564		Fiddlehead Joe's	◈◈	$10-$22	596
52 / p. 564		Chilli House Thai Bistro	◈◈	$11-$16	594
53 / p. 564		Il Giardino	◈◈◈	$16-$40	596
54 / p. 564		Blue Water Cafe	◈◈◈	$30-$45	594
55 / p. 564	CAA	**A Kettle Of Fish**	◈◈	$20-$39	593
56 / p. 564	CAA	**Glowbal Grill & Satay Bar**	◈◈◈	$10-$35	596
57 / p. 564		Brix Restaurant & Wine Bar	◈◈◈	$22-$39	594
58 / p. 564		Yaletown Brewing Company	◈◈	$9-$29	600
59 / p. 564		Elixir Restaurant - Opus Bar	◈◈◈	$16-$38	595
60 / p. 564		La Terrazza	◈◈◈	$18-$38	597
61 / p. 564		C Restaurant	◈◈◈	$18-$39	595
62 / p. 564		Nu	◈◈◈	$13-$37	598
63 / p. 564		Provence Marinaside	◈◈◈	$9-$35	598
64 / p. 564		The Sandbar Seafood Restaurant	◈◈	$10-$30	599
65 / p. 564		Dockside Restaurant & Brewing Company	◈◈	$10-$30	595

1803-B

© 2007 NAVTEQ

Vancouver
Lodging & Dining

RAPID TRANSIT

STATIONS

✈ Airport Accommodations

Spotter/Map Page Number	OA	VANCOUVER	Diamond Rating	Rate Range High Season	Listing Page
49 / p. 568	CAA	Accent Inns, 5 km e of airport	◆◆	$99-$169 SAVE	623
45 / p. 568	CAA	Best Western Abercorn Inn, 2.4 mi (4 km) e of airport	◆◆	$119-$219 SAVE	623
54 / p. 568	CAA	Best Western Richmond Hotel & Convention Center, 3 mi (5 km) se of airport	◆◆◆	Rates not provided SAVE	624
42 / p. 568	CAA	Days Inn Vancouver Airport, 1.8 mi (3 km) e of airport	◆◆	$125-$139 SAVE	624
47 / p. 568	CAA	Delta Vancouver Airport, 2.4 km e of airport	◆◆◆	$149-$300 SAVE	624
41 / p. 568	CAA	The Fairmont Vancouver Airport, at airport	◆◆◆◆	$279-$379 SAVE	625
52 / p. 568	CAA	Four Points by Sheraton Vancouver Airport, 5 km se of airport	◆◆◆	$135-$180 SAVE	625
44 / p. 568	CAA	Hampton Inn Vancouver Airport, 1.8 mi (3 km) e of airport	◆◆◆	$119-$209 SAVE	625
53 / p. 568	CAA	Hilton Vancouver Airport, 3 mi (5 km) se of airport	◆◆◆	$269-$289 SAVE	625
43 / p. 568	CAA	Holiday Inn Express Vancouver-Airport, 4 km e of airport	◆◆◆	$109-$179 SAVE	625
51 / p. 568	CAA	Holiday Inn International Vancouver Airport, 5 km e of airport	◆◆◆	$109-$179 SAVE	626
56 / p. 568	CAA	Quality Hotel Airport (South), 3 mi (5 km) se of airport	◆◆	$89-$179 SAVE	626
50 / p. 568	CAA	Radisson President Hotel & Suites, 4 km se of airport	[fyi]	$139-$199 SAVE	626
40 / p. 568	CAA	River Rock Casino Resort, 5 km e of airport	◆◆◆◆	Rates not provided SAVE	626
48 / p. 568		Sandman Hotel Vancouver Airport, 5 km e of airport	◆◆	$119-$159	626
46 / p. 568	CAA	Travelodge Hotel Vancouver Airport, 5 km e of airport	◆◆	$119-$179 SAVE	627
55 / p. 568	CAA	Vancouver Airport Marriott, (5 km) se of airport	◆◆◆	$219-$263 SAVE	627
8 / p. 568	CAA	Quality Inn Airport, 9 km ne of airport	◆◆	$79-$149 SAVE	605

Vancouver and Vicinity

This index helps you "spot" where approved lodgings and restaurants are located on the corresponding detailed maps. Lodging daily rate range is for comparison only and show the property's high season. Restaurant rate range is a combination of lunch and/or dinner. Turn to the listing page for more detailed rate information and consult display ads for special promotions.

Spotter/Map Page Number	OA	VANCOUVER - Lodgings	Diamond Rating	Rate Range High Season	Listing Page
1 / p. 568	CAA	Holiday Inn Express Vancouver - see color ad on insert, p 582	◆◆◆	$89-$209 SAVE	603
2 / p. 568	CAA	Best Western Exhibition Park	◆◆	$99-$179 SAVE	601
3 / p. 568		Holiday Inn Vancouver-Centre (Broadway) - see color ad on insert	◆◆◆	$179-$209	604
4 / p. 568	CAA	Best Western Uptown - see color ad p 601	◆◆◆	$85-$179 SAVE	602
5 / p. 568	CAA	Plaza 500 Hotel & Convention Centre	◆◆◆	$144-$199 SAVE	604
6 / p. 568	CAA	Days Inn-Vancouver Metro - see color ad p 603	◆◆	$79-$189 SAVE	603

Spotter/Map Page Number	OA	**VANCOUVER** - Lodgings (continued)	Diamond Rating	Rate Range High Season	Listing Page
7 / p. 568		2400 Motel	◈	$85-$110	601
8 / p. 568	(AAA)	**Quality Inn Airport** - see color ad on insert, p 606	◈ ◈	$79-$149 [SAVE]	605
		VANCOUVER - Restaurants			
① / p. 568	(AAA)	**Sequoia Grill at the Tea House**	◈ ◈ ◈	$12-$39	610
② / p. 568	(AAA)	**The Cannery**	◈ ◈ ◈	$15-$30	608
③ / p. 568		Pink Pearl Chinese Restaurant	◈ ◈	$4-$19	610
④ / p. 568		Abigail's Party	◈ ◈	$8-$15	608
⑤ / p. 568		Lombardo's Ristorante Pizzeria	◈	$9-$25	609
⑥ / p. 568		Quattro on Fourth	◈ ◈ ◈	$18-$38	610
⑦ / p. 568		Bishop's	◈ ◈ ◈ ◈	$34-$40	608
⑧ / p. 568		Monk McQueen's	◈ ◈	$12-$30	609
⑨ / p. 568	(AAA)	**Sophie's Cosmic Cafe**	◈	$6-$10	611
⑩ / p. 568		Hell's Kitchen	◈ ◈	$9-$24	608
⑪ / p. 568		Las Margaritas Restaurante & Cantina	◈ ◈	$8-$17	609
⑫ / p. 568		Feenie's	◈ ◈ ◈	$16-$28	608
⑬ / p. 568		Mistral French Bistro	◈ ◈ ◈	$14-$29	609
⑭ / p. 568	(AAA)	**Lumiere**	◈ ◈ ◈ ◈ ◈	$37-$45	609
⑮ / p. 568		Provence Mediterranean Grill	◈ ◈ ◈	$10-$29	610
⑯ / p. 568		Maurya Indian Cuisine	◈ ◈	$11-$22	609
⑰ / p. 568		Wild Garlic	◈ ◈ ◈	$8-$28	611
⑱ / p. 568		Aurora Bistro	◈ ◈ ◈	$16-$26	608
⑲ / p. 568		Rasputin	◈ ◈	$13-$25	610
⑳ / p. 568		Tojo's Restaurant	◈ ◈	$22-$30	611
㉑ / p. 568		Rugby Beach Club Grille	◈ ◈	$8-$13	610
㉒ / p. 568		Gramercy Grill	◈ ◈	$9-$33	608
㉓ / p. 568		Star Anise	◈ ◈ ◈	$18-$30	611
㉔ / p. 568		West Restaurant & Bar	◈ ◈ ◈	$11-$45	611
㉕ / p. 568		Red Door Pan Asian Grill	◈ ◈	$7-$18	610
㉖ / p. 568		The Ouisi Bistro	◈ ◈	$8-$22	609
㉗ / p. 568		Trafalgars Bistro	◈ ◈	$10-$25	611
㉘ / p. 568		Sawasdee Thai Restaurant	◈ ◈	$8-$15	610
㉙ / p. 568		Seasons Hilltop Bistro	◈ ◈ ◈	$11-$32	610
㉚ / p. 568		Shaughnessy Restaurant At VanDusen Garden	◈ ◈	$11-$28	610
㉛ / p. 568		Avenue Grill	◈ ◈	$8-$22	608

Spotter/Map Page Number	OA	BOWEN ISLAND - Lodgings	Diamond Rating	Rate Range High Season	Listing Page
11 / p. 568		Wildwood Lane Cottages	◆◆	Rates not provided	489
		NORTH VANCOUVER - Lodgings			
14 / p. 568	CAA	North Vancouver Hotel - see color ad p 605	◆◆	$109-$159 SAVE	621
15 / p. 568	CAA	Comfort Inn and Suites - see color ad on insert	◆◆	$79-$269 SAVE	621
16 / p. 568		Lionsgate Travelodge	◆	$69-$149	621
17 / p. 568		Grouse Inn - see color ad p 580	◆◆	$75-$175	621
18 / p. 568	CAA	Best Western Capilano Inn & Suites	◆◆	$99-$169 SAVE	620
19 / p. 568	CAA	Holiday Inn Hotel & Suites North Vancouver - see color ad on insert, p 606, p 621	◆◆◆	$199-$329 SAVE	621
		NORTH VANCOUVER - Restaurants			
40 / p. 568		The Edge Bistro	◆◆	$8-$26	622
41 / p. 568		Moustache Cafe	◆◆◆	$10-$32	622
42 / p. 568		Jagerhof Schnitzel House	◆◆	$9-$17	622
43 / p. 568		Gusto di Quattro	◆◆◆	$10-$31	622
		BURNABY - Lodgings			
22 / p. 568		Lake City Motor Inn	◆◆	$94-$179	613
23 / p. 568	CAA	Accent Inns - see color ad p 639	◆◆	$119-$179 SAVE	612
24 / p. 568	CAA	Hilton Vancouver Metrotown - see color ad p 612	◆◆◆	$140-$239 SAVE	613
25 / p. 568		Holiday Inn Express Metrotown	◆◆◆	$149-$179	613
26 / p. 568	CAA	Best Western Kings Inn and Conference Centre	◆◆◆	Rates not provided SAVE	612
		BURNABY - Restaurants			
46 / p. 568		HORIZONS	◆◆◆	$12-$30	613
47 / p. 568	CAA	Hart House on Deer Lake	◆◆◆	$14-$36	613
48 / p. 568	CAA	Crystal Bar and Grille - see color ad p 612	◆◆	$9-$30	613
		PITT MEADOWS - Lodgings			
29 / p. 568		Ramada Inn & Suites Hotel Royale	◆◆	$112	622
		COQUITLAM - Lodgings			
32 / p. 568	CAA	Best Western Coquitlam Inn Convention Centre	◆◆◆	$132-$289 SAVE	614
33 / p. 568		Ramada Inn Coquitlam	◆◆	$110-$150	614
34 / p. 568	CAA	Best Western Chelsea Inn	◆◆◆	$119-$139 SAVE	614
		COQUITLAM - Restaurant			
51 / p. 568		Pacific Rim Grille	◆◆◆	$10-$30	615
		NEW WESTMINSTER - Lodgings			
37 / p. 568	CAA	Inn at Westminster Quay	◆◆	$200-$235 SAVE	620

Spotter/Map Page Number	OA	NEW WESTMINSTER - Restaurants	Diamond Rating	Rate Range High Season	Listing Page
54 / p. 568		La Rustica Ristorante	◆◆	$10-$24	620
55 / p. 568		Burger Heaven	◆	$7-$18	620
		RICHMOND - Lodgings			
40 / p. 568	CAA	**River Rock Casino Resort**	◆◆◆	Rates not provided SAVE	626
41 / p. 568	CAA	**The Fairmont Vancouver Airport** - see color ad p 603	◆◆◆	$279-$379 SAVE	625
42 / p. 568	CAA	**Days Inn Vancouver Airport**	◆◆	$125-$139 SAVE	624
43 / p. 568	CAA	**Holiday Inn Express Vancouver-Airport**	◆◆◆	$109-$179 SAVE	625
44 / p. 568	CAA	**Hampton Inn Vancouver Airport**	◆◆◆	$119-$209 SAVE	625
45 / p. 568	CAA	**Best Western Abercorn Inn**	◆◆	$119-$219 SAVE	623
46 / p. 568	CAA	**Travelodge Hotel Vancouver Airport**	◆◆	$119-$179 SAVE	627
47 / p. 568	CAA	**Delta Vancouver Airport**	◆◆◆	$149-$300 SAVE	624
48 / p. 568		Sandman Hotel Vancouver Airport	◆◆	$119-$159	626
49 / p. 568	CAA	**Accent Inns** - see color ad p 639	◆◆	$99-$169 SAVE	623
50 / p. 568	CAA	**Radisson President Hotel & Suites** - see color ad p 626	fyi	$139-$199 SAVE	626
51 / p. 568	CAA	**Holiday Inn International Vancouver Airport** - see color ad p 604	◆◆◆	$109-$179 SAVE	626
52 / p. 568	CAA	**Four Points by Sheraton Vancouver Airport**	◆◆◆	$135-$180 SAVE	625
53 / p. 568	CAA	**Hilton Vancouver Airport** - see color ad p 605	◆◆◆	$269-$289 SAVE	625
54 / p. 568	CAA	**Best Western Richmond Hotel & Convention Center** - see color ad p 602	◆◆◆	Rates not provided SAVE	624
55 / p. 568	CAA	**Vancouver Airport Marriott**	◆◆◆	$219-$263 SAVE	627
56 / p. 568	CAA	**Quality Hotel Airport (South)** - see color ad on insert	◆◆	$89-$179 SAVE	626
		RICHMOND - Restaurants			
58 / p. 568		Tramonto	◆◆◆	$25-$40	628
59 / p. 568		Globe @ YVR	◆◆◆	$15-$30	627
60 / p. 568		Flying Beaver	◆◆	$9-$20	627
61 / p. 568	CAA	**Steveston Seafood House**	◆◆◆	$18-$43	628
62 / p. 568		Tapenade Bistro	◆◆	$10-$26	628
63 / p. 568		Correlis Restaurant	◆◆	$7-$21	627
		DELTA - Lodgings			
59 / p. 568	CAA	**Delta Town & Country Inn**	◆◆◆	$94-$101 SAVE	616
60 / p. 568	CAA	**Clair's Bed & Breakfast**	◆◆	$125-$185 SAVE	615
61 / p. 568		River Run Cottages	◆◆◆	$150-$210	616
62 / p. 568	CAA	**The Coast Tsawwassen Inn** - see color ad p 602	◆◆◆	$130-$240 SAVE	616
		DELTA - Restaurant			
66 / p. 568	CAA	**La Belle Auberge**	◆◆◆	$30-$35	616

Spotter/Map Page Number	OA	SURREY - Lodgings	Diamond Rating	Rate Range High Season	Listing Page
65 / p. 568	CAA	Howard Johnson Express Inn & Suites	◆◆	$85-$100 SAVE	629
66 / p. 568	CAA	Sheraton Vancouver Guildford Hotel - see color ad p 629	◆◆◆	Rates not provided SAVE	629
67 / p. 568		Ramada Hotel & Suites Surrey/Guildford	◆◆	$99-$159	629
68 / p. 568		Holiday Inn Express Hotel & Suites - see color ad on insert	◆◆◆	$149-$189	628
69 / p. 568		Days Inn Surrey	◆◆	Rates not provided	628
70 / p. 568	CAA	Best Western King George Inn & Suites - see color ad p 601	◆◆◆	$89-$149 SAVE	628
71 / p. 568		Hampton Inn & Suites - see color ad p 617	◆◆◆	Rates not provided	628
72 / p. 568		Ramada Inn Langley-Surrey	◆◆	Rates not provided	629
73 / p. 568	CAA	Best Western Peace Arch Inn - see color ad on insert	◆◆	$100-$130 SAVE	628
		SURREY - Restaurants			
69 / p. 568		Yokohama Japanese Restaurant	◆	$7-$21	630
70 / p. 568		Villa Verdi Ristorante Italiano	◆◆	$15-$32	630
71 / p. 568		Crescent Beach Bistro	◆◆	$10-$26	630
72 / p. 568		The Turkey House & Deli	◆	$7-$10	630
		LANGLEY - Lodgings			
76 / p. 568		Sandman Hotel Langley	◆◆	Rates not provided	618
77 / p. 568	CAA	Holiday Inn Express Hotel & Suites Langley - see color ad on insert	◆◆◆	$114-$144 SAVE	618
78 / p. 568	CAA	Best Value Westward Inn	◆	$75-$95 SAVE	616
79 / p. 568	CAA	Best Western Langley Inn - see color ad p 617	◆◆◆	Rates not provided SAVE	617
80 / p. 568	CAA	Coast Hotel & Convention Centre	◆◆◆	$125-$165 SAVE	618
		WHITE ROCK - Lodgings			
83 / p. 568	CAA	Ocean Promenade Hotel - see color ad p 631	◆◆◆	$139-$469 SAVE	631
		WHITE ROCK - Restaurants			
75 / p. 568	CAA	Pearl On The Rock	◆◆◆◆	$10-$34	632
76 / p. 568		Giraffe	◆◆◆	$10-$28	631
77 / p. 568		La Baia Italian Restaurant	◆◆	$12-$22	632
		WEST VANCOUVER - Restaurants			
34 / p. 568		Salmon House on the Hill	◆◆	$12-$34	631
35 / p. 568	CAA	The Beach House at Dundarave Pier	◆◆◆	$13-$30	630
36 / p. 568		La Regalade French Bistro	◆◆	$12-$25	631
37 / p. 568		Beach Side Cafe	◆◆◆	$12-$36	631

DOWNTOWN VANCOUVER   (See map and index starting on p. 564)

─── WHERE TO STAY ───

BARCLAY HOUSE IN THE WEST END   *Book at AAA.com*   **Phone: 604/605-1351**

Historic Bed
& Breakfast
Rates not provided

Address: 1351 Barclay St V6E 1H6 **Location:** Between Broughton and Jervis sts. Located in a residential area in West End. **Facility:** The Victorian home is on a tree-lined street in the West End district; a lovely front porch overlooks the garden, and rooms have a masculine motif. Smoke free premises. 6 one-bedroom standard units. 3 stories (no elevator), interior/exterior corridors. *Bath:* combo or shower only. **Parking:** on-site. **Terms:** office hours 7 am-7 pm, age restrictions may apply. **Amenities:** video library, DVD players, CD players, voice mail, irons, hair dryers. **Guest Services:** wireless Internet.

BEST WESTERN CHATEAU GRANVILLE   *Book great rates at AAA.com*   **Phone: (604)669-7070**   **31**

(CAA) SAVE

Small-scale Hotel
$99-$249 All Year

Address: 1100 Granville St V6Z 2B6 **Location:** Between Davie and Helmcken sts. **Facility:** 150 units. 55 one-bedroom standard units. 95 one-bedroom suites. 3-15 stories, interior corridors. **Parking:** on-site (fee). **Terms:** cancellation fee imposed. **Amenities:** dual phone lines, voice mail, irons, hair dryers. **Guest Services:** valet laundry, wireless Internet. **Business Services:** meeting rooms. **Cards:** AX, CB, DC, DS, JC, MC, VI. **Free Special Amenities:** early check-in/late check-out and room upgrade (subject to availability with advance reservations).

Best Western

AAA Benefit:
Members save 10%
everyday, plus an
exclusive frequent
stay program.

▼ See AAA listing p 589 ▼

Sunset
Inn & Suites

The Comfort of Home. Completely renovated spacious suites in Downtown Vancouver.

- Fully Renovated
- Spacious suites
- Free wireless Internet
- Continental breakfast served every morning
- Free gated parking
- Short or longer stays

Located in downtown Vancouver's scenic West End, where you can walk to the beach, Stanley Park & Robson Street. We offer fully equipped kitchens, separate living rooms and bedrooms, and your own balcony.

Call 1-800-786-1997 or visit www.sunsetinn.com
1111 Burnaby St., Vancouver, BC Canada

(See map and index starting on p. 564)

BEST WESTERN DOWNTOWN VANCOUVER   *Book great rates at AAA.com*   Phone: (604)669-9888   **38**

Small-scale Hotel
$103-$206 All Year

AAA Benefit:
Members save 10% everyday, plus an exclusive frequent stay program.

Address: 718 Drake St V6Z 2W6 **Location:** Corner of Drake and Granville sts. Located in the Granville Street Entertainment District. **Facility:** Smoke free premises. 143 one-bedroom standard units, some with efficiencies and/or whirlpools. 12 stories, interior corridors. **Parking:** on-site (fee). **Amenities:** voice mail, safes, irons, hair dryers. **Leisure Activities:** saunas; whirlpool, limited exercise equipment. **Guest Services:** valet and coin laundry, area transportation-within downtown, wireless Internet. **Business Services:** meeting rooms. **Cards:** AX, DC, DS, JC, MC, VI. **Free Special Amenities:** early check-in/late check-out and room upgrade (subject to availability with advance reservations). *(See color ad p 577)*

BEST WESTERN SANDS   *Book great rates at AAA.com*   Phone: (604)682-1831   **9**

Small-scale Hotel
$119-$259 All Year

AAA Benefit:
Members save 10% everyday, plus an exclusive frequent stay program.

Address: 1755 Davie St V6G 1W5 **Location:** Between Bidwell and Denman sts. **Facility:** Smoke free premises. 121 one-bedroom standard units, some with efficiencies. 6 stories, interior corridors. **Parking:** on-site (fee). **Terms:** check-in 4 pm. **Amenities:** video games (fee), voice mail, irons, hair dryers. **Leisure Activities:** sauna, limited exercise equipment. **Guest Services:** valet and coin laundry, wireless Internet. **Business Services:** meeting rooms. **Cards:** AX, CB, DC, DS, JC, MC, VI. **Free Special Amenities:** room upgrade (subject to availability with advance reservations) and high-speed Internet. *(See color ad below)*

BLUE HORIZON HOTEL   *Book great rates at AAA.com*   Phone: (604)688-1411   **12**

Small-scale Hotel
$99-$319 All Year

Address: 1225 Robson St V6E 1C3 **Location:** Between Jervis and Bute sts. **Facility:** Smoke free premises. 214 one-bedroom standard units. 31 stories, interior corridors. **Parking:** on-site (fee). **Terms:** cancellation fee imposed. **Amenities:** high-speed Internet, voice mail, safes, irons, hair dryers. *Some:* honor bars. **Pool(s):** heated indoor. **Leisure Activities:** sauna, whirlpool, limited exercise equipment. **Guest Services:** valet laundry. **Business Services:** meeting rooms. **Cards:** AX, DC, MC, VI. **Free Special Amenities:** high-speed Internet. *(See color ad p 578)*

(See map and index starting on p. 564)

DAYS INN VANCOUVER DOWNTOWN   *Book great rates at AAA.com*   Phone: (604)681-4335

Small-scale Hotel
$115-$295 All Year

Address: 921 W Pender St V6C 1M2 **Location:** Between Burrard and Hornby sts. Located in the financial district. **Facility:** Smoke free premises. 85 one-bedroom standard units. 6 stories, interior corridors. *Bath:* combo or shower only. **Parking:** on-site (fee) and valet. **Terms:** cancellation fee imposed. **Amenities:** high-speed Internet, voice mail, safes, irons, hair dryers. **Guest Services:** valet and coin laundry, wireless Internet. **Business Services:** meeting rooms. **Cards:** AX, CB, DC, DS, JC, MC, VI. **Free Special Amenities:** room upgrade (subject to availability with advance reservations) and high-speed Internet. *(See color ad below)*

▼ See AAA listing p 585 ▼

(See map and index starting on p. 564)

DELTA VANCOUVER SUITES *Book great rates at AAA.com* Phone: 604/689-8188 **17**

CAA SAVE

Small-scale Hotel
$174-$234 All Year

Address: 550 W Hastings St V6B 1L6 **Location:** Between Seymour and Richards sts; entrance in alley way. **Facility:** 225 units. 40 one-bedroom standard units. 185 one-bedroom suites. 23 stories, interior corridors. **Parking:** on-site (fee) and valet. **Terms:** cancellation fee imposed. **Amenities:** dual phone lines, voice mail, honor bars, irons, hair dryers. **Fee:** video games, high-speed Internet. **Some:** CD players. **Pool(s):** heated indoor. **Leisure Activities:** sauna, whirlpool, exercise room. **Guest Services:** valet laundry. **Business Services:** meeting rooms, business center. **Cards:** AX, DC, DS, JC, MC, VI.

    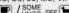

THE FAIRMONT HOTEL VANCOUVER *Book great rates at AAA.com* Phone: (604)684-3131 **18**

CAA SAVE

Classic Historic
Large-scale Hotel
$229-$429 All Year

Address: 900 W Georgia St V6C 2W6 **Location:** Corner of Burrard at W Georgia St; enter from Hornby St. **Facility:** Opened by the Queen Mother in 1938, this historic downtown landmark hotel features elegantly restored rooms and suites as well as lobby boutiques. 556 units. 527 one-bedroom standard units. 29 one-bedroom suites. 21 stories, interior corridors. **Parking:** on-site (fee) and valet. **Terms:** cancellation fee imposed. **Amenities:** voice mail, honor bars, irons, hair dryers. **Fee:** video games, high-speed Internet. **Some:** dual phone lines. **Dining:** entertainment. **Pool(s):** heated indoor. **Leisure Activities:** saunas, whirlpool, spa. **Guest Services:** valet laundry. **Business Services:** conference facilities, business center. **Cards:** AX, DC, DS, JC, MC, VI.

THE FAIRMONT WATERFRONT *Book great rates at AAA.com* Phone: (604)691-1991 **6**

CAA SAVE

Large-scale Hotel
$249-$429 All Year

Address: 900 Canada Place Way V6C 3L5 **Location:** Howe St at Cordova St. Located opposite Canada Place. **Facility:** Near the cruise ship terminal and convention center, this guest-oriented property features attractive guest rooms with either a city or harbor view. 489 units. 478 one-bedroom standard units. 11 one-bedroom suites. 23 stories, interior corridors. **Parking:** on-site (fee) and valet. **Terms:** cancellation fee imposed. **Amenities:** voice mail, honor bars, irons, hair dryers. **Fee:** video games, high-speed Internet. **Some:** CD players, safes. **Dining:** Herons Restaurant, see separate listing. **Pool(s):** heated outdoor. **Leisure Activities:** whirlpool, steamrooms. **Fee:** massage. **Guest Services:** valet laundry. **Business Services:** conference facilities, business center. **Cards:** AX, DC, DS, JC, MC, VI. **Free Special Amenities:** newspaper.

▼ See AAA listing p 621 ▼

(See map and index starting on p. 564)

FOUR SEASONS HOTEL VANCOUVER *Book great rates at AAA.com* Phone: (604)689-9333 **21**

(CAA) (SAVE)

▽▽▽ ▽▽▽

Large-scale Hotel
$240-$815 All Year

Address: 791 W Georgia St V6C 2T4 **Location:** Between Howe and W Georgia sts. Connected to a shopping complex. **Facility:** Known for providing luxury accommodations and impeccable service, this downtown hotel is connected to a large shopping complex. 376 units. 308 one-bedroom standard units. 68 one-bedroom suites. 28 stories, interior corridors. **Parking:** on-site (fee) and valet. **Terms:** cancellation fee imposed. **Amenities:** dual phone lines, voice mail, safes, honor bars, irons, hair dryers. **Fee:** video games, high-speed Internet. **Pool(s):** heated indoor/outdoor. **Leisure Activities:** saunas, whirlpool. **Guest Services:** valet laundry. **Business Services:** conference facilities, business center. **Cards:** AX, CB, DC, DS, JC, MC, VI.

🍴 24 🍸 CALL 🛄 🍽 👶 🎥 / SOME UNITS 🐾 ✕

THE GEORGIAN COURT HOTEL *Book great rates at AAA.com* Phone: (604)682-5555 **32**

(CAA) (SAVE)

▽▽▽

Small-scale Hotel
$189-$359 All Year

Address: 773 Beatty St V6B 2M4 **Location:** Between Georgia and Robson sts. Located opposite BC Place Stadium. **Facility:** 180 units. 179 one- and 1 two-bedroom standard units. 12 stories, interior corridors. **Parking:** on-site (fee). **Terms:** cancellation fee imposed. **Amenities:** high-speed Internet, voice mail, safes, honor bars, irons, hair dryers. **Dining:** 2 restaurants, also, The William Tell, see separate listing. **Leisure Activities:** whirlpool, steamroom, exercise room. **Guest Services:** valet laundry, wireless Internet. **Business Services:** meeting rooms. **Cards:** AX, CB, DC, JC, MC, VI. **Free Special Amenities: newspaper and high-speed Internet.**

🍴 🍸 CALL 🛄 ✕ 👶 💻 / SOME UNITS FEE 🐾 ✕

GRANVILLE ISLAND HOTEL *Book great rates at AAA.com* Phone: (604)683-7373 **39**

(CAA) (SAVE)

▽▽▽

Small-scale Hotel
$160-$475 All Year

Address: 1253 Johnston St V6H 3R9 **Location:** Granville Island; below the bridge, follow signs. **Facility:** 82 one-bedroom standard units, some with whirlpools. 3-4 stories, interior corridors. **Parking:** on-site (fee). **Terms:** cancellation fee imposed. **Amenities:** high-speed Internet, dual phone lines, voice mail, honor bars, irons, hair dryers. **Dining:** Dockside Restaurant & Brewing Company, see separate listing. **Leisure Activities:** sauna, whirlpool, rental bicycles, limited exercise equipment. **Guest Services:** valet laundry. **Business Services:** meeting rooms, PC. **Cards:** AX, DC, DS, JC, MC, VI. **Free Special Amenities: newspaper and high-speed Internet.** *(See color ad below)*

🆂🅳 🍴 CALL 🛄 💻 👶 💻 / SOME UNITS FEE 🐾 ✕ 🍳

HAMPTON INN & SUITES BY HILTON, DOWNTOWN VANCOUVER *Book great rates at AAA.com* Phone: (604)602-1008 **34**

(CAA) (SAVE)

▽▽▽

Small-scale Hotel
$159-$269 All Year

Address: 111 Robson St V6B 2A8 **Location:** Between Cambie and Beatty sts. Located opposite BC Place Stadium. **Facility:** 132 units. 110 one-bedroom standard units, some with whirlpools. 22 one-bedroom suites with kitchens. 16 stories, interior corridors. **Parking:** on-site (fee). **Terms:** cancellation fee imposed. **Amenities:** video games (fee), high-speed Internet, dual phone lines, voice mail, safes, irons, hair dryers. **Leisure Activities:** sauna, whirlpool, limited exercise equipment. **Guest Services:** valet and coin laundry, area transportation-downtown. **Business Services:** meeting rooms. **Cards:** AX, CB, DC, DS, JC, MC, VI. *(See color ad p 577)*

🆂🅳 🍴 CALL 🛄 ✕ 👶 📠 📺 💻 / SOME UNITS ✕

(See map and index starting on p. 564)

**HOLIDAY INN HOTEL & SUITES
VANCOUVER-DOWNTOWN** *Book great rates at AAA.com*   **Phone:** (604)684-2151

Large-scale Hotel
$199-$379 3/1-10/15
$119-$199 10/16-2/28

Address: 1110 Howe St V6Z 1R2 **Location:** Between Helmcken and Davie sts. **Facility:** 245 one-bedroom standard units, some with efficiencies, kitchens and/or whirlpools. 7 stories, interior corridors. *Bath:* combo or shower only. **Parking:** on-site (fee). **Terms:** cancellation fee imposed. **Amenities:** voice mail, irons, hair dryers. *Some:* honor bars. **Pool(s):** heated indoor. **Leisure Activities:** saunas, unsupervised children playroom, exercise room. **Guest Services:** valet and coin laundry, wireless Internet. **Business Services:** meeting rooms, PC (fee). **Cards:** AX, CB, DC, DS, JC, MC, VI. **Free Special Amenities:** newspaper and high-speed Internet. *(See color ad on insert)*

▼ See AAA listing p 603 ▼

▼ See AAA listing p 583 ▼

(See map and index starting on p. 564)

HOTEL LE SOLEIL   *Book great rates at AAA.com*   Phone: (604)632-3000   **16**

(CAA) [SAVE]

▼▼▼ ▼▼▼

Small-scale Hotel
$365-$465 All Year

Address: 567 Hornby St V6C 2E8 **Location:** Between Dunsmuir and Pender sts. **Facility:** One of Vancouver's most exclusive boutique hotels, the Hotel Le Soleil prides itself on its amazing attention to detail; the hotel pampers each guest. 100 units. 9 one-bedroom standard units. 91 one-bedroom suites, some with whirlpools. 16 stories, interior corridors. *Bath:* combo or shower only. **Parking:** valet. **Terms:** cancellation fee imposed. **Amenities:** high-speed Internet, dual phone lines, voice mail, safes, honor bars, irons, hair dryers. **Dining:** Copper Chimney, see separate listing. **Guest Services:** valet laundry, wireless Internet. **Business Services:** meeting rooms, business center. **Cards:** AX, MC, VI. **Free Special Amenities: newspaper and high-speed Internet.** *(See color ad p 582)*

[icons] CALL / SOME UNITS FEE

HOWARD JOHNSON HOTEL   *Book great rates at AAA.com*   Phone: (604)688-8701   **35**

(CAA) [SAVE]

▼▼▼

Small-scale Hotel
$149-$259 3/1-9/30
$79-$169 10/1-2/28

Address: 1176 Granville St V6Z 1L8 **Location:** Between Davie and Helmcken sts. Located in the Granville Street Entertainment District. **Facility:** Smoke free premises. 110 units. 105 one-bedroom standard units. 5 one-bedroom suites. 5 stories, interior corridors. **Parking:** on-site (fee). **Terms:** cancellation fee imposed. **Amenities:** voice mail, hair dryers. *Some:* fax, irons. **Guest Services:** valet and coin laundry, wireless Internet. **Cards:** AX, CB, DC, JC, MC, VI. **Free Special Amenities: newspaper and high-speed Internet.** *(See color ad below)*

[icons] / SOME UNITS FEE

(See map and index starting on p. 564)

HYATT REGENCY VANCOUVER   *Book great rates at AAA.com*   Phone: (604)683-1234   **15**

Large-scale Hotel
$159-$439 All Year

Address: 655 Burrard St V6C 2R7 **Location:** Between W Georgia and Melville sts. Connected to shopping centre. **Facility:** Room renovations are expected to be complete in the spring of 2007, but the higher floors of this 34-story hotel in downtown Vancouver are finished. 644 units. 634 one-bedroom standard units. 10 one-bedroom suites. 34 stories, interior corridors. *Bath:* combo or shower only. **Parking:** on-site (fee) and valet. **Terms:** check-in 4 pm, cancellation fee imposed. **Amenities:** high-speed Internet (fee), dual phone lines, voice mail, honor bars, irons, hair dryers. *Some:* DVD players, CD players, safes. **Pool(s):** heated outdoor. **Leisure Activities:** whirlpool, exercise room. **Guest Services:** valet laundry, wireless Internet. **Business Services:** conference facilities, business center. **Cards:** AX, CB, DC, DS, JC, MC, VI. *(See color ad below)*

AAA Benefit:
Ask for the AAA rate and save 10%.

LANDIS HOTEL & SUITES   *Book great rates at AAA.com*   Phone: (604)681-3555   **30**

Small-scale Hotel
$169-$349 3/1-8/31
$169-$249 9/1-2/28

Address: 1200 Hornby St V6Z 1W2 **Location:** Between Drake and Davie sts. **Facility:** Smoke free premises. 50 two-bedroom standard units with kitchens. 18 stories, interior corridors. **Parking:** on-site (fee). **Amenities:** high-speed Internet, dual phone lines, voice mail, irons, hair dryers. **Pool(s):** heated indoor. **Leisure Activities:** whirlpool, exercise room. **Guest Services:** valet and coin laundry, area transportation-within downtown. **Cards:** AX, CB, DC, DS, JC, MC, VI. **Free Special Amenities: continental breakfast and high-speed Internet.** *(See color ad p 585)*

THE LISTEL HOTEL   *Book great rates at AAA.com*   Phone: (604)684-8461   **7**

Small-scale Hotel
$149-$399 All Year

Address: 1300 Robson St V6E 1C5 **Location:** Between Broughton and Jervis sts. **Facility:** Smoke free premises. 130 one-bedroom standard units. 6 stories, interior corridors. **Parking:** valet. **Terms:** cancellation fee imposed. **Amenities:** high-speed Internet (fee), dual phone lines, voice mail, honor bars, irons, hair dryers. *Some:* DVD players, CD players. **Leisure Activities:** whirlpool, exercise room. **Guest Services:** valet laundry, wireless Internet. **Business Services:** meeting rooms. **Cards:** AX, CB, DC, DS, JC, MC, VI. **Free Special Amenities: newspaper and early check-in/late check-out.**

'O CANADA' HOUSE B&B   Phone: 604/688-0555   **22**

Historic Bed
& Breakfast
Rates not provided

Address: 1114 Barclay St V6E 1H1 **Location:** Between Thurlow and Bute sts. Located in a residential area in West End. **Facility:** This beautifully restored 1897 Victorian home is located in the West End, within easy walking distance to many restaurants and shops. Smoke free premises. 7 units. 6 one-bedroom standard units. 1 cottage. 3 stories (no elevator), interior corridors. *Bath:* combo or shower only. **Parking:** on-site. **Terms:** office hours 7 am-7 pm, age restrictions may apply. **Amenities:** video library, DVD players. *Some:* hair dryers. **Guest Services:** wireless Internet.

(See map and index starting on p. 564)

PACIFIC PALISADES HOTEL   *Book great rates at AAA.com*   Phone: (604)688-0461   **8**

Large-scale Hotel
$370-$420 All Year

Address: 1277 Robson St V6E 1C4 **Location:** Between Jervis and Bute sts. **Facility:** 233 one-bedroom standard units, some with kitchens. 20-23 stories, interior corridors. **Parking:** on-site (fee) and valet. **Terms:** cancellation fee imposed. **Amenities:** video games (fee), high-speed Internet, dual phone lines, voice mail, honor bars, irons, hair dryers. **Dining:** Zin, see separate listing. **Pool(s):** heated indoor. **Leisure Activities:** whirlpool, steamroom, spa. **Guest Services:** valet and coin laundry. **Business Services:** meeting rooms, business center. **Cards:** AX, CB, DC, DS, JC, MC, VI. **Free Special Amenities: newspaper and early check-in/late check-out.** *(See color ad p 579)*

PAN PACIFIC VANCOUVER   *Book great rates at AAA.com*   Phone: (604)662-8111   **4**

Large-scale Hotel
$269-$449 3/1-10/31
$179-$359 11/1-2/28

Address: 300-999 Canada Place V6C 3B5 **Location:** Motor entrance off Burrard St. Located at Canada Place. **Facility:** This service-oriented hotel is attached to the convention center as well as a pier where huge cruise ships dock during summer months. 504 units. 473 one-bedroom standard units. 29 one- and 2 two-bedroom suites, some with kitchens and/or whirlpools. 23 stories, interior corridors. **Parking:** on-site (fee) and valet. **Terms:** check-in 4 pm. **Amenities:** CD players, dual phone lines, voice mail, safes, honor bars, irons, hair dryers. *Fee:* video games, high-speed Internet. *Some:* DVD players, fax. **Dining:** 2 restaurants, also, Five Sails Restaurant, see separate listing, entertainment. **Pool(s):** heated outdoor. **Leisure Activities:** saunas, whirlpool, steamrooms, spa. **Guest Services:** valet laundry. **Business Services:** conference facilities, business center. **Cards:** AX, DC, JC, MC, VI. **Free Special Amenities: local telephone calls and newspaper.** *(See color ad p 586)*

QUALITY HOTEL DOWNTOWN-THE INN AT FALSE CREEK   *Book great rates at AAA.com*   Phone: (604)682-0229   **37**

Small-scale Hotel
$89-$209 All Year

Address: 1335 Howe St V6Z 1R7 **Location:** Between Drake and Pacific sts. **Facility:** Smoke free premises. 157 units. 137 one-bedroom standard units. 20 one-bedroom suites, some with kitchens. 7 stories, interior corridors. **Parking:** on-site (fee). **Amenities:** voice mail, irons, hair dryers. **Pool(s):** heated outdoor. **Guest Services:** valet laundry, wireless Internet. **Business Services:** meeting rooms. **Cards:** AX, DC, DS, JC, MC, VI. *(See color ad on insert)*

▼ See AAA listing p 584 ▼

(See map and index starting on p. 564)

RAMADA INN & SUITES DOWNTOWN VANCOUVER — *Book great rates at AAA.com* — **Phone:** (604)685-1111

Small-scale Hotel
$129-$259 3/1-9/30
$79-$189 10/1-2/28

Address: 1221 Granville St V6Z 1M6 **Location:** Between Davie and Drake sts. Located in the Granville Street Entertainment District. **Facility:** 116 one-bedroom standard units, some with efficiencies. 6 stories, interior corridors. *Bath:* combo or shower only. **Parking:** on-site (fee) and valet. **Terms:** check-in 4 pm, cancellation fee imposed. **Amenities:** voice mail, irons, hair dryers. **Guest Services:** valet laundry, wireless Internet. **Business Services:** meeting rooms. **Cards:** AX, CB, DC, DS, JC, MC, VI. **Free Special Amenities:** newspaper and high-speed Internet. *(See color ad below)*

(See map and index starting on p. 564)

RAMADA LIMITED DOWNTOWN VANCOUVER   *Book great rates at AAA.com*   Phone: (604)488-1088   **19**

Small-scale Hotel
$129-$229 All Year

Address: 435 W Pender St V6B 1V2 **Location:** Between Homer and Richards sts. **Facility:** Smoke free premises. 80 one-bedroom standard units. 6 stories, interior corridors. **Parking:** valet. **Amenities:** voice mail, irons, hair dryers. **Guest Services:** valet and coin laundry, wireless Internet. **Business Services:** meeting rooms, PC. **Cards:** AX, DS, MC, VI. *(See color ad below)*

ASK SD ⊞ CALL &M ✕ 🎦 📺 / SOME UNITS FEE 🐾

RENAISSANCE VANCOUVER HOTEL
HARBOURSIDE   Phone: 604/689-9211   **3**

CAA SAVE
[fyi]

Large-scale Hotel
$219-$329 All Year

Under major renovation, scheduled to be completed April 2008. Last rated: ▽▽▽ **Address:** 1133 W Hastings St V6E 3T3 **Location:** Between Bute and Thurlow sts. **Facility:** Smoke free premises. 438 units. 426 one-bedroom standard units. 12 one-bedroom suites. 19 stories, interior corridors. **Parking:** on-site (fee) and valet. **Amenities:** high-speed Internet (fee), voice mail, safes, irons, hair dryers. **Dining:** Vistas Revolving Restaurant, see separate listing. **Pool(s):** heated indoor. **Leisure Activities:** sauna, whirlpool. **Guest Services:** valet laundry. **Business Services:** meeting rooms, business center. **Cards:** AX, DC, DS, JC, MC, VI. **Free Special Amenities: newspaper and room upgrade (subject to availability with advance reservations).** *(See color ad p 588)*

SD ⊞ ⊤ CALL &M 🏊 👪 ✕ 🎦 📺 / SOME UNITS FEE 🐾

RENAISSANCE.
HOTELS & RESORTS

AAA Benefit:

Members save 5% off of the best available rate.

RESIDENCE INN BY MARRIOTT VANCOUVER   *Book great rates at AAA.com*   Phone: 604/688-1234   **33**

CAA SAVE
▽▽▽

Small-scale Hotel
$252-$384 All Year

Address: 1234 Hornby St V6Z 1W2 **Location:** Between Drake and Davie sts. **Facility:** Smoke free premises. 200 one-bedroom standard units, some with efficiencies or kitchens. 22 stories, interior corridors. **Parking:** on-site (fee). **Terms:** check-in 4 pm. **Amenities:** high-speed Internet, voice mail, irons, hair dryers. **Pool(s):** heated indoor. **Leisure Activities:** whirlpool, exercise room. **Guest Services:** valet and coin laundry. **Business Services:** meeting rooms, PC. **Cards:** AX, DC, DS, JC, MC, VI. **Free Special Amenities: full breakfast and high-speed Internet.**

SD ⊞ CALL &M 🏊 ✕ 🎦 🔌 📺 📺 / SOME UNITS FEE 🐾

Residence
Inn
Marriott

AAA Benefit:

Members save 5% off of the best available rate.

▼ *See AAA listing above* ▼

(See map and index starting on p. 564)

ST REGIS HOTEL   *Book great rates at AAA.com*   Phone: (604)681-1135

Address: 602 Dunsmuir St V6B 1Y6 **Location:** Between Granville and Seymour sts. **Facility:** Smoke free premises. 72 one-bedroom standard units. 5 stories, interior corridors. *Bath:* combo or shower only. **Parking:** street. **Terms:** 3 day cancellation notice, in summer-fee imposed. **Amenities:** irons, hair dryers. **Guest Services:** wireless Internet. **Business Services:** business center. **Cards:** AX, JC, MC, VI. **Free Special Amenities: continental breakfast and high-speed Internet.**

Small-scale Hotel
$129-$199 All Year

SANDMAN HOTEL VANCOUVER CITY CENTER   *Book at AAA.com*   Phone: 604/681-2211

Large-scale Hotel
Rates not provided

Address: 180 W Georgia St V6B 4P4 **Location:** Between Cambie and Beatty sts. **Facility:** 303 one-bedroom standard units. 11-14 stories, interior corridors. **Parking:** on-site (fee). **Amenities:** voice mail, hair dryers, high-speed Internet. *Some:* irons. **Dining:** Moxie's Classic Grill, see separate listing. **Pool(s):** heated indoor. **Leisure Activities:** whirlpool. **Guest Services:** valet laundry. **Business Services:** meeting rooms, business center.

SHERATON VANCOUVER WALL CENTRE HOTEL   *Book great rates at AAA.com* . Phone: (604)331-1000

Large-scale Hotel
$459 3/1-10/31
$359 11/1-2/28

Address: 1088 Burrard St V6Z 2R9 **Location:** Between Helmcken and Nelson sts. **Facility:** The hotel's two tall black towers rise above Vancouver's skyline; inside, rooms offer floor-to-ceiling windows and wonderful views of the city. 735 units. 662 one-bedroom standard units, some with whirlpools. 39 one-, 30 two- and 4 three-bedroom suites, some with kitchens. 28-35 stories, interior corridors. *Bath:* combo or shower only. **Parking:** on-site (fee) and valet. **Terms:** cancellation fee imposed. **Amenities:** high-speed Internet (fee), dual phone lines, voice mail, safes, irons, hair dryers. **Dining:** 2 restaurants. **Pool(s):** heated indoor. **Leisure Activities:** sauna, whirlpools, steamroom, spa. **Guest Services:** valet laundry, area transportation-downtown. **Business Services:** conference facilities, business center. **Cards:** AX, CB, DC, MC, VI. **Free Special Amenities: newspaper.** *(See color ad p 589)*

Ⓢ Sheraton
HOTELS & RESORTS

AAA Benefit:
Members get up to 15% off, plus Starwood Preferred Guest® bonuses.

▼ See AAA listing p 587 ▼

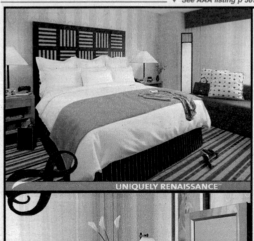

UNIQUELY RENAISSANCE™

- ⊛ 300 thread count sheets
- ⊛ Freshly laundered duvet covers
- ⊛ Plusher mattresses and more pillows
- ⊛ Oversized artistic headboard is a brand standard
- ⊛ Flat-panel, high definition LCD television
- ⊛ Sleek sofa chaise lounge with accent pillows
- ⊛ Combination dresser and desk
- ⊛ High speed Internet access
- ⊛ Sophisticated bathroom lighting
- ⊛ Luxury branded bath amenities

RENAISSANCE.
VANCOUVER HOTEL
HARBOURSIDE

**1133 West Hastings Street
Vancouver, BC V6E 3T3**

**For Reservations, call:
1-800-905-8582**

RenaissanceVancouver.com

(See map and index starting on p. 564)

SUNSET INN & SUITES   *Book great rates at AAA.com*   Phone: (604)688-2474

Small-scale Hotel
$99-$475 All Year

Address: 1111 Burnaby St V6E 1P4 **Location:** Between Thurlow and Bute sts. **Facility:** 50 units. 10 one-bedroom standard units with kitchens. 40 one-bedroom suites with kitchens. 11 stories, interior corridors. *Bath:* combo or shower only. **Parking:** on-site. **Terms:** cancellation fee imposed. **Amenities:** voice mail, safes, irons, hair dryers. *Some:* DVD players. **Leisure Activities:** limited exercise equipment. **Guest Services:** coin laundry, wireless Internet. **Cards:** AX, DC, JC, MC, VI. **Free Special Amenities: continental breakfast and high-speed Internet.** *(See color ad p 575)*

THE SUTTON PLACE HOTEL   *Book great rates at AAA.com*   Phone: (604)682-5511

Large-scale Hotel
$209-$599 All Year

Address: 845 Burrard St V6Z 2K6 **Location:** Between Smithe and Robson sts. **Facility:** Find attractive, yet understated, rooms with superior residential-style furnishings at this wonderful, service-oriented hotel near Robson St. 397 units. 350 one-bedroom standard units. 47 one-bedroom suites. 21 stories, interior corridors. **Parking:** on-site (fee) and valet. **Terms:** cancellation fee imposed. **Amenities:** video library, DVD players, CD players, dual phone lines, voice mail, safes, honor bars, irons, hair dryers. *Fee:* video games, high-speed Internet. **Dining:** Fleuri Restaurant, see separate listing. **Pool(s):** heated indoor. **Leisure Activities:** sauna, whirlpool, steamrooms, exercise room, spa. **Guest Services:** valet laundry, area transportation-downtown, wireless Internet. **Business Services:** meeting rooms, business center. **Cards:** AX, DC, DS, JC, MC, VI. **Free Special Amenities:** newspaper. *(See color ad p 590)*

▼ See AAA listing p 588 ▼

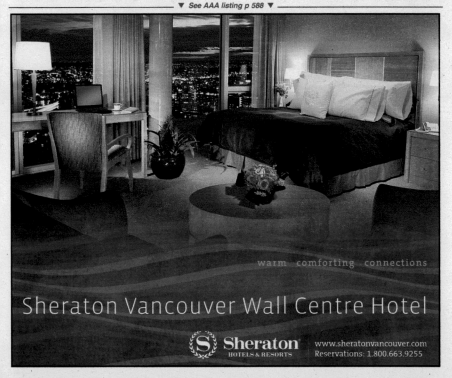

(See map and index starting on p. 564)

SYLVIA HOTEL — *Book at AAA.com*

Historic
Small-scale Hotel
$115-$200 All Year

Phone: (604)681-9321 **2**

Address: 1154 Gilford St V6G 2P6 **Location:** Beach Ave and Gilford St; across from English Bay. **Facility:** An English Bay landmark, the 1912 hotel is popular due to its rates; ask to hear the story about the resident cats, Mr. Gottago and Ms. Gottastay. 120 one-bedroom standard units, some with efficiencies or kitchens. 8 stories, interior corridors. **Parking:** on-site (fee). **Terms:** 30 day cancellation notice. **Amenities:** voice mail, hair dryers. **Guest Services:** valet laundry. **Business Services:** meeting rooms, PC. **Cards:** AX, DC, MC, VI.

TERMINAL CITY TOWER HOTEL — *Book at AAA.com*

Small-scale Hotel
Rates not provided

Phone: 604/681-4121 **11**

Address: 837 W Hastings St V6C 1B6 **Location:** Between Howe and Hornby sts. **Facility:** Smoke free premises. 60 units. 30 one-bedroom standard units. 30 one-bedroom suites. 30 stories, interior corridors. **Parking:** on-site (fee). **Amenities:** high-speed Internet (fee), dual phone lines, voice mail, irons, hair dryers. **Pool(s):** heated indoor. **Leisure Activities:** saunas, whirlpool, steamrooms, racquetball courts. **Guest Services:** valet laundry. **Business Services:** meeting rooms.

VANCOUVER MARRIOTT PINNACLE DOWNTOWN — *Book great rates at AAA.com*

(CAA) (SAVE)

Large-scale Hotel
$219-$340 All Year

Phone: 604/684-1128 **5**

Address: 1128 W Hastings St V6E 4R5 **Location:** Between Thurlow and Bute sts. **Facility:** Located in the heart of the downtown business district, guest rooms offer breathtaking views of the mountains, water and downtown Vancouver. Smoke free premises. 434 one-bedroom standard units. 31 stories, interior corridors. **Parking:** on-site (fee) and valet. **Terms:** check-in 4 pm. **Amenities:** dual phone lines, voice mail, safes, irons, hair dryers. *Fee:* video games, high-speed Internet. *Some:* CD players. **Dining:** Show Case Restaurant, see separate listing. **Pool(s):** heated indoor. **Leisure Activities:** sauna, whirlpool, steamroom, exercise room. **Guest Services:** valet laundry. **Business Services:** conference facilities, business center. **Cards:** AX, DC, DS, JC, MC, VI. **Free Special Amenities:** newspaper.

Marriott.
HOTELS & RESORTS

AAA Benefit:
Members save 5% off of the best available rate.

THE WEDGEWOOD HOTEL & SPA — *Book great rates at AAA.com*

(CAA) (SAVE)

Small-scale Hotel
$450-$600 3/1-10/31
$350-$600 11/1-2/28

Phone: (604)689-7777 **24**

Address: 845 Hornby St V6Z 1V1 **Location:** Between Smithe and Robson sts. **Facility:** An intimate and very stylish boutique hotel, the Wedgewood is a must-visit thanks to a wonderfully attentive staff. Smoke free premises. 83 units. 45 one-bedroom standard units. 38 one-bedroom suites, some with whirlpools. 13 stories, interior corridors. **Parking:** valet. **Terms:** cancellation fee imposed. **Amenities:** video games (fee), CD players, high-speed Internet, dual phone lines, voice mail, safes, honor bars, irons, hair dryers. **Dining:** Bacchus Restaurant, see separate listing, entertainment. **Leisure Activities:** steamroom, exercise room, spa. **Guest Services:** valet laundry, wireless Internet. **Business Services:** meeting rooms, business center. **Cards:** AX, DC, DS, JC, MC, VI. **Free Special Amenities:** newspaper and high-speed Internet.

WEST END GUEST HOUSE

(CAA) (SAVE)

Historic Bed
& Breakfast
$160-$285 All Year

Phone: (604)681-2889 **10**

Address: 1362 Haro St V6E 1G2 **Location:** Between Broughton and Jervis sts. **Facility:** Inquire about the resident ghost that allegedly lives in this well-preserved Victorian home in the residential neighborhood known as the West End. Smoke free premises. 8 one-bedroom standard units. 2 stories (no elevator), interior corridors. *Bath:* combo or shower only. **Parking:** on-site. **Terms:** office hours 8 am-10 pm, cancellation fee imposed. **Amenities:** video library, DVD players, hair dryers. **Leisure Activities:** bicycles. **Guest Services:** wireless Internet. **Cards:** AX, DS, MC, VI.

▼ See AAA listing p 589 ▼

▼ See AAA listing p 593 ▼

(See map and index starting on p. 564)

THE WESTIN BAYSHORE VANCOUVER   *Book great rates at AAA.com*   **Phone:** (604)682-3377

CAA SAVE

▼▼▼ ▼▼▼

Large-scale Hotel
$460 All Year

Address: 1601 Bayshore Dr V6G 2V4 **Location:** W Georgia and Cardero sts. **Facility:** Manicured grounds surround this downtown, harborside hotel where every room offers excellent views; an outdoor pool is set amid lush landscaping. Smoke free premises. 510 units. 482 one-bedroom standard units. 28 one-bedroom suites. 9-16 stories, interior corridors. **Parking:** on-site (fee) and valet. **Terms:** check-in 4 pm, cancellation fee imposed. **Amenities:** video games (fee), dual phone lines, voice mail, safes, honor bars, irons, hair dryers. *Some:* high-speed Internet (fee). *Dining:* 2 restaurants. **Pool(s):** heated outdoor, heated indoor. **Leisure Activities:** saunas, whirlpool, steamroom, jogging, exercise room. *Fee:* massage. **Guest Services:** valet laundry, area transportation-downtown, wireless Internet. **Business Services:** conference facilities, business center. **Cards:** AX, DC, DS, JC, MC, VI. *(See color ad p 591)*

AAA Benefit:

Members get up to 15% off, plus Starwood Preferred Guest® bonuses.

      / SOME UNITS

THE WESTIN GRAND, VANCOUVER   *Book great rates at AAA.com*   **Phone:** (604)602-1999

CAA SAVE

▼▼▼ ▼▼▼

Large-scale Hotel
$429-$749 All Year

Address: 433 Robson St V6B 6L9 **Location:** Between Homer and Richards sts. **Facility:** Shaped like a baby grand piano, this chic, all-suite hotel on trendy Robson St. has floor-to-ceiling windows, offering city views from every unit. Smoke free premises. 207 units. 23 one-bedroom standard units. 184 one-bedroom suites. 26 stories, interior corridors. **Parking:** on-site (fee) and valet. **Terms:** cancellation fee imposed. **Amenities:** dual phone lines, voice mail, safes, honor bars, irons, hair dryers. *Fee:* video games, high-speed Internet. **Pool(s):** heated outdoor. **Leisure Activities:** sauna, whirlpool, steamroom, exercise room. *Fee:* massage. **Guest Services:** valet laundry, wireless Internet. **Business Services:** meeting rooms, business center. **Cards:** AX, DC, DS, JC, MC, VI.

AAA Benefit:

Members get up to 15% off, plus Starwood Preferred Guest® bonuses.

 CALL / SOME UNITS FEE

———— WHERE TO DINE ————

A KETTLE OF FISH   *Menu on AAA.com*   **Phone:** 604/682-6661   **55**

CAA

▼▼▼

Seafood
$20-$39

You'll enjoy this restaurant's enchanting, casually elegant atmosphere and lush garden setting. They are known for their commitment to fresh seafood, and the "kettle" fish soup is their specialty. Visitors and locals alike dine here. Fun, friendly staff. Casual dress. **Bar:** Full bar. **Reservations:** suggested. **Hours:** 5 pm-9:30 pm. Closed major holidays. **Address:** 900 Pacific St V6Z 2E3 **Location:** Corner of Hornby and Pacific sts. **Parking:** on-site (fee). **Cards:** AX, DC, JC, MC, VI.

AL PORTO RISTORANTE   **Phone:** 604/683-8376   **29**

▼▼ ▼▼

Northern Italian
$12-$27

Located in the heart of Old Gastown, this restaurant is housed in a century-old Hudson Bay Trading Company warehouse. Tables upstairs offer a great harbor view; the downstairs area is like dining in a Tuscan villa. The prosciutto di parma is excellent. Note: Parking can be found in a nearby lot or at street meters. Casual dress. **Bar:** Full bar. **Reservations:** suggested. **Hours:** 11:30 am-10:30 pm, Sat & Sun from 5:30 pm. Closed: 1/1, 12/25, 12/26; also for lunch holidays. **Address:** 321 Water St V6B 1B8 **Location:** Between Richards and Cambie sts; in Gastown. **Parking:** street. **Cards:** AX, DC, JC, MC, VI.

AQUA RIVA   **Phone:** 604/683-5599   **20**

▼▼ ▼▼

Peruvian
$12-$35

Wood-fired pizza and Pacific tuna stand out on a menu of rotisserie and seafood dishes. Casual dress. **Bar:** Full bar. **Reservations:** suggested. **Hours:** 11:30 am-2:30 & 5-10 pm. Closed: 12/24, 12/25. **Address:** 200 Granville St V6C 1S4 **Location:** Between Cordova and Howe sts. **Parking:** on-site (fee). **Cards:** AX, DC, JC, MC, VI.

BACCHUS RESTAURANT   **Phone:** 604/608-5319   **37**

CAA

▼▼▼ ▼▼▼

French
$9-$35

The elegant establishment occupies a wonderful, boutique-style downtown hotel. On warm summer evenings, the windows are opened so diners can people-watch. The creative menu reflects a heavy French influence, and each night a special entree is prepared in the classical French style along with a la carte menu items. A signature appetizer is the caramelized pan-seared sea scallops. The staff is highly attentive. Dressy casual. Entertainment. **Bar:** Full bar. **Reservations:** suggested. **Hours:** 6:30 am-11 pm. **Address:** 845 Hornby St V6Z 1V1 **Location:** Between Smithe and Robson sts; in The Wedgewood Hotel & Spa. **Parking:** valet. **Cards:** AX, CB, DC, DS, JC, MC, VI.

BALTHAZAR   **Phone:** 604/689-8822   **19**

▼▼ ▼▼

Continental
$13-$24

Open nightly for dinner, the funky restaurant offers not only great food but live DJs during the week as well as Monday and Tuesday comedy nights. On the weekends, you'll find a dance floor at the back with hip and happening music. Parking is limited, so use the valet on the weekends or try the self-park lots around the neighborhood. Casual dress. **Bar:** Full bar. **Reservations:** suggested, weekends. **Hours:** 5:30 pm-midnight. Closed: 12/25. **Address:** 1215 Bidwell St V6G 2K7 **Location:** Between Davie and Burnaby sts. **Parking:** street. **Cards:** AX, DC, DS, MC, VI.

(See map and index starting on p. 564)

BLUE WATER CAFE

Seafood
$30-$45

Phone: 604/688-8078 ⑤④

In the hip Yaletown district, the cafe has a wonderful oyster bar, fresh fish, live lobster and crab tank, as well as premium steaks and sushi items. During warm weather, the patio is a hot spot for people-watching. Casual dress. **Bar:** Full bar. **Reservations:** suggested. **Hours:** 5 pm-midnight. Closed: 1/1, 12/25. **Address:** 1095 Hamilton St V6B 5T4 **Location:** Between Nelson and Helmcken sts. **Parking:** valet and street. **Cards:** AX, MC, VI.

THE BOATHOUSE RESTAURANT

Seafood
$10-$25

Phone: 604/669-2225

The restaurant's fantastic heated and covered patio, which is open all year and in all kinds of weather, affords spectacular views of English Bay. Casual bar food makes up the menu in the downstairs pub, while the more formal upstairs dining room serves fresh seafood. Casual dress. **Bar:** Full bar. **Reservations:** suggested. **Hours:** 11 am-11 pm. Closed: 12/25. **Address:** 1795 Beach Ave V6G 1Y9 **Location:** Between Bidwell and Denman sts. **Parking:** valet and street. **Cards:** AX, DC, DS, MC, VI.

BRIX RESTAURANT & WINE BAR

Pacific Rim
$22-$39

Phone: 604/915-9463 ⑤⑦

A nice place to drop in for a glass of wine and a bite, the restaurant is pure Yaletown—a funky old space with wood floors and high ceilings. A wine list with 50-odd by-the-glass choices complements the tapas selections, as well as items on the varied main menu. Casual dress. **Bar:** Full bar. **Reservations:** required. **Hours:** 5 pm-1 am. Closed: 12/25, 12/26; also Sun. **Address:** 1138 Homer St V6B 2X6 **Location:** Between Helmcken and Davie sts. **Parking:** street. **Cards:** AX, MC, VI.

CACTUS CLUB CAFE

Canadian
$9-$29

Phone: 604/685-8070

This bustling, casual restaurant serves huge burgers, sandwiches, pasta, salads, soups, quesadillas, fajitas, vegetarian dishes, steak, ribs, chicken and fish. Featured are certified Angus beef and fresh wild British Columbia salmon. The thick and creamy milk shakes come highly recommended. Casual dress. **Bar:** Full bar. **Hours:** 11 am-midnight, Fri & Sat-1 am. Closed: 12/25. **Address:** 357 Davie St V6B 1R2 **Location:** Between Homer and Hamilton sts. **Parking:** street. **Cards:** AX, MC, VI.

CACTUS CLUB CAFE

Canadian
$9-$29

Phone: 604/687-3278

This bustling, casual restaurant serves huge burgers, sandwiches, pasta, salads, soups, quesadillas, fajitas, vegetarian dishes, steak, ribs, chicken and fish. Featured are certified Angus beef and fresh wild British Columbia salmon. The thick and creamy milk shakes come highly recommended. Casual dress. **Bar:** Full bar. **Hours:** 11 am-midnight, Fri & Sat-1 am. Closed: 12/25. **Address:** 1136 Robson St V6E 1B2 **Location:** Between Bute and Thurlow sts. **Parking:** street. **Cards:** AX, MC, VI.

CAFE DE MEDICI

Italian
$15-$40

Phone: 604/669-9322 ㉝

On fashionable Robson Street, the distinctive restaurant is tucked away in a small courtyard. On sunny days, patrons linger on the large patio deck. Included on a menu of primarily traditional fare are antipasto, wonderful pasta preparations, lighter fare and larger main dishes. A nice wine list accents the menu. Casual dress. **Bar:** Full bar. **Reservations:** suggested. **Hours:** noon-2:30 & 5:30-10 pm, Sat & Sun from 5:30 pm. Closed major holidays. **Address:** 109-1025 Robson St V6E 1A9 **Location:** Between Burrard and Thurlow sts. **Parking:** street. **Cards:** AX, DC, JC, MC, VI.

CAFE DE PARIS
French
$13-$30

Phone: 604/687-1418 ③

A West End staple since 1977, the bistro-style French restaurant lets guests choose from among longtime menu favorites and daily chef's creations. The wonderful wine list includes a nice selection of both French and British Columbia wines. Guests who can't find a spot in the free lot behind the building can feed a meter on the street. Casual dress. **Bar:** Full bar. **Reservations:** suggested. **Hours:** 11:30 am-2 & 5:30-10 pm, Sat from 5:30 pm, Sun 5 pm-9 pm. Closed: 1/1, 12/25, 12/26. **Address:** 751 Denman St V6G 2L6 **Location:** Between Robson and Alberni sts. **Parking:** on-site and street. **Cards:** AX, MC, VI.

CAFE PRESTO PANINI   *Menu on AAA.com*

Italian
$9-$10

Phone: 604/684-4445 ㊴

The small cafe satisfies cravings for reasonably priced homemade food, from delicious grilled panini sandwiches on focaccia bread to penne or linguine pasta with any of six sauces. Vegetarian choices also are available. Parking is at street meters or in nearby lots. Casual dress. **Bar:** Beer & wine. **Reservations:** suggested, for lunch. **Hours:** 11:30 am-2 & 5-8 pm, Sat from 5 pm. Closed major holidays; also Sun. **Address:** 895 Hornby St V6Z 1T9 **Location:** Between Robson and Smithe sts. **Parking:** street. **Cards:** AX, MC, VI.

CARDERO'S RESTAURANT
Pacific Rim
$9-$25

Phone: 604/669-7666 ④

The waterfront restaurant presents a selection of fresh grilled fish, juicy rib-eye steaks, wok squid and wood oven pizzas. Casual dress. **Bar:** Full bar. **Reservations:** suggested. **Hours:** 11:30 am-11 pm, Sun-10 pm. Closed: 12/25. **Address:** 1583 Coal Harbour Quay V6G 3E7 **Location:** Between Cardero and Nicola sts. **Parking:** valet and street. **Cards:** AX, MC, VI.

CHILLI HOUSE THAI BISTRO
Thai
$11-$16

Phone: 604/685-8989 ㊾

Just under the Burrard Street Bridge and along the picturesque marina, the restaurant prepares spicy Thai favorites, including satays, pad thai noodles and coconut rice. The friendly staff will help guests pick dishes, which can be requested in milder varieties. Free underground parking is available. Casual dress. **Bar:** Full bar. **Reservations:** suggested. **Hours:** 11 am-10 pm. Closed: 12/25. **Address:** 1018 Beach Ave V6E 3N9 **Location:** Between Thurlow and Hornby sts. **Parking:** on-site. **Cards:** AX, MC, VI.

CIAO BELLA RISTORANTE
Italian
$8-$29

Phone: 604/688-5771 ②

Patrons can taste some excellent Italian food. Convenient parking is at the rear of the building, just off Alberni Street. The menu lists many classics—including pasta dishes with authentic sauces and hearty main courses. This place is well worth the stop. Casual dress. **Bar:** Full bar. **Reservations:** suggested. **Hours:** 11:30 am-2:30 & 5-10:30 pm. **Address:** 703 Denman St V6G 2L6 **Location:** Between Robson and Alberni sts. **Parking:** on-site. **Cards:** AX, DC, MC, VI.

(See map and index starting on p. 564)

CINCIN

▼▼▼▼
Mediterranean
$18-$45

Phone: 604/688-7338 24

The menu at this restaurant features homemade sausage, pasta and thin-crust, wood-oven pizza. The bustling atmosphere is known as a trendy place—sometimes film stars dine here. The service is prompt and attentive. Casual dress. **Bar:** Full bar. **Reservations:** suggested. **Hours:** 11:30 am-11 pm, Sat & Sun from 5 pm. Closed: 1/1, 12/25, 12/26. **Address:** 1154 Robson St V6E 1B5 **Location:** Between Bute and Thurlow sts. **Parking:** street. **Cards:** AX, DC, JC, MC, VI.

COPPER CHIMNEY

▼▼▼▼
Continental
$14-$30

Phone: 604/689-8862 22

French and Italian influences fuse to create a wonderful blend of interesting flavors. The bustling bi-level dining room features a large, open kitchen, a pleasant bar area and a loft dining area overlooking an artistic hanging light fixture. Casual dress. **Bar:** Full bar. **Reservations:** suggested. **Hours:** 6:30 am-10 pm, Sat & Sun 6:30 am-11:30 & 5-10 pm. **Address:** 567 Hornby St V6C 2E8 **Location:** Between Dunsmuir and Pender sts; in Hotel Le Soleil. **Parking:** valet. **Cards:** AX, MC, VI.

C RESTAURANT

▼▼▼▼
Seafood
$18-$39

Phone: 604/681-1164 61

Located along the seawall just at the end of Howe St, one of the biggest treats is dining on the outdoor patio during the summer. This restaurant features a wonderful array of fresh fish and seafood along with an extensive wine list that will compliment each of every dish. Recommend using valet parking since parking is limited in this area. Casual dress. **Bar:** Full bar. **Reservations:** required, for dinner. **Hours:** 11:30 am-2:30 & 5:30-10 pm, Sat & Sun from 5:30 pm. Closed: 12/25, 12/26. **Address:** 2-1600 Howe St V6Z 2L9 **Location:** 1 blk below Beach Ave. **Parking:** valet and street. **Cards:** AX, DC, MC, VI.

DELILAH'S

▼▼ ▼▼
Pacific Rim
$29-$39

Phone: 604/687-3424 7

Just off trendy Denman Street, the tucked-away restaurant is known for its martinis and over-the-top atmosphere. All dinners—from the small, two-course selection to the full, four-course feast—are prix fixe. Casual dress. **Bar:** Full bar. **Reservations:** suggested. **Hours:** 5:30 pm-10 pm, Fri & Sat-11 pm. Closed: 1/1, 12/25, 12/26; also Mon. **Address:** 1789 Comox St V6G 1P5 **Location:** Between Denman and Bidwell sts. **Parking:** street. **Cards:** AX, DC, MC, VI.

DIVA AT THE MET

▼▼ ▼▼
Regional
Canadian
$12-$42

Phone: 604/602-7788 32

An affluent clientele patronizes the fashionable fine-dining establishment. Creative nouvelle cuisine, which is equal parts health-conscious and delicious, is elevated to an art form. Dressy casual. **Bar:** Full bar. **Reservations:** suggested. **Hours:** 6:30 am-10 pm. **Address:** 645 Howe St V6C 2Y9 **Location:** Between Georgia and Dunsmuir sts; in Metropolitan Hotel. **Parking:** on-site and valet. **Cards:** AX, CB, DC, JC, MC, VI.

DOCKSIDE RESTAURANT & BREWING COMPANY

▼▼ ▼
Canadian
$10-$30

Phone: 604/685-7070 65

Floor-to-ceiling windows offer views of the marina, and a 50-foot aquarium adds to the restaurant's charm. In the heart of the kitchen is a wood-fired grill where breakfast, lunch and dinner dishes are prepared. Casual dress. **Bar:** Full bar. **Reservations:** suggested. **Hours:** 7 am-10 pm; Sunday brunch. **Address:** 1253 Johnston St V6H 3R9 **Location:** Granville Island; below the bridge, follow signs; in Granville Island Hotel. **Parking:** on-site and valet. **Cards:** AX, DC, MC, VI.

DON FRANCESCO RISTORANTE   *Menu on AAA.com*

(AA)

▼▼▼▼
Italian
$14-$40

Phone: 604/685-7770 36

Located in heart of Vancouver's vibrant downtown area, this wonderful Italian restaurant offers market-fresh specialties prepared with a Mediterranean flare, served in a warm and inviting atmosphere. Dressy casual. **Bar:** Full bar. **Reservations:** suggested. **Hours:** 11:30 am-11 pm, Sat & Sun from 5 pm. Closed: 1/1, 7/1, 12/26. **Address:** 860 Burrard St V6Z 1X9 **Location:** Between Smithe and Robson sts. **Parking:** on-site (fee). **Cards:** AX, DC, MC, VI.

EARLS ON TOP

▼▼ ▼▼
Canadian
$10-$19

Phone: 604/669-0020

Offering an experience that falls between fast food and fine dining, the fun, relaxed restaurant prepares great food at a great price. Choices range from juicy burgers, hearty sandwiches, fresh salads, wings and pizza to full entrees of steak, chops and seafood. Made-from-scratch soups and assorted breads, as well as a nice choice of wines and beers, round out the offerings. This is a fitting spot for impromptu get-togethers and festive occasions. Casual dress. **Bar:** Full bar. **Hours:** 11:30 am-midnight, Fri & Sat-1 am. Closed: 12/25. **Address:** 1185 Robson St V6E 1B5 **Location:** Between Bute and Thurlow sts. **Parking:** street. **Cards:** AX, DC, MC, VI.

EARLS PARAMOUNT

▼▼ ▼▼
Canadian
$8-$20

Phone: 604/682-6700

Offering an experience that falls between fast food and fine dining, the fun, relaxed restaurant prepares great food at a great price. Choices range from juicy burgers, hearty sandwiches, fresh salads, wings and pizza to full entrees of steak, chops and seafood. Made-from-scratch soups and assorted breads, as well as a nice choice of wines and beers, round out the offerings. This is a fitting spot for impromptu get-togethers and festive occasions. Casual dress. **Bar:** Full bar. **Hours:** 11:30 am-midnight. Closed: 12/25. **Address:** 905 Hornby St V6Z 1V3 **Location:** Corner of Hornby and Smithe sts. **Parking:** street. **Cards:** AX, DC, MC, VI.

ELIXIR RESTAURANT - OPUS BAR

▼▼▼▼
French
$16-$38

Phone: 604/642-0557 59

Guests feel as if they have been transported to Paris. The design is pure Parisian, and the funky lounge is known for its martinis. Delightful surprises abound on the classic French brasserie menu. Casual dress. **Bar:** Full bar. **Reservations:** suggested. **Hours:** 6:30 am-11 pm. **Address:** 350 Davie St V6B 5Z6 **Location:** Between Hamilton and Mainland sts. **Parking:** valet and street. **Cards:** AX, DC, MC, VI.

EZOGIKU NOODLE CAFE

▼
Japanese
$6-$9

Phone: 604/685-8606 13

The Japanese noodle shop offers something different from standard restaurants. For less than $10, diners can order a steaming bowl of egg noodles served with a choice of three mouthwatering broths and a choice of such complementary items as teriyaki chicken, wontons or seafood. Cash is the only acceptable method of payment at the restaurant, which offers mostly counter service. Casual dress. **Hours:** 11 am-10 pm. Closed major holidays. **Address:** 1329 Robson St V6E 1C6 **Location:** Between Jervis and Broughton. **Parking:** street.

(See map and index starting on p. 564)

FIDDLEHEAD JOE'S
Phone: 604/688-1969 `51`

Continental
$10-$22

Tucked away on a seawall curve in a labyrinth of waterfront condominiums, the unassuming little restaurant turns out some delicious food. Panini and gourmet sandwiches and eight-inch personal pizzas are good, but lamb lasagna is a favorite. The view of the marina is breathtaking. Complimentary underground parking is available. Casual dress. **Bar:** Full bar. **Reservations:** suggested. **Hours:** 11 am-10 pm, Sat & Sun from 10 am; Saturday & Sunday brunch. Closed: 12/24-12/26. **Address:** 1A-1012 Beach Ave V6E 1T7 **Location:** Between Thurlow and Hornby sts; under Burrard Bridge by Aquatic Centre. **Parking:** on-site. **Cards:** AX, MC, VI.

THE FISH HOUSE IN STANLEY PARK   *Menu on AAA.com*
Phone: 604/681-7275 `1`

Seafood
$10-$30

Located in the lush and quiet surroundings of Stanley Park, this restaurant features a wide variety of fresh seafood wonderfully prepared with a Canadian West Coast influence. Its casual atmosphere offers patio dining in season. Pay parking lot in effect at all times. Casual dress. **Bar:** Full bar. **Reservations:** suggested. **Hours:** 11:30 am-10 pm, Sun from 11 am; Sunday brunch. Closed: 12/25, 12/26. **Address:** 8901 Stanley Park Dr V6G 3E2 **Location:** Beach Ave entrance to Stanley Park; next to tennis courts. **Parking:** on-site (fee). **Cards:** AX, DC, JC, MC, VI.

FIVE SAILS RESTAURANT
Phone: 604/844-2855 `9`

Canadian
$32-$42

Long hailed as one of the city's finest restaurants, this place is a must for its unbeatable combination of stunning waterfront views and spectacular food. Patrons can watch cruise ships docking in the summer or just take in the water and mountain vistas from window tables. The sea inspires exquisite menu choices, which celebrate the best seafood the Pacific Rim has to offer. Complementing the food are diverse hand-selected wines from both distant vineyards and British Columbia wineries. Dressy casual. **Bar:** Full bar. **Reservations:** suggested. **Hours:** 5:30 pm-10 pm. Closed: 1/1, 12/26; also 01/01-01/15. **Address:** 999 Canada Pl V6C 3B5 **Location:** Motor entrance off Burrard St; in The Pan Pacific Vancouver. **Parking:** on-site and valet. **Cards:** AX, DC, JC, MC, VI.

FLEURI RESTAURANT
Phone: 604/682-5511 `35`

Pacific Rim
$16-$46

In the elegant hotel, the restaurant offers quiet seclusion from the bustling city streets. Diners enjoy consistently professional, personable service and a fine Continental menu, which includes both a la carte choices and a chef's tasting selection. Dressy casual. **Bar:** Full bar. **Reservations:** suggested. **Hours:** 6:30 am-10:30 pm. **Address:** 845 Burrard St V6Z 2K6 **Location:** Between Smithe and Robson sts; in The Sutton Place Hotel. **Parking:** on-site and valet. **Cards:** AX, CB, DC, DS, JC, MC, VI. *(See color ad p 590)*

GLOWBAL GRILL & SATAY BAR
Phone: 604/602-0835 `56`

International
$10-$35

In the funky Yaletown district, the hip grill might make visitors feel like they've stepped back into the 70s. Lending to the mood are amazing hanging lamps that look like sea anemones and great 70s-like carpet. The satay bar offers a nice selection of individually priced items, as well as a $20 sampler. Some fun wines are not badly priced, as is also the case with the entrees. Dressy casual. **Bar:** Full bar. **Reservations:** suggested. **Hours:** 11:30 am-midnight, Sat & Sun from 10:30 am; Saturday & Sunday brunch. Closed: 1/1, 12/25. **Address:** 1079 Mainland St V6B 5P9 **Location:** Between Helmcken and Nelson sts. **Parking:** street. **Cards:** AX, DC, MC, VI.

THE HERMITAGE   *Menu on AAA.com*
Phone: 604/689-3237 `23`

Traditional French
$12-$36

A former chef to King Leopold of Belgium, the chef/owner offers a menu that includes delicious rack of lamb, crepes Suzette and many French specialties. Servers are trained to be proper and exact. Patio dining is available in fair weather. The restaurant sits along trendy Robson Street. Casual dress. **Bar:** Full bar. **Reservations:** suggested. **Hours:** 11:30 am-2:30 & 5:30-10 pm, Sat & Sun from 5:30 pm. Closed: 1/1, 12/25, 12/26; also for lunch holidays. **Address:** 115/1025 Robson St V6E 4A9 **Location:** Between Thurlow and Burrard sts; in courtyard area. **Parking:** street. **Cards:** AX, DC, MC, VI.

HERONS RESTAURANT
Phone: 604/691-1991 `15`

Pacific Rim
$12-$35

Patrons are treated to panoramic views of the harbor, the mountains and distant Stanley Park. The restaurant's menu is a showcase for the best of seasonal British Columbian cuisine. The open kitchen enables guests to view the chefs as they create magic for breakfast, lunch and dinner. Try the popular Sunday brunch. Dressy casual. **Bar:** Full bar. **Reservations:** suggested. **Hours:** 6:30 am-10 pm. **Address:** 900 Canada Place Way V6C 3L5 **Location:** Howe St at Cordova St; in The Fairmont Waterfront. **Parking:** on-site (fee) and valet. **Cards:** AX, DC, DS, JC, MC, VI.

CALL

IL GIARDINO
Phone: 604/669-2422 `53`

Italian
$16-$40

This very nice restaurant, which specializes in game, fowl and pasta, is designed to look like the Tusca Villa of the owner, Umberto Menghi. The very charming decor has bright colors, open beams and exquisite furniture. Wonderful wine, good service. Casual dress. **Bar:** Full bar. **Reservations:** suggested. **Hours:** 11:30 am-3:30 & 5:30-11 pm, Sat from 5:30 pm. Closed major holidays; also Sun. **Address:** 1382 Hornby St V6Z 1W5 **Location:** Corner of Pacific and Hornby sts. **Parking:** valet and street. **Cards:** AX, JC, MC, VI.

IMPERIAL CHINESE SEAFOOD RESTAURANT
Phone: 604/688-8191 `12`

Chinese
$15-$58

Diners at the long-established restaurant should request a table next to one of the floor-to-ceiling windows. Also lending appeal to the dining room are fancy tablecloths with matching napkins and chandeliers hanging from the soaring ceilings. Choices include fresh lobster and crab, shark fin and bird's Chinese dishes, with prices that can range from $15 to $300 for shark fin soup. Casual dress. **Bar:** Full bar. **Reservations:** suggested. **Hours:** 11 am-10 pm, Sat & Sun from 10:30 am. **Address:** 355 Burrard St V6C 2G8 **Location:** Between W Hastings and Cordova sts. **Parking:** street. **Cards:** DC, MC, VI.

(See map and index starting on p. 564)

INDIA BISTRO — Indian — $8-$13
Phone: 604/684-6342   ㊶
In the area of Davie Street known as the "gay village," the wonderful Indian restaurant serves well-known and reasonably priced favorites, including naan bread, savory tandoori chicken and a good choice of vegetarian options. Friendly servers circulate through the bright, colorful dining area. Parking is at street meters or in nearby pay lots. Casual dress. **Bar:** Full bar. **Reservations:** suggested, weekend evenings. **Hours:** 11:30 am-11 pm. Closed: 1/1, 12/25. **Address:** 1157 Davie St V6E 1N2 **Location:** Between Bute and Thurlow sts. **Parking:** street. **Cards:** AX, MC, VI.

JOE FORTES SEAFOOD & CHOP HOUSE   *Menu on AAA.com* — Seafood — $9-$35
Phone: 604/669-1940   ㉘
Along trendy Robson Street, the San Francisco-style seafood grill allows for delightful rooftop garden dining in season. Also on site are a popular oyster bar and fireplace lounge. Diners are encouraged to ask about turn-of-the-20th-century legend Joe Fortes. Valet service begins at 6 p.m. Casual dress. Entertainment. **Bar:** Full bar. **Reservations:** suggested. **Hours:** 11 am-11 pm. Closed: 12/25. **Address:** 777 Thurlow St V6E 3V5 **Location:** Between Robson and Alberni sts. **Parking:** valet and street. **Cards:** AX, DC, DS, JC, MC, VI.

KAM'S PLACE SINGAPOREAN CUISINE — Asian — $9-$15
Phone: 604/669-3389   ㊺
In the part of West End known as Davie Village, the restaurant dishes up food in huge portions. Lines are not uncommon, and reservations are taken only for large groups. Don't forget to ask about lunch and dinner specials. Casual dress. **Bar:** Full bar. **Hours:** 11 am-2:30 & 5-9:30 pm. Closed: 12/25. **Address:** 1043 Davie St V6E 1M5 **Location:** Between Thurlow and Burrard sts. **Parking:** street. **Cards:** AX, DC, JC, MC, VI.

KINGSTON TAPHOUSE & GRILLE — Canadian — $10-$19
Phone: 604/681-7011   ㊷
Casual dress. **Bar:** Full bar. **Hours:** 11:30 am-midnight. Closed: 12/25. **Address:** 755 Richards St V6B 3A6 **Location:** Between Robson and W Georgia sts. **Parking:** street. **Cards:** AX, MC, VI.

KOBE JAPANESE STEAK HOUSE — Steak & Seafood — $30-$56
Phone: 604/684-2451   ㉚
Visitors and locals alike enjoy this restaurant's style of dinner, which seats several guests at a teppan table where the chef prepares your meal of steak, chicken, shrimp or lobster on the grill in front of you. Valet parking is available Friday-Saturday only. Casual dress. **Bar:** Full bar. **Reservations:** required. **Hours:** 5 pm-9:30 pm, Thurs-Sat to 10 pm. Closed major holidays. **Address:** 1042 Alberni St V6E 1A3 **Location:** Between Burrard and Thurlow sts. **Parking:** on-site (fee) and valet. **Cards:** AX, DC, DS, JC, MC, VI.

LA TERRAZZA — Northern Italian — $18-$38
Phone: 604/899-4449   ㊻
Near the Cambie Street bridge in Yaletown, the lovely restaurant features an impressive wine list with many bottles displayed in a huge rack against one wall. On the menu is an array of meat dishes—such as grilled venison, rack of lamb and Cornish game hen—along with some seafood and a choice of pasta. Dressy casual. **Bar:** Full bar. **Reservations:** suggested. **Hours:** 5 pm-11 pm. Closed: 3/24, 12/24-12/26. **Address:** 1088 Cambie St & Pacific Blvd V6B 6J5 **Location:** By Cambie St Bridge. **Parking:** valet and street. **Cards:** AX, DC, MC, VI.

LE CROCODILE — French — $15-$36
Phone: 604/669-4298   ㊳
The French restaurant's menu shows an emphasis on beef and seafood. The signature dish is Alsatian onion pie; other offerings include grilled lamb chops and pan-fried Dover sole filleted tableside. The atmosphere is bustling, and the servers keep busy. Dressy casual. **Bar:** Full bar. **Reservations:** suggested. **Hours:** 11:30 am-2 & 5:30-10 pm, Sat from 5:30 pm. Closed major holidays; also Sun. **Address:** 100-909 Burrard St V6Z 2N2 **Location:** Smithe and Burrard sts. **Parking:** on-site (fee) and valet. **Cards:** AX, MC, VI.

LE GAVROCHE RESTAURANT FRANCAIS — French — $13-$45
Phone: 604/685-3924   ⑥
In a small, character house, the charming French restaurant's second-floor dining room affords views of the harbor and North Shore. Try the lamb, beef tenderloin, veal or veal sweetbread. For seafood lovers, there are salmon, prawns and the ever-popular lobster. Dressy casual. **Bar:** Full bar. **Reservations:** suggested. **Hours:** 11:30 am-2:30 & 5:30-10:30 pm, Sat & Sun from 5:30 pm. Closed: 1/1, 12/25, 12/26. **Address:** 1616 Alberni St V6G 1A6 **Location:** Between Cardero and Bidwell sts. **Parking:** street. **Cards:** AX, DC, MC, VI.

LICKERISH — Pacific Rim — $15-$25
Phone: 604/696-0725   ㊽
One of several trendy restaurants on Davie Street, this place sets itself apart by emphasizing food rather than decor. On the menu are reasonably priced entrees, such as grilled venison burger, Mandarin beef and tiger prawns, wild British Columbia salmon and vegetarian dishes. Casual dress. **Bar:** Full bar. **Reservations:** suggested. **Hours:** 11 am-2:30 & 5-midnight, Thurs-Sun to 1 am. Closed: 12/25. **Address:** 903 Davie St V62 1B8 **Location:** Between Burrard and Hornby sts. **Parking:** street. **Cards:** AX, MC, VI.

LUCY MAE BROWN RESTAURANT AND LOUNGE — Nouvelle French — $20-$30
Phone: 604/899-9199   ㊻
Fifty years ago, an American widow named Lucy Mae Brown ran a bordello den in Vancouver, and today it's one of many of the city's distinctive dining destinations. The restaurant's menu centers on modern French-Mediterranean food, while the lower-level lounge, which is open late and employs funky DJs, serves tasty tapas and inventive cocktails. Dressy casual. **Bar:** Full bar. **Reservations:** required. **Hours:** 5:30 pm-1:30 am. Closed: 12/25. **Address:** 862 Richards St V6B 3A7 **Location:** Between Robson and Smithe sts. **Parking:** street. **Cards:** AX, DC, JC, MC, VI.

MILESTONE'S GRILL & BAR — Canadian — $12-$28
Phone: 604/684-9111
Popular with locals, the bustling eatery is a great gathering place. Diners enjoy the relaxed setting and casual menu featuring pasta, pizza, roasted chicken and a tasty choice of egg and brunch options. A nice wine list complements the food choices. Casual dress. **Bar:** Full bar. **Reservations:** accepted. **Hours:** 11 am-10 pm, Fri-midnight, Sat 10 am-midnight, Sun 9:30 am-10 pm. Closed: 12/25. **Address:** 1109 Hamilton St V6B 2Y1 **Location:** Between Helmcken and Davie sts. **Parking:** street. **Cards:** AX, DC, MC, VI.

(See map and index starting on p. 564)

MILESTONE'S RESTAURANT   Phone: 604/682-4477

Canadian
$12-$28

Popular with locals, the bustling eatery is a great gathering place. Diners enjoy the relaxed setting and casual menu featuring pasta, pizza, roasted chicken and a tasty choice of egg and brunch options. A nice wine list complements the food choices. Casual dress. **Bar:** Full bar. **Reservations:** suggested, evenings. **Hours:** 11 am-10 pm, Fri-midnight, Sat 10 am-midnight, Sun 9:30 am-10 pm. Closed: 12/25. **Address:** 1145 Robson St V6E 1B5 **Location:** Between Bute and Thurlow sts. **Parking:** street. **Cards:** AX, DC, MC, VI.

MOXIE'S CLASSIC GRILL   Phone: 604/678-8043

Canadian
$9-$25

This sleek, funky and popular restaurant presents an extensive menu of creatively prepared dishes, including pizza, pasta, rice, noodles, signature salads and burgers. Other menus include one for children and one for Sunday brunch. Lending to the upbeat, stylish decor are dark wood appointments and river rock fireplaces. Casual dress. **Entertainment. Hours:** 6:30 am-1 am, Sun-midnight. Closed: 12/25. **Address:** 1160 Davie St V6E 1N1 **Location:** Between Bute and Thurlow sts. **Parking:** on-site (fee) and street. **Cards:** AX, MC, VI.

CALL

MOXIE'S CLASSIC GRILL   Phone: 604/684-8434

Canadian
$8-$18

This sleek, funky and popular restaurant presents an extensive menu of creatively prepared dishes, including pizza, pasta, rice, noodles, signature salads and burgers. Other menus include one for children and one for Sunday brunch. Lending to the upbeat, stylish decor are dark wood appointments and river rock fireplaces. Casual dress. **Bar:** Full bar. **Hours:** 6 am-midnight, Fri & Sat-1 am. Closed: 12/25. **Address:** 180 W Georgia St V6B 4P4 **Location:** Between Cambie and Beatty sts; in Sandman Hotel Downtown Vancouver. **Parking:** street. **Cards:** AX, MC, VI.

MOXIE'S CLASSIC GRILL   Phone: 604/696-9986

Canadian
$8-$18

This sleek, funky and popular restaurant presents an extensive menu of creatively prepared dishes, including pizza, pasta, rice, noodles, signature salads and burgers. Other menus include one for children and one for Sunday brunch. Lending to the upbeat, stylish decor are dark wood appointments and river rock fireplaces. Casual dress. **Bar:** Full bar. **Hours:** 11 am-midnight, Sat & Sun from 9:30 am. Closed: 12/25. **Address:** 808 Bute St V6E 1Y4 **Location:** Between Robson and Haro sts. **Parking:** street. **Cards:** AX, MC, VI.

NU   Phone: 604/646-4668   (62)

Continental
$13-$37

Casual dress. **Bar:** Full bar. **Reservations:** suggested. **Hours:** 11:30 am-11 pm, Sat & Sun from 10:30 am. Closed: 12/25. **Address:** 1661 Granville St V6Z 1N3 **Location:** Just off Beach Crescent; under the Granville Street Bridge. **Parking:** on-site. **Cards:** AX, MC, VI.

OYSI OYSI JAPANESE RESTAURANT   Phone: 604/682-0011   (21)

Japanese
$7-$19

The downtown restaurant's menu lists fresh seafood, barbecue and sushi, as well as take-out combination trays. Guests can park in metered street spots or in a limited number of free spaces in underground parking lot stalls 200 through 300. Casual dress. **Bar:** Beer & wine. **Reservations:** accepted. **Hours:** 11 am-10:30 pm, Fri-11:30 pm, Sat noon-11:30 pm, Sun noon-10 pm. **Address:** 1136 Alberni St V6E 1A5 **Location:** Between Bute and Thurlow sts. **Parking:** on-site (fee) and street. **Cards:** AX, DC, JC, MC, VI.

PACIFIC CRAB COMPANY OYSTER BAR & GRILL   Phone: 604/633-2722   (16)

Seafood
$9-$40

With its second floor vantage point, this restaurant features great views of English Bay. Open for lunch during the spring and summer months and really late for night owls, it serves delightful Asian fusion seafood with a twist. Casual dress. **Bar:** Full bar. **Reservations:** suggested. **Hours:** 11 am-11 pm; from 5 pm 1/1-4/30. Closed: 12/25. **Address:** 1184 Denman St V6G 4M9 **Location:** Corner of Davie and Denman sts, 2nd level. **Parking:** street. **Cards:** AX, MC, VI.

PARKSIDE ON HARO STREET   Phone: 604/683-6912   (5)

Regional
Continental
$45-$52

In the lower level of the Buccan Hotel in Vancouver's West End, the restaurant presents a daily changing menu based on the freshest available ingredients. On the wine list are 60 carefully chosen wines of less than $79. Although valet parking is recommended, public pay parking can be found under the West End Community Centre at Haro and Denman streets. Dressy casual. **Bar:** Full bar. **Reservations:** suggested. **Hours:** 6 pm-10 pm, Fri & Sat-11 pm. Closed: 10/13, 12/25, 12/26. **Address:** 1906 Haro St V6G 1H7 **Location:** Between Gilford and Chilco sts. **Parking:** valet and street. **Cards:** MC, VI.

PROVENCE MARINASIDE   Phone: 604/681-4144   (63)

Pacific Rim
$9-$35

The delightful restaurant faces the seawall and a small marina in an area known as Falsecreek. The menu spans breakfast, lunch and dinner, so guests can fit this place into any part of their day. In addition to choices from the antipasto display case, selections include wonderful pasta and panini, as well as beef, chicken and fish entrees. Casual dress. **Bar:** Full bar. **Reservations:** suggested. **Hours:** 8 am-10:30 pm, Fri & Sat-11 pm. Closed: 12/25. **Address:** 1177 Marinaside Crescent V6Z 2Y3 **Location:** End of Davie St, towards water. **Parking:** street. **Cards:** AX, DC, MC, VI.

RAIN CITY GRILL   Phone: 604/685-7337   (11)

Continental
$22-$32

You'll enjoy the Rain City's Pacific Northwest cuisine with a menu that includes fresh ingredients and weekly changes. The atmosphere is simple yet stately, the server staff is attentive and nicely attired, and the wine list is extensive. Limited seating. Dressy casual. **Bar:** Full bar. **Reservations:** suggested. **Hours:** 5 pm-11 pm, Sat & Sun also 10:30 am-2:30 pm. Closed: 12/25, 12/26. **Address:** 1193 Denman St V6G 2N1 **Location:** Just n of jct Denman and Davie sts. **Parking:** valet and street. **Cards:** AX, DC, MC, VI.

RELISH-THE RESTAURANT & LOUNGE   Phone: 604/669-1962   (44)

Continental
$12-$25

In a downtown courtyard-like setting, the restaurant has an outdoor waterfall that greets patio diners. Plates are meant for sharing, and the martini menu is extensive. Many nearby offices help make this a popular lunchtime haunt; reservations are a must at midday. Walk-ins are more readily accommodated during less-busy dinner hours. Casual dress. **Bar:** Full bar. **Reservations:** suggested. **Hours:** 11 am-midnight. Closed: 12/25. **Address:** 888 Nelson St V6Z 2H2 **Location:** Between Hornby and Howe sts. **Parking:** on-site (fee). **Cards:** AX, MC, VI.

(See map and index starting on p. 564)

REX ROTISSERIE & GRILL
Phone: 604/683-7390 (18)

▽▽▽
Southwestern
$11-$30

Featuring hot rotisserie chicken and prime rib, also fresh made sandwiches and some pasta. Patio dining in season. Validated parking after 5 pm. Casual dress. **Bar:** Full bar. **Reservations:** required, for lunch. **Hours:** 11:30 am-3 & 5-9:30 pm. Closed major holidays; also Sat & Sun. **Address:** 1055 Dunsmuir St V7X 1G4 **Location:** Between Thurlow and Burrard sts; plaza level of Bentall Centre. **Parking:** street. **Cards:** AX, DC, MC, VI.

RICKY'S ALL DAY GRILL
Phone: 604/602-9233

▽▽▽ ▽▽
Canadian
$6-$15

The comfortable eatery, which employs friendly servers, presents a varied menu that includes pasta dishes, wraps, omelets, stir-fry preparations and burgers. Portions are generous. Children's and senior selections are offered. Guests can request seating in a booth or at a table. Casual dress. **Bar:** Full bar. **Hours:** 6:30 am-8 pm, Sat & Sun from 7:30 am. **Address:** 1-111 Dunsmuir St V6B 6A3 **Location:** Corner of Dunsmuir and Beatty sts. **Parking:** on-site (fee). **Cards:** MC, VI.

RICKY'S ALL DAY GRILL
Phone: 604/669-2781

▽▽▽ ▽▽
Canadian
$6-$15

The comfortable eatery, which employs friendly servers, presents a varied menu that includes pasta dishes, wraps, omelets, stir-fry preparations and burgers. Portions are generous. Children's and senior selections are offered. Guests can request seating in a booth or at a table. Casual dress. **Bar:** Full bar. **Hours:** 7 am-7 pm, Sat & Sun from 8 am. **Address:** 23-200 Burraro St V6C 3L6 **Location:** Between W Hastings and Cordova sts. **Parking:** on-site (fee). **Cards:** MC, VI.

THE SANDBAR SEAFOOD RESTAURANT
Phone: 604/669-9030 (64)

▽▽ ▽▽
Seafood
$10-$30

More than a century ago, Granville Island was known as "the great sandbar," where native tribes came to fish. Today, the 300-seat fresh seafood restaurant perches on the waterfront and offers great views from every seat. Complimentary parking is available for three hours during the day and all night after 7 pm. Casual dress. **Bar:** Full bar. **Reservations:** suggested, for dinner. **Hours:** 11:30 am-11 pm, Sun-10 pm. Closed: 12/25. **Address:** #9 The Creekhouse, 1535 Johnston St V6H 3R9 **Location:** Below the bridge, follow signs to Granville Island. **Parking:** on-site. **Cards:** AX, MC, VI.

CALL ⓑⓜ

SAVEUR
Phone: 604/688-1633 (34)

▽▽ ▽▽▽
Northern French
$9-$38

Patrons can savor the tastes of France through the restaurant's three-course tasting menu, which offers a choice of six appetizers, six entrees and six desserts for a set price of $38. The only available parking is at metered street spots or in a nearby pay lot. Dressy casual. **Bar:** Full bar. **Reservations:** suggested. **Hours:** 11:30 am-2 & 6-10 pm, Sat from 6 pm. Closed major holidays; also Sun. **Address:** 850 Thurlow St V6E 1W2 **Location:** Between Robson and Haro sts. **Parking:** street. **Cards:** AX, JC, MC, VI.

SAVORY COAST
Phone: 604/642-6278 (25)

▽▽▽▽
Mediterranean
$13-$35

Casual dress. **Bar:** Full bar. **Reservations:** suggested. **Hours:** 11:30 am-11 pm, Sat & Sun from 2 pm. Closed: 12/25. **Address:** 1133 Robson St, Second Floor V6E 1B5 **Location:** Between Thurlow and Bute sts. **Parking:** street. **Cards:** AX, MC, VI.

SHOW CASE RESTAURANT
Phone: 604/639-4040 (10)

▽▽▽▽
Pacific Rim
$15-$30

Natural light shining through floor-to-ceiling windows illuminates the restaurant and adjoining bar. Distinctive presentations characterize offerings of West Coast cuisine. Breakfast, lunch and dinner are available daily. Casual dress. **Bar:** Full bar. **Reservations:** suggested. **Hours:** 6:30 am-2 & 5-10 pm. **Address:** 1128 W Hastings St V6E 4R5 **Location:** Between Bute and Thurlow sts; in Vancouver Marriott Pinnacle Downtown. **Parking:** on-site and valet. **Cards:** AX, DC, DS, JC, MC, VI.

CALL ⓑⓜ

STEPHO'S SOUVLAKI GREEK TAVERNA
Phone: 604/683-2555 (43)

▽▽ ▽▽
Greek
$7-$10

On bustling Davie Street, the longstanding restaurant is a favorite for its generous plates of rice, roasted potatoes, souvlaki, lamb and chicken. There's often a line, so diners are encouraged to arrive early. Casual dress. **Bar:** Full bar. **Hours:** 11:30 am-11:30 pm. Closed: 12/25. **Address:** 1124 Davie St V6E 1N1 **Location:** Between Bute and Thurlow sts. **Parking:** street. **Cards:** AX, MC, VI.

SUBEEZ CAFE
Phone: 604/687-6107 (47)

▽▽ ▽▽
Canadian
$10-$23

Around for more than 10 years, the restaurant serves casual fare to the masses. On the menu are sandwiches, all-day breakfast items, pasta, salads and larger entrees for those who are particularly hungry. The patio opens on warmer days. Casual dress. **Bar:** Full bar. **Hours:** 11 am-1 am, Sun-midnight. Closed: 12/25. **Address:** 891 Homer St V6B 2W2 **Location:** Between Smithe and Robson sts. **Parking:** street. **Cards:** AX, MC, VI.

TROPIKA MALAYSIAN & THAI CUISINE
Phone: 604/737-6002 (27)

ⒸⒶⒶ

▽▽ ▽▽
Asian
$8-$20

A quick trip through the extensive menu, which combines Malaysian, Thai and Singapore cuisine, turns up Thai curries that are eight hours in preparation, pan-fried roti bread that disappears within seconds of reaching the table and Malaysian chili sauce dishes. The restaurant is on trendy Robson Street. Casual dress. **Bar:** Full bar. **Reservations:** suggested. **Hours:** 11:30 am-10:30 pm. **Address:** 1128 Robson St V6E 1B2 **Location:** Between Bute and Thurlow sts. **Parking:** street. **Cards:** AX, DC, JC, MC, VI.

VERA'S BURGER SHACK
Phone: 604/893-8372

▽▽
Canadian
$5-$9

This Davie Village location, Vera's third and newest, joins others in Kitsilano and Dundarave. The local favorite is known for fresh ground beef burgers, juicy hot dogs, huge onion rings and thick milk shakes. This place is great for something different. Guests can eat in or order for take-out. Casual dress. **Hours:** 11 am-11 pm, Thurs-Sat to 2 am. Closed: 1/1, 12/25. **Address:** 1030 Davie St V6E 1M3 **Location:** Between Thurlow and Burrard sts. **Parking:** street. **Cards:** MC, VI.

(See map and index starting on p. 564)

VERA'S BURGER SHACK
Phone: 604/228-8372

Canadian
$5-$9

Vera's, as it has come to be known, has received kudos for its burgers for the past few years. The secret to its success is simple, fresh ground beef that's cooked to perfection. In addition to burgers, guests might want to try the dogs, fries, onion rings or daily specials. A children's menu is available. Casual dress. **Hours:** 11 am-11 pm. Closed: 1/1, 12/25. **Address:** 1935 Cornwall Ave V6J 1C8 **Location:** Between Walnut and Cypress sts. **Parking:** street. **Cards:** MC, VI.

VILLA DE LUPO RESTAURANT
Phone: 604/688-7436   **49**

Italian
$20-$36

You'll enjoy the fine cuisine at this restaurant; all meals—such as homemade pasta and the lamb osso bucco—are prepared with fresh, local ingredients. The menu also features a wide range of fine wines, and the lovely atmosphere has a romantic feel. Casual dress. **Bar:** Full bar. **Reservations:** required. **Hours:** 5:30 pm-10 pm. Closed: 1/1, 12/25, 12/26. **Address:** 869 Hamilton St V6B 2R7 **Location:** Between Robson and Smithe sts. **Parking:** on-site and street. **Cards:** AX, DC, MC, VI.

VISTAS REVOLVING RESTAURANT
Phone: 604/691-2777   **8**

Pacific Rim
$28-$40

The revolving restaurant couples an elegant setting with majestic views of the harbor, city and North Shore Mountains. Guests palates are tantalized with delectable seafood, along with some chicken and steak items. Dressy casual. **Bar:** Full bar. **Reservations:** suggested. **Hours:** 5:30 pm-10 pm, Thurs-Sat to 11 pm. **Address:** 1133 W Hastings St V6E 3T3 **Location:** Between Bute and Thurlow sts; in Renaissance Vancouver Hotel Harbourside. **Parking:** on-site and valet. **Cards:** AX, DC, DS, JC, MC, VI.
(See color ad p 588)

WATER ST. CAFE
Phone: 604/689-2832   **31**

Italian
$11-$24

Located in a Victorian building across the street from Old Gastown's steam clock landmark, the Water Street Cafe features elegant yet casual dining with a Continental and Italian cuisine inspired with British Columbia and Canadian West Coast touches. Casual dress. **Bar:** Full bar. **Reservations:** suggested. **Hours:** 11:30 am-10 pm. Closed: 1/1, 12/24, 12/25. **Address:** 300 Water St V6B 1B6 **Location:** Corner of Cambie and Water sts; in Gastown. **Parking:** street. **Cards:** AX, DC, JC, MC, VI.

WHITE SPOT
Phone: 604/681-8034

Canadian
$8-$18

Open for three meals a day, the popular casual restaurant prepares offerings such as sandwiches and burgers, fresh salads, pastas and stir-fries, fish and chips, chargrilled sirloin steaks and chicken, in addition to a selection of yummy desserts. Casual dress. **Bar:** Full bar. **Hours:** 6 am-11 pm, Fri & Sat-midnight. Closed: 12/25. **Address:** 1616 W Georgia St V6G 2V5 **Location:** Corner of W Georgia and Cardero sts. **Parking:** on-site. **Cards:** AX, DC, MC, VI.

WHITE SPOT
Phone: 604/605-0045

Canadian
$8-$18

Open for three meals a day, the popular casual restaurant prepares offerings such as sandwiches and burgers, fresh salads, pastas and stir-fries, fish and chips, chargrilled sirloin steaks and chicken, in addition to a selection of yummy desserts. Casual dress. **Bar:** Full bar. **Hours:** 7 am-10 pm. Closed: 12/25. **Address:** 718 Drake St V6Z 2W6 **Location:** Between Granville and Hornby sts. **Parking:** street. **Cards:** AX, DC, DS, MC, VI.

WHITE SPOT
Phone: 604/662-3066

Canadian
$8-$18

Open for three meals a day, the popular casual restaurant prepares offerings such as sandwiches and burgers, fresh salads, pastas and stir-fries, fish and chips, chargrilled sirloin steaks and chicken, in addition to a selection of yummy desserts. Casual dress. **Bar:** Full bar. **Hours:** 6:30 am-11 pm. Closed: 12/25. **Address:** 580 W Georgia St V6B 2A3 **Location:** Corner of W Georgia and Seymour sts. **Parking:** on-site (fee). **Cards:** AX, DS, MC, VI.

WILD RICE
Phone: 604/642-2882   **40**

Asian
$10-$19

The funky downtown bar and eatery caters to the nightclub crowd looking for appetizers to share with fancy and innovative drinks. Just up the street from Tinseltown Cinema, this place is a great pre- or post-movie stop. Street parking is limited, but spots are ample in the nearby parkade. Casual dress. **Bar:** Full bar. **Hours:** 11:30 am-midnight, Fri-1 am, Sat 5 pm-1 am, Sun 5 pm-11 pm. Closed: 12/25. **Address:** 117 W Pender St V6B 1S4 **Location:** Between Beatty and Abbott sts. **Parking:** street. **Cards:** MC, VI.

THE WILLIAM TELL   *Menu on AAA.com*
Phone: 604/688-3504   **50**

Swiss
$23-$38

Tiger prawns, rainbow trout, rack of lamb and steak tartare are the favorites at the established, popular William Tell's. The restaurant displays an attractive, European-style elegance. Sunday night features a Swiss-style buffet. Casual dress. **Bar:** Full bar. **Reservations:** suggested. **Hours:** 5:30 pm-9 pm, Sun-8 pm; Sunday brunch 11 am-1:30 pm. Closed major holidays; also Mon. **Address:** 765 Beatty St V6B 2M4 **Location:** Between Georgia and Robson sts; in The Georgian Court Hotel. **Parking:** on-site (fee) and valet. **Cards:** AX, DC, MC, VI.

WON MORE SZECHUAN CUISINE
Phone: 604/688-8856   **14**

Chinese
$7-$16

On the corner of Davie and Denman streets, the second-floor restaurant overlooks English Bay. The wonderful eatery is known for its dry ginger beef and salt and pepper squid. Those who like it hot and spicy should look for the highlighted items on the menu. Casual dress. **Bar:** Beer & wine. **Hours:** 4 pm-10 pm. Closed: 12/25; also Tues. **Address:** 201-1184 Denman St V6G 2M9 **Location:** Between Davie and Pendrell sts. **Parking:** street. **Cards:** MC, VI.

YALETOWN BREWING COMPANY
Phone: 604/681-2739   **58**

Canadian
$9-$29

In the trendy Yaletown area, the distinctive brew pub offers homemade beers to accompany its thin-crust pizzas and wonderful burgers. On warm days, patrons can unwind on the large outdoor patio. Casual dress. **Bar:** Full bar. **Reservations:** suggested. **Hours:** 11:30 am-midnight, Thurs-1 am, Fri & Sat-2 am. Closed: 12/25. **Address:** 1111 Mainland St V6B 2T9 **Location:** Between Helmcken and Davie sts. **Parking:** street. **Cards:** AX, MC, VI.

(See map and index starting on p. 564)

ZEFFERELLI'S RESTAURANT   Phone: 604/687-0655   26

Italian
$8-$25

Casual dress. **Bar:** Full bar. **Reservations:** suggested. **Hours:** 11:30 am-11 pm, Sat from 5 pm, Sun 5 pm-10 pm. Closed: 1/1, 12/25, 12/26. **Address:** 1136 Robson St V6E 1B2 **Location:** Between Bute and Thurlow sts. **Parking:** street. **Cards:** AX, MC, VI.

ZIN   Phone: 604/408-1700   17

International
$10-$28

On trendy Robson Street, the funky restaurant gets its name from zinfandel wines, which servers say pair well with the global cuisine on the wonderful, meant-for-sharing tapas menu. Casual dress. **Bar:** Full bar. **Reservations:** suggested. **Hours:** 7 am-midnight, Sat & Sun from 8 am. Closed: 12/25. **Address:** 1277 Robson St V6E 1C4 **Location:** Between Jervis and Bute sts; in Pacific Palisades Hotel. **Parking:** on-site (fee) and valet. **Cards:** AX, DC, JC, MC, VI.

VANCOUVER pop. 578,041   (See map and index starting on p. 568)

——— WHERE TO STAY ———

2400 MOTEL   *Book at AAA.com*   Phone: 604/434-2464   7

Motel
$85-$110 5/1-2/28
$70-$85 3/1-4/30

Address: 2400 Kingsway V5R 5G9 **Location:** 4.5 mi (7.2 km) se on Hwy 1A and 99A (Kingsway and 33rd Ave). **Facility:** 65 units. 32 one- and 33 two-bedroom standard units, some with kitchens. 1 story, exterior corridors. *Bath:* combo or shower only. **Parking:** on-site. **Cards:** AX, JC, MC, VI.

BEST WESTERN EXHIBITION PARK   *Book great rates at AAA.com*   Phone: 604/294-4751   2

Small-scale Hotel
$99-$179 All Year

Address: 3475 E Hastings St V5K 2A5 **Location:** Trans-Canada Hwy 1, exit 26; jct Trans-Canada Hwy 1 and 7A. **Facility:** 58 one-bedroom standard units. 3 stories, interior corridors. **Parking:** on-site. **Amenities:** voice mail, irons, hair dryers. **Leisure Activities:** saunas, whirlpool. **Guest Services:** valet and coin laundry, wireless Internet. **Cards:** AX, CB, DC, DS, JC, MC, VI. **Free Special Amenities:** early check-in/late check-out and preferred room (subject to availability with advance reservations).

AAA Benefit:
Members save 10% everyday, plus an exclusive frequent stay program.

(See map and index starting on p. 568)

BEST WESTERN UPTOWN   *Book great rates at AAA.com*   Phone: 604/267-2000

Small-scale Hotel
$85-$179 All Year

Address: 205 Kingsway V5T 3J5 **Location:** Corner of E 10th St. **Facility:** 69 one-bedroom standard units, some with whirlpools. 4 stories, interior corridors. **Parking:** on-site. **Terms:** cancellation fee imposed. **Amenities:** high-speed Internet, voice mail, irons, hair dryers. *Some:* dual phone lines. **Leisure Activities:** limited exercise equipment. **Guest Services:** valet laundry. **Business Services:** meeting rooms, PC. **Cards:** AX, DC, DS, JC, MC, VI. **Free Special Amenities:** continental breakfast and high-speed Internet. *(See color ad p 601)*

AAA Benefit:
Members save 10% everyday, plus an exclusive frequent stay program.

▼ See AAA listing p 624 ▼

▼ See AAA listing p 616 ▼

(See map and index starting on p. 568)

DAYS INN-VANCOUVER METRO

Book great rates at AAA.com   **Phone:** (604)876-5531   **6**

Motel

$79-$189 3/1-9/30
$59-$129 10/1-2/28

Address: 2075 Kingsway V5N 2T2 **Location:** 3.8 mi (6 km) se on Hwy 1A and 99A (Kingsway and Victoria Dr). **Facility:** 66 one-bedroom standard units. 2 stories (no elevator), exterior corridors. *Bath:* combo or shower only. **Parking:** on-site. **Terms:** cancellation fee imposed. **Amenities:** irons, hair dryers. *Some:* high-speed Internet. **Guest Services:** wireless Internet. **Cards:** AX, DC, DS, JC, MC, VI. **Free Special Amenities: continental breakfast and high-speed Internet.**
(See color ad below)

HOLIDAY INN EXPRESS VANCOUVER

Book great rates at AAA.com   **Phone:** 604/254-1000   **1**

Small-scale Hotel

$89-$209 3/1-9/30
$89-$129 10/1-2/28

Address: 2889 E Hastings St V5K 2A1 **Location:** Between Renfrew and Kaslo sts. **Facility:** Smoke free premises. 100 units. 99 one-bedroom standard units. 1 one-bedroom suite. 4 stories, interior corridors. **Parking:** on-site. **Terms:** check-in 4 pm, cancellation fee imposed. **Amenities:** video games (fee), dual phone lines, voice mail, irons, hair dryers. **Leisure Activities:** sauna, exercise room. **Guest Services:** valet and coin laundry, wireless Internet. **Business Services:** meeting rooms. **Cards:** AX, CB, DC, DS, JC, MC, VI. **Free Special Amenities: expanded continental breakfast and high-speed Internet.**
(See color ad on insert & p 582)

(See map and index starting on p. 568)

HOLIDAY INN VANCOUVER-CENTRE (BROADWAY) *Book great rates at AAA.com* Phone: 604/879-0511

Small-scale Hotel
$179-$209 3/1-10/16
$119-$135 10/17-2/28

Address: 711 W Broadway V5Z 3Y2 **Location:** Between Heather and Willow sts. **Facility:** 200 one-bedroom standard units. 16 stories, interior corridors. **Parking:** on-site (fee). **Terms:** cancellation fee imposed. **Amenities:** high-speed Internet, voice mail, irons, hair dryers. **Pool(s):** heated indoor. **Leisure Activities:** sauna, exercise room. **Guest Services:** valet and coin laundry. **Business Services:** meeting rooms, PC (fee). **Cards:** AX, DC, DS, JC, MC, VI.
(See color ad on insert)

PLAZA 500 HOTEL & CONVENTION CENTRE *Book great rates at AAA.com* Phone: 604/873-1811

Small-scale Hotel
$144-$199 All Year

Address: 500 W 12th Ave V5Z 1M2 **Location:** Corner of W 12th Ave at Cambie St. **Facility:** 153 one-bedroom standard units. 17 stories, interior corridors. **Parking:** on-site (fee). **Terms:** check-in 4 pm. **Amenities:** dual phone lines, voice mail, irons, hair dryers. *Some:* high-speed Internet (fee). **Guest Services:** valet laundry, area transportation-downtown, wireless Internet. **Business Services:** conference facilities, business center. **Cards:** AX, CB, DC, DS, JC, MC, VI. **Free Special Amenities:** newspaper and high-speed Internet.

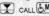

▼ See AAA listing p 626 ▼

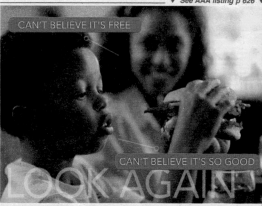

CAN'T BELIEVE IT'S FREE

CAN'T BELIEVE IT'S SO GOOD

LOOK AGAIN

- Kids Stay and Eat Free*
- Vancouver's Prime Location to Airport, Highways and Ferries
- Kid Themed Bunk Bed Rooms
- Fogg 'N Suds Restaurant Onsite
- Free High Speed Wireless Internet
- Discover Richmond - Especially for Asian Shopping & Dining

Holiday Inn
International
Vancouver Airport

PRIORITY**CLUB** REWARDS | 1·800·holiday | holidayinn.com

*Kids Eat Free is available for kids age 12 and under. Call hotel or visit www.holidayinn.com for details. See www.priorityclub.com for reward details. ©2007 InterContinental® Hotels Group. All rights reserved. Most hotels are independently owned and/or operated.

Richmond, BC | 10720 Cambie Road 800-465-4329

(See map and index starting on p. 568)

QUALITY INN AIRPORT   *Book great rates at AAA.com*   Phone: (604)321-6611

Small-scale Hotel
$79-$149 All Year

Address: 725 SE Marine Dr V5X 2T9 **Location:** Corner of SE Marine Dr and Fraser St. **Facility:** 100 one-bedroom standard units. 6 stories, interior corridors. **Parking:** on-site. **Terms:** cancellation fee imposed. **Amenities:** voice mail, irons, hair dryers. **Leisure Activities:** bowling centre. **Guest Services:** valet laundry, wireless Internet. **Business Services:** meeting rooms, PC (fee). **Cards:** AX, CB, DC, DS, JC, MC, VI. **Free Special Amenities: continental breakfast and high-speed Internet.** *(See color ad on insert & p 606)*

▼ See AAA listing p 621 ▼

▼ See AAA listing p 605 ▼

(See map and index starting on p. 568)

——— WHERE TO DINE ———

ABIGAIL'S PARTY

Canadian
$8–$15

Phone: 604/739-4677   ④
The owners of the cheeky Kitsilano tapas eatery chose its name because it's fun and sexy, as is the warm interior with low lighting and cool music. Selections from the small and selective wine list complement the monthly changing menu. Tapas dishes are big enough to share, and servers are attentive and friendly. Parking is at street meters or in two-hour spots around the neighborhood. Casual dress. **Bar:** Full bar. **Reservations:** suggested. **Hours:** 5:30 pm-2 am, Sat also 9:30 am-2:30 pm, Sun 9:30 am-2:30 pm; Saturday & Sunday brunch. Closed: 1/1, 12/25. **Address:** 1685 Yew St V6K 3E6 **Location:** Between Cornwall and 1st Ave; in Kitsiland District. **Parking:** street. **Cards:** AX, MC, VI.

AURORA BISTRO
Continental
$16–$26

Phone: 604/873-9944   ⑱
Rising out of the ashes of an old Chinese restaurant, the bistro is the belle of this still-gritty section of Main Street, just north of Broadway. The impressively inventive chef/owner adds a seductive allure to what is essentially comfort food. The owner has opted for all British Columbia choices on the modest wine list. Casual dress. **Bar:** Full bar. **Reservations:** suggested. **Hours:** 5:30 pm-10 pm, Fri & Sat-11 pm. Closed: 1/1, 12/25, 12/26. **Address:** 2420 Main St V5T 3E2 **Location:** Between Broadway and E 8th St. **Parking:** street. **Cards:** AX, MC, VI.

AVENUE GRILL
Italian
$8–$22

Phone: 604/266-8183   ㉛
In the trendy Kerrisdale neighborhood, the long-established restaurant has limited space, making reservations a good idea, especially on weekends. Tables are tightly spaced, but seating is comfortable. The main draw is the food: standard breakfast selections, fresh sandwiches, daily soups and blue-plate specials for lunch; and many pasta dishes made from more than 40 toppings on the dinner menu. Most parking is along the street. Casual dress. **Bar:** Full bar. **Reservations:** required, weekends. **Hours:** 8 am-9:30 pm. Closed: 12/25. **Address:** 2114 W 41st Ave V6M 1Z1 **Location:** Between Yew St and W Boulevard. **Parking:** street. **Cards:** AX, DC, MC, VI.

BISHOP'S
Continental
$34–$40

Phone: 604/738-2025   ⑦
The long-established restaurant has been serving wonderful contemporary North American cuisine for more than 20 years. The weekly changing menu highlights the season's freshest ingredients, such as British Columbia salmon, which has a short season. Try the signature death by chocolate dessert. Dressy casual. **Bar:** Full bar. **Reservations:** required. **Hours:** 5:30 pm-11 pm, Sun-10 pm. Closed: 12/24-12/26; also 1/1-1/15. **Address:** 2183 W 4th Ave V6K 1N7 **Location:** Between Arbutus and Yew sts. **Parking:** street. **Cards:** AX, DC, MC, VI.

CACTUS CLUB CAFE
Canadian
$9–$29

Phone: 604/733-0434
This bustling, casual restaurant serves huge burgers, sandwiches, pasta, salads, soups, quesadillas, fajitas, vegetarian dishes, steak, ribs, chicken and fish. Featured are certified Angus beef and fresh wild British Columbia salmon. The thick and creamy milk shakes come highly recommended. Casual dress. **Bar:** Full bar. **Hours:** 11 am-midnight, Fri & Sat-1 am. Closed: 12/25. **Address:** 1530 W Broadway V6J 5K9 **Location:** Between W Broadway and Fir St. **Parking:** street. **Cards:** AX, MC, VI.

CACTUS CLUB CAFE
Canadian
$9–$29

Phone: 604/714-6000
This bustling, casual restaurant serves huge burgers, sandwiches, pasta, salads, soups, quesadillas, fajitas, vegetarian dishes, steak, ribs, chicken and fish. Featured are certified Angus beef and fresh wild British Columbia salmon. The thick and creamy milk shakes come highly recommended. Casual dress. **Bar:** Full bar. **Hours:** 11 am-midnight, Fri & Sat-1 am. Closed: 12/25. **Address:** 575 W Broadway V5Z 1E6 **Location:** Corner of W Broadway and Ash St. **Parking:** street. **Cards:** AX, MC, VI.

THE CANNERY

Seafood
$15–$30

Menu on AAA.com   **Phone: 604/254-9606**   ②
For 34 years, the seafood restaurant has set the standards for fresh seafood. In an industrial section of town, it's well worth the visit. The setting offers a memorable view of the harbor, mountains and sea lions at play. The many fresh seafood dishes, such as salmon Wellington, and local wines are excellent. Casual dress. **Bar:** Full bar. **Reservations:** required. **Hours:** 11:30 am-2:30 & 5:30-9 pm, Fri-9:30 pm, Sat 5 pm-9:30 pm, Sun 5 pm-9 pm. Closed: 12/24-12/26. **Address:** 2205 Commissioner St V5L 1A4 **Location:** E Hastings St to Renfrew St, just n to McGill, just e to Commissioner St, then 0.9 mi (1.5 km) n. **Parking:** on-site. **Cards:** AX, DC, DS, JC, MC, VI.

FEENIE'S
Canadian
$16–$28

Phone: 604/739-7115   ⑫
Casual dress. **Bar:** Full bar. **Reservations:** suggested. **Hours:** 11:30 am-11 pm, Sat & Sun from 10:30 am. Closed: 1/1, 12/25. **Address:** 2563 W Broadway V6K 2E9 **Location:** Between Trafalgar and Larch sts. **Parking:** valet and street. **Cards:** AX, DC, MC, VI.

GRAMERCY GRILL
Canadian
$9–$33

Phone: 604/730-5666   ㉒
Named after a New York district, the restaurant offers a dark-wood interior, comfortable booths and tables and a showpiece bar. During warm days and evenings, patrons gather on the pleasant patio. Prices for such dishes as osso buco, roast lamb sirloin, game hen and, of course, West Coast salmon are reasonable. Several wines by the glass are available. Casual dress. **Bar:** Full bar. **Reservations:** suggested. **Hours:** 11:30 am-2:30 & 5-11 pm, Sat & Sun from 11 am. Closed: 12/25. **Address:** 2685 Arbutus St V6J 3Y4 **Location:** Between W 10th and W 11th aves. **Parking:** street. **Cards:** AX, DC, JC, MC, VI.

HELL'S KITCHEN
Canadian
$9–$24

Phone: 604/736-4355   ⑩
This busy publike restaurant features hearty food to go with the beers on tap. Try a burger with sweet yam fries and a delightful dipping sauce, or go for the "Pizza from Hell" made in the classic New York thin crust-style. Choose from a wide array of toppings (perhaps the "Daisy Duke" or "The Naked Chef" appeal to you?), or create your own. Note: Parking is in metered street spots only. Casual dress. **Bar:** Full bar. **Hours:** 11:30 am-1 am, Fri-2 am, Sat & Sun 10 am-2 am. Closed: 12/25. **Address:** 2041 W 4th Ave V6J 1N3 **Location:** Between Arbutus and Maple sts. **Parking:** street. **Cards:** AX, MC, VI.

(See map and index starting on p. 568)

LAS MARGARITAS RESTAURANTE & CANTINA

Mexican
$8–$17

Phone: 604/734-7117   11

Mexican appointments accent the bright, festive dining room, where diners scan a menu of healthy choices, as well as fajitas, grilled salmon burritos and chipotle chicken. Servers are prompt and attentive. Those who don't secure one of the six parking stalls behind the building can opt for metered street parking. Casual dress. **Bar:** Full bar. **Reservations:** suggested, except Fri-Sun. **Hours:** 11:30 am-10 pm, Fri & Sat-11 pm. Closed: 12/25. **Address:** 1999 W 4th Ave V6J 1M7 **Location:** Between Cypress and Maple sts. **Parking:** on-site and street. **Cards:** AX, MC, VI.

LOMBARDO'S RISTORANTE PIZZERIA

Pizza
$9–$25

Phone: 604/251-2240   5

Located in the Mercata Mall, Lombardo's is known as one of the oldest brick-oven pizza houses in town, and it offers 15 types of pizza. The lasagna is very good also. Locals and visitors alike enjoy the family-style atmosphere. Seating is a bit limited. Casual dress. **Bar:** Beer & wine. **Hours:** 11 am-11 pm, Sun-10 pm. Closed major holidays. **Address:** 120 1641 Commercial Dr V5L 3A4 **Location:** Corner of 1st St and Commercial Dr; in Il Mercato Mall. **Cards:** AX, DC, MC, VI.

LUMIERE

CAA
French
$37–$45

Phone: 604/739-8185   14

The restaurant merges European elegance, North American flair and Asian minimalism. Food critics worldwide have bestowed accolades on this place, a must for visitors to the city. Prices for the chef's tasting menu, which consists of 6 or 10 courses, range from $88 to $180; wine pairings are extra. The menu changes monthly. Dressy casual. **Bar:** Full bar. **Reservations:** suggested. **Hours:** 5:30 pm-10:30 pm. Closed: 1/1, 12/25, 12/26; also Mon. **Address:** 2551 W Broadway V6K 2E9 **Location:** Between Trafalgar and Larch sts. **Parking:** valet and street. **Cards:** AX, DC, MC, VI.

MAURYA INDIAN CUISINE

Indian
$11–$22

Phone: 604/742-0622   16

Representative of the cuisine are moist, flavorful tandoori chicken, vindaloo lamb and a number of vegetarian dishes. Yummy naan bread comes with three dipping sauces. Lending to the warm, inviting atmosphere are rich wood accents and professional decoration down to the last detail. Parking is at the back of the restaurant or at street meters. Casual dress. **Bar:** Full bar. **Reservations:** suggested. **Hours:** 11:30 am-2:30 & 5-11 pm, Sun 11:30 am-3:30 & 5-11 pm. Closed: 12/25. **Address:** 1643 W Broadway V6J 1W9 **Location:** Between Fir and Pine sts. **Parking:** on-site and street. **Cards:** AX, MC, VI.

MEMPHIS BLUES BARBEQUE HOUSE

Barbecue
$7–$19

Phone: 604/215-2599

A sure sign that diners are likely to get messy fingers and faces is the roll of paper towels at each table. Savory favorites include slabs of ribs, pulled pork, Cornish game hens and, of course, heaps of barbecue wings. Locations are on Broadway at Granville Street and on Commercial Drive. Casual dress. **Bar:** Beer & wine. **Hours:** 11 am-10 pm, Fri-midnight, Sat noon-midnight, Sun noon-10 pm. Closed: 12/25. **Address:** 1342 Commercial Dr V5L 3X6 **Location:** Between Kitchener and Charles sts. **Parking:** street. **Cards:** AX, DC, MC, VI.

MEMPHIS BLUES BARBEQUE HOUSE

Barbecue
$7–$19

Phone: 604/738-6806

A sure sign that diners are likely to get messy fingers and faces is the roll of paper towels at each table. Savory favorites include slabs of ribs, pulled pork, Cornish game hens and, of course, heaps of barbecue wings. Locations are on Broadway at Granville Street and on Commercial Drive. Casual dress. **Bar:** Beer & wine. **Hours:** 11 am-10 pm, Fri-midnight, Sat noon-midnight, Sun noon-10 pm. Closed: 12/25, 12/26. **Address:** 1465 W Broadway V6H 1H6 **Location:** Between Granville and Hemlock sts. **Parking:** street. **Cards:** AX, DC, MC, VI.

MISTRAL FRENCH BISTRO

French
$14–$29

Phone: 604/733-0046   13

The quaint French bistro serves wonderful lunches and dinners with a heavy reliance on such meats as roast chicken, veal and New York grade A beef. Amazing desserts made on the premises are the highlight here. Parking is offered at metered spots along the street. Casual dress. **Bar:** Full bar. **Reservations:** suggested. **Hours:** 11:30 am-2 & 5:30-10:30 pm. Closed: 12/25, 12/26; also Sun & Mon. **Address:** 2585 W Broadway V6K 2E9 **Location:** Between Trafalgar and Larch sts. **Parking:** street. **Cards:** AX, DC, MC, VI.

MONK MCQUEEN'S

Seafood
$12–$30

Phone: 604/877-1351   8

The restaurant affords great views of the mountains and the south shore of False Creek, with its numerous moored sailboats and condominiums. Two moods are sustained: casual in the downstairs area and more upscale upstairs, where the sounds of live jazz filter out on Wednesday through Sunday evenings in summer and on weekends in winter. Casual dress. **Bar:** Full bar. **Reservations:** suggested. **Hours:** 11:30 am-10 pm, Sat & Sun from 11 am. Closed: 12/25. **Address:** 601 Stamps Landing V5Z 3Z1 **Location:** W 6th Ave and Moberly Rd; just w of Cambie St Bridge. **Parking:** valet and street. **Cards:** AX, DC, JC, MC, VI.

MOXIE'S CLASSIC GRILL

Canadian
$8–$18

Phone: 604/678-9973

This sleek, funky and popular restaurant presents an extensive menu of creatively prepared dishes, including pizza, pasta, rice, noodles, signature salads and burgers. Other menus include one for children and one for Sunday brunch. Lending to the upbeat, stylish decor are dark wood appointments and river rock fireplaces. Casual dress. **Bar:** Full bar. **Hours:** 11 am-midnight, Fri & Sat-1 am. **Address:** 1759 W Broadway V6J 4S5 **Location:** Between Burrard and Pine sts; in Sandman Hotel Vancouver City Center. **Parking:** on-site (fee). **Cards:** AX, MC, VI.

THE OUISI BISTRO

Cajun
$8–$22

Phone: 604/732-7550   26

In the mix of high-end shops and restaurants along trendy Granville Street, the low-key restaurant serves Louisiana Creole and Cajun dishes from its open kitchen. Certain times of the year usher in live jazz in the evenings. Parking is at street meters. Casual dress. **Bar:** Full bar. **Reservations:** suggested. **Hours:** 11 am-1 am, Sat & Sun from 9 am. Closed: 12/25. **Address:** 3014 Granville St V6H 3J8 **Location:** Between W 15th and W 14th sts. **Parking:** street. **Cards:** MC, VI.

(See map and index starting on p. 568)

PINK PEARL CHINESE RESTAURANT   Phone: 604/253-4316   ③
▼▼ ▼▼
Chinese
$4-$19
Pink Pearl's focus is on fresh ingredients, local produce and West Coast seafood. An excellent and varied array of dim sum items is offered 9 am-3 pm This restaurant has received numerous write-ups in newspapers, magazines and travel guides. Casual dress. **Bar:** Full bar. **Reservations:** accepted. **Hours:** 9 am-10 pm, Fri & Sat-11 pm, Sun-10 pm. **Address:** 1132 E Hastings St V6A 1S2 **Location:** Just w of Clark St. **Parking:** on-site. **Cards:** AX, DC, MC, VI.

PROVENCE MEDITERRANEAN GRILL   Phone: 604/222-1980   ⑮
▼▼▼▼▼
Continental
$10-$29
The pleasant restaurant serves casual southern French and Italian cuisine in a warm neighborhood atmosphere. At the end of the month, the owners have a culinary tasting or chef's sampling at a set price. Guests can walk off their meal afterward by checking out the nearby shops. One-hour street parking is available. Casual dress. **Bar:** Full bar. **Reservations:** suggested. **Hours:** 11:30 am-10 pm, Sat-11 pm, Sun 10 am-10 pm. Closed: 12/25. **Address:** 100-4473 W 10th Ave V6R 2H2 **Location:** Between Sasamat and Trimble sts. **Parking:** street. **Cards:** AX, DC, MC, VI.

QUATTRO ON FOURTH   Phone: 604/734-4444   ⑥
▼▼▼▼▼
Italian
$18-$38
This restaurant features an airy, fun and lively decor; it makes you feel like you're in Tuscany. This place has a great local reputation, as its pasta and other dishes are heartful, full-flavored and created with healthy ingredients. Good service, too. Casual dress. **Bar:** Full bar. **Reservations:** suggested. **Hours:** 5 pm-11 pm, Sun-10 pm. Closed: 1/1, 12/25, 12/26. **Address:** 2611 W 4th Ave V6K 1P8 **Location:** Between MacDonald and Trafalgar sts. **Parking:** street. **Cards:** AX, DC, MC, VI.

RASPUTIN   Phone: 604/879-6675   ⑲
▼▼ ▼▼
Russian
$13-$25
The restaurant's Russian cuisine is as rich and varied as the land it comes from. A typical meal usually features several appetizers accompanied by shots of vodka. Representative of the fare are Ukrainian borscht, black caviar and pirozhki, Russia's famous stuffed buns. Dinner entrees include kebabs, chicken Kiev and "the feast," a mixed grill of several items. Casual dress. **Bar:** Full bar. **Reservations:** suggested, weekends. **Hours:** 5 pm-11 pm, Fri & Sat-midnight. Closed: 1/1, 12/25; also Mon. **Address:** 457 W Broadway V5Y 1R4 **Location:** Between Cambie and Yukon sts. **Parking:** street. **Cards:** AX, MC, VI.

RED DOOR PAN ASIAN GRILL   Phone: 604/733-5699   ㉕
▼▼▼ ▼▼▼
Asian
$7-$18
Across the bridge from downtown and along a trendy part of Granville Street, the distinctive Asian restaurant designs plates for sharing, which allows patrons to sample a variety of reasonably priced dishes. The decor incorporates plenty of black and red, and service is fast and friendly. Casual dress. **Bar:** Full bar. **Hours:** 11:30 am-11 pm, Fri & Sat-midnight, Sun 11:30 am-10 pm. Closed: 12/25. **Address:** 2996 Granville St V6H 3J7 **Location:** Corner of W 14th St. **Parking:** on-site. **Cards:** AX, MC, VI.

CALL ⑤M

RUGBY BEACH CLUB GRILLE   Phone: 604/736-2438   ㉑
▼▼▼ ▼▼▼
Continental
$8-$13
The 250-seat restaurant is spacious and comfortable, but when this place gets going, it also gets noisy. The energy buzz is a big part of the appeal, as is the food, which is priced a la carte. Drink prices are among the cheapest in town. Pay parking can be found on the street or in lots. Casual dress. **Bar:** Full bar. **Reservations:** suggested. **Hours:** 4:24 pm-midnight, Fri-1 am, Sat 11 am-1 am, Sun 11 am-11 pm. Closed: 12/25. **Address:** 201-950 W Broadway V5Z 1K7 **Location:** Between Oak and Laurel sts. **Parking:** street. **Cards:** AX, MC, VI.

SAWASDEE THAI RESTAURANT   Phone: 604/876-4030   ㉘
▼▼▼ ▼▼
Thai
$8-$15
Flavorful food and pleasant service are hallmarks of the popular restaurant, which is outside the downtown core on a street with various other shops and restaurants. Decor includes pale walls with various framed posters of Thailand, and clean, comfortable surroundings. Casual dress. **Bar:** Full bar. **Reservations:** suggested, weekends. **Hours:** 11:30 am-2:30 & 5-10 pm, Sat & Sun from 5 pm. Closed: 12/24, 12/25. **Address:** 4250 Main St V5V 3P9 **Location:** Main St and 27th Ave. **Parking:** street. **Cards:** MC, VI.

SEASONS HILLTOP BISTRO   Phone: 604/874-8008   ㉙
▼▼▼ ▼▼▼
Continental
$11-$32
Atop a small hill in Queen Elizabeth Park, the restaurant affords lovely views of the park and its flowers. Fish and meat preparations stand out on the menu. Because of construction on Cambie Street for a future rapid transit line, diners are advised to use Main Street then 33rd Avenue to access the park. Dressy casual. **Bar:** Full bar. **Reservations:** suggested. **Hours:** 11:30 am-10 pm, Sun from 10:30 am. Closed: 12/25. **Address:** 1583 Coal Harbour Quay V6G 3E7 **Location:** Between Main and Cambie sts; at 33rd Ave; in Queen Elizabeth Park. **Parking:** on-site (fee) and valet. **Cards:** AX, MC, VI.

SEQUOIA GRILL AT THE TEA HOUSE   *Menu on AAA.com*   Phone: 604/669-3281   ①
Ⓐ
▼▼▼ ▼▼▼
Pacific Rim
$12-$39
In the charming country-garden setting of Stanley Park, the restaurant affords spectacular views of English Bay and the mountains. The menu standout is the fabulous roasted rack of lamb. Couples and visitors especially enjoy the atmosphere of casual elegance. Pay parking is in effect. Casual dress. **Bar:** Full bar. **Reservations:** suggested. **Hours:** 11:30 am-2:30 & 5-9:45 pm, Sat-3 pm, Sun 10:30 am-3 pm; Saturday & Sunday brunch. Closed: 12/25. **Address:** 7501 Stanley Park Dr V6G 3E2 **Location:** Ferguson Point; in Stanley Park. **Parking:** on-site (fee). **Cards:** AX, MC, VI.

SHAUGHNESSY RESTAURANT AT VANDUSEN GARDEN   Phone: 604/261-0011   ㉚
▼▼▼ ▼▼▼
Pacific Rim
$11-$28
Overlooking the wonderful Vandusen Gardens, the quiet haven uses fresh ingredients in beautiful lunch and dinner entrees. Among daily specials are homemade soups. Ask about the chicken pot pie, a longtime favorite. After the meal, enjoy a stroll through the gardens. Casual dress. **Bar:** Full bar. **Reservations:** suggested. **Hours:** 11:30 am-9 pm, Sat & Sun from 11 am. Closed: 12/25. **Address:** 5251 Oak St V6M 4H1 **Location:** Between W 33rd and W 37th aves. **Parking:** on-site. **Cards:** AX, DC, MC, VI.

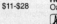

(See map and index starting on p. 568)

SOPHIE'S COSMIC CAFE

Canadian

$6-$10

Phone: 604/732-6810　⑨

Guests should be prepared to stand in line for this popular restaurant, the walls of which are covered with decorations that serve as reminders of a bygone time. Breakfast is the specialty meal, but burgers and sandwiches rarely disappoint. Casual dress. **Bar:** Full bar. **Hours:** 8 am-9:30 pm. Closed: 12/25. **Address:** 2095 W 4th Ave V6J 1N3 **Location:** Between Arbutus and Maple sts. **Parking:** street. **Cards:** MC, VI.

STAR ANISE

Regional
Canadian

$18-$30

Phone: 604/737-1485　㉓

Superb Pacific Rim cuisine reflects West Coast Canadian touches. Excellent local wines pair with local seafood and such meat dishes as Alberta pork chops. Guests should inquire about free parking when making a reservation. Casual dress. **Bar:** Full bar. **Reservations:** suggested. **Hours:** 5:30 pm-10 pm. Closed: 12/25. **Address:** 1485 W 12th Ave V6H 1M6 **Location:** Between Hemlock and Granville sts. **Parking:** on-site. **Cards:** AX, MC, VI.

SWISS CHALET ROTISSERIE & GRILL

Swiss

$6-$19

Phone: 604/732-8100

The popular restaurant is known for its rotisserie chicken and ribs and the tangy Chalet sauce that gives food its special zip. Diners munch on a half or quarter chicken with sides such as steamed vegetables, fries, baked potatoes and salads. Lunch guests often go for the great soup and sandwich combination. Take-out and delivery service are popular options. Casual dress. **Bar:** Beer & wine. **Hours:** 11 am-10 pm, Fri & Sat-11 pm. Closed: 12/25. **Address:** 3204 W Broadway V6K 2H4 **Location:** Between Blenheim and Trutch sts. **Parking:** on-site. **Cards:** AX, DC, MC, VI.

TOJO'S RESTAURANT

Japanese

$22-$30

Phone: 604/872-8050　⑳

Each dish at the second-floor restaurant is prepared using traditional Japanese methods and only the freshest ingredients (which never include monosodium glutamate). There's not much to the decor, but the food clearly is the focus here anyway. Guests can park at street meters or in an underground lot. Casual dress. **Bar:** Full bar. **Reservations:** required. **Hours:** 5 pm-10 pm. Closed: 12/25; also Sun & 1/1-1/15. **Address:** 202-777 W Broadway V5Z 4J7 **Location:** Between Heather and Willow sts. **Parking:** on-site (fee) and street. **Cards:** AX, DC, MC, VI.

TRAFALGARS BISTRO

Regional Pacific
Rim

$10-$25

Phone: 604/739-0555　㉗

If you covet one of the limited seats at dinnertime, be sure to reserve ahead since table spacing is a little tight. Trafalgars Bistro occupies a small neighborhood shopping complex and serves brunch daily. The owners describe the food as being "French based with some Asian influences," but you'll likely describe it as being good and reasonably priced. The lamb and ground pork burger, fresh-made soups of the day and all-day egg dishes are popular choices. Casual dress. **Bar:** Full bar. **Reservations:** required, evenings. **Hours:** 11 am-10 pm, Sat & Sun 10 am-11 pm. Closed: 12/25, 12/26. **Address:** 2603 W 16th Ave V6K 3C2 **Location:** Between Trafalgar and Stephens sts. **Parking:** street. **Cards:** MC, VI.

WEST RESTAURANT & BAR

International

$11-$45

Phone: 604/738-8938　㉔

On trendy South Granville Street, this restaurant has been recognized with several awards, especially for its innovative wine list and magnificent "wall of wine," which holds some 3,000 wines from 750 labels. The menu highlights British Columbia's finest seafood, game, organic and local ingredients. The in-house pastry chef makes all the fresh breads, sorbets, ice creams, chocolates and desserts. Dressy casual. **Bar:** Full bar. **Reservations:** suggested. **Hours:** 11:30 am-2:30 & 5:30-11 pm, Sat & Sun from 5:30 pm. Closed: 1/1, 12/25. **Address:** 2881 Granville St V6H 3J4 **Location:** Between 12th and 13th aves. **Parking:** valet and street. **Cards:** AX, DC, MC, VI.

WHITE SPOT

Canadian

$8-$18

Phone: 604/261-2820

Open for three meals a day, the popular casual restaurant prepares offerings such as sandwiches and burgers, fresh salads, pastas and stir-fries, fish and chips, chargrilled sirloin steaks and chicken, in addition to a selection of yummy desserts. Casual dress. **Bar:** Full bar. **Hours:** 7:30 am-10 pm, Fri & Sat-11 pm. Closed: 12/25. **Address:** 613A-650 41st Ave V5Z 2M9 **Location:** 41st Ave and Cambie St; in Oakridge Mall. **Parking:** on-site. **Cards:** AX, DC, MC, VI.

WHITE SPOT

Canadian

$8-$12

Phone: 604/873-1252

Open for three meals a day, the popular casual restaurant prepares offerings such as sandwiches and burgers, fresh salads, pastas and stir-fries, fish and chips, chargrilled sirloin steaks and chicken, in addition to a selection of yummy desserts. Casual dress. **Bar:** Full bar. **Hours:** 6:30 am-10 pm, Fri & Sat-11 pm. Closed: 12/25. **Address:** 2850 Cambie St V5Z 1V5 **Location:** Corner of Cambie and 13th sts. **Parking:** on-site and street. **Cards:** AX, DC, MC, VI.

WILD GARLIC

Asian

$8-$28

Phone: 604/730-0880　⑰

Garlic is strictly supported in spicy dishes that blend Asian and European influences. Parking in the busy Broadway commercial district is a challenge, and street spots should be grabbed upon sight. Casual dress. **Bar:** Full bar. **Reservations:** suggested. **Hours:** 5 pm-10 pm, Wed-Fri also 11 am-2 pm. Closed: 12/25. **Address:** 2120 W Broadway V6K 2C8 **Location:** Between Arbutus and Yew sts. **Parking:** street. **Cards:** AX, DC, DS, MC, VI.

The Vancouver Vicinity

ALDERGROVE pop. 12,363

——— WHERE TO STAY ———

BEST WESTERN COUNTRY MEADOWS   *Book great rates at AAA.com*   **Phone: (604)856-9880**

Small-scale Hotel
$95-$229 3/1-9/5
$89-$129 9/6-2/28

Address: 3070 264th St V4W 3E1 **Location:** Trans-Canada Hwy 1, exit 73 (264th St/Aldergrove), 3.1 mi (5 km) s on 264th St (Hwy 13). **Facility:** 78 units. 77 one-bedroom standard units, some with efficiencies and/or whirlpools. 1 two-bedroom suite with kitchen and whirlpool. 2 stories (no elevator), interior corridors. **Parking:** on-site (fee). **Terms:** check-in 4 pm. **Amenities:** voice mail, irons, hair dryers. *Some:* high-speed Internet. **Pool(s):** heated indoor. **Leisure Activities:** whirlpool, limited exercise equipment. **Guest Services:** valet and coin laundry, wireless Internet. **Business Services:** meeting rooms, business center. **Cards:** AX, CB, DC, DS, MC, VI. **Free Special Amenities: expanded continental breakfast and high-speed Internet.** *(See color ad p 617)*

AAA Benefit:
Members save 10% everyday, plus an exclusive frequent stay program.

BURNABY pop. 202,799   (See map and index starting on p. 568)

——— WHERE TO STAY ———

ACCENT INNS   *Book great rates at AAA.com*   **Phone: (604)473-5000**   **23**

Motel
$119-$179 All Year

Address: 3777 Henning Dr V5C 6N5 **Location:** Trans-Canada Hwy 1, exit 28 (Grandview Hwy), just n on Boundary Rd. **Facility:** Smoke free premises. 128 one-bedroom standard units, some with efficiencies. 3 stories, exterior corridors. **Parking:** on-site. **Amenities:** voice mail, irons, hair dryers. *Some:* dual phone lines. **Leisure Activities:** sauna, whirlpool, limited exercise equipment. **Guest Services:** valet and coin laundry, wireless Internet. **Business Services:** meeting rooms, business center. **Cards:** AX, CB, DC, DS, MC, VI. **Free Special Amenities: newspaper and high-speed Internet.** *(See color ad p 639)*

BEST WESTERN KINGS INN AND CONFERENCE CENTRE   *Book great rates at AAA.com*   **Phone: 604/438-1383**   **26**

Small-scale Hotel
Rates not provided

Address: 5411 Kingsway V5H 2G1 **Location:** Trans-Canada Hwy 1, exit 29 (Willingdon Ave), 1.9 mi (3 km) s to Kingsway, then 1.2 mi (2 km) e. **Facility:** 132 one-bedroom standard units, some with efficiencies, kitchens and/or whirlpools. 2 stories (no elevator), exterior corridors. **Parking:** on-site. **Amenities:** high-speed Internet, voice mail, irons, hair dryers. **Pool(s):** heated outdoor. **Guest Services:** valet and coin laundry, wireless Internet. **Business Services:** meeting rooms. **Free Special Amenities: continental breakfast and high-speed Internet.**

AAA Benefit:
Members save 10% everyday, plus an exclusive frequent stay program.

(See map and index starting on p. 568)

HILTON VANCOUVER METROTOWN *Book great rates at AAA.com*   Phone: (604)438-1200   24

Large-scale Hotel
$140-$239 All Year

Address: 6083 McKay Ave V5H 2W7 **Location:** Trans-Canada Hwy 1, exit 29 (Willingdon Ave), 1.8 mi (3 km) s to Kingsway, then just e. Located next to Metrotown Shopping Mall. **Facility:** 283 one-bedroom standard units. 18 stories, interior corridors. **Parking:** on-site and valet. **Terms:** cancellation fee imposed. **Amenities:** video games (fee), high-speed Internet, dual phone lines, voice mail, irons, hair dryers. **Dining:** Crystal Bar and Grille, see separate listing. **Pool(s):** heated outdoor. **Leisure Activities:** whirlpool, exercise room. **Guest Services:** valet laundry. **Business Services:** conference facilities, business center. **Cards:** AX, DC, DS, MC, VI. **Free Special Amenities: high-speed Internet.** *(See color ad p 612)*

HOLIDAY INN EXPRESS METROTOWN *Book at AAA.com*   Phone: (604)438-1881   25

Small-scale Hotel
$149-$179 All Year

Address: 4405 Central Blvd V5H 4M3 **Location:** Trans-Canada Hwy 1, exit 29 (Willingdon Ave), 3.1 mi (5 km) s to Central Blvd, then just e. Located adjacent to a large shopping centre. **Facility:** 100 one-bedroom standard units. 6 stories, interior corridors. **Parking:** on-site. **Terms:** check-in 4 pm, cancellation fee imposed. **Amenities:** video games (fee), voice mail, irons, hair dryers. **Pool(s):** heated outdoor. **Leisure Activities:** limited exercise equipment. **Guest Services:** valet and coin laundry, wireless Internet. **Business Services:** meeting rooms, PC (fee). **Cards:** AX, DC, DS, JC, MC, VI.

LAKE CITY MOTOR INN   Phone: (604)294-5331   22

Motel
$94-$179 All Year

Address: 5415 Lougheed Hwy V5B 2Z7 **Location:** Trans-Canada Hwy 1, exit 29 (Willingdon Ave), just n, 0.6 mi (1 km) e on Lougheed Hwy, just n on Springer Ave, then just e on Broadway. Located in a residential area. **Facility:** 48 units. 42 one- and 6 two-bedroom standard units, some with efficiencies. 2 stories (no elevator), exterior corridors. **Parking:** on-site. **Terms:** cancellation fee imposed. **Amenities:** voice mail, irons. **Pool(s):** heated outdoor. **Leisure Activities:** whirlpool. **Guest Services:** coin laundry, wireless Internet. **Business Services:** meeting rooms. **Cards:** AX, MC, VI.

——— WHERE TO DINE ———

CACTUS CLUB CAFE   Phone: 604/291-6606

Canadian
$9-$29

This bustling, casual restaurant serves huge burgers, sandwiches, pasta, salads, soups, quesadillas, fajitas, vegetarian dishes, steak, ribs, chicken and fish. Featured are certified Angus beef and fresh wild British Columbia salmon. The thick and creamy milk shakes come highly recommended. Casual dress. **Bar:** Full bar. **Hours:** 11 am-midnight, Fri & Sat-1 am. Closed: 12/25. **Address:** 4219B Lougheed Hwy V5C 3Y6 **Location:** Between Gillmore and Madison aves. **Parking:** on-site. **Cards:** AX, MC, VI.

CRYSTAL BAR AND GRILLE   Phone: 604/438-1200   48

Continental
$9-$30

On the third floor of the Hilton Vancouver Metrotown, the 80-seat restaurant is open for breakfast, lunch and dinner and also serves a fabulous Sunday brunch. Creative dishes center on fish, beef or pasta. Casual dress. **Bar:** Full bar. **Reservations:** suggested. **Hours:** 6 am-11 pm. **Address:** 6083 McKay Ave V5H 2W7 **Location:** Trans-Canada Hwy 1, exit 29 (Willingdon Ave), 1.8 mi (3 km) s to Kingsway, then just e; in Hilton Vancouver Metrotown. **Parking:** on-site (fee) and valet. **Cards:** AX, DC, DS, JC, MC, VI. *(See color ad p 612)*

EARLS   Phone: 604/205-5025

Canadian
$10-$28

Offering an experience that falls between fast food and fine dining, the fun, relaxed restaurant prepares great food at a great price. Choices range from juicy burgers, hearty sandwiches, fresh salads, wings and pizza to full entrees of steak, chops and seafood. Made-from-scratch soups and assorted breads, as well as a nice choice of wines and beers, round out the offerings. This is a fitting spot for impromptu get-togethers and festive occasions. Casual dress. **Bar:** Full bar. **Hours:** 11:30 am-11 pm, Fri & Sat-midnight. Closed: 12/25. **Address:** 3838 Lougheed Hwy V5C 6N4 **Location:** Just e of Boundary Rd. **Parking:** on-site. **Cards:** AX, DC, MC, VI.

HART HOUSE ON DEER LAKE   Phone: 604/298-4278   47

Pacific Rim
$14-$36

The turn-of-the-20th-century, Tudor-style country home has been turned into a lovely restaurant overlooking Deer Lake and two acres of lush lawn. The menu features rack of lamb, fish and pasta, along with lighter fare for lunch. Casual dress. **Bar:** Full bar. **Reservations:** suggested. **Hours:** 11:30 am-2:30 & 5:30-9 pm, Fri-10 pm, Sat 5:30 pm-10 pm, Sun 11 am-2 & 5:30-9 pm; Sunday brunch. Closed: 1/1, 12/26; also Mon. **Address:** 6664 Deer Lake Ave V5E 4H3 **Location:** Trans-Canada Hwy 1, exit 33 (Kensington S), 0.6 mi (1 km) e on Canada Way to Sperling Ave, follow signs to Burnaby Village Museum. **Parking:** on-site. **Cards:** AX, MC, VI.

HORIZONS   Phone: 604/299-1155   46

Pacific Rim
$12-$30

Horizon's hilltop location in Burnaby Mountain Park gives you a spectacular view of the city and mountains. Its menu specializes in alderwood-fired fresh seafood and steak as well as rack of lamb and roasted duck. This is a casual, fine-dining experience. Dressy casual. **Bar:** Full bar. **Reservations:** suggested. **Hours:** 11:30 am-2 & 5-close, Sun from 11 am; Sunday brunch. Closed: 12/24, 12/25. **Address:** 100 Centennial Way V5A 2X9 **Location:** Lougheed Hwy, 3.1 mi (5 km) n on Gaglardi Way, 0.6 mi (1 km) w on University Dr, then just n, follow signs. **Parking:** on-site. **Cards:** AX, JC, MC, VI.

(See map and index starting on p. 568)

MILESTONE'S GRILL & BAR
Phone: 604/291-7393

Canadian
$12-$28

Popular with locals, the bustling eatery is a great gathering place. Diners enjoy the relaxed setting and casual menu featuring pasta, pizza, roasted chicken and a tasty choice of egg and brunch options. A nice wine list complements the food choices. Casual dress. **Bar:** Full bar. **Hours:** 11 am-10 pm, Fri-midnight, Sat 10 am-midnight, Sun 9:30 am-10 pm. Closed: 12/25. **Address:** 4420 Lougheed Hwy V5C 3Z3 **Location:** Between Rosser and Willingdon aves. **Parking:** on-site. **Cards:** AX, DC, MC, VI.

RICKY'S ALL DAY GRILL
Phone: 604/451-3400

Canadian
$6-$15

The comfortable eatery, which employs friendly servers, presents a varied menu that includes pasta dishes, wraps, omelets, stir-fry preparations and burgers. Portions are generous. Children's and senior selections are offered. Guests can request seating in a booth or at a table. Casual dress. **Bar:** Full bar. **Hours:** 7 am-9 pm, Sun-8 pm. **Address:** 259-4820 Kingsway V5H 4P1 **Location:** Between McMurray and Miller aves; in Metrotown Centre Mall. **Parking:** on-site. **Cards:** MC, VI.

SWISS CHALET
Phone: 604/299-1761

Canadian
$6-$18

The popular restaurant is known for its rotisserie chicken and ribs and the tangy Chalet sauce that gives food its special zip. Diners munch on a half or quarter chicken with sides such as steamed vegetables, fries, baked potatoes and salads. Lunch guests often go for the great soup and sandwich combination. Take-out and delivery service are popular options. Casual dress. **Bar:** Full bar. **Hours:** 11 am-10 pm, Fri & Sat-11 pm. Closed: 12/25. **Address:** 3860 Lougheed Hwy V5C 6N4 **Location:** Lougheed Hwy at Boundary Rd. **Parking:** on-site. **Cards:** AX, MC, VI.

COQUITLAM pop. 114,565   (See map and index starting on p. 568)

--- **WHERE TO STAY** ---

BEST WESTERN CHELSEA INN
Book great rates at AAA.com   **Phone:** (604)525-7777   **34**

Small-scale Hotel
$119-$139 3/1-9/30
$109-$129 10/1-2/28

Address: 725 Brunette Ave V3K 1C3 **Location:** Trans-Canada Hwy 1, exit 40B (Brunette Ave N). **Facility:** 61 units. 60 one-bedroom standard units, some with efficiencies and/or whirlpools. 1 two-bedroom suite with kitchen and whirlpool. 3 stories, interior corridors. **Parking:** on-site. **Amenities:** voice mail, irons, hair dryers. **Pool(s):** heated outdoor. **Leisure Activities:** sauna, whirlpool. **Guest Services:** valet and coin laundry, wireless Internet. **Cards:** AX, DC, DS, MC, VI. **Free Special Amenities:** continental breakfast and high-speed Internet.

AAA Benefit:
Members save 10% everyday, plus an exclusive frequent stay program.

BEST WESTERN COQUITLAM INN CONVENTION CENTRE
Book great rates at AAA.com   **Phone:** (604)931-9011   **32**

Small-scale Hotel
$132-$289 All Year

Address: 319 North Rd V3K 3V8 **Location:** Trans-Canada Hwy 1, exit 37 (Cariboo Rd/Gaglardi Way), 1.2 mi (2 km) e on Lougheed Hwy (Hwy 7), then just s. **Facility:** Smoke free premises. 106 units. 90 one-bedroom standard units, some with whirlpools. 16 two-bedroom suites with kitchens. 2 stories, interior/exterior corridors. **Parking:** on-site. **Terms:** cancellation fee imposed. **Amenities:** voice mail, irons, hair dryers. **Dining:** 2 restaurants. **Pool(s):** heated indoor. **Leisure Activities:** sauna, whirlpool, limited exercise equipment. **Guest Services:** valet laundry, wireless Internet. **Business Services:** conference facilities. **Cards:** AX, CB, DC, DS, JC, MC, VI. **Free Special Amenities:** local telephone calls and newspaper.

AAA Benefit:
Members save 10% everyday, plus an exclusive frequent stay program.

RAMADA INN COQUITLAM
Book at AAA.com   **Phone:** (604)931-4433   **33**

Small-scale Hotel
$110-$150 3/1-9/30
$90-$120 10/1-2/28

Address: 631 Lougheed Hwy V3K 3S5 **Location:** Trans-Canada Hwy 1, exit 44 (Coquitlam), 1.9 mi (3 km) w on Lougheed Hwy (Hwy 7). **Facility:** 84 one-bedroom standard units, some with whirlpools. 2 stories (no elevator), interior/exterior corridors. **Parking:** on-site. **Amenities:** voice mail, irons, hair dryers. **Pool(s):** heated indoor. **Leisure Activities:** whirlpool. **Guest Services:** valet and coin laundry. **Business Services:** meeting rooms. **Cards:** AX, CB, DC, DS, JC, MC, VI.

--- **WHERE TO DINE** ---

CACTUS CLUB CAFE
Phone: 604/777-0440

Canadian
$9-$29

This bustling, casual restaurant serves huge burgers, sandwiches, pasta, salads, soups, quesadillas, fajitas, vegetarian dishes, steak, ribs, chicken and fish. Featured are certified Angus beef and fresh wild British Columbia salmon. The thick and creamy milk shakes come highly recommended. Casual dress. **Bar:** Full bar. **Hours:** 11 am-midnight, Fri & Sat-1 am. Closed: 12/25. **Address:** 110-101 Schoolhouse St V3K 4X8 **Location:** From Lougheed Hwy, just n. **Parking:** on-site. **Cards:** AX, MC, VI.

JOEY TOMATO'S MEDITERRANEAN GRILL
Phone: 604/939-3077

Canadian
$8-$24

The cuisine blends Mediterranean and Asian cooking styles and emphasizes finger foods for sharing. Those who aren't big fans of tapas can consider full meal offerings centered on steaks and chops. Casual dress. **Bar:** Full bar. **Hours:** 11 am-1 am, Sun & Mon-midnight. Closed: 12/25. **Address:** 550 Lougheed Hwy V3K 353 **Location:** Trans-Canada Hwy 1, exit 37 (Gaglardi Way) eastbound, 2.3 mi (3.8 km) e on Longhead Hwy (Hwy 7); exit 44 (Coquitlam) westbound, 1.9 mi (3.2 km) w. **Parking:** on-site. **Cards:** AX, MC, VI.

(See map and index starting on p. 568)

MONTANA'S COOKHOUSE
Phone: 604/472-7772
Steak House $7-$25 — Pine boards, exposed beams, a fireplace and Western gear displayed about the dining room give the feeling of a back-country setting. The menu lists hearty portions of comfort fare, such as Yankee pot roast. While the focus is on steaks, ribs and chicken, some seafood entrees also are among offerings. Service is efficient and friendly. Casual dress. **Bar:** Full bar. **Hours:** 11 am-11 pm, Fri & Sat-midnight. **Address:** 2929 Barnet Hwy, Unit 1046 V3B 5R5 **Location:** Corner of Barnet and Lougheed hwys; in Coquitlam Centre Mall. **Parking:** on-site. **Cards:** AX, MC, VI.

PACIFIC RIM GRILLE
Phone: 604/939-4000 51
Pacific Rim $10-$30 — Located in a simple strip mall where there is plenty of free parking at the back of the building, the restaurant features a wonderful assortment of fresh seafood with their signature meat dish being wild boar. There is a fine selection of BC wines by the glass, both white and red, to complement your meal. Casual dress. **Bar:** Full bar. **Reservations:** suggested, for dinner. **Hours:** 11:30 am-2:30 & 5:30-9:30 pm, Fri-10 pm, Sat 5:30 pm-10 pm, Sun 5:30 pm-9 pm. Closed: 1/1, 12/25, 12/26; also Mon. **Address:** 1126 C Austin Ave V3K 3P5 **Location:** From Trans-Canada Hwy 1, exit 40B (Brunette Ave), 0.6 mi (1 km) n on Blue Mountain St, then just e; between Marmont and Gatensbury sts. **Parking:** on-site. **Cards:** AX, MC, VI.

RICKY'S ALL DAY GRILL
Phone: 604/468-8000
Canadian $6-$15 — The comfortable eatery, which employs friendly servers, presents a varied menu that includes pasta dishes, wraps, omelets, stir-fry preparations and burgers. Portions are generous. Children's and senior selections are offered. Guests can request seating in a booth or at a table. Casual dress. **Bar:** Full bar. **Hours:** 7:30 am-8 pm, Wed & Thurs-9 pm, Fri & Sat-10 pm. **Address:** 2929 Barnet Hwy, Unit 2660 V3B 5R5 **Location:** Just off Barnet Hwy; in Coquitlam Centre Mall. **Parking:** on-site. **Cards:** MC, VI.

DELTA pop. 96,723 (See map and index starting on p. 568)

—— WHERE TO STAY ——

CLAIR'S BED & BREAKFAST
Phone: 604/940-8867 60
Historic Bed & Breakfast $125-$185 3/1-9/30 $105-$145 10/1-2/28 — **Address:** 4919 48th Ave V4K 1V4 **Location:** Hwy 17, 1.1 mi (1.8 km) w on Ladner Trunk Rd to Elliott St, just n on 48th Ave. Located in Ladner Village. **Facility:** Built in 1913, this Edwardian-style house served as a family home for its first 60 years. In 1994 the home was purchased and converted into a B&B. Smoke free premises. 6 one-bedroom standard units, some with whirlpools. 2 stories (no elevator), interior corridors. **Bath:** combo, shower or tub only. **Parking:** on-site. **Terms:** office hours 8 am-8 pm, check-in 4 pm, 10 day cancellation notice-fee imposed. **Cards:** MC, VI. **Free Special Amenities:** full breakfast and high-speed Internet.

(See map and index starting on p. 568)

THE COAST TSAWWASSEN INN
Book great rates at AAA.com   Phone: (604)943-8221

Small-scale Hotel
$130-$240 3/1-9/30
$122-$232 10/1-2/28

Address: 1665 56th St V4L 2B2 **Location:** Hwy 99, exit 28 (Tsawwassen Ferries), 5 mi (8 km) w on Hwy 17; 3.1 mi (5 km) from the BC ferry terminal. **Facility:** 90 one-bedroom suites, some with kitchens and/or whirlpools. 3 stories, interior corridors. **Parking:** on-site. **Amenities:** video games (fee), voice mail, irons, hair dryers. *Some:* high-speed Internet. **Pool(s):** heated indoor. **Leisure Activities:** sauna, whirlpool, exercise room. **Guest Services:** valet and coin laundry, area transportation-ferry terminal, wireless Internet. **Business Services:** conference facilities, business center. **Cards:** AX, CB, DC, DS, JC, MC, VI. **Free Special Amenities: local telephone calls and newspaper.** *(See color ad p 602)*

DELTA TOWN & COUNTRY INN
Book great rates at AAA.com   Phone: (604)946-4404

Small-scale Hotel
$94-$101 All Year

Address: 6005 Hwy 17 at Hwy 99 V4K 5B8 **Location:** Hwy 17 at Hwy 99, exit 28 (River Rd). Located in a quiet rural area. **Facility:** 49 one-bedroom standard units. 2 stories (no elevator), interior corridors. **Parking:** on-site. **Terms:** cancellation fee imposed. **Amenities:** voice mail, irons, hair dryers. *Some:* high-speed Internet (fee). **Pool(s):** heated outdoor. **Leisure Activities:** exercise room. *Fee:* 5 tennis courts (4 indoor, 5 lighted). **Guest Services:** valet and coin laundry. **Business Services:** meeting rooms, business center. **Cards:** AX, CB, DC, MC, VI. **Free Special Amenities: local telephone calls and high-speed Internet.**

RIVER RUN COTTAGES
Phone: (604)946-7778

Bed & Breakfast
$150-$210 3/1-9/30
$129-$180 10/1-2/28

Address: 4551 River Rd W V4K 1R9 **Location:** Hwy 17, 1.6 mi (2.5 km) n on Ladner Trunk Rd (which becomes 47A St, then becomes River Rd W). Located in Ladner Village. **Facility:** These three self-contained cottages with decks are built on pillars over tidal mud flats on the Fraser River; one floating cottage is tied to a dock. Smoke free premises. 4 one-bedroom standard units. 1 story, exterior corridors. **Bath:** combo or shower only. **Parking:** on-site. **Terms:** office hours 7 am-10 pm, check-in 4 pm, 21 day cancellation notice-fee imposed. **Amenities:** CD players, hair dryers. **Leisure Activities:** bicycles. **Cards:** MC, VI.

──────── **WHERE TO DINE** ────────

CACTUS CLUB CAFE
Phone: 604/591-1707

Canadian
$9-$29

This bustling, casual restaurant serves huge burgers, sandwiches, pasta, salads, soups, quesadillas, fajitas, vegetarian dishes, steak, ribs, chicken and fish. Featured are certified Angus beef and fresh wild British Columbia salmon. The thick and creamy milk shakes come highly recommended. Casual dress. **Bar:** Full bar. **Hours:** 11 am-midnight, Fri & Sat-1 am. Closed: 12/25. **Address:** 7907 120th St V4C 6P6 **Location:** Just s from 80th Ave. **Parking:** on-site. **Cards:** AX, MC, VI.

LA BELLE AUBERGE
Menu on AAA.com   Phone: 604/946-7717

French
$30-$35

For more than 25 years, the charming Ladner home has served as a comfortable inn serving fine French cuisine. The restaurant is owned and operated by a chef who competed with the Canadian Culinary Olympic team in the '80s and judged the competition in the '90s. A six-course meal costs $80; a la carte ordering is another option. Casual dress. **Bar:** Full bar. **Reservations:** suggested. **Hours:** 6 pm-11 pm. Closed: Sun, Mon & 1/1-1/15. **Address:** 4856 48th Ave V4K 1V2 **Location:** Hwy 17, 1.1 mi (1.8 km) w on Ladner Trunk Rd to Elliott St, then just n. **Parking:** on-site. **Cards:** AX, DC, MC, VI.

RICKY'S ALL DAY GRILL
Phone: 604/599-1784

Canadian
$6-$15

The comfortable eatery, which employs friendly servers, presents a varied menu that includes pasta dishes, wraps, omelets, stir-fry preparations and burgers. Portions are generous. Children's and senior selections are offered. Guests can request seating in a booth or at a table. Casual dress. **Bar:** Full bar. **Hours:** 6 am-9 pm, Sun from 7 am. **Address:** 7135 120th St V4E 2A9 **Location:** Just s of 72nd Ave. **Parking:** on-site. **Cards:** MC, VI.

LANGLEY pop. 23,606   (See map and index starting on p. 568)

──────── **WHERE TO STAY** ────────

BEST VALUE WESTWARD INN
Book great rates at AAA.com   Phone: 604/534-9238

Motel
$75-$95 All Year

Address: 19650 Fraser Hwy V3A 4C7 **Location:** Trans-Canada Hwy 1, exit 58 (200th St/Langley City), 3.1 mi (5 km) s on 200th St, 0.6 mi (1 km) w on Hwy 10, then just w. **Facility:** 55 one-bedroom standard units, some with kitchens. 1 story, exterior corridors. **Parking:** on-site. **Guest Services:** coin laundry. **Business Services:** PC. **Cards:** AX, MC, VI. **Free Special Amenities: local telephone calls and early check-in/late check-out.**

(See map and index starting on p. 568)

BEST WESTERN LANGLEY INN *Book great rates at AAA.com* Phone: 604/530-9311

Small-scale Hotel
Rates not provided

Address: 5978 Glover Rd V3A 4H9 **Location:** Trans-Canada Hwy 1, exit 66 (232nd St), 6 km s, follow signs. **Facility:** 78 units. 77 one-bedroom standard units, some with efficiencies. 1 two-bedroom suite with kitchen. 2 stories (no elevator), interior corridors. **Parking:** on-site. **Amenities:** video games (fee), voice mail, irons, hair dryers. **Pool(s):** heated indoor. **Leisure Activities:** whirlpool, limited exercise equipment. **Guest Services:** valet and coin laundry, wireless Internet. **Business Services:** meeting rooms, business center. **Free Special Amenities:** expanded continental breakfast and high-speed Internet. *(See color ad below)*

AAA Benefit:
Members save 10% everyday, plus an exclusive frequent stay program.

    / SOME UNITS FEE

(See map and index starting on p. 568)

COAST HOTEL & CONVENTION CENTRE — *Book great rates at AAA.com*
Phone: (604)530-1500 **80**

(CAA) [SAVE]

◆◆◆◆

Small-scale Hotel
$125-$165 3/1-9/30
$115-$155 10/1-2/28

Address: 20393 Fraser Hwy V3A 7N2 **Location:** Trans-Canada Hwy 1, exit 58 (200th St/Langley City), 3.9 mi (6.3 km) s on 200th St, then just e. **Facility:** 77 one-bedroom standard units. 6 stories, interior corridors. **Parking:** on-site. **Amenities:** CD players, high-speed Internet, dual phone lines, voice mail, irons, hair dryers. **Dining:** 2 restaurants. **Leisure Activities:** steamrooms, exercise room. **Guest Services:** valet laundry. **Business Services:** conference facilities, business center. **Cards:** AX, DC, MC, VI. **Free Special Amenities: local telephone calls and newspaper.**

[icons]

HOLIDAY INN EXPRESS HOTEL & SUITES LANGLEY — *Book great rates at AAA.com*
Phone: (604)882-2000 **77**

(CAA) [SAVE]

◆◆◆

Small-scale Hotel
$114-$144 All Year

Address: 8750 204th St V1M 2Y5 **Location:** Trans-Canada Hwy 1, exit 58 (200th St/Langley City), just e on 88th Ave. **Facility:** Smoke free premises. 85 one-bedroom standard units, some with whirlpools. 4 stories, interior corridors. **Parking:** on-site. **Amenities:** video games (fee), high-speed Internet, dual phone lines, voice mail, irons, hair dryers. **Pool(s):** heated indoor. **Leisure Activities:** sauna, whirlpool, steamroom, limited exercise equipment. **Business Services:** meeting rooms, PC (fee). **Cards:** AX, CB, DC, DS, JC, MC, VI. **Free Special Amenities: continental breakfast and high-speed Internet.** *(See color ad on insert)*

[icons]

SANDMAN HOTEL LANGLEY
Phone: 604/888-7263 **76**

◆◆◆

Small-scale Hotel
Rates not provided

Address: 8855 202nd St V1M 2N9 **Location:** Trans-Canada Hwy 1, exit 58 (200th St/Langley City), just e on 88th Ave. **Facility:** 145 units. 129 one-bedroom standard units, some with efficiencies. 16 one-bedroom suites. 4 stories, interior corridors. **Parking:** on-site. **Amenities:** high-speed Internet, voice mail, irons, hair dryers. **Leisure Activities:** limited exercise equipment. **Guest Services:** valet laundry. **Business Services:** meeting rooms, PC.

[icons]

SUPER 8 LANGLEY/ALDERGROVE — *Book at AAA.com*
Phone: (604)856-8288

◆◆◆

Motel
$89-$99 3/1-10/31
$71-$79 11/1-2/28

Address: 26574 Gloucester Way V4W 4A8 **Location:** Trans-Canada Hwy 1, exit 73 (264th St/Aldergrove), just e on 56th Ave. **Facility:** Smoke free premises. 81 units. 69 one-bedroom standard units. 12 one-bedroom suites. 4 stories, interior corridors. **Parking:** on-site. **Amenities:** high-speed Internet, voice mail, hair dryers. **Pool(s):** heated indoor. **Leisure Activities:** whirlpool, waterslide, limited exercise equipment. **Guest Services:** valet and coin laundry, wireless Internet. **Business Services:** meeting rooms, PC (fee). **Cards:** AX, CB, DC, DS, JC, MC, VI.

[icons]

SUPER 8 LANGLEY CITY — *Book great rates at AAA.com*
Phone: (604)514-3111

◆◆◆

Motel
$80-$90 All Year

Address: 6722 Glover Rd V2Y 1S6 **Location:** Trans-Canada Hwy 1, exit 66 (232nd St), 2.5 mi (4 km) s on Glover Rd, follow signs. Located close to railroad tracks. **Facility:** 46 one-bedroom standard units. 2 stories, interior corridors. **Bath:** combo or shower only. **Parking:** on-site. **Amenities:** voice mail. **Leisure Activities:** sauna, limited exercise equipment. **Guest Services:** valet laundry, wireless Internet. **Business Services:** meeting rooms. **Cards:** AX, DC, MC, VI. *(See color ad on insert)*

[icons]

--------- **WHERE TO DINE** ---------

KELSEY'S
Phone: 604/514-9100

◆◆

Canadian
$7-$21

A fun, relaxed atmosphere and tasty menu of casual fare make the restaurant a popular favorite with locals. Diners might start a meal with some tempting appetizers, such as wings, loaded potato skins or nachos, and follow them with an old-time favorite, such as a burger, wrap, pizza or pasta dish. For a heartier meal, it's hard to beat pork back ribs or a steak. The diverse menu has broad appeal. Casual dress. **Bar:** Full bar. **Hours:** 11 am-11 pm, Fri & Sat-midnight. **Address:** 300-20020 Willowbrook Rd V2Y 2T4 **Location:** Between 64th Ave and Hwy 10. **Parking:** on-site. **Cards:** AX, MC, VI.

MONTANA'S COOKHOUSE
Phone: 604/532-6799

◆◆

Steak House
$7-$25

Pine boards, exposed beams, a fireplace and Western gear displayed about the dining room give the feeling of a back-country setting. The menu lists hearty portions of comfort fare, such as Yankee pot roast. While the focus is on steaks, ribs and chicken, some seafood entrees also are among offerings. Service is efficient and friendly. Casual dress. **Bar:** Full bar. **Hours:** 11 am-11 pm, Fri & Sat-midnight. Closed: 12/25. **Address:** 20100 Langley Bypass V3A 9J7 **Location:** Trans-Canada Hwy 1, exit 58 (200th St/Langley City), 3.4 mi (5.5 km) s, then just e on Hwy 10. **Parking:** on-site. **Cards:** AX, MC, VI.

MOXIE'S CLASSIC GRILL
Phone: 604/539-9491

◆◆

Canadian
$8-$18

This sleek, funky and popular restaurant presents an extensive menu of creatively prepared dishes, including pizza, pasta, rice, noodles, signature salads and burgers. Other menus include one for children and one for Sunday brunch. Lending to the upbeat, stylish decor are dark wood appointments and river rock fireplaces. Casual dress. **Bar:** Full bar. **Hours:** 11 am-midnight, Fri & Sat-1 am. **Address:** 19777 Willowbrook Dr V3A 8H2 **Location:** Trans-Canada Hwy 1, exit 58 (200th St/Langley City), just e on 88th Ave. **Parking:** on-site. **Cards:** AX, MC, VI.

RICKY'S ALL DAY GRILL
Phone: 604/530-4317

◆◆

Canadian
$6-$15

The comfortable eatery, which employs friendly servers, presents a varied menu that includes pasta dishes, wraps, omelets, stir-fry preparations and burgers. Portions are generous. Children's and senior selections are offered. Guests can request seating in a booth or at a table. Casual dress. **Bar:** Full bar. **Hours:** 6:30 am-9 pm, Fri & Sat-10 pm. **Address:** 22314 Fraser Hwy V3A 8M6 **Location:** Between 222nd and 223A sts. **Parking:** on-site. **Cards:** MC, VI.

(See map and index starting on p. 568)

RICKY'S RESTAURANT   Phone: 604/888-4211

▼▼▼ ▼▼▼
Canadian
$9-$22

The comfortable eatery, which employs friendly servers, presents a varied menu that includes pasta dishes, wraps, omelets, stir-fry preparations and burgers. Portions are generous. Children's and senior selections are offered. Guests can request seating in a booth or at a table. Casual dress. **Bar:** Full bar. **Hours:** 6 am-9 pm. Closed: 12/25. **Address:** 8720 204th St V3A 8G5 **Location:** Trans-Canada Hwy 1, exit 58 (200th St/Langley City), just e on 88th Ave. **Parking:** on-site. **Cards:** MC, VI.

SWISS CHALET   Phone: 604/530-6007

▼▼ ▼▼
Canadian
$6-$18

The popular restaurant is known for its rotisserie chicken and ribs and the tangy Chalet sauce that gives food its special zip. Diners munch on a half or quarter chicken with sides such as steamed vegetables, fries, baked potatoes and salads. Lunch guests often go for the great soup and sandwich combination. Take-out and delivery service are popular options. Casual dress. **Bar:** Full bar. **Hours:** 11 am-10 pm. Closed: 12/25. **Address:** 20065 Langley Bypass V3A 8R6 **Location:** Langley Bypass at 200th St. **Parking:** on-site. **Cards:** AX, MC, VI.

MAPLE RIDGE pop. 68,949

——— WHERE TO STAY ———

BEST WESTERN MAPLE RIDGE   *Book great rates at AAA.com*   Phone: 604/463-5111

(CAA) (SAVE)

◆◆◆
Small-scale Hotel
Rates not provided

Address: 21735 Lougheed Hwy V2X 2S2 **Location:** 1.2 mi (2 km) w on Lougheed Hwy (Hwy 7). **Facility:** 61 one-bedroom standard units, some with kitchens and/or whirlpools. 2 stories (no elevator), exterior corridors. **Parking:** on-site. **Amenities:** high-speed Internet, voice mail, irons, hair dryers. **Leisure Activities:** whirlpool, limited exercise equipment. **Guest Services:** coin laundry. **Business Services:** meeting rooms. **Free Special Amenities:** local telephone calls and high-speed Internet.

AAA Benefit:

Members save 10% everyday, plus an exclusive frequent stay program.

🍴 💻 / SOME UNITS FEE 🐕 ✕ 🗄 🖨

TRAVELODGE MAPLE RIDGE   *Book great rates at AAA.com*   Phone: (604)467-1511

(CAA) (SAVE)

◆◆ ◆
Motel
$99-$110 3/1-9/30
$90-$100 10/1-2/28

Address: 21650 Lougheed Hwy V2X 2S1 **Location:** 1.2 mi (2 km) w on Lougheed Hwy (Hwy 7). **Facility:** 56 one-bedroom standard units, some with efficiencies. 2 stories (no elevator), interior corridors. **Parking:** on-site. **Terms:** cancellation fee imposed. **Amenities:** hair dryers. **Leisure Activities:** sauna, whirlpool, limited exercise equipment. **Guest Services:** valet and coin laundry, wireless Internet. **Business Services:** meeting rooms. **Cards:** AX, DC, JC, MC, VI. **Free Special Amenities:** continental breakfast and local telephone calls.

S/D 🍴 ✕ 💻 / SOME UNITS FEE 🐕 ✕ 🗄 🖨

——— WHERE TO DINE ———

SWISS CHALET   Phone: 604/460-8033

▼▼▼
Canadian
$6-$18

The popular restaurant is known for its rotisserie chicken and ribs and the tangy Chalet sauce that gives food its special zip. Diners munch on a half or quarter chicken with sides such as steamed vegetables, fries, baked potatoes and salads. Lunch guests often go for the great soup and sandwich combination. Take-out and delivery service are popular options. Casual dress. **Bar:** Full bar. **Hours:** 11 am-9 pm, Fri & Sat-10 pm. Closed: 12/25. **Address:** 20395 Lougheed Hwy V2X 2P9 **Location:** Lougheed Hwy (Hwy 7) at 203rd St. **Parking:** on-site. **Cards:** AX, MC, VI.

MISSION pop. 34,505

———— WHERE TO STAY ————

BEST WESTERN MISSION CITY LODGE   *Book great rates at AAA.com*   Phone: 604/820-5500

Small-scale Hotel
Rates not provided

Address: 32281 Lougheed Hwy V2V 1A3 **Location:** Just w of Hwy 11; corner of Lougheed Hwy (Hwy 7) and Hurd St. **Facility:** 80 one-bedroom standard units, some with efficiencies and/or whirlpools. 4 stories, interior corridors. *Bath:* combo or shower only. **Parking:** on-site. **Amenities:** high-speed Internet, voice mail, irons, hair dryers. **Pool(s):** heated indoor. **Leisure Activities:** sauna, whirlpool, limited exercise equipment. **Guest Services:** coin laundry. **Business Services:** meeting rooms. **Free Special Amenities:** local telephone calls and high-speed Internet.

AAA Benefit:
Members save 10% everyday, plus an exclusive frequent stay program.

———— WHERE TO DINE ————

SPURS GRILL HOUSE   Phone: 604/820-8525

Canadian
$7-$23

In a large shopping complex, the family-oriented restaurant treats guests to fine dining at affordable prices. Daily lunch specials are offered until 3 pm and daily appetizer and beer specials from 3 pm to 6 pm. Free parking is plentiful. Casual dress. **Bar:** Full bar. **Hours:** 11 am-10 pm, Fri & Sat-11 pm. Closed: 12/25. **Address:** 32555 London Ave, #130 V2V 6M7 **Location:** Jct Hwy 7 and 11; in Junction Shopping Centre. **Parking:** on-site. **Cards:** AX, MC, VI.

NEW WESTMINSTER pop. 58,549   (See map and index starting on p. 568)

———— WHERE TO STAY ————

INN AT WESTMINSTER QUAY   *Book great rates at AAA.com*   Phone: (604)520-1776   **37**

Small-scale Hotel
$200-$235 3/1-9/30
$192-$225 10/1-2/28

Address: 900 Quayside Dr V3M 6G1 **Location:** Along waterfront, follow signs to Westminster Quay. Located adjacent to public market. **Facility:** 126 one-bedroom standard units, some with whirlpools. 9 stories, interior corridors. *Bath:* combo or shower only. **Amenities:** video games (fee), voice mail, honor bars, irons, hair dryers. **Leisure Activities:** sauna, whirlpool, exercise room. **Guest Services:** valet laundry, wireless Internet. **Business Services:** conference facilities. **Cards:** AX, DC, DS, JC, MC, VI. **Free Special Amenities:** newspaper and high-speed Internet.

———— WHERE TO DINE ————

THE BOATHOUSE RESTAURANT   Phone: 604/525-3474

Seafood
$10-$37

Along the water at Westminster Quay, the relaxed restaurant lets diners look out over the Fraser River. An extensive selection of wines and cocktails complements the great seafood dishes. Casual dress. **Bar:** Full bar. **Reservations:** suggested. **Hours:** 6:30 am-3 & 5-10 pm, Sat from 11:30 am, Sun 8 am-3 & 5-9 pm. Closed: 12/25. **Address:** 900 Quayside Dr V3M 6G1 **Location:** Along the waterfront, follow signs to Westminster Quay. **Parking:** on-site (fee). **Cards:** AX, DC, MC, VI.

BURGER HEAVEN   Phone: 604/522-8339   **55**

American
$7-$18

This locally popular dining spot features all kinds of burgers—chicken, veggie, beef—cooked to order and served with many different fresh toppings. They also have a wide variety of sandwiches, a living-room atmosphere, beer, wine and coolers. Casual dress. **Bar:** Beer & wine. **Hours:** 11:30 am-9 pm, Fri & Sat-10 pm. Closed: 12/25. **Address:** 77 10th St V3M 3X4 **Location:** From Royal Ave, just e. **Parking:** street. **Cards:** AX, MC, VI.

LA RUSTICA RISTORANTE   Phone: 604/525-6355   **54**

Italian
$10-$24

This restaurant's traditional homemade cuisine is complemented by French and Continental dishes. The veal piccata and pepper steak are good choices. The setting was converted from two older side-by-side houses. The servers are pleasant and friendly. Casual dress. **Bar:** Full bar. **Reservations:** suggested, weekends. **Hours:** 11:30 am-2 & 5-10 pm, Fri-10:30 pm, Sat 5 pm-10:30 pm, Sun 5 pm-10 pm. Closed: 12/25. **Address:** 228 6th St V3L 3A4 **Location:** Between 3rd and 2nd aves. **Parking:** on-site and street. **Cards:** AX, DC, MC, VI.

NORTH VANCOUVER pop. 44,303   (See map and index starting on p. 568)

———— WHERE TO STAY ————

BEST WESTERN CAPILANO INN & SUITES   *Book great rates at AAA.com*   Phone: (604)987-8185   **18**

Motel
$99-$169 All Year

Address: 1634 Capilano Rd V7P 3B4 **Location:** Trans-Canada Hwy 1, exit 14 (Capilano Rd), 0.9 mi (1.5 km) s; from north end of Lions Gate Bridge, 0.6 mi (1 km) e on Marine Dr, then just n. **Facility:** 74 units. 73 one- and 1 two-bedroom standard units, some with efficiencies, kitchens and/or whirlpools. 2 stories (no elevator), exterior corridors. **Parking:** on-site. **Amenities:** voice mail, irons, hair dryers. *Some:* high-speed Internet. **Pool(s):** heated outdoor. **Guest Services:** coin laundry, wireless Internet. **Business Services:** meeting rooms. **Cards:** AX, DS, MC, VI. **Free Special Amenities:** local telephone calls and high-speed Internet.

AAA Benefit:
Members save 10% everyday, plus an exclusive frequent stay program.

(See map and index starting on p. 568)

COMFORT INN AND SUITES   *Book great rates at AAA.com*   Phone: 604-988-3181   **15**

Motel
$79-$269 All Year

Address: 1748 Capilano Rd V7P 3B4 **Location:** Trans-Canada Hwy 1, exit 14 (Capilano Rd), 0.9 mi (1.5 km) s; from north end of Lions Gate Bridge, 0.6 mi (1 km) e on Marine Dr, then just n. **Facility:** 94 units. 91 one- and 3 two-bedroom standard units, some with efficiencies or kitchens. 2 stories (no elevator), exterior corridors. **Parking:** on-site. **Terms:** cancellation fee imposed. **Amenities:** voice mail, hair dryers. *Some:* high-speed Internet. **Pool(s):** heated outdoor. **Leisure Activities:** whirlpool. **Guest Services:** coin laundry, wireless Internet. **Business Services:** meeting rooms. **Cards:** AX, DC, DS, MC, VI. **Free Special Amenities: continental breakfast and local telephone calls.**
(See color ad on insert)

GROUSE INN   *Book great rates at AAA.com*   Phone: (604)988-7101   **17**

Motel
$75-$175 All Year

Address: 1633 Capilano Rd V7P 3B3 **Location:** Trans-Canada Hwy 1, exit 14 (Capilano Rd), 0.9 mi (1.5 km) s; from north end of Lions Gate Bridge, 0.6 mi (1 km) e on Marine Dr. **Facility:** 73 one- and 7 two-bedroom standard units, some with efficiencies, kitchens and/or whirlpools. 2 stories (no elevator), exterior corridors. **Parking:** on-site. **Terms:** cancellation fee imposed. **Amenities:** voice mail, irons, hair dryers. **Pool(s):** heated outdoor. **Guest Services:** coin laundry, wireless Internet. **Business Services:** meeting rooms, PC (fee). **Cards:** AX, CB, DC, DS, JC, MC, VI.
(See color ad p 580)

HOLIDAY INN HOTEL & SUITES NORTH VANCOUVER   *Book great rates at AAA.com*   Phone: (604)985-3111   **19**

Large-scale Hotel
$199-$329 All Year

Address: 700 Old Lillooet Rd V7J 2H5 **Location:** Trans-Canada Hwy 1, exit 22 (Mt Seymour Pkwy), follow signs. **Facility:** 162 one-bedroom standard units, some with efficiencies and/or whirlpools. 6 stories, interior corridors. **Parking:** on-site. **Amenities:** video games (fee), high-speed Internet, dual phone lines, voice mail, safes, irons, hair dryers. **Pool(s):** heated indoor. **Leisure Activities:** sauna, whirlpool, exercise room. **Guest Services:** valet and coin laundry. **Business Services:** meeting rooms. **Cards:** AX, DC, DS, JC, MC, VI. **Free Special Amenities: newspaper and high-speed Internet.**
(See color ad on insert, p 606 & below)

LIONSGATE TRAVELODGE   *Book at AAA.com*   Phone: (604)985-5311   **16**

Motel
$69-$149 All Year

Address: 2060 Marine Dr V7P 1V7 **Location:** Trans-Canada Hwy 1, exit 14 (Capilano Rd), 0.9 mi (1.5 km) s, then just w; from north end of Lions Gate Bridge, just e. **Facility:** 61 one-bedroom standard units. 2 stories (no elevator), exterior corridors. *Bath:* combo or shower only. **Parking:** on-site. **Amenities:** irons, hair dryers. **Pool(s):** heated outdoor. **Cards:** AX, DC, MC, VI.

NORTH VANCOUVER HOTEL   *Book great rates at AAA.com*   Phone: (604)987-4461   **14**

Motel
$109-$159 3/1-8/31
$79-$109 9/1-2/28

Address: 1800 Capilano Rd V7P 3B6 **Location:** Trans-Canada Hwy 1, exit 14 (Capilano Rd), 0.9 mi (1.5 km) s; from north end of Lions Gate Bridge, 0.6 mi (1 km) e on Marine Dr, then just n. **Facility:** 72 one-bedroom standard units, some with kitchens. 2 stories (no elevator), exterior corridors. **Parking:** on-site. **Amenities:** high-speed Internet, voice mail, irons, hair dryers. **Pool(s):** heated outdoor. **Guest Services:** valet and coin laundry. **Cards:** AX, DC, JC, MC, VI. **Free Special Amenities: continental breakfast and high-speed Internet.**
(See color ad p 605)

(See map and index starting on p. 568)

———— **WHERE TO DINE** ————

CACTUS CLUB CAFE

Canadian
$9-$29

Phone: 604/986-5776

This bustling, casual restaurant serves huge burgers, sandwiches, pasta, salads, soups, quesadillas, fajitas, vegetarian dishes, steak, ribs, chicken and fish. Featured are certified Angus beef and fresh wild British Columbia salmon. The thick and creamy milk shakes come highly recommended. Casual dress. **Bar:** Full bar. **Hours:** 11 am-midnight, Fri & Sat-1 am. Closed: 12/25. **Address:** 1598 Pemberton Ave V7P 2S2 **Location:** From Marine Dr, just w at W 16th St. **Parking:** on-site. **Cards:** AX, MC, VI.

THE EDGE BISTRO

Mediterranean
$8-$26

Phone: 604/985-9125   40

In the quaint Edgemont Shopping Village on the road to Grouse Mountain, the quaint restaurant prepares a large selection of pastas in the $14 range and poultry, meats and seafood in the $20 range. Selections from the primarily Italian wine list are reasonably priced. Don't leave without trying the amazing tiramisu. Casual dress. **Bar:** Full bar. **Reservations:** suggested. **Hours:** 11 am-2:30 & 5-close, Sat & Sun from 5 pm. Closed 12/25. **Address:** 3135 Edgemont Blvd V7R 2N7 **Location:** 1.1 mi (1.8 km) n on Capilano Rd, 0.6 mi (1 km) e on Ridgewood Dr, then just s; in Edgemont Village. **Parking:** street. **Cards:** AX, MC, VI.

GUSTO DI QUATTRO

Italian
$10-$31

Phone: 604/924-4444   43

Translated, Gusto di Quattro means "a taste of Quattro." The North Shore favorite, which has a small dining space, is by Lonsdale Quay Market. Wonderful pastas and freshly made breads await. Patrons likely will have to wait for a table if they didn't make a reservation. A pay parking lot is right across the street. Casual dress. **Bar:** Full bar. **Reservations:** suggested. **Hours:** 11 am-2:30 & 5-10 pm, Sat & Sun from 5 pm. Closed: 1/1, 12/25, 12/26. **Address:** 1 Lonsdale Ave V7M 2E4 **Location:** Trans-Canada Hwy 1, exit 18 (Lonsdale Ave), 1.6 mi (2.5 km) s to Lonsdale Quay Market. **Parking:** street. **Cards:** AX, DC, MC, VI.

JAGERHOF SCHNITZEL HOUSE

German
$9-$17

Phone: 604/980-4316   42

Just north of the Sea Bus terminal on Lonsdale and near the shops of Lonsdale Quay Market, the cozy little restaurant lures a loyal clientele for wonderful schnitzels. The only available parking is on the street. Casual dress. **Bar:** Full bar. **Reservations:** suggested, for dinner. **Hours:** 11:30 am-1:30 & 5-9:30 pm, Sat & Sun from 5 pm. Closed: 12/25, 12/26; also Mon. **Address:** 71 Lonsdale Ave V7M 2E5 **Location:** Between 1st St and Esplanade. **Parking:** street. **Cards:** AX, DC, MC, VI.

KELSEY'S

Canadian
$7-$21

Phone: 604/924-5100

A fun, relaxed atmosphere and tasty menu of casual fare make the restaurant a popular favorite with locals. Diners might start a meal with some tempting appetizers, such as wings, loaded potato skins or nachos, and follow them with an old-time favorite, such as a burger, wrap, pizza or pasta dish. For a heartier meal, it's hard to beat pork back ribs or a steak. The diverse menu has broad appeal. Casual dress. **Bar:** Full bar. **Hours:** 11 am-10 pm, Fri & Sat-midnight. **Address:** 1378 Main St V7J 1C6 **Location:** Main St and Harbour Rd. **Parking:** on-site. **Cards:** AX, MC, VI.

MOUSTACHE CAFE

Pacific Rim
$10-$32

Phone: 604/987-8461   41

The decor is bright and colorful inside the cozy 1918 home that serves as the setting for this cafe. A West Coast flair is evident in preparations made from ingredients found only in British Columbia. Limited parking is found in the rear. Casual dress. **Bar:** Full bar. **Reservations:** suggested. **Hours:** 11:30 am-2:30 & 5:30-10:30 pm, Sat & Sun from 5:30 pm. Closed major holidays; also Mon. **Address:** 1265 Marine Dr V7P 1T3 **Location:** Between Bridgman and Pemberton aves. **Parking:** on-site. **Cards:** AX, MC, VI.

RICKY'S ALL DAY GRILL

Canadian
$6-$15

Phone: 604/904-4430

The comfortable eatery, which employs friendly servers, presents a varied menu that includes pasta dishes, wraps, omelets, stir-fry preparations and burgers. Portions are generous. Children's and senior selections are offered. Guests can request seating in a booth or at a table. Casual dress. **Bar:** Full bar. **Hours:** 7 am-9 pm, Fri & Sat-10 pm. **Address:** 1995 Lonsdale Ave V7M 2K3 **Location:** Between 20th and 19th sts. **Parking:** on-site. **Cards:** MC, VI.

SWISS CHALET
Canadian
$6-$18

Phone: 604/986-1858

The popular restaurant is known for its rotisserie chicken and ribs and the tangy Chalet sauce that gives food its special zip. Diners munch on a half or quarter chicken with sides such as steamed vegetables, fries, baked potatoes and salads. Lunch guests often go for the great soup and sandwich combination. Take-out and delivery service are popular options. Casual dress. **Bar:** Full bar. **Hours:** 11 am-10 pm. Closed: 12/25. **Address:** 801 Marine Dr V7P 3K6 **Location:** Marine Dr at Fell Ave. **Parking:** on-site. **Cards:** AX, MC, VI.

PITT MEADOWS pop. 15,623   (See map and index starting on p. 568)

———— **WHERE TO STAY** ————

RAMADA INN & SUITES HOTEL ROYALE
Book at AAA.com
Small-scale Hotel
$112 3/1-9/30
$89 10/1-2/28

Phone: (604)460-9859   29

Address: 19267 Lougheed Hwy V3Y 2J5 **Location:** Lougheed Hwy (Hwy 7) and Harris Rd. **Facility:** 80 one-bedroom standard units, some with efficiencies and/or whirlpools. 3 stories, interior corridors. **Parking:** on-site. **Terms:** check-in 4 pm. **Amenities:** high-speed Internet, voice mail, irons, hair dryers. **Pool(s):** heated outdoor. **Leisure Activities:** whirlpool, limited exercise equipment. **Guest Services:** valet and coin laundry, wireless Internet. **Business Services:** meeting rooms. **Cards:** AX, CB, DC, DS, JC, MC, VI.

PORT COQUITLAM pop. 52,687

——— WHERE TO DINE ———

EARLS

Canadian
$8-$15

Phone: 604/941-1733

Offering an experience that falls between fast food and fine dining, the fun, relaxed restaurant prepares great food at a great price. Choices range from juicy burgers, hearty sandwiches, fresh salads, wings and pizza to full entrees of steak, chops and seafood. Made-from-scratch soups and assorted breads, as well as a nice choice of wines and beers, round out the offerings. This is a fitting spot for impromptu get-togethers and festive occasions. Casual dress. **Bar:** Full bar. **Hours:** 11:30 am-10:30 pm, Fri & Sat-11 pm. Closed: 12/25. **Address:** 5100 Lougheed Hwy V3C 6K5 **Location:** Corner of Shaughnessy St and Lougheed Hwy (Hwy 7). **Parking:** on-site. **Cards:** AX, MC, VI.

RICHMOND pop. 174,461   (See map and index starting on p. 568)

——— WHERE TO STAY ———

ACCENT INNS   *Book great rates at AAA.com*   **Phone: (604)273-3311**

Small-scale Hotel
$99-$169 All Year

Address: 10551 St. Edwards Dr V6X 3L8 **Location:** Hwy 99, exit 39 (Bridgeport/Airport) northbound to St. Edwards Dr; exit 39A (Richmond/Airport) southbound to St. Edwards Dr. **Facility:** 206 one-bedroom standard units, some with efficiencies. 3 stories, exterior corridors. **Parking:** on-site. **Amenities:** voice mail, irons, hair dryers. *Some:* high-speed Internet. **Leisure Activities:** whirlpool, limited exercise equipment. **Guest Services:** valet and coin laundry, wireless Internet. **Business Services:** meeting rooms, PC. **Cards:** AX, CB, DC, DS, MC, VI. **Free Special Amenities; newspaper and high-speed Internet.** *(See color ad p 639)*

BEST WESTERN ABERCORN INN   *Book great rates at AAA.com*   **Phone: (604)270-7576**

Small-scale Hotel
$119-$219 All Year

Address: 9260 Bridgeport Rd V6X 1S1 **Location:** Hwy 99, exit 39 (Bridgeport/Airport) northbound; exit 39A (Richmond/Airport) southbound. **Facility:** Smoke free premises. 99 one-bedroom standard units, some with whirlpools. 3 stories, interior corridors. **Parking:** on-site. **Amenities:** voice mail, irons, hair dryers. **Leisure Activities:** limited exercise equipment. **Guest Services:** valet laundry, wireless Internet. **Business Services:** meeting rooms, business center. **Cards:** AX, DC, DS, JC, MC, VI. **Free Special Amenities: continental breakfast and local telephone calls.**

Best Western

AAA Benefit: Members save 10% everyday, plus an exclusive frequent stay program.

(See map and index starting on p. 568)

BEST WESTERN RICHMOND HOTEL & CONVENTION CENTER   *Book great rates at AAA.com*

Phone: 604/273-7878   **54**

CAA SAVE

Large-scale Hotel
Rates not provided

Address: 7551 Westminster Hwy V6X 1A3 **Location:** Corner of Minoru Blvd and Westminster Hwy. **Facility:** 390 one-bedroom standard units, some with whirlpools. 6-7 stories, interior corridors. **Parking:** on-site (fee). **Amenities:** voice mail, irons, hair dryers. *Some:* high-speed Internet. **Pool(s):** heated outdoor. **Leisure Activities:** saunas, whirlpool, exercise room. **Guest Services:** valet and coin laundry, wireless Internet. **Business Services:** conference facilities, business center. **Free Special Amenities: local telephone calls and high-speed Internet.** *(See color ad p 602)*

AAA Benefit:
Members save 10% everyday, plus an exclusive frequent stay program.

DAYS INN VANCOUVER AIRPORT   *Book great rates at AAA.com*

Phone: (604)207-8000   **42**

CAA SAVE

Small-scale Hotel
$126-$139 3/1-9/30
$81-$89 10/1-2/28

Address: 2840 Sexsmith Rd V6X 2H3 **Location:** Hwy 99, exit 39 (Bridgeport Rd/Airport) northbound; exit 39A (Richmond/Airport) southbound, just w on Bridgeport Rd. **Facility:** Smoke free premises. 66 one-bedroom standard units. 5 stories, interior corridors. **Parking:** on-site. **Terms:** check-in 4 pm. **Amenities:** high-speed Internet, voice mail, safes, irons, hair dryers. **Leisure Activities:** limited exercise equipment. **Guest Services:** valet laundry, wireless Internet. **Business Services:** PC (fee). **Cards:** AX, DC, DS, MC, VI. **Free Special Amenities: continental breakfast and high-speed Internet.**

DELTA VANCOUVER AIRPORT   *Book great rates at AAA.com*

Phone: 604/278-1241   **47**

CAA SAVE

Large-scale Hotel
$149-$300 All Year

Address: 3500 Cessna Dr V7B 1C7 **Location:** Corner of Russ Baker Way and Cessna Dr; near Moray Bridge. **Facility:** 415 one-bedroom standard units. 10 stories, interior corridors. **Parking:** on-site (fee) and valet. **Amenities:** voice mail, irons, hair dryers. *Fee:* video games, high-speed Internet. **Dining:** 2 restaurants. **Pool(s):** heated outdoor. **Leisure Activities:** exercise room. **Guest Services:** valet laundry. **Business Services:** conference facilities, business center. **Cards:** AX, CB, DC, DS, JC, MC, VI.

(See map and index starting on p. 568)

THE FAIRMONT VANCOUVER AIRPORT

Phone: (604)207-5200   41

CAA SAVE

▼▼▼▼▼

Large-scale Hotel
$279-$379 All Year

Address: 3111 Grant McConachie Way V7B 1X9 **Location:** In Vancouver International Airport. **Facility:** Luxurious rooms feature sound-insulated windows and high-tech temperature and lighting controls; a full spa and jetted lap pool are on property. 392 one-bedroom standard units, some with whirlpools. 14 stories, interior corridors. **Parking:** on-site (fee) and valet. **Terms:** cancellation fee imposed. **Amenities:** dual phone lines, voice mail, safes, honor bars, irons, hair dryers. *Fee:* video games, high-speed Internet. *Some:* CD players. **Dining:** Globe @ YVR, see separate listing. **Pool(s):** heated indoor. **Leisure Activities:** saunas, whirlpool, spa. **Guest Services:** valet laundry. **Business Services:** meeting rooms, business center. **Cards:** AX, DC, DS, JC, MC, VI. **Free Special Amenities:** newspaper. *(See color ad p 603)*

[icons]

FOUR POINTS BY SHERATON VANCOUVER AIRPORT   *Book great rates at AAA.com*

Phone: (604)214-0888 52

CAA SAVE

▼▼▼

Small-scale Hotel
$135-$180 All Year

Address: 8368 Alexandra Rd V6X 4A6 **Location:** No. 3 Rd, just e on Alderbridge Way, then just n on Hazelbridge Way. **Facility:** 139 one-bedroom standard units. 6 stories, interior corridors. **Parking:** on-site (fee). **Amenities:** video games (fee), high-speed Internet, dual phone lines, voice mail, irons, hair dryers. **Pool(s):** heated indoor. **Leisure Activities:** whirlpool, limited exercise equipment. **Guest Services:** valet laundry. **Business Services:** meeting rooms, business center. **Cards:** AX, DC, DS, MC, VI. **Free Special Amenities:** newspaper and high-speed Internet.

[icons]

FOUR ❖ POINTS
BY SHERATON

AAA Benefit:

Members get up to 15% off, plus Starwood Preferred Guest® bonuses.

HAMPTON INN VANCOUVER AIRPORT   *Book great rates at AAA.com*

Phone: (604)232-5505 44

CAA SAVE

▼▼▼

Small-scale Hotel
$119-$209 All Year

Address: 8811 Bridgeport Rd V6X 1R9 **Location:** Hwy 99, exit 39 (Bridgeport Rd/Airport) northbound; exit 39A (Richmond/Airport) southbound. **Facility:** 112 one-bedroom standard units. 5 stories, interior corridors. **Parking:** on-site. **Terms:** cancellation fee imposed. **Amenities:** video games (fee), voice mail, irons, hair dryers. *Some:* dual phone lines. **Leisure Activities:** limited exercise equipment. **Guest Services:** valet laundry, wireless Internet. **Business Services:** business center. **Cards:** AX, DC, DS, MC, VI. **Free Special Amenities:** expanded continental breakfast and high-speed Internet.

[icons]

HILTON VANCOUVER AIRPORT   *Book great rates at AAA.com*

Phone: (604)273-6336 53

CAA SAVE

▼▼▼

Small-scale Hotel
$269-$289 6/1-2/28
$229-$249 3/1-5/31

Address: 5911 Minoru Blvd V6X 4C7 **Location:** Corner of Minoru Blvd and Westminster Hwy. **Facility:** 237 units. 235 one-bedroom standard units. 2 two-bedroom suites. 15 stories, interior corridors. **Parking:** on-site (fee). **Terms:** cancellation fee imposed. **Amenities:** high-speed Internet (fee), dual phone lines, voice mail, irons, hair dryers. **Pool(s):** heated outdoor. **Leisure Activities:** whirlpool, tennis court, limited exercise equipment. **Guest Services:** valet laundry. **Business Services:** meeting rooms, business center. **Cards:** AX, CB, DC, DS, JC, MC, VI. *(See color ad p 605)*

[icons]

HOLIDAY INN EXPRESS VANCOUVER-AIRPORT   *Book great rates at AAA.com*

Phone: (604)273-8080 43

CAA SAVE

▼▼▼

Small-scale Hotel
$109-$179 All Year

Address: 9351 Bridgeport Rd V6X 1S3 **Location:** Hwy 99, exit 39 (Bridgeport Rd/Airport) northbound; exit 39A (Richmond/Airport) southbound. **Facility:** 107 one-bedroom standard units, some with whirlpools. 8 stories, interior corridors. **Parking:** on-site. **Terms:** check-in 4 pm, cancellation fee imposed. **Amenities:** dual phone lines, voice mail, irons, hair dryers. **Guest Services:** valet laundry, wireless Internet. **Business Services:** meeting rooms. **Cards:** AX, DC, DS, MC, VI. **Free Special Amenities:** expanded continental breakfast and high-speed Internet.

[icons]

(See map and index starting on p. 568)

HOLIDAY INN INTERNATIONAL VANCOUVER AIRPORT   *Book great rates at AAA.com*   Phone: (604)821-1818   [51]

Small-scale Hotel
$109-$179 All Year

Address: 10720 Cambie Rd V6X 1K8 **Location:** Hwy 99, exit 39 (Bridgeport Rd/Airport) northbound to St. Edwards Dr, just 0.6 mi (1 km) n; southbound exit 39B (No. 4 Rd), just e. **Facility:** 162 one-bedroom standard units. 6 stories, interior corridors. **Parking:** on-site. **Terms:** check-in 4 pm, cancellation fee imposed. **Amenities:** high-speed Internet, dual phone lines, voice mail, irons, hair dryers. **Leisure Activities:** whirlpool, limited exercise equipment. **Guest Services:** valet laundry. **Business Services:** meeting rooms, PC (fee). **Cards:** AX, DC, DS, MC, VI. **Free Special Amenities:** newspaper and high-speed Internet. *(See color ad p 604)*

QUALITY HOTEL AIRPORT (SOUTH)   *Book great rates at AAA.com*   Phone: (604)244-3051   [56]

Small-scale Hotel
$89-$179 All Year

Address: 7228 Westminster Hwy V6X 1A1 **Location:** Between Gilbert Rd and Alderbridge Way. **Facility:** 70 one-bedroom standard units, some with whirlpools. 4 stories, interior corridors. **Parking:** on-site. **Terms:** cancellation fee imposed. **Amenities:** high-speed Internet, voice mail, irons, hair dryers. **Guest Services:** valet laundry. **Business Services:** meeting rooms. **Cards:** AX, DC, JC, MC, VI. **Free Special Amenities:** continental breakfast and high-speed Internet. *(See color ad on insert)*

RADISSON PRESIDENT HOTEL & SUITES   Phone: (604)276-8181   [50]

Large-scale Hotel
$139-$199 All Year

Under major renovation, scheduled to be completed June 2008. Last rated: ▼▼▼ **Address:** 8181 Cambie Rd V6X 3X9 **Location:** Corner of No. 3 and Cambie rds. **Facility:** 184 one-bedroom standard units, some with whirlpools. 12 stories, interior corridors. **Parking:** on-site (fee). **Amenities:** high-speed Internet, voice mail, safes, irons, hair dryers. **Pool(s):** heated indoor. **Leisure Activities:** whirlpool, exercise room. **Guest Services:** valet laundry. **Business Services:** conference facilities, PC (fee). **Cards:** AX, DC, DS, JC, MC, VI. **Free Special Amenities:** full breakfast and high-speed Internet. *(See color ad below)*

RIVER ROCK CASINO RESORT   *Book great rates at AAA.com*   Phone: 604/247-8900   [40]

Large-scale Hotel
Rates not provided

Address: 8831 River Rd V6X 3P8 **Location:** Hwy 99, exit 39 (Bridgeport Rd/Airport) northbound; exit 39A (Richmond/Airport) southbound, just w on Bridgeport Rd, then just n on Great Canadian Way. **Facility:** Features include a large show lounge, conference facilities, a full-service spa and a 24-hour casino; kids love the pool's water slide. 220 units. 192 one- and 28 two-bedroom suites. 9-11 stories, interior corridors. **Bath:** combo or shower only. **Parking:** on-site and valet. **Terms:** check-in 4 pm. **Amenities:** video games (fee), CD players, high-speed Internet, dual phone lines, voice mail, safes, honor bars, irons, hair dryers. **Dining:** 2 restaurants, also, Tramonto, see separate listing, entertainment. **Pool(s):** heated indoor. **Leisure Activities:** whirlpool, waterslide, exercise room, spa. **Fee:** marina. **Guest Services:** valet laundry. **Business Services:** conference facilities, business center. **Free Special Amenities:** newspaper and high-speed Internet.

SANDMAN HOTEL VANCOUVER AIRPORT   *Book at AAA.com*   Phone: (604)303-8888   [48]

Small-scale Hotel
$119-$159 3/1-9/30
$99-$139 10/1-2/28

Address: 3233 St. Edwards Dr V6X 3K4 **Location:** Hwy 99, exit 39 (Bridgeport Rd/Airport) northbound to St. Edwards Dr; exit 39A (Richmond/Airport) southbound. **Facility:** 172 one-bedroom standard units, some with whirlpools. 5 stories, interior corridors. **Parking:** on-site. **Terms:** cancellation fee imposed. **Amenities:** video games (fee), high-speed Internet, voice mail, irons, hair dryers. **Dining:** Moxie's Classic Grill, see separate listing. **Pool(s):** heated indoor. **Leisure Activities:** whirlpool, limited exercise equipment. **Guest Services:** valet laundry. **Business Services:** meeting rooms, business center. **Cards:** AX, DC, DS, MC, VI.

(See map and index starting on p. 568)

TRAVELODGE HOTEL VANCOUVER AIRPORT   *Book great rates at AAA.com*   Phone: (604)278-5155   46

CAA SAVE

Small-scale Hotel
$119-$179 7/1-2/28
$99-$149 3/1-6/30

Address: 3071 St Edwards Dr V6X 3K4 **Location:** Hwy 99, exit 39 (Bridgeport Rd/Airport) northbound to St Edwards Dr; exit 39A (Richmond Rd/Airport) southbound. **Facility:** 160 one-bedroom standard units. 10 stories, interior corridors. **Parking:** on-site. **Terms:** cancellation fee imposed. **Amenities:** video games (fee), voice mail, irons, hair dryers. **Pool(s):** heated indoor. **Leisure Activities:** whirlpool. **Guest Services:** valet laundry, wireless Internet. **Business Services:** meeting rooms. **Cards:** AX, DC, DS, MC, VI.

VANCOUVER AIRPORT MARRIOTT   *Book great rates at AAA.com*   Phone: 604/276-2112   55

CAA SAVE

Small-scale Hotel
$219-$263 All Year

Address: 7571 Westminster Hwy V6X 1A3 **Location:** Corner of Minoru Blvd and Westminster Hwy. **Facility:** Smoke free premises. 237 units. 235 one-bedroom standard units. 2 two-bedroom suites. 18 stories, interior corridors. **Parking:** on-site (fee). **Amenities:** dual phone lines, voice mail, irons, hair dryers. **Fee:** video games, high-speed Internet. **Pool(s):** heated outdoor. **Leisure Activities:** whirlpool, exercise room. **Guest Services:** valet and coin laundry. **Business Services:** meeting rooms, business center. **Cards:** AX, DC, DS, JC, MC, VI. **Free Special Amenities:** newspaper and preferred room (subject to availability with advance reservations).

Marriott
HOTELS & RESORTS

AAA Benefit:
Members save 5% off of the best available rate.

——— WHERE TO DINE ———

CACTUS CLUB CAFE   Phone: 604/244-9969
Canadian
$9-$29
This bustling, casual restaurant serves huge burgers, sandwiches, pasta, salads, soups, quesadillas, fajitas, vegetarian dishes, steak, ribs, chicken and fish. Featured are certified Angus beef and fresh wild British Columbia salmon. The thick and creamy milk shakes come highly recommended. Casual dress. **Bar:** Full bar. **Hours:** 11 am-midnight, Fri & Sat-1 am. Closed: 12/25. **Address:** 5500 No 3 Rd V6X 2C8 **Location:** Corner of No. 3 and Lansdowne rds. **Parking:** on-site. **Cards:** AX, MC, VI.

CORRELIS RESTAURANT   Phone: 604/272-7264   63
Greek
$7-$21
Traditional Greek dishes with a hint of Italian influence are what guests will find at Correlis. This spot specializes in large portions of fresh local seafood, lamb and chicken. Modern decor, a casual atmosphere and friendly service all add up to a good dining experience. Guests may dine on the patio in warmer weather. Casual dress. **Bar:** Full bar. **Reservations:** accepted. **Hours:** 11 am-10 pm; seasonal hours may vary. Closed: 12/25. **Address:** 160-3900 Bayview St V7E 4R7 **Location:** At No. 1 Rd. **Parking:** on-site. **Cards:** MC, VI.

FLYING BEAVER   Phone: 604/273-0278   60
Canadian
$9-$20
The pub is in the terminal of Harbour Air, a small float plane operation. While chowing down on a good burger or some appetizers, patrons can gaze through large bay windows to watch planes land and take off. Signs to the South Terminal lead to this place, where there's plenty of free parking. Casual dress. **Bar:** Full bar. **Hours:** 11 am-midnight, Sat & Sun from 8 am. Closed: 1/1, 12/25. **Address:** 4760 Inglis Dr V7B 1W4 **Location:** Russ Baker Way, 0.6 mi (1 km) w on Inglis Dr towards south terminal. **Parking:** on-site. **Cards:** AX, MC, VI.

GLOBE @ YVR   Phone: 604/207-5200   59
Regional Pacific Rim
$15-$30
This restaurant treats diners to a memorable view of air traffic creeping in and out of the gates as service vehicles buzz around like bees. In addition to complete lunch and dinner service, the restaurant offers a wonderful Sunday brunch. The skilled culinary team keeps up the pace in the open-activity kitchen. Casual dress. **Bar:** Full bar. **Reservations:** suggested. **Hours:** 6 am-11 pm. **Location:** In Vancouver International Airport; in The Fairmont Vancouver Airport. **Parking:** on-site (fee) and valet. **Cards:** AX, DC, DS, JC, MC, VI.

KELSEY'S   Phone: 604/274-7404
Canadian
$7-$21
A fun, relaxed atmosphere and tasty menu of casual fare make the restaurant a popular favorite with locals. Diners might start a meal with some tempting appetizers, such as wings, loaded potato skins or nachos, and follow them with an old-time favorite, such as a burger, wrap, pizza or pasta dish. For a heartier meal, it's hard to beat pork back ribs or a steak. The diverse menu has broad appeal. Casual dress. **Bar:** Full bar. **Hours:** 11 am-10 pm, Wed & Thurs-11 pm, Fri & Sat-midnight. **Address:** 100-11300 Steveston Hwy V7A 5J5 **Location:** Steveston Hwy and No. 5 Rd; in Ironwood Plaza. **Parking:** on-site. **Cards:** AX, MC, VI.

MOXIE'S CLASSIC GRILL   Phone: 604/303-1111
Canadian
$8-$18
This sleek, funky and popular restaurant presents an extensive menu of creatively prepared dishes, including pizza, pasta, rice, noodles, signature salads and burgers. Other menus include one for children and one for Sunday brunch. Lending to the upbeat, stylish decor are dark wood appointments and river rock fireplaces. Casual dress. **Bar:** Full bar. **Hours:** 6 am-midnight. **Address:** 3233 St Edwards Dr V6X 3K4 **Location:** Hwy 99, exit 39 (Bridgeport Rd/Airport) northbound to St. Edwards; exit 39A (Richmond/Airport) southbound; in Sandman Hotel Vancouver Airport. **Parking:** on-site. **Cards:** AX, MC, VI.

RICKY'S ALL DAY GRILL   Phone: 604/233-7705
Canadian
$6-$15
The comfortable eatery, which employs friendly servers, presents a varied menu that includes pasta dishes, wraps, omelets, stir-fry preparations and burgers. Portions are generous. Children's and senior selections are offered. Guests can request seating in a booth or at a table. Casual dress. **Bar:** Full bar. **Hours:** 7 am-8 pm, Fri & Sat-9 pm. **Address:** 9100 Blundell Rd, #490 V6V 1K3 **Location:** Between Garden City Rd and Heather St. **Parking:** on-site. **Cards:** MC, VI.

(See map and index starting on p. 568)

STEVESTON SEAFOOD HOUSE

Phone: 604/271-5252   61

(AAA)

You'll enjoy your fine-dining experience at this restaurant located in the historic village of Steveston. The menu offers ocean-fresh seafood based on availability. The prawns and scallops are delicious, and the warm and friendly decor is quite pleasant. Casual dress. **Bar:** Full bar. **Reservations:** suggested. **Hours:** 5:30 pm-9 pm, Fri & Sat-10 pm. Closed major holidays. **Address:** 3951 Moncton St V7E 3A2 **Location:** Jct Moncton St and No. 1 Rd; in Steveston Village. **Parking:** street. **Cards:** AX, DC, MC, VI.

Seafood
$18-$43

TAPENADE BISTRO

Phone: 604/275-5188   62

Casual dress. **Bar:** Full bar. **Hours:** 11:30 am-2:30 & 5-9 pm, Sat & Sun 11 am-9 pm. Closed: 12/25; also Mon. **Address:** 3711 Bayview St V7E 3B6 **Location:** Between 2nd and 3rd aves; in Historic Steveston. **Parking:** street. **Cards:** AX, MC, VI.

Continental
$10-$26

TRAMONTO

Phone: 604/247-8900   58

Spectacular views of the Fraser River await those who dine at this third-floor dining room, which is perfect for an intimate evening or entertaining an important client. The menu lines up a selection of delicious Southern Italian cuisine, and the extensive wine cellar boasts more than 500 red and white wines from many wine-producing countries. Dressy casual. **Bar:** Full bar. **Reservations:** suggested. **Hours:** 5 pm-11 pm. **Address:** 8831 River Rd V6X 3P8 **Location:** Hwy 99, exit 39 (Bridgeport Rd/Airport) northbound; exit 39A (Richmond/Airport) southbound, just w on Bridgeport Rd, then just n on Great Canadian Way; in River Rock Casino Resort. **Parking:** on-site and valet. **Cards:** AX, MC, VI.

South Italian
$25-$40

CALL [M]

SURREY pop. 347,825   (See map and index starting on p. 568)

——— **WHERE TO STAY** ———

BEST WESTERN KING GEORGE INN & SUITES   *Book great rates at AAA.com*   Phone: (604)502-9000   70

(AAA) [SAVE]

Address: 8033 King George Hwy V3W 5B4 **Location:** Jct Fraser Hwy (Hwy 1A), 2.5 mi (4 km) s to 80th Ave. **Facility:** 72 one-bedroom standard units, some with efficiencies. 3 stories, interior corridors. **Parking:** on-site. **Terms:** cancellation fee imposed. **Amenities:** high-speed Internet, voice mail, irons, hair dryers. *Some:* dual phone lines. **Pool(s):** heated indoor. **Leisure Activities:** whirlpool, limited exercise equipment. **Guest Services:** valet and coin laundry. **Business Services:** meeting rooms, PC (fee). **Cards:** AX, DC, DS, MC, VI. **Free Special Amenities:** continental breakfast and high-speed Internet. *(See color ad p 601)*

Small-scale Hotel
$89-$149 All Year

AAA Benefit:
Members save 10% everyday, plus an exclusive frequent stay program.

[icons] CALL [M] [icons] / SOME UNITS [X]

BEST WESTERN PEACE ARCH INN   *Book great rates at AAA.com*   Phone: (604)541-8100   73

(AAA) [SAVE]

Address: 2293 King George Hwy V4A 5A4 **Location:** Hwy 99, exit 10 southbound, 2.8 mi (4.5 km) s; exit 2 northbound, 2.1 mi (3.5 km) n. **Facility:** Smoke free premises. 42 one-bedroom standard units, some with whirlpools. 3 stories, interior corridors. **Parking:** on-site. **Amenities:** high-speed Internet, voice mail, irons, hair dryers. **Pool(s):** indoor. **Leisure Activities:** sauna, whirlpool, limited exercise equipment. **Guest Services:** coin laundry. **Business Services:** meeting rooms. **Cards:** AX, MC, VI. **Free Special Amenities:** continental breakfast and high-speed Internet. *(See color ad on insert)*

Motel
$100-$130 3/1-9/30
$90-$110 10/1-2/28

AAA Benefit:
Members save 10% everyday, plus an exclusive frequent stay program.

[icons]

DAYS INN SURREY   *Book great rates at AAA.com*   Phone: 604/588-9511   69

Address: 9850 King George Hwy V3T 4Y3 **Location:** Jct Fraser Hwy (Hwy 1A) and Hwy 99A (King George Hwy). **Facility:** Smoke free premises. 81 one-bedroom standard units. 6 stories, interior corridors. *Bath:* combo or shower only. **Parking:** on-site. **Amenities:** voice mail, irons, hair dryers. **Pool(s):** heated indoor. **Leisure Activities:** whirlpool, limited exercise equipment. **Guest Services:** valet and coin laundry, wireless Internet. **Business Services:** meeting rooms.

Small-scale Hotel
Rates not provided

[icons] CALL [M] [icons] / SOME UNITS FEE [icons]

HAMPTON INN & SUITES   *Book great rates at AAA.com*   Phone: 604/530-6545   71

Address: 19500 Langley Bypass V3S 7R2 **Location:** Trans-Canada Hwy 1, exit 58 (200th St/Langley City), 3.1 mi (5 km) s, then 0.7 mi (1.2 km) w on Hwy 10. **Facility:** 96 units. 78 one-bedroom standard units. 18 one-bedroom suites with efficiencies. 4 stories, interior corridors. **Parking:** on-site. **Amenities:** video games (fee), high-speed Internet, voice mail, irons, hair dryers. *Some:* dual phone lines. **Pool(s):** heated indoor. **Leisure Activities:** whirlpool, waterslide, limited exercise equipment. **Guest Services:** valet and coin laundry. **Business Services:** meeting rooms, business center. *(See color ad p 617)*

Small-scale Hotel
Rates not provided

[icons] CALL [M] [icons] / SOME UNITS [X] [icons]

HOLIDAY INN EXPRESS HOTEL & SUITES   *Book great rates at AAA.com*   Phone: (604)930-8510   68

Address: 15808 104th Ave V4N 5L2 **Location:** Trans-Canada Hwy 1, exit 50 (160th St), just w. **Facility:** 86 one-bedroom standard units, some with whirlpools. 4 stories, interior corridors. **Parking:** on-site. **Terms:** check-in 4 pm, 7 day cancellation notice-fee imposed. **Amenities:** video games (fee), high-speed Internet, voice mail, irons, hair dryers. **Pool(s):** heated indoor. **Leisure Activities:** whirlpool, limited exercise equipment. **Guest Services:** coin laundry, wireless Internet. **Business Services:** meeting rooms, business center. **Cards:** AX, DC, DS, MC, VI. *(See color ad on insert)*

Small-scale Hotel
$149-$189 3/1-8/31
$109-$139 9/1-2/28

[ASK] [icons] CALL [M] [icons] / SOME UNITS [X]

(See map and index starting on p. 568)

HOWARD JOHNSON EXPRESS INN & SUITES   *Book great rates at AAA.com*   Phone: (604)588-0181   **65**

Motel
$85-$100 All Year

Address: 13245 King George Hwy V3T 2T3 **Location:** Southbound from the Pattullo Bridge to 112th Ave; northbound 3.1 mi (5 km) from jct Frasier Hwy (Hwy 1A). **Facility:** 54 units. 42 one- and 12 two-bedroom standard units, some with efficiencies and/or whirlpools. 2 stories (no elevator), exterior corridors. *Bath:* combo or shower only. **Parking:** on-site. **Guest Services:** coin laundry, wireless Internet. **Cards:** AX, CB, DC, DS, MC, VI. **Free Special Amenities: continental breakfast and high-speed Internet.**

RAMADA HOTEL & SUITES SURREY/GUILDFORD   *Book at AAA.com*   Phone: (604)930-4700   **67**

Small-scale Hotel
$99-$159 3/1-9/30
$99-$149 10/1-2/28

Address: 10410 158th St V4N 5C2 **Location:** Trans-Canada Hwy 1, exit 50 (160th St), just w on 104th Ave. **Facility:** 77 one-bedroom standard units. 3 stories, interior corridors. *Bath:* combo or shower only. **Parking:** on-site. **Amenities:** high-speed Internet, voice mail, irons, hair dryers. **Pool(s):** heated outdoor. **Leisure Activities:** whirlpool, limited exercise equipment. **Guest Services:** valet laundry, area transportation (fee). **Business Services:** meeting rooms, PC (fee). **Cards:** AX, MC, VI.

RAMADA INN LANGLEY-SURREY   *Book at AAA.com*   Phone: 604/576-8388   **72**

Small-scale Hotel
Rates not provided

Address: 19225 Hwy 10 V3S 8V9 **Location:** Trans-Canada Hwy 1, exit 58, 3.1 mi (5 km) s on 200th St, then 1.2 mi (2 km) w on Rt 10; corner of 192nd St and Rt 10. **Facility:** 85 one-bedroom standard units, some with efficiencies. 3 stories, interior corridors. **Amenities:** voice mail, irons, hair dryers. *Some:* high-speed Internet. **Pool(s):** heated indoor. **Leisure Activities:** whirlpool, limited exercise equipment. **Guest Services:** valet and coin laundry. **Business Services:** meeting rooms, PC (fee).

SHERATON VANCOUVER GUILDFORD HOTEL   *Book great rates at AAA.com*   Phone: 604/582-9288   **66**

Large-scale Hotel
Rates not provided

Address: 15269 104th Ave V3R 1N5 **Location:** Trans-Canada Hwy 1, exit 48 eastbound, 0.6 mi (1 km) s on 152nd St, then just e; exit 50 westbound, 104th Ave, then just w. **Facility:** Smoke free premises. 279 one-bedroom standard units, some with whirlpools. 20 stories, interior corridors. **Parking:** on-site (fee). **Amenities:** voice mail. *Some:* video games (fee), irons, hair dryers. **Pool(s):** heated outdoor. **Leisure Activities:** whirlpool, limited exercise equipment. **Guest Services:** valet laundry, wireless Internet. **Business Services:** meeting rooms, business center. **Free Special Amenities: newspaper and preferred room (subject to availability with advance reservations).** *(See color ad below)*

(S) Sheraton
HOTELS & RESORTS

AAA Benefit:
Members get up to 15% off, plus Starwood Preferred Guest® bonuses.

▼ *See AAA listing above* ▼

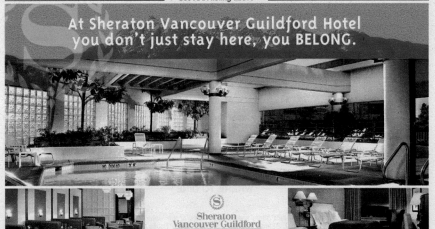

At Sheraton Vancouver Guildford Hotel you don't just stay here, you BELONG.

Sheraton
Vancouver Guildford
HOTEL
BRITISH COLUMBIA

15269-104th Avenue, Surrey, BC V3R 1N5 Canada   P. 604.582.9288   1.800.325.3535   www.sheraton.com/guildford

(See map and index starting on p. 568)

———— WHERE TO DINE ————

CRESCENT BEACH BISTRO   Phone: 604/531-1882   (71)

Seafood
$10-$26
Diners here enjoy a delightful setting either on the lovely outdoor terrace or the quaint indoor dining room. Plants adorn both sections and the lively Mediterranean background music adds to the atmosphere. Menu highlights include Spanish paella, shrimp and scallops with tangy mango chutney, or a more traditional rack of lamb. Its best to phone ahead for reservations as it's very popular with the locals. Casual dress. **Bar:** Full bar. **Reservations:** suggested. **Hours:** 11:30 am-2 & 5-10 pm, Sat from 5 pm. Closed major holidays; also Sun. **Address:** 12251 Beecher St V4A 3A4 **Location:** 2 blks from Crescent Beach at McKenzie Ave. **Parking:** street. **Cards:** MC, VI.

MOXIES CLASSIC GRILL   Phone: 604/495-7020

Canadian
$8-$18
This sleek, funky and popular restaurant presents an extensive menu of creatively prepared dishes, including pizza, pasta, rice, noodles, signature salads and burgers. Other menus include one for children and one for Sunday brunch. Lending to the upbeat, stylish decor are dark wood appointments and river rock fireplaces. Casual dress. **Bar:** Full bar. **Hours:** 11 am-midnight, Fri & Sat-1 am. **Address:** 10608 151A St V3R 1J8 **Location:** Trans-Canada Hwy 1, exit 48 eastbound, 0.6 mi (1 km) s on 152 St; exit 50 westbound, 0.6 mi (1 km) s on 104 Ave. **Parking:** on-site. **Cards:** AX, MC, VI.

RICKY'S ALL DAY GRILL   Phone: 604/582-2545

Canadian
$6-$15
The comfortable eatery, which employs friendly servers, presents a varied menu that includes pasta dishes, wraps, omelets, stir-fry preparations and burgers. Portions are generous. Children's and senior selections are offered. Guests can request seating in a booth or at a table. Casual dress. **Bar:** Full bar. **Hours:** 7 am-9 pm, Mon & Tues-8 pm. **Address:** 1076 Central City V3T 2W1 **Location:** Between King George Hwy and 100th Ave. **Parking:** on-site. **Cards:** MC, VI.

RICKY'S ALL DAY GRILL   Phone: 604/581-3212

Canadian
$6-$15
The comfortable eatery, which employs friendly servers, presents a varied menu that includes pasta dishes, wraps, omelets, stir-fry preparations and burgers. Portions are generous. Children's and senior selections are offered. Guests can request seating in a booth or at a table. Casual dress. **Bar:** Full bar. **Hours:** 6 am-9 pm. **Address:** 8958 152nd St V3R 4L7 **Location:** Between Fraser Hwy and 88th Ave. **Parking:** on-site. **Cards:** MC, VI.

RICKY'S ALL DAY GRILL   Phone: 604/535-1789

Canadian
$6-$15
The comfortable eatery, which employs friendly servers, presents a varied menu that includes pasta dishes, wraps, omelets, stir-fry preparations and burgers. Portions are generous. Children's and senior selections are offered. Guests can request seating in a booth or at a table. Casual dress. **Bar:** Full bar. **Hours:** 6 am-9 pm. **Address:** 3189 King George Hwy V4P 1B8 **Location:** Hwy 99, exit 10, 1.9 mi (3 km) s. **Parking:** on-site. **Cards:** MC, VI.

SWISS CHALET   Phone: 604/583-0883

Canadian
$6-$18
The popular restaurant is known for its rotisserie chicken and ribs and the tangy Chalet sauce that gives food its special zip. Diners munch on a half or quarter chicken with sides such as steamed vegetables, fries, baked potatoes and salads. Lunch guests often go for the great soup and sandwich combination. Take-out and delivery service are popular options. Casual dress. **Bar:** Full bar. **Hours:** 11 am-10 pm, Fri & Sat-11 pm. Closed: 12/25. **Address:** 9666 King George Hwy V3T 2V4 **Location:** King George Hwy at 96th Ave. **Parking:** on-site. **Cards:** AX, MC, VI.

THE TURKEY HOUSE & DELI   Phone: 604/531-6222   (72)

Deli/Subs
Sandwiches
$7-$10
Since 1973, the distinctive combination restaurant and delicatessen has been serving 100 percent turkey products and unforgettable home-cooked meals. On the menu are varied sandwiches and soups, as well as hot items that can be eaten here or taken out. Visitors can purchase turkey deli meats and pre-made dishes that can be warmed at home, including turkey pies, sausage rolls and lasagna. Casual dress. **Hours:** 9 am-7 pm, Sat-6 pm. Closed major holidays; also Sun & Mon. **Address:** 1433 King George Hwy V4A 4Z5 **Location:** Hwy 99, exit 2B southbound; from Canada/US border, exit 2 northbound, then 0.6 (1 km) n. **Parking:** on-site. **Cards:** AX, MC, VI.

VILLA VERDI RISTORANTE ITALIANO   Phone: 604/591-2123   (70)

Italian
$15-$32
Open for lunch and dinner, the Italian restaurant offers a choice among a wide selection of pasta dishes, including a pasta bar option that lets patrons customize a specialty dish from a list of pastas and sauces. Free parking is plentiful. Casual dress. **Bar:** Full bar. **Reservations:** suggested. **Hours:** 11:30 am-2 & 5:30-10 pm, Sat from 5:30 pm. Closed major holidays; also Sun. **Address:** 13620 80th Ave V3W 6M1 **Location:** Jct Fraser Hwy (Hwy 1A), 2.5 mi (4 km) s on King George Hwy. **Parking:** on-site. **Cards:** AX, MC, VI.

YOKOHAMA JAPANESE RESTAURANT   Phone: 604/584-4555   (69)

Japanese
$7-$21
Tatami rooms and a full sushi bar contribute to the cozy environment. The combination dinner includes beef teriyaki, tempura, noodles, rice and dessert. Another option is the all-you-can-eat lunch and dinner menu. Service is pleasant. Casual dress. **Bar:** Full bar. **Reservations:** suggested, weekends. **Hours:** 11:30 am-2:30 & 5-10 pm, Fri & Sat-10:30 pm, Sun 5 pm-10 pm. Closed: 1/1, 12/24, 12/25. **Address:** 10356 137th St V3T 4H4 **Location:** Just e off Hwy 99A (King George Hwy) at 104th Ave on Whalley Ring Rd. **Parking:** on-site. **Cards:** AX, MC, VI.

WEST VANCOUVER pop. 42,131 (See map and index starting on p. 568)

———— WHERE TO DINE ————

THE BEACH HOUSE AT DUNDARAVE
PIER   Phone: 604/922-1414   (35)

Seafood
$13-$30
The oceanfront restaurant offers spectacular views of the water and entices guests to walk along the sea wall after a filling meal. Seafood dishes suit every taste. Those who can't find a parking spot in the small lot behind this place should park wherever possible along the street. Casual dress. **Bar:** Full bar. **Reservations:** suggested. **Hours:** 11:30 am-11 pm, Fri & Sat-midnight, Sun 10:30 am-10 pm. Closed: 12/25. **Address:** 150 25th St V7V 4H8 **Location:** Marine Dr at 25th St, towards ocean. **Parking:** street. **Cards:** AX, DC, MC, VI.

(See map and index starting on p. 568)

BEACH SIDE CAFE
Phase: 604/925-1945 **37**

Pacific Rim
$12-$36

At the entrance of the trendy area known as Dundurave, the lovely restaurant has large bay windows that overlook the distant inlet and a front section that overlooks the active street with its many unique shops. On the menu is a mix of fish, meat and pasta dishes, including risotto, lasagna and gnocchi, while the dinner menu lists rack of lamb, free-range chicken and Fraser Valley duck. Parking is on the street or in the public lot right behind the restaurant, where it's free for two hours. Casual dress. **Bar:** Full bar. **Reservations:** suggested. **Hours:** 11:30 am-3 & 5:30-10 pm. Closed: 12/25, 12/26. **Address:** 1362 Marine Dr V7T 1B5 **Location:** Between 13th and 14th sts. **Parking:** street. **Cards:** AX, MC, VI.

CACTUS CLUB CAFE
Phone: 604/922-1707

Canadian
$9-$29

This bustling, casual restaurant serves huge burgers, sandwiches, pasta, salads, soups, quesadillas, fajitas, vegetarian dishes, steak, ribs, chicken and fish. Featured are certified Angus beef and fresh wild British Columbia salmon. The thick and creamy milk shakes come highly recommended. Casual dress. **Bar:** Full bar. **Hours:** 11 am-midnight, Fri & Sat-1 am. Closed: 12/25. **Address:** 855 Main St V7T 2Z3 **Location:** Just off Marine Dr; in Village at Park Royal. **Parking:** on-site. **Cards:** AX, MC, VI.

LA REGALADE FRENCH BISTRO
Phone: 604/921-2228 **36**

French
$12-$25

The tiny, family-run bistro blends fantastically fresh ingredients in heaping plates of great food. The chef/owner hails from France and has cooked at fine restaurants both in France and here in the city. Daily specials are listed on the wall chalkboard. Don't leave without trying one of the many homemade desserts on display. Casual dress. **Bar:** Full bar. **Reservations:** required. **Hours:** 11:30 am-2 & 5:30-10 pm, Sat from 5:30 pm. Closed: major holidays, 12/26; also Sun & Mon. **Address:** #103 2232 Marine Dr V7V 1K4 **Location:** Trans-Canada Hwy 1, exit 10 (22nd St), 0.9 mi (1.5 km) s, then just w. **Parking:** street. **Cards:** MC, VI.

SALMON HOUSE ON THE HILL
Phone: 604/926-3212 **34**

Seafood
$12-$34

You'll certainly appreciate the incredible panoramic view of the city and harbor from the Salmon House's hilltop location. The restaurant's cuisine specializes in Pacific Rim influences, with fresh British Columbia salmon as the house specialty. Casual dress. **Bar:** Full bar. **Reservations:** suggested, for dinner. **Hours:** 11:30 am-2 & 5-10 pm, Fri & Sat-11 pm, Sun 11 am-2 & 5-10 pm; Sunday brunch. Closed: 12/24, 12/25. **Address:** 2229 Folkestone Way V7S 2Y6 **Location:** Trans-Canada Hwy 1, exit 10 (21st St), follow signs. **Parking:** on-site. **Cards:** AX, DC, MC, VI.

WHITE ROCK pop. 18,755 (See map and index starting on p. 568)

——— **WHERE TO STAY** ———

OCEAN PROMENADE HOTEL
Book great rates at AAA.com   Phone: (604)542-0102 **83**

Small-scale Hotel
$139-$469 3/1-10/1
$129-$469 10/2-2/28

Address: 15611 Marine Dr V4B 1E1 **Location:** Hwy 99, exit 2B southbound; exit 2 (White Rock/8th Ave) northbound, 1.3 mi (2 km) w. **Facility:** 51 one-bedroom standard units, some with kitchens and/or whirlpools. 3 stories, interior/exterior corridors. **Parking:** on-site. **Terms:** check-in 4 pm, cancellation fee imposed. **Amenities:** DVD players, high-speed Internet, voice mail, safes, irons, hair dryers. **Leisure Activities:** limited exercise equipment. **Guest Services:** valet and coin laundry. **Business Services:** meeting rooms. **Cards:** AX, MC, VI. **Free Special Amenities:** local telephone calls and high-speed Internet. *(See color ad below)*

——— **WHERE TO DINE** ———

GIRAFFE
Phone: 604/538-6878 **76**

Pacific Rim
$10-$28

All tables at the lovely, intimate restaurant face the water. Giraffe-centric decor, including the noteworthy napkin holders, suits this place's name. Daily specials, which are printed on a blackboard at the entrance, are can't-miss choices. The dining room's small size accounts for tight table spacing. Pay parking is in effect at all times. Casual dress. **Bar:** Full bar. **Reservations:** suggested. **Hours:** 5:30 pm-9 pm, Thurs-Sat also 11:30 am-2 pm, Sun 11 am-2 & 5:30-9 pm; Sunday brunch. Closed major holidays. **Address:** 15053 Marine Dr V4B 1C5 **Location:** Hwy 99, exit 2B southbound; exit 2 northbound, 1.8 mi (3 km) w. **Parking:** street. **Cards:** MC, VI.

▼ *See AAA listing above* ▼

(See map and index starting on p. 568)

LA BAIA ITALIAN RESTAURANT

Italian

$12-$22

Phone: 604/531-6261   ⑦

Delicious rack of lamb and veal Marsala are among choices at the bright and airy restaurant, which displays antiques and offers a nice view of the park. The atmosphere is cozy, and service is friendly and attentive. Those who can't nab a free parking spot at the back can pay to park on the street. Casual dress. **Bar:** Full bar. **Reservations:** suggested. **Hours:** 5 pm-10 pm. Closed: 12/25. **Address:** 15791 Marine Dr V4B 1E5 **Location:** Hwy 99, exit 2B southbound; exit 2 northbound, 0.9 mi (1.5 km) w. **Parking:** on-site. **Cards:** AX, MC, VI.

PEARL ON THE ROCK   *Menu on AAA.com*

Seafood

$10-$34

Phone: 604/542-1064   ⑦⑤

Across from the beach, where there is plenty of pay parking in lots or at street meters, the restaurant has an open patio that makes it a hot spot for people-watching. However, one sampling from the spectacular menu makes clear the real draw: the food. With or without wine pairings, the tasting menu highlights wonderfully creative seafood dishes. Casual dress. **Bar:** Full bar. **Reservations:** suggested. **Hours:** 11:30 am-2:30 & 5-9 pm. Closed major holidays. **Address:** 14955 Marine Dr V4B 1C3 **Location:** Hwy 99, exit 2B southbound; exit 2 northbound, 2.1 mi (3.5 km) w. **Parking:** street. **Cards:** AX, MC, VI.

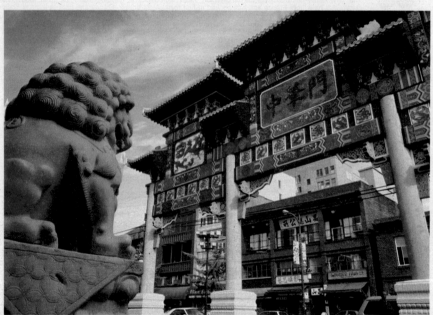

Chinese Cultural Centre Museum & Archives, Chinatown / Connie Coleman / Getty Images

This ends listings for the Vancouver Vicinity.
The following page resumes the alphabetical listings of cities in British Columbia.

VANDERHOOF pop. 4,064

——— WHERE TO DINE ———

RICKY'S ALL DAY GRILL
Canadian
$6-$15

Phone: 250/567-6080
The comfortable eatery, which employs friendly servers, presents a varied menu that includes pasta dishes, wraps, omelets, stir-fry preparations and burgers. Portions are generous. Children's and senior selections are offered. Guests can request seating in a booth or at a table. Casual dress. **Bar:** Full bar. **Hours:** 7 am-8 pm, Fri & Sat-9 pm. **Address:** 2351 Church St V0J 3A0 **Location:** Corner of Church St and Stewart Ave. **Parking:** on-site.

VERNON —See Okanagan Valley p. 539.

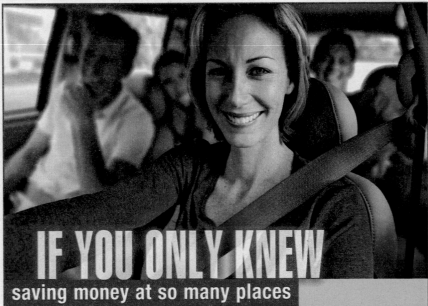

Destination Victoria

pop. 74,125

The Trans-Canada Highway ends in Victoria, but your journey isn't complete until you've seen the city and its surroundings.

Wander down cobblestone streets lined with Victorian lampposts. Tour one glorious English garden after another. Do the town in a double-decker bus. Or cruise to neighboring islands.

© Richard Cummins / SuperStock

Butchart Gardens, Brentwood Bay. A symphony of colors combines to produce spectacular floral displays within this 22-hectare (55-acre) garden. (See listing page 194)

© Chuck Pefley / Alamy

Bastion Square, Victoria. A folk musician entertains in Bastion Square, a popular site for summer festivals. (See listing page 186)

Shopping in Victoria. Craft markets and specialty shops afford opportunities to purchase that special item.

BRITISH COLUMBIA
WASHINGTON

Sidney

Brentwood Bay

Malahat   Saanich

Esquimalt   Oak Bay

Sooke

Victoria

CANADA
UNITED STATES

See Vicinity map page 635

Tourism Victoria

Tourism Victoria

Whale-watching in Victoria. Whale-watching excursions allow visitors to view majestic whales in their natural environment.

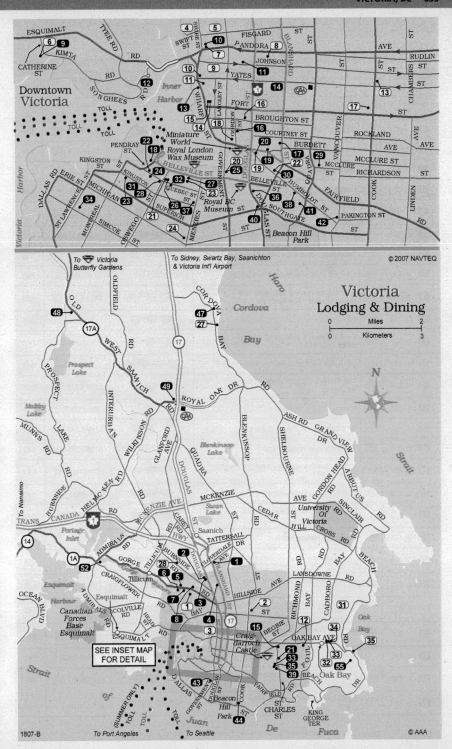

Downtown Victoria

Miniature World
Royal London
Wax Museum

Royal BC
Museum

Beacon Hill
Park

© 2007 NAVTEQ

Victoria
Lodging & Dining

To Victoria
Butterfly Gardens

To Sidney, Swartz Bay, Saanichton
& Victoria Int'l Airport

Miles 0 — 2
Kilometers 0 — 3

N

Cordova
Bay

Haro
Strait

Prospect
Lake

Maltby
Lake

Munns
Lake

Blenkinsop
Lake

University
Of
Victoria

Swan
Lake

Saanich

Portage
Inlet

To Nanaimo

Tillicum

Esquimalt
Harbour

Canadian
Forces
Base
Esquimalt

OCEAN BLVD

SEE INSET MAP
FOR DETAIL

Craig-
darroch
Castle

Oak
Bay

Oak Bay

Beacon
Hill
Park

Strait
of
Juan
de
Fuca

(SUMMER ONLY)
TOLL

To Port Angeles

To Seattle

1807-B

© AAA

Victoria

This index helps you "spot" where approved lodgings and restaurants are located on the corresponding detailed maps. Lodging daily rate range is for comparison only and show the property's high season. Restaurant rate range is a combination of lunch and/or dinner. Turn to the listing page for more detailed rate information and consult display ads for special promotions.

Spotter/Map Page Number	OA	VICTORIA - Lodgings	Diamond Rating	Rate Range High Season	Listing Page
1 / p. 635	CAA	**Accent Inns** - see color ad p 639	◆◆	$99-$179 SAVE	639
2 / p. 635	CAA	**Mayfair Motel**	◆◆	$49-$119 SAVE	649
3 / p. 635	CAA	**Blue Ridge Inns**	◆◆	$69-$129 SAVE	644
4 / p. 635	CAA	**Holiday Inn Victoria**	◆◆	$90-$179 SAVE	648
5 / p. 635	CAA	**Robin Hood Motel** - see color ad p 653	◆◆	$66-$104 SAVE	652
6 / p. 635		Ramada Victoria - see color ad p 653	◆◆	$135-$185	652
7 / p. 635	CAA	**Travelodge Victoria** - see color ad p 656	◆◆◆	$144-$174 SAVE	656
8 / p. 635	CAA	**Howard Johnson Hotel-City Centre**	◆◆	$69-$159 SAVE	648
9 / p. 635	CAA	**Spinnakers Gastro Brewpub and Guesthouses** - see color ad p 655	◆◆	$129-$249 SAVE	653
10 / p. 635		Swans Hotel	◆◆◆	$149-$359	655
11 / p. 635	CAA	**Best Western Carlton Plaza Hotel** - see color ad p 642	◆◆◆	$89-$189 SAVE	642
12 / p. 635		Delta Victoria Ocean Pointe Resort & Spa	◆◆◆◆	$265-$398	645
13 / p. 635	CAA	**The Victoria Regent Hotel** - see color ad p 657	◆◆◆	$139-$309 SAVE	657
14 / p. 635	CAA	**Dalton Hotel & Suites**	◆	$66-$178 SAVE	644
15 / p. 635	CAA	**Amethyst Inn at Regents Park**	◆◆◆	$149-$249 SAVE	641
16 / p. 635	CAA	**The Magnolia Hotel & Spa**	◆◆◆◆	$175-$335 SAVE	649
17 / p. 635	CAA	**Quality Inn Downtown** - see color ad on insert, p 651	◆◆◆	$79-$169 SAVE	651
18 / p. 635	CAA	**Admiral Inn** - see color ad p 640	◆◆◆	$99-$609 SAVE	640
19 / p. 635		Chateau Victoria Hotel and Suites - see color ad p 644	◆◆◆	$159-$229	644
20 / p. 635	CAA	**Executive House Hotel**	◆◆	$195-$215 SAVE	645
21 / p. 635		Villa Marco Polo Inn	◆◆◆	Rates not provided	658
22 / p. 635	CAA	**Huntingdon Hotel & Suites** - see color ad p 648	◆◆	$99-$379 SAVE	649
23 / p. 635		A Haterleigh Heritage Inn	◆◆◆	Rates not provided	640
24 / p. 635	CAA	**Harbour Towers Hotel & Suites** - see color ad p 646	◆◆◆	$94-$450 SAVE	647
25 / p. 635		The Fairmont Empress - see color ad p 646	◆◆◆◆	$169-$569	646
26 / p. 635	CAA	**Best Western Inner Harbour** - see color ad p 643	◆◆◆	$109-$279 SAVE	643
27 / p. 635	CAA	**Hotel Grand Pacific** - see color ad p 647	◆◆◆◆	$149-$319 SAVE	648

Spotter/Map Page Number	OA	VICTORIA - Lodgings (continued)	Diamond Rating	Rate Range High Season	Listing Page
28 / p. 635	⊛	The Oswego Hotel - see color ad p 651	▽▽▽	$275-$650 [SAVE]	650
29 / p. 635	⊛	Abigail's Hotel	▽▽▽	$209-$450 [SAVE]	639
30 / p. 635	⊛	Marriott Victoria Inner Harbour - see color ad p 650	▽▽▽▽	$208-$307 [SAVE]	649
31 / p. 635		Andersen House Bed & Breakfast	▽▽▽	Rates not provided	642
32 / p. 635	⊛	Royal Scot Suite Hotel - see color ad p 654	▽▽▽	$175-$249 [SAVE]	653
33 / p. 635		Abbeymoore Manor Bed & Breakfast Inn	▽▽	$139-$249	639
34 / p. 635		Heathergate House Bed & Breakfast	▽▽	$85-$145	647
35 / p. 635		Fairholme Manor	▽▽▽	$175-$325	645
36 / p. 635	⊛	Queen Victoria Hotel and Suites - see color ad p 652	▽▽▽	$130-$450	651
37 / p. 635	⊛	Embassy Inn - see color ad p 645	▽▽	$89-$349 [SAVE]	645
38 / p. 635		Humboldt House Bed & Breakfast	▽▽▽	$147-$315	648
39 / p. 635	⊛	Prior House B&B Inn	▽▽▽▽	$129-$299 [SAVE]	650
40 / p. 635	⊛	Helm's Inn	▽▽▽	Rates not provided [SAVE]	647
41 / p. 635		Ambrosia Historic Bed & Breakfast Retreat	▽▽	$115-$255	640
42 / p. 635		Beaconsfield Inn	▽▽▽	Rates not provided	642
43 / p. 635	⊛	James Bay Inn Hotel & Suites - see color ad p 649	▽	$130-$164 [SAVE]	649
44 / p. 635		Dashwood Seaside Heritage Manor	▽▽	Rates not provided	644
		VICTORIA - Restaurants			
1 / p. 635		Glo Euro Pub	▽▽	$9-$20	660
2 / p. 635		Haultain's Fish & Chips	▽	$10-$18	660
3 / p. 635		Herald Street Cafe	▽▽▽	$9-$28	660
4 / p. 635		Canoe Brewpub Marina Restaurant	▽▽	$9-$28	660
5 / p. 635		Hunan Village	▽▽	$8-$15	660
6 / p. 635	⊛	Spinnakers Gastro Brewpub & Restaurant	▽▽	$8-$23	662
7 / p. 635		Wild Saffron Bistro & Wine Bar	▽▽▽	$15-$34	663
8 / p. 635	⊛	The Black Olive	▽▽▽	$9-$34	660
9 / p. 635		Il Terrazzo	▽▽▽	$10-$35	661
10 / p. 635		Restaurant Matisse	▽▽▽	$20-$30	662
11 / p. 635		Periklis Greek Restaurant	▽▽	$12-$30	662
12 / p. 635		White Heather Tea Room	▽▽	$8-$14	663
13 / p. 635		Passero's Mediterranean Cuisine	▽▽	$7-$19	661

Spotter/Map Page Number	OA	VICTORIA - Restaurants (continued)	Diamond Rating	Rate Range High Season	Listing Page
⑭ / p. 635		Siam Thai Restaurant	◆◆	$8-$18	662
⑮ / p. 635		Koto Japanese Restaurant	◆◆	$6-$20	661
⑯ / p. 635		Pagliacci's	◆◆	$6-$24	661
⑰ / p. 635		Pluto's	◆◆	$7-$15	662
⑱ / p. 635		Pescatore's Seafood & Grill	◆◆	$9-$30	662
⑲ / p. 635		Barkley's Steak & Seafood	◆◆◆	$20-$45	660
⑳ / p. 635		The Empress Room	◆◆◆◆	$25-$40	660
㉑ / p. 635		Victoria Harbour House Restaurant	◆◆	$16-$35	662
㉒ / p. 635	CAA	**Fire & Water Fish & Chop House** - see color ad p 650	◆◆◆	$7-$36	660
㉓ / p. 635	CAA	**The Mark**	◆◆◆◆	$30-$40	661
㉔ / p. 635	CAA	**James Bay Tea Room & Restaurant**	◆	$8-$14	661
		SAANICH - Lodgings			
㊼ / p. 635		Sunnymeade House B&B	◆◆	$89-$165	665
㊽ / p. 635		Iris Garden Country Manor Bed & Breakfast	◆◆	Rates not provided	665
㊾ / p. 635		Howard Johnson Hotel & Suites	◆◆◆	Rates not provided	665
		SAANICH - Restaurants			
㉗ / p. 635	CAA	**Charter's Restaurant at McMorran's Beach House**	◆◆	$9-$30	665
㉘ / p. 635		Brady's Fish & Chips	◆	$7-$13	665
		ESQUIMALT - Lodgings			
㊷ / p. 635	CAA	**Comfort Inn & Suites** - see color ad on insert	◆◆◆	$89-$299 SAVE	663
		OAK BAY - Lodgings			
㊵ / p. 635		Oak Bay Guest House Bed & Breakfast	◆◆	$139-$199	664
		OAK BAY - Restaurants			
㉛ / p. 635		Paprika Bistro	◆◆◆	$20-$29	665
㉜ / p. 635		Penny Farthing Public House	◆◆	$8-$17	665
㉝ / p. 635		The Blethering Place Tea Room & Restaurant	◆◆	$6-$17	664
㉞ / p. 635		Ottavio Italian Bakery & Delicatessen	◆◆	$7-$14	664
㉟ / p. 635		The Marina Restaurant	◆◆	$10-$32	664

VICTORIA pop. 78,057 (See map and index starting on p. 635)

―――――― WHERE TO STAY ――――――

ABBEYMOORE MANOR BED & BREAKFAST INN

♦♦♦ ♦♦♦
Historic Bed
& Breakfast
$139-$249 3/1-10/28
$109-$219 10/29-2/28

Phone: 250/370-1470 **33**

Address: 1470 Rockland Ave V8S 1W2 **Location:** Blanshard St (Hwy 17), 1.2 mi (2 km) e on Fort St, just s on St. Charles St, then just w. **Facility:** Once the residence of a lieutenant governor, this renovated B&B is in a neighborhood dotted with stately Victorian homes. Smoke free premises. 7 units. 5 one-bedroom standard units. 2 one-bedroom suites with efficiencies and whirlpools. 3 stories (no elevator), interior/exterior corridors. **Bath:** combo or shower only. **Parking:** on-site. **Terms:** office hours 7 am-10 pm, 14 day cancellation notice-fee imposed. **Amenities:** CD players, hair dryers. **Guest Services:** wireless Internet. **Business Services:** PC. **Cards:** MC, VI.

⊠ 🐾 / SOME UNITS 📺 ⓩ 🖥 📷 📭

ABIGAIL'S HOTEL

Ⓐ SAVE

♦♦♦ ♦♦♦
Bed & Breakfast
$209-$450 All Year

Book great rates at AAA.com **Phone:** (250)388-5363 **29**

Address: 906 McClure St V8V 3E7 **Location:** Blanshard St (Hwy 17), just n on Fairfield Rd, then just n on Vancouver St. Located in a quiet residential area. **Facility:** The European-style boutique hotel has newer rooms with TVs, refrigerators and coffee makers; older rooms boast fireplaces and large, claw-foot tubs. Smoke free premises. 23 one-bedroom standard units, some with whirlpools. 2-3 stories (no elevator), interior corridors. **Bath:** combo or shower only. **Parking:** on-site. **Terms:** age restrictions may apply, 7 day cancellation notice-fee imposed. **Amenities:** video library, DVD players, voice mail, hair dryers. **Leisure Activities:** spa. **Guest Services:** valet laundry, wireless Internet. **Cards:** AX, MC, VI. **Free Special Amenities:** full breakfast and high-speed Internet.

🅂🄳 🛟 ⊠ / SOME UNITS FEE 🐾 🖥 📭

ACCENT INNS

Ⓐ SAVE

♦♦♦ ♦♦♦
Small-scale Hotel
$99-$179 All Year

Book great rates at AAA.com **Phone:** (250)475-7500 **1**

Address: 3233 Maple St V8X 4Y9 **Location:** 1.9 mi (3 km) n on Blanshard St (Hwy 17); corner of Blanchard St and Cloverdale Ave. **Facility:** 118 one-bedroom standard units, some with efficiencies (utensils extra charge). 3 stories, exterior corridors. **Parking:** on-site. **Amenities:** high-speed Internet, voice mail, irons, hair dryers. **Guest Services:** valet and coin laundry, wireless Internet. **Business Services:** meeting rooms. **Cards:** AX, CB, DC, DS, MC, VI. **Free Special Amenities:** newspaper and high-speed Internet. *(See color ad below)*

🅂🄳 🍽 CALL 🄲🄼 🛟 🎥 🖥 📭 / SOME UNITS FEE 🐾 ⊠ 📷

"Everywhere in BC you want to be."

When you stay with us, you always arrive at a great deal. We provide quality where it counts. Enjoy our famously comfy beds, spotlessly clean rooms and friendly service. Please visit our website for details on our special offers. See you down the road.

Accent Inns™
quality where it counts

1-800-663-0298
accentinns.com

Vancouver Airport • Vancouver Burnaby • Victoria • Kamloops • Kelowna

(See map and index starting on p. 635)

ADMIRAL INN
Phone: (250)388-6267 **18**

Motel
$99-$609 All Year

Address: 257 Belleville St V8V 1X1 **Location:** Corner of Belleville and Quebec sts. **Facility:** Smoke free premises. 32 units. 21 one-bedroom standard units, some with kitchens. 11 one-bedroom suites with kitchens. 3 stories, exterior corridors. **Parking:** on-site. **Terms:** office hours 7:30 am-11 pm, cancellation fee imposed. **Amenities:** video library (fee), irons, hair dryers. **Guest Services:** valet and coin laundry, wireless Internet. **Business Services:** PC. **Cards:** AX, DS, MC, VI. **Free Special Amenities: continental breakfast and high-speed Internet.**
(See color ad below)

A HATERLEIGH HERITAGE INN
Book at AAA.com
Phone: 250-384-9995 **23**

Historic Bed
& Breakfast
Rates not provided

Address: 243 Kingston St V8V 1V5 **Location:** Corner of Pendray and Kingston sts. Located in the Inner Harbour. **Facility:** A sweeping staircase, semicircular porch and stained-glass and leaded windows distinguish this restored, early 20th-century Victorian home. Smoke free premises. 7 one-bedroom standard units, some with whirlpools. 2 stories (no elevator), interior corridors. **Parking:** on-site. **Terms:** office hours 8 am-9 pm, check-in 4 pm, age restrictions may apply. **Amenities:** hair dryers. **Business Services:** PC.

AMBROSIA HISTORIC BED & BREAKFAST RETREAT
Phone: 250-380-7705 **41**

Historic Bed
& Breakfast
$115-$255 All Year

Address: 522 Quadra St V8V 3S3 **Location:** Between Southgate and Humboldt sts. **Facility:** Located within walking distance of Beacon Hill Park and downtown, the inn offers spacious rooms in a fully restored Victorian style home. Smoke free premises. 4 one-bedroom standard units, some with whirlpools. 2 stories (no elevator), interior corridors. *Bath:* combo or shower only. **Parking:** on-site. **Terms:** office hours 8 am-10 pm, check-in 4 pm, age restrictions may apply, 14 day cancellation notice-fee imposed. **Amenities:** CD players, hair dryers. **Guest Services:** wireless Internet. **Cards:** AX, JC, MC, VI.

─────────── ▼ *See AAA listing above* ▼ ───────────

(See map and index starting on p. 635)

AMETHYST INN AT REGENTS PARK   Phone: (250)595-2053   **15**

**Historic Bed
& Breakfast**

$149-$249 4/1-2/28
$119-$189 3/1-3/31

Address: 1501 Fort St V8S 1Z6 **Location:** Blanshard St (Hwy 17), 1.2 mi (2 km) e on Fort St to St. Charles St. Located in a residential area. **Facility:** With antiques, stained glass and a magnificent staircase, this authentic Victorian mansion is located in a charming neighborhood of stately homes. Smoke free premises. 13 one-bedroom standard units, some with whirlpools. 3 stories (no elevator), interior/exterior corridors. **Parking:** on-site. **Terms:** office hours 7 am-11 pm, age restrictions may apply, 14 day cancellation notice-fee imposed. **Amenities:** hair dryers. *Some:* CD players. **Cards:** AX, MC, VI. **Free Special Amenities:** full breakfast and high-speed Internet.

▼ See AAA listing p 666 ▼

(See map and index starting on p. 635)

ANDERSEN HOUSE BED & BREAKFAST   Phone: 250/388-4565   **31**

Historic Bed
& Breakfast

Rates not provided

Address: 301 Kingston St V8V 1V5 **Location:** Between Pendray and Montreal sts. Located in the Inner Harbour. **Facility:** This 1891 home in Victoria's Inner Harbour blends rich historic details with comfortable, contemporary furnishings and original artwork. Smoke free premises. 4 one-bedroom standard units, some with whirlpools. 3 stories (no elevator), interior/exterior corridors. *Bath:* combo or shower only. **Parking:** on-site. **Terms:** office hours 8 am-10 pm, age restrictions may apply. **Amenities:** CD players, hair dryers. **Guest Services:** wireless Internet.

BEACONSFIELD INN   Phone: 250/384-4044   **42**

Historic Bed
& Breakfast

Rates not provided

Address: 998 Humboldt St V8V 2Z8 **Location:** Blanshard St (Hwy 17), just e on Fairfield Rd, then just s on Vancouver St. Located in a quiet residential area. **Facility:** This 1905 Edwardian mansion features richly paneled walls, mahogany floors and tall, beamed ceilings; some rooms have fireplaces or whirlpool tubs. Smoke free premises. 9 one-bedroom standard units, some with whirlpools. 4 stories (no elevator), interior corridors. *Bath:* combo or shower only. **Parking:** on-site. **Terms:** office hours 7 am-10 pm, age restrictions may apply. **Amenities:** CD players, hair dryers.

BEST WESTERN CARLTON PLAZA HOTEL   *Book great rates at AAA.com*   Phone: (250)388-5513   **11**

Small-scale Hotel
$89-$189 All Year

Address: 642 Johnson St V8W 1M6 **Location:** Between Douglas and Broad sts. **Facility:** Smoke free premises. 103 units. 97 one-bedroom standard units, some with efficiencies or kitchens. 6 one-bedroom suites with kitchens. 7 stories, interior corridors. **Parking:** on-site (fee) and valet. **Terms:** cancellation fee imposed. **Amenities:** voice mail, safes, irons, hair dryers. *Some:* high-speed Internet. **Leisure Activities:** exercise room. **Guest Services:** valet and coin laundry, wireless Internet. **Business Services:** PC. **Cards:** AX, CB, DC, DS, JC, MC, VI. **Free Special Amenities:** newspaper and room upgrade (subject to availability with advance reservations). *(See color ad below)*

AAA Benefit:
Members save 10% everyday, plus an exclusive frequent stay program.

(See map and index starting on p. 635)

BEST WESTERN INNER HARBOUR   *Book great rates at AAA.com*   **Phone:** (250)384-5122

Small-scale Hotel
$109-$279 3/1-10/12
$89-$169 10/13-2/28

Address: 412 Quebec St V8V 1W5 **Location:** Between Oswego and Menzies sts. **Facility:** Smoke free premises. 74 units. 66 one-bedroom standard units, some with efficiencies (utensils extra charge). 7 one- and 1 two-bedroom suites with whirlpools, some with efficiencies or kitchens (utensils extra charge). 8 stories, interior corridors. **Parking:** on-site. **Terms:** check-in 4 pm. **Amenities:** video library (fee), high-speed Internet, voice mail, irons, hair dryers. *Some:* DVD players (fee). **Pool(s):** heated outdoor. **Leisure Activities:** sauna, whirlpool, steamroom, limited exercise equipment. **Guest Services:** valet and coin laundry. **Cards:** AX, DC, DS, MC, VI. **Free Special Amenities: expanded continental breakfast and newspaper.** *(See color ad below)*

AAA Benefit:
Members save 10% everyday, plus an exclusive frequent stay program.

     / SOME UNITS FEE VCR

(See map and index starting on p. 635)

BLUE RIDGE INNS *Book great rates at AAA.com*   Phone: (250)388-4345 **3**

Motel
$69-$129 All Year

Address: 3110 Douglas St V8Z 3K4 **Location:** Between Finlayson St and Speed Ave. **Facility:** 63 units. 61 one- and 1 two-bedroom standard units, some with efficiencies or kitchens. 1 cottage. 2 stories (no elevator), exterior corridors. *Bath:* combo or shower only. **Parking:** on-site. **Amenities:** voice mail. *Some:* high-speed Internet (fee). **Pool(s):** heated indoor. **Leisure Activities:** sauna. **Guest Services:** coin laundry, wireless Internet. **Business Services:** meeting rooms, PC. **Cards:** AX, CB, DC, DS, MC, VI. **Free Special Amenities:** newspaper and high-speed Internet.

CHATEAU VICTORIA HOTEL AND SUITES   *Book great rates at AAA.com*   Phone: (250)382-4221 **19**

Large-scale Hotel
$159-$229 3/1-9/30
$89-$115 10/1-2/28

Address: 740 Burdett Ave V8W 1B2 **Location:** Between Douglas and Blanshard sts. **Facility:** 177 units. 59 one-bedroom standard units. 111 one- and 7 two-bedroom suites, some with efficiencies, kitchens and/or whirlpools. 19 stories, interior corridors. **Parking:** on-site. **Amenities:** video games (fee), voice mail, safes, irons, hair dryers. **Pool(s):** heated indoor. **Leisure Activities:** whirlpool, limited exercise equipment. **Guest Services:** valet laundry, area transportation, wireless Internet. **Business Services:** meeting rooms, PC. **Cards:** AX, CB, DC, DS, JC, MC, VI. *(See color ad below)*

DALTON HOTEL & SUITES   *Book great rates at AAA.com*   Phone: (250)384-4136 **14**

Small-scale Hotel
$66-$178 All Year

Address: 759 Yates St V8W 1L6 **Location:** Between Blanchard and Douglas sts. **Facility:** Smoke free premises. 93 units. 89 one-bedroom standard units. 4 one-bedroom suites with efficiencies. 4 stories, interior corridors. *Bath:* combo or shower only. **Parking:** on-site (fee). **Terms:** cancellation fee imposed. **Amenities:** voice mail. **Guest Services:** wireless Internet. **Cards:** AX, MC, VI. **Free Special Amenities:** local telephone calls and high-speed Internet.

DASHWOOD SEASIDE HERITAGE MANOR   Phone: 250/385-5517 **44**

Historic Bed
& Breakfast
Rates not provided

Address: 1 Cook St V8V 3W6 **Location:** 0.6 mi (1 km) e of Douglas St on Dallas Rd. Located in a residential area across from Beacon Hill Park. **Facility:** Built in 1912, this charming Tudor-style mansion sits at the end of Cook Street and is the only B&B with an ocean view and a peek at Mt. Baker. Smoke free premises. 11 one-bedroom standard units, some with whirlpools. 3 stories (no elevator), interior corridors. **Parking:** on-site. **Terms:** office hours 8 am-9 pm, check-in 4 pm, age restrictions may apply. **Amenities:** hair dryers. **Guest Services:** wireless Internet.

(See map and index starting on p. 635)

DELTA VICTORIA OCEAN POINTE RESORT & SPA   *Book great rates at AAA.com*   **Phone:** 250/360-2999

Large-scale Hotel
$265-$398 10/1-2/28
$159-$328 3/1-9/30

Address: 45 Songhees Rd V9A 6T3 **Location:** Just w of Johnson St Bridge, Esquimalt at Tyee Rd. **Facility:** Rooms with city and Inner Harbour views are featured at this waterfront hotel; guests may observe sea planes land and take off right from the harbor. 244 units. 239 one-bedroom standard units, some with efficiencies. 5 one-bedroom suites, some with efficiencies and/or whirlpools. 8 stories, interior corridors. **Parking:** on-site (fee) and valet. **Terms:** check-in 4 pm. **Amenities:** CD players, dual phone lines, voice mail, honor bars, irons, hair dryers. *Fee:* video games, high-speed Internet. **Pool(s):** heated indoor. **Leisure Activities:** sauna, whirlpool, 2 lighted tennis courts, racquetball court, spa. **Guest Services:** valet laundry, area transportation. **Business Services:** conference facilities, business center. **Cards:** AX, CB, DC, DS, JC, MC, VI.

EMBASSY INN   **Phone:** (250)382-8161   **37**

Small-scale Hotel
$89-$349 All Year

Address: 520 Menzies St V8V 2H4 **Location:** Corner of Quebec St. Located adjacent to Parliament buildings. **Facility:** Smoke free premises. 103 one-bedroom standard units, some with efficiencies or kitchens. 3-4 stories, interior/exterior corridors. **Parking:** on-site. **Terms:** check-in 4 pm, cancellation fee imposed. **Amenities:** voice mail, hair dryers. *Some:* irons. **Pool(s):** heated outdoor. **Leisure Activities:** sauna. **Guest Services:** valet and coin laundry, wireless Internet. **Business Services:** meeting rooms. **Cards:** AX, CB, DC, MC, VI. **Free Special Amenities:** preferred room (subject to availability with advance reservations) and high-speed Internet.
(See color ad below)

EXECUTIVE HOUSE HOTEL   *Book great rates at AAA.com*   **Phone:** 250/388-5111   **20**

Small-scale Hotel
$195-$215 All Year

Address: 777 Douglas St V8W 2B5 **Location:** Between Blanshard and Douglas sts; downtown. **Facility:** 181 units. 98 one-bedroom standard units, some with efficiencies and/or whirlpools. 78 one- and 5 two-bedroom suites, some with kitchens and/or whirlpools. 17 stories, interior corridors. **Parking:** on-site (fee) and valet. **Terms:** cancellation fee imposed. **Amenities:** high-speed Internet, voice mail, irons, hair dryers. *Some:* CD players. **Dining:** Barkley's Steak & Seafood, see separate listing. **Leisure Activities:** whirlpool, steamroom, exercise room. **Guest Services:** valet and coin laundry, area transportation-Inner Harbour/downtown. **Business Services:** meeting rooms. **Cards:** AX, DC, DS, JC, MC, VI. **Free Special Amenities:** local telephone calls and high-speed Internet.

FAIRHOLME MANOR   **Phone:** (250)598-3240   **35**

Historic Bed
& Breakfast
$175-$325 3/1-10/15
$135-$250 10/16-2/28

Address: 638 Rockland Pl V8S 3R2 **Location:** Blanshard St (Hwy 17), 1.2 mi (2 km) e on Fort St, just s on St. Charles St to Rockland Ave, look for Rockland Pl sign, then down alley. Located in historic Rockland District. **Facility:** Built in 1885, this restored mansion surrounded by an acre of parklike gardens and lawn has been converted into luxury suites with upscale bathrooms. Smoke free premises. 6 units. 5 one- and 1 two-bedroom standard units. 2 stories (no elevator), interior/exterior corridors. **Parking:** on-site. **Terms:** office hours 8 am-10 pm, check-in 4 pm, age restrictions may apply, 14 day cancellation notice-fee imposed. **Amenities:** video library, DVD players, CD players, irons, hair dryers. **Guest Services:** wireless Internet. **Cards:** AX, MC, VI.

(See map and index starting on p. 635)

THE FAIRMONT EMPRESS   *Book great rates at AAA.com*   **Phone:** (250)384-8111   25

Historic
Large-scale Hotel
$169-$569 All Year

Address: 721 Government St V8W 1W5 **Location:** Between Belleville and Humboldt sts. Located on the Inner Harbour. **Facility:** Known for its tradition of afternoon tea, this landmark Victorian property offers views of the harbor; rooms vary in size and style, as do the views. 476 one-bedroom standard units, some with whirlpools. 8 stories, interior corridors. **Parking:** on-site (fee) and valet. **Terms:** check-in 4 pm. **Amenities:** video games (fee), voice mail, irons, hair dryers. *Some:* CD players, high-speed Internet (fee), dual phone lines, safes. **Dining:** The Empress Room, see separate listing. **Pool(s):** heated indoor. **Leisure Activities:** saunas, whirlpool, exercise room, spa. **Guest Services:** valet laundry. **Business Services:** conference facilities, business center. **Cards:** AX, DC, DS, JC, MC, VI. *(See color ad below)*

(See map and index starting on p. 635)

HARBOUR TOWERS HOTEL & SUITES   *Book great rates at AAA.com*   **Phone:** (250)385-2405

Large-scale Hotel
$94-$450 All Year

Address: 345 Quebec St V8V 1W4 **Location:** Between Oswego and Pendray sts. **Facility:** Smoke free premises. 196 units. 123 one-bedroom standard units, some with efficiencies. 45 one- and 28 two-bedroom suites, some with efficiencies, kitchens and/or whirlpools. 12 stories, interior corridors. **Parking:** on-site (fee). **Terms:** cancellation fee imposed. **Amenities:** video games (fee), high-speed Internet, voice mail, irons, hair dryers. *Some:* CD players. **Pool(s):** heated indoor. **Leisure Activities:** sauna, whirlpool, spa. **Guest Services:** valet and coin laundry, area transportation-downtown, beauty salon. **Business Services:** meeting rooms, PC. **Cards:** AX, DC, JC, MC, VI. **Free Special Amenities:** newspaper and high-speed Internet. *(See color ad p 646)*

HEATHERGATE HOUSE BED & BREAKFAST   **Phone:** (250)383-0068

Bed & Breakfast
$85-$145 3/1-9/1
$90-$125 9/2-2/28

Address: 122 Simcoe St V8V 1K4 **Location:** Between St. Lawrence and Montreal sts. **Facility:** Smoke free premises. 5 units. 4 one- and 1 two-bedroom standard units. 2 stories (no elevator), interior/exterior corridors. *Bath:* combo or shower only. **Parking:** on-site. **Terms:** office hours 8 am-11 pm, 2 night minimum stay - seasonal, 14 day cancellation notice-fee imposed. **Amenities:** hair dryers. **Cards:** AX, DS, JC, MC, VI.

HELM'S INN   *Book great rates at AAA.com*   **Phone:** 250/385-5767

Small-scale Hotel
Rates not provided

Address: 600 Douglas St V8V 2P8 **Location:** Corner of Douglas and Superior sts. **Facility:** Smoke free premises. 42 units. 36 one-bedroom standard units, some with kitchens. 6 one-bedroom suites, some with kitchens. 3 stories (no elevator), interior corridors. **Parking:** on-site (fee). **Terms:** office hours 7 am-11 pm, check-in 4 pm. **Amenities:** voice mail, irons, hair dryers. **Guest Services:** coin laundry, wireless Internet. **Free Special Amenities:** newspaper and high-speed Internet.

▼ See AAA listing p 648 ▼

(See map and index starting on p. 635)

HOLIDAY INN VICTORIA   *Book great rates at AAA.com*   Phone: (250)382-4400   **4**

Small-scale Hotel
$90-$179 All Year

Address: 3020 Blanshard St V8T 5C7 **Location:** 1.6 mi (2.6) km n on Blanshard St (Hwy 17), just s of Finlayson St. **Facility:** Smoke free premises. 152 units. 143 one-bedroom standard units, some with efficiencies. 9 one-bedroom suites, some with efficiencies. 3-4 stories, interior/exterior corridors. **Parking:** on-site. **Amenities:** video games (fee), voice mail, irons, hair dryers. *Some:* high-speed Internet. **Leisure Activities:** sauna, whirlpool, limited exercise equipment. **Guest Services:** valet and coin laundry, wireless Internet. **Business Services:** meeting rooms. **Cards:** AX, CB, DC, DS, JC, MC, VI. **Free Special Amenities: local telephone calls and high-speed Internet.**

HOTEL GRAND PACIFIC   *Book great rates at AAA.com*   Phone: (250)386-0450   **27**

Large-scale Hotel
$149-$319 All Year

Address: 463 Belleville St V8V 1X3 **Location:** Between Oswego and Menzies sts. **Facility:** The upscale high-rise building offers a variety of views, and modern rooms with private balconies overlook the Olympic Mountains or the Inner Harbour. Smoke free premises. 304 units. 266 one-bedroom standard units. 38 one-bedroom suites, some with whirlpools. 10 stories, interior corridors. **Parking:** on-site (fee) and valet. **Terms:** cancellation fee imposed. **Amenities:** video games (fee), high-speed Internet, voice mail, safes, honor bars, irons, hair dryers. **Dining:** 2 restaurants, also, The Mark, see separate listing. **Pool(s):** heated indoor. **Leisure Activities:** sauna, whirlpool, steamroom, spa. *Fee:* racquetball court. **Guest Services:** valet laundry. **Business Services:** conference facilities, business center. **Cards:** AX, DC, DS, JC, MC, VI. **Free Special Amenities: newspaper and high-speed Internet.** *(See color ad p 647)*

HOWARD JOHNSON HOTEL-CITY CENTRE   *Book great rates at AAA.com*   Phone: 250/382-2151   **8**

Small-scale Hotel
$69-$159 3/1-9/30
$59-$119 10/1-2/28

Address: 310 Gorge Rd E V8T 2W2 **Location:** From Douglas St, 0.6 mi (1.4 km) w; between Jutland St and Washington Ave. **Facility:** Smoke free premises. 80 one-bedroom standard units, some with kitchens. 3 stories, interior corridors. **Parking:** on-site. **Terms:** cancellation fee imposed. **Amenities:** voice mail, irons, hair dryers. *Some:* high-speed Internet. **Pool(s):** heated indoor. **Leisure Activities:** saunas, exercise room. **Guest Services:** valet and coin laundry, wireless Internet. **Business Services:** meeting rooms, PC. **Cards:** AX, DS, MC, VI. **Free Special Amenities: newspaper and early check-in/late check-out.**

HUMBOLDT HOUSE BED & BREAKFAST   Phone: (250)383-0152   **38**

Historic Bed
& Breakfast
$147-$315 All Year

Address: 867 Humboldt St V8V 2Z6 **Location:** Humboldt and Quadra sts. Located in a quiet area. **Facility:** A retreat-like ambience makes this B&B well-suited for romantic getaways. Smoke free premises. 6 one-bedroom standard units, some with whirlpools. 2 stories (no elevator), interior corridors. *Bath:* combo or shower only. **Parking:** on-site. **Terms:** office hours 7 am-11 pm, 7 day cancellation notice-fee imposed. **Amenities:** CD players, hair dryers. **Cards:** AX, JC, MC, VI.

▼ See AAA listing p 649 ▼

(See map and index starting on p. 635)

HUNTINGDON HOTEL & SUITES   *Book great rates at AAA.com*   Phone: (250)381-3456   **22**

Small-scale Hotel
$99-$379 All Year

Address: 330 Quebec St V8V 1W3 **Location:** Between Oswego and Pendray sts. **Facility:** Smoke free premises. 115 units. 114 one- and 1 two-bedroom standard units, some with kitchens (utensils extra charge). 3 stories, interior corridors. **Parking:** on-site (fee). **Amenities:** video games (fee), voice mail, irons, hair dryers. **Leisure Activities:** sauna, whirlpool. **Guest Services:** valet and coin laundry, wireless Internet. **Business Services:** meeting rooms. **Cards:** AX, CB, DC, DS, JC, MC, VI. **Free Special Amenities:** preferred room (subject to availability with advance reservations). *(See color ad p 648)*

JAMES BAY INN HOTEL & SUITES   *Book great rates at AAA.com*   Phone: (250)384-7151   **43**

Small-scale Hotel
$130-$164 3/1-10/15
$75-$85 10/16-2/28

Address: 270 Government St V8V 2L2 **Location:** Between Toronto and Marifield sts. **Facility:** 45 one-bedroom standard units, some with kitchens. 4 stories (no elevator), interior corridors. **Bath:** combo or shower only. **Parking:** on-site. **Terms:** cancellation fee imposed. **Guest Services:** wireless Internet. **Business Services:** PC. **Cards:** AX, MC, VI. **Free Special Amenities:** early check-in/late check-out and room upgrade (subject to availability with advance reservations). *(See color ad below)*

THE MAGNOLIA HOTEL & SPA   *Book great rates at AAA.com*   Phone: (250)381-0999   **16**

Small-scale Hotel
$175-$335 All Year

Address: 623 Courtney St V8W 1B8 **Location:** Corner of Courtney and Gordon sts. Located on the Inner Harbour. **Facility:** A luxury hotel offering elegant rooms with large bay windows, The Magnolia is in Victoria's Inner Harbour area, convenient for strolling and shopping. Smoke free premises. 63 one-bedroom standard units. 7 stories, interior corridors. **Parking:** valet. **Terms:** cancellation fee imposed. **Amenities:** CD players, high-speed Internet, dual phone lines, voice mail, honor bars, irons, hair dryers. **Dining:** 2 restaurants. **Leisure Activities:** limited exercise equipment, spa. **Guest Services:** valet laundry. **Business Services:** meeting rooms. **Cards:** AX, CB, DC, DS, JC, MC, VI. **Free Special Amenities:** expanded continental breakfast and high-speed Internet.

MARRIOTT VICTORIA INNER HARBOUR   *Book great rates at AAA.com*   Phone: 250/480-3800   **30**

Large-scale Hotel
$208-$307 All Year

Address: 728 Humboldt St V8W 3Z5 **Location:** Between Blanshard and Douglas sts. **Facility:** Newest full-service hotel located near the Inner Harbor and downtown; guest units are spacious and offer wonderful views of the downtown area. Smoke free premises. 236 units. 228 one-bedroom standard units. 8 one-bedroom suites. 16 stories, interior corridors. **Parking:** on-site (fee) and valet. **Terms:** check-in 4 pm. **Amenities:** CD players, high-speed Internet, dual phone lines, voice mail, safes, irons, hair dryers. **Dining:** Fire & Water Fish & Chop House, see separate listing. **Pool(s):** heated indoor. **Leisure Activities:** whirlpool, steamroom, exercise room. **Guest Services:** valet and coin laundry. **Business Services:** meeting rooms, business center. **Cards:** AX, DC, DS, MC, VI. **Free Special Amenities:** newspaper and room upgrade (subject to availability with advance reservations). *(See color ad p 650)*

Marriott
HOTELS & RESORTS

AAA Benefit:
Members save 5% off of the best available rate.

MAYFAIR MOTEL   Phone: (250)388-7337   **2**

Motel
$49-$119 All Year

Address: 650 Speed Ave V8Z 1A4 **Location:** From downtown, 1.6 mi (2.5 km) n on Douglas St. **Facility:** Smoke free premises. 22 one-bedroom standard units with kitchens (utensils extra charge). 4 stories, interior corridors. **Parking:** on-site. **Terms:** office hours 8 am-11:30 pm. **Guest Services:** coin laundry. **Cards:** AX, MC, VI. **Free Special Amenities:** local telephone calls and preferred room (subject to availability with advance reservations).

▼ *See AAA listing above* ▼

JAMES BAY INN HOTEL & SUITES
TURN OF THE CENTURY

- Quaint, quiet, charming
- Great dining and friendly pub
- Ample free parking
- A short walk to the Inner Harbour, Parliament buildings and downtown
- Guests receive 15% off all meals

THE JAMES BAY INN

270 Government St. Victoria BC ▸ Tel: 250-384-7151 ▸ Toll Free: 1-800-836-2649 ▸ www.jamesbayinn.com

(See map and index starting on p. 635)

THE OSWEGO HOTEL

Small-scale Hotel
$275-$650 3/1-9/21
$195-$445 9/22-2/28

Book great rates at AAA.com   Phone: (250)294-7500 28

Address: 500 Oswego St V8V 5C1 **Location:** Between Kingston and Quebec sts. **Facility:** Smoke free premises. 80 units. 21 one-bedroom standard units with efficiencies. 44 one- and 15 two-bedroom suites with kitchens. 10 stories, interior corridors. **Parking:** on-site (fee) and valet. **Terms:** cancellation fee imposed. **Amenities:** CD players, high-speed Internet, voice mail, irons, hair dryers. **Leisure Activities:** whirlpool, exercise room. **Guest Services:** valet and coin laundry. **Business Services:** meeting rooms, PC. **Cards:** AX, DS, MC, VI. **Free Special Amenities:** expanded continental breakfast and early check-in/late check-out. *(See color ad p 651)*

PRIOR HOUSE B&B INN

Historic Bed
& Breakfast
$129-$299 All Year

Phone: (250)592-8847 39

Address: 620 St. Charles St V8S 3N7 **Location:** Blanshard St (Hwy 17), 1.2 mi (2 km) e on Fort St, then just s. Located in a quiet area. **Facility:** Set on lush, landscaped grounds in a tree-lined neighborhood, the Prior House is a wonderfully restored 1912 manor home featuring antique furnishings. Smoke free premises. 6 units. 2 one-bedroom standard units with whirlpools. 2 one- and 2 two-bedroom suites with whirlpools. 3 stories (no elevator), interior corridors. **Parking:** on-site. **Terms:** office hours 7 am-9 pm, age restrictions may apply, 14 day cancellation notice-fee imposed. **Amenities:** video library, CD players, high-speed Internet, voice mail, irons, hair dryers. **Guest Services:** valet and coin laundry. **Business Services:** PC. **Cards:** MC, VI. **Free Special Amenities:** full breakfast and high-speed Internet.

(See map and index starting on p. 635)

QUALITY INN DOWNTOWN   *Book great rates at AAA.com*   Phone: (250)385-6787

Small-scale Hotel
$79-$169 3/1-9/30
$79-$119 10/1-2/28

Address: 850 Blanshard St V8W 2H2 **Location:** Between Courtney St and Burnett Ave; downtown. **Facility:** 63 units. 61 one-bedroom standard units, some with efficiencies and/or whirlpools. 2 one-bedroom suites with whirlpools. 3 stories, interior corridors. **Parking:** on-site. **Terms:** cancellation fee imposed. **Amenities:** voice mail, irons, hair dryers. *Some:* high-speed Internet. **Pool(s):** heated indoor. **Leisure Activities:** steamroom, limited exercise equipment. **Guest Services:** valet and coin laundry, wireless Internet. **Business Services:** meeting rooms. **Cards:** AX, DC, DS, MC, VI. **Free Special Amenities: local telephone calls and high-speed Internet.** *(See color ad on insert & below)*

QUEEN VICTORIA HOTEL AND SUITES   *Book great rates at AAA.com*   Phone: (250)386-1312 36

Small-scale Hotel
$130-$450 All Year

Address: 655 Douglas St V8V 2P9 **Location:** Between Belleville and Superior sts. **Facility:** Smoke free premises. 146 units. 125 one-bedroom standard units, some with efficiencies and/or whirlpools. 14 one- and 7 two-bedroom suites, some with whirlpools. 7 stories, interior corridors. **Parking:** on-site (fee). **Terms:** cancellation fee imposed. **Amenities:** voice mail, irons, hair dryers. **Pool(s):** heated indoor. **Leisure Activities:** sauna, whirlpool, exercise room. **Guest Services:** valet and coin laundry, area transportation-downtown area, wireless Internet. **Cards:** AX, DS, MC, VI. **Free Special Amenities: room upgrade (subject to availability with advance reservations).** *(See color ad p 652)*

(See map and index starting on p. 635)

RAMADA VICTORIA **Phone:** (250)386-1422 **6**

Small-scale Hotel
$135-$185 3/1-9/30
$65-$130 10/1-2/28

Address: 123 Gorge Rd E V9A 1L1 **Location:** From Douglas St, 1.2 mi (2.4 km) w. **Facility:** 94 one-bedroom standard units, some with efficiencies or kitchens. 4 stories, interior corridors. **Parking:** on-site. **Terms:** cancellation fee imposed. **Amenities:** voice mail, irons, hair dryers. **Pool(s):** heated outdoor. **Guest Services:** valet and coin laundry, wireless Internet. **Business Services:** meeting rooms, PC. **Cards:** AX, DC, DS, MC, VI. *(See color ad p 653)*

[ASK] [S/D] [🍽] [🍸] [🏊] [🎥] [💻]
/SOME UNITS FEE [🐕] [✕] [📠] [🛄]

ROBIN HOOD MOTEL **Phone:** (250)388-4302 **5**

Motel
$66-$104 3/1-9/30
$66-$79 10/1-2/28

Address: 136 Gorge Rd E V9A 1L4 **Location:** Douglas St, 1.2 mi (2.4 km) w. **Facility:** 55 one-bedroom standard units, some with kitchens. 3 stories (no elevator), exterior corridors. **Parking:** on-site. **Terms:** office hours 8 am-11 pm. **Guest Services:** coin laundry, wireless Internet. **Cards:** AX, CB, DC, JC, MC, VI. **Free Special Amenities:** local telephone calls and preferred room (subject to availability with advance reservations). *(See color ad p 653)*

[S/D] [🍽] [💻] /SOME UNITS FEE [🐕] [✕] [📶] [📠]

▼ See AAA listing p 651 ▼

(See map and index starting on p. 635)

ROYAL SCOT SUITE HOTEL   *Book great rates at AAA.com*   Phone: (250)388-5463   32

Small-scale Hotel
$175-$249 3/1-9/30
$109-$149 10/1-2/28

Address: 425 Quebec St V8V 1W7 **Location:** Between Menzies and Oswego sts. **Facility:** Smoke free premises. 176 units. 94 one-bedroom standard units, some with kitchens. 78 one- and 4 two-bedroom suites with kitchens. 4 stories, interior corridors. **Parking:** on-site. **Terms:** cancellation fee imposed. **Amenities:** high-speed Internet (fee), voice mail, safes, irons, hair dryers. **Pool(s):** heated indoor. **Leisure Activities:** saunas, whirlpool, billiards, limited exercise equipment, game room. **Guest Services:** valet and coin laundry, area transportation-downtown. **Business Services:** meeting rooms, PC (fee). **Cards:** AX, DC, DS, JC, MC, VI. **Free Special Amenities:** newspaper. *(See color ad p 654)*

   / SOME UNITS

SPINNAKERS GASTRO BREWPUB AND
   GUESTHOUSES   Phone: (250)386-2739   9

Small-scale Hotel
$129-$249 All Year

Address: 308 Catherine St V9A 3S8 **Location:** 1.3 mi (2 km) nw over Johnson St Bridge, then just s. **Facility:** Smoke free premises. 9 one-bedroom standard units, some with efficiencies, kitchens and/or whirlpools. 2 stories (no elevator), interior/exterior corridors. *Bath:* combo or shower only. **Parking:** on-site. **Terms:** office hours 8 am-11 pm, age restrictions may apply, 7 day cancellation notice-fee imposed. **Amenities:** voice mail, irons, hair dryers. **Dining:** Spinnakers Gastro Brewpub & Restaurant, see separate listing. **Guest Services:** wireless Internet. **Cards:** AX, MC, VI. **Free Special Amenities:** expanded continental breakfast and local telephone calls. *(See color ad p 655)*

     / SOME UNITS

▼ See AAA listing p 653 ▼

By the Harbour in the Beautiful City of Victoria, BC

Full service suite hotel surrounded by beautiful gardens. Located 1 block from downtown, by the Inner Harbour. 146 Suites, 30 rooms. Queen & king beds, spacious studios, 1 & 2 bedroom suites with living room & complete kitchens. Many balconies, 4 stories, interior corridors, 100% non-smoking, no A/C. Children under 16 stay free; no pets.

SERVICES AVAILABLE - Licensed restaurant, room service, gift shop featuring original artwork & a selection of fine foods, meeting rooms, high speed internet, above ground surface parking, valet service, coin laundry, Nintendo, babysitting services, business centre, 24 hour security patrols.

SERVICES - NO CHARGE - Indoor heated pool, sauna, whirlpool, games and exercise rooms, billiards room, shuttle service to downtown, bicycle lock-up, newspaper, data phones, in-suite coffee, tea & cookies, bathrobes, microwaves, iron & ironing boards, hair dryers, electronic safes, 25" remote TV in living room, additional TV in one and two bedroom suites, cable. Seasonal Guest Services coordinator. Join us for whale watching, golfing, fishing, eco-tours & much more!
Visit Victoria through our website at www.royalscot.com

AAA SPECIAL VALUE RATES

ROYAL SCOT SUITE HOTEL
VICTORIA

425 Quebec Street
1-800-663-7515 • www.royalscot.com

(See map and index starting on p. 635)

SWANS HOTEL

Small-scale Hotel
$149-$359 All Year

Phone: (250)361-3310 **10**

Address: 506 Pandora Ave V8W 1N6 **Location:** Corner of Pandora Ave and Store St. **Facility:** Smoke free premises. 30 units. 18 one- and 12 two-bedroom suites with kitchens, some with whirlpools. 2 stories, interior corridors. **Parking:** on-site (fee). **Terms:** check-in 4 pm, 7 day cancellation notice, 6/1-9/30-fee imposed. **Amenities:** video library, DVD players, voice mail, irons, hair dryers. *Some:* high-speed Internet. **Guest Services:** valet and coin laundry, wireless Internet. **Business Services:** meeting rooms. **Cards:** AX, DC, DS, MC, VI.

welcome

Experience Spinnakers at every level, be it the luxury GuestHouses or Gastro Brewpub with oceanfront patios, multi-tiered restaurant and comfortable upper-level taproom. In close proximity to Spinnakers waterfront location are an intimate cluster of handsome adult-oriented GuestHouses.

Spinnakers GuestHouses are one of Victoria's best kept secrets!

 Approved

308 Catherine Street, Victoria • Toll Free 877.838.2739 www.spinnakers.com

(See map and index starting on p. 635)

TRAVELODGE VICTORIA   *Book great rates at AAA.com*   Phone: (250)388-6611

Small-scale Hotel
$144-$174 3/1-10/12
$74-$94 10/13-2/28

Address: 229 Gorge Rd E V9A 1L1 **Location:** From Douglas St, 1.2 mi (2 km) w on Gorge Rd E; at Washington Ave. **Facility:** 73 one-bedroom standard units, some with efficiencies or kitchens. 3 stories (no elevator), exterior corridors. **Parking:** on-site. **Terms:** cancellation fee imposed. **Amenities:** voice mail, safes, hair dryers. **Pool(s):** heated indoor. **Leisure Activities:** saunas, exercise room. **Guest Services:** valet and coin laundry, wireless Internet. **Business Services:** meeting rooms. **Cards:** AX, CB, DC, DS, JC, MC, VI. **Free Special Amenities:** local telephone calls and high-speed Internet. *(See color ad below)*

     SOME UNITS FEE

▼ *See AAA listing above* ▼

CLOSE TO VICTORIA'S INNER HARBOUR & DOWNTOWN SHOPPING DISTRICTS.

♦ Situated on the scenic Gorge Waterway, just a five-minute drive from downtown
♦ Spacious, air-conditioned guest rooms & family suites
♦ Complimentary in-room coffee, tea, local calls and wireless Internet access
♦ Indoor heated pool, sauna and fitness facilities
♦ Free parking - room for buses and motorhomes
♦ Restaurant and Lounge

 WE FEATURE THE WORLD'S BEST MATTRESS.™

Call Toll Free 1-800-565-3777 U.S. and Canada

Travelodge Victoria
229 Gorge Road East, Victoria
Tel: (250) 388-6611 ♦ www.travelodgevictoria.com

Approved

(See map and index starting on p. 635)

THE VICTORIA REGENT HOTEL — *Book great rates at AAA.com* — **Phone:** (250)386-2211

Vacation Rental Condominium
$139-$309 All Year

Address: 1234 Wharf St V8W 3H9 **Location:** Wharf and Yates sts. Located on the Inner Harbour. **Facility:** These wonderful downtown condo units all have spectacular harbor views, modern, full kitchens and super large bedrooms. Smoke free premises. 49 units. 23 one- and 26 two-bedroom standard units, some with kitchens and/or whirlpools. 8 stories, interior corridors. **Parking:** on-site. **Terms:** cancellation fee imposed. **Amenities:** high-speed Internet, voice mail, honor bars, irons, hair dryers. **Guest Services:** valet and coin laundry. **Business Services:** meeting rooms, PC. **Cards:** AX, CB, DC, DS, JC, MC, VI. **Free Special Amenities:** expanded continental breakfast and high-speed Internet. *(See color ad below)*

──── ▼ See AAA listing above ▼ ────

(See map and index starting on p. 635)

VILLA MARCO POLO INN

Bed & Breakfast
Rates not provided

Phone: 250/370-1524 **21**

Address: 1524 Shasta Pl V8S 1X9 **Location:** Blanshard St (Hwy 17), 1.3 mi (2 km) e on Fort St, then just s on St. Charles St. Located in a residential area. **Facility:** This recently renovated home is in one of Victoria's oldest neighborhoods; many of the spacious bedrooms overlook manicured grounds. Smoke free premises. 4 one-bedroom standard units, some with whirlpools. 2 stories (no elevator), interior corridors. **Parking:** on-site. **Terms:** office hours 7 am-11 pm, check-in 4 pm, age restrictions may apply. **Amenities:** voice mail, hair dryers. **Guest Services:** wireless Internet.

THE WESTIN BEAR MOUNTAIN VICTORIA GOLF
RESORT & SPA   *Book great rates at AAA.com*

Resort
Small-scale Hotel
$189-$419 3/1-9/30
$169-$359 10/1-2/28

Phone: (250)391-7160

Address: 1999 Country Club Way V9B 6R3 **Location:** Trans-Canada Hwy 1, exit 14 (Highlands), 1.1 mi (1.7 km) n on Millstream Rd, then 1.9 mi (3 km) ne on Bear Mountain Pkwy, follow signs. **Facility:** In an up-and-coming area called Bear Mountain, Victoria's newest resort offers standard-style rooms or large, one-bedroom suites with full kitchens. Smoke free premises. 156 units. 83 one-bedroom standard units. 73 one-bedroom suites with kitchens. 3-5 stories, interior corridors. **Parking:** on-site and valet. **Amenities:** DVD players, video games (fee), high-speed Internet, voice mail, safes, honor bars, irons, hair dryers. *Some:* dual phone lines. **Dining:** 4 restaurants. **Pool(s):** heated outdoor. **Leisure Activities:** sauna, whirlpool, spa. *Fee:* golf-19 holes. **Guest Services:** complimentary and valet laundry, wireless Internet. **Business Services:** meeting rooms, business center. **Cards:** AX, DC, DS, JC, MC, VI. *(See color ad below)*

WESTIN
HOTELS & RESORTS

AAA Benefit:
Members get up to 15% off, plus Starwood Preferred Guest® bonuses.

(See map and index starting on p. 635)

——— **WHERE TO DINE** ———

BARKLEY'S STEAK & SEAFOOD
Phone: 250/382-7111 [19]

Steak & Seafood
$20-$45

Barkley's has an elegant, Victorian atmosphere and an attentive, professional service staff. The restaurant's dishes include steak and seafood, of course, but the menu also offers pasta selections and a choice o Continental dishes. Dressy casual. **Bar:** Full bar. **Reservations:** suggested. **Hours:** 4:30 pm-10:30 pm, Fr & Sat-11 pm, Sun-10 pm. Closed: 12/26. **Address:** 777 Douglas St V8W 2B5 **Location:** Between Blanshard and Douglas sts; downtown; in Executive House Hotel. **Parking:** on-site (fee) and valet **Cards:** AX, DC, MC, VI.

THE BLACK OLIVE
Phone: 250/384-6060 [8]

CAA

Mediterranean
$9-$34

This quaint restaurant is located downtown, serving an interesting mix of Mediterranean and Italian influenced west coast food. Parking is available on the street or in nearby pay lots. Casual dress. **Bar:** Ful bar. **Reservations:** suggested. **Hours:** 11:30 am-2:30 & 5-10 pm, Sat & Sun from 5 pm. Closed: 12/25 12/26. **Address:** 739 Pandora Ave V8W 1N9 **Location:** Between Douglas and Blanshard (Hwy 17) sts **Parking:** street. **Cards:** AX, DC, DS, JC, MC, VI.

CACTUS CLUB CAFE
Phone: 250/361-3233

Canadian
$9-$29

This bustling, casual restaurant serves huge burgers, sandwiches, pasta, salads, soups, quesadillas, fajitas, vegetarian dishes, steak, ribs, chicken and fish. Featured are certified Angus beef and fresh wild British Columbia salmon. The thick and creamy milk shakes come highly recommended. Casual dress. **Bar:** Full bar. **Hours:** 11 am-midnight, Fri & Sat-1 am. Closed: 12/25. **Address:** 1125 Douglas St V8W 3L7 **Location:** Between Fort and View sts. **Parking:** street. **Cards:** AX, MC, VI.

CANOE BREWPUB MARINA RESTAURANT
Phone: 250/361-1940 [4]

Canadian
$9-$28

The waterfront brew pub offers freshly brewed beers along with fresh fish, tasty pasta, burgers, sandwiches and pizza. Casual dress. **Bar:** Full bar. **Reservations:** suggested. **Hours:** 11:30 am-11 pm, Thurs-midnight, Fri & Sat-1 am. Closed: 1/1, 12/25. **Address:** 450 Swift St V8W 1S3 **Location:** Corner of Stone and Fisgard sts. **Parking:** on-site. **Cards:** AX, MC, VI.

THE EMPRESS ROOM
Phone: 250/384-8111 [20]

Regional
Canadian
$25-$40

Topping the list for fine dining in Victoria, the restaurant enables guests to dine surrounded by tapestry walls and richly carved ceilings that are amazing to see. The menu changes seasonally to showcase the best cuisine the province has to offer. Other aspects that contribute to the experience include the exceptional staff and an outstanding wine list with many flavorful British Columbia vintages. Semi-formal attire. Entertainment. **Bar:** Full bar. **Reservations:** suggested. **Hours:** 6 pm-10 pm. **Address:** 721 Government St V8W 1W5 **Location:** Between Belleville and Humboldt sts; in The Fairmont Empress. **Parking:** on-site (fee) and valet. **Cards:** AX, DC, DS, JC, MC, VI. **Historic**

FIRE & WATER FISH & CHOP HOUSE
Phone: 250/480-3828 [22]

CAA

Steak & Seafood
$7-$36

The all-day restaurant offers a comfortable, casual atmosphere. On the menu are premium-quality steaks and seasonal local seafood, such as Pacific rockfish, halibut and wild British Columbia salmon. Dishes are served with a choice of signature sauces and accompaniments, which makes every entree distinctive. Dressy casual. **Bar:** Full bar. **Reservations:** suggested. **Hours:** 6:30 am-3 & 5-10 pm; Sunday brunch. **Address:** 728 Humboldt St V8W 3Z5 **Location:** Between Blanshard and Douglas sts; in Marriott Victoria Inner Harbour. **Parking:** on-site and valet. **Cards:** AX, DC, DS, MC, VI. *(See color ad p 650)*

GLO EURO PUB
Phone: 250/385-5643 [1]

Canadian
$9-$20

Open late every night, this distinctive pub/restaurant is a little tricky to find, but it's well worth the trouble. All tables in the dining room and on the large patio overlook the Gorge Waterway. Fun and tasty food choices range from flat-bread pizza, entree salads and burgers to sandwiches and pasta. Parking is along the street, but the pub will validate tickets for those who use pay lots. Casual dress. **Bar:** Full bar. **Reservations:** accepted. **Hours:** 11 am-close. Closed: 12/25. **Address:** 104-2940 Jutland Rd V8T 5K6 **Location:** Just sw of Gorge Rd. **Parking:** street. **Cards:** AX, MC, VI.

HAULTAIN'S FISH & CHIPS
Phone: 250/383-8332 [2]

English
$10-$18

Patrons can dine in or take out from this small, neighborhood-favorite restaurant that's been in the same quiet residential area for 32 years. Fish 'n' chips is the specialty, but burgers and specialty dinners also are served. Seating can be limited, but it's well worth the wait. Casual dress. **Bar:** Beer & wine. **Hours:** 11:30 am-8 pm, Sun 3:30 pm-7:30 pm. Closed: 1/1, 12/25, 12/26; also Mon. **Address:** 1127 Haultain St V8T 1V4 **Location:** From Blanshard St (Hwy 17), 0.6 mi (1 km) e on Bay St, then just n on Cook St. **Parking:** on-site. **Cards:** AX, MC, VI.

HERALD STREET CAFE
Phone: 250/381-1441 [3]

Regional
Canadian
$9-$28

In a historic downtown warehouse, the cafe presents an eclectic menu of such West Coast favorites as fresh wild British Columbia Coho salmon, Alberta beef, venison and lamb. Guests can visit the sports bar for excellent pub food and wide-screen TVs showing the latest sports events. The only parking is at street meters. Casual dress. **Bar:** Full bar. **Reservations:** required. **Hours:** 11:30 am-2:30 & 5-10 pm. Closed: 1/1, 12/25. **Address:** 546 Herald St V8W 1S6 **Location:** Between Government and Store sts. **Parking:** street. **Cards:** AX, MC, VI.

HUNAN VILLAGE
Phone: 250/382-0661 [5]

Chinese
$8-$15

Located in Victoria's Chinatown district, this restaurant specializes in Hunan and Cantonese meals. Hot and spicy beef, smoked duck or ham dishes are the local favorites. There's metered street parking or spaces nearby in pay parking lots. Casual dress. **Bar:** Full bar. **Hours:** 11 am-11 pm, Sun 5 pm-10 pm. Closed: 10/13, 12/25. **Address:** 546 Fisgard St V8W 1R4 **Location:** Between Government and Store sts. **Parking:** street. **Cards:** AX, DC, MC, VI.

(See map and index starting on p. 635)

IL TERRAZZO   Phone: 250/361-0028   **9**

Italian
$10-$35

Situated in an old courtyard, Il Terrazzo offers excellent meals such as Australian lamb, ostrich, pasta and seafood, with emphasis on wood-burning oven specialties. Wine choices are extensive, with a nice by-the-glass selection. Fast, friendly service. Casual dress. **Bar:** Full bar. **Reservations:** suggested. **Hours:** 11:30 am-3 & 5-10 pm, Fri & Sat-10:30 pm, Sun 5 pm-10 pm. Closed: 12/25; also for lunch Sat 10/1-4/1. **Address:** 555 Johnson St V8W 1M2 **Location:** Jct Wharf St; near Market Square; main entrance off Waddington Alley. **Parking:** street. **Cards:** AX, DC, MC, VI.

JAMES BAY TEA ROOM &
RESTAURANT   *Menu on AAA.com*   Phone: 250/382-8282   **24**

CAA

Canadian
$8-$14

Inside a 1907 home, the popular restaurant displays memorabilia and photographs of Britain's royal family. The menu lists omelets, pot pies, bangers and kidney pie. Afternoon tea is $11 and high tea, $15. Casual dress. **Bar:** Beer & wine. **Reservations:** suggested. **Hours:** 7 am-5 pm, Sun from 8 am. Closed: 12/24-12/26. **Address:** 332 Menzies St V8V 2G9 **Location:** Corner of Superior; just s of the Parliament buildings. **Parking:** street. **Cards:** AX, DC, MC, VI.

KELSEY'S   Phone: 250/978-5550

Canadian
$7-$21

A fun, relaxed atmosphere and tasty menu of casual fare make the restaurant a popular favorite with locals. Diners might start a meal with some tempting appetizers, such as wings, loaded potato skins or nachos, and follow them with an old-time favorite, such as a burger, wrap, pizza or pasta dish. For a heartier meal, it's hard to beat pork back ribs or a steak. The diverse menu has broad appeal. Casual dress. **Bar:** Full bar. **Hours:** 10:30 am-11 pm, Fri & Sat-midnight. **Address:** 325 Burnside Rd W V8Z 7L6 **Location:** Burnside and Tillicum rds. **Parking:** on-site. **Cards:** AX, MC, VI.

KOTO JAPANESE RESTAURANT   Phone: 250/382-1514   **15**

Japanese
$6-$20

Offerings include an extensive array of sushi and sashimi dishes, as well as teriyaki steak, ginger pork and a wide selection of tempura. Casual dress. **Bar:** Full bar. **Reservations:** suggested. **Hours:** 11:30 am-2 & 5-10 pm, Sat & Sun from 5 pm. Closed: 1/1, 12/25. **Address:** 510 Fort St V8W 1E6 **Location:** Between Government and Wharf sts. **Parking:** street. **Cards:** AX, MC, VI.

THE MARK   *Menu on AAA.com*   Phone: 250/386-0450   **23**

CAA
Regional
Canadian
$30-$40

With only 28 seats, the restaurant offers the discriminating guest a very intimate dining experience. The menu is constantly changing, but it always offers the finest in local ingredients. An excellent selection of wines will complement any meal. Dressy casual. **Bar:** Full bar. **Reservations:** required. **Hours:** 6 pm-10 pm. **Address:** 463 Belleville St V8V 1X3 **Location:** Between Oswego and Menzies sts; in Hotel Grand Pacific. **Parking:** on-site and valet. **Cards:** AX, DC, DS, JC, MC, VI.

MILESTONE'S BAR & GRILL   Phone: 250/381-2244

Canadian
$12-$28

Popular with locals, the bustling eatery is a great gathering place. Diners enjoy the relaxed setting and casual menu featuring pasta, pizza, roasted chicken and a tasty choice of egg and brunch options. A nice wine list complements the food choices. Casual dress. **Bar:** Full bar. **Reservations:** suggested, evenings. **Hours:** 11 am-10 pm, Fri-midnight, Sat 10 am-midnight, Sun 9:30 am-10 pm. Closed: 12/25. **Address:** 812 Wharf St V8W 1T3 **Location:** Corner of Government and Humboldt sts. **Parking:** street. **Cards:** AX, DC, MC, VI.

MONTANA'S COOKHOUSE   Phone: 250/978-9333

Steak House
$7-$25

Pine boards, exposed beams, a fireplace and Western gear displayed about the dining room give the feeling of a back-country setting. The menu lists hearty portions of comfort fare, such as Yankee pot roast. While the focus is on steaks, ribs and chicken, some seafood entrees also are among offerings. Service is efficient and friendly. Casual dress. **Bar:** Full bar. **Hours:** 11 am-11 pm, Fri & Sat-midnight. Closed: 12/25. **Address:** 315 Burnside Rd W V8Z 7L6 **Location:** From Trans-Canada Hwy 1 N, just s to Tillicum Rd. **Parking:** on-site. **Cards:** AX, MC, VI.

MOXIE'S CLASSIC GRILL   Phone: 250/360-1660

Canadian
$8-$18

This sleek, funky and popular restaurant presents an extensive menu of creatively prepared dishes, including pizza, pasta, rice, noodles, signature salads and burgers. Other menus include one for children and one for Sunday brunch. Lending to the upbeat, stylish decor are dark wood appointments and river rock fireplaces. Casual dress. **Bar:** Full bar. **Hours:** 11 am-11 pm, Fri & Sat-midnight. **Address:** 1010 Yates St, #1 V8V 3M6 **Location:** Between Vancouver and Cook sts. **Parking:** on-site. **Cards:** AX, MC, VI.

PAGLIACCI'S   Phone: 250/386-1662   **16**

Italian
$6-$24

A New York style Italian eatery with a bustling Big Apple ambience, and food to match. Enjoy their flavorful pasta dishes. The ravioli is exceptional, or if you're a tomato sauce fan, the Spaghetti Western may be the ticket, made with fresh tomatoes and topped with a couple of large meatballs, it's as Italian as it gets. Casual dress. **Bar:** Full bar. **Hours:** 11:30 am-3 & 5:30-10 pm, Fri & Sat-11 pm, Sun 10 am-3 & 5:30-11 pm; Sunday brunch. Closed: 12/25; also Yom Kippur. **Address:** 1011 Broad St V8W 2A1 **Location:** Between Fort and Broughton sts. **Parking:** street. **Cards:** AX, MC, VI.

PASSERO'S MEDITERRANEAN CUISINE   Phone: 250/384-6474   **13**

Mediterranean
$7-$19

The family-run restaurant serves a fine combination of Greek and Italian cuisine in large portions. Lending to the bistro theme are lots of color and live plants. The patio opens seasonally. Casual dress. **Bar:** Full bar. **Reservations:** accepted. **Hours:** 11 am-9 pm, Fri & Sat-10 pm. Closed major holidays; also Sun. **Address:** 1102 Yates St V8V 3M8 **Location:** Corner of Cook St. **Parking:** on-site. **Cards:** MC, VI.

(See map and index starting on p. 635)

PERIKLIS GREEK RESTAURANT

Phone: 250/386-3313   ⑪

Greek
$12-$30

An open, airy taverna style restaurant, located near the harbour in Victoria's historic area, Periklis Restaurant is a favorite of the locals and tourists alike. A wide variety of Greek dishes, like roast lamb, mousaka, and souvlaki are prepared using authentic recipes from Greece. Enjoy a tasty meal, followed by their exceptional baklava and coffee for dessert. Casual dress. **Bar:** Full bar. **Reservations:** suggested. **Hours:** 4:30 pm-11:30 pm. Closed: 1/1, 12/25. **Address:** 531 Yates St V8W 1K7 **Location:** Between Wharf and Langley sts. **Parking:** street. **Cards:** AX, MC, VI.

PESCATORE'S SEAFOOD & GRILL

Phone: 250/385-4512   ⑱

Seafood
$9-$30

Pescatore's is a chic bistro with excellent fresh seafood such as salmon Wellington and trout stuffed with crab and brie, and great beverage choices such as espresso, cappuccino and martinis. This is hip and funky fine dining, with live jazz on weekends (seasonal). Blue plate specials from 4:30 pm-6:30 pm. Parking at street meters or pay lots. Casual dress. **Bar:** Full bar. **Reservations:** suggested. **Hours:** 11:30 am-midnight, Sat & Sun from 11 am; Saturday and Sunday brunch. Closed: 12/25. **Address:** 614 Humboldt St V8W 1A4 **Location:** Between Gordon and Government sts. **Parking:** street. **Cards:** DC, JC, MC, VI.

PLUTO'S

Phone: 250/385-4747   ⑰

Canadian
$7-$15

The funky-looking, turquoise and pink art deco structure used to be a gas station. In addition to the extensive breakfast menu, which is served until 2 pm, there are also varied wraps and burgers and a few Mexican items. Casual dress. **Bar:** Full bar. **Hours:** 8 am-10 pm, Sun & Mon-9 pm. Closed: 12/25. **Address:** 1150 Cook St V8V 3Z9 **Location:** Corner of Cook and View sts. **Parking:** on-site. **Cards:** MC, VI.

RESTAURANT MATISSE

Phone: 250/480-0883   ⑩

French
$20-$30

This eatery is a wonderful French restaurant located downtown. The first thing you'll notice is the bright sunlight-yellow decor that is warm and inviting. Daily specials along with what they do best include duck, beef and fish. Casual dress. **Bar:** Full bar. **Reservations:** required. **Hours:** 5:30 pm-10 pm. Closed: 12/25; also Mon & Tues. **Address:** 512 Yates St V8W 1K8 **Location:** Between Government and Wharf sts. **Parking:** street. **Cards:** AX, MC, VI.

RICKY'S ALL DAY GRILL

Phone: 250/383-9925

Canadian
$6-$15

The comfortable eatery, which employs friendly servers, presents a varied menu that includes pasta dishes, wraps, omelets, stir-fry preparations and burgers. Portions are generous. Children's and senior selections are offered. Guests can request seating in a booth or at a table. Casual dress. **Bar:** Full bar. **Hours:** 7 am-9 pm. **Address:** 1501 Admirals Rd V9A 2P8 **Location:** Corner of Admirals and Glentana rds; on Admirals Walk Mall. **Parking:** on-site. **Cards:** AX, MC, VI.

SIAM THAI RESTAURANT

Phone: 250/383-9911   ⑭

Thai
$8-$18

The secret of Thai cooking is to maintain a delicate balance between the spices and main ingredients. The restaurant accomplishes this in its soups, as well as dishes of fried rice, noodles, chicken, beef, pork, seafood and vegetarian items. Lunch specials are available. Casual dress. **Bar:** Full bar. **Reservations:** suggested. **Hours:** 11:30 am-2 & 5-10 pm, Sun from 5 pm. Closed: 12/25. **Address:** 512 Fort St V8W 1E6 **Location:** Between Government and Wharf sts. **Parking:** street. **Cards:** AX, DC, MC, VI.

SMITTY'S FAMILY RESTAURANT

Phone: 250/383-5612

Canadian
$6-$18

The family-oriented restaurant satisfies patrons with its ever-popular all-day breakfast items, as well as tasty and wholesome soups and salads at lunchtime. A relaxed mood characterizes the dining space. Casual dress. **Bar:** Full bar. **Hours:** 6:30 am-9 pm. Closed: 12/25. **Address:** 850 Douglas St V8W 2B6 **Location:** Between Burdett Ave and Courtney St. **Parking:** on-site. **Cards:** AX, MC, VI.

SPINNAKERS GASTRO BREWPUB & RESTAURANT

Phone: 250/386-2739   ⑥

Canadian
$8-$23

The fun and lively pub, which has a stand-up bar area, prepares terrific breads, a wonderful mile-high apple pie and homemade soup. Guests can tour the brew house or bring home treats from the on-site bakery. Casual dress. **Bar:** Full bar. **Reservations:** suggested. **Hours:** 11 am-11 pm. Closed: 12/25. **Address:** 308 Catherine St V9A 3S8 **Location:** 1.3 mi (2 km) nw over Johnson St Bridge, then just s; in Spinnakers Gastro Brewpub and Guesthouses. **Parking:** on-site. **Cards:** AX, MC, VI.

SWISS CHALET ROTISSERIE & GRILL

Phone: 250/475-0334

Canadian
$7-$19

The popular restaurant is known for its rotisserie chicken and ribs and the tangy Chalet sauce that gives food its special zip. Diners munch on a half or quarter chicken with sides such as steamed vegetables, fries, baked potatoes and salads. Lunch guests often go for the great soup and sandwich combination. Take-out and delivery service are popular options. Casual dress. **Bar:** Full bar. **Hours:** 11 am-10 pm. Closed: 12/25. **Address:** 3233 Douglas St V8Z 3K8 **Location:** Between Tolmie and Roderick sts. **Parking:** on-site. **Cards:** AX, DC, MC, VI.

VICTORIA HARBOUR HOUSE RESTAURANT

Phone: 250/386-1244   ㉑

Steak & Seafood
$16-$35

Just up from the U.S. Ferry terminal in Victoria's Inner Harbour and surrounded by many hotels sits this long-established restaurant that serves fresh seafood and fine steaks. If on-site parking is full, diners can park along the street. Casual dress. **Bar:** Full bar. **Reservations:** suggested. **Hours:** 4:30 pm-11:30 pm. **Address:** 607 Oswego St V8V 4W9 **Location:** Corner of Oswego and Quebec sts. **Parking:** on-site. **Cards:** AX, MC, VI.

(See map and index starting on p. 635)

WHITE HEATHER TEA ROOM
Phone: 250/595-8020   (12)

Bakery/Desserts
$8-$14

On Oak Bay, the wonderful tea room serves lunch and afternoon tea starting at 1:30 p.m. Among choices are wee tea for $12.45, not-so-wee tea for $15.95 and the big muckle $37.95 for hearty appetites. Among favorites are the sconewiches, freshly baked scones with varied fillings. Everything is baked on site. Casual dress. **Bar:** Beer & wine. **Reservations:** required, for lunch. **Hours:** 10 am-5 pm. Closed: 12/25, 12/26; also Sun & Mon. **Address:** 1885 Oak Bay Ave V8R 1C6 **Location:** Corner of Davie St. **Parking:** on-site. **Cards:** MC, VI.

WILD SAFFRON BISTRO & WINE BAR
Phone: 250/361-3150   (7)

Pacific Rim
$15-$34

The warm, contemporary bistro pairs innovative West Coast cuisine with an attractive selection of local and international wines. Seafood, delectable vegetarian preparations and lamb, game and poultry entrees all are presented with artistic flair. A brewery is on site. Casual dress. **Bar:** Full bar. **Reservations:** suggested. **Hours:** 5 pm-10 pm. Closed: Sun & Mon. **Address:** 1605 Store St V8W 1N6 **Location:** At Pandora St. **Parking:** street. **Cards:** AX, MC, VI.

The Victoria Vicinity

BRENTWOOD BAY

——— WHERE TO STAY ———

BRENTWOOD BAY LODGE & SPA   *Book at AAA.com*
Phone: (250)544-2079

Small-scale Hotel
$429-$729 All Year

Address: 849 Verdier Ave V8M 1C5 **Location:** Hwy 17, exit Brentwood Bay, 1.8 mi (3 km) w on Keating Rd, 0.9 mi (1.5 km) n on W Saanich Rd, then 0.6 mi (1 km) w to the Mill Bay Ferry. **Facility:** Smoke free premises. 33 units. 30 one-bedroom standard units with whirlpools. 3 one-bedroom suites with whirlpools. 3 stories, exterior corridors. **Parking:** on-site. **Terms:** 7 day cancellation notice-fee imposed. **Amenities:** video library, DVD players, CD players, high-speed Internet, voice mail, safes, honor bars, irons, hair dryers. **Dining:** Seagrille, see separate listing. **Pool(s):** heated outdoor. **Leisure Activities:** whirlpool, exercise room, spa. *Fee:* marina. **Guest Services:** valet and coin laundry, wireless Internet. **Business Services:** meeting rooms. **Cards:** MC, VI.

——— WHERE TO DINE ———

SEAGRILLE
Phone: 250/544-2079

Seafood
$15-$30

In the city's newest luxury oceanfront resort, the restaurant is just minutes from famous Butchart Gardens. Fresh fish, Alberta beef and local produce factor in exquisite, creatively prepared dishes. An extensive wine list features many award-winning British Columbia wines. Dressy casual. **Bar:** Full bar. **Reservations:** suggested, required Fri & Sat nights. **Hours:** 5:30 pm-10 pm. **Address:** 849 Verdier Ave V8M 1C5 **Location:** Hwy 17, exit Brentwood Bay, 1.8 mi (3 km) w on Keating Rd, 0.9 mi (1.5 km) n on W Saanich Rd, then 0.6 mi (1 km) w to the Mill Bay Ferry; in Brentwood Bay Lodge & Spa. **Parking:** on-site. **Cards:** AX, DS, MC, VI.

SMITTY'S FAMILY RESTAURANT
Phone: 250/652-1764

Canadian
$6-$18

The family-oriented restaurant satisfies patrons with its ever-popular all-day breakfast items, as well as tasty and wholesome soups and salads at lunchtime. A relaxed mood characterizes the dining space. Casual dress. **Bar:** Full bar. **Hours:** 6:30 am-8 pm. Closed: 12/25. **Address:** Box 249, 6719 W Saanich Rd V0S 1A0 **Location:** Corner of Saanich and Keating Cross rds. **Parking:** on-site. **Cards:** MC, VI.

ESQUIMALT pop. 16,840   (See map and index starting on p. 635)

——— WHERE TO STAY ———

COMFORT INN & SUITES   *Book great rates at AAA.com*
Phone: (250)388-7861   (52)

Motel
$89-$299 All Year

Address: 101 Island Hwy V8W 2L9 **Location:** Douglas St, 3.1 mi (5 km) w on Gorge Rd, then just s on Admirals Rd. **Facility:** 106 units. 96 one- and 10 two-bedroom standard units, some with efficiencies or kitchens. 2 stories (no elevator), interior/exterior corridors. **Parking:** on-site. **Amenities:** irons, hair dryers. **Pool(s):** heated outdoor. **Leisure Activities:** rental bicycles. *Fee:* kayaks. **Guest Services:** valet and coin laundry, wireless Internet. **Business Services:** meeting rooms, PC (fee). **Cards:** AX, DC, MC, VI. **Free Special Amenities:** continental breakfast and high-speed Internet. *(See color ad on insert)*

MALAHAT

——— WHERE TO STAY ———

THE AERIE RESORT

(CAA) (SAVE)

▽▽▽ ▽▽▽

Country Inn
$175-$825 All Year

Phone: (250)743-7115

Address: 600 Ebadora Ln V0R 2L0 **Location:** 20 mi (32 km) n of Victoria off Trans-Canada Hwy 1, use Spectacle Lake turn off, follow signs. Located in a quiet area. **Facility:** This high-end, luxury retreat offers sweeping ocean and mountain views, rococo furnishings an elegant dining room and an on-site spa. Smoke free premises. 35 units. 10 one-bedroom standard units, some with whirlpools. 23 one- and 2 two-bedroom suites, some with whirlpools. 2-3 stories (no elevator), interior corridors. **Parking:** on-site. **Terms:** office hours 7 am-10 pm, 7 day cancellation notice-fee imposed. **Amenities:** video library, DVD players, CD players, voice mail, honor bars, irons, hair dryers. **Dining:** The Aerie Dining Room, see separate listing. **Leisure Activities:** whirlpool, tennis court, cooking instruction, exercise room, spa. **Guest Services:** valet laundry, wireless Internet. **Business Services:** meeting rooms, PC. **Cards:** AX, MC, VI. **Free Special Amenities: continental breakfast and local telephone calls.**

(icons) / SOME UNITS FEE

MALAHAT BUNGALOWS MOTEL

▽

Motel
$62-$500 All Year

Phone: (250)478-3011

Address: 300 Trans-Canada Hwy V0R 2L0 **Location:** Trans-Canada Hwy 1, 16.3 mi (26 km) n of Victoria, watch for signs. **Facility:** 18 units. 13 one-bedroom standard units, some with kitchens. 5 two-bedroom suites with kitchens. 1 story, exterior corridors. *Bath:* combo or shower only. **Parking:** on-site. **Terms:** office hours 8 am-midnight, 3 day cancellation notice-fee imposed. **Leisure Activities:** whirlpool. **Guest Services:** coin laundry. **Cards:** MC, VI. *(See color ad p 650)*

(icons) / SOME UNITS FEE

——— WHERE TO DINE ———

THE AERIE DINING ROOM

(CAA)

▽▽▽ ▽▽▽

Nouvelle French
$18-$45

Phone: 250/743-7115

The elegant, formal restaurant prepares Northwest-influenced cuisine with many local fresh ingredients. Guests can order a la carte or request five- or nine-course tasting menus at $85 and $105, respectively. Perched high atop a mountain, the unusual and comfortable resort location affords outstanding views. The wine list is outstanding, and service is top notch. Casual dress. **Bar:** Full bar. **Reservations:** required. **Hours:** noon-2 & 5:30-8:30 pm. **Address:** 600 Ebadora Ln V0R 2L0 **Location:** 20 mi (32 km) n of Victoria off Trans-Canada Hwy 1, use Spectacle Lake turn off, follow signs; in The Aerie Resort. **Parking:** on-site. **Cards:** AX, DC, MC, VI.

MALAHAT MOUNTAIN INN

▽▽ ▽▽

Regional Canadian
$11-$35

Phone: 250/478-1944

Gourmet dining is the mode in the relaxed setting. Set 600 feet above Saanich Inlet, the dining room affords a stunning view of the mountains and ocean. Food choices exhibit a delightful Pacific Northwest influence. Casual dress. **Bar:** Full bar. **Reservations:** suggested. **Hours:** 11:30 am-8 pm, Sat 11 am-9 pm, Sun 10 am-8 pm. Closed: 12/25. **Address:** 265 Trans-Canada Hwy 1 V0R 2L0 **Location:** Trans-Canada Hwy 1, 16 mi (26 km) n of Victoria, watch for signs. **Parking:** on-site. **Cards:** AX, MC, VI.

OAK BAY pop. 17,908   (See map and index starting on p. 635)

——— WHERE TO STAY ———

OAK BAY GUEST HOUSE BED & BREAKFAST

▽▽ ▽▽

Historic Bed & Breakfast
$139-$199 3/1-9/15
$99-$179 9/16-2/28

Phone: (250)598-3812   [55]

Address: 1052 Newport Ave V8S 5E2 **Location:** 3 mi (4.8 km) e on Oak Bay Ave (which becomes Newport Ave). **Facility:** In keeping with the age of this historic building, the guest rooms are average-size and some bathrooms are compact. Smoke free premises. 11 one-bedroom standard units. 2 stories (no elevator), interior corridors. *Bath:* combo or shower only. **Parking:** on-site. **Terms:** office hours 8 am-10 pm, 7 day cancellation notice imposed. **Amenities:** hair dryers. **Cards:** AX, DS, MC, VI.

(ASK) (icons)

——— WHERE TO DINE ———

THE BLETHERING PLACE TEA ROOM & RESTAURANT

▽▽ ▽▽

Canadian
$6-$17

Phone: 250/598-1413   [33]

Built in 1912, this building is the oldest in the "village." Its English-style decor matches its English-style fare featuring roast beef and Yorkshire pudding and Welsh rarebit. Afternoon tea is served 11 am-7:30 pm Families are welcomed here. Casual dress. **Bar:** Beer & wine. **Reservations:** accepted. **Hours:** 8 am-9 pm. **Address:** 2250 Oak Bay Ave V8R 1G5 **Location:** Corner of Monterey and Oak Bay aves; in Oak Bay Village. **Parking:** on-site. **Cards:** AX, DC, JC, MC, VI.

(icon)

THE MARINA RESTAURANT

▽▽ ▽▽

Seafood
$10-$32

Phone: 250/598-8555   [35]

Located in the Oak Bay Marina, this restaurant provides beautiful sweeping views of the ocean, harbor and mountains. Its menu features a Pacific Northwest cuisine, showcasing fresh local and exotic seafood, sushi bar and cafe deli. Casual dress. **Bar:** Full bar. **Reservations:** suggested. **Hours:** 11:30 am-2:30 & 5-10 pm, Fri & Sat-11 pm, Sun 9:30 am-9 pm. Closed: 12/25. **Address:** 1327 Beach Dr V8S 2N4 **Location:** 3.8 mi (6 km) e via Oak Bay Ave, just s. **Parking:** on-site. **Cards:** AX, DC, MC, VI.

OTTAVIO ITALIAN BAKERY & DELICATESSEN

▽▽ ▽▽

Italian
$7-$14

Phone: 250/592-4080   [34]

This pleasant cafe in the heart of Oak Bay offers a wide variety of fresh salads, grilled panini sandwiches and wonderful soups. The homemade gelato with fresh fruit is a hit. Choose dining inside or out on a lovely terrazzo overlooking a busy street scene. Casual dress. **Bar:** Beer & wine. **Hours:** 8 am-6 pm, Sun from 10 am. Closed: 12/25, 12/26; also Mon. **Address:** 2272 Oak Bay Ave V8R 1G7 **Location:** At Monterey Ave. **Parking:** on-site. **Cards:** MC, VI.

CALL (icons)

(See map and index starting on p. 635)

PAPRIKA BISTRO
Phone: 250/592-7424   31

Continental
$20-$29

In the small Estevan Shopping Centre, the bistro prepares some superb dishes from fresh ingredients. Because this place can be tricky to find, it's wise to ask a concierge or other hotel staffer for directions. The drive is worthwhile. Casual dress. **Bar:** Full bar. **Reservations:** suggested. **Hours:** 5 pm-10 pm. Closed major holidays; also Sun. **Address:** 2524 Estevan Ave V8R 2S7 **Location:** Between Dunlevy and Musgrave sts; in Estevan Shopping Centre; in Oak Bay area. **Parking:** street. **Cards:** AX, MC, VI.

PENNY FARTHING PUBLIC HOUSE
Phone: 250/370-9008   32

Canadian
$8-$17

The classic and relaxed British-style pub is decorated in rich dark wood with brass accents. Fine pub fare pairs with a wide selection of stouts, ales and lagers. Patrons younger than age 19 are not permitted. Casual dress. **Bar:** Full bar. **Hours:** 11 am-midnight, Sun & Mon-11 pm. Closed: 12/25. **Address:** 2228 Oak Bay Ave V8R 1G5 **Location:** Between Monterey Ave and Hampshire Rd. **Parking:** street. **Cards:** AX, MC, VI.

SAANICH   (See map and index starting on p. 635)

-------- WHERE TO STAY --------

HOWARD JOHNSON HOTEL & SUITES   *Book at AAA.com*
Phone: 250/704-4656   49

Small-scale Hotel
Rates not provided

Address: 4670 Elk Lake Dr V8Z 5M1 **Location:** Blanshard St (Hwy 17), just w on Royal Oak Dr, then just n. **Facility:** Smoke free premises. 88 one-bedroom standard units, some with kitchens. 3 stories, interior/exterior corridors. *Bath:* combo or shower only. **Parking:** on-site. **Amenities:** high-speed Internet, voice mail, irons, hair dryers. **Pool(s):** heated outdoor. **Leisure Activities:** whirlpool, limited exercise equipment. **Guest Services:** valet and coin laundry. **Business Services:** meeting rooms.

IRIS GARDEN COUNTRY MANOR BED & BREAKFAST
Phone: 250/744-2253   48

Bed & Breakfast
Rates not provided

Address: 5360 W Saanich Rd V9E 1J8 **Location:** Blanshard St (Hwy 17), exit Royal Oak Dr, just w, then 2.7 mi (4.5 km) n on W Saanich Rd (Hwy 17A N), watch for signs. **Facility:** Smoke free premises. 4 one-bedroom standard units, some with whirlpools. 2 stories (no elevator), interior corridors. *Bath:* combo or shower only. **Parking:** on-site. **Terms:** office hours 8 am-10 pm, check-in 4 pm, age restrictions may apply. **Amenities:** hair dryers.

QUALITY INN WADDLING DOG   *Book great rates at AAA.com*
Phone: (250)652-1146

Small-scale Hotel
$99-$169 All Year

Address: 2476 Mt Newton Crossroad V8M 2B8 **Location:** Corner of Hwy 17 and Mt Newton Crossroad. **Facility:** Smoke free premises. 30 one-bedroom standard units. 3 stories, interior corridors. **Parking:** on-site. **Amenities:** irons, hair dryers. **Guest Services:** wireless Internet. **Business Services:** meeting rooms. **Cards:** AX, DC, MC, VI. *(See color ad on insert)*

SUNNYMEADE HOUSE B&B
Phone: (250)658-1414   47

Bed & Breakfast
$89-$165 3/1-11/1

Address: 1002 Fenn Ave V8Y 1P3 **Location:** 7.2 mi (12 km) n on Hwy 17, exit Cordova Bay Rd, then 1.8 mi (3 km) e on Sayward/Cordova Bay Rd; across from service station. **Facility:** Smoke free premises. 4 one-bedroom standard units, some with whirlpools. 2 stories (no elevator), interior corridors. *Bath:* combo or shower only. **Parking:** on-site. **Terms:** open 3/1-11/1, office hours 9 am-10 pm, 2 night minimum stay - seasonal and/or weekends, age restrictions may apply, 7 day cancellation notice. **Amenities:** hair dryers. **Cards:** MC, VI.

VICTORIA AIRPORT SUPER 8   *Book great rates at AAA.com*
Phone: 250/652-6888

Small-scale Hotel
Rates not provided

Address: 2477 Mt Newton Crossroad V8M 2B7 **Location:** Just e of Hwy 17. **Facility:** 51 one-bedroom standard units, some with whirlpools. 2 stories (no elevator), interior corridors. **Parking:** on-site. **Amenities:** safes, hair dryers. **Guest Services:** wireless Internet. **Free Special Amenities:** continental breakfast and high-speed Internet.

-------- WHERE TO DINE --------

BRADY'S FISH & CHIPS
Phone: 250/382-3695   28

Seafood
$7-$13

The casual family restaurant serves English-style fish and chips, as well as mouthwatering halibut and cod and fine chowder. Guests can order for dine-in or take-out. Casual dress. **Bar:** Beer & wine. **Hours:** 11 am-7 pm, Fri & Sat-8 pm, Sun noon-7 pm. Closed: 10/13, 12/25. **Address:** 1-50 Burnside Rd W V9A 1B9 **Location:** Just w of Harriet Rd; in Albion Mall. **Parking:** on-site. **Cards:** AX, MC, VI.

CHARTER'S RESTAURANT AT McMORRAN'S BEACH HOUSE   *Menu on AAA.com*
Phone: 250-658-5527   27

Seafood
$9-$30

If this place were any closer to the ocean, guests would need a bathing suit. On the city's outskirts, the restaurant has been a local landmark for decades. Although the focus is on fresh seafood, the menu also lines up varied meat dishes and lighter fare for lunch. Patio seating is popular in season. Casual dress. **Bar:** Full bar. **Reservations:** suggested. **Hours:** 11 am-9 pm. Closed: 12/25, 12/26. **Address:** 5109 Cordova Bay Rd V8Y 2K1 **Location:** Blanshard St (Hwy 17), exit Royal Oak Dr, 1.3 mi (2 km) e on Royal Oak Dr, then 1.4 mi (2.3 km) n. **Parking:** on-site. **Cards:** AX, MC, VI.

SIDNEY pop. 11,315

—— WHERE TO STAY ——

BEACON INN AT SIDNEY

Bed & Breakfast
$119-$259 All Year

Phone: (250)655-3288

Address: 9724 3rd St V8L 3A2 **Location:** Hwy 17, exit Sidney, 0.6 mi (1 km) e on Beacon Ave, then just s. **Facility:** Royally appointed guest rooms have rich wood furnishings, plush velvet trim and regal feather beds; set on a quiet residential street near the harbor. Smoke free premises. 9 one-bedroom standard units, some with whirlpools. 3 stories (no elevator), interior corridors. **Parking:** on-site. **Terms:** office hours 8 am-8 pm, age restrictions may apply. **Amenities:** CD players, hair dryers. **Guest Services:** wireless Internet. **Cards:** MC, VI.

BEST WESTERN EMERALD ISLE MOTOR INN   *Book great rates at AAA.com*

(CAA) (SAVE)

Small-scale Hotel
$135-$181 3/1-9/30
$99-$126 10/1-2/28

Phone: (250)656-4441

Address: 2306 Beacon Ave V8L 1X2 **Location:** Hwy 17, exit Sidney, just e. **Facility:** 65 one-bedroom standard units, some with efficiencies, kitchens and/or whirlpools. 2 stories, interior corridors. **Parking:** on-site. **Terms:** cancellation fee imposed. **Amenities:** voice mail, irons, hair dryers. *Some:* high-speed Internet. **Dining:** Smitty's Family Restaurant, see separate listing. **Leisure Activities:** sauna, whirlpool. **Guest Services:** valet and coin laundry, wireless Internet. **Business Services:** meeting rooms. **Cards:** AX, DC, DS, MC, VI. **Free Special Amenities:** local telephone calls and newspaper. *(See color ad p 641)*

AAA Benefit:
Members save 10% everyday, plus an exclusive frequent stay program.

THE CEDARWOOD INN & SUITES   *Book at AAA.com*

Small-scale Hotel
$85-$249 All Year

Phone: (250)656-5551

Address: 9522 Lochside Dr V8L 1N8 **Location:** Hwy 17, just e on McTavish Rd, then 0.8 mi (1.4 km) n. **Facility:** Smoke free premises. 46 units. 45 one- and 1 two-bedroom standard units, some with efficiencies, kitchens and/or whirlpools. 2 stories (no elevator), exterior corridors. **Parking:** on-site. **Terms:** office hours 7 am-11 pm. **Amenities:** video library (fee), irons, hair dryers. *Some:* high-speed Internet. **Guest Services:** coin laundry, wireless Internet. **Cards:** AX, DC, DS, MC, VI.

MIRALOMA ON THE COVE

Small-scale Hotel
$119-$399 All Year

Phone: (250)656-6622

Address: 2326 Harbour Rd V8L 2P8 **Location:** Beacon Ave, 1.3 mi (2 km) n then 0.6 mi (1 km) e. **Facility:** Smoke free premises. 22 units. 9 one-bedroom standard units. 9 one- and 4 two-bedroom suites, some with efficiencies, kitchens and/or whirlpools. 3 stories, interior corridors. *Bath:* combo or shower only. **Parking:** on-site. **Terms:** 1-2 night minimum stay - seasonal, cancellation fee imposed. **Amenities:** video library, DVD players, CD players, high-speed Internet, voice mail, irons, hair dryers. **Leisure Activities:** sauna, whirlpool, limited exercise equipment. **Guest Services:** valet laundry. **Business Services:** meeting rooms. **Cards:** AX, MC, VI.

THE SIDNEY PIER HOTEL & SPA   *Book great rates at AAA.com*

Small-scale Hotel
$109-$649 All Year

Phone: (250)655-9445

Address: 9805 Seaport Pl V8L 4X3 **Location:** From Hwy 17, 0.6 mi (1 km) e on Beacon Ave. **Facility:** Smoke free premises. 55 units. 46 one-bedroom standard units. 9 one-bedroom suites with kitchens. 3 stories, interior corridors. *Bath:* combo or shower only. **Parking:** on-site. **Terms:** check-in 4 pm, cancellation fee imposed. **Amenities:** video library, DVD players, high-speed Internet, voice mail, safes, irons, hair dryers. **Dining:** Haro's Waterfront Dining, see separate listing. **Leisure Activities:** steamrooms, exercise room, spa. **Guest Services:** valet and coin laundry. **Business Services:** meeting rooms, PC. **Cards:** AX, DC, MC, VI.

VICTORIA AIRPORT TRAVELODGE SIDNEY   *Book great rates at AAA.com*

(CAA) (SAVE)

Small-scale Hotel
$129-$199 3/1-9/30
$99-$169 10/1-2/28

Phone: (250)656-1176

Address: 2280 Beacon Ave V8L 1X1 **Location:** Just e of Hwy 17, exit Sidney. **Facility:** 90 one-bedroom standard units, some with efficiencies (utensils extra charge). 2-4 stories, interior corridors. *Bath:* combo or shower only. **Parking:** on-site. **Amenities:** voice mail, hair dryers. *Some:* high-speed Internet. **Pool(s):** heated outdoor. **Guest Services:** valet laundry, wireless Internet. **Business Services:** meeting rooms. **Cards:** AX, DS, MC, VI. **Free Special Amenities:** early check-in/late check-out and room upgrade (subject to availability with advance reservations).

—— WHERE TO DINE ——

BLUE PETER PUB & RESTAURANT

Canadian
$7-$17

Phone: 250/656-4551

This pub located along the wharf has a great view of the harbor. Fresh seafood, steak and pasta are featured, and the laid-back environment offers two sections: one for families with kids and one pub side with a fireplace. Outdoor patio dining in warm weather. Casual dress. **Bar:** Full bar. **Hours:** 11 am-10 pm, Fri & Sat-midnight. **Address:** 2270 Harbour Rd V8L 2P6 **Location:** Beacon Ave, 1.3 mi (2 km) n on Resthaven Dr to Harbour Rd, then just e. **Parking:** on-site. **Cards:** AX, MC, VI.

DEEP COVE CHALET

French
$15-$45

Phone: 250/656-3541

Visitors and locals alike enjoy this delightful restaurant hidden away in a setting that offers a spectacular view of the inlet. The menu features country French cuisine plus fresh seafood, lamb, ostrich, caribou, wild boar, and a nice variety of wines. Casual dress. **Bar:** Full bar. **Reservations:** suggested. **Hours:** 5:30 pm-10 pm, Wed-Sun noon-2:30 pm. Closed: 12/24 & Mon. **Address:** 11190 Chalet Rd V8L 4R4 **Location:** Hwy 17, exit Wain Rd/Deep Cove, 0.6 mi (1 km) w on Wain Rd, then 1.8 mi (3 km) nw on Tatlow Rd. **Parking:** on-site. **Cards:** AX, MC, VI.

HARO'S WATERFRONT DINING

Pacific Rim
$14-$38

Phone: 250/655-9700

Casual dress. **Bar:** Full bar. **Reservations:** suggested. **Hours:** 11 am-9 pm. **Address:** 9805 Seaport Pl V8L 4X3 **Location:** From Hwy 17, 0.6 mi (1 km) e on Beacon Ave; In The Sidney Pier Hotel & Spa. **Parking:** on-site. **Cards:** AX, MC, VI.

SMITTY'S FAMILY RESTAURANT

Canadian
$6-$18

Phone: 250/656-2423

The family-oriented restaurant satisfies patrons with its ever-popular all-day breakfast items, as well as tasty and wholesome soups and salads at lunchtime. A relaxed mood characterizes the dining space. Casual dress. **Bar:** Full bar. **Hours:** 7 am-8 pm. Closed: 12/25. **Address:** 2306 Beacon Ave V8L 1X2 **Location:** Hwy 17, exit Sidney, just e; in Best Western Emerald Isle Motor Inn. **Parking:** on-site. **Cards:** MC, VI.

SOOKE pop. 9,704

--------- **WHERE TO STAY** ---------

MARKHAM HOUSE BED & BREAKFAST

Bed & Breakfast
$120-$250 All Year

Phone: (250)642-7542

Address: 1775 Connie Rd V9C 4C2 **Location:** 6.2 mi (10 km) e on Hwy 14. Located in a quiet rural area. **Facility:** Just a short drive from Victoria, the 10-acre, Tudor estate is home to three large, elegant rooms; a private cottage features its own outdoor hot tub. Smoke free premises. 4 one-bedroom standard units, some with whirlpools. 2 stories (no elevator), interior corridors. *Bath:* combo or shower only. **Parking:** on-site. **Terms:** 7 day cancellation notice-fee imposed. **Amenities:** video library, DVD players, CD players, hair dryers. **Leisure Activities:** whirlpool. **Guest Services:** complimentary laundry, wireless Internet. **Cards:** AX, CB, DC, DS, JC, MC, VI. **Free Special Amenities:** full breakfast and high-speed Internet.

OCEAN WILDERNESS INN

Bed & Breakfast
$120-$210 All Year

Phone: (250)646-2116

Address: 9171 W Coast Rd V0S 1N0 **Location:** 8.6 mi (14 km) w on Hwy 14. Located in a secluded area. **Facility:** Smoke free premises. 7 one-bedroom standard units. 2 stories (no elevator), interior/exterior corridors. **Parking:** on-site. **Terms:** office hours 8 am-8 pm, 7 day cancellation notice-fee imposed. **Amenities:** hair dryers. **Leisure Activities:** whirlpool. **Guest Services:** wireless Internet. **Cards:** AX, MC, VI.

SOOKE HARBOUR HOUSE

Country Inn
$339-$599 3/1-10/15
$269-$439 10/16-2/28

Phone: (250)642-3421

Address: 1528 Whiffen Spit Rd V0S 1N0 **Location:** 1.2 mi (2 km) w on Hwy 14. **Facility:** A colorful garden enhances this small inn, where guest rooms are cozy—many have wood fireplaces, and all feature gorgeous views of the ocean. Smoke free premises. 28 one-bedroom standard units, some with whirlpools. 4 stories, interior/exterior corridors. *Bath:* combo or shower only. **Parking:** on-site. **Terms:** office hours 8 am-1 am, 7 day cancellation notice-fee imposed. **Amenities:** CD players, voice mail, irons, hair dryers. **Leisure Activities:** saunas. **Guest Services:** wireless Internet. **Business Services:** meeting rooms, PC. **Cards:** AX, MC, VI.

--------- WHERE TO DINE ---------

STONE PIPE GRILL

Canadian
$7-$19

Phone: 250/642-0566

The casual restaurant offers homestyle cooking with flair. The menu includes options from burgers and sandwiches to fine steaks and seafood, plus daily specials and homemade desserts. Portions are ample and incorporate the use of local ingredients in season. Casual dress. **Bar:** Full bar. **Hours:** 11 am-9 pm, Thurs-Sat to 10 pm. Closed: 12/25. **Address:** 2038 Otter Point Rd V0S 1N0 **Location:** Hwy 14; center. **Parking:** on-site. **Cards:** MC, VI.

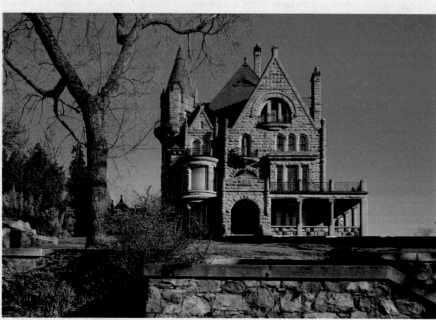

Craigdarroch Castle / © Eero Sorila

This ends listings for the Victoria Vicinity.
The following page resumes the alphabetical listings of cities in British Columbia.

WESTBANK —*See Okanagan Valley p. 541.*

WEST VANCOUVER —*See Vancouver p. 630.*

WHISTLER pop. 9,248

————— WHERE TO STAY —————

THE ASPENS ON BLACKCOMB   *Book at AAA.com*   **Phone:** 604/932-7222

🔷🔷🔷
Condominium
Rates not provided

Address: 4800 Spearhead Dr V0N 1B4 **Location:** Hwy 99, 0.6 (1 km) e on Lorimer Rd (Upper Village), just se on Blackcomb Way, then just w. **Facility:** Smoke free premises. 77 units. 56 one- and 21 two-bedroom suites with kitchens. 3 stories, interior corridors. **Parking:** on-site (fee). **Terms:** check-in 4 pm. **Amenities:** video library (fee), DVD players, voice mail, irons, hair dryers. **Pool(s):** heated outdoor. **Leisure Activities:** sauna, whirlpools. **Guest Services:** coin laundry, wireless Internet. **Business Services:** meeting rooms, PC (fee).

🏊 ✕ 🏋 📶 🍽 💻

BEST WESTERN LISTEL WHISTLER HOTEL   *Book great rates at AAA.com*   **Phone:** 604/932-1133

(CAA) (SAVE)
🔷🔷🔷
Small-scale Hotel
Rates not provided

Address: 4121 Village Green V0N 1B4 **Location:** Hwy 99, just e on Village Gate Blvd, then follow Whistler Way. **Facility:** Smoke free premises. 98 units. 96 one-bedroom standard units. 2 one-bedroom suites with whirlpools. 3 stories, interior corridors. **Parking:** on-site (fee). **Terms:** check-in 4 pm. **Amenities:** video games (fee), voice mail, safes, irons, hair dryers. **Dining:** Bear Foot Bistro, see separate listing. **Pool(s):** heated outdoor. **Leisure Activities:** saunas, whirlpool. **Guest Services:** valet and coin laundry, wireless Internet. **Business Services:** meeting rooms. **Free Special Amenities:** local telephone calls and newspaper.

AAA Benefit:
Members save 10% everyday, plus an exclusive frequent stay program.

🛎 🍸 🏊 ✕ 📷 📶 💻 / SOME UNITS FEE 🐕 🏋

BLACKCOMB LODGE & SPA   *Book great rates at AAA.com*   **Phone:** 604/932-4155

(CAA) (SAVE)
🔷🔷🔷
Small-scale Hotel
Rates not provided

Address: 4220 Gateway Dr V0N 1B4 **Location:** Hwy 99, just e on Village Gate Blvd, then just s. **Facility:** Smoke free premises. 71 one-bedroom standard units, some with efficiencies. 3 stories, interior corridors. **Parking:** on-site (fee). **Terms:** check-in 4 pm. **Amenities:** DVD players, voice mail, safes, irons, hair dryers. **Pool(s):** heated indoor. **Leisure Activities:** sauna, whirlpool, spa. **Guest Services:** coin laundry, wireless Internet. **Business Services:** meeting rooms. **Free Special Amenities:** local telephone calls and room upgrade (subject to availability with advance reservations).

🛎 🏊 ✕ ✕ 💻 / SOME UNITS 📶

CHALET LUISE   **Phone:** 604/932-4187

🔷🔷
Bed & Breakfast
Rates not provided

Address: 7461 Ambassador Crescent V0N 1B7 **Location:** Hwy 99, exit Nancy Green Dr, follow to Ambassador Crescent. Located in a residential area. **Facility:** Smoke free premises. 8 one-bedroom standard units. 2 stories (no elevator), interior corridors. *Bath:* combo or shower only. **Parking:** on-site. **Terms:** open 5/1-11/30, office hours 8 am-10 pm. **Amenities:** hair dryers. **Leisure Activities:** sauna, whirlpool. **Guest Services:** coin laundry.

✕ 🏋 📺 🖂 / SOME UNITS 📶

▼ See AAA listing p 556 ▼

CRYSTAL LODGE

Small-scale Hotel
$108-$1225 All Year

Book great rates at AAA.com

Phone: 604/932-2221

Address: 4154 Village Green V0N 1B0 **Location:** Hwy 99, just e on Village Gate Blvd, then follow Whistler Way. **Facility:** Smoke free premises. 159 units. 145 one-bedroom standard units, some with efficiencies and/or whirlpools. 3 one-, 8 two- and 3 three-bedroom suites with kitchens, some with whirlpools. 5 stories, interior corridors. **Parking:** on-site (fee). **Terms:** check-in 4 pm, cancellation fee imposed. **Amenities:** video games (fee), voice mail, hair dryers. *Some:* high-speed Internet (fee), safes, irons. **Dining:** Ric's Grill, see separate listing. **Pool(s):** heated outdoor. **Leisure Activities:** sauna, whirlpool, limited exercise equipment. **Guest Services:** valet and coin laundry. **Business Services:** meeting rooms, business center. **Cards:** AX, DC, DS, MC, VI. **Free Special Amenities:** newspaper.

DELTA WHISTLER VILLAGE SUITES

Large-scale Hotel
$99-$399 All Year

Book great rates at AAA.com

Phone: (604)905-3987

Address: 4308 Main St V0N 1B4 **Location:** Hwy 99, just e on Village Gate Blvd, just n on Northlands Blvd, then just e. **Facility:** Smoke free premises. 205 units. 22 one-bedroom standard units. 131 one- and 52 two-bedroom suites with kitchens. 6 stories, interior corridors. **Parking:** on-site (fee) and valet. **Terms:** check-in 4 pm, 45 day cancellation notice-fee imposed. **Amenities:** video games (fee), voice mail, irons, hair dryers. **Dining:** 2 restaurants. **Pool(s):** heated outdoor. **Leisure Activities:** sauna, whirlpools, rental bicycles, exercise room, spa. **Fee:** ski equipment. **Guest Services:** coin laundry, wireless Internet. **Business Services:** meeting rooms, PC (fee). **Cards:** AX, DC, JC, MC, VI. *(See color ad below)*

THE DURLACHER HOF ALPINE INN

Bed & Breakfast
$129-$359 All Year

Phone: (604)932-1924

Address: 7055 Nesters Rd V0N 1B7 **Location:** 0.9 mi (1.5 km) n on Hwy 99. **Facility:** Goose-down duvets and hand-carved pine furniture are featured in the guest rooms, which are kept meticulous thanks to a caring housekeeping staff. Smoke free premises. 8 one-bedroom standard units, some with whirlpools. 3 stories (no elevator), interior corridors. *Bath:* combo or shower only. **Parking:** on-site. **Terms:** office hours 7 am-8 pm, 14 day cancellation notice, 30 day in winter-fee imposed. **Amenities:** hair dryers. **Leisure Activities:** sauna, whirlpool. **Guest Services:** wireless Internet. **Cards:** MC, VI.

EDGEWATER LODGE

Motel
$124-$225 All Year

Phone: (604)932-0688

Address: 8020 Alpine Way V0N 1B0 **Location:** 2.5 mi (4 km) n of Whistler Village via Hwy 99, then e. **Facility:** Smoke free premises. 12 one-bedroom standard units. 1 story, exterior corridors. *Bath:* combo or shower only. **Parking:** on-site. **Terms:** office hours 8 am-10 pm, age restrictions may apply, 14 day cancellation notice-fee imposed. **Amenities:** video library, hair dryers. **Leisure Activities:** whirlpool. **Cards:** AX, MC, VI. **Free Special Amenities:** expanded continental breakfast and high-speed Internet. *(See color ad p 671)*

THE FAIRMONT CHATEAU WHISTLER

Large-scale Hotel
$199-$3099 All Year

Book great rates at AAA.com

Phone: (604)938-8000

Address: 4599 Chateau Blvd V0N 1B4 **Location:** Hwy 99, 0.6 mi (1 km) e on Lorimer Rd (Upper Village), just w on Blackcomb Way. **Facility:** A luxurious chateau at the number-one rated ski resort in North America, the property includes such added amenities as a spa and golf course. 550 units. 490 one-bedroom standard units, some with whirlpools. 55 one- and 5 two-bedroom suites, some with whirlpools. 12 stories, interior corridors. **Parking:** on-site (fee) and valet. **Terms:** check-in 4 pm, 3 day cancellation notice-fee imposed. **Amenities:** voice mail, safes, irons, hair dryers. **Fee:** video games, high-speed Internet. *Some:* DVD players, CD players, honor bars. **Pool(s):** 2 heated outdoor. **Leisure Activities:** sauna, whirlpools, steamrooms, 3 tennis courts, spa. **Fee:** golf-18 holes, tennis instruction, ski & sports equipment. **Guest Services:** valet and coin laundry, area transportation-Whistler Township and Golf Course. **Business Services:** conference facilities, business center. **Cards:** AX, CB, DC, DS, JC, MC, VI.

FOUR SEASONS RESORT WHISTLER

Phone: 604/935-3400

Large-scale Hotel
Rates not provided

Address: 4591 Blackcomb Way V0N 1B4 **Location:** Hwy 99, 0.6 mi (1 km) e on Lorimer Rd (Upper Village). **Facility:** This new lodging near Blackcomb Mountain offers stunning guest rooms warmly decorated in rich wood accents, with fireplaces and balconies. 298 units. 178 one-bedroom standard units. 90 one-, 20 two- and 10 three-bedroom suites, some with kitchens and/or whirlpools. 6-9 stories, interior corridors. **Parking:** on-site (fee) and valet. **Amenities:** video library, DVD players, CD players, dual phone lines, voice mail, safes, irons, hair dryers. *Fee:* video games, high-speed Internet. **Dining:** Fifty Two 80 Bistro & Bar, see separate listing. **Pool(s):** heated outdoor. **Leisure Activities:** whirlpools, steamrooms, rental bicycles, jogging, spa. **Guest Services:** valet laundry, area transportation-Whistler Village & golf course. **Business Services:** meeting rooms, business center.

GLACIER LODGE

Phone: 604/905-0518

Condominium
Rates not provided

Address: 4573 Chateau Blvd V0N 1B4 **Location:** Hwy 99, 0.6 mi (1 km) e on Lorimer Rd (upper village), then just w on Blackcomb Way. **Facility:** This lodge offers proximity to the mountain and is well-suited for groups. Smoke free premises. 99 units. 36 one-bedroom standard units, some with efficiencies. 53 one-, 9 two- and 1 three-bedroom suites with kitchens. 3 stories, interior corridors. **Parking:** on-site (fee). **Terms:** check-in 4 pm. **Amenities:** video library, DVD players, voice mail, irons, hair dryers. **Pool(s):** heated outdoor. **Leisure Activities:** whirlpools, exercise room. **Guest Services:** coin laundry, wireless Internet. **Business Services:** meeting rooms, PC (fee).

HILTON WHISTLER RESORT & SPA

Phone: (604)932-1982

Large-scale Hotel
$149-$899 All Year

Address: 4050 Whistler Way V0N 1B4 **Location:** Hwy 99, just e on Village Gate Blvd, then follow Whistler Way. **Facility:** The newly renovated hotel boasts some of the largest hotel rooms in Whistler; the chair lifts at Whistler Mountain are within easy walking distance. Smoke free premises. 289 units. 265 one-bedroom standard units, some with efficiencies. 15 one- and 9 two-bedroom suites, some with kitchens. 5-8 stories, interior corridors. **Parking:** on-site (fee) and valet. **Terms:** check-in 4 pm. **Amenities:** dual phone lines, voice mail, safes, irons, hair dryers. *Fee:* video games, high-speed Internet. **Pool(s):** heated outdoor. **Leisure Activities:** sauna, whirlpools, exercise room, spa. **Guest Services:** valet and coin laundry, wireless Internet. **Business Services:** conference facilities, business center. **Cards:** AX, CB, DC, DS, JC, MC, VI. *(See color ad p 672)*

HOLIDAY INN SUNSPREE RESORT WHISTLER VILLAGE CENTRE

Phone: 604/938-0878

Small-scale Hotel
$119-$499 All Year

Address: 4295 Blackcomb Way V0N 1B4 **Location:** Hwy 99, just e on Village Gate Blvd. **Facility:** Smoke free premises. 115 units. 105 one- and 10 two-bedroom standard units with whirlpools, some with efficiencies or kitchens. 6 stories, interior corridors. **Parking:** on-site (fee). **Terms:** check-in 4 pm, 2-7 night minimum stay - seasonal, 30 day cancellation notice-fee imposed. **Amenities:** video games (fee), high-speed Internet, voice mail, irons, hair dryers. **Leisure Activities:** whirlpool, limited exercise equipment. **Guest Services:** valet laundry, wireless Internet. **Cards:** AX, DC, DS, JC, MC, VI. **Free Special Amenities:** local telephone calls and high-speed Internet. *(See color ad on insert)*

LE CHAMOIS

Phone: (604)932-8700

Small-scale Hotel
$165-$577 11/24-2/28
$105-$165 3/1-11/23

Address: 4557 Blackcomb Way V0N 1B0 **Location:** Hwy 99, 0.6 mi (1 km) e on Lorimer Rd (Upper Village), then just w. **Facility:** Smoke free premises. 45 units. 44 one-bedroom standard units, some with whirlpools. 1 three-bedroom suite with kitchen and whirlpool. 6 stories, interior corridors. **Parking:** on-site (fee). **Terms:** check-in 4 pm, 2-7 night minimum stay - seasonal, 30 day cancellation notice-fee imposed. **Amenities:** DVD players, voice mail, irons, hair dryers. **Dining:** La Rua Restaurante, see separate listing. **Pool(s):** heated outdoor. **Leisure Activities:** whirlpool, limited exercise equipment. **Guest Services:** coin laundry, wireless Internet. **Business Services:** meeting rooms. **Cards:** AX, MC, VI. **Free Special Amenities:** local telephone calls and high-speed Internet.

▼ See AAA listing p 670 ▼

LOST LAKE LODGE

Vacation Rental
Condominium

Rates not provided

Book at AAA.com **Phone:** 604/905-7631
Address: 4660 Blackcomb Way V0N 1B4 **Location:** Hwy 99, 0.6 mi (1 km) e on Lorimer Rd (Upper Village), 0.6 mi (1 km) ne. **Facility:** Situated in a quiet residential area closer to Blackcomb Mountain, these are very modern and wonderfully decorated condos. Smoke free premises. 70 units. 4 one-bedroom standard units with efficiencies. 48 one- and 18 two-bedroom suites with kitchens. 5 stories, interior corridors. **Parking:** on-site (fee). **Terms:** office hours 8 am-midnight, off-site registration, check-in 4 pm. **Amenities:** video library, voice mail, irons, hair dryers. **Pool(s):** heated outdoor. **Leisure Activities:** whirlpool, exercise room. **Guest Services:** coin laundry. **Business Services:** meeting rooms, PC (fee).

PAN PACIFIC WHISTLER MOUNTAINSIDE *Book at AAA.com*   **Phone:** (604)905-2999

Small-scale Hotel
$139-$1509 All Year

Address: 4320 Sundial Crescent V0N 1B4 **Location:** Hwy 99, just e on Village Gate Blvd, then just s on Blackcomb Way. **Facility:** Smoke free premises. 121 units. 45 one-bedroom standard units with kitchens. 51 one- and 25 two-bedroom suites with kitchens. 8 stories, interior corridors. **Parking:** on-site (fee) and valet. **Terms:** 1-5 night minimum stay - seasonal and/or weekends, 7 day cancellation notice, 30 day in winter-fee imposed. **Amenities:** CD players, dual phone lines, voice mail, safes, irons, hair dryers. *Fee:* video games, high-speed Internet. **Pool(s):** heated outdoor. **Leisure Activities:** whirlpools, steamroom, limited exercise equipment. **Guest Services:** valet and coin laundry, area transportation, wireless Internet. **Business Services:** meeting rooms, PC (fee). **Cards:** AX, DC, MC, VI.

PAN PACIFIC WHISTLER VILLAGE CENTRE *Book at AAA.com*   **Phone:** 604/966-5500

Small-scale Hotel
$159-$2699 All Year

Address: 4299 Blackcomb Way V0N 1B4 **Location:** Hwy 99, just e on Village Gate Blvd. **Facility:** Smoke free premises. 83 units. 45 one-, 35 two- and 3 three-bedroom suites with kitchens. 8 stories, interior corridors. **Parking:** on-site (fee) and valet. **Terms:** 1-5 night minimum stay - seasonal and/or weekends, 7 day cancellation notice, 30 day in winter-fee imposed. **Amenities:** CD players, dual phone lines, voice mail, safes, irons, hair dryers. *Fee:* video games, high-speed Internet. **Pool(s):** heated outdoor. **Leisure Activities:** sauna, whirlpools, limited exercise equipment, massage. **Guest Services:** valet and coin laundry, area transportation, wireless Internet. **Business Services:** meeting rooms, business center. **Cards:** AX, DC, MC, VI.

RESIDENCE INN BY MARRIOTT *Book great rates at AAA.com*   **Phone:** 604/905-3400

Vacation Rental
Condominium
$164-$329 All Year

Address: 4899 Painted Cliff Rd V0N 1B4 **Location:** Hwy 99, 0.6 mi (1 km) e on Lorimer Rd (Upper Village), just se on Blackcomb Way, then just w, follow road all the way to the end. **Facility:** Smoke free premises. 186 units. 141 one- and 45 two-bedroom suites with kitchens. 6 stories, interior corridors. **Parking:** on-site (fee). **Terms:** check-in 4 pm. **Amenities:** voice mail, irons, hair dryers. **Pool(s):** heated outdoor. **Leisure Activities:** whirlpools, limited exercise equipment. **Guest Services:** valet and coin laundry, wireless Internet. **Business Services:** meeting rooms, PC (fee). **Cards:** AX, MC, VI.

AAA Benefit:
Members save 5% off of the best available rate.

SUMMIT LODGE & SPA *Book great rates at AAA.com* Phone: (604)932-2778

CAA SAVE

▼▼▼▼

Small-scale Hotel
$139-$425 3/1-4/30
$119-$425 5/1-2/28

Address: 4359 Main St V0N 1B4 **Location:** Hwy 99, just n on Village Gate Blvd, just w on Northlands Blvd. **Facility:** Smoke free premises. 81 units. 75 one-bedroom standard units with efficiencies. 6 one-bedroom suites with efficiencies. 5 stories, interior corridors. **Parking:** on-site (fee). **Terms:** check-in 4 pm, 1-7 night minimum stay - seasonal, 30 day cancellation notice-fee imposed. **Amenities:** high-speed Internet, voice mail, irons, hair dryers. **Dining:** Sachi Sushi, see separate listing. **Pool(s):** heated outdoor. **Leisure Activities:** sauna, whirlpool, spa. **Guest Services:** valet and coin laundry. **Business Services:** meeting rooms, PC (fee). **Cards:** AX, DC, DS, JC, MC, VI. **Free Special Amenities:** newspaper and early check-in/late check-out.

⬛ ⬛ ⬛ CALL ⬛ ⬛ ⬛ ⬛ ⬛ ⬛ ⬛ ⬛ / SOME UNITS ⬛

SUNDIAL BOUTIQUE HOTEL *Book great rates at AAA.com* Phone: (604)932-2321

▼▼▼ ▼▼▼

Small-scale Hotel
$199-$1149 All Year

Address: 4340 Sundial Crescent V0N 1B4 **Location:** Hwy 99, just e on Village Gate Blvd, then just s on Blackcomb Way. **Facility:** Smoke free premises. 49 units. 27 one- and 22 two-bedroom suites with kitchens, some with whirlpools. 6 stories, interior corridors. **Parking:** on-site (fee). **Terms:** check-in 4 pm, 45 day cancellation notice-fee imposed. **Amenities:** voice mail, safes, irons, hair dryers. **Leisure Activities:** whirlpool. **Guest Services:** coin laundry, wireless Internet. **Business Services:** meeting rooms. **Cards:** AX, MC, VI.

⬛ CALL ⬛ ⬛ ⬛ ⬛ ⬛ ⬛

TANTALUS RESORT LODGE *Book at AAA.com* Phone: (604)932-4146

▼▼▼ ▼▼

Vacation Rental
Condominium

$199-$829 11/16-2/28
$129-$299 3/1-11/15

Address: 4200 Whistler Way V0N 1B4 **Location:** Hwy 99, just e on Village Gate Blvd, then follow Whistler Way to the end. **Facility:** Smoke free premises. 64 two-bedroom suites with kitchens. 5 stories, interior corridors. **Parking:** on-site (fee). **Terms:** check-in 4 pm, 1-7 night minimum stay - seasonal, cancellation fee imposed. **Amenities:** voice mail, hair dryers. **Pool(s):** heated outdoor. **Leisure Activities:** sauna, whirlpools, 2 tennis courts, playground, volleyball. **Guest Services:** coin laundry, area transportation. **Business Services:** meeting rooms, PC (fee). **Cards:** AX, JC, MC, VI.

(ASK) ⬛ ⬛ ⬛ ⬛ ⬛ ⬛ ⬛ ⬛ ⬛ / SOME UNITS FEE ⬛

THE WESTIN RESORT & SPA *Book great rates at AAA.com* Phone: 604/905-5000

CAA SAVE

▼▼▼ ▼▼▼

Large-scale Hotel
Rates not provided

Address: 4090 Whistler Way V0N 1B4 **Location:** Hwy 99, just e on Village Gate Blvd, then s. **Facility:** The upscale lodging comprises shops, conference facilities, a spa and health club and ski-in, ski-out convenience to Whistler Mountain. Smoke free premises. 419 units. 218 one-bedroom standard units with efficiencies. 183 one- and 18 two-bedroom suites with kitchens, some with whirlpools. 11 stories, interior corridors. **Parking:** on-site (fee) and valet. **Terms:** check-in 4 pm. **Amenities:** dual phone lines, voice mail, safes, honor bars, irons, hair dryers. **Fee:** video games, high-speed Internet. **Dining:** The Aubergine Grille, see separate listing. **Pool(s):** heated indoor/outdoor. **Leisure Activities:** sauna, whirlpools, steamrooms, spa. **Guest Services:** valet and coin laundry, area transportation-within Whistler Township, wireless Internet. **Business Services:** conference facilities, business center. **Free Special Amenities:** local telephone calls and newspaper.

WESTIN
HOTELS & RESORTS

AAA Benefit:
Members get up to
15% off, plus
Starwood Preferred
Guest® bonuses.

⬛ 24⬛ ⬛ CALL ⬛ ⬛ FEE ⬛ ⬛ ⬛ ⬛ ⬛ ⬛ ⬛ / SOME UNITS ⬛

▼ See AAA listing p 676 ▼

WHISTLER CASCADE LODGE

Vacation Rental
Condominium
Rates not provided

Phone: 604/905-4875

Address: 4315 Northlands Blvd V0N 1B0 **Location:** Hwy 99, just e on Village Gate Blvd, then just n. **Facility:** Smoke free premises. 112 units. 30 one-bedroom standard units with efficiencies. 80 one-and 2 two-bedroom suites with kitchens. 6 stories, interior corridors. **Parking:** on-site (fee). **Terms:** check-in 4 pm. **Amenities:** video library, DVD players, voice mail, irons, hair dryers. **Pool(s):** heated outdoor. **Leisure Activities:** saunas, whirlpools, limited exercise equipment. **Guest Services:** coin laundry, wireless Internet. **Business Services:** meeting rooms, PC (fee).

WHISTLER VILLAGE INN + SUITES

CAA SAVE

Small-scale Hotel
$119-$389 All Year

Phone: (604)932-4004

Address: 4429 Sundial Pl V0N 1B4 **Location:** Hwy 99, just e on Village Gate Blvd, then just s on Blackcomb Way to Sundial Pl. **Facility:** 87 units. 83 one-bedroom standard units, some with efficiencies. 4 one-bedroom suites with efficiencies. 3 stories, interior corridors. **Parking:** on-site (fee). **Terms:** check-in 4 pm, 14 day cancellation notice-fee imposed. **Amenities:** DVD players, voice mail, hair dryers. **Pool(s):** heated outdoor. **Leisure Activities:** saunas, whirlpools, exercise room. **Guest Services:** valet and coin laundry, wireless Internet. **Business Services:** meeting rooms, PC. **Cards:** AX, DC, DS, MC, VI. *(See color ad p 674)*

———— WHERE TO DINE ————

ARAXI RESTAURANT & BAR

Continental
$12-$46

Phone: 604/932-4540

You'll enjoy Araxi's exceptionally diverse and creative menu that includes tuna tartare, tofino salmon filet and smoked pork loin. They also have an impressive wine list and enticing desserts. The vibrant and theatrical atmosphere has summer patio dining. Casual dress. **Bar:** Full bar. **Reservations:** suggested. **Hours:** 11 am-3 & 5-11 pm; from 5 pm 9/30-5/31. **Address:** 4222 Village Square V0N 1B4 **Location:** In Whistler Village Square, by the Blackcomb Lodge. **Parking:** on-site (fee). **Cards:** AX, DC, JC, MC, VI.

THE AUBERGINE GRILLE

Pacific Rim
$10-$36

Phone: 604/905-5000

French for "eggplant," Aubergine houses a show kitchen where guests can watch chefs assemble breakfast, lunch and dinner selections. The eclectic menu centers on West Coast seafood, including British Columbia salmon, but it also lists such comfort foods as steak, pizza and pasta. Casual dress. **Bar:** Full bar. **Reservations:** suggested, dinner & in winter. **Hours:** 7 am-10 pm. **Address:** 4090 Whistler Way V0N 1B4 **Location:** Hwy 99, just e on Village Gate Blvd, then s; in The Westin Resort & Spa. **Parking:** on-site (fee) and valet. **Cards:** AX, DC, DS, JC, MC, VI.

BAVARIA RESTAURANT

CAA

German
$21-$39

Phone: 604/932-7518

German beers and schnapps complement pork and veal schnitzels and fondues. The three-course dinner includes an appetizer, choice of schnitzel and dessert. Metered street parking is in effect at all times. Casual dress. **Bar:** Full bar. **Reservations:** suggested. **Hours:** 5:30 pm-10 pm. **Address:** 101-4369 Main St V0N 1B4 **Location:** Hwy 99, just n on Village Gate Blvd, then just w on Northland Blvd; in Alpenglow Lodge. **Parking:** street. **Cards:** AX, MC, VI.

BEAR FOOT BISTRO

CAA

Continental
$85-$125

Phone: 604/932-3433

The bistro features what is reputed to be the city's largest wine cellar, with more than 1,100 bottles. The dining room's strictly table d'hote menu lists a three-course meal at $40 summer and $85 winter and a five-course meal at $75 summer and $125 winter. Those not inclined to eat in the dining room can visit the wine bar, where meals often are served with by-the-glass wines, or the cigar room, which features cigars from around the world. Casual dress. **Bar:** Full bar. **Reservations:** required. **Hours:** 5:30 pm-10 pm. **Address:** 4121 Village Green V0N 1B4 **Location:** Hwy 99, just e on Village Gate Blvd, then follow Whistler Way; in Best Western Listel Whistler Hotel. **Parking:** valet. **Cards:** AX, DC, MC, VI.

BREW HOUSE

Canadian
$12-$37

Phone: 604/905-2739

This "brewpub" brews beer solely for consumption on the premises. There are six flagship brews which are always available, their menu features a fine selection of pizza, pasta and rotisserie foods chosen to go with their fine selection of beers. Casual dress. **Bar:** Full bar. **Reservations:** suggested. **Hours:** 11:30 am-midnight, Fri & Sat-1 am. **Address:** 4355 Blackcomb Way V0N 1B4 **Location:** Hwy 99, 0.6 mi (1 km) e on Lorimer Rd (Upper Village), then just w. **Parking:** on-site (fee). **Cards:** MC, VI.

THE DEN RESTAURANT ON THE LAKE

Canadian
$11-$35

Phone: 604/938-9898

Open for breakfast, lunch and dinner, the publike restaurant overlooks the golf course and nearby lake. Offerings range from tapas, burgers and sandwiches at lunch to more sophisticated dinner fare, including preparations of Alberta beef and great seafood. Many microbrews are on tap. **Bar:** Full bar. **Reservations:** suggested. **Hours:** Open 3/1-10/14 & 12/1-2/28; 6:30 am-10 pm; from 5 pm 12/1-3/31. **Address:** 8080 Nicklaus North Blvd V0N 1B8 **Location:** 3.5 km n of Whistler Village via Hwy 99, then just e; in The Nicklaus North Golf Course Clubhouse. **Parking:** on-site. **Cards:** AX, DC, MC, VI.

EARL'S

Canadian
$10-$28

Phone: 604/935-3222

Offering an experience that falls between fast food and fine dining, the fun, relaxed restaurant prepares great food at a great price. Choices range from juicy burgers, hearty sandwiches, fresh salads, wings and pizza to full entrees of steak, chops and seafood. Made-from-scratch soups and assorted breads, as well as a nice choice of wines and beers, round out the offerings. This is a fitting spot for impromptu get-togethers and festive occasions. Casual dress. **Bar:** Full bar. **Hours:** 11:30 am-11 pm. **Address:** 220/221, 4295 Blackcomb Way V0N 1B4 **Location:** Hwy 99, just e on Village Gate Blvd, then just s. **Parking:** street. **Cards:** AX, DC, MC, VI.

FIFTY TWO 80 BISTRO & BAR

Seafood
$12-$40

Phone: 604/966-5280

The restaurant is named for the number of feet in the vertical mile that can be skied on Blackcomb Mountain. The casual bistro welcomes guests for breakfast, lunch and dinner. British Columbia wines match with items from the seafood bar, including freshly shucked oysters, crab, lobster and prawns. Stylish, casual resort wear is recommended for evenings. Casual dress. **Bar:** Full bar. **Reservations:** suggested. **Hours:** 6:30 am-10 pm. **Address:** 4591 Blackcomb Way V0N 1B4 **Location:** Hwy 99, 0.6 mi (1 km) e on Lorimer Rd (Upper Village); in Four Seasons Resort Whistler. **Parking:** on-site and valet. **Cards:** AX, CB, DC, DS, JC, MC, VI.

LABOCCA RESTAURANT & BAR

Canadian
$7-$30

Phone: 604/932-2112

This restaurant is busy and popular with both the young and mature. The menu features fondue, rack of lamb, pizza, pasta and wok cooking—a real mix of different items to suit almost every taste. The huge outdoor patio is open during the summer. Casual dress. **Bar:** Full bar. **Reservations:** suggested, during ski season. **Hours:** 10 am-11 pm. **Address:** 4232 Village Stroll V0N 1B0 **Location:** In Whistler Village Square. **Parking:** no self-parking. **Cards:** AX, MC, VI.

LA RUA RESTAURANTE

Steak & Seafood
$19-$45

Phone: 604/932-5011

In the Upper Village, the wonderful restaurant affords wonderful views of Blackcomb Mountain. This place is known for its wild game and fish. Complimentary parking is available in Le Chamois Hotel. Casual dress. **Bar:** Full bar. **Reservations:** required. **Hours:** 6 pm-10 pm. Closed: Tues. **Address:** 4557 Blackcomb Way V0N 1B0 **Location:** Hwy 99, 0.6 mi (1 km) e on Lorimer Rd (Upper Village), then just w; in Le Chamois. **Parking:** on-site. **Cards:** AX, DC, MC, VI.

THE MOUNTAIN CLUB

Canadian
$9-$30

Phone: 604/932-6009

Casual dress. **Bar:** Full bar. **Reservations:** suggested. **Hours:** 5 pm-1 am, Sun-midnight; 11 am-1 am 6/15-9/15. **Address:** 40 4314 Main St V0N 1B4 **Location:** In Whistler Village North; just n of Village Gate Blvd. **Parking:** street. **Cards:** AX, DC, MC, VI.

QUATTRO AT WHISTLER

Italian
$20-$40

Phone: 604/905-4844

Next to Pinnacle International Resort, the restaurant offers a cozy atmosphere and a wonderful wine list that represents several regions and includes some reasonably priced selections. Adventurous diners might try Fraser Valley duck, rack of lamb, pan-seared beef tenderloin, baked salmon wrapped in phyllo pastry or pazza a pezzi—a combination of five pastas. Two-hour free parking is available in the lot next to Whistler Public Library. Casual dress. **Bar:** Full bar. **Reservations:** suggested. **Hours:** 5:30 pm-11 pm. **Address:** 4319 Main St V0N 1B4 **Location:** Hwy 99, just e on Village Gate Blvd, then just n on Northlands Blvd. **Parking:** street. **Cards:** AX, DC, MC, VI.

RIC'S GRILL

Steak & Seafood
$20-$35

Phone: 604/932-7427

"Funky and modern" describes the decor and the food at the upscale steakhouse, which bustles with activity. Reservations are definitely recommended. Steaks are well worth it, but then again, so are the salmon, chicken and pasta dishes. A wide variety of distinctive appetizers rounds out the menu. Servers are friendly and attentive. Casual dress. **Bar:** Full bar. **Reservations:** suggested, for dinner. **Hours:** 4:30 pm-midnight. **Address:** 4154 Village Green V0N 1B4 **Location:** Hwy 99, just e on Village Gate Blvd, then follow Whistler Way; in Crystal Lodge. **Parking:** street. **Cards:** AX, DC, MC, VI.

RIMROCK CAFE

Seafood
$32-$52

Phone: 604/932-5565

The hidden gem may be hard to find, but the locals know and love this place. Open for dinner, the restaurant serves many seafood items, including swordfish, salmon and halibut, in addition to an interesting selection of such wild game as buffalo and grilled caribou. Reservations are a must at this spot, which is well worth the jog outside of Whistler township. Casual dress. **Bar:** Full bar. **Reservations:** required. **Hours:** 6 pm-9:30 pm. Closed: 10/15-11/20. **Address:** 2117 Whistler Rd V0N 1B0 **Location:** From Whistler Village; Village Gate Blvd, 2.1 mi (3.5 km) s on Hwy 99, just e on Whistler Rd; in The Highland Lodge. **Parking:** on-site. **Cards:** AX, DC, MC, VI.

SACHI SUSHI

Japanese
$6-$24

Phone: 604/935-5649

At Summit Lodge, the cozy Japanese restaurant prepares interesting fresh sushi selections. Diners can pay for street parking for 2 hours. Casual dress. **Bar:** Full bar. **Hours:** noon-2:30 & 5:30-10 pm. **Address:** 106-4359 Main St V0N 1B4 **Location:** Hwy 99, just n on Village Gate Blvd, then just w on Northlands Blvd; in Summit Lodge & Spa. **Parking:** street. **Cards:** MC, VI.

SUSHI VILLAGE JAPANESE CUISINE

Japanese
$6-$38

Phone: 604/932-3330

Located opposite the Blackcomb Gondola, this restaurant specializes in fresh, tasty sushi and sashimi. They also have tatami rooms for small or large groups. The relaxed and friendly setting was one of the original six restaurants in Whistler. Features green salad, steamed rice, steamed vegatables and ice cream. Casual dress. **Bar:** Full bar. **Hours:** 5:30 pm-10 pm, Fri-Sun also noon-2:30 pm; 5 pm-10 pm, Fri-Sun also noon-2:30 pm in winter. **Address:** 4272 Mountain Sq V0N 1B4 **Location:** In Whistler Village; in Westbrook Whistler Hotel. **Parking:** street. **Cards:** AX, JC, MC, VI.

VAL D'ISERE BRASSERIE

French
$9-$38

Phone: 604/932-4666

The French brasserie is a must-stop. West Coast touches punctuate the wonderfully creative European menu. Casual comfort food is "simply French." Guests should ask about the daily specials and remarkable wine list. Patio seating is a great option in summer. Casual dress. **Bar:** Full bar. **Reservations:** suggested. **Hours:** 11:30 am-11 pm; from 5 pm 11/15-5/31. **Address:** #8-4314 Main St V0N 1B0 **Location:** In Whistler's Town Plaza; in The Bear Lodge. **Parking:** on-site (fee). **Cards:** AX, DC, JC, MC, VI.

WHITE ROCK —*See Vancouver p. 631.*

WILLIAMS LAKE pop. 10,744

─────── **WHERE TO STAY** ───────

DRUMMOND LODGE MOTEL
Phone: 250/392-5334

Motel
$69-$135 All Year

Address: 1405 Cariboo Hwy V2G 2W3 **Location:** 0.6 mi (1 km) s on Hwy 97. **Facility:** 24 units. 23 one-bedroom standard units, some with efficiencies or kitchens (utensils extra charge). 1 one-bedroom suite with kitchen (utensils extra charge). 1-2 stories (no elevator), exterior corridors. **Parking:** on-site, winter plug-ins. **Terms:** office hours 7:30 am-11 pm. **Amenities:** high-speed Internet. **Guest Services:** coin laundry. **Cards:** AX, MC, VI.

🍽️ 📷 🎧 / SOME UNITS FEE 🛏️ ⊠ 🛢️

WILLIAMS LAKE SUPER 8 MOTEL   *Book great rates at AAA.com*
Phone: 250/398-8884

(AAA) SAVE

Motel
$92-$120 3/1-10/31
$85-$110 11/1-2/28

Address: 1712 Broadway Ave S V2G 2W4 **Location:** 1.2 mi (2 km) s on Hwy 97. **Facility:** 54 one-bedroom standard units, some with whirlpools. 3 stories (no elevator), interior corridors. **Parking:** on-site, winter plug-ins. **Amenities:** high-speed Internet (fee), hair dryers. **Guest Services:** coin laundry, wireless Internet. **Cards:** AX, CB, DC, DS, JC, MC, VI. **Free Special Amenities: continental breakfast and high-speed Internet.**

S/D 🍽️ CALL 📶M 🎧 / SOME UNITS FEE 🛏️ ⊠ 🛢️ 📷

WINDERMERE pop. 1,259

─────── **WHERE TO STAY** ───────

WINDERMERE CREEK BED AND BREAKFAST
CABINS
Phone: (250)342-0356

Cabin
$109-$149 All Year

Address: 1658 Windermere Loop Rd V0B 2L0 **Location:** Hwy 95, 5.3 mi (8.2 km) ne on Kootenay 3 Rd, keep left at fork. Located in a quiet area. **Facility:** Set in a mountain valley, the B&B offers four modern cabins with kitchenettes as well as one rustic yet well-appointed 1887 cabin. Smoke free premises. 5 cabins with whirlpools. 1 story, interior/exterior corridors. **Parking:** on-site, winter plug-ins. **Terms:** age restrictions may apply, 30 day cancellation notice. **Amenities:** CD players, hair dryers. **Leisure Activities:** cross country skiing, hiking trails. **Cards:** MC, VI.

⊠ 🎿 📺 ☎️ 🛢️ 🎧 / SOME UNITS 📺 VCR 📷

Manitoba

Churchill
© Milse / age fotostock

BEAUSEJOUR pop. 2,823

---------- WHERE TO STAY ----------

SUPERIOR INN *Book at AAA.com*

Small-scale Hotel
$90-$95 All Year

Phone: (204)268-9050
Address: 1055 Park Ave R0E 0C0 **Location:** Jct Hwy 44, 12 and 302. Located in a rural area. **Facility:** 36 units. 32 one-bedroom standard units. 4 one-bedroom suites with whirlpools. 2 stories (no elevator), interior corridors. **Parking:** on-site, winter plug-ins. **Terms:** cancellation fee imposed. **Amenities:** high-speed Internet, voice mail, hair dryers. **Pool(s):** heated indoor. **Leisure Activities:** sauna, whirlpool. **Guest Services:** coin laundry. **Business Services:** meeting rooms. **Cards:** AX, DS, MC, VI.

ASK (S) (swim) (movie) (computer) / SOME UNITS FEE (pet) (X) FEE (VCR) FEE (fridge) (microwave)

BRANDON pop. 41,511

---------- WHERE TO STAY ----------

CANAD INNS-BRANDON *Book great rates at AAA.com*
(CAA) (SAVE)

Small-scale Hotel
$109-$159 All Year

Phone: (204)727-1422
Address: 1125 18th St R7A 7C5 **Location:** On Hwy 10 (18th St) at jct Brandon Ave. **Facility:** Smoke free premises. 159 units. 150 one-bedroom standard units, some with whirlpools. 9 one-bedroom suites. 11 stories, interior corridors. *Bath:* combo or shower only. **Parking:** on-site, winter plug-ins. **Amenities:** high-speed Internet, voice mail, irons, hair dryers. **Dining:** 2 restaurants, nightclub. **Pool(s):** heated indoor. **Leisure Activities:** waterslide, hot tub, exercise room. **Guest Services:** valet laundry, wireless Internet. **Business Services:** meeting rooms, business center. **Cards:** AX, CB, DC, DS, JC, MC, VI. **Free Special Amenities: newspaper and high-speed Internet.**

(S) (restaurant) (chair) CALL (GM) (swim) (X) (X) (movie) (fridge) (computer) / SOME UNITS FEE (pet) (microwave)

COLONIAL INN

Small-scale Hotel
$62-$76 All Year

Phone: 204/728-8532
Address: 1944 Queens Ave R7B 0T1 **Location:** Jct Hwy 10 (18th St), just w. Located in a commercial area. **Facility:** 73 units. 72 one-bedroom standard units, some with efficiencies. 1 one-bedroom suite. 2 stories (no elevator), interior/exterior corridors. **Parking:** on-site, winter plug-ins. **Amenities:** hair dryers. **Pool(s):** heated indoor. **Leisure Activities:** whirlpool. **Guest Services:** wireless Internet. **Business Services:** meeting rooms, PC. **Cards:** AX; DC, MC, VI.

ASK (S) (restaurant) (swim) (fridge) (microwave) (computer) / SOME UNITS FEE (pet) (X) FEE (VCR)

COMFORT INN *Book great rates at AAA.com*

Small-scale Hotel
$99-$130 5/1-2/28
$98-$125 3/1-4/30

Phone: (204)727-6232
Address: 925 Middleton Ave R7C 1A8 **Location:** Northside Trans-Canada Hwy 1 service road; between Hwy 10 N and 10 S; just e of McDonald's Restaurant. Located in a commercial area. **Facility:** 81 one-bedroom standard units. 2 stories (no elevator), interior corridors. **Parking:** on-site, winter plug-ins. **Amenities:** irons, hair dryers. **Guest Services:** valet laundry, wireless Internet. **Business Services:** meeting rooms, PC. **Cards:** AX, CB, DC, DS, JC, MC, VI. *(See color ad on insert)*

ASK (S) (restaurant) CALL (GM) (movie) (computer) / SOME UNITS FEE (pet) (X) FEE (fridge) (microwave)

DAYS INN *Book great rates at AAA.com*
(CAA) (SAVE)

Small-scale Hotel
$90-$104 All Year

Phone: (204)727-3600
Address: 2130 Currie Blvd R7B 4E7 **Location:** Jct Trans-Canada Hwy 1, 5 mi (8 km) s on Hwy 10 S (18th St). Located in a commercial area. **Facility:** 61 units. 58 one-bedroom standard units. 3 one-bedroom suites. 3 stories, interior corridors. **Parking:** on-site, winter plug-ins. **Terms:** check-in 4 pm, cancellation fee imposed. **Amenities:** video library (fee), high-speed Internet, voice mail, hair dryers. *Some:* DVD players (fee), irons. **Pool(s):** heated indoor. **Leisure Activities:** whirlpool, limited exercise equipment. **Guest Services:** valet and coin laundry, wireless Internet. **Business Services:** meeting rooms. **Cards:** AX, CB, DC, MC, VI. **Free Special Amenities: continental breakfast and high-speed Internet.**

(S) (restaurant) (swim) (computer) / SOME UNITS FEE (pet) (X) (fridge) (microwave)

LAKEVIEW INNS & SUITES-BRANDON *Book great rates at AAA.com*

Small-scale Hotel
$90-$135 All Year

Phone: (204)728-1880
Address: 1880 18th St N R7C 1A5 **Location:** Just s of jct Trans-Canada Hwy 1 and Hwy 10. Located in a commercial area. **Facility:** 66 units. 50 one-bedroom standard units, some with whirlpools. 16 one-bedroom suites. 3 stories, interior corridors. **Parking:** on-site, winter plug-ins. **Terms:** cancellation fee imposed. **Amenities:** video library, DVD players, voice mail, irons, hair dryers. *Some:* dual phone lines. **Pool(s):** heated indoor. **Leisure Activities:** exercise room. **Guest Services:** valet and coin laundry, wireless Internet. **Business Services:** meeting rooms. **Cards:** AX, CB, DC, DS, JC, MC, VI. *(See color ad p 362)*

ASK (S) (restaurant) (swim) (fridge) (microwave) (computer) / SOME UNITS (X)

ROYAL OAK INN & SUITES

Book at AAA.com ▼▼ ▼▼
Small-scale Hotel
$122 All Year

Phone: (204)728-5775

Address: 3130 Victoria Ave R7B 0N2 **Location:** 3 mi (5 km) s of Trans-Canada Hwy 1; 0.9 mi (1.4 km) w of jct Hwy 10 (18th St) and 1A (Victoria Ave). Located in a commercial area. **Facility:** 156 units. 96 one-bedroom standard units, some with whirlpools. 60 one-bedroom suites, some with whirlpools. 2-5 stories, interior corridors. **Parking:** on-site, winter plug-ins. **Amenities:** video games (fee), high-speed Internet, voice mail, irons, hair dryers. **Pool(s):** heated indoor. **Leisure Activities:** whirlpool, waterslide, exercise room. **Guest Services:** valet and coin laundry, wireless Internet. **Business Services:** conference facilities, PC. **Cards:** AX, MC, VI.

(ASK) ⊞ ▼ ➋ ✕ ☎ ▣ / SOME UNITS FEE 🐾 ✕ 🛗 🖼

SUPER 8 MOTEL BRANDON

Book at AAA.com ▼▼ ▼▼
Small-scale Hotel
$91-$101 3/1-9/30
$86-$96 10/1-2/28

Phone: (204)729-8024

Address: 1570 Highland Ave R7C 1A7 **Location:** On Trans-Canada Hwy 1, south service road, just e of Hwy 10 (18th St). Located in a commercial area. **Facility:** 80 units. 78 one-bedroom standard units. 2 one-bedroom suites. 2 stories (no elevator), interior corridors. **Parking:** on-site, winter plug-ins. **Amenities:** video library (fee), voice mail, hair dryers. *Some: Fee:* DVD players. **Pool(s):** heated indoor. **Leisure Activities:** whirlpool. **Guest Services:** valet and coin laundry, wireless Internet. **Business Services:** meeting rooms. **Cards:** AX, CB, DC, DS, MC, VI.

(ASK) ⊞ CALL 🄼 ➋ 🛗 ▣ / SOME UNITS FEE 🐾 ✕ FEE 🖼

VICTORIA INN

Book at AAA.com ▼▼ ▼▼
Small-scale Hotel
$131 All Year

Phone: (204)725-1532

Address: 3550 Victoria Ave R7B 2R4 **Location:** 3 mi (5 km) s of Trans-Canada Hwy 1; 1.1 mi (1.8 km) w of jct Hwy 10 (18th St) and 1A (Victoria Ave). Located in a residential/commercial area. **Facility:** 131 one-bedroom standard units, some with whirlpools. 2 stories (no elevator), interior corridors. **Parking:** on-site, winter plug-ins. **Terms:** cancellation fee imposed. **Amenities:** video library, DVD players, high-speed Internet, voice mail, irons, hair dryers. **Pool(s):** heated indoor. **Leisure Activities:** whirlpool, exercise room. *Fee:* massage. **Guest Services:** valet and coin laundry, wireless Internet. **Business Services:** conference facilities. **Cards:** AX, MC, VI.

(ASK) 🅂 ⊞ ▼ ➋ ✕ 🛗 ▣ / SOME UNITS FEE 🐾 ✕ 🖼

------- WHERE TO DINE -------

ALBERT'S BISTRO

▼▼ ▼▼
Canadian
$7-$33

Phone: 204-727-3911

Casual dress. **Bar:** Full bar. **Hours:** 9 am-9 pm, Sat from 11:30 am, Sun 11:30 am-8 pm. Closed: 12/25. **Address:** 2000 Highland Ave R7C 1A7 **Location:** Jct Trans-Canada Hwy 1 and Hwy 10 (18th St), just sw. **Parking:** on-site. **Cards:** AX, DC, DS, MC, VI.

DOUBLE HAPPINESS RESTAURANT

▼▼ ▼▼
Chinese
$6-$12

Phone: 204-728-6388

Bright and clean, the little spot is where locals head when they get a craving for Chinese food. Casual dress. **Bar:** Full bar. **Reservations:** accepted. **Hours:** 11 am-10 pm, Fri & Sat-11 pm, Sun 4 pm-10 pm. Closed: 12/25. **Address:** 608 Rosser Ave R7A 0K7 **Location:** Between 7th and 6th sts. **Parking:** street. **Cards:** MC, VI.

CHURCHILL pop. 923

------- WHERE TO STAY -------

POLAR INN & SUITES

▼▼ ▼▼
Motel
$135 All Year

Phone: (204)675-8878

Address: 153 Kelsey Blvd R0B 0E0 **Location:** Centre. **Facility:** 26 units. 23 one-bedroom standard units, some with kitchens. 3 one-bedroom suites with kitchens. 1 story, interior corridors. **Parking:** on-site, winter plug-ins. **Terms:** office hours 8 am-8 pm. **Amenities:** video library, voice mail, hair dryers. *Some:* irons. **Guest Services:** valet laundry, wireless Internet. **Cards:** AX, MC, VI.

(ASK) ⊞ 🄺 🐾 🛗 ▣ / SOME UNITS 🐾 ✕ (VCR) 🖼

THE TUNDRA INN

▼▼ ▼▼
Small-scale Hotel
$95-$205 All Year

Phone: (204)675-8831

Address: 34 Franklin St R0B 0E0 **Location:** Centre. Located in a commercial area. **Facility:** 31 one-bedroom standard units. 2 stories (no elevator), interior corridors. **Parking:** on-site, winter plug-ins. **Terms:** office hours 8 am-5 pm. **Amenities:** high-speed Internet, hair dryers. **Guest Services:** valet laundry. **Cards:** AX, DS, MC, VI.

🅂 🄺 🐾 🛗 ▣ / SOME UNITS 🐾 ✕ (VCR)

------- *The following lodgings were either not evaluated or did not meet AAA rating requirements but are listed for your information only.* -------

BEAR COUNTRY INN

[fyi]

Phone: 204/675-8299

Not evaluated. **Address:** 126 Kelsey Blvd R0B 0E0 **Location:** Just w of train station. Facilities, services, and decor characterize a basic property.

CHURCHILL MOTEL

[fyi]

Phone: 204/675-8853

Not evaluated. **Address:** 152 Kelsey Blvd R0B 0E0 **Location:** Centre. Located in a commercial area. Facilities, services, and decor characterize a basic property.

SEAPORT HOTEL

[fyi]

Phone: 204/675-8807

Not evaluated. **Address:** 215 Kelsey Blvd R0B 0E0 **Location:** Centre. Facilities, services, and decor characterize a mid-range property.

──── WHERE TO DINE ────

GYPSY BAKERY & COFFEE SHOP

American
$4-$19

Phone: 204/675-2322

This incredibly popular eatery features an extensive selection of fresh baked goods, steak, shrimp, fish, chicken, sandwiches, soup, salad, pizza and pirogies. It is THE place for to-go lunches. Fine wines and cigars are also available. Polite service. Casual dress. **Bar:** Full bar. **Hours:** 7 am-midnight. Closed major holidays. **Address:** 253 Kelsey Blvd R0B 0E0 **Location:** Centre. **Parking:** on-site. **Cards:** AX, DC, MC, VI.

FLIN FLON pop. 5,836

──── WHERE TO STAY ────

VICTORIA INN NORTH

Small-scale Hotel
Rates not provided

Phone: 204/687-7555

Address: 160 Hwy 10A N R8A 0C6 **Location:** Jct Hwy 10 and 10A, 0.6 mi (1 km) nw (eastern approach to city). Located in a commercial area. **Facility:** 93 one-bedroom standard units, some with whirlpools. 3 stories (no elevator), interior corridors. **Parking:** on-site, winter plug-ins. **Amenities:** video games (fee), irons, hair dryers. *Some:* voice mail. **Dining:** The Kelsey Dining Room, see separate listing. **Pool(s):** heated indoor. **Leisure Activities:** whirlpool, exercise room. **Guest Services:** valet and coin laundry, wireless Internet. **Business Services:** meeting rooms.

──── WHERE TO DINE ────

THE KELSEY DINING ROOM

Canadian
$6-$21

Phone: 204/687-7555

Friendly, efficient service and generous portions keep locals and visitors returning to this restaurant. The menu is varied and offers selections such as steak, chicken, fish and pasta. Booth and table seating are available. Casual dress. **Bar:** Full bar. **Reservations:** accepted. **Hours:** 6:30 am-10 pm, Sat & Sun from 8 am. Closed: 12/25. **Address:** 160 Hwy 10A N R8A 0C6 **Location:** Jct Hwy 10 and 10A, 0.6 mi (1 km) nw (eastern approach to city); in Victoria Inn North. **Parking:** on-site. **Cards:** AX, DC, MC, VI.

GIMLI pop. 1,891

──── WHERE TO STAY ────

LAKEVIEW RESORT   *Book great rates at AAA.com*

Small-scale Hotel
$92-$285 All Year

Phone: (204)642-8565

Address: 10 Centre St R0C 1B0 **Location:** Centre. **Facility:** 99 units. 42 one-bedroom standard units. 52 one- and 5 two-bedroom suites, some with efficiencies, kitchens and/or whirlpools. 3 stories, interior corridors. **Parking:** on-site, winter plug-ins. **Terms:** cancellation fee imposed. **Amenities:** video library, DVD players, voice mail, irons, hair dryers. **Pool(s):** heated outdoor, heated indoor. **Leisure Activities:** sauna, whirlpool, exercise room. *Fee:* game room. **Guest Services:** coin laundry, wireless Internet. **Business Services:** conference facilities, PC. **Cards:** AX, DC, DS, MC, VI.
(See color ad p 362)

HECLA

──── WHERE TO STAY ────

SOLMUNDSON GESTA HUS

Bed & Breakfast
$75-$90 All Year

Phone: (204)279-2088

Address: Village on Hecla Island R0C 2R0 **Location:** On Hwy 8. Located in Hecla Provincial Park. **Facility:** Smoke free premises. 4 one-bedroom standard units. 2 stories (no elevator), interior corridors. *Bath:* some shared or private, combo or shower only. **Parking:** on-site, winter plug-ins. **Terms:** office hours 8 am-9 pm. **Amenities:** video library, hair dryers. *Some:* DVD players. **Leisure Activities:** bicycles, hiking trails. **Cards:** AX, MC, VI.

NEEPAWA pop. 3,298

──── WHERE TO STAY ────

BAY HILL INNS & SUITES

Motel
Rates not provided

Phone: 204/476-8888

Address: 160 Main St W R0J 1H0 **Location:** Hwy 16, just w of jct Rt 5. Located in a quiet area. **Facility:** 34 units. 32 one-bedroom standard units. 2 one-bedroom suites, some with whirlpools. 2 stories (no elevator), interior corridors. **Parking:** on-site, winter plug-ins. **Pool(s):** heated indoor. **Leisure Activities:** whirlpool. **Guest Services:** wireless Internet. **Business Services:** PC.

PORTAGE LA PRAIRIE pop. 12,728

──── WHERE TO STAY ────

CANAD INNS-PORTAGE LA PRAIRIE

Small-scale Hotel
$94-$130 All Year

Phone: (204)857-9745

Address: 2401 Saskatchewan Ave W R1N 3L5 **Location:** Jct Hwy 1A and 24th St W. Located in a commerical area. **Facility:** Smoke free premises. 92 units. 71 one-bedroom standard units. 21 one-bedroom suites, some with whirlpools. 2 stories, interior corridors. *Bath:* combo or shower only. **Parking:** on-site, winter plug-ins. **Amenities:** irons, hair dryers. *Some:* high-speed Internet. **Pool(s):** heated indoor. **Leisure Activities:** sauna, whirlpool, waterslide. **Guest Services:** valet laundry. **Business Services:** conference facilities. **Cards:** AX, CB, DC, DS, JC, MC, VI. **Free Special Amenities:** newspaper and high-speed Internet.

SUPER 8   **Phone:** 204/857-8883

Motel
Rates not provided

Address: 2668 Hwy 1A W R1N 3B9 **Location:** 0.9 mi (1.5 km) w on Trans-Canada Hwy 1A. Located in a commercial area. **Facility:** 58 units. 56 one-bedroom standard units. 2 two-bedroom suites. 2 stories (no elevator), interior corridors. **Parking:** on-site, winter plug-ins. **Amenities:** voice mail, hair dryers. *Some:* high-speed Internet. **Pool(s):** heated indoor. **Leisure Activities:** whirlpool, waterslide. **Guest Services:** valet and coin laundry, wireless Internet. **Business Services:** meeting rooms, PC.

WESTGATE INN MOTEL   **Phone:** (204)239-5200

Motel
$60-$89 All Year

Address: 1010 Saskatchewan Ave E R1N 0K1 **Location:** 0.6 mi (1 km) e on Trans-Canada Hwy 1A. Located in a commercial area. **Facility:** 25 one-bedroom standard units, some with efficiencies. 2 stories (no elevator), exterior corridors. **Parking:** on-site, winter plug-ins. **Terms:** office hours 7 am-midnight. **Cards:** AX, DC, DS, MC, VI.

—————— WHERE TO DINE ——————

BILL'S STICKY FINGERS   **Phone:** 204/857-9999

Canadian
$6-$20

The comfortable, casual, older restaurant offers a wide-ranging menu that includes ribs, chicken, steak, lasagna, gyros and pizza, as well as daily specials. The service is friendly and prompt. Casual dress. **Bar:** Full bar. **Reservations:** accepted. **Hours:** 11 am-midnight, Sat & Sun from 4 pm. Closed: 1/1, 12/25. **Address:** 210 Saskatchewan Ave E R1N 0K9 **Location:** Just w of Main St. **Parking:** on-site. **Cards:** AX, DC, MC, VI.

RUSSELL pop. 1,428

—————— WHERE TO STAY ——————

THE RUSSELL INN HOTEL & CONFERENCE
CENTRE   **Phone:** (204)773-2186

Small-scale Hotel
$98-$158 12/1-2/28
$89-$108 3/1-11/30

Address: Hwy 16 Russell R0J 1W0 **Location:** 0.8 mi (1.2 km) se on Hwy 16 and 83. Located in a commercial area. **Facility:** 70 units. 47 one-bedroom standard units, some with whirlpools. 23 one-bedroom suites, some with efficiencies. 1 story, interior/exterior corridors. **Parking:** on-site, winter plug-ins. **Terms:** cancellation fee imposed. **Amenities:** video library, voice mail, hair dryers. *Some:* DVD players, video games (fee), high-speed Internet, irons. **Dining:** Russell Inn Dining Room, see separate listing. **Pool(s):** heated indoor. **Leisure Activities:** whirlpool, waterslide, playground, exercise room. *Fee:* game room. **Guest Services:** wireless Internet. **Business Services:** conference facilities. **Cards:** AX, MC, VI.

—————— WHERE TO DINE ——————

RUSSELL INN DINING ROOM   **Phone:** 204/773-7507

Canadian
$7-$23

This popular local dining room offers generous portions and efficient service in a family atmosphere. The varied menu includes such items as pasta, seafood, chicken and ribs, as well as veal, steaks and quesadillas. Some light meals are also available. Casual dress. **Bar:** Full bar. **Reservations:** accepted. **Hours:** 7 am-10 pm, Sun-9 pm. Closed: 12/25. **Address:** Hwy 16 Russell R0J 1W0 **Location:** 0.8 mi (1.2 km) se on Hwy 16 and 83; in The Russell Inn Hotel & Conference Centre. **Parking:** on-site. **Cards:** AX, DC, MC, VI.

STEINBACH pop. 11,066

—————— WHERE TO STAY ——————

DAYS INN   **Phone:** 204/320-9200

Small-scale Hotel
Rates not provided

Address: 75 Hwy 12 N R5G 1T3 **Location:** Jct Trans-Canada Hwy 1 and 12, 12.5 mi (20 km) s. Located in a commercial area. **Facility:** 49 one-bedroom standard units. 3 stories, interior corridors. **Bath:** combo or shower only. **Parking:** on-site, winter plug-ins. **Amenities:** voice mail, irons. *Some:* dual phone lines, irons. **Pool(s):** heated indoor. **Leisure Activities:** whirlpool, waterslide, exercise room. **Guest Services:** valet and coin laundry, wireless Internet. **Business Services:** meeting rooms, PC (fee).

THE PAS pop. 5,589

—————— WHERE TO STAY ——————

KIKIWAK INN   **Phone:** 204/623-1800

Small-scale Hotel
Rates not provided

Address: Hwy 10 N R0B 2J0 **Location:** On Hwy 10, 0.4 mi (0.6 km) n. Located in a commercial area. **Facility:** 60 one-bedroom standard units, some with whirlpools. 3 stories, interior corridors. **Parking:** on-site, winter plug-ins. **Amenities:** voice mail, irons, hair dryers. *Some:* DVD players, high-speed Internet. **Dining:** Niska Dining Room, see separate listing. **Pool(s):** heated indoor. **Leisure Activities:** whirlpool, exercise room. **Guest Services:** valet laundry. **Business Services:** conference facilities, fax (fee).

SUPER 8 *Book at AAA.com*

Small-scale Hotel
Rates not provided

Phone: 204/623-1888

Address: 1717 Gordon Ave R9A 1K3 **Location:** At southern approach to town. Located in a commercial area. **Facility:** 70 units. 53 one-bedroom standard units. 17 one-bedroom suites. 2 stories (no elevator), interior corridors. **Parking:** on-site, winter plug-ins. **Amenities:** voice mail, hair dryers. *Some:* DVD players (fee). **Pool(s):** heated indoor. **Leisure Activities:** whirlpool, waterslide. **Guest Services:** valet and coin laundry, wireless Internet. **Business Services:** meeting rooms.

WESCANA INN   *Book great rates at AAA.com*

(AAA) SAVE

Small-scale Hotel
$106 All Year

Phone: (204)623-5446

Address: 439 Fischer Ave R9A 1M3 **Location:** On Hwy 10; centre. Located in a commercial area. **Facility:** 76 units. 75 one-bedroom standard units. 1 one-bedroom suite. 2 stories (no elevator), interior/exterior corridors. **Parking:** on-site, winter plug-ins. **Terms:** cancellation fee imposed. **Amenities:** video library (fee). *Some:* high-speed Internet. **Dining:** restaurant, see separate listing. **Guest Services:** coin laundry, wireless Internet. **Business Services:** meeting rooms. **Cards:** AX, MC, VI. **Free Special Amenities:** local telephone calls and high-speed Internet.

───── WHERE TO DINE ─────

NISKA DINING ROOM

Canadian
$9-$23

Phone: 204/623-1800

The menu lists such choices as pickerel, stir-fried beef, steak, chicken, ribs, pasta and salads. Also offered are heart-healthy choices and dishes recommended for diabetics. Native art is displayed in the dining room. Casual dress. **Bar:** Full bar. **Reservations:** accepted. **Hours:** 6 am-10 pm, Sun 8 am-8 pm; from 7 am 10/1-4/30. Closed: 12/25. **Address:** Hwy 10 N R0B 2J0 **Location:** On Hwy 10, 0.4 mi (0.6 km) n; in Kikiwak Inn. **Parking:** on-site. **Cards:** AX, DC, MC, VI.

WESCANA DINING ROOM

Canadian
$7-$18

Phone: 204/623-5446

Unpretentious dining in a casual setting is found at this restaurant, which features an extensive menu with a good selection of prime rib, steak, chicken, fish and pasta combinations. The lunch menu includes sandwiches, burgers and salads. Casual dress. **Bar:** Full bar. **Hours:** 6:30 am-10 pm, Sun 7 am-2 pm. Closed: 12/25. **Address:** 439 Fischer Ave R9A 1M3 **Location:** On Hwy 10; centre; in Wescana Inn. **Parking:** on-site. **Cards:** AX, DC, MC, VI.

THOMPSON pop. 13,446

───── WHERE TO STAY ─────

COUNTRY INN & SUITES BY CARLSON   *Book great rates at AAA.com*

Small-scale Hotel
$108 All Year

Phone: (204)778-8879

Address: 70 Thompson Dr N R8N 1Y8 **Location:** Just w of Hwy 6. Located in a commercial area. **Facility:** 60 units. 23 one-bedroom standard units. 37 one-bedroom suites. 2 stories (no elevator), interior corridors. **Parking:** on-site, winter plug-ins. **Amenities:** video library, DVD players, irons, hair dryers. **Leisure Activities:** sauna, exercise room. **Guest Services:** coin laundry, wireless Internet. **Business Services:** meeting rooms. **Cards:** AX, MC, VI. *(See color ad p 362)*

DAYS INN   *Book at AAA.com*

Small-scale Hotel
Rates not provided

Phone: 204/778-6000

Address: 21 Thompson Dr N R8N 2B5 **Location:** Just e of Hwy 6. Located in a commercial area. **Facility:** Smoke free premises. 44 units. 41 one-bedroom standard units. 3 one-bedroom suites, some with whirlpools. 2 stories (no elevator), interior corridors. **Parking:** on-site, winter plug-ins. **Amenities:** video library (fee), DVD players, high-speed Internet, voice mail, irons, hair dryers. **Leisure Activities:** limited exercise equipment. **Guest Services:** coin laundry, wireless Internet. **Business Services:** business center.

───── The following lodgings were either not evaluated or did not ─────
meet AAA rating requirements but are listed for your information only.

INTERIOR INN

[fyi]

Phone: 204/778-5535

Not evaluated. **Address:** 180 Thompson Dr R8N 1Y8 **Location:** Thompson Dr at Riverside St. Facilities, services, and decor characterize a mid-range property.

BURNTWOOD HOTEL

[fyi]

Phone: 204/677-4551

Not evaluated. **Address:** 146 Selkirk Ave R8N 0N1 **Location:** Jct Cree Rd. Facilities, services, and decor characterize a mid-range property.

───── WHERE TO DINE ─────

THE HUB

Canadian
$7-$27

Phone: 204/778-5630

The restaurant is a meeting spot for local folks. Fish and chips, burgers, sandwiches, salads and pizza are served in generous portions. Casual dress. **Bar:** Full bar. **Reservations:** accepted. **Hours:** 11 am-10 pm. Closed major holidays. **Address:** 111 Churchill Dr R8N 1M9 **Location:** Centre. **Parking:** street. **Cards:** AX, MC, VI.

WINKLER pop. 9,106

WHERE TO STAY

DAYS INN & SUITES

Small-scale Hotel
Rates not provided

Phone: 204/325-8888

Address: 395 Boundary Tr R6W 4B1 **Location:** Main St and Hwy 14; centre. Located in a commercial area. **Facility:** 52 units. 40 one-bedroom standard units. 12 one-bedroom suites, some with whirlpools. 3 stories, interior corridors. **Parking:** on-site, winter plug-ins. **Amenities:** high-speed Internet, voice mail, hair dryers. *Some:* irons. **Pool(s):** heated indoor. **Leisure Activities:** whirlpool, waterslide, limited exercise equipment. **Guest Services:** coin laundry, wireless Internet. **Business Services:** meeting rooms.

© 2007 NAVTEQ   © AAA

Downtown
Winnipeg
Lodging & Dining

The Forks

FORKS MARKET RD

Manitoba Children's Museum

Dalnavert Museum

The Manitoba Museum

1809-B

Downtown Winnipeg

This index helps you "spot" where approved lodgings and restaurants are located on the corresponding detailed maps. Lodging daily rate range is for comparison only and show the property's high season. Restaurant rate range is a combination of lunch and/or dinner. Turn to the listing page for more detailed rate information and consult display ads for special promotions.

Spotter/Map Page Number	OA	DOWNTOWN WINNIPEG - Lodgings	Diamond Rating	Rate Range High Season	Listing Page
1 / p. 686		The Fairmont Winnipeg	▼▼▼	$149-$399	691
2 / p. 686		The Marlborough Hotel	▼▼	Rates not provided	693
3 / p. 686		Radisson Hotel Winnipeg Downtown	▼▼▼	Rates not provided	693
4 / p. 686		Hampton Inn & Suites	▼▼▼	$129-$169	693
5 / p. 686	CAA	Holiday Inn Hotel & Suites Winnipeg-Downtown	▼▼▼	$140 SAVE	693
6 / p. 686		Place Louis Riel All-Suite Hotel	▼▼	$125-$300	693
7 / p. 686	CAA	Delta Winnipeg - see color ad p 691	▼▼▼	$89-$349 SAVE	691
8 / p. 686	CAA	Best Western Charterhouse Hotel Downtown Winnipeg	▼▼	$119-$149 SAVE	691
9 / p. 686	CAA	Inn at the Forks	▼▼▼	$135-$249 SAVE	693
10 / p. 686	CAA	Norwood Hotel	▼▼	$111-$135 SAVE	693
		DOWNTOWN WINNIPEG - Restaurants			
1 / p. 686	CAA	The Velvet Glove	▼▼▼▼	$16-$45	695
2 / p. 686		Pasta La Vista	▼▼	$6-$20	694
3 / p. 686		Ivory Restaurant & Bar	▼▼	$12-$20	694
4 / p. 686		Blaze Bistro & Lounge	▼▼▼	$8-$32	694
5 / p. 686		Ichiban Japanese Steak House & Sushi Bar	▼▼▼	$13-$35	694
6 / p. 686		Brio Restaurant & Catering	▼▼	$9-$15	694
7 / p. 686		The Current	▼▼▼	$10-$37	694
8 / p. 686		Beachcombers	▼▼	$10-$37	694
9 / p. 686		Amici	▼▼▼	$10-$38	694
10 / p. 686		Restaurant Dubrovnik	▼▼▼	$28-$46	694

Winnipeg
Lodging & Dining

© AAA   1808-B

✈ Airport Accommodations

Spotter/Map Page Number	OA	WINNIPEG INTERNATIONAL AIRPORT	Diamond Rating	Rate Range High Season	Listing Page
8 / p. 688		Comfort Inn Airport, 1.4 mi (2.3 km) e of airport	◈◈	$116-$135	696
7 / p. 688		Country Inn & Suites By Carlson, 1.2 mi (1.9 km) e of airport	◈◈	$91-$99	696
3 / p. 688	CAA	**Four Points Sheraton Winnipeg International Airport, at airport**	◈◈◈	$125-$229 SAVE	697
4 / p. 688		Greenwood Inn & Suites, 0.9 mi (1.5 km) e of airport	◈◈◈	Rates not provided	697
5 / p. 688	CAA	**Hilton Suites Winnipeg Airport, 1 mi (1.6 km) e of airport**	◈◈◈	$119-$189 SAVE	698
6 / p. 688	CAA	**Victoria Inn Hotel & Convention Centre, 0.9 mi (1.4 km) e of airport**	◈◈◈	$95-$160 SAVE	699

Winnipeg

This index helps you "spot" where approved lodgings and restaurants are located on the corresponding detailed maps. Lodging daily rate range is for comparison only and show the property's high season. Restaurant rate range is a combination of lunch and/or dinner. Turn to the listing page for more detailed rate information and consult display ads for special promotions.

Spotter/Map Page Number	OA	WINNIPEG - Lodgings	Diamond Rating	Rate Range High Season	Listing Page
1 / p. 688	CAA	**Canad Inns Garden City**	◈◈	$94-$130 SAVE	696
2 / p. 688	CAA	**Days Inn**	◈◈	$119-$139 SAVE	697
3 / p. 688	CAA	**Four Points Sheraton Winnipeg International Airport**	◈◈◈	$125-$229 SAVE	697
4 / p. 688		Greenwood Inn & Suites	◈◈◈	Rates not provided	697
5 / p. 688	CAA	**Hilton Suites Winnipeg Airport - see color ad p 698**	◈◈◈	$119-$189 SAVE	698
6 / p. 688	CAA	**Victoria Inn Hotel & Convention Centre**	◈◈◈	$95-$160 SAVE	699
7 / p. 688		Country Inn & Suites By Carlson - see color ad p 362	◈◈	$91-$99	696
8 / p. 688		Comfort Inn Airport - see color ad on insert	◈◈	$116-$135	696
9 / p. 688	CAA	**Canad Inns Club Regent Casino**	◈◈◈	$109-$159 SAVE	695
10 / p. 688	CAA	**Canad Inns-Transcona**	◈◈	$94-$130 SAVE	696
11 / p. 688	CAA	**Canad Inns Polo Park**	◈◈◈	$109-$159 SAVE	696
12 / p. 688		Clarion Hotel & Suites - see color ad on insert	◈◈◈	$139-$299	696
13 / p. 688	CAA	**Viscount Gort Hotel**	◈◈	$87 SAVE	699
14 / p. 688	CAA	**Holiday Inn Winnipeg Airport/West - see color ad on insert**	◈◈◈	Rates not provided SAVE	698
15 / p. 688	CAA	**Canad Inns Windsor Park**	◈◈	$94-$130 SAVE	696
16 / p. 688	CAA	**Quality Inn & Suites - see color ad p 699**	◈◈	$90-$270 SAVE	699
17 / p. 688		Travelodge	◈◈	$76-$119	699
18 / p. 688	CAA	**Holiday Inn Winnipeg-South - see color ad on insert**	◈◈◈	$115-$139 SAVE	698
19 / p. 688	CAA	**Best Western Pembina Inn & Suites**	◈◈	$89-$160 SAVE	695

Spotter/Map Page Number	OA	WINNIPEG - Lodgings (continued)	Diamond Rating	Rate Range High Season	Listing Page
20 / p. 688	CAA	**Canad Inns Express Fort Garry**	▽▽	$78-$108 SAVE	695
21 / p. 688	CAA	**Canad Inns Fort Garry**	▽▽▽	$109-$159 SAVE	695
22 / p. 688	CAA	**Comfort Inn South** - see color ad on insert	▽▽	$105-$130 SAVE	696
		WINNIPEG - Restaurants			
1 / p. 688		Branigan's	▽▽	$10-$30	700
2 / p. 688		India Palace	▽▽	$10-$21	700
3 / p. 688		529 Wellington	▽▽▽	$12-$49	700
4 / p. 688		Fusion Grill	▽▽▽	$10-$39	700
5 / p. 688		Spuntino Cafe	▽▽	$12-$22	701
6 / p. 688		Tavern In The Park	▽▽▽	$12-$41	701
7 / p. 688		Mona Lisa Ristorante	▽▽	$7-$29	700
8 / p. 688	CAA	**Bonfire Bistro**	▽▽	$9-$23	700
9 / p. 688		Lux Sole	▽▽	$6-$23	700
10 / p. 688		The Round Table Steak House & Pub	▽▽	$9-$39	701
11 / p. 688		Maxime	▽▽	$7-$22	700

DOWNTOWN WINNIPEG   (See map and index starting on p. 686)

——— WHERE TO STAY ———

BEST WESTERN CHARTERHOUSE HOTEL
DOWNTOWN WINNIPEG   *Book great rates at AAA.com*   Phone: (204)942-0101

Small-scale Hotel
$119-$149 3/1-11/30
$109-$149 12/1-2/28

Address: 330 York Ave R3C 0N9 **Location:** Between Hargrave and Donald sts. Located in the business district. **Facility:** 86 one-bedroom standard units. 5 stories, interior corridors. **Parking:** on-site (fee), winter plug-ins. **Amenities:** high-speed Internet, voice mail, irons, hair dryers. **Leisure Activities:** exercise room. **Guest Services:** valet and coin laundry, area transportation-bus depot & train station, wireless Internet. **Business Services:** meeting rooms, PC. **Cards:** AX, DC, DS, MC, VI. **Free Special Amenities:** newspaper and early check-in/late check-out.

AAA Benefit: Members save 10% everyday, plus an exclusive frequent stay program.

DELTA WINNIPEG   *Book great rates at AAA.com*   Phone: 204/942-0551   7

Large-scale Hotel
$89-$349 All Year

Address: 350 St. Mary Ave R3C 3J2 **Location:** At Hargrave St. Located adjacent to convention centre. **Facility:** 393 units. 377 one- and 6 two-bedroom standard units. 10 one-bedroom suites, some with whirlpools. 18 stories, interior corridors. *Bath:* combo or shower only. **Parking:** on-site (fee) and valet. **Amenities:** video games (fee), high-speed Internet, voice mail, irons, hair dryers. *Some:* CD players. *Fee:* DVD players. **Dining:** Blaze Bistro & Lounge, Elephant & Castle, see separate listings. **Pool(s):** heated outdoor, heated indoor. **Leisure Activities:** sauna, whirlpool. **Guest Services:** valet and coin laundry. **Business Services:** conference facilities, business center. **Cards:** AX, DC, DS, JC, MC, VI. *(See color ad below)*

THE FAIRMONT WINNIPEG   *Book at AAA.com*   Phone: (204)957-1350   1

Large-scale Hotel
$149-$399 All Year

Address: 2 Lombard Pl R3B 0Y3 **Location:** Just e of corner Portage Ave and Main St. Located in a commerical area. **Facility:** 340 units. 334 one-bedroom standard units, some with whirlpools. 6 one-bedroom suites, some with whirlpools. 21 stories, interior corridors. **Parking:** on-site (fee) and valet, winter plug-ins. **Amenities:** voice mail, honor bars, irons, hair dryers. *Fee:* video games, high-speed Internet. *Some:* DVD players (fee), CD players. **Dining:** The Velvet Glove, see separate listing. **Pool(s):** heated indoor. **Leisure Activities:** whirlpool, steamroom, exercise room. *Fee:* massage. **Guest Services:** valet laundry, wireless Internet. **Business Services:** conference facilities, business center. **Cards:** AX, DC, DS, JC, MC, VI.

——— ▼ *See AAA listing above* ▼ ———

- Delta Winnipeg is the largest hotel in the province, located in the heart of downtown Winnipeg
- Only steps away from cityplace and Portage Place shopping centres, MTS Centre and Imax Theatre, with easy access to The Forks Market, Winnipeg Art Gallery, Millennium Library and many other Winnipeg attractions
- Odyssey Health Club
- Three restaurants and lounges
- Heated underground parking
- Pet-friendly

350 St. Mary Avenue, Winnipeg, MB R3C 3J2   1-888-311-4990   www.deltawinnipeg.com

(See map and index starting on p. 686)

HAMPTON INN & SUITES — *Book great rates at AAA.com*
Phone: (204)942-4222 **4**

Small-scale Hotel
$129-$169 All Year

Address: 260 Main St R3C 1A9 **Location:** Corner of St. Mary Ave. Located in the business district. **Facility:** 128 one-bedroom standard units, some with whirlpools. 6 stories, interior corridors. *Bath:* combo or shower only. **Parking:** on-site, winter plug-ins. **Amenities:** high-speed Internet, dual phone lines, voice mail, irons, hair dryers. **Pool(s):** heated indoor. **Leisure Activities:** whirlpool, steamroom, exercise room. **Guest Services:** valet and coin laundry, wireless Internet. **Business Services:** meeting rooms, business center. **Cards:** AX, DS, MC, VI.

HOLIDAY INN HOTEL & SUITES WINNIPEG-DOWNTOWN — *Book great rates at AAA.com*
Phone: (204)786-7011 **5**

Small-scale Hotel
$140 All Year

Address: 360 Colony St R3B 2P3 **Location:** Corner of Portage Ave and Colony St. **Facility:** 140 units. 120 one-bedroom standard units. 20 one-bedroom suites. 11 stories, interior corridors. *Bath:* combo or shower only. **Parking:** on-site (fee), winter plug-ins. **Terms:** cancellation fee imposed. **Amenities:** video games (fee), high-speed Internet, dual phone lines, voice mail, irons, hair dryers. **Pool(s):** heated indoor. **Leisure Activities:** whirlpool, exercise room. **Guest Services:** valet and coin laundry, wireless Internet. **Business Services:** meeting rooms, PC (fee). **Cards:** AX, DC, MC, VI.

INN AT THE FORKS — *Book great rates at AAA.com*
Phone: (204)942-6555 **9**

Small-scale Hotel
$135-$249 All Year

Address: 75 Forks Market Rd R3C 0A2 **Location:** At the Forks. Located in a park and entertainment area. **Facility:** Smoke free premises. 117 units. 107 one-bedroom standard units. 10 one-bedroom suites, some with whirlpools. 5 stories, interior corridors. **Parking:** on-site (fee) and valet, winter plug-ins. **Amenities:** video games (fee), high-speed Internet, dual phone lines, voice mail, safes, irons, hair dryers. *Some:* CD players. **Dining:** The Current, see separate listing. **Leisure Activities:** exercise room, spa. **Guest Services:** valet laundry, wireless Internet. **Business Services:** conference facilities, PC. **Cards:** AX, DC, MC, VI. **Free Special Amenities:** newspaper and early check-in/late check-out.

THE MARLBOROUGH HOTEL — *Book at AAA.com*
Phone: 204/942-6411 **2**

Small-scale Hotel
Rates not provided

Address: 331 Smith St R3B 2G9 **Location:** Just n off Metro Rt 85 (Portage Ave). Located in a commercial area. **Facility:** 148 units. 140 one-bedroom standard units. 8 one-bedroom suites, some with whirlpools. 9 stories, interior corridors. **Parking:** on-site (fee), winter plug-ins. **Amenities:** video games (fee), voice mail, irons, hair dryers. *Some:* high-speed Internet. **Pool(s):** heated indoor. **Leisure Activities:** whirlpool, waterslide, exercise room. *Fee:* game room. **Guest Services:** valet and coin laundry, wireless Internet. **Business Services:** conference facilities.

NORWOOD HOTEL — *Book great rates at AAA.com*
Phone: (204)233-4475 **10**

Small-scale Hotel
$111-$135 All Year

Address: 112 Marion St R2H 0T1 **Location:** On Metro Rt 115, just e of St. Mary's Rd. Located in a commercial area. **Facility:** 52 one-bedroom standard units. 5 stories, interior corridors. **Parking:** on-site, winter plug-ins. **Amenities:** voice mail, irons, hair dryers. *Some:* DVD players (fee), high-speed Internet. **Guest Services:** valet laundry, wireless Internet. **Business Services:** meeting rooms. **Cards:** AX, DC, JC, MC, VI. **Free Special Amenities:** newspaper and early check-in/late check-out.

PLACE LOUIS RIEL ALL-SUITE HOTEL — *Book at AAA.com*
Phone: (204)947-6961 **6**

Small-scale Hotel
$125-$300 All Year

Address: 190 Smith St R3C 1J8 **Location:** At St. Mary Ave. **Facility:** 294 units. 105 one-bedroom standard units with kitchens. 172 one- and 17 two-bedroom suites with kitchens. 23 stories, interior corridors. **Parking:** on-site (fee), winter plug-ins. **Terms:** cancellation fee imposed. **Amenities:** video games (fee), high-speed Internet, voice mail, irons, hair dryers. *Some:* CD players. **Leisure Activities:** exercise room. *Fee:* game room. **Guest Services:** valet and coin laundry. **Business Services:** meeting rooms, business center. **Cards:** AX, DC, MC, VI.

RADISSON HOTEL WINNIPEG DOWNTOWN — *Book great rates at AAA.com*
Phone: 204/956-0410 **3**

Large-scale Hotel
Rates not provided

Address: 288 Portage Ave R3C 0B8 **Location:** At Smith St. Located in a commercial area. **Facility:** 272 units. 261 one-bedroom standard units. 11 one-bedroom suites. 29 stories, interior corridors. **Parking:** on-site (fee) and valet, winter plug-ins. **Amenities:** video games (fee), high-speed Internet, voice mail, irons, hair dryers. *Some: Fee:* DVD players. **Pool(s):** heated indoor. **Leisure Activities:** saunas, whirlpool, exercise room. **Guest Services:** valet laundry, area transportation, wireless Internet. **Business Services:** conference facilities, business center.

The following lodging was either not evaluated or did not meet AAA rating requirements but is listed for your information only.

THE FORT GARRY
Phone: 204/942-8251

Not evaluated. Address: 222 Broadway Ave R3C 0R3 **Location:** Just w of jct Main St and Broadway Ave. Facilities, services, and decor characterize a mid-range property.

(See map and index starting on p. 686)

——————— **WHERE TO DINE** ———————

AMICI

▼▼▼▼

Italian
$10-$38

Phone: 204/943-4997   ⑨

You'll find this restaurant offers fine dining in contemporary surroundings upstairs, and casual dining and more moderate pricing at the Bombolini Wine Bar downstairs. The innovative menu features dishes with complex preparation and creative presentation. Dressy casual. **Bar:** Full bar. **Reservations:** suggested. **Hours:** 11:30 am-2 & 5-10 pm, Sat from 5 pm. Closed major holidays; also Sun. **Address:** 326 Broadway R3C 0S5 **Location:** At Hargrave St. **Parking:** street. **Cards:** AX, DC, MC, VI.

BEACHCOMBERS

▼▼ ▼▼

Canadian
$10-$37

Phone: 204/948-0020   ⑧

You'll enjoy the very good menu at this restaurant; it offers daily made soups and breads, fresh salad, classic and unique sandwiches, creative pasta, tender chicken and veal dishes, mouthwatering ribs, sizzling steaks and succulent seafood. Located in a bustling market, it also has outdoor seating. Casual dress. **Bar:** Full bar. **Reservations:** accepted. **Hours:** 11 am-midnight, Fri & Sat-1 am. Closed: 12/25. **Address:** 162-1 Forks Market Rd R3C 4L8 **Location:** Behind Union Station. **Parking:** on-site. **Cards:** AX, DC, MC, VI.

BLAZE BISTRO & LOUNGE

▼▼▼▼

Canadian
$8-$32

Phone: 204/944-7259   ④

This bistro offers an inviting atmosphere with oil paintings that truly depict the prairies. The menu is also regionally inspired and draws on local products for dishes such as Manitoba pickerel bruschetta and corn crusted turkey medallions. Casual dress. **Bar:** Full bar. **Reservations:** accepted. **Hours:** 6:30 am-10 pm, Sat 7 am-noon & 5-10 pm, Sun 7 am-noon. **Address:** 350 St. Mary Ave R3C 3J2 **Location:** At Hargrave St; in Delta Winnipeg. **Parking:** on-site (fee) and valet. **Cards:** AX, DC, DS, JC, MC, VI.

BRIO RESTAURANT & CATERING

▼▼▼▼

Canadian
$9-$15

Phone: 204/948-0085   ⑥

This restaurant features a progressive menu with some Pacific Rim influences. The Caesar salad and barbecue chicken wrap with salsa are delightful choices, with attractive presentations. The decor is funky, with an open kitchen and outdoor patio. Casual dress. **Bar:** Full bar. **Reservations:** suggested. **Hours:** 11:30 am-2:30 pm, Sat & Sun from 11 am. Closed major holidays; also Mon. **Address:** 300 Memorial Blvd R3C 1V1 **Location:** Just s of Portage Ave; top floor in the Winnipeg Art Gallery. **Parking:** street. **Cards:** AX, DC, MC, VI.

CALL

THE CURRENT

▼▼▼▼

Canadian
$10-$37

Phone: 204/944-2445   ⑦

Large windows in the rear section of the dining room allow guests to view part of the interesting Forks Market area. Service is attentive and professional and the menu offers a good variety of items that are carefully and creatively prepared. Casual dress. **Bar:** Full bar. **Reservations:** accepted. **Hours:** 6:30 am-11 pm, Fri & Sat-midnight, Sun 7:30 am-11 pm. **Address:** 75 Forks Market Rd R3C 0A2 **Location:** At the Forks; in Inn at the Forks. **Parking:** on-site. **Cards:** AX, DC, MC, VI.

ELEPHANT & CASTLE

▼▼ ▼▼

English
$10-$18

Phone: 204/942-5555

Exposed beams, brick and decorative accents that suggest jolly old England surround patrons at the comfortable pub. The menu lists traditional dishes, such as shepherd's pie, steak and kidney pie and roast beef. Casual dress. **Bar:** Full bar. **Hours:** 11 am-11 pm. **Address:** 350 St. Mary Ave R3C 3J2 **Location:** At Hargrave St; in Delta Winnipeg. **Parking:** on-site (fee). **Cards:** AX, CB, DC, MC, VI.

HY'S STEAKHOUSE

▼▼ ▼▼

Steak House
$10-$50

Phone: 204/942-1000

A popular and long-established dining tradition, the steakhouse lines up a good selection of grilled steaks, most of which are cut large. However, a lighter filet is likely to appeal to diners with lesser appetites. The pleasingly varied wine list includes some by-the-glass choices. The upscale decor resembles that of a private club, but the atmosphere remains warm and friendly. Dressy casual. **Bar:** Full bar. **Reservations:** suggested. **Hours:** 11:30 am-2 & 5-9 pm, Sat-10 pm, Sun 5 pm-9 pm. Closed major holidays. **Address:** 1 Lombard Pl R3B 0X3 **Location:** Jct Main St and Portage Ave; main floor of Richardson Building. **Parking:** on-site. **Cards:** AX, DC, MC, VI.

ICHIBAN JAPANESE STEAK HOUSE & SUSHI BAR

▼▼▼▼

Japanese
$13-$35

Phone: 204/925-7400   ⑤

Ichiban features a sushi bar and teppan-style cooking, where your meal is prepared in an entertaining manner at your table. Offerings also include North American dishes of steak, chicken and seafood. The server staff is pleasant, cordial and attentive. Casual dress. **Bar:** Full bar. **Reservations:** accepted. **Hours:** 4:30 pm-10 pm. Closed major holidays. **Address:** 189 Carlton St R3C 3H7 **Location:** Corner of St. Mary Ave and Carlton St. **Parking:** on-site. **Cards:** AX, DC, MC, VI.

IVORY RESTAURANT & BAR

▼▼▼▼

Indian
$12-$20

Phone: 204/944-1600   ③

An East Indian treat, the restaurant offers diners the option of choices from a nicely developed menu or from the buffet line, which is a showcase for high-quality, well-presented, hot and cold dishes. Food is delightfully seasoned and reflects the diner's preference for spiciness. The decor blends "art gallery" and "bistro." Dressy casual. **Bar:** Full bar. **Reservations:** required. **Hours:** 11 am-11 pm, Sat from 5 pm, Sun 5 pm-10 pm. Closed: 3/24, 10/13, 12/25; also Sun, for lunch 11/11 & Good Fri. **Address:** 200 Main St R3C 1A8 **Location:** Between St. Mary and York aves. **Parking:** on-site. **Cards:** AX, DC, MC, VI.

PASTA LA VISTA

▼▼ ▼▼

Italian
$6-$20

Phone: 204/956-2229   ②

Join in the fun, lively atmosphere where the casual, friendly service is caring and professional. The food is served in generous portions and the variety is good, including fresh salads, hearty sandwiches and pizza from the hearth of an oak-fired oven. A rotisserie is used for cooking chicken, ribs, pork and prime rib. And, of course, there is plenty of pasta. Casual dress. **Bar:** Full bar. **Reservations:** accepted. **Hours:** 11 am-11 pm, Sun 4 pm-10 pm. Closed: 12/25. **Address:** 66-333 St. Mary Ave R3C 4A5 **Location:** At Hargrave St. **Parking:** street. **Cards:** AX, DC, MC, VI.

RESTAURANT DUBROVNIK

▼▼▼▼

Continental
$28-$46

Phone: 204/944-0594   ⑩

Located in a beautifully restored mansion near the Assiniboine River, this restaurant provides a warm and inviting dining room and an excellent menu with 20 artfully presented entrees such as pork tenderloin, chicken goyko with shrimp, beef and seafood. Dressy casual. **Bar:** Full bar. **Reservations:** suggested. **Hours:** 5 pm-10:30 pm. Closed: 12/25; also Sun. **Address:** 390 Assiniboine Ave R3C 0Y1 **Location:** Between Carlton and Hargrave sts. **Parking:** on-site. **Cards:** AX, DC, MC, VI. **Historic**

(See map and index starting on p. 686)

THE VELVET GLOVE   *Menu on AAA.com*   Phone: 204/957-1350   ①

Continental
$16-$45

The dining room has a warm finish of wood, large chandeliers and a fireplace. Unpretentious servers are attentive, professional and keen to share their knowledge of the well-developed wine list. Guests can order from the main menu, which lists favorite steak and fish dishes, or the seasonal menu, which centers on creative and artistically presented alternatives. Dressy casual. **Bar:** Full bar. **Reservations:** suggested. **Hours:** 6:30 am-2 & 5:30-10 pm, Sat 7 am-11 & 6-10 pm, Sun 7 am-2 & 6-10 pm. **Address:** 2 Lombard Pl R3B 0Y3 **Location:** Just e of corner of Portage Ave and Main St; in The Fairmont Winnipeg. **Parking:** on-site (fee) and valet. **Cards:** AX, DC, DS, MC, VI.

WINNIPEG pop. 633,451   (See map and index starting on p. 688)

──────── **WHERE TO STAY** ────────

BEST WESTERN PEMBINA INN & SUITES   *Book great rates at AAA.com*   Phone: (204)269-8888   ⑲

Small-scale Hotel
$89-$160 All Year

Address: 1714 Pembina Hwy R3T 2G2 **Location:** 0.6 mi (1 km) n of jct Bishop Grandin Blvd. Located in a commercial area. **Facility:** 104 units. 91 one-bedroom standard units. 13 one-bedroom suites, some with whirlpools. 4 stories, interior corridors. **Parking:** on-site, winter plug-ins. **Terms:** 7 day cancellation notice. **Amenities:** high-speed Internet, voice mail, safes, irons, hair dryers. *Some:* dual phone lines. **Pool(s):** heated indoor. **Leisure Activities:** whirlpool, waterslide, exercise room. **Guest Services:** valet and coin laundry, wireless Internet. **Business Services:** meeting rooms, PC. **Cards:** AX, DS, MC, VI. **Free Special Amenities: expanded continental breakfast and high-speed Internet.**

AAA Benefit:
Members save 10% everyday, plus an exclusive frequent stay program.

CANAD INNS CLUB REGENT CASINO   *Book great rates at AAA.com*   Phone: (204)667-5560   ⑨

Small-scale Hotel
$109-$159 All Year

Address: 1415 Regent Ave W R2C 3B2 **Location:** Just w of Plessis Rd. **Facility:** With direct access to an adjacent casino, this property offers well-appointed guest units. Smoke free premises. 146 units. 142 one-bedroom standard units. 4 one-bedroom suites with whirlpools. 6 stories, interior corridors. *Bath:* combo or shower only. **Parking:** on-site, winter plug-ins. **Amenities:** video games (fee), high-speed Internet, dual phone lines, voice mail, irons, hair dryers. **Dining:** nightclub. **Pool(s):** heated indoor. **Leisure Activities:** whirlpool, exercise room. **Guest Services:** valet laundry. **Business Services:** meeting rooms. **Cards:** AX, CB, DC, DS, JC, MC, VI. **Free Special Amenities: newspaper and high-speed Internet.**

CANAD INNS EXPRESS FORT GARRY   Phone: (204)269-6955   ⑳

Small-scale Hotel
$78-$108 All Year

Address: 1792 Pembina Hwy R3T 2G2 **Location:** Just n of Bishop Grandin Blvd. **Facility:** Smoke free premises. 36 one-bedroom standard units. 2 stories (no elevator), interior/exterior corridors. **Parking:** on-site, winter plug-ins. **Amenities:** voice mail, irons, hair dryers. **Dining:** nightclub. **Guest Services:** valet laundry, wireless Internet. **Business Services:** meeting rooms. **Cards:** AX, CB, DC, DS, JC, MC, VI. **Free Special Amenities: newspaper and high-speed Internet.**

CANAD INNS FORT GARRY   *Book great rates at AAA.com*   Phone: (204)261-7450   ㉑

Small-scale Hotel
$109-$159 All Year

Address: 1824 Pembina Hwy R3T 2G2 **Location:** Just n of Bishop Grandin Blvd. **Facility:** Smoke free premises. 107 units. 64 one-bedroom standard units, some with whirlpools. 39 one- and 4 two-bedroom suites. 2 stories, interior corridors. *Bath:* combo or shower only. **Parking:** on-site, winter plug-ins. **Amenities:** high-speed Internet (fee), voice mail, irons, hair dryers. *Some:* DVD players, video games, CD players. **Dining:** nightclub. **Pool(s):** heated indoor. **Leisure Activities:** whirlpool, waterslide. **Guest Services:** valet laundry, wireless Internet. **Business Services:** meeting rooms. **Cards:** AX, CB, DC, DS, JC, MC, VI. **Free Special Amenities: newspaper and high-speed Internet.**

(See map and index starting on p. 688)

CANAD INNS GARDEN CITY

CAA SAVE

Small-scale Hotel
$94-$130 All Year

Phone: (204)633-0024   **1**

Address: 2100 McPhillips St R2V 3T9 **Location:** McPhillips St at Jefferson Ave. Located in a residential commercial area. **Facility:** Smoke free premises. 55 units. 46 one-bedroom standard units. 7 one- and 2 two-bedroom suites. 2 stories (no elevator), interior corridors. **Parking:** on-site, winter plug-ins. **Amenities:** voice mail, irons, hair dryers. *Some:* DVD players, video games, CD players. **Dining:** nightclub. **Pool(s):** heated indoor. **Leisure Activities:** whirlpool, waterslide. **Guest Services:** wireless Internet. **Business Services:** meeting rooms. **Cards:** AX, CB, DC, DS, JC, MC, VI. **Free Special Amenities: newspaper and high-speed Internet.**

CANAD INNS POLO PARK

CAA SAVE

Small-scale Hotel
$109-$159 All Year

Book great rates at AAA.com

Phone: (204)775-8791   **11**

Address: 1405 St. Matthews Ave R3G 0K5 **Location:** Just e of St James St. Located opposite Canad Inns Stadium. **Facility:** Smoke free premises. 111 units. 108 one-bedroom standard units, some with whirlpools. 3 one-bedroom suites. 6 stories, interior corridors. *Bath:* combo or shower only. **Facility:** Parking: on-site, winter plug-ins. **Amenities:** video games (fee), high-speed Internet, voice mail, irons, hair dryers. **Pool(s):** heated indoor. **Leisure Activities:** whirlpool, waterslide, exercise room. **Guest Services:** valet laundry, area transportation, wireless Internet. **Business Services:** conference facilities, PC. **Cards:** AX, CB, DC, DS, JC, MC, VI. **Free Special Amenities: newspaper and high-speed Internet.**

CANAD INNS-TRANSCONA

CAA SAVE

Small-scale Hotel
$94-$130 All Year

Phone: (204)224-1681   **10**

Address: 826 Regent Ave W R2C 3A8 **Location:** Regent Ave at Plessis Rd. **Facility:** Smoke free premises. 50 units. 43 one- and 4 two-bedroom standard units. 3 two-bedroom suites. 2 stories, interior corridors. **Parking:** on-site, winter plug-ins. **Amenities:** voice mail, irons, hair dryers. *Some:* DVD players, video games. **Dining:** nightclub. **Pool(s):** heated indoor. **Leisure Activities:** whirlpool, waterslide. **Guest Services:** valet laundry, wireless Internet. **Business Services:** conference facilities. **Cards:** AX, CB, DC, DS, JC, MC, VI. **Free Special Amenities: newspaper and high-speed Internet.**

CANAD INNS WINDSOR PARK

CAA SAVE

Small-scale Hotel
$94-$130 All Year

Phone: (204)253-2641   **15**

Address: 1034 Elizabeth Rd R2J 1B3 **Location:** At Lagimodiere Blvd. Located in a residential/commercial area. **Facility:** Smoke free premises. 54 units. 47 one- and 5 two-bedroom standard units. 2 two-bedroom suites. 2 stories (no elevator), interior corridors. **Parking:** on-site, winter plug-ins. **Amenities:** voice mail, irons, hair dryers. *Some:* DVD players. **Dining:** nightclub. **Pool(s):** heated indoor. **Leisure Activities:** whirlpool, waterslide. **Guest Services:** valet laundry, wireless Internet. **Business Services:** meeting rooms. **Cards:** AX, CB, DC, DS, JC, MC, VI. **Free Special Amenities: newspaper and high-speed Internet.**

CLARION HOTEL & SUITES

Book great rates at AAA.com

Small-scale Hotel
$139-$299 All Year

Phone: (204)774-5110   **12**

Address: 1445 Portage Ave R3G 3P4 **Location:** Jct Empress St. Located in a commercial area. **Facility:** 139 units. 89 one-bedroom standard units, some with whirlpools. 50 one-bedroom suites. 4 stories, interior corridors. **Parking:** on-site, winter plug-ins. **Amenities:** video games (fee), high-speed Internet, dual phone lines, voice mail, irons, hair dryers. *Some:* safes. *Fee:* DVD players. **Pool(s):** heated indoor. **Leisure Activities:** whirlpool, steamroom, waterslide, exercise room, spa. **Guest Services:** valet laundry, wireless Internet. **Business Services:** conference facilities, business center. **Cards:** AX, CB, DC, DS, JC, MC, VI. *(See color ad on insert)*

COMFORT INN AIRPORT

Book at AAA.com

Small-scale Hotel
$116-$135 All Year

Phone: (204)783-5627   **8**

Address: 1770 Sargent Ave R3H 0C8 **Location:** At Sargent Ave and King Edward St. Located in a commercial area. **Facility:** 81 one-bedroom standard units. 2 stories (no elevator), interior corridors. **Parking:** on-site, winter plug-ins. **Amenities:** high-speed Internet, irons, hair dryers. **Guest Services:** valet laundry. **Business Services:** PC. **Cards:** AX, CB, DC, DS, JC, MC, VI. *(See color ad on insert)*

COMFORT INN SOUTH

Book great rates at AAA.com

CAA SAVE

Small-scale Hotel
$105-$130 All Year

Phone: (204)269-7390   **22**

Address: 3109 Pembina Hwy R3T 4R6 **Location:** Just n of jct Perimeter Hwy 100 and 75. Located in a residential commercial area. **Facility:** 85 one-bedroom standard units, some with whirlpools. 2 stories (no elevator), interior corridors. **Parking:** on-site, winter plug-ins. **Amenities:** irons, hair dryers. **Guest Services:** valet laundry, wireless Internet. **Cards:** AX, CB, DC, DS, JC, MC, VI. *(See color ad on insert)*

COUNTRY INN & SUITES BY CARLSON

Book great rates at AAA.com

Small-scale Hotel
$91-$99 All Year

Phone: (204)783-6900   **7**

Address: 730 King Edward St R3H 1B4 **Location:** Just s of jct Wellington Ave. Located in a commercial area. **Facility:** Smoke free premises. 76 units. 40 one-bedroom standard units. 36 one-bedroom suites. 3 stories, interior corridors. **Parking:** on-site, winter plug-ins. **Terms:** 4 day cancellation notice. **Amenities:** video library, DVD players, voice mail, irons, hair dryers. **Leisure Activities:** exercise room. **Guest Services:** valet and coin laundry, wireless Internet. **Business Services:** PC. **Cards:** AX, CB, DC, DS, JC, MC, VI. *(See color ad p 362)*

(See map and index starting on p. 688)

DAYS INN
Book great rates at AAA.com   Phone: (204)586-8525 **2**

Small-scale Hotel
$119-$139 3/1-8/31
$109-$129 9/1-2/28

Address: 550 McPhillips St R2X 2H2 **Location:** Just n of Logan Ave. Located in a commercial area. **Facility:** 66 one-bedroom standard units. 2 stories (no elevator), interior corridors. **Parking:** on-site, winter plug-ins. **Terms:** cancellation fee imposed. **Amenities:** voice mail, irons, hair dryers. **Pool(s):** heated indoor. **Leisure Activities:** whirlpool, waterslide. **Guest Services:** wireless Internet. **Business Services:** meeting rooms. **Cards:** AX, MC, VI.

FOUR POINTS SHERATON WINNIPEG
INTERNATIONAL AIRPORT   *Book great rates at AAA.com*   Phone: 204/775-5222 **3**

Small-scale Hotel
$125-$229 All Year

Address: 1999 Wellington Ave R3H 1H5 **Location:** At Winnipeg International Airport. **Facility:** Smoke free premises. 132 units. 114 one-bedroom standard units. 18 one-bedroom suites, some with whirlpools. 7 stories, interior corridors. *Bath:* combo or shower only. **Parking:** on-site (fee), winter plug-ins. **Amenities:** video library, high-speed Internet, voice mail, irons, hair dryers. **Leisure Activities:** exercise room. *Fee:* pool tables. **Guest Services:** valet laundry, wireless Internet. **Business Services:** meeting rooms, business center. **Cards:** AX, DC, DS, JC, MC, VI. **Free Special Amenities:** local telephone calls and high-speed Internet.

> FOUR POINTS BY SHERATON
>
> **AAA Benefit:**
> Members get up to 15% off, plus Starwood Preferred Guest® bonuses.

GREENWOOD INN & SUITES   *Book great rates at AAA.com*   Phone: 204/775-9889 **4**

Small-scale Hotel
Rates not provided

Address: 1715 Wellington Ave R3H 0G1 **Location:** Wellington Ave at Century St. Located in a commercial area. **Facility:** 213 units. 203 one-bedroom standard units. 10 one-bedroom suites, some with whirlpools. 6 stories, interior corridors. *Bath:* combo or shower only. **Parking:** on-site, winter plug-ins. **Amenities:** video games (fee), high-speed Internet, voice mail, irons, hair dryers. *Some:* CD players. **Pool(s):** heated indoor. **Leisure Activities:** whirlpool, steamroom, exercise room. **Guest Services:** valet laundry, wireless Internet. **Business Services:** conference facilities, PC.

(See map and index starting on p. 688)

HILTON SUITES WINNIPEG AIRPORT   *Book great rates at AAA.com*   Phone: (204)783-1700

Small-scale Hotel
$119-$189 All Year

Address: 1800 Wellington Ave R3H 1B2 **Location:** At Berry St. Located in a commercial area. **Facility:** Smoke free premises. 160 units. 11 one-bedroom standard units. 149 one-bedroom suites, some with whirlpools. 6 stories, interior corridors. **Parking:** on-site, winter plug-ins. **Amenities:** video games (fee), dual phone lines, voice mail, irons, hair dryers. **Pool(s):** heated outdoor, heated indoor. **Leisure Activities:** sauna, whirlpool, exercise room. **Guest Services:** valet laundry, wireless Internet. **Business Services:** conference facilities. **Cards:** AX, CB, DC, DS, JC, MC, VI. *(See color ad below)*

HOLIDAY INN WINNIPEG AIRPORT/WEST   *Book great rates at AAA.com*   Phone: 204/885-4478

Small-scale Hotel
Rates not provided

Address: 2520 Portage Ave W R3J 3T6 **Location:** Just e of Moray St. Located in a residential/commercial area. **Facility:** 226 units. 208 one-bedroom standard units. 18 one-bedroom suites, some with kitchens and/or whirlpools. 15 stories, interior corridors. *Bath:* combo or shower only. **Parking:** on-site, winter plug-ins. **Amenities:** video games (fee), dual phone lines, voice mail, irons, hair dryers. *Some:* DVD players, CD players. **Pool(s):** heated indoor. **Leisure Activities:** saunas, whirlpool, children's activity centre, exercise room. *Fee:* game room. **Guest Services:** valet and coin laundry, area transportation-Polo Park, wireless Internet. **Business Services:** conference facilities, business center. **Free Special Amenities:** local telephone calls and high-speed Internet. *(See color ad on insert)*

HOLIDAY INN WINNIPEG-SOUTH   *Book great rates at AAA.com*   Phone: (204)452-4747

Small-scale Hotel
$115-$139 All Year

Address: 1330 Pembina Hwy R3T 2B4 **Location:** At McGillivray Blvd. Located in a residential/commercial area. **Facility:** 170 units. 169 one-bedroom standard units. 1 one-bedroom suite with whirlpool. 15 stories, interior corridors. **Parking:** on-site, winter plug-ins. **Amenities:** dual phone lines, voice mail, irons, hair dryers. *Some:* CD players. **Pool(s):** heated indoor. **Leisure Activities:** whirlpool, children's activity play centre, exercise room. *Fee:* game room. **Guest Services:** valet and coin laundry, wireless Internet. **Business Services:** conference facilities, PC. **Cards:** AX, CB, DC, DS, JC, MC, VI. **Free Special Amenities:** newspaper and high-speed Internet. *(See color ad on insert)*

▼ See AAA listing above ▼

(See map and index starting on p. 688)

QUALITY INN & SUITES *Book great rates at AAA.com*
Phone: (204)453-8247

Small-scale Hotel
$90-$270 All Year

Address: 635 Pembina Hwy R3M 2L4 **Location:** Jct Grant Ave, just s. **Facility:** 69 units. 55 one-bedroom standard units, some with whirlpools. 14 one-bedroom suites with efficiencies. 4 stories, interior corridors. **Parking:** on-site, winter plug-ins. **Terms:** 30 day cancellation notice. **Amenities:** voice mail, irons, hair dryers. *Some:* DVD players, high-speed Internet, dual phone lines. **Guest Services:** valet laundry, wireless Internet. **Business Services:** meeting rooms, business center. **Cards:** AX, CB, DC, DS, JC, MC, VI. **Free Special Amenities: full breakfast and high-speed Internet.** *(See color ad below)*

TRAVELODGE *Book at AAA.com*
Phone: (204)255-6000

Small-scale Hotel
$76-$119 All Year

Address: 20 Alpine Ave R2M 0Y5 **Location:** Just e of jct Fermor Ave and St. Anne's Rd. Located in a residential/commercial area. **Facility:** 75 units. 71 one-bedroom standard units. 4 one-bedroom suites, some with whirlpools. 2 stories (no elevator), interior corridors. **Parking:** on-site, winter plug-ins. **Amenities:** voice mail, hair dryers. *Some:* irons. **Pool(s):** heated indoor. **Leisure Activities:** sauna, whirlpool. *Fee:* game room. **Guest Services:** valet laundry, wireless Internet. **Business Services:** meeting rooms. **Cards:** AX, MC, VI.

VICTORIA INN HOTEL & CONVENTION CENTRE *Book great rates at AAA.com*
Phone: (204)786-4801

Small-scale Hotel
$95-$160 All Year

Address: 1808 Wellington Ave R3H 0G3 **Location:** At Berry St. Located in a commercial area. **Facility:** 259 units. 246 one-bedroom standard units. 13 one-bedroom suites. 5 stories, interior corridors. *Bath:* combo or shower only. **Parking:** on-site, winter plug-ins. **Terms:** cancellation fee imposed. **Amenities:** video games (fee), high-speed Internet, voice mail, irons, hair dryers. *Some:* CD players. **Pool(s):** heated indoor. **Leisure Activities:** whirlpool, waterslide, exercise room. *Fee:* massage. **Guest Services:** valet and coin laundry, wireless Internet. **Business Services:** conference facilities, business center. **Cards:** AX, MC, VI. **Free Special Amenities: local telephone calls and high-speed Internet.**

VISCOUNT GORT HOTEL *Book great rates at AAA.com*
Phone: (204)775-0451

Small-scale Hotel
$87 All Year

Address: 1670 Portage Ave R3J 0C9 **Location:** Portage Ave at Rt 90. Located in a commercial area. **Facility:** 135 units. 129 one-bedroom standard units. 6 one-bedroom suites, some with whirlpools. 4-6 stories, interior corridors. **Parking:** on-site, winter plug-ins. **Amenities:** video games (fee), voice mail, irons, hair dryers. **Dining:** 2 restaurants. **Pool(s):** heated indoor. **Leisure Activities:** sauna, whirlpool, waterslide, limited exercise equipment. **Guest Services:** valet laundry, area transportation-bus & train station, wireless Internet. **Business Services:** conference facilities, PC. **Cards:** AX, DC, MC, VI. **Free Special Amenities: full breakfast and high-speed Internet.**

▼ See AAA listing above ▼

(See map and index starting on p. 688)

——— **WHERE TO DINE** ———

529 WELLINGTON

Steak & Seafood
$12-$49

Phone: 204/487-8325   ③

The restaurant encourages patrons to think big: big steaks, that is. Also huge on quality are lobster and jumbo prawns. Only Canadian Prime certified Alberta beef is served. Service matches the detailed old dining rooms, which are paneled in rich wood and fitting of a grand old mansion. Dressy casual. **Bar:** Full bar. **Reservations:** accepted. **Hours:** 11:30 am-2 & 5-11 pm, Sat from 5 pm, Sun 5 pm-10 pm. Closed: 1/1, 12/25. **Address:** 529 Wellington Cresent R3M 0A5 **Location:** Jct Acadamy Ave, just s. **Parking:** on-site. **Cards:** AX, DC, MC, VI.

BONFIRE BISTRO   *Menu on AAA.com*

Italian
$9-$23

Phone: 204/487-4440   ⑧

Diners can expect comfortable, simple decor and a friendly atmosphere. Management and staff are focused on creating well-prepared dishes. Among choices are wonderful thin-crust gourmet pizzas baked in a wood-fired oven, assorted pasta creations and varied daily specials posted on a blackboard. Casual dress. **Bar:** Beer & wine. **Hours:** 11:30 am-2:30 & 5-10 pm, Fri & Sat-11 pm. Closed major holidays; also Sun. **Address:** 1433 Corydon Ave R3N 0J2 **Location:** Jct Waterloo St. **Parking:** on-site. **Cards:** MC, VI.

BRANIGAN'S
Canadian
$10-$30

Phone: 204/948-0040   ①

The family restaurant's menu offers a wide variety to cater to varied tastes. The convenient shopping center location has lots of parking. Casual dress. **Bar:** Full bar. **Reservations:** accepted. **Hours:** 11 am-10 pm, Thurs-Sat to 11 pm, Sun-8 pm. Closed: 12/25. **Address:** 1555 Regent Ave R2C 4J2 **Location:** Just e of Lagimodiere Blvd (Metro Rt 20); in Kildonan Place Mall. **Parking:** on-site. **Cards:** AX, DC, MC, VI.

CORA'S BREAKFAST & LUNCH
Canadian
$6-$11

Phone: 204/928-1200

Although this place specializes in breakfast, it offers a varied daytime menu that includes bacon, eggs, sausages, crepes, grilled cheese, sandwiches, freshly prepared quiches, salads, fruit platters and freshly squeezed juices. The family-friendly dining room is casual and modern. Casual dress. **Hours:** 6 am-3 pm, Sun from 7 am. Closed: 12/25. **Address:** 840 Waverley St R3T 5Z7 **Location:** Jct Wilkes Ave. **Parking:** on-site. **Cards:** AX, MC, VI.

EARL'S
Canadian
$10-$32

Phone: 204/275-1250

Offering an experience that falls between fast food and fine dining, the fun, relaxed restaurant prepares great food at a great price. Choices range from juicy burgers, hearty sandwiches, fresh salads, wings and pizza to full entrees of steak, chops and seafood. Made-from-scratch soups and assorted breads, as well as a nice choice of wines and beers, round out the offerings. This is a fitting spot for impromptu get-togethers and festive occasions. Casual dress. **Bar:** Full bar. **Hours:** 11 am-midnight, Wed-Sat to 1 am. Closed: 12/25. **Address:** 2005 Pembina Hwy R3T 5W7 **Location:** From jct Bishop Grandin Blvd, just s. **Parking:** on-site. **Cards:** AX, DC, MC, VI.

FUSION GRILL

Canadian
$10-$39

Phone: 204/489-6963   ④

This comfortable little restaurant affords a wonderful opportunity to experience fine Canadian food. Manitoba produce is often used and the list of Canadian wines is notable. Casual dress. **Bar:** Full bar. **Reservations:** suggested. **Hours:** 11:30 am-2 & 5:30-10 pm. Closed major holidays; also Sun & Mon. **Address:** 550 Academy Rd R3N 0E3 **Location:** Just e of jct Kenaston Blvd. **Parking:** street. **Cards:** AX, DC, MC, VI.

INDIA PALACE

Indian
$10-$21

Phone: 204/774-6061   ②

You'll enjoy the fresh, flavorful cuisine at this restaurant, where the tandoori chicken is exceptional. The menu is so extensive that it will satisfy the most discerning tastes. It has a softly lit decor and warm, caring and friendly service. Casual dress. **Bar:** Full bar. **Reservations:** suggested. **Hours:** 11 am-10 pm, Sun from 2 pm. Closed: 12/25. **Address:** 770 Ellice Ave R3G 0B8 **Location:** Corner of Simcoe St. **Parking:** street. **Cards:** AX, DC, MC, VI.

KELSEY'S

Canadian
$7-$20

Phone: 204/668-6689

A fun, relaxed atmosphere and tasty menu of casual fare make the restaurant a popular favorite with locals. Diners might start a meal with some tempting appetizers, such as wings, loaded potato skins or nachos, and follow them with an old-time favorite, such as a burger, wrap, pizza or pasta dish. For a heartier meal, it's hard to beat pork back ribs or a steak. The diverse menu has broad appeal. Casual dress. **Bar:** Full bar. **Hours:** 11 am-midnight, Thurs-Sat to 1 am, Sun-11 pm. Closed: 12/25. **Address:** 1582 Regent Ave W R2C 3B4 **Location:** Just e of jct Lagimodiere Blvd. **Parking:** on-site. **Cards:** MC, VI.

LUX SOLE

International
$6-$23

Phone: 204/453-0222   ⑨

Hallmarks of this cafe include a friendly staff and a menu that demonstrates International ingenuity and imagination. Casual dress. **Bar:** Full bar. **Reservations:** accepted. **Hours:** 11:30 am-10 pm, Thurs-11 pm, Fri & Sat-midnight, Sun 5 pm-9 pm. Closed major holidays. **Address:** 726 Osborne St S R3L 2C2 **Location:** Jct Beresford Ave. **Parking:** street. **Cards:** MC, VI.

MAXIME
Continental
$7-$22

Phone: 204/257-1521   ⑪

This restaurant is a favorite with locals. Its menu features pasta, pizza, Greek specialties, steak, chicken and seafood entrees, which are served in large portions. The service is polite, professional and efficient, and the decor is upscale. Casual dress. **Bar:** Full bar. **Reservations:** accepted. **Hours:** 11 am-midnight, Sun 10:30 am-10 pm. Closed: 1/1, 12/25, 12/26. **Address:** 1131 St Mary Rd R2M 3T9 **Location:** Corner of St. Mary's Rd and Bishop Grandin Blvd. **Parking:** on-site. **Cards:** AX, MC, VI.

MONA LISA RISTORANTE

Italian
$7-$29

Phone: 204/488-3687   ⑦

This popular neighborhood restaurant features an extensive cuisine of Northern Italian fare, including mezza lune, melengane alla parmigiana, veal and jumbo prawns. Local hockey hero memorabilia adorn the walls in the lounge, and there's a sidewalk patio. Casual dress. **Bar:** Full bar. **Reservations:** suggested. **Hours:** 11:30 am-11 pm, Fri & Sat-midnight, Sun 4 pm-10 pm. Closed: 12/25. **Address:** 1697 Corydon Ave R3N 0J9 **Location:** Corner of Renfrew St. **Parking:** street. **Cards:** AX, DC, MC, VI.

MONTANA'S COOKHOUSE
Canadian
$8-$25

Phone: 204/789-9939

Pine boards, exposed beams, a fireplace and Western gear displayed about the dining room give the feeling of a back-country setting. The menu lists hearty portions of comfort fare, such as Yankee pot roast. While the focus is on steaks, ribs and chicken, some seafood entrees also are among offerings. Service is efficient and friendly. Casual dress. **Bar:** Full bar. **Hours:** 11 am-11 pm, Fri & Sat-1 am. Closed: 12/25. **Address:** 665 Empress St R3G 3P7 **Location:** N of Hwy 85 (Portage Ave). **Parking:** on-site. **Cards:** AX, MC, VI.

(See map and index starting on p. 688)

MONTANA'S COOKHOUSE

Canadian
$7-$26

Phone: 204/254-2128

Pine boards, exposed beams, a fireplace and Western gear displayed about the dining room give the feeling of a back-country setting. The menu lists hearty portions of comfort fare, such as Yankee pot roast. While the focus is on steaks, ribs and chicken, some seafood entrees also are among offerings. Service is efficient and friendly. Casual dress. **Bar:** Full bar. **Hours:** 11 am-midnight, Fri & Sat-1 am, Sun 11 am-11 pm. Closed: 12/25. **Address:** 1221 St. Mary's Rd R2M 5E5 **Location:** From Bishop Grandin Blvd, just s. **Parking:** on-site. **Cards:** MC, VI.

MONTANA'S COOKHOUSE

Canadian
$7-$26

Phone: 204/668-2723

Pine boards, exposed beams, a fireplace and Western gear displayed about the dining room give the feeling of a back-country setting. The menu lists hearty portions of comfort fare, such as Yankee pot roast. While the focus is on steaks, ribs and chicken, some seafood entrees also are among offerings. Service is efficient and friendly. Casual dress. **Bar:** Full bar. **Hours:** 11 am-midnight, Fri & Sat-1 am, Sun-11 pm. Closed: 12/25. **Address:** 1574 Regent Ave W R2C 3B4 **Location:** From jct Lagimodiere Blvd; in Crossroads Shopping Centre. **Parking:** on-site. **Cards:** MC, VI.

THE ROUND TABLE STEAK HOUSE & PUB

Steak House
$9-$39

Phone: 204/453-3631 ⑩

You'll enjoy the casual atmosphere at this restaurant, which has an English-manor decor that includes glowing fireplaces. The house specialty is prime rib, and the menu also offers a very good variety of steak, seafood, chicken and pasta dishes. Casual dress. **Bar:** Full bar. **Reservations:** accepted. **Hours:** 11:30 am-10 pm. Closed: 1/1, 9/1, 12/25; also 5/19. **Address:** 800 Pembina Hwy R3M 2M7 **Location:** Just s of Taylor St. **Parking:** on-site. **Cards:** AX, DC, MC, VI.

ROYAL FORK BUFFET RESTAURANT

American
$10-$13

Phone: 204/668-1960

The Royal Fork features buffet-style dining with a wide variety of freshly made choices, including sugar-free desserts. Families can be fed for an excellent value. Dinner prices are in effect starting at 4 p.m. Monday through Saturday and all day on Sunday and major holidays. Casual dress. **Hours:** 11 am-8:30 pm, Fri & Sat-9 pm, Sun 10 am-8 pm. Closed: 12/25. **Address:** 1615 Regent Ave W R2C 5C6 **Location:** Jct Lagimodiere Blvd (Metro Rt 20) and Regent Ave W; in Kildonan Crossing Shopping Centre. **Parking:** on-site. **Cards:** MC, VI.

SPUNTINO CAFE

Italian
$12-$22

Phone: 204-475-4447 ⑤

The delightful little cafe features wonderful pasta dishes, veal and some seafood, which are accompanied by fresh bread that's prepared in-house. Desserts are not to be ignored. Casual dress. **Bar:** Full bar. **Reservations:** suggested. **Hours:** 11 am-close, Sat from noon, Sun from 5 pm. Closed: 12/25; also Mon. **Address:** 926 Grosvenor Ave R3M 0N4 **Location:** Jct Stafford St. **Parking:** street. **Cards:** AX, DC, MC, VI.

TAVERN IN THE PARK

Continental
$12-$41

Phone: 204/896-7275 ⑥

Set in the city's most famous park, this restaurant's dining room is bright, airy and upscale. Be ready to savor its meals, which are delectable, progressive Continental fare. Its server staff is charming and knowledgeable. One of the city's better spots. Dressy casual. **Bar:** Full bar. **Reservations:** required. **Hours:** 11:30 am-2:30 & 5-10 pm, Sun 10 am-2 & 5-9 pm. Closed major holidays; also Mon. **Address:** 55 Pavilion Cres R3P 2N6 **Location:** In Assiniboine Park. **Parking:** on-site. **Cards:** AX, DC, MC, VI.

CALL 🅖Ⓜ

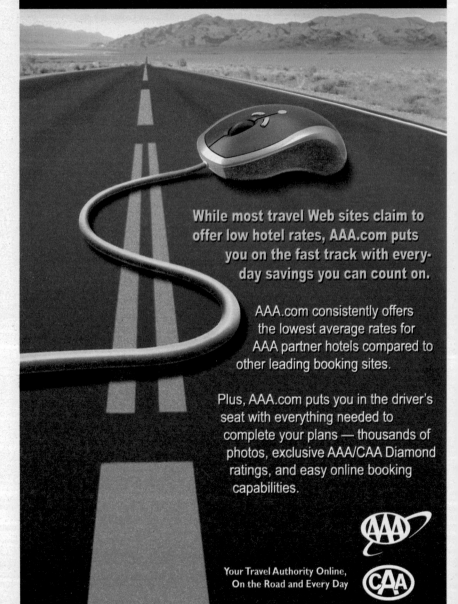

Northwest Territories and Nunavut

Hood River, near Bathurst
Inlet, Arctic Circle
© Brian Sytnyk
Masterfile

YELLOWKNIFE pop. 18,700

──── WHERE TO STAY ────

CHATEAU NOVA

CAA SAVE

▽▽▽
Small-scale Hotel
$189 All Year

Book great rates at AAA.com

Phone: (867)873-9700

Address: 4401 50th Ave X1A 2N2 **Location:** Downtown. **Facility:** 60 one-bedroom standard units, some with efficiencies and/or whirlpools. 4 stories, interior corridors. **Parking:** on-site, winter plug-ins. **Terms:** cancellation fee imposed. **Amenities:** high-speed Internet, voice mail, irons, hair dryers. **Leisure Activities:** whirlpool, steamroom, exercise room, spa. **Guest Services:** valet laundry. **Business Services:** meeting rooms, business center. **Cards:** AX, DS, MC, VI. **Free Special Amenities:** local telephone calls and high-speed Internet.

THE EXPLORER HOTEL
▽▽▽
Large-scale Hotel
Rates not provided

Book at AAA.com

Phone: 867/873-3531

Address: 4825 49th Ave X1A 2R3 **Location:** Downtown. **Facility:** 127 units. 125 one-bedroom standard units. 2 one-bedroom suites. 8 stories, interior corridors. **Parking:** on-site, winter plug-ins. **Amenities:** high-speed Internet, voice mail, hair dryers. **Leisure Activities:** exercise room. **Guest Services:** valet laundry, wireless Internet. **Business Services:** conference facilities, business center.

FRASER TOWER SUITE HOTEL
▽▽▽
Small-scale Hotel
$156-$185 All Year

Book at AAA.com

Phone: (867)873-8700

Address: 5303 52nd St X1A 1V1 **Location:** Corner of 52nd St and 53rd Ave. **Facility:** 58 units. 40 one- and 18 two-bedroom standard units with kitchens. 10 stories, interior corridors. **Parking:** on-site, winter plug-ins. **Amenities:** high-speed Internet, dual phone lines, voice mail, irons, hair dryers. **Leisure Activities:** steamroom, exercise room. **Guest Services:** valet and coin laundry. **Business Services:** meeting rooms. **Cards:** AX, DC, DS, MC, VI.

YELLOWKNIFE SUPER 8 MOTEL
▽▽▽ ▽▽▽
Motel
$169-$199 All Year

Book at AAA.com

Phone: (867)669-8888

Address: 308 Old Airport Rd X1A 3G3 **Location:** 1.2 mi (2 km) s on Franklin, 0.6 mi (1 km) w; in WalMart Plaza. **Facility:** Smoke free premises. 66 units. 41 one-bedroom standard units. 25 one-bedroom suites. 4 stories, interior corridors. **Parking:** on-site, winter plug-ins. **Terms:** cancellation fee imposed. **Amenities:** high-speed Internet, voice mail, irons, hair dryers. **Leisure Activities:** exercise room. **Guest Services:** valet and coin laundry. **Cards:** AX, DC, DS, JC, MC, VI.

──── WHERE TO DINE ────

BULLOCK'S BISTRO
▽
Regional
Canadian
$18-$30

Phone: 867/873-3474

Ask any local for a place to eat, and the seafood joint is usually one of the first names mentioned. They also are likely to point out the unusual service, which includes some self-service aspects. Patrons get their own beverages and may clear their own plates. The menu lists many local dishes, including freshly caught pike and cod and caribou. Although what service is provided can be slow, a visit here is well worth it. The distinctive decor provides ample things to view while waiting. Casual dress. **Bar:** Beer & wine. **Reservations:** suggested. **Hours:** Open 4/15-10/15; 11 am-10 pm. Closed major holidays. **Address:** 3534 Weaver Dr X1A 2H2 **Location:** In Old Town. **Parking:** on-site. **Cards:** MC, VI.

LE FROLIC BISTRO/BAR
CAA
▽▽▽
French
$10-$30

Phone: 867/669-9852

Creative, colorful and regionally inspired cuisine is on the menu at the bustling bistro, beneath L'Heritage Restaurant. Locals frequent the restaurant after work and on weekends for its casual, relaxed environment. Guests can mingle with the locals and sample entrees ranging from venison to Arctic char. Casual dress. **Bar:** Full bar. **Hours:** 11 am-1 am. Closed major holidays; also Sun. **Address:** 5019 49th St X1A 2N6 **Location:** Downtown; underneath L'Heritage Restaurant Francais. **Parking:** street. **Cards:** AX, DC, JC, MC, VI.

L'HERITAGE RESTAURANT FRANCAIS
CAA
▽▽▽
French
$20-$37

Phone: 867/873-9561

One of the city's best-kept downtown secrets, the quaint French restaurant is a pleasant surprise. Small touches of France are incorporated into the decor. Each dish is a delight, with creativity and color, and the menu is heavily influenced with regional ingredients. This spot shouldn't be missed for a fine, elegant meal in lovely surroundings. Casual dress. **Bar:** Full bar. **Reservations:** suggested. **Hours:** 5 pm-10 pm. Closed major holidays; also Sun. **Address:** 5019 49th St X1A 2N6 **Location:** Downtown. **Parking:** street. **Cards:** AX, DC, JC, MC, VI.

WILDCAT CAFE

▽
Regional
Canadian
$6-$15

Phone: 867/873-8850

In the heart of Old Town, the historic cafe is a popular spot at meal times, both with locals and tourists. One of the city's original buildings, the small log cabin has large picnic tables inside, and guests who can't find their own are invited to partake in a city tradition and join another party's table. Among offerings of regional cuisine are musk-ox stew and awesome milkshakes. Casual dress. **Bar:** Full bar. **Hours:** Open 6/1-9/30; 11 am-10 pm, Sat & Sun from 10 am. Closed: 7/14/06. **Address:** 3904 Wiley Rd X1A 2N2 **Location:** In Old Town. **Parking:** on-site. **Cards:** VI. **Historic**

Saskatchewan

North Saskatchewan
Canadian Tourism
Commission

CARONPORT pop. 919

THE PILGRIM INN

Small-scale Hotel
$80 3/1-12/15
$70 12/16-2/28

Phone: 306/756-5002

Address: Hwy 1 W S0H 0S0 **Location:** Jct Main Access; on Trans-Canada Hwy 1. Located adjacent to a truck stop. **Facility:** Smoke free premises. 41 units. 40 one-bedroom standard units, some with kitchens. 1 one-bedroom suite with efficiency. 2 stories (no elevator), interior corridors. **Parking:** on-site, winter plug-ins. **Terms:** office hours 7 am-11 pm. **Leisure Activities:** 4 tennis courts. **Guest Services:** complimentary laundry, wireless Internet. **Business Services:** meeting rooms. **Cards:** AX, DC, DS, MC, VI.

(A$K) (X) (💻) / SOME UNITS (🛏) FEE (🚪) FEE (🖥)

DAVIDSON pop. 958

——— WHERE TO DINE ———

KEEPER'S RESTAURANT & LOUNGE
American
$6-$15

Phone: 306/567-4225

This popular local eatery and truck stop offers hearty fare, served up in generous portions, in an atmosphere of collectibles, bric-a-brac and antiques. Casual dress. **Bar:** Full bar. **Reservations:** accepted. **Hours:** 6 am-midnight. **Address:** Hwy 11, Davidson S0G 1A0 **Location:** Shell Station Hwy 11, south approach to town. **Parking:** on-site. **Cards:** MC, VI.

ELBOW pop. 294

——— WHERE TO DINE ———

BACK HOME BAKERY & DELI
Bakery/Desserts
$5-$9

Phone: 306/854-2244

Locals sample fresh bread, buns and other sweets that are prepared daily. In addition, there are delicatessen goods, soups and sandwiches. Casual dress. **Hours:** 6 am-4 pm; from 8 am, Sat & Sun-2 pm in winter. Closed: 12/24-1/2. **Address:** 431 Saskatchewan St S0H 1J0 **Location:** Jct Pfeffer Ave. **Parking:** on-site. **Cards:** AX, MC, VI.

ESTEVAN pop. 10,084

——— WHERE TO STAY ———

DAYS INN

Small-scale Hotel
Rates not provided

Phone: 306/634-6456

Address: 1305 9th St S4A 1J1 **Location:** Centre. Located in a commercial area. **Facility:** 75 units. 68 one-bedroom standard units, some with whirlpools. 7 one-bedroom suites, some with whirlpools. 3 stories, interior corridors. **Parking:** on-site, winter plug-ins. **Amenities:** high-speed Internet, voice mail, irons, hair dryers. **Dining:** 2 restaurants. **Leisure Activities:** whirlpool, exercise room. **Business Services:** meeting rooms. **Free Special Amenities: continental breakfast and high-speed Internet.**

(🍽) (Y) (🚪) (💻) / SOME UNITS (X) (VCR) (🖥)

PERFECT INNS & SUITES
(CAA) (SAVE)

Small-scale Hotel
$83-$110 All Year

Phone: (306)634-8585

Address: 134 2nd Ave S4A 2W6 **Location:** Just n of jct Hwy 39 E and 2nd Ave. Located next to Tim Horton's. **Facility:** 70 units. 65 one-bedroom standard units. 5 one-bedroom suites, some with whirlpools. 3 stories, interior corridors. **Parking:** on-site, winter plug-ins. **Amenities:** high-speed Internet, voice mail, irons, hair dryers. *Some:* dual phone lines. **Leisure Activities:** whirlpool, exercise room. **Guest Services:** coin laundry. **Business Services:** meeting rooms. **Cards:** AX, DC, DS, MC, VI. **Free Special Amenities: expanded continental breakfast and high-speed Internet.**

(🍽) (🦽) (🚪) (💻) / SOME UNITS FEE (🛏) (X) FEE (VCR) FEE (🖥)

——— WHERE TO DINE ———

EDDIE WEBSTER'S GRILL & BAR
Canadian
$6-$27

Phone: 306/634-5656

The popular, casual restaurant provides efficient, friendly service in a pleasant atmosphere. The menu offers good variety. Patio seating can be requested in season. Casual dress. **Bar:** Full bar. **Reservations:** accepted. **Hours:** 11 am-11 pm. Closed: 12/25. **Address:** 2015 Mayfair Bay S4A 1X7 **Location:** Just e of jct Hwy 39 E and 2nd Ave. **Parking:** on-site. **Cards:** AX, MC, VI.

KINDERSLEY pop. 4,412

——— WHERE TO STAY ———

BEST WESTERN WESTRIDGE INN
(CAA) (SAVE)

Small-scale Hotel
Rates not provided

Phone: 306/463-4687

Address: 100 12th Ave NW S0L 1S0 **Location:** Jct of Hwy 7 and 21. Located in a commercial area. **Facility:** 43 one-bedroom standard units. 2 stories (no elevator), interior/exterior corridors. **Parking:** on-site, winter plug-ins. **Amenities:** high-speed Internet, voice mail, irons, hair dryers. **Leisure Activities:** sauna, exercise room. **Guest Services:** valet laundry, wireless Internet. **Business Services:** meeting rooms. **Free Special Amenities: newspaper and high-speed Internet.**

(🍽) (Y) (🦽) (🚪) (💻) / SOME UNITS (🛏) (X) (🖥)

AAA Benefit:

Members save 10% everyday, plus an exclusive frequent stay program.

LANGENBURG pop. 1,048

——— WHERE TO STAY ———

LANGENBURG COUNTRY INN

◆

Motel

$55-$65 All Year

Address: 1041 Kaiser William Ave E S0A 2A0 **Location:** On Hwy 16, 0.6 mi (1 km) e. Located in a rural area. **Facility:** 14 one-bedroom standard units. 1 story, exterior corridors. **Parking:** on-site, winter plug-ins. **Terms:** office hours 7:30 am-10 pm. **Guest Services:** wireless Internet. **Cards:** AX, MC, VI.

Phone: 306/743-2638

ASK ⬤ ⬤ ⬤ ⬤ / SOME UNITS ⊗

LLOYDMINSTER —See also LLOYDMINSTER, AB

——— WHERE TO DINE ———

SPIRO'S STEAK & PIZZA

◆◆

Steak House

$7-$16

A great place to take a family for a meal, the steak and pizza house has something for everyone on its menu. In addition to the requisites, this place serves sandwiches and some Greek dishes. Casual dress. **Bar:** Full bar. **Hours:** 10 am-10 pm, Sun 4 pm-9 pm. Closed: 1/1, 12/25, 12/26; also Mon. **Address:** 3425 50th Ave S9V 0N9 **Location:** Hwy 16 (Yellowhead Hwy), 0.6 mi (1 km) s. **Parking:** on-site. **Cards:** AX, MC, VI.

Phone: 306/825-9787

◥

MOOSE JAW pop. 32,132

——— WHERE TO STAY ———

COMFORT INN *Book at AAA.com*

◆◆

Small-scale Hotel

Rates not provided

Address: 155 Thatcher Dr W S6J 1M1 **Location:** Just w of jct Main St. Located in a commercial area. **Facility:** 60 units. 58 one-bedroom standard units, some with whirlpools. 2 one-bedroom suites with whirlpools. 3 stories, interior corridors. **Parking:** on-site, winter plug-ins. **Amenities:** voice mail, hair dryers. *Some:* high-speed Internet, irons. **Leisure Activities:** limited exercise equipment. **Guest Services:** valet and coin laundry. *(See color ad on insert)*

Phone: 306/692-2100

⬤ ⬤ / SOME UNITS FEE ⬤ ⊗ FEE ⬤ FEE ⬤

DAYS INN *Book at AAA.com*

◆◆

Small-scale Hotel

$120-$130 3/1-6/30

$101-$110 7/1-2/28

Address: 1720 Main St N S6J 1L4 **Location:** From jct Trans-Canada Hwy 1, just s. Located in a commercial area. **Facility:** 80 units. 69 one- and 11 two-bedroom standard units, some with whirlpools. 4 stories, interior corridors. **Parking:** on-site, winter plug-ins. **Terms:** 1-5 night minimum stay, cancellation fee imposed. **Amenities:** high-speed Internet, voice mail, irons, hair dryers. **Pool(s):** heated indoor. **Leisure Activities:** whirlpool, waterslide, exercise room. **Guest Services:** valet and coin laundry. **Business Services:** PC. **Cards:** AX, MC, VI.

Phone: (306)691-5777

ASK ⬤ ⬤ ⬤ ⬤ / SOME UNITS FEE ⬤ ⊗ FEE ⬤ ⬤

HERITAGE INN *Book at AAA.com*

◆◆

Small-scale Hotel

Rates not provided

Address: 1590 Main St N S6J 1L3 **Location:** 0.9 mi (1.5 km) s of jct Trans-Canada Hwy 1 and 2; access from Hwy 2 via Thatcher Dr. Located in a commercial area. **Facility:** 104 units. 102 one-bedroom standard units. 2 one-bedroom suites with whirlpools. 2 stories (no elevator), interior corridors. **Parking:** on-site, winter plug-ins. **Amenities:** voice mail, irons, hair dryers. *Some:* DVD players (fee), high-speed Internet. **Pool(s):** heated indoor. **Leisure Activities:** whirlpool. **Guest Services:** valet laundry, wireless Internet. **Business Services:** conference facilities, PC.

Phone: 306/693-7550

⬤ ⬤ ⬤ ⬤ / SOME UNITS FEE ⬤ ⊗ FEE VCR ⬤ ⬤

PRAIRIE OASIS MOTEL

CAA SAVE

◆◆

Motel

$80-$84 All Year

Address: 955 Thatcher Dr E S6H 4N9 **Location:** Just s of jct Trans-Canada Hwy 1 and Thatcher Dr E. Located in a rural area. **Facility:** 40 units. 36 one-bedroom standard units, some with efficiencies. 4 one-bedroom suites with efficiencies. 1 story, exterior corridors. **Parking:** on-site, winter plug-ins. **Terms:** check-in 4 pm. **Pool(s):** heated indoor. **Leisure Activities:** whirlpool, waterslide, playground. *Fee:* miniature golf. **Guest Services:** coin laundry, wireless Internet. **Business Services:** meeting rooms. **Cards:** AX, MC, VI. **Free Special Amenities:** local telephone calls and high-speed Internet.

Phone: (306)692-4894

 ⬤ ⊗ ⬤ / SOME UNITS ⬤ ⊗ ⬤ ⬤

SUPER 8 MOTEL-MOOSE JAW *Book at AAA.com*

◆◆

Motel

$99 All Year

Address: 1706 Main St N S6J 1L4 **Location:** 0.9 mi (1.5 km) s of jct Trans-Canada Hwy 1; access from Hwy 2 via Thatcher Dr. Located in a commercial area. **Facility:** 60 units. 58 one-bedroom standard units, some with whirlpools. 2 one-bedroom suites. 3 stories, interior corridors. **Parking:** on-site, winter plug-ins. **Amenities:** high-speed Internet, hair dryers. **Guest Services:** coin laundry, wireless Internet. **Cards:** AX, MC, VI.

Phone: 306/692-8888

 CALL ⬤ ⬤ ⬤ / SOME UNITS FEE ⬤ ⊗ ⬤

TEMPLE GARDENS MINERAL SPA RESORT HOTEL *Book great rates at AAA.com*

CAA SAVE

◆◆◆

Small-scale Hotel

$139 All Year

Address: 24 Fairford St E S6H 0C7 **Location:** Main St, next to Crescent Park; 2 mi (3.2 km) s of Trans-Canada Hwy 1. Located in a commercial area. **Facility:** Smoke free premises. 179 units. 166 one-bedroom standard units, some with whirlpools. 13 one-bedroom suites, some with whirlpools. 5 stories, interior corridors. **Parking:** on-site (fee), winter plug-ins. **Terms:** check-in 4 pm, cancellation fee imposed. **Amenities:** video games (fee), high-speed Internet, voice mail, hair dryers. *Some:* irons. **Dining:** Harwood's, see separate listing. **Pool(s):** heated indoor/outdoor. **Leisure Activities:** steamroom, mineral spa pool, rental bicycles, exercise room, spa. **Guest Services:** valet laundry, wireless Internet. **Business Services:** conference facilities. **Cards:** AX, DC, DS, MC, VI.

Phone: 306/694-5055

⬤ ⬤ ⬤ ⊗ ⊗ ⬤ ⬤ / SOME UNITS ⬤

—— WHERE TO DINE ——

HARWOOD'S

Steak & Seafood
$7-$45

Phone: 306/693-7778
Known for its high-quality cuts of beef, the restaurant is a popular spot with locals. Casual dress. **Bar:** Full bar. **Reservations:** suggested. **Hours:** 7 am-11 pm. **Address:** 24 Fairford St E S6H 0C7 **Location:** Main St, next to Crescent Park; 2 mi (3.2 km) s of Trans-Canada Hwy 1; in Temple Gardens Mineral Spa Resort Hotel. **Parking:** street. **Cards:** AX, DC, MC, VI.

HOUSTON PIZZA

American
$6-$20

Phone: 306/693-3934
A nice spot for couples or families, the restaurant presents a menu of steaks, spaghetti, lasagna, ribs, barbecue chicken, seafood, stir-fry and salads, as well as yummy pizza. Servers are prompt. Casual dress. **Bar:** Full bar. **Reservations:** accepted. **Hours:** 11 am-11 pm, Fri & Sat-midnight. Closed: 12/25. **Address:** 117 Main St N S6H 0V9 **Location:** Just s of High St; 2 mi (3.5 km) s of Trans-Canada Hwy 1. **Parking:** street. **Cards:** AX, MC, VI.

WAYNE & LAVERNE'S PIZZA & STEAK HOUSE

American
$6-$30

Phone: 306/694-1777
The family-oriented eatery offers good value and features an Italian buffet, buffalo burgers and heart-smart entrees. The menu includes dishes for small appetites and children's meals. The decor is inviting, and the service staff is cordial and prompt. Casual dress. **Bar:** Full bar. **Reservations:** accepted. **Hours:** 11 am-8:30 pm, Fri & Sat-9:30 pm, Sun 4 pm-8:30 pm. Closed: 12/25. **Address:** 622 Main St N S6H 3K4 **Location:** Just s of Hochelaga St; centre. **Parking:** street. **Cards:** AX, DC, MC, VI.

NORTH BATTLEFORD pop. 13,190

—— WHERE TO STAY ——

GOLD EAGLE LODGE   *Book great rates at AAA.com*
(CAA) (SAVE)

Small-scale Hotel
$96-$109 All Year

Phone: (306)446-8877
Address: 12004 Railway Ave E S9A 3W3 **Location:** Jct Hwy 46 and 16 (Yellowhead Hwy), just w. Located in a commercial area. **Facility:** Smoke free premises. 112 units. 93 one- and 10 two-bedroom standard units. 9 one-bedroom suites, some with kitchens and/or whirlpools. 4 stories, interior corridors. *Bath:* combo or shower only. **Parking:** on-site, winter plug-ins. **Amenities:** high-speed Internet, voice mail, irons, hair dryers. **Pool(s):** heated indoor. **Leisure Activities:** sauna, whirlpools, steamroom, exercise room. **Guest Services:** coin laundry. **Business Services:** meeting rooms, business center. **Cards:** AX, MC, VI. **Free Special Amenities: expanded continental breakfast and high-speed Internet.**

[icons] S/D CALL &M 🏊 ✖ ✕ 📠 💻 / SOME UNITS FEE 📦

SUPER 8 MOTEL   *Book at AAA.com*
[diamond]
Small-scale Hotel
$80-$100 All Year

Phone: (306)446-8888
Address: 1006 Hwy 16 Bypass S9A 3W2 **Location:** 0.3 mi (0.5 km) nw of jct Hwy 16. Located in a commercial area. **Facility:** 39 one-bedroom standard units. 2 stories (no elevator), interior corridors. **Parking:** on-site, winter plug-ins. **Terms:** cancellation fee imposed. **Amenities:** high-speed Internet, hair dryers. **Cards:** AX, DC, MC, VI.

[icons] ASK S/D / SOME UNITS FEE 🐾 ✕ FEE VCR 📦

TROPICAL INN

Small-scale Hotel
Rates not provided

Phone: 306/446-4700
Address: 1001 Hwy 16 Bypass S9A 3W2 **Location:** Corner of Battleford Rd and Hwy 16 Bypass. Located in a commercial area. **Facility:** 119 units. 115 one- and 2 two-bedroom standard units, some with whirlpools. 2 one-bedroom suites with whirlpools. 2 stories, interior corridors. **Parking:** on-site, winter plug-ins. **Amenities:** video games (fee), voice mail, irons, hair dryers. **Pool(s):** heated indoor. **Leisure Activities:** sauna, whirlpool, waterslide. **Guest Services:** valet laundry, wireless Internet. **Business Services:** meeting rooms, PC (fee).

[icons] 🍴 🍸 🏊 ✖ 📷 💻 / SOME UNITS FEE 🐾 ✕ 📠 📦

PRINCE ALBERT pop. 34,138

—— WHERE TO STAY ——

COMFORT INN   *Book at AAA.com*
[diamonds]
Small-scale Hotel
$109 All Year

Phone: (306)763-4466
Address: 3863 2nd Ave W S6W 1A1 **Location:** 1.4 mi (2.3 km) s at jct Hwy 2 and Marquis Rd. Located in a commercial area. **Facility:** 62 one-bedroom standard units. 2 stories (no elevator), interior corridors. **Parking:** on-site, winter plug-ins. **Guest Services:** valet laundry, wireless Internet. **Cards:** AX, CB, DC, DS, JC, MC, VI. *(See color ad on insert)*

[icons] ASK S/D 🍴 ♿ 📷 💻 / SOME UNITS 🐾 ✕ 📠 📦

DAYS INN   *Book at AAA.com*
[diamonds]
Small-scale Hotel
Rates not provided

Phone: 306/763-8988
Address: 150 34th St W S6V 8E9 **Location:** Hwy 2, jct Marquis Rd, just n. Located in a commercial area. **Facility:** 80 units. 72 one-bedroom standard units, some with whirlpools. 8 one-bedroom suites. 4 stories, interior corridors. **Parking:** on-site, winter plug-ins. **Amenities:** high-speed Internet, voice mail, irons, hair dryers. **Pool(s):** heated indoor. **Leisure Activities:** whirlpool, waterslide, limited exercise equipment. **Guest Services:** valet and coin laundry. **Business Services:** business center.

[icons] 🍴 🏊 ✖ 💻 / SOME UNITS ✕ 📠 📦

SUPER 8   *Book at AAA.com*
[diamonds]
Small-scale Hotel
$87-$97 All Year

Phone: (306)953-0088
Address: 4444 2nd Ave W S6V 5R7 **Location:** Just s of jct Hwy 2 and Marquis Rd. Located in a commercial area. **Facility:** 60 one-bedroom standard units. 3 stories, interior corridors. **Parking:** on-site, winter plug-ins. **Amenities:** voice mail, irons, hair dryers. **Guest Services:** valet and coin laundry, wireless Internet. **Cards:** AX, CB, DC, DS, JC, MC, VI.

[icons] ASK S/D ♿ 💻 / SOME UNITS 🐾 ✕ VCR 📠 📦
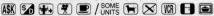

TRAVELODGE PRINCE ALBERT *Book at AAA.com* Phone: 306/764-6441

Small-scale Hotel
Rates not provided

Address: 3551 2nd Ave W S6V 5G1 **Location:** 1.4 mi (2.2 km) s at jct Hwy 2 and Marquis Rd. Located in a commercial area. **Facility:** 80 units. 57 one-bedroom standard units. 23 one-bedroom suites, some with whirlpools. 2 stories (no elevator), interior/exterior corridors. **Parking:** on-site, winter plug-ins. **Amenities:** hair dryers. *Some:* DVD players, high-speed Internet, irons. **Leisure Activities:** limited exercise equipment. **Guest Services:** valet laundry, wireless Internet. **Business Services:** meeting rooms.

WHERE TO DINE

AMY'S ON SECOND RESTAURANT Phone: 306/763-1515

Continental
$9-$27

You'll discover a warm and intimate setting here. Amy's menu specializes in the freshest ingredients for the homemade food and many regional specialties including wild rice soup, rack of lamb, excellent Saskatchewan pickerel, and cheesecake. Casual dress. **Bar:** Full bar. **Reservations:** suggested. **Hours:** 11 am-9 pm. Closed major holidays; also Sun. **Address:** 2990 2nd Ave W S6V 7E9 **Location:** 0.9 mi (1.5 km) s on 2nd Ave W; at 30th St W. **Parking:** on-site. **Cards:** AX, DC, MC, VI.

VENICE HOUSE RESTAURANT Phone: 306/764-6555

Greek
$8-$39

A casual, family-dining experience awaits you at the Venice House. The menu offers steak, pizza, spaghetti and seafood dishes, but their house specialty is Greek-style ribs. The very relaxed atmosphere is quite comfortable and appealing. Lightside senior menu offered. Casual dress. **Bar:** Full bar. **Reservations:** accepted. **Hours:** 11 am-10 pm, Fri & Sat-11 pm. Closed: 12/25; also for lunch holidays. **Address:** 1498 Central Ave S6V 4W5 **Location:** 15th St and Central Ave. **Parking:** on-site and street. **Cards:** AX, MC, VI.

REGINA pop. 179,246

WHERE TO STAY

BEST WESTERN SEVEN OAKS INN *Book great rates at AAA.com* Phone: 306/757-0121

Small-scale Hotel
Rates not provided

Address: 777 Albert St S4R 2P6 **Location:** Jct 2nd Ave. Located in a commercial area. **Facility:** 157 units. 154 one-bedroom standard units. 3 one-bedroom suites. 3 stories, interior corridors. **Parking:** on-site, winter plug-ins. **Amenities:** high-speed Internet, voice mail, irons, hair dryers. **Pool(s):** heated indoor. **Leisure Activities:** sauna, whirlpool, waterslide, exercise room. **Guest Services:** valet and coin laundry. **Business Services:** conference facilities, PC. **Free Special Amenities:** local telephone calls and newspaper. *(See color ad below)*

AAA Benefit:
Members save 10% everyday, plus an exclusive frequent stay program.

COMFORT INN *Book great rates at AAA.com* Phone: (306)789-5522

Small-scale Hotel
$115-$122 All Year

Address: 3221 E Eastgate Dr S4Z 1A4 **Location:** Trans-Canada Hwy 1, 1.3 mi (2 km) e of Ring Rd; at eastern approach to city. Located in a commercial area. **Facility:** 99 one-bedroom standard units. 2 stories (no elevator), interior corridors. **Parking:** on-site, winter plug-ins. **Amenities:** irons, hair dryers. **Guest Services:** valet laundry, wireless Internet. **Business Services:** PC. **Cards:** AX, DC, DS, JC, MC, VI. *(See color ad on insert)*

▼ *See AAA listing above* ▼

COUNTRY INN & SUITES BY CARLSON   *Book great rates at AAA.com*   Phone: 306/789-9117

Small-scale Hotel
Rates not provided

Address: 3321 Eastgate Bay S4Z 1A4 **Location:** Trans-Canada Hwy 1, 1.3 mi (2 km) e of Ring Rd; at eastern approach to city. Located in a commercial area. **Facility:** 76 units. 39 one-bedroom standard units. 37 one-bedroom suites. 3 stories, interior corridors. **Parking:** on-site, winter plug-ins. **Amenities:** video library, DVD players, voice mail, irons, hair dryers. *Some:* high-speed Internet, dual phone lines. **Leisure Activities:** exercise room. **Guest Services:** valet and coin laundry. **Business Services:** PC. *(See color ad p 362)*

[icons] CALL / SOME UNITS FEE

DAYS INN   *Book at AAA.com*   Phone: (306)522-3297

Small-scale Hotel
$110-$120 All Year

Address: 3875 Eastgate Dr S4Z 1A4 **Location:** Trans-Canada Hwy 1, exit Eastgate Dr; at eastern approach to city. Located in a commercial area. **Facility:** 96 one-bedroom standard units, some with whirlpools. 3 stories, interior corridors. **Parking:** on-site, winter plug-ins. **Terms:** check-in 4 pm, cancellation fee imposed. **Amenities:** high-speed Internet, voice mail, irons, hair dryers. **Pool(s):** heated indoor. **Leisure Activities:** whirlpool, waterslide. **Guest Services:** valet and coin laundry, wireless Internet. **Cards:** AX, DC, DS, MC, VI.

[icons] / SOME UNITS

DELTA REGINA   *Book at AAA.com*   Phone: 306/525-5255

Large-scale Hotel
$165-$230 All Year

Address: 1919 Saskatchewan Dr S4P 4H2 **Location:** At Rose St; centre. Located opposite Casino Regina. **Facility:** 274 units. 251 one-bedroom standard units. 23 one-bedroom suites, some with whirlpools. 25 stories, interior corridors. **Parking:** on-site (fee), winter plug-ins. **Amenities:** high-speed Internet, voice mail, irons, hair dryers. *Some:* CD players. **Pool(s):** heated indoor. **Leisure Activities:** whirlpool, waterslide, exercise room. **Guest Services:** valet laundry. **Business Services:** conference facilities, business center. **Cards:** AX, DC, MC, VI.

[icons] / SOME UNITS FEE

HOLIDAY INN EXPRESS HOTEL & SUITES REGINA   *Book great rates at AAA.com*   Phone: (306)569-4600

(CAA) SAVE

Small-scale Hotel
$130 All Year

Address: 1907 11th Ave S4P 0J2 **Location:** Corner of Rose St; centre of downtown. Located in a commercial area. **Facility:** 78 units. 70 one-bedroom standard units. 8 one-bedroom suites, some with whirlpools. 5 stories, interior corridors. **Parking:** on-site, winter plug-ins. **Amenities:** dual phone lines, voice mail, irons, hair dryers. **Leisure Activities:** whirlpool, exercise room. **Guest Services:** valet laundry, wireless Internet. **Business Services:** meeting rooms, business center. **Cards:** AX, MC, VI. **Free Special Amenities:** continental breakfast and local telephone calls. *(See color ad on insert)*

[icons] / SOME UNITS FEE

HOLIDAY INN HOTEL & SUITES   *Book at AAA.com*   Phone: 306/789-3883

[diamond icons]

Small-scale Hotel
$115-$185 All Year

Address: 1800 Prince of Wales Dr S4Z 1A4 **Location:** From jct Trans-Canada Hwy 1, just n; at eastern approach to city. Located in a commercial area. **Facility:** 120 one-bedroom standard units, some with whirlpools. 4 stories, interior corridors. **Parking:** on-site, winter plug-ins. **Amenities:** high-speed Internet, voice mail, irons, hair dryers. **Pool(s):** heated indoor. **Leisure Activities:** whirlpool, waterslide, exercise room. **Guest Services:** valet and coin laundry. **Business Services:** meeting rooms, business center. **Cards:** AX, DS, MC, VI.

[icons] ASK / SOME UNITS FEE

HOWARD JOHNSON INN   *Book great rates at AAA.com*   Phone: (306)565-0455

(CAA) SAVE

[diamond icons]

Small-scale Hotel
$100-$130 All Year

Address: 1110 Victoria Ave E S4N 7A9 **Location:** Trans-Canada Hwy 1, just w of Ring Rd; at eastern approach to city. Located in a commercial area. **Facility:** Smoke free premises. 127 units. 120 one-bedroom standard units. 7 one-bedroom suites, some with whirlpools. 3 stories, interior corridors. **Parking:** on-site, winter plug-ins. **Amenities:** voice mail, irons, hair dryers. **Pool(s):** heated indoor. **Leisure Activities:** whirlpool. **Guest Services:** valet and coin laundry, wireless Internet. **Business Services:** meeting rooms, business center. **Cards:** AX, MC, VI. **Free Special Amenities:** local telephone calls and high-speed Internet.

[icons] / SOME UNITS VCR FEE

▼ See AAA listing p 711 ▼

QUALITY HOTEL
Phone: (306)569-4656

▼▼▼▼
Small-scale Hotel
$109-$149 All Year

Address: 1717 Victoria Ave S4P 0P9 **Location:** Just e of Broad St; downtown. Located in a commercial area. **Facility:** 126 one-bedroom standard units. 7 stories, interior corridors. **Parking:** on-site, winter plug-ins. **Amenities:** video games (fee), voice mail, irons, hair dryers. **Leisure Activities:** sauna, exercise room. **Guest Services:** valet and coin laundry, wireless Internet. **Business Services:** meeting rooms. **Cards:** AX, DS, MC, VI. *(See color ad on insert)*

ASK SD ⒯⒯ 🏊 🖥 / SOME UNITS 🐾 ✕ FEE 🖥

RADISSON PLAZA HOTEL SASKATCHEWAN
Phone: (306)522-7691

CAA SAVE
▼▼ ▼▼ ▼▼
Large-scale Hotel
$135-$178 All Year

Address: 2125 Victoria Ave S4P 0S3 **Location:** Victoria Ave at Scarth St; centre. Located adjacent to the business district. **Facility:** This elegantly restored, 1927 hotel has an impressive lobby. Guest rooms are decorated in Victorian style. Smoke free premises. 224 units. 198 one-bedroom standard units. 26 one-bedroom suites, some with whirlpools. 10 stories, interior corridors. **Parking:** on-site and valet, winter plug-ins. **Amenities:** high-speed Internet, voice mail, honor bars, irons, hair dryers. *Some:* DVD players, CD players. **Dining:** Cortland Hall Dining Room, see separate listing. **Leisure Activities:** whirlpool, steamroom, spa. **Guest Services:** valet laundry, barber shop, beauty salon, wireless Internet. **Fee:** airport transportation-Regina International Airport, area transportation-within city limits. **Business Services:** conference facilities, business center. **Cards:** AX, DC, MC, VI. *(See color ad p 710)*

SD FEE ⤦ ⒯⒯ ⓘ CALL Ⓜ 🛏 ✕ 🖥 / SOME UNITS FEE 🐾 🖥 🖥 🖥

RAMADA HOTEL & CONVENTION CENTRE
Phone: 306/569-1666

▼▼▼ ▼▼
Large-scale Hotel
Rates not provided

Address: 1818 Victoria Ave and Broad St; **Location:** Victoria Ave and Broad St. Located in a commercial area. **Facility:** 232 units. 226 one-bedroom standard units. 6 one-bedroom suites, some with whirlpools. 15 stories, interior corridors. **Parking:** on-site (fee). **Amenities:** voice mail, irons, hair dryers. *Some:* high-speed Internet. **Pool(s):** heated indoor. **Leisure Activities:** sauna, whirlpool, exercise room. **Guest Services:** complimentary and valet laundry, wireless Internet. **Business Services:** conference facilities, PC.

⒯⒯ ⓘ 🏊 🖥 / SOME UNITS FEE 🐾 ✕ FEE 🖥 FEE 🖥

REGINA INN HOTEL & CONFERENCE CENTRE
Phone: (306)525-6767

CAA SAVE
▼▼▼ ▼▼
Large-scale Hotel
$119-$195 All Year

Address: 1975 Broad St S4P 1Y2 **Location:** Jct Victoria Ave; centre of downtown. Located in a commercial area. **Facility:** 235 units. 230 one-bedroom standard units. 5 one-bedroom suites, some with whirlpools. 15 stories, interior corridors. **Parking:** on-site and valet. **Terms:** check-in 4 pm, cancellation fee imposed. **Amenities:** video games (fee), high-speed Internet, voice mail, irons, hair dryers. *Some:* CD players. **Leisure Activities:** exercise room. **Guest Services:** valet laundry, wireless Internet. **Business Services:** meeting rooms, business center. **Free Special Amenities: local telephone calls and high-speed Internet.**

SD ⒯⒯ ⓘ 🏊 🖥 / SOME UNITS FEE 🐾 ✕ 🖥 🖥

REGINA SUPER 8
Phone: 306/789-8833

▼▼
Small-scale Hotel
Rates not provided

Address: 2730 Victoria Ave E S4N 6M5 **Location:** Trans-Canada Hwy 1, 1 mi (1.6 km) e of Ring Rd; at eastern approach to city. Located in a commercial area. **Facility:** 59 units. 58 one-bedroom standard units. 1 one-bedroom suite. 3 stories (no elevator), interior corridors. **Parking:** on-site, winter plug-ins. **Terms:** check-in 4 pm. **Guest Services:** wireless Internet.

CALL Ⓜ 🖥 / SOME UNITS FEE 🐾 ✕ 🖥

REGINA TRAVELODGE HOTEL
Phone: (306)586-3443

CAA SAVE
▼▼▼ ▼▼
Small-scale Hotel
$106-$150 All Year

Address: 4177 Albert St S S4S 3R6 **Location:** 0.9 mi (1.5 km) n of jct Trans-Canada Hwy 1 and Albert St (Hwy 6). Located in a commercial area. **Facility:** 200 one-bedroom standard units. 4 stories, interior corridors. **Parking:** on-site, winter plug-ins. **Amenities:** high-speed Internet, voice mail, irons, hair dryers. *Some:* dual phone lines. **Pool(s):** heated indoor. **Leisure Activities:** whirlpool, waterslide, children's play cave, exercise room. **Guest Services:** valet laundry, wireless Internet. **Business Services:** conference facilities, business center. **Cards:** AX, DC, MC, VI. **Free Special Amenities: local telephone calls and high-speed Internet.**

SD ⒯⒯ ⓘ CALL Ⓜ 🏊 ✕ 🖥 🖥 / SOME UNITS ✕

SANDMAN HOTEL SUITES AND SPA
Phone: 306/757-2444

▼▼▼ ▼▼
Small-scale Hotel
Rates not provided

Address: 1800 Victoria Ave E S4N 7K3 **Location:** Just e of Ring Rd; at eastern approach to city. Located in a commercial area. **Facility:** 132 units. 49 one-bedroom standard units. 83 one-bedroom suites, some with whirlpools. 4 stories, interior corridors. **Bath:** combo or shower only. **Parking:** on-site, winter plug-ins. **Terms:** check-in 4 pm. **Amenities:** video games (fee), high-speed Internet, voice mail, irons, hair dryers. **Pool(s):** heated indoor. **Leisure Activities:** whirlpool, exercise room. **Guest Services:** valet laundry. **Business Services:** business center.

⒯⒯ CALL Ⓜ 🏊 🖥 🖥 / SOME UNITS FEE 🐾 ✕ 🖥

WEST HARVEST INN
Phone: 306/586-6755

▼▼▼ ▼▼
Small-scale Hotel
Rates not provided

Address: 4025 Albert St S S4S 3R6 **Location:** 1 mi (1.6 km) n of jct Trans-Canada Hwy 1. Located in a commercial area. **Facility:** Smoke free premises. 105 one-bedroom standard units, some with whirlpools. 5 stories, interior corridors. **Parking:** on-site, winter plug-ins. **Amenities:** video games (fee), voice mail, hair dryers. **Leisure Activities:** whirlpools, steamrooms, exercise room. **Guest Services:** valet laundry, wireless Internet. **Business Services:** meeting rooms, PC.

⒯⒯ ⓘ ✕ ✕ 🖥 🖥 / SOME UNITS 🖥

——— WHERE TO DINE ———

ALFREDO'S ON SCARTH
Phone: 306/522-3366

▼▼ ▼▼
Italian
$5-$21

The extremely popular Alfredo's features a trendy-looking dining room and a separate wine bar. The restaurant's extensive menu offers an endless number of fresh pasta dishes. Good service. The downtown location is close to theatres and boutiques. Casual dress. **Bar:** Full bar. **Reservations:** suggested. **Hours:** 11 am-2 & 5-10 pm. Closed major holidays; also Sun. **Address:** 1801 Scarth St S4P 2G9 **Location:** Corner of 11th Ave; centre. **Parking:** street. **Cards:** AX, DC, MC, VI.

CATHEDRAL VILLAGE FREE HOUSE

Phone: 306/359-1661

Canadian
$8-$22

The young and young at heart appreciate the sometimes boisterous atmosphere at the upscale tavern. Servers are friendly. The menu lists an interesting mix of dishes, such as ribs, steak, burritos, tandoori chicken stir fry, soups, salads, sandwiches and pizzas cooked in a wood-fired oven. The patio is open seasonally. Casual dress. **Bar:** Full bar. **Reservations:** accepted. **Hours:** 11:30 am-midnight, Wed-Sat to 1 am. Closed: 12/25. **Address:** 2062 Albert St S4P 2T7 **Location:** Jct 13th Ave. **Parking:** street. **Cards:** AX, MC, VI.

CORTLAND HALL DINING ROOM

Phone: 306/522-7691

Canadian
$8-$38

The award-winning chefs at this restaurant prepare a wide-ranging menu of delicious meals served with pleasing presentation and a good selection of in-house dessert and pastries. The attractive Victorian decor provides for intimate dining. Casual dress. **Bar:** Full bar. **Reservations:** accepted. **Hours:** 6:30 am-10 pm, Sun-9 pm. **Address:** 2125 Victoria Ave S4P 0S3 **Location:** Victoria Ave at Scarth St; centre; in Radisson Plaza Hotel Saskatchewan. **Parking:** on-site. **Cards:** AX, DC, MC, VI.

THE CREEK IN CATHEDRAL BISTRO

Phone: 306/352-4448

Continental
$10-$29

The charming bistro has a tasteful decor and friendly, capable servers. Creatively prepared and artfully presented food keeps the locals returning. Dressy casual. **Bar:** Full bar. **Reservations:** suggested. **Hours:** 11 am-4 & 5-9 pm, Fri-close, Sat 10 am-4 pm. Closed: 7/1, 9/1, 12/25; also Sun. **Address:** 3414 13th Ave S4T 1P7 **Location:** Just e of Elphinstone St. **Parking:** street. **Cards:** AX, DC, MC, VI.

THE DIPLOMAT

Phone: 306/359-3366

Steak & Seafood
$8-$50

You're sure to appreciate the excellent treatment you'll receive at this restaurant, which offers wonderful steak, filet mignon, coq au vin and seafood, as well as an impressive choice of wine and cognac. Elegant surroundings and knowledgeable servers. Dressy casual. **Bar:** Full bar. **Reservations:** suggested, weekends. **Hours:** 11 am-2 & 4-midnight, Sat from 4 pm, Sun 4 pm-9 pm. Closed: 7/1, 12/25. **Address:** 2032 Broad St S4P 1Y3 **Location:** Just s of jct Broad St and Victoria Ave. **Parking:** on-site. **Cards:** AX, DC, MC, VI.

EARL'S

Phone: 306/584-7733

Canadian
$10-$28

Offering an experience that falls between fast food and fine dining, the fun, relaxed restaurant prepares great food at a great price. Choices range from juicy burgers, hearty sandwiches, fresh salads, wings and pizza to full entrees of steak, chops and seafood. Made-from-scratch soups and assorted breads, as well as a nice choice of wines and beers, round out the offerings. This is a fitting spot for impromptu get-togethers and festive occasions. Casual dress. **Bar:** Full bar. **Reservations:** accepted, except Fri & Sat for dinner. **Hours:** 11:30 am-midnight, Fri & Sat-1 am. Closed: 12/25. **Address:** 2606 28th Ave S4S 6P3 **Location:** Jct Albert St S. **Parking:** on-site. **Cards:** AX, DC, MC, VI.

FIRESIDE BISTRO

Phone: 306/761-2305

Canadian
$9-$27

The menu lists creative choices alongside such favorites as pasta, chicken, fish and steak. The bistro's dining areas are in the rooms of a large old house. The patio opens seasonally. Casual dress. **Bar:** Full bar. **Reservations:** suggested. **Hours:** 11 am-10 pm. Closed: 1/1, 12/25; also Good Fri. **Address:** 2305 Smith St S4P 2P7 **Location:** 3 blks s of Victoria Ave. **Parking:** street. **Cards:** AX, DC, MC, VI.

GOLF'S STEAK HOUSE

Phone: 306/525-5808

Steak & Seafood
$9-$40

This restaurant features hearty portions of very good steak, seafood and rack of lamb dishes that are quite tasty and served in large portions. There's a good variety to the menu. The restaurant has traditional formal decor and professional service. When the torch in front of the restaurant is burning, they are open for business. Casual dress. **Bar:** Full bar. **Reservations:** accepted. **Hours:** 11 am-11 pm, Sat from 4 pm, Sun 4 pm-10 pm. Closed: 12/25. **Address:** 1945 Victoria Ave S4P 0R3 **Location:** Corner of Victoria Ave and Hamilton St. **Parking:** on-site. **Cards:** AX, DC, MC, VI.

KELSEY'S

Phone: 306/761-9000

Canadian
$7-$20

A fun, relaxed atmosphere and tasty menu of casual fare make the restaurant a popular favorite with locals. Diners might start a meal with some tempting appetizers, such as wings, loaded potato skins or nachos, and follow them with an old-time favorite, such as a burger, wrap, pizza or pasta dish. For a heartier meal, it's hard to beat pork back ribs or a steak. The diverse menu has broad appeal. Casual dress. **Bar:** Full bar. **Hours:** 11 am-11 pm, Fri & Sat-midnight. Closed: 12/25. **Address:** 1875 Victoria Ave E S4N 7K3 **Location:** Just e of Ring Rd; at eastern approach to city. **Parking:** on-site. **Cards:** MC, VI.

LA BODEGA

Phone: 306/546-3660

Mediterranean
$8-$40

Those who enjoy a variety of taste sensations surely will be pleased with the varied tapas menu. The atmosphere is cozy in the dining room and on the seasonal patio. Casual dress. **Bar:** Full bar. **Reservations:** accepted. **Hours:** 11 am-1 am, Sun 10:30 am-midnight. Closed: 12/25, 12/26. **Address:** 2228 Albert St S4P 2V2 **Location:** Just n of jct 15th Ave. **Parking:** street. **Cards:** AX, MC, VI.

THE LAST SPIKE

Phone: 306/781-7000

American
$8-$20

In the old Regina train station, the restaurant has one dining room section in a rail passenger car. Reservations are required to dine in the car. The menu centers on simple, filling fare along the lines of ribs, chicken and fish 'n' chips. Casual dress. **Bar:** Full bar. **Reservations:** accepted. **Hours:** 9 am-10:30 pm, Fri & Sat-midnight. Closed: 12/24, 12/25. **Address:** 1880 Saskatchewan Dr S4P 0A8 **Location:** Centre; in Casino Regina. **Parking:** on-site (fee). **Cards:** AX, DC, MC, VI.

LUIGGI'S PASTA HOUSE

Phone: 306/949-7427

Italian
$7-$18

The family-oriented eatery serves traditional Italian food in a fun and lively atmosphere. Casual dress. **Bar:** Full bar. **Reservations:** accepted. **Hours:** 11 am-9 pm, Fri & Sat-10 pm, Sun 4 pm-9 pm. Closed: 3/24, 12/25; also 10/8. **Address:** 470 Albert St N S4R 3C1 **Location:** Corner of 9th Ave. **Parking:** on-site. **Cards:** AX, DC, MC, VI.

MEDITERRANEAN BISTRO

Continental
$6-$32

Phone: 306/757-1666

At this casual yet upscale bistro market, fresh products are used to offer a good varity of fish, chicken, red meat and pasta dishes which are all carefully prepared and creatively presented. Dressy casual. **Bar:** Full bar. **Reservations:** suggested. **Hours:** 11 am-close, Sun from 5 pm. Closed major holidays. **Address:** 2589 Quance St E S4V 2Y7 **Location:** Trans-Canada Hwy 1, just se of jct Fleet St; at eastern approach to city. **Parking:** on-site. **Cards:** AX, CB, DC, MC, VI.

MOJO

International
$9-$26

Phone: 306/569-5555

This restaurant offers diners an opportunity to experience carefully selected, fresh ingredients that are creatively combined to produce unusual and delightful dishes. The wine list has also been carefully created. Casual dress. **Bar:** Full bar. **Reservations:** accepted. **Hours:** 11 am-3 & 5-10 pm, Sat from 5 pm. Closed major holidays; also Sun. **Address:** 2330 Albert St S4P 2V7 **Location:** Just s of jct 15th Ave. **Parking:** street. **Cards:** MC, VI.

MONTANA'S COOKHOUSE

Canadian
$7-$24

Phone: 306/569-1557

Pine boards, exposed beams, a fireplace and Western gear displayed about the dining room give the feeling of a back-country setting. The menu lists hearty portions of comfort fare, such as Yankee pot roast. While the focus is on steaks, ribs and chicken, some seafood entrees also are among offerings. Service is efficient and friendly. Casual dress. **Bar:** Full bar. **Reservations:** accepted, Mon-Thurs. **Hours:** 11 am-11 pm, Fri & Sat-1 am, Sun noon-11 pm. Closed: 12/25. **Address:** 2655 Gordon Rd S4S 6H7 **Location:** Just n of jct Trans-Canada Hwy 1 and Albert St; in Rio-Can Shopping Plaza. **Parking:** on-site. **Cards:** MC, VI.

MOXIE'S CLASSIC GRILL

Canadian
$8-$23

Phone: 306/781-5655

This sleek, funky and popular restaurant presents an extensive menu of creatively prepared dishes, including pizza, pasta, rice, noodles, signature salads and burgers. Other menus include one for children and one for Sunday brunch. Lending to the upbeat, stylish decor are dark wood appointments and river rock fireplaces. Casual dress. **Bar:** Full bar. **Hours:** 11 am-11 pm, Thurs-Sat to 1 am. Closed: 12/25. **Address:** 1800A Victoria Ave S4N 7K3 **Location:** Jct Glen Carin Rd, just nw. **Parking:** on-site. **Cards:** AX, MC, VI.

THE WILLOW ON WASCANA

Canadian
$9-$39

Phone: 306/585-3663

Here is an opportunity to enjoy a cozy restaurant in a park setting with super river views. Service is skilled and friendly and the menu offers a good variety of beautifully prepared dishes; a patio is available in season. Casual dress. **Bar:** Full bar. **Reservations:** suggested. **Hours:** 11 am-11 pm. Closed: 10/13, 12/25, 12/26; also First 2 weeks in Jan. **Address:** 3000 Wascana Dr S4P 3B2 **Location:** Jct S Broad St and Wascana Pkwy; next to marina. **Parking:** on-site. **Cards:** AX, MC, VI.

SASKATOON pop. 202,425

✈ Airport Accommodations

OA	SASKATOON	Diamond Rating	Rate Range High Season	Listing Page
	Best Western Inn & Suites, 2.5 mi (4 km) se of airport	▽▽ ▽▽	$120-$160 [SAVE]	713
	Comfort Inn, 1.9 mi (3 km) se of airport	▽▽ ▽▽	$109	714
	Country Inn & Suites By Carlson, 1.6 mi (2.5 km) se of airport	▽▽ ▽▽	$100	714
	Days Inn, 1.9 mi (3 km) se of airport	▽▽ ▽▽	Rates not provided [SAVE]	714
	Sandman Hotel, 1.6 mi (2.5 km) se of airport	▽▽ ▽▽	Rates not provided	715
	Saskatoon Travelodge Hotel, 1.9 mi (3 km) se of airport	▽▽ ▽▽	$129-$169	715
	Super 8, 2.5 mi (4 km) se of airport	▽▽ ▽▽	$110-$122	715

─── WHERE TO STAY ───

BEST WESTERN INN & SUITES

Book great rates at AAA.com

Phone: (306)244-5552

Ⓒ [SAVE]
▽▽ ▽▽
Small-scale Hotel
$120-$160 All Year

Address: 1715 Idylwyld Dr N S7L 1B4 **Location:** 1.6 mi (2.6 km) n on Hwy 11 (Idylwyld Dr). Located in a strip mall. **Facility:** 91 units. 82 one-bedroom standard units. 9 one-bedroom suites. 2 stories, interior/exterior corridors. **Parking:** on-site, winter plug-ins. **Amenities:** high-speed Internet, voice mail, irons, hair dryers. **Dining:** Ricky's All Day Grill, see separate listing. **Leisure Activities:** whirlpool, exercise room. **Guest Services:** valet laundry. **Business Services:** meeting rooms. **Cards:** AX, DC, DS, MC, VI. **Free Special Amenities: local telephone calls and high-speed Internet.**

AAA Benefit:
Members save 10% everyday, plus an exclusive frequent stay program.

(icons)

COLONIAL SQUARE MOTEL & SUITES

Phone: (306)343-1676

Ⓒ [SAVE]
▽▽ ▽▽
Small-scale Hotel
$99-$109 All Year

Address: 1301 8th St E S7H 0S7 **Location:** Just w of Cumberland Ave. Located in a commercial area. **Facility:** 80 one-bedroom standard units. 2 stories (no elevator), interior/exterior corridors. **Parking:** on-site, winter plug-ins. **Amenities:** voice mail, irons, hair dryers. **Guest Services:** valet laundry, wireless Internet. **Business Services:** meeting rooms. **Cards:** AX, MC, VI. **Free Special Amenities: local telephone calls and high-speed Internet.**

COMFORT INN
Book at AAA.com

Phone: (306)934-1122

▼▼▼ ▼▼▼
Small-scale Hotel
$109 All Year

Address: 2155 Northridge Dr S7L 6X6 **Location:** 1.9 mi (3 km) n; just ne of jct Hwy 11 (Idylwyld Dr) and Circle Dr. Located in a commercial area. **Facility:** 80 one-bedroom standard units. 2 stories (no elevator), interior corridors. **Parking:** on-site, winter plug-ins. **Terms:** 7 day cancellation notice. **Amenities:** irons, hair dryers. **Guest Services:** valet laundry, wireless Internet. **Business Services:** meeting rooms, PC. **Cards:** AX, DC, DS, MC, VI. *(See color ad on insert)*

ASK SÓ ¶↑ CALL ⑤M ⚡ ▥ / SOME UNITS 🐾 ✕ 🖥 🖾

COUNTRY INN & SUITES BY CARLSON
Book great rates at AAA.com

Phone: (306)934-3900

▼▼▼ ▼▼▼
Small-scale Hotel
$100 1/1-2/28
$97 3/1-12/31

Address: 617 Cynthia St S7L 6B7 **Location:** Just w of jct Hwy 11 (Idylwyld Dr) and Circle Dr. Located in a commercial area. **Facility:** Smoke free premises. 76 units. 37 one-bedroom standard units. 39 one-bedroom suites. 3 stories, interior corridors. **Parking:** on-site, winter plug-ins. **Amenities:** video library, DVD players, voice mail, irons, hair dryers. **Leisure Activities:** exercise room. **Guest Services:** coin laundry, wireless Internet. **Business Services:** meeting rooms, PC. **Cards:** AX, CB, DC, DS, JC, MC, VI. *(See color ad p 362)*

ASK SÓ ⑪ CALL ⑤M ✕ 🖥 ▥ / SOME UNITS FEE 🐾 🖾

DAYS INN
Book great rates at AAA.com

Phone: 306/242-3297

ⒶⒶ SAVE
▼▼▼ ▼▼▼
Small-scale Hotel
Rates not provided

Address: 2000 Idylwyld Dr N S7L 7M7 **Location:** Just nw of jct Hwy 11 (Idylwyld Dr) and Circle Dr. Located in a commercial area. **Facility:** 102 units. 96 one-bedroom standard units, some with whirlpools. 6 one-bedroom suites. 4 stories, interior corridors. *Bath:* combo or shower only. **Parking:** on-site, winter plug-ins. **Amenities:** high-speed Internet, voice mail, irons, hair dryers. *Some:* safes (fee). **Pool(s):** heated indoor. **Leisure Activities:** whirlpool, waterslide, exercise room. **Guest Services:** valet and coin laundry. **Free Special Amenities: expanded continental breakfast and high-speed Internet.**

✈ ¶↑ CALL ⑤M 🛋 ✕ ⚡ 🖥 ▥ / SOME UNITS ✕ FEE VCR 🖾

DELTA BESSBOROUGH
Book at AAA.com

Phone: (306)244-5521

▼▼▼▼▼▼
Large-scale Hotel
$122-$340 7/1-2/28
$142-$290 3/1-6/30

Address: 601 Spadina Crescent E S7K 3G8 **Location:** At 21st St E; centre of downtown. Located beside park and river. **Facility:** 225 units. 216 one-bedroom standard units, some with whirlpools. 9 one-bedroom suites, some with whirlpools. 6 stories, interior corridors. **Parking:** on-site (fee), winter plug-ins. **Amenities:** video games (fee), high-speed Internet, voice mail, irons, hair dryers. *Some:* CD players, dual phone lines, honor bars. **Dining:** Samurai Japanese Restaurant, see separate listing. **Pool(s):** heated indoor. **Leisure Activities:** sauna, whirlpool, steamroom, recreation programs, jogging, exercise room, spa. **Guest Services:** valet laundry, wireless Internet. **Business Services:** conference facilities, business center. **Cards:** AX, MC, VI.

ASK ⑪ ⍖ ⑴ 🛋 ✕ ⚡ ▥ / SOME UNITS FEE 🐾 ✕ 🖥 🖾

HILTON GARDEN INN
Book great rates at AAA.com

Phone: (306)244-2311

▼▼▼ ▼▼▼
Small-scale Hotel
$109-$209 All Year

Address: 90 22nd St E S7K 3X6 **Location:** Just e of jct Hwy 11 (Idylwyld Dr), 1st and 22nd sts. Located in the downtown business district. **Facility:** 180 units. 166 one-bedroom standard units. 14 one-bedroom suites, some with whirlpools. 16 stories, interior corridors. **Parking:** on-site (fee). **Amenities:** high-speed Internet, voice mail, irons, hair dryers. **Pool(s):** heated indoor. **Leisure Activities:** whirlpool, exercise room. **Guest Services:** valet laundry, wireless Internet. **Business Services:** conference facilities, business center. **Cards:** AX, CB, DC, DS, JC, MC, VI.

ASK ⑪ ⍖ CALL ⑤M 🛋 ✕ ⚡ 🖥 🖾 ▥ / SOME UNITS ✕

HOLIDAY INN EXPRESS HOTEL & SUITES
SASKATOON *Book at AAA.com*

Phone: (306)384-8844

▼▼▼ ▼▼▼
Small-scale Hotel
$114 All Year

Address: 315 Idylwyld Dr N S7L 0Z1 **Location:** Jct 25th St W. Located in a commercial area. **Facility:** 120 units. 114 one-bedroom standard units. 5 one- and 1 two-bedroom suites. 4 stories, interior corridors. **Parking:** on-site, winter plug-ins. **Amenities:** high-speed Internet, dual phone lines, voice mail, irons, hair dryers. **Pool(s):** heated indoor. **Leisure Activities:** whirlpool, exercise room. **Guest Services:** valet laundry, wireless Internet. **Business Services:** meeting rooms, business center. **Cards:** AX, CB, DC, DS, JC, MC, VI.

ASK ✈ ¶↑ CALL ⑤M 🛋 ⚡ ▥ / SOME UNITS FEE 🐾 ✕ FEE 🖥 🖾

MOTEL 6 SASKATOON

Phone: 306/665-6688

▼▼▼ ▼▼▼
Small-scale Hotel
$81-$101 6/1-2/28
$79-$99 3/1-5/31

Address: 231 Marquis Dr S7R 1B7 **Location:** Jct Trans Canada Hwy 16 W (Yellowhead Hwy). **Facility:** 67 one-bedroom standard units. 3 stories, interior corridors. *Bath:* combo or shower only. **Parking:** on-site, winter plug-ins. **Terms:** cancellation fee imposed. **Amenities:** high-speed Internet, voice mail. **Pool(s):** heated indoor. **Leisure Activities:** whirlpool. **Guest Services:** coin laundry, wireless Internet. **Business Services:** PC (fee). **Cards:** AX, DC, DS, MC, VI. *(See color ad p 258)*

ASK SÓ 🛋 / SOME UNITS 🐾 ✕ 🖥

RADISSON HOTEL SASKATOON
Book at AAA.com

Phone: (306)665-3322

▼▼▼ ▼▼▼
Small-scale Hotel
$129-$199 All Year

Address: 405 20th St E S7K 6X6 **Location:** At 4th Ave S; centre. Located close to a river-side park. **Facility:** 291 units. 283 one-bedroom standard units. 8 one-bedroom suites with whirlpools. 19 stories, interior corridors. **Parking:** on-site (fee). **Amenities:** video games (fee), high-speed Internet, dual phone lines, voice mail, irons, hair dryers. **Pool(s):** heated indoor. **Leisure Activities:** sauna, whirlpool, waterslide, jogging, exercise room. *Fee:* game room. **Guest Services:** valet laundry, wireless Internet. **Business Services:** conference facilities, PC. **Cards:** AX, DC, DS, MC, VI.

ASK SÓ ⑪ ⍖ CALL ⑤M 🛋 ✕ ⚡ ▥ / SOME UNITS FEE 🐾 ✕ 🖥 🖾

SANDMAN HOTEL

Small-scale Hotel
Rates not provided

Phone: 306/477-4844

Address: 310 Circle Dr W S7L 2Y5 **Location:** Jct Ave C N. Located in a commercial area. **Facility:** 190 units. 178 one-bedroom standard units, some with whirlpools. 12 one-bedroom suites. 4 stories, interior corridors. **Parking:** on-site, winter plug-ins. **Terms:** check-in 4 pm. **Amenities:** video games (fee), high-speed Internet, voice mail, irons, hair dryers. **Pool(s):** heated indoor. **Leisure Activities:** whirlpool, exercise room. **Guest Services:** valet laundry. **Business Services:** meeting rooms, business center.

SASKATOON TRAVELODGE HOTEL

Small-scale Hotel
$129-$169 All Year

Phone: (306)242-8881

Address: 106 Circle Dr W S7L 4L6 **Location:** 1.9 mi (3 km) n, then just w of jct Hwy 11 (Idylwyld Dr). Located in a commercial area. **Facility:** 265 one-bedroom standard units, some with whirlpools. 2-6 stories, interior corridors. **Parking:** on-site, winter plug-ins. **Terms:** 30 day cancellation notice. **Amenities:** voice mail, irons, hair dryers. *Some:* DVD players. **Pool(s):** 2 heated indoor. **Leisure Activities:** whirlpools, waterslide, exercise room. *Fee:* game room. **Guest Services:** valet and coin laundry, wireless Internet. **Business Services:** conference facilities, business center. **Cards:** AX, CB, DC, DS, JC, MC, VI.

SHERATON CAVALIER

Small-scale Hotel
$219 All Year

Phone: (306)652-6770

Address: 612 Spadina Crescent E S7K 3G9 **Location:** At 21st St E; centre of downtown. Located opposite park and river. **Facility:** Smoke free premises. 249 units. 243 one-bedroom standard units, some with whirlpools. 6 one-bedroom suites with whirlpools. 8 stories, interior corridors. **Parking:** on-site (fee), winter plug-ins. **Terms:** cancellation fee imposed. **Amenities:** high-speed Internet, dual phone lines, voice mail, honor bars, irons, hair dryers. **Dining:** Carver's Steak House, see separate listing. **Pool(s):** heated indoor. **Leisure Activities:** whirlpools, waterslide, exercise room. **Guest Services:** valet laundry, wireless Internet. **Business Services:** conference facilities, business center. **Cards:** AX, CB, DC, DS, MC, VI.

AAA Benefit:
Members get up to 15% off, plus Starwood Preferred Guest® bonuses.

SUPER 8
Book at AAA.com

Small-scale Hotel
$110-$122 All Year

Phone: (306)384-8989

Address: 706 Circle Dr E S7K 3T7 **Location:** 1.3 mi (2 km) e of jct Hwy 11 (Idylwyld Dr). Located in a commercial area. **Facility:** 69 one-bedroom standard units, some with whirlpools. 3 stories, interior/exterior corridors. **Bath:** combo or shower only. **Parking:** on-site, winter plug-ins. **Amenities:** voice mail, hair dryers. *Some:* irons. **Guest Services:** valet laundry, wireless Internet. **Cards:** AX, MC, VI.

──────── **WHERE TO DINE** ────────

2ND AVE GRILL

American
$7-$33

Phone: 306/244-9899

In the heart of the downtown business district, the upscale grill offers an inviting atmosphere and attentive service. The varied menu features items that range from soups and salads to jambalaya. Casual dress. **Bar:** Full bar. **Reservations:** accepted. **Hours:** 11:30 am-10 pm, Fri & Sat-midnight. Closed: 12/25, 12/26; also Sun. **Address:** 10-123 2nd Ave S S7K 7E6 **Location:** Just w of jct 22nd St; centre. **Parking:** street. **Cards:** AX, MC, VI.

CARVER'S STEAK HOUSE

Steak & Seafood
$26-$48

Phone: 306/652-8292

This popular restaurant serves Caesar salads that are prepared at the table to your taste, and top quality steaks are delivered sizzling on a skillet. Dressy casual. **Bar:** Full bar. **Reservations:** suggested. **Hours:** 5:30 pm-10 pm. Closed major holidays. **Address:** 612 Spadina Crescent E S7K 3G9 **Location:** At 21st St E; centre of downtown; in Sheraton Cavalier. **Parking:** on-site (fee). **Cards:** AX, CB, DC, DS, MC, VI.

CHIANTI

Italian
$5-$16

Phone: 306/665-8466

Lining the menu is a good selection of fresh pasta creations, as well as veal, seafood and chicken dishes. Personable servers circulate in an atmosphere that suits families and couples. Casual dress. **Bar:** Full bar. **Reservations:** suggested. **Hours:** 11 am-10 pm, Fri & Sat-11 pm. Closed: 12/25. **Address:** 102 Idylwyld Dr N S7L 0Y7 **Location:** Corner of 22nd St E; centre. **Parking:** on-site. **Cards:** AX, DC, MC, VI.

EARL'S

Canadian
$10-$28

Phone: 306/664-4060

Offering an experience that falls between fast food and fine dining, the fun, relaxed restaurant prepares great food at a great price. Choices range from juicy burgers, hearty sandwiches, fresh salads, wings and pizza to full entrees of steak, chops and seafood. Made-from-scratch soups and assorted breads, as well as a nice choice of wines and beers, round out the offerings. This is a fitting spot for impromptu get-togethers and festive occasions. Casual dress. **Bar:** Full bar. **Reservations:** accepted, except Fri & Sat dinner. **Hours:** 11 am-midnight, Fri & Sat-1 am. Closed: 12/25. **Address:** 610 2nd Ave N S7K 2C8 **Location:** Jct Queen St. **Parking:** street. **Cards:** AX, MC, VI.

GENESIS FAMILY RESTAURANT

Chinese
$6-$16

Phone: 306/244-5516

The Genesis features a progressive Chinese menu offering many healthy choices—all made with fresh ingredients. Portions are large, and the diverse and creative menu includes Western dishes. Dim sum is served 11 am-2:30 pm each day. Friendly service. Casual dress. **Bar:** Full bar. **Reservations:** accepted. **Hours:** 11 am-10 pm. Closed major holidays. **Address:** 901 D 22nd St W S7M 0R9 **Location:** 0.6 mi (1 km) w of Hwy 11 (Idylwyld Dr). **Parking:** on-site. **Cards:** AX, MC, VI.

JOHN'S PRIME RIB HOUSE

Phone: 306/244-6384

◆◆◆

Steak & Seafood
$9-$50

A longstanding city favorite, the restaurant is known for top-quality prime rib and steak. Service is professional, and the rich wood paneling in the dining room creates a pleasant atmosphere. Casual dress. **Bar:** Full bar. **Reservations:** accepted. **Hours:** 11:30 am-11:30 pm, Sat from 4:30 pm. Closed: 7/1, 12/25; also Sun. **Address:** 401 21st St E S7K 0C5 **Location:** Just s of 4th Ave S; centre. **Parking:** street. **Cards:** AX, DC, MC, VI.

MONTANA'S COOKHOUSE

Phone: 306/384-9340

◆◆

Canadian
$7-$24

Pine boards, exposed beams, a fireplace and Western gear displayed about the dining room give the feeling of a back-country setting. The menu lists hearty portions of comfort fare, such as Yankee pot roast. While the focus is on steaks, ribs and chicken, some seafood entrees also are among offerings. Service is efficient and friendly. Casual dress. **Bar:** Full bar. **Hours:** 11 am-midnight, Fri & Sat-1 am, Sun-11 pm. Closed: 12/25. **Address:** 1510 8th St E S7H 0T3 **Location:** From jct Cumberland Ave, just e. **Parking:** on-site. **Cards:** AX, MC, VI.

MOXIE'S CLASSIC GRILL

Phone: 306/374-9800

◆◆

Canadian
$11-$26

This sleek, funky and popular restaurant presents an extensive menu of creatively prepared dishes, including pizza, pasta, rice, noodles, signature salads and burgers. Other menus include one for children and one for Sunday brunch. Lending to the upbeat, stylish decor are dark wood appointments and river rock fireplaces. Casual dress. **Bar:** Full bar. **Hours:** 11 am-midnight, Fri & Sat-1 am, Sun 10 am-midnight. Closed: 12/25. **Address:** 3134 8th St E S7H 0W2 **Location:** Jct Circle Dr, just se. **Parking:** on-site. **Cards:** AX, MC, VI.

RICKY'S ALL DAY GRILL

Phone: 306/652-3222

◆◆

Canadian
$7-$25

The comfortable eatery, which employs friendly servers, presents a varied menu that includes pasta dishes, wraps, omelets, stir-fry preparations and burgers. Portions are generous. Children's and senior selections are offered. Guests can request seating in a booth or at a table. Casual dress. **Bar:** Full bar. **Reservations:** accepted. **Hours:** 7 am-9 pm, Fri & Sat-10 pm. **Address:** 1715 Idylwyld Dr N S7L 1B4 **Location:** 1.6 mi (2.6 km) n on Hwy 11 (Idylwyld Dr); in Best Western Inn & Suites. **Parking:** on-site. **Cards:** AX, MC, VI.

SAMURAI JAPANESE RESTAURANT

Phone: 306/683-6926

◆◆◆

Japanese
$17-$36

Finely crafted sushi and authentic tableside Teppanyaki cuisine are featured at this dining room. Casual dress. **Bar:** Full bar. **Reservations:** suggested. **Hours:** 5 pm-10 pm. Closed: 7/1, 12/25. **Address:** 601 Spadina Cres E S7K 3G8 **Location:** At 21st St E; centre of downtown; in Delta Bessborough Hotel. **Parking:** on-site (fee). **Cards:** AX, DC, MC, VI.

THE WILLOWS DINING ROOM

Phone: 306/956-1100

◆◆

Canadian
$8-$36

Grand golf course views, friendly servers and a varied menu make this restaurant a good place to simply relax and enjoy. Casual dress. **Bar:** Full bar. **Reservations:** accepted. **Hours:** 11 am-9 pm; hours vary in winter. Closed: 12/25. **Address:** 382 Cartwright St S7T 1B1 **Location:** Jct Clarence and Cartwright St, just w. **Parking:** on-site. **Cards:** AX, DC, MC, VI.

SHAUNAVON pop. 1,691

—— WHERE TO STAY ——

HIDDEN HILTEN MOTEL

Phone: 306/297-4166

◆

Motel
$58-$73 All Year

Address: 352 5th St W S0N 2M0 **Location:** 0.3 mi (0.5 km) e from jct Hwy 13 and 37, just n. Located in a quiet area. **Facility:** 13 one-bedroom standard units, some with whirlpools. 1 story, exterior corridors. **Parking:** on-site, winter plug-ins. **Terms:** office hours 7 am-11 pm. **Guest Services:** wireless Internet. **Cards:** MC, VI.

SWIFT CURRENT pop. 14,946

—— WHERE TO STAY ——

COMFORT INN

Book great rates at AAA.com

Phone: (306)778-3994

◆◆

Small-scale Hotel
$103-$144 All Year

Address: 1510 S Service Rd E S9H 3X6 **Location:** Trans-Canada Hwy 1, just w of 22nd Ave NE. Located in a commercial area. **Facility:** 74 one-bedroom standard units. 2 stories (no elevator), interior corridors. **Parking:** on-site, winter plug-ins. **Amenities:** irons, hair dryers. **Guest Services:** valet laundry, wireless Internet. **Business Services:** PC. **Cards:** AX, CB, DC, DS, JC, MC, VI.
(See color ad on insert)

GREEN HECTARES BED & BREAKFAST

Phone: 306/773-7632

◆◆

Bed & Breakfast
$85-$105 All Year

Address: Waker Rd S9H 4M7 **Location:** Trans-Canada Hwy 1, exit 22nd Ave NE, just n to Saskatchewan Dr, just ne to Adams St, then just e to Waker Rd, follow signs. Located in a rural area. **Facility:** Smoke free premises. 6 one-bedroom standard units. 1 story, interior/exterior corridors. *Bath:* some shared or private, combo or shower only. **Parking:** on-site, winter plug-ins. **Terms:** office hours 7 am-10 pm. **Leisure Activities:** *Fee:* horseback riding. **Guest Services:** TV in common area, coin laundry. **Business Services:** meeting rooms.

RODEWAY INN MOTEL

Phone: 306/773-4664

(CAA) (SAVE)

◆

Small-scale Hotel
$57-$65 All Year

Address: 1200 S Service Rd E S9H 3X6 **Location:** Trans-Canada Hwy 1, just w of 22nd Ave NE. Located in a commercial area. **Facility:** 28 one-bedroom standard units. 1 story, interior/exterior corridors. **Parking:** on-site, winter plug-ins. **Terms:** office hours 7 am-11 pm, cancellation fee imposed. **Amenities:** high-speed Internet. **Guest Services:** valet laundry. **Business Services:** meeting rooms. **Cards:** AX, DC, MC, VI. **Free Special Amenities:** local telephone calls and high-speed Internet.

SAFARI INN MOTEL

Motel
$62-$67 All Year

Phone: (306)773-4608

Address: 810 S Service Rd E S9H 3T9 **Location:** 0.6 mi (1 km) w of jct Hwy 1 and 4. Located in a commercial area. **Facility:** 18 units. 16 one- and 2 two-bedroom standard units, some with efficiencies. 1 story, exterior corridors. **Parking:** on-site, winter plug-ins. **Terms:** office hours 7 am-11 pm. **Guest Services:** wireless Internet. **Business Services:** PC. **Cards:** AX, DC, MC, VI. **Free Special Amenities: local telephone calls and high-speed Internet.**

SUPER 8 MOTEL

Book at AAA.com

Small-scale Hotel
$120-$130 All Year

Phone: (306)778-6088

Address: 405 N Service Rd E S9H 3X6 **Location:** Just e of Central Ave. Located in a commercial area. **Facility:** 63 one-bedroom standard units, some with whirlpools. 2 stories (no elevator), interior corridors. **Parking:** on-site, winter plug-ins. **Terms:** cancellation fee imposed. **Amenities:** voice mail, hair dryers. *Some:* DVD players. **Pool(s):** heated indoor. **Leisure Activities:** whirlpool, exercise room. **Guest Services:** coin laundry, wireless Internet. **Cards:** AX, CB, DC, DS, MC, VI.

WESTWIND MOTEL

Motel
$60-$78 All Year

Phone: (306)773-1441

Address: 155 N Service Rd W S9H 3X6 **Location:** Trans-Canada Hwy 1, 0.3 mi (0.5 km) w of Central Ave. Located in a commercial area. **Facility:** 20 one-bedroom standard units, some with kitchens. 1 story, exterior corridors. **Parking:** on-site, winter plug-ins. **Terms:** office hours 8 am-midnight. **Amenities:** voice mail. **Dining:** TNT Family Restaurant, see separate listing. **Pool(s):** heated outdoor. **Guest Services:** coin laundry, wireless Internet. **Cards:** AX, MC, VI. **Free Special Amenities: local telephone calls and newspaper.**

——— WHERE TO DINE ———

SPRINGS GARDEN RESTAURANT

American
$7-$28

Phone: 306/773-2021

The Springs Garden's decor is casual, contemporary, bright and cheerful. The menu includes a variety of popular dishes: soup, steak, chicken, seafood, pizza, ribs and Greek specialties. The server staff is friendly, efficient and prompt. Casual dress. **Reservations:** suggested, Thurs-Sun. **Hours:** 8:30 am-9 pm, Fri & Sat-10 pm, Sun 9 am-9 pm. Closed major holidays. **Address:** 323 1 Springs Dr S9H 3X6 **Location:** Trans-Canada Hwy 1, on north service road; in Swift Current Shopping Mall. **Parking:** on-site. **Cards:** AX, DC, MC, VI.

TNT FAMILY RESTAURANT

Menu on AAA.com

Canadian
$7-$20

Phone: 306/773-1441

Casual dress. **Bar:** Full bar. **Reservations:** accepted. **Hours:** 8 am-10 pm, Sun 9 am-8 pm. Closed major holidays. **Address:** 155 N Service Rd W S9H 3X6 **Location:** Trans-Canada Hwy 1, 0.3 mi (0.5 km) w of Central Ave; in Westwind Motel. **Parking:** on-site. **Cards:** AX, DC, MC, VI.

WONG'S KITCHEN

Chinese
$6-$20

Phone: 306/773-4636

Wong's Kitchen is one of the best spots in town to visit. The locally popular restaurant features Cantonese-style preparation of its dishes. The menu also offers steak and seafood selections. A smorgasbord is served noon-2 pm each day. Helpful staff. Casual dress. **Bar:** Full bar. **Reservations:** accepted. **Hours:** 11:30 am-11 pm, Sun-9 pm. Closed: 12/25, 12/26. **Address:** 320 S Service Rd E S9H 3T6 **Location:** Trans-Canada Hwy 1, just w of 22nd Ave NE. **Parking:** on-site. **Cards:** AX, DC, MC, VI.

WEYBURN pop. 9,433

——— WHERE TO STAY ———

PERFECT INNS & SUITES

Motel
$60-$120 All Year

Phone: 306/842-2691

Address: 238 Sims Ave S4H 2J8 **Location:** 0.3 mi (0.5 km) w of jct Hwy 35 and 39. Located next to McDonalds. **Facility:** 59 units. 55 one-bedroom standard units. 4 one-bedroom suites with kitchens. 1 story, interior/exterior corridors. **Parking:** on-site, winter plug-ins. **Amenities:** high-speed Internet. *Some:* irons, hair dryers. **Guest Services:** valet laundry. **Cards:** AX, MC, VI. **Free Special Amenities: expanded continental breakfast and high-speed Internet.**

——— WHERE TO DINE ———

T & C FAMILY RESTAURANT/DALLAS PIZZA

American
$6-$25

Phone: 306/842-2933

This restaurant offers family dining in contemporary and friendly surroundings. The menu features a wide variety of sandwiches, stir-fry, steak, seafood, pizza, souvlakia and Greek ribs. Families, couples and business people alike enjoy this eatery. Casual dress. **Bar:** Full bar. **Reservations:** accepted. **Hours:** 10 am-10 pm. Closed: 12/25. **Address:** 72 3rd St NE S4H 0V9 **Location:** Just n of Hwy 39; centre. **Parking:** street. **Cards:** AX, MC, VI.

YORKTON pop. 15,038

BEST WESTERN PARKLAND INN
Book great rates at AAA.com

Phone: 306/783-9781

Small-scale Hotel
Rates not provided

Address: 100 Broadway St E S3N 0K9 **Location:** On Hwy 9, 10, and 16 (Yellowhead Hwy); downtown. Located in a commercial area. **Facility:** 80 units. 79 one-bedroom standard units, some with whirlpools. 1 one-bedroom suite. 2 stories (no elevator), interior corridors. **Parking:** on-site, winter plug-ins. **Amenities:** high-speed Internet, voice mail, irons, hair dryers. *Some:* DVD players. **Pool(s):** heated indoor. **Leisure Activities:** sauna, whirlpool, waterslide, exercise room. **Guest Services:** valet and coin laundry, wireless Internet. **Business Services:** conference facilities.

AAA Benefit:
Members save 10% everyday, plus an exclusive frequent stay program.

COMFORT INN & SUITES
Book at AAA.com

Phone: (306)783-0333

Small-scale Hotel
$110-$199 All Year

Address: 22 Dracup Ave S3N 3W1 **Location:** Just w of jct Hwy 9, 10 and 16 (Yellowhead Hwy). Located in a commercial area. **Facility:** 80 units. 64 one-bedroom standard units. 16 one-bedroom suites, some with whirlpools. 4 stories, interior corridors. **Parking:** on-site, winter plug-ins. **Amenities:** voice mail, irons, hair dryers. *Some:* DVD players, high-speed Internet. **Pool(s):** heated indoor. **Leisure Activities:** whirlpool, exercise room. **Guest Services:** coin laundry, wireless Internet. **Business Services:** meeting rooms. **Cards:** AX, CB, DC, DS, JC, MC, VI. *(See color ad on insert)*

DAYS INN
Book at AAA.com

Phone: 306/783-3297

Small-scale Hotel
$95 All Year

Address: 2 Kelsey Bay S3N 3Z4 **Location:** Just e of jct Hwy 9, 10 and 16 (Yellowhead Hwy). Located in a commercial area. **Facility:** 74 one-bedroom standard units, some with whirlpools. 3 stories, interior corridors. **Parking:** on-site, winter plug-ins. **Terms:** check-in 4 pm. **Amenities:** voice mail, irons, hair dryers. *Some:* high-speed Internet. **Pool(s):** heated indoor. **Leisure Activities:** whirlpool, waterslide. **Guest Services:** wireless Internet. **Business Services:** PC. **Cards:** AX, MC, VI.

Yukon Territory

DAWSON CITY pop. 1,327

------ **WHERE TO STAY** ------

BONANZA GOLD MOTEL
Phone: 867/993-6789

Motel
$89-$189 All Year

Address: Bonanza Creek Rd Y0B-1G0 **Location:** 1.5 mi (2.4 km) s on Hwy 2. **Facility:** 45 one-bedroom standard units, some with efficiencies, kitchens and/or whirlpools. 2 stories (no elevator), exterior corridors. *Bath:* combo or shower only. **Parking:** on-site, winter plug-ins. **Terms:** office hours 7 am-10 pm. **Amenities:** *Some:* hair dryers. **Leisure Activities:** hiking trails. **Guest Services:** coin laundry, wireless Internet. **Business Services:** PC (fee). **Cards:** MC, VI.

DAWSON CITY BED & BREAKFAST
Phone: 867/993-5649

Bed & Breakfast
$115-$155 All Year

Address: 451 Craig St Y0B 1G0 **Location:** Just off 7th Ave. **Facility:** Smoke free premises. 7 units. 6 one-bedroom standard units. 1 one-bedroom suite. 2 stories (no elevator), interior corridors. *Bath:* some shared or private, combo or shower only. **Parking:** on-site, winter plug-ins. **Amenities:** video library. *Some:* DVD players, CD players, hair dryers. **Leisure Activities:** library. **Guest Services:** area transportation-bus station & town dock. **Business Services:** PC. **Cards:** DC, MC, VI. **Free Special Amenities:** full breakfast and high-speed Internet.

THE ELDORADO HOTEL
Phone: (867)993-5451

[fyi]
Motel
$105-$165 All Year

Under major renovation, scheduled to be completed June 2008. Last rated: ♥ **Address:** 3rd Ave & Princess St Y0B 1G0 **Location:** Downtown. **Facility:** 46 one-bedroom standard units, some with kitchens. 2 stories (no elevator), interior/exterior corridors. **Parking:** on-site, winter plug-ins. **Terms:** cancellation fee imposed. **Amenities:** voice mail. *Some:* honor bars, irons, hair dryers. **Guest Services:** coin laundry. **Business Services:** PC. **Cards:** AX, DC, DS, JC, MC, VI. **Free Special Amenities:** local telephone calls and high-speed Internet.

KLONDIKE KATE'S CABINS
Phone: (867)993-6527

Cabin
$95-$140 4/4-9/30

Address: 1103 3rd Ave & King St Y0B 1G0 **Location:** Corner of 3rd Ave and King St. **Facility:** 15 cabins. 1 story. *Bath:* combo or shower only. **Parking:** on-site. **Terms:** open 4/4-9/30. **Amenities:** voice mail. **Dining:** Klondike Kate's Restaurant, see separate listing. **Guest Services:** valet laundry. **Cards:** MC, VI.

WESTMARK INN DAWSON CITY
Book great rates at AAA.com
Phone: (867)993-5542

Motel
$155 5/16-9/5

Address: 5th St & Harper Y0B 1G0 **Location:** At 5th and Harper sts; downtown. **Facility:** Smoke free premises. 177 one-bedroom standard units. 2 stories (no elevator), interior/exterior corridors. *Bath:* combo or shower only. **Parking:** on-site. **Terms:** open 5/16-9/5, cancellation fee imposed. **Amenities:** voice mail, hair dryers. **Guest Services:** coin laundry. **Business Services:** PC. **Cards:** AX, MC, VI. **Free Special Amenities:** local telephone calls.

YUKON HOTEL
Phone: (867)993-5451

Small-scale Hotel
$150 3/1-12/19 & 2/1-2/28

Address: 5th Ave & Princess St Y0B 1G0 **Location:** Corner of 5th Ave; downtown. **Facility:** Smoke free premises. 6 one-bedroom standard units with efficiencies. 2 stories (no elevator), interior corridors. **Parking:** on-site, winter plug-ins. **Terms:** open 3/1-12/19 & 2/1-2/28, off-site registration. **Amenities:** voice mail. **Guest Services:** coin laundry. **Cards:** AX, DC, DS, MC, VI.

------ **WHERE TO DINE** ------

KLONDIKE KATE'S RESTAURANT
Menu on AAA.com
Phone: 867/993-6527

American
$7-$32

Along the city's main drag and just a few blocks from the theater, the restaurant captures a sense of history and the gold rush era. During summer, guests can choose to eat inside or on the heated patio. The menu features an array of sandwiches, wraps and seafood and meat dishes. Casual dress. **Bar:** Full bar. **Reservations:** suggested. **Hours:** Open 4/15-9/15; 6:30 am-11 pm. Closed major holidays. **Address:** 3rd Ave & King St Y0B 1G0 **Location:** Corner of 3rd Ave and King St; in Klondike Kate's Cabins. **Parking:** on-site. **Cards:** MC, VI. **Historic**

TINTINA BAKERY
Phone: 867/993-5558

Bakery/Desserts
$5-$7

Follow the signs to get to this intimate art gallery/bakery. Featuring a range of baked goods and samosas, this is an excellent stop before heading out to explore the Dempster Highway or any of the other nearby attractions. Casual dress. **Hours:** 7 am-6 pm; seasonal hours may vary. Closed major holidays. **Location:** 12.4 mi (20 km) s on Hwy 2, follow signs; in Henderson Corner. **Parking:** on-site. **Cards:** MC, VI.

HAINES JUNCTION pop. 589

------ WHERE TO STAY ------

ALCAN MOTOR INN

Motel
$110-$160 All Year

Phone: (867)634-2371
Address: Alaska & Haines Hwys Y0B 1L0 **Location:** Jct Hwy 1 (Alaska Hwy) and 3 (Haines Hwy). **Facility:** 22 units. 19 one-bedroom standard units, some with whirlpools. 3 one-bedroom suites, some with efficiencies. 2 stories (no elevator), exterior corridors. **Parking:** on-site, winter plug-ins. **Terms:** 3 day cancellation notice-fee imposed. **Amenities:** irons, hair dryers. **Guest Services:** coin laundry, wireless Internet. **Cards:** AX, MC, VI. **Free Special Amenities: local telephone calls and early check-in/late check-out.**

TESLIN pop. 141

------ WHERE TO DINE ------

DAWSON PEAKS RESORT

Canadian
$6-$22

Phone: 867/390-2244
Just outside of town, this rustic but comfortable restaurant has earned international acclaim for being one of the settings in a well known mystery novel and, more importantly, its freshly made rhubarb pies. Casual dress. **Hours:** Open 5/15-9/30; 8 am-8 pm. **Address:** Box 80 Y0A 1B0 **Location:** 6 mi (10 km) s of town at KM 1232. **Parking:** on-site. **Cards:** MC, VI.

WHITEHORSE pop. 20,461

------ WHERE TO STAY ------

EDGEWATER HOTEL

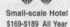
Small-scale Hotel
$169-$189 All Year

Phone: (867)667-2572
Address: 101 Main St Y1A 2A7 **Location:** Opposite White Pass Rail Depot. **Facility:** 30 units. 27 one-bedroom standard units. 3 one-bedroom suites with kitchens. 3 stories (no elevator), interior corridors. **Parking:** on-site, winter plug-ins. **Amenities:** high-speed Internet, dual phone lines, irons, hair dryers. **Dining:** The Cellar Steakhouse and Wine Bar, see separate listing. **Guest Services:** valet laundry. **Business Services:** meeting rooms. **Cards:** AX, MC, VI. **Free Special Amenities: local telephone calls and high-speed Internet.**

HIGH COUNTRY INN

Small-scale Hotel
$149-$259 All Year

Book great rates at AAA.com
Phone: (867)667-4471
Address: 4051 4th Ave Y1A 1H1 **Location:** 0.4 mi (0.6 km) e of Main St. **Facility:** 84 one-bedroom standard units, some with efficiencies, kitchens and/or whirlpools. 4 stories, interior corridors. *Bath:* combo or shower only. **Parking:** on-site, winter plug-ins. **Terms:** 3 day cancellation notice, in summer-fee imposed. **Amenities:** voice mail, irons, hair dryers. *Some:* high-speed Internet. **Leisure Activities:** exercise room. **Guest Services:** valet and coin laundry. **Business Services:** conference facilities, PC. **Cards:** AX, DC, DS, MC, VI.

MIDNIGHT SUN INN/BED & BREAKFAST
Phone: (867)667-2255

Bed & Breakfast
$99-$140 All Year

Address: 6188 6th Ave Y1A 1N8 **Location:** Corner of Cook St. Located in a residential area. **Facility:** In a residential area just outside of the downtown core, this modern B&B is walking distance from shops and offers guest rooms with themed decor. Smoke free premises. 4 one-bedroom standard units. 3 stories (no elevator), interior corridors. **Parking:** on-site, winter plug-ins. **Terms:** check-in 4 pm, 2 night minimum stay - seasonal, 7 day cancellation notice-fee imposed. **Amenities:** hair dryers. *Some:* high-speed Internet, voice mail. **Guest Services:** coin laundry. **Business Services:** meeting rooms. **Cards:** AX, JC, MC, VI.

WESTMARK WHITEHORSE HOTEL & CONFERENCE CENTRE
Book great rates at AAA.com
Phone: (867)393-9700

Small-scale Hotel
$169-$179 1/1-2/28
$159-$169 3/1-12/31

Address: 201 Wood St Y1A 2E4 **Location:** At 2nd Ave; centre. **Facility:** 180 units. 172 one-bedroom standard units. 8 one-bedroom suites, some with whirlpools. 3 stories, interior corridors. *Bath:* combo or shower only. **Parking:** on-site, winter plug-ins. **Terms:** cancellation fee imposed. **Amenities:** voice mail, irons, hair dryers. *Some:* high-speed Internet. **Leisure Activities:** *Fee:* Frantic Follies Vaudeville Revue. **Guest Services:** valet and coin laundry, barber shop. **Business Services:** conference facilities, PC. **Cards:** AX, MC, VI. **Free Special Amenities:** local telephone calls and high-speed Internet.

─────── **WHERE TO DINE** ───────

ALPINE BAKERY
Phone: 867/668-6871

Bakery/Desserts
$5-$8

A short walk from the downtown core, this organic bakery features a handcrafted masonry oven that produces a whole range of fresh breads, pizzas and other baked goods. Casual dress. **Hours:** 7 am-6 pm. Closed major holidays; also Sun & Mon. **Address:** 411 Alexander St Y1A 2L8 **Location:** Jct 4th Ave. **Parking:** on-site. **Cards:** AX, MC, VI.

THE CELLAR STEAKHOUSE AND WINE BAR
Phone: 867/667-2572

Steak & Seafood
$26-$45

You'll enjoy the Cellar Dining Room's offerings of prime rib, halibut, Alaskan king crab, steak, salmon, baby back ribs, chicken, as well as a good selection of wine by the glass. Its well-appointed dining room is one of the hot spots in town. Dressy casual. **Bar:** Full bar. **Reservations:** accepted. **Hours:** 5 pm-10 pm. Closed: Sun & Mon. **Address:** 101 Main St Y1A 2A7 **Location:** Opposite White Pass Rail Depot; in Edgewater Hotel. **Parking:** on-site and street. **Cards:** AX, DC, MC, VI.

THE CHOCOLATE CLAIM
Phone: 867/667-2202

Bakery/Desserts
$5-$8

Tucked away on a side street a short distance from the downtown core, this small art gallery-style dining offers a range of delicious cakes and other dessert items. Casual dress. **Hours:** 7:30 am-6 pm, Sat from 8:30 am. Closed major holidays; also Sun. **Address:** 305 Strickland St Y1A 2J9 **Location:** Jct 4th Ave, just e. **Parking:** on-site. **Cards:** AX, MC, VI.

THE DELI
Phone: 867/667-7583

Deli/Subs
Sandwiches
$5-$7

A short walk from the downtown core, this unassuming little butcher shop offers a wide variety of prepackaged items, such as locally made sausages, pates and baked goods. Also tempting are traditional delicatessen salads and meats, which the sandwich corner uses in custom-made sandwiches that can be enjoyed on the limited tables inside or at picnic tables at the SS Klondike a few blocks away. Casual dress. **Hours:** 7:30 am-5:30 pm. Closed major holidays; also Sun. **Address:** 203 Hanson St Y1A 1Y3 **Location:** Corner of 2nd Ave. **Parking:** street. **Cards:** MC, VI.

GIORGIO'S CUCCINA
Phone: 867/668-4050

Italian
$8-$45

The attractive dining room serves up Italian food, including thin crust pizza, fish, seafood, pasta and steaks. Many dishes are prepared on a mesquite-flavoring charbroiler. Fresh fruit smoothies and a wide selection of wines round out the menu. Casual dress. **Bar:** Full bar. **Reservations:** accepted. **Hours:** 11:30 am-2 & 4:30-11 pm. Closed: 12/25. **Address:** 206 Jarvis St Y1A 2H1 **Location:** Between 2nd and 3rd aves; downtown. **Parking:** on-site. **Cards:** MC, VI.

KLONDIKE RIB & SALMON BBQ
Phone: 867/667-7554

Seafood
$10-$25

The popular restaurant opens seasonally each year to serve regional cuisine prepared in memorable and creative manners. On the menu are Arctic char, halibut and salmon, as well as entree-size salads and pasta. Guests can eat inside, where they might share a table with other diners, or enjoy the midnight sun on the patio. **Bar:** Beer & wine. **Reservations:** suggested. **Hours:** 11 am-9 pm. **Address:** 2116 2nd Ave Y1A 2B9 **Location:** Jct Main St; downtown. **Parking:** street. **Cards:** MC, VI.

LA GOURMANDISE CREPERIE & WORLD CUISINE
Phone: 867/456-4127

Continental
$9-$36

One of the newer additions to the town's dining scene, this charming and somewhat theatrical looking, Gaelic-inspired country inn offers an extensive menu that features selections of steaks, local game and fresh produce. Casual dress. **Bar:** Full bar. **Reservations:** suggested. **Hours:** 11 am-11 pm; Sunday brunch. Closed major holidays. **Address:** 4121 4th Ave Y1A 2E4 **Location:** Jct Steele St and 4th Ave. **Parking:** street. **Cards:** AX, MC, VI.

MAINSTREET BACKEREI KAFFEE HAUS

Phone: 867/633-6291

Deli/Subs
Sandwiches
$5-$7

Primarily an organic bakery, this main street mainstay is a popular gathering spot for those looking to enjoy a freshly baked pastry while sipping on a locally roasted cup of coffee. Casual dress. **Hours:** 7:30 am-9:30 pm. Closed major holidays. **Address:** 108-100 Main St Y1A 2A8 **Location:** Centre. **Parking:** street. **Cards:** MC, VI.

MIDNIGHT SUN COFFEE ROASTERS

Phone: 867/633-4563

Coffee/Espresso
$4-$6

Distributing all over the Yukon and even in northeastern Alaska, the funky, casual coffeehouse roasts outstanding coffee beans. This is a great place to catch up with local happenings and enjoy a panini, salad or tasty dessert from the display case. In season, patrons can sit outside and enjoy the midnight sun. Internet access is available, and the staff is exceedingly friendly. **Reservations:** not accepted. **Hours:** 8 am-10 pm; seasonal hours vary. Closed: 12/25, 12/26. **Address:** 9002 Quartz Rd Y1A 2Z5 **Location:** From jct 2nd Ave, 0.4 mi n on Quartz Rd. **Parking:** on-site. **Cards:** VI.

SANCHEZ CANTINA

Phone: 867/668-5858

Mexican
$12-$20

This casual restaurant with a seasonal terrace offers a variety of house-prepared authentic Mexican dishes, including tacos and enchiladas. Casual dress. **Bar:** Full bar. **Reservations:** suggested. **Hours:** 11:30 am-3:30 & 4:30-9 pm. Closed: Sun. **Address:** 211 Hanson St Y1A 1Y3 **Location:** Corner of 3rd Ave; downtown. **Parking:** street. **Cards:** MC, VI.

TALISMAN CAFE AT THE RIVERVIEW HOTEL

Phone: 867/667-2736

International
$8-$19

While Talisman was voted in the top ten favorites of all vegetarian restaurants in Canada, there's also something for meat eaters, especially the buffalo burgers. Vegetarian offerings are simply the best around, creatively prepared using legumes, veggies, fruits and wonderful spices. The menu is as eclectic as the decor, and service is extremely friendly. Casual dress. **Bar:** Beer & wine. **Hours:** 7 am-8 pm, Sun 8 am-4 pm; 8 am-4 pm, Thurs & Fri-7 pm, Sun-2 pm in winter. Closed major holidays. **Address:** 102 Wood St Y1A 1B9 **Location:** Jct 2nd Ave and Wood St; downtown. **Parking:** street. **Cards:** AX, MC, VI.

Savings for all Seasons

Hertz rents Fords and other fine cars. ® REG. U.S. PAT. OFF. © HERTZ SYSTEM INC., 1999/2006-99.

No matter the season, Hertz offers CAA members exclusive discounts and benefits.

Operating in 150 countries at over 7,600 locations, Hertz makes traveling more convenient and efficient wherever and whenever you go. Hertz offers CAA members discounts up to 20% on car rentals worldwide.

To receive your exclusive CAA member discounts and benefits, mention your CAA membership card at time of reservation and present it at time of rental. **In addition**, to receive a free one car class upgrade on daily, weekly or weekend rental in the United States, Puerto Rico and Canada, mention PC# 969194 at the time of reservation. Offer is valid for vehicle pick-up on or before 12/15/08.

For reservations and program details, call your CAA Travel centre or the Hertz/CAA Desk at **1-800-654-3080.**

Receive a free One Car Class Upgrade on a Hertz daily, weekly or weekend rental when reserving a Compact through Full-Size four-door car (Class B-F) and take advantage of your AAA/CAA discount as well. Highest obtainable upgrade is to a Premium vehicle (Car Class G). Your AAA CDP# and the applicable PC# (above) must be included in the reservation. This offer is available at participating Hertz locations in the U.S., Canada, and Puerto Rico and is subject to availability. Advance reservations are required. Offer may be limited in some cities at some times, especially during periods of peak demand. Blackout periods may apply. If a blackout period does occur, you are still entitled to your member discount. This offer may only be used with a AAA/CAA CDP#, has no cash value and may not be used with any other coupon, discount or promotion. Hertz age, driver and credit qualifications and daily, weekend, and weekly rate requirements for the renting location apply. The car must be returned to that location. Taxes, tax reimbursement, fees and optional service charges, such as refueling, are not subject to discount. Discounts apply to time and mileage only. Offer value in local currency upon redemption. Offer is valid for vehicle pick-up on or before 12/15/2008. Call for details.

Alaska

Katmai National Park and
Preserve / © ImageState
Diomedia Stock Images

Downtown Anchorage

Anchorage
Lodging & Dining

0   Miles   2.6

Fort Richardson

SEE INSET MAP FOR DETAIL

Alaska Native Heritage Center

1695-B   © 2007 NAVTEQ   © AAA

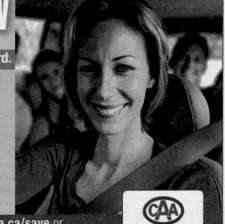

✈ Airport Accommodations

Spotter/Map Page Number	OA	ANCHORAGE INTERNATIONAL	Diamond Rating	Rate Range High Season	Listing Page
22 / p. 726	AAA	Best Western Barratt Inn, 1.8 mi e of airport	◆◆	Rates not provided SAVE	730
32 / p. 726		Coast International Inn, 1.8 mi e of airport	◆◆◆	$84-$169	731
19 / p. 726		Holiday Inn Express Anchorage Airport, 1.9 mi e of airport	◆◆◆	Rates not provided	734
18 / p. 726	AAA	Long House Alaskan Hotel, 2 mi ne of airport	◆	Rates not provided SAVE	734
26 / p. 726		Microtel Inn & Suites, 1.7 mi e of airport	◆◆	$160-$170	735
23 / p. 726	AAA	Millennium Alaskan Hotel Anchorage, 1.8 mi e of airport	◆◆◆	$290-$310 SAVE	735

Anchorage

This index helps you "spot" where approved lodgings and restaurants are located on the corresponding detailed maps. Lodging daily rate range is for comparison only and show the property's high season. Restaurant rate range is a combination of lunch and/or dinner. Turn to the listing page for more detailed rate information and consult display ads for special promotions.

Spotter/Map Page Number	OA	ANCHORAGE - Lodgings	Diamond Rating	Rate Range High Season	Listing Page
1 / p. 726		Comfort Inn Ship Creek	◆◆◆	Rates not provided	731
2 / p. 726	AAA	Anchorage Grand Hotel - see color ad p 729	◆◆	$210 SAVE	729
3 / p. 726	AAA	Ramada Anchorage Downtown	◆◆	$79-$249 SAVE	735
4 / p. 726		Hilton Anchorage	◆◆◆	Rates not provided	733
5 / p. 726	AAA	Historic Anchorage Hotel	◆◆	$149-$269 SAVE	734
6 / p. 726	AAA	Howard Johnson Plaza Hotel - see color ad p 734	◆◆	$85-$149 SAVE	734
8 / p. 726	AAA	Westmark Anchorage Hotel	◆◆◆	$139-$239 SAVE	737
9 / p. 726		Red Roof Inn	◆◆	Rates not provided	735
10 / p. 726	AAA	The Voyager Hotel - see color ad p 736	◆◆	$99-$189 SAVE	736
11 / p. 726	AAA	Sheraton Anchorage Hotel - see color ad p 735	◆◆◆	$349 SAVE	736
12 / p. 726		Anchorage Marriott Downtown	◆◆◆	$187-$308	730
13 / p. 726		Anchorage Clarion Suites	◆◆◆	$140-$233	729
14 / p. 726	AAA	Hawthorn Suites Ltd	◆◆◆	$149-$240 SAVE	733
15 / p. 726		Camai Bed & Breakfast	◆◆◆	$55-$149	731
16 / p. 726	AAA	Chugach Bed & Breakfast	◆	$105-$140 SAVE	731
17 / p. 726		Hampton Inn-Anchorage	◆◆◆	Rates not provided	733
18 / p. 726	AAA	Long House Alaskan Hotel	◆	Rates not provided SAVE	734
19 / p. 726		Holiday Inn Express Anchorage Airport	◆◆◆	Rates not provided	734
20 / p. 726		Homewood Suites-Anchorage	◆◆◆	Rates not provided	734
21 / p. 726		Hilton Garden Inn	◆◆◆	Rates not provided	734
22 / p. 726	AAA	Best Western Barratt Inn	◆◆	Rates not provided SAVE	730
23 / p. 726	AAA	Millennium Alaskan Hotel Anchorage - see color ad p 729	◆◆◆	$290-$310 SAVE	735
24 / p. 726		Motel 6 - 4216	◆	Rates not provided	735
25 / p. 726		Fairfield Inn and Suites by Marriott	◆◆◆	$98-$197	732
26 / p. 726		Microtel Inn & Suites	◆◆	$160-$170	735

Spotter/Map Page Number	OA	ANCHORAGE - Lodgings (continued)	Diamond Rating	Rate Range High Season	Listing Page
27 / p. 726	◆◆◆	Dimond Center Hotel - see color ad p 732	◆◆◆	$124-$269 SAVE	732
28 / p. 726	◆◆◆	Highland Glen Lodge B&B	◆◆◆	$100-$189 SAVE	733
29 / p. 726		15 Chandeliers Alaska B & B	◆◆◆	$150-$300	729
30 / p. 726		Copper Whale Inn	◆◆	$95-$210	732
31 / p. 726	◆◆◆	Best Western Golden Lion Hotel - see color ad p 730	◆◆	Rates not provided SAVE	731
32 / p. 726		Coast International Inn	◆◆◆	$84-$169	731
		ANCHORAGE - Restaurants			
1 / p. 726		How How Chinese Restaurant	◆	$7-$18	738
2 / p. 726		Snow Goose Restaurant	◆◆	$9-$30	740
3 / p. 726		Marx Bros. Cafe	◆◆◆◆	$25-$42	738
4 / p. 726		The Top of the World	◆◆	$21-$29	740
5 / p. 726		Sack's Cafe & Restaurant	◆◆◆	$10-$34	739
6 / p. 726		Sweet Basil Cafe	◆	$6-$10	740
7 / p. 726		Downtown Deli & Cafe	◆	$6-$12	737
8 / p. 726		Phyllis's Cafe and Salmon Bake	◆◆	$8-$39	739
9 / p. 726		Simon & Seaforts	◆◆◆	$8-$48	740
10 / p. 726		Snow City Cafe	◆◆	$5-$10	740
11 / p. 726		Club Paris	◆◆	$5-$42	737
12 / p. 726	◆◆◆	**Crow's Nest Restaurant**	◆◆◆◆	$28-$50	737
13 / p. 726		Sullivan's Steakhouse	◆◆◆	$8-$39	740
14 / p. 726		Glacier Brewhouse	◆◆	$9-$38	738
15 / p. 726		Ristorante ORSO	◆◆	$9-$37	739
16 / p. 726		Corsair Restaurant	◆◆◆	$22-$42	737
17 / p. 726		Humpy's Great Alaskan Ale House	◆	$7-$16	738
18 / p. 726		The Greek Corner	◆◆	$6-$15	738
19 / p. 726		Middle Way Cafe	◆	$5-$10	739
20 / p. 726		Moose's Tooth Pub & Pizzeria	◆◆	$6-$10	739
21 / p. 726		Yen King Chinese Restaurant	◆	$8-$20	741
22 / p. 726	◆◆◆	**Jens' Restaurant**	◆◆◆	$7-$33	738
23 / p. 726		Campobello Bistro	◆◆◆	$11-$25	737
24 / p. 726		Sea Galley	◆◆	$9-$55	739
25 / p. 726		Pepper Mill	◆◆	$14-$40	739
26 / p. 726		Peter's Sushi Spot	◆◆◆	$8-$20	739
27 / p. 726		Gwennie's Old Alaska Restaurant	◆	$6-$23	738
28 / p. 726		Fu Do Chinese Restaurant	◆◆	$6-$18	738
29 / p. 726		Skyfire Cafe	◆	$8-$10	740
30 / p. 726		Kincaid Grill	◆◆◆	$22-$32	738
31 / p. 726		Las Margaritas	◆◆	$9-$16	738
32 / p. 726		Sushi Ya Japanese Restaurant	◆◆	$8-$23	740
33 / p. 726		Royal Fork Buffet	◆	$9-$13	739
34 / p. 726	◆◆◆	**Southside Bistro**	◆◆◆	$8-$33	740

ANCHORAGE pop. 260,283 (See map and index starting on p. 726)

———— **WHERE TO STAY** ————

15 CHANDELIERS ALASKA B & B **Phone:** 907/345-3032 🔲29

Bed & Breakfast
$150-$300 3/1-9/15
$125-$250 9/16-2/28
Address: 14020 Sabine St 99516 **Location:** S of Anchorage on US 1 (New Seward Hwy), exit e on DeArmoun, then just s. **Facility:** True to this upscale B&B's name, ornate chandeliers light the common areas and guest rooms; a gourmet breakfast is offered. Smoke free premises. 5 units. 4 one-bedroom standard units. 1 two-bedroom suite. 3 stories (no elevator), interior corridors. *Bath:* shower only. **Parking:** on-site, winter plug-ins. **Terms:** age restrictions may apply, 30 day cancellation notice. **Amenities:** irons, hair dryers. **Cards:** MC, VI.

ANCHORAGE CLARION SUITES   *Book at AAA.com*   **Phone:** (907)274-1000 🔲13
Small-scale Hotel
$140-$233 All Year
Address: 325 W 8th Ave 99501 **Location:** Corner of C St and W 8th Ave. **Facility:** 111 one-bedroom suites. 3 stories, interior corridors. *Bath:* combo or shower only. **Parking:** on-site, winter plug-ins. **Terms:** 3 day cancellation notice-fee imposed. **Amenities:** video games (fee), high-speed Internet, dual phone lines, voice mail, irons, hair dryers. **Pool(s):** heated indoor. **Leisure Activities:** whirlpool, exercise room. **Guest Services:** valet and coin laundry, area transportation. **Business Services:** meeting rooms, business center. **Cards:** AX, CB, DC, DS, JC, MC, VI.

ANCHORAGE GRAND HOTEL   *Book great rates at AAA.com*   **Phone:** (907)929-8888 🔲2
Condominium
$210 3/1-8/31
$99 9/1-2/28
Address: 505 W 2nd Ave 99501 **Location:** Corner of 2nd Ave and E St; downtown. Located across from Anchorage Market. **Facility:** Smoke free premises. 31 units. 6 one-bedroom standard units with kitchens. 25 one-bedroom suites with kitchens. 5 stories, interior corridors. **Parking:** on-site and street. **Amenities:** high-speed Internet, dual phone lines, voice mail, irons, hair dryers. **Guest Services:** valet and coin laundry. **Business Services:** business center. **Cards:** AX, DS, MC, VI. **Free Special Amenities:** continental breakfast and high-speed Internet. *(See color ad below)*

———— ▼ See AAA listing p 735 ▼ ————

———— ▼ See AAA listing above ▼ ————

(See map and index starting on p. 726)

ANCHORAGE MARRIOTT DOWNTOWN   *Book great rates at AAA.com*   Phone: 907/279-8000   12

Large-scale Hotel
$187-$308 All Year

Address: 820 W. 7th Ave 99501 **Location:** Between I and H sts. **Facility:** Smoke free premises. 392 units. 389 one-bedroom standard units. 3 one-bedroom suites. 20 stories, interior corridors. *Bath:* combo or shower only. **Parking:** on-site (fee) and valet. **Amenities:** high-speed Internet (fee), dual phone lines, voice mail, irons, hair dryers. **Pool(s):** indoor. **Leisure Activities:** whirlpool, exercise room. **Guest Services:** valet and coin laundry. **Business Services:** conference facilities, business center. **Cards:** AX, DC, DS, JC, MC, VI.

Marriott
HOTELS & RESORTS

AAA Benefit:
Members save 5%
off of the best
available rate.

BEST WESTERN BARRATT INN   *Book great rates at AAA.com*   Phone: 907/243-3131   22

Small-scale Hotel
Rates not provided

Address: 4616 Spenard Rd 99517-3299 **Location:** International Airport Rd; just ne of jct Jewel Lake and Spenard rds. **Facility:** 122 one-bedroom standard units, some with efficiencies. 2-5 stories, interior/exterior corridors. **Parking:** on-site, winter plug-ins. **Amenities:** video games (fee), voice mail, irons, hair dryers. *Some:* high-speed Internet. **Leisure Activities:** exercise room. **Guest Services:** valet and coin laundry, area transportation-train station. **Business Services:** meeting rooms, PC. **Free Special Amenities:** continental breakfast and local telephone calls.

AAA Benefit:
Members save 10%
everyday, plus an
exclusive frequent
stay program.

▼ See AAA listing p 771 ▼

Only 45 miles North of Anchorage

On the way to Denali National Park. Superb location on beautiful Lake Lucille. Breathtaking views of Chugach Mountains. Elegant Restaurant, Lounge, Convention facilities. Fitness room, Hot tub and Sauna.

LakeLucilleInn
1300 W. Lake Lucille Dr., Wasilla, AK 99654

907-373-1776 • Fax: 907-376-6199 • www.bestwesternlakelucilleinn.com

(See map and index starting on p. 726)

BEST WESTERN GOLDEN LION HOTEL
Book great rates at AAA.com   Phone: 907/561-1522   **31**

Small-scale Hotel
Rates not provided

Address: 1000 E 36th Ave 99508 **Location:** US 1 (New Seward Hwy) and 36th Ave. **Facility:** 83 one-bedroom standard units. 3 stories, interior corridors. *Bath:* combo or shower only. **Parking:** on-site. **Amenities:** voice mail, irons, hair dryers. *Some:* high-speed Internet, dual phone lines. **Leisure Activities:** sauna, exercise room. **Guest Services:** valet and coin laundry, wireless Internet. **Business Services:** meeting rooms, business center. **Free Special Amenities: local telephone calls and high-speed Internet.** *(See color ad below)*

AAA Benefit:
Members save 10% everyday, plus an exclusive frequent stay program.

CAMAI BED & BREAKFAST
Phone: (907)333-2219   **15**

Bed & Breakfast
$55-$149 All Year

Address: 3838 Westminster Way 99508-4834 **Location:** US 1 (New Seward Hwy), 2.8 mi e on Benson/Northern Lights Blvd, 0.6 mi s on Wesleyn Ave to Queen Ct, then just e. Located in a residential area. **Facility:** This B&B is located in a quiet residential area and provides guests with spacious, well equipped rooms with a homey, comfortable decor. In the summer months guests enjoy the lovely back garden. Smoke free premises. 3 one-bedroom suites, some with efficiencies. 2 stories (no elevator), interior/exterior corridors. **Parking:** on-site, winter plug-ins. **Terms:** cancellation fee imposed. **Amenities:** video library, DVD players, high-speed Internet, voice mail, irons, hair dryers. **Guest Services:** wireless Internet. **Business Services:** PC.

CHUGACH BED & BREAKFAST
Phone: (907)333-4615   **16**

Bed & Breakfast
$105-$140 5/1-9/30

Address: 3901 Laron Ln 99504 **Location:** US 1 (New Seward Hwy), exit Tudor Rd, 5 mi e to Patterson Rd, just n to Madelynne, then just e on Madellyne to Laron Ln. **Facility:** Smoke free premises. 4 one-bedroom standard units, some with whirlpools. 2 stories (no elevator), interior corridors. *Bath:* some shared or private. **Parking:** on-site. **Terms:** open 5/1-9/30, check-in 4 pm, 2 night minimum stay, 7 day cancellation notice. **Amenities:** video library, CD players, high-speed Internet, irons, hair dryers. **Leisure Activities:** sauna, exercise room. **Cards:** AX, DS, MC, VI. **Free Special Amenities: full breakfast and high-speed Internet.**

COAST INTERNATIONAL INN
Book at AAA.com   Phone: (907)243-2233   **32**

Small-scale Hotel
$84-$169 All Year

Address: 3450 Aviation Ave 99502 **Location:** Just ne of jct International Airport and Spenard rds, then just w. **Facility:** 141 one-bedroom standard units. 2 stories (no elevator), interior corridors. *Bath:* combo or shower only. **Parking:** on-site, winter plug-ins. **Terms:** cancellation fee imposed. **Amenities:** video games (fee), high-speed Internet, dual phone lines, voice mail, irons, hair dryers. **Leisure Activities:** sauna, exercise room. **Guest Services:** valet and coin laundry. **Business Services:** meeting rooms, PC. **Cards:** AX, CB, DC, DS, MC, VI.

COMFORT INN SHIP CREEK
Book at AAA.com   Phone: 907/277-6887   **1**

Small-scale Hotel
Rates not provided

Address: 111 W Ship Creek Ave 99501 **Location:** At 3rd and E sts, 0.3 mi n on E St, across the railway, just e on Ship Creek Ave; downtown. **Facility:** 100 units. 98 one-bedroom standard units, some with kitchens and/or whirlpools. 2 two-bedroom suites with kitchens and whirlpools. 3 stories, interior corridors. *Bath:* combo or shower only. **Parking:** on-site. **Terms:** check-in 4 pm. **Amenities:** video games (fee), dual phone lines, voice mail, irons, hair dryers. **Pool(s):** heated indoor. **Leisure Activities:** fishing, exercise room. **Guest Services:** valet and coin laundry, area transportation, wireless Internet. **Business Services:** business center.

─────── ▼ *See AAA listing above* ▼ ───────

(See map and index starting on p. 726)

COPPER WHALE INN
Phone: (907)258-7999

Bed & Breakfast
$95-$210 All Year

Address: 440 L St 99501 **Location:** Jct W 4th Ave; downtown. Located in a commercial area. **Facility:** Smoke free premises. 14 one-bedroom standard units. 2 stories (no elevator), interior corridors. *Bath:* some tub only. **Parking:** no self-parking. **Terms:** 14 day cancellation notice. **Amenities:** *Some:* irons. **Guest Services:** coin laundry, wireless Internet. **Business Services:** PC. **Cards:** AX, DC, DS, MC, VI.

[ASK] [S] [X] [AC] [W]

DIMOND CENTER HOTEL　*Book great rates at AAA.com*
Phone: (907)770-5000

Small-scale Hotel
$124-$269 All Year

Address: 700 E Dimond Blvd 99515 **Location:** US 1 (New Seward Hwy), exit Dimond Blvd, just w to E Dimond Blvd, then s. **Facility:** 109 one-bedroom standard units, some with whirlpools. 3 stories, interior corridors. **Parking:** on-site. **Terms:** cancellation fee imposed. **Amenities:** CD players, high-speed Internet, dual phone lines, voice mail, irons, hair dryers. **Leisure Activities:** chess, limited exercise equipment. **Guest Services:** valet and coin laundry, area transportation-downtown. **Business Services:** meeting rooms, PC. **Cards:** AX, DC, DS, MC, VI. **Free Special Amenities: expanded continental breakfast and high-speed Internet.** *(See color ad below)*

  CALL / SOME UNITS

FAIRFIELD INN AND SUITES BY MARRIOTT　*Book great rates at AAA.com*
Phone: 907/222-9000

Small-scale Hotel
$98-$197 All Year

Address: 5060 A St 99503 **Location:** Jct C St and International Airport Rd. **Facility:** Smoke free premises. 106 one-bedroom standard units, some with whirlpools. 4 stories, interior corridors. *Bath:* combo or shower only. **Parking:** on-site. **Amenities:** high-speed Internet, dual phone lines, voice mail, irons, hair dryers. **Pool(s):** heated outdoor. **Leisure Activities:** whirlpool, limited exercise equipment. **Guest Services:** valet and coin laundry. **Business Services:** PC. **Cards:** AX, DS, MC, VI.

AAA Benefit:
Members save 5% off of the best available rate.

[ASK] [S] [+] [↕+] CALL [M] [≈] [X] [CTV] [□] / SOME UNITS [□] [□]

▼ See AAA listing above ▼

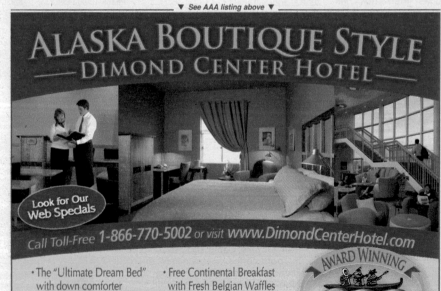

(See map and index starting on p. 726)

HAMPTON INN-ANCHORAGE *Book great rates at AAA.com* Phone: 907/550-7000 **17**

Small-scale Hotel
Rates not provided

Address: 4301 Credit Union Dr 99503 **Location:** Corner of Tudor Rd and C St. **Facility:** 101 one-bedroom standard units, some with whirlpools. 3 stories, interior corridors. *Bath:* combo or shower only. **Parking:** on-site. **Amenities:** video games, high-speed Internet, dual phone lines, voice mail, irons, hair dryers. **Pool(s):** heated indoor. **Leisure Activities:** whirlpool, exercise room. **Guest Services:** valet and coin laundry, area transportation, wireless Internet. **Business Services:** meeting rooms, business center.

HAWTHORN SUITES LTD *Book great rates at AAA.com* Phone: (907)222-5005 **14**

[AAA] [SAVE]
Small-scale Hotel
$149-$240 All Year

Address: 1110 W 8th Ave 99501 **Location:** Corner of L St and W 8th Ave. **Facility:** 111 one-bedroom suites. 3 stories, interior corridors. *Bath:* combo or shower only. **Parking:** on-site. **Terms:** 3 day cancellation notice-fee imposed. **Amenities:** video games (fee), dual phone lines, voice mail, irons, hair dryers. **Pool(s):** heated indoor. **Leisure Activities:** whirlpool, limited exercise equipment. **Guest Services:** valet and coin laundry, airport transportation-Ted Stevens Airport, area transportation-train depot, wireless Internet. **Business Services:** meeting rooms, business center. **Cards:** AX, CB, DC, DS, JC, MC, VI. **Free Special Amenities: continental breakfast and high-speed Internet.**

HIGHLAND GLEN LODGE B&B Phone: (907)336-2312 **28**

[AAA] [SAVE]
Bed & Breakfast
$100-$189 All Year

Address: 11651 Hillside Dr 99507 **Location:** US 1 (New Seward Hwy), exit O'Mally, 4 mi e to Hillside Dr, then 0.5 mi s. **Facility:** This lovely Tudor-style home offers guests comfortable accommodations in an attractive country setting; the rooms are spacious and well equipped and there are several comfortable sitting areas. Smoke free premises. 4 units. 3 one- and 1 two-bedroom standard units, some with whirlpools. 2 stories (no elevator), interior corridors. *Bath:* combo or shower only. **Parking:** on-site. **Terms:** office hours 6 am-8 pm, check-in 5 pm, 14 day cancellation notice-fee imposed. **Amenities:** video library, DVD players, hair dryers. **Leisure Activities:** hot tub. **Cards:** AX, MC, VI. **Free Special Amenities: full breakfast and high-speed Internet.**

HILTON ANCHORAGE *Book great rates at AAA.com* Phone: 907/272-7411 **4**

Large-scale Hotel
Rates not provided

Address: 500 W 3rd Ave 99501 **Location:** At E St; downtown. **Facility:** 605 units. 595 one-bedroom standard units. 10 one-bedroom suites. 15-22 stories, interior corridors. *Bath:* combo or shower only. **Parking:** on-site (fee) and valet. **Amenities:** dual phone lines, voice mail, irons, hair dryers. *Fee:* video games, high-speed Internet. **Dining:** The Top of the World, see separate listing. **Pool(s):** heated indoor. **Leisure Activities:** whirlpool, steamrooms. **Guest Services:** valet laundry. **Business Services:** conference facilities, business center.

▼ See AAA listing p 751 ▼

(See map and index starting on p. 726)

HILTON GARDEN INN　　*Book great rates at AAA.com*　　Phone: 907/729-7000　**21**

▼▼▼▼

Small-scale Hotel
Rates not provided

Address: 100 W Tudor Rd 99503 **Location:** Corner of Tudor Rd and A St. **Facility:** 125 one-bedroom standard units, some with whirlpools. 4 stories, interior corridors. *Bath:* combo or shower only. **Parking:** on-site. **Amenities:** video games (fee), high-speed Internet, dual phone lines, voice mail, irons, hair dryers. **Pool(s):** heated indoor. **Leisure Activities:** whirlpool, exercise room. **Guest Services:** valet and coin laundry, area transportation. **Business Services:** meeting rooms, business center.

HISTORIC ANCHORAGE HOTEL　　*Book great rates at AAA.com*　　Phone: (907)272-4553　**5**

(AAA) (SAVE)

▼▼ ▼▼

Small-scale Hotel
$149-$269 All Year

Address: 330 E St 99501 **Location:** Between 4th and 3rd sts. **Facility:** Smoke free premises. 26 one-bedroom standard units. 3 stories, interior corridors. **Parking:** no self-parking. **Terms:** 7 day cancellation notice-fee imposed. **Amenities:** irons, hair dryers. **Guest Services:** wireless Internet. **Business Services:** meeting rooms. **Cards:** AX, CB, DC, DS, JC, MC, VI. **Free Special Amenities: continental breakfast and high-speed Internet.**

HOLIDAY INN EXPRESS ANCHORAGE AIRPORT　　*Book at AAA.com*　　Phone: 907/248-8848　**19**

▼▼▼▼

Small-scale Hotel
Rates not provided

Address: 4411 Spenard Rd 99517 **Location:** 0.5 mi ne of Jewell Lake and International Airport rds. **Facility:** 128 one-bedroom standard units, some with whirlpools. 3 stories, interior corridors. *Bath:* combo or shower only. **Parking:** on-site. **Amenities:** video games (fee), high-speed Internet, dual phone lines, voice mail, irons, hair dryers. **Pool(s):** heated indoor. **Leisure Activities:** whirlpool, exercise room. **Guest Services:** valet and coin laundry, wireless Internet. **Business Services:** business center.

HOMEWOOD SUITES-ANCHORAGE　　*Book great rates at AAA.com*　　Phone: 907/762-7000　**20**

▼▼▼▼

Small-scale Hotel
Rates not provided

Address: 140 W Tudor Rd 99503 **Location:** US 1 (New Seward Hwy), exit Tudor Rd W, turn on C St. **Facility:** 122 units. 47 one-bedroom standard units with efficiencies. 71 one- and 4 two-bedroom suites with efficiencies. 4 stories, interior corridors. *Bath:* combo or shower only. **Parking:** on-site. **Amenities:** video games (fee), high-speed Internet, dual phone lines, voice mail, irons, hair dryers. *Some:* DVD players (fee). **Pool(s):** heated indoor. **Leisure Activities:** whirlpool, exercise room, basketball. **Guest Services:** valet and coin laundry, area transportation, wireless Internet. **Business Services:** meeting rooms, business center.

HOWARD JOHNSON PLAZA HOTEL　　*Book great rates at AAA.com*　　Phone: (907)793-5500　**6**

(AAA) (SAVE)

▼▼ ▼▼

Small-scale Hotel
$85-$149 All Year

Address: 239 W 4th Ave 99501 **Location:** At 3rd Ave and C St; downtown. **Facility:** 246 one-bedroom standard units. 3 stories, interior corridors. *Bath:* combo or shower only. **Parking:** on-site. **Amenities:** video games (fee), voice mail, safes, irons. **Pool(s):** heated indoor. **Leisure Activities:** exercise room. **Guest Services:** valet and coin laundry, wireless Internet. **Business Services:** meeting rooms, PC. **Cards:** AX, MC, VI. **Free Special Amenities: full breakfast and high-speed Internet.** *(See color ad below)*

LONG HOUSE ALASKAN HOTEL　　*Book great rates at AAA.com*　　Phone: 907/243-2133　**18**

(AAA) (SAVE)

▼▼

Small-scale Hotel
Rates not provided

Address: 4335 Wisconsin St 99517 **Location:** International Airport Rd, 1.5 mi ne on Spenard Rd, nw on Wisconsin St at 43rd Ave, then just e. **Facility:** 54 one-bedroom standard units. 2 stories (no elevator), interior corridors. *Bath:* combo or shower only. **Parking:** on-site, winter plug-ins. **Terms:** check-in 4 pm. **Amenities:** voice mail, hair dryers. **Leisure Activities:** walk-in fish freezer. **Guest Services:** valet and coin laundry, airport transportation-Ted Stevens Airport, area transportation, wireless Internet. **Free Special Amenities: continental breakfast and local telephone calls.**

▼ *See AAA listing above* ▼

(See map and index starting on p. 726)

MICROTEL INN & SUITES   *Book at AAA.com*   Phone: (907)245-5002   26

Small-scale Hotel
$160-$170 3/1-9/30
$75-$85 10/1-2/28

Address: 5205 Northwood Dr 99517 **Location:** 1.7 mi e of airport. **Facility:** 79 one-bedroom standard units, some with whirlpools. 3 stories, interior corridors. *Bath:* combo or shower only. **Parking:** on-site. **Amenities:** video games (fee). *Some:* irons, hair dryers. **Leisure Activities:** whirlpools. **Guest Services:** valet and coin laundry, wireless Internet. **Business Services:** PC. **Cards:** AX, DC, DS, MC, VI.

[ASK] [✈] CALL [&M] [🛗] [📺] [💻] / SOME UNITS FEE [🐕] [✗] [🛗] [🖨]

MILLENNIUM ALASKAN HOTEL ANCHORAGE   *Book great rates at AAA.com*   Phone: (907)243-2300   23

[AAA] [SAVE]
Large-scale Hotel
$290-$310 3/1-9/20
$170-$190 9/21-2/28

Address: 4800 Spenard Rd 99517 **Location:** International Airport Rd; just ne from jct Jewel Lake and Spenard rds. **Facility:** 247 units. 245 one-bedroom standard units. 2 one-bedroom suites with whirlpools. 4 stories, interior corridors. *Bath:* combo or shower only. **Parking:** on-site. **Amenities:** video games (fee), dual phone lines, voice mail, irons, hair dryers. *Some:* high-speed Internet (fee). **Leisure Activities:** sauna, whirlpool, steamroom, exercise room. **Guest Services:** valet and coin laundry, airport transportation-Ted Stevens Airport, area transportation-Diamond Mall and downtown. **Business Services:** conference facilities, business center. **Cards:** AX, CB, DC, DS, JC, MC, VI.
(See color ad p 729)

[S🌙] [✈] [🍴] [24] [Y] CALL [&M] [✗] [📺] [🛗] [💻] / SOME UNITS FEE [🐕] [✗]

MOTEL 6 - 4216   Phone: 907/677-8000   24

Motel
Rates not provided

Address: 5000 A St 99503 **Location:** Jct C St and International Airport Rd. **Facility:** 85 one-bedroom standard units. 3 stories, interior corridors. *Bath:* combo or shower only. **Parking:** on-site. **Amenities:** voice mail. **Guest Services:** wireless Internet.

[✈] CALL [&M] [📺] / SOME UNITS [✗]

RAMADA ANCHORAGE DOWNTOWN   *Book great rates at AAA.com*   Phone: (907)272-7561   3

[AAA] [SAVE]
Small-scale Hotel
$79-$249 All Year

Address: 115 E 3rd Ave 99501 **Location:** Jct Barrow St; downtown. **Facility:** 90 one-bedroom standard units, some with whirlpools. 3 stories, interior/exterior corridors. *Bath:* combo or shower only. **Parking:** on-site. **Terms:** cancellation fee imposed. **Amenities:** voice mail, irons, hair dryers. **Leisure Activities:** limited exercise equipment. **Guest Services:** valet and coin laundry, wireless Internet. **Business Services:** meeting rooms, PC. **Cards:** AX, DC, DS, MC, VI. **Free Special Amenities:** expanded continental breakfast and local telephone calls.

[S🌙] [📶] [💻] / SOME UNITS FEE [🐕] [✗] [🍴] [🛗] [🖨]

RED ROOF INN   *Book at AAA.com*   Phone: 907/274-1650   9

Motel
Rates not provided

Address: 1104 E 5th Ave 99501 **Location:** At Karluk St. **Facility:** 55 one-bedroom standard units. 2-3 stories (no elevator), interior/exterior corridors. *Bath:* combo or shower only. **Parking:** on-site. **Amenities:** high-speed Internet, voice mail, hair dryers. **Guest Services:** complimentary laundry, area transportation.

[✈] [📶] CALL [&M] [📺] / SOME UNITS [🐕] [✗] [🛗] [🖨] [💻]

▼ See AAA listing p 736 ▼

(See map and index starting on p. 726)

SHERATON ANCHORAGE HOTEL Phone: (907)276-8700 **11**

Large-scale Hotel
$349 3/1-9/14
$209 9/15-2/28

Address: 401 E 6th Ave 99501 **Location:** 6th Ave and Denali St. **Facility:** 375 units. 370 one- and 1 two-bedroom standard units. 4 one-bedroom suites, some with whirlpools. 16 stories, interior corridors. *Bath:* combo or shower only. **Parking:** on-site and valet. **Terms:** cancellation fee imposed. **Amenities:** voice mail, irons, hair dryers. *Fee:* video games, high-speed Internet. *Some:* fax. **Leisure Activities:** saunas, whirlpool, steamrooms, exercise room. **Guest Services:** valet laundry, area transportation-downtown. **Business Services:** conference facilities, business center. **Cards:** AX, CB, DC, DS, JC, MC, VI. *(See color ad p 735)*

AAA Benefit:
Members get up to 15% off, plus Starwood Preferred Guest® bonuses.

THE VOYAGER HOTEL Phone: (907)277-9501 **10**

Small-scale Hotel
$99-$189 All Year

Address: 501 K St 99501 **Location:** At K St and 5th Ave; downtown. **Facility:** Smoke free premises. 40 one-bedroom standard units. 4 stories, interior corridors. *Bath:* combo or shower only. **Parking:** on-site (fee). **Amenities:** high-speed Internet, dual phone lines, voice mail, hair dryers. **Dining:** Corsair Restaurant, see separate listing. **Guest Services:** valet laundry. **Cards:** AX, CB, DC, DS, JC, MC, VI. **Free Special Amenities: continental breakfast and high-speed Internet.** *(See color ad below)*

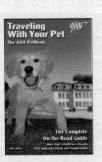

(See map and index starting on p. 726)

WESTMARK ANCHORAGE HOTEL   *Book great rates at AAA.com*   Phone: (907)276-7676   **8**

AAA [SAVE]

▼▼▼▼
Large-scale Hotel
$139-$239 All Year

Address: 720 W 5th Ave 99501 **Location:** At G St and W 5th Ave; downtown. **Facility:** Smoke free premises. 200 one-bedroom standard units. 14 stories, interior corridors. *Bath:* combo or shower only. **Parking:** on-site. **Terms:** cancellation fee imposed. **Amenities:** video games (fee), dual phone lines, voice mail, irons, hair dryers. **Dining:** 2 restaurants. **Leisure Activities:** exercise room. **Guest Services:** valet laundry, wireless Internet. **Business Services:** meeting rooms, PC. **Cards:** AX, DC, DS, MC, VI. **Free Special Amenities:** local telephone calls and high-speed Internet.

[icons: ▯ ▾ CALL ♿M 🛍 🖥 / SOME UNITS 🐾 ✕ 🛗]

─────── *The following lodgings were either not evaluated or did not* ───────
meet AAA rating requirements but are listed for your information only.

ANCHORAGE AIRPORT COURTYARD BY MARRIOTT   Phone: 907/245-0322

[fyi]
Small-scale Hotel

Did not meet all AAA rating requirements for some property operations at time of last evaluation on 10/11/2006. **Address:** 4901 Spenard Rd 99517 **Location:** Just ne of Jewell Lake and International Airport rds. Facilities, services, and decor characterize a mid-range property.

RESIDENCE INN BY MARRIOTT   Phone: 907/563-9844

[fyi]
Small-scale Hotel

Did not meet all AAA rating requirements for some property operations at time of last evaluation on 10/10/2006. **Address:** 1025 E 35th Ave 99508 **Location:** Corner of US 1 (New Seward Hwy) and 36th Ave. Facilities, services, and decor characterize a mid-range property.

SPRINGHILL SUITES BY MARRIOTT   Phone: 907/562-3247

[fyi]
Small-scale Hotel

Did not meet all AAA rating requirements for some property operations at time of last evaluation on 10/09/2006. **Address:** 3401 A St 99503 **Location:** Corner of 36th Ave and A St. Facilities, services, and decor characterize a mid-range property.

─────── **WHERE TO DINE** ───────

CAMPOBELLO BISTRO   Phone: 907/563-2040   **23**

▼▼▼
Italian
$11-$25

A true gem is hidden in the Midtown roadside mall. The elegantly simple dining room is a perfect place for a casual yet romantic meal. Italian cooking, including various preparations of pasta and seafood, reflects an Alaskan flair. Casual dress. **Bar:** Beer & wine. **Reservations:** suggested. **Hours:** 11 am-2:30 & 5-close, Sat from 5 pm, Mon 11 am-2:30 pm. Closed major holidays; also Sun. **Address:** 601 W 36th Ave 99503 **Location:** Just w at Arctic Blvd. **Parking:** on-site. **Cards:** DC, MC, VI.

[icon: 🅰C]

CLUB PARIS   Phone: 907/277-6332   **11**

▼▼▼
Steak House
$5-$42

Home to the locally renowned four-inch filet mignon, the longstanding downtown restaurant—said to be the oldest steakhouse in the city—is a favorite of visitors and locals alike. The dimly lit dining room, with its dark upholstery and padded booths, has a loungelike feel. In addition to a good selection of steaks, the menu also lists Alaskan seafood options. Casual dress. **Bar:** Full bar. **Hours:** 11:30 am-2:30 & 5-11 pm, Sun 5 pm-10 pm. Closed: 11/27, 12/25. **Address:** 417 W 5th Ave 99501 **Location:** Between D and E sts; downtown. **Parking:** street. **Cards:** AX, CB, DC, DS, MC, VI.

[icons: CALL ♿M 🅰C]

CORSAIR RESTAURANT   Phone: 907/278-4502   **16**

▼▼▼
Continental
$22-$42

The restaurant provides its guests a fine dining experience featuring fresh Alaskan seafood, veal, steak and rack of lamb. The dining room decor is nautical but romantic, with impressive, fabric-upholstered booths acting as a focal point. Sweeping curves resemble ocean waves. The award-winning wine list offers an excellent selection of domestic and imported vintages. This eatery opens for lunch the last Friday of each month. Dressy casual. **Bar:** Full bar. **Reservations:** suggested. **Hours:** 5 pm-10 pm, Fri & Sat-11 pm. Closed major holidays; also Sun. **Address:** 944 W 5th Ave 99501 **Location:** At K St and 5th Ave; downtown; in The Voyager Hotel. **Parking:** street. **Cards:** AX, DC, DS, MC, VI.

CROW'S NEST RESTAURANT   *Menu on AAA.com*   Phone: 907/276-6000   **12**

AAA

▼▼▼ ▼▼
Continental
$28-$50

Perched high on the 20th floor of The Hotel Captain Cook, the restaurant affords panoramic mountain and Cook Inlet views, especially on long summer days. Service is attentive and formal but unstuffy. The menu's accent is on seafood although it also offers an excellent variety of meats and exotic foods, such as Caspian Sea caviar, truffles, foie gras and seaweed. The excellent wine cellar houses more than 10,000 bottles. Casual dress. **Bar:** Full bar. **Reservations:** suggested. **Hours:** 5:30 pm-9:30 pm. Closed major holidays; also Sun. **Location:** Just w of centre at K St; in The Hotel Captain Cook. **Parking:** on-site and valet. **Cards:** AX, DC, DS, JC, MC, VI.

[icon: CALL ♿M]

DOWNTOWN DELI & CAFE   Phone: 907/276-7116   **7**

◆
Deli/Subs
Sandwiches
$6-$12

Across from the log cabin visitor center downtown, the popular eatery is known for its huge portions and all-day breakfast items. Such offerings as the quiche of the day, eggs with reindeer sausage and fish and chips will satisfy any appetite. Casual dress. **Bar:** Wine only. **Reservations:** not accepted. **Hours:** 6 am-10 pm; 7 am-3 pm 10/1-4/30. Closed major holidays. **Address:** 525 W 4th Ave 99501-2211 **Location:** Downtown; across from Log Cabin Visitors Centre. **Parking:** street. **Cards:** AX, DC, DS, MC, VI.

(See map and index starting on p. 726)

FU DO CHINESE RESTAURANT
Phone: 907/561-6611
Chinese
$6-$18
A good mix of Mandarin, Cantonese and Szechuan selections is offered at this restaurant. The crispy duck, orange beef and sesame chicken are good choices. The attractive dining room is situated in a brightly decorated building in a commercial area. Casual dress. **Bar:** Full bar. **Reservations:** suggested. **Hours:** 11 am-10 pm, Fri & Sat-11 pm. **Address:** 2600 E Tudor Rd 99507 **Location:** Jct Old Seward Hwy, 1 mi e. **Parking:** on-site. **Cards:** AX, DC, DS, MC, VI.

GLACIER BREWHOUSE
Phone: 907-274-2739
American
$9-$38
Characterized by a large stone fireplace as its focal point, the decor blends contemporary, industrial and rustic themes. Large beer-brewing vats, which produce a number of tasty brews, loom behind glass walls. Varied seafood and roasted meat dishes, pizzas, sandwiches, salads and pastas are served in generous portions. Seasonal salmon is the standout, but other preparations—including dinner prime rib, tangy barbecue pork ribs, bread pudding and peanut butter pie—are plenty tempting. Casual dress. **Bar:** Full bar. **Reservations:** suggested. **Hours:** 11 am-10 pm, Fri & Sat-11 pm. Closed: 7/4, 11/27, 12/25. **Address:** 737 W 5th Ave, Suite 110 99501 **Location:** At H St; downtown. **Parking:** street. **Cards:** AX, DC, DS, MC, VI.

THE GREEK CORNER
Phone: 907/276-2820
Greek
$6-$15
Folks might miss the small, family-run restaurant, one of the city's best-kept secrets. The menu lists both Greek and Italian cuisine, and there is something for everyone. Guests are greeted warmly, whether they are there all the time or for their first visit, and the service is friendly. Portions are hearty. The casual, traditional atmosphere is family-friendly. **Bar:** Beer & wine. **Hours:** 11 am-10 pm, Sat from noon, Sun from 4 pm. Closed major holidays. **Address:** 302 W Fireweed Ln 99503 **Location:** Corner of W Fireweed Ln and C St. **Parking:** on-site. **Cards:** AX, MC, VI.

GWENNIE'S OLD ALASKA RESTAURANT
Phone: 907-243-2090
American
$6-$23
For a taste of the Alaskan experience, the popular family restaurant serves huge portions in a dining room bedecked with authentic Alaskan paraphernalia, including black and white photographs, dog sleds and even snowshoes. Service is attentive, and patrons get great value for the dollar. Casual dress. **Bar:** Full bar. **Reservations:** not accepted. **Hours:** 6 am-10 pm, Sun 8 am-9 pm. Closed: 11/27, 12/25. **Address:** 4333 Spenard Rd 99517 **Location:** International Airport Rd, just ne of jct Jewel Lake and Spenard rds. **Parking:** on-site. **Cards:** AX, CB, DC, DS, MC, VI.

HOW HOW CHINESE RESTAURANT
Phone: 907/337-2116
Chinese
$7-$18
Attached to the Howard Johnson at the east end of town, the popular restaurant is one of the oldest in Anchorage. This place bustles during lunch, when an all-you-can-eat buffet is featured. Dinner guests can expect traditional a la carte menu items, as well as some Western fare. Glance overhead to admire the traditional Chinese panels. **Bar:** Full bar. **Hours:** 11 am-10 pm. Closed: 1/1, 11/27, 12/25. **Address:** 207 Muldoon Rd 99504 **Location:** 5 mi ne on US 1 (Glenn Hwy), just s; in Ramada Limited Hotel of Anchorage. **Parking:** on-site. **Cards:** AX, DC, DS, MC, VI.

HUMPY'S GREAT ALASKAN ALE HOUSE
Phone: 907/276-2337
American
$7-$16
With an impressive selection of Alaskan microbrewed beers, the casual ale house is a favorite among locals. Guests can choose from a variety of sandwiches, burgers and pastas. Patio seating can be requested in season, and often local bands perform to an enthusiastic crowd. Casual dress. Entertainment. **Bar:** Full bar. **Reservations:** not accepted. **Hours:** 9 am-1 am. Closed: 1/1, 3/23, 12/25. **Address:** 610 W 6th Ave 99501 **Location:** Between F and G sts; downtown. **Parking:** street. **Cards:** AX, CB, DC, DS, MC, VI.

JENS' RESTAURANT
Phone: 907/561-5367
Continental
$7-$33
Danish by day and French by night, the cozy, bistro-style restaurant, which includes a casual tapas bar, is one of the city's finest. Local artists are featured, and the casual side has a stool bar where guests can enjoy a glass of wine from the extensive wine list. The eclectic, monthly changing menu relies heavily on local ingredients and flavors, which the talented chef prepares with a Danish and French twist. Casual dress. **Bar:** Full bar. **Reservations:** suggested. **Hours:** Open 3/1-12/31 & 2/1-2/28; 11:30 am-2 & 6-midnight, Mon from 6 pm. Closed: 12/24, 12/25; also Sun. **Address:** 701 W 36th Ave 99503 **Location:** Just e of Arctic Blvd and W 36th Ave; in Olympic Center. **Parking:** on-site. **Cards:** AX, DC, DS, MC, VI.

KINCAID GRILL
Phone: 907/243-0507
Continental
$22-$32
It's no surprise that locals flock to this popular restaurant featuring a contemporary decor and innovative menu. Diners enjoy the carefully planned a la carte options or the chef's changing tasting menu paired with wines from the extensive wine list. Highlights include Alaska oyster or Kodiak scallops to start, followed by a seafood fusion soup or Caprese salad. A wide selection of local fish and seafood is paired with some creative sauces or try the meat, game and poultry offerings. Casual dress. **Bar:** Full bar. **Reservations:** suggested. **Hours:** 5 pm-10 pm. Closed major holidays; also Sun & Mon. **Address:** 6700 Jewel Lake Rd 99502 **Location:** Jct Raspberry. **Parking:** on-site. **Cards:** AX, MC, VI.

LAS MARGARITAS
Phone: 907/349-4922
Mexican
$9-$16
This restaurant is a little out of the way, but it's worth the drive. The restaurant has a charming and casual country-style ambience, and its cuisine features popular Mexican and Italian specialties including burritos, spaghetti, pizza, steak and shrimp. Casual dress. **Bar:** Full bar. **Reservations:** suggested. **Hours:** 4 pm-10:30 pm, Sat-10 pm. Closed major holidays. **Address:** 541 W Dimond 99515 **Location:** Between Artic Blvd and C St. **Parking:** on-site. **Cards:** AX, MC, VI.

MARX BROS. CAFE
Phone: 907/278-2133
Nouvelle American
$25-$42
For a truly exquisite meal, look no further than the dining rooms of this renovated 1916 home. Innovative and artistic selections of Alaskan seafood highlight the menu, and the locally renowned Caesar salad is prepared tableside. Choices include not only a wide selection of seafood, such as oysters, salmon and halibut, but also lamb and other meats. Save room for one of the divine desserts. The atmosphere is delightful, and the service friendly and genuine. Dressy casual. **Bar:** Beer & wine. **Reservations:** suggested. **Hours:** 6 pm-9:30 pm, Fri & Sat 5:30 pm-10 pm; 5:30 pm-10 pm 5/31-9/6. Closed major holidays; also Sun & Mon. **Address:** 627 3rd Ave W 99501 **Location:** At F St; downtown. **Parking:** street. **Cards:** AX, DC, MC, VI. **Historic**

(See map and index starting on p. 726)

MIDDLE WAY CAFE
Phone: 907/272-6433   (19)

Vegetarian
$5-$10

Considered one of the city's best vegetarian restaurants, the casual coffeehouse is tucked away from crowds in a small shopping plaza. Patrons can look to the blackboard for a choice of sandwiches, smoothies and homemade soups, most of which are organic. The funky, upbeat atmosphere draws on a variety of characters. It's not unusual to stumble upon musicians playing an impromptu concert out front. Casual dress. **Reservations:** not accepted. **Hours:** 7 am-6:30 pm, Sat from 8 am, Sun 9 am-5 pm. Closed major holidays. **Address:** 1200 W Northern Lights Blvd 99503 **Location:** Jct Arctic and Northern Lights blvds; in shopping plaza. **Parking:** on-site. **Cards:** MC, VI.

MOOSE'S TOOTH PUB & PIZZERIA
Phone: 907/258-2537   (20)

American
$6-$10

This rustic hangout with a bustling, casual atmosphere is popular with locals and tourists alike, so expect a long wait as no reservations are accepted. The specialty is gourmet pizzas, and they come with regular or thick crust; red sauce, green sauce or sauceless; assorted meats, steak, chicken, seafood or vegetable toppings; cheeses ranging from mozzarella and provolone to gorganzola, parmesan, cheddar and feta. Also featured are sodas and beers brewed in their own brewery. Casual dress. **Bar:** Beer & wine. **Hours:** 11 am-11:30 pm, Fri & Sat-midnight. Closed: 3/23, 11/27, 12/25. **Address:** 3300 Old Seward Hwy 99503 **Location:** Old Seward Hwy at 34th St. **Parking:** on-site. **Cards:** AX, DC, DS, MC, VI.

PEPPER MILL
Phone: 907/561-0800   (25)

Steak House
$14-$40

This unique steakhouse offers up hearty portions of sizzling steaks and prime rib that can be topped off with their wide variety of exotic peppers. Each table has a series of pepper mills that are filled with a selection of peppercorns from around the world — a perfect way to experiment with different taste sensations. The owner has also collected some interesting pepper shakers that are displayed throughout the dining room. Casual dress. **Bar:** Full bar. **Hours:** 4 pm-10 pm, Fri & Sat-11 pm. Closed: 11/27, 12/25. **Address:** 4101 Credit Union Dr 99503 **Location:** Jct C and 40th sts. **Parking:** on-site. **Cards:** AX, DC, DS, MC, VI.

PETER'S SUSHI SPOT
Phone: 907/276-5188   (26)

Japanese
$8-$20

A real gem offering some of the most delightful sushi around. The menu is made up of a wide variety of specialty and imported ingredients and served by a casual but friendly staff. Patrons can enjoy dining either at the sushi bar or at a traditional table. Casual dress. **Bar:** Beer & wine. **Hours:** 11 am-10 pm, Fri-11 pm, Sat 4 pm-11 pm, Sun 4 pm-10 pm. Closed major holidays. **Address:** 4140 13 St 99503 **Location:** Just n of E Tudor Rd. **Parking:** on-site. **Cards:** MC, VI.

PHYLLIS'S CAFE AND SALMON BAKE
Phone: 907/274-6576   (8)

American
$8-$39

Diners will enjoy the great menu variety of hearty portions of home-cooked fare for breakfast, lunch or dinner. The large covered outdoor patio lets guests enjoy the long days in the summer months. The menu features a good selection of hot and cold appetizers, the ever-popular chowder in a bread bowl, a variety of pastas, steaks and ribs and of course the fresh Alaska halibut and salmon. A tasting of local beers is a great way to dine like Alaskans. Casual dress. **Bar:** Full bar. **Hours:** 8 am-11 pm; hours may vary off season. Closed: 1/1, 11/27, 12/25. **Address:** 436 D St 99501 **Location:** Jct 5th Ave. **Parking:** street. **Cards:** AX, DC, DS, MC, VI.

RISTORANTE ORSO
Phone: 907/222-3232   (15)

Regional Italian
$9-$37

You'll enjoy the regional Italian cuisine in this newest addition to the downtown Anchorage restaurant scene. The chef's creativity shines with dishes such as prosciutto-wrapped halibut with carmelized onion relish. Pasta lovers would enjoy the wild mushroom ravioli. Please save room for the in-house prepared desserts, especially the marscapone chocolate cheesecake. Casual dress. **Bar:** Full bar. **Reservations:** suggested. **Hours:** 11:30 am-4 & 5-10 pm, Fri-11 pm, Sat 5 pm-11 pm, Sun 5 pm-10 pm. Closed: 7/4, 11/27, 12/25. **Address:** 737 W 5th Ave 99501 **Location:** Centre. **Parking:** on-site (fee) and street. **Cards:** AX, DC, DS, MC, VI.

CALL

ROYAL FORK BUFFET
Phone: 907/522-5600   (33)

American
$9-$13

The Royal Fork features buffet-style dining with a wide variety of freshly made choices, including sugar-free desserts. Families can be fed for an excellent value. Dinner prices are in effect starting at 4 pm Monday through Saturday and all day on Sunday and major holidays. Casual dress. **Hours:** 11 am-8:30 pm, Fri & Sat-9 pm, Sun 10 am-8 pm. Closed major holidays. **Address:** 9220 Old Seward Hwy 99515 **Location:** Just s of E Dimond Blvd. **Parking:** on-site. **Cards:** DS, MC, VI.

SACK'S CAFE & RESTAURANT
Phone: 907/274-4022   (5)

International
$10-$34

In a word, the restaurant is delightful. The chic choice's menu draws largely on area ingredients, including fresh salmon, scallops and halibut. Thai and Asian influences are abundant. At lunch, sandwiches and casual fare are at the heart of the offerings; dinner is a bit more complex, with several entrees that change nightly as the season changes. Casual dress. **Bar:** Beer & wine. **Reservations:** suggested. **Hours:** 11 am-2:30 & 5-9 pm, Fri-10:30 pm, Sat 10 am-2:30 & 5-10:30 pm, Sun 10 am-2:30 & 5-9:30 pm; Sun-Thurs to 9 pm 10/1-5/31. Closed: major holidays, 12/24. **Address:** 328 G St 99501 **Location:** Between 3rd and 4th aves; downtown. **Parking:** street. **Cards:** AX, DC, MC, VI.

SEA GALLEY
Phone: 907/563-3520   (24)

Seafood
$9-$55

A great place to dine for those in the mood for seafood, the restaurant features a distinct nautical decor complete with fish nets and a wide selection of fresh fish and seafood cooked up in a variety of ways. Dinners include tasty chowder or an all-you-can-eat salad bar. Desserts are a highlight here; a huge display case filled with sweet treats sits near the dining room entrance. Casual dress. **Bar:** Full bar. **Hours:** 11 am-11 pm, Fri & Sat-1 am, Sun noon-10 pm. **Address:** 4101 Credit Union Dr 99503 **Location:** Jct C St and 40th. **Parking:** on-site. **Cards:** AX, DC, DS, MC, VI.

(See map and index starting on p. 726)

SIMON & SEAFORTS
Phone: 907/274-3502 — 9

▽▽▽

Regional American
$8-$48

This local favorite specializes in fresh, creatively prepared seafood flown in daily from Homer. Angus beef from Nebraska, pasta and chicken are also good. The dining room has a scenic inlet view. Try their world-famous sipping dessert, brandy ice! Casual dress. **Bar:** Full bar. **Reservations:** suggested. **Hours:** 11 am-2:30 & 5-9:30 pm, Fri-10 pm, Sat 4:30 pm-10 pm, Sun 4:30 pm-9 pm. Closed: 11/27, 12/25. **Address:** 420 L St 99501 **Location:** Between 4th and 5th aves; downtown; overlooking Cook Inlet. **Parking:** street. **Cards:** AX, DC, MC, VI.

CALL 🔊M

SKYFIRE CAFE
Phone: 907/561-2969 — 29

▽

American
$8-$10

In a small roadside mall, the simple cafe and bakery serves fantastic breakfasts and great sandwiches for lunch. Patrons find great value for the dollar. The menu offers a choice of various omelets and hearty sandwiches. Those in a hurry can grab one of the massive cinnamon buns or muffins. **Reservations:** not accepted. **Hours:** 11 am-3 pm; Sunday brunch 10 am-2 pm. Closed major holidays; also Sat. **Address:** 5701 Lake Otis Pkwy, Suite 600 99507 **Location:** Old Seward Hwy, exit 36th Ave, 2 mi e, then 2 mi s. **Parking:** on-site. **Cards:** DS, MC, VI.

SNOW CITY CAFE
Phone: 907/272-2489 — 10

▽▽▽ ▽▽▽

American
$5-$10

It's all but guaranteed that a line will form on Saturday morning at the popular spot, and it is definitely worth the wait. Home to an all-day breakfast, this one has been ranked highly by city residents. The cafe bustles with energy during the breakfast and lunch hours and provides an upbeat atmosphere in which to enjoy hearty, delicious food. Casual dress. **Bar:** Beer & wine. **Reservations:** not accepted. **Hours:** 7 am-3 pm, Sat & Sun-4 pm. Closed major holidays. **Address:** 1034 W 4th Ave 99501 **Location:** Jct L St; downtown. **Parking:** street. **Cards:** AX, DS, MC, VI.

🅰🅲

SNOW GOOSE RESTAURANT
Phone: 907/277-7727 — 2

▽▽▽ ▽▽

American
$9-$30

Those looking for a pint of locally brewed beer might visit this great stop, which also offers views of the Cook Inlet and shipyard. Upstairs is a casual pub-type atmosphere, and downstairs, though still casual, is more of a restaurant. Service can be unpredictable, but the food and view make a visit worthwhile. Casual dress. **Bar:** Full bar. **Reservations:** suggested. **Hours:** 11:30 am-midnight, Sat & Sun 5 pm-11 pm. Closed: 11/27, 12/25. **Address:** 717 W 3rd Ave 99501 **Location:** Corner of 3rd Ave and G St; downtown. **Parking:** street. **Cards:** AX, DC, DS, MC, VI.

SOUTHSIDE BISTRO — *Menu on AAA.com*
Phone: 907/348-0088 — 34

Ⓐ

▽▽▽▽ ▽

American
$8-$33

Located in the heart of a southside Anchorage business park is this little strip mall eatery with an upbeat and contemporary decor. The menu offers a wide variety of items to suit all tastes with cooking styles that defy classification. Fresh seafood, assorted meat dishes, pastas and thin crust pizzas are offered, all oozing with flavor and a creative bent. Lunch menus offer an additional selection of sandwiches. The wine list focuses mainly on western U.S. product. Casual dress. **Bar:** Beer & wine. **Reservations:** suggested. **Hours:** 11:30 am-10 pm, Fri & Sat-11 pm. Closed major holidays; also Sun & Mon. **Address:** 1320 Huffman Park Dr 99515 **Location:** 0.6 mi nw of US 1 (New Seward Hwy), exit Huffman Rd. **Parking:** on-site. **Cards:** AX, DS, MC, VI.

CALL 🔊M

SULLIVAN'S STEAKHOUSE
Phone: 907/258-2882 — 13

▽▽▽ ▽

Steak House
$8-$39

Named for John L. Sullivan, heavyweight champion of the world in the 1880s, the upscale steak house prepares a wide selection of steaks, chops and seafood. Decorated with black-and-white photographs of Sullivan, Jack Dempsey and other boxing legends. Casual dress. **Bar:** Full bar. **Reservations:** suggested. **Hours:** 11 am-10 pm. Closed: 11/27, 12/25. **Address:** 320 W 5th Ave 99501 **Location:** 5th Ave at C St. **Parking:** street. **Cards:** AX, MC, VI.

SUSHI YA JAPANESE RESTAURANT
Phone: 907/522-2244 — 32

▽▽▽ ▽▽

Japanese
$8-$23

This delightful restaurant features a distinct Japanese decor complete with sushi bar and fine Asian ornamental artifacts throughout. In addition to an outstanding sushi selection, diners can also choose from traditional favorites such as tempura and teriyaki entrees and combination plates. Most entrees include miso soup and salad. Casual dress. **Bar:** Full bar. **Hours:** 11:30 am-11 pm, Sat from noon, Sun 2 pm-10 pm. Closed: 7/4, 12/25. **Address:** 1111 E Dimond Blvd 99515 **Location:** Jct Old Seward Hwy. **Parking:** on-site. **Cards:** MC, VI.

SWEET BASIL CAFE
Phone: 907/274-0070 — 6

▽▽▽

Coffee/Espresso
$6-$10

Diners who enjoy homemade soups, freshly squeezed juices, large sandwiches and salads, and sumptuous desserts might find the casual, cozy cafe an appealing spot. Locals and visitors alike frequent this place. Casual dress. **Bar:** Full bar. **Reservations:** not accepted. **Hours:** 7:45 am-3 pm, Sat 9 am-4 pm. Closed major holidays; also Sun. **Address:** 335 E St 99501 **Location:** Downtown; across from Hilton Anchorage. **Parking:** street. **Cards:** AX, DC, MC, VI.

🅰🅲

THE TOP OF THE WORLD
Phone: 907/265-7111 — 4

▽▽▽ ▽▽

American
$21-$29

On the 15th floor of Westward Tower, the tiered dining room offers an excellent view of Anchorage Harbor and Ship Creek. The elegant yet casual atmosphere enables diners to enjoy a relaxing dinner after an active day of touring or shopping. On the menu are selections of seafood, beef and game with cooking twists that touch on an eclectic variety of International influences. If driving to the Hilton, inquire about validated valet parking. Dressy casual. **Bar:** Full bar. **Reservations:** suggested. **Hours:** 6 pm-10 pm. Closed: 11/27, 12/25. **Address:** 500 W 3rd Ave 99501 **Location:** At E St; downtown; in Hilton Anchorage. **Parking:** on-site (fee) and valet. **Cards:** AX, DC, DS, JC, MC, VI.

(See map and index starting on p. 726)

TURNAGAIN HOUSE

Steak & Seafood
$25-$35

Phone: 907/653-7500

The top reason to visit the restaurant is its coastal location. Although a bit of a drive from Anchorage, this place is well worth it for the steak and seafood, as well as the view. Guests who time their visit right might catch the tide coming in, which is a sight to see. Casual dress. **Bar:** Full bar. **Reservations:** suggested. **Hours:** Open 3/1-10/31 & 2/1-2/28; 5 pm-10 pm. Closed: Mon & Tues. **Address:** Milepost 103.1 New Seward Hwy 99511 **Location:** 16 mi s on US 1 (New Seward Hwy), Milepost 103.1. **Parking:** on-site. **Cards:** AX, DC, DS, MC, VI.

CALL

YEN KING CHINESE RESTAURANT

Chinese
$8-$20

Phone: 907/563-2627 21

A distinct Oriental decor and an expansive buffet of tasty Chinese cuisine make this place a favorite of both locals and tourists. The all-day buffet lines up a selection of soups, salads and Chinese favorites, including stir-fries, mixed Chinese greens and preparations of noodles, beef, chicken and pork. Those not in the mood for a buffet can browse the full a la carte menu or request food for takeout or hotel delivery. Casual dress. **Bar:** Full bar. **Hours:** 11 am-10 pm, Fri & Sat-11 pm. **Address:** 3501 Old Seaward Hwy 99503 **Location:** Jct 36th St. **Parking:** on-site. **Cards:** AX, DS, MC, VI.

CANTWELL pop. 222—See also DENALI NATIONAL PARK AND PRESERVE.

——— **WHERE TO STAY** ———

BACKWOODS LODGE

Motel
$130-$160 3/1-8/31
$100-$130 9/1-2/28

Phone: 907/768-2232

Address: Denali Hwy MM 133.8 99729 **Location:** Parks Hwy, (Milepost 210), just e on Denali Hwy. Located in a quiet area. **Facility:** Smoke free premises. 10 units. 9 one-bedroom standard units. 1 one-bedroom suite with kitchen. 1 story, exterior corridors. **Bath:** combo or shower only. **Parking:** on-site, winter plug-ins. **Terms:** 10 day cancellation notice-fee imposed. **Amenities:** hair dryers. **Leisure Activities:** pond with campfire area, shared barbecue on exterior walkway, hiking trails. **Cards:** AX, MC, VI. **Free Special Amenities:** local telephone calls and preferred room (subject to availability with advance reservations).** *(See color ad below)*

COOPER LANDING pop. 369

——— **WHERE TO STAY** ———

KENAI PRINCESS WILDERNESS LODGE   *Book at AAA.com*

Small-scale Hotel
$159-$239 5/17-9/14

Phone: (907)595-1425

Address: Mile 2 Bean Creek Rd 99572 **Location:** SR 1 (Sterling Hwy) at Milepost 47.8, just n of bridge, then 2.1 mi w. **Facility:** Smoke free premises. 86 one-bedroom standard units. 1 story, exterior corridors. **Bath:** combo or shower only. **Parking:** on-site. **Terms:** open 5/17-9/14, check-in 3:30 pm, 7 day cancellation notice-fee imposed. **Amenities:** hair dryers. **Dining:** Eagle's Crest Restaurant, see separate listing. **Leisure Activities:** whirlpools, fishing, hiking trails, limited exercise equipment, horseshoes, shuffleboard. **Fee:** charter fishing. **Guest Services:** coin laundry. **Business Services:** meeting rooms, PC. **Cards:** AX, DS, MC, VI.

——— **WHERE TO DINE** ———

EAGLE'S CREST RESTAURANT

Continental
$9-$30

Phone: 907/595-1425

Diners will enjoy the rustic lodge ambiance complete with country pine walls and ceilings and a huge stone fireplace. The main focus of the dining room is, however, the large panoramic windows that offer spectacular views of the mountains on a clear day. Light luncheon fare is featured including lots of salads, sandwiches and local fish and chips, and a more upscale dinner menu is also offered. Casual dress. **Bar:** Full bar. **Reservations:** suggested. **Hours:** Open 5/15-9/12; 7 am-11:30, noon-2:30 & 5:30-9:30 pm; hours may vary off season. **Address:** Mile 2, Bean Creek Rd 99572 **Location:** SR 1 (Sterling Hwy) at Milepost 47.8, just n of bridge, then 2.1 mi w; in Kenai Princess Wilderness Lodge. **Parking:** on-site. **Cards:** AX, MC, VI.

——— ▼ *See AAA listing above* ▼ ———

DENALI NATIONAL PARK AND PRESERVE —*See also CANTWELL & HEALY.*

——— **WHERE TO STAY** ———

DENALI BACKCOUNTRY LODGE   Phone: (907)376-1900
Cabin
$663-$900 6/4-9/12

Address: MM 95 Denali Park Rd 99755 **Location:** End of the 90 mi Denali National Park Rd. Located in Denali National Park. **Facility:** Smoke free premises. 38 one-bedroom standard units. 2 stories (no elevator), exterior corridors. *Bath:* shower only. **Parking:** on-site. **Terms:** open 6/4-9/12, check-out 6:15 am, cancellation fee imposed. **Leisure Activities:** fishing, recreation programs, bicycles, hiking trails. **Guest Services:** area transportation. **Cards:** MC, VI. *(See color ad p 319 & p 322)*

DENALI BLUFFS HOTEL   *Book great rates at AAA.com*   Phone: 907/683-7000
Small-scale Hotel
Rates not provided

Address: Milepost 238.4 Parks Hwy 99755 **Location:** 1 mi n of park entrance. **Facility:** Smoke free premises. 112 one-bedroom standard units. 2 stories (no elevator), exterior corridors. **Parking:** on-site. **Terms:** open 5/28-9/7. **Amenities:** voice mail, hair dryers. **Dining:** Mountaineer Bar & Grill, see separate listing. **Leisure Activities:** *Fee:* dinner theater. **Guest Services:** coin laundry, area transportation. *(See color ad p 744)*

DENALI CABINS   Phone: (907)683-2643
Cabin
$149-$249 6/1-9/4
$127-$212 9/5-9/12

Address: Milepost 229 Parks Hwy 99755 **Location:** 9 mi s of park entrance. **Facility:** Smoke free premises. 46 cabins. 1 story, exterior corridors. *Bath:* shower or tub only. **Parking:** on-site. **Terms:** open 6/1-9/12, office hours 6 am-10 pm, 60 day cancellation notice-fee imposed. **Amenities:** voice mail. **Leisure Activities:** whirlpools, hiking trails. **Guest Services:** area transportation. **Cards:** MC, VI.

DENALI PRINCESS LODGE   *Book at AAA.com*   Phone: (907)683-2282
Large-scale Hotel
$179-$269 5/14-9/21

Address: Milepost 238.5 99755 **Location:** SR 3 (Parks Hwy), 1.5 mi n of park entrance. **Facility:** Smoke free premises. 652 units. 649 one-bedroom standard units, some with whirlpools. 3 one-bedroom suites with whirlpools. 2-3 stories, interior/exterior corridors. *Bath:* combo or shower only. **Parking:** on-site. **Terms:** open 5/14-9/21, check-in 3:30 pm, 7 day cancellation notice-fee imposed. **Amenities:** voice mail, hair dryers. **Dining:** King Salmon, see separate listing. **Leisure Activities:** whirlpools, exercise room. *Fee:* massage. **Guest Services:** coin laundry, area transportation, beauty salon, tanning facilities. **Business Services:** meeting rooms, PC. **Cards:** AX, DC, DS, MC, VI.

AAA.com TripTik® Travel Planner

Makes It Easy

So you can take it easy

Whether your favorite getaway spot is the beach, the mountains or Main Street, the newly enhanced **AAA.com TripTik Travel Planner** tool is simply the best link to a great road trip:

- Use the exclusive Modify My Route tool to select preferred roadways.
- Book Diamond rated hotels at great member rates.
- Peruse destinations and find the best things to see and do.
- Get a heads-up on detours and road construction, and so much more.

TripTik Travel Planner is simply better...
Plan on it!

AAA.com

GRANDE DENALI LODGE   *Book great rates at AAA.com*
Phone: 907/683-8500

AAA (SAVE)

▼▼ ▼▼

Small-scale Hotel
Rates not provided

Address: Milepost 238.2 George Parks Hwy 99755 **Location:** SR 3 (Parks Hwy), at Milepost 238.2, on east side of road, ne on Grande Dr. Located in a rustic area. **Facility:** 165 units. 159 one-bedroom standard units. 6 cabins. 4 stories, interior/exterior corridors. **Bath:** combo or shower only. **Parking:** on-site. **Terms:** open 5/18-9/13. **Amenities:** voice mail, hair dryers. **Dining:** Alpenglow, see separate listing. **Leisure Activities:** hiking trails. *Fee:* dinner theater. **Guest Services:** coin laundry, area transportation-within 5 mi. **Business Services:** meeting rooms, PC. *(See color ad below)*

🛏️ 🍽️ CALL 📞M ✕ 💻 / SOME UNITS 🛎️

MCKINLEY CHALET RESORT   *Book great rates at AAA.com*
Phone: (907)683-8200

AAA (SAVE)

▼▼ ▼▼

Large-scale Hotel
$279 5/13-9/18

Address: Milepost 238 (Parks Hwy) 99755 **Location:** Milepost 238.5 on SR 3 (Parks Hwy). **Facility:** 480 units. 190 one-bedroom standard units. 290 one-bedroom suites. 2-3 stories, interior/exterior corridors. **Bath:** combo or shower only. **Parking:** on-site, winter plug-ins. **Terms:** open 5/13-9/18, 30 day cancellation notice-fee imposed. **Amenities:** voice mail, hair dryers. **Dining:** Nenana View Grille, see separate listing. **Leisure Activities:** recreation programs, hiking trails, basketball, horseshoes, volleyball. *Fee:* rafting, massage. **Guest Services:** coin laundry, area transportation. **Cards:** AX, DS, MC, VI. **Free Special Amenities:** local telephone calls. *(See color ad below)*

$🛏️ 🛏️ 🍽️ CALL 📞M ✕ ✕ 🎿 💻 / SOME UNITS 🐾 🛎️

MCKINLEY CREEKSIDE CABINS   *Book great rates at AAA.com*
Phone: (907)683-2277

AAA (SAVE)

▼▼ ▼▼

Cabin
$139-$199 6/1-9/15
$89-$149 5/15-5/31

Address: Milepost 224 Parks Hwy 99755 **Location:** 13 mi s; Milepost 224 on SR 3 (Parks Hwy). **Facility:** Smoke free premises. 30 cabins. 1 story, exterior corridors. **Bath:** shower only. **Parking:** on-site. **Terms:** open 5/15-9/15, office hours 6 am-11 pm, 14 day cancellation notice. **Dining:** Creekside Cafe, see separate listing. **Leisure Activities:** hiking trails, playground, horseshoes. **Cards:** DS, MC, VI. **Free Special Amenities:** high-speed Internet.

$🛏️ 🛏️ CALL 📞M ✕ ✕ 🎿 📺 🚭 / SOME UNITS 🛎️ 🖥️ 💻

NORTH FACE LODGE
Phone: (907)683-2290

▼▼ ▼▼

Motel
$2730 6/6-9/12

Address: Milepost 89 Denali National Park Rd 99755 **Location:** Milepost 89 Denali National Park Rd. **Facility:** Smoke free premises. 15 units. 14 one- and 1 two-bedroom standard units. 1 story, exterior corridors. **Parking:** on-site. **Terms:** open 6/6-9/12, office hours 8 am-4 pm, check-out 6:45 am, 3-4 night minimum stay - seasonal, 60 day cancellation notice, rate reflects 3 night all inclusive-fee imposed. **Leisure Activities:** canoeing, boat dock, fishing, recreation programs, bicycles, hiking trails, jogging. **Guest Services:** area transportation.

✕ ✕ 🎿 📺 🚭

——— **The following lodging was either not evaluated or did not** ———
meet AAA rating requirements but is listed for your information only.

CAMP DENALI   Phone: 907/683-2290
[fyi]   Not evaluated. **Address:** Milepost 89 Denali National Park Rd 99755 Facilities, services, and decor
characterize a basic property.

——— **WHERE TO DINE** ———

ALPENGLOW   Phone: 907/683-8720
▼▼ ▼▼   Take the drive one mile up to enjoy this restaurant perched on the side of a mountain, featuring a full
windowed dining room with spectacular panoramic views of Denali. Grilled fresh Alaskan Salmon is a
Regional American   favorite of many diners. Casual dress. **Bar:** Full bar. **Reservations:** accepted. **Hours:** Open 5/15-9/14; 5-
$7-$32   10:30 am, 11-2:30 & 5-11 pm. **Address:** Milepost 238.2 Parks Hwy 99707 **Location:** SR 3 (Parks Hwy), at
Milepost 238.2, on east side of road on Grande Dr; in Grande Denali Lodge. **Parking:** on-site. **Cards:** AX,
CB, DC, DS, MC, VI.
CALL [&M]

CREEKSIDE CAFE   Phone: 907/683-2277
(AAA)   Though the decor and service is simple, the cafe's food is hearty and delicious. You'll find a wide selection
of sandwiches and salads, as well as one of the best breakfasts in the park. At the front of the restaurant is
▼▼   a large dessert case featuring selections such as cookies, squares, cinnamon buns and cakes. Casual
dress. **Bar:** Beer & wine. **Hours:** Open 5/15-9/15; 6 am-10 pm. **Address:** Milepost 224 Parks Hwy 99755
Regional   **Location:** 13 mi s; Milepost 224 on SR 3 (Parks Hwy); in McKinley Creekside Cabins. **Parking:** on-site.
American   **Cards:** DS, MC, VI.
$7-$24   [Ⓚ]

KING SALMON   Phone: 907/683-2282
▼▼▼▼   This spacious restaurant adjacent to the Princess Lodge satisfies those looking to feast on tasty Alaskan
seafood dishes while enjoying a view that is spectacular. Sure to be a favorite at your table, the seafood
Regional American   sampler consists of tempura prawns, pan seared halibut and Alaskan crab cake. Casual dress.
$5-$30   Entertainment. **Bar:** Full bar. **Reservations:** accepted. **Hours:** Open 5/15-9/16; 5-10:30 am, 11-2 & 5-10
pm. **Address:** Milepost 238.5 99755 **Location:** 1.5 mi n of park entrance; in Denali Princess Lodge.
Parking: on-site. **Cards:** AX, DC, DS, MC, VI.
[Ⓚ]

MORINO GRILL   Phone: 907/683-2294
▼▼ ▼▼   This grill located adjacent to the Denali Visitor Center is comprised of a full-service coffeeshop barista
station, a grill area in which your selection is made to order featuring grilled panini and a premade pack-
American   and-go station for your picnic lunch in the park. Casual dress. **Hours:** Open 5/15-9/15; 8 am-7 pm.
$5-$10   **Address:** Denali Visitor Center 99755 **Location:** At Denali Visitor Center. **Parking:** on-site. **Cards:** MC, VI.
CALL [&M] [Ⓚ]

MOUNTAINEER BAR & GRILL   Phone: 907/683-8889
▼▼ ▼▼   The restaurant offers a nice change of pace with Italian selections. Items are freshly prepared and flavorful.
The dining room has an early 1900s theme with log walls, antique outdoor decorative items and windows for
Italian   viewing the mountains. Casual dress. **Bar:** Full bar. **Hours:** Open 5/15-9/15; 5 am-10 pm.
$6-$24   **Address:** Milepost 238.4 George Parks Hwy 99755 **Location:** 1 mi n of park entrance; in Denali Bluffs
Hotel. **Parking:** on-site. **Cards:** AX, DC, DS, MC, VI.

NENANA VIEW GRILLE   Phone: 907/683-8258
▼▼▼▼   This contemporary restaurant, one of the newest in Denali, features a wide variety of Alaskan fare, ranging
from salmon to chowder and delectable desserts; the lounge is a great place to relax and unwind. Casual
American   dress. **Bar:** Full bar. **Reservations:** suggested. **Hours:** Open 5/15-9/15; 6 am-10:30 pm. **Address:** Milepost
$12-$28   238 Parks Hwy 99755 **Location:** Milepost 238.5 on SR 3 (Parks Hwy); in McKinley Chalet Resort. **Parking:**
on-site. **Cards:** AX, DC, DS, MC, VI.
CALL [&M]

THE PERCH   Phone: 907/683-2523
▼▼ ▼▼   As the name suggests, The Perch sits nestled on a side of a mountain, offering incredible views of the
Denali Mountain Range. The fragrance of freshly baked bread envelops you as you approach the dining
Regional American   room, and again as a loaf is placed on your table. The planked Salmon and halibut with herbed butter
$7-$31   melting on top is the specialty of the house. Casual dress. **Bar:** Full bar. **Hours:** 6 am-10 pm; Fri & Sat from
5 pm 5/1-9/15. **Address:** Milepost 224 (George Parks Hwy) 99755 **Location:** 11 mi s of Denali National
Park entrance; follow signs up hill. **Parking:** on-site. **Cards:** AX, DS, MC, VI.
[Ⓚ]

DENALI STATE PARK

──────── **WHERE TO STAY** ────────

MT. MCKINLEY PRINCESS WILDERNESS LODGE   *Book at AAA.com*   Phone: 907/733-2900

▼▼▼
Resort
Large-scale Hotel
$149-$189 5/15-9/16

Address: Milepost 133.1 99683 **Location:** SR 3 (George Parks Hwy), Milepost 133.1, 1 mi e on Mt McKinley View Rd. **Facility:** The hotel and some of the guest rooms offer exceptional views of Mt. McKinley when the mountain is not shrouded in clouds; the guest rooms feature a contemporary, mountain-wilderness motif. Smoke free premises. 460 units. 454 one-bedroom standard units. 6 one-bedroom suites with whirlpools. 2 stories (no elevator), interior/exterior corridors. *Bath:* combo or shower only. **Parking:** on-site. **Terms:** open 5/15-9/16, check-in 3:30 pm, cancellation fee imposed. **Amenities:** voice mail, hair dryers. **Leisure Activities:** whirlpools, recreation programs, hiking trails, playground, limited exercise equipment. *Fee:* horseback riding. **Guest Services:** coin laundry, area transportation (fee). **Cards:** AX, DS, MC, VI.

🛏️ 🍽️ CALL 🅼 ⊗ ⊠ 🏌️ 📺 📷 🍽️ 🖥️ / SOME UNITS ♿

EAGLE RIVER

──────── **WHERE TO STAY** ────────

EAGLE RIVER MICROTEL INN & SUITES   *Book great rates at AAA.com*   Phone: (907)622-6000

🅰🅰🅰 SAVE
▼▼▼
Small-scale Hotel
$120-$160 All Year

Address: 13049 Old Glenn Hwy 99577 **Location:** Jct Glenn Hwy (SR 1), exit Eagle River, just e, then just s. **Facility:** 60 one-bedroom standard units. 3 stories, interior corridors. **Parking:** on-site, winter plug-ins. **Amenities:** high-speed Internet, voice mail. **Leisure Activities:** exercise room. **Business Services:** meeting rooms. **Cards:** AX, DC, DS, MC, VI. **Free Special Amenities: continental breakfast and high-speed Internet.**

🆂🅳 🏌️ 📷 / SOME UNITS FEE 🐾 ⊠ ♿ 🖥️ 🖥️

EAGLE RIVER MOTEL   Phone: 907/694-5000

🅰🅰🅰 SAVE
▼
Motel
$54-$169 All Year

Address: 11111 Old Eagle River Rd 99577 **Location:** Glenn Hwy, exit Eagle River, just e; center. Located in a residential area. **Facility:** Smoke free premises. 14 one-bedroom standard units, some with efficiencies or kitchens. 3 stories (no elevator), exterior corridors. **Parking:** on-site, winter plug-ins. **Terms:** 3 day cancellation notice. **Amenities:** video library (fee), high-speed Internet, voice mail. *Some:* DVD players (fee). **Guest Services:** complimentary laundry, wireless Internet. **Business Services:** PC. **Cards:** AX, DS, MC, VI. **Free Special Amenities: local telephone calls and high-speed Internet.**

⊠ 🏌️ 📷 ♿ 🖥️ 🖥️ / SOME UNITS FEE 🐾

──────── **WHERE TO DINE** ────────

HAUTE QUARTER GRILL   Phone: 907/622-4745

▼▼▼
American
$8-$30

This locally-popular restaurant offers upscale cuisine in a relaxed, casual atmosphere. Food is well prepared using fresh ingredients and the kitchen shows its creative and innovative talent in many of the preparations. The flavorful creations and attentive staff combine to make this an enjoyable experience. Casual dress. **Bar:** Full bar. **Reservations:** accepted. **Hours:** 11 am-2 & 5-10 pm, Sat from 5 pm. Closed major holidays; also Sun & Mon. **Address:** 11221 Old Glenn Hwy 99577 **Location:** Jct Glenn Hwy (SR 1), exit Eagle River, just e. **Parking:** on-site. **Cards:** AX, DS, MC, VI.

FAIRBANKS pop. 30,224

──────── **WHERE TO STAY** ────────

A BED AND BREAKFAST INN ON MINNIE STREET   *Book great rates at AAA.com*   Phone: (907)456-1802

🅰🅰🅰 SAVE
▼▼▼
Bed & Breakfast
$129-$249 3/1-9/30
$75-$199 10/1-2/28

Address: 345 Minnie St 99701 **Location:** Just n of downtown, follow Cushman St over Bridge to Illinois St, 0.5 mi n, then just e. Located in a residential area. **Facility:** Contemporary rooms that vary in size and style are offered at this B&B, which is made up of two detached houses connected by a lovely private garden area and deck. Smoke free premises. 12 units. 9 one-bedroom standard units, some with kitchens and/or whirlpools. 3 one-bedroom suites, some with kitchens. 2 stories (no elevator), interior/exterior corridors. *Bath:* combo or shower only. **Parking:** on-site, winter plug-ins. **Terms:** 21 day cancellation notice-fee imposed. **Amenities:** video library. *Some:* DVD players, CD players, irons. **Leisure Activities:** whirlpool, barbecue. **Guest Services:** coin laundry. **Business Services:** PC. **Cards:** AX, DC, DS, MC, VI. **Free Special Amenities: full breakfast and high-speed Internet.**

⊠ 📷 / SOME UNITS 🏌️ VCR ♿ 🖥️ 🖥️

ALL SEASONS INN   *Book great rates at AAA.com*   Phone: (907)451-6649

🅰🅰🅰 SAVE
▼▼▼
Bed & Breakfast
$85-$195 All Year

Address: 763 7th Ave 99701 **Location:** Just w of Barnette St; downtown. Located in a residential area. **Facility:** This well-tended, European-style property features an attractive lobby and is within walking distance of shopping and restaurants; rooms vary in size yet all are pleasantly and comfortably decorated. Smoke free premises. 8 one-bedroom standard units. 2 stories (no elevator), interior corridors. **Parking:** on-site, winter plug-ins. **Terms:** office hours 8 am-6 pm, check-in 4 pm, 21 day cancellation notice-fee imposed. **Amenities:** video library. **Leisure Activities:** board games in sun room, library. **Guest Services:** coin laundry. **Business Services:** meeting rooms, PC. **Cards:** AX, CB, DC, DS, JC, MC, VI. **Free Special Amenities: full breakfast and high-speed Internet.**

CALL 🅼 ⊠ 📷 / SOME UNITS VCR

ALPINE LODGE, LLC   *Book at AAA.com*   Phone: (907)455-4413

▼▼▼
Small-scale Hotel
$89-$199 All Year

Address: 4920 Dale Rd 99709 **Location:** 0.3 mi from Fairbanks International Airport. **Facility:** 113 units. 111 one-bedroom standard units, some with efficiencies and/or whirlpools. 2 one-bedroom suites with efficiencies and whirlpools. 3 stories, interior corridors. *Bath:* combo or shower only. **Parking:** on-site, winter plug-ins. **Terms:** 3 day cancellation notice-fee imposed. **Amenities:** voice mail, irons, hair dryers. **Leisure Activities:** sauna, limited exercise equipment. **Guest Services:** valet and coin laundry, wireless Internet. **Cards:** AX, DC, DS, MC, VI.

 🆂🅳 ⊷ ⊠ 📷 ♿ 🖥️ 🖥️

A TASTE OF ALASKA LODGE   *Book great rates at AAA.com*   Phone: (907)488-7855

Bed & Breakfast
$185-$235 All Year

Address: 551 Eberhardt Rd 99712 **Location:** 4.5 mi ne on US 2 (Steese Hwy), 5.3 mi e on Chena Hot Springs Rd, 0.5 mi s, then follow signs. Located in a quiet secluded area. **Facility:** Seclusion and a rustic elegance characterize this B&B, which is located on the outskirts of town; from the main lodge and breakfast room you can take in breaktaking views of an endless rolling Alaskan landscape. Smoke free premises. 10 units. 8 one-bedroom standard units. 2 cabins, some with whirlpools. 2 stories (no elevator), interior/exterior corridors. *Bath:* combo or shower only. **Parking:** on-site, winter plug-ins. **Terms:** cancellation fee imposed. **Amenities:** video library, high-speed Internet, voice mail, hair dryers. *Some:* CD players, irons. **Leisure Activities:** sauna, whirlpool, cross country skiing, hiking trails, limited exercise equipment, horseshoes. *Fee:* dog mushing, gold panning. **Business Services:** meeting rooms. **Cards:** AX, MC, VI. **Free Special Amenities:** full breakfast and high-speed Internet.

CALL ⓂⒶ ⊗ ⊠ ⒶⒸ / SOME UNITS Ⓥ🅒🅡 ▯ 🖼 ▯

BEST WESTERN FAIRBANKS INN   *Book great rates at AAA.com*   Phone: 907/456-6602

Small-scale Hotel
Rates not provided

Address: 1521 S Cushman St 99701 **Location:** Just s of Airport Way. **Facility:** Smoke free premises. 102 one-bedroom standard units, some with whirlpools. 2 stories (no elevator), interior corridors. **Parking:** on-site, winter plug-ins. **Amenities:** voice mail, irons, hair dryers. *Some:* high-speed Internet. **Guest Services:** valet and coin laundry, area transportation, wireless Internet. **Business Services:** PC.

🛬 🍴 Ⓨ CALL ⓂⒶ 🚶‍♂️ ⊠ 🎥 ▯ 🖼 ▯
/ SOME UNITS FEE 🐕

AAA Benefit:
Members save 10% everyday, plus an exclusive frequent stay program.

BRIDGEWATER HOTEL   *Book at AAA.com*   Phone: (907)452-6661

Small-scale Hotel
$169 5/15-9/15

Address: 723 1st Ave 99701 **Location:** Just w of Cushman St; downtown. **Facility:** Smoke free premises. 94 one-bedroom standard units. 5 stories, interior corridors. *Bath:* combo or shower only. **Parking:** on-site, winter plug-ins. **Terms:** open 5/15-9/15. **Amenities:** hair dryers. **Guest Services:** valet laundry, area transportation. **Cards:** AX, DC, DS, MC, VI.

ⒶⓈⓀ 🅢🅓 🛬 🍴 CALL ⓂⒶ FEE 🚶‍♂️ ⊠ 🎥 ▯

COMFORT INN-CHENA RIVER   *Book at AAA.com*   Phone: (907)479-8080

Small-scale Hotel
Rates not provided

Address: 1908 Chena Landings Loop 99701 **Location:** Airport Way, just n on Peger Rd, then just e on Phillips Field Rd, follow signs in wooded area south of road. Located in a quiet area. **Facility:** 74 one-bedroom standard units, some with whirlpools. 3 stories, interior corridors. *Bath:* combo or shower only. **Parking:** on-site, winter plug-ins. **Terms:** check-in 4 pm. **Amenities:** video games (fee), irons, hair dryers. **Pool(s):** heated indoor. **Leisure Activities:** whirlpool. **Guest Services:** valet and coin laundry, area transportation, wireless Internet. **Business Services:** meeting rooms, PC.

🛬 CALL ⓂⒶ 🏊 🎥 ▯ / SOME UNITS FEE 🐕 ⊠ ▯ 🖼

EXTENDED STAY DELUXE   *Book at AAA.com*   Phone: (907)457-2288

Small-scale Hotel
$167-$185 3/1-9/16
$113-$125 9/17-2/28

Address: 4580 Old Airport Rd 99709 **Location:** Near jct Parks Hwy and Airport Rd. **Facility:** 97 units. 94 one- and 2 two-bedroom standard units, some with whirlpools. 1 one-bedroom suite with efficiency (no utensils). 2 stories, interior corridors. *Bath:* combo or shower only. **Parking:** on-site. **Amenities:** voice mail, irons, hair dryers. *Fee:* video library, high-speed Internet. *Some:* video games. **Pool(s):** heated indoor. **Leisure Activities:** whirlpool, limited exercise equipment. **Guest Services:** valet and coin laundry, area transportation. **Business Services:** meeting rooms, PC, Cards: AX, DC, DS, JC, MC, VI.

ⒶⓈⓀ 🅢🅓 🛬 🍴 CALL ⓂⒶ 🏊 Ⓥ🅒🅡 🎥 ▯ 🖼 ▯ / SOME UNITS ⊠

FAIRBANKS DOWNTOWN BED & BREAKFAST

Bed & Breakfast
$115-$120 5/15-9/1

Book great rates at AAA.com

Phone: (907)452-7700

Address: 1461 Gillam Way 99701 **Location:** Jct Airport and Gillam ways, just s. Located in a residential area. **Facility:** Smoke free premises. 5 one-bedroom standard units. 2 stories (no elevator), interior corridors. *Bath:* combo or shower only. **Parking:** on-site, winter plug-ins. **Terms:** open 5/15-9/1, 14 day cancellation notice. **Cards:** AX, DS, MC, VI. **Free Special Amenities: continental breakfast and high-speed Internet.**

FAIRBANKS PRINCESS RIVERSIDE LODGE

Large-scale Hotel
$99-$199 All Year

Book at AAA.com

Phone: (907)455-4477

Address: 4477 Pikes Landing Rd 99709 **Location:** Jct Airport and Pikes Landing rds, just nw. **Facility:** 325 units. 322 one-bedroom standard units, some with whirlpools. 3 one-bedroom suites, some with efficiencies and/or whirlpools. 3 stories, interior corridors. *Bath:* combo or shower only. **Parking:** on-site, winter plug-ins. **Terms:** check-in 3:30 pm, 7 day cancellation notice-fee imposed. **Amenities:** voice mail, irons, hair dryers. *Some:* fax. **Leisure Activities:** steamrooms, hiking trails, exercise room, horseshoes. **Guest Services:** valet and coin laundry, area transportation, wireless Internet. **Business Services:** conference facilities, PC. **Cards:** AX, DC, MC, VI.

PIKE'S WATERFRONT LODGE

Small-scale Hotel
$75-$550 All Year

Book great rates at AAA.com

Phone: (907)456-4500

Address: 1850 Hoselton Rd 99709 **Location:** Jct Airport and Hoselton rds. **Facility:** 208 units. 179 one-bedroom standard units, some with whirlpools. 1 one-bedroom suite. 28 cabins. 1-3 stories, interior/exterior corridors. *Bath:* combo or shower only. **Parking:** on-site, winter plug-ins. **Terms:** cancellation fee imposed. **Amenities:** voice mail, irons, hair dryers. *Some:* video games (fee), high-speed Internet. **Leisure Activities:** sauna, steamroom, exercise room. *Fee:* game room. **Guest Services:** valet and coin laundry, area transportation-train station, wireless Internet. **Business Services:** meeting rooms, PC. **Cards:** AX, CB, DC, DS, MC, VI. **Free Special Amenities: local telephone calls and high-speed Internet.** *(See color ad below)*

REGENCY FAIRBANKS HOTEL

Small-scale Hotel
Rates not provided

Phone: 907/459-2700

Address: 95 10th Ave 99701 **Location:** Just w of SR 2 (Steese Expwy). **Facility:** 128 units. 114 one-and 2 two-bedroom standard units with efficiencies, some with whirlpools. 9 one- and 3 two-bedroom suites with kitchens, some with whirlpools. 3 stories, interior corridors. **Parking:** on-site, winter plug-ins. **Amenities:** high-speed Internet, voice mail, hair dryers. **Leisure Activities:** exercise room. **Guest Services:** valet and coin laundry, area transportation-train station. **Business Services:** meeting rooms, PC.

RIVER'S EDGE RESORT   *Book great rates at AAA.com*   Phone: (907)474-0286

Cabin
$149-$240 6/1-9/12
$109-$194 5/19-5/31

Address: 4200 Boat St 99709 **Location:** Airport Way, just n on Sportsman Way, then 0.5 mi w. **Facility:** 94 units. 8 one-bedroom standard units. 86 cabins. 2 stories (no elevator), interior/exterior corridors. **Parking:** on-site, winter plug-ins. **Terms:** open 5/19-9/12. **Amenities:** voice mail, hair dryers. **Dining:** Chena's Fine Dining & Deck, see separate listing. **Guest Services:** coin laundry, area transportation-train station, wireless Internet. **Business Services:** meeting rooms, business center. **Cards:** AX, DS, MC, VI. *(See color ad below)*

SOPHIE STATION HOTEL   *Book at AAA.com*   Phone: (907)479-3650

Condominium
$120-$235 All Year

Address: 1717 University Ave S 99709 **Location:** Airport Way, just s. **Facility:** 148 units. 8 one-bedroom standard units with kitchens, some with whirlpools. 140 one-bedroom suites with kitchens. 3 stories, interior corridors. *Bath:* combo or shower only. **Parking:** on-site, winter plug-ins. **Terms:** cancellation fee imposed. **Amenities:** voice mail, irons, hair dryers. *Some:* high-speed Internet (fee). **Guest Services:** valet and coin laundry, area transportation, wireless Internet. **Business Services:** meeting rooms, PC. **Cards:** AX, DC, DS, MC, VI.

SUPER 8 MOTEL   *Book at AAA.com*   Phone: 907/451-8888

Motel
Rates not provided

Address: 1909 Airport Way 99701 **Location:** Airport Way at Wilbur St. Located near Pioneer Park. **Facility:** 77 one-bedroom standard units. 3 stories (no elevator), interior corridors. **Parking:** on-site, winter plug-ins. **Amenities:** video games (fee), safes. **Guest Services:** coin laundry, area transportation. **Business Services:** meeting rooms.

WEDGEWOOD RESORT   *Book at AAA.com*   Phone: (907)452-1442

Condominium
$95-$195 All Year

Address: 212 Wedgewood Dr 99701 **Location:** Johanson Expwy, 1 mi w on College Rd to Margaret Dr, then just n. **Facility:** 460 units. 155 one-bedroom standard units. 233 one- and 72 two-bedroom suites with kitchens. 3 stories (no elevator), interior/exterior corridors. *Bath:* combo or shower only. **Parking:** on-site, winter plug-ins. **Terms:** check-in 4 pm, cancellation fee imposed. **Amenities:** voice mail, irons, hair dryers. *Some:* DVD players, high-speed Internet (fee). **Leisure Activities:** cross country skiing. **Guest Services:** valet and coin laundry, area transportation. **Business Services:** conference facilities, PC. **Cards:** AX, DC, DS, MC, VI.

WESTMARK FAIRBANKS HOTEL & CONFERENCE CENTER   *Book great rates at AAA.com*   Phone: (907)456-7722

Small-scale Hotel
$210-$500 3/1-9/15
$89-$500 9/16-2/28

Address: 813 Noble St 99701 **Location:** Just n of Airport Way at 10th Ave; just w of SR 2; downtown. **Facility:** Smoke free premises. 400 units. 391 one-bedroom standard units. 9 one-bedroom suites. 4-8 stories, interior corridors. *Bath:* combo or shower only. **Parking:** on-site, winter plug-ins. **Terms:** cancellation fee imposed. **Amenities:** voice mail, irons, hair dryers. *Some:* high-speed Internet, dual phone lines. **Dining:** 2 restaurants. **Leisure Activities:** exercise room. *Fee:* massage. **Guest Services:** valet and coin laundry, area transportation-train station. **Business Services:** conference facilities, PC. **Cards:** AX, CB, DC, DS, JC, MC, VI. **Free Special Amenities: local telephone calls and high-speed Internet.**

▼ *See AAA listing above* ▼

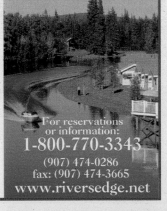

─────── *The following lodging was either not evaluated or did not* ───────
meet AAA rating requirements but is listed for your information only.

SPRINGHILL SUITES BY MARRIOTT
Phone: 907/451-6552

fyi

Did not meet all AAA rating requirements for. **Address:** 575 1st Ave 99701 **Location:** Downtown. Located across from visitors center. Facilities, services, and decor characterize a mid-range property.

Small-scale Hotel

─────── **WHERE TO DINE** ───────

ALASKA COFFEE ROASTING CO
Phone: 907/457-5282

Coffee/Espresso
$4-$6

Known for its huge selection of coffee roasted on the premises, this funky, upbeat and contemporary coffeehouse also serves a variety of light lunches. You can enjoy vegetable empanadas, wraps and pizzas, and there is a large dessert case to tempt your sweet tooth. You order at the counter and can either get your food to go or linger in the cafe at this locally popular spot. Casual dress. **Hours:** 7 am-10 pm, Sat from 8 am, Sun from 9 am. Closed major holidays. **Address:** 4001 Geist Rd, Suite 2 99709 **Location:** Just w of University Ave; in West Valley Plaza. **Parking:** on-site. **Cards:** MC, VI.

CALL

ALASKA SALMON BAKE
Phone: 907/452-7274

American
$28-$31

This traditional salmon bake has an excellent salad bar and the option of the salmon dinner or a prime rib dinner. Pay for your ticket at the counter and serve yourself at the salad bar, fish barbecue and dessert cabin. You can either eat at the picnic tables outside or inside the covered area; either way, you can satisfy any appetite. Casual dress. **Bar:** Beer & wine. **Hours:** Open 5/15-9/10; 5 pm-9 pm; show offered at 8:15 pm. **Address:** 3175 College Rd, #1 99709 **Location:** Airport Way; in Pioneer Park. **Parking:** on-site. **Cards:** AX, DS, MC, VI.

CHENA'S FINE DINING & DECK
Phone: 907/474-3644

American
$10-$28

Antiques and upscale appointments are used in creating a decor that suggests early 1900s Alaska. The menu emphasizes steaks and seafood and items are very well prepared and nicely presented. Dining is casual and leisurely, with outside deck dining available in season. Casual dress. **Bar:** Full bar. **Reservations:** suggested, for dinner. **Hours:** Open 5/15-10/31; 6 am-9, noon-2 & 5-10 pm; hours vary off season. **Address:** 4200 Boat St 99709 **Location:** Airport Way, just n on Sportsman Way, then 0.5 mi w; in River's Edge Resort. **Parking:** on-site. **Cards:** AX, DS, MC, VI.

CALL

THE COOKIE JAR RESTAURANT
Phone: 907/479-8319

American
$6-$17

Enjoy leisurely dining in a casual and relaxed atmosphere. The kitchen turns out a variety of selections prepared using fresh ingredients. Much is made on-site and when ordered. Save room for indulging in the restaurant's homemade cookies and pastries. Casual dress. **Reservations:** accepted. **Hours:** 6:30 am-9 pm, Mon-8:30 pm, Sun 8 am-7 pm. Closed: 11/27, 12/25. **Address:** 1006 Cadillac Ct 99701 **Location:** Jct Johanson Expwy, just n on Danby St. **Parking:** on-site. **Cards:** AX, DS, MC, VI.

GAMBARDELLA'S PASTA BELLA
Phone: 907/456-3417

Italian
$6-$25

Business travelers and couples enjoy the excellent lasagna and tiramisu at the warm, comfortable restaurant. Among other good choices are homemade pizza, bread, pie, cheesecake, espresso and cappuccino. Seating is available on the covered patio in season. Casual dress. **Bar:** Beer & wine. **Reservations:** accepted. **Hours:** 11 am-9 pm, Fri & Sat-10 pm, Sun 4 pm-9 pm. Closed major holidays. **Address:** 706 2nd Ave 99701 **Location:** Downtown. **Parking:** on-site and street. **Cards:** AX, MC, VI.

LAVELLE'S BISTRO
Phone: 907/450-0555

Regional American
$19-$28

This restaurant features an impressive and extensive wine list, a funky modern interior and a varied menu that can range from halibut and salmon to lamb and pasta. Casual dress. **Bar:** Full bar. **Hours:** 4:30 pm-10 pm, Sun & Mon-9 pm. Closed major holidays. **Address:** 575 1st Ave 99701 **Location:** Downtown; in SpringHill Suites by Marriott. **Parking:** on-site. **Cards:** AX, CB, DS, JC, MC, VI.

CALL

PIKE'S LANDING RESTAURANT & LOUNGE
Phone: 907/479-6500

Regional American
$9-$45

One nice thing about Alaska in the summer is endless nights under the midnight sun, and one of the city's best places to enjoy this is on the patio of the restaurant, which is set along the riverbank. Patrons find an extensive selection of Alaskan seafood and can eat inside or out. Because it is such a popular place, prepare yourself for a lingering meal. Service is exceptionally friendly. Casual dress. **Bar:** Full bar. **Hours:** 11 am-10 pm; hours vary in winter. Closed: 12/25. **Address:** 4438 Airport Way 99709 **Location:** Jct Airport Way and Hoselton; next to Pike's Waterfront Lodge. **Parking:** on-site. **Cards:** AX, DC, DS, MC, VI.

CALL

THE PUMP HOUSE RESTAURANT & SALOON
Phone: 907/479-8452

American
$12-$42

An authentic former tin pumphouse used in gold-mining operations, the restaurant is listed on the National Register of Historic Places. The deck affords a great view of the Chena River. The decor exudes a warm Victorian charm. Casual dress. **Bar:** Full bar. **Reservations:** suggested. **Hours:** 11:30 am-2 & 5-10 pm; Sunday brunch 10 am-2 pm. **Address:** 796 Chena Pump Rd 99708 **Location:** Jct Parks Hwy and Geist Rd (Chena Pump Rd), just e to Chena Pump Rd, then 1.3 mi s. **Parking:** on-site. **Cards:** AX, MC, VI. **Historic**

THAI HOUSE RESTAURANT

Thai
$7-$14

Phone: 907/452-6123

This cozy, unassuming downtown spot is very popular with locals. Yellow curry powder, onion, egg, fresh ginger, chili and garlic are a few of the ingredients that bring the cuisine to life. The kitchen staff can accommodate your preferred level of spiciness. The servers dress in authentic and ornate Thai gowns and provide instructions and hints for first-time Thai diners. Casual dress. **Bar:** Beer & wine. **Reservations:** accepted. **Hours:** Open 3/1-12/31 & 1/15-2/28; 11 am-4 & 5-10 pm. Closed major holidays; also Sun. **Address:** 526 5th Ave 99701 **Location:** Downtown. **Parking:** street. **Cards:** MC, VI.

THE TURTLE CLUB

Steak & Seafood
$19-$31

Phone: 907/457-3883

Although menu selections are limited, the restaurant uses quality products. While specializing in prime rib and seafood, one of the restaurant's signature items is giant prawns. Throughout the restaurant are curio cabinets filled with turtle knick-knacks. Casual dress. **Bar:** Full bar. **Reservations:** suggested. **Hours:** 6 pm-10 pm, Sun 5 pm-9 pm. Closed: 1/1, 11/27, 12/25; also 11/25 & 11/26. **Address:** 10 Mile Old Steese Hwy 99712 **Location:** 10 mi n on SR 2 (Steese Expwy), 0.6 mi w on SR 6 (Old Steese Hwy). **Parking:** on-site. **Cards:** AX, DS, MC, VI.

CALL [&M] [⊗]

WOLF RUN RESTAURANT

American
$5-$25

Phone: 907/458-0636

Known for its sinful and decadent desserts, this cozy and comfortable dessert house also features a good selection of homemade soups, sandwiches and salads. You may not want to come in for anything but dessert, as you'll have to choose from a list of 20 creations! Originally designed as a private home, the restaurant still maintains the coziness with its simple decor. A very popular spot with the locals, this is a great place to sit and lounge over a cup of coffee and dessert. Casual dress. **Bar:** Beer & wine. **Reservations:** suggested. **Hours:** 11 am-9 pm, Fri & Sat-11 pm, Sun noon-8:30 pm, Mon 11 am-3 pm. Closed: 11/27, 12/25. **Address:** 3360 Wolf Run 99709 **Location:** Jct Johanssen Expwy and University Ave. **Parking:** on-site. **Cards:** AX, CB, DC, DS, JC, MC, VI.

CALL [&M] [⊛]

GIRDWOOD

——— WHERE TO STAY ———

HOTEL ALYESKA

🅐🅐🅐 [SAVE]

▼▼▼
Resort
Large-scale Hotel
$149-$500 All Year

Book great rates at AAA.com

Phone: (907)754-1111

Address: 1000 Arlberg Ave 99587 **Location:** 2 mi n on Alyeska Blvd from SR 1 (Seward Hwy), then 0.9 mi e. Located in a quiet area. **Facility:** Fine dining, upscale rooms and attention to service are featured at this resort-style hotel set in a valley next to ski hills. 307 units. 303 one-bedroom standard units. 4 one-bedroom suites. 8 stories, interior corridors. *Bath:* combo or shower only. **Parking:** on-site and valet. **Terms:** check-in 4 pm. **Amenities:** video games (fee), voice mail, safes, irons, hair dryers. **Dining:** 5 restaurants, also, Seven Glaciers Restaurant, see separate listing. **Pool(s):** heated indoor. **Leisure Activities:** sauna, whirlpool, cross country skiing, snowmobiling, ice skating, hiking trails, exercise room. *Fee:* downhill skiing, bicycles, massage. **Guest Services:** valet laundry, area transportation-within Girdwood. **Cards:** AX, CB, DC, DS, JC, MC, VI. **Free Special Amenities:** local telephone calls and high-speed Internet. *(See color ad p 733)*

[icons] /SOME UNITS

——— WHERE TO DINE ———

DOUBLE MUSKY INN

▼▼
Regional Cajun
$25-$40

Phone: 907/783-2822

You're sure to enjoy the twist on New Orleans dishes prepared with fresh Alaskan seafood. Many savory delights such as crab meat dressing stuffed halibut served with Creole burre blanc or shrimp etouffee are among the favorites of the local crowds. Unique decor of Mardi Gras beads and masks surrounding locally made framed stained glass create a festive atmosphere for you to dine in. Casual dress. **Bar:** Full bar. **Reservations:** not accepted. **Hours:** Open 3/1-11/1 & 12/1-2/28; 5 pm-10 pm, Fri-Sun from 4:30 pm. Closed: Mon. **Address:** Milepost 0.3 (Crow Creek Rd) 99587 **Location:** 1.9 mi n on Alyeska Blvd from SR 1 (Seward Hwy), 0.3 mi w. **Parking:** on-site. **Cards:** CB, DC, DS, MC, VI.

SEVEN GLACIERS RESTAURANT

🅐🅐🅐

▼▼▼▼
Regional
American
$24-$42

Phone: 907/754-2249

The unusual mountaintop location is a spectacular setting, accessible only by an aerial tram from the hotel. The menu centers on creative Alaskan and West Coast preparations of seafood, beef and more exotic game. Seasonal salmon and halibut are always popular. Although the ambience is elegant, diners are at home either dressed up or in more casual resort attire. A reservation will ensure a free tram ride to the dining room. Casual dress. **Bar:** Full bar. **Reservations:** suggested. **Hours:** Open 3/1-4/14 & 5/6-2/28; 5:30 pm-9:30 pm. Closed: 10/1-11/15, Tues & Wed 5/1-5/31 & 9/1-9/30. **Address:** 1000 Arlberg Ave 99587 **Location:** 2 mi n on Alyeska Blvd from SR 1 (Seward Hwy), then 0.9 mi e; in Hotel Alyeska. **Parking:** on-site and valet. **Cards:** AX, CB, DC, DS, JC, MC, VI. *(See color ad p 733)*

GLENNALLEN pop. 554

──────── WHERE TO STAY ────────

LAKE LOUISE LODGE

Small-scale Hotel
$95-$140 All Year

Phone: (907)822-3311
Address: Mile 16.1 Lake Louise Rd 99588 **Location:** 27.7 mi w on US 1, 16.1 mi n. **Facility:** Designated smoking area. 7 one-bedroom standard units. 2 stories (no elevator), interior/exterior corridors. *Bath:* shower only. **Parking:** on-site, winter plug-ins. **Terms:** check-in 4 pm, 14 day cancellation notice-fee imposed. **Amenities:** *Some:* hair dryers. **Leisure Activities:** rental boats, boat dock, fishing, hiking trails. *Fee:* charter fishing. **Guest Services:** TV in common area. **Cards:** AX, MC, VI.

[ASK] [S] [†]] [↓] [×] [×] [火] [W] [🎥] [🏁] / SOME UNITS [▣]

GUSTAVUS pop. 429

──────── WHERE TO STAY ────────

ANNIE MAE LODGE

Country Inn
$125-$190 All Year

Phone: (907)697-2346
Address: #2 Grandpa Rd 99826 **Location:** From airport, 3 mi w to Good River Rd, 0.5 mi to Grandpa's Farm Rd. Located in a quiet area. **Facility:** Smoke free premises. 11 one-bedroom standard units. 2 stories (no elevator), interior/exterior corridors. *Bath:* some shared or private, combo or shower only. **Parking:** on-site. **Terms:** office hours 5:30 am-10:30 pm, 30 day cancellation notice-fee imposed. **Leisure Activities:** fishing, bicycles, hiking trails. **Guest Services:** valet laundry, area transportation. **Cards:** AX, DS, MC, VI.

[ASK] [✈] [†]] CALL [S] [×] [×] [火] [W] [🏁]

GLACIER BAY LODGE

Motel
Rates not provided

Phone: 907/697-4000
Address: 199 Bartlett Cove 99826 **Location:** 9 mi w of airport. **Facility:** Smoke free premises. 54 one-bedroom standard units. 2 stories (no elevator), exterior corridors. **Parking:** on-site. **Terms:** open 5/15-9/5, office hours 5 am-11 pm. **Dining:** Fairweather Dining Room, see separate listing. **Leisure Activities:** boat dock, hiking trails. **Guest Services:** coin laundry.

[†]] [×] [火] [W]

GLACIER BAY'S BEAR TRACK INN

Small-scale Hotel
Rates not provided

Phone: 907/697-3017
Address: 255 Rink Creek Rd 99826 **Location:** 7 mi e of airport; at end of Rink Creek Rd. Located in a quiet area. **Facility:** Smoke free premises. 14 one-bedroom standard units. 2 stories (no elevator), interior corridors. **Parking:** on-site. **Terms:** open 5/15-9/10, office hours 7 am-10 pm. **Amenities:** hair dryers. **Leisure Activities:** hiking trails. **Guest Services:** valet laundry, area transportation. **Business Services:** meeting rooms, PC.

[✈] [†]] [×] [火] [W] [🏁] / SOME UNITS FEE [🛏]

──────── WHERE TO DINE ────────

FAIRWEATHER DINING ROOM

American
$10-$30

Phone: 907/697-4000
The hotel dining room offers both a wonderful view of the inlet and creatively prepared, locally caught seafood, as well as a variety of standards ranging from sandwiches to steaks. Casual dress. **Bar:** Full bar. **Reservations:** accepted. **Hours:** Open 5/20-9/30; 6-9:30 am, 11:30-2:30 & 5:30-10 pm. **Address:** 199 Bartlett Cove 99826 **Location:** 9 mi w of airport; in Glacier Bay Lodge. **Parking:** on-site. **Cards:** AX, DS, MC, VI.

CALL [S] [火]

HAINES pop. 1,811

──────── WHERE TO STAY ────────

CAPTAIN'S CHOICE INC MOTEL

[AAA] [SAVE]

Motel
$86-$182 All Year

Phone: (907)766-3111
Address: 108 2nd Ave N 99827 **Location:** Jct 2nd Ave and Dalton St. **Facility:** 39 units. 37 one- and 1 two-bedroom standard units, some with whirlpools. 1 one-bedroom suite. 2 stories (no elevator), exterior corridors. **Parking:** on-site. **Amenities:** voice mail, hair dryers. *Some:* irons. **Leisure Activities:** sun deck. **Guest Services:** coin laundry, area transportation-ferry. **Cards:** AX, CB, DC, DS, MC, VI. **Free Special Amenities:** continental breakfast and high-speed Internet.

[✈] [†]↑] [火] [🎥] [🔲] [▤] [▣] / SOME UNITS FEE [🛏] [×] FEE [VCR]

──────── WHERE TO DINE ────────

CHILKAT RESTAURANT & BAKERY

[AAA]

American
$3-$12

Phone: 907/766-3653
A few steps away from downtown, this local favorite offers a variety of well prepared and hearty dishes and features in-house bakery items. Casual dress. **Reservations:** accepted. **Hours:** 7 am-3 pm. Closed: 7/4, 11/27, 12/25; also Sun. **Address:** 25 5th Ave 99827 **Location:** Jct 5th Ave and Dalton St. **Parking:** on-site and street. **Cards:** MC, VI.

[火]

FORT SEWARD LODGE RESTAURANT & SALOON

American
$9-$25

Phone: 907-766-2009

The casual dining room has been restored to reflect its former gold rush saloon days and offers a variety of bar favorites including hamburgers and locally caught seafood. Dressy casual. **Bar:** Full bar. **Reservations:** suggested. **Hours:** Open 5/1-10/11; 5:30 pm-9 pm. Closed: Sun 9/1-10/11. **Address:** 39 Mud Bay Rd 99827 **Location:** In Fort William H Seward. **Parking:** on-site. **Cards:** DS, MC, VI.

[AC]

LIGHTHOUSE RESTAURANT

Seafood
$7-$30

Phone: 907-766-2442

Casual dress. **Bar:** Full bar. **Reservations:** suggested. **Hours:** Open 3/1-12/31; 8-10:45 am, 11-3 & 4-9:30 pm. Closed: 11/27, 12/25. **Address:** 101 Front St 99827 **Location:** Waterfront; town center. **Parking:** on-site. **Cards:** AX, DS, MC, VI.

[AC]

HEALY pop. 1,000—*See also DENALI NATIONAL PARK AND PRESERVE.*

——— **WHERE TO STAY** ———

DENALI DOME HOME BED & BREAKFAST

Bed & Breakfast
$90-$185 All Year

Phone: 907-683-1239

Address: 137 Healy Spur Rd 99743 **Location:** Jct SR 3 and Healy Spur Rd, 0.5 mi e. Located in a quiet area. **Facility:** In a scenic area, this unusual dome-shaped B&B offers cozy, comfortable rooms and spacious living areas. Smoke free premises. 7 one-bedroom standard units, some with whirlpools. 3 stories (no elevator), interior/exterior corridors. *Bath:* combo or shower only. **Parking:** on-site, winter plug-ins. **Terms:** check-in 4 pm, 30 day cancellation notice-fee imposed. **Amenities:** video library, DVD players, hair dryers. **Leisure Activities:** hiking trails, jogging. **Business Services:** business center. **Cards:** DS, MC, VI. **Free Special Amenities: full breakfast and high-speed Internet.**

[icons] CALL

DENALI LAKESIDE LODGING

Bed & Breakfast
Rates not provided

Phone: 907-683-2511

Address: Mile 1.4 Otto Lake Rd 99743 **Location:** SR 3, 1.4 mi w at Milepost 247, follow signs. **Facility:** Smoke free premises. 4 units. 2 one- and 1 two-bedroom standard units with kitchens. 1 cabin. 2 stories, interior/exterior corridors. *Bath:* combo or shower only. **Parking:** on-site, winter plug-ins. **Terms:** check-in 4 pm. **Amenities:** video library, hair dryers. **Leisure Activities:** whirlpool, canoeing, boat dock, fishing, hiking trails, jogging. **Guest Services:** coin laundry.

[icons]

DENALI LAKEVIEW INN

Bed & Breakfast
$69-$185 All Year

Phone: 907-683-4035

Address: Mile 1.2 Otto Lake Rd 99743 **Location:** SR 3, Milepost 247, 1.2 mi w. **Facility:** Guest rooms at this modern inn, which fronts on a tranquil lake, all feature cheery decor and have decks. Smoke free premises. 19 one-bedroom standard units, some with kitchens and/or whirlpools. 2-3 stories (no elevator), interior/exterior corridors. **Parking:** on-site, winter plug-ins. **Terms:** check-in 4 pm, cancellation fee imposed. **Amenities:** hair dryers. **Leisure Activities:** fishing, hiking trails, jogging. *Fee:* canoes. **Guest Services:** coin laundry. **Cards:** MC, VI. **Free Special Amenities: expanded continental breakfast and local telephone calls.**

[icons]

HEALY HEIGHTS FAMILY CABINS

Cabin
$130-$220 6/1-9/20
$100-$180 5/15-5/31

Phone: (907)683-2639

Address: Hill Top Rd 99743 **Location:** SR 3, Milepost 247; 0.9 mi w on Otto Lake Rd, 1.5 mi n, follow signs. **Facility:** Smoke free premises. 6 cabins. 1 story, exterior corridors. *Bath:* combo or shower only. **Parking:** on-site, winter plug-ins. **Terms:** open 5/15-9/20, check-in 4 pm, 15 day cancellation notice-fee imposed. **Amenities:** *Some:* irons, hair dryers. **Leisure Activities:** hiking trails, jogging. **Cards:** MC, VI.

[icons]

HOMER pop. 3,946

——— **WHERE TO STAY** ———

BEST WESTERN BIDARKA INN   *Book great rates at AAA.com*

Motel
$89-$189 All Year

Phone: (907)235-8148

Address: 575 Sterling Hwy 99603 **Location:** 0.3 mi n on (SR 1) Sterling Hwy. **Facility:** 74 one-bedroom standard units, some with whirlpools. 2 stories (no elevator), interior/exterior corridors. **Parking:** on-site, winter plug-ins. **Terms:** check-in 4 pm. **Amenities:** high-speed Internet, irons, hair dryers. **Dining:** 2 restaurants. **Leisure Activities:** exercise room. **Guest Services:** coin laundry, area transportation-ferry, wireless Internet. **Business Services:** meeting rooms, PC. **Cards:** AX, CB, DC, DS, JC, MC, VI. **Free Special Amenities: local telephone calls and high-speed Internet.**

[icons] FEE

AAA Benefit:
Members save 10% everyday, plus an exclusive frequent stay program.

KIANA B&B

Bed & Breakfast
$110-$160 5/1-9/10

Phone: (907)235-8824

Address: 58856 E End Rd 99603 **Location:** Jct Pioneer and Lake aves, 5 mi e. **Facility:** Smoke free premises. 6 units. 4 one-bedroom standard units. 1 vacation home and 1 cabin, some with whirlpools. 2 stories (no elevator), interior/exterior corridors. *Bath:* combo or shower only. **Parking:** on-site. **Terms:** open 5/1-9/10, 10 day cancellation notice-fee imposed. **Amenities:** video library, hair dryers. **Leisure Activities:** whirlpool, gas & charcoal grills. **Guest Services:** TV in common area, wireless Internet. **Cards:** MC, VI.

[icons]

LANDS END RESORT   *Book at AAA.com*

Phone: (907)235-0400

Resort
Small-scale Hotel
$79-$235 All Year

Address: 4786 Homer Spit Rd 99603 **Location:** Oceanfront. 5 mi se; at end of Homer Spit Rd. **Facility:** Smoke free premises. 108 units. 97 one-bedroom standard units. 2 one-, 2 two- and 7 three-bedroom suites with kitchens, some with whirlpools. 3 stories, interior/exterior corridors. *Bath:* combo or shower only. **Parking:** on-site. **Terms:** check-in 4 pm. **Amenities:** video library (fee), hair dryers. *Some:* DVD players. **Leisure Activities:** sauna, whirlpool, limited exercise equipment, spa. *Fee:* fishing, charter fishing, bicycles. **Business Services:** conference facilities, PC. **Cards:** AX, CB, DC, DS, MC, VI.

PIONEER INN   *Book at AAA.com*

Phone: 907/235-5670

Motel
$99-$119 3/1-9/15
$59-$89 9/16-2/28

Address: 244 W Pioneer Ave 99603 **Location:** Just e off Sterling Hwy (SR 1); at entrance of town. **Facility:** Smoke free premises. 7 units. 2 one-bedroom standard units. 5 one-bedroom suites with kitchens. 2 stories (no elevator), exterior corridors. **Parking:** on-site. **Terms:** 7 day cancellation notice. **Guest Services:** wireless Internet. **Cards:** AX, MC, VI.

TUTKA BAY WILDERNESS LODGE

Phone: (907)235-3905

Small-scale Hotel
$790-$896 5/15-9/15

Address: Tutka Bay 99603 **Location:** Tutka Bay; accessible by water taxi or Lodge boat only. **Facility:** Smoke free premises. 6 units. 4 one-bedroom standard units. 2 two-bedroom suites. *Bath:* combo or shower only. **Parking:** on-site. **Terms:** open 5/15-9/15, check-in 4 pm, 2 night minimum stay, cancellation fee imposed. **Leisure Activities:** sauna, whirlpool, limited beach access, fishing, guided sea kayaking, hiking trails. *Fee:* charter fishing. **Guest Services:** wireless Internet. **Cards:** AX, DS, MC, VI. **Free Special Amenities:** full breakfast and high-speed Internet.

VICTORIAN HEIGHTS BED AND BREAKFAST

Phone: (907)235-6357

Bed & Breakfast
$135-$165 5/15-9/30

Address: 1585 Race Rd 99603 **Location:** Sterling Hwy (SR 1), 1.8 mi ne on Pioneer Ave (which becomes East End Rd), 2.1 mi nw on East Hill Rd, 0.3 mi e on Cottonwood, then follow signs. **Facility:** This tastefully decorated, spacious B&B offers two rooms with private balconies overlooking the bay and mountains. Smoke free premises. 4 one-bedroom standard units, some with whirlpools. 2 stories (no elevator), interior corridors. *Bath:* combo or shower only. **Parking:** on-site, winter plug-ins. **Terms:** open 5/15-9/30, office hours 7 am-11 pm, check-in 4 pm, 2 night minimum stay, 14 day cancellation notice. **Amenities:** hair dryers. **Leisure Activities:** cross country skiing, snowmobile trails. **Guest Services:** TV in common area, coin laundry, wireless Internet. **Business Services:** PC. **Cards:** MC, VI. **Free Special Amenities:** full breakfast and high-speed Internet.

--------- WHERE TO DINE ---------

CAFE CUPS

Phone: 907/235-8330

American
$7-$23

Considered to be one of the best places in town, this eclectic, funky restaurant serves up a variety of homemade goods, and is well-known for its seafood options. There are only about fifteen tables at this funky place, which features a unique mosaic wall around the door. You can choose from salmon, shrimp and other seafood dishes, or try the feature of the day. The servers are efficient and personable. Casual dress. **Bar:** Beer & wine. **Reservations:** suggested. **Hours:** 11 am-10 pm, Sat from 5 pm. Closed: 12/25; also Sun & Mon. **Address:** 162 W Pioneer Ave 99603 **Location:** Center. **Parking:** on-site. **Cards:** MC, VI.

CAPTAIN PATTIE'S FISH HOUSE

Phone: 907/235-5135

Regional Seafood
$7-$27

Those who spent the day fishing and can't wait to eat their catch can bring it in to the restaurant for preparation and cooking. Alaskan art contributes to the simple decor. The ever-changing menu boasts freshly caught fish dishes, along the lines of halibut, scallops and salmon. Early birds can take advantage of specials from 5 pm to 6 pm. On the famous Homer Spit, this spot is distinctive and casual. Casual dress. **Bar:** Beer & wine. **Reservations:** suggested. **Hours:** Open 3/20-10/31; 11 am-10 pm. Closed major holidays. **Address:** 4241 Homer Spit Rd 99603 **Location:** 5 mi along Homer Spit Rd. **Parking:** on-site. **Cards:** DS, MC, VI.

DUNCAN HOUSE DINER

Phone: 907/235-5344

American
$4-$12

Well worth the visit for the hearty homestyle fare and the atmosphere, this country cozy diner is known for their all-day breakfast that features hearty portions of freshly cooked fare — a great way to start the day, and service starts at 5 am for early risers. In addition to the breakfast options, a light lunch menu is offered from 7 am which features hearty burgers, sandwiches, fresh soups and entree salads. The decor is delightful with a true rustic Alaskan feel with a homey touch. Casual dress. **Hours:** 5 am-3 pm; from 7 am 11/1-6/30. Closed: 1/1, 12/25. **Address:** 125 E Pioneer Ave 99603 **Location:** Center. **Parking:** on-site. **Cards:** MC, VI.

FRESH SOURDOUGH EXPRESS BAKERY & CAFE

Phone: 907/235-7571

Bakery/Desserts
$6-$25

A popular spot with the locals, the Sourdough Express is a warm, inviting place serving up locally produced and some organic fare. Whether you're stopping in for a big breakfast, a sandwich for lunch or an evening bite to eat, you might also be tempted by the display case in the bakery, which features a wide array of delicious desserts. In the summer, outdoor patio dining is available, complete with a small play area for the kids. Casual dress. **Bar:** Beer & wine. **Reservations:** accepted. **Hours:** Open 3/1-10/31; 7 am-9 pm; 9 am-3 pm in fall & spring. Closed major holidays. **Address:** 1316 Ocean Dr 99603 **Location:** 3 mi sw on Sterling Hwy (SR 1). **Parking:** on-site. **Cards:** DS, MC, VI.

THE HOMESTEAD RESTAURANT

Phone: 907/235-8723

American
$19-$53

Diners can enjoy views of the Homer Spit in this lively restaurant, which centers its menu on innovative preparations of fresh seafood. Casual dress. **Bar:** Full bar. **Reservations:** suggested. **Hours:** Open 3/15-1/1; 5 pm-10 pm. **Address:** Mile 8.2 East End Rd 99603 **Location:** 8.2 mi s. **Parking:** on-site. **Cards:** AX, MC, VI.

TWO SISTERS BAKERY

Phone: 907/235-2280

Bakery/Desserts
$3-$8

For healthy, organic baked goods and light lunches, the three sisters at the Two Sisters Bakery have what it takes. Located in a big house just on the outskirts of downtown, and near several galleries, the eatery offers giant cinnamon buns, scones, quiches, breakfast granola and, of course, a fine selection of fresh breads. Lounge for a few hours, or take your baked goods to go. Either way, you'll receive service with a smile. Casual dress. **Reservations:** not accepted. **Hours:** 7 am-8 pm, Sun 9 am-4 pm; hours vary in winter. Closed: 12/25. **Address:** 233 E Bunnell 99603 **Location:** Sterling Hwy (SR 1), just s at Main St, then just e. **Parking:** on-site. **Cards:** MC, VI.

JUNEAU pop. 30,711

OA	JUNEAU	Diamond Rating	Rate Range High Season	Listing Page
AAA	Best Western Country Lane Inn, n of terminal	◈◈	Rates not provided SAVE	755
AAA	Best Western Grandma's Feather Bed, 1 mi n of terminal	◈◈	Rates not provided SAVE	755
	Extended Stay Deluxe Juneau, n of terminal	◈◈	$180-$200	756

——— **WHERE TO STAY** ———

AK FIREWEED HOUSE BED & BREAKFAST

Phone: 907/586-3885

Bed & Breakfast
$109-$399 All Year

Address: 8530 N Douglas Hwy 99801 **Location:** From airport, 12 mi s on Egan Dr to Juneau/Douglas bridge; across bridge, 5.1 mi n. Located in a secluded area on Douglas Island. **Facility:** A two-story home and a cedar-beamed guest house are featured at this B&B on four acres of rain forest wetlands. Smoke free premises. 4 units. 3 one-bedroom standard units, some with whirlpools. 1 vacation home with whirlpool. 1-2 stories (no elevator), interior/exterior corridors. *Bath:* combo or shower only. **Parking:** on-site. **Terms:** 30 day cancellation notice-fee imposed. **Amenities:** video library, DVD players, high-speed Internet, voice mail, irons, hair dryers. **Leisure Activities:** hiking trails, playground. **Guest Services:** coin laundry. **Business Services:** PC. **Cards:** AX, DS, MC, VI.

ALASKA WOLF LODGE

Phone: 907/586-2422

Bed & Breakfast
$95-$325 All Year

Address: 1900 Wickersham Dr 99801 **Location:** 2 mi n of downtown; from Highland Ave, 0.9 mi n on Glacier Ave, just e. Located in a quiet residential area. **Facility:** Smoke free premises. 6 one-bedroom standard units, some with kitchens and/or whirlpools. 2 stories (no elevator), interior corridors. *Bath:* some shared or private, combo or shower only. **Parking:** on-site. **Terms:** 30 day cancellation notice. **Amenities:** video library, hair dryers. *Some:* DVD players. **Cards:** MC, VI.

BEST WESTERN COUNTRY LANE INN   *Book great rates at AAA.com*

Phone: 907/789-5005

Motel
Rates not provided

Address: 9300 Glacier Hwy 99801 **Location:** Just e off Egan Dr. **Facility:** Smoke free premises. 55 units. 50 one-bedroom standard units, some with efficiencies and/or whirlpools. 5 one-bedroom suites with efficiencies. 2 stories (no elevator), exterior corridors. **Parking:** on-site. **Amenities:** high-speed Internet, irons, hair dryers. **Guest Services:** valet and coin laundry, area transportation-within 10 mi. **Business Services:** business center. **Free Special Amenities: expanded continental breakfast and high-speed Internet.**

AAA Benefit:
Members save 10% everyday, plus an exclusive frequent stay program.

BEST WESTERN GRANDMA'S FEATHER BED   *Book great rates at AAA.com*

Phone: 907/789-5566

Country Inn
Rates not provided

Address: 2358 Mendenhall Loop Rd 99801 **Location:** Just e off Egan Dr. **Facility:** Smoke free premises. 14 one-bedroom standard units with whirlpools. 2 stories, interior corridors. **Parking:** on-site. **Terms:** off-site registration. **Amenities:** high-speed Internet, irons, hair dryers. **Guest Services:** valet laundry, area transportation-within 10 mi. **Business Services:** PC. **Free Special Amenities: full breakfast and high-speed Internet.**

AAA Benefit:
Members save 10% everyday, plus an exclusive frequent stay program.

EXTENDED STAY DELUXE JUNEAU *Book at AAA.com* Phone: (907)790-6435

Small-scale Hotel
$180-$200 3/1-9/16
$95-$105 9/17-2/28

Address: 1800 Shell Simmons Dr 99801 **Location:** At Juneau International Airport. **Facility:** 94 units. 91 one-bedroom standard units, some with whirlpools. 3 one-bedroom suites with efficiencies. 2 stories, interior corridors. *Bath:* combo or shower only. **Parking:** on-site. **Amenities:** high-speed Internet (fee), voice mail, irons, hair dryers. **Pool(s):** heated indoor. **Leisure Activities:** whirlpool, exercise room. **Guest Services:** valet and coin laundry, area transportation. **Business Services:** meeting rooms, PC. **Cards:** AX, DC, DS, JC, MC, VI.

[ASK] [🛏️] [✈️] [🍴] CALL [🔥M] [🏊] [VCR] [🎿] [🖥️] [📠] [💻] / SOME UNITS [✕]

GOLDBELT HOTEL JUNEAU *Book great rates at AAA.com* Phone: (907)586-6900

[AAA] [SAVE]

Small-scale Hotel
$139-$189 All Year

Address: 51 Egan Dr 99801 **Location:** Just n of Main St; downtown. **Facility:** 105 one-bedroom standard units. 7 stories, interior corridors. **Parking:** on-site. **Terms:** cancellation fee imposed. **Amenities:** high-speed Internet, voice mail, irons, hair dryers. **Guest Services:** valet laundry. **Business Services:** meeting rooms. **Cards:** AX, CB, DC, DS, MC, VI. **Free Special Amenities:** local telephone calls and high-speed Internet. *(See color ad below)*

[✈️] [🍴] [🍷] [🦮] [🎿] [💻] / SOME UNITS [✕] [📠]

PEARSON'S POND LUXURY INN & ADVENTURE SPA *Book great rates at AAA.com* Phone: (907)789-3772

[AAA] [SAVE]

Bed & Breakfast
$249-$499 All Year

Address: 4541 Sawa Cir 99801-8723 **Location:** From Egan Dr, 2.2 mi n on Mendenhall Loop Rd, 1.2 mi w on Mendenhall Loop Rd, 0.3 mi s on River Rd, just w on Kelly Ct, then just s. Located in a quiet residential area. **Facility:** A placid pond beautifies the property's grounds, while guest rooms offer luxurious amenities; hosts can assist with activity planning. Smoke free premises. 5 one-bedroom standard units with efficiencies, some with whirlpools. 2 stories (no elevator), interior/exterior corridors. *Bath:* combo or shower only. **Parking:** on-site. **Terms:** 2 night minimum stay - seasonal, age restrictions may apply, 21 day cancellation notice-fee imposed. **Amenities:** video library, DVD players, CD players, high-speed Internet, dual phone lines, voice mail, irons, hair dryers. *Some:* fax. **Leisure Activities:** whirlpools, boating, paddleboats, boat dock, fishing, fishing equipment, cross country skiing, barbecue facility, yoga instruction, bicycles, hiking trails, exercise room. *Fee:* massage. **Guest Services:** complimentary laundry. **Business Services:** meeting rooms, PC. **Cards:** AX, CB, DC, DS, JC, MC, VI. **Free Special Amenities:** expanded continental breakfast and high-speed Internet.

[✕] [✕] [🦮] [🎿] [📠] [📧] [💻]

THE SILVERBOW INN BAKERY & RESTAURANT *Book at AAA.com* Phone: (907)586-4146

Historic Bed
& Breakfast
$78-$188 All Year

Address: 120 2nd St 99801 **Location:** Downtown. **Facility:** This restored 1914 building has quaint guest rooms with cheery, bright decor. Smoke free premises. 6 one-bedroom standard units. 3 stories (no elevator), interior corridors. **Parking:** on-site. **Terms:** 7 day cancellation notice. **Amenities:** video library, high-speed Internet, voice mail, hair dryers. *Some:* DVD players. **Guest Services:** valet laundry. **Cards:** AX, DS, VI.

[ASK] [🍴] [✕] [🦮] [🎿] / SOME UNITS [VCR]

WESTMARK BARANOF *Book great rates at AAA.com* Phone: (907)586-2660

[AAA] [SAVE]

Small-scale Hotel
$149-$279 All Year

Address: 127 N Franklin St 99801 **Location:** At 2nd and Franklin sts; downtown. **Facility:** 195 units. 181 one-bedroom standard units, some with kitchens. 14 one-bedroom suites, some with efficiencies. 9 stories, interior corridors. *Bath:* combo or shower only. **Parking:** on-site. **Amenities:** high-speed Internet (fee), voice mail, irons, hair dryers. **Dining:** 2 restaurants. **Guest Services:** valet laundry. **Business Services:** conference facilities, PC. **Cards:** AX, DC, DS, MC, VI. **Free Special Amenities:** local telephone calls.

[🍴] [🍷] CALL [🔥M] [🦮] [💻] / SOME UNITS [🐾] [✕] [📠]

▼ *See AAA listing above* ▼

─────── **WHERE TO DINE** ───────

BREAKWATER INN RESTAURANT   Phone: 907/586-6303

Located on the second floor, this nautical-themed restaurant commands an impressive view of the harbor where the chef purchases the daily specials such as fresh salmon, king crabs and clams as they are brought in by fishermen. Casual dress. **Bar:** Full bar. **Reservations:** accepted. **Hours:** 7 am-10 pm, Fri & Sat-midnight. **Address:** 1711 Glacier Ave 99801 **Location:** Jct Highland Dr; in Breakwater Inn Hotel.
Steak & Seafood
$15-$30
Parking: on-site. **Cards:** AX, DC, DS, MC, VI.

CHAN'S THAI KITCHEN   Phone: 907/789-9777

This non-descript eatery tucked away in a small strip mall across from Auke Bay Marina will be worth finding. Authentic Thai cooking is served up hot and spicy. The spring rolls are some of the best to be had. This extremely popular restaurant does not take reservations and the seating is limited, so expect a wait for a table in the evening. Casual dress. **Reservations:** not accepted. **Hours:** 11:30 am-2 & 4:30-8:30 pm, Sat from 4:30 pm, Sun 4:30 pm-8 pm. Closed: 7/4, 11/27, 12/25. **Address:** 11820 Glacier Hwy 99801
Thai
$8-$15
Location: 12 mi nw on Glacier Hwy; at Auke Bay, across from harbor. **Parking:** on-site. **Cards:** MC, VI.

GOLD CREEK SALMON BAKE   Phone: 907/586-1424

Catering to cruise ship customers, this outdoor buffet offers all-you-can-eat wood-grilled salmon filets in a forest mining camp setting. Casual dress. **Bar:** Full bar. **Hours:** Open 5/15-9/21; 11 am-2 & 5-8 pm.
American
$29
Address: 1061 Salmon Creek Ln 99801 **Location:** Jct Glacier Hwy and Hospital Dr, just n. **Parking:** on-site. **Cards:** AX, DS, MC, VI.

THE GOLD ROOM   Phone: 907/586-2660

Casual dress. **Bar:** Full bar. **Reservations:** suggested. **Hours:** 5 pm-9:30 pm. **Address:** 127 N Franklin St 99801 **Location:** At 2nd and Franklin sts; downtown; at Westmark Baranof. **Parking:** on-site. **Cards:** AX, MC, VI.
Steak & Seafood
$25-$39

THE HANGAR ON THE WHARF   Phone: 907/586-5018

Located on the wharf and popular with locals, the vibrant eatery offers no-frills dining. Guests can watch seaplanes take off and land while munching on fried halibut fingers and sipping an Alaskan Brewing Company amber ale. Casual dress. **Bar:** Full bar. **Hours:** 11 am-10 pm; hours may vary in winter. Closed: 11/27, 12/25. **Address:** #2 Marine Way, Suite 106 99801 **Location:** Downtown; on the wharf at the Sea Plane runway. **Parking:** on-site. **Cards:** AX, DS, MC, VI.
American
$7-$27

MI CASA MEXICAN CUISINE   Phone: 907/789-3636

Casual dress. **Bar:** Full bar. **Hours:** 6:30 am-9 pm, Fri & Sat-9:30 pm, Sun 9 am-2 & 3-9 pm. **Address:** 9200 Glacier Hwy 99801 **Location:** Just e off Egan. **Parking:** on-site. **Cards:** AX, DS, MC, VI.
Mexican
$6-$25

SILVERBOW BAGELS   Phone: 907/586-4146

You'll have fun at the Silverbow, a restored historical structure, with its funky decor and classic and golden oldies films shown two nights a week. Kids can color on the table covers too. A New York-style bakery is adjacent and offers sinful desserts. Casual dress. **Bar:** Beer & wine. **Reservations:** not accepted. **Hours:** 6 am-8 pm, Sat & Sun from 8 am. Closed: 1/1, 12/25. **Address:** 120 2nd St 99801 **Location:** Jct Main and 2nd sts; downtown. **Parking:** on-site. **Cards:** DC, MC, VI.
Deli/Subs
Sandwiches
$5-$10

TIMBERLINE BAR & GRILL   Phone: 907/463-3412

Take a six-minute cable car ride to the top of Mount Roberts—$21.95 for adults and $10.95 for children— from which you'll be treated to stunning views of Juneau and the Gastineau Channel below. It also takes you to this restaurant, which would be equally worthy at sea level. The Alaskan Alpine experience is sure to be memorable. Casual dress. **Bar:** Full bar. **Hours:** Open 5/10-9/30; 11 am-9 pm. **Address:** 490 S Franklin 99801 **Location:** Downtown; at the top of Mount Roberts Tramway. **Parking:** on-site. **Cards:** AX, CB, DC, DS, MC, VI.
American
$8-$29

TWISTED FISH COMPANY   Phone: 907/463-5033
Alaskan seafood is the specialty at this restaurant, located on the pier near the cruise ship landing areas. Service is quick and friendly, and on those sunny days enjoy dining al fresco. Casual dress. **Bar:** Beer & wine. **Hours:** Open 5/1-9/30; 11 am-10 pm. **Address:** 550 S Franklin St 99801 **Location:** Downtown. **Parking:** on-site. **Cards:** AX, DS, MC, VI.
Seafood
$7-$30

KENAI pop. 6,942

———— WHERE TO STAY ————

HARBORSIDE COTTAGES

Cottage
$150-$180 5/1-10/1

Phone: (907)283-6162
Address: 813 Riverview Dr 99611 **Location:** Just s on Main St, then just e; center. **Facility:** Smoke free premises. 5 cottages. 1 story, exterior corridors. *Bath:* shower only. **Parking:** on-site. **Terms:** open 5/1-10/1, check-in 4 pm, 3 night minimum stay - seasonal, 30 day cancellation notice. **Amenities:** irons. **Leisure Activities:** barbecue deck with picnic table, breakfast basket. **Cards:** AX, DS, MC, VI. **Free Special Amenities:** local telephone calls and high-speed Internet.

———— WHERE TO DINE ————

PARADISOS RESTAURANT

Italian
$5-$29

Greek, Mexican and Italian selections round out this restaurant's extensive menu, which also offers steak and fresh local seafood such as halibut and Alaskan king crab legs. Expect to be served good-size portions in a bustling, welcoming ambience. Casual dress. **Bar:** Full bar. **Reservations:** suggested. **Hours:** 11 am-11 pm, Fri & Sat-midnight. Closed: 11/27, 12/25. **Address:** Main St & Frontage Rd 99611 **Location:** Downtown. **Parking:** on-site. **Cards:** AX, DS, MC, VI.

Phone: 907/283-2222

VERONICA'S

American
$6-$23

This charming bistro is the perfect spot to savor a homemade pastry with an aromatic cup of coffee or tea. Available until the early evening, delicious specialty lunch dishes—such as salmon in puff pastry, creative soups and pecan chicken salad—are made in-house. Casual dress. **Hours:** 10 am-4 pm, Thurs-Sat to 9:30 pm; 9 am-8 pm, Thurs-Sat to 9:30 pm, Sun 11 am-5 pm in summer. Closed major holidays; also Sun in winter. **Address:** 604 Peterson Way 99611 **Location:** In historic district. **Parking:** on-site. **Cards:** DS, MC, VI. **Historic**

Phone: 907/283-2725

KETCHIKAN pop. 7,922

———— WHERE TO STAY ————

BEST WESTERN LANDING

Book great rates at AAA.com

Small-scale Hotel
$142-$230 All Year

Phone: (907)225-5166
Address: 3434 Tongass Ave 99901 **Location:** Across from the Alaska Marine Hwy ferry terminal. **Facility:** 107 units. 90 one-bedroom standard units. 17 one-bedroom suites. 2-4 stories, interior/exterior corridors. *Bath:* combo or shower only. **Parking:** on-site. **Amenities:** high-speed Internet (fee), voice mail, irons, hair dryers. **Dining:** 2 restaurants, also, The Landing, see separate listing. **Leisure Activities:** exercise room. **Guest Services:** valet and coin laundry, area transportation-within city limits. **Business Services:** meeting rooms, PC (fee). **Cards:** AX, CB, DC, DS, JC, MC, VI. **Free Special Amenities:** early check-in/late check-out and room upgrade (subject to availability with advance reservations).

AAA Benefit:
Members save 10% everyday, plus an exclusive frequent stay program.

CAPE FOX LODGE

Book great rates at AAA.com

Large-scale Hotel
$110-$200 All Year

Phone: (907)225-8001
Address: 800 Venetia Way 99901 **Location:** Above Creek St (Tramway from Creek St). **Facility:** 72 units. 70 one-bedroom standard units. 2 one-bedroom suites with whirlpools. 3 stories, interior/exterior corridors. *Bath:* combo or shower only. **Parking:** on-site. **Amenities:** voice mail, irons, hair dryers. *Fee:* video games, high-speed Internet. **Dining:** Cape Fox Lodge Dining Room & Lodge, see separate listing. **Guest Services:** valet laundry. **Business Services:** meeting rooms, PC (fee). **Cards:** AX, CB, DC, DS, MC, VI. **Free Special Amenities:** local telephone calls.

———— WHERE TO DINE ————

ANNABELLE'S FAMOUS KEG & CHOWDER HOUSE

Seafood
$10-$39

Located directly across from the cruise ship docks, diners can enjoy freshly caught seasonal seafood such as fresh salmon, clam chowder or halibut cheeks in either an attractive bar or classy dining room. Casual dress. **Bar:** Full bar. **Reservations:** suggested. **Hours:** 11 am-9 pm, Fri-Sun to 9:30 pm. Closed major holidays; also Sun 10/1-4/30. **Address:** 326 Front St 99901 **Location:** Center; across from cruise ship docks; in Gilmore Hotel. **Parking:** street. **Cards:** AX, MC, VI.

Phone: 907/225-9423

CAPE FOX LODGE DINING ROOM & LODGE

American
$8-$53

Perched 130 feet above Creek Street and high above the busy cruise ship harbor is the Westcoast Cape Fox Lodge and its reputable dining room, Heen Kahidi—meaning "house by the creek." This place is legendary for celebrating special events. Local seafood anchors the menu, which also includes aged beef, chicken and pasta. Spectacular views of the harbor are framed by pine boughs just outside the windows. Dressy casual. **Bar:** Full bar. **Reservations:** suggested. **Hours:** 7 am-9 pm, Fri & Sat-9:30 pm. Closed: 11/27, 12/24, 12/25; also 11/22. **Address:** 800 Venetia Way 99901 **Location:** Above Creek St (Tramway from Creek St); in Cape Fox Lodge. **Parking:** on-site. **Cards:** AX, DC, DS, MC, VI.

Phone: 907/225-8001

THE LANDING

Continental
$8-$25

Phone: 907/225-5166

Located across from the Marine Ferry terminal, this 1950s-style diner offers an extensive menu of comfort foods as well as some of the best pies in the area. Casual dress. **Bar:** Beer only. **Hours:** 6 am-11 pm; seasonal hours may vary. **Address:** 3434 Tongass Ave 99901 **Location:** Across from Alaska Marine Hwy ferry terminal; in Best Western Landing. **Parking:** on-site. **Cards:** AX, MC, VI.

THE NARROWS INN RESTAURANT
American
$7-$25

Phone: 907/247-2600

Named for the Tongass Narrows on whose shores it is located, the restaurant offers casual dining about 1.5 miles north of town. The quiet rain-forest setting is adjacent to The Narrows Inn. The menu features fresh local seafood as well as pasta, steaks and chops. Casual dress. **Bar:** Full bar. **Reservations:** accepted. **Hours:** 9 am-2 & 5-9 pm, Sun-2 pm; seasonal hours may vary. Closed: 12/25; also Sun 10/1-5/1. **Address:** 4871 N Tongass Hwy 99901 **Location:** 1.6 mi n from Alaska Marine Hwy ferry terminal; 1.2 mi n from Airport ferry terminal. **Parking:** on-site. **Cards:** AX, CB, DC, DS, MC, VI.

NEW YORK CAFE
American
$8-$12

Phone: 907/225-0246

Popular with the local crowd, this casual storefront restaurant is located steps away from the historic town. While not wide ranging, the menu offers a variety of creatively prepared dishes including fresh, locally caught seafood. Casual dress. **Hours:** 7 am-9 pm. Closed major holidays. **Address:** 211 Stedman St 99901 **Location:** Adjacent to Creek St; center. **Parking:** street. **Cards:** AX, MC, VI.

SALMON FALLS RESORT
Steak & Seafood
$21-$55

Phone: 907/225-2752

Overlooking the Clarence Straits and Behm Canal of the Inland Passageway, the restaurant serves fresh northern water seafood and grilled steaks. Casual dress. **Bar:** Full bar. **Reservations:** suggested. **Hours:** Open 5/27-9/30; 5 pm-9 pm. **Address:** 16707 Tongass Hwy 99901 **Location:** 14.5 mi n from Alaska Marine Hwy ferry terminal; 14.1 mi n from Airport ferry terminal. **Parking:** on-site. **Cards:** AX, MC, VI.

STEAMERS ON THE DOCK
Seafood
$13-$40

Phone: 907/225-1600

The casual third floor restaurant commands a magnificent view of Ketchikan harbor and features a variety of locally caught seafood including salmon and clams. Casual dress. **Bar:** Full bar. **Hours:** 10 am-10 pm; 11 am-9 pm off season. Closed major holidays; also Sun. **Address:** 76 Front St 99901 **Location:** Across from cruise ship dock; on 3rd floor of Commercial Building; center. **Parking:** street. **Cards:** AX, DS, MC, VI.

CALL

KLAWOCK pop. 854

—— WHERE TO STAY ——

—— *The following lodging was either not evaluated or did not meet AAA rating requirements but is listed for your information only.* ——

FIREWEED LODGE
[fyi]

Phone: 907/755-2930

Not evaluated. **Address:** 6863 Klawock/Hollis Hwy 99925 **Location:** 4.5 mi w of Hollis ferry terminal. Facilities, services, and decor characterize a mid-range property.

KODIAK pop. 6,334

✈ Airport Accommodations			
KODIAK AIRPORT	Diamond Rating	Rate Range High Season	Listing Page
Comfort Inn Kodiak, adjacent to airport	◆◆	$166-$235	760

—— WHERE TO STAY ——

BEST WESTERN KODIAK INN   *Book great rates at AAA.com*

Small-scale Hotel
$109-$219 All Year

Phone: (907)486-5712

Address: 236 W Rezanof Dr 99615 **Location:** 0.3 mi w of ferry terminal; center. **Facility:** 80 units. 78 one-bedroom standard units, some with whirlpools. 2 one-bedroom suites. 3 stories, interior/exterior corridors. **Parking:** on-site. **Terms:** cancellation fee imposed. **Amenities:** DVD players, voice mail, irons, hair dryers. *Some:* high-speed Internet. **Dining:** Chart Room Restaurant and Lounge, see separate listing. **Leisure Activities:** whirlpool, fish and game freezer. **Guest Services:** coin laundry, area transportation-ferry, wireless Internet. **Business Services:** meeting rooms, PC, fax (fee). **Cards:** AX, DC, DS, MC, VI. **Free Special Amenities:** expanded continental breakfast and high-speed Internet.

AAA Benefit:
Members save 10% everyday, plus an exclusive frequent stay program.

COMFORT INN KODIAK

Book at AAA.com

Small-scale Hotel
$166-$235 3/1-9/30
$110-$200 10/1-2/28

Phone: (907)487-2700

Address: 1395 Airport Way 99615 **Location:** Adjacent to airport. **Facility:** 50 one-bedroom standard units, some with whirlpools. 2 stories, interior corridors. **Parking:** on-site. **Terms:** cancellation fee imposed. **Amenities:** voice mail, irons, hair dryers. *Some:* high-speed Internet. **Leisure Activities:** exercise room. **Guest Services:** coin laundry, area transportation, wireless Internet. **Business Services:** meeting rooms, PC. **Cards:** AX, CB, DC, DS, MC, VI.

——— WHERE TO DINE ———

CHART ROOM RESTAURANT AND LOUNGE

Continental
$9-$40

Phone: 907/486-5712

Diners enjoy a lovely view from the large panoramic windows of this second-floor restaurant. The luncheon menu has a nice variety of casual fare including fresh chowder, tasty salads, sandwiches, pastas and burgers, as well as the ever-popular halibut and chips. Dinner features an extensive fish and seafood selection that is sure to please. Casual dress. **Bar:** Full bar. **Reservations:** suggested. **Hours:** 6:30 am-2 & 5-9:30 pm, Fri & Sat-10 pm; 7 am-2 & 5-9 pm, Fri & Sat-10 pm off season. Closed: 11/27. **Address:** 236 W Rezanof Dr 99615 **Location:** 0.3 mi w of ferry terminal; center; in Best Western Kodiak Inn. **Parking:** on-site. **Cards:** AX, MC, VI.

MOOSE PASS pop. 206

——— WHERE TO STAY ———

TRAIL LAKE LODGE

Book great rates at AAA.com

AAA SAVE

Motel
$89-$115 3/1-9/30
$59 10/1-2/28

Phone: (907)288-3101

Address: MM 29.5 Seward Hwy 99631 **Location:** US 9 (Seward Hwy) at MM 29.5. **Facility:** Designated smoking area. 22 one-bedroom standard units. 1-2 stories (no elevator), exterior corridors. *Bath:* shower only. **Parking:** on-site. **Terms:** 7 day cancellation notice-fee imposed. **Cards:** AX, DS, MC, VI.

PALMER pop. 4,533

——— WHERE TO STAY ———

PEAK INN MOTEL

AAA SAVE

Motel
$80-$105 3/1-9/14
$55-$80 9/15-2/28

Phone: (907)746-5757

Address: 775 W Evergreen Ave 99645 **Location:** Just w of Glenn Hwy (SR 1). **Facility:** 21 one-bedroom standard units, some with efficiencies (utensils extra charge). 1 story, exterior corridors. **Parking:** on-site. **Terms:** 7 day cancellation notice. **Cards:** AX, DS, MC, VI. **Free Special Amenities:** local telephone calls and high-speed Internet.

——— WHERE TO DINE ———

THE INN CAFE

American
$7-$9

Phone: 907/746-6118

Just a short distance from the tourist information center, this small restaurant overflows the lobby of the Inn B&B. Immensely popular with locals, the casual place is well known for its tastily prepared meals. Using a mix of local and seasonal ingredients, the chef/owner creates approachable food, such as daily quiches, light sandwiches and salads that are strong on flavor. Casual dress. **Reservations:** not accepted. **Hours:** 11 am-3 pm, Sun 9 am-2 pm. Closed major holidays; also Sat. **Address:** 325 E Elmwood Ave 99645 **Location:** 1 mi e of Glenn Hwy (SR 1) along Evergreen Ave (which becomes E Elmwood Ave); centre. **Parking:** on-site. **Cards:** MC, VI.

SELDOVIA pop. 286

——— WHERE TO DINE ———

THE MAD FISH RESTAURANT

American
$8-$28

Phone: 907/234-7676

A fun and vibrant eatery serving creative fare ranging from seafood to vegetarian dishes and homemade gourmet desserts. Casual dress. **Bar:** Beer & wine. **Reservations:** suggested. **Hours:** Open 5/1-9/5; noon-4 & 5:30-9 pm. Closed: Wed. **Address:** 221 Main St 99663 **Location:** Center. **Parking:** on-site. **Cards:** MC, VI.

SEWARD pop. 2,830

——— WHERE TO STAY ———

BOX CANYON CABINS

Cabin
$150-$260 5/1-10/31

Phone: (907)224-5046

Address: 31515 Lois Way 99664 **Location:** 3.5 mi n on SR 9, just w on Herman Leirer Rd; 1 mi n on Old Exit Glacier Rd, just e. **Facility:** Smoke free premises. 6 cabins. 1 story, exterior corridors. *Bath:* shower only. **Parking:** on-site, winter plug-ins. **Terms:** open 5/1-10/31, check-in 4 pm, 45 day cancellation notice-fee imposed. **Amenities:** hair dryers. **Leisure Activities:** hiking trails. *Fee:* charter fishing. **Guest Services:** coin laundry, wireless Internet. **Cards:** MC, VI.

HARBORVIEW INN

Motel
$59-$144 All Year

Book great rates at AAA.com   Phone: (907)224-3217
Address: 804 Third Ave 99664 **Location:** Just n of the Alaska Sealife Center. **Facility:** Smoke free premises. 39 units. 36 one-bedroom standard units. 2 two- and 1 three-bedroom suites with kitchens. 2 stories (no elevator), exterior corridors. *Bath:* combo or shower only. **Parking:** on-site, winter plug-ins. **Terms:** office hours 8 am-10 pm, check-in 4 pm, 3 day cancellation notice. **Amenities:** hair dryers. **Guest Services:** wireless Internet. **Cards:** AX, DS, MC, VI. **Free Special Amenities: local telephone calls and high-speed Internet.** *(See color ad below)*

HOLIDAY INN EXPRESS SEWARD HARBOR HOTEL   *Book at AAA.com*   Phone: (907)224-2550

Small-scale Hotel
$69-$299 All Year

Address: 1412 4th Ave 99664 **Location:** At Small Boat Harbor. **Facility:** Smoke free premises. 82 one-bedroom standard units. 3 stories, interior corridors. *Bath:* combo or shower only. **Parking:** on-site, winter plug-ins. **Amenities:** high-speed Internet, voice mail. *Some:* irons, hair dryers. **Pool(s):** indoor, heated indoor. **Leisure Activities:** whirlpool. **Guest Services:** coin laundry. **Cards:** AX, DC, DS, MC, VI.

▼ See AAA listing p 762 ▼

HOTEL EDGEWATER

Small-scale Hotel
$99-$359 3/1-9/30

Book great rates at AAA.com

Phone: (907)224-2700

Address: 200 5th Ave 99664 **Location:** Just n of Alaska Sealife Center. **Facility:** 76 one-bedroom standard units. 3 stories, interior corridors. *Bath:* combo or shower only. **Parking:** on-site and valet. **Terms:** open 3/1-9/30, 3 day cancellation notice-fee imposed. **Amenities:** video library, dual phone lines, hair dryers. **Leisure Activities:** sauna, whirlpool, limited exercise equipment. **Guest Services:** valet and coin laundry, airport transportation-Seward Airport, area transportation-within 5 mi & train depot, wireless Internet. **Business Services:** meeting rooms, PC. **Cards:** AX, CB, DC, DS, JC, MC, VI. **Free Special Amenities: continental breakfast and high-speed Internet.**
(See color ad p 761)

SEWARD WINDSONG LODGE

Small-scale Hotel
Rates not provided

Phone: 907/224-7116

Address: Milepost 0.5 Herman Leirer Rd 99664 **Location:** 3.5 mi n on SR 9, 0.5 mi w on Herman Leirer Rd (former exit Glacier Rd). **Facility:** Smoke free premises. 144 one-bedroom standard units, some with whirlpools. 2 stories (no elevator), exterior corridors. *Bath:* combo or shower only. **Parking:** on-site. **Terms:** open 5/12-9/9. **Amenities:** video library, voice mail, hair dryers. **Dining:** Resurrection Roadhouse, see separate listing. **Guest Services:** airport transportation-Seward Airport, area transportation-downtown & harbor. **Business Services:** meeting rooms, PC (fee). **Free Special Amenities: local telephone calls.**

——— WHERE TO DINE ———

CHINOOKS WATERFRONT RESTAURANT

Steak & Seafood
$8-$35

Phone: 907/224-2207

Diners will enjoy, on a clear day, the spectacular views of the mountains and harbor from the large panoramic windows. A great choice for both family and special occasion dining, the restaurant features two floors of dining with great views from all tables. The view is complemented by the chef's selection of fresh local seafood, pasta and steak selections. Casual dress. **Bar:** Full bar. **Hours:** Open 5/1-9/30; 11:30 am-10 pm. **Address:** 1404 4th Ave 99664 **Location:** At Small Boat Harbor. **Parking:** street. **Cards:** AX, DC, DS, MC, VI.

THE CRAB POT RESTAURANT Phone: 907/224-2200
◆◆◆ ◆◆◆
Steak & Seafood
$15-$46

A relaxed ambiance and friendly service complement the varied menu of freshly prepared cuisine. Fresh local fish and seafood is the specialty here, including live Alaskan king crab in season. Other choices include oysters, clams and local salmon and halibut. For those not in the mood for seafood, an excellent selection of pastas, stir-fries and sizzling steaks are available. All entrees include a choice of salad or homemade chowder. Casual dress. **Reservations:** not accepted. **Hours:** Open 6/1-8/31; 4 pm-midnight. **Address:** 303 Adams St 99664 **Location:** Just n of Alaska Sealife Center; downtown. **Parking:** street. **Cards:** DS, MC, VI.

GREEK ISLANDS Phone: 907/224-4433
◆◆◆ ◆◆◆
Greek
$9-$24

Diners enjoy a mixed menu that's great for families. In addition to Greek specialties, the menu lists made-to-order pizza and pasta, as well as fresh local seafood and steak. Locally made cheesecake is a dessert favorite. Casual dress. **Hours:** 11 am-midnight. **Address:** 308 N Harbor St 99664 **Location:** Just n of Alaska Sealife Center. **Parking:** on-site. **Cards:** AX, DS, JC, MC, VI.

ORIENTAL GARDEN Phone: 907/224-7677
◆◆◆ ◆◆◆
Chinese
$8-$18

This casual restaurant has a very authentic Oriental decor complete with Chinese lanterns and a comfortable ambiance. A tasty luncheon buffet is featured Monday through Saturday in addition to the full a la carte selections. Both Japanese and Chinese cuisine are featured here with some very reasonably priced combination meals being popular choices. Casual dress. **Bar:** Full bar. **Hours:** 11 am-10 pm. **Address:** 313 4th Ave 99664 **Location:** Just n of Alaska Sealife Center; downtown. **Parking:** street. **Cards:** AX, DS, MC, VI.

PEKING RESTAURANT Phone: 907/224-5444
◆◆◆ ◆◆◆
Chinese
$7-$15

The traditional restaurant serves a variety of dishes, including chicken balls and lemon chicken and rice, as well as dishes inspired by the area. For a new twist, try the kung pao halibut, a tasty dish that is sure to please. At lunch you satisfy any hunger at the all-you-can-eat buffet, or order a la carte off the menu. Casual dress. **Bar:** Full bar. **Reservations:** accepted. **Hours:** 10 am-11 pm. Closed major holidays. **Address:** 338 4th Ave 99664 **Location:** Downtown. **Parking:** street. **Cards:** AX, CB, DC, DS, JC, MC, VI.

RESURRECTION ROADHOUSE Phone: 907/224-7116
◆◆◆ ◆◆◆
Regional American
$5-$28

Continuing the theme of the adjacent lodge, you'll be seated in a dining room with a natural wood decor while enjoying the views of the wooded setting overlooking a glacial stream. Heaping portions of tasty Alaskan seafood is the standout here. Dressy casual. **Bar:** Full bar. **Reservations:** suggested. **Hours:** Open 5/14-9/30; 7 am-2 & 5-9 pm. **Address:** Milepost 0.6 (Herman Leirer Rd) 99664 **Location:** 3.5 mi n on SR 9, 0.5 mi w on Herman Leirer Rd (formerly exit Glacier Rd); in Seward Windsong Lodge. **Parking:** on-site. **Cards:** AX, MC, VI.

CALL 👍M

YOLY'S BISTRO Phone: 907/224-3295
◆◆◆ ◆◆◆
Regional American
$5-$26

The eclectic menu features fresh regional seafood flavored with innovative sauces. Fresh fruit smoothies are delicious. Wood accents mark the bright, airy interior, which displays the original work of local artists on the walls. Casual dress. **Bar:** Beer & wine. **Hours:** 11 am-4 & 5-10 pm. Closed major holidays. **Address:** 220 4th Ave 99664 **Location:** Center; 2 blks n of Alaska Sea Life Center. **Parking:** street. **Cards:** MC, VI.

SITKA pop. 8,835

——— **WHERE TO STAY** ———

ALASKA OCEAN VIEW BED AND BREAKFAST INN *Book at AAA.com* Phone: (907)747-8310
◆◆◆◆
Bed & Breakfast
$99-$249 All Year

Address: 1101 Edgecumbe Dr 99835 **Location:** 1 mi n on Halibut Point Rd; 5.7 mi s of Alaska Marine Hwy ferry terminal, just e on Kashevarof St, then just s. Located in a residential area. **Facility:** Attractively decorated rooms with excellent amenities are offered at this ocean-view B&B; a garden pond enhances the setting. Smoke free premises. 3 one-bedroom standard units, some with whirlpools. 2 stories (no elevator), interior corridors. **Parking:** on-site. **Terms:** cancellation fee imposed. **Amenities:** video library, DVD players, CD players, high-speed Internet, irons, hair dryers. **Leisure Activities:** whirlpool, horseshoes. **Business Services:** PC. **Cards:** AX, CB, DC, DS, MC, VI.

(ASK) ✕ 👍 (VCR) ▯ ▱ ▭

HELGA'S BED & BREAKFAST BY THE SEA Phone: (907)747-5497
◆◆◆ ◆◆◆
Bed & Breakfast
Rates not provided

Address: 2827 Halibut Point Rd 99835 **Location:** 3 mi n on Halibut Point Rd; 3.4 mi s of Alaska Marine Hwy ferry terminal. **Facility:** Smoke free premises. 4 units. 3 one-bedroom standard units. 1 two-bedroom suite. 2 stories (no elevator), interior corridors. *Bath:* combo or shower only. **Parking:** on-site. **Terms:** age restrictions may apply. **Guest Services:** coin laundry.

🍴 ✕ 👍 ▯ ▱ ▭

SHEE ATIKA TOTEM SQUARE INN *Book great rates at AAA.com* Phone: (907)747-3693
(AAA) (SAVE)
◆◆◆ ◆◆◆
Small-scale Hotel
$159-$169 3/1-9/30
$99-$109 10/1-2/28

Address: 201 Katlian St 99835 **Location:** Center; in Totem Square Complex, near Municipal Office. **Facility:** Smoke free premises. 68 one-bedroom standard units. 4 stories, interior corridors. *Bath:* combo or shower only. **Parking:** on-site. **Terms:** cancellation fee imposed. **Amenities:** high-speed Internet, voice mail, hair dryers. **Guest Services:** coin laundry, wireless Internet. **Business Services:** meeting rooms, PC. **Cards:** AX, DS, MC, VI. **Free Special Amenities:** expanded continental breakfast and high-speed Internet.

🍴 ✕ 👍 ▭ / SOME UNITS FEE 🐾

WESTMARK SITKA

Small-scale Hotel
$159 3/1-9/15
$129 9/16-2/28

Book great rates at AAA.com Phone: (907)747-6241

Address: 330 Seward St 99835 **Location:** Center. **Facility:** Smoke free premises. 101 one-bedroom standard units, some with kitchens. 4 stories, interior corridors. *Bath:* combo or shower only. **Parking:** on-site. **Amenities:** video library (fee), high-speed Internet, voice mail, irons, hair dryers. **Guest Services:** valet laundry. **Business Services:** meeting rooms, PC. **Cards:** AX, CB, DC, DS, JC, MC, VI. **Free Special Amenities: local telephone calls and high-speed Internet.**

WILD STRAWBERRY LODGE FISHING RESORT Phone: 907/747-3232

Resort Motel
$95-$135 3/1-9/1
$75-$95 9/2-2/28

Address: 724 Siginaka Way 99835 **Location:** 1 mi n on Halibut Point Rd, just w on Katlian (only traffic light on island). Located at Thomsen Harbor. **Facility:** This is not your typical "fishing lodge," as the owners encourage males and females of all ages to try their hand at catching "the big one". Smoke free premises. 10 units. 8 one-bedroom standard units. 1 two-bedroom suite with kitchen. 1 vacation home. 1 story, interior/exterior corridors. *Bath:* combo or shower only. **Parking:** on-site. **Leisure Activities:** *Fee:* charter fishing. **Guest Services:** complimentary laundry, area transportation. **Business Services:** PC. **Cards:** AX, DS, MC, VI.

——— WHERE TO DINE ———

BAYVIEW RESTAURANT Phone: 907/747-5440

American
$8-$28

The second floor location can be difficult to find, but this casual restaurant offers an extensive menu ranging from sandwiches to fresh seafood and steak as well as a large variety of daily made desserts. Casual dress. **Bar:** Full bar. **Reservations:** accepted. **Hours:** 5 am-10 pm, Sun-3 pm; 7 am-3 pm off season. **Address:** 407 Lincoln St 99835 **Location:** Center; on 2nd floor of Mac Donald Trading Company Building. **Parking:** street. **Cards:** AX, DS, MC, VI.

LITTLE TOKYO Phone: 907/747-5699

Sushi
$8-$15

A short walk from the marina will bring you to this small restaurant that features a sushi bar. Diners can watch chefs prepare sushi and sashimi or they can order from the standard menu. Casual dress. **Bar:** Beer only. **Hours:** 11 am-9 pm. **Closed:** 11/27, 12/25. **Address:** 315 Lincoln St 99835 **Location:** Center. **Parking:** street. **Cards:** AX, MC, VI.

LUDVIG'S BISTRO Phone: 907/966-3663

Mediterranean
$19-$32

A popular choice with locals and visitors alike, the restaurant serves a variety of Mediterranean fare prepared with a regional influence. Dressy casual. **Bar:** Beer & wine. **Reservations:** suggested. **Hours:** 2 pm-10 pm. Closed major holidays; also Sun & Mon. **Address:** 256 Katlian St 99835 **Location:** Center; 0.3 mi n of Totem Square. **Parking:** street. **Cards:** MC, VI.

RAVEN DINING ROOM Phone: 907/747-6241

American
$9-$32

This casual restaurant has long served as the training kitchen for chefs who later go on to work on the cruise ships that the restaurant overlooks. Diners can expect standard items ranging from sandwiches to steak as well as creative touches to locally caught and seasonal seafood. Casual dress. **Bar:** Full bar. **Reservations:** suggested. **Hours:** 6:30 am-2 & 5-9 pm, Fri & Sat-10 pm; 6:30 am-2 & 5-10 pm 5/15-9/15. Closed: 12/25; also for dinner 12/24. **Address:** 330 Seward St 99835 **Location:** Center; in Westmark Shee Atika. **Parking:** on-site and street. **Cards:** AX, CB, DC, DS, JC, MC, VI.

TEA-LICIOUS TEA HOUSE & BAKERY Phone: 907/747-4535

Deli/Subs
Sandwiches
$5-$7

Not surprisingly, this casually upscale restaurant is the scene of many afternoon tea parties. As well as offering an extensive selection of both hot and iced teas, the restaurant features a variety of delicate deli sandwiches and bakery items. Casual dress. **Reservations:** not accepted. **Hours:** 11 am-6 pm. Closed: 3/23, 11/27, 12/25; also Sun. **Address:** 315 Lincoln St, Suite 110 99835 **Location:** Center. **Parking:** street. **Cards:** AX, DS, MC, VI.

VAN WINKLE & SONS Phone: 907/747-7652

American
$7-$26

Tasty regional cuisine awaits you at this popular eatery. Alaskan art adorns the walls, and you can gaze at the water while dining. Located upstairs of a small shopping mall near the bridge, the restaurant's view of the bay is spectacular and the food well prepared. Casual dress. **Bar:** Full bar. **Reservations:** suggested, in summer. **Hours:** 11:30 am-1:45 & 5-9:30 pm, Sat from 5 pm. Closed: 12/25; also Sun. **Address:** 205 Harbor Dr 99835 **Location:** Downtown; across from Crescent Harbor, just before O'Connell Bridge. **Parking:** on-site. **Cards:** AX, MC, VI.

SKAGWAY pop. 862

——— WHERE TO STAY ———

WESTMARK INN SKAGWAY *Book great rates at AAA.com* Phone: 907/983-6000

Small-scale Hotel
$135-$145 5/11-9/15

Address: 3rd & Spring St 99840 **Location:** Downtown. **Facility:** 151 one-bedroom standard units. 2 stories (no elevator), interior/exterior corridors. **Parking:** on-site. **Terms:** open 5/11-9/15, cancellation fee imposed. **Amenities:** irons, hair dryers. **Dining:** 2 restaurants. **Guest Services:** coin laundry, area transportation-local area. **Business Services:** meeting rooms, PC. **Cards:** AX, MC, VI. **Free Special Amenities: local telephone calls.**

------ WHERE TO DINE ------

BONANZA BAR & GRILL
American
$7-$15

Phone: 907/983-6214

Open seasonally, this sports bar can be loud and boisterous and is a popular spot for those looking for a wide selection of bar favorites. Casual dress. **Bar:** Full bar. **Reservations:** not accepted. **Hours:** Open 5/10-9/15; 10 am-midnight. **Address:** 3rd & Spring St 99840 **Location:** Jct 3rd and Broadway sts; downtown. **Parking:** street. **Cards:** AX, DC, DS, JC, MC, VI.

HAVEN CAFE
Coffee/Espresso
$3-$8

Phone: 907/983-3553

Off the beaten track from downtown, the upscale coffeehouse brews a great cup of coffee, which patrons often sip with one of the varied breakfast options, salads, panini sandwiches, shakes or desserts. The cozy refuge is attached to a health-food store. A few coveted tables are outside. Casual dress. **Reservations:** not accepted. **Hours:** 6 am-10 pm; seasonal hours vary. Closed major holidays. **Location:** 9th St and State. **Parking:** street. **Cards:** MC, VI.

SWEET TOOTH CAFE
American
$7-$15

Phone: 907/983-2405

A local favorite, this casual Victorian-style restaurant offers few surprises but is well regarded for its well-prepared breakfasts and lunches. Casual dress. **Reservations:** accepted. **Hours:** 6 am-2 pm. Closed: 1/1, 11/27, 12/25. **Address:** 315 Broadway St 99840 **Location:** Jct 3rd St; downtown. **Parking:** street. **Cards:** MC, VI.

SOLDOTNA pop. 3,759

------ WHERE TO STAY ------

ALASKAN SERENITY BED AND BREAKFAST
Bed & Breakfast
$59-$180 All Year

Phone: (907)262-6648

Address: 41598 Aksala Ln 99669 **Location:** Sterling Hwy (SR 1), 1.5 mi e, 1.6 mi n on Mackey Lake Rd, then 0.5 mi e on Denise Lake Rd. **Facility:** Smoke free premises. 5 units. 2 one- and 1 two-bedroom standard units. 2 cabins. 2 stories (no elevator), interior/exterior corridors. *Bath:* combo or shower only. **Parking:** on-site, winter plug-ins. **Terms:** check-in 4 pm, 2 night minimum stay, 30 day cancellation notice-fee imposed. **Amenities:** video library. **Leisure Activities:** whirlpool. **Cards:** AX, DS, MC, VI.

ASPEN HOTEL-SOLDOTNA *Book at AAA.com*
Small-scale Hotel
$89-$179 All Year

Phone: (907)260-7736

Address: 326 Binkley Cir 99669 **Location:** Sterling Hwy (SR 1) at Binkley Cir; center. **Facility:** 63 units. 58 one- and 2 two-bedroom standard units, some with whirlpools. 3 one-bedroom suites with efficiencies. 2 stories, interior corridors. *Bath:* combo or shower only. **Parking:** on-site, winter plug-ins. **Terms:** cancellation fee imposed. **Amenities:** video library (fee), DVD players, dual phone lines, voice mail, irons, hair dryers. *Some:* video games. **Pool(s):** heated indoor. **Leisure Activities:** whirlpool, limited exercise equipment. **Guest Services:** valet and coin laundry, wireless Internet. **Business Services:** meeting rooms, business center. **Cards:** AX, DC, DS, MC, VI.

BEST WESTERN KING SALMON MOTEL *Book great rates at AAA.com*
Motel
Rates not provided

Phone: 907-262-5857

Address: 35546 A Kenai Spur Hwy 99669 **Location:** 1 mi nw on Kenai Spur Hwy. **Facility:** 48 one-bedroom standard units, some with efficiencies (no utensils). 2 stories (no elevator), exterior corridors. **Parking:** on-site, winter plug-ins. **Terms:** office hours 7 am-11 pm, check-in 4 pm. **Amenities:** high-speed Internet, dual phone lines, voice mail, irons, hair dryers. **Guest Services:** coin laundry. **Business Services:** meeting rooms, fax. **Free Special Amenities:** local telephone calls and high-speed Internet.

AAA Benefit:
Members save 10% everyday, plus an exclusive frequent stay program.

KENAI JIM'S LODGE & GUIDE SERVICE
Condominium
Rates not provided

Phone: 907/262-1324

Address: Polar St, Bldg A 99669 **Location:** Sterling Hwy (SR 1), 0.3 mi w on Kalifornsky Beach Rd, then s on Polar St. Located in a quiet area. **Facility:** Smoke free premises. 3 two-bedroom suites with kitchens. 2 stories (no elevator), interior corridors. **Parking:** on-site, winter plug-ins. **Terms:** open 5/1-9/30. **Leisure Activities:** *Fee:* charter fishing. **Guest Services:** coin laundry.

KENAI RIVER RAVEN LODGE
Bed & Breakfast
$175-$240 3/1-8/31
$120-$130 9/1-2/28

Phone: 907/262-5818

Address: Mile 0.2 Funny River Rd 99669 **Location:** Sterling Hwy (SR 1) at Milepost 96.5, just e. **Facility:** A modern log home in a secluded wooded area near the river, this B&B offers bright guest rooms; the breakfast room has a stone fireplace. Smoke free premises. 8 one-bedroom standard units, some with efficiencies and/or whirlpools. 3 stories (no elevator), interior corridors. **Parking:** on-site. **Terms:** check-in 4 pm, age restrictions may apply. **Leisure Activities:** boat dock, fishing, river access. *Fee:* fishing guides. **Guest Services:** wireless Internet. **Cards:** AX, MC, VI. **Free Special Amenities:** full breakfast and high-speed Internet.

LONGMERE LAKE LODGE B & B

Phone: (907)262-9799

 AAA SAVE

WWW WWW

Bed & Breakfast
$115-$290 5/25-8/31

Address: 35955 Ryan Ln 99669 **Location:** 5 mi e of town at Milepost 88 on Sterling Hwy (SR 1), 1 mi s on St. Theresa Rd, then just w. Located in a quiet secluded area. **Facility:** Smoke free premises. 6 units. 5 one-bedroom standard units, some with whirlpools. 1 one-bedroom suite with kitchen. 2 stories (no elevator), interior corridors. *Bath:* combo or shower only. **Parking:** on-site, winter plug-ins. **Terms:** open 5/25-8/31, check-in 4 pm, 30 day cancellation notice-fee imposed. **Amenities:** video library, hair dryers. **Leisure Activities:** canoeing, paddleboats, boat dock, fishing, fish freezing facilities, barbecue, croquet, horseshoes. **Guest Services:** wireless Internet. **Business Services:** PC. **Cards:** AX, MC, VI. **Free Special Amenities:** expanded continental breakfast and high-speed Internet.

[icons: ⊠ ⊠ K CTV VCR / SOME UNITS ☎ 🛄 🖼 🖵]

ORCA LODGE

Phone: (907)262-5649

WWW

Cottage
$190 5/1-9/30

Address: 44250 Oehler Dr 99669 **Location:** Sterling Hwy (SR 1) at Milepost 96.5, 0.8 mi e on Funny River Rd, just n. **Facility:** Smoke free premises. 6 cottages. 1 story, exterior corridors. **Parking:** on-site. **Terms:** open 5/1-9/30, 30 day cancellation notice. **Leisure Activities:** *Fee:* charter fishing. **Business Services:** PC. **Cards:** AX, MC, VI.

[icons: ASK SD ⊠ K W ☎ 🛄 🖵]

SPURRVIEW HOUSE BED & BREAKFAST

Phone: 907/260-6961

WWW WWW

Bed & Breakfast
$100-$275 All Year

Address: 36725 Jim Dahler Rd 99669 **Location:** Sterling Hwy SR1, 1 mi n. **Facility:** Smoke free premises. 3 units. 2 one-bedroom standard units. 1 two-bedroom suite with kitchen. 2 stories (no elevator), interior corridors. *Bath:* shower or tub only. **Parking:** on-site. **Terms:** 2 night minimum stay - seasonal, 30 day cancellation notice. **Amenities:** hair dryers. *Some:* DVD players, irons. **Leisure Activities:** cross country skiing, jogging. **Guest Services:** complimentary laundry, wireless Internet.

[icons: ASK SD ⊠ K 🌳 ☎ / SOME UNITS VCR 🛄 🖼 🖵]

——— **WHERE TO DINE** ———

CHARLOTTE'S RESTAURANT

Phone: 907/283-2777

WWW WWW

American
$7-$10

Tucked in the back of a bookstore, the restaurant is one of the city's best-kept secrets. Healthy, hearty fare cooked by Charlotte is sure to please. The limited menu lists a choice of sandwiches, wraps, soups and often a quiche of the day. Guests might linger over dessert, then browse the bookstore. Casual dress. **Reservations:** accepted. **Hours:** 7 am-4 pm; 8 am-3 pm in winter. Closed major holidays. **Address:** 115 S Willow St, Suite 102 99611 **Location:** Jct Sterling Hwy (SR 1) and Kenai Spur Hwy; adjacent to bookstore. **Parking:** on-site. **Cards:** AX, MC, VI.

[icon: K]

CHINA SEA RESTAURANT

Phone: 907/262-5033

WWW

Chinese
$8-$15

A local favorite for the all-day all-you-can-eat Chinese buffet, this restaurant offers a nice mix of casual fare in a relaxed setting. The buffet includes a tasty salad bar, a choice of soups and mixed Chinese fare, including noodles, stir-fry, sweet and sour pork, chicken wings and rice. Self-serve soft ice cream is a great finish. Casual dress. **Hours:** 11 am-9 pm. Closed: 12/25. **Address:** 44539 Sterling Hwy, Suite 210 99669 **Location:** Sterling Hwy (SR 1); center at Blazy Mall, 2nd Floor. **Parking:** on-site. **Cards:** AX, MC, VI.

THE CROSSING

Phone: 907/262-1906

WWW WWW

Regional American
-$6-$28

Guests can look out to the Kenai River through a large wall of windows in the upscale dining room, which has high beamed ceilings and wood accents. Fresh local seafood factors prominently on the menu. Outdoor seating is an option when the weather permits. Dressy casual. **Bar:** Full bar. **Reservations:** suggested. **Hours:** 11 am-9 pm, Fri & Sat-10 pm. Closed major holidays; also Sun. **Address:** 44789 Sterling Hwy 99669 **Location:** South end of bridge. **Parking:** on-site. **Cards:** AX, DS, MC, VI.

CALL [icon: &M]

FROSO'S FAMILY DINING

Phone: 907/262-5306

WWW WWW

Continental
$8-$36

The family-oriented restaurant has a distinct Greek influence in its decor and menu selections. Guests enjoy the comfortable booths and ornate chandeliers that adorn the ceilings. The extensive menu includes fine steak and seafood options, freshly made pizzas and pasta dishes, and a full Mexican section. All entrees include soup or salad, or for an additional charge, diners can indulge in the salad bar. Casual dress. **Bar:** Full bar. **Hours:** 11 am-midnight. Closed major holidays. **Address:** 35433 Kenai Spur Hwy 99669 **Location:** Jct Marydale Ave. **Parking:** on-site. **Cards:** AX, DC, DS, MC, VI.

STERLING pop. 4,705

——— **WHERE TO DINE** ———

SUZIE'S CAFE

Phone: 907/260-5751

WWW

American
$7-$14

Ask anyone in Sterling for a great, inexpensive place to eat, and this eatery will be mentioned again and again. This diner-style eatery is conveniently located on the highway, so whether you're passing through town or staying a few days, you can stop and enjoy huge burgers, fish and chips, sandwiches and salads. Breakfast is available on weekends, and the service is prompt and attentive. Casual dress. **Bar:** Beer & wine. **Reservations:** not accepted. **Hours:** 11:30 am-9 pm. Closed: 12/25. **Address:** Milepost 82.7, Sterling Hwy 99672 **Location:** Milepost 83, Sterling Hwy (SR 1). **Parking:** on-site. **Cards:** AX, MC, VI.

[icon: K]

TALKEETNA pop. 772

——— WHERE TO STAY ———

TALKEETNA ALASKAN LODGE
Phone: 907/733-9500

(AAA) [SAVE]

▼▼▼

Small-scale Hotel
$149-$559 5/14-9/18

Address: Mile 12.5 Talkeetna Spur Rd 99676 **Location:** 3.5 mi s of Talkeetna. **Facility:** Smoke free premises. 212 units. 209 one-bedroom standard units, some with whirlpools. 3 one-bedroom suites with whirlpools. 3 stories, interior/exterior corridors. *Bath:* combo or shower only. **Parking:** on-site, winter plug-ins. **Terms:** open 5/14-9/18, 14 day cancellation notice-fee imposed. **Amenities:** voice mail, hair dryers. **Dining:** 2 restaurants. **Leisure Activities:** outdoor viewing deck, hiking trails. **Guest Services:** airport transportation-Talkeetna Airport, area transportation-train depot, wireless Internet. **Business Services:** meeting rooms, PC (fee). **Cards:** AX, DS, MC, VI. **Free Special Amenities:** local telephone calls.

——— WHERE TO DINE ———

CAFE' MICHELE
Phone: 907/733-5300

▼▼▼

Regional American
$9-$27

A meal at Michele's is a must when traveling to Talkeetna. The atmosphere is casual and fitting for this "Northern Exposure" town. You may have a difficult time choosing between fresh Alaskan seafood on pasta and the king crab legs served with the freshest vegetables this side of Anchorage! Your basket of freshly baked bread will be refilled often, but save room for one of the homemade desserts, such as the delicious and light chocolate ricotta cheesecake. Casual dress. **Bar:** Beer & wine. **Reservations:** accepted. **Hours:** Open 5/1-10/1; 11 am-4 & 5:30-10 pm. **Address:** 13.75 Talkeetna Spur Rd 99676 **Location:** Milepost 13.5 (Talkeetna Spur Rd) and Second St. **Parking:** on-site. **Cards:** MC, VI.

TALKEETNA ROADHOUSE
Phone: 907/733-1351

▼▼

Coffee/Espresso
$4-$12

The food is simple and the decor basic, but the atmosphere and desserts are unforgettable. A city stop is not complete without a stop to the historic roadhouse. The dessert case is stocked with fresh, homemade goodies, ranging from huge hiker cookies to pies to the ultimate cinnamon bun. Guests seat themselves as they walk in the door and are entertained by the banter of the staff. Casual dress. **Bar:** Beer & wine. **Reservations:** not accepted. **Hours:** 6:30 am-3 & 5-9 pm; Sat & Sun 8 am-2 pm in winter. Closed major holidays. **Location:** Downtown; in historic district. **Parking:** on-site. **Cards:** MC, VI. **Historic**

TOK pop. 1,393

——— WHERE TO STAY ———

CLEFT OF THE ROCK BED & BREAKFAST
Phone: (907)883-4219

(AAA) [SAVE]

▼▼

Cabin
$95-$145 3/1-9/30
$75-$85 10/1-2/28

Address: 122 Sundog Tr 99780 **Location:** Jct SR 1 and 2 (Alaskan Hwy), 3 mi w on SR 2 (Alaskan Hwy) to Sundog Trail, then 0.5 mi n. **Facility:** Smoke free premises. 8 units. 3 one-bedroom standard units, some with whirlpools. 5 cabins. 2 stories (no elevator), interior/exterior corridors. *Bath:* some shared or private, combo or shower only. **Parking:** on-site, winter plug-ins. **Terms:** check-in 5 pm, 3 day cancellation notice-fee imposed. **Amenities:** video library. *Some:* DVD players. **Leisure Activities:** cross country skiing, play area, hiking trails, basketball. **Business Services:** business center. **Cards:** DS, MC, VI. **Free Special Amenities:** full breakfast and high-speed Internet.

WESTMARK INN TOK
Book great rates at AAA.com
Phone: (907)883-5174

(AAA) [SAVE]

▼▼

Motel
$139 5/15-9/9

Address: Jct Alaska Hwy & Glenn Hwy 99780 **Location:** On SR 1; jct SR 2 (Alaskan Hwy). **Facility:** 93 one-bedroom standard units. 2 stories (no elevator), exterior corridors. **Parking:** on-site. **Terms:** open 5/15-9/9, cancellation fee imposed. **Amenities:** voice mail, irons, hair dryers. **Guest Services:** coin laundry. **Business Services:** PC. **Cards:** AX, DS, MC, VI. **Free Special Amenities:** local telephone calls.

——— WHERE TO DINE ———

FAST EDDY'S RESTAURANT
Phone: 907/883-4411

▼▼▼

American
$4-$30

Decorated in contemporary appointments, the comfortable, family-oriented restaurant specializes in hoagies, steaks, halibut and handmade pizzas. The key word is "fast"—meals are served with remarkable speed. Also on the diverse menu are gourmet burgers, sandwiches and pasta. Casual dress. **Bar:** Beer & wine. **Reservations:** accepted. **Hours:** 6 am-11 pm; seasonal hours may vary. Closed: 1/1, 11/27, 12/25. **Address:** 1313 Alaska Hwy 99780 **Location:** Jct SR 1 and 2 (Alaskan Hwy), 1 mi e on SR 2 (Alaska Hwy). **Parking:** on-site. **Cards:** AX, DS, MC, VI.

GATEWAY SALMON BAKE & RV CAMPGROUND
Phone: 907/883-5555

▼

American
$7-$19

A trip to Tok would not be complete without a stop at Gateway Salmon Bake, an Alaskan treat. Guests order a choice of reindeer, buffalo, salmon or halibut at the office, then unwind on the outdoor patio or in the cabin while their selection is being barbecued. Seafood chowder and a salad bar round out the meal. The restaurant offers great value for the dollar. Casual dress. **Reservations:** accepted. **Hours:** Open 5/25-8/31; 11 am-9 pm. **Address:** Mile 1313.1 Alaska Hwy 99780 **Location:** Jct SR 1 and 2 (Alaska Hwy), 1 mi e on SR 2 (Alaska Hwy). **Parking:** on-site. **Cards:** AX, DS, MC, VI.

TRAPPER CREEK pop. 423

---------- WHERE TO STAY ----------

GATE CREEK CABINS

Cottage
$130 All Year

Phone: (907)733-1393

Address: Mile 10.5 Petersville Rd 99683 **Location:** From MM 114 (Parks Hwy), 10.5 mi w at Petersville Rd. **Facility:** Smoke free premises. 8 cottages. 2 stories (no elevator), exterior corridors. *Bath:* combo or shower only. **Parking:** on-site, winter plug-ins. **Terms:** check-in 4 pm, 2 night minimum stay - seasonal and/or weekends, 10 day cancellation notice. **Amenities:** video library (fee). **Leisure Activities:** sauna, canoeing, paddleboats, bicycles, playground. *Fee:* snowmobiling. **Cards:** AX, MC, VI. *(See color ad below)*

VALDEZ pop. 4,036

---------- WHERE TO STAY ----------

ASPEN HOTEL   *Book at AAA.com*

Small-scale Hotel
Rates not provided

Phone: 907/835-4445

Address: 100 Meals Ave 99686 **Location:** Richardson Hwy to Egan Dr; center. **Facility:** 102 units. 95 one- and 2 two-bedroom standard units, some with whirlpools. 5 one-bedroom suites with efficiencies. 3 stories (no elevator), interior corridors. *Bath:* combo or shower only. **Parking:** on-site. **Amenities:** video library (fee), voice mail, irons, hair dryers. **Pool(s):** heated indoor. **Leisure Activities:** whirlpool, limited exercise equipment. **Guest Services:** coin laundry, wireless Internet. **Business Services:** meeting rooms, PC.

BEST WESTERN VALDEZ HARBOR INN   *Book great rates at AAA.com*

Phone: (907)835-3434

Small-scale Hotel
$99-$169 All Year

Address: 100 N Harbor Dr 99686 **Location:** Just s at Meals Dr. At small boat Harbour. **Facility:** 88 one-bedroom standard units. 2 stories (no elevator), interior corridors. *Bath:* combo or shower only. **Parking:** on-site. **Amenities:** video library (fee), DVD players, voice mail, irons, hair dryers. *Some:* high-speed Internet. **Dining:** Alaska's Bistro, see separate listing. **Leisure Activities:** exercise room. *Fee:* massage. **Guest Services:** coin laundry, area transportation-ferry. **Business Services:** meeting rooms. **Cards:** AX, DS, MC, VI. **Free Special Amenities:** local telephone calls and room upgrade (subject to availability with advance reservations).

AAA Benefit:
Members save 10% everyday, plus an exclusive frequent stay program.

---------- ▼ *See AAA listing above* ▼ ----------

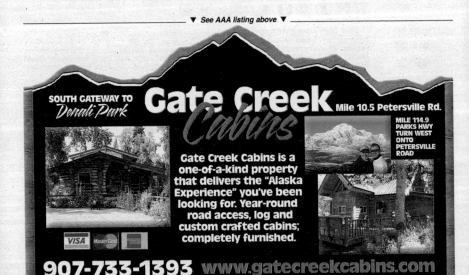

——— WHERE TO DINE ———

ALASKA HALIBUT HOUSE   Phone: 907/835-2788

American
$7-$10

This restaurant located just steps from the harbor features fresh seafood, primarily halibut and salmon, prepared breaded and deep fried. Casual dress. **Hours:** 6 am-10 pm. Closed major holidays. **Address:** 208 Meals Ave 99686 **Location:** Just n. **Parking:** on-site. **Cards:** MC, VI.

ALASKA'S BISTRO   Phone: 907/835-5688

🔺🔺🔺

Mediterranean
$9-$30

The nice restaurant offers fine service, a casually upscale atmosphere and a menu that centers on local seafood prepared with Italian influences. Casual dress. **Bar:** Full bar. **Hours:** 7 am-2 & 5-9 pm. Closed: 12/25. **Address:** 100 N Harbor Dr 99686 **Location:** Just s at Meals Dr; in Best Western Valdez Harbor Inn. **Parking:** on-site. **Cards:** AX, DS, MC, VI.

MIKE'S PALACE RISTORANTE   Phone: 907/835-2365

Italian
$9-$25

This eatery offers a menu of Italian, Greek and Mexican selections, as well as some sandwiches, steaks and seafood. Dining is casual and the service informal. Casual dress. **Bar:** Beer & wine. **Hours:** 11 am-11 pm. Closed: 11/27. **Address:** 201 N Harbor Dr 99686 **Location:** On the harbor. **Parking:** street. **Cards:** MC, VI.

WASILLA pop. 5,469

——— WHERE TO STAY ———

AGATE INN   *Book at AAA.com*   Phone: (907)373-2290

Condominium
$99-$225 All Year

Address: 4725 Begich Cir 99654 **Location:** (2.7 mi) e of George Parks Hwy (SR 3) on Palmer-Wasilla Hwy, just s on Begich, then just e. **Facility:** Smoke free premises. 13 units. 8 one-bedroom standard units, some with whirlpools. 3 two- and 1 three-bedroom suites with kitchens. 1 cottage with whirlpool. 2 stories (no elevator), interior/exterior corridors. *Bath:* combo or shower only. **Parking:** on-site, winter plug-ins. **Terms:** check-in 4 pm, 14 day cancellation notice-fee imposed. **Amenities:** video library, high-speed Internet, voice mail, hair dryers. *Some:* irons. **Leisure Activities:** horseshoes. **Guest Services:** coin laundry. **Business Services:** meeting rooms, PC. **Cards:** AX, DS, MC, VI.

BEST WESTERN LAKE LUCILLE INN   *Book great rates at AAA.com*   Phone: 907/373-1776

🔺🔺🔺 [SAVE]
🔻🔻 🔻🔻

Small-scale Hotel
Rates not provided

Address: 1300 W Lake Lucille Dr 99654 **Location:** George Parks Hwy (SR 3), just w on Hallea Ln; center. **Facility:** Smoke free premises. 54 units. 50 one-bedroom standard units. 4 one-bedroom suites with whirlpools. 2 stories (no elevator), interior corridors. **Parking:** on-site. **Amenities:** voice mail, irons, hair dryers. *Some:* high-speed Internet. **Leisure Activities:** sauna, whirlpool, fishing, hiking trails, exercise room. *Fee:* boat dock. **Guest Services:** coin laundry, wireless Internet. **Business Services:** meeting rooms. **Free Special Amenities:** expanded continental breakfast and high-speed Internet.
(See color ad p 730 & p 323)

AAA Benefit:
Members save 10% everyday, plus an exclusive frequent stay program.

GRANDVIEW INN & SUITES   *Book great rates at AAA.com*   Phone: (907)357-7666

🔺🔺🔺 [SAVE]
🔻🔻 🔻🔻

Small-scale Hotel
$80-$160 All Year

Address: 2900 E Parks Hwy 99654 **Location:** 1 mi n of jct Parks Hwy and Fairview Loop exit. **Facility:** Smoke free premises. 134 units. 78 one-bedroom standard units, some with whirlpools. 40 one- and two-bedroom suites with kitchens. 3 stories, interior corridors. *Bath:* combo or shower only. **Parking:** on-site, winter plug-ins. **Terms:** cancellation fee imposed. **Amenities:** high-speed Internet, voice mail, irons, hair dryers. **Pool(s):** heated indoor. **Leisure Activities:** whirlpool, exercise room. **Guest Services:** coin laundry. **Business Services:** meeting rooms. **Cards:** AX, DS, MC, VI.

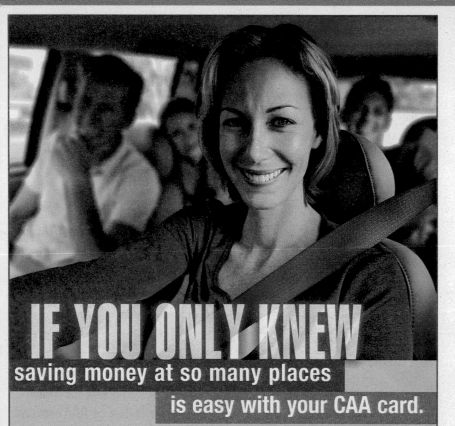

IF YOU ONLY KNEW

saving money at so many places

is easy with your CAA card.

Shopping. Playing. Traveling. Dining. Living life to its fullest and with savings galore! It's what the CAA membership card is all about!

With special deals on everything from shoes and school supplies to hotel rooms and theme park tickets. You'll receive immediate savings, or at some locations in Canada, will earn CAA Dollars - simply by presenting your CAA membership card.

Save at more than 150,000 merchant locations worldwide. CAA is your shopping source for living the good life. It pays to belong to CAA.

Discover your savings at **caa.ca/save** or visit one of **148 CAA locations.**

Offices

Cities with main offices are listed in **BOLD TYPE** and toll-free member service numbers in *ITALIC TYPE*.
All are closed Saturdays, Sundays and holidays unless otherwise indicated.
The type of service provided is designated below the name of the city where the office is located:

+ Auto travel services, including books/maps, marked maps and on-demand TripTik® maps
● Auto travel services, including books/maps, marked maps, but no on-demand TripTik® maps
■ Provides books/maps only. No marked maps or on-demand TripTik® maps available
▲ Travel agency services

AAA NATIONAL OFFICE: 1000 AAA DRIVE, HEATHROW, FLORIDA 32746-5063, (407) 444-7000

ALASKA

ANCHORAGE—AAA MOUNTAINWEST, 1005 E DIMOND BLVD ST 2A, 99515. MON-FRI 8:30-5:30. (907) 344-4310, *(800) 391-4222.*+▲

PROVINCE OF ALBERTA

CALGARY—ALBERTA MOTOR ASSOCIATION, #100 530 8TH AVE SW, T2P 3S8. MON-FRI 9-5. (403) 262-2345, *(800) 642-3810.*▲

CALGARY—ALBERTA MOTOR ASSOCIATION, 3650 20 AVE NE, T1Y 6E8. MON-FRI 9-5, SAT 9-5. (403) 590-0001, *(800) 642-3810.*●▲

CALGARY—ALBERTA MOTOR ASSOCIATION, 10816 MACLEOD TRL SE, T2J 5N8. MON-FRI 9-5, SAT 9-5. (403) 278-3530, *(800) 642-3810.*●▲

CALGARY—ALBERTA MOTOR ASSOCIATION, 220 CROWFOOT CRES NW, T3G 3N5. MON-FRI 9-5, SAT 9-5. (403) 239-6644, *(800) 642-3810.*●▲

CALGARY—ALBERTA MOTOR ASSOCIATION, #600 85 SHAWVILLE BLVD SE, T2Y 3W5. MON-FRI 9-5, SAT 9-5. (403) 254-2447.●▲

CALGARY—ALBERTA MOTOR ASSOCIATION, 4700 17TH AVE SW, T3E 0E3. MON-FRI 9-5, SAT 9-5. (403) 240-5300, *(800) 642-3810.*●▲

CAMROSE—ALBERTA MOTOR ASSOCIATION, 6702 48 AVE, T4V 4S3. MON-FRI 9-5, SAT 9-1. (780) 672-3391, *(800) 642-3810.*●▲

EDMONTON—ALBERTA MOTOR ASSOCIATION, 10310 GA MACDONALD AVE, T6J 6R7. MON-FRI 9-5:30, SAT 9-5. (780) 430-5555, *(800) 642-3810.*●▲

EDMONTON—ALBERTA MOTOR ASSOCIATION, 9938 170 ST, T5T 6G7. MON-FRI 9-5:30, SAT 9-5. (780) 484-1221, *(800) 642-3810.*●▲

EDMONTON—ALBERTA MOTOR ASSOCIATION, 5040 MANNING DR NW, T5A 5B4. MON-FRI 9-5, SAT 9-5. (780) 473-3112, *(800) 642-3810.*●▲

EDMONTON—ALBERTA MOTOR ASSOCIATION, 11220 109 ST, T5G 2T6. MON-FRI 9-5, SAT 9-5. (780) 474-8601, *(800) 642-3810.*+▲

FORT MCMURRAY—ALBERTA MOTOR ASSOCIATION, #4 HOSPITAL ST, T9H 5E4. MON-FRI 9-5. (780) 743-2433, *(800) 642-3810.*●▲

GRANDE PRAIRIE—ALBERTA MOTOR ASSOCIATION, 11401 99 ST, T8V 2H6. MON-FRI 9-5, SAT 9-2. (780) 532-4421, *(800) 642-3810.*●▲

LETHBRIDGE—ALBERTA MOTOR ASSOCIATION, 120 SCENIC DR S, T1J 4R4. MON-FRI 8:30-5, SAT 9-12:30. (403) 328-1181, *(800) 642-3810.*●▲

MEDICINE HAT—ALBERTA MOTOR ASSOCIATION, 2710 13 AVE SE, T1A 3P8. MON-FRI 9-5, SAT 9-12:30. (403) 527-1166, *(800) 642-3810.*●▲

RED DEER—ALBERTA MOTOR ASSOCIATION, 141 2004 50TH AVE, T4R 3A2. MON-FRI 9-5, SAT 9-12:30. (403) 342-6633.+▲

PROVINCE OF BRITISH COLUMBIA

ABBOTSFORD—CAA BRITISH COLUMBIA, 33310 S FRASER WAY, V2S 2B4. MON-FRI 9-5:30, SAT 9-5. (604) 870-3850, *(800) 663-1956.*■▲

BURNABY—CAA BRITISH COLUMBIA, 4567 CANADA WAY, V5G 4T1. MON-FRI 9-5:30, SAT 9-5. (604) 268-5000, *(800) 663-1956.*+▲

CHILLIWACK—CAA BRITISH COLUMBIA, #190-45428 LUCKAKUCK WAY, V2R 3S9. MON-FRI 9-5:30, SAT 9-5. (604) 824-2720, *(800) 663-1956.*■▲

COQUITLAM—CAA BRITISH COLUMBIA, 50-2773 BARNET HWY, V3B 1C2. MON-FRI 9-6, SAT 9-5. (604) 268-5750, *(800) 663-1956.*■▲

COURTENAY—CAA BRITISH COLUMBIA, 17-1599 CLIFFE AVE, V9N 2K6. MON-FRI 9-5:30, SAT 9-5. (250) 703-2328, *(800) 663-1956.*■▲

DELTA—CAA BRITISH COLUMBIA, SCOTT 72 CTR 7343-120 ST, V4C 6P5. MON-FRI 9-6, SAT 9-5. (604) 268-5900, *(800) 663-1956.*■▲

KAMLOOPS—CAA BRITISH COLUMBIA, 400-500 NOTRE DAME DR, V2C 6T6. MON-FRI 9-6, SAT 9-5. (250) 852-4600, *(800) 663-1956.*■▲

KELOWNA—CAA BRITISH COLUMBIA, #18-1470 HARVEY AVE, V1Y 9K8. MON-FRI 9-6, SAT 9-5. (250) 870-4900, *(800) 663-1956.*■▲

LANGLEY—CAA BRITISH COLUMBIA, 10 - 20190 LANGLEY BYPASS, V3A 9J9. MON-FRI 9-6, THU 9-8, SAT 9-5. (604) 268-5950, *(800) 663-1956.*■▲

MAPLE RIDGE—CAA BRITISH COLUMBIA, #500 20395 LOUGHEED HWY, V2X 2P9. MON-FRI 9-5:30, SAT 9-5. (604) 205-1200.■▲

NANAIMO—CAA BRITISH COLUMBIA, METRAL PL-6581 AULDS RD, V9T 6J6. MON-FRI 9-6, SAT 9-5. (250) 390-7700, *(800) 663-1956.*■▲

NELSON—CAA BRITISH COLUMBIA, 596 BAKER ST, V1L 4H9. MON-FRI 9-5, SAT 9-5. (250) 505-1720, *(800) 663-1956.*■▲

NEW WESTMINSTER—CAA BRITISH COLUMBIA, 501 SIXTH ST, V3L 3B9. MON-FRI 9-5:30, SAT 9-5. (604) 268-5700, *(800) 663-1956.*■▲

NORTH VANCOUVER—CAA BRITISH COLUMBIA, 333 BROOKSBANK AVE, V7J 3S8. MON-FRI 9-6, SAT 9-5, SUN 10-5. (604) 205-1050, *(800) 663-1956.*■▲

PENTICTON—CAA BRITISH COLUMBIA, 100-2100 MAIN ST, V2A 5H7. MON-FRI 9-5:30, SAT 9-5. (250) 487-2450, *(800) 663-1956.*■▲

PRINCE GEORGE—CAA BRITISH COLUMBIA, 492 VICTORIA ST, V2L 2J7. MON-FRI 9-5, SAT 9-5. (250) 649-2399, *(800) 663-1956.*■▲

RICHMOND—CAA BRITISH COLUMBIA, 180-5951 NO 3 RD, V6X 2E3. MON-FRI 9-5:30, SAT 9-5. (604) 268-5850, *(800) 663-1956.*■▲

SURREY—CAA BRITISH COLUMBIA, 130 2655 KING GEORGE HWY, V4P 1H7. MON-FRI 9-6, SAT 9-5. (604) 205-1150, *(800) 663-1956.*■▲

SURREY—CAA BRITISH COLUMBIA, #C4-15285 101 AVE, V3R 9V8. MON-FRI 9-6, SAT 9-5. (604) 205-1000, *(800) 663-1956.*■▲

VANCOUVER—CAA BRITISH COLUMBIA, 2347 W 41ST AVE, V6M 2A3. MON-FRI 9-5:30, SAT 9-5. (604) 268-5800, *(800) 663-1956.*■▲

VANCOUVER—CAA BRITISH COLUMBIA, 999 W BROADWAY, V5Z 1K5. MON-FRI 9-5:30, SAT 9-5. (604) 268-5600, *(800) 663-1956.*■▲

VERNON—CAA BRITISH COLUMBIA, #520 4400 32ND ST, V1T 9H2. MON-FRI 9-6, SAT 9-5. (250) 550-2400, *(800) 663-1956.*■▲

VICTORIA—CAA BRITISH COLUMBIA, 1262 QUADRA ST, V8W 2K7. MON-FRI 9-5, SAT 9-5. (250) 414-8320, *(800) 663-1956.*■▲

VICTORIA—CAA BRITISH COLUMBIA, #120-777 ROYAL OAK DR, V8X 4V1. MON-FRI 8:30-5:30, FRI 8:30-6:30, SAT 9-5. (250) 704-1750, *(800) 663-1956.*■▲

VICTORIA—CAA BRITISH COLUMBIA, 160 2401C MILLSTREAM RD, V9B 3R5. MON-FRI 9-5:30, SAT 9-5. (250) 391-3250.✦▲

WEST VANCOUVER—CAA BRITISH COLUMBIA, 608 PARK ROYAL N, V7T 1H9. MON-FRI 9-6, SAT 9-5. (604) 268-5650, *(800) 663-1956.*■▲

WESTBANK—CAA BRITISH COLUMBIA, 301 3550 CARRINGTON RD, V4T 2Z1. MON-FRI 9-5:30. (250) 707-4800.■▲

PROVINCE OF MANITOBA

ALTONA—CAA MANITOBA, 61 2ND AVE NE, R0G 0B0. MON-FRI 9-5, SAT 9-1. (204) 324-8474.●▲

BRANDON—CAA MANITOBA, 305 - 18TH ST. N, R7A 6Z2. MON-FRI 9-5, SAT 10-3. (204) 571-4111, *(877) 222-1321.*✦▲

WINNIPEG—CAA MANITOBA, 870 EMPRESS ST, R3G 3H3. MON-FRI 9-6, SAT 10-4. (204) 262-6161.✦▲

WINNIPEG—CAA MANITOBA, 2211 MCPHILLIPS ST UNIT C, R2V 3M5. MON-FRI 9-6, SAT 10-4. (204) 262-6223.●▲

WINNIPEG—CAA MANITOBA, 501 ST ANNES RD, R2M 3E5. MON-FRI 9-6, SAT 10-4. (204) 262-6201.●▲

PROVINCE OF SASKATCHEWAN

ESTEVAN—CAA SASKATCHEWAN, 1340-400 KING ST, S4A 2B4. MON-FRI 9-5:30, SAT 9-5:30. (306) 637-2185, *(800) 564-6222.*✦▲

MOOSE JAW—CAA SASKATCHEWAN, 80 CARIBOU ST W, S6H 2J6. MON-FRI 9-5:30, SAT 9-5:30. (306) 693-5195, *(800) 564-6222.*✦▲

NORTH BATTLEFORD—CAA SASKATCHEWAN, 2002-100TH ST, S9A 0X5. MON-FRI 9-5:30, SAT 9-5:30. (306) 445-9451, *(800) 564-6222.*✦▲

PRINCE ALBERT—CAA SASKATCHEWAN, #29 2995 2ND AVE W, S6V 5V5. MON-FRI 9-5:30, SAT 9-5:30. (306) 764-6818, *(800) 564-6222.*✦▲

REGINA—CAA SASKATCHEWAN, 200 ALBERT ST N, S4R 5E2. MON-FRI 9-5:30, SAT 9-5:30. (306) 791-4321, *(800) 564-6222.*✦▲

REGINA—CAA SASKATCHEWAN, 2510 E QUANCE ST, S4V 2X5. MON-FRI 9-5:30, SAT 9-5:30. (306) 791-4323, *(800) 564-6222.*●▲

REGINA—CAA SASKATCHEWAN, 4528 ALBERT ST, S4S 6B4. MON-FRI 9-5:30, SAT 9-5:30. (306) 791-4322, *(800) 564-6222.*✦▲

SASKATOON—CAA SASKATCHEWAN, 150 - 1ST AVE S, S7K 2L9. MON-FRI 9-5:30, SAT 9-5:30. (306) 668-3737, *(800) 564-6222.*●▲

SASKATOON—CAA SASKATCHEWAN, 3110 8TH ST EAST #1, S7H 0W2. MON-FRI 9-5:30, SAT 9-5:30. (306) 668-3770, *(800) 564-6222.*●▲

SWIFT CURRENT—CAA SASKATCHEWAN, 15 DUFFERIN ST W, S9H 5A1. MON-FRI 9-5:30, SAT 9-5:30. (306) 773-3193, *(800) 564-6222.*✦▲

WEYBURN—CAA SASKATCHEWAN, 110 SOURIS AVE, S4H 2Z8. MON-FRI 9-5:30, SAT 9-5:30. (306) 842-6651, *(800) 564-6222.*●▲

YORKTON—CAA SASKATCHEWAN, 159 BROADWAY ST E, S3N 3K6. MON-FRI 9-5:30, SAT 9-5:30. (306) 783-6536, *(800) 564-6222.*✦▲

Population

Canadian population figures—Statistics Canada's 2001 GeoSuite, by permission of Canadian Minister of Industry.

Metric Equivalents Chart

TEMPERATURE

To convert Fahrenheit to Celsius, subtract 32 from the Fahrenheit temperature, multiply by 5 and divide by 9.
To convert Celsius to Fahrenheit, multipy by 9, divide by 5 and add 32.

ACRES

1 acre = 0.4 hectare (ha)	1 hectare = 2.47 acres

MILES AND KILOMETRES

Note: A kilometre is approximately 5/8 or 0.6 of a mile.
To convert kilometres to miles multiply by 0.6.

Miles/Kilometres		Kilometres/Miles	
15	24.1	30	18.6
20	32.2	35	21.7
25	40.2	40	24.8
30	48.3	45	27.9
35	56.3	50	31.0
40	64.4	55	34.1
45	72.4	60	37.2
50	80.5	65	40.3
55	88.5	70	43.4
60	96.6	75	46.6
65	104.6	80	49.7
70	112.7	85	52.8
75	120.7	90	55.9
80	128.7	95	59.0
85	136.8	100	62.1
90	144.8	105	65.2
95	152.9	110	68.3
100	160.9	115	71.4

Celsius °		Fahrenheit °
100	BOILING	212
37		100
35		95
32		90
29		85
27		80
24		75
21		70
18		65
16		60
13		55
10		50
7		45
4		40
2		35
0	FREEZING	32
-4		25
-7		20
-9		15
-12		10
-15		5
-18		0
-21		-5
-24		-10
-27		-15

LINEAR MEASURE

Customary	Metric
1 inch = 2.54 centimetres	1 centimetre = 0.4 inches
1 foot = 30 centimetres	1 metre = 3.3 feet
1 yard = 0.91 metres	1 metre = 1.09 yards
1 mile = 1.6 kilometres	1 kilometre = .62 miles

WEIGHT

If You Know:	Multiply By:	To Find:
Ounces	28.000	Grams
Pounds	0.450	Kilograms
Grams	0.035	Ounces
Kilograms	2.200	Pounds

LIQUID MEASURE

Customary	Metric
1 fluid ounce = 30 millilitres	1 millilitre = .03 fluid ounces
1 cup = .24 litres	1 litre = 2.1 pints
1 pint = .47 litres	1 litre = 1.06 quarts
1 quart = .95 litres	1 litre = .26 gallons
1 gallon = 3.8 litres	

PRESSURE

Air pressure in automobile tires is expressed in kilopascals. Multiply pound-force per square inch (psi) by 6.89 to find kilopascals (kPa).

24 psi = 165 kPa	28 psi = 193 kPa
26 psi = 179 kPa	30 psi = 207 kPa

GALLON AND LITRES

Gallons/Litres				Litres/Gallons			
5	19.0	12	45.6	10	2.6	40	10.4
6	22.8	14	53.2	15	3.9	50	13.0
7	26.6	16	60.8	20	5.2	60	15.6
8	30.4	18	68.4	25	6.5	70	18.2
9	34.2	20	76.0	30	7.8	80	20.8
10	38.0	25	95.0	35	9.1	90	23.4

WESTERN CANADA
AND ALASKA
DRIVING DISTANCES

100 MILES IN US/KILOMETERS IN CANADA
2:00 AVERAGE TIME (EXCLUDING STOPS)

© AAA

OCEAN

Sea

Horton River

ARCTIC

Great
Bear
Lake

Mackenzie

River

CIRCLE

NUNAVUT

NORTHWEST TERRITORIES

YELLOWKNIFE

Fort
Simpson   315
              4:44

              367   178
Fort   4:48   2:12
Providence

528   Hay River
              51
              0:47
Enterprise

Great
Slave Lake

Hudson
Bay

UMBIA   NORTHWEST   TERRITORIES   NUNAVUT
              ALBERTA   SASKATCHEWAN   MANITOBA

Fort
Nelson

BRITISH COLUMBIA   552
ALBERTA   3:38

360
3:27

Fort
St. John

71
0:41
Dawson
Creek

6:39

Peace River   141   246
               1:33   3:47   Slave Lake

251
2:41

Valleyview   351
               3:40   241
                      3:33

Lake
Athabasca

Wollaston
Lake

ALBERTA SASKATCHEWAN

SASKATCHEWAN

Reindeer
Lake

KILOMETERS
IN CANADA

Churchill   River

Nelson   River

MANITOBA

Flin
Flon

270
:38

Tete
Jaune
Cache

116
1:09

405
5:13

364
3:57

608
2:54

524
5:27

EDMONTON   591
            6:45

Prince
Albert

408
4:24

537
5:57

Grand
Rapids

Lake
Manitoba

Lake Winnipeg

MANITOBA

ONTARIO

Jasper

ache
reek

5:10

53

592

SASKATOON   140
             1:42

503
6:06

586
6:27

336
3:45

432
4:50

WINNIPEG   209
             2:29

Kenora

CALGARY   621
             6:35

268
3:30

260
2:38

Dauphin

162
2:02

211
2:25

108
1:03

203
2:46

208
2:04

ON

KAMLOOPS   5:42

290
2:53

REGINA   360
            3:55

Brandon

MN

ope   272
       3:55

Cranbrook   460
             6:48

47:35
4:35

219
2:04

243
2:35

241
2:50

Swift Current

101
1:10

75

2:30   International
        Falls

232
29

Osoyoos   6:02

449

Medicine
Hat

3:49

ALBERTA   CANADA
MONTANA   UNITED STATES

1:32   101

206
3:45   Grand Forks

Omak

WASHINGTON
IDAHO

IDAHO
MONTANA

8
0:12   Eureka

Havre   83
             1:46

428
10:22

MONTANA

Minot

MINNESOTA
NORTH DAKOTA

NORTH DAKOTA

MILES
IN U.S.

3665-B

Border Information

FOR UNITED STATES RESIDENTS TRAVELING TO CANADA

Passports for air travel are now required for travel to Canada. As early as January 1, 2008, U.S. citizens traveling between the U.S. and Canada, Mexico, the Caribbean, and Bermuda by land or sea (including ferries), could be required to present a valid U.S. passport. Please refer to the U.S. Department of State's Web site travel.state.gov for the most current information on these requirements.

Native-born citizens of the United States:
- Passport not required (but is recommended)
- Proof of citizenship required (a birth certificate and photo ID)
- Proof of residence may be required

Naturalized citizens: naturalization certificate required

U.S. resident aliens: Alien Registration Receipt Card (Green Card) required

Single parents, grandparents or guardians traveling with a minor must show documentation of legal custody and provide proof of citizenship for each child (the minor's passport or a parent's passport that includes the child).

When a child is traveling with only 1 parent that parent should have a notarized letter of consent from the other parent or legal custody documents.

When a child is traveling alone or with an individual other than a parent the minor should have a notarized letter of consent with phone number(s) from both parents or a custody document.

Legal Issues: Persons with felony convictions, driving while intoxicated records or other offenses may be denied admittance into Canada. Contact the Canadian embassy or nearest consulate before travel.

Canadian Goods and Services Tax (GST):
- 6 percent GST levied on most items sold and most services rendered in Canada
- 15 percent Harmonized Sales Tax (HST) (7 percent GST and 8 percent provincial component) charged on most goods and services in Nova Scotia, New Brunswick and Newfoundland
- Apply for GST/HST rebate on items including short-term accommodations (less than 1 month in 1 location)
- Claim a rebate on a minimum of $200 of eligible purchases prior to taxes provided the goods are exported 60 days from purchase date

- GST/HST rebate not refundable on alcohol, food and beverages, tobacco, transportation, entertainment, automobile fuel and such services as dry cleaning
- Submit original receipts (amount must be at least $50 before tax)

Free GST brochures with rebate form available in Canada at land border and airport duty-free shops, tourist information centres, customs offices, hotels. Allow 4 to 6 weeks for claim processing. For information contact: Visitor Rebate Program, Summerside Tax Centre, Canada Revenue Agency, 275 Pope Road, Suite 104, Summerside, P.E., Canada C1N 6C6; 902-432-5608 outside Canada; 800-668-4748 in Canada.

Firearms: Canada has strict laws regarding the importing, exporting, possession, use, storage, display and transportation of firearms. These are federal laws that apply across the country.

Classes of Firearms:
- Non-restricted (most ordinary rifles and shotguns)
- Restricted (mainly handguns)
- Prohibited (full automatics, converted automatics, handguns with a barrel length of 105 m ($\approx$4 inches) or less, and .25 or .32 caliber handguns, among others)

Certain handguns used in International Shooting Union sporting competition are classified as restricted even though they meet the prohibited handgun definition.

Yes: To bring a non-restricted or restricted firearm into Canada you must:
- Be 18 years of age or older
- Declare firearm(s) at first point of entry
- Get an Authorization to Transport (ATT) from a provincial or territorial Chief Firearms Officer before arriving at point of entry (Note: ATT not issued for hunting or self-protection purposes)

No: You may not bring into Canada a prohibited firearm or replica firearm, except replicas of firearms classified as antiques (a replica that looks exactly, or almost exactly, like a firearm but is not a firearm; it cannot discharge projectiles or discharges only harmless projectiles).

The Canada Border Services Agency is responsible for all customs procedures.

Yes:
- You may import non-restricted firearms for legitimate purposes: sporting or hunting; use in competitions; transit movement; or personal protection against wildlife in remote areas (customs officer must agree that circumstances warrant firearm possession)
- Register weapons with U.S. Customs before departure
- Upon return you must show proof that you had the weapon before departure
- Under certain circumstances individuals and businesses may import firearms

No: Non-residents may not import prohibited items.

Fees (in Canadian funds):
- Non-Resident Firearm Declaration – $50 covers all firearms listed on declaration
- Possession and acquisition license – $60 for non-restricted firearms; valid for 5 years
- Temporary Firearms Borrowing License (for non-residents) – $30; may renew once in a 12-month period at no extra cost; $30 thereafter (800-731-4000)
- Imported firearm registration fee – $25 per firearm registered in Canada

Prohibited: Any large capacity cartridge magazine (limited to 5 rounds for semiautomatic rifles or shotguns, 10 rounds for handguns), any device designed to stop the sound of a firearm, any knife with a blade opened by spring pressure (e.g., switchblade), martial arts weapons (e.g., shuriken (shooting stars), nunchaku sticks), mace, blowguns, hand-held compact crossbows and any other weapons declared prohibited by regulation.

Yes: Hunters may bring in, duty-free, 200 rounds of ammunition; competition participants 1,500 rounds. Must show valid license or declaration to purchase ammunition. If planning to hunt in multiple provinces or territories, you must obtain a hunting license from each one.
No: Firearms forbidden in many of Canada's national and provincial parks, game reserves and adjacent areas.

Parks and Hunting Regulation Information: Newfoundland and Labrador 800-563-6353 or 709-729-2830; Prince Edward Island 888-734-7529 or 902-629-2400; Nova Scotia 800-565-0000 ext 998 or 902-425-5781; New Brunswick 800-561-0123 or 506-789-4982; Quebec 800-363-7777 or 514-873-2015; Ontario 800-668-2746 or 416-314-0944; Manitoba 800-665-0040 or 204-945-3777; Saskatchewan 877-237-2273 or 306-787-2300; Alberta 800-661-8888 or 780-427-4321; British Columbia 800-663-6000 or 250-387-1642; Northwest Territories (Western NWT) 800-661-0788 or 867-873-4059; Nunavut (Eastern NWT) 800-491-7910 or 867-979-1261; Yukon 867-667-5340.

Note: Provinces and territories also have their own laws regulating the transportation of firearms through their areas, usually in connection with their hunting regulations. For further information on the entry of firearms, applying for a license or to obtain authorization to transport a firearm, contact: Canadian Firearms Centre at 800-731-4000.

Personal Baggage:
- Admissible into Canada on a temporary basis without payment of duty and taxes
- Customs may require a refundable security deposit at time of entry
- Deposits not normally required for health- or pleasure-related visits as long as all items are exported at trip's end

Personal baggage that may be taken into Canada on a duty- and tax-free basis includes clothing and personal items, sporting goods, automobiles, vessels, aircraft, snowmobiles, cameras, personal computers, food products and other items appropriate for the purpose and duration of the visit.

Tobacco products – Those meeting age requirements (18 years in Alberta, Manitoba, Northwest Territories and Nunavut, Saskatchewan, Quebec and Yukon Territory; 19 years in other provinces) may bring in 50 cigars, 200 cigarettes, 200 grams of tobacco and 200 tobacco sticks. **Alcohol** – Those meeting age requirements (18 years in Alberta, Manitoba and Quebec; 19 years in other provinces and territories) may bring in limited alcoholic beverages: 40 ounces (1.14 L) of liquor, 1.6 quarts (1.5 L) of wine or 9 quarts (8.6 L) of beer or ale (equivalent to 24 12-ounce bottles or cans).
- Generally, a minimum 24-hour stay is required to transport any liquor or tobacco into Canada

- Amounts exceeding the allowable quantities noted above are subject to federal duty and taxes, and provincial/territorial liquor fees
- Pay provincial fees at customs at the time of entry in all provinces and the Yukon Territory
- Illegal to bring more than the allowable alcohol quantity into the Northwest Territories and Nunavut

Articles purchased at Canadian duty-free shops are subject to U.S. Customs exemptions and restrictions; those purchased at U.S. duty-free shops before entering Canada are subject to duty if brought back into the United States.

Prescription Drugs: Persons requiring medication while visiting Canada are permitted to bring it for their own use. Clearly identify and carry in original packaging with a label listing the drug and its intended use. Have a copy of the prescription and prescribing doctor's phone number.

Gifts: Items not exceeding $60 (CAN) in value, excluding tobacco, alcoholic beverages and advertising matter, taken into or mailed to Canada are allowed free entry. Gifts valued at more than $60 are subject to regular duty and taxes on the excess amount.

Pets and Plants: You must have a certificate for a dog or cat age 3 months and older. It must clearly describe the animal, declare that the animal has been vaccinated against rabies within the past 36 months, and have a licensed veterinarian signature.

- Collar tags are not sufficient proof of immunization
- Be sure the vaccination does not expire while traveling in Canada
- The certificate is also required to bring the animal back into the United States

Exempt From These Rules: Assist dogs; healthy puppies and kittens under 3 months old with a health certificate, signed by a licensed veterinarian, indicating that the animal is too young to vaccinate.

Plants or plant material must be declared. For information, contact: Canadian Food Inspection Agency (CFIA), 59 Camelot Dr., Ottawa, ON K1A 0Y9; 613-225-2342.

Radio Communication Equipment
- Cell phone, PCS phone, citizens band (CB) or Family Radio Service radio allowed without prior registration
- Use of aircraft, marine or amateur radio allowed without prior authorization
- All other types of radio transmitting stations allowed with authorization letter from Industry Canada's Radiocommunication and Broadcasting Regulatory Branch

Special Permits: A CITIES (Convention on International Trade in Endangered Species) permit is required for any endangered species brought into Canada, including those kept as pets, and for any items made from them (e.g., coats, handbags, shoes). For information contact: Environment Canada, Canadian Wildlife Service at 819-997-1840.

An Export Permit may be required to take out of Canada objects more than 50 years old (e.g., fossils, archaeological artifacts, fine and decorative art, technological objects or books and archival material). Contact: Movable Cultural Property Program of Canadian Heritage, 15 Eddy St., 3rd Floor, Hull, Quebec, Canada K1A 0M5; 819-997-7761.

An Import Permit may be required for the importation of clothing, textiles, steel and certain agricultural products in excess of minimum quantities. For information contact: Department of Foreign Affairs and Int'l Trade, Export and Import Controls Bureau, Tower C, 4th Floor, LB Pearson Bldg, 125 Sussex Dr., Ottawa, ON K1A 0G2.

Vehicles
- Vehicles entering Canada for touring, including trailers not exceeding 8 feet 6 inches (2.6 m) in width are generally subject to quick and routine entry procedures.
- To leave or store a car, trailer or other goods in Canada while you leave the country you must pay import duty and taxes or present a valid permit. Canadian Customs officials issue permits at point of entry.
- You may not store a vacation trailer in Canada during the off-season.
- Vehicle registration cards required for Canadian travel.
- If driving a car other than your own, you must have written permission from the owner to use it.
- If driving a rented car, you must possess a copy of the contract.
- A valid U.S. driver's license is valid in Canada for time period specified by the individual provinces and territories.

- In all Canadian provinces and territories it is illegal to use radar detectors.
- Seat belts required for the driver and all passengers throughout Canada.

Headlights: Driving with vehicle headlights on for extended periods after dawn and before dusk is a statutory requirement in provinces and territories.

- In Alberta, British Columbia, New Brunswick, Ontario and Prince Edward Island, lights must be turned on when light conditions restrict visibility to 500 feet (150 m).
- In Manitoba, lights must be turned on when light conditions restrict visibility to 200 feet (60 m).
- In Alberta, Yukon Territory, Northwest Territories and Nunavut, headlights must remain on at all times.
- Elsewhere in Canada, driving with headlights on during all hours of the day is advised.

FINANCIAL RESPONSIBILITY LAWS IN CANADA

When an accident involves death, injury or property damage, Canadian provinces and territories require evidence of financial responsibility. You may be asked to show this evidence at any time.

U.S. motorists should obtain from their own U.S. insurance companies a yellow Non-Resident Inter-Province Motor Vehicle Liability Insurance Card (accepted as evidence of financial responsibility throughout Canada). Those not carrying proper proof may be subject to a substantial fine (minimum $575). Fine varies in each province. If renting a vehicle, check with the rental car company.

The minimum liability insurance requirement is $200,000 in all provinces and territories except Quebec, which requires $50,000. Should the courts' judgments exceed these figures, motorists held accountable are responsible for paying the full amount.

If traveling in Québec, discuss your collision, disability and bodily injury coverages with your insurance agent. Since Québec's minimum requirement does not include bodily injury, coverage of $200,000 or more is recommended. Consider additional coverage (i.e., trip accident policy).

FOR UNITED STATES RESIDENTS RETURNING TO THE UNITED STATES

Everyone who seeks entry into the United States – whether foreign visitors, U.S. citizens, or U.S. lawful permanent residents – must be inspected at the point of entry. Random searches may be conducted by U.S. Customs and Border Protection agents.

U.S. Exemptions for a Stay in Canada No Less Than 48 hours

- You may bring back tax- and duty-free articles not exceeding $800 in retail value
- Any amount over the $800 exemption is subject to duty
- The exemption is allowed once every 30 days
- A family (related persons living in the same household) may combine its exemptions (a family of 6 is entitled to $4,800 worth of goods duty-free on 1 declaration, even if articles claimed by 1 member exceed that individual's $800 amount)
- Exemptions based on fair retail value (keep receipts of all purchases as proof of fair retail value)
- Exemptions apply to articles acquired only for personal or household use or as gifts, but not intended for sale
- The exemption may include 100 cigars, 200 cigarettes and 1 liter of liquor per person over age 21 (customs enforces state liquor laws)
- All articles claimed under this exemption must accompany you on your return

U.S. Exemptions for a Stay in Canada Less Than 48 hours

- You may bring back tax- and duty-free articles not exceeding $200 in retail value
- The exemption may include no more than 50 cigarettes, 10 cigars, 4 fluid ounces (150 milliliters) of alcoholic beverage or 150 milliliters of perfume containing alcohol
- A family may not combine purchases
- If purchases exceed the $200 exemption, you lose the exemption and all purchases become subject to duty
- All goods must be declared
- All articles claimed under this exemption must accompany you on your return

Gifts

- Gifts up to $100 fair retail value may be sent to friends or relatives in the United States provided no recipient receives more than 1 gift per day (need not be included in the $800 exemption)

- Gifts containing tobacco products, alcoholic beverages or perfume containing alcohol valued at more than $5 retail are excluded from this provision
- Write on outside of package the contents, retail value and "Unsolicited Gift"

Prohibited: Articles considered detrimental to the general welfare of the United States are prohibited entry: narcotics and dangerous drugs, drug paraphernalia, obscene articles and publications, seditious or treasonable matter, lottery tickets, hazardous items (fireworks, dangerous toys, toxic or poisonous substances) and switchblade knives. Any goods originating in the following countries are prohibited: Balkans, Burma, Cuba, Iran, Iraq, Liberia, Libya, North Korea, Sudan, Syria and Zimbabwe. Please note embargoes are not limited to these countries.

Restricted items include automobiles, biological materials (disease organisms and vectors for research), ceramic tableware, cultural treasures, firearms and ammunition, articles bearing marks or names copying or simulating trademarked articles or trade names (watches, cameras, perfumes), pirated copies of copyrighted articles (books, CDs, DVDs, audio- and video-tapes, computer programs), agricultural goods (plants and animal products) and pets, wildlife and fish.

You may bring into or take out of the United States an unlimited amount of money, however, if you transport more than $10,000 you must file a Form 4790 with U.S. Customs. Failure to comply can result in civil, criminal and/or forfeiture penalties. Monies include currency, traveler's checks, U.S. or foreign coins in circulation, money orders and negotiable instruments or investment securities in bearer form. For a currency reporting flier contact: U.S. Customs, P.O. Box 7407, Washington, D.C. 20044.

While some agricultural products of Canadian origin (fruits, some plants with phyto-sanitary certificates, meats, etc.) may be brought into the United States, many are restricted to prevent the introduction of plant and animal pests and diseases. All must be declared at the U.S. border. Write to APHIS, Dept. of Agriculture, 6505 Belcrest Rd., Hyattsville, MD 20782, for a free copy of *Traveler's Tips*. Write to U.S. Customs, P.O. Box 7407, Washington, D.C. 20044 for other

helpful leaflets: *Visiting the U.S.: Requirements for Non-Residents*, *Know Before You Go*, *Importing a Car*, and *Pets, Wildlife and U.S. Customs*.

FOR CANADA RESIDENTS TRAVELING TO THE UNITED STATES

Passports for air travel are now required for travel to the U.S. As early as January 1, 2008, Canada residents traveling between the U.S. and Canada, Mexico, the Caribbean, and Bermuda by land or sea (including ferries), could be required to present a valid passport. Please refer to the U.S. Department of State's Web site travel.state.gov for the most current information on these requirements.

Native-born citizens of Canada:
- Passport not required (but is recommended)
- Proof of citizenship required (a birth certificate and photo ID)
- Proof of residence may be required

If traveling to the United States with a child, carry documentation proving your custodial rights. A person under age 18 traveling to the United States alone or with only 1 parent or another adult, must have certified documentation proving that the trip is permitted by both parents.

United States Customs permits Canadian residents to bring, free of duty, for personal use and not intended for sale: clothing, personal items and equipment appropriate to the trip, including 200 cigarettes, 50 cigars or 2 kilograms of tobacco, or proportionate amounts of each, and 1 liter of alcoholic beverage.

Visitors in the United States for at least 72 hours who have not claimed this exemption in the preceding 6 months may bring gifts totaling $100 (US) retail value. Perfume containing alcohol and valued at more than $5 retail, tobacco products and alcoholic beverages excluded from the gift provision.

Use of cell phones and General Radio Service Station (CB) is unrestricted.

FOR CANADA RESIDENTS RETURNING TO CANADA

The Canada Border Services Agency allows Canadian residents to bring, free of duty and taxes, goods valued up to $200 (CAN) any number of times a year, provided the visit to the United States is 48 hours or more and all goods accompany the purchaser (written declaration may be required).

You may claim a $50 (CAN) exemption on goods, excluding alcoholic beverages and tobacco products, if returning after an absence of 24 hours or more and are not using any other exemption. If bringing back more than $50 worth of goods, the regular duty and tax rate is levied on the entire value. This exemption may apply any number of times in a year.

If returning after 7 days or more in the United States (not counting departure day from Canada) you may claim up to a $750 (CAN) exemption on goods. Goods, other than alcohol and tobacco products, need not accompany you (written declaration may be required).

Permitted within the $200 and $750 exemptions: up to 50 cigars, 200 cigarettes, 200 tobacco sticks and 200 grams (6.4 oz) of tobacco, and up to 1.14 liters (40 oz) of liquor or 1.5 liters (1.6 qts) of wine or 8.5 liters (9 qts) of beer or ale (or its equivalent of 24 12-ounce bottles or cans). You must meet the minimum age requirement of the province or territory entered to claim alcohol or tobacco products.

Special Tariff: When exceeding the $200 or $750 exemption, a special rate of 7 percent combined duty and taxes is levied on the next $300 value in goods (except

tobacco and alcohol) exceeding the maximum exemptible amounts, provided goods are of U.S origin. Regular duties apply on any additional amount. A 15 percent Harmonized Sales Tax (HST) (7 percent Goods and Services Tax (GST) and 8 percent provincial component) is charged on most goods and services supplied in Nova Scotia, New Brunswick and Newfoundland and Labrador. For information contact the Canada Border Services Agency before departing Canada. All extra goods must accompany you.

All exemptions are individual and may not be combined with those of other people. You may be asked to verify the length of your visit. Dated receipts normally constitute proof. Gifts (excluding alcoholic beverages, tobacco products and advertising matter) up to $60 (CAN) retail may be sent from abroad free of duty or taxes. For gifts valued at more than $60 (CAN), duty and taxes apply to amount exceeding $60. Gifts sent from abroad do not count against personal exemptions; gifts brought back must be included in exemptions.

NATIONAL PARKS ENTRANCE FEES

At Canada's national parks, the basic per person or per family entry fee gives visitors access to the park, scenic outlooks, picnic areas and a variety of facilities. Additional fees are charged for visitors who choose to use other recreational services such as campgrounds, special interpretation programs and golf courses.

To receive a free Parks Canada vacation planner, phone (888) 773-8888. Detailed information about the services, benefits, entry fees and discounts at all national parks and historic sites is available by calling the following numbers:

- (800) 748-7275 for Alberta;
- (902) 426-3436 for Atlantic provinces (Newfoundland and Labrador, New Brunswick, Nova Scotia and Prince Edward Island);
- (604) 513-4777 for British Columbia;
- (888)748-2928 for Manitoba;
- (800) 748-7275 for Saskatchewan;
- (800) 463-6769 for Québec;
- (800) 661-0486 for Yukon Territory.

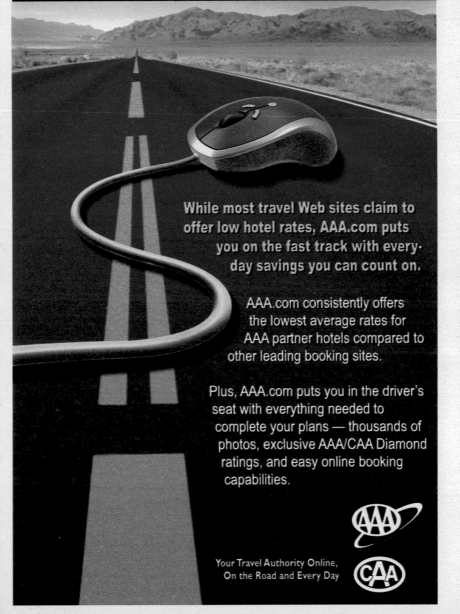

Savings for all Seasons

Hertz rents Fords and other fine cars. ® REG. U.S. PAT. OFF. © HERTZ SYSTEM INC., 1999/2006-09.

No matter the season, Hertz offers CAA members exclusive discounts and benefits.

Operating in 150 countries at over 7,600 locations, Hertz makes traveling more convenient and efficient wherever and whenever you go. Hertz offers CAA members discounts up to 20% on car rentals worldwide.

To receive your exclusive CAA member discounts and benefits, mention your CAA membership card at time of reservation and present it at time of rental. **In addition**, to receive a free one car class upgrade on daily, weekly or weekend rental in the United States, Puerto Rico and Canada, mention PC# 969194 at the time of reservation. Offer is valid for vehicle pick-up on or before 12/15/08.

For reservations and program details, call your CAA Travel centre or the Hertz/CAA Desk at **1-800-654-3080.**

Points of Interest Index

Index Legend

NB.	national battlefield	NR.	national river
NBP.	national battlefield park	NS.	national seashore
NC.	national cemetery	NWR.	national wildlife refuge
NF.	national forest	PHP.	provincial historic(al) park
NHM.	national historic(al) monument	PHS.	provincial historic(al) site
NHP.	national historic(al) park	PP.	provincial park
NHS.	national historic(al) site	SF.	state forest
NL.	national lakeshore	SHM.	state historic(al) monument
NME.	national memorial	SHP.	state historic(al) park
NMO.	national monument	SHS.	state historic(al) site
NMP.	national military park	SME.	state memorial
NP.	national park	SP.	state park
NRA.	national recreation area	SRA.	state recreation area

▽ GEM: Points of Interest Offering a *Great Experience for Members*®

EXHIBITS & COLLECTIONS-INDIAN

EXHIBITS & COLLECTIONS-RELIGIOUS ITEMS

EXHIBITS & COLLECTIONS-SCIENCE

EXHIBITS & COLLECTIONS-SPORTS

EXHIBITS & COLLECTIONS-VEHICLES

MUSIC HALLS & OPERA HOUSES

MYTHICAL PERSONS & ANIMALS

NATIONALITIES & ETHNIC AREAS

NATURAL PHENOMENA

NATURE CENTERS

NATURE TRAILS

OBSERVATORIES

PAINTINGS

PARKS, CITY; STATE; PROVINCIAL

VISITOR INFORMATION

WALKING TOURS

822

We Never Leave You Hanging

There's no need to worry when you book your travel plans on AAA.com.

Our online services are backed by knowledgeable travel professionals ready to help.

AAA.com is the only travel Web site backed by 10,000 travel professionals in more than 1,100 AAA Travel offices across the country. If you have changes, questions, or just want to talk to a real person, we're there for you.

Clear ratings, best prices, reliable bookings, custom routes, real photos and facts.

24/7 on AAA.com

 Your Travel Authority
Online, On the Road and Every Day

SAVE *Attraction Admission Discount Index*

Bed & Breakfast Lodgings Index

Some bed and breakfasts listed below might have historical significance.
Those properties are also referenced in the Historical index.

Country Inns Index

Some of the following country inns can also be considered as bed-and-breakfast operations.

Historical Lodgings & Restaurants Index

Some of the following historical lodgings can also be considered as bed-and-breakfast operations.

Resorts Index

Many establishments are located in resort areas; however, the following places have extensive on-premises recreational facilities.

Comprehensive City Index

Here is an alphabetical list of all cities appearing in this TourBook® guide. Cities are presented by state/province. Page numbers under the POI column indicate where points of interest text begins. Page numbers under the L&R column indicate where lodging and restaurant listings begin.

828

Comprehensive City Index (cont'd)

Comprehensive City Index (cont'd)